THE WORLD ATLAS OF ARCHITECTURE

Foreword by
John Julius Norwich

THE WORLD
ARCHIT

ATLAS OF
ECTURE

Mitchell Beazley

Edited by Mitchell Beazley International Ltd.,
Artists House, 14–15 Manette Street, London W1V 5LB

© Mitchell Beazley Publishers, 1984
French edition *Le Grand Atlas de l'Architecture Mondiale*
© Encyclopædia Universalis France S.A., 1981
Partly based on *Great Architecture of the World* © Mitchell Beazley, 1975
and some illustrations © International Visual Resource, 1973
English translation © Mitchell Beazley Publishers, 1984
Reprinted 1988

ISBN 0 85533 540 8

Filmset in Eastleigh, England by Vantage Photosetting Co. Ltd.
Printed and bound in Spain by Printer Industria Grafica S.A., Barcelona
DLB 5648–1988

The World Atlas of Architecture

is the English edition of

Le Grand Atlas de l'Architecture Mondiale

created by Encyclopaedia Universalis and derived from Mitchell Beazley's

Great Architecture of the World

Contributors to the original, French edition:

CHRISTINE FLON (editor)

**CATHERINE BRISAC, FRÉDÉRIQUE DE CAGNY, ANDRÉ CHASTEL,
JEAN DEVISSE, ALAIN ERLANDE-BRANDENBURG, ROBERT FOHR,
JOSÉ GARANGER, BERNARD PHILIPPE GROSLIER,
JEAN GUILLAUME, BERNARD HOLTZMANN, JEAN-LOUIS HUOT, BERNARD JEANNEL,
CHANTAL KOZYREFF, DANIÈLE LAVALLÉE, FRANÇOIS LOYER,
DOMINIQUE MICHELET, CLAUDE MIGNOT, MONIQUE MOSSER,
JEAN-PIERRE MOUILLESEAUX, LUC PFIRSCH, DANIEL RABREAU,
MICHEL TERRASSE**

English translation,
arranged through Rosetta Translations, by:

**CHRISTOPHER DUFTON, JAMES DUNNETT, JOHN GILBERT,
MARK HELSTON, WILFRED LASCELLES, MICHÈLE OSBORNE,
JANE PEPPEREL, ANTHEA RIDETT, HELEN TOPSFIELD,
MALCOLM WARNER**

Additional editing by:

**JAMES CHAMBERS, JANE CRAWLEY, MARGARET CROWTHER,
PAUL DAVIES, ROGER HEARN,
PAUL HOLBERTON**

Contents

THE MIDDLE AGES

THE MODERN ERA

THE AGE OF CLASSICISM

Foreword

In the great family of the arts, architecture has always been something of a poor relation. Even the ancient Greeks, who were responsible for several buildings which are still after some two and a half thousand years among the most beautiful in the world, never allotted it a Muse of its own. They did at least record the names of a few of their architects: we know for example that a certain Ictinus built the Parthenon – and, quite possibly, the temple of Apollo at Bassae as well. Two other men of genius, Anthemius of Tralles and Isidore of Miletus, have gone down in history as the designers, a thousand years later, of another *tour de force*, the Church of the Holy Wisdom – St. Sophia – in Constantinople. But these were fortunate exceptions. The melancholy truth is that very nearly all the architects of the civilized world working in the years before the Renaissance – and that includes the builders of virtually every medieval cathedral – are to us nameless, faceless men. Nor is it just the individuals who have gone unrecognized. Throughout the Middle Ages the architect's profession scarcely existed in its own right, merging as it did with that of the master mason. Perhaps the first important *début* of an architect as such was that of Arnolfo di Cambio, who drew up the original plan for the cathedral at Florence between 1294 and 1302. (Giotto's *campanile* came only in 1334, and Brunelleschi's dome a century later still.) In England, however, we were a good deal slower off the mark: the architect was not really recognized until the beginning of the 17th century.

But why, one wonders, were both the art of architecture and the men who practised it so consistently underrated? There are – or so it seems to me – two principal reasons. The first is that the art is not a pure one. This is not to suggest that in the hands of a consummate master it cannot attain heights every bit as sublime as any other of the visual arts, or even music; but whereas the others – though they may on occasion be used to point a moral or adorn a tale – in their essence exist only for themselves, in architecture the situation is not so simple: here every creation has a serious and specific job to do. It is not enough for an architect to produce a beautiful building, as a painter might paint a canvas or a composer conceive a symphony; that building must also serve its designated purpose. If it fails to do so, if the architect allows himself to be carried away by his desire to create a work of art to the point where that work can no longer adequately perform the function for which it was intended, then – however beguiling it may be to the eye – it is bad architecture. There is no good architecture that is not successful architecture too.

In the very earliest times one purpose only was recognized for a building: to provide shelter from the elements and protection from wild beasts. Gradually, however, as the millennia succeeded one another, man became more ambitious; and as his ambitions developed, so did his skills. He began to turn his mind to new ideas and concepts, each of which seemed to demand new architectural forms: to tombs in which to be buried, monuments by which to be remembered, palaces from which to be governed and – most important of all – shrines in which he could worship his gods.

Here were challenges indeed; and the way in which these challenges have been met by different peoples at different moments of their history forms one of the principal themes of this book. But, it must be remembered, these tombs and monuments, these palaces and shrines represented only an infinitesimal fraction of the structures erected in any given period. The vast majority were the ordinary, unassuming buildings in which most people have nearly always spent most of their lives: for town dwellers, the shops and workshops and offices in which they earned their daily bread; for countrymen, the barns, stables and cattle-sheds; for everyone, everywhere, the houses in which they lived. As a general rule, the life-span of these buildings was relatively short – sometimes a century or two, more often than not considerably less. Only very occasionally did one of them manage to survive for long enough beyond its expected term to take on a certain rarity value; but where such exist today they are usually of interest more to the social historian than to the lover of architecture. Few of them find a place in the pages that follow.

And so we come to the second reason why architecture has received less respect than it deserves. There is too much of it. We see it all around us, and therefore do not see it at all. Our sensibilities become blunted, and no longer react as they would if we were confronted with a painting or a piece of sculpture. Often, alas, this is just as well. It is given to few of us – unless we have the luck to live in Rome, or Venice, or Bath – to spend our lives surrounded by really beautiful architecture. For the rest, condemned as we are to an environment that ranges, all too often, from the mediocre to the frankly atrocious, some dulling of our aesthetic sense is both necessary and beneficial. But this does not mean that we should not be able to resharpen it at will.

The problem is how to do so. Some years ago, entirely for my own benefit, I drew up a few general rules which may be worth enumerating here. Rule Number One, when you are confronted with any building of real quality, is: *Do not attempt to photograph it for at least five minutes.* All too many people, nowadays, see great works of architecture merely as compositions in a viewfinder; how much they miss! Buildings were not made for snapshots; they must be looked at long and hard. John Ruskin, who for all his idiosyncrasy and quirkiness knew more about fine architecture than most people, went even further; and in doing so framed what I suggest should be Rule Number Two. "*Don't look at buildings,*" he said, "*Watch them.*"

Rule Number Three applies particularly to churches and cathedrals, which are usually free-standing; though it is equally valid for all buildings, whenever circumstances permit. *Do not be content to look at just the show front of a building; walk, if you can, all the way round it.* Architecture is essentially a three-dimensional art and must be treated as such. Like all of us, it has a particular face which it likes to present to the world, but it is not to be known by that face alone; others can be a good deal more revealing. And, speaking of revelations, it has always been astonishing to me how much can be gained by returning for a second visit, if possible within 24 hours of the first, at a different time of day. A building that can look grim and menacing at ten o'clock in the morning with the light behind it can completely change its character when bathed in a gentle afternoon sun. Rule Number Four may not, as I know from long experience, be always possible to obey; but it is none the less important for that: *Go back.*

The fifth and last rule is to submit oneself to a brief questionnaire. The questions themselves will inevitably depend to some extent on the building concerned and also, perhaps, on the individual tastes and interest of the beholder; but here are a few suggestions to be getting on with. What are the principal materials used? Are they local, or did they have to be brought from afar? If the latter, then why? Is the building all of one date, or are there signs that it has been added to or altered? Does it hang together as a single composition, with a well-defined centre and other lesser focal points? How good is the detailing, and the workmanship? Does it, or did it, serve its purpose really well? And – enormously important – *do I like it?* This list is, I repeat, by no means exhaustive and can be extended at will; and it is no bad thing to end up by trying, more for the sake of amusement than anything else, to find one little subtlety, refinement or *jeu d'esprit* which you are confident that you would never have spotted if you had not deliberately set out to look for it.

Now the point of this questionnaire is not just to elicit the answers to the questions; it is above all to develop one's architectural eye. There are many stories told of the offence regularly given by the late Sir Nikolaus Pevsner who, when compiling his monumental series on *The Buildings of England*, would stride purposefully through a medium-sized house in 20 minutes and then be off to the next on his list, brushing aside all attempts to make him stay for tea. But for him those 20 minutes were enough. A year later the relevant volume would appear and there would be the entry on the house: two-thirds of a page, with everything just right, and not a single feature that mattered left out. Few of us, of course, can hope to develop an eye like Professor Pevsner's; but we could, nearly all of us, become a good deal more receptive than we are at present – simply by looking, consciously, at the buildings we pass every day and asking ourselves, equally consciously, what we think of them.

For with architecture, even more than its sister arts, the secret of enjoyment is understanding; and it is in an attempt to increase that understanding that this book has been designed. It has had a curious history. Its first incarnation was a volume of a relatively modest size – though, even then, considerable ambition – of which I was the general editor and to which Professor Pevsner himself contributed a foreword. That was published in 1975, and has since been translated into ten languages. In France, however, as well as appearing in translation, it formed the nucleus of a very much larger and more comprehensive survey, completely rewritten and supplemented by whole new sections on areas such as Black Africa, Korea and South-East Asia which had been omitted from the earlier volume. This enlarged version also contained nearly twice the number of illustrations – photographs, reconstructions, sections, plans, isometric and perspective cutaways. Its increased scope was made clear in the title: whereas the English parent was called, simply, *Great Architecture of the World*, the French offspring could describe itself with complete justification *Le Grand Atlas de l'Architecture Mondiale*; and it is this volume, newly translated, that you now have in your hands.

In my introduction to the former work I wrote: "Clearly it is impossible to encapsulate the whole of architectural history throughout the world in a single volume of manageable size." The present book is unanswerable proof of how wrong I was; and if the greater number of its pages are concerned with the architecture of Europe and the Western World, that is only because it is there that the most important and influential developments have occurred. Those civilizations which do not form part of this mainstream are grouped together in the first hundred pages, since they cover a wider time span and do not lend themselves to such comfortable concepts as antiquity or the Middle Ages, Renaissance or Baroque. In the remaining three-quarters of the book, the architecture of the West is treated chronologically, so that we can follow not only the development of building styles but also that of the actual techniques of construction.

At least in the earlier centuries with which we have to deal, this technical development is every bit as fascinating to me as is the strictly art-historical. Looking at the stupendous stonemasonry of Cuzco or Sacsayhuamán, for example, one finds it hard to believe that these monuments could have been built by a people who had not yet invented the wheel, who had no beasts of burden other than the highly unsatisfactory llama, no scales or weights, and no tools other than those made of the same stone as that which had to be worked. The arch, too, was unknown to the builders of pre-Hispanic America, as it was to the ancient Greeks. To this day its origins are uncertain, but its invention was to prove the most important single breakthrough in the whole history of architecture, leading as it did to the vault and thence to that noblest and most majestic of all architectural forms, the dome.

The reason for the unfailing impressiveness of any great dome is a simple one: architecture is first and foremost about the enclosure of space, and the hemispherical form will enclose more space than any other. It should not be foregotten, however, that the famous domes of Europe testify not only to the genius of the men who built them but also to their courage. Sir Christopher Wren, when he designed St. Paul's, had only seen one dome in his life, Mansart's very much smaller one on the Val de Grâce in Paris. Brunelleschi, working in Florence two and a half centuries earlier, may well have studied ancient Roman domes like that of the Pantheon; but this, being built on a circular base rather than a square one, posed far fewer technical problems than those he was so triumphantly to surmount in the cathedral of his native city. Most remarkable of all were those two architects of St. Sophia in Constantinople, whom I have already mentioned in the first paragraph of this foreword. To have contrived, as early as the 6th century, a dome some 35 metres (115 feet) across, to have given it a curve as shallow as a saucer and then to have pierced it around the base with no less than 40 windows was an achievement not far short of miraculous. When a contemporary wrote that it seemed to be suspended from heaven by a golden chain, he was speaking no more than the truth.

All these buildings, and well over a thousand others, are described and illustrated here. Each can of course be studied as an individual work of art; for myself, however, I prefer to see them as constituent parts of a long and magnificent story. That story began when early man first fashioned for himself a settled habitation. It continued as he taught himself, by trial and error, the fundamental principles of construction; as he invented better and better tools, and the techniques by which to make them; as he gradually acquired and refined his manual skills; as he discovered new materials and developed means of transporting them from forest, mine or quarry; and as, little by little, he established his mastery over them – first mud, then wood, then brick, then stone and, finally, marble.

Long before that process was complete, he had become not only a builder but an artist. From earliest times he had been accustomed to decorate the walls of his dwelling with paintings, often of remarkable power, just as in later chapters of the story he would turn to painters and sculptors, plaster-workers and mosaicists to embellish his work after its completion; but he had also perceived the possibility of creating another beauty, purely architectural – a beauty that was inherent in the lines and proportions and perspectives of the building itself and not merely applied to its surface. With that perception, true architecture was born.

Whatever the cynics may say, it is not yet dead. The last quarter-century has seen the construction of several masterpieces that can stand comparison with any of those of the past: the East Wing of the National Gallery of Art in Washington D.C. or the superb Olympic Stadium in Tokyo, to name but two of the examples included in this book. And the story remains unfinished. Somewhere, in their various corners of the world, the great architects of tomorrow are already at work, crouched on their school-room floors, slowly and with infinite care laying one wooden brick on top of another.

9

Introduction

Architecture is perhaps the most familiar of all the arts, but at the same time the least well understood. Some of the reasons for this have already been suggested in the foreword to this book. Another major cause of ignorance and indifference is the virtual absence of architectural history and aesthetics from the curricula of our schools and colleges. The essentially literary outlook of our culture is largely to blame for this neglect (the practical teaching of art being no substitute for proper instruction in architectural appreciation). Such disregard cannot, however, be justified, for only a little groundwork is required to make architecture as accessible and rewarding as any of the other arts.

This book in part hopes to remedy the situation, beginning with a few guidelines on how to approach and "read" a building – a habit which, once acquired, will greatly enrich the experience both of the traveller through time, who explores architecture through books and illustrations, and of the real-life traveller, who has the good fortune to visit and study at first hand some of the world's great monuments. It then goes on to provide plentiful examples for study, arranged for the most part chronologically and geographically so that the reader can appreciate not only the social and cultural forces that led to the creation of various styles, but also the technical and practical considerations that shaped their development.

Understanding what a building is

A building does not express its meaning in the same way as a picture or a sculpture, because it is by nature much more complex. It demands a prior effort of analysis. In the first place, we never see a building in its totality: we can never obtain more than partial views both of the exterior and interior, with the result that we are always obliged to relate what we can see to what we cannot see to form a clear picture of the whole. It is impossible simply to indulge the pleasure of the eye: one has to think as well as look. To help us in this intellectual exercise we have an important tool to hand, the plan, which informs us simultaneously about exterior and interior, the whole and the part. Together with the cross section, which reveals the structure, it gives in abstract form a composite image of the building which photographs – in whatever number – could never give (fig. 1). It is therefore necessary, before anything else, to learn to read a plan and to familiarize oneself in a general way with the various means of graphic expression used in architecture (cross section, elevation, axonometric plan).

The transformations to which buildings are subject constitute a second difficulty. Very often we can no longer see today what the builders would have wished: projects are abandoned or modified

fig. 1 – *The importance of drawings: the plan (left) reveals the perfectly unified organization of the dome of Les Invalides; the section (right) opens to view the complex structure of the inner domes (in stone) and the outer dome (in wood): the first inner dome is open at the top, allowing the upper part of the second inner dome to be seen – illuminated by windows concealed at a lower level behind the first dome. (See p. 304 for an exterior view of the building.)*

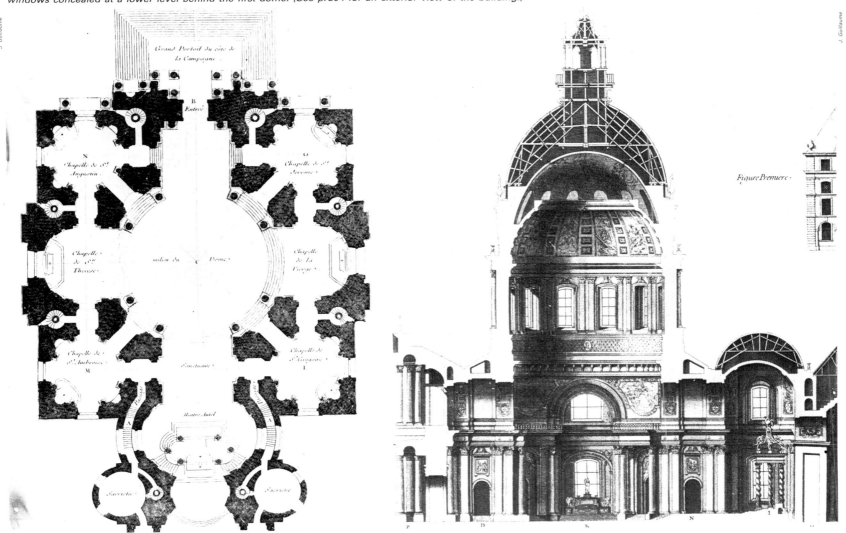

11

Introduction

before completion, parts that were complete are demolished, others, added later, are of a different character. Time, it is true, alters all works of art, but its effect on architecture is more noticeable because the construction of a major building takes a long time, and because buildings – always intended for use – must be adapted to the changing needs of men. We should not, therefore, look at a building completed at one stretch and still more or less intact, such as Salisbury Cathedral, in the same way as we regard an incomplete château, such as Brissac, or a building that has been continuously altered, such as Versailles. In the first unusual case, we are immediately in a position to appreciate the work of the builders; in the second, we have to imagine what was intended (fig. 2); and in the third case, we have to discover the successive stages of building to interpret correctly what we see, and not attribute to the intention of a single architect what was the product of several building campaigns.

Finally, it should never be forgotten that even the most magnificent buildings were never intended simply as works of art, and that they are incomprehensible if one is unaware of their purpose, whether utilitarian or symbolic. The particular forms of religious buildings, houses and palaces, are always a reflection of the demands of religious cult, of everyday life, or of the exercise of power in any given society. Less independent than other artists, the architect exercises his powers of invention within a framework strictly defined by the society to which he belongs and the individuals to whom he owes each commission. Such constraints, compelling to a degree dependent on the particular age and social level (the Greek temple, the urban dwelling, are highly standardized types), impose limits on invention, but also confer on architecture an important social significance: buildings are a unique embodiment – the most durable, the most manifest – of the needs and dreams of men.

All these observations lead to the same conclusion: a work of architecture is too complex to be understood at first glance: one has simultaneously to be aware of all its elements, to imagine its successive states (including those that were never completed), and to know what it signified to those who built it. This initial analysis must precede aesthetic appreciation. It enables one to form a clear picture of the building and to differentiate between what is due to constraints (structural necessity, existing buildings, stylistic conventions, demands of the client), and what is the product of purely artistic creation, the play of forms.

Reading the form of a building

We take an interest in a building to the degree to which we see in it "effects" of volume, space, rhythm and colour that please us. In certain cases – an urban dwelling or rural architecture, for example – these effects are very simple and result above all from harmony between a building and its environment. In other cases – the most interesting – these effects are extremely complex and can be attributed to one or more creative individuals who have deliberately contrived them. Between these two extremes – architecture without

architects and the architecture of great masters – there are numerous degrees, but it would be pointless to distinguish them. It is more worthwhile to identify the various means of expression available to architecture: only in this way can we enrich our perception of the buildings we encounter.

Volumes

Seen from the outside, a building first of all appears as a volume or, more often, as a combination of different volumes – horizontal or vertical, compact or spread out. The Greek temple and the Gothic cathedral represent two entirely opposed conceptions of volume. Let us, however, draw attention to less striking contrasts. The château of St. Loup-sur-Thouet, for example, illustrates perfectly the French taste for volumes that are alternately upright and horizontal, each one identified by a high roof (fig. 3). Under the influence of Italian architecture, which favoured simple, square volumes (see Palazzo Strozzi, p. 273), the central and corner pavilions little by little lost their independence – without ever completely disappearing. Starting at Maisons (see p. 305), this evolution was completed by the 18th century, when all that remained were slight projections below a single low roof: harsh contrasts and emphatic rhythms had given way to a more fluent grouping of elements (Hôtel Matignon, fig. 3).

The individual form of each volume plays an equally important part: the straight, cylindrical volumes of the dome of Les Invalides, Paris and the Taj Mahal (see fig. 1, p. 62 and p. 304) appear perfectly stable and serene – conveying an impression of eternity – while the concave and protuberant forms of Sant' Ivo della Sapienza, Rome (see p. 303) seem to interrelate in such a way as never to achieve stability. The materials used in 20th century architecture have opened up a number of expressive possibilities: cantilevered projections, sloping walls and "free" volumes treated like sculpture, are just some of these original effects (see Notre-Dame-du-Haut, Ronchamp, p. 381).

Façades

No architectural volume, except for a pyramid, has completely smooth and "blind" surfaces. Façades are always animated by openings, by recessed or projecting features, or by contrasts of colour. The elements which are thus brought together can be of many types, but it is possible to divide them into three groups – relating to the wall, to the structure, and to decoration.

Solids and voids

The number, shape and distribution of openings to a large degree determines the character of a façade. Italian *palazzi* appear massive because their windows are relatively small, whereas houses in northern Europe are more open, and appear lighter. At the Hôtel Matignon for example (fig. 3), the architect has incorporated a great

fig. 2 – *A drawn reconstruction enables the initial project to be "seen" and an incomplete building to be appreciated at its true worth: the château of Brissac as it is and as it was supposed to be.*

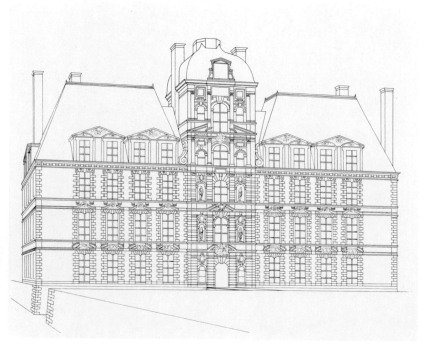

J. Feuillie, Arch. Phot. Paris/S.P.A.D.E.M.

12

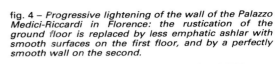

fig. 4 – Progressive lightening of the wall of the Palazzo Medici-Riccardi in Florence: the rustication of the ground floor is replaced by less emphatic ashlar with smooth surfaces on the first floor, and by a perfectly smooth wall on the second.

fig. 3 – Château of St. Loup-sur-Thouet (top) and the Hôtel Matignon in Paris. A radical change in the play of volumes can be seen within the same type of composition with five elements: in the later building, the central and corner pavilions become no more than slight projections and the verticality disappears.

fig. 5 – Effects created by surfaces: transparent glass at the Illinois Institute of Technology (Mies van der Rohe), and rugged concrete at Boston City Hall (Paul Rudolph).

13

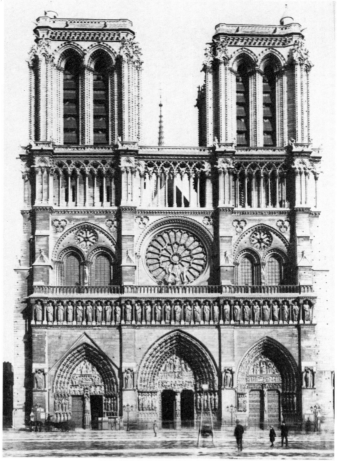

fig. 6 – *Multiplication of vertical lines makes the façade of Reims Cathedral appear more extended than that of Notre-Dame, Paris, even though their general proportions are roughly similar.*

number of windows whose tall, narrow proportions contrast happily with the horizontality of the mass of the building; by slightly modifying their spacing he has varied the rhythm and given greater "weight" to the lateral pavilions that terminate the façade.

The solid areas themselves appear more or less weighty depending on the physical surface of the wall: smooth, shiny or coloured surfaces lighten a building whereas rusticated surfaces (roughened and marked by sunk joints) give an effect of solidity (fig. 4). Rustication is often used on the ground floor to form a base (see also Palazzo Caprini, p. 278), or in the form of quoins, to emphasize the corners (fig. 3). Modern architects are also aware of the effects that can be obtained through materials alone – or, rather, through their appearance: rough concrete and faceted claddings emphasize the strength of a wall, while glass walls give buildings an insubstantial character – an effect well known to Gothic architects (fig. 5).

Lines of force

Most façades are articulated by some kind of membering, standing out either in relief or in colour, to provide accents and set up rhythms. Members are generally horizontal or vertical; they can even be free-standing and independent when the wall becomes simply a row of supports (in a colonnade, for instance). The façades of

fig. 7 – *Windows breaking through the entablature are evidence of a conflict between horizontal and vertical emphasis: the little château of Chantilly (engraving by Du Cerceau).*

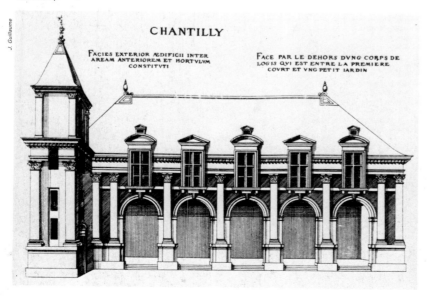

cathedrals clearly show the importance of membering: Reims Cathedral appears taller, more slender and more rhythmic than Notre-Dame, Paris, because its vertical members are thinner, more numerous and set closer together, and because they rise uninterrupted to the top of the towers (fig. 6). Architecture in antiquity and the Renaissance had no sense of this dynamic linearity: classical buildings emphasize the horizontal mouldings dividing the storeys and the topmost cornice – a sharply projecting feature that clearly defines the upper limit of the volume (fig. 4). The two traditions, Gothic and classical, came into conflict when Italian forms penetrated northwards in the 16th century: such hybrid features as windows cut through the main entablature and extending into the roof created a new, animated effect (fig. 7).

By adjusting the horizontal and vertical members (especially secondary ones, since the primary members are always more or less bound by the storeys), by moving them closer together or further apart, by giving them different emphasis, interesting and varied rhythms can be obtained. Architects from the Renaissance onwards have systematically explored these possibilities, using the classical system of pilasters, columns and entablatures in all manner of combinations, developing numerous kinds of bay unit and interpenetrating the Orders (fig. 8).

Members can also be accentuated or attenuated in relief. Gothic architects used progressively finer and more ductile mouldings which seemed endowed with a life of their own on the surface of the wall (see Santa Maria del Mar, Barcelona, p. 223), while Renaissance and later architects employed heavier, fuller members which were integral with the wall and were able to express its internal strength and tensions (see the upper part of the façade of Santa Maria della Pace, p. 303). Somerset House in London or the example of the Louvre shown here (fig. 9) indicate the varying effects that can be produced by slight alterations of relief or rhythm.

Ornament

Ornament can be natural or geometric, coloured or in relief, consisting in mouldings or developed across a flat surface, confined within a frame or freely disposed. Formed of small-scale and disparate elements, ornament sets up a subtle play of light and shade, or of colour, very different from the bolder architectural effects. When it reproduces animal, vegetable, or human forms, it also brings a literal animation into the abstract world of architecture. It plays very different roles, in different times and places: it can proliferate (see the Alhambra of Granada, p. 259), obscure the structure (see sacristy of the Carthusians, Granada, p. 324) or underline it (see tholos of

fig. 8 – Complex rhythms. On the left, a syncopated rhythm of bays (Ancy-le-Franc): the pilasters are grouped in pairs, separated by a niche, instead of following one after another at equal intervals. On the right, interpenetration of Orders (Campidoglio, Rome): two small Ionic Orders contend with the major Corinthian Order.

fig. 9 – Variation in the use of the Orders on the first floor of the Louvre. The corner pavilion is required to unite two very different façades: on the left, pilasters with regular spacing, on the right, free-standing columns grouped in pairs set forward from the wall. The left-hand façade of the pavilion only has pilasters, like the neighbouring façade, but these are doubled at the corners. The right-hand façade has paired members, like the colonnade beside it, but these are mainly pilasters, not columns; also, the rhythm is interrupted at the centre to allow room for a large window. Notice the reappearance of columns on either side of this window; the setting back of the central bay and the resultant play of shadow imparts to the pavilion a remarkable plasticity and establishes a continuity between this "flat" volume and the colonnade.

fig. 10 – Two types of spatial dynamism: the vertical and horizontal thrust of Bourges Cathedral, the progressive expansion of the internal spaces of St. Peter's in Rome.

15

fig. 11 – *The Piazza and Piazzetta, Venice: the* campanile *and basilica define the space and determine the disposition of the two squares. The arrangement of these areas invites movement, because there is no single privileged viewpoint: the façades are revealed in succession and the shape of the space changes with each step.*

Epidaurus, p. 131). In all cases it creates its own effects which reinforce, elaborate or oppose the strictly architectural effects.

Internal space

Volumes and façades determine the external appearance of a building. It remains to discover what is enclosed behind those walls, that "reverse space" which is unique to architecture: "in giving definitive form to this spatial void architecture is in truth creating its own world" (Henri Focillon). No photograph, unfortunately, can reproduce the impression made by a space that completely envelops the spectator and which he discovers gradually as he moves around and explores a building.

Anyone who has entered a great Gothic church has experienced the dynamic quality of its space – the predominance of vertical members, the virtual disappearance of walls, the lightness of the vaults, the rapid succession of bays; all these direct our gaze both upwards and towards the apse without any intervening obstruction (fig. 10, left). This taste for dynamic space recurred in another form in the domed churches of the Renaissance and the Baroque (in contrast with the internal space of the Pantheon in Rome, which is strictly static). At St. Peter's in Rome the immense space becomes ever more vast as one moves up the nave, and the broadening out at the crossing (achieved by the use of cut-away piers) and the prodigious volume of the dome (made to seem still larger by the handling of light) are gradually revealed (fig. 10, right). Far from weighing down on its supports, the dome appears suspended, held up by an irresistible force. The sense of movement is not the product of uninterrupted lines, but of the skilful coordination of increasingly large spaces.

The forms of St. Peter's are perfectly clear, with the result that the spaces, however vast, are always exactly defined. In German Baroque churches, on the other hand, space appears elusive and subject to continuous movement: the walls lose all solidity, articulation disappears, lines undulate, and an all-pervasive light sets stucco and paintings aglow: we are transported into an insubstantial, animated, vibrant world, with undefined limits (see the abbey church at Ottobeuren, p. 322).

Thus each major style has its own spatial qualities that can stimulate sensations beyond those of everyday experience. In the West, the most important examples are in religious architecture because it commandeered the largest spaces, but spatial effects were also created in secular architecture – by successions of rooms of different shapes and by the elaboration of staircases. What an extraordinary sequence of this kind is afforded by the Paris Opéra! After passing through two relatively low entrance foyers, the visitor suddenly finds himself in the immense space of the staircase, open to further space on three sides. As he climbs the steps and follows the staircase round, he is made aware of all that is around him, and he perceives more and more clearly the secondary spaces that extend the principal space beyond the screen of columns: before he has even entered the auditorium, he is already in the magic world of theatre (see p. 351).

External space

Streets and squares are open-air spaces enclosed by architecture in much the same way as internal spaces. In some cases – once rare, now common – an architect uses the elements of a city to create an urban composition: he calculates his effects, places the elements in relation to one another and, if he is capable of it, contrives surprises – in compositions of this type the danger is always monotony and overstatement. In older cities, on the other hand, the layout is generally the product of many years of history. Made up of small-scale elements and disposed in a very haphazard fashion, the streets and squares give rise to a constant succession of spatial experiences – quite independent of the interest of the buildings that border them. Rather than impose an artificial regularity on such spaces, architects have often drawn inspiration from them: they have kept the site and existing buildings in mind when building anew. In this way the most interesting urban compositions have been built up gradually over the centuries – for example, the Piazza and Piazzetta of Venice, perfectly disposed around the *campanile* (fig. 11).

A systematic introduction to the art of architecture would require a book in itself. But the preceding remarks should at least be of assistance when it comes to identifying some of the architect's means of expression and hence in perceiving his effects.

This perception should not be equated with aesthetic appreciation, but it is a necessary precondition. Without it, spontaneous judgments which appear to be expressions of personal opinion do no more than repeat preconceived ideas – on the "bareness" of the Romanesque, the "excesses" of the Baroque, the "frigidity" of classical churches. . . . Thus we could not recommend to the reader too strongly to forget such prejudices and to look with a fresh eye and open mind in order to appreciate the objectives peculiar to each style. Works of art cannot, in fact, be appreciated absolutely, but only within their own context, by reference to the most original and expressive works of their type. Hence the importance of the history of art and the importance of this book, which gathers together a great number of examples of high quality. Now it is up to the reader to make his or her own exploration of architecture and so to learn to love it.

16

NON-EUROPEAN CIVILIZATIONS

M. Arnaud

Tower of the Four Doors at the old Buddhist monastery of Shendong Si, Shandong

A religious building, this small stone edifice dates from the Wei dynasty (386–534). Like all pagodas, it has great symbolic significance. Standing in the grounds of the Temple of Shendong Si, one of the great religious centres in 6th century China, the tower expresses architectural mastery over space: its four doors face the four cardinal points. Inside, four statues of the Buddha sit in the lotus position, symbolizing the four stages in his life; they gaze radiantly in the four directions defined by the building's orientation.

Chinese architecture is not merely the art of construction, it is the art of ordering space. It is not only the product but also a kind of guarantee of the social and historical context in which it developed over a long period of time. Concerned with town planning and the creation of gardens, patterns of building were dictated only to a limited extent by the function of the construction. Towns and buildings were conceived in the image of the cosmos, and their planning and design were intended to reflect both its permanence and movement. Because of an animistic conception of the universe, space was invested with a dynamic quality, and this had to be captured, in architecture in particular, which thus became an applied magic or geomancy. An analysis of urban construction and architectural design on the level of form is therefore inconceivable without taking into account the concepts of space, both global and dynamic, which condition all Chinese architecture.

The cosmic analogy dictates Chinese design, from the grandest to the humblest buildings; this can be seen in the similarity of methods and materials used in every construction, be it funerary, religious or residential. However, the forms used, derived from a blend of interwoven modular design and a strict regularity of structural support, are free enough to permit supple variation in the appearance of buildings. The logical and flexible approach of Chinese architects meant that they developed the potential of wooden structures to a remarkable degree; the complex bracketed capital stands as the symbol of this. Their nature and techniques ensured continuity, and a unity of style was created by their constant reference to tradition. In every building project the decoration was subject to a rigorous canon, determined primarily by function. Constant reference was made over the centuries to the magnificent buildings of the past, though the freshness of the original designs was never recaptured.

In spite of this relative homogeneity it is essential "to emphasize the clearly defined differences between northern and southern China" (M. Pirazzoli). In the north, a land of windswept steppes, vast plateaux, open plains, and where the climate moves from one extreme to another, people are fairly mobile. Towns are laid out in regular grid patterns, their wide streets lined with single-storeyed houses. Stonework, often massive, is the most widespread means of construction. The traditional use of wood has long been restricted because of progressive deforestation. On the other hand, the temperate, humid climate of southern China provides the builder with a wide choice of good-quality timber. When masonry is called for, southern Chinese architects tend to make play with geometric forms, exploiting curves and taking advantage of the transparency of lattice panelling to let cool breezes circulate through the rooms; wide windows open out on to artistically landscaped gardens. Plant life is prolific in these towns that cling to craggy and tormented landscapes; it decorates the narrow, winding streets or lines the busy waterways.

The economic use of local building materials, architectural features ingeniously designed to withstand the rigours of the climate and central heating by warm air circulating under the floor are just some of the traditional ideas that are being revived by contemporary Chinese architects responsible for building programmes and environmental planning.

The history of Chinese architecture can be traced back nearly 4,000 years. Recent archaeological excavations in the Yellow River region have revealed the typical disposition of the earliest Bronze Age settlements. During the Shang dynasty (c.1765–1122BC) urban fortifications made of mud began to appear, and a clear distinction between religious and domestic buildings emerged. In Henan province, first at Zhengzhou (16th–14th century BC) and later at Anyang (14th–11th century BC), the most important towns testify to a hierarchical social order which was essentially religious. The symmetrical construction of the Ancestral Temple and of the shrine to the god of the soil, standing on either side of the town's southern axis, is the first indication of a balancing division of space. According to E. von Erdberg Comsten, "Chinese builders also confronted technical problems. How were they to erect a framework that could support a roof and that would allow the spaces in between the pillars to be filled in by walls?"

Corner pavilion, Forbidden City, Peking. Four corner pavilions punctuate the high wall surrounding the ancient imperial residence. The fortifications, dating from the 15th to 18th centuries, are reinforced by a wide moat.

B. Jeannel

Wooden pillars rested on stone or bronze discs with cross beams joining them at their highest point. Roofs were usually gabled, with the ridge set longitudinally. In larger rooms an interior row of wooden pillars was erected along the longitudinal axis to forestall any weakening in the cross beams under the heavy weight of the roof. The building's main entrance was set in the centre of the south façade, with the gable-ends facing east and west. Stone foundations, pisé (or mud infill) walls, simple wooden jointing and thatch roofs were all characteristic of Chinese architecture before the discovery of iron.

During the Zhou dynasty (1122–221BC) architecture was stimulated by the dissemination of new building methods, although there was no real break with traditional concepts: rather, affirmation of the same principles and a desire to improve upon the past. There was now a masonry-hewn stone or moulded brick. Thanks to mortise and tenon joints, buildings could be much wider, in spite of the increased weight of the roofs which from this time onwards were tiled. The dimensions of palaces, which consisted of several buildings surrounding a paved courtyard, demonstrate the enormous progress being made: the palace at Handan (Hebei), built at the beginning of the 4th century BC, has a courtyard 300 metres (330 yards) in circumference, whereas the perimeter of the courtyard of the 3rd century BC palace of Afang Gong is 1,200 metres (some 1,300 yards).

The design of the Zhou dynasty's capital city, as described in the Zhou rituals, was based on an initial square outline and a centralized, strictly axial plan. Land belonging to the city is defined by a series of concentric circles. These begin at the wall surrounding the palace and encompass both the fortified area of the city and its adjacent farmland. The principal axis, leading to the south-facing Audience Hall, enters the city through the monumental gate in the south wall. To balance the composition, the markets are situated in the northern part of the city between the palace and the wall. Placed symmetrically on either side of the Royal Approach, to the south-east and south-west of the palace, stand the Ancestral Temple and the Altar of the Soil, the former on a square podium, the latter on a circular foundation.

The Zhou ceremonial effectively establishes a relationship between architectural form, a building's function and its use of space. The cosmic symbolism of the city is characterized by 12 gates, placed at regular intervals along the four walls and representing the 12 phases of the

Pavilion of Rest in the garden of the Humble Administrator (Zhuozheng Yuan), Suzhou, 16th century. Architectural form and design encourage a greater intimacy with nature, thus echoing the cosmic harmony expressed by the symbolic composition of the landscaped garden.

moon in the cycle of the zodiac. The architectural symbolism embodies the bond between the universe and humanity, expressing the relationship between time and space: the east is associated with spring, the south with summer, the west with autumn and the north with winter. Thus the ritual may be considered to be part of the architectural design: it is the first stage in the application of geometry to form. A site is chosen not only for practical considerations but also for its health-giving and aesthetic qualities.

During this period, the Chinese first built ramparts of rocks and stones along the mountain crests to the north to protect themselves against barbarous tribes, thus reinforcing the unity of their sacred domain. Rituals for building these followed an identical pattern, and their construction involved official state architects, who could devote their time exclusively to the study of construction techniques and the preparation of sites. These rituals sought to join the earth's positive and negative energies, which were themselves dependent on the four factors governing the movements of the heavens. These four factors corresponded to the succession of seasons that governed human activity. The first energy, which gives rise to yin (light) and yang (shade), is called qi (spirit). The cyclical relationships of yin and yang obey certain rules known as li or natural order.

These relationships are mathematically quantifiable by numbers placed in "magic squares". These three components determine the "aspect" of nature, the forms and features of which cannot be directly perceived by the senses.

The division of the zodiac into 12 animal signs, featured on ritual compasses, established a relationship between time and space which was, however, slightly upset by the precession of the equinoxes. Also featured were the four animals corresponding to the cardinal points and the qualities belonging to them – their colours, matter, form, stars and plants. The purpose of the ritual was to calculate the most favourable conjunctions between certain figures taken from the "magic squares" and the principal heavenly bodies: the sun, the moon and the five planets. This dynamic and cyclical conception of nature was connected with the theory of the five elements, which were associated with the four cardinal points and the central point. They were correlated with the seasons and years and possessed a creative or destructive power, depending on the direction in which they travelled through space. Ceremonies in the temples and palaces were governed by these principles; the centre was known as the "yellow earth", and here the emperor would sit. The ceremonies that took place in the Temple of Heaven under the last Chinese

and 13th centuries AD refer to the Chinese originals. In the case of the "shinden" residences of the Japanese princes, as in those of their Chinese equivalents, garden composition conformed to geomantic ritual. The stream or river was channelled from the landscaped garden and flowed into the lake around the islands of Paradise. Flowing in the direction of the cosmos, the river bore the nature spirits under the building, thus purifying the home and blessing the inhabitants. As the world of the dead was often thought to be an inversion of this world, the direction of the river was sometimes reversed in temples dedicated to the protection of the dead.

The text of the Sakutei-ki, the earliest manual of Japanese gardens, was copied, according to its author, from a manuscript brought over by a Chinese Buddhist monk who was wellknown for his designs of temple gardens in China. Its detailed instructions on how to respect nature's laws

The Great Wall at Badaling, north of Peking. Started in the 5th century BC during the period of the Warring States, the Great Wall, which with its many branches is more than 6,000 kilometres (3,700 miles) long, owes its present appearance to restoration work undertaken by the Ming Emperors between the 15th and 17th centuries.

dynasty were echoed by those held by the Han rulers in the Ming Tang. *Both performed ritual "journeys" to the "four countries" and the "nine provinces" which were bordered by the sacred "mountains" at which they would rest. Mountains corresponded to stars, and large expanses of water to the Milky Way. The "Middle Empire" lay at the centre of the "four seas" beyond the mountains. But, although generally observed by most of the dynasties, these rituals were not always considered to be infallible. Some modifications to the laws governing the siting of a building are known. In the 6th century, the Emperor Wendi pronounced: "I cannot deny that the site of my father's tomb is auspicious, because I have come to the throne; but I cannot affirm that it is, either, because my brother has died in battle."*

Dili fengshui, *or geomancy, which was*

Pavilion of Introspection, Fragrant Hills, Peking. An example of a charming woodland retreat (17th–19th century); a circular gallery runs along the edge of the pool, which is situated in the middle of the buildings.

applied and developed during the Song period, could also be translated as "the geography of wind and water". There is an interesting parallel with the 6th century BC treatise called Waters, Arts and Places *by* Hippocrates, *which described the procedure of the Greeks before they constructed their towns.*

In the same way, the five elements – air, water, fire, wood and metal – cited in I Ching (The Book of Changes) *are also the essential substances used in Western alchemy. They were familiar to the Middle East of the day and Vitruvius's architectural treatise also speaks of their influence. Nevertheless the practice of geomancy was much more widespread in China than in the West; indeed, it is still practised today, especially in Taiwan, Korea and Japan. In the People's Republic it is allowed only at burial rites. The work of a geomancer involved assessing the character of the landscape, with which he then tried to harmonize the forms and arrangement of the buildings: so far his duties were similar to those of an architect. However, his work also included the management and organization of various ceremonies and the calculation of a calendar for the project's execution. Once the project was completed the geomancer checked the building's conformity to the original plan and to its environment. It was also his more difficult task to listen to nature's subtle "spirits", conveyed by the wind and the rivers, and to distinguish auguries of good or bad fortune. When considering a site he was guided by the ideal configurations set out in his handbook: for instance, if the site were bordered by a chain of mountains to the east whose outline resembled that of a green dragon, then it might be considered appropriate. To the west he expected the white tiger, symbol of liberation, and to the north the black tortoise, symbol of death. The beneficent south was symbolized by a red phoenix. To counteract the influence of an environment that did not conform to the ritual, there was a range of options open to the geomancer – architect—he could build a pagoda, redirect the course of a river, or plant trees.*

In the art of garden composition, geomancy again dictated the principles of the design. The original Chinese documents are lost, but Japanese texts and designs of the 12th

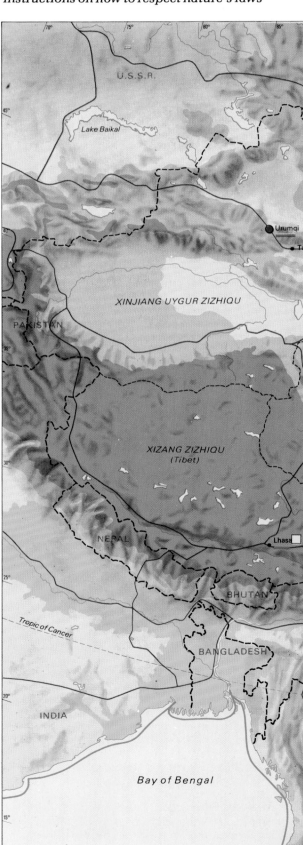

and apply Chinese geomancy are all the more useful as contemporary Chinese texts have disappeared. The treatise dictates that stones should be positioned just as they were found in their natural state, before being transported to the garden; "they should never be positioned upside down, and stones found on their side should never be placed upright." Groups of stones designed to represent sacred mountains should not be placed to the north-east of the home, although this is the situation recommended for temple gardens. The axes of the groups of stones must not be aligned with the columns of the building. The rules of the Sakutei-ki on planting trees and shrubs exactly correspond to those mentioned in Chinese treatises of domestic geomancy. "If there is no road to the west then seven mulberry trees should be planted; if there are no mountains to the north then plant three cypress trees; if there is no pond to the south then plant nine camphor trees; if there is no river to the east

then plant nine willows." The ideal ritual procedure and the suggested designs relate to the numbers and symbols of the Book of Changes and correspond to the criteria used in the siting of ancient Chinese capitals where orientation, layout, materials, numbers, attributes and symbols were all important. Time was also included since mulberry trees recall the season of silk-worm breeding which lasts until the end of the autumn; evergreen cypresses symbolize immortality during the winter; camphor trees are associated with summer; and the willow signifies spring.

Founded upon these principles, which indicate the perfectionism of Chinese thought, architecture and town planning needed the support of a strong government to evolve fully. It was during the reign of Emperor Qin, who reunited the country in 221BC, and under the Han dynasty (206BC–AD220), that building activity flourished in the region around Chang'an

(now Xi'an) and Luoyang. With the building of several capitals of geometric design, the Han dynasty developed the habit of constantly changing their seat of government, thus creating rivalry between capitals. The construction of identical towns and buildings based on previous designs assured mastery in composition and technique.

Han palaces comprise a series of buildings arranged in geometrical order. The state apartments lie on the principal axis, with secondary buildings on either side. The latter are smaller replicas of the state apartments and are made up of a succession of courtyards and galleries. Taken together, the buildings clearly express both their unity and diversity, and the hierarchy of their functions. From this time onwards architects planned larger and larger structures, and designs became more and more complicated, though the basic concept conformed to tradition.

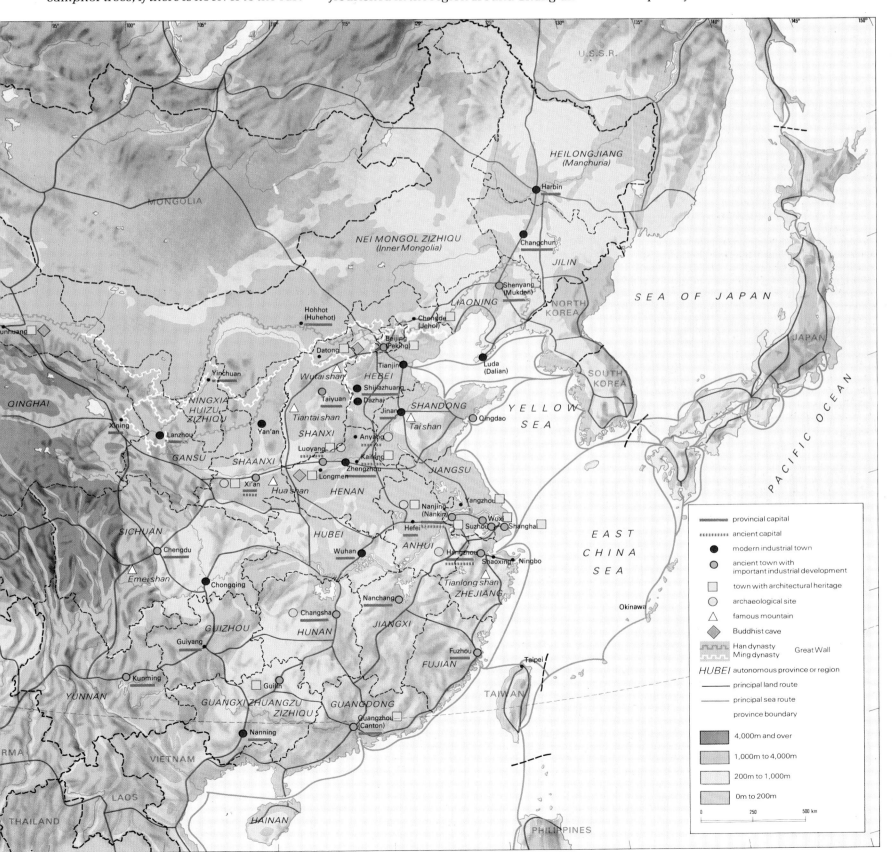

	provincial capital
	ancient capital
●	modern industrial town
◐	ancient town with important industrial development
◻	town with architectural heritage
○	archaeological site
△	famous mountain
◇	Buddhist cave
	Han dynasty / Ming dynasty — Great Wall
HUBEI	autonomous province or region
——	principal land route
——	principal sea route
	province boundary

4,000m and over
1,000m to 4,000m
200m to 1,000m
0m to 200m

0   250   500 km

Civilization	Architecture

500,000–200,000BC Palaeolithic period. Traces of man at Zhoukoudian near Peking; stone tools.

200,000–10,000BC Remains of civilization in Shanxi and Shaanxi provinces.

10,000–5,000BC Neolithic period. Microlithic industry, painted pottery, cultivated grains, hunting and fishing.

3,000–2,000BC Agriculture at Yangshao and Longshan. Use of wood.

2,000–1,900BC End of the neolithic period. Legendary Xia dynasty. Relations with the Middle East.

1,800–900BC Bronze Age. Shang (1,800–1,100) and Zhou (1,100–300) dynasties. Middle Eastern influence on craft industry. Religious power divided between states. Contrast between urban aristocracy and peasants. Invention of writing.

800–500BC Period of the Spring and Autumn Annals.

500–300BC Period of the Warring States. Agriculture on deforested land. Emergence of ritual codes and state hierarchies. Growth in commercial activity. Iron Age: radical changes through use of metal tools. Field irrigation. Developments in armaments and transport (wheeled cart). Progress made in silkworm breeding. Growth of towns and trade. Establishment of traditional political structures. Historical and philosophical writings.

300–200BC Qin Shi Huangdi achieved Chinese unity (221BC). Construction of road network. Destruction of ancient books. Revolts.

206BC–AD8 Early Han dynasty. Large landed estates. Reorganization of the imperial government.

AD9–25 Xin dynasty.

25–220 Late Han dynasty. Spread of Taoism. Revolts.

221–581 Period of the Three Kingdoms and the dynasties of the North and South. Incursions from barbarian nomads. Advent of Buddhism. Relations with Korea. Progress in craft industry. Distribution of agricultural land.

386–534 Wei dynasty (Toba).

495 Revival of Luoyang under Emperor Xiaowen Di.

581–618 Sui dynasty. First official relations with Japan.

618–907 Tang dynasty. Enforcement of imperial power throughout the country. Culture, religion and art flourish. Reform of farming statute (624): collective system introduced.

907–60 Period of the Five Dynasties and the Ten Kingdoms. The country divided, with the Liao occupying the Peking region (916).

960–1276 Northern and Southern Song dynasties. Period of the Northern Song in Kaifeng (960–1127): the height of Chinese civilization.

10,000–5,000BC Signs of cave dwellers, particularly to the south-west of Peking.

5,000BC Remains of habitation in northern China and the valley of the Yellow River (Banpo).

2,000BC Remains at Banpo (upper level).

1,700BC Shang capitals at Zhengzhou (1,600–1,400) and Anyang (1,400–1,100) (Henan province).

1,500–800BC Feudal cities of rectangular plan. Earth forts and buildings with foundations. Wooden structures, *pisé* (mud) walls and thatched roofs. Underground or sunken houses and pole-and-branch huts. Tombs of aristocrats with human victims. Remains at the sites of Xi'an and Luoyang (750).

800–200BC Metal tools advance building with wood (mortise frameworks). Use of baked building materials: bricks, tiles and paints. Progress in fortification: Great Wall and city walls. Palace and popular dwellings differentiated by construction statutes. Capital established at Xianyang (site of present Xi'an, Shaanxi, 221–206BC). Palace and gardens at Afang Gong. Tumulus of Qin Shi Huangdi (210BC). Reinforcement of the Great Wall.

200BC–AD200 Few architectural remains but objects found in burial chambers have yielded information. Remains at Chang'an (site of Xi'an). First examples of "Islands of Paradise" in ornamental gardens.

AD200–400 Remains at Luoyang.

400–800 Buddhist structures. Caves at Dunhuang, Yungang and Longmen (4th and 5th centuries), pagodas and temples of Song Shan (Henan) and Licheng (Shandong, AD544), symbolic, landscaped temple gardens (7th century).

500–600 Tombs around Nankin.

581–618 Rebuilding of capitals Chang'an and Luoyang. Building of the Grand Canal. Anji Qiao, vaulted stone bridge in Zhaoxian (Hebei).

634 Building of Daming Gong palace in Chang'an.

652–707 Great and Small Goose pagodas in Chang'an.

End of 8th century Poets' gardens at Chang'an and Luoyang.

857–77 Great hall of Buddhist temple Foguang Si in Wutai Shan (Shanxi).

916 New plan of Peking by the Liao.

918 Tomb of Wang Jian at Chengdu, (Sichuan).

937 Pagoda of Heli Ta in Nankin.

960 The Song arrive at Kaifeng, Henan (new plan of the city, palaces and gardens).

Civilization	Architecture

1115–1234 Jin dynasty in Peking. Capture of Kaifeng.

1127–1276 Government of the Southern Song dynasty in Hangzhou. Cultural revival (schools, academies, fine arts). Literate and merchant middle class.

1264 Kublai Khan settles in Peking. The arrival of Marco Polo and the first European missionaries.

1276–1368 Yuan dynasty. Genghis Khan captures China.

1368–1644 Ming dynasty. Nankin becomes capital city (1368–1409). Expulsion of the Mongols. Restructuring of the country. Naval expeditions. Increase in population. Political influence of the eunuchs and localized rebellions.

1644–1911 Manchurian Qing dynasty. Growth in the population from 150 million in 1680 to 450 million in 1860. Arrival of Europeans, colonial wars. Contrast between industrial prosperity and the social misery of the towns and especially the country. The Opium War (1839–42). The Taiping Revolt (1848–64). Capture of Peking by Western forces (1860). The Boxers' Revolt (1900).

1911 Republic.

1921 Founding of the Chinese Communist Party.

1934 Japanese colonization.

1945–49 Civil War.

1949 Founding of the People's Republic.

1966 Beginning of the Cultural Revolution.

1976 Death of Chou En-lai and Mao Tse-tung.

961–1049 Huqiu pagoda, twin pagodas and Buddhist temple Ruigang Si in Suzhou (Jiangsu, 961–84). Hall of Buddhist temple Lingyin Si in Hangzhou (Zhejiang, 969). Buddhist temple Longxing Si and Taoist temple Xianwen Miao in Zhending (Hebei, 971). Buddhist temple Dule Si in Jixian (Hebei, 984). Buddhist temples Shanhua Si in Datong (Shanxi, 11th–12th centuries). Buddhist temple Xiangguo Si and iron pagoda Tie Ta in Kaifeng (1049).

1053–59 The Luoyang bridge (Luoyang Qiao).

1100–1145 Publication of the *Yingzao fashi* or "Methods and Designs of Architecture" by Li Jie.

1125 Peking capital of the Jin dynasty. Chuzu An hall at Buddhist temple Shaolin Si in Song Shan (Henan).

1127–1279 Hangzhou becomes capital of the Southern Song dynasty. Building of palaces and gardens; decorative improvement of the city. Building of the pagoda Liuhe Ta (1153) and temple Xuanmiao Guan (1179). White Dagoba at Tibetan temple Miaoying Si, Peking (1271). New plan of Peking and the construction of palaces in the "Forbidden City" (1276). Palace of Yongle Gong in Ruicheng (Shanxi, 13th–14th centuries).

1170 New plan of Nankin, identical to that of Chang'an by the Tang.

1175 Pagodas of Tianning Si in Peking and Baima Si in Luoyang. Lugou Qiao (said to be Marco Polo's bridge) in Peking.

1368–1500 Refurbishing of Nankin and the construction of the tomb of Hong Wu. Rebuilding of the Great Wall.

1409–1643 Peking becomes new capital (rebuilding of the Forbidden City, reinforcement of the earth wall around the city). Building of the Drum Tower in Xi'an. Building of tombs for 13 Ming rulers near Peking (15th–17th centuries). In Peking, the building of the Temple of Heaven and the Drum Tower (1420). Buddhist temples of Zihua Si and Wuta Si (1443–73), and the White Dagoba at the lama temple of Biyun Si (16th century).

Beginning of the 16th century Temple of Confucius in Qufu (Shandong). Vaulted hall of Wulian Dian at the Temple of Kaiyuan Si in Suzhou.

1617 Publication of the *Yuanye* ("Garden Manual") by Ji Cheng.

1644–1911 Peking, capital of the Qing. Building of the Summer Palace at Jehol (now Chengde, Hebei, 1660–1709).
Building work in Peking: strengthening of the city wall; the White Dagoba at Beihai park in the "Forbidden City" (1652); the Summer Palace with gardens (1709–51); the Buddhist Temple Dazhong Si (1733); the Belltower (1745); the dagoba at the Buddhist Temple Huang Si (1780).
Destruction of the Summer Palace in Peking by Anglo-French troops (1860). The first Chinese students of architecture sent abroad (1872). Building of the present Summer Palace in Peking by the Empress Cixi (1903).

1920–31 Restoration of Peking palaces. First concrete skyscrapers in Shanghai.

1930 Research committee for Chinese architecture formed.

1957–58 Movement for the reform of architectural construction.

1978–1983 Receptiveness to foreign architectural influences, but also a new approach to traditional architecture.

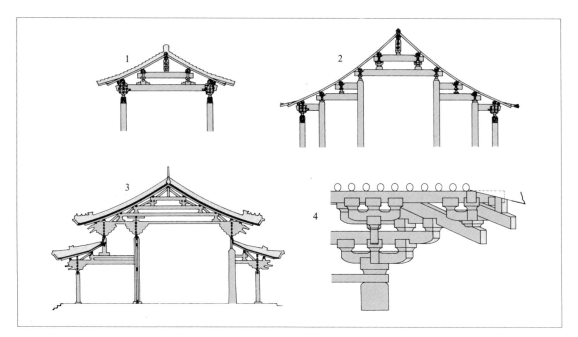

The evolution of Chinese roof construction

The most striking feature of the roof is the absence of triangular tied frames. To increase the size of a room, it was necessary to introduce more pillars.

1. The archaic design consisted of narrow eaves and span.

2. With an increased number of pillars, the interior became cluttered.

3. A system of brackets opened up the space of the room while reinforcing the structure.

4. From the 8th century, cantilevers were introduced, penetrating the bracket clusters and supporting a further series of brackets.

During the short Sui dynasty (589–618), governmental decree restored the official status of architecture and town planning. The cities of Chang'an, Luoyang, and later Hangzhou, were redesigned and given vast governmental buildings. Monumental, civil and religious architecture became more refined while domestic building began to take on forms and dimensions that were more suited to its function. The construction of the Grand Canal, lined with some 40 palaces, marks a decisive point in the development of communications to be enjoyed by succeeding dynasties. The first years of the Tang dynasty (618–907) mark one of the peaks in Chinese architecture, when Chang'an (now Xi'an) and Luoyang were totally rebuilt; both cities were laid out according to a geometric design. The imperial palaces and gardens reveal the increasing taste for refinement and luxury in architecture and urban development. Among the genuinely Chinese buildings such as the Altar of Heaven, the Altar of the Soil, and Taoist and Confucian temples, stand Buddhist pagodas and monasteries and Nestorian temples and mosques. The style, design and structure of these various buildings are, however, relatively similar. Foreign cultural influences, originating principally in Persia and India and introduced by increasing commercial activity, encouraged a great renaissance in the arts which, mainly through Buddhism, spread to Korea and Japan.

After the fall of the Tang dynasty, the Song established themselves in Kaifeng towards the end of a succession of five short-lived and chaotic dynasties (907–60) while the Liao built the first northern capital, to a geometric design, on the site of the modern city of Peking. In 1124, on the ashes of the former Liao capital, the Jin dynasty rebuilt a much bigger city in the form of a square surrounded by a wall. Two years later they moved into the sumptuous palaces built by the Song in Kaifeng. Having first withdrawn to Nankin and later to Hangzhou where they wanted to build their new capital, in 1145 the Song reprinted the great authority on Chinese architectural methods and designs known as the Yingzao fashi, *first published in 1100. This was a treatise covering every aspect of construction work from the measurements of the timber framework to the proportions of decorative motifs.*

In 1264 the Mongol emperor Shi Zong (Kubilai) moved his capital from Karakorum to Peking. He rebuilt the city once again and enlarged it even further. The emperor, who had by then adopted Chinese

customs, revived the use of wood in architecture which had been neglected in favour of stone under the Liao and Jin dynasties. During the same period the arrival of Tibetan lamas gave rise to the massive Buddhist temples and white dagobas on prominent sites in and around the capital. The return of the Chinese Ming dynasty may have served to recapture the aesthetics of ancient China and its past architectural elegance. However, the scarcity of wood and the customs inherited from the previous dynasty prevented any return to the ways of the past. When stone was being used on the reinforcement of the Great Wall, the use of grey brick became more and more widespread. Buildings lost their finesse and once-beautiful wooden corbels became nothing more than decorative friezes. The last reigning dynasty of the Manchurian Qing (1644–1911) failed to recapture any of the delicacy of Chinese architecture. As

adherence to tradition weakened, buildings became cumbersome, decorations obtrusive and the quality of building materials deteriorated progressively. The increase in population and the rise in commerce encouraged uncontrolled growth in towns and cities. Economic and practical considerations were reflected in the style of construction without, however, eclipsing the traditional designs or geomantic ritual. With the coming of the Europeans, Chinese architecture became a symbol of nationalism; the present Summer Palace in Peking, built by the last empress, Cixi, at the start of the 20th century, is the best example. In the words of Liu Dunzhen, Chinese architecture "is the result of a long cooperation between the craftsman and his skill and the natural resources of his environment; such traditional methods should now be developed using scientific techniques."

Belltower, Xi'an. Built during the Tang dynasty, moved in the 16th century and restored several times since, the belltower lay on the axis of the Imperial Way that led to the palace of the former capital, Chang'an.

The origins of Chinese architecture

According to ancient chronicles, there were two categories of early Chinese habitation: pole-and-branch huts and domed houses similar to clay ovens, dug deep into the earth. Recent archaeological excavations, particularly at Banpo village (dated first half of the third millennium), have corroborated these descriptions and provided greater insight into their practical and ritualistic significance. They confirm that the early Chinese, like many other primitive peoples, lived in caves and huts; but also that the form of these first dwellings was strongly governed by Shamanist ritual. The pole-and-branch huts were lived in during the warm season, while the underground houses sheltered the inhabitants from the severe winters. In Shamanism the earth was subordinated to the heavens because the earth was dependent on rainfall for its fertility: in response to the heaven-sent gift of rain, the people instituted the ritual of the domestic fire. Openings in the roofs of the huts and "wells of heaven" in the sunken dwellings recall this ritual exchange. The sunken dwellings, which were either round or square with an entrance porch at the front, represent an intermediary stage in the development of the house. Their construction was similar to that of ancient burial chambers and was intended to symbolize the link between the houses of the living and the houses of the dead. In Banpo, the entrance porches all face the centre of the village, probably the site of the temple or sacred granary.

The ancient Chinese system of astronomy named the stars according to certain human activities that corresponded to the time of year the stars reached their highest point in the firmament. According to some interpretations, building work should begin in the autumn and be finished by the following spring, before work in the fields was resumed. The building of a home followed a sequence of five different stages: marking out the plan on the ground, banking up the earth, building the wooden framework, ramming the earth into the wall spaces (the *pisé* system) and thatching the roof.

Yu the Great, founder of the legendary Xia dynasty (second millennium), is thought to have been the first to drain the Chinese plains, digging the canals and irrigation channels that enabled the farms and towns to prosper. When a site had been chosen, taking due account of topography and ritual, the emperor had the land cleared by fire; it was then distributed among his ministers and military leaders. The first part of the city to be constructed was its fortifications, a broad rampart of earth around the perimeter. Social and religious order was expressed by the construction of prominent palaces and temples in the centre. The Ancestral Temple was the first to be built, symbolizing the people's ties to the city and the emperor. It was followed by the palace, then by aristocratic residences and finally the homes of the people. The latter were often given a plot of land for growing vegetables which lay on the outskirts of the city yet within the protection of its walls. In the same way as the house, which served not only practical and decorative functions but also as a reflection of an individual's social status, the institutions of the city contributed to maintaining the social hierarchy.

Since urban architecture reflected social status in a feudal system, the palace gradually took pride of place over all other buildings in size, quality of building material and location. Since the ritual involved in building developed at the same time as techniques of construction and concepts of design, a close relationship remained betwen ritual and building methods. By the 14th century BC, the construction of a palace might be divided into nine stages: orientation according to the cardinal points, planting of hazel and chestnut trees (for offerings), planting of catalpa and three varieties of sumac (the first has a symbolic function and the latter three were used in the making of lutes), a study of the shadows cast on to the land by the adjacent mountains, a search for plains suitable for growing mulberry trees (for silk), ritual consultation of tortoise shells, successful completion of building work, waiting for the rain to bring fertility, and finally the presence of the emperor in the centre of the composition as the "son of heaven". Round houses and towns surrounded by circular walls gradually began to disappear. As the rectangular plan became widespread the application of geometry brought about a more rhythmic urban plan within which buildings of more harmonious proportions were erected. Through the constant repetition of architectural forms and the perfection of techniques (introduction of the mortise joint, baked bricks and tiles) the classical style gradually began to emerge; the first bracketed capitals were to span the inner and outer colonnades and support the heavy frame of the earliest curved roofs (2nd century BC). Finally, painted decoration increased and eventually extended over the entire building.

Tang watchtower

This detail of an 8th century mural shows the characteristics of the first wave of classical Chinese architecture. The pavilion is a wooden structure built on a relatively primitive system of brackets; the roofs, already markedly curved, are covered in tiles; the foundation is massive and richly decorated.

Pottery model of a farmstead (1st–2nd century BC)

Placed as offerings in tombs, these pottery models are faithful replicas of contemporary buildings; walls were framed with timber, filled with bricks and then smeared with plaster (*pisé* method). The roofs were tiled. The different farm buildings, all of them south-facing, were built symmetrically around a courtyard. The outer walls are windowless for reasons of defence.

Tumulus in the Valley of the Thirteen Tombs, north of Peking

Ever since the Shang dynasty (19th–11th century BC), the underground tombs of the aristocracy and military leaders had been covered by tumuli. Planted with evergreens, symbols of eternity, the "Thirteen Tombs" of the Ming dynasty (15th–17th century) followed the ancient design used for imperial tombs.

**Diagram reconstruction
of an ancient capital city**

1 *wall surrounding the aristocratic quarter*
2 *wall surrounding semi-urbanized agricultural zone*
3 *imperial gates*
4 *fortified gates*
5 *markets*
6 *palaces and shrines*
7 *field boundaries*

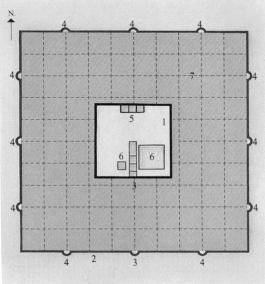

**Garden of palace
at Luoyang**

1 *diverted river*
2 *lake of the "Nine Islands" of Paradise*
3 *pond*
4 *flower garden*
5 *palace and pavilions*
6 *fortified external wall*

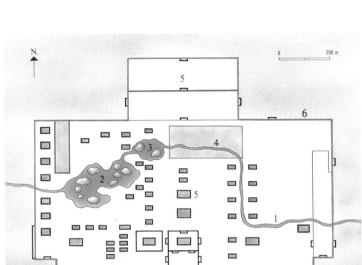

**Buddhist caves at Longmen near Luoyang
(4th–7th century AD)**

Similar to their Indian counterparts, the Buddhist caves are chapels dug into cliffs and house colossal statues. At Longmen, the "Gate of the Dragons", the classical temple, now destroyed, once clung to the rock face and protected the statues of the guardian deities and the cave of the Buddha.

**Five-tiered pagoda on Lake Suzhou
(9th–13th century AD)**

The origins of the word pagoda are uncertain, but the building is simply called *ta* in Chinese, which means tower. Over the centuries pagodas have had many functions – as commemorative or funerary edifices, watchtowers, shrines or simply as decoration. Geomancy gives the pagoda its protective power. This decorative pagoda, built in glazed brickwork, recaptures the forms of the wooden towers of the Han period.

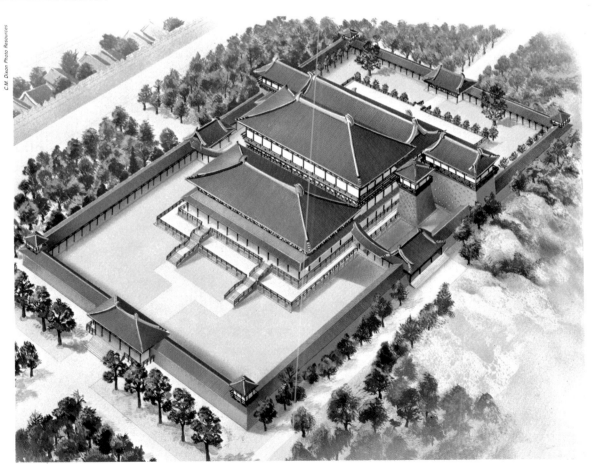

Audience chamber at the Palace of Daming Gong in Chang'an

The palace of Daming Gong (634) was built outside the capital city in the middle of the "Forbidden Garden". It centres on the imperial courtyard and the audience hall, built on stepped terraces. The Forbidden City in Peking, if surrounded by abundant vegetation, would give some idea of the Palace of Daming Gong during the Tang dynasty.

Urban architecture

Architecture in China's cities and towns owes its success to experience and determination. The plans of the capital cities that were built with each successive dynasty reflect the quest for an ideal urban design. As an image of the cosmos, the ideal capital would serve as an example of organization and hierarchical structure to society.

The repetition of one architectural style culminated in a perfection of design that can be seen in Chang'an (Xi'an today), rebuilt in 617 during the Tang dynasty. Luoyang in 618, Nankin in 1130 and, in Japan, Nara in 710 and Kyoto in 794, are all replicas of Chang'an. All these cities were completed within a given time and peopled at the emperor's behest. More than one million people lived within the walls of these capitals, in which each of the four walls measured 14 kilometres (9 miles).

The first capitals built according to a geometric design were the Shang cities of Zhengzhou (16th century BC) and Anyang (14th century BC). In the second Shang capital the burial grounds were located in the north and separated from the city by a river; this feature was later adopted by the Han in Chang'an. The numerous capitals built between the 9th and the 5th centuries BC show a progression in dimensions and quality. In the 4th century, Nanda, in Hebei province, was planned to a square design. Two groups of three parallel roads that cross each other at right angles led to the 12 gates of the fortified town. They divided the city into 16 square residential precincts. This trial plan, adopted by the Zhou dynasty in the 4th century, was transposed to Xiadu in Hebei.

Xianyang, built in 221BC and the capital of the Qin dynasty, was a fortified city with a perimeter wall 24 kilometres (15 miles) long. To protect the population of about 40,000, the city gates as well as the gates to different quarters within the city were locked and guarded at night. Built on the site of the future Chang'an of the Han and the Tang dynasties, Xianyang is a fine example of the changing location of imperial and governmental buildings within the urban framework. Palaces which hitherto had been clustered around the city centre now occupied nearly two-thirds of the city's southern half. Chang'an's plan evokes the layouts used in the capitals of Central Asia: it is centred along the Imperial Way that leads from the palace in the north of the city to the Imperial Gate in the south wall. The two markets lie in the middle of the chequered composition on either side of the axis, a position once occupied by the ancient temples of the Zhou capitals. Chang'an, although less famous for its design than Peking, which consists only of a succession of juxtaposed enclosures, is more representative of the quality of Chinese design in terms of urban development. The relationship between the architectural environment and the social structure is clearly a reflection of cosmic harmony.

Chang'an ("Long Peace"), like many other capitals, derives its name from the aspirations of its political institutions towards eternity. The magnificence of the city is evident above all in its size: 9,780 kilometres (6,073 miles) from east to west and 8,550 kilometres (5,309 miles) from north to south; the Imperial Way is 176 metres (192 yards) wide and the main streets 140 metres (153 yards) and 90 metres (98 yards) wide. Both the city, and the governmental offices within it, are surrounded by a rampart with a moat on either side. The "Sacred Park" site of the imperial tombs was also a pleasure garden for the emperor and his court. After 637 the new, permanent residence of the Tang emperors was placed within its walls. The grandeur of the architecture and the quality of its design make Chang'an the epitome of the splendours of China's feudal era.

Like Chang'an, Luoyang and Nankin, Peking, "Capital of the North", underwent a series of successive changes in design, all more or less superimposed. First a centre of trade and then capital of the temporary states, it was not until the 9th century, when it was captured by the Liao, that Peking was rebuilt according to a geometric design; included in the design was the imperial palace, which was later enlarged by the Jin at the beginning of the 12th century. Kublai Khan must have first built his palace within a circular city in 1261 before building the great square capital known as the Tartar city which surrounded the "Forbidden City". After 1368 the Ming added to the fortifications of the Mongol city. In 1524 the commercial districts that had grown up outside the south wall were included in the city by extending a rampart.

At the same time as the construction of the ideal capitals, completed in a given period of time in symbolic sequence and in adherence to a rigorous system of chequered geometric designs, many Chinese towns and cities were built without a master plan. Nevertheless the architectural ideals of the day did much to conserve the rectangular street plan. The absence of a main square, the modest height of the buildings and the respect for the surrounding countryside as dictated by geomantic ritual, gave each district a village atmosphere.

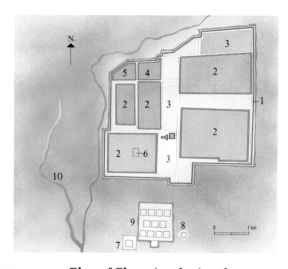

Plan of Chang'an during the Han era (2nd century AD)

1 fortified town wall
2 aristocratic palaces
3 residential areas
4 market of the east
5 market of the west
6 altar on circular foundations
7 altar on square foundations
8 Altar of Lights (Ming Tang)
9 tombs
10 water courses, natural and channelled

Plan of Chang'an during the Tang dynasty (7th century AD)

1 walled enclosure
2 Taiji Imperial Palace
3 government offices
4 Imperial Way
5 Mingde Gate (main gate)
6 fortified gates
7 market of the east
8 market of the west
9 residential district
10 Pagoda of the Great Goose
11 Pagoda of the Small Goose
12 Xing Qing Palace
13 Daming Gong Palace
14 Sacred Park (created under the Han)
15 Public Hibiscus Garden
16 channelled rivers

Great Goose Pagoda in Xi'an

The Pagoda of the Great Goose (Dayan Ta) which towers 60 metres (200 feet) above the city, was built in the Buddhist temple by the pilgrim monk Xuanzang. The pagoda was originally called the Pagoda of the Classics. It was built in 652 to house holy texts brought from India.

Evolution of the plan of Peking from the 10th to the 20th century

A Liao dynasty (947)

B Jin dynasty (1115)

C Mongol dynasty
(Peking becomes capital in 1264)

D Ming dynasty (1368)

E Qing dynasty (1644)

F Peking today (1981)

G water courses and lakes

1 Tartar city (13th century)

2 Chinese city (14th–16th century)

3 Forbidden City

4 Park of the "Three Seas" (San Hai)

5 Gate of "Heavenly Peace" (Tian'an Men)

6 Imperial Way

7 Temple of Heaven (Ming era)

8 present Summer Palace (1903)
on the site of Yuan Ming Yuan (18th century)

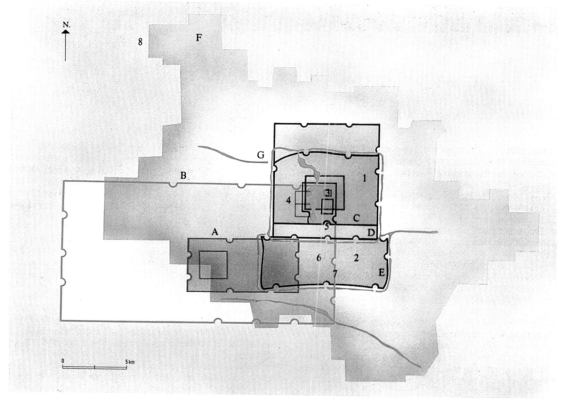

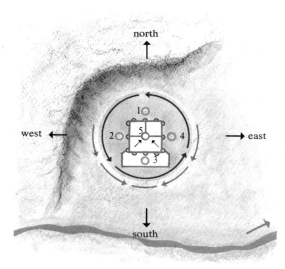

Interpretation of the site of Peking according to geomantic ritual

A capital of the Sons of Heaven

B twenty peripheral districts

C countryside

D curved mountain chain protecting
the north and the west aspects

E river lying to the south
flowing towards the east

1 Altar of the Earth   a most suitable directions for
entrance into the palace

2 Altar of the Moon

3 Altar of the Sky   b most suitable direction to
mount to the throne

4 Altar of the Sun

5 Throne Room

Suzhou, city of canals

Suzhou (13th–17th century), the city where the reigning Song took refuge in the 13th century, was well known for the quality of its urban development and its luxurious architecture. Known as Kinsay or Suzhou in the West, the capital of the southern Song dynasty has often been praised by Chinese poets, and enchanted the Venetian traveller Marco Polo. The canals in Suzhou are still used for transportation.

Wooden bridge

Wooden framed bridge, called "the Rainbow Bridge", in the capital of Kaifeng during the era of the northern Song (960–1127). Detail from a painted silk scroll dating from the Ming dynasty (1368–1644).

The Metropolitan Museum of Art, Fletcher Fund, 1947, A.W. Bahr Collection.

Monumental architecture

Monumental architecture in China consists of palaces, altars, temples and monasteries that served a residential, ceremonial or communal purpose. The wooden framework of these buildings dictated their structure and design, limiting the freedom with which Chinese architects could arrange groups of buildings within the walls of a fortification. The precision of their designs is evident in the geometrical clarity of the plans, which also reflect the grading of the buildings' functions. A classic form, subtle contrast of shape and material, and consistent rationality – these are the salient features of Chinese monumental architecture, which has consistently pursued a single ideal since the second millennium BC.

The palaces of the Shang capitals (Zhengzhou, 16th century; Anyang, 14th century) were made up of a series of interconnected buildings surrounding a courtyard, within a walled enclosure. The foundations were of rammed earth and the columns simply rested on stone discs. The Weiyang palace in Chang'an (199BC), built during the Han dynasty, is like a "city within a city". Built to house the imperial court and the government, it, too, was intended, by its size and splendour, to affirm the importance of the "Son of Heaven". Also at this time the numerous, vast palaces to be found throughout the city of Chang'an began to differentiate between imperial residences and government offices. But it was not until the building of the Daming Gong palace (637), in the Forbidden Park to the north of the new Tang capital of Chang'an, that luxurious imperial mansions, to be used from then on as permanent residences, began to appear outside the fortified walls of the city amidst landscaped gardens. From the 10th century onwards, the refinement of the Song palaces brought an added dimension to Tang architecture – notably in their coloured ornament and curvacious roofs, so popular in the southern provinces. Yu Hao, a native of Hangzhou, was the architect responsible for the introduction of this new style to Kaifeng, capital of northern Song. Painted views of the era demonstrate the degree of attention paid to architectural delicacy and refinement. Artists may even have collaborated in the design and decoration of the palaces at Kaifeng.

In contrast to the finesse of Tang and Song architecture, the ensemble of buildings that make up the Forbidden City in Peking appears somewhat less refined. Built in 1406 by the Ming on the site of the palace of Kublai Khan, this complex has been renovated several times since then. Oriented to the south, the Forbidden City is protected to the north by Coal Hill, crowned with its five red pavilions. To the west of the palace stretches the Park of the Three Seas, which consists of numerous islands, pavilions built above the water and open, latticework galleries. The design of the entire palace is centred on the Audience Hall which is raised on a white marble platform and dominates all the other buildings. The Imperial Way begins at the southern gate of the city, and crosses the fortified palace enclosure and the sacred river before leading up to the imperial staircase and the Throne Room. The residential apartments of the emperor and his court lie to the north of the palace, with servants' quarters on either side of the axis. All buildings, irrespective of their function, look out on to a courtyard decorated with ceremonial objects or plants. The Ancestral Altar is situated to the south-east of the layout whereas the Altar of the Sun God lies to the south-west. Two white marble pillars, known as the Heavenly Gate (*Tian'an Men*), mark the entrance to the Forbidden City. Stretching for 3 kilometres (2 miles) through the northern suburbs of Peking lies the palace of Yuanming Yuan, built in the mid-17th century as an imperial residence. Including the palaces of Jehol (now Cheng'de), it made up the largest gathering of palaces and gardens ever built in China.

The temples of the three major Chinese religions, Taoism, Confucianism and Buddhism, are all fairly similar in design to palaces. They are again symmetrical or at least balanced, and most temples also have a southerly orientation. Their construction calls for the same materials, methods and techniques: they are built around a courtyard, which is also surrounded by a wall, and the prayer rooms open to the worshippers are arranged around the axis of the design. The pagoda, whose positioning varied according to the period, was originally a reliquary; its original form, derived from the Indian *stupa*, gradually became lost as the design of the many-roofed Chinese look-out tower began to predominate. Religious buildings in wood developed up until the 13th century much like residential constructions; both show a similar progress towards structural grace and an improvement in technique.

The vast funerary building projects of China have origins as far back as the second millennium BC. They were built in solid stone and surrounded by defensive moats. Underground burial chambers reserved for the aristocracy were developed under the Shang dynasty. Funerary architecture reached its peak with the building of the tomb of Qin Shi Huangdi (near Xi'an, Shaanxi), whose mound measures more than 500 metres (1,640 feet) at the base and rises to a height of 78 metres (255 feet) above ground. The road leading up to the tomb is bordered by statues and pillars, a permanent guard of honour. The tomb was placed under the protection of a chain of mountains that formed an arc on its northern side. This arrangement, already common during the Han dynasty, was to be used again in the 15th century for the Thirteen Tombs of the Ming to the north of Peking.

Winding over more than 3,000 kilometres (1,800 miles), with two or even three ramifications over some stretches, the Great Wall is a symbol of the magnitude of the utilitarian projects of ancient China. The construction of the Great Wall and the Grand Canal (from the 6th century), and the great undertakings of city fortification, illustrate the constant necessity of external defence and the maintenance of public order. Built and rebuilt over a period of more than 2,000 years the "Wall of Ten Thousand Leagues" was once a simple rampart of pebbles and earth. After reinforcement in the 3rd century BC by the Qin and later by the Han and the Sui, it gradually took on the appearance of a hewn stone wall with slightly sloping sides and foundations that followed the contours of the land. Restoration in the 14th and 16th centuries gave it its present appearance of a rampart-walk punctuated by small forts.

Robert Harding Associates

Forbidden City, Peking (1406)

The five bridges of the Imperial Way cross the Golden River between the South Gate and the Imperial Courtyard. The sculpted clouds of the balustrades evoke the celestial lineage of the emperor.

Axonometric pla of the Forbidden Ci

1 *South Gate (Wu Men), third fortified gate of the palace*

2 *the five marble bridg of the Golden River*

3 *Gate of Supreme Harmony (Taihe Men), protecting the Imperial Courtyard*

4 *Palace of Supreme Harmony (Taihe Dian), Audience H*

5 *Intermediary Hall a Palace for the Preservation of Harmony (Baohe Dian)*

6 *side pavilions*

7 *side galleries*

8 *corner pavilions*

Varieties of Chinese temples

Although consecrated to different cults, Chinese temples all adopt the traditional arrangements of monumental architecture. They are made up of a series of different buildings situated round a court-yard and linked together by galleries.

1. *main gate, known as the Mountain Gate*
2. *central building (reliquary)*
3. *prayer room (with statues)*
4. *secondary altars*
5. *portico*
6. *Gate of the Guardians (demons)*
7. *sacred pond*
8. *courtyard (gallery)*
9. *gallery*
10. *pagoda*

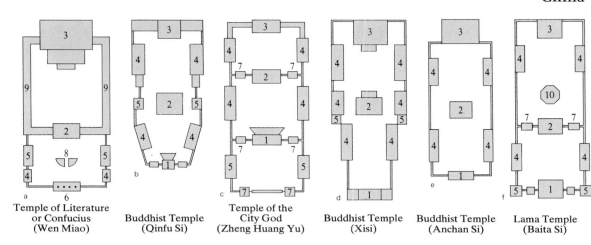

Temple of Literature or Confucius (Wen Miao)

Buddhist Temple (Qinfu Si)

Temple of the City God (Zheng Huang Yu)

Buddhist Temple (Xisi)

Buddhist Temple (Anchan Si)

Lama Temple (Baita Si)

Pavilion of Pleasure in the Forbidden City, Peking

Built in the 17th century as a place where the em-peror could entertain, this two-storeyed pavilion dominates the roofline of the Forbidden City. Ex-posed to the winds yet sheltered by surrounding vegetation, the room was used especially for night-time festivities during the summer. The courtyard is protected by high, thick walls and a screen of masonry in front of the gates.

Courtyard of the Temple of Benevolence (Dacien Si, 7th century) in Xi'an

Dominated by the Great Goose Pagoda, the temple was built by the Emperor Taizong in honour of his mother and entrusted to the pilgrim Buddhist monk Xuanzang on his return from India. Once situated to the south-east of the Tang capital, Chang'an (now Xi'an), and destroyed in the 10th century, the temple now lies amid open fields.

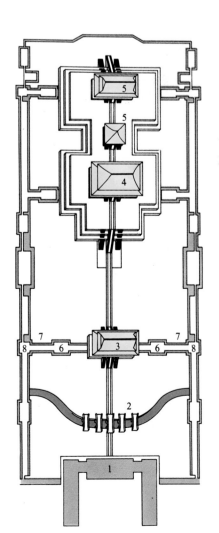

Temple of Heaven, Peking

Built by the Ming and restored under the Qing, the Temple of Heaven (15th century) is a ceremonial building where emperors came to celebrate seasonal rites. Surrounded by a walled enclosure, the setting consists of a circular mound, a vault of heaven and an altar of prayer for the harvests. The architectural components of the temple, the circular form and the number of columns and terraces symbolize the structure of the cosmos.

Houses, parks and gardens

The form and structure of traditional Chinese houses followed well-defined models. Aesthetic canons and geomantic or climatic requirements were more important than the architect's plan or the occupant's wishes. The homes of China's many ethnic minorities were designed according to the principle of a symbolic arrangement of space. A walled enclosure was a common feature in rural areas; in towns and cities, most houses were built with an inner courtyard. Simple in appearance and structure, these often precarious homes nevertheless afforded the occupants sufficient protection for their way of life; the modest yet elegant appearance of these houses was the outcome of gradual evolution. Particularly fine illustrations of this are the Mongolian tents and their system of underground heating, or the houses raised on piles, rebuilt each year by the migrating populations of the mountainous regions to the south. Others include the Tibetan houses built on mountainside terraces or the village communities of the minorities living in Hakka in Fujian province where all the families of each community were housed on different floors within a round or square citadel, sharing a communal area below.

For the Chinese, the concept of the garden was inseparable from that of the house. Also, because the political hierarchy dictated not only place in society but also residential quarter within the city, there was a tendency to designate people by their address. Similarly, in Chinese, the same word, made up of two picture symbols, means both "family" and "home". When considered separately, symbols represent "house" and "courtyard" respectively. The first represents a roof with a pig beneath it; the second is a picture of an enclosure surrounded by a portico. The former is reminiscent of the little pot-tery houses that were offered up to the dead, in which a pig, most prized of farm animals in China, stood in the middle of the courtyard as a symbol of wealth. This was the design adopted in most of China's towns. The number, shape, size and arrangement of the courtyards within the different units that made up the house varied from city to city. In Peking, as a result of laws laid down by the Ming and the Qing, buildings that surrounded a generally square courtyard were practically identical in size throughout the city. The number of courtyards and units chosen was the one that allowed the fullest use of the building land available. In the districts where living quarters were surrounded by walls, the street served as both meeting-place and recreation area.

As a sacred enclosure, a place for meditation or a scenic walk, the Chinese landscaped garden, originally the representation of the Paradise of Taoist legend, later came to reflect the artistic or philosophical concepts of nature evolved by the great writers. The composition of the earlier garden followed a strictly ritualistic pattern: surrounding their tombs, it presented the departed souls with a harmonious image of the perfect world. In a departure from this design, emperors and writers wanted to recreate Paradise in their parks (the former by religious necessity, the latter because they considered themselves immortal); Paradise was symbolized by a mountain surrounded by water. The creation of the landscaped garden therefore began with the contrast between mountain (*shan*) and water (*shui*) – *shanshui* means "landscape" in Chinese – and resulted in a harmonious, subtle and sometimes suggestive composition. The orientation of the garden, the harmony of its size and form with the architecture, the positioning of the ornamental stones and shrubs were all perfectly balanced, combining geomantic ritual with freedom of design.

The sacred enclosures of the Zhou, the Qin and the Han were as large as their capitals. As well as tombs, there were lakes, islands, animals, flowers and evergreen plants (symbols of immortality). The fragrance of the flowers and the surrounding countryside were a foil to the luxurious palaces, built on raised ground within the garden. Music and the aroma of alcohol would accompany those who walked along the terraces to admire the dragon-shaped boats or the view.

Chinese poetry and historical records extol the early gardens that were to serve as a model for later designs, in particular the imperial summer residences like the Yuanming Yuan, built in the 17th century to the north-west of Peking or the parks in Jehol (now Cheng'de). In the private gardens of the civil servants or merchants of the cities of Hangzhou, Suzhou and Wuxi there is often an element of fantasy in the design of the rock-gardens. In the large cities of Nankin, Peking or Shanghai it is difficult to find any of the respect for nature that characterized the lush, colourful gardens of the Tang and Song periods. Courtyards, however, are often decorated with landscapes or miniature trees standing on plinths surrounded by seasonal flowers.

At the time of the Tang and Song dynasties, first Korea and then Japan began to adopt Chinese techniques. The Anglo-Chinese garden combines European naturalist ideals with a taste for the exoticism of Chinese art. It recalls the imperial decree that palaces and gardens be built in the European style of the Yuanming Yuan, the old palace of Peking built by the Jesuits and destroyed by Anglo-French forces during the last century.

The Garden of Harmony, Suzhou

Landscaped in the traditional style, the Garden of Harmony (18th century) embellished the home of a rich government official. The artificial lake lies between the pavilions, galleries and courtyards decorated with rock-gardens.

1 *entrance pavilion*
2 *Pavilion of the Little Waves*
3 *artificial grottoes*
4 *Summer-house of the Lotus Perfume*
5 *rock-gardens*
6 *covered galleries*
7 *rooms*
8 *boat-shaped room*

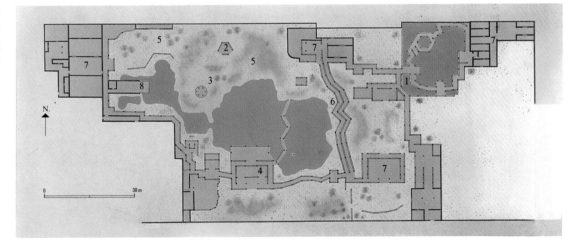

Pavilion in the garden of Peking's Summer Palace

Built at the beginning of the 20th century by the Chinese Empress Cixi on the shores of the lake in the Yihe Yuan garden, this traditionally styled pavilion was a quiet retreat for contemplation.

Entrance courtyard

In a house once resided in by a Buddhist priest of the Chan sect, the planted courtyard is surrounded by covered galleries that lead to the "Garden of the Forest of Stone Lions". The arrangement of rock-gardens and plants around an artificial lake lay, at the time of its construction, within the walls of a Buddhist temple. The house underwent alterations in the 18th century when it was bought by a wealthy merchant.

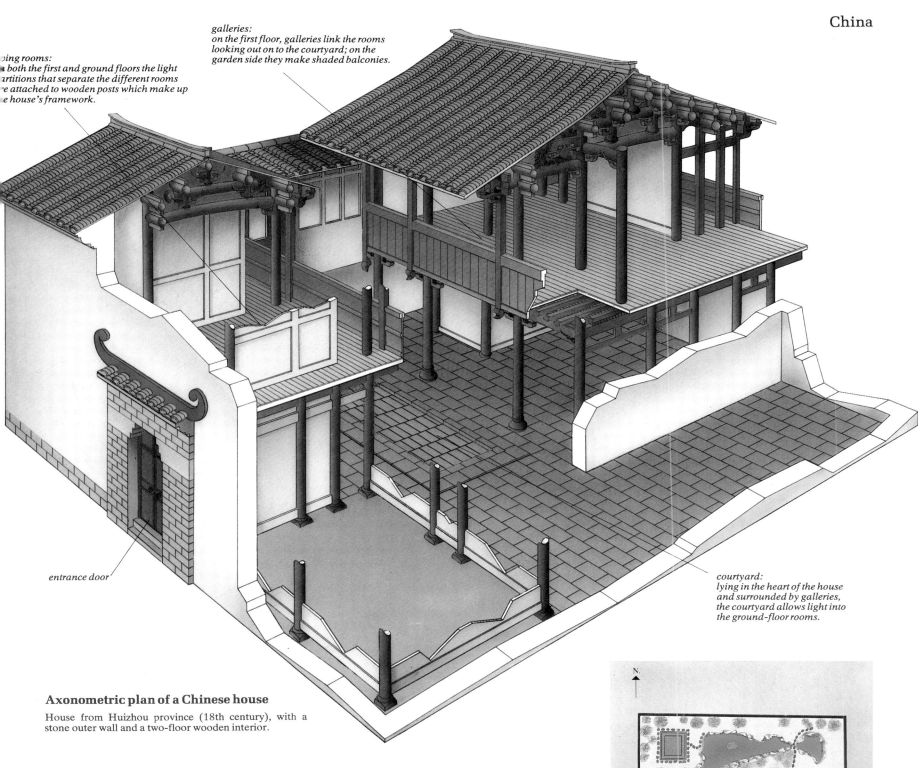

ping rooms:
both the first and ground floors the light
artitions that separate the different rooms
re attached to wooden posts which make up
e house's framework.

galleries:
on the first floor, galleries link the rooms
looking out on to the courtyard; on the
garden side they make shaded balconies.

entrance door

courtyard:
lying in the heart of the house
and surrounded by galleries,
the courtyard allows light into
the ground-floor rooms.

Axonometric plan of a Chinese house

House from Huizhou province (18th century), with a
stone outer wall and a two-floor wooden interior.

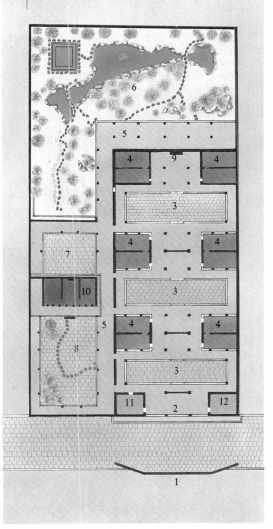

N.

Plan of an 18th century Chinese house

Layout of an urban dwelling with
several courtyards and a pleasure
garden at the back.

1 _protective screen_
2 _entrance_
3 _inner courtyards_
4 _living quarters_
5 _outer gallery_
6 _pleasure garden_
7 _servants' courtyard_
8 _the master's garden_
9 _ancestral altar_
10 _Confucian altar_
11 _doorkeeper's room_
12 _lavatory_

31

Pagoda of the Popchu-sa temple

The wooden pagodas of Korean Buddhist temples show that, in the repertoire of architectural forms, Korean structures are dependent on Chinese models. The elegance of the curve of the roofs has a threefold origin: technique, aesthetics and symbolism. The sweep of the line of rafters in this 17th century example demonstrates the perfection of these wooden structures. All the elements of the framework are cut in advance using the carpenter's calibrated square. The curves are seen by the Koreans as an image of the wings of the phoenix – the sacred bird and symbol of eternity.

*B*ecause of the homogeneity of its population, which could not be assimilated into the populations of neighbouring countries, and owing to the link established by its Uralo-Altaic language, Korea was able to build an original civilization little by little over the centuries. Even though numerous cultural and artistic concepts were imported from China, such as handwriting, Buddhism and construction techniques, and although these were transmitted to Japan, the Korean peninsula was destined to ensure the flourishing of its own art rather than simply acting as an intermediary. The "Country of the Calm Morning" can be divided into four great regions whose geographical characteristics have historical repercussions. The plains of the north saw the establishment of the first migrant populations and came under strong influence from the mainland. Adjacent to the west coast, which is very jagged, there is a region of hills which was the cradle of former capitals, such as Puyo and ancient Seoul. The south and east are more mountainous and had a later, more original cultural development, which is well preserved: the city of Kyongju, the former capital of Silla, a veritable open-air museum, is located in the centre of a region where the best preserved Buddhist temples are found. The abundance of forests and granite throughout the territory must have provided Korean builders with the materials for improving the quality of their structures and techniques.

In Korea, the oldest building remains date back to the megalithic era and are found all over the territory: they comprise stone tables, reminiscent of the dolmens found in Europe, and can be divided into two groups. The northern type takes the form of a stone slab, resting on four upright rocks and describing a geometric, oriented architectural area. The "table" of Enyul in the province of Hwanghae is 9 metres (25 feet) long. On Mount Sokchon, in the province of P'yongan, the largest of the 12 "tables" measures 6 by 4 metres (20 by 13 feet) and stands 2 metres (7 feet) high. These tables used to cover graves, but no traces remain of the latter. The southern type is reminiscent of the thick tables of the oriental game of chess: the slab lay flat on the ground and bore tombs of various shapes and orientations, which in some cases have been well preserved. These structures, which did not require any metal tools, characterize the transition period between the Bronze Age and Iron Age (3rd century BC). The religion connected with their construction is similar to Siberian Shamanism. Already it implies a division of social functions and a differentiation between religious and secular areas.

Compared with the legend of Tanjun, celestial founder of the Korean nation, the story of Kija, who came from China at the end of the Shang period (the Chinese dynasty reigning up to the 11th century BC) and who was said to have founded a kingdom in Korea – known as the kingdom of Chosen – seems rather more credible. Chinese historical sources also mention a certain Wiman, of the kingdom of Yan (in the region of Peking), who seized Chosen at the end of the 3rd century BC. However, it was in 109BC that Korean history began, with the occupation of the northern half of Korea by the Emperor Wu of the Chinese Han dynasty. China therefore played a very important role during the dawn of civilization in the "Country of the Calm Morning", one of the centres of which was Lelang, the region of present-day P'yongyang. The numerous tombs scattered around the town highlight the different aspects of culture and the arts at the time, revealing a close dependence on the contemporary works of the Chinese Han dynasty. The Chinese culture of Lelang progressively spread to all the Korean people, whose techniques belonged to the civilization of the Bronze Age. According to the Chinese, the southern Koreans lived "in huts similar to tombs, with the entrance at the top. They lived in them without distinction of sex or age. Some of these huts, which were made of wood, were

reminiscent of Chinese gaols" (Chewon Kim, 1964). Semi-subterranean houses were common in the north of ancient China and widespread too in prehistoric Japan.

In contrast with these primitive, aboriginal dwellings, the Korean capitals of the period of the Three Kingdoms (57BC–AD668) show evidence of a more structured organization and improved construction techniques, imported from China. The royal towns were similar to the fortified cities in the north of China: they were surrounded by a defensive earthen rampart and a moat. The urban areas were divided up to reflect the social hierarchy, with the palace in the centre and facing south. Grid-like street plans marked off the residential quarters allotted to people of eminence. The capital of the kingdom of Koguryo (founded in 37BC), T'onggu, on the river Yalu, and the capital which replaced it in the 5th century, P'yongyang, were the first examples of urban architecture worthy of the name. The successive capitals of the kingdom of Paekche (founded in 8BC), like those of the kingdom of Silla (founded in 57BC) in the east, were not so strongly influenced by the Chinese.

The graves in Koguryo, scattered around the town of T'onggu, on the border of Manchuria and Korea, are stonework tombs, a number of which are covered by

Burial mound of Kwoe nung, Kyongju. One of the finest royal graves in Korea, the tomb of Kwoe nung (8th century) is enclosed by a stonework surrounding wall, which has 12 images of the zodiac on it, intended to protect the spirit of the deceased.

KOREA

tumuli. The General's Tomb, at the foot of Mount Tukouzou, is a conical pyramid of granite slabs in horizontal layers. It was surrounded by many other tombs, fairly similar in structure, but of smaller dimensions. About half of the tombs scattered over the plain of T'onggu have the classic shape of the Far-Eastern tumulus, that is, square or circular. The decoration of the burial chamber, often very well preserved, teaches us about the state of the arts in the 5th century. The similarity between Korean and Chinese tombs is underlined by the shape of the triangular corbelling on the stonework cupolas. On the ceiling the paintings depict the vault of heaven and the stars. On the walls, ritual animals symbolize the four points of the compass: the blue dragon in the east, the red bird in the south, the white tiger in the west and the black tortoise in the north. These pictures stress the divine relationship between the macrocosm and the microcosm that presides over the destinies of individuals.

In the region of P'yongyang, later tombs show the increased mastery of the Korean builders. Thus, in the granite block tombs of Uhyon-ri pillars support the internal vault: it is the first example in Korea of a differentiation, in stonework constructions, between the bearing function and the isolating function. As in the case of wooden structures, stone piers act as point-shaped bearing members, whereas walls, which are continuous linear supports, are also screens which obstruct movement as well as view. The monumental buildings, palaces and religious structures were erected on banks of earth held in position by stonework walls in horizontal layers. The wooden structures, the shape of the roofs and the arrangement of the plan are similar to the architecture of ancient China.

The other two kingdoms, of Paekche and Silla, which have fewer burial remains, have preserved a great deal of evidence of Buddhist buildings: examples are the tomb of Songsan-ri near Kongju and the various graves in the vicinity of Puyo. The pagoda of Chongnim-sa in Puyo is the only example in Paekche to have remained more or less intact. It originally stood in front of the Golden Hall of the wooden temple, which has long been destroyed. The plan of the temple, centred and aligned with the prayer-hall, placed the pagoda in the middle of the courtyard linking the prayer-hall to the entrance porch. A covered gallery formed the rectangular enclosure of the temple, as in Kunsu-ri near Puyo. The Shitenno-ji, built in Osaka by Korean craftsmen invited to Japan, is a replica of Korean Buddhist temples. Thus, by repetition of identical constructions based on models previously formulated, the Asian carpenters were able to perfect their construction techniques. The pagoda of the Buddhist temple of Miroksa in Iksan in North Korea consists of nine storeys and its stone architecture is based on the familiar wooden structures of the Chinese pagodas, also imitated by Japan. The greatest number of remains of early Buddhist architecture are at Kyongju, the capital of the kingdom of Silla. Amid the 50 aristocratic tombs scattered over the valley, there are 200 stone pagodas, formerly situated inside temples, the majority of which were destroyed between the 13th and 16th centuries. The design of the Kyongju tombs was not influenced by Buddhism. They are nevertheless of large dimensions: the Punghwang dae burial mound measures 85 metres (278 feet) in diameter and is 21 metres (69 feet) high – a size which is still quite modest compared with Chinese or Japanese tombs. Also in Kyongju, the Chomsong dae observatory (7th century), in the shape of a bottle surmounted by a group of stones arranged like the square opening of a Chinese well, constitutes a unique Asian monument. The 365 blocks of granite which form the main part of the building are arranged in 12 groups and clearly indicate the celestial function of this utilitarian structure.

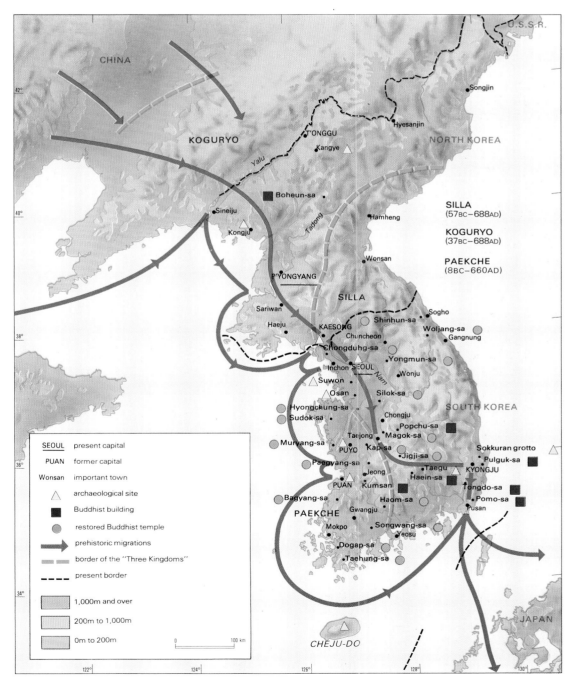

Civilization	Architecture	Civilization	Architecture
50,000BC First remains of tools and every-day objects.			**9th century** Construction of the Buddhist temple of HAEIN-SA. Mansubang (812), Pyonghui (812) and Wolchi (823) palaces in KYONGJU.
8000BC Palaeolithic era. Migrations from central Asia as far as Japan.	**2650BC** CHEJU-DO island: Grotto of the Three Gods, emblems of the country.	**918–1392** Koryo period. Manchu menace. Governmental hierarchy and universities of Confucian inspiration.	**10th century** Building and rebuilding of numerous Buddhist temples throughout the country, and of the Monwoldae palace in KAESONG, restoration of the Posok jong pavilion and of the "River of the Floating Cups" in KYONGJU (936), remodelling of the Anap pond into the shape of united Korea.
2333BC Mythological foundation of the country of Chogun by Tangun.	**2000BC** Onung tombs in KYONGJU.	**927** Destruction of Kyongju.	
1000BC Arrival of nomadic tribes of Uralo-Altaic origin.	**800BC** Semi-subterranean houses.	**935** Fall of Silla.	
5th–3rd centuries BC Bronze Age, then Iron Age.	**400BC** Underfloor heating in houses and palaces.	**936** New capital in Songdo (Kaesong).	
108BC First Chinese colonization.		**1011** First printing of Buddhist texts *Tripitaka Koreana*.	**1012** Reconstruction of the wall of KYONG-JU (restored in 14th and 18th centuries).
75BC Chinese kingdom of Lelang in the north of the country.		**1018** Three Mongol invasions repelled.	**1042** Construction of the Buddhist temple and of the pagoda of BOYOEN-SA (North Korea).
57BC–AD668 Period of the Three Kingdoms.		**1145** The annals of the Three Kingdoms are written.	
57BC Foundation of the kingdom of Silla (capital Kyongju).		**13th century** Genghis Khan in China (1213). Invasion of Korea by the army of Kublai Khan (1231). Printing works with movable type imported from China (1234). Reprint of *Tripitaka Koreana* burned by the Mongols (1251). Peace treaty and Mongol occupation (1270). Mongol and Korean military expeditions against Japan (1272–81).	
37BC Foundation of the kingdom of Koguryo (capital T'onggu).			
8BC Foundation of the kingdom of Paekche (capital near Seoul).	**8BC** Foundation of SEOUL, capital of the kingdom of Paekche. Tombs.		
	AD4 First tombs in KYONGJU.		
	AD57–59 Tomb of King Tnailae at the foot of Mount TOHAM.	**1390–91** Burning of land registers. New distribution of land.	**1365–72** Tomb of King Kong Min in KAESONG.
AD65 Legend of King Kim.	**AD284** Tomb of Michu I, king of the Kim clan, in KYONGJU.	**1392–1910** Yi dynasty. Seoul again becomes the capital.	**1392–96** Reconstruction of the capital, SEOUL, fortified gates and Kyongbok palace.
4th–5th centuries AD Introduction of Buddhism into Korea. Arrival of Chinese Buddhist monk Sundo in the kingdom of Koguryo (372) and of the Indian monk, Marnananta. Coexistence of Shamanism and Buddhism.	**4th century** Foundation of the Buddhist temple of POMOSA to the north of Pusan (the present buildings date from the 17th century), and of the temple of CH'OMUN.	**1406–50** Buddhist temples restricted. The Korean phonetic alphabet invented by King Sejong.	**1400–18** Gardens of the Ch'angdok palace and of the Haeon pavilion (SEOUL).
391 Japanese ambassador arrives in Korea.	**357** Anak tomb.	**16th century** Conflict of bourgeois factions.	
	5th century Palaces of Kuknae in T'ONGGU, Anhak near P'YONGYANG. Tombs and burial mounds in KYONGJU, P'YONGYANG and TAEGU.	**1545–67** Reign of King Myongjong.	**1543** Spread of geomantic practices.
427 P'yongyang capital of the kingdom of Koguryo.	**c.425** First Buddhist temple in KYONGJU (Hungnyun-sa).	**1572** Revival of Confucianist schools.	**1572** Confucianist school Oksan Sowan is built in KYONGJU.
475 Kongju capital of the kingdom of Paekche.		**1592–98** Japanese invasion.	**1592** Chang gyong and Chang bok palaces in SEOUL are destroyed.
Beginning of 6th century First Confucian universities. Introduction of Confucianist rite of human victims in royal tombs.	**6th century** Triple statue of Buddha and tombs in KYONGJU.		**17th century** Five-storeyed wooden pagoda of the Buddhist temple of POPCHU-SA.
528 Introduction of Buddhism into Silla.	**525** First construction of Buddhist temple Pulguk-sa in KYONGJU.	**1627–36** Manchu invasion.	
538–660 Puyo capital of the kingdom of Paekche.	**554** New palace of Panwol Song in KYONGJU.	**1644** Manchus take Peking (Qing dynasty).	
		end of 17th century Korean border is closed until 1880.	
632–50 The Buddhist monks Myong Nang and Won Hyo visit China.	**7th century** Foundation of the Buddhist temple TONGDO-SA, comprising 65 buildings, 13 hermitages and a sacred pond called the Pond of the Nine Dragons (616). Building in KYONGJU (634–43): cosmic observatory Chomsong dae. Yaksa Yorae altar, great nine-storeyed wooden pagoda (by the priest Chajan on his return from China). Construction of the Buddhist temple SACHONG WANG by Chajan. Building in KYONGJU, reign of Munmu (661–81): Imhae palace and Anap garden, royal tombs, twin multi-storeyed pagodas.	**17th–18th centuries** Movement of the Science of the Real (*Sil Hak*).	**18th century** Temple of the ancestors Song Hye jon is built in SEOUL (1750), a memorial altar to the first king of Silla, Sungdok jon (1759).
668–935 Korea unified: fall of Koguryo, kingdom of "Great Silla" with Kyongju as the capital (one million inhabitants). Buddhism official religion. Introduction of writings of Lao-tseu and Chuang-tseu.			**1789** Construction in SEOUL of the "Bridge of Thirty-Eight Boats" by the architect Chong Yag-gong.
			1796 Construction of the fortified town of SUWON to the south of SEOUL.
	8th century In KYONGJU, construction of the "3,000-foot Wall", of stonework pagodas, of the Yongchong (727) and Yongmyong (748) palaces, and reconstruction of the Pulguk-sa temple (after 742) with its meditation hall and Sokkatap and Sabotap pagodas; restoration of the "Serpentine River" (Posok jong) and masonry work directed by Chinese.		**19th century** Influence of Western construction methods.
737 Casting of the bronze bell "Emille", Korean national treasure (737).		**1905–45** Protectorate and Japanese occupation.	**20th century** Coexistence of the traditional style (mainly in houses) and international style.
		1945 Foundation of the Republic of Korea.	
		1954 Division of the country into two states: North Korea and South Korea.	

In 668 the period of "Great Silla" began in Korea: this was the peak of Korean cultural refinement, because of the close contacts established with the China of the Tang period. As a result of Buddhism being adopted as the official religion and Confucianism as the political philosophy, numerous residential and religious buildings were constructed. Kyongju, which wished to compete with Chang'an, the Chinese capital, was adorned with luxurious palaces and landscaped gardens. Because of the abundance of stone, large terraces could be built to support the wooden-structured buildings, with bracketed capitals and curved roofs covered with moulded tiles. The Buddhist temple of Pulguk-sa was rebuilt for King Kyongbok (742–64). The present structure, altered several times over the centuries, rests on the foundations of a more modest temple built 200 years earlier. It takes the form of a classic mountain temple: terraces climb the slope and culminate in the pavilion containing the statue of the Buddha Kwannon, which dominates the whole composition. After passing under the porch of the precinct and having crossed the Bridge of White Clouds, which indicates that the temple, symbolizing the sky, was originally surrounded by a moat, and having passed under the Chaha Gate, the pilgrim discovers the courtyard which surrounds the prayer-hall and the gallery around it. Two pagodas situated on either side of the central passage, the Pagoda of the Buddha (Sokkatap) and the Pagoda of the Treasures (Tabotap), replace the single pagoda formerly situated on the axis of the

Chomsong dae observatory, Kyongju. The Chomsong dae observatory (7th century) enabled the ancient Koreans to study the evolution of the sky, whose cycles determined earthly matters. The square window was used to observe the heavens, which were reflected in the sheet of water at the foot of the tower.

buildings. This new plan is found both in China and Japan. It seems to be due to an evolution in religious doctrine. The western part of the temple, which is smaller, shows the same separation of areas and functions. The western courtyard, surrounded by a gallery, is adjoined by a hall dedicated to the Buddha Amitabha. A number of structures of secondary importance – belltower, Fountain of the Ablutions, stelae – surround the temple in no particular order. The building of the Sokkuran grotto is attributed to the minister Taesong Kim. This grotto, which is similar to Indian and Chinese Buddhist grottoes, contains a statue of the Buddha sitting facing the east. Like the mausoleum under the sea of King Munmu, the Sokkuran grotto was intended to protect Korea from its island neighbour, Japan. Together with the Munmu temple, the temples of Pulguk-sa and Kamung-sa, with similar plans, are the three most characteristic buildings of the Great Silla period (668–918).

The Koryo dynasty, founded in 918, ruled Korea for nearly five centuries. Buddhism remained the predominant religion and numerous temples were built, particularly in the capital, Kaesong. The sovereigns, benefiting from the wealth of the country, lived in sumptuous palaces. Two different styles of wooden construction, found in China and Japan, coexisted at that time in Korea: the Chusimp'o style corresponds to the Japanese Tenjikuyo, and to the Chinese style originating in the province of Fujian. The Tap'o style (Karayo in Japanese) corresponds to the style of northern China. With the former style, the most widespread in Korea, the bracketing systems are arranged solely at the top of the columns, whereas with the latter style they are placed next to each other on horizontal joists linking the columns to one another. The presence of joists in the latter style promoted the building of coffered ceilings, generally absent in the Chusimp'o style. The main pavilion of the Pusok-sa in the province of Kyongsang, in North Korea, is the oldest surviving building in the Chusimp'o style. It is thought to have been built in the 13th and 14th centuries. Observance of the rituals of geomancy,

which was established in China under the Song dynasty, spread into Korea (it is still very important today in South Korea). The geographical situation, the orientation of the buildings, the towns and the houses of the dead and the living had, according to the rites, an influence on the destiny of individuals. The town of Kaesong and the palace of Manwol dae, symbols of authority and intended to ensure the prosperity of the country and of the dynasty, were built according to the rules and architectural provisions recommended in the geomancy manuals.

The Yi dynasty (1392–1910) was also based on Confucianism, but it sought to restrict the influence of Buddhism. The first sovereign decided in 1392 to move the capital from Kaesong to Seoul, which was then rebuilt and fortified. The building of the Kyongbok palace began in the same year. This palace comprises a number of buildings and pavilions spaced out in

gardens landscaped with lakes and other artificial features. A large number of Confucian schools and altars were built in Korea, but many were destroyed between 1592 and 1598 during the Japanese invasion. The painted decoration of Confucian palaces must have fascinated the Japanese, who drew inspiration from it, particularly at Nikko. By contrast, the Confucian altar, Taesong jong, and the Buddhist temples, relegated to the countryside, are soberly decorated (Haein-sa temple in the province of Kyongsang and Kakhwangjon temple in the province of Cholla in South Korea). The wooden bridge built in Seoul in 1789 by the architect Chong Yag yong, using 38 boats, is an example of utilitarian construction, under the influence of the sect of the Science of the Real, Sil Hak. This structure clearly shows that Korean architects were able to master the association between functional forms and aesthetic refinement.

Pagoda of the Popchu-sa temple. The only wooden pagoda dating from the Li dynasty (17th century), the five-storeyed pagoda of the Buddhist temple of Popchu-sa is based on models erected in China and Korea between the 6th and 8th centuries.

Palaces and temples

Residence of kings, deified symbol of power, the palace in Korea fulfils a representative function which is duly expressed in its architecture, ground plan and chosen location. The governmental palaces were built at the same time as the new capitals when each dynasty was established. The earliest techniques used in palace architecture are known to us from written texts and tomb paintings. The more recent structures – the Kyongbok palace, for example, which was begun in the 14th century – show us several aspects of the construction methods.

Of the earliest palaces of the Three Kingdoms period (57BC–AD668), those of Koguryo are the best known: the two Yi palaces of the Ryang and Ko valleys, like the Kuje palace, are mentioned in the Korean chronicles, but their exact location and construction date remain hypothetical. By examining the frescos in burial chambers, recently excavated, information was gathered about the Kuknae palaces in T'onggu (5th century), the Anhak palace, built near P'yongyang and the palace situated near Moran-bong. The pictures in the burial chambers confirm that in ancient times tiles were reserved for the royal family's buildings, administrative buildings and temples. In the tumulus of the Liaotung rampart (late 4th/early 5th century), a picture of the imperial palaces of the capital was discovered in 1953. The fresco shows two rectangular enclosures, equipped with towers, pavilions and battlements. The gateways are surmounted by pavilions. There are a number of buildings in the picture, including a structure centred in the so-called external part, and a single-storeyed pavilion, probably reserved for the king's leisure pursuits, in the inner enclosure.

However, the layout of the walls and the architecture of the palaces are reminiscent of the imperial buildings of the Chinese capitals of the Han dynasty in Chang'an.

The Ch'omun-sa temple is the oldest Buddhist temple of the Koguryo kingdom. The pillars are wooden and rest on round foundation stones at regular intervals. They supported a roof covered with tiles, which had the curved appearance symbolizing the wings of the phoenix. With the rounded ends of the beams joined to the posts by a complicated system of brackets, this early temple already possesses a number of the characteristics of Korean monumental architecture. As for the palaces of the Paekche kingdom, which have now disappeared, they were built at the foot of mountains, in accordance with the rituals, and included a number of pavilions decorated with floral and animal motifs. The evolution of Paekche temple and palace styles may be summarized as a gradual improvement of techniques, resulting in the increased elegance of buildings, rather than as a series of construction styles characterizing different periods. Our knowledge of their architecture is based on the Horyuji temple, which was built in Japan at the beginning of the 7th century in the region of Nara, under the supervision of Korean carpenters. Finally in the kingdom of Silla, the earliest palaces mentioned in the texts date from the 1st century. In the 5th century, King Soji (479–500) built the royal palaces and laid down a number of regulations about the dimensions suitable for the dwellings of the nobility, the middle classes and the common people. King Munmu (661–81) was attracted by the buildings of the Y'ang dynasty. He ordered the construction of the Imhae palace and the Anap garden in Kyongju, whose luxury was compared by the Chinese themselves to that of the Daming gong palace in Chang'an.

The biggest palace in the kingdom of Koryo (918–1392) was built in Manwol dae in the new capital of Kaesong. It comprised a group of well-ordered buildings and pavilions, arranged around square courtyards and surrounded by a stonework rampart. The buildings were made of wood; their frameworks of posts, arranged in spans and surrounded by colonnades, rested on stepped honorific terraces. The chosen location and orientation of the buildings "enjoyed good conditions as regards water and mountains" (Tonghyon Kim), which appears to be a reference to the ancient legends of the first Korean capitals. The Kyongbok palace, the residence of the Li dynasty, first built in 1392 in Seoul, is the biggest of the Korean royal palaces. Surrounded by a wall 4 metres (13 feet) high, it forms a true governmental city, organized around the audience hall, which is in turn surrounded by a wall with a covered gallery. The hall, raised on an honorific terrace, faces south. It is the culminating point of the royal way which, after crossing the palace courtyards and the sacred river, leads beyond the main gateway into the capital. The octagonal pavilion, built in the 19th century in the middle of an artificial pond, in accordance with the traditional principle of Korean architectural composition – "palace in front, garden behind" – clearly expresses the wish of the Korean constructors to establish a harmonious relationship between the buildings and their natural environment.

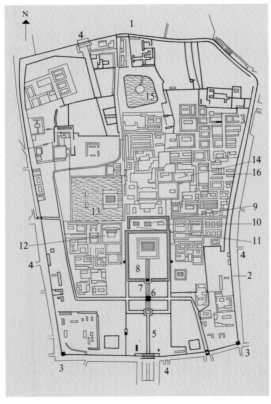

1 *Mount Pukak*	9 *Council palace*
2 *surrounding wall*	10 *Autumn pavilion*
3 *watchtowers*	11 *Spring pavilion*
4 *main gates*	12 *governmental palace*
5 *royal way*	13 *Kyonghoe pavilion*
6 *bridge and sacred river*	14 *Changgyong palace*
7 *inner gates and precincts*	15 *Perfume pavilion*
8 *main courtyard and audience hall*	16 *administration*

Kyongbok palace, Seoul

This palace was rebuilt in the 19th century on the model of 14th and 15th century palaces.

Tabotap (pagoda of the Buddha of the Treasures), temple of Pulguk-sa, Kyongju

Attributed to Asa Dal, architect from the kingdom of Paekche (and possibly even from China of the Tang period), this 7th century structure is a typical example of Korean pagodas. Standing on eight stones, arranged like the petals of the lotus, it contains the sacred texts of Buddhism.

Paved courtyard in the "secret gardens" of the Ch'angdok palace, Seoul

The "secret gardens" (Biwon) of the Ch'angdok palace contain several pavilions, a number of which were intended for the ladies of the Court. The landscaped gardens are situated behind the buildings and a gallery borders the paved area which is exposed to the south.

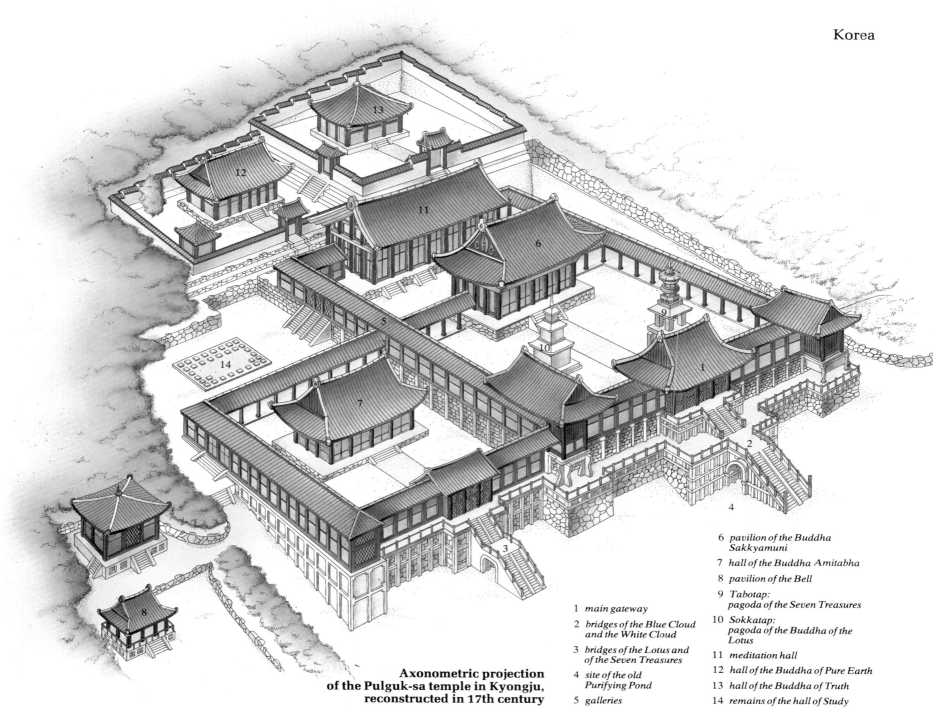

**Axonometric projection
of the Pulguk-sa temple in Kyongju,
reconstructed in 17th century**

1 *main gateway*

2 *bridges of the Blue Cloud
and the White Cloud*

3 *bridges of the Lotus and
of the Seven Treasures*

4 *site of the old
Purifying Pond*

5 *galleries*

6 *pavilion of the Buddha
Sakkyamuni*

7 *hall of the Buddha Amitabha*

8 *pavilion of the Bell*

9 *Tabotap:
pagoda of the Seven Treasures*

10 *Sokkatap:
pagoda of the Buddha of the
Lotus*

11 *meditation hall*

12 *hall of the Buddha of Pure Earth*

13 *hall of the Buddha of Truth*

14 *remains of the hall of Study*

Corner capital, Popchu-sa temple

In this 17th century example from the Popchu-sa temple, as elsewhere in Korea, the corner capital – a fundamental element in the wooden structure of buildings – is simultaneously crossed by the architrave beams, the arms of the brackets, the rafters and the oblique members of the hip of the roof.

Cross section of a building with galleries

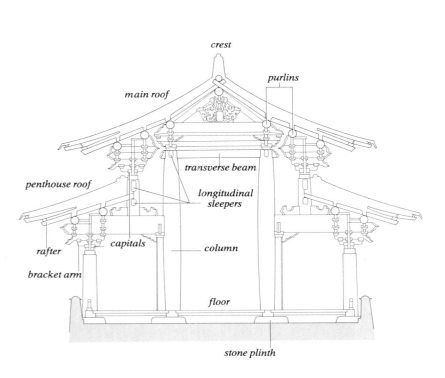

crest

purlins

main roof

transverse beam

penthouse roof

*longitudinal
sleepers*

rafter

capitals

column

bracket arm

floor

stone plinth

Houses and gardens

Since ancient times, the Korean house has been based on a wooden structure, with the posts resting on stones aligned on a mud platform. The walls are made of clay infill and the roof is covered with tiles or straw. Although methods have evolved little over the centuries, the quality of construction has continually improved. Even today, the traditional Korean house is appreciated for the natural appearance of its materials and for the ingenuity of its layout, fixtures and fittings. The shape, the slope and the projection of the roofs vary from one region to another according to climatic conditions. They protect the house from the cold winters and hot summers. The height of the pillars and the solidity and pliability of the timber framework offer the best conditions for withstanding typhoons and earthquakes.

The impression that, in the Korean countryside, nature, villages and farms are fused in a harmonious composition, reminiscent of the prettiest of pictures, is attributable to the rites of geomancy which came from China. The 17th century *Treatise on the Ideal House* outlines the method for choosing a site for houses, before describing the layout and arrangement of the buildings. "After building the framework, you make a pair of doors, then you make the rear terrace supporting a weatherboard. You add a stable to the east, a shelter to the west, a pavilion for the head of the house and, beyond the central door, a cowshed for the yellow cattle. You keep sows as well as geese to warn against thieves." (Sin Yong hun).

This description does not apply to town dwellings, the architectural parameters of which have been strongly influenced by royal buildings and government regulations (ensuring, for example, that dimensions correspond to social status). Consisting of only one habitable storey, Korean town houses are organized around one or more courtyards. They comprise a main building, which contains the ancestral altar, and several secondary buildings. In the buildings used for accommodation, the main living areas are raised, whereas the utility areas for the kitchen, cellar and bath retain a mud floor. For more than 20 centuries, Korean houses have had a system of underfloor heating in addition to heating from a brick-built hearth.

In the eyes of the Koreans, the garden forms part of the house. Evergreen trees are the precious symbols of immortality; formerly, they were planted around the sacred enclosures sheltering the graves of royalty or commoners. In landscaped parks and gardens, trees with colourful blossoms and foliage reflect the harmony of nature and express the cycle of the seasons. The first Korean gardens mentioned in the country's chronicles were created during the 1st century AD by King P'asa, of the kingdom of Silla, to embellish the palaces of his capital, Kyongju. Arranged around a diverted river, the royal gardens included an artificial mountain with nine peaks, a symbol of the heavenly paradise. In the 7th century, King Munmu (661–81) built the splendid rock gardens of Anap, comprising 12 wooded hills and encompassing an artificial lake. In the same period, in the kingdom of Paekche, King Mu (601–41) built an artificial lake in the garden of his palace. The Korean gardeners who planned the gardens for the aristocratic residences built around Nara in Japan originated from the kingdom of Paekche. In the 8th century, on the basis of a Chinese idea later adopted by Japan, the "River of the Floating Cups" was created in the royal gardens of Kyongju, near the Posok jong pavilion. Poets gathered around the river and organized poetry competitions, the prize being a cup of alcohol left to drift downstream. Under the Koryo dynasty, several landscape gardens were constructed in the town of Kaesong. In the Buddhist temples "seated meditation" was practised overlooking the rock gardens and one retired for the tea ceremony to pavilions built in the shrubberies. Between 1450 and 1820, about 20 fine gardens were built around the capital, Seoul. Most of them were constructed by the princes of the Li dynasty. The garden of the Ch'angdok palace, built after 1406 by King T'aejong (1400–18), is the most representative of Korean gardens. It was altered a few years later by King Sejo (1456–68) and new pavilions were added. The pond was enlarged to enable musical boat trips to take place. The gardens were destroyed during the Japanese invasion of 1591 by the populace rebelling against the extravagance and corruption of the Court. During the 17th century the gardens of the Ch'angdok palace were named the "secret gardens". New pavilions were built over the stretches of water, in highly geometric shapes. Garden architecture still forms part of the idyllic Korean landscape and seems to invite the traveller to rest and daydream.

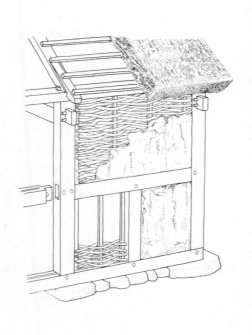

Traditional house on the outskirts of Suwon

In the vicinity of towns, the influence of monumental architecture on 20th century houses is stronger than regional trends. Middle-class houses, while retaining great simplicity, reflect, as a result of building regulations, the social standing of families.

Structure and materials

The wooden structure and clay walls of the houses are protected from the sun and rain by the projection of the roof. In the countryside, houses have thatched roofs whereas in the towns grey tiles are used. The construction materials (wood, thatch, clay, pebbles), used for their aesthetic qualities, are abundant in all the provinces of the country. They give the Korean towns and villages their architectural unity.

Kyonghoe pavilion, Kyongbok palace, Seoul

Situated overlooking a large ornamental pond and shaded by the trees of the royal garden, the 19th century Kyonghoe pavilion is a wooden structure resting on stonework piles.

Plans of typical urban and rural dwellings in the 18th–19th century period

Left: plan of a town house surrounded by an enclosure wall and divided into two parts – one for men, the other for women. Right: plan of a country house with several principal buildings, similarly divided into two parts – one for each sex.

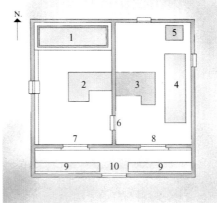
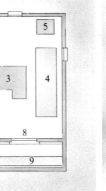

1	kitchen
2	women's house
3	men's house
4	library
5	kiosk
6	internal door
7	women's door
8	men's door
9	servants' quarters
10	main door

1	mistress's house	9	master's house
2	stand for jars	10	pigsty
3	kiosk under the pines	11	servants' quarters
4	well	12	entrance gate
5	grain chest	13	stream
6	shelter	14	pond
7	fields	15	willows
8	stable		

Hyangwon jung pavilion, garden of the Kyongbok palace, Seoul

Among the numerous pavilions of the "secret garden" of the recently restored royal palace, the Hyangwon jung pavilion (16th–19th century) is reached by a bridge, as recommended by the architectural rules for landscape gardens.

Geomancy of the Korean house, 17th century
(according to the *Treatise on the Ideal House*)

1	protective mountains
2	main mountain
3	ideal house
4	internal "blue dragon"
5	internal "white tiger"
6	external "blue dragon"
7	external "white tiger"
8	table-shaped hill
9	stream
10	stream outlet
11	mountain trapping "the energy of the earth"

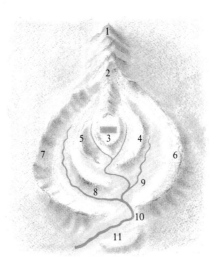

General view of Itsukushima jinja, Hiroshima

The unusual placing of the shrines at Itsukushima, on this narrow shore between the sea and the mountains, is in keeping with the sacred character of the buildings. High tide makes them look as though they are floating on the water and enhances their famous layout. Although a precise date is not known, this group must have been founded in the Heian period, since in 1168–69 the buildings were the subject of a massive restoration programme, and they probably assumed their present appearance then. But the oldest pavilions still to be seen date from a later reconstruction (1241), which was made necessary by a number of fires.

Japan owes much to China for the basis and structure of her civilization. But it would be wrong to conclude from this that Japan does not really have an art form of her own, and that she has been restricted to imitating or even counterfeiting China. As far as architecture is concerned, Japan is certainly indebted to China for fundamental principles and a number of models; and it is also true that she often failed to grasp their true meaning or, in some ways, how to use them. But, in the first place, if Japan did not understand the Chinese message, it was because she received it through the bias of Buddhism and then applied it over the centuries under Buddhist control. In Chinese architecture and technology, shaped and developed as they were by Buddhism, fundamental notions and concepts had become blurred, impoverished, or even corrupted. And secondly, it should be remembered that these distortions actually gave Japan a chance, by allowing her to dress this foreign heritage in her own characteristic manner, to go outside the taboos and restrictions in order to give free rein to her own creativity, and to allow herself to adopt original solutions which China would have regarded as heresies.

The Japanese variations of the Chinese norms can be demonstrated in many ways. From all the materials used in architecture on the Chinese mainland, for example, Japan chose to use wood almost exclusively. In contrast to Chinese symmetry, she substituted dissymmetry as often as possible, since this was better suited to her temperament. On the technical level, she thought up new and ingenious schemes in answer to her own needs. And in an attempt to integrate the buildings with their environment, she deliberately rejected Chinese magnificence and the grand scale of Chinese architecture. Finally, where China has been quite casual in her attitude towards her architectural wealth, allowing herself the luxury of destroying evidence of a long history after each political upheaval, Japan on the contrary has been deeply conservative. Indeed, Japan has preserved her heritage at all costs, and because of this it is today a veritable museum of national architecture and a conservatory of mainland archetypes which have long since vanished from their place of origin.

The evolution of dwelling places during Japanese prehistory and protohistory, the end of which is usually dated around AD552, can be followed quite easily. The first signs of habitation date back to around 8000BC. In the cold climate of those days, men naturally sought shelter in caves, and they continued to live in these or under overhanging rocks, which offered the same

kind of shelter, until the Early Jomon period. As the climate warmed up, a new kind of dwelling began to spread – the half-buried house, designed to last for many years. This was a pit, which, although it was quite shallow, still lessened the extremes of temperature; and the posts that supported its superstructure were driven into it. The whole history of semi-buried living quarters runs parallel to the history of agriculture and reflects its development. In the pre-agricultural settlements on high ground, the houses were not uniform in shape, and none of them had a hearth. This did not become common until the end of the Early Jomon period (C.3400–3000BC). With the introduction of very primitive agriculture in the Middle Jomon period (C.3000–2000BC), bigger buildings with better layouts were constructed further down on the low plateaux and the alluvial soil; the pits, which were round or rectangular with rounded corners, were surrounded by a low wall, which in turn was surrounded by a gutter. From this period onwards, but especially from the Late Jomon period (C.2000–300BC), the development of agriculture, with its socio-cultural consequences as well as its need for appropriate land, inevitably led to architectural diversity – much larger pits were added to the small domestic ones, which, judging by the many objects that were buried there, had some religious purpose. Next, in the Yayoi era (C.300BC–AD250), the development of rice-growing pushed the villages towards the warm valleys. From then on it was necessary to protect the houses from damp; and to avoid direct contact with the ground, matting was laid on a bed of branches or bamboo, or else a floor was attached to the posts with its edges resting on the sides of the pit.

But the spread of rice-growing during the Yayoi period had not only given rise to massive agricultural development, it had also led to the manufacture of a rather specialized iron tool, as well as the relevant technology. And architecture profited from this to produce a great innovation – the granary on stilts. This, a tangible sign of wealth and the most important building in the village, was the object of the greatest technical attention and research. With its very long stilts, its plain supporting walls made of planks, and its overhanging roof – emphasized by large projections above the gable walls – the Yayoi granary echoes the architecture of Sumatra and the Celebes, although its roots appear to lie in southern or central China.

Finally, during the Tumuli period (C.250–550), the stratification of society was deeply imprinted on building

patterns. While semi-buried houses remained the norm among the lower classes, the ruling classes adopted the one-storey houses on stilts which probably appeared at the end of the Yayoi period. Although these houses have left very few traces in the ground, their outlines have been found on haniwa (pottery drains which were at first cylindrical and then became miniature and symbolic representations of houses, animals and people), which offer a wealth of information on the main architectural tendencies at the dawn of history. Through them it was discovered that technological progress had made it possible to build rafters on a framework without supporting walls, and to erect hipped or half-hipped roofs, even though there was a preference for gabled roofs. These, which were hog-backed, projected a long way out over the gabled walls, but they no longer needed, as before, to be supported by extra non-aligned posts. Finally, and this is characteristic of the Japanese mentality, the primitive functional elements were preserved in a decorative and symbolic form as signs of authority and power.

But of all the creations that belong to this lengthy period, the most remarkable is funerary architecture. Although the burial practices of primitive Japan were on the whole related to the practices of those neighbours who had reached the same level of civilization, the ties were broken during the last stages of her protohistory. In fact, Japanese tumuli, which are definitely Chinese in origin, were more closely related to the land of the living than to the land of the dead. They were essentially an instrument to create prestige among the clans, as can be seen from the way they were built. The Japanese did not consider the tomb of their dead chief to be his new home. Unlike the Chinese builders, they raised a round mound first, with a rectangular platform in front of it, and from the top they dug out the cavity which was to hold the coffin. This type of tomb reached impressive proportions and took the entirely original shape of a keyhole, while the platform was lengthened into a trapeze shape and built higher to correspond to the height of the mound. For a short time the burial place, with a design that had no equivalent on the mainland, became the sacred monument par excellence and the ostensible sign of the clan's power.

Japan's decisive integration with the civilization of the Far East took place in the 6th century, at a time when the country had just acquired a framework of states and was already quite centralized. In a crisis of both political and cultural conscience, Japan evaluated her backwardness and understandably decided to assimilate the values which had been perfected in China through the medium of Buddhism. Officially introduced in 552, Buddhism brought with it a whole infrastructure, generated in China but modified as it passed through Korea. The meeting of the two cultures led the Japanese to follow back along the path by which Buddhism had reached them. Thus, having obtained their basic knowledge from Korean artisans, they went on from the end of the 7th century to learn more in China itself; this period – lasting until 794 – was the only one in which they practised a religion that conformed to the contemporary Chinese model and was not just an extraction of a previous phase.

This cultural progression is perfectly illustrated in the development of the general plan of Buddhist foundations between the 6th and 8th centuries, which can be restricted here to the cloistered holy area (garan), with its middle gate (chumon), the pagoda, the main sacred pavilion (kondo) and, next to it, the assembly pavilion (kodo). The Japanese faithfully copied the Chinese architectural system – a wooden structure, built on a terrace of packed earth with stone facings, with a hipped or half-hipped roof, which stands on rafters laid on top of each other and is supported by a system of consoles and pillars resting on stone pedestals. But they were not very concerned at first about conforming to the strict north-south axis.

According to archaeological findings, the earliest monasteries show not just one, but at least two architectural traditions whose equivalents may be found in Korea. The first is reminiscent of the central plan from India. As if to emphasize its holiness further, the pagoda was built in the centre of the square between the middle gate and the kondo, on a north-south axis, and was flanked by two extra kondo on the cross axis. The second model, more popular at the end of the 6th century and the beginning of the 7th, was closer to the orthodox Chinese style, with all the important buildings lined up on a north-south axis, including the assembly pavilion.

Towards the middle of the 7th century, another very widely adopted formula took over. Better suited to the Japanese temperament and allowing for numerous variations, it consisted of two symmetrical buildings standing on a north-south axis and merging with the cloisters, together with two independent buildings on the transverse axis. All these experiments, interesting for their attempts to create a volumetric harmony, found fulfilment in the western holy area (saiin) at Horyuji (after 670), where only three buildings were retained in the plan: the middle gate, the kondo on the east, and the pagoda on the west. To increase the distance between the kondo and pagoda and to create a more harmonious space around the kondo, the builders extended the cloisters asymmetrically north and south, with a line of columns stretching east from the middle gate. In order to balance the volumes and masses elsewhere, the middle gate and the kondo were built on two levels. Furthermore, the height of the pagoda was exactly twice that of the kondo, and the two buildings had the same volume. Finally, breaking all the rules, the middle gate had two pathways, instead of the one or three that were normally built, in accordance with the fashion for uneven numbers. Thus, from the third quarter of the 7th century, this spatial layout became unique in its dissymmetry and freed itself from the rigid Chinese plan.

From the last quarter of the 7th century, a revival of Chinese influence strongly imposed mainland orthodoxy in Japan, with the alignment of major buildings on the north-south axis and the building of a second pagoda. This duplication was maintained throughout the first half of the 8th century, but the pagodas were taken out of the holy area, and the kondo and the middle gate were merged into the cloisters. This transformed the holy area into a completely empty courtyard, so that it could be used for two purposes: as a place of prayer and as a setting for religious ceremonies. This rigorous observation of mainland rules did not create any sense of monotony, however, since each monastery had its own individual characteristics.

The architectural fever reached its climax in the middle of the 8th century with the construction of Todaiji, on which work began in 747 and continued until 789. This massive undertaking proved the skill of Japanese carpenters, since the original kondo was the biggest wooden structure that has ever been built; and it symbolized the power and influence of the monks. But in the second half of the century building programmes were considerably reduced by economic recession and political rivalry

Back of a bronze mirror decorated with images of four buildings, found in a tumulus at Samida, Nara. The first building, on stilts, is generally assumed to be a granary despite the absence of supporting walls. The second, on long stilts, is a chief's dwelling, with an entrance in the gable wall and a surrounding balcony, which are reached by a ramp-like staircase. The third is a single-storey building at ground level, which had an unknown purpose. And the fourth is clearly a semi-buried house.

Shogakukan, Zoto

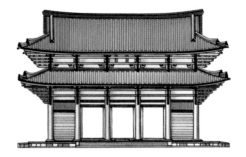

Todaiji Monastery, the great south gate or "nandaimon", Nara. When Minamoto Yoritomo decided, in 1181, to reconstruct Todaiji, which had been reduced to ashes, he entrusted the work to Chogen (1121–1206), a monk of the Jodo sect. Concerned above all to ensure the rigidity necessary for a building of such great size, Chogen rationalized the construction and, taking his inspiration from a regional Chinese style, put some revolutionary ideas into practice without worrying about any refinement. Extra buildings were standardized; visible pillars were strengthened – in both directions and right up to the level of the purlins – by cross-beams placed at regular intervals; the small cross-beams in the aisles were linked by false middle posts; and the main beams were supported by a system of protruding consoles inserted into the pillars. On the outside, the roof overhang was supported by an original corbelling system, as can be seen in the "nandaimon" (1199): some of the cross-beams extend outside the building to join up with the consoles (all perpendicular to the wall except for the last layer), rails catch the free butts of several consoles and, in the protruding angles of the roof, radiating rafters near the joists allow better weight distribution.

between the high aristocracy and the Buddhist clergy. New foundations assumed smaller proportions, having only one pagoda; public or residential buildings were often used for the purpose after minor alterations, as can be seen from a number of important pavilions in Toshadaiji (founded in 759). Thus the period which had turned completely towards China and centred itself on Buddhism came to an end.

In reaction to the pervading Buddhism, Shinto – the indigenous religion, which encompassed all the country's primitive beliefs and practices – began as early as the 6th century to devise its own sacred architecture. In order to express its antiquity and its native origins, Shinto was to develop its first buildings in rejection of new or foreign values and to turn quite naturally to the most dominant forms of ancient architecture. Among the most venerable and ancient establishments, there are three which illustrate this perfectly. These are Ise jingu, a building which has echoes of a granary – the most important building of the ancient agricultural communities – Izumo taisha, derived from the palace structure – the most majestic construction of the ancient tribal groups – and finally Sumiyoshi taisha, a development of the temporary shrines which were built for religious festivals and official ceremonies.

One of the major manifestations of Chinese influence was the foundation of the first capitals. Before the 7th century, Japan had no real urban tradition; and indeed she never had any areas containing a population large enough to create one. But the situation changed when the increasingly important administration required a fixed urban seat, and the Japanese were naturally inspired by the plan of the Chinese capital, Chang'an – based on a quadrilateral with rectangular

divisions, separated into two districts by a wide central street running from north to south. The copy did not entirely conform to its model, however. In contrast to Chang'an, the length of the rectangular Japanese plan ran from north to south, and the width east to west, while the shape of the districts was square rather than rectangular, in response to a pre-existing system of land registration. Furthermore, whether it be at Heijokyo (Nara) or later at Heiankyo (Kyoto), the spontaneous development of the houses and the immediate addition of new districts thwarted the symmetry intended by the town planners. Without regard to the original plan, these towns stretched out to the east, where the lie of the land and the nature of the soil made it easier to expand. Hence, in spite of its respect for China, town planning in the ancient Japanese capitals was characterized by its asymmetry, a very typical mark of the native temperament.

When the emperor moved his capital to Heiankyo, a phase of classical balance began (794–1185). The withdrawal of ambassadors at the court of Tang, ordered by Japan in 894, was the signal for cultural emancipation: real national tendencies made an attempt to flourish, but even so they were based on ideals which were Chinese, and which were already obsolete in China. Although architectural development is still difficult to define because time has spared so little evidence, it does seem that, in style and technique, this era cultivated characteristics which dated from before the previous era rather than any that were new. Nevertheless, simply through the abolition of stone and tile pavings in favour of boards and bark coverings, the pavilions governed by the ancient mainland formulas assumed a specifically Japanese appearance.

Finally, what makes this period unique is that the distinguishing characteristics of each architectural type merged into each other: a monastery is seen to resemble a palace in its layout, a Shinto shrine borrows details from civic and Buddhist buildings, a dwelling is inspired by Shinto simplicity and is expressive of the Buddhist sentiment of universal transience.

Residential architecture was very reluctant to accept mainland teaching, and from the beginning of the 7th century it developed a style which was to culminate during the Heian period in Shinden zukuri, about which, alas, our knowledge is limited to literary and pictorial evidence. The plan consisted of a group of detached pavilions, of which the principal one, for the master of the household, constituted the structural pivot. Each pavilion formed an autonomous residential unit which had a great deal of spatial flexibility, and they were linked by single or double galleries and corridors which were extended southwards as covered passages to fishing pavilions and artificial lakes. Due to its symmetry, the ground plan was at first reminiscent of the Chinese imperial parks, but it very quickly veered towards asymmetry by eliminating the secondary pavilions; and the general design continued to be simplified by the successive removal of different buildings until it was finally reduced to a single pavilion.

Of the many schools of thought which then influenced Buddhist architecture, the most inventive was undoubtedly Amitabha Buddhism. This faith, which was completely incompatible with the teachings of other sects, particularly recommended

circumambulation, and followers of Amitabha therefore required a building with a central choir. This need was fulfilled by two types of temple: the first, a square building with a development of three rows of columns down the side, was adopted by small and provincial monasteries; and the second, oblong in shape with 11 rows of columns by three – required by Amitabha in his nine manifestations – was preferred in the large foundations built during the 11th and 12th centuries.

In addition, the high nobility, prompted by the hope of rebirth in the Paradise of Western thinking, attempted to create on earth the ideal beauty of the world beyond, and especially of the palace of Amitabha. This longing was fulfilled above all in the Hoodo (1053) of Byodoin at Uji. The plan consists of a central structure with a gallery in the middle leading from the rear façade and two lateral galleries which extend the front façade and project forward in a right-angle. It derives directly from the ancient pictorial descriptions of the Amitabha palace which were circulating in China and Japan from the 8th century onwards. An abstraction of the elements required in Buddhism, the general appearance of Hoodo is reminiscent of imperial Chinese parks, as well as evocative of the style of early Shinden zukuri.

But it was also in the Heian period that Shinto architecture blossomed to the full and defined its fundamental styles: Kasuga zukuri, Nagare zukuri and Hachiman zukuri. Under the influence of Buddhism, all three sought extra space both outside and inside. Kasuga zukuri and the Nagare style, which was widely adopted, shared the techniques of using plate-foundations and gable roofs and of extending a canopy over the main façade. Nagare zukuri also inspired different ways of enlarging the façades without altering the shrine. Hachiman zukuri was a pairing of both Buddhist and residential styles in which two buildings of equal length were set one behind the other with a gutter at the junction of the two roofs. The linking area developed into a slightly dugout passage, and in this form the style was greatly developed from the 16th century onwards, when it was revived for the mausoleums of national heroes with the new name of Gongen zukuri.

In spite of socio-political instability, the Japanese Middle Ages (1185–1573) were one of the most creative architectural eras, with Buddhism as the guiding force as before, but now quickened by the impact of Zen. Profound changes in society had forced Buddhism to offer new doctrinal options and to diversify its teachings; this led, aesthetically, to a profusion of new directions. At this time also, architecture found a happy balance between functional plan and monumental decoration, under the influence of a growing mannerism, which was the outcome of a native inclination for refinement.

In analysing the architectural tendencies of the time, it is possible to distinguish four main styles, which can then be grouped into twos according to whether or not they derive from national tradition. The two national styles contrast as much in their reaction to contemporary conditions as in their diffusion. The one (Wayo zukuri), which is conservative, is confined to the Nara region, the birthplace of Buddhism, and tries to reproduce as accurately as possible models from the Golden Age, shunning all

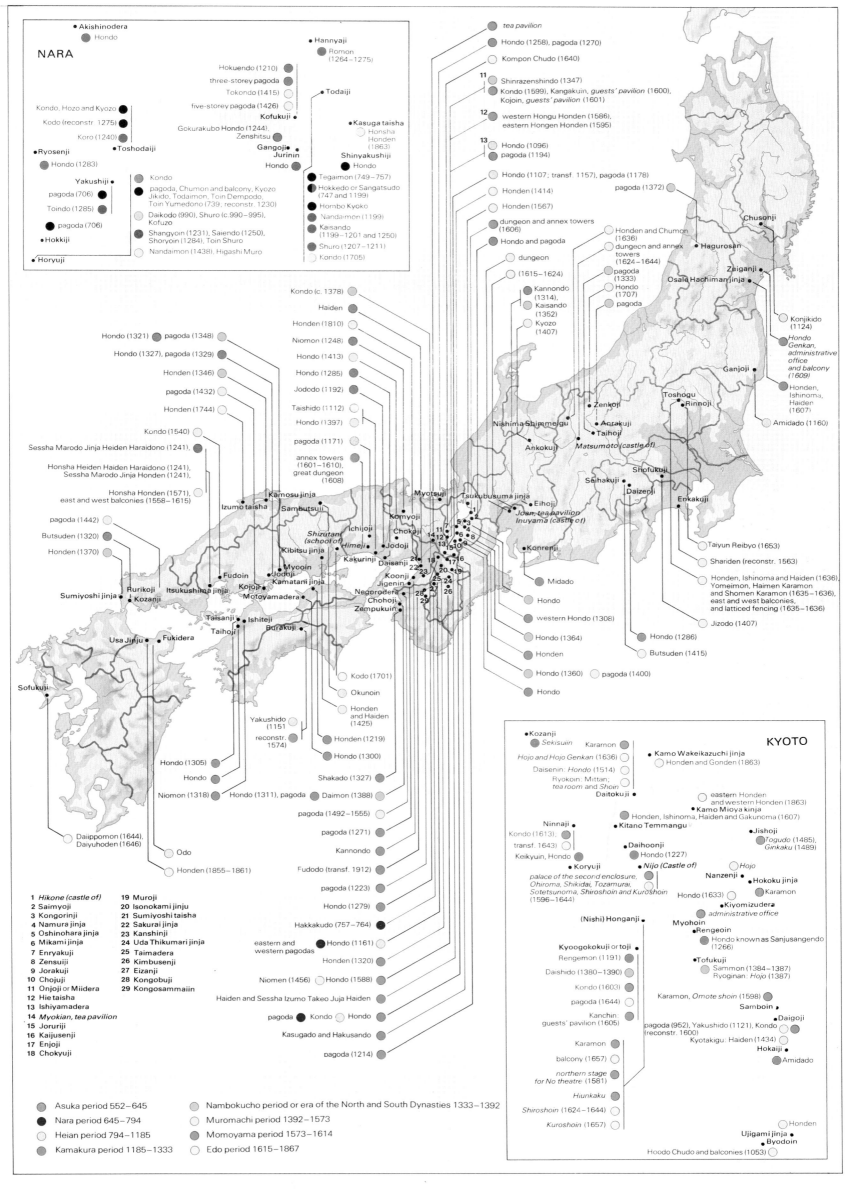

NARA

- Akishinodera
- Hondo

- Hannyaji
  Romon
  (1264–1275)
- Hokuendo (1210)
- three-storey pagoda
- Tokondo (1415)
- five-storey pagoda (1426)
- Todaiji
- Kondo, Hozo and Kyozo
- Kodo (reconstr. 1275)
- Koro (1240)
- Gokurakubo Hondo (1244), Zenshitsu
- Kofukuji
- Kasuga taisha
  Honsha Honden (1863)
- Ryosenji
- Hondo (1283)
- Toshodaiji
- Gangoji Jurinin
  Hondo
- Shinyakushiji
  Hondo
- Yakushiji
- pagoda (706)
- Toindo (1285)
- pagoda (706)
- Hokkiji
- Horyuji
- Kondo
- pagoda, Chumon and balcony, Kyozo Jikido, Todaimon, Toin Dempodo, Toin Yumedono (739; reconstr. 1230)
- Daikodo (990), Shuro (c.990–995), Kofuzo
- Shangyoin (1231), Saiendo (1250), Shoryoin (1284), Toin Shuro
- Nandaimon (1438), Higashi Muro
- Tegaimon (749–757)
- Hokkedo or Sangatsudo (747 and 1199)
- Hombo Kyoko
- Nandaimon (1199)
- Kaisando (1199–1201 and 1250)
- Shuro (1207–1211)
- Kondo (1705)

- tea pavilion
- Hondo (1258), pagoda (1270)
- Kompon Chudo (1640)
- 11
  - Shinrazenshindo (1347)
  - Kondo (1599), Kangakuin, guests' pavilion (1600), Kojoin, guests' pavilion (1601)
- 12
  - western Hongu Honden (1586), eastern Hongen Honden (1595)
- 13
  - Hondo (1096)
  - pagoda (1194)
- Hondo (1107; transf. 1157), pagoda (1178)
- Honden (1414)
- Honden (1567)
- dungeon and annex towers (1606)
- Hondo and pagoda
- dungeon
- (1615–1624)
- Honden and Chumon (1636)
- dungeon and annex towers (1624–1644)
- pagoda (1333)
- Hondo (1707)
- pagoda
- Chusonji
- Haidden
- Zuiganji
- Osale Hachiman jinja
- Konjikido (1124)
- Hondo Genkan, administrative office and balcony (1609)
- Ganjoji
- Honden, Ishinoma, Haiden (1607)
- Amidado (1160)

- Kondo (c. 1378)
- Haiden
- Honden (1810)
- Niomon (1248)
- Hondo (1413)
- Hondo (1285)
- Jododo (1192)
- Taishido (1112)
- Hondo (1397)
- pagoda (1171)
- annex towers (1601–1610), great dungeon (1608)
- Kannondo (1314), Kaisando (1352)
- Kyozo (1407)

- Hondo (1321) pagoda (1348)
- Hondo (1327), pagoda (1329)
- Honden (1346)
- pagoda (1432)
- Honden (1744)
- Kondo (1540)
- Sessha Marodo Jinja Heiden Haraidono (1241)
- Honsha Heiden Haiden Haraidono (1241), Sessha Marodo Jinja Honden (1241),
- Honsha Honden (1571), east and west balconies (1558–1615)
- pagoda (1442)
- Butsuden (1320)
- Honden (1370)

Sumiyoshi jinja

Rurikoji
Kozanji
Fudoin
Myoin
Jodoji
Kamatani jinja
Motoyamadera
Taisanji
Ishiteji
Taihoji
Burakuji
Usa Jinju
Fukidera

Sofukuji

Izumo taisha
Kamosu jinja
Sambutsuji
Ichijoji
Shizutani (school of)
Kibitsu jinja
Himeji
Kojoji
Jodoji
Kakurinji
Daisanji

Myotsuji
Komyoji
Chokoji
Jodoji
Koonji
Jigenin
Negorodera
Chohoji
Zempukuin

Tsukubusuma jinja
Eihoji
Joan, tea pavilion
Inuyama (castle of)

Nishima Shimmeigu
Zenkoji
Anrakuji
Taihoji
Matsumoto (castle of)
Ankokuji

Toshogu
Rinnoji
Saihakuji
Shofukuji
Daizenji
Enkakuji

Seikihaku ji

Taiyun Reibyo (1653)
Shariden (reconstr. 1563)
Honden, Ishinoma and Haiden (1636), Yomeimon, Haimen Karamon and Shomen Karamon (1635–1636), east and west balconies, and latticed fencing (1635–1636)

Jizodo (1407)

Konrenji
Midado
Hondo
western Hondo (1308)
Hondo (1364)
Honden
Hondo (1360)
Hondo

Hondo (1286)
Butsuden (1415)
pagoda (1400)

- Kodo (1701)
- Okunoin
- Honden and Haiden (1425)
- Yakushido (1151) reconstr. 1574
- Honden (1219)
- Hondo (1300)
- Shakado (1327)
- Daimon (1388)
- pagoda (1492–1555)
- pagoda (1271)
- Kannondo
- Fudodo (transf. 1912)
- pagoda (1223)
- Hondo (1279)
- Hakkakudo (757–764)
- Hondo (1161)
- Honden (1320)
- Hondo (1588)
- Haiden and Sessha Izumo Takeo Juja Haiden
- pagoda Kondo Hondo
- Kasugado and Hakusando
- pagoda (1214)

- Hondo (1305)
- Hondo
- Niomon (1318)
- Hondo (1311), pagoda

- Daiippomon (1644), Daiyuhoden (1646)
- Odo
- Honden (1855–1861)

- eastern and western pagodas
- Niomen (1456)

1 Hikone (castle of)
2 Saimyoji
3 Kongorinji
4 Namura jinja
5 Oshinohara jinja
6 Mikami jinja
7 Enryakuji
8 Zensuiji
9 Jorakuji
10 Chojuji
11 Onjoji or Miidera
12 Hie taisha
13 Ishiyamadera
14 Myokian, tea pavilion
15 Joruriji
16 Kaijusenji
17 Enjoji
18 Chokyuji
19 Muroji
20 Isonokami jinju
21 Sumiyoshi taisha
22 Sakurai jinja
23 Kanshinji
24 Uda Thikumari jinja
25 Taimadera
26 Kimbusenji
27 Eizanji
28 Kongobuji
29 Kongosammaiin

KYOTO

- Kozanji
- Sekisuiin
- Karamon
- Hojo and Hojo Genkan (1636)
- Daisenin: Hondo (1514)
- Ryokoin: Mittan; tea room and Shoin
- Daitokuji
- Kamo Wakeikazuchi jinja
- Honden and Gonden (1863)
- eastern Honden and western Honden (1863)
- Kamo Mioya kinja
- Honden, Ishinoma, Haiden and Gakunoma (1607)
- Kitano Temmangu
- Ninnaji
- Kondo (1613); transf. 1643
- Keikyuin, Hondo
- Koryuji
- Daihoonji
- Hondo (1227)
- Jishoji
- Togudo (1485), Ginkaku (1489)
- Nijo (Castle of)
- palace of the second enclosure, Ohiroma, Shikidai, Tozamurai, Sotetsunoma, Shiroshoin and Kuroshoin (1596–1644)
- Hojo
- Nanzenji
- Hondo (1633)
- Hokoku jinja
- Hokoku jinja
- Karamon
- Kiyomizudera administrative office
- Myohoin
- Rengeoin
- Hondo known as Sanjusangendo (1266)
- (Nishi) Honganji
- Kyoogokokuji or toji
- Rengemon (1191)
- Daishido (1380–1390)
- Kondo (1603)
- pagoda (1644)
- Kanchin: guests' pavilion (1605)
- Tofukuji
- Sammon (1384–1387)
- Ryoginan: Hojo (1387)
- Karamon, Omote shoin (1598)
- Samboin
- Daigoji
- pagoda (952), Yakushido (1121), Kondo (reconstr. 1600)
- Kyotakigu: Haiden (1434)
- Hokaiji
- Amidado
- Karamon
- balcony (1657)
- northern stage for No theatre (1581)
- Hiunkaku
- Shiroshoin (1624–1644)
- Kuroshoin (1657)
- Honden
- Ujigami jinja
- Byodoin
- Hoodo Chudo and balconies (1053)

- Asuka period 552–645
- Nara period 645–794
- Heian period 794–1185
- Kamakura period 1185–1333
- Nambokucho period or era of the North and South Dynasties 1333–1392
- Muromachi period 1392–1573
- Momoyama period 1573–1614
- Edo period 1615–1867

Civilization	Architecture
ASUKA period (538–645)	
592 Shotoku taishi elected as regent.	
	593 Construction work begun on Shitennoji, OSAKA.
NARA period (645–794)	
	670 Construction work begun on Horyuji, NARA.
710 Capital established at HEIJOKYO (Nara).	
	730 Oriental pagoda of Yakushiji, HEIJOKYO (Nara).
752 Official consecration of Todaiji.	
	759 Foundation of Toshodaiji, NARA.
HEIAN period (794–1185)	
794 Capital transferred to HEIANKYO (Kyoto).	
1016–74 Apogee of power of the Fujiwara clan.	
	1053 Phoenix Pavilion at Byodoin, KYOTO.
	1124 Konjikido of Chusonji, IWATE.
KAMAKURA period (1185–1333)	
1192 Institution of first shogun rulers: the Minamoto.	
	1199 Great south gate of Todaiji, NARA.
	1241 The oldest surviving buildings of Itsukushima jinja, HIROSHIMA.
1274 and 1281 Mongol attacks.	
NAMBOKUCHO period (1333–92)	
1338 Institution of second shogun rulers: the Ashikaga.	
	1346 Kamosu jinja, SHIMANE.
MUROMACHI period (1392–1573)	
	1489 Silver Pavilion, KYOTO.
1543 Arrival of the first Portuguese.	
AZUCHI-MOMOYAMA period (1573–1615)	
1573 Oda Nobunaga takes power.	
1582 Toyotomi Hideyoshi takes power.	
	1598 Omote Shoin of Samboin, KYOTO.
	1601–10 Himeji stronghold, HYOGO.
1603 Institution of third shogun rulers: the Tokugawa.	
EDO period (1615–1867)	
	1616–63 Katsura Palace, KYOTO.
1635 Frontiers closed.	**1635–36** Toshogu of Nikko, TOCHIGI.
1853 Arrival of Commodore Perry's ships in Edo Bay (Tokyo).	

innovations. The other (Shinwayo zukuri), progressive and very widely spread, manages to respect tradition while still taking socio-religious reform into account. Thus, as much to answer the often esoteric imperatives of ritual as to assist the participation of the believers, it takes its final form in sacred pavilions that have a dissymmetrical design and contain a shrine and prayer-room which are separated from each other by a clerestory. Although it was roughly mapped out during the Heian period, the most characteristic example of Shinwayo zukuri is perhaps the tahoto, a variation of the pagoda inspired by the Indian stupa. It consists of a central cylindrical core on two levels, covered with a pyramid-shaped roof and partially shrouded by a sloping roof running around the ground floor.

In spite of their common Chinese origins, the two foreign styles developed in ways which were respectively just as different as the two national styles. Introduced by the monk, Chogen (1121–1206), Daibutsuyo zukuri grew from a regional Chinese style which seems to have been favoured in the southern coastal regions. Concerned above all with structure, Chogen opted firmly for rationalization by standardizing the extra buildings, and for putting function before refinement. As well as retaining the symmetry and the stacked, gable-roof timbers of the classical Chinese tradition, he perfected a revolutionary building system, notably with an original corbelling technique: sunk straight into the pillars, the consoles were placed at regular intervals perpendicular to the wall, except for the last one, which ran lengthwise and took the ridge-pole. But this sudden break with all

the old customs offended Japanese sensibilities and the Daibutsuyo style had little influence. The Song style, on the other hand, which was introduced by the Zen sect and treated as official, had a novel elegance which was the perfect answer to contemporary aspirations. In a building that was totally sophisticated, the finest feature was the corbelling – consoles were placed on top of the pillars and between them as well, giving the effect of an ornamental cornice. The success of this style, known as Zenshuyo, was due perhaps to the fact that it absorbed a great many formulas which had been known for a long time in Japan but had either been abandoned or diverted from their original function. It brought back stone terraces, paved grounds, thicker pillars and covered passageways in the sacred areas – all features which had disappeared after the Nara period. It also increased the number of two-storeyed buildings; although these had been quite popular, judging by the kondo and the middle gate at Horyuji, they had had absolutely no use, but now, in Zenshuyo zukuri, the second storey became practicable. Furthermore, in important buildings, the oblong shape which had been fashionable until then was replaced by a square plan, which had only been used previously in small secondary temples. And finally, the Zenshuyo style extended the whole of the ground floor with a sloping roof attached to the walls, a practice which had lapsed at the end of the 12th century.

Until now, Buddhism had catalysed and controlled the arts, but after 1573 the new political leaders had no qualms about eliminating this Chinese element. From now on, two apparently contradictory

tendencies were to emerge and predominate during the Azuchi-Momoyama and Edo periods (1573–1867). The first, retained by the leaders of the country and fairly generally by the religious sects, was expressed in an ostentatious architecture, in which the decorative arts played a leading role. The second developed from the tea ceremony and ended in a style of supreme refinement which relied totally on simplicity and lack of artifice. Eventually the interaction of these two streams gave birth to a style of residence which was free from official restrictions and had more of fantasy than the tea ceremony tolerated.

Both a fortress and a residence, the castle is one of the most spectacular creations of the Japanese feudal system. In its general appearance it seems to violate all traditional values. In contrast to other buildings of primary importance, such as palaces and monasteries, where modesty and simplicity prevailed, the castle adopted triumphant height, massive dimensions and complex plans to express its splendour. It also sets itself apart because it was made principally of stone, which was hardly used anywhere else at all, and because its walls were made to look extremely solid, whereas in all other buildings they were reduced to a minimum. It seems rather surprising that the brief flourishing of castles happened during the early 17th century, when Japan was returning to peace, and that, contrary to all logic, it did not happen during troubled times but was instead a kind of survivor of them. The reason is that the lords wanted castles less to defend themselves than to proclaim their power and to signify their prestige.

In the residential sectors of the castle a sumptuous palatial style developed, the Shoin zukuri, which was not only admired by the nobility, but was also taken up, with certain modifications, by other levels of society. In fact, the term shoin has had different meanings in different social spheres and periods. For a long time it was a corner for reading and writing in a monastery study, constructed on a projection above the external gallery. During the Muromachi era it was an entire living room, first envisaged for the monk in his convent, then for the daimyo in his castle. During the Momoyama period the term was stretched to include the whole of the rear section of a building, where the master of the household lived. Finally, in the middle of the 17th century, names such as "little shoin" and "big shoin" appeared, describing buildings in front of the house which were used for meeting people and for official receptions. Above all, the Shoin style is characterized by the presence of four elements in its interior layout: the tokonoma (a kind of niche), the tsukeshoin (a work desk under the window) and the chigaidana (shelves), all borrowed from the monastic residences of the Middle Ages, and finally, the chodaigamae (a door of four sliding panels) taken from the Shinden zukuri. Another of its characteristics is the more rigid partitioning of the internal area: a specific function is allocated to each unit and each is immediately obvious from its position in the building. This functional specialization spread to the pavilions in the richest homes. In its ideal form – the best example of which is the palace in the second enclosure of the Nijo stronghold at Kyoto (restored 1624–26) – the Shoin zukuri has the system of detached pavilions of the Shinden style but these are built along a diagonal line and each is given a precise and unique function. At a time that was marked by a taste for show, the buildings for receptions and official gatherings became the most important: they were placed in front of the property and were sumptuously decorated.

In reaction to all this pomposity, "tea architecture" was established. The master Sen no Rikyu (1528–92) gave the tea ceremony its classic form, with an austerity and refinement which could not in any way adapt themselves to the residential style in common use at that time. He therefore invented a framework, inspired by rural architecture, which would recreate the atmosphere of a mountain hermitage. It was a spartan place with cob walls and a solid appearance, generally without shoji (the translucent mobile screens which act as an element of union between the interior and the environment) or balconies (related to

the shoji), but with small windows; because of their positions, these windows were able to throw varied lighting into the interior, according to the time of day and the seasons. In short, it was a studiously bare setting, with a refined beauty that consisted in acknowledging the materials and functional elements. Furthermore, the basic formula allowed for many completely different interpretations. The tea ceremony could thus be carried out in the home itself, either in a specially arranged separate room, or in a dual-purpose room, treated partly according to the tea-ceremony style and partly in the sober Shoin style. It could also be celebrated in a house designed exclusively for the purpose, containing an anteroom, a pantry and a tea room, or even in a garden pavilion which had an inward-facing section for the tea ceremony but also drawing rooms and a rest area that were wide open on the outside.

The influence of tea architecture on the classical Shoin zukuri provoked the development of a new kind of residence, characterized by less ponderous structures, more sober decorations, and a freedom of design and appearance which resulted in a more flexible interior, as in the Shinden zukuri. This trend, Sukiyafu shoin zukuri, took shape just as the Shoin style reached its peak, during the Kanei era (1624–44). It began in the garden pavilions which were used as residences and then blossomed in palaces and town houses, in so far as protocol permitted. The Katsura palace complex provides the most brilliantly successful example of this eclectic style, full of dignity, simplicity and the unexpected. A synthesis of the most striking developments of the tradition, Sukiyafu shoin zukuri was in turn to be the father of what we usually consider to be Japanese architecture proper.

Reconstruction of ground plans of Buddhist monasteries, late 6th – mid 8th centuries. Study of these plans shows above all how the roles of importance reversed between the main sacred buildings, the pagoda and the kondo. Of all the buildings in a monastery, the pagoda was initially considered the essential one: consequently it was built either immediately behind the middle gate, hiding the kondo from view, or in the centre of the square, as the commanding pivot for the other pavilions. But the kondo gradually gained in sacred value and acquired a status equal to that of the pagoda, before supplanting it altogether. Indeed, during the next phase, the duplication of pagodas (of which only one held the sacred relics) simply indicated a concern for symmetry; and their withdrawal towards the corners showed subordination to the kondo. In the end, their removal from the sacred area brought the process to its final conclusion. (From *Genshoku*, 2 and 3.)

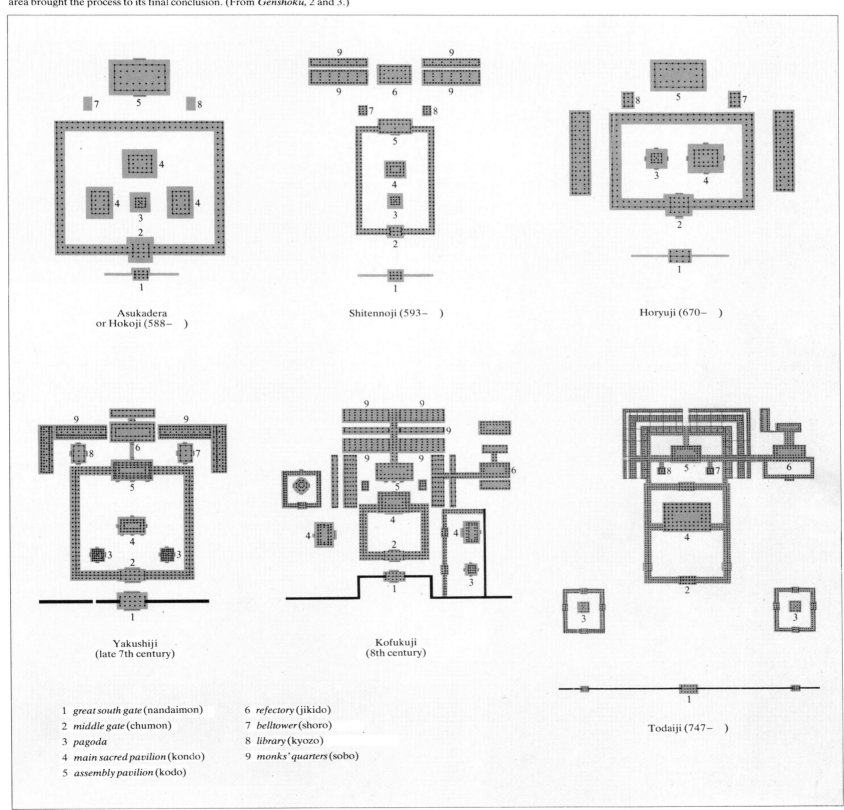

Asukadera
or Hokoji (588–)

Shitennoji (593–)

Horyuji (670–)

Yakushiji
(late 7th century)

Kofukuji
(8th century)

Todaiji (747–)

1 great south gate (nandaimon)
2 middle gate (chumon)
3 pagoda
4 main sacred pavilion (kondo)
5 assembly pavilion (kodo)
6 refectory (jikido)
7 belltower (shoro)
8 library (kyozo)
9 monks' quarters (sobo)

The Shinto shrine, an expression of national tradition

At the end of the 6th century the national religion, Shinto, was a synthesis of all the primitive beliefs and practices centred around the cult of the "superior beings" or "higher beings" (*kami*). In a country where the awareness of nature is profound, the *kami* were initially the deification of crude natural forms. With the introduction of agriculture they also appeared as spirits who controlled the seasons, presiding over work in the fields and bringing prosperity. Then the changing social structure brought about totemic *kami*: implacable and fearsome, they all lived on the fringes of the profane world, but some of them condescended nonetheless to participate in time in the activities of man and even, in an ultimate phase of togetherness, to take on human form.

A sacred architecture slowly developed with the changing relationships between *kami* and man. Hence, for the *kami* who periodically joined the life of man it became customary to build a temporary house and to take it down immediately after the *kami*'s departure. Then, for the *kami* who consented to be anthropomorphic, permanent houses were required. Buddhist temples, which suggest that the gods have a way of life similar to man's, would certainly have influenced this tendency for Shinto shrines to become solid and durable buildings. These structures cut themselves off immediately (from the 6th century) from their contemporary environment. In giving itself an architecture, Shinto turned to an older fashion for its models. And it is this that enables us today to imagine the protohistoric buildings with all their variations. From these distant sources the Shinto shrine retained a roofing of plant material – *miscanthus sinensis* (*kaya*) or, more generally, cypress bark which lasted longer – wood as the sole material for the rest, except for the occasional use of stone pedestals to prevent the poles from rotting, and finally, highly raised floors. Furthermore, because the Shinto *kami* date from prehistory, when their territory or living quarters were taboo, the shrine was completely closed. Inaccessible to the profane, it could even be hidden from sight by homocentric palisades, such as at Ise, although this is an extreme case.

In order to protect the original beauty and purity of the shrines against the ravages of time, and to retain the original design, regular reconstructions took place. This practice encouraged in particular the introduction of plate foundations, which, in the *Kasuga* and *Nagare* styles, was done with scrupulous respect for the primitive proportions; in the case of the *Kasuga zukuri*, where the building was prefabricated, this allowed for the constant reassurance that the deity would be sheltered while the work was in progress. The result of this practice of constant reconstruction, applied fairly strictly, was that the earliest examples of Shinto architecture are relatively recent. At Ise, where the 20 year reconstruction cycle has been most strictly observed, the shrines were rebuilt for the sixtieth time in 1973, but their present style was probably perfected at the end of the 7th century.

Of course, under the imperious influence of Buddhism, the Shinto constructions were sometimes subject to modifications – the curvature of the roofs, the abandoning of the traditional gable, the development of the ground plans – but these foreign borrowings did not basically alter the ancient character. This respect for tradition was already manifesting itself in the oldest buildings. For example, at Ise, the pavilion of daily offerings (*mikeden*) of Geku, built in an early style, returns in a perfected form to the building methods used for ancient storehouses, with non-aligned posts directly propping up the roof and supporting walls made of overlapping planks, which made it necessary to cut the entrance into the side wall. In contrast, the main shrines (*shoden*) and the two treasure houses (*honden*) of Naiku and Geku at Ise are built on the entirely different principle of a framework with screen walls; nevertheless, in keeping with tradition, they still have their entrance in a side wall, as well as ridge poles. The same respect for tradition is responsible for the retention of wooden components which no longer serve any functional purpose, but which were once needed to secure the roof-timbers, such as the *muchikake* (protruding elements reminiscent of the laths used only in the *Shimmei* style), the *chigi* (angle-rafters in the *Shimmei* style; crossed timbers placed on the roof in the other styles) and the *katsuogi* (roof logs). These survivors of an era when there were no dowels to hold structures together are the most characteristic details of Shinto architecture and the ones that were most widely used no matter what the style was.

In short, although it made no gestures to technological progress and was influenced by Buddhist styles, Shinto architecture still managed to remain faithful to itself, and to retain the authenticity of its ancient heritage.

Main shrine or "honden" of Nishima shimmeigu, Nagano

Constructed in 1636, the present *honden* is the oldest preserved example of the *Shimmei* style. It has all the main characteristics: ground plan with four pillars by three, surrounding balcony on tall stilts, door cut into the centre of a side wall, free-standing post placed beyond the gable end and decorative roof elements (*muchikake*, *chigi* and *katsuogi*). Compared to the famous *shoden* or major shrines at Ise, however, there are certain differences: the pillars rest on stone pedestals, the balcony struts are separated by low mortised stringers and, finally, the area allocated to rituals is protected by a roof integrated with the structure, which is of solid appearance, conforming to the *honden* style. Foreign influence can be seen in the introduction of the primitive hull-shaped console (*funa hijiki*).

Main shrine or "honden" of Kamosu jinja, Shimane

The *honden* of Kamosu dates from 1346, making it the oldest shrine of the *Taisha* style existing today. It shares with the present *honden* of Izumo the square shape with three pillars on the sides, the symbolic central pillar rising up to the roof, the entrance in the gable wall located off-centre to the right, the surrounding balcony with long cross-braced piles, the stairway covered with a small independent roof and the gently curving roofing. However, there are certain points of difference. The struts are completely visible; the two posts directly supporting the edges of the roofing project from the gable walls instead of being built into them; the sacred section outlined inside by a partition stretched between the central pillar and one of the side walls is on the left instead of on the right.

   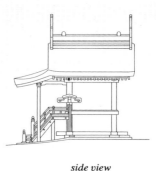

| *main façade* | *side view* | *main façade* | *side view* |

Nagare style: eastern shrine
of Kamo mioya jinja at Kyoto (1863)

Kasuga style: one of the four main shrines
of Kasuga taisha honsha at Nara (1863)

Elevation of a Shinto shrine

Among all the styles practised in Shinto architecture, the *Nagare zukuri* and *Kasuga zukuri* predominate. Indeed, out of 451 *honden* so far listed as national treasures, 260 are of the *Nagare* style and 90 of the *Kasuga* style. Both are characterized by a gable roof and by a structure consisting exclusively of the cella or central body (*moya*), without any through passages. They can be identified from each other above all by the choice of gable wall or eave wall for the main façade. Otherwise, Buddhist influence has persuaded both forms to have a covered area accessible to worshippers; the answer was to cover the entrance stairway either by extending one of the roof overhangs (*Nagare* style) or by raising a canopy held up by two pillars (*Kasuga* style). Finally, they have discreetly adopted a system of consoles which, more often than not, takes the very early form of a ship's hull (*funa hijiki*).

The Kasugado and Hakusando of Enjoji, Nara

Dating from the Kamakura period, these two shrines, linked to each other by a wooden partition 2 metres (7 feet) high, are the most ancient surviving examples of the *Kasuga* style. Although the canopies above the stairway are still independent structures, from face on they give the impression of being part of a half-hipped roof. In fact, *Kasuga*-style canopies were very quickly integrated with the roof, thanks to linking angle-rafters (*sumigi*). But here they have the distinguishing feature of resting on a corbelling system of very simple consoles surmounted by three little blocks (*hira mitsudo*), and on an extra support between the pillars, called a "frog's leg" (*kaerumata*). This element is the perfected Japanese development of the inverted 'Y' support; it was already being used in the decor at Yungang in China, and was later used on the second floor of the *kondo* of Horyuji.

Main shrine or "honden" of Kamitani jinja, Kagawa

Erected in 1219, this building is the oldest example of the *Nagare* style. Although relatively small, it has the unusual feature of a supplementary entrance to the cella through a side door. Moreover, it proves that, from the beginning of the Kamakura period, Shinto architecture had assimilated an entirely foreign system of consoles. Like the two *Kasuga*-style shrines of Enjoji, it uses the primitive hull-shaped console (*funa hijiki*), mainly to support the tie-beam, and the *hira mitsudo* system to hold up the winged purlin in the main façade.

Main shrines or "honden" of Usa jingu, Oita

In the search for extra space, Shinto made use of a solution supplied by Buddhist temples: the twin structures of the *Raido zukuri*. Identical in principle, but known under the name of *Hachiman zukuri*, the three *honden* of Usa jingu (whose present construction only dates from 1855–61) are the earliest examples. They consist of two buildings stuck together, one behind the other, each four pillars long and supporting a gable roof. The back building, used as the cella, is three pillars wide and the front one only two, although it has a wider span. Beneath the slopes of the two roofs, which join in a communal gutter, the front building has another two pillars, making it bigger (about 39 sq. metres/47 sq. yards as opposed to 30 sq. metres/36 sq. yards). One feature of this style is that the front façade is completely closed by shutters (*shitomido*). Also, the two buildings share the same access – two doors opposite each other under the communal gutter in the side façades. This kind of construction has a weak point because of the absence of any architectural link between the two structures. To remedy this, a cross roof was built to cover the place of junction and to improve water drainage. The Kitano tenmangu (1607) at Kyoto is an example of this progress.

47

The Buddhist temple and technical progress

Through Buddhism Japan inherited all the Chinese principles of building in wood. But, in applying these principles, the Japanese tried to perfect them to make them more suitable for their own needs. In the Far East, the beauty of a building lies above all in the majesty of its roof, and the first step to be accomplished involved the system of consoles used to support the overhang. At Horyuji, a singularly large overhang rests on an archaic corbelling system (which had already disappeared from the stone Chinese temples), where the consoles on one level are all placed lengthwise and imitate the shape of a cloud. The protruding angle of the roof presented an extremely tricky problem of weight. In a technically better developed system, the console placed at an angle of 45 degrees is usually helped by others at 90 degrees. But in this case these are absent, and the auxiliary supporting role is taken up by consoles lodged to the right of the pillars, which, in the angled sections of the building, are built very close to each other. A precautionary measure, which no doubt existed from the start, is an extra non-aligned pillar directly supporting the angle of the roof. This system was very quickly abandoned in favour of more efficient and more developed corbelling systems commonly used in China. One of these formulas reached perfection at Toshodaiji in the form of the *mitesaki*, or a system of consoles wedged on three levels. But at the beginning of the 13th century the function of the corbelling was transferred to a system of overhangs which introduced big lever arms (*hanegi*) into the roof-timbers, and these were capable of bearing the weight of the roofing canopies by themselves. Corbelling was not dropped, however – on the contrary, its use was increased, although only as decoration.

Japan is often troubled by earthquakes, and builders were therefore concerned to improve bracing. Until the Middle Ages this had been done mainly with purlins and, at wall level, with a kind of beam (*kashiranuki*) which ran between the notches in the tops of the pillars; to a lesser degree it was also done with stringers (*nageshi*), mortised at the ends and pegged into the pillars. After that the corner pillars were more firmly secured by crossing the butts of the *kashiranuki*. And in the end the external pillars were linked on several planes by *kashiranuki* which crossed from one to another. This produced a solid assembly which removed the structural role from the walls.

In addition, it soon became evident that there was a need for a greater spiritual quality and for the increased participation of the laity in the liturgy. This made it necessary to rethink the internal space. In cross-section the Chinese prototype of the main pavilion offered perfect symmetry, with a system of roof-timbers meeting at the base of the leaning point. It provided a central section, which acted as the shrine, and clear areas on the sides, acting as lateral naves or circumambulatories. But when the buildings were finally opened to worshippers, supplementary space was required. There were three early and immature solutions – to pull back the platform bearing the statues, to extend the canopy roof of the main façade into a kind of porch (*magobisashi*), or to double the structure by sticking together two similar buildings, each with its own roof (*Raido zukuri*), the first building acting as a prayer-room and the other as a shrine. These experiments culminated in the provision of a single building with the dual function of shrine and prayer-room, which was dissymmetrical because of the positioning and spacing of the pillars. In fact, in the section provided for the public, the removal of some pillars brought with it a change in the positioning of the others. The secondary square temples had a peripheral ambulatory and a central choir surrounded by four interior pillars. The expansion of the area provided for the public here involved drawing back the pillars, or else removing two of them, or even widening the first transverse bay.

This versatility of design and rejection of symmetry in the leaning points and supports for the roof were only possible thanks to a kind of roof trussing which was very different to the Chinese model. In the Japanese design, artificial rafters (*keshoyane*) or just the ends of them were left showing, resting on the pillars; they were surmounted by other roof timbers, which were invisible but carried the weight. Above the lower visible beams, whose span corresponded to the spacing of the pillars, the upper beams were now held by false king-posts, placed at regular intervals without any relation to the positioning of the pillars. The purlin timbers did not always have the combined support of the false king-posts and the ends of the stretchers; they often rested only on the false king-posts, which were of varying heights and linked together by narrow stretchers in the upper rafters.

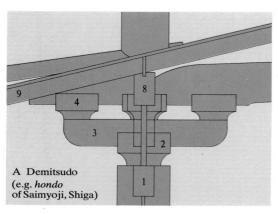

A Demitsudo
(e.g. *hondo* of Saimyoji, Shiga)

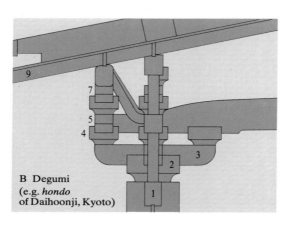

B Degumi
(e.g. *hondo* of Daihoonji, Kyoto)

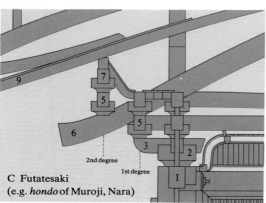

C Futatesaki
(e.g. *hondo* of Muroji, Nara)

D Mitesaki
(e.g. *tokondo* of Kofukuji, Kyoto)

1 *beam crossing the top of the pillar* (kashiranuki)
2 *main support block* (daito)
3 *console* (hijiki)
4 *little support block* (makito)
5 *balancing console* (hakari hijiki)
6 *small lever arm* (odaruki)
7 *extra console* (sane hijiki)
8 *purlin*
9 *rafter* (jidaruki)

The most commonly used system of consoles in Japan (from *Genshoku*, 9). The earliest system is merely a console cut in the shape of a ship's hull (*funa hijiki*), placed between the pillar and the element to be supported. The other systems are elaborations based on the following elements: the support block (*daito*) at the top of the pillar, the console (or the arm of the console) and, grafted on to this, little support blocks (*makito*). This structure forms the *hira mitsudo*. The *demitsudo* (A) is the first development: it has two consoles on the main support block (one parallel with the wall and the other perpendicular to it), fitted one into the other and carrying a little block at the ends and at their intersection. By adding to the end of the perpendicular console a balancing protruding console (*hakari hijiki*), parallel to the wall and surmounted or not by an extra console without a block (*sane hijiki*), a system in one degree and two tiers called *degumi* or *hitotesaki* is created (B). Generally using a small lever arm (*odaruki*), a system of a second balancing console can be added and fitted with the extra console without a block: this is the *futatesaki* (C) with two degrees and three tiers. Finally, breaking up the *mitesaki* system (D) with its three degrees, there are, from the main base block upwards, two crossed consoles fitted one into the other (first degree), a second perpendicular console (second degree), a balancing console with a lever arm wedged into it (third degree) and a second balancing console.

The main sacred pavilion or "kondo" of Horyuji, Nara

The *kondo* of Horyuji is the oldest wooden building in the world. Built to replace the Wakakusadera (late 6th–early 7th century), which was burnt in 670, it perpetuates a technology already out-dated at the time of its construction. The system of measurement and the balconies on two levels belong to the Korean tradition. The width and pronounced bulge of the pillars, as well as their narrower spacing as they reach the corners, are survivors of the primitive style, as is the absence of *kashiranuki* on the top level. The *saraita* (abacuses) are examples of a Chinese custom of the 5th and 6th centuries. The shape of the parapet is based on an ancient Chinese system of supporting the eaves.

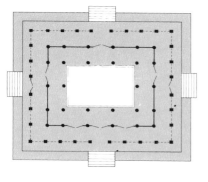
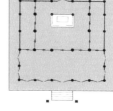
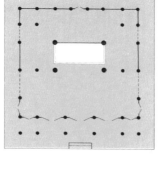
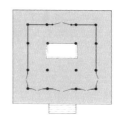
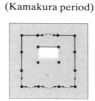

E *Amidado* of Myodoji, Kumamoto (Kamakura period)

A *Kondo* of Horyuji, Nara (*c.*670)

B *Hondo* of Myooin, Hiroshima (1321)

C *Kondo* of Fudoin, Hiroshima (1540)

D *Amidado* of Ganjoji, Fukushima (1160)

F *Butsuden* of Saionji, Yamanashi (Nambokucho period)

Evolution of ground plans (from *Kenzobutsu*, vol. 1)

In the sacred pavilions, both major and minor, the evolution of ground plans indicates the same quest for extra space, to satisfy the needs of ritual as well as to accommodate the congregation. From the beginning until the middle of the 8th century, the only function of the *kondo*, or main sacred pavilion, had been as a sanctuary for the Buddhist statues: as a result it simply consisted of a space defined by the statue platform and ambulatory. However, the existence of a surrounding sloping roof can already be seen at Horyuji (A) – a kind of passageway lit by daylight from windows. Then, in the Middle Ages, when worshippers were allowed in, it became necessary to arrange an area distinct from the shrine, which sometimes included the classic column structuring. The front part was therefore enlarged with a cross nave and this area was freed of pillars, partially at first and then totally (B). Elsewhere the same result was obtained by placing the pillars asymmetrically and removing them from the front part of the building, which was enlarged even further with more doors and the addition of a porch (C). In the secondary temples, which since the Heian period had mainly adopted the square shape, pillars were at first placed at regular intervals (D), but to facilitate circulation, more doors were added. Next, the four central pillars were drawn back, thus outlining a rectangular surface for the statuary instead of a square one (E). Finally, not only were the two pillars left out, but the span between the remaining pillars was varied to obtain a maximum area of clear space in the front part (F).

J.P. Ziolo, Zauho Press

Ksitigarbha Pavilion or Jizodo at Shofukuji, Tokyo

The Jizodo is the oldest main sacred pavilion in the Zen style to have survived; and its date of construction is known for certain (1407). It has the characteristics of a building of the first order in the *Zenshuyo* style: a square shape with six pillars on each side, a sloping roof all the way round, decorative corbelling forming a continuous cornice, radiating rafters below the eaves, arched windows (*katomado*), free imposts forming a frieze (*yumi ramma*), and framed panelled doors (*sankarado*).

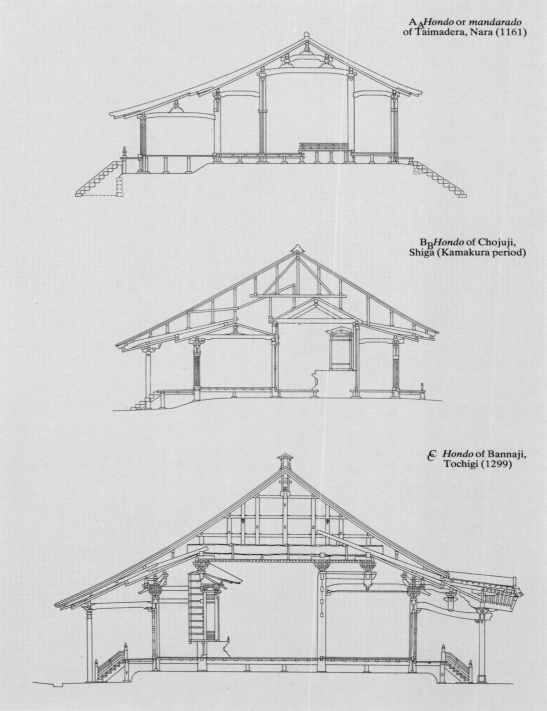

A *Hondo* or *mandarado* of Taimadera, Nara (1161)

B *Hondo* of Chojuji, Shiga (Kamakura period)

C *Hondo* of Bannaji, Tochigi (1299)

Cross-sections showing the development in distribution of space
(from *Genshoku*, 9; *Kenzobutsu*, vol. 1)

Cross-sections show better than ground plans how the interior space was adapted to the new rules, since they show the results at the level of the roof timbers. The internal area had to hold a central section (*moya*) and lateral or surrounding clearways (*hisashi*), with the respective duties of shrine (*naijin*) and side naves or ambulatory (*gejin*). To hold all the people while still maintaining the classic pillar spacing and rafters (A), the simplest answer was to add a porch or a supplementary peripheral passage (*magobisashi*). Later, the Japanese arranged the *gejin* for the worshippers by giving it a dissymmetrical structure, for which they set about inventing an appropriate roof: this was composed of two superimposed structures (B). The final version, with its highly elaborate roofing section, could have all the technical refinements of *Zenshuyo zukuri* without having to conform to Zen (C). Sometimes, however, the ceilings of this later period were relatively simple.

The castle, an exception to the rules of architecture

Traditional Japanese architecture is essentially characterized by the emphasis of horizontal elements. From time to time, under foreign influence, stark contradictions broke out within this basic tendency. The castle is one of these contradictions, although not the only one.

In the far-off times of Yayoi, the only buildings of any height were on stilts. This applied particularly to the granary, which was raised on very high stilts, not only as a protection against predators and damp, but also to make it a symbol of the wealth of the community. Ancient texts also refer to a considerably raised building with an uncertain function, known as a *takadono*. There is an illustration which may be of the *takadono* in the decoration of a *dotaku* of the 1st and 2nd centuries which has come to light in the province of Kagawa: it is a construction on tall stilts, but it is impossible to decide whether it is a granary, a residence or an ornamental tower. A more interesting case from this period is the Izumo taisha sanctuary, whose origin lies buried in the sacred myths of Japan. Legend initially describes its *honden* or main shrine as being 93 metres (300 feet) high – impossible for the primitive methods of the time – and texts from the Heian period reduce this to 46 metres (150 feet). Even without aspiring to such heights, the shrine was in all events high enough to strike the imagination. But this massiveness was the reason for its decline. It was impossible to carry out the regular reconstructions that it required, since these needed to be staggered over several years and also presented difficult architectural problems. As a result, the present shrine (1744) had to be reduced down to 24

metres (80 feet) by shortening the stilts and the structure had to be altered too.

Later, by introducing the knowledge of Chinese technology, Buddhism prompted the Japanese to construct buildings of several storeys, although these at first had no practical use. Whatever its appearance, height and shape, the only practical level of the pagoda was the ground floor; all the other levels (made use of in China) were no more than external structural elements, arranged independently around the central pillar. The same goes for other sacred two-storeyed buildings: the Japanese only realized their functional potential with the revival of Zen. Zen also imported the fashion for garden pavilions with several storeys. The oldest of these still standing, the Ginkaku of Jishoji, bears the mark of sobriety and refinement, and the equally famous Hiunkaku in the Tekisuien garden of Nishi Honganji has the baroque appearance typical of its period. In the latter example, maximum exploitation of the three levels has made it possible to have larger floor plans, irregular tiers and varied rooftops.

These diverse experiments in building up in stages were to be pursued in military architecture and were to achieve their most spectacular results in the "donjons" and towers of castles. The castle had its beginnings in the Middle Ages, against the background of feudal wars, as a military retreat in the mountains. Later, it became the lord's residence and the political and economic centre of the region. As a result, it moved to an inhabited area, on a hill or even on a plain, which deprived it of its former natural defences, but it made up for this vulnera-

bility with the thickness and complexity of its walls. It was the donjon in particular which conveyed prestige and authority as well as offering defence. Apart from the great stone pedestals, the materials used – wood and plaster – were not of the sort to give the building any air of grandeur. Nevertheless, it did assume an awesome appearance thanks to the emphasis on height, which was both accentuated and modulated by the complex roof structures.

At the end of the Muromachi period, the donjon's form was hybrid: it was a building of several storeys, capped with a half-hipped roof, which had a long slope embellished with gables, and it was surmounted by a watchtower. After this the preoccupation was to find a structural unit that was more resistant to earth tremors, and this was done as soon as technological progress made it possible to level the rocky base. It was then feasible to build on a rectangular plan on the lower level, to place hipped roofs on top of the building and to adjust their incline to ensure that rain would run off and snow would slide off. In addition, the balustrade and balcony of the watchtower were omitted so that the ascending line would not be broken. Finally, the standardization of measures, the mass-production of materials, and the simplification of construction methods all led to a system of prefabrication which flung the doors open wide to variation. Thus, little by little, a coherent design of a massive tower of several storeys was perfected, with an outline punctuated by a series of rooftops, canopies, gables, façades and penthouse roofs, which were mostly decorative features and bore no relation to the internal layout. The final result is highly impressive.

Japon Information, Londres

Oriental pagoda of Yakushiji, Nara

At the end of prehistoric times, foreign influence had made itself felt in architecture, notably by the verticality of buildings on tall stilts. Buddhism, also from the mainland, was to develop this tendency in pagodas. The strangest pagoda was erected at the end of the 7th century in the old capital of Fujiwarakyo. Although it has now disappeared, its type survives in the oriental pagoda (730) of present day Yakushiji, which is a scrupulous copy. The building has three storeys which are much higher than usual and each is made double by a surrounding penthouse roof, with the result that, while not going beyond the traditional height of five levels, the building seems to have six. In fact, these sloping roofs have no structural function: their only role is to harmonize the whole. The division between the real storey and the fake storey is clearly pointed out by the corbelling system. Like most pagodas, the Yakushiji looks like a tiered tower because it narrows regularly at each level, but the presence of the penthouse roofs increases this effect. Naturally, such decisive verticality, although non-functional, was loaded with significance: it symbolized the faith, the relics of which were (usually) left in the pagoda, by providing concrete evidence of this, and showed the authority which Buddhism enjoyed at that time as the State religion.

Shogakukan, Ziolo

Gate of Salvation or Sammon of Tofukuji, Kyoto

In contrast to its opposite number, the "middle gate" of the 7th century, the "gate of Salvation" of the Zen sects put its first floor to practical use. This was conceived as a sumptuous chapel, consecrated to Sakyamuni, to Avalokitesvara or to the *arhats*, and it was reached by a staircase in a tower. In addition, the gate was framed by the belltower and the *sutra* tower, which were also built on two levels. Later, like all the major buildings of sects which went in for systematic reconstruction, the gate of Salvation became smaller, and access to the first floor was by a side stair, all but the bottom steps of which were open, while the two neighbouring towers disappeared. The Sammon of Tofukuji, built around 1384–87, already shows the new modifications, but it has retained the astounding proportions of earlier models. The most interesting contribution made by Zen to architecture is that it finally revealed to the Japanese the practical possibilities of buildings of more than one storey, an advantage which was to be exploited in civic and military buildings.

Silver Pavilion or Ginkaku at Jishoji, Kyoto

Ginkaku is the name given to a building which was originally called Kannonden or the Avalokitesvara Pavilion.
With the Togudo, it is the only building left practically
intact from the residence which the shogun Ashikaga
Yoshimasa (1436–90) had built at Higashiyama. This
illustrious home formerly comprised a number of pavilions, spread around the grounds and centred around a
lake, integrating the natural environment into the plan.
Yoshimasa decided on the construction of the Ginkaku
when the garden was almost finished, but died before
seeing the result. This pavilion is an example not only of
garden architecture during the Muromachi period, but
also of residential architecture which had reached a bridg-
ing point between the *Shinden* and the *Shoin* styles, and
even also of religious architecture which, under the influences of Jodo and Zen, had taken to laying out its sacred
buildings in secluded gardens. The Ginkaku is a two-
storey building. Its ground floor, called the *shikuden*, is
more or less rectangular with dimensions of 8 by 6 metres
(25 by 20 feet) and with its main façade facing the lake.
The façade is closely linked with the garden through a
veranda (*hiroen*), a slightly lower exterior balcony
(*ochien*) and sliding partitions decorated with *shoji*
(*koshidaka akarishoji*), all details evoking the *Shoin
zukuri*. The first floor, called the *choonkaku*, acts as a
chapel for a statue of Kannon (*Avalokitesvara*). Its style
returns to *Zenshuyo zukuri*, notably because of its square
shape, its box ceiling, its two framed panelled doors
(*sankarado*) opening on to the external balcony, and its
basket-handle arched windows (*katomado*) beneath
which runs a bench for the practice of *zazen*. This kind of
architecture was to undergo remarkable developments
later on in military architecture.

Donjon of Inuyama Castle, Aichi

The only remaining part of the castle, the donjon, is a two-storey building covered with a
half-hipped roof which is itself surmounted by a watchtower. From its external appearance –
well-defined masses, exterior balcony, balustrade and basket-handle arched windows – this
observatory is derived from constructions similar to the Golden Pavilion (Kinkaku) and the
Silver Pavilion (Ginkaku). Because of its hybrid nature and the technique of mounting it on a
stone structure, it conforms to the early type of castle. In fact, it was built at the end of the
Muromachi period. But during the Genna era (1615–24), to give it a more decorative
character, a gable with sinuous lines (*karahafu*) was fixed to the north and south slopes of the
half-hipped roof.

Himeji Castle, Hyogo

A masterpiece of military architecture, the castle of Himeji is also the largest and
the best preserved in Japan. Begun in 1346, it has been altered during the course
of the centuries, partly by time and partly by occupants. One of these was
Toyotomi Hideyoshi, who took possession of the building in 1577 and built
several additions, notably a three-storey donjon in 1581 (the foundations have
recently been found). But it is no longer possible to have any clear idea of the
appearance of the castle then, since a later occupant, Ikeda Terumasa, made
great alterations between 1601–10. Today, there remain 37 buildings dispersed
within four enclosures, and 16 gates. Architecturally, the donjon (1608) is the
most remarkable of the constructions. Donjons were conceived as final refuges
for beleaguered garrisons, and their access was always carefully defended.
Sometimes they were surrounded by a special rampart at the centre of the main
enclosure (*hommaru*); more often, an annexe tower (*tsukeyagura*) was attached
to the donjon, as at Inuyama, or yet again, as at Matsumoto, a fortified gate tower
(*watari yagura*) linked it with a secondary donjon. But the most elaborate
solution was devised at Himeji: the tall main donjon and three smaller ones are
joined to each other by fortified corridors; these are arranged to form a
quadrangle which had to be crossed by assailants.

Houses and pavilions, precursors of contemporary architecture

Although they were slow to mature, Japanese residential styles have undoubtedly influenced modern Western architecture. The phenomenon began in the second half of the 19th century, when China was withdrawing from international affairs and Japan was taking part in them again. Some ideas which were then in the process of shaking Western architecture coincided oddly with Japanese tradition: flexibility of ground plan, framework structure, modular system, awareness of materials and the aesthetic exploitation of their contrasting qualities. Of course it would be difficult to point precisely to Japanese contributions to modern architecture, since inventions such as reinforced concrete and metal frameworks were themselves sufficient to stimulate development. But it is certain that, when they came into contact with the Japanese arts, Western architects were taught much about relationships with nature and about harmony, simplicity and spatial freedom.

Japanese architecture has always been thought of as being in close communion with its environment. It is this that explains, for example, the opening walls and the external balconies, which provide both internal and external spaces. This tendency dates back a great many years, as can be seen from a building as old as the Dempodo of Horyuji (first half of the 8th century) at a time when it was used as a residential pavilion; it then consisted of a room surrounded by permanent walls and by a larger area which opened out on to the exterior and was further extended by a huge platform. During the Heian period, the *Shinden zukuri* emphasized the relationship with nature: indeed, the central body of the pavilion raised on stilts was surrounded by covered balconies (ultimate development of the early portico), which were later widened by verandas. The

relationship between the garden and its corollary, natural lighting, was further improved in the *Shoin zukuri*, at the end of the 16th century, with the invention of *amado* (detachable blinds). Until then, light had only been able to penetrate through half columns, since the blinds could only be drawn from one pillar to the next; but by bringing them back to the extreme edge of the eaves it was possible to draw them without meeting any pillars, and even to fold them away at will. From then on, the *shoji* (translucent screens) were all that occupied the spaces between the pillars; the light flowed in, and the barrier with the outside world was diminished.

The sense of harmony in Japanese houses was greatly increased when *Shoin zukuri* defined its modular system based on *tatami* (matting fixed on a compressed straw mattress). The use of *tatami* had previously been restricted, but it was now used more generally until it covered all the internal surfaces. Since it had a standard size, it served as a module: the dimensions and proportions of a room were expressed in terms of *tatami*. But for the very small rooms reserved for the tea ceremony it became necessary to introduce a new dimensional unit, the "three-quarter *tatami*".

"Tea architecture" brought with it an aesthetic appreciation of raw materials, not only for structural purposes, but also for interior decoration. Tree trunks were often used as supporting elements, still with their bark, never trimmed to shape, and barely changed if it was possible to emphasize the beauty of a knot, a vein or a profile. The wall cob was bare or, at the most, bore a decorative paper. The ceiling was sometimes composed of slats of different woods, but more often it was made of a layer of reeds or bamboo; sometimes it was omitted altogether, and the rafters were left bare and ex-

posed. The *Sukiyafu shoin zukuri* style profited from this refined simplicity, based on natural materials and functional logic. However, it removed some of its austerity by infusing a little discreet fantasy, thereby creating a synthesis which has seduced European designers.

But the most precious thing the West has learnt from the Japanese tradition is perhaps its conception of internal space. The first residential pavilions at the beginning of the 8th century were composed of one large room with multiple uses. The area was given further freedom in the *Shinden zukuri* by the addition of more open spaces: on the north side these were separated from the central room by removable partitions, but on the south side the transition was indicated only by an uneven layer of floorboards. Open as it was, the living area was nonetheless varied by curtains, folding partitions, screens, and the occasional piece of furniture. All these elements could, moreover, be moved according to circumstances. Later, however, *Shoin zukuri* advocated a break-up of the internal space: partitions appeared, which were generally sliding (*fusuma*), but there were never very many of them and they never gave the impression of a closed-in area. The purpose or the importance of a room was indicated not so much by the partitioning as by its height from the ground and the appearance of the ceiling. The relationship between adjoining rooms, separated by *fusama* or linked by wide openings, could be seen in the treatment of the gap between the ceiling and the lintel or the *fusuma*: a drop in the wall indicated a clear demarcation; a transom or a sculptured lintel indicated a close relationship.

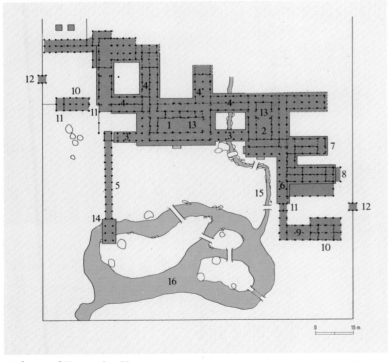

1	*main pavilion* (shinden)
2	*secondary pavilion* (tainoya)
3, 5	*open galleries*
4, 7	*single or double corridors*
6	*covered passage leading to the middle gate*
8	*guardroom*
9	*coach house*
10	*service pavilions*
11	*middle gates*
12	*outside gates*
13	*bedrooms*
14	*fishing pavilion*
15	*stream*
16	*lake*

Palace of Tosanjo, Kyoto (from *Japanese Architecture and Gardens*, 1966)

The home of the chiefs of the Fujiwara clan at Tosanjo seems to have been the most prestigious example of *Shinden zukuri* (it often served as a temporary residence for the emperors when the imperial palace was undergoing restoration or reconstruction after fires). It is therefore interesting to study the ground plan in so far as it has been possible to reconstruct it. It centres around the pavilion of the chief (*shinden*): with its adjoining buildings (*tainoya*) this pavilion forms an alignment which leads into projections of opposing right angles, one towards the north, the other towards the south; through an interlacing of open galleries (*sukiwataridono*) and single or double corridors (*futamunero*), the various pavilions are combined within a continuous architectural network connected to the fishing pavilion (*tsuridono*) on the lake. The lake, with its artificial islands and meandering shape, seems to be the heart of the property.

Whether it was of the *shinden* or *tainoya* type, the pavilion always consisted of one room (*moya*) with surrounding clear passages (*hisashi*) – a constant in Japanese architecture – on a flooring outlined only by pillars. The function of the different parts of the pavilion was marked only by mobile elements whose arrangement varied according to the circumstances. However, there was one defined area between the partitions and the fixed doors, either in the *moya* or in the clear passages – the *nurigome*, which was initially a bedroom, then a repository for precious objects. The pavilion could have been further enlarged because of the clear areas parallel to the inside passages, and because of the large covered spaces or verandas. The fundamental principles of the *Shinden zukuri* were perpetuated for many years after this style of residence had disappeared.

Tea pavilion of Yurakuen Joan, Aichi

When he decided to disappear from public view in 1618, Oda Urakusai had a house built in Kyoto which included a tea pavilion. The pavilion, which was transferred to its present site in 1972, perfectly embodies the ideal of Sen no Rikyu. From the Nara era, residential architecture had followed two very distinct lines: one was for aristocratic city-dwellers, the other for ordinary country folk. The first kind culminated in very open houses which were cool in summer; the other kind led to closed houses to protect the occupants from bad weather. Because he wanted to give his tea pavilions the atmosphere of mountain hermitages, Rikyu took his inspiration from rural architecture. And in addition, to encourage the participants to meditate, he created a very confined area inside, which had low ceilings, was completely isolated and had a beauty that was always based on the simplicity of raw materials. The most characteristic feature is perhaps the guests' door (*nijiriguchi*): it is so small that people had to enter on their knees. Symbolically, it represents the ultimate stage of the spiritual preparation, since the ceremony was meant to eliminate all class distinctions.

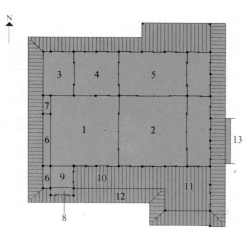

1 *main room or* Shoza no ma
2 *second room or* Tsugi no ma
3 *cloakroom reached from the* chodaigamae *or* nando
4 *room of 8* tatami
5 *room of 12* tatami
6 tokonoma
7 chigaidana
8 tsukeshoin
9 *raised platform area or* jodan
10 *covered area/veranda or* hiroen
11 *covered area/middle gate or* chumon
12 *surrounding balcony or* ochien
13 *coach halt or* kurumayose

Guests' pavilion or "kyakuden" of Kojoin, Shiga

The guests' pavilion of Kojoin in the monastery of Onjoji (or Miidera) is a more or less faithful illustration of the classic plan of a *shuden* or main pavilion in the *Shoin zukuri* architectural style. Built in 1601, it includes two lines of adjoining rooms, one on the south side, the other on the north side. The south rooms, bordered by a huge veranda (*hiroen*) opening out into the *chumon*, were used for meetings or official receptions, the north rooms being reserved as living quarters. Placed accordingly in the south, the main room (with a surface area of 18 *tatami*, like the next room) is arranged in the usual manner: the *tokonoma* and *chigaidana* on the far wall, the *chodaigamae* (although rare in a monastic complex) in the internal partition and the *tsukeshoin* along the front wall. Here, the *jodan* area (the raised platform section in the main room reserved for important people) projects on to the veranda, even forcing the *tsukeshoin* to encroach on to the gallery – reminiscent of the early projecting *shoin*. In addition, the façade overlooking the courtyard has a stopping place for coaches (*kurumayose*) beneath a sinuous gable. Nevertheless, this pavilion has certain elements which differ from the prototype: the *jodan* does not extend into the main room and, having itself become an independent room, is provided both with a *tsukeshoin* and with a *tokonoma*; the entrance hall (*shikidai*) is also different. There are also surviving elements from another era: the complete closure of the east façade by shutters (*shitomido*) and solid doors (*karado*).

Interior of the Omote "shoin" of Samboin, Kyoto

Reorganized in 1598 for the visit of Toyotomi Hideyoshi, the Omote *shoin* constitutes – especially in its extremely innovatory layout – a precious link between past and future. The outside of the pavilion shows the influence of the *Shinden zukuri*. The size of the *chumon* is reminiscent of the Pavilion of the Spring; a short balustrade runs along the balcony and a staircase protected by an awning descends from the middle of the front façade to the garden. The interior, on the other hand, perfectly answers to the norms imposed by *Shoin zukuri* for a *shuden* whose function is exclusively official. It has only three adjoining rooms, a layout which became standard from the Meireki era (1655–58), and adheres to rationalization and simplicity. The impost (*ramma*) above the sliding partitions (*fusuma*) shows the close relation between the different rooms, the *tokonoma* and the *chigaidana* identify the main room, and the *jodan* dominates the second room, making it stand out from the third.

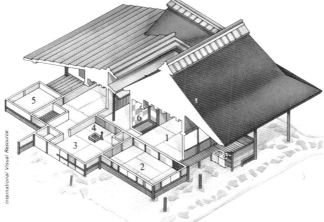

1 *first room*
2 *second room*
3 *tea room*
4 *lobby*
5 *pantry section*
6 tokonoma

The Shokintei, garden pavilion of palace of Katsura, Kyoto

Situated beyond the lake right opposite the house, the Shokintei (or Pavilion of the Lute and Pine) was used for nocturnal celebrations and for meetings to observe the moon. The varying roof levels and the diversity of roofing materials clearly translate the plan and spatial composition: the central body has a half-hipped roof covered in a sort of thatch (*miscanthus*), the tea room has a roof of cyprus bark and the pantry has a tiled roof. In fact such wide differentiation is explained by the lack of continuity in construction. The central section with the open pantry under the north eaves was probably the original building erected around 1641. Its two large rooms closely linked with the garden form a vast L-shaped room with a surface area of 17 *tatami*. In the first room, equipped only with removable *shoji*, lighting is restricted because of the deep eaves. These are supported by posts of oak logs which, from the inside, look like live trees (an example of the "recreation of nature" which was very important to the *Sukiya* style). The tea room seems to have been introduced around 1647. Conforming to the classic rules, it retains an enclosed appearance.

Palace of Katsura, Kyoto

This princely hermitage is the best example of the *Sukiya* style. It is made up of four main pavilions built on a staggered diagonal line: the Old Shoin (*Koshoin*), the Central Shoin (*Chushoin*), the Music Room (*Gakinoma*) and the New Palace (*Shingoten*). A layout like this, which had already been adopted for the palace of Nijo, permits large bays to be cut into the east and south façades, thus providing varied outlooks on to the gardens. The Old Shoin could have been built as long ago as 1616 and was reconstructed in its present form to be attached to the Central Shoin, which dates from approximately 1641, as does the Music Room. As for the New Palace, it seems to have been built around 1655, then restored and no doubt partially modified in 1663. The different dates of the buildings are apparent in their varying styles. The tall struts, common to all the buildings, are left uncovered under all the balconies except in the Old Shoin, where they are surrounded by masonry. However, the Old Shoin is the only building whose balcony has retained its external character, to the extent of becoming a platform which juts out on to the garden and is used for observing the moon. In the Central Shoin and the New Palace, the original balconies have been changed into corridors, closed by a series of *shoji* and shutters. The balcony of the Music Room has taken on the appearance of a spectators' gallery with a bench from which to watch ball games. Inside, the layout of the Old Shoin is extremely simple. The Central Shoin has a raised floor to indicate the boundaries of the private quarters. Whereas the Old Shoin is relatively open and official because of its function to receive guests, the private quarters of the Central Shoin bathe in a calm atmosphere, personalized by discreet decoration and wash-drawings. Finally, in the New Palace, spatial flexibility reminiscent of the *Shinden* style can be observed.

Sun Temple, Konarak

Built by Narasimha I (1238–64), this temple was the final achievement of the Orissan style. It takes the form, on a colossal scale, of the wooden processional cars in which the gods were paraded on holy days. In front, the base of a huge hall of dance stands in isolation. The magnificent hall of worship in the temple itself has survived, with its celebrated female figures on the roof slabs. The incomplete sanctuary tower must have risen to a height of more than 66 metres (215 feet). The vitality of the sculpture that fills every surface of the building draws the eye of the spectator from one delight to the next.

T he study of Indian architecture is difficult since, because of the time-honoured use of wood as a building material, very little has survived from the earliest period. Excavation has made it possible to reconstruct some of the ground plans of towns; the Buddhist monasteries, which were constructed in brick from a very early date, were to retain certain arrangements found in domestic architecture. It was only in the centuries immediately preceding our era that craftsmen began to hollow out rock or to build in brick, and then only for religious establishments such as temples or monasteries. Although we know from literary sources that vast public buildings and royal palaces existed at this time, these have with rare exceptions disappeared. They reappear only in wall paintings or in their remote descendants of the Islamic period.

The earliest structure was a single four-sided cell. Its image is preserved in the Draupadi ratha at Mahabalipuram and is still found today in the peasant dwellings of Bengal. It was built on posts with walls of planks or puddled clay and covered with a roof of thick thatch in the form of a mitre supported by a radiating framework. As India is the land of teak, Indian craftsmen excelled at a very early stage in the use of timber framing (to which we may apply the terminology of our own Middle Ages), which enabled them to cover large spaces, to vary the forms, approaches and lighting of their buildings and finally to build on upper storeys. The roofing, which was ribbed in the form of a horse-shoe, carried purlins and thus resembled the inverted hull of a ship, protected by flat over-lapping tiles. To judge from surviving reproductions in stone, Indian carpenters achieved an extraordinary versatility of style from at least the 6th century BC. The cities of Rajagrha and Kausambi (6th–5th century BC) have left the remains of an impressive teak enclosure (which was later reconstructed in stone). The palace of Pataliputra, capital of the Maurya dynasty (324–184BC) included an audience hall on a vast brick terrace with 80 pillars in which Achaemenid, and hence also some Hellenistic influences can be discerned.

The earliest buildings, in which the Hindu form of worship was elaborated and around which the life of the community revolved, had thus become the orthodox model, sanctioned as it were by success. Later buildings could only continue this tradition. The adoption of brick and subsequently of stone only represented a technical improvement, but, requiring a greater effort to implement, it earned more merit for the donor. New materials and technology were adapted to the forms of sacred architecture, rather than vice versa. To us this may seem illogical – but only within the terms of our own quite relative "logic": the Greek temple, for example, was also from column to pediment only a repetition of the original timbering or, if one prefers, a metaphor in marble for the wooden structure.

In appearance, the Indian temple has one main building, usually square or rectangular, which is sometimes extended around the image at the west end by the addition of a domed apse. It sits on a plinth which is crossed at the east end by an axial staircase between curved string-walls. The frames for the supporting beams and the joists of the original woodwork can be traced in the form of a moulded plinth. The projection of the coping was dictated by the remembered forms of the stringers. The corner posts as well as those reinforcing the partitions and framing the openings were transformed into pilasters. The vaulting is usually corbelled on the inside, while the extrados is given a cylindrical curve, recalling the ancient ribbed wooden structures. These have been interpreted as gables in the form of vast horse-shoe arches with a pierced tympanum or ornamental balcony. The upper storeys, if any, are artificial and lit by false windows, always in a horse-shoe form which echoes that of the ribbed roofing. The decoration emphasizes the underlying framework; it covers the mouldings on the plinth and coping, pilasters, columns and lintels, in imitation of the original wood and its festoons of foliage. The internal walls are undecorated. The bays of the false storeys are blind and filled with relief figures which appear to be leaning outwards like living persons. Except for the entrance at the east end, the doors are usually false, carved to give the impression of wooden panels.

The rigidity and persistence of this design is explicable if we bear in mind that the only buildings known to us from this period are temples. For Hindus the temple is the abode of the god on earth. He is present in the form of a linga (phallus) for Siva, or of an image. The observances of life itself are the form of worship offered to the god: food, music and dance, offerings of flowers, perfumes and fine clothing. The priest alone is permitted to approach the god, while the donor may attend the sacrifice by remaining in the anteroom or by completing a circumambulation of the exterior. The god is only revealed to the world on festival days; he is then brought out on a portable shrine or a processional car and paraded through the streets to refresh himself in the sacred tank. All is arranged so that the god may live in a manner befitting the Lord of the Universe and so may in return bestow his bounty upon his servants.

In Hindu mythology the gods reside at the summit of the superimposed worlds and heavens, in the Himalaya, which is also the axis of the universe. Thus, at a very early stage, three, five or seven storeys of identical plan and elevation but of regularly diminishing size were erected over the sanctuary, the whole assuming the form of a stepped pyramid and crowned with a roof in the form of a mitre, a bulb or a barrel vault. Each false storey is decorated with the creatures which inhabit the different worlds and thus indicates, as a function of acquired merit, the successive levels of reincarnation, up to the supreme heaven. This form of architecture is in fact a spatial sculpture or a reduced model of the Universe. The whole structure is strictly oriented to the cardinal axes. The tower, with its foundations and pinnacle, marks the nadir and zenith. The quadrants of the sacred area correspond to the path of the sun and to the seasons. The ground plans were drawn according to elaborate diagrams corresponding to the astronomical concepts of the Brahmins. The whole building subtends and therefore gives order to the dimensions of space and time. This function of sacred architecture is so fundamental that it is found in an almost identical form in later Buddhist architecture.

The temple is also seen as a city inhabited by the family and celestial attendants of the deity, or, more literally, by the Brahmins and their worldly servants. Other shrines were added for the heavenly pantheon. Each one adhered to the same plan but they were grouped in increasingly intricate networks. Often in the course of time new halls of worship, propylaea or tanks for the use of the devotees were added to a famous sanctuary by donors. A surrounding wall with gateways at each of the four cardinal points encompassed and protected this labyrinth, so that the temple became a city within a city.

It is difficult to establish why and at what period wood was finally given up in favour of brick and then stone. Brick had been in use as a building material for more than a thousand years: in the far west of India it was used in the construction of the impressive cities of the Indus valley, from Mohenjo-daro to Harappa. The Vedic altar was itself constructed in brick. We may also remember the prestige of the great Persian cities in the eyes of the dynasties that were trying to unite India from the 3rd century BC onwards.

The technique is simple: solid masses of

INDIA

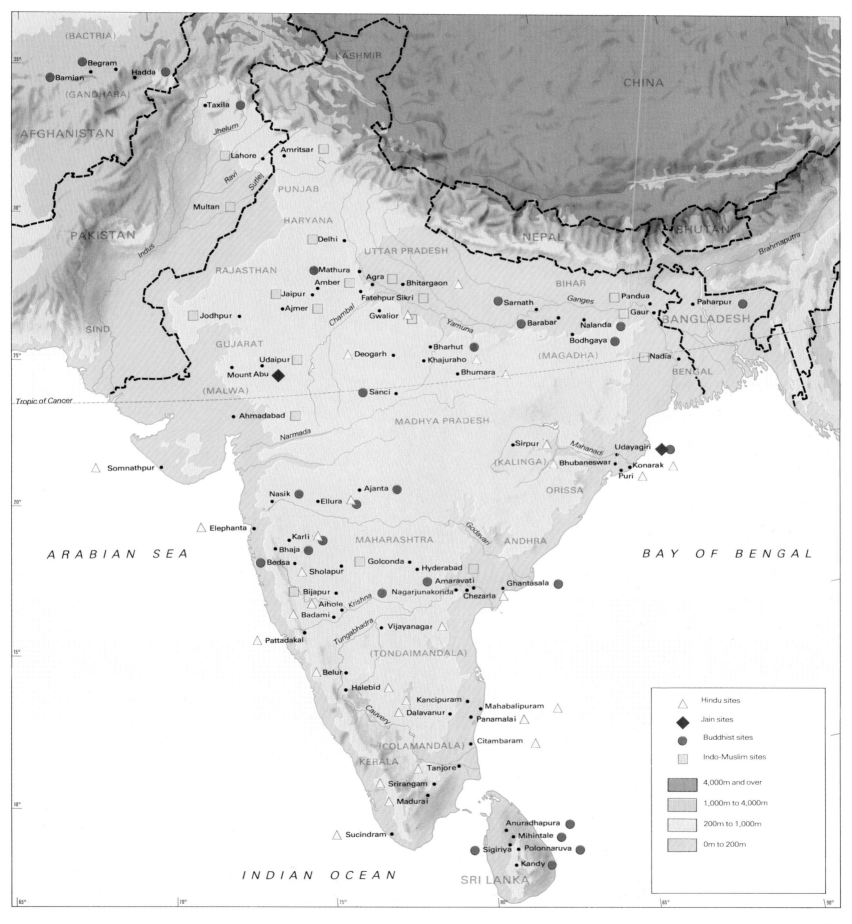

REGIONS OF INDIA

	Gandhara, Punjab, Sind, Rajasthan	Uttar Pradesh, Bihar, Bengal, Madhya Pradesh, Magadha	Gujarat, Kalinga, Orissa, Maharastra, Andhra	Colamandala, Kerala, Pandiya	Ceylon	
500BC	DARIUS	BUDDHA c. 566–486	MAHAVIRA † c. 468			500BC
400BC	XERXES	NANDA 364–324	*Rajagrha, Kausambi*		VIJAYA	400BC
300BC	ALEXANDER	MAURYA 324–184 CANDRAGUPTA 324–300 *Pataliputra* ASOKA c. 273–236			Anuradhapura	300BC
200BC	BACTRIAN GREEKS	*Barabar, Dhauli, Asokan pillars* *Bharut* SUNGA 187–75			Buddhist missions	200BC
100BC		*Sanci* KANVA 75–30	*Ajanta, Bhaja, Karli* Amaravati		*Abhayagiri*	100BC
0	SCYTHIANS PARTHIANS GONDOPHARIANS	*Sanci sculptures*	*Kanheri, Udayagiri*			0
50	KUSAN *Taxila, Sirkap*		SATAVAHANA 50–195			50
100	*Jandial Peshawar*	KUSANA 78–240 KANISKA *Mathura Bodh Gaya*	*Ajanta, Nasik, Karli* *Bedsa, Goli* *Amaravati sculptures*			100
200	SASSANIANS *Surkh Kotal Hadda*		*Nagar junakonda* VAKATAKA 275–558			200
300		IKSAKU 225–321			*Jetavana*	300
400	SHAPUR *Bamiyan* WHITE HUNS	GUPTA 320–510	*Ajanta, Aihole, Ellura,*	PALLAVA 325–892	MAHASENA	400
500		*Chezarla, Sanci,* *Sarnath, Bhitargaon* *Deogarh*	*Aurangabad, Bagh, Ter*		KASSAPA I *Sigiriya*	500
600	CHOSROES *Fundukistan*	*Bhumara, Mahabodhi* VARDHAMANA	CALUKYA 535–753 *Ellura* *Aihole*	*Dalavanur Mahavalipuram Shore Temple Kancipuram*	Tamil incursions *Vatadage* AGRABODHI	600
700	MAHOMET † 632 VALABHI ARABS in Sind	HARSA 606–647 *Elephanta, Nalanda* PRATIHARA 740 PALA 765	*Badami* RASTRAKUTA 752–973 *Pattadakal, Alampur, Kailasa of Ellura*	PANDYA 740–920 *Panaimalai Narttamalai*	Tamil incursions	700
800		*Gwalior* *Paharpur*	*Bhubaneswar* *Malkhed, Mansura*	COLA 846–1173		800
900	*Osia Jodhpur*	*Deogarh Maribagh Chamba*		RAJARAJA *Erumbur*	Cola incursions end of the Anuradhapura	900
1000	MAHMUD OF GHAZNI *Mt. Abu, Solanki, Sunak*	CANDELLA 941 *Khajuraho* *Ajmer* *Gwalior* SENA 1095	EASTERN CALUKYA 973 *Lingaraja of Bhubaneswar, Puri*	*Srinivasanalur Tanjore, Gangai-colakondapuram Darasuram*	VIJAYABAHU *Polonnaruva*	1000
1100	RAJPUT STATES *Osia, Jalor*		HOYSALA 1047	PANDIYA 1100 *Madurai*	PARAKRAMABAHU	1100
1200	MAHMUD OF GHOR *Modhera*	GHURI SULTANS Qutb-Minar' Ajmer	*Belur, Halebid* *Konarak* *Somnathpur, Palampet*	*Tirunandikkari*	*Thuparama Lankatilaka*	1200
1300		KHILJI				1300
1400	Broach Cambay TIMUR	TUGHLUQ 1320 Lalkot, Delhi	VIJAYANAGAR 1336–1565		GAMPOLA	1400
1500	SAFAVIDS	LODI 1451 Siri, Ahmadabad, Khairpur, Jaunpur, Mandu MUGHAL BABUR 1504–1530	*Hampi*	*Srisailan Cidambaram Srirangam Vellure*	CHINESE KINGDOM OF KOTTE KINGDOM OF KANDY	1500
1600		AKBAR 1556–1605 Ajmer, Agra, Fatehpur Sikri, Lahore, Gwalior JAHANGIR 1605–1627 Agra, Sikandra	Bijapur, Golconda, Hyderabad, Bidar EAST INDIA COMPANY	NAYAK *Trichinopoly Ramesvaram*	PORTUGUESE	1600
1700		SHAH JAHAN 1628–1658 Taj Mahal of Agra, Shalimar, Lahore AURANGZEB 1658–1707		*Kumbakonam Madurai*	DUTCH	1700

SCYTHIANS: peoples, dynasties, great powers, sovereigns; *Taxila*: Buddhist sites; *Pataliputra*: Hindu sites; Ahmadabad: Islamic sites.

bricks are erected, carefully lapped against each other and cemented, as it were, with a liquid mortar. As for the apertures, Indian craftsmen were aware of the use of brick lintels with keystones set on edge, and even, for the interior, of vaulting which made use of brick arch-stones. The most usual method, however, was that of corbelling, which involved a series of overhanging ledges, each one projecting beyond the one below. The external ornament was carved in a lime mortar or on slabs of stone, set in for this purpose, and the brick was thus obscured. The interior of the building was decorated with wall paintings.

With rock, Indian craftsmen made use of a remarkable technique which has never been surpassed or even equalled. The earliest examples are the temples hollowed out of the living rock, perhaps in imitation of the rock tombs of Persia. This process is astonishing in its disregard for the effort involved. The rock face was tackled from the front. Pilot galleries were bored to the height of the future ceiling and to the desired depth. They were then hollowed out layer by layer to the required floor level. Massive bodies of rock were removed one at a time, their circumference marked by a line of holes into which pegs of hard wood were driven. When moistened, these swelled and split the rock along the desired outline. Clearance of the rock was completed with the aid of the miner's bar and pickaxe. Sections of rock were left in place for the shaping of the columns which would "support" the ceiling in imitation of wooden structures, and in some cases, of the cult object, the stupa or linga. Finally, the decoration is planed and chiselled. Beginning with modest rectangular chambers fronted by access porches of only two pillars, Indian craftsmen were able by the 5th to 6th centuries AD to fashion impressive sanctuaries: the caitya at Karli measures some 40 metres (130 feet) in length and 15 metres (50 feet) in width and height; the main hall at Elephanta has sides of 30 metres (100 feet). The Kailasa temple at Ellura remains the most remarkable of all; its volume, hewn from the cliff face, is some 150,000 cubic metres (200,000 cubic yards), while to achieve this some 200,000 cubic metres (260,000 cubic yards) of rock had to be cut away and cleared. At Mahabalipuram enormous erratic blocks left on the beach by the moraine were used as they lay. Apart from the sheer labour involved, the planning and flawless execution of such works are still astonishing.

Because of the adherence to ancient prototypes, the original woodwork was reproduced in the most minute detail in these rock-cut temples, almost to the point of trompe l'oeil. In fact it seems that the earliest caves had wooden façades and even interior revetments of wood. This is the case at the excavated sanctuary of Bhaja (2nd century BC) where the nave, on plain octagonal pillars, has been cut from the rock, but the façade must have been of wood. On that of the caitya at Karli the pillars cut from rock reserved for this purpose supported a wooden balcony. The oldest and most numerous of these rock-cut temples are Buddhist, but their wooden prototypes were Hindu, predating the time of the Buddha. Their plan is simple: a huge rectangular hall for worship, often extended by a hemispherical apse which was used in the circumambulation of the stupa, or, in the case of the Hindus, by a simple cella for the linga. The nave is "supported" by a double row of columns which demarcate quite narrow aisles. Monks' cells of a simple cube form and, later, lateral shrines open on to this great assembly hall. The vaulting reproduces the primitive ribs and purlins. For the façade, an imposing horse-shoe arch is carved to imitate the timbering, with windows in the tympanum or else a balcony above a portico.

This arrangement is found from the 2nd to 1st century BC at Bhaja, in the earliest caves at Ajanta (nos. 8, 9, 10, 12; 1st century BC) and at Nasik and Karli. Yet this design was to develop quite quickly. The columns became more ornate; the base took on a bulbous shape, the capital became bell-shaped and the shafts, which now decreased in length, became octagonal. They were much closer together and supported a high architrave, which was itself heavily decorated. The imitation of earlier wooden structures became less skilful as they passed further into history and the decoration became increasingly enriched for its own sake. This may be observed in the flowering of the rock-cut temples of the Gupta period (320–510AD), for example in caves 1, 16, 17, 19 at Ajanta (c.450–550AD) and cave 10 at Ellura (late 6th, early 7th century AD): the great arch of the façade gradually disappears beneath the decoration and the "timber framing" of the nave is no longer indicated. This evolution becomes pronounced in the 7th and 8th centuries. At Ellura, under the first of the Calukya kings (535–753AD) this disorganization of the original motifs is completed. Moreover, although the old cutting techniques were employed in removing the volumes of rock necessary for the realization of the Kailasa temple at Ellura, the model for the temple itself (end of the 8th century) was to be a temple built in stone. In fact the Kailasa temple, the most gigantic endeavour in the dressing of rock known to us, marks the end of this genre.

The Buddhist sites of the north-west of the subcontinent enable us to some extent to trace the origins of constructional architecture and to detect foreign influences. Parts of buildings which still exist, such as the base of the stupa known as the "shrine of the double-headed eagle" of Sirkap (1st century AD) or the Fire Temple of Jandial (of the same period), bear witness to the role played by Achaemenid and hence by Greek models. Brick or quarry-stone is the base material used, and the entire surface is plastered. Certain parts (smaller columns, lintels) may be in dressed stone. The arch of bonded brickwork and the cupola resting on pendentives were both taken from Iranian models. Nevertheless timber framing was still the rule. Literary texts describe the famous stupa erected in the 2nd century AD by Kaniska at Peshawar; from a stone base, measuring 77 metres (250 feet) at the sides and 46 metres (150 feet) in height, rises a wooden structure of 13 storeys, 122 metres (400 feet) high and crowned with an iron mast supporting umbrellas. A knowledge of these structures is essential to an understanding of the origin and form of the Chinese pagoda, which was based upon them. In spite of these remains, it is difficult to follow in any detail the early development of free-standing architecture in durable materials. The earliest buildings known to us go back only to the 4th century AD; our account of

them can only be unduly schematic and no doubt over-emphasizes the part played by external influences, in view of the dearth of indigenous evidence.

If brick was familiar to Indian builders, stone, although cut and worked with extraordinary skill, was less easy to use in the construction of free-standing buildings. At all events, it was initially used only cautiously and for very modest buildings. It was usually dressed before being placed in position, except for the portion reserved for later, chiselled decoration. It was at first treated in the same manner as wood: pillar and post, architrave, monolithic lintels, thin slabs for wall panels set in edgewise, the whole structure fixed by tenon and mortise joints, or set into grooves. No mortar was ever employed. The cutting and polishing were excellent, producing a perfect join however hard the stone. Indian craftsmen made use of all the local veins of rock, from granite to schist, with equal success. Very soon increasingly large stone buildings were being constructed, for which the simple method of fitting was no longer adequate. It thus became necessary to reduce the size of the unit. But the stability of these unpointed blocks posed a problem. Each block was given a slightly trapezoidal slant and then placed top to bottom in such a way as to hold them against each other. A wedge, cut to the required shape and then driven in, became necessary every five or six blocks to secure this self-locking system. Copper clamps sealed with lead were used to reinforce the corners.

The roofing was at first made up of large flat slabs which rested on architraves and monolithic pillars and were reinforced with battens; the monsoon rains were drained off by stone gargoyles which were, however, only suitable for very narrow buildings. The solution was to corbel out the walls. In the case of the cella of the deity, the small surface area and the existence above it of a pyramid of false storeys enabled the builder to give a slight overhang to each successive course. This technique was safe because, due to the square plan, the four walls would jam and secure each other, above a relatively small space. For the rather wider hall preceding the sanctuary, the number of internal columns supporting architraves was increased so as to create three naves, and the whole was covered with large slabs superimposed in the manner of corbelling, giving the exterior the silhouette of a low stepped pyramid.

The earliest temples seem to have been built in brick, as in the case of the original state of the Mahabodhi Temple at Bodh Gaya (end of the 2nd century AD) and the small sanctuaries with corbelled vaulting which may still be seen at Chezarla (Guntur; 4th century AD). These culminate in the 5th century with the beautiful temple at Bhitargaon. The cella is surmounted by superimposed and diminishing false storeys, covered by a hull-shaped vault on a north–south axis and thus at right angles to the axis of entrance. It is decorated with terracotta panels. The modelling shows the influence of wood-built architecture. This building is all the more interesting because it is almost identical with the type which the Indians were to introduce in South-East Asia; it is thus the origin of all the architecture of that region.

By the end of the 5th century, the basic formula of the Hindu temple comprises the following definitive features: an east–west axis, an entrance porch or portico, a

rectangular hall of worship (often with three pillared naves and side-entrances), a narrow passage and finally the cella of the deity, sometimes surrounded by an ambulatory which may be extended in the form of a hemispherical apse (or "elephant's back" as the Indians engagingly term it). A pyramid of false storeys, diminishing in plan and elevation in the same manner as the main part, surmounts the cella and terminates in a bulb, a four-sided dome or a short barrel on a north–south axis, as the case may be. Decoration is, as a rule, limited to mouldings. It may also consist of relief panels narrating the life of the god, on the exterior of the cella, sometimes on a balustrade around the plinth, or else in the ambulatory, a formula which was to be exported overseas, notably to Java.

In the 7th century a proliferation of forms took place, the most remarkable developments occurring in the south-east of the country, under the aegis of the Pallava kings (especially from 600–740). Having hollowed out cave temples which were modest in themselves but decorated with wonderful reliefs, they went on to fashion the rocks of Mahabalipuram in imitation of wood-built sanctuaries (630–68), thus

Temple of Gangaikondacolapuram. This was built by Rajaraja the Great (985–1014), as was the great temple at Tanjore. The sanctuary tower (33 sq. metres/110 sq. feet at ground level, height 52 metres/170 feet) overhangs the imposing hall of worship (31 metres by 57 metres/100 feet by 190 feet). A descendant of the Pallava temples, this powerful building has preserved their clear definition and plastic vigour.

leaving us a faithful image of their prototypes. From the end of the 7th century, with the Shore Temple on the same site, and then during the 8th century at Panaimalai and above all at Kancipuram, they erected a number of beautiful sanctuaries, which became very influential – notably the Meguti temple at Aihole (c.634); the Sivalaya temple at Badami (c.700); the Virupaksa at Pattadakal; and finally the Kailasa temple of Ellura (between 758 and 773), which, although an excavated temple, is nevertheless the unquestionable masterpiece of the period. From the end of the 8th century, increasingly huge and ornate buildings were constructed. We shall try to distinguish the main trends among them; but we shall confine ourselves to their cult functions and relationship to religious beliefs rather than their architectural qualities.

The tomb of earthly desires

In this study of the origins of Indian architecture little distinction has been made between Buddhist and Hindu monuments. This is because the earliest rock sanctuaries were above all places of assembly, copied from the wooden structures that were common to all the different sects. They were distinguished only by their particular cult object, the *stupa* or the *linga*, and later by their figurative reliefs. As a simple rule, the apsidal ambulatory seems to be a Buddhist feature. For the rest, the rock-cut sanctuaries were mostly Buddhist, since the communities of monks tended to choose for their places of retreat isolated valleys flanked by suitable cliffs; it was they who were able to provide the man-power coupled with sufficient will and enthusiasm for the work. The Buddhists also built monasteries in brick and quarry-stone overlaid with stucco, with their cells grouped around a courtyard-patio, which was often decorated with a *stupa* as an aid to meditation. They developed a number of refined fittings, notably for the circulation of water.

The Buddhist faith was able to evolve its own particular architectural forms. The reliefs tell us that among the earliest of these were the temple-railings built around the Bodhi tree, beneath which the Buddha attained enlightenment. Unfortunately they have now all disappeared and we only know of this polygonal wooden enclosure from the great sculptural reliefs. Nevertheless they must have played an important part in the development of the *stupa*. Originally a funerary monument, a simple tumulus, whose form is said to have been prescribed by the Buddha at the moment of his extinction, the *stupa* is the supreme symbol of his teaching; the renunciation of worldly desires, which are impossi-ble to satisfy and hence the source of all suffering. The erection of a *stupa* reliquary to house the relics of the Teacher or his great disciples was to become the chief missionary activity of Buddhism.

But the *stupa* is also a cosmic symbol and an aid to meditation. The base, often decorated with narrative reliefs, is our own world, teeming with life. The dome is the "egg", the celestial dome or the Universe. The mast which pierces it from nadir to zenith is the cosmic axis. The square balcony at the summit of the dome represents the 33 heavens inhabited by the Hindu pantheon, presided over by Siva. Above this, parasols in tiers symbolically shelter the Buddha, who, having passed beyond all the delusions of reality, is liberated from suffering, but only after he has set in motion the "Wheel of the Law", which teaches his example to men. The internal structure of the dome repeats the form of a wheel with its hub and spokes.

Literary texts and sculptural reliefs, as well as surviving votive *stupas* in metal, all support the idea that the earliest type was essentially a timber-framed tower, like that at Peshawar. The symbolism, moreover, is identical. However, at a very early stage the *stupa* became a hemispherical mound built of brick and later of stone. To protect it and to direct the worshippers, a railing was built around it with gateways at the four cardinal points. Originally of wood, this railing was soon executed in stone, and then decorated with medallions and suppliant figures, and finally with scenes from the lives of the Buddha. The gateways – two tall uprights bearing three slightly curved cross-bars – provided a suitable ground for religious imagery. When space ran out, stone plaques carved with narrative reliefs began to be set around the base of the dome.

The *stupas* at Sanci, which were founded from the end of the 3rd century BC, but with decoration dating from between the end of the 2nd century BC and the 1st century AD, are among the most famous examples. In the south-east, there survive above all the narrative panels of the great *stupas* of Amaravati (2nd century BC–2nd AD) and Nagar-junakonda (3rd–4th century AD), whose vast brick domes were supported by internal structures in the form of wheel-spokes. Meanwhile, the monks also began to hollow out assembly halls such as we have already seen at Bhaja, at Ajanta and subsequently throughout the Gupta period. In the north-west, there was an increase in the number of brick-built *stupas*, whose bases were decorated with arched niches containing images of the Teacher, sharing the distant but determining influence of Graeco-Roman sculpture. In the north-east, for example at the Buddhist university of Nalanda (mainly 7th century AD), the dome rises from a double octagon-al base ornamented with blind arches. The principal monastery at Paharpur (late 8th, early 9th century) is notable for an enormous monument in the form of a Greek cross, with passages for circumambula-tion at different levels and possibly crowned by either a *stupa* or sanctuary. These are models which would reappear in South-East Asia.

Because Buddhism was in the end driven out of the country of its birth – the ravages of the Muslim era cannot be dwelt on here – no evidence of it survives in India after the 11th century. But from an early period it had spread to other countries, initial-ly to Ceylon, where it still flourishes. The great *stupas* of Anuradhapura are majestic examples.

Monastery of Bhaja

Excavated at the beginning of the 2nd century BC, this is an outstanding example of the great rock-cut Buddhist monasteries. The reconstruction by Percy Brown (below) shows the original wooden framework. The axial vault, which is of the barrel (or inverted hull) type, is supported by 27 octagonal pillars and made up of purlins (originally, tiles) supported on hoops. The two lateral aisles are covered in the same way, but only with half-vaults. The main timberframe projects freely from the façade, forming a porch roof. Its tympanum is of latticework for ventilation and opens on to a balcony. This is reinforced by pillars and shelters a covered porch or veranda. In front there is a terrace with balustrade. Two lines of corbelling, supported by brackets at two levels and with a balcony, correspond to the lateral aisles. To the left is the façade of the monks' cells, with upper storey, balcony and veranda. Doors and windows are protected by porch roofs of hooped woodwork. These details, deriving from woodwork, faithfully copied in the rock, enable us to understand the composition and hence the development of the later free-standing architecture, in which they continued to appear for a long time. Moreover at Bhaja, the original façade of the cave was itself probably of wood.

1 *principal nave with barrel vault*

2 *lateral naves with half-vaulting*

3 *porch roof, tympanum and balcony of principal nave*

4 *covered porch and terrace*

5 *corbelling of façade of lateral naves*

6 *façade of monks' cells, with balcony and veranda*

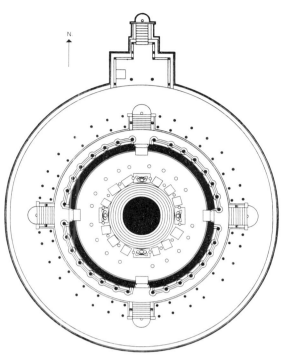

Thuparama, Anuradhapura, and plan of Vatadage, Polonnaruva (Sri Lanka)

The *stupa* indicates the tomb of the Buddha, the spread of his teaching in the concrete form of his relics, and ultimately, the Cosmos. The primitive tumulus thus becomes a complex representation (see diagram below). The dome is the celestial arc. It is pierced by the cosmic axis, which emerges at the summit in the form of a mast. This surmounts a platform with balustrade which symbolizes the 33 heavens inhabited by the gods of the Hindu pantheon; it carries parasols, a mark of royalty and so of the presence of the Buddha. The dome is encompassed by an ambulatory for the faithful which, in India, would be decorated with relief panels illustrating the legend of Sakyamuni. A railing with four gateways protects the monument. The Thuparama (founded in the 2nd century BC and restored in the 7th) and the Vatadage (restored at the end of the 12th century) are examples of a more developed formula: an enclosing wall and four altars flank the base of the dome. Formerly the ambulatory was covered with a wooden structure supported by pillars. The parasols at the summit are set into a conical mass of masonry.

1 *dome or* anda: "egg"

2 *platform or* harmika

3 *shaft or* chattravali, *carrying the parasols, or* chattra

4 *relief panels*

5 *paved ambulatory*

6 *railing or* vedika

7 *gateway or* torana

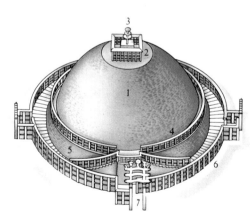

Northern gateway of the great "stupa", Sanci

This brick *stupa* was erected by Asoka in the 3rd century BC and enlarged in the 1st century BC. The gateways were added in the 1st century AD, in the following order: south, north, east and west. Copied from wooden structures, they consist of two square pillars with three built-in cross-bars (total height 11 metres/36 feet). The brackets of the cross-bars are superbly carved in the form of female figures or animals. Scenes from the previous lives of the Buddha and his preaching, or from the spread of his teaching, are carved in low relief on both sides, in small panels on the pillars, and in long bands along the cross-bars. The Teacher himself is not yet represented except in symbolic forms. The liveliness and sense of movement are remarkable, as is the naturalistic decoration of the ends. As in cartoon strips, the same character may be represented twice in order to relate two succeeding phases of the action. But it is also the start of a new development. Formerly it was the pure form of the architecture that carried the message. Now the imagery takes over the expressive function, and the structure tends to become simply a support for it.

The abode of the gods

The form of the Hindu temple seems to have become set after the 8th century. As the abode of the god and hence a representation of the layered universe over which he presided, it had found in the sanctuary tower its definitive form. Thanks to a building technique perfectly suited to the task, it was possible to build the temples ever larger and taller; to ornament them to the point where their forms dissolved in decoration, and to increase the number of lateral shrines, courtyards, gateways, tanks and railings. But, in architectural terms, hardly anything new was created and the basic forms remained the same.

In fact these remarks could apply equally well to the whole of Indian art and thought, which gradually crystallized around their respective traditions, albeit with an infinite richness of expression. And, of course, no further social or philosophical upheaval occurred which was comparable with that occasioned by Buddhism. Politically, the country disintegrated. If some vigorous local dynasties may still have sought to distinguish themselves by erecting grandiose buildings, no truly imperial dynasty, setting its stamp on the art of the whole country, was to emerge until the period of Muslim conquest.

On the other hand, Hinduism sustains and gives perfect order to a coherent and harmonious social system in which each member has his place and is persuaded that it is for the best. In each village there stands a stone temple which is as important in this context as the most lofty royal foundation elsewhere. Furthermore, it is often surprisingly substantial and well made. It is proof that in the service of a living religion architecture may be anonymous, almost spontaneous, and yet nonetheless effective.

The evolution of the Hindu temple is characterized by two distinct tendencies which can be said to belong respectively to southern and northern India. The main difference between them is in the appearance of the sanctuary tower. In the south, the superimposed storeys, even though reduced in scale, are seen quite distinctly as individual architectural features. If the ground plan is square, a four-sided bulb generally appears at the summit; if it is rectangular, it has a barrel vault on a north–south axis. Most often, the one or more halls of worship which precede the cella are hypostyles with a flat roof of stone slabs. In the major capitals, the temple stands at the heart of the city and forms a distinct complex of its own. This pattern becomes established with the great buildings erected at Kancipuram by the later Pallava kings in the 8th century. The finest buildings were erected by the powerful Cola rulers (846–1173), such as the great temple at Tanjore (1009) which rose to a height of more than 63 metres (205 feet), or that of Gangaikondacolapuram. The Pandya kings (1100–1350) and above all the rulers of Vijayanagar (1336–1565) further elaborated upon this model. A proliferation of sculpture occurred, unfortunately causing a dissolution of forms. The Vitthala temple (1513) at Hampi marks a final stage in this process: the carving has become so overcrowded that it is hardly possible to distinguish the plan of the building. Nevertheless, the sacred cities of southern India such as those of its last rulers, the Nayaks (from 1600), still continue to fascinate: probably because they have remained living cities. A curious inversion of hierarchy has taken place: the main sanctuary is now a modest cella, almost invisible but for its gold tiles. The sanctuary towers are now erected over the gateways and appear more impressive the further one goes towards the outside of the temple. This pattern, which is especially striking when viewed as a whole, is found at Madurai, Cidambaram, Srirangam and Tiruvannamalai. For thousands of years a strong sense of devotion has existed in these heavenly cities.

In the north, developments are first seen in the temples of Orissa from the 8th century onwards. Above the cella, the sanctuary tower becomes a stack of false storeys compressed into single rows of blind windows; this is the only trace of the original design. Its plan follows the outlines of the cella, including its projecting parts and porches. Through a progressive reduction in these indentations and distinct levels, the tower takes on the form of a beehive, culminating in a flattened and ribbed fruit-shaped bulb. The hall of worship is covered by a low stepped pyramid made up of flat slabs. This progression is illustrated at Bhubaneswar, from the Mukteshvara temple (9th century) to the huge Lingaraja temple (c.1100) and especially the Surya (Sun) temple at Konarak (13th century), where the architectural mass, with immense wheels sculpted on the plinth, represents the processional chariot of the deity. This style is found again in the sanctuaries at Khajuraho, built by the Candella kings (941–1203). On the raised plinths, the line of recession of the towers is accentuated by the subsidiary towers built over the lateral cellas. This pattern was adopted in the whole of the north and north-west of the country, usually with a hall of worship supported by columns: it can be traced from the Surya temple at Osia (10th century) to the Surya temple at Modhera (13th century). The Jains, in their sanctuaries on Mount Abu (11th–13th centuries), erected cupolas on arcatures and pillars with great skill – carving them, however, with such a profusion of ornament that the architectural forms are no longer discernible. A similar development took place in Mysore under the Hoysalas from the 11th to 14th centuries, notably at the temples of Somnathpur. Henceforth, in all regions, decorative effect supplants mass; there is no longer an architecture as such, only masons piling up stones to be turned into ornament. From the 13th century onwards sculptors, too, lacked creative talent. Thenceforth architecture was more of an industry than a form of religious art.

Kailasa, Ellura

Mainly the work of King Krishna of the Rastrakuta dynasty which dominated the Deccan, the temple (50 by 33 metres/165 by 110 feet) and its subsidiary buildings were cut from the rock between 758 and 773. The required masses of rock were hewn out of the cliff, then fashioned into the shape of buildings and carved; to the sides, vast assembly halls were hollowed out of the cliff face at different levels. The sanctuary tower above the cella is based on Pallava models, with its three diminishing false storeys terminating in a lotiform bulb. Sixteen pillars arranged in the form of a cross support the flat roof slabs of the hall of worship. In front, a small pavilion shelters the sacred bull of Siva, flanked by two monolithic pillars carrying the trident of the god. Access to the court is by a building on two levels, barrel-roofed, which is the first of the entrance pavilions. Besides the truly colossal amount of work necessary to produce this form of "sculptural architecture", most admirable of all are the relief carvings (guardians and attendants ornament the walls, great mythological panels the assembly halls, and elephants and lion caryatids the plinths): these are the finest achievement of late post-Gupta art and the point of departure for all the medieval styles of India.

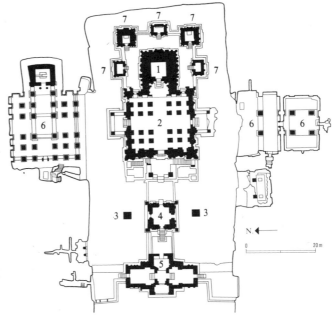

1 *cella and sanctuary tower or* vimana

2 *hall of worship or* mandapa

3 *monolithic pillars or* stambha

4 *shelter for Siva's bull*

5 *entrance pavilion or* gopuram

6 *assembly halls in the cliff*

7 *subsidiary shrines*

Mukteshvara, Bhubaneswar

This tiny building (the tower rises only 11.5 metres/38 feet), probably dating from the beginning of the 9th century, epitomizes the form of the Orissan temple, one of the finest of its kind in medieval India. On the outside walls of the cella there is a wide double projection which is decorated with model buildings. Because of all its accretions, the sanctuary tower assumes a curvilinear outline which only ends at the flat bulb with which it is crowned. The hall of worship and the antechamber which precedes it are both covered by low pyramids of flat slabs. The perfection of the carving, notably of the human figures on the gateway, enclosure wall and tower, is exceptional.

Lingaraja, Bhubaneswar

This was constructed *c*.1100, but halls 4 and 5 were added about a century later (plan and cross-section after Percy Brown).

1 *sanctuary of Siva or* deul
2 *sanctuary tower or* gandi
3 *audience hall or* jagamohana
4 *dancing hall or* nata-mandapa
5 *refectory or* bhoga-mandapa

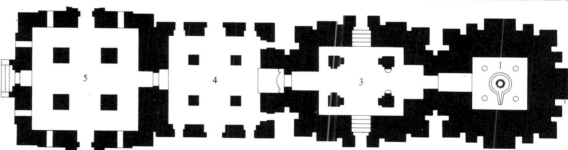

Mahabalipuram

Pallava art reaches its peak at this site. The *rathas* were fashioned between 630 and 669, from enormous outcrops of rock deposited on the beach. The Draupadi *ratha* (right) perpetuates the primitive type of local dwelling: a simple cube with umbrella-shaped radiating framework supporting a thick thatched roof in the form of a four-sided mitre. The careful reproduction of this primitive wooden structure demonstrates the persistence of ancient forms. At the end of the same century, the Shore Temple (left) was begun. Details of the earlier woodwork still continue to be carved, and the sandstone is worked as though it were wood: nevertheless this is a free-standing building and no longer a form of sculpted architecture. The cella is crowned by five diminishing false storeys; the hall of worship, by a roof of flat slabs. The design, vigorous and clean, was to be an inspiration not only to the whole of medieval Indian architecture, but also to that of South East Asia, beginning with Java.

The house and palaces of the faithful

From the 11th to 14th centuries the Muslim conquerors occupied northern India and imposed on it the architecture of Islam. An abstract art, formed in desert countries, was thus to make a strange marriage with the teeming life of the land of monsoons. In the service of new concepts and new patrons, Islamic buildings at first derived little from the country itself except materials and labour. The mosque was obviously the supreme symbol of conquest: a house where the faithful gathered to pray had hardly any local precedent, unless in the Buddhist monasteries in their function as teaching centres. The earliest plan was as follows: a courtyard enclosed by pillared halls with brick domes, a monumental entrance to the east, and to the west a hall with three naves, also covered by domes, and flanked by two (later four) minarets.

Together with their fortresses, Muslim sovereigns erected palaces which were a symbol of their might. These were like cities, arranged according to three dichotomies: between public life (audiences, processions) and private life; between the men and youths and the women and children; and, finally, between life in summer and winter, with cool chambers sunk below ground level or raised above it. In India the newcomers also rediscovered older wooden forms of architecture which have perished and cannot now be studied. Furthermore the Hindu princes, and principally the Rajputs, were to show themselves quite ready to imitate the palaces of their conquerors. In the end Mughal architecture became so closely identified with the Raj or "power" that the British, in their turn, adopted the style.

The final great architectural form to be imported from abroad was that of the tomb, a funerary palace which preserved for posterity the majesty of the commander of the faithful or else the memory of his passions. The simple, basic theme, of a cubic or polygonal mass surmounted by a cupola, would be decorated on every conceivable surface and lit by the same effects of light and shade as are seen in the formal gardens surrounding it. This proud, not to say, arrogant monument contrasts unhappily with the spirit of renunciation and anonymity represented by the Buddhist *stupa*. Yet, with the passage of time, they are in a sense united: the forms of architecture continue long after the religions, emotions and powers that gave rise to them have disappeared.

It was Mahmud Aibak who, having taken Delhi, began the first of the great mosques of India with the Qutb-Minar (1199), based on Afghan prototypes from Ghazni. The Tughluq sultans (1320–1412), the greatest of whom was Firoz (1351–88), broke with the purely Islamic tradition and began to make use of local craftsmen for their fortress-palaces. The Lodi sultans (1451–1526) produced a great number of tombs, both cubic and octagonal, as well as mosques and palaces which were richly decorated with ceramic tiles inspired by Timurid Persia. The various regional styles of the 15th and 16th centuries have their origins in these buildings. Three groups may be defined: the Delhi tradition with its rich glazed tile decoration; the styles of Bengal, Kashmir and Gujarat, which were more influenced by Indian traditions and which culminate in the finely carved sandstone buildings of Ahmadabad; and, lastly, the heavily Persianized styles of the Deccan, which also show borrowings from the arts of Vijayanagar (conquered in the mid-16th century), as can be seen in the palaces and mosques at Golconda, Bijapur and Hyderabad.

Following the conquest by Babur in 1526, imperial power was re-established by the Mughals in northern India, bringing with it influences from Samarkand and Bukhara. Their architecture at first showed a fondness for light pavilions, opening spaciously on to gardens, like the tents of the desert nomads. However, Akbar (1556–1605) anchored the dynasty at Delhi, where Humayun's tomb (1572) borrows its stone mosaics, columns, balconies and cloisters from India. This fusion of styles appears again in the mosque at Ajmer and in the palaces of Agra and Fatehpur Sikri. Under Jahangir (1605–27), Mughal forms, Rajput plans and Indian craftsmanship combined to produce a harmonious unity as in Akbar's tomb at Sikandra (1614). The reign of Shah Jahan (1628–58) saw a brief return to architectural orthodoxy and thus to Safavid forms, although these were as always interpreted by Indian craftsmen: of special note are the tombs of Lahore and above all the Taj Mahal at Agra (1632), which with the several Shalimar gardens at Delhi, Lahore and Kashmir became the best known symbol of Indian architecture, until the archaeological rediscovery of Sanci and Ellura. This triumphant and harmonious union of imperial Mughal and Indian art was short-lived. The religious bigotry of Aurangzeb (1658–1707) provoked tensions which were to undermine Mughal power and to prepare the way for British domination.

This imported international style of architecture had spread across the whole of the Mediterranean, the Middle East and Central Asia in the service of a unique faith and of the ruling powers of those regions. But it must be said that it also drew from the well-springs of Indian culture, and while in the south the Indian tradition increasingly hardened into a formal aridity, in the north, in the service of a new religious fervour, it rediscovered its technical virtuosity in the treatment of stone, its decorative vitality, its serenity and its acceptance of the silence of the tomb.

Central doorway, Humayun's tomb, Delhi

Erected by his widow between 1564 and 1572 and enclosed by an octagonal courtyard, the tomb itself measures 51 metres (165 feet) at the sides while the dome rises to a height of more than 41 metres (135 feet). An imposing arch frames each doorway. The pink sandstone of the façade is enhanced with geometric motifs in white marble. The windows are screened with remarkable trelliswork in stucco and marble. The building is in fact modelled on the Timurid architecture of Samarkand and Bukhara.

Taj Mahal, Agra

This was built between 1632 and 1647 by Shah Jahan to house the remains of his favourite queen, Mumtaz Mahal; he too was later buried here. Set on a raised site, between a mosque and a rest-house for pilgrims, the tomb is clearly visible from every point. Long water-courses constantly draw the eye towards it. It rises from a terrace of pink sandstone 103 metres (112 yards) square with a minaret at each corner. It is designed within a cube, with a base of 61 metres (200 feet) and a height of 62 metres (203 feet). The four axial archways lead into the great central octagon, where the two cenotaphs are enclosed within a perforated marble screen; the actual tombs lie in a vaulted chamber further below. Private apartments lie at an angle within the corners, on two levels, their great arches opening on to both the interior and exterior; they are crowned with arcaded kiosks. The decoration consists of Qur'anic texts and *pietra dura* inlay of flowers, following Safavid models.

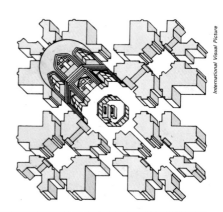

Jami Masjid, Ahmadabad

This mosque was constructed in 1423, in the reign of Ahmed I, founder of the city. Originally the minarets were double their present height, but they were partially destroyed by an earthquake. The beginnings of Islamic art in Gujarat are discernible in the rather ponderous style with its irregular elements, and more particularly in its poorly integrated use of decoration. The mosque forms the west side of a square court with the corners cut off, bordered by cloisters; 260 columns, arranged in squares, support 15 depressed cupolas, the central bay overhanging the side aisles. The façade is a high Persian arch, flanked by smaller arches which correspond to the aisles, in pink sandstone with geometric decorative mouldings. Indian craftsmanship is recognizable behind the Muslim schema. The slightly pyramidal design of the façade, with its columns and the disposition of elements in the minarets, perhaps recalls the general silhouette of the sanctuary tower of the Hindu temple. Although a little heavy in effect, this is the beginning of an important regional style, which subsequently produced some fine buildings, in the capital itself as well as at Sarkhej and Champaner. (From an English watercolour of 1809.)

Gol Gumbaz, Bijapur (Deccan)

Constructed in 1660 as a mausoleum for the Sultan Adil Shah (1627–56) on a plan 64 metres (210 feet) square and beneath a dome 41 metres (135 feet) in diameter, this is one of the largest surface areas ever covered by an architect. The dome is flanked by four towers, each eight storeys and crowned by a cupola, which give access to the roof by spiral staircases. The great cupola overwhelms these: by its size it is the dominant feature of the building – hence its popular name of "Round Dome". It is possible that this building was influenced by contemporary Ottoman Turkish architecture, and that Hagia Sophia at Instanbul may have served as a model. This would explain the predominance of the cupola, and the shrewd disposition of the pendentives which both secure it and support a circular gallery at the junction with the dome. This arrangement was a relatively isolated creation and without any direct heir. The period of British domination was, of course, soon to begin.

Fatehpur Sikri, near Agra

Built on the site of a famous hermitage, the new capital, standing perched on the top of a cliff, was begun in 1569 by Akbar. The exceptional site, together with the determination of the emperor, produced an appropriately imperial architecture. The entrance to the great mosque, the Buland Darwaza (right) clearly earns its name, the "High Gate". It is built in pink sandstone to a height of 44 metres (144 feet) at the top of an impressive flight of steps. The combination of the great Persian arch opening on to a half-cupola, which allows it to descend once more to the level of the true doorways, is remarkable. While the exterior of the Diwan-i-Khas (above), the hall of Private Audience, gives the illusion of a building with an upper storey, the interior encloses a single integral space. A gallery runs around the building at the upper level. Each of the corners is connected diagonally by pathways which meet in the wide capital of a splendid marble column rising from floor level. There the great Mughal sat enthroned. These buildings were arranged according to a symbolic system: Akbar was to spend his whole life in search of a harmonious synthesis of the mystical elements in Islam and Hinduism.

63

Temple of Chandi Lara Jonggrang (Prambanan), Java

Built between 832 and 856. At the heart of three concentric courtyards and surrounded by a constellation of minor shrines, rise three tower-sanctuaries, dedicated to Siva, Vishnu and Brahma. Siva's dominant central tower stands on a plinth and is approached by stairways and entrance pavilions; superb low reliefs adorn the inner face of the balustrade. In its vigour, this monument is certainly the supreme mountain of the gods.

*P*erhaps as early as the 2nd century, but certainly during the 4th and 5th centuries, when the Gupta empire was at the height of its power and its arts were flourishing, Indians settled almost everywhere along the coasts of South-East Asia. They came in search of rare goods, particularly gold and spices, which were highly prized in their homeland and could also be sold at great profit in Alexandria, the bazaar of the Roman empire.

In this way, distinct centres of Indian culture grew up, with all their attendant elements, from Hindu temples and their brahmins to zealous Buddhist missionaries. But the Indian grafting did not take hold everywhere; it only grew on the wide, open, fertile planes, where people were able to form themselves readily into nations. These "colonies" – in the Greek sense of the word – would not have become established, nor have prospered and expanded, if they had not met with friendly indigenous populations that were already firmly settled. Unfortunately, very little is known about these various peoples, except that they had progressed as far as the Bronze and Metal Ages. However, we do know that there was a whole succession of "Indianized" states which appeared during the 4th century and flourished from the 5th century onwards: Sriksetra, in middle Burma, with its Pyu (Burmese) people living around Prome and later Pagan; Pegu, in lower Burma, around Thaton, although its Mon people, who were also found in the kingdom of Dvaravati (in the Menam delta) were centred on Nakhon Pathom; Fou Nan, on the eastern shores of the gulf of Siam, which laid the foundations of the powerful Angkor empire; the Sumatran empire of Srivijaya, which more or less controlled the Malay peninsula and, briefly, western Java as well; the kingdoms of central Java, which began with the powerful Sailendra dynasty; and lastly, the kingdom of Champa, which was also an Indonesian-speaking state, and which flourished from Hué to Saigon, in the area which later became Annam.

All the Indianized countries, which had at first built in wood, were to construct free-standing buildings in brick; and Cambodia and Java were later to build in stone as well. These stone structures were not erected until the end of the 6th century, by which time the Indian art of building had improved considerably, and it is probably because of this that there are none of those slightly clumsy assemblies of huge monolithic slabs which marked the beginnings of architecture in India. The people of Cambodia and Java built from the outset with small blocks; they built quickly and well, and almost from the first attempt produced impressive monuments.

Using brick and stone as the Indians had taught them, these different countries began by reproducing the buildings which had been made before out of wood, and they adhered to these models for a long time. Indian methods of roofing were strange to them, particularly the ribbed barrel vault, and almost everywhere they seem to have preferred a pitched roof supported on a triangular frame with a king-post. Initially they copied the Indian system of overlapping tiles, but in Indo-China, under Sino-Vietnamese influence, they soon adopted flat-grooved tiles and curved-batten tiles (similar to the Roman type). The twofold influence of woodwork on masonry can be seen in 9th century Cambodian architecture: on the one hand there are reminders of the Indian prototypes, with timber framing and ribbed barrel vaulting, and, on the other hand, brick-walled buildings, with tiled roofs on a triangular timber frame – which was later copied in stone. Brickwork was all the more readily adopted because it suited these countries perfectly: there was a plentiful supply of clay and firewood; bricks were simple to make and safe to use; they had excellent resistance to the climate, and were easily decorated. Burma, Siam and Champa were all to persist in using brickwork but between the 6th and 10th centuries Cambodia and Java came to prefer stone – although Java never completely abandoned bricks and returned to them at a later stage. The Burmese used them with exceptional skill, probably copying from nearby Bengal, where brick architecture flourished until the late Middle Ages. They were familiar with all the most effective methods: corbelled arches made with bricks and specially shaped keystones; bonded lintel courses; load-bearing arches which were superimposed or built into the brickwork above; and alternating layers of bricks set square or at an angle, to distribute the load more evenly. Indian formulas were used in the beginning, but these were probably perfected by copying from China, where all such methods had been practised since before the time of Christ. The stone used in Cambodia and Java was either andesite (a volcanic rock) or sandstone; it was cut and ground, then dry-jointed with quoins, a technique learned from the Indians. Starting from the Indian patterns, with roughly the same technical means, the various countries of South-East Asia erected monuments which soon rivalled their models and which finally, in some cases, surpassed them.

Champa, the most remote and least known of the Indianized states, created an architecture that appears poor at first glance. But it is actually both vigorous and powerful. Although there is evidence of

brick-built structures with sandstone facings that date from the end of the 7th century, it is not until the third quarter of the 9th century that we find the first intact Cham tower at Hoa-lai. The central part of the building is a rectangular mass reinforced at the corners by double pilasters, with doorways surmounted by double undulating arches, which are derived from the curved lintels of Indian wooden gateways. The keystone of the ornamental arcade is decorated with a monster's head, spitting out garlands of the same foliage that appears on the pilasters. The brick panels are brought to life by carvings of protective deities and, in the same way, beneath the arcade, demons guard the blind doorways (only the eastern door is a real one). The sanctuary is crowned by three blank storeys, stepped back one above the other, and terminates in a lotus bud.

In 875 King Indravarman II, a devotee of Mahayana Buddhism, erected the great monastery of Dông-düöng. It covers a large area, with successive courtyards and entrance pavilions, a vast building with a wooden roof for the monks, and finally the main tower-sanctuary, which opens out on all sides. The tower contains a feature peculiar to Cham architecture – great stepped altars, built in stone and superbly carved. Under King Indravarman III (c.918–59) Champa reached the summit of its power, and so did its architecture – in the style of Mi-sön A 1. These fine monuments, built within a circle of mountains which are still uninhabited and marvellously serene, were the religious capital of the kingdom for centuries. At tower A 1, from which the style takes its name, the main body of the building is a powerful mass of brick, more than 20 metres (60 feet) high, discreetly offset by the rhythms of the corner pilasters and the carved floral decoration. The projecting section, which runs round all four sides and is blind to the north, south and west, has false side windows and a door beneath a double pediment; it is crowned by a blank storey. The main part of the building is surmounted by three more blank storeys, their sharply diminishing proportions accentuated by scaled-down decorative details at the corners. The whole building has the outline of a pyramid and is almost perfectly preserved: only the facings have been damaged.

This basic type did not evolve much. But the projecting section that housed the entrance gradually became more accentuated and, finally, a small building in its own right; the pilasters and pediments atrophied into simple brick bands; and the corner decorations assumed such importance that they began to encroach on the blank storeys, which were reduced to mere cubes. By the 13th and 14th centuries, the Cham tower-sanctuary had become only a caricature of its original classical design. There were innovations from time to time which varied the basic concept, such as hexagonal towers with roofs in the shape of bishop's mitres, but these were rare. The composition was always simple: there was a tower at the centre of an enclosure and an entrance pavilion preceded by up to three towers on one large plinth; the plinth was decorated with figure sculptures in arched niches.

Like the Javanese, who shared their language, the Cham seem to have developed a cult devoted to their dead monarchs. They built tower-sanctuaries in their honour, and represented each by a statue endowed with the appearance and attributes of a Hindu god. But the Cham were divided, and they were attacked and eventually driven back by the Vietnamese; they never had a chance to build an empire, or to develop their own truly distinctive art.

The earliest monuments in Java, which lie on the plateau of Dieng, are Hindu and date from the middle of the 7th century. They are simple cellas, surmounted by one or two storeys of similar shape but smaller scale, and derive directly from Pallavan models. Between 780 and 820, however, a magnificent group of Buddhist temples was erected in central Java by the powerful Sailendra dynasty. (The finest of these, Borobudur, is described in a later feature.) They follow the lines of the tower-sanctuary, generally standing on a high plinth, which is breached on the eastern side by an elegant stairway. The tower itself is often cruciform in plan, like Chandi Kalassan (in its final state at the beginning of the 9th century). Each wing carries a blank storey crowned by six little stupas; the main body of the tower supports an octagonal drum and another, final stupa. More original are buildings such as Chandi Sari (c.800), which has a rectangular ground plan consisting of a row of three temples facing east; a wooden stairway leads to the storey above, which is the same size as the ground plan; this upper storey is in turn surmounted by three blank storeys, one over each temple and thus perpendicular to the main axis; these have barrel vaults and little stupas. The Mahayana Buddhist cult, which was at that time in favour, inspired the construction of astonishing stone mandalas, symbols of an ordered universe which served as guides and stimuli to the meditations of the Buddha's disciples.

From 830 to the end of the century the Sanjaya dynasty built beautiful Hindu buildings beside the Buddhist creations of

their overlords. The high point of this art was Prambanan, which we shall examine in detail later. But to understand the evolution of this style we must first take a look at earlier examples. The tower-sanctuaries at Dieng and at other early sites bore distinctive decorations on their corners and summits, in the form of cubical blocks crowned by ribbed, bell-shaped bulbs. There was often a balustrade along the edge of the plinth and the entrance steps were treated as a major feature, with decorated rails and, frequently, an overhanging pavilion. The body of the tower was sometimes designed to look as if it were composed of two storeys, by being given two rows of windows even though the main sanctuary inside rose through its whole height. Inside the encircling walls and their pavilions, the tower-sanctuaries, whether single or in groups of three, are practically the only features of these compositions that have survived. There must have been subsidiary buildings in timber, but they have all long since disappeared.

By the time this art had reached its final stage, the tower-sanctuary of central Java had become no more than a sort of withered lantern with a simple, shallow-stepped pyramid on top. The only parts that are still of any interest are the powerful monsters' heads which protect the doors from evil spirits, like those at Singasari (c.1300) and Panataran (c.1370); and the low reliefs which, adorning the walls of the plinth, are always enchanting in their narrative imagination and vitality. Sculpture at least was to retain its formal power for longer.

The earliest buildings in Cambodia are simple sandstone cells, designed to house lingas (phallic emblems); they were constructed on the frontiers of the empire by its founder, Bhavavarman, at the end of the 6th century. At the beginning of the following century, at Sambor Prei Kuk, then the capital of the empire, King Isanavarman I built some imposing brick tower-sanctuaries, of varied and harmonious shapes and set in vast courtyards with surrounding walls and entrance pavilions. They are not very different from the Indian models, but the Khmers' discipline, sense of order and breadth of conception are already evident.

The Khmer tower-sanctuary acquired its definitive form at the beginning of the 9th century, with the establishment of the capital in the Angkor region. The square body of the tower stands on a plain plinth and is open towards the east, with blind doors on the other faces. There is a deity on either side of each door, and the cella is surmounted by a tall stack of corbelling in the shape of a bishop's mitre. The blank

storeys are exact scaled-down replicas of the main storey, each one smaller than the one below, with the result that the levels of the building look as though they have been drawn out of each other, like the tubular sections of an old marine telescope. There are usually three of these blank storeys, and they are crowned by a lotus bud. The temple is protected on the ground by statues of guardians and animals, which reappear sculpted on the antefixes of the blank storeys. The towers are most often grouped in a line of three, with Siva enthroned in the centre, Vishnu to the north and Brahma to the south. The towers and their pavilions have barrel vaults, based on Indian models. In general, however, the Khmers preferred pitched roofs, using this type for certain subsidiary structures; the gables are made into fine triangular pediments, first of brick and then of stone, and the roof itself is covered with enamelled tiles.

By combining these various elements, the Khmers finally arrived at the temple-mountain, which we shall consider later. But they also built temples "on the flat", in some of the provincial cities for example, and these are no less remarkable. The tower-sanctuaries that were built during the 11th century or after are preceded by a ritual chamber, which has three naves, a central axial barrel vault and two flanking half-vaults, all made of sandstone; and there are one or two annexes in the courtyard which repeat the shape of the ritual chamber. The main entrance pavilion, on the east, is generally a tower with blank storeys flanked by two vaulted wings aligned with the axis of the enclosing wall. Rooms and galleries are lit by windows with bars to filter the sunlight; the same windows appear on the drum that rises above the axial nave. The undersides of the vaults are masked by ceilings of carved and gilded wood; and the sandstone blocks, already ground into shape, provided an ideal surface for decorative sculpture – the celestial nymphs, or apsaras, on the walls of Angkor are particularly famous. In the clarity and precision of their plan, the vigour of their profile and the perfection of their decoration, these buildings are all models of harmony.

The kings built huge temples for their ancestors, where hundreds of priests held rites for the redemption of their souls. The central sanctuary was of the type already described and stood in a series of concentrically placed courtyards, each surrounded by a gallery. This formula began with Preah Vihear at the beginning of the 11th century and was developed at Beng Mealea at the start of the 12th. At the end of that century Jayavarman VII built two similar foundations – Preah Khan and Ta

	Burma	Siam	Cambodia	Champa	Indonesia	China	
0							0
100	Indian expansion *Suvannabhumi* PYU		Indian expansion		Indian expansion	HAN	100
200	*Beikhtano*		FOU NAN SRI MARA	LIN YI		THREE KINGDOMS	200
300		DVARAVATI	TCHAN-TAN *Oc-èo*	FAN-YI FAN-WEN	*Tambralinga* *Lankasuka*		300
400	*Sriksetra* Thaton	*Nakhon Sri Thammarat*	KAUNDINYA JAYAVARMAN	BHADRAVARMAN	*P'an P'an*	SIX DYNASTIES	400
500	Halin Hmawza	Chaiya *Sri Tep*	*Phnom Da* TCHEN LA BHAVAVARMAN	*Mi-sön*			500
600		Khmer attacks Phum Pon	*North Sambor* ISANAVARMAN I *South Sambor*	RUDRAVARMAN SAMBHUVARMAN PRAKASADHARMA *Mi-sön E 1*	WALAING *Dieng*	SOUEI T'ANG Protectorate of Annam	600
700	Prome	*Phong Tük* *Phnom Pathom* U Thong	*Phnom Bayang* *Prei Kmeng* *Kompong Preah*	CHAMPA SATYAVARMAN	SRIVIJAYA *Palembang* SANJAYA		700
	NAN TCHAO KO-LO-FONG	Chaiya Ligor			SAILENDRA *Chandi Lumbung*		
			Javan incursions				
800	PAGAN	Ku Bua	ANGKOR JAYAVARMAN II *Trapeang Phong*	INDRAPURA *Hoa-lai* INDRAVARMAN II *Dông-düöng*	Chandi Sewu, Chandi Sari *Borobudur* *Mendut, Pawon* MATARAM *Prambanan*		800
	PEGU HAMSAVATI	Takuapa *Candi Batu Pahat* Wieng Sa	INDRAVARMAN Bakong				
900			YASOVARMAN *Bakhêng* *Koh Ker*	*Khuong-my*	BALITUNG	FIVE DYNASTIES	900
1000	*Zeitleik* *Bupaya* *Thagyapaya* ANORATHA *Shwezigon* KYANZITTHA	Khmer conquest *Muang Tham* *Panom Van* *Preah Vihear* *Primay* *Lopburi*	RAJENDRAVARM *Prè Rup, Banteay Srei* *Ta Kèo* SURYAVARMAN I *Vat Ek, Vat Banon* *Baphuon* SURYAVARMAN II	INDRAVARMAN III *Mi-sön A 1* Vietnamese attacks VIJAYA *Po-nagar* *Chanh-lo*	SINDOK *Djalatunda* Cola raids AIRLANGA *Belahan* *Tampaksiring* KADIRI	NORTHERN SONG	1000
1100							1100
	Ananda *Schwegugyi* *Thatbyinyu*	*Panom Van* *Sri Kharaphum*	*Angkor Wat* *Beng Mealea* *Preah Pithu*	Khmer conquest *Binh-dinh*		SOUTHERN SONG	
	Dhammayangyi		Capture of Angkor by the Chams				
	Gawdawpalin		JAYAVARMAN VII	JAYA INDRAVARMAN IV			
1200	*Sulamani* *Htilominlo*	*Lopburi* *Muong Sing*	Ta Prohm, Preah Khan, Bayon	Khmer conquest	*Chandi Sawentar* ANGROK		1200
	Mingalazedi MONGOLS SAGAING	Liberation CHEFFERIES THAI RAMA KAMHENG Sukhothai Sri Sajanalai	Terraces	*Hung-thanh* Mongol incursions *Thap-man* Po Klaung Garai	*Bahal* *Chandi Kidal* *Chandi Blitar, Chandi Jago* *Singasari* MOJOPAHIT *Chandi Djâbung*	AN NAM GENGHIS KHAN YUAN MING	1300
1300	TAGAUNG						
	TAUNGU AVA	SIAM Ayuthya	Thai attacks Angkor abandoned	Vietnamese attacks	Islam *Panataran*		
1400	HAMSAVATI *Shwedagon*	LAN NA	CAMBODIA *Lovék* ANG CHAN	Vietnamese conquest	*Chandi Tigawangi*	Islam in Java	1400
1500					PORTUGUESE at Malacca		1500

PYU: *dynasties and sovereigns*; Halin: *Buddhist sites*; *Phong Tük*: *Hindu sites*

Prohm, great temples that lie lost in the jungle, casting their spells over the pilgrims who wander in their labyrinths.

Burma never deviated from Buddhism, nor from using brick architecture in its service. The earliest remains are the monasteries of Beikhtano (2nd century), which are evidence of Indian influence on the Pyu (the first Burmese) and of their conversion to Buddhism. Then, at Sriksetra during the 6th and 7th centuries, the earliest cylindrical stupas appeared, such as the Bawbawgyi and the Payagyi, and also the earliest temples – simple brick cubes surmounted by stupas, as at Bebe (5th–6th centuries). The Mon of lower Burma and the delta of Siam were converted to Buddhism at the same time and expressed their faith in similar fashion, but they soon developed a remarkable art of their own, in the form of decorative stucco relief.

A truly Burmese architecture emerged for the first time at Pagan, which became the capital when the country was unified by Anawratha (1044–77). The stupa is at first cylindrical, then hemispherical or bell-shaped, and crowned by parasol-like forms of gilt metal. It is raised on a number of plinths of regularly decreasing size, which are generally square but can also be polygonal. Axial stairways give access to the different levels. Reliefs of enamelled terracotta are frequently set into the retaining walls. Later structures are further enriched by the incorporation into the base of caryatid elephants and by the addition of an enclosure wall with entrance pavilions. The great stupas of Pagan – from the most famous, the Shwezigon (11th century), to the most developed, the Dhammayanzika (1196) – are the most beautiful in South-East Asia. They were the models for the stupas of the Thai states, and the famous Shwedagon of Rangoon (15th century), with its gold-leaf revetment, has kept their glory and opulence alive to this day. The kings and high dignitaries of Pagan added continuously to the number of monasteries, which had many buildings, mostly in wood. The monks gathered in a central brick structure, which was inspired by Hindu temples. About a third of the way between this building and the edge of the monastery, rather than at the edge itself, the statue of Buddha was enthroned beneath a brick canopy. An ambulatory encircled it to the west, and in front of it there was a huge hall for the monks, lit by narrow windows and entered through a porch. This hall was roofed by corbelled vaults, but on the outside it appeared as a pitched roof. Above the Buddha, on top of the canopy, there was either a tower-sanctuary with several blank storeys, often terminated by a little stupa, or else simply a stupa on a pyramidal plinth. The architects of Pagan gave access to the upper levels by fitting staircases into the considerable thickness of the walls. As a result the first floor, in the base of the tower, became a sanctuary. The white chalk facings of these harmonious compositions were decorated with shallow carvings, which glittered brilliantly in the sunlight.

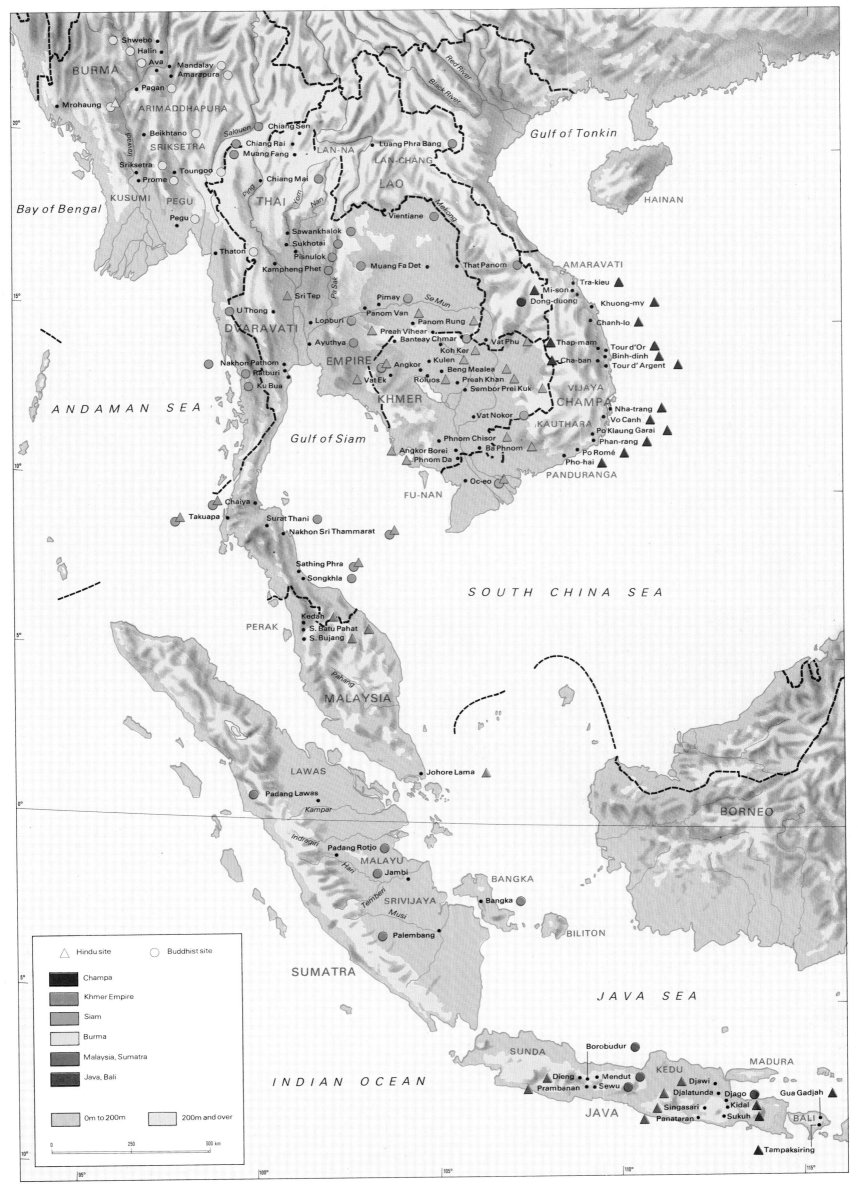

BURMA
Shwebo
Halin
Ava
Mandalay
Amarapura
Pagan
Mrohaung
ARIMADDHAPURA
Beikhtano
SRIKSETRA
Sriksetra
Prome
Toungoo
KUSUMI
PEGU
Pegu
Thaton

Bay of Bengal

Chiang Sen
Chiang Rai
Muang Fang
LAN-NA
Chiang Mai
THAI
Luang Phra Bang
LAN-CHANG
LAO

Gulf of Tonkin

HAINAN

Red River
Black River

Vientiane
Sawankhalok
Sukhotai
Pisnulok
Kampheng Phet
Sri Tep
U Thong
DVARAVATI
Lopburi
Ayuthya
Muang Fa Det
Pimay
Panom Van
Panom Rung
Preah Vihear
Banteay Chmar
EMPIRE
Koh Ker
Angkor
Kulen
Vat Ek
Roluos
Beng Mealea
Preah Khan
KHMER
Sembor Prei Kuk
Vat Nokor
That Panom
AMARAVATI
Mi-son
Dong-duong
Vat Phu
Thap-mam
Cha-ban
Tra-kieu
Khuong-my
Chanh-lo
Tour d'Or
Binh-dinh
Tour d'Argent
VIJAYA
CHAMPA
KAUTHARA
Nha-trang
Vo Canh
Po Klaung Garai
Phan-rang
Po Romé
Pho-hai
PANDURANGA

ANDAMAN SEA

Nakhon Pathom
Ratburi
Ku Bua

Gulf of Siam

Phnom Chisor
Angkor Borei
Phnom Da
Ba Phnom
Oc-eo
FU-NAN

Chaiya
Takuapa
Surat Thani
Nakhon Sri Thammarat
Sathing Phra
Songkhla

SOUTH CHINA SEA

PERAK
Kedah
S. Batu Pahat
S. Bujang

Pahang
MALAYSIA

Johore Lama

BORNEO

LAWAS
Padang Lawas
Kampar

Indragiri
Padang Rotjo
MALAYU
Hari
Jambi

BANGKA

Temberi
SRIVIJAYA
Musi
Bangka
BILITON

Palembang

SUMATRA

JAVA SEA

INDIAN OCEAN

Borobudur
SUNDA
Dieng
Prambanan
Mendut
Sewu
KEDU
Djawi
Djalatunda
Singasari
Panataran
Djago
Kidal
Sukuh
MADURA
Gua Gadjah
BALI

JAVA

Tampaksiring

Hindu site
Buddhist site

Champa
Khmer Empire
Siam
Burma
Malaysia, Sumatra
Java, Bali

0m to 200m
200m and over

0   250   500 km

The mountain of the gods

In India, as we have seen, the tower-sanctuary is a physical expression of the cosmos, represented as superimposed worlds with the master, Siva, occupying the cella. All the South-East Asian nations which converted to Hinduism adopted this architectural formula, but they gave it a scale that was never to be attained in its country of origin.

The most noble expression of the concept of the mountain of the gods is Prambanan (or Chandi Lara Jonggrang) in Java, built between 832 and 856 and therefore suggesting a desire to affirm the concept immediately after the ending of the Buddhist period. The temple consists of three concentric courtyards, each one raised to form a podium; there are 200 secondary shrines within them, and at the centre three tower-sanctuaries stand in a line, with three smaller towers in front of them, guarding the shrines of the great trinity – Vishnu, Siva and Brahma. The central tower of Siva, which has recently been restored, rises to a height of 40 metres (130 feet). The balustrade on the high plinth is decorated on its inner face with reliefs which illustrate the Javanese version of the Ramayana. Three small pavilions shelter the tops of the axial stairways. The main body of the building has two levels of windows, giving the impression of two storeys. It is cruciform in plan and contains the image of Siva. Three other, independent cellas open directly on to the plinth. Their blank storeys repeat the design of the main body and they are crowned by the traditional ribbed and bell-shaped ornament. Vitality but equilibrium, power but harmony – it would be impossible to wish for a more precise architectural expression of a concept. The plasticity, the fire and the refinement of the reliefs make Prambanan the counterpart to the Kailasa at Ellura.

It was at Angkor that the Khmers were to build real mountains for their gods. The first endeavour was that of Bakong, built by King Indravarman (881). Here, a tower-sanctuary (replaced in the 12th century by the present building) stood on three terraces of cut sandstone, regularly decreasing in size. The walls and concentric moats that surround the whole composition were an essential means of irrigation for the city as well as a fine setting for the temple-mountain, which here reached its apogee in all senses of the term.

Around 900, in the Bakheng, Yasovarman improved the formula and gave it additional scale by building on a hill. Five terraces carried five tower-sanctuaries, which were arranged in a quincunx on the summit; on the lower terraces and at the foot of the monument stood 103 little tower-sanctuaries, corresponding to the great cycle of Jupiter, the basis of Indian astronomical computation. As the believer stood facing this mountain of stone, he could see 33 temples at a glance, building up in a perfect pyramid to the central tower and the throne of Siva, the lord of the 32 other gods who lived in the subsidiary temples. Around 961, the temple of Prè Rup, which was similar in conception, was enhanced on its first level by the addition of elongated structures with wooden roofs. This development was taken further around the year 1000 at Ta Keo, where the second terrace was given a continuous gallery with sandstone walls, brick vaulting and axial pavilions at the top of the stairways. The formula was developed to the full at Baphuon (c.1060–66). Although this has only one tower-sanctuary at the summit, it has galleries vaulted in sandstone around its three main storeys, which have towers at each corner and in the centre of each side,

decorated with charming panels of narrative relief sculpture; there is also a fine sandstone causeway, punctuated by pavilions, leading to the eastern stairway.

The culmination of the temple-mountain is Angkor Wat, which was built by the greatest of the Khmer monarchs, Suryavarman II (1113–c.1150). The temple, dedicated to Vishnu, stands facing west in the centre of a vast enclosure, measuring 1,000 by 800 metres (1,100 by 900 yards). Beyond the surrounding wall is a moat 200 metres (220 yards) wide. A causeway, bordered by a balustrade representing the body of the mythical serpent, leads over the moat to a noble entrance portico, and from here an interior causeway crosses the enclosure to the platform where the temple rises. This mass of stone, which seems equal in size to the pyramid of Chephren, rises in three terraces, each with vaulted galleries, corner tower-sanctuaries and axial pavilions over the stairways. The principal approach – from the west – is distinguished by colonnaded galleries linking the first and second levels. On the third level, the central tower-sanctuary is linked to all four stairways by vaulted arcades; like the galleries on the first level, these allow light to flood through and illuminate the sumptuous low reliefs on the inner walls, which narrate the lives of the gods and the king. The stonework is enriched throughout by refined drapery-like decoration and by female deities who people the upper reaches in their thousands. Nowhere was the mountain of the gods given more perfect form or decoration. There can be no doubt that this is the finest architectural achievement in the whole of Indianized Asia.

Temple of Angkor Wat, 1113 – c.1150

Only an aerial view can show the simplicity and power of the plan. Describing a rectangle of 187 by 215 metres (600 by 700 feet) the temple rises in three steps. Each one is punctuated by corner towers and stairways rising to axial pavilions, with encircling galleries linking them. On the west, the principal approach between the first and second levels is indicated by covered porticoes; on the third level, the central tower is linked to the four axial pavilions in the same way. The plan is simple, even repetitive, but the sureness of proportions makes this colossal structure the high point of Asian architecture.

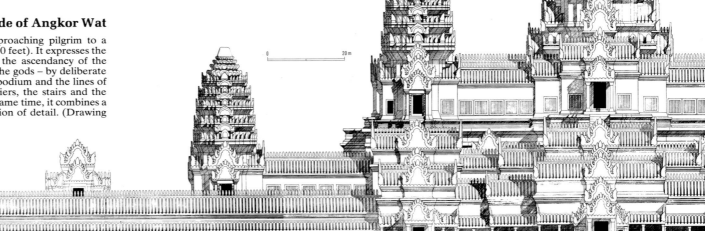

West façade of Angkor Wat

The temple soars above the approaching pilgrim to a height of more than 65 metres (210 feet). It expresses the three superimposed worlds, and the ascendancy of the central mountain – the home of the gods – by deliberate contrasts: the horizontals of the podium and the lines of the vaults; the verticals of the piers, the stairs and the towers. Powerful and light at the same time, it combines a majesty of volume with a perfection of detail. (Drawing after Guy Nafilyan.)

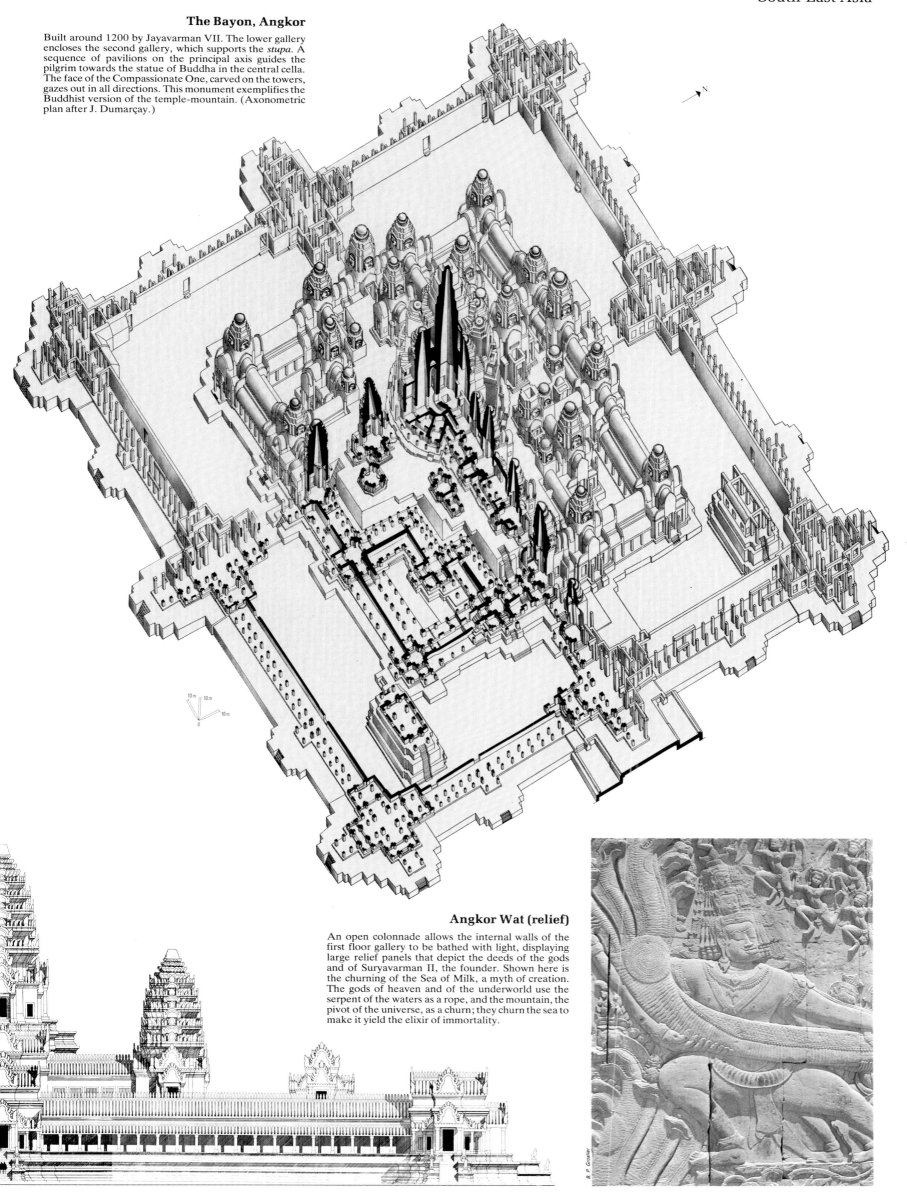

The Bayon, Angkor

Built around 1200 by Jayavarman VII. The lower gallery encloses the second gallery, which supports the *stupa*. A sequence of pavilions on the principal axis guides the pilgrim towards the statue of Buddha in the central cella. The face of the Compassionate One, carved on the towers, gazes out in all directions. This monument exemplifies the Buddhist version of the temple-mountain. (Axonometric plan after J. Dumarçay.)

Angkor Wat (relief)

An open colonnade allows the internal walls of the first floor gallery to be bathed with light, displaying large relief panels that depict the deeds of the gods and of Suryavarman II, the founder. Shown here is the churning of the Sea of Milk, a myth of creation. The gods of heaven and of the underworld use the serpent of the waters as a rope, and the mountain, the pivot of the universe, as a churn; they churn the sea to make it yield the elixir of immortality.

Labyrinths of meditation

In the same way as they began with the lessons of the Indians and went on to build the Hindu mountain of the gods, it was again the peoples of South-East Asia who were to build the most extraordinary of the Buddhist monuments. The earliest of them, Borobudur in central Java, was inspired by the Sailendra dynasty, devotees of Mahayana Buddhism. It stands on a hilltop in a magnificent amphitheatre of volcanoes, but is only the centrepiece of a huge group – at least two other monuments, Pawon and Mendut, mark its east–west axis over a distance of several kilometres. The temple was altered in the course of construction, and remodelled thereafter: most of what we admire today must have been built between 792 and 824. The plan of the base is an indented square with sides measuring 100 metres (300 feet). It is a powerful podium carrying four successive terraces, linked by axial staircases. From the second to the fifth level, the outer parapets and the walls supporting the level above are decorated with reliefs describing the previous existences of Buddha, then the story of his life and, finally, the quest of a believer consulting the Buddhas of the future. Above these square terraces are three circular storeys, which bear perforated *stupas* containing Buddhas; a final *stupa* crowns the summit. A total of 504 Buddhas can be counted on the circular storeys and in the niches over the balustrades. The significance of Borobudur has never been entirely clear. It could be said that it is a gigantic instrument of meditation, which guides the disciple towards liberation through sacred history and the symbols of the cosmos and the soul. At first the pilgrim is virtually imprisoned in a labyrinth of images, where all that he can see of the sky is above him, but then he comes out on to the circular terraces, which stand open to the sky, silently poised at the centre of a circle of volcanoes.

When a country has been as constantly Buddhist as Burma, it can be no surprise to find that it contains one of the most beautiful architectural expressions of that faith: the Ananda at Pagan. Built around 1091 by King Kyanzittha (1084–1113), it is said to have been inspired by some of the hermitages that lie in the heart of the Himalayas. But no less evident is the genius of the architect who here broke completely with the somewhat banal traditions of the Pagan temples. At the heart of the Ananda is an enormous brick cube with four gigantic statues of the Teacher on its faces; around it, in the square body of the building, run two concentric corridors, lit by two levels of windows. Four large vestibules, each with three naves, transform this square into a Greek cross with a span of 65 metres (210 feet). The roofs are vaulted, although their outer shell is pitched. The four terraces above the main body of the building carry a tower-sanctuary with numerous blank storeys and a slender spire in the form of a *stupa*. The only decorations on the exterior are reliefs in enamelled terracotta narrating the previous incarnations of the Buddha; the same story is told by the restrained sandstone slabs which are set into the walls of the corridors.

The Ananda was the starting point for a whole series of temples which were no less colossal. The Thatbyinnyu (mid 12th century) is on two levels, with a huge seated Buddha on the first level. This was followed by the Dhammayangyi (mid 12th century), the Sulamani (1183) and, finally, the Htilominlo (1211). In all these temples, long corridors and dark staircases lead the pilgrim to the calm image of the Teacher, at the end of the labyrinth of desires and illusions.

The last of the great kings of Angkor, Jayavarman VII (1181–c.1219), who became a convert to Buddhism, was the builder of the Bayon (see page 69). This temple marked the centre of a big city, the axial gates of which reproduced the general silhouette of the monument. In its first state the temple was planned on a Greek cross, but sections of gallery were subsequently built between the arms, transforming it into a rectangle surrounded by an external gallery. The first two terraces carry peripheral galleries, punctuated by towers and pavilions at the centre and corners. The galleries on the first level are decorated with low reliefs depicting the life of the king (Hindu scenes were added on the second level later). The circular mass in the middle has eight chapels radiating from its central cella, like the petals of a lotus in flower. Above rises a powerful tower-*stupa* on three levels. The towers on the terraces and in the centre, numbering 49 in all, display an enormous face on each side, surmounted by classic blank storeys. As a result, animated by the changing light of day, almost 200 faces appear to be turning in the sky. It is a colossal representation of the great miracle of Sravasti, in which the Buddha confounded the Brahmins by multiplying himself and whirling and flickering across all the horizons, like a thousand suns.

B. P. Groslier

Ananda, Pagan

This highly original Burmese creation is the work of Kyanzittha (*c.*1091). At the heart of its labyrinth of corridors, the powerful cubical body of the building houses four colossal images of Buddha. Four wings extend the cube into a Greek cross. Above rise the superimposed worlds, then the peak of the mountain which is their pivot and, finally, the crowning *stupa* which rides serene, like the supreme lesson of the Teacher, above all transitory realities. The austere force of this mass contrasts with the luminous paths that pass through it: it is one of the greatest achievements of Buddhist architecture.

Borobudur, Java

Built principally between the years 792 and 824 by the Sailendra kings, this is the most astonishing manifestation of esoteric architecture in Asia. Hundreds of Buddhas, meditating in their niches, line the first five levels of terracing, like ramparts. Only the course of the axial stairways indicates a way through. The path leads along each level, sheltered from view behind reliefs depicting the various stages of spiritual attainment. Above lie rings of little *stupas* with diamond-shaped perforations and, finally, the austere culminating *stupa*, enclosing the silence of deliverance. (Drawing after J. Dumarçay.)

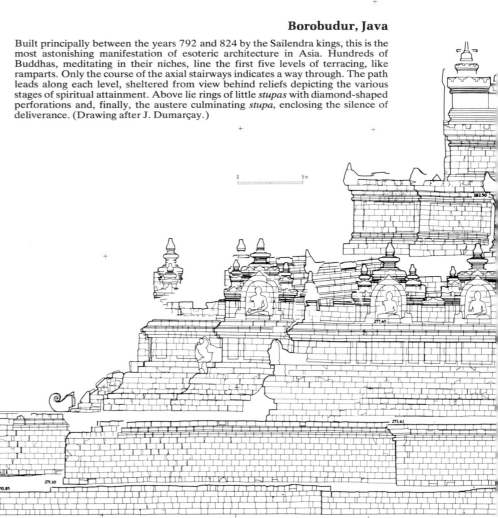

Sulamani, Pagan

(far left)

A building constructed by King Narapatisithu in 1183. A first storey ringed by corridors and surmounted by terraces carries the sanctuary with its colossal image of Buddha. A second series of terraces supports the final tower. The austere masses of brickwork are enlivened by warmly coloured enamelling. The design is derived from the Ananda but does not have its vigour.

Dhammayanzika, Pagan

(near left)

Another building by Narapatisithu, dated 1196. A pentagonal enclosure with five doors surrounds a podium with a small temple attached to each face. Three terraces rise above this, adorned with enamelled plaques narrating the previous lives of Buddha. A bell-shaped *stupa* crowns the ensemble.

Fachi Oasis (Niger)

The surrounding clay wall protects the family granaries, which are also built of clay. This image typifies both the nature of building and the collective organization of space in Africa.

I n Europe, the word "architecture", which has been defined as "the art of constructing buildings", suggests royal palaces, stately homes or religious buildings rather than modest houses. Thus it has assumed a social and cultural significance that is inappropriate to Africa. In Africa, the "art of building" is generally no more than the organization of living space, and only very occasionally amounts to the construction of monumental forms destined to last. For cultures which attach much less importance to display and appearance than to the survival of the soul, and which put collective needs above individual concerns, the construction of buildings has different aims and objectives from those of the West.

Christian Europe and the Muslim world, both heirs in their own way to Mediterranean antiquity, have both given priority to urban space, symbol of progress and liberation. This centuries-old Mediterranean way of thinking was summed up in the 14th century by Ibn Khaldun when he identified the city with civilization: by contrast, he said, the people from intertropical Africa and those from the northern regions of the world "... are equally far removed from any harmony or unity in their ways of life. Their dwellings are made of clay and reeds ... Most of the Sudanese, living between the tropics, apparently inhabit caves or live in the bush ... They are savages without any civilization." (Ibn Khaldun, "Muqaddima", in Recueil des sources arabes concernant l'Afrique occidentale du VIIIᵉ au XVIᵉ siècle, Paris, 1975.) The realm of wealth and culture, the town is also the stage for monumental forms – the stone forms of grand patrician houses, designed to accentuate social differences, or forms raised for the glorification of the one God, buildings for prayer required to resist the test of time.

The industrial civilizations have abandoned cathedrals, but have retained a taste for urban and symbolic monumentality. Industrial, communal and official buildings sometimes now occupy the central locations once given to religious edifices – although the mosque has retained more forcefully its central significance in Muslim towns. Generally, however, urban land has become the property of individuals or of companies; everywhere it attracts speculation and rapid development, and yields vast profits. Such commercial ramifications were foreign to the ancient African cultures, in so far as these are known to us today. To understand their context, one has first of all to look beneath the urban incrustations formed under European influence and often, too,

beneath earlier remodellings occasioned by Islam. Archaeology alone can provide an insight into the essential outlook of the African peoples.

In architecture, as in so many other spheres, Africans have left us no observed, explicit or written information; their perceptions were always implicitly transmitted from generation to generation, through the organization of their space or the construction of their buildings. It is only by painstaking decoding of archaeological remains (the historical method) or by anthropological interpretation of present ways of life that we can understand the true role of architecture in African culture. Archaeological research in the black world has only just started; it is only in recent years that the study of cultural anthropology has taken over from ethnological studies, which were often based on inverse comparisons with Europeans. These diverse findings probably explain why today there is no general view of African architecture and why published works on this subject are only at the stage of analysis.

The Mediterranean type of urban settlement has no counterpart in Africa. Hence, in the past there was a tendency to come to the hasty conclusion that the African peoples were incapable of

organizing their social space. Because of the absence of any towns, it was hastily concluded that the Africans had been ignorant of any "urban" system. Today, archaeology directs us towards other conclusions.

From the third millennium BC traces appear of organized groups of people living on the cliffs overlooking an important residual lake in eastern Mauritania. These people were not farmers, but subsisted from hunting, fishing and gathering. Vast stone enclosures of different shapes constituted living quarters whose exact nature is still a mystery to us. Between these enclosures, open spaces allowed free passage. From a bird's-eye view, the whole area seems to consist of adjacent spots of habitation spread without any geometric precision over an area of more than 100 kilometres (60 miles). What should one call an agglomeration like this in which thousands of people lived side by side? The excavations of Tegdaoust have shown that in the 10th century, before the arrival of Muslim towns – with their streets, squares and mosques – there existed a series of enclosures of stone or sun-dried bricks, delimiting areas fairly comparable with those of eastern Mauritania. Research carried out in Ghana has revealed the antiquity of such phenomena; the cluster in Begho dates from the 11th century.

Mofou massif, Gouele (Cameroon). The grouping of the houses respects social and family hierarchies; it delimits the small area suitable for cultivation, on the flatter areas of the steep, rocky slope.

BLACK AFRICA

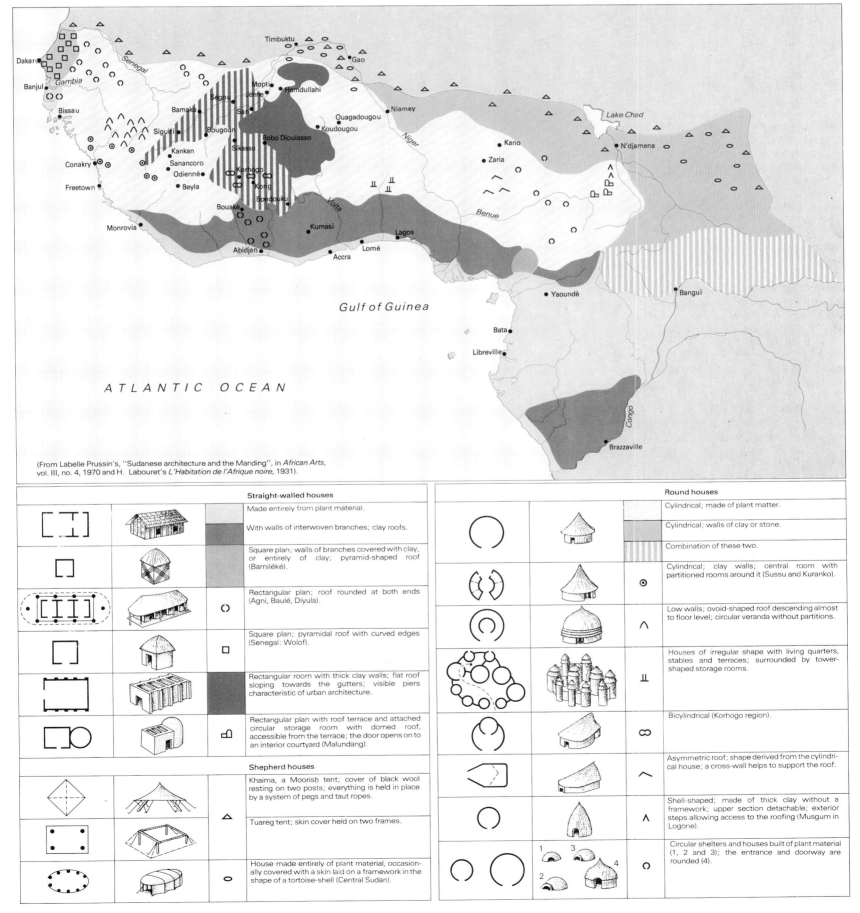

(From Labelle Prussin's, "Sudanese architecture and the Manding", in *African Arts*, vol. III, no. 4, 1970 and H. Labouret's *L'Habitation de l'Afrique noire*, 1931).

Straight-walled houses

			Made entirely from plant material.
			With walls of interwoven branches; clay roofs.
			Square plan; walls of branches covered with clay, or entirely of clay; pyramid-shaped roof (Bamiléké).
		◌	Rectangular plan; roof rounded at both ends (Agni, Baulé, Diyula).
		▫	Square plan; pyramidal roof with curved edges (Senegal: Wolof).
			Rectangular room with thick clay walls; flat roof sloping towards the gutters; visible piers characteristic of urban architecture.
			Rectangular plan with roof terrace and attached circular storage room with domed roof, accessible from the terrace; the door opens on to an interior courtyard (Malundang).

Shepherd houses

		△	Khaima, a Moorish tent; cover of black wool resting on two posts; everything is held in place by a system of pegs and taut ropes.
			Tuareg tent; skin cover held on two frames.
		○	House made entirely of plant material, occasionally covered with a skin laid on a framework in the shape of a tortoise-shell (Central Sudan).

Round houses

			Cylindrical; made of plant matter.
			Cylindrical; walls of clay or stone.
			Combination of these two.
		⊙	Cylindrical; clay walls; central room with partitioned rooms around it (Sussu and Kuranko).
		∧	Low walls; ovoid-shaped roof descending almost to floor level; circular veranda without partitions.
		⫪	Houses of irregular shape with living quarters, stables and terraces; surrounded by tower-shaped storage rooms.
		∞	Bicylindrical (Korhogo region).
		⌒	Asymmetric roof; shape derived from the cylindrical house; a cross-wall helps to support the roof.
		∧	Shell-shaped; made of thick clay without a framework; upper section detachable; exterior steps allowing access to the roofing (Musgum in Logone).
		◌	Circular shelters and houses built of plant material (1, 2 and 3); the entrance and doorway are rounded (4).

Tegdaoust (Mauritania). Archaeological exploration has uncovered the remains of the ancient town of Audaghost. A pair of houses built of sandstone can be seen in the foreground; in the background are other houses with vast courtyards and wells. Two roads have been excavated.

Work that has been undertaken in the ancient towns of Ifé and Benin in Nigeria shows that the organization of open spaces in vast enclosing walls seems to have followed a set pattern, at least in West Africa, both in the method used and in the "systematic" irregularity of the wall lines. It seems as though a deliberate decision was taken not to build in straight lines and angles. Other research on the more recent Yoruba towns serves only to confirm this theory. Everything points to the conclusion that external influences had no effect on the African organization of dense living areas, which were determined both by family relationships and by function. It also seems clear that this "social occupation" of space is not really comparable with any other

Doll's house, Oualata (Mauritania). This "toy" shows the layout of the rooms in relation to the road and the central courtyard. The colours imitate those used by the Mauritanians to paint their walls.

system, because it derives from a unique cultural background. It would be interesting to know if the developments at Kilwa that preceded "Islamic" organization bore any relation to this system; unfortunately there is still nothing in the published accounts of excavations that can help to answer this question.

It is at least apparent in the case of Kilwa, as in so many other places, that the reshaping of urban space was carried out in a cultural climate different from that of the preceding black culture. It follows that Muslim towns such as Audaghost (dating from the 10th century at the latest, and probably built on top of a non-Muslim settlement of an earlier date and of a completely different style), Gao (from the 11th century), Koumbi Saleh (where the oldest parts of the large mosque appear to date back to the 11th century), and Kilwa

(probably dating from the 12th century) cannot be cited as faithful examples of the ancient African concept of organized space.

L. Prussin, in an excellent study of Jenne, posed these very questions about the layout of the town – the relationship of the years before to the years after the introduction of Muslim architectural influence; recent findings in the Jenne region all confirm the existence of differences (McIntosh, S. Keach and J. Roderick, "Prehistoric Investigations at Jenne, Mali", in Cambridge Monographs in African Archaeology, no. 2, 1980). Even if it is still difficult to put forward an overall hypothesis with any degree of confidence, at least it seems that an indigenous African style of organized agglomeration did once exist. Family or ethnic "nuclei" were juxtaposed as much as the environment would permit; between the nuclei were "natural" spaces, often used for religious purposes. In these agglomerations, the temptation to build upwards scarcely existed: apart from the fact that this kind of construction required technical effort which was not worthwhile – although it could be done – there was plenty of land and, in principle, no private property marked off surface space as unavailable. Should it happen that the balance with nature was threatened, a section of the group emigrated to build a new nucleus elsewhere.

Arab sources insist on the polynuclear character of African "towns" – at least in Ghana and Mali. But whether this means lack of organization is another question. One could say that the character of all pre-Islamic or pre-Christian African agglomerations is necessarily polynuclear: family and ethnic groups organized themselves without wasting space and expanded as much as they felt was necessary; essentially there were very few public monuments which could compare with the church or with the mosque and which therefore constituted a central urban attraction; sometimes a sacred grove would play this role, standing as a symbol of cultural unity. But the polynuclear principle was also well suited to the coexistence of "ghettoes" of different traditions and religions; for example, it would have been perfectly feasible for one of these nuclei to be handed over to the Muslims even if the majority of the population and the ruling power remained faithful to African religion. Again, the polynuclear principle did not prevent the area reserved for the leader from being a

privileged one: this could be placed right in the heart of the grouping of nuclei and could be indicated by differences of decoration or disposition. The "palace" of the ruler in many cases represented the organization not only of the agglomeration but also of whole territory. Symbolic area planning also exists among recent African cultures. Quite remarkable developments have been reported on in the following two works: C. Tardits, Le Royaume Bamoum, Paris, 1980, and E. Mworoha, Peuples et rois de l'Afrique des lacs, Dakar-Abidjan, 1977.

This striking use of polynuclearity seems to constitute an essential characteristic of African organization of space. But it also makes it difficult to perceive the transition from "village" to "town". Because of the present absence of material, it is also hard to assess the relationship between polynuclearity and the division of labour inside the agglomeration, between different agglomerations, and between "town" and "country".

Assuming that such a concept existed, the practice of polynuclear social space was subsequently challenged by the external influences that affected black Africa. Sometimes this happened dramatically, when total remodelling took place, due to Islamic or European colonial influences; sometimes it came about by the more subtle means of exchange, infiltration and gradual acceptance. Wherever Islam took root, the remodelling was spectacular. This is clear at Audaghost and on the eastern coast of Africa. Apparently, in Audaghost the changes took place in a few years; they affected spatial organization without fundamentally altering the size of the town.

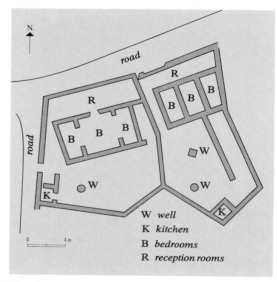

W well
K kitchen
B bedrooms
R reception rooms

Tegdaoust. Plan of the two houses seen in the photograph above and of the access roads (10th–11th century). The living area is generally smaller than the courtyard, which plays an important role in everyday life.

This is particularly clear from the study of ceramics from the 10th century onward. The disposition of the new dwelling places, built in stone from this time on, bore no relation to the structures of the old enclosures, while the introduction of streets, squares, markets and, most importantly, the construction of at least one mosque shows us that we are dealing with a completely different type of town.

In the same way, before the development of the famous "Sudanese" style of mosque, other, perhaps less spectacular, architectural influences were at work. Their effects are apparent, for instance, in the first Muslim prayer houses erected in the southern part of the Sahara. Study of these

Political or cultural group	Area Nature of remains	Date	Sources of information		
			written reports	archaeology	remains
Neolithic agglomerations	MAURITANIA Stone enclosures at Tichitt and Akrejit.	2nd millennium		•	•
NAPATA MEROE	SUDAN Pyramids. Palaces of stone and dried brick.	1st millennium–4th century AD	•	•	•
YEHA	ETHIOPIA Stone temple.	5th–8th centuries		•	•
NUBIA	SUDAN Churches and towns (Faras).	4th–12th centuries		•	
AXUM	ETHIOPIA Palaces. Monumental tombs. Obelisks.	1st–10th centuries	•	•	•
AUDAGHOST	MAURITANIA Pre-Islamic constructions in dried brick. Muslim towns of stone cut more than 6 metres (20 feet) thick.	8th–14th centuries	•	•	•
GHANA	MAURITANIAN MALI Impressive remains buried more than 7 metres (23 feet) deep. Schist constructions at Koumbi Saleh.	8th–17th centuries	•	•	•
MALI	GUINEAN MALI Excavations at Niani (Guinea). Remains of superimposed constructions becoming more elaborate from 13th–14th centuries.	6th–16th centuries	•	•	•
SONGHAY	MALI Remains of mosque, large necropolis at Gao.	11th–16th centuries		•	
NIGER VALLEY	MALI Dried-brick houses, often restored, at Jenne. Comparable houses at Segou, Mopti.	15th–20th centuries			•
HAUSA	NIGERIA Towns to be excavated by archaeologists in the north of the country.	11th–20th centuries			•
LALIBELA	ETHIOPIA Underground churches dug into the rock.	since the 13th century?		•	•
KILWA	KENYA Muslim city-state. Stone buildings and large mosque on ancient African substrata.	11th–16th centuries		•	•
GEDI	KENYA Ruins of houses and stone tombs.	14th–16th centuries	•		•
ZIMBABWE	ZIMBABWE (formerly Rhodesia) Important stone ruins.	11th–16th centuries		•	•
MBANZA KONGO (São Salvador)	ANGOLA Capital of the kingdom of Kongo.	16th century	•		

Naturally this chart is far from complete. It takes into account most of the recent research work carried out, but there is a large number of architectural remains, some ancient, still to be discovered or excavated.

Agglomerations of constructed remains

The map below shows sites that are of significance in the history of Africa.

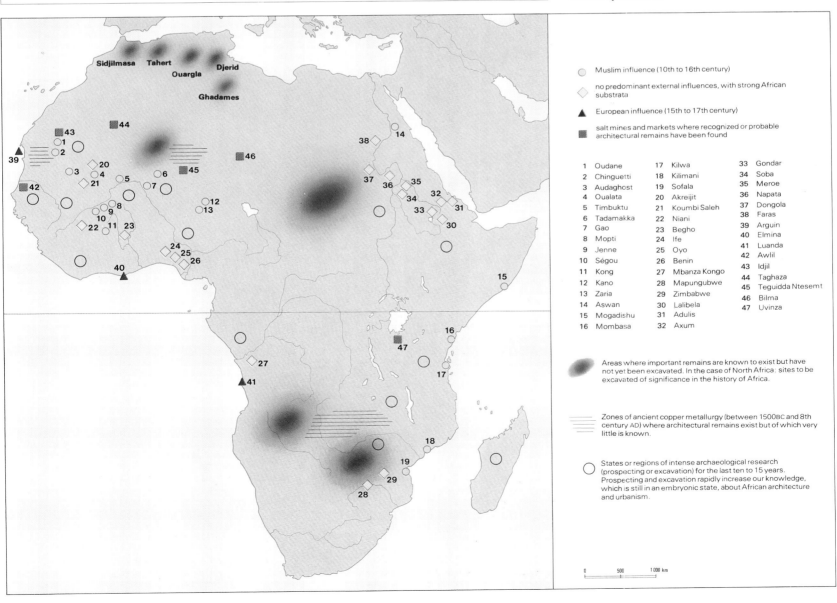

○ Muslim influence (10th to 16th century)

◇ no predominant external influences, with strong African substrata

▲ European influence (15th to 17th century)

■ salt mines and markets where recognized or probable architectural remains have been found

1	Oudane	17	Kilwa	33	Gondar
2	Chinguetti	18	Kilimani	34	Soba
3	Audaghost	19	Sofala	35	Meroe
4	Oualata	20	Akreijit	36	Napata
5	Timbuktu	21	Koumbi Saleh	37	Dongola
6	Tadamakka	22	Niani	38	Faras
7	Gao	23	Begho	39	Arguin
8	Mopti	24	Ife	40	Elmina
9	Jenne	25	Oyo	41	Luanda
10	Ségou	26	Benin	42	Awlil
11	Kong	27	Mbanza Kongo	43	Idjil
12	Kano	28	Mapungubwe	44	Taghaza
13	Zaria	29	Zimbabwe	45	Teguidda Ntesemt
14	Aswan	30	Lalibela	46	Bilma
15	Mogadishu	31	Adulis	47	Uvinza
16	Mombasa	32	Axum		

Areas where important remains are known to exist but have not yet been excavated. In the case of North Africa: sites to be excavated of significance in the history of Africa.

Zones of ancient copper metallurgy (between 1500BC and 8th century AD) where architectural remains exist but of which very little is known.

States or regions of intense archaeological research (prospecting or excavation) for the last ten to 15 years. Prospecting and excavation rapidly increase our knowledge, which is still in an embryonic state, about African architecture and urbanism.

Cameroon. The monumental entrance to important houses is decorated with pillars of wood which are often sculpted. The heavy straw roof also plays a decorative role.

changes in African architecture has barely begun; but it is essential if the more ancient traditions are to be understood. For example, we do not know what traditional methods of construction were available when it came to the building of new types of houses and mosques. Was it necessary to import advisers, architects and plans, or even perhaps materials and techniques? (In the old mosque of the ancient city of Ouadane, in Mauritania, there are still one or two stone arcades built according to techniques which have not yet been studied, but which apparently have parallels, though rare, in the southern Sahara.) It is also possible that, at first, the Africans refused to apply their own methods of construction to "foreign" buildings. Nevertheless, black Africa did not passively accept the introduction of foreign building types. Africa has moved slowly but in a definite direction over the years. Its economic evolution has become much better understood. By making feasible comparisons between peasant societies (after taking into account fundamental ecological differences) it becomes apparent that the gaps between black Africa, the Islamic regions and the West were not so very wide in the 12th century. The accelerating development in Europe of a monetary economy, bringing with it the means of expansion and domination, only gradually created the global differences which are so forcefully apparent in the 20th century. The disparity developed over eight centuries and not over thousands of years. Even in the 14th century, the West African economy was expanding, at least from the commercial point of view. The gap begins to appear in the 15th century. It was aggravated by the slave trade which emptied Africa of the best part of its manpower, quantitively and qualitatively, just when the fever for apparently limitless expansion seized Europe and held it for the following four centuries.

For thousands of years there was a give-and-take relationship between Africa and other parts of the world. This was certainly the case in the field of architecture. For example, it would be hard to believe that contact with the Muslim type of town had no effect on the African village. The deepening sense of insecurity brought about by the increase in the slave trade must have had some bearing on the fact that towns and agglomerations of all kinds came to be more

deliberately enclosed behind ditches and earth walls: in this context, the Chad region offers material for further research (H.D. Bivar and P.L. Shinnie, "Old Kanuri Capitals", in Journal of African History, vol. III, 1962). At some stage, also, a new system of organizing urban space appeared, the ruling power becoming more assertive and monopolistic in character.

In fact, area planning in Africa underwent a number of changes, under diverse influences that remain to be studied; unfortunately, research on these matters is still sparse. For example, in the case of Tegdaoust it is more or less clear that the type of square stone house found there was imported by settlers from Ifriqiya. From the 10th century a certain type of domestic interior, developed from Mediterranean, oriental and Muslim influences, infiltrated the area south of the Sahara. As we shall see later, it conflicted with the traditional disposition of the African house, both in the organization of space and in the use of rooms. In the square Muslim house, domestic life was divided off from street life by walls and by the provision of a special room in which visitors were received when they entered; the importance of the role of this "hall" made it the most developed room in the house. Finally, from the way these square houses were organized it is probable that, at least in certain examples in Tegdaoust, roof terraces were constructed to give extra space to the inhabitants. Dating these presumed architectural borrowings and trying to ascertain to what degree the square houses antedate the establishment of Islam can prove problematic. So many questions remain unanswered.

Monumental gateway, Jenne (Mali). Access to certain quarters is indicated by such gateways, even when there is no wall. The complexity of the construction techniques is apparent.

To study the modification of architecture by borrowing or exchange, it is worth having a close look at Sahel, at the Chad area and at the country of the Hausa, all places where the indications seem to be that exchange and innovation proceeded at a rapid pace. To what kind of synthesis between ancient and imported traditions do the superb houses of the merchants and intellectuals of Oualata in Mauritania, Kano in Nigeria, Khartoum in Sudan, and Jenne or Segou in Mali, bear witness? However, it would be wrong to put the main emphasis on these places; they have been successfully

Mali. The architecture of the Senoufo people remains one of the most representative in Africa. The collective buildings are larger and more carefully constructed than the homes. This photograph shows a building where masks and cult objects are kept. The clay walls are decorated with vegetable or mineral paints.

Tichitt (Mauritania). Decorative nooks are arranged, often in sequences, in the stone walls. In this case, they play no architectural role; in other sections of the building, they serve as cupboards set in the piers.

investigated already and in this respect reference should be made to the works of L. Prussin. However, on the whole, the chronological study of architecture in black Africa has not tempted researchers up to now.

Even if the materials available necessarily determine the form of a house to some extent, it is not true that they provide the sole determining factor. The occupations of the people – agricultural and sedentary, pastoral and semi- or wholly nomadic – play an equally significant part: a close look at the map is enough to show this. Nevertheless, although research into styles of construction often allows us to characterize ethnic groups and although ornamental details serve to distinguish families or hierarchies, still the lack of variety in building materials throughout Africa is remarkable – even if the use of these materials reveals deep thought and careful adaptation to the environment, particularly as regards drainage and water supply. Until now, little attention has been focused on the relationship between water and architecture, but there are many details to make us more aware of it: the use of sloping roofs, the choice of the best materials for rain to run off, the use of gullies and drains and all kinds of gargoyles, the collecting of water by systems of covered gullies leading down to a water tank.

Even today, between 85 and 90 per cent of black Africans live away from towns; a good number of these still live in houses constructed in traditional styles. These styles, which are the result of deliberation and choice, deserve neither to be forgotten nor to be despised as they were until the end of the 19th century. In addition, the grouping of such houses provides a telling guide to social and cultural relationships in Africa, and even to economic structure. There is always an underlying logic beneath the apparently random and haphazard groupings. M.A. Fassussi recently remarked that, in black Africa, the courtyard constitutes the open area of collective habitation which bonds the groups together, whereas the buildings themselves are areas in which the social groups are dispersed in rest or in work. This is a fundamental observation which sheds light on the whole system. The houses are broken up into little cells, the number of which directly reflects

the structure of the group. A "hall" is often found, but not always; we do not know if this is a borrowed feature. The head man occupies a dwelling which is strategically positioned. Each wife must have her own living quarters and work place; every boy past the age of puberty and no longer attached to his mother must have his own place for sleeping; every married son or daughter must be given lodgings; each coherent sub-group has its own place where food may be prepared. There are individual eating areas – one for each little group – also, storage spaces of all sizes, kitchens, chicken runs, washing places and latrines, and areas where the whole group may gather. These numerous components, united by the daily routines of the people that live in the agglomeration, are dispersed around courtyards which vary in size and in the number of trees grown in them, in the ways in which they are divided up and in the number of points of access. The fragmented nature of the whole permits greater economy in building materials: none of the dwellings is destined to last; all of them are rearranged from time to time according to the current needs of the community. Although there is little variation in architectural formulae, methods of construction are by no means mediocre. The size of each base cell imposes a simple plan, and – in appearance – simplifies the problem of roofing. However, methods of providing protection against the African sun, heat and wind have proved, on investigation, to be highly sophisticated and often difficult to build and to maintain. Nevertheless, there is no need for specialists in the art of construction – in other words, architects – although one person within each group may well prove himself to be especially skilful in this field: the task of building is one in which every member of the family or village participates and which no one can shirk.

space becomes more complex. And should the living space itself become scarce, buildings are constructed in storeys; the extraordinary tiered constructions of the Dogon people, on the cliffs of Bandiagara, merit their own architectural monograph. When serious danger threatens the group, it shelters behind a magical or physical barrier. This may be no more than a space allocated to gardens and rubbish tips, separating the houses from the bush – the place where "wild" and menacing things could lurk; or it may be an impenetrable hedge of bushes especially planted for the purpose; or an enclosure in the centre of the group of buildings, designed to protect the community's most precious possessions – for example, the cattle. The Somba people of Benin and the Lobi tribe of the Upper Volta took protection a step further, by modifying the design of the square house, making access difficult or "fortified".

Layouts may appear haphazard but in reality nothing is left to chance in the African habitat. In one region the dwellings may be carefully established along a certain contour-line; in another they are arranged along either side of a central alley separating the married from the unmarried. Study of the architectural landscape will prepare the visitor for the kind of society he is about to encounter; and the fact that there is so much variation in no way calls into question the existence of a fundamental "strategy". Gratuitous decoration is an individual right, widely exercised but subject also to well-defined restrictions. Anyone may decorate his wall or lovingly varnish his doorframe, his clay bed or his support pillars. However, in these societies which so jealously guard their social symbols, not everyone may erect the sort of roof that belongs to a woman who has just married off her children, or have the kind of pottery ridge-tiles which identify the house

Senegal. Villages of Casamance. In this region where rainwater is abundant, the collective houses are organized around a central rainwater tank supplied by water draining from the sloping roof. The houses are built of clay.

The apparent uniformity of construction in fact conceals a variety of forms determined by social needs. When Islam, directly or indirectly, made its influence felt, the courtyard became surrounded by an enclosure which protected it from the eyes of onlookers. Whenever the family overflows the simple nucleus, the collective

of an eminent person, or set a floor above the "hall" in a way which indicates a prestigious residence. And, of course, in the complex web of signs which constitutes the code of every society, those signs associated with living areas are, in Africa, all the more important because of the rustic simplicity of the basic building materials.

Materials and building methods

In general, Africa is not short of stone: there are mountainous ranges or rocky outcrops everywhere. Stonecutting was mastered by Africans tens of thousands of years ago, as can be proved by the impressive cutting tools that have been found. The Africans have built stone walls, great and small, both in proud cities and humble villages. However, particularly where the construction of houses is concerned, they have used stone very little. This may seem strange, considering that they are fully aware of the advantages of the material for such uses as making a clean coping for wells, reinforcing the base of clay walls, or building raised paths above flood level in courtyards. This contradiction is not due to any technical inability. All the remains of stone constructions known today reveal skills equal to those of any other region in the world; and architectural remains from Sahel in Mauritania to Zimbabwe prove how adept the Africans were at constructing in stone before any contact with Europeans.

The materials universally used in black Africa are plants, wood and clay. Not surprisingly, the nature of these materials affects the arrangement of living accommodation. The traditional use of plant material in forest regions has by no means readily been supplanted by corrugated iron. Wood still plays a major role, not only as a framework for walls but also as an invisible strengthening for complex structures (such as those built by the Hausas) and as the main material in exterior facings (in Cameroon, for example). Detailed research into the use of wood in ancient African architecture would certainly give contemporary architects some interesting ideas; indeed, certain schools of architecture have already returned to the use of wood as a building material, even for important buildings.

In 1974, when René Gardy opened his absorbing book on African houses with the statement, "Houses may also be of clay", he immediately raised the very interesting issue of why the Africans deliberately chose clay for most of their building needs. We could not even begin to list all the names which have been given to the various ways in which they have used clay, from *tub* in the north, to *banco* in the west, to *daga* in the south east. The innumerable variants not only correspond to natural linguistic diversities, but also reveal a highly refined technical knowledge of the potential of clay. Applied to the construction of living, sleeping or storage areas, clay imparts its own colours and shapes, and even its own spatial consequences, on African architecture; it is also, of course, omnipresent in pottery.

As Labelle Prussin has observed, the finished results differ markedly, depending on the technique used. This may be modelling (related to pottery techniques) or construction (employing prefabricated material in the form of bricks). With the use of modelling, there is complete freedom in the lines of the building: curves eradicate all the monotony created by uniformly shaped materials, and the circular plan creates a distinctive space to which the straw conical roof seems particularly suited. Without going quite so far as to say that the material used determines the shape, we can see that round houses predominate in areas where the modelling technique is used. Raw brick, dried in the sun, was used in Nubia well over 2,000 years ago. It has been discovered in the most ancient strata at Tegdaoust (8th–9th century) and was probably used in West Africa well before this period. Everything leads us to believe that it was part of the ancient stock of techniques employed by the black people. Brick frees the builder of curves without necessarily imposing angles. In Nubia during the first millennium AD, large civic and religious monuments were built of brick and some of them also had brick vaults. The use of brick made possible the construction of larger façades, as at Jenne and Segou, and the creation of rectangular or square rooms, thus developing a completely new domestic layout. But it also did away with the interesting rhythms of bends and curves that characterize, for example, a Gurunsi village. It is not difficult to evolve from sun-dried brick to oven-baked brick, yet the Africans rarely made this transition; archaeological evidence of oven-baked brick has, however, been found in Gao and Chad.

In short, the prime material of African architecture, clay, deserves more detailed study. Despite its vulnerability to water, this medium attracted the Africans above all because of its resistance to severe changes in temperature. It would be rash to dismiss it as a "primitive" material without first having understood why it responded so well and for so long to the needs of an entire people.

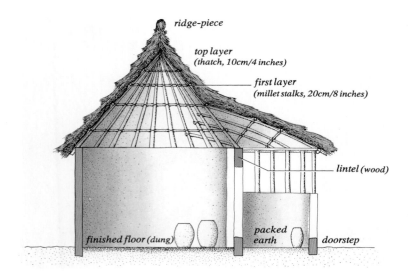

ridge-piece

top layer
(thatch, 10cm/4 inches)

first layer
(millet stalks, 20cm/8 inches)

lintel (wood)

finished floor (dung)

packed earth

doorstep

Cross section of an individual home (Senoufo, Ivory Coast)

(After Tana Coulibaly.)

A high doorstep isolates the interior from the outside. Due to its shape and thickness, the roof should not generally let rainwater in. There is a cooking hearth inside, but the main bulk of the cooking is done outside or in an anteroom. The diameter of the room is usually around 3 to 4 metres (10 to 13 feet), which provides a living area for several people.

Decorative construction techniques

These six examples, taken from a book by Maurice Delafosse, are based on the work of the Senoufo people, who model bricks and then dry them in the sun. The seventh example (photograph, far right) comes from Zimbabwe: a similar ornamental motif has here been realized in stone. Many other regions offer comparable forms. Beautiful architectural ornamentation is abundant in the Sahel zone, in Mauritania, Mali, the Ivory Coast and Nigeria.

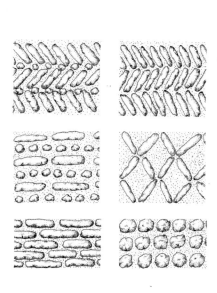

Mabas houses (Cameroon)

A good example of the intelligent use of available materials. The piled up stones delineate abutting enclosures, each of which marks off the living area of a coherent group. The group is further divided into smaller units, the members of which live in raised houses of *banco*, a malleable material that is easy both to work and to repair. Here the use of layered straw roofing is also very much in evidence. The simple first layer is covered with a more solid and ornate plaited layer; a third straw roof sometimes tops the first two layers.

Oualata (Mauritania)

Here the concealment of the building material under layers of fine clay and paint has been made into a fine art. In this small town, both the courtyards and the rooms are used as living areas, and both are decorated in order to be pleasing to the eye. The designs, executed in white on a red ochre background, are regularly repainted by the women. The solids and voids of beds, nooks and crannies, and door frames, are accentuated by the way they are painted. Northern Nigeria and the Sudan offer equally beautiful examples of painted or sculpted designs made of fine *banco*.

Gurunsi house (Upper Volta)

The large rectangular room and roof terrace are typical of the architecture widespread in the Gurunsi region. The monotony of blank surfaces is relieved by alternating completely flat areas with others decorated in patterns scratched on by bundles of canes. Ibn Battuta, who visited Africa in the middle of the 14th century, remarked that the Africans took great care of their walls: they would roughcast them with a mixture of earth and oil.

The stone walls of Zimbabwe

In Zimbabwe (formerly Rhodesia), there are about 150 sites that have monumental stone walls. Only eight of these have been excavated; eleven have been dated by the radiocarbon technique. After much controversy, archaeologists and historians are now agreed that they were built between the 14th and 18th centuries; they are also agreed on their chronology. The most ancient walls were built in a rather rudimentary way and later required reconstruction or reinforcement. Those of the finest quality were erected during the 15th century: the highest and most beautiful walls, made of rubble sandwiched between two external facings, date from this era. At that time, the available workforce must have been larger or more continuously exploited. From the beginning of the 16th century, the quality deteriorated. Recent detailed research has finally quashed the highly fantastic theories that attributed these monuments to anyone except the black population. The cultural identity of the builders and of the techniques they used has been proven: the creators of these walls were Bantus.

The best-known and richest of all these agglomerations is the site of Zimbabwe (from which the country takes its name), near the upper valleys of the Sabi. It grew slowly from the 10th and 11th centuries onward. The evolution of spatial and architectural planning accompanied economic and social developments. The life of the inhabitants, at first dependent on cattle-raising and very similar to that of many other agglomerations in Mashonaland, was led simply enough for three or four centuries:

essential buildings for man or beast (huts, stores, *kraals* for the cattle) were made of clay, heaped up stones or plant material. Little trace has been left of these ancient constructions or of those that followed in the 13th century, which were built of clay mixed with wood matting to strengthen the walls. However, comparable structures have been better preserved on other sites and it is these findings that help us to interpret the inadequate evidence of Zimbabwe itself. The existence of clay buildings proves these sites with stone walls to belong to the development of African architecture as a whole.

After the 13th century, economic evolution changed this society and its way of life. Exportation of gold via the Sabi and Sofala rivers, from the plateau to the Indian Ocean, created a wealthy aristocracy and occasioned the emergence of a "king" who dominated and then monopolized transactions. These *nouveaux riches* appeared from the 14th century onward; in the 15th century, they became extremely powerful. The stone walls that date from this period are symbolic of this power. Of little military use but spectacularly ostentatious, they encircled the "sacred" areas where the "king" lived, where the nobles were buried, and perhaps also where religious ceremonies were celebrated – the large elliptical enclosure probably had some ceremonial function. In this new type of urban landscape, in this town perhaps inhabited by thousands of people, decorative elements enlivened the massive expanses of the walls, and a taste for imported objects reflected the wealth of the nobles.

The combination of clay and stone – for platforms and steps – and the careful provision of curves in the stonework, to soften the look of this "mineral world", coincided with the appearance of imported Chinese celadon and ornate glass from the Muslim world. Remains of these wares have been found among the ruins.

Zimbabwe architecture, a manifestation of political power, was imitated in all the regions dominated by the ruler of this town: one can easily imagine the setting up of an administrative network run by officials who answered only to the ruler of Zimbabwe. However, from the traces of house walls found within the city walls, it seems that domestic architecture was never built of stone: once again, the Africans remained faithful to clay. The city walls, far too big to have been covered over, constitute the only obvious signs of Zimbabwe's past power and greatness.

The eclipse of Zimbabwe in the 16th century is universally recognized, but those who have studied this period do not all agree on the reasons for this decline. Be that as it may, the building of great stone walls in this region came to an end with the history of Zimbabwe. New ones were built further to the north, near the valley of the Zambezi: they herald the emergence of Monomotapa on to the historical map.

There is still much to be discovered from archaeology in this region of Africa. Only then can we come to a definitive conclusion about these spectacular products of African architecture.

The Zimbabwe site

The map on the facing page includes the spot from which this photograph was taken. It was taken from the hill to the north of the site, looking down one of several carefully paved paths that descend towards the plain, where a larger number of remains can be found. The raised ground on the horizon is the Mashonaland plateau. This plateau, which has remained untouched by the tsetsefly throughout its history, is a prime cattle-grazing area; it also harbours gold mines from the "medieval" period. Zimbabwe was built on the first foothills of this plateau, about 1,000 metres (3,000 feet) above sea-level.

Fragment of the wall of the western enclosure of Zimbabwe

Leaning heavily on the granite of the north hill, this wall probably dates from the second half of the 14th century; it has the only ancient doorway in the town still intact. A stone stairway leads up through it – the first steps can be seen here outside the wall – and a stone lintel is fixed into the rounded jambs. Although aesthetically satisfying, the wall would not have been able to play a serious defensive role.

1 *granite hill,*
north of the site

2 *western enclosure*
on the hill

3 *eastern enclosure*

4 *large, oval*
enclosure wall

5 *conical tower*

6 *traces of habitation*

General plan of the Zimbabwe ruins

The stone ruins, covering an area of more than half a sq. kilometre (500 sq. yards), date from the 14th and 15th centuries. The hill to the north was used for places of worship, tombs, and workshops where iron, copper and gold were worked. Traces of buildings have been found on the plain (particularly at **6**): they consisted of a series of round clay structures joined by little stone walls. The large oval wall, rebuilt on several occasions, was encircled by great walls in the 15th century, 10 metres (30 feet) high in places. There are three unfortified entrances leading to the interior. Other stone walls, some of which are even older, were built inside and outside the enclosure: their purpose is not clear. Similarly, the significance of the 10 metre (30 feet) high conical tower hidden by trees is not clear. It is often supposed to be the symbol of a granary containing tributes paid in kind to the "king".

The symbolism of the granary

Granaries, although in some regions rather primitive, made of straw or of plant screens on stone bases, are generally highly regarded in Africa and consequently very carefully constructed. It should also be noted that grains are often better preserved in buildings of plant material than in clay structures where the grain may ferment.

The Pharaohs of ancient Egypt, as part of their general responsibility for the well-being of their people, built granaries in which surplus grain could be accumulated during good years. In this way, they managed to survive years of bad harvest. With similar intentions, other ancient societies evolved rather different arrangements. In black Africa, food storage was organized at a local level, without the regulation of the economy by a central political power. The granary was all the more important in rural areas, where the pattern of life was relatively simple and unsophisticated. It formed (and in some cases still forms) the main feature of many villages, not only sheltering the year's food supply and seed-corn but also, just as importantly, holding the grain used for the various ceremonies that bonded the village community at all levels. These ceremonies still survive in many places, even where the Africans have officially converted to monotheism. The granary is part of the culture and spirit of Africa.

The granary contributes to ethnic, clan or group identity, and so naturally becomes a centre for creative activity, artistry, craftsmanship and decoration. When visiting a village, one studies the granaries to assess the nature of the society, and perhaps even its religious outlook. The place where the granaries are situated may also reveal something about social history. Granaries isolated on roof-tops, like those of the Somba people, or hidden in houses, like those of the Lobi or the Kirdi, reveal a lack of confidence in neighbours, perhaps of ancient origin but still not forgotten. When the storehouses are grouped together within a guarded enclosure, a fear of pillage is indicated; when they are dispersed outside the dwelling area between the houses and the bush, a sense of security is implied; more often than not, they are grouped within an area of houses. Granaries also indicate the hierarchy of each society and relations between its different members: the Massa people of Cameroon have a large storehouse for the men and a much smaller one for each woman; she uses it but does not own it since the contents of the granaries are nearly always redistributed periodically among the members of the group. The shape and size of the granary are also interesting: there is an important difference between the large collective storehouses of the Songhay people in Mali or of the Marka people in the Upper Volta and the small storage spaces, almost individualized, of the Gurunsi, also in the Upper Volta. However, in every case, the relationship between the storehouse and the environment is carefully balanced. Some of the methods used for organizing the interior of the granary for the best conservation of grain are highly ingenious and deserve systematic research.

Carefully constructed and maintained, the granary is not individual property in the sense that we understand it. This communal store proudly bears the signs and symbols of the people who use it – a lizard or some other guardian animal, an abstract mark, imprinted ornamentation to set off the main lines of the "monument", or painting with different types of ochre. Decorative devices like these help to give an individual identity to each storehouse. In other cases, for instance that of the Dogon people, wooden doors and their locks take on a decorative function.

Thus it is not only family or collective altars, or buildings where cult objects are kept, but also granaries, which provide a good basis for studying the architecture and decoration of black Africa.

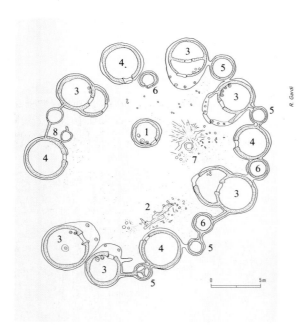

1 *building where cult objects are kept*

2 *bench*

3 *women's living quarters*

4 *men's living quarters*

5 *granaries*

6 *enclosures for small livestock*

7 *working area for women*

8 *washing area*

Collective Senoufo dwelling

(Plan by Tana Coulibaly.)

It can be seen that the granaries are closely mingled with the other buildings; this is usually the case. In the same way as the houses, the granaries are regularly "redistributed" among the people of the agglomeration.

Mandara region, Cameroon

The iron furnaces are built with the same materials and using the same techniques as the granaries and houses.

Somba tripod granaries, Benin

Agricultural communities have gradually perfected the most efficient kinds of granary. Although always made of the same materials, the shapes vary enormously: every people and region has its own style; similarly, each granary usually has its own particular decoration. The three- and four-legged storehouses of the Somba people, despite their essentially functional role, are exceptionally beautiful.

Perched granary of the Somba people, Benin

The Somba build their collective dwellings like veritable fortresses, blind on the exterior. In this case, the granary is safeguarded by being incorporated into the house; access is only possible from the roof. The shape and quality of the granary is remarkable. This detail shows the care given to decoration – note the two-tone colour and the stamped patterning of the lower part – indicating the importance of the granary to these people.

Marka granaries, Upper Volta

Like the bases of very tall pyramids, Marka granaries stand on grids of crossed branches. Built of dried brick held together by wood, they resemble wicker or wooden storehouses more than do those of the people further south. They surround the villages, an instant guide to the identity of the occupants.

Collective granaries, Mali

Another region, another way of life, another way of organizing granaries. This large group provides efficient protection.

Temple of the Sun, Palenque

Built at the end of the 7th century during the reign of the successor to the famous Pacal, this building belongs to an architectural group which also includes the Temple of the Cross and the Temple of the Leafed Cross. Beneath an apparent simplicity, the architecture of these buildings is very subtle and innovatory. The numerous decorative elements, especially on the interior, evoke the double aspect, dynastic and mythological, of these constructions.

If a survey of pre-Hispanic architecture were to take in not only monumental buildings but also other types of construction, including the homes of the common people ("primitive houses" and "native houses", as Amos Rapoport has called them), it would have to range over practically every area of the double continent that is America. From a more limited point of view there is no doubt that, next to central America and the region around the middle of the Andes, south-west America, with its Hohokam, Mogollon and Anasazi traditions, and even the Mississippi Valley, where there are types of pyramid, take a prominent place in pre-Columbian architecture. The exclusive attention that is paid here to the Mesoamerican culture, and to the sector that stretches from San Augustín in Colombia to Tiahuanaco in Bolivia, can be justified for two reasons. In the first place, these two regions acquired a special stature in the course of their prehistory; and in the second place, the rich complexity of their culture was manifested in their architecture, in spite of the technical limitations that have all too often been over-emphasized. The fact that the men who built the Maya cities and the Inca fortresses

the time of the Spanish conquest, spread to the south of modern Mexico and to the north-west of central America, he was not just offering a neat suggestion for solving a terminological problem: he was making a precise attempt to point out the existence of a cultural reality. Mesoamerica is indeed defined by a collection of common characteristics which it is possible to list in detail and which include certain architectural features – pyramids composed of superimposed elements, special courts for playing ball games, areas laid out for markets, buildings used as steam baths, floors coated with stucco.... It is hardly surprising that architecture figures in the formation of the concept of Mesoamerica, since it reflects the multiple components of the whole civilization. But the cultural unity described by the term does not signify uniformity: in the vast area that represented Mesoamerica in 1519 many ethnic groups coexisted, living in very varied environments. Naturally, this double source of diversity affected many aspects of the material culture, one of which was architecture. Furthermore, the cultural area of Mesoamerica did not appear suddenly just before the conquest; it evolved progressively, beginning around

architectural history of pre-Columbian Mesoamerica unfolds.

The first known example of building in the territory of Mesoamerica was found in the valley of Tehuacán and dates back to the Abejas era (3500–2300BC). It is an oval-shaped house, half underground and built of perishable materials (wood and thatch). In area it covers less than 6 sq. metres (7 sq. yards), but the remains that have been found there show that it was used as a permanent dwelling place, enabling R.S. MacNeish to talk about the beginnings of the rural hamlet way of life. It is possible, however, that future excavations elsewhere will reveal traces of much older houses. On a site at Zohapilco in the south of the Mexican basin, for example, there is evidence of settled occupation from the sixth millennium BC, although investigations may not be able to uncover any kind of dwelling. The concept of a public place for gatherings of the religious community probably made its appearance at a very early stage in the history of Mesoamerica. In the centre of the site at Gheo-Shih, near Mitla, which is thought to have been the seasonal camp of a group of between 15 and 30 people around 5000BC, there is a cleared space bordered by two parallel rows of stones, 20 metres (66 feet) long and 7 metres (23 feet) apart. As K.V. Flannery has emphasized, this could have been a ritual area, foreshadowing the religious buildings of the settled communities. In addition there is a fairly similar structure on the lowest levels of San José Mogote (Oaxaca valley), which dates from around 1700BC. This one has a double line of posts partially replacing the lines of stones; the area between them is the same size, and its main north-south axis appears to have been a conscious decision. During the centuries that followed, the same site at San José Mogote acquired several successive buildings which are clearly different from the houses and which are very likely to have had a public function. Structure 6 is a good example of these buildings: it consists of a single rectangular room, some 4 by 5 metres (14 by 18 feet), whose walls are made out of cob on a trellis of wood and a framework of pine posts, and are covered, as is the floor, by a smooth layer of stucco. Two other details which attract attention are the small, low, rectangular platform against the inside of the southern wall, which could well be interpreted as an altar, and the cylindrical cavity towards the centre of the room, which is meticulously covered with stucco. Stucco was also used as a finish on the earliest buildings in the central Mayan area. The first structure to be built at Cuello (Belize), discovered in 1976, dates from around 2500BC. It is a round building (3 metres/10

Labná Arch, from a drawing by F. Catherwood (1841). Situated about 50 kilometres (30 miles) south-east of Uxmal, the site of Labná offers several remarkable examples of the Puuc architectural style. With the exception of Yucatán, the corbelled vault is used only in the design of interior spaces.

used tools far inferior to those of the neolithic Europeans only makes their buildings all the more remarkable. In 1943, when the anthropologist Paul Kirchhoff coined the word "Mesoamerica" to describe the homogeneous cultural area which, at

the end of the second millennium BC with the appearance of the Olmec phenomenon. So far as we can tell today, some of the fundamental elements of subsequent architecture were first used by this civilization. It is from here that the

PRE-HISPANIC AMERICA

feet in diameter) and could well have been used for ceremonial purposes. Thus, during the thousand years preceding the flourishing of the Olmec style, while a village way of life was becoming general, a few modest architectural efforts heralded some of the developments of the future.

Erected in about 1200BC, the great Olmec centre at San Lorenzo marks an important stage in the architectural evolution of Mesoamerica. As M.D. Coe has demonstrated, it is built around a natural rise in the ground; but this rise has been enlarged to create a plateau of 50 hectares (120 acres) which stands about 50 metres (164 feet) above the neighbouring savanna. This impressive piece of work already evokes the monumental tendencies of some of the creations of the Middle Horizon. The numerous hillocks (more than 200) on the summit of this "acropolis" have not been given a precise date. They were the substructure for houses and other buildings, particularly temples, and in the period under consideration they were all made out of clay. It is also interesting to note the intentional orientation of everything, and the arrangement of courtyards in the residential areas and of squares between the

principal buildings. There is even a massive drainage system dating from this period, which was made out of basalt brought from distant mines: channels were cut through rows of basalt blocks and then covered over with slabs. The site at La Venta appears to have succeeded San Lorenzo as the capital of the Olmec region. Although it is almost totally ruined and has not been completely excavated, it reveals the same vigour and the same architectural care. Complex A, which lies towards the northern end of the main group, is arranged in perfect symmetry around a north-south axis (deviating from the north by only 8° westwards) and contains one of the most ancient examples of the square-based step pyramid. The most spectacular monument rises to the south of this group: it is 34 metres (112 feet) high and its general shape is conical, but it is conspicuous for its ten depressions separated by as many protruding sections. According to R.F. Heizer, it looks like a volcanic cone that has been furrowed by erosion. Here, as on the previous site, the main building material is clay, sometimes coloured, but adobe (sun-baked brick) can also be found, as well as prismatic columns of basalt, which were used for palisades and tombs. We are sure

now that the main zones of Mesoamerica were influenced by various aspects of the Olmec civilization, including its basic architectural concepts. The seven centuries which separated the collapse of La Venta from the beginning of the Middle Horizon formed a period of cultural consolidation, during which each region absorbed the Olmec heritage and experimented with new forms of architecture. In the Oaxaca valley, the foundation of Monte Albán, around 500BC, and its rapid evolution thereafter are clear proof of this process. From a technological point of view, hewed stone was now being used for the foundations of important buildings and for the lower parts of tall structures, where adobe was still used in the upper walls; masonry columns also began to appear. Temples, consisting of a single room slightly raised above the porch in front, began to take on a distinctive appearance, and the ball-game court came into being, as well as other structures whose function is less obvious – such as structure J, which some have suggested was an observatory, but which, judging by the iconographic details that are sculpted on to the slabs on its side, must have played a political role. Related but distinct architectural currents appeared in other

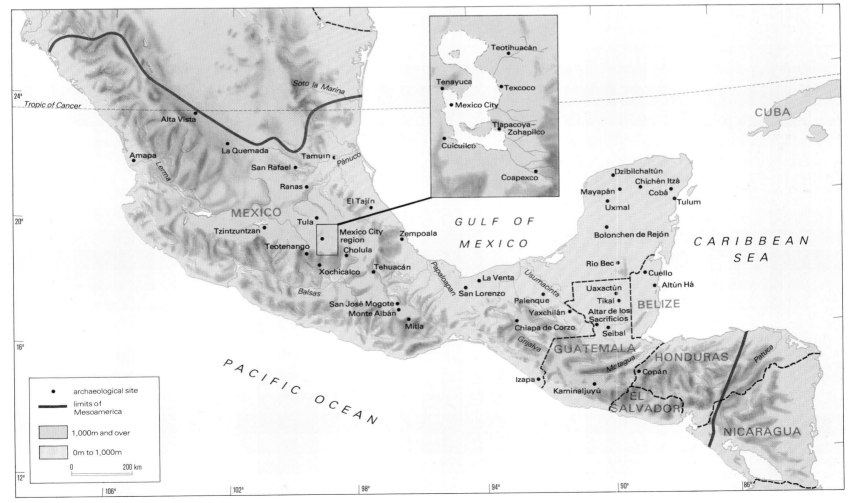

regions. On the site at Cuicuilco, in the Mexican basin, where there may have been as many as 20,000 inhabitants around the time of Christ, there is a pyramid with a circular base and two ramps leading to the summit, which underwent two or three stages of construction before reaching its final form. Remains of some particularly dynamic cities of the same period can be found on the high ground in the south of the Mayan region. These include Izapa, where there are about 80 huge earth structures all faced with stone, and Kaminaljuyú, where no stone has been used but where the architectural activity was intense. In the lowlands of the centre and the north the buildings appear to be more limited, but there are already several notable experiments – Dzibilchaltún, Acancéh, Uaxactún, Tikal and, perhaps the most important, El Mirador, where systematic excavations were begun in 1979. For a little while longer, the building of permanent structures coexisted with the simple use of clay and stucco. It seems as though the principle of the corbelled vault was used before the beginning of the Middle Horizon, initially to cover tombs. And so it was that, around the time of Christ, an architectural skill was acquired which was to find its full expression with the growth of the civilizations of the Middle Horizon.

The architectural unity of Mesoamerica between AD200 and the Spanish conquest can be discerned in several ways: in some of the building practices (the general use of cut stone, the use of lime mortar to coat surfaces and periodic reconstructions in which new buildings were erected over old ones), in the shape of most of the ordinary houses, in the recurrence of types of building with similar functions (pyramid-based temples, ball-game courts, "palaces"), and in certain principles of spatial organization (concern for orientation, the importance of open spaces). But this fundamental unity is expressed in eminently varied ways, and the eye, even the untrained eye, can easily pick out the regional, and sometimes local, styles, which are the signs of true schools of architecture, like the very characteristic one at Palenque. In western Mesoamerica, the first seven centuries AD were dominated by Teotihuacán. At its height, around AD450, this rapidly developing city contained about 150,000 inhabitants, and it is one of the finest examples of pre-industrial urban architecture. The positioning of the central axis of the town, known as the "Street of the Dead", and its division into four quadrants by a secondary axis running east to west, seem to have been established since the Tzacualli period (from around the time of the birth of Christ to AD150). It was at this time that the Pyramid of the Sun was built, representing an accumulation of two and a half million tons of material, and also the first stages of the Moon Pyramid. During the following era the centre of the town was moved further to the south, as a result of the erection of the "Citadel" and the Pyramid of Quetzalcoatl, in front of which the "Large Group" was to be established a few decades later. During a vast programme of urban renewal, which took place shortly afterwards, the dwellings were systematically rebuilt in more durable materials. They were arranged in complexes of single-storey flats, each complex built within a roughly square area surrounded by an almost solid wall. The architects of Teotihuacán are celebrated for their particular system of construction: on each platform level there was a lower, sloping part and, attached to this, a vertical panel bordered by a talud-tablero or jutting cornice. The talud-tablero, which has been studied in detail by P. Gendrop, was possibly invented in the Puebla valley, but it is regarded as a sign of Teotihuacán's influence on contemporary sites elsewhere (on the high plateau of Mexico and right up in the Mayan region) and it was to be perpetuated on later sites with modifications (at El Tajín, for example).

At the height of their development, the cities of the central Mayan region appear to have been completely different. The main difference is due to the fact that the dwelling places here are more spread out. Although "Great Tikal" covers an area of 160 sq. kilometres (62 sq. miles), it never contained more than 50,000 inhabitants. But the centres of these cities are not lacking in monumental structures (temple IV at Tikal is 72 metres/236 feet high). Nor do they lack symmetry, even though this is often very subtle. There are two factors which possibly explain the distinctive style of the most notable Mayan buildings: first, architectonic development which does not follow any preconceived plan but which tries to make use of pre-existing elements (topographical accidents, as in the case of Piedras Negras, and/or earlier structures, as is suggested by the sequence of building at the palace in Palenque); and second, a particular accent on architectural decoration, which is especially exaggerated in the styles of Río Bec, Chenes and Puuc in central Yucatán. The interpretation of these

Western Mesoamerica	Eastern Mesoamerica	Periods	
August 14, 1521 : end of the MEXICO-TENOCHTITLÁN siege.	**March 1517** : discovery of YUCATÁN (expedition led by F. Hernández de Córdoba).	Colonial	
MEXICO-TENOCHTITLÁN ⎡ 1487 4th (?) dedication of the main temple. ⎣ 1369 (?) foundation.		Late Horizon (postclassical)	AD1500
	MAYAPÁN (north Maya zone) : 1283, beginning of hegemony.		
MITLA (Oaxaca valley) : groups of columns. TULA (north of the Mexican basin) : apogee.	CHICHÉN ITZÁ (north Maya zone) : Maya-Toltec buildings.	Second Intermediate	
	Zones of RÍO BEC, CHENES, PUUC : apogee.		
EL TAJÍN (Gulf coast) : apogee.	TIKAL ⎡ Temple IV ⎣ beginnings of the construction of twin groups.		
MONTE ALBÁN (Oaxaca valley) : apogee.		Middle Horizon (classical)	AD500
TEOTIHUACÁN (Mexican basin) ⎡ urban renovation, Citadel, ⎢ Pyramid of Quetzalcoatl, ⎢ Pyramid of the Sun and ⎣ Pyramid of the Moon.	Central Maya zone : vaults used to cover tombs. Southern Maya zone (KAMINALJUYÚ, IZAPA) : rapid development, especially in architecture.		
CUICUILCO (Mexican basin) : last stage in the construction of the main edifice.	UAXACTÚN : structure E-VII sub, TIKAL : structure 5c-54. CHIAPA DE CORZO : building 1-H. DZIBILCHALTÚN (north Maya zone) : complex 450. ALTAR DE SACRIFICIOS (central Maya zone) : group B.	First Intermediate (middle and upper formatives)	
MONTE ALBÁN (Oaxaca valley) : foundation of the site.			500BC
	SEIBAL, ALTAR DE SACRIFICIOS, BARTON RAMIE, TIKAL... (central Maya zone) : first signs of settlement.		
LA VENTA (Gulf coast) : complex C (?).			
SAN LORENZO (Gulf coast) : artificial plateau of about 50 hectares (120 acres). COAPEXCO (Mexican basin) : site covering about 50 hectares (120 acres). SAN JOSÉ MOGOTE (Oaxaca valley) : structure 6, public edifice.		Early Horizon (lower formative)	1500BC
	Development of village life on the Pacific coast.		
Development of village life.		Initial (initial formative)	
	CUELLO (Belize) : house on circular platform.		2500BC
TEHUACÁN valley : permanent hamlets, semi-buried houses.		Pre-ceramic (archaic)	
ZOHAPILCO (Mexican basin) : permanent occupation from 5500BC.			3500BC

general tendencies is extremely complex. The comparison of elements such as vaults or roof ridges (cresteria) between one site and another, or even between one building and another, inevitably calls to mind the musical metaphor of theme and variations.

It is certainly no paradox if some of the greatest architectural achievements in pre-Columbian Mesoamerica (those, for example in Uxmal or in Sayil to the north of Yucatán) testify not only to an exceptional morphological and decorative inventiveness, but also to a mastery of conception and execution which included techniques of prefabrication. Such a combination implies the existence of great architects, even if their names have not survived.

The western territories of South America, from around the Equator to about 20° south, are grouped under the title of Central Andes. Lying along the mountain range and in its coastal and Amazonian foothills, they obviously include a great variety of natural surroundings and ethnic groups. But the history of their cultural development over about 20,000 years reveals a certain unity. In fact they form one of those "nuclear zones" like Mesoamerica where settled, hierarchical societies evolved and flourished, not only socially and politically, but also religiously and aesthetically. These societies are at the origin of what is commonly called the Andean classical culture; and one of the most striking characteristics of this culture

is the early development of its elaborate civil and religious architecture. Their creations, as complex as they were rich, have sadly been ignored for too long, in favour of the buildings of the Inca era, which, although impressive, are very recent (15th–16th century AD). Yet they invented original and practical ways of making up for the scarcity of raw materials (particularly on the Peruvian side) and for their own lack of technological knowledge – although this was not always as rudimentary as people have often suggested. Large ceremonial centres existed in Peru from the 3rd millennium BC, and real towns from the 2nd millennium, long before the appearance of pottery and the development of any real agriculture.

Periods	Pacific Coast	High Andean ground
Late Horizon (Inca empire)	**1527** : Landing of F. Pizarro at Tumbes. TAMBO COLORADO; PACHACAMAC : Temple of the Sun and Mamakona.	**November 15, 1532** : capture of CAJAMARCA. CUZCO and neighbouring sites, HUANUCO VIEJO, VILCAS HUAMÁN.
Late Intermediate (regional states)	Fortress-temple of PARAMONGA, towns of CHAN-CHÁN, PACATNAMÚ (Chimu culture, north coast).	
Middle Horizon (Wari empire)	Town of CAJAMARQUILLA (Lima culture). PACHACAMAC : Temple and town of Pachacamac (Lima culture, central coast).	PIKILLACTA : town and stores. WARI : extension of the town. TIAHUANACO : Akapana and Door of the Sun (around AD600?). TIAHUANACO : first buildings. WARI : first constructions.
Early Intermediate (regional classical)	"Temple" of PAÑAMARCA; Pyramid of the Sun and Pyramid of the Moon at MOCHE (Mochica culture). Town of CAHUACHI (Nazco culture, south coast).	City of PUCARA (Pucara culture).
Early Horizon (formative)	"Temples" of PALLKA, MOXEC, CERRO BLANCO, PUNKURI.	CHAVÍN : New Temple or Castillo (between 800 and 500BC?). CHAVÍN DE HUANTAR : Temple of Lanzón and buried square (between 900 and 800BC?).
Initial (ancient formative)	CERRO SECHÍN : stela temples? LAS ALDAS : pyramidal structures and buried square (1200–900BC). CULEBRAS : step pyramid and square. LA FLORIDA : pyramid. EL PARAÍSO : unit 1 (1620BC). CULEBRAS : terraced village. LAS ALDAS : first construction?	KOTOSH : White Temple, then Temple of the Crossed Hands and Temple of the Niches (between 2000 and 1800BC?).
Pre-ceramic (archaic)	HUACA PRIETA : semi-buried stone dwellings. CHILCA : first known houses (between 3400 and 3000BC).	

The oldest example of a constructed dwelling dates from about 3400BC. It was discovered in the coastal village of Chilca, where there may then have been about 500 inhabitants, and is only a simple conical hut, slightly over 2 metres (6 feet) in diameter, built out of clumps of rushes which are joined together at the top and supported by a framework of large reeds and whale ribs. On another part of the coast, at Huaca Prieta, there are groups of little oval or quadrangular houses built around 2500BC. They are half underground, with pebble walls, and roofs made of wooden poles or whale ribs; in all, they too must have housed several hundred people. But the most spectacular example of this Pre-ceramic domestic architecture is the development at Culebras, which was built around 2000BC. The entire side of a hill was laid out in terraces supported by retaining walls made out of basalt blocks, each terrace carrying a series of little, quadrangular, half-buried buildings. The lower parts of these buildings were also made out of basalt blocks, this time grouted with clay, but the upper parts must have been adobe or else clay-coated rush matting. The settled population of a site such as this could well have been as many as a thousand.

Monumental architecture had not yet appeared, and these three sites reveal no signs of any real village community, or of buildings that were used as anything other than the homes of individuals or families. It seems as though the first obviously public buildings, which are generally termed "ceremonial" even though their actual purpose is uncertain, were erected on a few sites in Peru before the appearance of any pottery. The most famous examples of these are at Río Seco and El Paraíso, both dating from around 1600BC. The architecture of the two communities is radically different. At Río Seco, there are the remains of two pyramidal monuments, truncated at a height of 4 metres (13 feet). The base for each of these monuments was made by filling an adobe structure of several sections with stones collected from the river nearby. A second adobe structure, similarly filled, was erected on the top of the first, and then the whole building was covered in gravel, and several still-unexplained monoliths were set upright on the top platform. The group of buildings at El Paraíso is much larger, covering between 50 and 60 hectares (125 to 150 acres). It is made up of eight large platforms, each carrying a complex superstructure. One of them, which has been excavated and restored – perhaps a little too daringly – by F. Engel, is a huge rectangular building, 60 by 50 metres (200 by 165 feet), containing 25 separate rooms or internal courtyards. This structure must have gone through several stages of

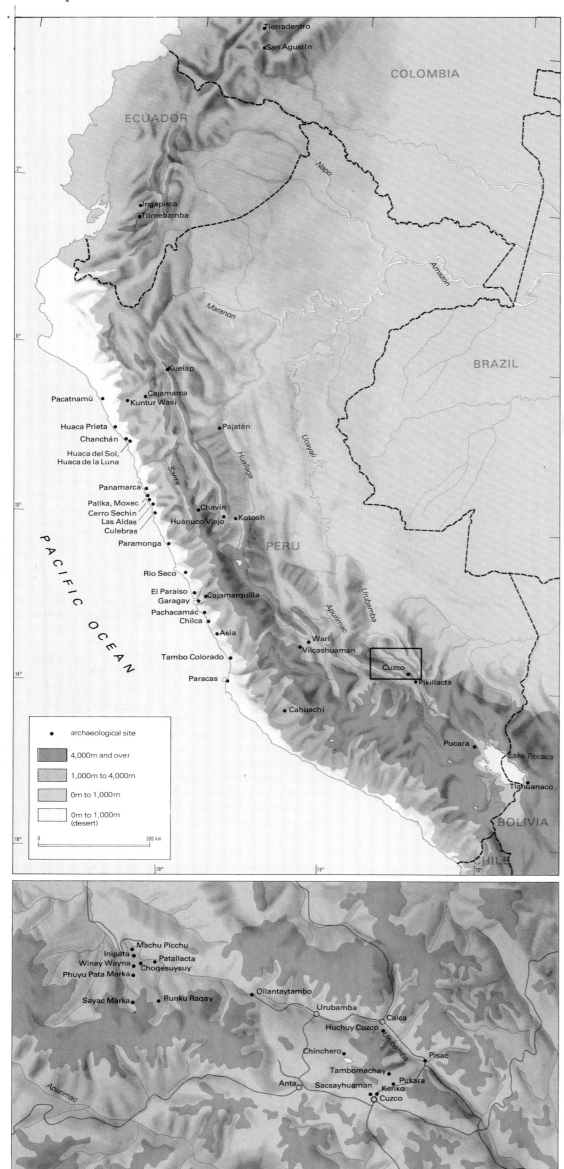

construction and it is only the last one that is represented by the restoration. The walls are double screens of flat stones filled in with earth and pebbles, and were originally covered with a layer of smoothed clay painted in white and red ochre. According to F. Engel, the structure had many functions and was lived in at the same time as being used as a place of worship; he suggests that the population of all eight platforms could have been as great as 1,500. The construction of a group such as this, which used around 100,000 tons of stone, would have required a much larger workforce than any that could have been found locally in an economy based on fishing and rudimentary agriculture.

It seems therefore that the Pacific coast was densely populated from the Pre-ceramic era. On the heights of the Andes, paradoxically, the known sites and architectural creations are still very few and far between, although agricultural development was certainly more advanced. A mound, 100 metres (330 feet) in diameter and 13 metres (43 feet) high, has recently been discovered at Kotosh. It is composed of ten separate structures, one on top of the other, of which the three lowest belong to the Pre-ceramic period. The best known of these three "temples" is the Temple of the Crossed Hands, a rectangular building with rubble-stone walls held together by a clay binding and covered by a smoothed clay facing. The interior walls are adorned with a series of niches, and the pairs of crossed human forearms carved in low relief beneath two of them, from which the temple takes its name, are the oldest known examples of Andean architectural decoration (about 1800BC).

It is not impossible that the earliest structures in the vast architectural group at Las Aldas, on the north coast, were built in the Pre-ceramic period, but it seems as though the majority of the buildings still visible date from no earlier than 1300–1200BC, towards the middle of the Initial period (the beginning of which coincides with the appearance of pottery). This site is the earliest example of the large ceremonial groups with stepped pyramids, courtyards and huge esplanades that were built along the coast right up until the Spanish conquest. Measuring about 700 by 200 metres (770 by 220 yards), the complex consists of a series of seven superposed platforms and of two large courtyards separated by an esplanade. A kind of half-buried circular well – whose purpose is still obscure – has been dug at the centre of the esplanade with two sets of steps leading into it. The walls that surround the buildings are made out of stone and a clay mortar mixed with sea water, which has given them exceptional strength. An ingenious method, characteristic of the period, was used for banking up the platforms: large nets, made of woven rushes, were filled with stones and then piled up behind the retaining walls. Another type of ceremonial building, which seems to be of a slightly later period, is in the shape of a U – with a pyramid-shaped central section and two lower lateral arms on either side of a rectangular court – and this also has a half-buried circular well.

The new styles of houses and the new architectural forms which appeared during the Early Horizon (beginning around 1000–900BC), were linked to the development of large politico-religious centres. The most famous – and certainly one of the most beautiful creations of

Sculpture, Chavín de Huantar. Sculpted head, fixed into the wall of the New Temple or Castillo at Chavín de Huantar (between 800 and 500BC).

ancient Peru – is Chavín de Huantar. This magnificent culmination of a long process of cultural evolution was probably built in stages, starting in 1000BC; and everything leads us to believe that, between 900 and 500BC, a religious system spread from this centre to influence a very large part of the Central Andes. The site covers about 12,000 sq. metres (14,000 sq. yards) and is composed of three major sections. The oldest part is the temple of El Lanzón. It was built in the shape of a U, opening towards the rising sun, and at its heart, at the crossing of two dark, narrow galleries, there stands a large slab of stone, about 4.5 metres (15 feet) high, engraved with a mythological figure, half human and half cat. A large truncated pyramid, known as the Castillo Pyramid, was built later on the south side. The central doorway, which is reached by a staircase, is flanked by two engraved and cylindrical columns, surmounted by a lintel engraved with jaguars and falcons. The whole building is profusely ornamented with cornices, engraved pillars and sculptures protruding from the walls. But quite apart from the magnificence of the engravings and the perfection of the external decor, the originality of Chavín lies in its extraordinary network of internal passages with communicating staircases and ventilation ducts.

The influence of Chavín can be seen along the coast, in the ceremonial centres of Pallka, Moxec and Sechín Alto among others. Their external facings are made of stone, combined with adobe, the traditional

material of the coastal regions, which is used here in the form of interlocking cones. These massive buildings, which are either stepped pyramids or adjoining towers and rise to a height of about 30 metres (100 feet), always have a central staircase leading to the upper platform, and they are decorated with sculpture in low relief and in the round, both forms typical of the Chavín style, only here they are modelled in clay.

Around 200BC, after the somewhat abrupt decline of the Chavín influence, there was a very marked period of development and regional diversification. During this time, owing to the apparent disappearance of all cultural and religious unity, the ceremonial centres and living areas were either abandoned or else reorganized, with the addition of new constructions which often used material from the earlier buildings. One of the characteristics of this Early Intermediate period seems to have been the construction of several towns, some of them fortified, and of a vast and complex irrigation system, built on the north coast of Peru to exploit as much fertile land as possible. Large buildings for cult worship were erected beside the living areas, as at Pañamarca and at Moche (the Pyramids of the Sun and Moon) – all vestiges of the Mochica civilization. The last of these monuments is an enormous stepped pyramid, resting on a rock base and made out of possibly more than 50 million parallelepiped adobes piled up in great columns. It was originally 50 metres (164 feet) tall and measured 228 by 136 metres (750 by 450 feet) at the base – and it is regarded as the largest dried brick monument in the world. Several similar but smaller buildings were erected during this period along the northern and central coasts of Peru (there are no less than 150 on the present site of Lima), suggesting not only a large population but also the existence of extremely powerful local military or theocratic authorities. Only the southern coast of Peru appears to have stayed apart from this rapid architectural development. It was probably around this time, in the highlands of the Andes, that building began on the cities of Wari and Tiahuanaco, and in particular – at Tiahuanaco – on the Kalasasaya and the large truncated pyramid of Akapana. The wall facings at Tiahuanaco make use of an ingenious technique in which carved and usually very large blocks are held together by copper crampons, made in the shape of a double T.

These two urban centres were at their peak during the Middle Horizon (8th–11th century), when each was the capital of an empire. Wari was a huge fortified city, composed of separate rectangular sectors, each surrounded by walls between 6 and 12 metres (20 and 40 feet) high and containing a series of squares, platforms and esplanades. The walls are made out of a double facing of small irregular stones, grouted with clay and filled in with pebbles and earth; they have no decoration other than a few internal niches. But the impressive beauty of the place is due to its geometric perfection and to the vast extent of its layout – foreshadowing the large coastal cities of the Late Intermediate period, of which Chanchán is the best example.

The urbanization of the Peruvian coast was completed during the 11th century. The city was used at that time to concentrate the population, as well as to play its usual role as a political, economic and social centre. Social or hierarchical organization is indicated by the existence of different sectors, each varying in size and in the sophistication of its architecture. The metropolis of Chanchán, capital of the Chimu empire, which is completely built of adobe, is certainly the largest planned city to be found in pre-Hispanic Peru, although many smaller but similar towns were built along the coastline during this period. It covers an area of about 20 sq. kilometres (8 sq. miles), and it has been calculated that the city could have housed a population of nearly 40,000. Chanchán reached its height when it was occupied by the Incas, who came from the southern Andes to conquer the coast. They apparently took it without a fight, but its dependence on irrigation would have put it at the mercy of anyone who could seize hold of the canals and springs.

From the beginning of the 15th century the Incas gradually spread their influence throughout those countries which are now called Peru, Ecuador and Bolivia, even reaching Colombia in the north and central Chile in the south. In all these areas, but particularly in the high Andes, they imposed architectural techniques and models which were to earn them the somewhat exaggerated reputation of being the greatest and even the only builders of South America.

Reconstruction of the temple of Cerro Sechín. Dating from the "formative" period, this building is notable for its surrounding wall, incorporating monoliths of engraved granite. The building itself is made of adobe. (After G. Willey, 1971.)

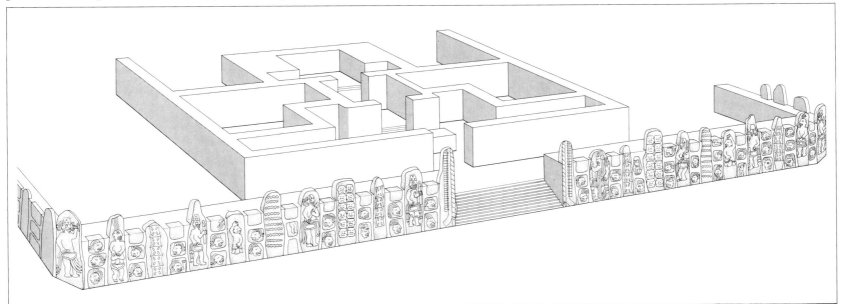

Domestic settlements and public architecture in Mesoamerica

The history of architecture has traditionally favoured monumental buildings. But from an anthropological point of view, domestic and public buildings cannot be dissociated, even if in the pre-industrial societies it was only the buildings of the greatest scope that received the attentions of really specialized architects.

The story of building in Mesoamerica begins with the appearance of houses made out of perishable materials, at least as early as the end of the Preceramic era and the beginning of the Initial period (3500–2500BC). In the subsequent great eras of architectural development (from the time of Christ to the Spanish conquest) groups of domestic buildings formed the context in which prestigious buildings were erected, not only on urban sites such as Teotihuacán – which, between AD400 and 600, had 150,000 inhabitants living in an area of 20 sq. kilometres (8 sq. miles) – but also in places where the dwellings were more dispersed. Throughout this period, from one end of Mesoamerica to another, the simplest houses were very similar, both in form and in the way they were built: they generally had some kind of cellar and were rectangular, single-storey structures, with walls and roofs made out of light materials (wood, cob and thatch). There were, nevertheless, certain differences, depending on the period, the region and above all, the social hierarchy and administrative organization of the site. For example, a number of historical developments and certain variations due to the status of the occupants have been brought to light in a paper by M. Winter on the residential groups at Monte Albán. From 500BC to AD600 the open, unstructured type of habitation gave way to the enclosed residential unit, in which the house and its dependent buildings were grouped around an internal courtyard or patio; at the same time there was a marked tendency towards standardization. Contrasts based on wealth or social position were apparent from the very beginning, but they reached their height shortly before this regional capital was abandoned and are particularly noticeable in the size of the patios: housing complexes at the lower end of the social scale surround courtyards of about 13 sq. metres (15 sq. yards), whereas the more important complexes have courtyards of more than 100 sq. metres (120 sq. yards).

Naturally, major differences are most obvious in the principal buildings. The cultural unity of Mesoamerica explains the regional and temporal recurrence of several categories of monumental structures – temples on top of pyramids, buildings developed on one or more horizontal plains, which are too often carelessly referred to as "palaces", ball-game courts, altars, esplanades and, later on, pillared halls, platforms bearing the skulls of sacrificial victims (*tzompantli*) and ceremonial enclosures or "snake walls" (*coatepantli*). There was even marked continuity in decorative styles; the fret theme, for example, was used copiously in the Oaxaca region, on the shores of the Gulf and in Yucatán. But beyond these formal affinities, which are basically functional and stylistic, there was considerable variety of architectural expression; this is immediately apparent in the treatment of individual forms and in the general organization of the whole. It is therefore easy to identify some of the great traditions, such as that of the Mayan region from AD300 to 900, but it is perhaps of greater interest to discuss here the local styles and their more limited spheres of influence. In the case of the central Mayan region, it is possible at first sight to identify the common characteristics of Tikal, Yaxchilán, Copán and Palenque, to name but four of the main capitals of Baktun 9 (435–829); it is enough to compare one single category of monuments, for example the temples. Even in the expression of certain pan-Mesoamerican ideas, such as the concepts of time and space, it is interesting to note how each city exercised its own choice. The main pyramid at El Tajín (Veracruz), which has 365 niches, is the only one to glorify the solar year. The Castillo at Chichén Itzá, with its four staircases and panelled decor, has been endowed in a less original way with rich spatio-temporal symbolism. And Tikal, which invented twin groupings to celebrate the end of each 20 year cycle, includes in a novel architectural composition the essentials of a vision of time and horizontal and vertical space. In fact, the monumental architecture of Mesoamerica clearly reflects the various elements that over the centuries have contributed to the cultural identity of the region. Beyond the differences caused by ethnic diversity, variety of terrain, socio-political changes and unequal rates of development, building styles were everywhere shaped by the wishes and ambitions of the elite; temples were conceived to glorify their builders as much as they were to honour the gods. The Aztec emperors loved to have their names associated with some prestigious new creation, and it is therefore not difficult to imagine that the architects of Mesoamerica held key positions in the society of their time and enjoyed the favour of their leaders – unless the leaders were themselves the architects, like Nezahualcoyotl, the great Texcoco prince, who was also an engineer and poet.

Pyramidal tower south of the main building, Xpujil

This kind of construction, known only in the Río Bec region, is a mock pyramid surmounted by a pseudo-temple. Generally, but not at Xpujil, the pyramidal towers are built in twos and flank the façade of a long low structure.

Palace interior, Palenque

This vast building, occupying an area of nearly 2 hectares (5 acres) in the centre of the site, has a complex layout. Its function is not entirely clear.

Ball-game court, Copán

The two long parallel structures, running north to south, outline the area of the game; here, there are markers both in the alley and at the top of the sloping benches (sculpted macaw heads). The complex that can be seen today covers two earlier successive courts. Structure 4, in the background, was uncovered and restored in 1978–79.

Main pyramid, Tenochtitlán

Surmounted by two temples, this building occupied a major position in the ceremonial enclosure of the Aztec capital. Its complete uncovering, undertaken in 1978, revealed a complex architectural history, albeit short (less than a century). About 60 offerings have been uncovered. Their placing often dates back to a time when an alteration to the structure was made.

Temple of Huitzilopochtli, patron of the Aztec tribe and sun god. The Huitzilopochtli cult was, together with the tribute system, one of the elements imposed by the Aztecs on conquered territories.

Temple of Tlaloc, god of rain and thunder, honoured for centuries on the high central plateau of Mexico. Its positioning next to the temple of Huitzilopochtli illustrates the religious syncretism of the Aztecs.

The practice of superposition (there are five main layers here) helped to preserve the two temples built during the first stages of construction.

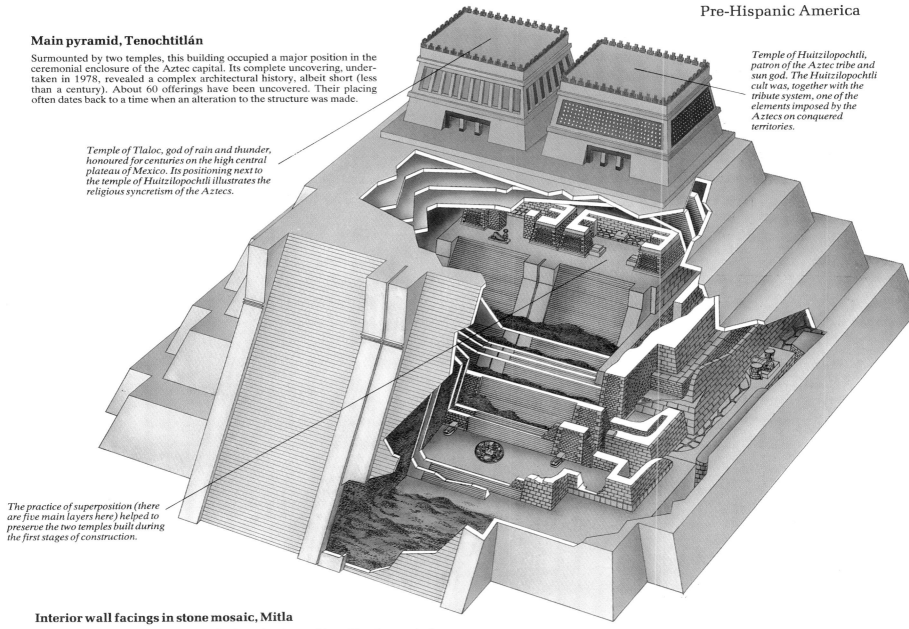

Interior wall facings in stone mosaic, Mitla

The stone mosaics spread out in three horizontal registers of frets. They form part of a structure that was probably residential. It appears to have been built at quite a late date (14th century at the earliest) and is thought to be representative of Mixtec architecture.

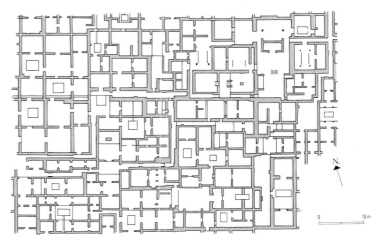

Pyramid of the Niches, El Tajín

In its final state, this square-based pyramid (35 metres/115 feet along each side) is made up of seven graded levels. The 365 niches that decorate the sides have a symbolic and decorative value. This monument, along with most of the public edifices in Mesoamerica, was originally painted in bright colours.

Plan of a residential complex, Teotihuacán

This is a very densely populated working-class zone in the Tlamimilolpa quarter. The residential centres in Teotihuacán are enclosed by walls of mainly similar dimensions and all face in the same direction. Inside, there are varying numbers of rooms, corridors and patios. (After S. Linné, 1942.)

Peruvian temples, cities and fortresses

If our introduction has devoted a large amount of space to the oldest of the Peruvian structures, those built before the Incas, it is because the Incas are usually regarded too highly and considered as the master builders of the pre-Hispanic Andean world. In fact they were not innovators, either in the domain of town planning, or (with one notable exception) in the field of construction engineering – the first irrigation systems, many of the roads and a number of terraced structures preceded them.

As far as town planning is concerned, it really appeared during the Middle Horizon. Until then agglomerations grew up around one of the ceremonial centres. And if the monuments already described – Chavín and the Mochica pyramids – seem isolated today, it is because the random groups of houses around them were built of perishable materials. The first large cities were built during the Middle Horizon on ground that was already occupied, but this time they followed a structured plan. Not only Wari and Tiahuanaco, but also Pikillacta and Cajamarquilla, the one built in stone and the other in adobe, prove the existence of a strong central power and an administrative organization which was in many ways similar to that of the Incas.

The urban centres of the Middle Horizon and then of the Late Intermediate period, of which Chanchán represents the ultimate and grandest achievement, are both residential areas and storage centres, where temples, if they are not outside the walls, occupy a secondary place – the Huaca del Dragón at Chanchán lies beyond the city perimeter. Many of these large cities were abandoned when their political power declined (Wari appears to have been deserted around AD1000–1100), and when the Incas arrived they found only ruins.

Unlike their predecessors, the Incas built religious and administrative centres, fortresses and garrisons. But, although they were evidently trying to regroup the population to make it easier to control it, they reduced the scale of residential centres, and rural living predominated. The largest Inca cities – Huánuco Viejo and Vilcashuamán – were never as big as Wari or Chanchán. When the Inca,

Pachakutec, rebuilt his capital at Cuzco between 1438 and 1471, he did so in accordance with a pre-established geometric plan (in the form of a clay model) and conceived it as a place for gods, nobles and priests – a majestic complex of palaces and temples from which the ordinary people were excluded.

What skills, therefore, did the Incas master? Only one: they were undoubtedly master stonemasons (although in some ways a structure like Chavín de Huantar can stand up well to comparison). A great deal of nonsense has been written about their gigantic constructions, suggesting that they required some sort of "cutting compound" or even a "mixture to soften stones". Admittedly some blocks weighing more than 100 tons were occasionally moved and put into place, but none of the structures, enormous as they seem, exceeded the physical or technical capabilities of the period.

In the region of Cuzco, the area where the greatest amount of building took place, the stones were taken from quarries which lay around the town within a radius of 35 kilometres (22 miles). They were initially broken off, using the natural cracks in the rocks, with the help of chisels and hammers (made of bronze and haematite). These tools were then used to make a row of holes, and the holes were filled with wedges of wood which, when they had been soaked and began to swell, made the rock crack along a predetermined line. Once they had been extracted and roughly cut to size, the blocks were transported on wooden logs, pulled along by ropes made of creepers and bark. Sometimes, if one of the blocks was too big, it would simply be abandoned on the way, giving rise to the legend of the "tired stones". (In the 16th century, the historian Garcilaso de La Vega described a block pulled by 20,000 men which killed 3,000 of them when it slipped.) When they arrived at the foot of the work, the blocks would be raised into position with the help of earth ramps and a rudimentary lifting system (like hoists). In the case of the so-called cyclopean structures, the same apparatus was used to adjust a polygonal block on top of the one that had

been laid before it (by putting wet sand between them and then swinging the top block backwards and forwards). Schemes such as these would naturally have required a very large labour force indeed, but this was no problem for the Inca rulers because of the system known as *mit'a* (the obligatory provision of manual labour).

This was how the dry-stone walls were made, and their perfect construction deserves admiration. But not all Inca buildings were so well-made: the regular or polygonal dry-stone method was reserved for temples, palaces and fortresses. In smaller towns and for less important monuments, rubble-stone and mortar were used, as in the past. The Incas built great administrative centres on the coast, where stone was replaced by the traditional coastal material – adobe. The best preserved example of this is Tambo Colorado. The characteristic trapezoidal shape of the doorways and niches definitely dates this building to the Inca era, and the parallelepiped adobes, joined together as they were in previous epochs, are here made in moulds, another example of the standardization of shapes and techniques that was so dear to the Incas.

Paradoxically, these elaborately constructed walls were merely covered with straw, resting on a rough wooden framework (although the false corbelled vault had been used in previous centuries for the burial places of the coastal and Andean populations). Inca buildings of more than two storeys are extremely rare (while some sites in the Andes north of Peru, dating from the Late Intermediate period, have buildings of five storeys or more).

The greatness of Inca architecture lies above all in its solidity and sense of balance – there are no embellishments. The rhythm is created simply by the calculated alternation of trapezoidal doors and niches. Thanks to their admirable and unique administration, the Incas were also the only people in pre-Hispanic America to impose uniform models across an area of 950,000 sq. kilometres/350,000 sq. miles (the citadels of Tomebamba and Ingapirca, at the extremes of the empire, were built only a few years before the Spanish conquest).

Detail of a door, Sacsayhuamán

A series of trapezoidal monumental doors gave access to three superposed levels of the fortress. In cases of danger, they were closed with the help of wooden panels secured by crossed posts. This is one of the most perfect examples of "cyclopean" dry-stone jointing, characteristic of Inca military constructions.

Wall bonding used in pre-Hispanic Peru

Various bonding techniques were employed from the Pre-ceramic age to the Inca period. During the Early Horizon, clay adobes moulded into cone shapes were used: Sechín Alto (1). Later, the adobes were parallelepipeds and the walls, coated with smoothed clay, sometimes carried moulded reliefs: Chanchán (2). The use of stone is also very old and some of the edifices from the Ancient Horizon consist of facings of irregular sized rubble: Sechín Alto (3). Even bonding of cut stone can be seen at Chavín de Huantar (4). Finally, Inca masonry is characterized by its dry-stone bonding, both regular: Pisac (5); and polygonal: Cuzco, stone of 12 angles (6).

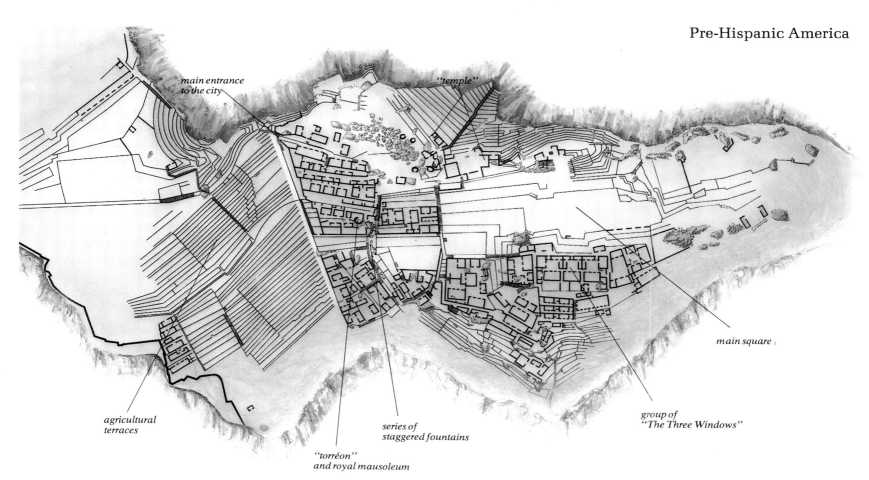

main entrance
to the city

"temple"

main square

agricultural
terraces

series of
staggered fountains

group of
"The Three Windows"

"torréon"
and royal mausoleum

General view and plan of Machu-Picchu

Built at an altitude of 2,450 metres (8,000 feet) on a ridge dominating the Urubamba, Machu-Picchu forms part of the network of cities built by the Incas towards the end of the 15th century on the road to the Amazon forest. Each section of the town can be clearly identified: to the south is a zone of terraces which played both an agricultural and defensive role; to the north, a dense residential area. This half is in turn divided into two sectors of differing architectural styles. The west sector has a concentration of beautifully built cutstone constructions (in the style of "imperial Cuzco"), which led H. Bingham who discovered the town to describe this part as the "noble quarter", whereas the east sector consists of layers of buildings made of granite rubble and clay mortar. A peculiarity of this sector is that it has an irrigation network consisting of a series of canals and staggered fountains dug into the granite. (After H. Bingham, 1912.)

Plan and view of the Tschudi quarter, Chanchán

The metropolis of Chanchán, capital of the Chimu kingdom on the north coast of Peru, was divided into a dozen rectangular "quarters", measuring as much as 500 by 300 metres (550 by 330 yards) and encircled by an enormous wall (from 7 to 9 metres/23 to 30 feet high and more than 4 metres/13 feet thick at the base), built of huge blocks of *tapia* (a mixture of clay and gravel). Within each of these enclosures were dwellings separated by roads and courtyards, stores, irrigated gardens, huge reservoir tanks and cemeteries, as well as a large square which must have been used as a meeting place. The exact purpose of these enclosures is not known: the residences of family clans? of specialized artisan groups? of a certain social category? In the "rich" quarters, of which the Tschudi group is the best preserved, the adobe walls were coated with a layer of smoothed clay and decorated with friezes in relief made by moulding of the thick layer of clay while still wet.

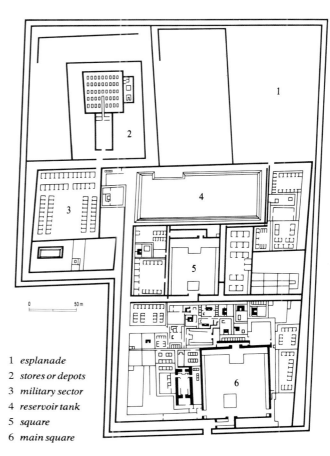

1 esplanade
2 stores or depots
3 military sector
4 reservoir tank
5 square
6 main square

93

J. Garanger

Melanese grave

Long before the era of large architectural constructions, the people of the Pacific islands erected the most basic monuments possible – prism-shaped slabs of basalt planted vertically in the ground to mark an event, the site of a ritual or a grave. This tradition continued for a long time in Melanesia and here, in Vanuatu (formerly the New Hebrides), it has been applied to the grave of an important chief. He was buried with his three companions and the dignitary of the clan (on his right), who had the task of keeping him in peace on earth and in the beyond. These stones established a link between the dwelling places of the dead and of the living and allowed them to communicate with each other. Later, they can be seen in the great Polynesian monuments, such as the *marae*. Three stones were erected next to the *ahu*, the central one being higher than the other two (an ancestral symbol). The ancestors were supposed to sit there during ceremonies.

There was nothing that could be described as architecture among the aborigines of Australia: their huts were no more than crude, temporary shelters, enough to protect them from the elements, and their ceremonial sites were in caves, under overhanging rocks or in open spaces that had simply been cleared and levelled. And in the distant days of its pre-history, the architecture of New Guinea was no more elaborate. But for several thousand years New Guinea was influenced by the Austronesian peoples who came from Asia and gradually colonized the islands of the Pacific. These peoples had not discovered the wheel, and they did not know how to extract metal from ore, but they could build monuments, sometimes so well that they astonished the first Europeans to see them.

Since the days of Admiral Dumont d' Urville, the islands of the Pacific have been divided into three groups – Melanesia, Micronesia and Polynesia. The famous French navigator based his divisions on general anthropological and cultural observations, but the ethnic boundaries defined in this way are less clearly marked in reality. The older the population of an island, the more complex the situation becomes; as is the case with the western Pacific, which was colonized at least 4,000 years ago. Eastern Polynesia, which was only reached during the first centuries AD, is more homogeneous, but, even here, different aspects of the ancestral culture have evolved in each region in relative isolation. We know almost nothing about the ancient architecture of the Pacific. Nevertheless, there are certain types of building which are so widespread that we can assume they are very old. These are, for the most part, dwellings, and buildings which have been styled incorrectly as "megalithic". It is also a little artificial to speak of architecture here without considering the countryside with which it is integrated and which its builders have altered. The New Caledonian village, for example, is not just a simple juxtaposing of huts. The huts are well ordered, like the society, and they are arranged along parallel, well-kept avenues. Trees have been planted, and their types and positions have been chosen in accordance with certain rules. And the architecture of the countryside is by no means limited to residential sites: there are few mountainous islands in Melanesia or Polynesia where the slopes have not been sculpted into stepped agricultural terraces, painstakingly supported by walls.

Apart from the eventual use of paving stones, mounds and foundation platforms, the houses of the Pacific islands were all built out of living materials, particularly wood. The method was simple: the pieces were merely strapped together. It was only in New Zealand that they were ever mortised, and then only in the most basic fashion. The ground plan of the houses varies, however; it may be circular, rectangular, oval, or simply with two short rounded sides. This plan determines the shape of the roof – conical, or with two main slopes. In Melanesia the most important huts, those of the village chiefs, are carefully decorated, with sculpted door frames and arrowed roof ridges. In northern Melanesia they are sometimes crowned with a pottery ornament, and the tapa (bark strips), which act as partitions in the gables of the large meeting huts, are decorated with multicoloured paintings. The large ceremonial houses of New Zealand are also remarkably decorated. Anthropomorphic sculptures, delicately embossed or in low relief, crowd the supporting pillars and the wooden framework. The house represents the body of the first ancestor: the two upper boards of the gable are his outstretched arms, and his head is sculpted at the intersection; the rafters are his ribs and the ridge pole is his backbone. In many places in the Pacific the huts are built on a mound or on a stone platform, and in the high islands of eastern Polynesia they usually have a paved veranda at the front. The lack of wood on Easter Island has led to a special architectural technique – the superstructure of the hut, made out of light material, is laid on a border of squared-off stones set out in an elongated oval. Other houses are simply built out of dry stone with a corbelled roof – a style unusual in the Pacific.

The most common and basic lithic (or stone-built) architecture consists of no more than stones planted in the ground. They can be seen everywhere in Melanesia, except on the high ground in New Guinea and in Australia. Isolated or grouped in threes, they mark the burial grounds, commemorate events, or are connected with some special rite. They can also be found in Polynesia, either isolated or adjoining pavements, or in the large religious buildings, such as the marae of central Polynesia. In Melanesia these standing stones are sometimes combined to form the rows and circles and quadrangles which outline ceremonial or funerary sites. More elaborate lithic monuments are rare, except on the islands of Fiji, where the prehistoric culture was Polynesian, and where the western Polynesian influence continued even after they were colonized by Melanesians around AD600. In the interior of the largest of these islands there are vast spaces surrounded by dry stone walls, which are sometimes divided by other walls internally. These enclosures, the nanga, and their immediate surroundings were consecrated to the dead and were reserved for initiation and propitiatory rites. The stone structures of the Fijian islands lead us on to examine the principal religious and secular buildings of Micronesia and Polynesia. These are very varied, but they have one common characteristic – they are all open to the sky. The only exceptions are, naturally, the huts (which, nevertheless, have some similarities) and the latte, a kind of monument peculiar to the Marianas Islands.

Western Micronesia – the Marianas Islands, Yap, Palau and the west of the Caroline Islands – forms a region which is culturally distinct from the rest of Micronesia. The latte of the Marianas Islands are coral or basalt pillars, some of them as tall as 5 metres (15 feet) high, surmounted by hemispheric capitals and laid out regularly in eights or tens along two parallel rows. The groups are either isolated or lie together near the beaches. Their purpose might still be uncertain today if the first Spanish navigators to see them had not recorded that they were no more than the supports for huge huts. Although the oldest of these latte date from the 9th century AD, this type of structure continued to be used until the 17th century. Central and eastern Micronesia have a more recent population and are culturally closer to Polynesia. Since the archipelagoes consist almost entirely of atolls and consequently have no stone for building, the only available material is coral. Nevertheless, there are some high islands, such as Kusaie and Ponape, which are rich in architectural remains. Kusaie is famous for its rectangular walled enclosures. This kind of construction is common enough throughout Micronesia, the Fiji Islands and Polynesia, but the walls here are unique for their thickness and height: some of them rise more than 10 metres (30 feet). In the interior of the little island of Ponape, which is uninhabited today, there are a great many structures which are also common in Polynesia – platforms for huts in stone or coral, tombs and burial grounds, cultivated terraces held up by walls, irrigation systems, wells built for storing food. But Ponape owes its fame to a site on the south-east coast – Nan Madol, where the architecture has given rise to almost as many wild theories as there are about the monuments on Easter Island. Nan Madol is a small city, entirely built on a lagoon and made up of 92 quadrangular platforms, which are surrounded by water at high tide. It has been described as the Venice of the Pacific. The platforms used to carry dwelling huts and ceremonial or funerary buildings, and they are surrounded by a long wall which holds in the coral block that supports them. Their

PACIFIC OCEAN

walls are striking and very beautiful: most of them are made out of courses of prism-shaped blocks of basalt, laid alternatately in stretchers and headers. The southern part of the city, Madol Pah, was reserved for religious buildings and the houses of the aristocracy. The most important of these is Pahn Kedira. Trapezoidal in shape, it is surmounted by a wall, 5 metres (15 feet) high, which encloses a three-tiered platform; and on the upper tier there is a huge hut, which was probably reserved for ancestral divinities and their worship. This enclosure was also the home of the "king" and his entourage, who even had a swimming pool, which was dug down to the

level of the lagoon. Apart from several other residential platforms, this southern sector contains a garden, where edible plants were grown as offerings, and a pond for rearing the sacred creatures, eels. The northern part of the city, Madol Powe, was reserved for funerary buildings and the houses of priests. The most important terrace here is Nan Douwas, which bore the royal tombs. The entire area is protected against the ocean by an independent wall which is tens of metres (up to 100 feet) thick. The top of the platform is surrounded by another, higher wall, and the walls inside this vast enclosure, which outline the positions of the tombs, are also made out of prism-

shaped basalt. The city was only built a few centuries ago, but it was gradually abandoned during the first years of Spanish colonization, due to the drop in population and the breach with the old society and traditions which followed soon after the European settlement.

The only clues that we have to the earliest history of Polynesia are a few household utensils, such as pottery in the Lapita tradition and tools made out of shell or stone. Apart from these, we know very little about it, other than that it dates back to around 1600BC. The oldest architectural structures which have been seen and

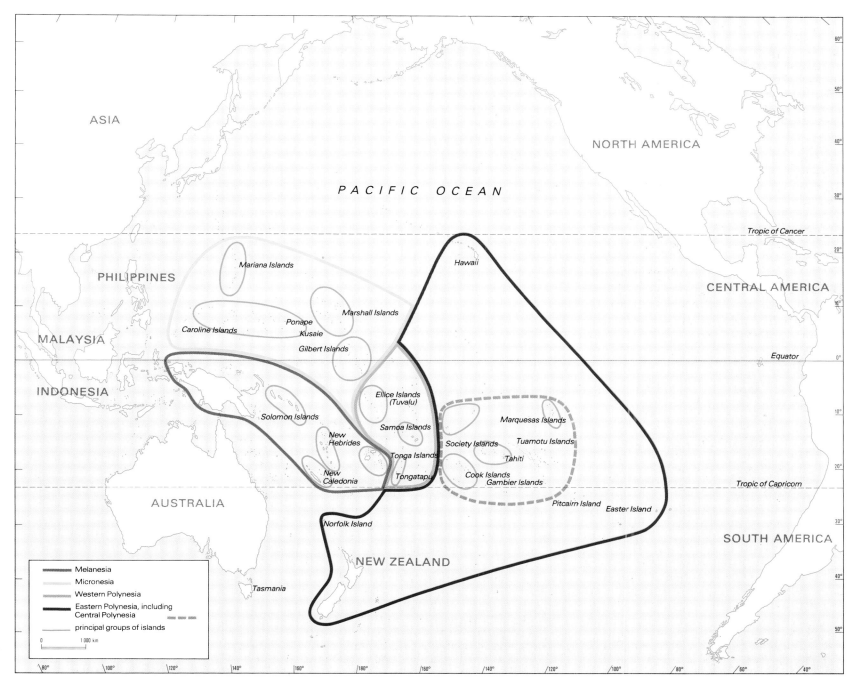

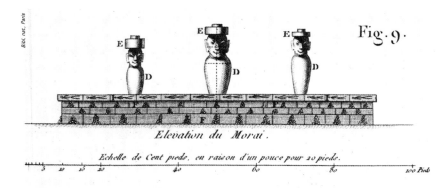

Elevation du Moraï.

Echelle de Cent pieds, en raison d'un pouce pour 20 pieds.

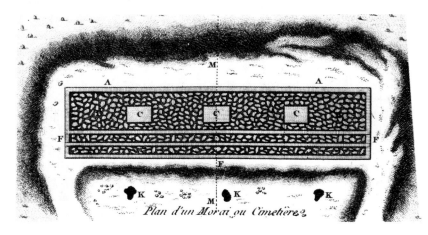

Plan d'un Moraï ou Cimetière.

Plan and elevation of a "marae"

Illustration taken from the *Atlas du Voyage autour du Monde* by J.F. de La Pérouse, Paris, 1797 (Bibliothèque Nationale, Paris). La Pérouse visited Easter Island in 1786 and made an important record of its architecture. The drawing facing represents an *ahu* where three giant statues, *moai*, have been erected.

examined, however, were built no more than a thousand years ago. The most remarkable of these are the huge mounds on which stood the huts for assembly and worship. Some of the mounds on the islands of Samoa are star shaped, and there is one on the north of Savai'i which is made out of blocks of rock and is roughly rectangular, with a flat top and paved ramps at either end. There are also quite a number of these mounds on the islands of Tonga, but here they were used generally as collective tombs. The graves are arranged on several levels, and the dimensions of the mounds are in direct proportion to the number of bodies that they eventually contained, which could sometimes be as many as a hundred. The tombs of the chiefs are on Tongatabu, the main island of the archipelago and the capital of the empire of the Tui Tonga. These men were buried, not in mounds, but in rectangular, stepped monuments, known as langi, which were made of huge blocks of calcareous coral, carefully shaped and fitted together. They had anything from two to five levels and were surmounted by ceremonial huts. According to tradition the most beautiful of them, the Paepae-o-Telea, was built during the 16th century. Tongatabu also contains the famous Ha'amonga-a-Maui. It is a trilith (two standing stones supporting a third, horizontally placed stone), and the story goes that it was erected by the eleventh Tui Tonga around the year 1200. The two calcareous coral pillars are said to represent his two sons. They are planted deep into the earth and weigh between 40 and 50 tons and the lintel that joins them at the top is carved out of the same material and fits into each pillar by means of a basic mortise, more than 4 metres (13 feet) above the ground.

So far as we know, the first islands to be settled in eastern Polynesia were the Marquesas, which were colonized by Samoans or Tongans around AD30. The population spread out rapidly to the other archipelagoes of central Polynesia and then on to the three points of the Polynesian triangle – Hawaii and Easter Island first, and New Zealand in the 8th or 9th century.

The archaeological remains which can be found almost everywhere are the same as those common in the western Pacific. But although some of the more recent stone structures (generally those built after AD1000) are clearly derived from these earlier buildings, they are, nevertheless, peculiar to their own area of eastern Polynesia – the monuments of the Marquesas, the marae of the Society Islands and their neighbouring archipelagoes, the heiau of the Hawaii Islands, and the ahu and moai of Easter Island. It was probably during the 13th or 14th century that the stone structures of the Marquesas Islands – the bases of the huts and the huge ceremonial centres – first took on their gigantic proportions. Some of the platforms, which were known as paepae, carried a hut with a paved veranda and a room carpeted in gravel. They could be 30 metres (100 feet) long, and their façades were made out of stone blocks, which were usually extremely large. The other important structures were the me'ae, the tall-roofed religious and funerary buildings, and these were sometimes integrated with the impressive ceremonial centres that were the forerunners of the tohua. The centres were originally no more than rectangular areas reserved for communal or socio-religious activities, but the monumental tohua is an immense rectangular earthwork, reminiscent of the mounds and meeting places of the western Pacific. The most elaborate are supported by high walls made out of enormous stone blocks, which are more or less squared off and are sometimes decorated with carvings. Some of them are 200 metres (650 feet) long and 30 metres (100 feet) wide, and it took tons of soil and stones to fill them. The arena in the middle was used for dancing and other ceremonies, and it was bordered by terraces where the different social groupings were seated in accordance with their rank. The terraces also carried stone platforms; the huts which were built on top of these were the homes of the civil and religious leaders, the temples of the ancestral deities (which were always placed at the end of the arena), and the store-houses for the sacred objects. There were also centres for dancing and

assemblies on the other archipelagoes of central Polynesia, but there were special kinds of centres, known as marae, which became increasingly important after the 14th century. At one end of a marae there was a stone platform or courtyard, the ahu, which was a temporary resting place for the gods and the spirits of ancestors. The ahu and its functions were derived from much older marae and from similar buildings which were sometimes known by other names in various parts of Polynesia, but the difference was that, as a meeting place, it was reserved exclusively for the priests and dignitaries of the clan that owned the marae: to the rest of the community it was taboo. The architecture and dimensions of these monuments evolved over the years: the society was competitive, and the building or enlarging of a marae was an excellent way for a dignitary to improve his prestige. It was probably this that provoked Princess Purea to build one of these monuments for her son in the district of Papara in 1767, which was to be the largest ever known in Tahiti – the Mahaiatea Marae. The quadrangular ahu, which covered an area of nearly 2,000 sq. metres (20,000 sq. feet), was shaped like a pyramid with 11 steps and rose to a height of more than 15 metres (50 feet) with a vast courtyard in front of it. This ostentatious marae was never consecrated – Purea was defeated by an alliance of island chiefs – and all that remains today are a few ruins.

Another very large marae, which is older and very famous in ancient central Polynesia, is that of Taputapuatea at Raiatea. The architecture of this one follows the style of those found on the Leeward Islands. The biggest ahu in the ceremonial group is based on the shape of a regular hexagon, measuring about 50 by 10 metres (160 by 30 feet). Its area is defined by a line of tall calcareous coral slabs planted in the ground, which average 2 metres (6 feet) in width and rise at least 3 metres (10 feet) above the ground. Marae are also numerous on the archipelagoes near to the Society Islands – the Tuamotu, Cook and Austral Islands. Their architecture varies in detail, but they all have an ahu with a courtyard and erected stones in front of it. The one with the most original design is the one on Tongareva, to the north of the Cook Islands, which is built in the shape of a man stretched out on the ground.

Many of the small islands beyond central Polynesia were uninhabited when the Europeans discovered them, but they preserve the ruins of comparatively modest monuments which testify to their earlier occupation. It may be that they were inhabited only sporadically during the great voyages between the islands, or that their populations dwindled slowly because there was not enough food. We do know at least that the islands of Necker and Nihoa, in the west of the Hawaiian archipelago, which have neither trees nor water, were abandoned for good around AD1500. They are particularly rich in architectural remains and some of their buildings are reminiscent of the marae of central Polynesia. This is also the case with some of the heiau on the larger islands of the archipelago, although they have other buildings as well which more closely resemble the Marquesian tohua. The large heiau were ceremonial centres, and their architectural complexity reflects the rites for which they were built. They are made up of several rectangular courtyards surrounded by walls and juxtaposed by sacrificial platforms, wooden statues, and

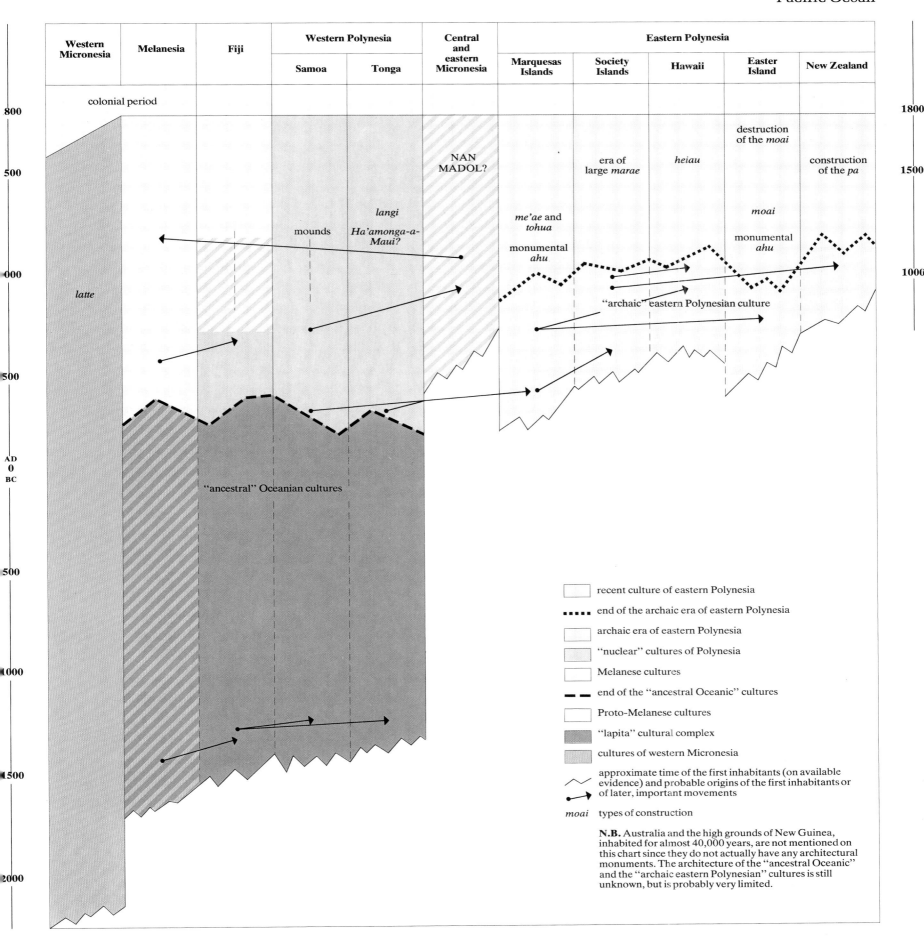

Western Micronesia	Melanesia	Fiji	Western Polynesia		Central and eastern Micronesia	Eastern Polynesia				
			Samoa	Tonga		Marquesas Islands	Society Islands	Hawaii	Easter Island	New Zealand

colonial period

NAN MADOL?

destruction of the *moai*

era of large *marae*

heiau

construction of the *pa*

langi

mounds

Ha'amonga-a-Maui?

me'ae and *tohua*

monumental *ahu*

moai

monumental *ahu*

latte

"archaic" eastern Polynesian culture

"ancestral" Oceanian cultures

800
500
000
500
AD 0 BC
500
000
500
000

1800
1500
1006

☐ recent culture of eastern Polynesia

▪▪▪▪ end of the archaic era of eastern Polynesia

▨ archaic era of eastern Polynesia

▨ "nuclear" cultures of Polynesia

☐ Melanese cultures

▬ ▬ end of the "ancestral Oceanic" cultures

☐ Proto-Melanese cultures

▨ "lapita" cultural complex

▨ cultures of western Micronesia

〰 approximate time of the first inhabitants (on available evidence) and probable origins of the first inhabitants or of later, important movements

→

moai types of construction

N.B. Australia and the high grounds of New Guinea, inhabited for almost 40,000 years, are not mentioned on this chart since they do not actually have any architectural monuments. The architecture of the "ancestral Oceanic" and the "archaic eastern Polynesian" cultures is still unknown, but is probably very limited.

sometimes by "oracle towers". These towers were tall, slim buildings made out of branches covered with tapa. It was inside these towers that the priests used to talk to their gods; and it was within the heiau that they buried their chiefs and the victims of their human sacrifices. The great monuments of Easter Island, the ahu and moai, are universally famous, and we shall examine them on the following pages. But there are much smaller structures on this little island as well, and since it has no large trees on it, they are all built out of stone, like the tupa. These were a type of tower with a vaulted chamber inside – and we still do not know exactly what they were used for. The Maoris of New Zealand, on the other hand,

rarely built anything out of stone. It is true that their ancestors had left central Polynesia before any of its large stone structures had been built, but in a far less humid climate they no longer needed to have paving and stone platforms to separate their houses from the ground, and besides, the New Zealand forests were inexhaustible and the Maoris were master-craftsmen with wood. They did, however, build huge defensive structures, known as pa, to protect themselves against invaders. Defence systems are known all over the Pacific – palissades, walls, fortified mounds, embankments and strongholds built into the crests of mountains like those on the Marquesas Islands and at Rapa. But

the New Zealand pa were particularly numerous: about 6,000 of them have been counted. And they were big: some of them covered as much as 50 hectares (120 acres). Their plans varied in order to make use of the natural features of their sites, but they always had several lines of defence, consisting alternately of ditches and embankments with palissades built on top of them, and there were tall platforms above the palissades, from which projectiles could be hurled at the enemy. Even at the end of the 19th century, when the traditional Pacific architecture was giving way to European styles, these formidable forts were able to hold out for a long time against British and colonial troops.

Easter Island

Easter Island is the most easterly of the Polynesian islands. This tiny island measuring only 117 sq. kilometres (45 sq. miles) and lying some 3,700 kilometres (2,300 miles) west of Chile is famous throughout the world for its strange monuments. The first Europeans to see them were astonished. Some of them could not believe that they had been made by the original inhabitants. Others, including Jacob Roggeveen, who discovered the island on Easter Day in 1722, were convinced that the giant statues, the *moai*, could not have been sculpted out of stone, since the islanders had no metal tools. They suggested instead that they had been modelled in clay and covered with a layer of gravel afterwards. The size of the *moai* is, indeed, astonishing: they weigh several tons and are 10 metres (30 feet) in height. Today there are more than 300 of them lying all over the island at the feet of *ahu*, or ceremonial platforms; and there are another 500 or so which are still upright or bedded down on the rocky slopes of Rano Raraku, the volcano from which their stone was taken.

A few of the *moai* were carved in basalt, but all the others were made out of volcanic rock, using the hard, handleless, stone picks which still lie scattered on the quarry floor. The giants have no lower limbs, and their heads are disproportionately large. Although many of them were carried to other parts of the island, several were erected permanently on the slopes of Rano Raraku, as if they were protecting it. It seems possible that the statues which still form part of the rock face were actually intended to remain there, in the words of Alfred Métraux, like the "recumbent statues in a cathedral". They have

been carved in places that are so inaccessible that it would have been impossible to remove them, and some of them are so big and cumbersome that it would also have been extremely difficult to transport them – there is one that measures 21 metres (70 feet) and must weigh more than 150 tons. These huge "recumbents", combined with the landscape that surrounds them and the upright giants on the slopes of the volcano, create a most impressive architectural effect.

The face of Rano Raraku carries traces of many other statues as well. Some of them still lie there abandoned, but others have been planted here and there across the island or erected on the platforms of the *ahu*. These ceremonial buildings are numerous and varied. The largest have hexagonal-shaped platforms with carefully paved ramps in front of them leading down into courtyards. The walls that support the platforms are often made out of very large stones, which are remarkably well fitted together, and the interiors are usually filled with stones as well, although a few of them have rooms inside, some of which contain tombs. The giant statues, which probably represented ancestors, were lined up on the paved summit, looking into the courtyard with their backs to the sea. Some, if not all, of them were painted in red or white ochre, and some carried an enormous cylindrical headpiece, which could be 3 metres (10 feet) tall and 2 metres (6 feet) in diameter, and which was cut from the red volcanic rock at Puna Pau. The transport and erection of these giants and their hats must indeed have been very difficult, but, even so, the technical problems that they presented can hardly justify the

irrational explanations which have all too often been put forward. The real problem lies in the fact that they have not been there very long. It is thought that the *moai* are only a few centuries old. The sudden halt in the activity of the sculptors at Rano Raraku and Puna Pau, and the toppling of all the statues from their pedestals, coincide with the disasters that befell the island after the 18th century. The population had grown too large to be supported by the island's meagre resources. The people starved, and the traditional chiefs could do nothing about it. There was no escape: they had no wood for building sea-going canoes. Inevitably the chiefs were held responsible, and so too, no doubt, were the images of their ancestors.

There is a large religious site at Orongo on the south-western point of the island which also dates from the last years of its pre-history. About 50 stone houses were built on a narrow rocky ridge, with the crater of Rano Kau on one side and a high cliff rising from the sea on the other. Their walls, which are decorated with painted motifs, are made out of sheets of salty rock, piled one on top of the other, and these also form the corbelled roofs, which are covered on the outside with earth. The interiors are oval-shaped and the narrow little entrances are only 50 centimetres (20 inches) high. This village was dedicated to the cult of the bird-man. Great ceremonies were organized at the end of the southern winter, when the terns came to lay their eggs on the little off-shore islands. The first man to possess one of these eggs became "Bird-Man" and war chief for a year.

Hut in the ceremonial centre of Tahai

Photograph of the base of an ancient hut; plan and reconstruction by the archaeologist, William Mulloy. If there were plenty of trees when the Polynesians landed, they must have been used up more quickly than nature could grow them, and soon there was no suitable wood left in a climate which was unfavourable to plant life; hence the need to resort to stone for building the important edifices. The roofing of the large huts like this one was of light plant material. The narrow proportions of the hut compared with its length compensated for the lack of large pieces of wood for the rafters. Basalt base stones, laid on their edges, reinforced the superstructure, whose main elements (single sticks or wooden stalks) were driven into special holes. The people slept either on the ground or on mats with their heads resting on stone pillows. The door was low and narrow and little statues placed in a kind of entrance hall protected the way in. The biggest of these houses sometimes reached several tens of metres in length (up to 100 feet).

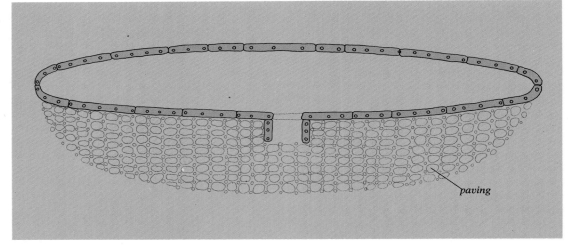

paving

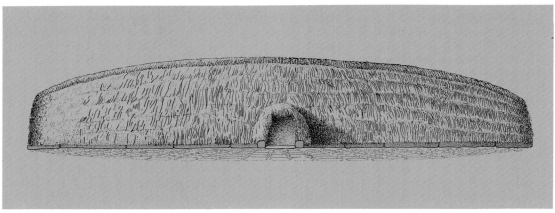

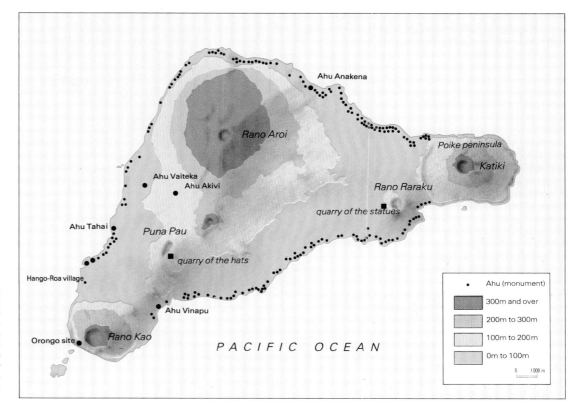

South face of Rano Raraku

The volcano, about 150 metres (500 feet) high, was used as the quarry for cutting out giant statues: the *moai*. In the foreground are some of the 465 statues cut out of the volcanic face, either standing or laid down. The rock face is pitted with holes, indications of the giants which were carved there. Many of them, incomplete, are still attached to the rock (note in particular the lower slope on the right). The exact number of these statues, complete or incomplete, is unknown. The relatively soft rock has, in fact, undergone the effects of erosion, and the sloping sediment has fossilized many of them at the foot of the volcano.

Giant on the side of the Rano Raraku quarry

Excavation carried out by Thor Heyerdahl's team in 1956 revealed that these statues, erected at the foot of the volcano and on the inside edge of its crater, were not meant, as were the others, to be carried to another part of the island. In fact, the base is placed on paving, or on a platform dug out of the natural slope of the ground. Here we can only see the upper part of the statue, barely half of its total height. The rest of the bust has been fossilized by the alluvial deposits of the volcanic slope. The same excavations reveal the care with which some of the details of the body hidden in the ground were treated: outlines of the arms and hands, a belt and carved tattoos. The uniformity in the general style of these statues shows that they were all carved in the same, rather brief, period.

"Ahu", Anakena Bay (north of the island)

According to history, it was here that the first Polynesians landed to colonize the island. Seven *moai* have been put back on their platform during the restoration of the site. Three of these statues were damaged when they were thrown to the ground during the revolts of the 18th century. Four of them are in better condition and have been restored with their "hats" of red tufa; their sizes vary, it is thought, in relation to the grade of the ancestor represented. It is here that the eyes of the statues were found, having been broken when they fell. A disc of red-brown coral, representing the iris, was inserted into an almond-shaped sclera carved out of white coral. These fine details and the painting of the body must have been done on the spot and gave life to the anonymous monoliths transported from the Rano Raraku quarry.

The "marae" of central Polynesia

In Polynesia, the term *marae* and its variants usually relate to the meeting places built in the open and used for various social activities. In central Polynesia, however, and notably on the Society Islands and their neighbouring archipelagoes, a *marae* is a dry stone monument which was a gathering place, not only for the living, but also for the protecting powers – the spirits of ancestors and the gods. All that remains of the most simple *marae*, those that belonged to the humblest families, are small paved areas, sometimes embellished by a few upright stones, and it is probable that they were never much more than this. But around the 14th century the architectural importance of the *marae* grew and became proportional to the importance of the chieftains who built them, symbolizing their ancestry and justifying their ownership of their lands.

The large *marae* is composed of a courtyard, which is more or less rectangular and which is often paved and enclosed by a wall. At one end of it there is a stone platform, the *ahu*, where the gods and ancestors were greeted and invited to participate in the ceremonies which took place in the courtyard. The structure was completed by additional buildings, made out of perishable materials, which were erected both inside and outside the courtyard – platforms for sacrifices, ceremonial huts and a hangar for the sacred canoe.

Starting from the basic plan of a courtyard with a sacred platform, the architecture of the *marae* varies according to its region or its period. The most common form on the Society Islands – and probably the oldest – contains a hexagonal *ahu* which is slightly raised and paved and separated from the surrounding wall, with several erect stones in the courtyard below it. The walls consist of two facings of irregular basalt, and the gap between them is filled with stones. The *marae* by the sea on the Leeward Islands are not surrounded by stone walls. The *ahu* here is outlined by tall slabs of calcareous coral, which are laid on edge and are sometimes decorated with carvings, and the interior is filled in with rubble. The *ahu* of the most recently built *marae* on the Windward Islands is a three-tiered platform. The construction of its walls alone is extraordinary: their facings are made of regularly spaced, oblong stones, which are arranged in courses and headers, and their base, and the base of the steps of the *ahu*, is a row of carefully adjusted quadrangular stones, some of them basalt and some of them coral.

Many *marae* on the coastal plains have been restored, and the profusion of others, which still lie in ruins in the uninhabited interiors of the islands, is evidence of the former density of their population and of the organization of pre-European society.

"Marae Ta'ata", Tahiti

This was one of the most important *marae* on the island; it has been rearranged and enlarged several times. On the left can be seen three kinds of bonding for the facings of the enclosure walls and their internal blocking. On the right is the *ahu* of the central enclosure; it is a single platform surrounded by paving, with three erect stones in front of it. The pebbles in the facing are evenly arranged; they were brought from the sea, which can be seen from the calcareous deposit still found on them. This *ahu* was later enlarged and then replaced by a three-stepped pyramid. The oldest *ahu* has been preserved and restored.

"Marae" of Tivaru, Rangiroa (Tuamotu)

The lack of stone material on the atolls means that the *marae* are smaller than they are on the higher islands. This structure is built of coral materials taken from the lagoon. The sides of the courtyard are marked by a single row of little slabs planted on their edge, and the *ahu* is a very low platform (here we can see the rear façade with three tall coral slabs). Three more, smaller slabs are planted in front of the *ahu*. Their presence is customary in the *marae*; it is thought that they have genealogical significance. In the centre of the courtyard is a seat with its back carved in calcareous coral. This was the place of the main officiating priest during the ceremonies. Such seats are only to be found in the Tuamotu *marae*; everywhere else there is nothing but a slab planted in the ground for the priest to lean against.

Ceremonial centre of Taputapuatea, Raiatea (Leeward Islands)

This is the *ahu* of the main *marae*. It measures 50 by 7.5 metres (160 by 25 feet). The coral slabs, which form the border and have been eroded by the weather, are still an average height of more than 4 metres (13 feet). This was the most important religious centre of eastern Polynesia. Chiefs and priests came from afar to sacrifice to the god Oro and to discuss religious matters.

THE ANCIENT WORLD

J.-L. Huot

Residential palace of Cyrus (called Palace P), Pasagadae

Palace P is the most recent of the three palaces in Pasagadae, and must have been built after 539BC. Here for the first time are *tori* (ringed column bases) with mouldings, showing Ionian influence. The ceiling of the central hypostyle hall was supported by five rows of six stone columns. The bases of the columns in this hall are among the most beautiful productions of Iranian masons. The contrasting colours, grey and white, give the whole a remarkable elegance. The interior of the hall measures 31 by 22 metres (102 by 72 feet).

As distinct from Egypt, the region commonly known as the Near East does not constitute any definite geographical unit. If we take it to comprise the countries extending from the Bosphorus to the Indus delta and from the Caucasus to the Persian gulf, its astonishing geographical variety is obvious. This enormous area has only once been unified politically, and then for just a short period, under the three Achaemenid kings.

At the centre of the Arabian Near East is the large Syrian-Arabian desert. This is an area which is hostile to life and a complete contrast to the fertile crescent that curves around it. Likewise, the centre of Iran is a desert, and there is also the Karakumy desert between the Caspian sea and the valley of the Amu Darya river. The scale of these vast areas must be borne in mind. The Syrian-Arabian desert extends nearly 3,000 kilometres (2,000 miles) in length and, at its widest point, is approximately 1,800 kilometres (1,000 miles) across. In these regions, rainfall is for all practical purposes nil and the number of inhabitants is extremely small. Thanks to the Tigris and the Euphrates, Mesopotamia, while having an arid climate, is not a desert; irrigation, and therefore agriculture, are possible. Similar conditions characterize Soviet central Asia and the Indus valley.

These regions were, in very early times, centres of brilliant urban civilizations. By contrast, the northern Orient consists of an enormous series of high plateaux surrounded by mountains. In these regions agriculture is difficult and communications poor. To the north of the central Iranian desert, the chain of the Elburz mountains, parallel to the southern side of the Caspian sea, rises at Mount Damavand to more than 5,600 metres (18,400 feet). To the east of Anatolia, the Pontic and Antitaurus chains join to form one single mountain range, dominated by Mount Ararat at 5,165 metres (17,000 feet). Finally there are the Mediterranean regions (known as the Levant): an area of hills and occasionally high mountains (Lebanon) with more or less straight coastal plains, all facing the Mediterranean. Lebanon and Hermon used to be covered with magnificent forests. The Near East is therefore a diverse world, where movement is relatively easy and the modern roads simply follow the tracks of the ancient ones.

Materials used in building were very varied. In several regions, and particularly in the large alluvial valleys (Mesopotamia, the Indus), the only materials were clayish muds and water. With this heavy soil and chopped straw, the people made (and are still making) an unlimited number of clay blocks or moulded bricks. These were, in most cases, simply dried in the sun; but sometimes they were baked in ovens, an operation that required skill and organization as well as considerable amounts of fuel. Such special materials were reserved for important buildings and for facing walls, courtyards, passages and doorways. If necessary, a coating of asphalt made the building watertight. In the open plains stone was rare, and in Babylon there was none at all. It was used nevertheless, and one must appreciate the engineering and management that brought such heavy material from so far away. In the early period of urban civilizations in Lower Mesopotamia, the huge temples of Uruk IV required enormous amounts of stone, which were probably carried by river. Stones were used for the foundations of certain buildings or, more astonishingly still, shaped into a kind of cone and placed side by side as a decorative covering. At this period – the end of the fourth millennium – when the inventive spirit of the first Sumerians was everywhere apparent, the builders of Uruk used an artificial material based on gypsum which they moulded into oblong blocks – the true ancestor of the modern breeze-block. It was a remarkable invention but was in use for only a very short time.

In fact, mudbrick was quite adequate for local architectural needs. It was cheap and was used extensively throughout the Near East in ancient times. There is no site on which traces of brick buildings are not to be found. They were easy to erect, easier still to pull down, and in the course of time the accumulated ruins have formed tells and hüyüks, which are spread throughout the countryside. But the fragility of the material must not be exaggerated. Certainly, an unmaintained crude brick building, deprived of its doorframes and of roof supports, will crumble in a few weeks and revert to the original soil. It is usually on remains of this kind that the archaeologist has to base his conclusions, and he is more often concerned with ground plans than elevations. But a brick building which has been carefully maintained, by re-painting the walls and repairing the roof at regular intervals, can last for decades, even centuries.

In the alluvial plains stone is a rarity, but it abounds in mountainous districts. Though it has never completely displaced brick, it has played a considerable part in most regions of the ancient Near East (the Levant, Anatolia, Iran) – although it has never had the importance it had in ancient Egypt. Very often people were content with badly quarried blocks, and we have to look to the end of the second millennium for the first carefully worked stones (the Hittites, or at Ras Shamra). Masonry masterpieces are to be found at Pasagadae and at Persepolis, where at the end of the 6th century BC and the beginning of the 5th, Greek, particularly Ionian, influence is undeniable. The use of wood was also limited. It was indispensable for door frames and for carpentry, and is sometimes found serving as a tie in walls. In the great alluvial plains it was a precious material which had to be imported (palm trees provided a very unsuitable wood for building). But its use should not be underestimated. Mesopotamian texts

THE NEAR EAST

reveal a veritable obsession with imported wood and, at least in the large public buildings, the use of wood for roofing was more common than has generally been supposed.

If the building materials of the ancient Near East were for the most part unsophisticated, they were at least flexible and adaptable. In general, the ruins we know about are not especially attractive or spectacular, but that is no reason to blame their architects, who were often inventive and painstaking, and occasionally brilliant.

According to one school of thought, the first house built in the open appeared in the Near East at the start of the 13th millennium BC (at Kebarien near Ein Guev in Israel). It consisted simply of a circular trench dug out of a slope, with a wall faced with stone. Before this period, the hunter-gatherers at the end of the Pleistocene era and the beginning of the Holocene era had used the very small amount of space provided by natural shelters. But far from living entirely in caves, as popular imagination would like us to believe, they also erected tents and built huts, either in the open country or

against natural hollows. Soon agglomerations were formed and man became a village dweller. The phenomenon of settling proceeded slowly, and was not necessarily linked with the development of agriculture. It is known, since the excavations at Mallaha, that in some regions the appearance of villages antedates the first traces of crop farming or stock raising. But it is necessary to wait until the sixth millennium before all the criteria of what is called a neolithic village finally emerge. An example is Byblos on the Lebanese coast, where construction of the

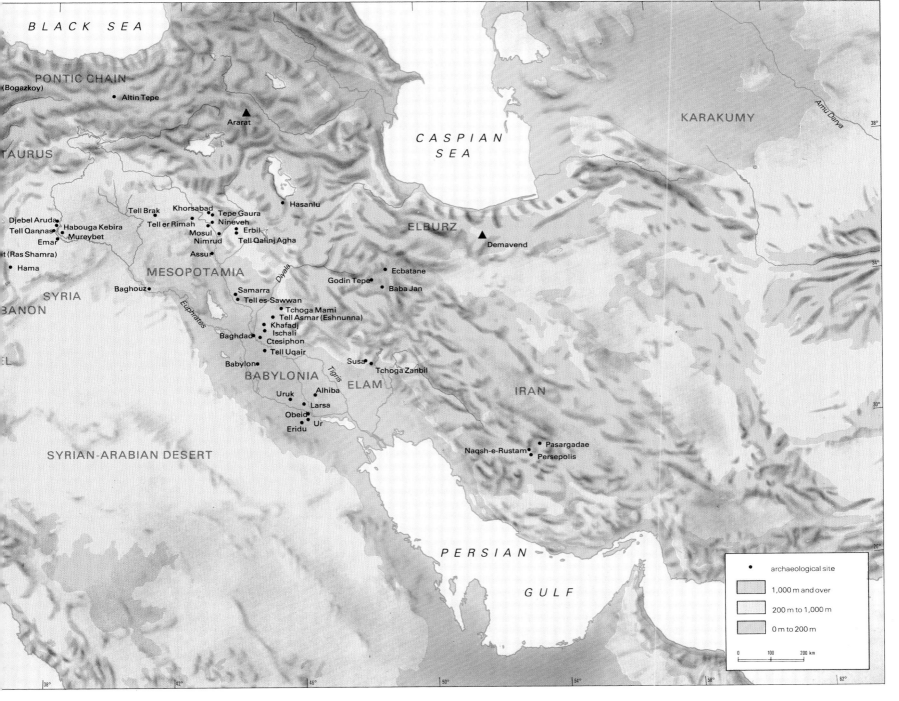

village was followed by subsistence farming, new technology and funeral rites.

Climatic factors do not seem to have played a vital part in the settling process. It may be that the climate of the Near East did grow warmer between 14,000 and 11,000BC, but prehistoric Levantine culture, known as Natuphian, is dated between 10,000 and 8300BC. This was the first period of organized villages. Natuphian houses are circular ditches of which the inner side is supported by a wall of stones, without any binding or plaster, set in layers, a single row thick, and with a kind of abutment continuing the line of the ditch out from the hollow.

The Natuphians were not really masons. Later, around 8000BC, the inhabitants of Jericho learnt how to build a large stone tower, rising to 8.5 metres (28 feet) with an inside staircase. It was clearly an important structure but its function is not clear. Also about 8000BC, the villagers of Mureybet III divided the interior of their round houses with straight walls that intersected at right angles. House XLVII of Mureybet is partly buried in sloping ground: one part of the circular wall is formed by the inner side of a trench, the other part is a cob wall built in the open air. The roof was of dried clay blocks set on joists placed side by side. Mureybet III was an agglomeration of round houses of varying dimensions arranged in tiers on a slope. Then came buildings in chequer pattern made of square cells, placed side by side, with walls made of clay blocks or stone. There was a progression from a round to a rectangular house which could be enlarged by the addition of new cells. This transition was made throughout the world, but at very different times. It seems that it occurred earlier on the Euphrates than anywhere else, having been initiated by the beginning of the eighth

millennium. During the seventh millennium rectangular dwellings became general. Between 7600 and 6000BC, complex constructions appeared in which the use of rough brick was widespread. New techniques such as the use of lime and plaster were tried. Villages became large agglomerations covering vast areas.

By 5600BC, a large variety of house types co-existed. Rooms became numerous and ground plans complicated. In Tell es-Sawwan (Iraq) several buildings followed an identical pattern: they consisted of a number of rooms (sometimes as many as 20) grouped around a central T-shaped space. Similar houses were to be found in Tchoga Mami and at Baghouz on the Euphrates. During this period, the so-called "Samarra" period, great use was made of moulded brick. This new material enabled the first steps to be taken in the systematic use of buttresses, internally and at the corners of buildings. We are now dealing with large dwellings attached to farms, perhaps partially covered by an upper storey. One of the rooms on the ground floor, judging by its size (larger than all the others), was probably used as a reception room. From the Obeid era (5000–4000BC), we see a truly architectural development based on a desire for symmetry. Rooms were grouped around a central area, which was either rectangular or T-shaped. In Eridu (southern Iraq) and at Tepe Gaura (western Iraq) there were buildings on a tripartite plan which have often been regarded as "temples", but it is probably more accurate to group them together with the large mudhifs of southern Iraq, which were meeting and reception rooms for travellers. The "temples" of the Obeid period were probably a development from the ordinary house, in which the part reserved as a reception area had been set aside. If we resist the temptation to assume that they were always the places of worship

that many later became, it is quite possible to imagine them as being originally community houses or, more probably, houses for the heads of communities. All that remained was to increase the size of these buildings and to improve the quality of the mural decorations, and a truly monumental architecture was born. Plans must have been based directly on Obeid examples, but the construction of such buildings must also have required a great deal of original work by professional architects, simply by virtue of the dimensions involved. The great temples of the Uruk era are the architectural expression of the advent of a much more complicated way of life than that of the simple village – the urban way of life. The appearance of figures, then writing, and some specific tools such as the cylinder seal, indicates the beginnings of an administration. Tangible signs of an urban revolution are seen in the appearance of a monumental architecture in southern Iraq during the second half of the fourth millennium.

Before discussing the architecture of public buildings, temples and palaces, it is as well to examine the more general aspects of ancient eastern towns. Very little is known about them. At the sites of excavations, private houses and residential quarters have often been neglected at the expense of public buildings which have been deemed more important. It may be supposed that the houses, residential quarters and roads would hardly be the same from town to town throughout the third, second and first millennia. But, apart from Habuba Kebira Süd in Syria and Qalinj Agha in Iraq from the end of the fourth millennium, the cities of the Indus and Hama in Syria from the end of the third millennium, Ur at the beginning of the second millennium and Babylon at the beginning of the 6th century BC, few ancient examples are known. However, the deeper one goes, the more clearly a recurrent pattern emerges. In other cases, as at Gournia in eastern Crete (15th century BC), it is hardly possible to discern the overall plan. Nowhere is there a public place or empty space capable of acting as a city centre, and people had to meet instead at the town gates.

Some oriental towns were very large. The population of Babylon in the neo-Babylonian era (6th century BC) has been estimated at about 80,000. Because of the abundance of brick and frequent destruction, towns were being continually expanded. Erbil in eastern Iraq is a good example: houses are still standing there, on the ancient tell, and were inhabited within living memory.

Private houses differed widely according to the wealth or poverty of the occupant. In the simplest examples, a room for multiple use led on to a small yard. Sometimes there were fine buildings, doubtless of only one storey, in which several rooms led on to a central tiled courtyard (Ur). Very often such houses shared a party wall. Except for dwellings in the Indus valley, sanitary installations and drainage of any kind seem to have been extremely rare.

The first big public buildings date from the middle of the fourth millennium. At this period, in the south of Mesopotamia, lifestyles changed considerably – a phenomenon which is often referred to as the urban revolution. The deeper causes of this revolution are still the subject of discussion, but the archaeological evidence

Mureybet. Round houses with interior divisions, eighth millennium. (J. Cauvin.)

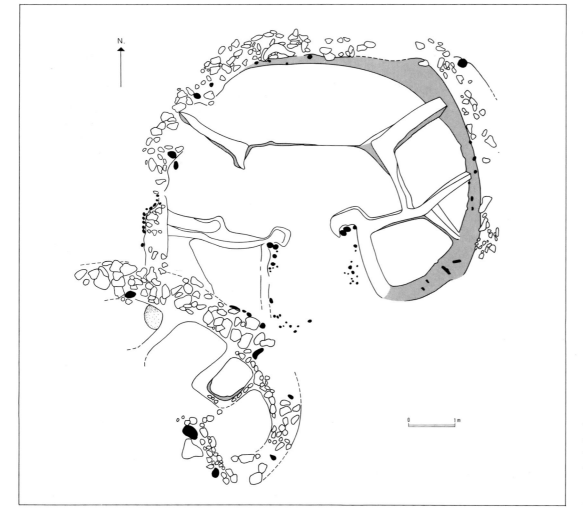

historical chronology					dates	civilization and architecture
Anatolia	**Syria**	**Palestine**	**Mesopotamia**	**Iran**		
BYZANTINE EMPIRE				SASSANIAN EMPIRE	AD600 / AD250	First domes on squinches.
ROMAN EMPIRE				PARTHIAN ARSACIDS	0 / −250BC	First *iwans*.
GREEK PERIOD					−330BC	Large hypostyle rooms. Greek influence on architecture.
ACHAEMENID EMPIRE					−550BC	
GREEK CITIES	LYDIAN KINGDOM	NEO-BABYLONIAN EMPIRE		KINGDOM OF THE MEDES	−600BC	Appearance of Greek alphabet. Neo-Assyrian royal palaces. Start of efforts to form a universal empire.
	NEO-ASSYRIAN EMPIRE			NEO-ELAMITE STATE	−900BC	
	ARAMAEAN KINGDOMS	ISRAEL JUDAH			−1000BC	Appearance of Phoenician alphabet.
	Aramaean invasions					First sculpted orthostats.
NEO-HITTITE EMPIRE HITTITE EMPIRE	cities of Canaan AMORITE KINGDOMS		CASSITE KINGS HAMMURABI	MIDDLE ELAMITE STATE	−2000BC	First ziggurats.
	Amorite invasions		UR III AKKAD SUMER URUK			Emergence of arches (small width).
	Bronze Age cities			SUSA	−3000BC	First urban agglomerations in lower Mesopotamia and Susian. Writing invented. Rise of monumental architecture. Large houses with numerous rooms (Samarra and Obeid periods).
	HABUBA KEBIRA					
CATAL HÜYÜK	prehistoric farming villages				−6000BC	Moulded bricks. First rectangular houses. At Mureybet, first houses with interior dimensions.
	Beginnings of farming and stock rearing				−7000BC / −8000BC	At Jericho, large stone tower.
	MUREYBET	JERICHO			−9000BC	First circular trenches with supporting wall.
	KEBARIAN					

is clear. In the architectural field, the change is marked by intense activity, as at Uruk.

Although the public buildings of Uruk seem to have been inspired by the tripartite plan of the private houses of the Obeid era, they now took on grandiose dimensions. The partitions were decorated with mosaics made up of cones of terracotta or sometimes of stone, of which the bases, the only parts visible, were variously coloured. These colours formed geometrical motifs – zigzags or lozenges. The buildings were laid out in an ordered manner. The religious buildings of Uruk IV, erected at the end of the fourth millennium, were set out in accordance with an overall plan. Similar buildings, without doubt contemporary, are known far from Uruk, in the centre of agglomerations which were probably commercial staging-posts of the great Sumerian empire. Temples are known which are similar to Tell Brak and to Tell Qannas in Syria. From the start of the first half of the fourth millennium, the inhabitants of Susa I in Elam erected an enormous terrace, some 10 metres (33 feet) high and about 24 metres (80 feet) long, in the middle of the agglomeration. It was intended to support one or more public buildings, but the use to which they were to be put is unknown. At the end of the fourth millennium, the inhabitants were able to restore this imposing structure after a period of neglect (Susa II). Such an undertaking was only equalled by Tell Qalinj Agha (near Erbil, in eastern Iraq) where, at the time of Uruk IV, a large terrace was built, 60 metres (197 feet) in length. Such buildings presuppose a complex, collective organization, of which the iconography of the sculpture of Uruk is further evidence. An important personage, with several duties, civil, military and religious, clearly guided the destiny of the

city. But public architecture, in the form in which we know it, remained exclusively religious. Royal palaces, clearly distinct from the religious buildings, did not appear until the third millennium. From that time on, the principal public buildings found in the excavations are, with the exception of the city ramparts, temples and palaces.

Sanctuary plans are varied, and their evolution is too complicated to describe here. In Mesopotamia it led to the "Babylonian" plan, in which buildings were arranged around a square courtyard, or to the "Assyrian" plan, in which the door, which was situated in the middle of a short side, faced the statue of worship. The buildings are sometimes enormous: the sanctuary of the god Nanna (Sin) at Ur measures nearly 400 by 200 metres (1,300 by 650 feet). In Mesopotamia there emerged a type of building unique in the field of religious architecture, the ziggurat, which was copied only by Elam among the neighbouring regions. It consisted of an enormous mass of bricks, leading by successive recesses or steps to several landings, the number of which could vary. In other regions, plans for sanctuaries varied considerably: Hittite sanctuaries bore no resemblance to Phoenician temples (of which Solomon's temple in Jerusalem, though it has completely disappeared, was the best example).

Palace architecture also took several forms. Again, little is known of its evolution. The stages have been carefully studied in Mesopotamia during the Bronze Age, but available evidence is very incomplete. It is only by the IIIrd dynasty of Ur (end of the third millennium) and the Amorite kingdoms (beginning of the second millennium) that one can describe a characteristic form of royal palace. It is by

then possible to identify a throne room, a distinctive feature of the type. From this time on, the palace is not simply an enlarged house or temple, but the place in which a king lived.

In the valleys of the great rivers, whatever the type of building, the architecture has certain common features due to the limitations imposed by materials. Crude brick could only be used to cover small spaces. Arches or domes were rare, and not large or prominent. Everywhere ceilings were constructed with horizontal wooden beams, even where it was necessary to import beams which were sufficiently long and strong from a great distance. For this reason rooms were always straight-walled. Within such limitations, the main variation was in their grouping. Lighting often posed difficult problems. Curious as it may seem, Mesopotamian architecture hardly ever employed columns or piers. Only decorative half-columns have been found (Tell er Rimah or Larsa, 18th century BC). Without central supports, the rectangular rooms were necessarily of small dimensions. The effect was often monotonous. Only the decorations succeeded in brightening the dreariness of the basic materials. There was an attempt to make light and shade play on the façades by multiplying the number of buttresses and niches. The walls were covered with plaster on which murals were painted, but most of these have disappeared with time. From the beginning of the 14th century BC the bases of walls were often protected by stone tiles; later, they came to be decorated with relief sculpture and, finally, by motifs in varnished brick.

On the periphery of the Mesopotamian world, in Anatolia, in Aegea and on the Iranian plateau, other building methods

Hirmer Fotoarchiv

Alaca Hüyük. Entrance to the temple, seen from the interior.

were explored. The mountainous countries quickly learnt about architecture in stone. In the second millennium, stone arches were being used in Anatolia and Aegea. The development of Mycenaean casemates and Hittite posterns should also be mentioned. In Crete and Syria during the second millennium, official buildings made use of numerous columns in porticoes and large windows. In Iran and Armenia, between the 9th and the 7th centuries BC, the first hypostyle rooms appeared, in which the roof was supported on wooden columns on stone plinths. This was the case at Hasanlu, Baba Jan, Godin Tepe and Altin Tepe, and it was an important invention. Rooms could attain a considerable size simply by the addition of rows of extra supports. The hypostyle rooms at Pasagadae, and later at Persepolis, were directly influenced by Iranian architecture at the start of the first millennium. It was only necessary to substitute stone columns for the wooden supports, and to use the skill of the stone masons of Ionia, which had recently been conquered, for the creation of the magnificent and sumptuous Achaemenid palaces.

After the fall of Persepolis and Susa to Alexander the Great in 331BC, the East came directly into contact with the Greek world, although communication between the two civilizations had been established earlier. The Greek conqueror died prematurely in 323BC, but his conquest was unaffected, and it spread Hellenism well beyond the future frontiers of the Roman Empire. His successor Seleucus and the Seleucid dynasty took over what he had left and founded a new capital, Seleucia, on the eastern shores of the Mediterranean.

Greek and Greco-Roman art was not fundamentally different in the Mediterranean countries, Anatolia or Syria, from what it was in Italy or Spain, but it was quite different from the art of Mesopotamia or Iran. The Parthians, who came from the steppes to the east of the Caspian Sea, drove the Macedonians out of Iran during the 3rd century BC, then later out of Mesopotamia too. These Arsacid Parthians (250BC to AD250), whose capital was Ctesiphon on the Euphrates, not very far from Baghdad,

established a quite distinctive culture. It was permeated by the Semitic religion but was also inspired by Greek ideas. Their art is well known from the remains of towns such as Uruk and Assur and, in particular, Hatra, which lies to the east of present-day Mosul.

The Parthians instituted a new architecture, in which remarkable use was made of the arch and the vault – to the extent of doing without the support of columns. Parthian architects invented the iwan, that is, a rectangular room entirely open on one of its short sides and covered by a vault. The Parthian era is extremely important in the history of oriental architecture. Recent researches have shown that the iwan, which became one of the major features of Sassanian and Islamic Iranian architecture, was first seen in Mesopotamia (Assur, Parthian palace, later Hatra) during the 1st or 2nd centuries AD. Then came the triumph of the barrel vault; but this was not followed up because of the preference, during the Sassanian period, for the domed vault. The dome was perhaps the most remarkable achievement of this latter period and its development merits a brief description. Even if the influence of Hellenism had at first gone deep, the ancient Orient rapidly recovered its traditions after the Macedonian conquest, and the history of the dome is an excellent illustration of this.

In AD224 the Persian Ardeshir, founder of the Sassanian empire, overthrew the Parthian Arsacid dynasty, which had appealed in vain to the legions of Rome. Shapur I, the son of Ardeshir, seized Hatra around 241, but the town was then abandoned in favour of the more central Ctesiphon on the Euphrates. Mesopotamia and the Iranian plateau remained under the dominion of the Sassanians for four centuries, until the Arab conquest. Sassanian architects built rooms roofed by domes, while also continuing to build the gigantic iwans of which Ctesiphon has preserved a magnificent example at Salman Pak.

Yet the dome was by no means a Sassanian invention. Circular buildings had appeared in the east since the fifth millennium BC (the

tholoi of the time of Halaf) and it seems reasonable to suppose that they had domed roofs. But then this form, though functional and economical in timber, seems to have disappeared. It is not until the tombs of the Ist dynasty in Ur, in the middle of the third millennium, that domes reappeared, in the roofing of subterranean funerary buildings. Dating from the end of the third millennium, the site of Tell er Rimah in northern Iraq provides evidence of domes over rectangular chambers. The domes were flattened, and were built by advancing in sections from the corners. Strangely, no other example of this form is known in the second and first millennia; the most recent archaeological evidence about domed vaults in ancient Mesopotamia dates them from the early second millennium (Tell Asmar). It is not until the Parthian era that they reappear. However, the shape of the dome had probably been preserved, although archaeology cannot document it, in popular rural architecture. This is suggested by some neo-Assyrian reliefs of the time of Sennacherib (704–681BC) which show domed houses in villages in the neighbourhood of Nineveh.

As has recently been shown, the first Sassanian dome appeared in Firuzabad, a town whose foundation is attributed to Ardeshir (AD224–41), and it is a dome built of rough stone on squinches. Its origin remains a mystery. There is nothing Greek about it, nor is it characteristic of the ancient Orient, which only made use of the vault for modest spans. Transposed into a masonry of rough stone, sealed by mortar, this vault shows the combination of two techniques; one, specific to brick, is that of squinches, built up vertically or on a slope; the other is that of the dome, built up from flat circular foundations.

Neither of these two components had appeared before in the eastern part of the Iranian plateau. If one looks elsewhere for their origin, it is in Mesopotamia that vaults on squinches of crude brick are to be found – at Tell Bardan (in the Djebel Hamrin in eastern Iraq) in the Parthian era, and at Dilberjin Tepe in Bactria, where the use of squinches was mastered in the 1st or 2nd centuries AD. As for the dome, it probably existed from the 4th to 2nd centuries BC in Balandy II in the Khorezm, but this is not certain. However, the use made in Buddhist architecture in eastern Afghanistan and in Bactria of domes on pendentives, on sites dating from the 3rd to the 7th centuries AD must not be forgotten. Their exact dating may have to be reviewed. R. Besenval has plausibly suggested as a working hypothesis that the dome on squinches is of oriental origin, developing from contact between the Bactrian and Buddhist worlds, in eastern Afghanistan, on sites dating from the 1st or 2nd centuries AD. This form of roofing did not extend west of the frontiers of the Iranian plateau during the Sassanian period, but it was used on the plateau up to the arrival of Islam.

Thus, south central Asia and Afghanistan seem to have played an essential role in the spreading of techniques and forms. At the frontiers of central Asia and of the Mesopotamian world, the Parthian world seems unique, and its architecture eloquently expresses its originality. Arsacid and then Sassanian architecture was not a simple continuation of the architecture of the Near East. It revitalized the possibilities of the materials it used, and left an indelible impression. Islamic architecture of the high plains is to a large extent derived directly from it.

Hattussas

Southern slope of the citadel of Büyükkale.

Hattussas

View towards building E and the north-west wall of the royal palace.

Palace P, Pasagadae

In the foreground is one of two porticoes, each 60 metres (197 feet) long, which run beside the central, hypostyle hall and were an innovation of the Achaemenid architects. The lower drums of some of the columns of the hall have been restored to their original positions: no upper drums have been recovered. It is not known if the palace was finished. While the foundations of the portico have remained intact, only some fragments of the upper tiling of white stones have remained. A line of black stones emphasizes the edge.

Sumerians, Elamites and Hittites

Monumental architecture was one of the major features of the Uruk period in lower Mesopotamia, during the second half of the fourth millennium. In a country rich only in water and soil, the favoured building material was brick dried in the sun. Wood, essential for the erection of flat roofs, had to be imported. Blocks of stone, which were sometimes used for foundations, and more rarely for lining walls, had also to be brought great distances. Some buildings were decorated with mosaics of clay cones, of which only the coloured base was visible. In order to brighten up the walls, otherwise monotonous and dreary, a careful arrangement of projections and recesses created varying light and shade. The temples of Uruk stood on high terraces reached by means of ramps or staircases. Now only traces remain of these huge buildings (the so-called limestone temple of Uruk V is more than 70 metres/230 feet long), excavated with great care by German archaeologists.

It is possible to follow the development of Sumerian religious architecture during the first part of the third millennium thanks to important American excavations in the lower valley of the Diyala, especially at Tell Asmar (the ancient Eshnunna) and Khafadj (possibly the ancient Tutub). From the end of the third millennium, the contours of the Mesopotamian city were dominated by high ziggurats, possibly distant descendants of the temples on terraces of the Uruk period. Thanks to the examples at Ur and Uruk, these massive brick buildings of several successively receding floors are well known; but it must not be forgotten that every large city in Mesopotamia had a ziggurat. The regions neighbouring Mesopotamia did not copy these monuments with the exception of the Elamite plain, where the great ziggurat of Tchoga Zanbil (13th century BC) is still standing. This is an excellent example of these gigantic structures which, though neither temple nor tomb, served a number of functions. By the beginning of the second millennium, the form of the Babylonian temples had been established; the temples of Ishtar-Kititum at Ischali (Diyala) or of E-Babbar at Larsa (southern Iraq) are good examples.

This architecture of brick and wood, remarkable though it may be, should not cause us to forget that the inhabitants of the plateaux and mountains could make masterful use of stone. Hittite architects turned it to excellent account at the site of their capital Hattussas, where the imposing ruins of temples and defensive works can still be seen. The royal gateway of Bogazköy and the gateway of the sphinxes at Alaca Hüyük are good examples of the vigour of Hittite architecture and stone sculpture. The architects of Hattussas also had imitators outside the Hittite world: a postern vaulted on corbels was built at Ugarit (14th–13th centuries) probably under the direction of Hittite architects. During the reign of King Mursil II (end of the 14th century BC) a new town was built at Emar in Syria, where extensive terracing was necessary to prepare a difficult site for buildings in the Hittite style.

Temple of E-Babbar, Larsa, Iraq

At the beginning of the second millennium BC Larsa was the capital of the Amorite kingdom. It was conquered by Hummurabi in 1761 BC. The main temple of the town, which was dedicated to the sun-god Shamash, has not been completely explored, but the walls indicated in black on the plan were the subject of a thorough excavation from 1969 to 1978. The shaded zones are reconstructions based on differences in the colour of the earth at the surface, while the dotted lines are conjectures. The complex of courtyards is dated by inscriptions from the early 18th century to the end of the 11th century BC. The rectangular temenos which surrounded the ziggurat (to the right of the courtyards) is not dated; but its perfect alignment with the rest of the building suggests that it dates from the same period. The whole of the known part of the building is 277 metres (900 feet) in length.

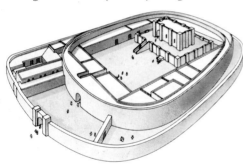

Temple of Khafadj

This site is located on the left bank of the Diyala, 16 kilometres (10 miles) to the east of Baghdad. The oval temple was built in three successive phases during the protodynastic periods II and III (2700–2500BC). The main entrance led through an exterior wall of 103 by 74 metres (113 by 81 yards) into a forecourt. After passing through an oval wall of 74 by 59 metres (81 by 65 yards), bordered by storehouses, one entered an inner court intended for cult practices. A staircase led up to the temple itself, standing on its own terrace. Nothing now remains of the complex and the restoration suggested here is hypothetical.

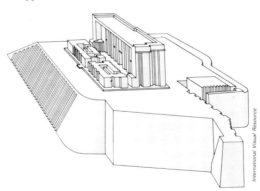

White Temple, Uruk

This temple was erected at Uruk, probably about 3000BC, in a quarter of the town already dedicated to worship for about 1,000 years. It stood on a brick terrace, formed by the construction of successive buildings on the site. The top was reached by a staircase. The temple measured 22 by 17 metres (73 by 57 feet). There was a podium with a staircase against one of the short sides, and another podium at the centre of one of the long sides. Access to the sanctuary was by three doors. The plan of the temple is similar to that of temple C in Uruk IV, and to that of Tell Uqair to the north of Babylon. Similar temples have been found recently in the central valley of the Euphrates in Syria, about 885 kilometres (550 miles) as the crow flies from Uruk (Tell Qannas and Djebel Aruda).

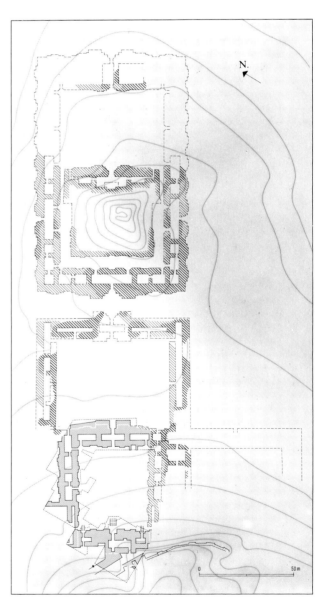

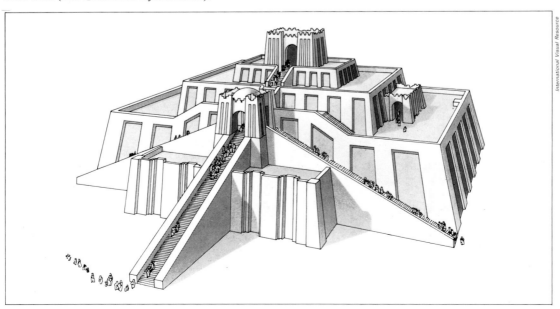

Ziggurat, Ur

The ziggurat at Ur is, along with that of Uruk, probably the best preserved of its kind in the whole of lower Mesopotamia. It was built by the kings of the IIIrd dynasty of Ur, Ur-Nammu and Shulgi (2111–2046BC) in honour of the god Sin (Nanna). The reconstruction proposed by the excavator, Sir Leonard Woolley, is probably basically correct, although nothing at all is known of the building beyond the base of the second storey and the battlements and domes are pure speculation. This enormous structure of crude bricks, covered by a facing of baked bricks, is rectangular in shape, and measures 62 by 43 metres (205 by 141 feet). The lower storey is 11 metres (36 feet) high. It is reached by three staircases that converge towards a main doorway leading to an intermediate terrace situated between the first and second storeys. The temple which stood at the top probably rested directly on the second storey.

Ziggurat, Tchoga Zanbil

The ancient town of Dur Untash was founded on a virgin site by King Untash-Napirisha, king of Anshan and Susa (1275–1240BC). It is situated about 32 kilometres (20 miles) to the south-east of Susa. It was discovered during an aerial geological survey in 1935, and was excavated by the Susa mission before the Second World War (R. de Mecquenem), then more completely by R. Ghirshman (1951–62). The religious temenos, dominated by an imposing three-storey ziggurat, stood in the middle of this new town. Access was gained by staircases incorporated into the brick itself. The antechamber to the staircase contained guardian animals made of enamelled terracotta. The temple at the top rose to 52 metres (173 feet). The accompanying aerial photograph gives a good idea of the impressive size of the monument, of which the reconstruction below is accepted as basically correct. The ziggurat was probably dedicated to the most important Elamite gods, Inshushinak and Napirisha. Of the town which was to extend around it, only three palaces and a temple were erected. Underneath the main palace were found the burial vaults of the royal family.

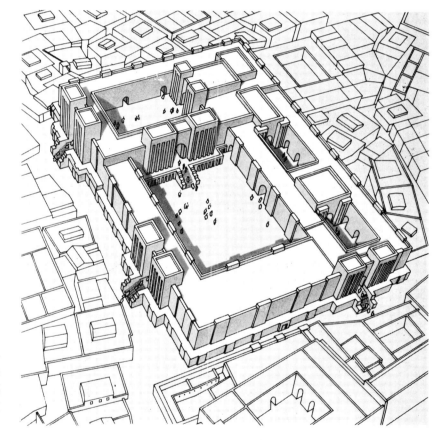

Temple of Ishtar-Kititum

Situated at Ischali, the ancient Neribtu, to the east of Baghdad, this temple was explored by an American team between 1934 and 1936. A huge structure, measuring more than 100 by 67 metres (330 by 220 feet), it was probably built during the second half of the 19th century BC by the Amorite king Ibiq-Adad II, who at that time ruled over the independent state of Eshunna. There were in fact three distinct temples of "Babylonian" plan grouped on the baked brick foundation, each with its own courtyard.

Royal gate, Bogazköy

Hattussas, the capital of the Hittite empire, known today as Bogazköy, had its heyday during the 14th and 13th centuries BC. Most of the monuments that German archaeologists have explored there date from this period: temples, palaces and a complex of fortified precincts, 6 kilometres (4 miles) in circumference. This rampart is an excellent example of Anatolian military architecture. The wall of "Cyclopean" stones was partly built at the top of an artificial embankment. There were five main gates: two were flanked by sculpted figures of lions and sphinxes and a third, called the royal gate, was decorated on the inside of one of the arches by a larger-than-life relief carving of a Hittite soldier. His battle dress gives us much useful information about the weaponry of the period: a helmet with protection for the cheeks, a curved sword in a scabbard and an axe. The horns on the front of the helmet almost certainly mean that this relief represents a divinity, not a king as had previously been thought. But the by-now familiar name of "royal gate" has stuck.

109

Assyrians and neo-Babylonians

At the beginning of the 9th century BC the small state of Assyria in northern Mesopotamia became possessed by what the historian P. Garelli called "a dream of universal domination". From the start of the reign of Assurnasirpal II (883–859BC), the Assyrian armies began a long series of raids towards the West and the Mediterranean coast. Successive rulers of genius managed to achieve for Assyria a long domination over the Near East, although the empire was never definitively established. The project was too ambitious, and the fall of the Assyrian empire in 612BC followed very rapidly on the capture of the city of Babylon by the greatest of its kings, Assurbanipal.

Most of the Assyrian kings were great builders, and left behind impressive palace complexes. It was these enormous buildings that the first Western archaeologists found in the middle of the last century as they began research into this part of the world. When P.E.Botta, the French consul in Mosul, opened his first dig at Nineveh in 1842, moving subsequently to Khorsabad, hardly more was known of the ancient East than what was in the Bible. Tradition placed the remains of the successive capital cities of the Assyrian empire in the north of Mesopotamia, and Botta quickly disco-

vered that he was exploring the capital of Sargon II (721–705BC). The English archaeologist Henry Layard soon joined him, basing his work at Nimrud to the south of Mosul.

Unfortunately, interest at that time was concentrated on relief sculpture and cuneiform tablets. Furthermore, all the buildings were built in rough brick, even if reliefs carved in stone decorated the greater part of the walls of the state rooms and doorways. They tended, therefore, to fall foul of excessively energetic digging projects. It was not until the arrival of German archaeologists with specialist training that excavations, in Babylon and Assur in particular, were properly conducted. This time brick architecture came in for much more attention.

Assurnasirpal II set up his capital in Nimrud, the ancient Kalkhu, known in the Bible as Kalakh. There he built an enormous palace which remained the prototype and model for all later royal buildings. Sargon II wanted to create his own new capital and opted for Dur Sharruken, the present Khorsabad, 16 kilometres (10 miles) north-east of Mosul. But Sennacherib (705–681BC) preferred to settle in Nineveh, on the eastern bank of the Tigris, opposite the present Mosul. When the old city (the

first occupants had settled on the site in the sixth millennium) became the capital of the Assyrian empire, Sennacherib fortified it and built his palace there. Assurbanipal also built his residence there. These two royal abodes were decorated with orthostats, or tiles placed against the base of the brick walls, which were decorated by reliefs glorifying the military might of Assyria and its king.

After the fall of Nineveh in 612BC to a coalition of Babylonians and Medes, the Babylonian kings inherited all the Mesopotamian territories of the Assyrian empire. The most remarkable of the kings of Babylonia, Nebuchadnezzar II (604–562 BC), is curiously the least known. He was intent on reviving the ancient glory of Babylonia, and more particularly of its capital, which had again become "the centre of the world" more than 1,100 years after Hammurabi. This was the neo-Babylonian town that the German excavators found in the last century. Thus the most celebrated and largest town in oriental antiquity, situated 100 kilometres (60 miles) to the south of Baghdad, briefly renewed its distant past, but without new inspiration. It remained for the Medes and the Persians, under the direction of the great Achaemenid kings, Cyrus and Darius, to inject a new vitality.

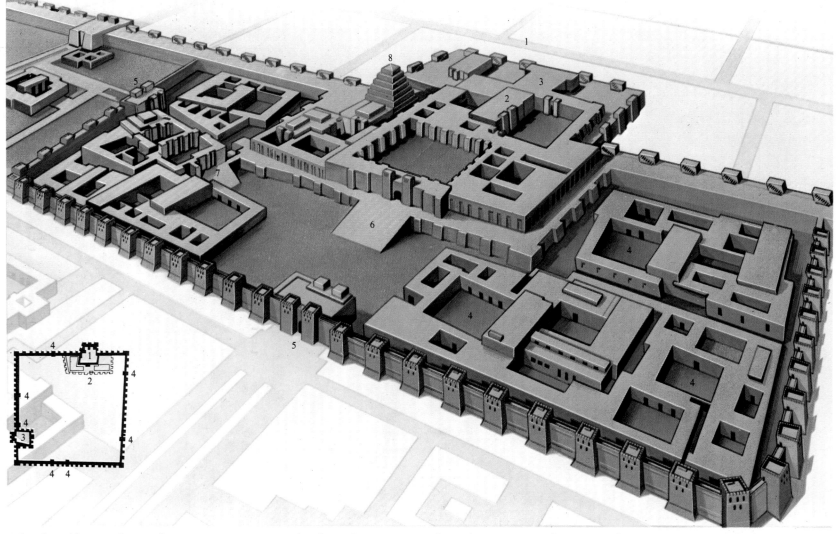

| 1 palace of Sargon | 3 arsenal | 1 palace on its terrace | 3 royal apartments | 5 monumental gate | 7 temple of Nabu |
| 2 citadel | 4 gates of the town | 2 throne room | 4 princes' apartments | 6 ramp to the royal palace | 8 ziggurat |

Khorsabad

Sargon II built his capital between 713 and 707BC but, with the exception of the ramparts, the royal palace and an arsenal, integrated into the defensive system, the town itself hardly seems to have been started. A rectangular curtain wall was entered by seven gates. The enormous royal palace straddled the north-west rampart. It was built on a terrace 12 metres (38 feet) high, and covered an area of nearly 10 hectares (25 acres). A vast ramp gave access to it. Beyond a large courtyard there was a ziggurat and a throne room, decorated by winged bulls and enormous genie figures. Grouped around the palace and on a lower level were the temple of Nabu, built on a terrace connected to that of the palace by a bridge, and the princes' apartments, built on the same principles as the royal palace. The throne room, or reception hall, was as usual situated between two courtyards; around the first courtyard, workshops, offices and all the departments accessible to the public were grouped. Beyond the throne room and around the second courtyard were private apartments. This architectural principle, perfected since the time of the palace of Assurnasirpal II in Nimrud, was still being followed in the much later royal palaces of Nineveh.

Bull on the exterior of the inner vestibule of the wall of the town, reign of Nebuchadnezzar II (604–562BC). The relief is in unvarnished bricks. Friezes of bulls alternate with those of dragons. At the end of the reign of Nebuchadnezzar, other reliefs of this type were covered with enamelled colours.

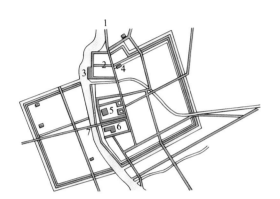

1 *processional route*
2 *Ishtar gate*
3 *palace of Nebuchadnezzar*
4 *temple of Ninmah*

5 *Etemenanki ziggurat*
6 *temple of Marduk*
7 *bridge leading to the new city*

The city of Babylon

The neo-Babylonian city consisted of a vast quadrilateral about 20 kilometres (12 miles) long; it was surrounded by a double wall and a canal. It extended on both banks of the Euphrates and the two parts were connected by a bridge. The city explored by the excavations was the one rebuilt after the destructions by Sennacherib in 689 and by Assurbanipal in 648. To the north stood the royal palace, forming the citadel. The palace was divided in two by a long processional route which started at the celebrated Ishtar gate, a double edifice corresponding to the double rampart. The façade of the outer gate was provided with two towers, decorated by bulls and horned dragons. In the reconstruction above (in which the two ramparts are shown), the three successive stages of the building of the outer gate are indicated; below, in yellow, the first stage, consisting of reliefs in unenamelled, baked brick; in the centre, in darker yellow, the second stage with enamelled decoration; finally, above, in blue, the final stage with enamelled reliefs. With this stage, the first two stages disappeared into the foundations. Traces of the final gate were removed by the German excavators in 1913, and rebuilt in the Pergamon Museum in Berlin.

After passing through the gates, the processional way led to the temple of Marduk, patron god of the city, situated in the town centre. Originally this road passed along the side of the great temple of Ninmah. The temple of Marduk was an enormous complex of sacred buildings, consisting of a ziggurat and the temple itself, which it has not been possible to explore completely. The ziggurat of Babylon, called Etemenanki or "foundation of the universe", was so thoroughly dug out in the search for building materials that it was completely razed. All that is known is that it was square, with sides 91 metres (100 yards) long and was approached by three staircases. According to the cuneiform texts it

possessed five floors. An accurate idea of the "tower of Babel" is provided in the excellent description of Babylon by Herodotus, following his visit there around 460BC: "The two sections of the city each have a fortified area in the centre: in one is the royal palace surrounded by a high and solid wall; in the other, the sanctuary of Zeus Belos with its ancient bronze gates. The sanctuary is a square two *stadia* long on each side; in the middle is a massive tower, one *stadium* square, on top of which is another tower which supports a third, and so on up to eight towers. An external ramp rises in a spiral to the last tower; about half way up is a balcony and some seats so that one can sit down and rest on the way. The last tower contains a large sanctuary in which there is a richly decorated bed, and beside it a golden table. But there is no statue, and only one person may sleep there: a native woman whom the god has chosen before all others, say the Chaldeans, who are priests of this divinity. Down below, the temenos contains another sanctuary in which there is a large statue in gold of Zeus seated; a golden table is placed beside it."

HERODOTUS, *Histories*

Apart from the temple of Marduk and that of Ninmah, Babylon contained more than 50 sanctuaries.

After the death of Nebuchadnezzar II, the city was delivered up to Cyrus in 539BC. It still played a major role in the Achaemenid era, but began to go into decline at the end of the Seleucid period. Its bricks were used to build the nearby modern town of Hilleh. But the memory of the most celebrated city of eastern antiquity will never be lost.

Decorative relief of a scene from a lion hunt

This alabaster relief from the time of Assurnasirpal II (883–859BC) decorated, with others like it, the throne room of the sovereign's palace at Nimrud; the king, clothed only in a tunic, kills the lions with a bow from the top of his chariot. The accuracy of sculpted relief during the neo-Assyrian period makes it an invaluable source of information, particularly regarding perishable articles such as wood, leather and textiles. (British Museum, London.)

Persians and Sassanians

Cyrus II, known as "the Great" (559–530BC), was of Persian origin and gained power over the Medes after the fall of Babylon in 539BC, thereby founding the Achaemenid dynasty. Some years later, he conceived the idea of a universal empire, yet he dealt generously with the peoples that he came to conquer. For example, he allowed the Jewish exiles "on the banks of the river of Babylon" to return to Jerusalem. It was here that they built the temple which was later destroyed by Nebuchadnezzar. As the archaeologist Jean Deshayes has explained, "the beginnings of the Achaemenid dynasty, the grandeur of its king, depended upon a new moral and political perspective". Lacking architectural traditions, the Achaemenids had to call on the artisans of the different nations of the empire. This eclecticism appears immediately and vigorously in the first royal buildings of the new imperial capital – Pasagadae, on the high inland plain of Fars. Their construction was carried on right through Cyrus' reign. In the remains of several of the palaces, all built with a grandeur made possible by hypostyle techniques, the influence of Ionian art is quickly recognized. This alone can explain the remarkable size of the blocks of limestone and the replacement of wooden pillars by beautiful columns of stone. In the first years of his reign, Cyrus had seized the Lydian kingdom of Croesus, a country which was largely hellenized and which kept closely in contact with the cities of Ionia. The subsequent inclusion of these cities in the Persian empire made the expansion of Greek influence into Achaemenid architecture much easier.

After the short reign of Cyrus' son, Cambyses, conqueror of Egypt (the artistic influence of this country on Achaemenid architecture was also considerable), the accession of Darius I (522–486BC), the greatest of the Persian kings, signalled the start of an immense architectural development: the building of Persepolis. Although the political capital remained Susa during the winter and Ecbatane during the summer, Persepolis was the most perfect example of royal Achaemenid architecture. Situated in the very heart of Fars on a plain surrounded by mountains it was built essentially by Darius and his son Xerxes.

As distinct from Pasagadae, which was spread over a wide area, Persepolis occupied a confined space, with all the buildings on a high terrace, partly artificial and partly cut out of the mountainside. It was reached by a vast staircase with two symmetrical double flights. Beyond there was a monumental propylaeum, the entrances of which were guarded in the Assyrian fashion by winged bulls with human heads; this opened on to a huge esplanade where numerous official buildings and large mansions stood. All these buildings consisted of square hypostyle rooms, flanked by porticoes with high wooden or stone columns. Although Egyptian influence is evident, in particular in the grooves decorating the lintels of the doors, and numerous details may well have been inspired by the Babylonian formal repertoire and iconography, still the main principle of the hypostyle room was in the direct line of Iranian tradition.

Even today, the ruins are impressive. The roofs have caved in, most of the columns have crumbled away and the brick walls, which were actually only partitions, have disappeared, yet the stone structures of buildings (columns, door- and window-frames and staircases) are still discernible. Passages and staircases are decorated with relief sculpture executed with particular care, representing the Achaemenid army, or the endless procession of bearers of tribute sent by people of the empire.

When Alexander occupied Persepolis in 330BC, an enormous fire, whether accidental or deliberate, destroyed this prestigious city. Yet even in its ruined state, Persepolis shows that Achaemenid art, though basically eclectic, was still capable of original creations.

Rock sculpture, Naqsh-i Rustam

After the reign of Darius I, the Achaemenid sovereigns had their tombs dug out of the rocks that overlooked the plain of Persepolis. The sculpted facings imitate those of the palaces. Above the colonnade is a large relief representing the king in front of the god Ahura Mazda. His passage is attended by subject peoples of the empire.

Column and capital

On a campaniform base, the Persepolitan column consists of a fluted drum surmounted by a crown of falling leaves, recalling some Ionic capitals. The double animal or monster capital is a wholly indigenous creation. A beam passed across the saddle back (the space separating the necks of the two animals) and another, perpendicular, rested on the animals' heads.

Persepolis

The main buildings which stand on the terrace of Persepolis have been given names by archaeologists that do not have any precise significance but are none the less useful. In the plan, it is easy to distinguish two parts connected by a monumental passage, the Tripylon. To the left is a public area with the Apadana or great audience hall of Darius and the "Palace of a Hundred Columns" or throne room of Xerxes; to the right is a private area consisting of the palaces of Darius and Xerxes, the "harem", which was probably the treasury of Xerxes, and the treasury of Darius.

1 *propylaeum of Xerxes*
2 *Apadana*
3 *incomplete monumental gate*
4 *"Palace of a Hundred Columns"*
5 *Tripylon*
6 *palace of Darius I*
7 *palace of Artaxerxes*
8 *palace of Xerxes*
9 *"harem"*
10 *treasury of Darius*

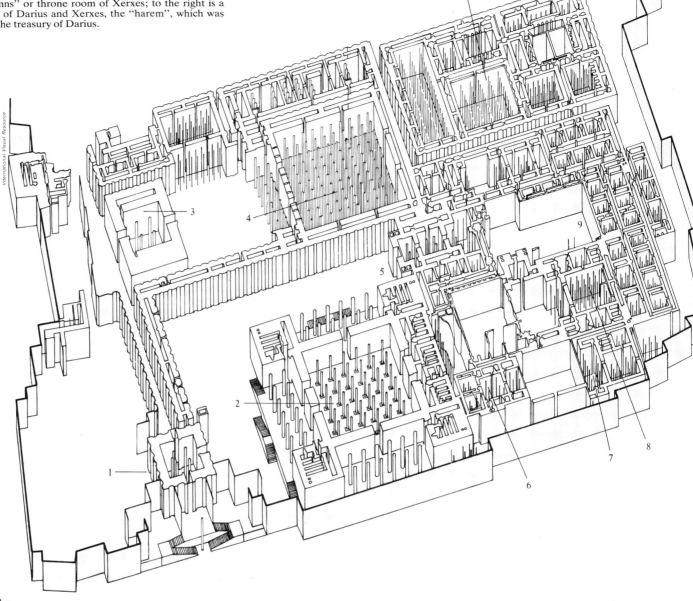

Tomb of Cyrus, Pasagadae

At the beginning of the Islamic era, this tomb was turned into a mosque, which explains its excellent state of preservation. It stands on a platform of six steps. Ornament has been reduced to a moulding, running along the top of the walls, and a rosette, in very poor condition, decorating the top of the pediment. The harmony of the proportions and the simplicity of the architectural lines make the tomb of Cyrus a remarkable monument. Other tombs of the Achaemenid period, all very small, were built on the same pattern.

Relief sculpture, Persepolis

The relief sculpture decorating the parapets of the staircases in Persepolis represents alternately Achaemenid, Persian and Median soldiers. In the corners, the motif of a lion attacking a bull from behind is an old Near-Eastern theme, found from the end of the fourth millennium on stone vases in Uruk III. Although the motif is almost standard, the meaning, after nearly 2,500 years of history, has changed considerably. Here the theme has probably only a simple apotropaic value.

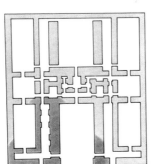

Plan of Ctesiphon

At the end of the great *iwan* which was used as an audience hall, a narrow door leads to a row of small rooms which give access to another hall almost as long as the *iwan* and probably once covered by a barrel vault. To the left and right of the complex are four other large, barrel-vaulted rooms, with smaller, square rooms between each pair.

Palace of Ctesiphon

The palace of Ctesiphon, on the Tigris near Baghdad, is currently attributed to the Sassanian king Chosroes I (531–79AD), but may be even older. In the centre of an ornate façade decorated with six tiers of arcades is an elliptical arch, 25 metres (84 feet) wide and 34 metres (110 feet) high, the main arch of an *iwan* 43 metres (140 feet) deep. This immense room, covered by a barrel vault, was the place in which the Sassanian king held his audiences. It covered a greater area than the throne room of the palace of Darius in Persepolis. The palace of Ctesiphon was the largest of the Sassanian royal residences and spread over an area of 12 hectares (30 acres). The arch of Chosroes is the only part remaining, a large part of the façade having collapsed in 1909.

L. Pfirsch

Ramesseum, Thebes, west bank

At the very edge of the valley, where the desert begins, the grandiose and romantic ruins of the "Castle of Millions of Years" of Ramesses II (XIXth dynasty) bear witness to the lust for eternal power of the most celebrated pharaoh of ancient Egypt. On the great pylon, now partly ruined, reliefs show the king's victories. The imposing and massive Osirian pillars, with mutilated heads, affirm his divinity. They fully express the monumentally imposing effects sought by the architects of the Ramessid era.

Egyptian civilization suddenly took several giant leaps forward about 3000BC. The country was unified under the powerful, centralized authority of a pharaoh. The agricultural exploitation of the Nile valley was greatly improved by a huge administration, which also developed the art of writing. Systematic irrigation made the best use of the annual flooding of the river. This "Egyptian miracle" was accompanied by the appearance of monumental brick buildings; around 2660BC construction in stone began as well.

In ancient Egypt, resplendent architecture was not only for the living, it was above all in the service of the dead and the gods. For the dead it was necessary to erect an "eternal dwelling", in which the corpse, carefully preserved by embalming and made ready for eternal life by the funeral rites, was sheltered. The tomb's furnishing and decoration and the power of the cult ceremonies provided the resurrected soul with all it needed to live again, enabling it to enter the region of the hereafter and take its place among the gods. During the whole of his life on earth, the ancient Egyptian cherished the hope of the greatest of all rewards, a fine burial in a permanent tomb. The gods, like the dead, also had a pressing need for a place on earth – a temple – to enable their presence to be truly effective. In their "divine palaces", thanks to offerings and rituals, their power to take action in the world was renewed and restored. Tombs and temples were thus essential elements in the functioning of the ancient Egyptian world: they guaranteed the continuation of life and maintained the original perfection of the world.

This perfection of things was ensured by the pharaohs, gods dwelling on earth, sole masters of the country and its inhabitants. The pharaohs initiated the great spiritual buildings – the long rows of monuments bordering the Nile in Egypt and Nubia were erected "on the orders of the king" or "at the king's wish". The pharaohs' role was not only spiritual, however; on the practical level, the king alone owned the resources of the country and the means for their use. Only the State could authorize expeditions to quarries and the carriage of materials. Only the royal administration had the trained manpower capable of designing and undertaking ambitious building projects. Finally, only the administration could organize the labour required on site. As a result, whenever royal power was weak there was a cessation of all important architectural activity. Monumental architecture in Egypt was therefore intimately bound up with both the religious and the temporal structures of this unique society.

dates (BC)	dynasties and principal kings	civilization	architecture
Early Dynastic period (c.3000–2660BC)			
*c.*3000	Ist dynasty Horus Narmer (Menes)	Capital: THIS Unification of Egypt. Establishment of pharaonic state. Development of writing and administration. Organized irrigation.	Saqqarah and Abydos: raw-brick tombs.
2800	IInd dynasty		Cut stone used for facings.
Old Kingdom (c.2660–2180BC)			
2660	IIIrd dynasty Zoser	Capital: MEMPHIS Elaboration of religious doctrine. Growing influence of Heliopolis and sun worship.	Imhotep, architect of Zoser, invents architecture in stone. Funerary monuments of Zoser at Saqqarah.
	Huni		Step pyramids of Meidoum.
2600	IVth dynasty Snefru		Rhomboidal pyramids, then first perfect pyramid (north pyramid, Dahchur).
	Cheops Chephren Mycerinus	Moral literature.	Pyramids and temples of Giza. Development of stone *mastabas*; Faraun *mastaba*.
	Chepseskaf	Religious crisis: movement against Heliopolis.	Non-pyramidal royal tombs.
2480	Vth dynasty Userkaf Sahure Nyuserre Isesi Ounas	Recovery and peak of Heliopolis' influence. Development of administration. Growing influence of scribes. Peak of moral literature. Development of Osirian cult. "Pyramid texts".	Smaller pyramids at Saqqarah and Abusir. Sun temples of Abu Gurab. Development of *mastabas* (Ti). Classic plan evolved for funerary temples; sophisticated internal plans for pyramids.
2330	VIth dynasty Teti Pepi I Merenre Pepi II	Alteration of royal land tax area. Strengthening of Osirian cult. Nomarchs gain power; autonomy in the provinces. Development of tomb biographies of functionaries.	Pyramids at Saqqarah. Great *mastabas* of Saqqarah (Mererouka). Development of rock necropolises for nomarchs.
First Intermediate period (c.2180–2040BC)			
2180	VIIth and VIIIth dynasties (Memphite) IXth and Xth dynasties	Serious troubles, sacking of the palace, pillage of the tombs. Capital: HERACLEOPOLIS Struggle against Theban princes. Peak of Osirian cult. Royal funeral practices extended to private sphere (sarcophagus texts).	General decline in monumental architecture. Nomarch rock tombs.
Middle Kingdom (c.2040–1780BC)			
2040	XIth dynasty Mentuhotep	Capital: THEBES Victory over Heracleopolis. Egypt reunified.	Architectural innovations. Tomb complex of Mentuhotep at Deir el-Bahari.
1990	XIIth dynasty Amenemhat I Sesostris I	Capital: LICHT Centralized government. Peak of Egyptian literature: royal pronouncements, loyalist literature, romances, stories.	The north returns to Memphite traditions. Massive pyramids of small stones or bricks. Continuation of new tendencies at Thebes (kiosks in Karnak, temple of Tod). Nubian fortresses.
	Amenemhat II	Beginning of the development of Fayum.	Great rock tombs of the nomarchs in middle Egypt and Aswan.

dates (BC)	dynasties and principal kings	civilization	architecture
	Sesostris II Sesostris III Amenemhat III	Town of Kahun. Struggle against the nomarchs. Scientific literature.	Decline of provincial necropolises. Last nomarch tombs (Qau el-Kebir).
Second Intermediate period (*c.*1780–1552)			
c.1780 **1660**	XIIIth and XIVth dynasties (Licht) XVth and XVIth dynasties (Hyksos) XVIIth dynasty (Theban)	Foreign infiltrators (Hyksos). Capital: Avaris Autonomy of Thebes and of upper Egypt.	General decline.
New Kingdom (*c.*1552–1070)			
1552 **1506** **1490**	XVIIIth dynasty Ahmosis and his successors Tutmosis I Hatshepsut Tutmosis III	Capital: Thebes Reunification of the country. Egyptian domination from Nubia to the Near East. Influence of the Amon-Re clergy. Peak of Egyptian imperialism. Epics of the campaigns in the Near East.	Foundation of the artisans' village of Deir el-Medineh. First hypogeums in the Valley of the Kings. Alterations to temple of Karnak. First rock temple (Speos Artemidos). Temple of Deir el-Bahari. Alterations and extensions at Karnak (Akh-Menu). Small "peripteral" temples.
1402	Amenophis III	Book of the Dead. Spreading influence of Egyptian civilization.	Temples of Luxor and Soleb. Brick funerary temples, colossi of Memnon. Palace of Malgatta. Funerary temple of Amenhotep, son of Hapu.
1364 **1347**	Amenophis IV Tutankamun	Capital: Tell el-Amarna (Akhetaten) Struggle against the Amon clergy. Henotheistic heresy. Cult of Aton (solar disc). Hymn to the sun. Thebes again Capital Worship of Amon-Re resumed.	Town, palace and temples of Amarna.
1306 **1304** **1290**	XIXth dynasty Seti I Ramesses II	Growing influence of the army. Renewal of external influence. Egyptian army at its height. Numerous foreign mercenaries employed. Epic peom of Pentaur (Qadech). Philosophical tales. Cults of Amon, Ptah (Memphis) and Re (Heliopolis).	Temple of Gurna. Grand temple of Abydos. Grand hypostyle hall of Karnak. Numerous buildings: development of the temple of Luxor, Ramesseum. Rock temples of Nubia (Abu Simbel).
1186 **1184** **1153–1070**	XXth dynasty Ramesses III Ramesses IV to IX	Stories of campaigns. Numerous troubles, clergy and civil service corrupted. Pillage of royal tombs.	Temple of Medinet-Habu.
Late period (1070 to the Christian era)			
713–664 **332**	XXVth dynasty (Ethiopian) Conquest by Alexander Ptolemaic and Roman rulers	Struggle of indigenous and foreign mercenary factions. Capital: Napata. Development of a pharaonic civilization in the Sudan. Continuance of pharaonic traditions up to the coming of Christianity.	Construction at Karnak. Temples of Gebel Barkal (Napata). Tombs in the form of pyramids. Temples of Philae, Edfu, Kom Ombo, Dendara, Esna.

Essential materials were provided by the Nile valley and the neighbouring deserts. Silt deposited by the annual flooding of the river gave the builder his commonest material, clay for moulding into bricks. Good quality wood was rare, and had to be imported, but stone abounded. Very often, the desert rock at close proximity to the sites provided a stone of average quality suitable for ordinary construction; but for facing, stone of superior quality had to be fetched from more distant quarries. So it was with the fine limestone of Turah, the alabaster of central Egypt (Hatnoub), the sandstone of Gebel Silsileh, and the pink and grey granite of Aswan. At the time of the annual flood, barges carried these materials great distances to the construction sites.

It was the intelligentsia, the aristocracy of scribes administering the kingdom, who conceived major building projects and directed the work. Their theological knowledge played an essential part in deciding both the general purpose and function of building programmes and the plan details to attain the spiritual effect required. Theological concepts determined the choice of site, the outline of the plan, and often even the selection of materials in the most essential parts. Certain rites were prescribed during the foundation of a building, during which votive offerings were deposited. These architect-theologians also decided on the decoration of buildings – determining the scenes and texts which were to be carved, incised or painted (low relief and painting inside, high relief on the outside). Architecture has seldom been a language and a symbol to such a degree. The search for perfection had nothing to do with aesthetics: it was intended as a magic formula to give immortality to the beneficiary – god or defunct mortal – of the monument. Hence the considerable prestige that the men of science who could so affect the course of nature obtained in the eyes of their king. The chief architects who left on the walls of their own tombs inscriptions of the very high honours and titles they received were numerous. Senenmout, the architect of the great temple of Deir el-Bahari, was also the favourite of Queen Hatshepsut. Some were even deified by later generations, such as Imhotep, the architect of Zoser and the inventor of stone architecture, and Amenhotep, son of Hapu, the architect employed by Amenophis III. Proud of their work, the great engineers, designers and architects of ancient Egypt frequently boasted in their memorials of having built monuments "which no one else had ever achieved before". However, their solicitous respect for theological tradition is without doubt a determining factor in the essential conservatism of the pharaohs' architecture.

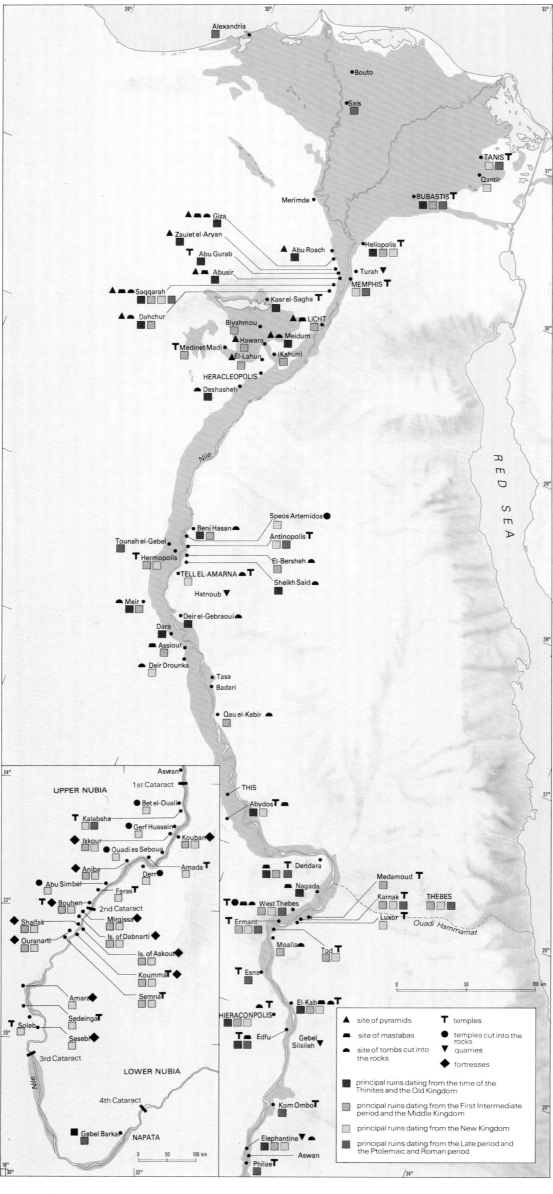

Under the orders of the architects, numerous labourers worked on a site. The craftsmen – masons, sculptors, painters – took precedence: they were the elite of the artisans in the service of the pharaoh and the temples, selected for their skill, and they passed the secrets of their trades on from father to son. Their social position was on the whole good. Then there came all the rest, the workforce responsible for the transport and shifting of materials. They were forced labour, including prisoners of war, and in particular countless peasants who could not cultivate the land during the flooding, and so were available for other work. Here again, we see how the Nile and its flood cycle dominated the life of ancient Egypt. The techniques used by the architects were rudimentary, but they were applied with patience, diligence and ingenuity. They used small forked sticks to obtain bearings on the stars by which they positioned the temples. The plans were then drawn roughly, indicating the essential parts of the building and the principal measurements. On site, the surveyor's tape fixed the alignments; plumb lines and set squares were used to check that the foundations were true.

The work was always kept on a level: as the building progressed, its centre was filled with sand and brick. When the walls were finished, the fill was cleared from the top downwards and the walls were decorated. Building materials were hauled up ramps of sand and brick. These ramps were covered with wet mud, sprinkled on to help the sledges carrying the stones to slide more easily, thus economizing considerably on labour. One could go on with examples of Egyptian ingenuity; the perfection we can still see in stone cutting and relief work was achieved with tools made of wood, flint, copper and bronze that hardly evolved during the entire length of the pharaonic period. What deserves our admiration in the ancient Egyptians' art of building is not a secret and mysterious science, but the remarkable ability of these men to exploit the very limited resources available to them. Patience and time overcame all difficulties; only the result was important, because it was indispensable both to the eternal life of the dead and to the prosperity of the nation.

The great royal tombs at Abydos and Saqqarah from the beginning of the Ist dynasty show a perfect mastery of building in brick and wood. Their upper parts contained numerous rooms for funerary furnishings and served to roof over the subterranean tomb. The oldest (Ist dynasty) had external walls of a stepped gable form, imitating fortified walls, in unbaked brick and indicating a Mesopotamian influence. This form of decoration disappeared with time, and tombs took on the traditional form of mastabas with sloping walls. But at the start of the Old Kingdom, under the reign of Zoser (IIIrd dynasty), Egyptian architecture underwent a dramatic change of scale. The mastaba, which traditionally rose only a little above the ground, merging into the desert, developed into a monumental symbol; it became huge and imposing, as is revealed in the magisterial forms of the great tomb complex of Zoser in Saqqarah. Here Imhotep invented the step pyramid, which remained the form of royal tomb throughout the IIIrd dynasty. There is no doubt that the influence of the sun-cult of Heliopolis had determined the idea that after death the pharaoh was called to join the sun in the skies. At the beginning of the IVth dynasty (about 2600BC), there was a tendency to represent the sun by *reproducing the image of the primordial hill illuminated by the first rays of the sun at the time of the creation of the world.*

Evolution towards the perfect pyramidal form was the great achievement of the reign of Snefru, and three monuments represent the enterprise. The first tentative one at Dahchur was never finished – the rhomboidal pyramid developed a crack in the slope when it was half built. The slope was then changed from 54°28' at the base to 43°. The king then transformed the step pyramid of Huni (the last king of the IIIrd dynasty) at Meidum into a true pyramid before undertaking the building of an even bigger monument – the pyramid to the north of Dahchur. He raised this to 104 metres (340 feet) in a uniform slope of 43°50'. These monuments at Meidum and at Dahchur are evidence of progress with construction in stone. They used immense blocks and remarkable corbelled arches, making it possible to introduce funeral apartments within the pyramid itself. The main elements associated with the royal tombs of the Old Kingdom – low temple, sloping access, upper temple, all with a role in the cult of the dead king – date from the reign of Snefru. Under his successors, Cheops and Chephren, the grand monuments erected at Giza seem to represent the culmination of this effort at the beginning of the IVth dynasty.

The period which follows the great pyramids in Giza was also remarkable. The end of the IVth dynasty was marked by a religious crisis which weakened the influence of Heliopolis, and the result was the construction of non-pyramidal royal tombs (the Faraun mastaba at Saqqarah). On the other hand, with the Vth dynasty came the return and consolidation of doctrinal domination by Heliopolis. The pyramids of the Vth and VIth dynasties were certainly smaller (between 45 and 80 metres/145 and 260 feet high), but they retained the excellent quality of workmanship. Today their appearance has changed completely as they have been used as stone quarries since the Middle Ages. Nevertheless it is still possible to appreciate the refinement of their architectural forms and the new importance of sculpted decoration. Elegant columns with floral motifs, which appeared for the first time in the temples of the pyramids of Abusir, replaced the massive piers of the temples of the IVth dynasty. Like the piers, the columns were of Aswan granite; they were dressed in the quarry and then transported on barges. In the VIth dynasty there was, however, a return to geometrically shaped supports of elegant proportions (square and polygonal piers). Finally the plans of temples and the internal arrangements of the pyramids were essentially fixed on models typical at the end of the Vth dynasty.

From the reign of Unas, the last king of the Vth dynasty, the inner walls of the pyramids were covered with texts that represent the oldest evidence of religious literature ("The Pyramid Texts"). This last period of the Old Kingdom is also very important for the evolution of private funerary architecture. At the end of the Vth dynasty and the beginning of the VIth, the mastabas that surrounded the royal tomb complexes were at the peak of their development. But after the reign of Teti, first king of the VIth dynasty, burial places for civil servants became fewer. On the other hand, from the Vth dynasty onwards as the regions became more powerful, important provincial burial places developed. In

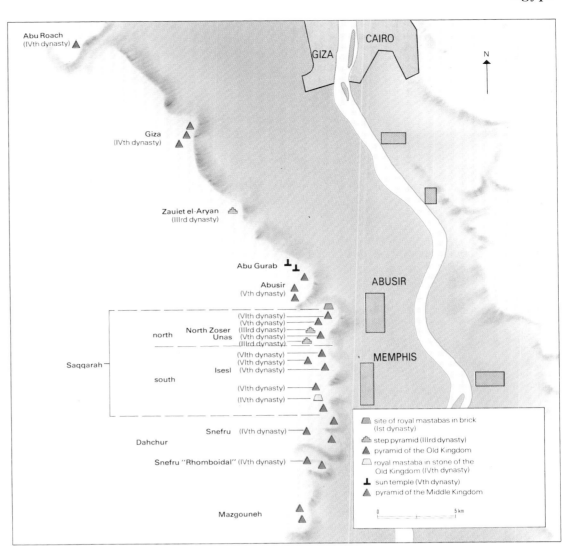

The royal tombs near Memphis

middle Egypt and around Aswan tombs were usually cut into the desert rock, like some of those found at Saqqarah and Giza.

It is much more difficult, because there are so few remains, to form an idea of the architecture of the temples of the Old Kingdom. Their central element was probably a main chamber with side chapels or sanctuaries. This was the scheme adopted in the temple of Kasr el-Sagha to the north of Fayum. This monument of unknown dedication and uncertain date was constructed of huge blocks which strongly recall the architecture of the IVth dynasty. It had a central chamber with seven sanctuaries in line. But most of the early sanctuaries were built of less durable materials. The temple of Pepi I (VIth dynasty) at Bubastis, built in brick, had a pillared façade with, inside, a chamber supported by eight columns giving access to a row of chapels. Much more imposing buildings were, without doubt, the sun temples of the Vth dynasty, which at this stage were associated with the royal funerary temples. They played an important role in the collection and preparation of offerings for the dead king, celebrating his affinity with the sun-god in the world beyond. Their monumentality was hardly less than that of the royal tomb complexes, with a low temple as an entrance gate and a road up to the sanctuary itself, which was set on the desert plateau. The terracing of the temple built by Neuserra at Abu Gurab, near his pyramid at Abusir, makes it possible to reconstruct the plan of the great temple of Heliopolis, about which very little is known. A massive stone obelisk stood in the centre of a vast courtyard on a platform in the shape of a truncated pyramid. The courtyard contained a monumental alabaster altar, which has been preserved, as well as

important sacrificial arrangements. It was surrounded by an enclosed, ill-lit ambulatory, of which one part led to a series of rooms and the other to a staircase which gave access to the terrace surrounding the foot of the obelisk.

And so during the Old Kingdom an architecture profoundly original both in its large and simple geometric volumes and in its strict planning and orderly design emerged. The pharaonic system had achieved a quality of building that has rarely been equalled. For the Egyptians of later eras this golden age was such a prestigious period that they made a veritable cult of ancient times, but about 2200BC everything that had made these remarkable developments possible collapsed in ruins. The foundations of Egyptian civilization were shaken by a political, social, economic and moral crisis. During this First Intermediate period, as Egyptologists call it, anarchy and disunity brought all important architectural activity to a halt. It was only about 2040BC, on the initiative of the princes of Thebes, that Egypt was eventually reunified. The foundation of the Middle Kingdom then made possible the restoration of the centralized state and reimposed the administrative structure necessary for great undertakings. The XIth dynasty shows some innovative architectural trends around its capital, Thebes. At Deir el-Bahri the funerary monument of Mentuhotep, today nearly a total ruin, was a complete reinterpretation of the tomb complex as it was known at the end of the Old Kingdom. It expressed a new architectural vision in which the pyramid crowns and unifies a larger complex. There was a small pyramid with a steep slope, built completely of stone, which rose from the centre of a terrace abutting the Theban mountains. Two storeys of pillared porticoes, one masking the retaining wall and framing the access ramp, the other surrounding the base of the pyramid on the terrace, created a balance between their horizontal lines and the vertical thrust of the piers that echoed the pyramidal crown. About five centuries later, this composition inspired the architecture of the temple of Hatshepsut, which was built on the same site. The use of numerous square and polygonal piers made it possible to create large covered spaces around and behind the pyramid; from these there was access to the sanctuary hollowed out in the cliff. This development heralded the great pillared or "hypostyle" halls of the New Kingdom. During the VIth dynasty pylons were erected to mark the entrance to the sacred precincts of funerary temples.

During the XIIth dynasty, monuments in the region of Thebes again show innovations. Kiosks – small monuments intended as resting places for divine statues during processions – achieved an astonishingly sensitive balance of proportion. That of Sesostris I at Karnak, which has been rebuilt from blocks found on the site, is an excellent example. The neat lines of the design are accentuated by the rounded mouldings at the corners and the concave cornice. The alternating white stone pillars and shaded areas in the bays emphasize the plastic qualities of the building. Interesting innovations also appeared in the plans of some divine temples. At Tod, south of Thebes, the temple of Montu anticipates the interior arrangement of temples of the New Kingdom. The sanctuary itself was treated like a kiosk and was surrounded by an ambulatory on to which the adjoining chapels or sanctuaries opened. This gives us some idea, despite the paucity of the evidence, of the importance of Middle Kingdom Theban building for the development of later Egyptian architecture. In the north, by contrast, when the XIIth dynasty transferred the capital to Licht, near Fayum, the return of the architectural traditions of Memphis became more clearly apparent. The kings of Licht built their funerary monuments on the model of those at the end of the Old Kingdom. Only the structure and the internal arrangements of these pyramids evolved. From now on, the whole body of the pyramid was made up of small stones or bricks supported by a framework of diagonally arranged walls. The arrangement of rooms varies, and is often very complicated in order to protect the tombs more effectively from pillage – something which had happened frequently during the crisis of the First Intermediate period. The same concern for tradition is found in the remaining fragments of the temples. The small temple of Medinet Madi, on the southern edge of Fayum, a region which exerted its greatest influence during this period, had a pillared portico and recalled the design of the sanctuary of Pepi I in Bubastis. On the sites of Fayum and in the delta, architects of the XIIth dynasty reverted to the use of columns with floral decoration.

The Middle Kingdom was a very productive period for private tombs, and notably the rock tombs of the provincial governors (nomarchs) of middle and upper Egypt. At Beni Hasan and at Aswan these tombs show real architectural quality. At Qua el-Kebir (end of the XIIth dynasty) in middle Egypt, an original arrangement combined the Memphite grouping (landing stage, rising ramp, temple) with successive terraces and colonnades, culminating in a sanctuary cut into the rock. This seems to reproduce the spirit of the Theban monuments of the XIth dynasty, but private tombs were soon to be exceptional: the reassertion of royal over provincial power meant that these great provincial tombs would cease to be built during the second part of the XIIth dynasty. The Middle Kingdom also extends our knowledge to civil and military architecture. By this time Egypt had annexed Lower Nubia, and in order to control the country built numerous imposing fortresses in unbaked brick. The fortress at Buhen, now submerged under Lake Nasser, had thick walls 15 metres (50 feet) high and a double curtain wall. The layout of the bastions, especially at the corners, reveals a very complicated method of fortification. These fortresses were reoccupied and systematically reconstructed during the New Kingdom after the unhappy times of the Second Intermediate period.

During the 18th and 17th centuries BC, a weak Middle Kingdom was unable to resist invasion by the foreign Hyksos. The conquerors took control of the delta and of middle Egypt, leaving some autonomy to the south, around Thebes. The Hyksos chiefs soon adopted pharaonic customs, while the Theban kings presented themselves as the legitimate successors of the pharaohs of the Middle Kingdom; neither the one nor the other had, however, the resources to undertake large architectural projects. But when the Thebans succeeded in liberating and

temples and royal temples became tenuous. Everywhere the pharaoh was revealed as the terrestrial manifestation of the god. These temples are characterized by the contrast between their large open courts and the shaded enclosed areas where the image of the god was housed. This corresponds to the two opposing principles of Egyptian religion – the importance of sun worship on the one hand, and the hidden and mysterious aspect of the divine presence on the other. Amon-Re retained these two features of the cult in his name: Amon ("the hidden one") and Re ("the sun god").

At the beginning of the New Kingdom, the role of the sun was given prominence, and was often expressed by a succession of courts and pylons, sometimes preceded by obelisks. At the time of the heresy of Akenhaten, exclusive devotion to the sun was taken to extremes in the temples of Amara, where the buildings extended into immense courtyards and pylons. But from the time of Hatshepsut and Tutmosis III, as the changes made in the sanctuary at Karnak show, there was gradual progress towards the worship of a hidden god, and the enclosed area was increased. Under Amenophis III, a balance was struck between the two, and this was consolidated under the Ramessids.

Under Hatshepsut and Tutmosis III numerous architects sought inspiration from the heritage of the Theban Middle

Kiosk of Sesostris I, Karnak. This remarkable little building of the XIIth dynasty, modest and perfectly proportioned, was rebuilt by the Egyptologist and architect H. Chevrier from blocks excavated in the foundations of the third pylon of the temple of Amon in Karnak (XVIIIth dynasty).

reunifying the country, they initiated a very prosperous period. For five centuries under the New Kingdom (about 1560 to 1070BC), Egypt reached the peak of her power and became frankly imperialistic. The kingdom extended its domination and influence from Nubia to the Euphrates, and grew wealthy on the tribute of subject peoples. Temples, in particular, were the beneficiaries of the pharaohs' prodigality, and the religious authorities were almost continually initiating projects. Thebes, the capital, where the god Amon-Re became the god of the empire, still offers today plenty of evidence of this intense activity. Theban tomb complexes had sung the praises of the kings of the Old Kingdom; the temples now proclaimed the grandeur of the pharaohs of the New. The distinction between divine

Kingdom – as in the magnificent temple of Hatshepsut at Deir el-Bahri, where the great terraces and colonnades mount in huge stages from the foot of the mountain. The kiosks of the Middle Kingdom became elegant colonnaded temples like those of Medinet Habu and Karnak (inside the Temple of Mut). The first rock temple, the Speos Artemidos, appeared in middle Egypt during the reign of Hatshepsut. And at Karnak, Tutmosis III built an entirely new type of structure behind the sanctuary, a large monumental complex, the Akh Menu, which was intended to celebrate the regeneration of royal power. The central motif was an immense basilical hall with five aisles terminating in sanctuaries; in the nave, the piers imitated wooden tent poles. Variety in types of pillar is characteristic of

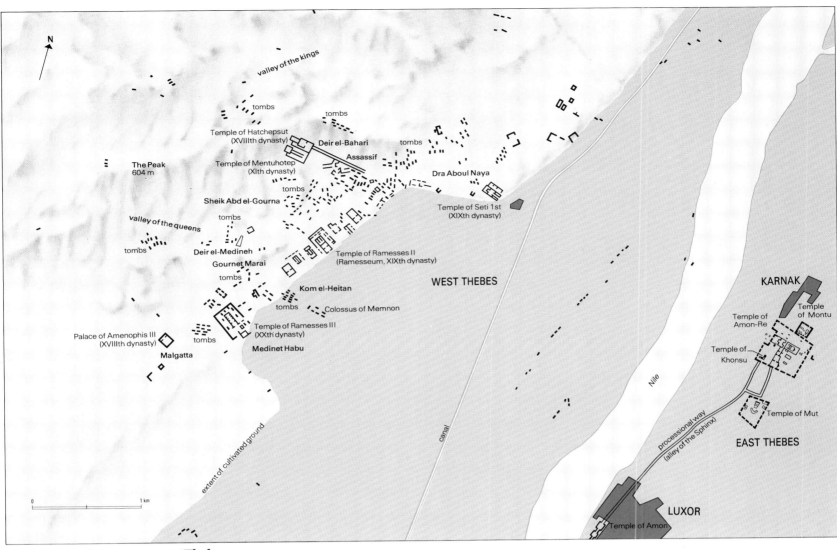

The principal monuments at Thebes.

the period. Most remained geometric
(square and polygonal pillars and proto-
Doric columns), but fasciculated,
papyriform columns were also used in
Karnak, and texts mentioned that they were
covered entirely in gold. Some columns in
the buildings associated with the goddess
Hathor reproduce her musical instrument,
the timbrel. But it was in the reign of
Amenophis III, urged on by his architect-
vizier, Amenhotep, son of Hapu, that sacred
Egyptian architecture found a perfect
balance of plan and its greatest formal
elegance. The peristyle court in Luxor and
the ruins of Soleb in Nubia still have
admirable papyriform or lotus-shaped
columns with proportions that are
particularly refined. Catching the light,
their shafts regimented and defined the
great entrance courtyards of the temples
and set the rhythm of the hypostyle halls.
Amenophis III was, however, unique in
adopting brick for his tomb temple in
western Thebes. There remain from it only
the two colossi of Memnon which today
stand solitary watch over the valley.

The Ramessids (XIXth and XXth dynasties)
sought above all effects of mass and power
in their architecture. This development is
still subdued in the temple at Abydos
erected by Seti I, but emerges clearly in the
huge hypostyle hall which the same
pharaoh built in Karnak. The power of
Ramessid architecture owed much to the
style of its supports and their grouping. For
interior spaces, two types of column were
used: stocky, monostyle columns
(papyriform with closed bud and a smooth
shaft) in the aisles emphasized the
verticality of the more slender
campaniform columns (papyriform with
open flower) of the nave, lit by the filtered
light of the clerestory windows. The axis

towards the sanctuary was clearly defined.
Lesser columns interposed added to the
impression of a dense forest of stone.

This tendency towards the monumental
reached its peak during the reign of
Ramesses II, without doubt the greatest
builder of ancient Egypt. The Ramesseum
consists of a series of massive pylons, with
courts lined by Osirian pillars bearing the
effigy of the king, and a stone forest of a
hypostyle hall. During the XXth dynasty,
the temple of Ramesses III in Medinet-Habu
faithfully followed the same principles. The
same superhuman proportions also appear
in the great Ramessid rock temples. At Abu
Simbel, the colossi at the entrance rose 20
metres (65 feet) above the terrace leading
to the temple. Saved from the waters of Lake
Nasser, the temple has now been entirely
rebuilt further up the cliff.

Besides temples, the architecture of the New
Kingdom included great underground
tombs for the kings and queens. These were
deliberately hidden from the world, and lie
concealed in the valleys to the west of
Thebes in order to escape the attention of
looters. Private tombs, although they are
often decorated with splendid paintings,
are with few exceptions very uninteresting
architecturally. The exceptions have the
peculiarity of being related to their owner's
occupation: Amenhotep, the son of Hapu,
built with his tomb a little model of a
temple, and the craftsmen of Deir el-
Medineh added cult chapels surmounted
by miniature pyramids. At the end of the
second millennium BC, Egypt again sank
into anarchy, and many different factions
disputed power. The country entered a long
period of depression and lost its
independence (the Late, Ptolemaic and
Roman periods). But the power of Egyptian

culture and its intellectual authority again
imposed itself on the various invaders.
Libyan, Nubian, Persian, Greek or Roman
invaders ruling over the conquered country
adopted pharaonic customs. The
"Ethiopian" (Sudanese) pharaohs even
took these traditions home with them to
their own capital, Napata, and maintained
them up until the 5th century AD.

Like the indigenous kings the new rulers
commissioned the temple clergy to erect
new buildings. These late works are
actually among the most beautiful and the
best preserved in Egypt, and strictly adhere
to the traditional canons of the New
Kingdom. Philae, Edfu and Dendara, to
mention only the most celebrated (there are
at least 100) have a remarkable clarity of
plan and perpetuate the clean shapes and
lines of pharaonic architecture. Their walls
are covered even more systematically with
scenes and texts, as if they had a duty to
preserve the achievements and the spirit of
Egyptian civilization. They confirm the
total rejection of any external influence,
even in techniques of construction. Greek
and Roman rulers were represented on the
walls of these last Egyptian temples in
costume which differs little from that of
Narmer, the first pharaoh. Only
Christianity and its intolerance of
paganism put an end to this activity,
sometimes by transforming the temples into
churches. And so, right up to the last
moment, the architecture of ancient Egypt
remained a vivid, detailed and enduring
expression of an inimitable civilization.

The pyramids and tombs of Memphis

During the IIIrd dynasty, Pharaoh Zoser set up his capital at Memphis, in the fortress of the "White Wall", founded according to tradition by the legendary Menes (Horus Narmer), who had united upper and lower Egypt in about 3000BC. Situated on the west bank of the Nile, about 25 kilometres (15 miles) south of Cairo, Memphis (now the village of Mit-Rahineh) has no detectable remains earlier than those of the New Kingdom. The important Ramessid ruins of the temple of Ptah, the local god, probably indicate nevertheless the older site of the religious centre of the town, situated opposite the most ancient and important of the royal burial places of Ancient Egypt – Saqqarah.

The burial places connected with the capital extend along the border of the Libyan desert for a distance of about 70 kilometres (43 miles), including, from north to south, the sites of Abu Roach (IVth dynasty), Giza (IVth), Zauiet el Aryan (IIIrd and IVth), Abusir (Vth), Saqqarah (Ist, IInd, IIIrd, Vth and VIth dynasties), Dahchur (IVth) and Meidum (IIIrd and IVth). So many different sites are the result, almost certainly, of the movement of the royal palace and political and administrative centres away from Memphis during the course of the Old Kingdom. The divergences from the ancient religious centre, furthermore, only date from the end of the IIIrd dynasty through the IVth; all other pharaohs of the Old Kingdom erected their pyramids at Saqqarah and at Abusir, opposite the traditional centre of the town. During the VIth dynasty the name of Mennefer (Memphis, in Greek), which had been that of the pyramid of Pepi I in southern Saqqarah and of the adjacent city development was applied to the whole city, replacing the ancient name of "White Wall".

The vast numbers of funerary monuments at Memphis were erected at the edge of the desert. They separated the living world, the fertile valley, from the hostile, inert world of the arid and silent Libyan desert.

At Saqqarah, the scribe Imhotep, Vizier to Pharaoh Zoser and High Priest of the sun-god Re in the temple of Heliopolis, whose reputation in letters, the arts and the sciences was without equal, and who was revered by the Greeks as a god of healing, created for the king the grandiose machinery for the exercise of his sovereignty over the hereafter. He designed the first collection of monumental buildings in stone, known by the Egyptians as the "material for eternity".

The central feature was the first step pyramid, of rectangular plan, which rose in six stages above the subterranean galleries of the funeral apartments. It reproduced the image of the great celestial staircase, and evoked the idea of the primordial hill from which the sun rose on the first morning. Around it, the buildings and courtyards were intended either for votive offerings or for the enactment of the series of ritual celebrations (Sed) which the king was believed to be performing in his celestial eternity much as he had done during his lifetime in his palace at Memphis. This vast collection of buildings covered 15 hectares (37 acres); it was surrounded by an imposing fortified wall which imitated in stone the brick fortifications of Memphis. This was the first time that the fundamental aim of the funerary architecture of Ancient Egypt – namely to deny the existence of time and of death by constructing a permanent and perfect building – had been expressed on this scale. The forms and techniques employed reveal the intention: they imitate in stone the traditional forms and techniques of architecture in brick and wattle which are thereby "eternalized".

The tendency towards the monumental in architecture in ancient Egypt reached its peak at Giza. The precision and the perfect shapes of the three pyramids of Cheops (145 metres/475 feet high), of Chephren (144 metres/470 feet) and Mycerinus (62 metres/200 feet), all guarded by the great sphinx of Chephren at the base of the plateau, are still a source of fascination and wonder. The mind boggles at the sheer size of these projects (about 2.6 million cu. metres/3.4 million cu. yards of stone for the pyramid of Cheops alone) and at the perfection of their masonry – there is not even the tiniest gap between the facing blocks, each of which weighs tens of tons).

The funeral apartments (after the plan had been changed several times) were finally placed in the very heart of the pyramid of Cheops. The corbelled vault of the great gallery and the arrangement of chambers above the ceiling of the hall of the sarcophagus to relieve the enormous load indicate the builders' supreme mastery of their art.

There are three further main features of the pyramids: at the bottom of the plateau a canal gave access to a large quay on which was the lower temple. This was connected by a covered way to the upper temple, intended for funeral ceremonies. These features are, in part, preserved in the funerary complex of Cheops, notably the lower temple to the south of the sphinx. This building shows the essential characteristics of the architecture of the IVth dynasty. Handling the massive monolithic granite pillars from Aswan that affirm the severity and majesty of the building required great skill, which is further evidenced in the perfect bonding of the walls' granite cladding.

From the time of Mycerinus the monuments became smaller, but their execution was still remarkable for its perfection. During the Vth dynasty, improved knowledge of the limitations and capacities of stone made it possible to refine architectural forms. Elegant columns in granite or limestone imitated wood and were variously shaped and decorated as palms, papyrus and lotus. The plans of the temples and of the apartments tended to become uniform. The funerary architecture of the Old Kingdom thus achieved a classic "Memphis" style that was to remain a reference point for all later periods.

All round these groupings of royal tombs, veritable towns of *mastabas* extended. *Mastabas* were the traditional tombs of rectangular plan with sloping walls. Originally of brick (the great royal *mastabas* of the Ist and IInd dynasties), the *mastabas* of high state functionaries were built in stone from the reign of Cheops onwards. The largest, which sometimes enclosed a courtyard, numerous rooms and a large sanctuary, date from the end of the Vth and the start of the VIth dynasties and are very richly decorated (for example, the *mastabas* of Ti and of Mereruka in northern Saqqarah).

At the end of the Old Kingdom, Memphis and its burial places were seriously damaged during the calamities of the First Intermediate period (about 2180BC). But though it ceased to be the capital, Memphis always remained one of the most important cities of ancient Egypt, even into the Late period, as Herodotus testified in the 5th century BC.

Step pyramid, Saqqarah

The pyramid of Zoser (IIIrd dynasty), the first such to be built, rises in six stages to a height of 60 metres (195 feet). Its plan is rectangular and measures 121 by 109 metres (390 by 350 feet). It was the outcome of three successive projects: Imhotep first designed a great *mastaba* in stone: then, almost certainly for theological reasons connected with the doctrine of Heliopolis, he decided to raise a four-step pyramid on the initial *mastaba*; finally he enlarged the base to permit the addition of two more steps.

The construction is solid; the courses are laid vertically, tapering towards the centre, which gives the monument great stability. Under the core, a shaft 28 metres (92 feet) deep leads to the subterranean galleries of the funeral apartment. This consists of several limestone chambers, the walls of which are covered with tiles of blue faience imitating reed wattling. The burial vault itself is made of Aswan granite. In the foreground, dummy (roomless) chapels run along the western edge of the Sed courtyard. Some façades, imitating timber-framed wattle-and-daub buildings, have been reconstructed from the great number of ancient stones on the site, thanks to the work over more than 50 years of J.-P. Lauer.

Perimeter wall of the monuments of Zoser, Saqqarah

This fortified curtain wall encloses an area 544 by 277 metres (595 by 300 yards). Built of stone, it imitates brick construction, but that is not the only illusion. There are 15 "gates" in the wall – all dummies: 14 of them are permanently closed; the remaining one, in the south-east, shown here, is permanently open. This enormous "fortification" cannot therefore be secured.

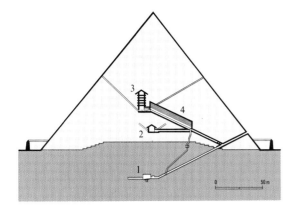

The sphinx, Giza

The sphinx is a natural rocky out-crop, the remains of a quarry that supplied a large number of blocks to the pyramid of Cheops, which the builders of the Chephren monuments had the idea of using to create a giant sphinx. The head was sculpted as an effigy of Chephren. The rock was covered with painted plaster to make it look like the body of a lion. The paws were carved separately and added on. The sphinx is 20 metres (65 feet) high and 71 metres (230 feet) long; its nose measures 1.70 metres (5 feet 6 inches).

Section through the pyramid of Cheops, Giza

There were in all three different plans for the location of the burial chamber: the subterranean solution (1) avoided the loading problems created by the huge mass of the pyramid, but almost certainly for theological reasons it was then decided to move the chamber above ground level.
This second chamber (2), 21 metres (68 feet) above the level of the base, was the first one vaulted by large monolithic blocks set in an inverted V, the method which was generally used thereafter for vaulting the inner chambers of pyramids.
The final project (3), the chamber near the centre of the pyramid, combined this construction method with the installation of upper chambers to discharge the load. The great gallery (4), 47 metres (154 feet) long, had a corbelled vault, a technique already mastered in the reign of Snefru.

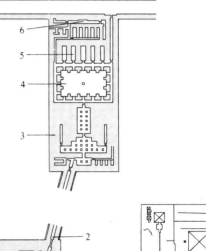
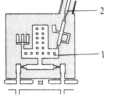
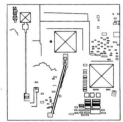

The pyramids, Giza

The three pyramids of Giza (IVth dynasty) remain a symbol of the architectural mastery of the ancient Egyptians. At the rear, that of Cheops, the biggest, measures 230.5 metres (756 feet) at the base against a height of 146 metres (479 feet), that is to say, a slope of 51° 52′. It is the oldest of the pyramids of Giza, adopting the smooth-sloping profile inaugurated by Cheops' predecessor Snefru, whose pyramid is to the south of Dahchur. In the centre, the pyramid of Chephren, though slightly smaller (143 by 215 metres/ 470 by 705 feet at the base) appears higher because of a steeper slope (52° 20′). At the top, it retains the capping of polished limestone that gave these monuments the appearance of veritable hills of light when the sun's rays shone on them, emphasizing their geometry by creating shadow. The burial chamber is slightly below ground level, which coincides with the monolithic blocks that form its roof. In the foreground, the pyramid of Mycerinus is the smallest of the three, measuring 108 metres (354 feet) at the base and 62 metres (203 feet) in height – a slope of 51°. The small pyramids are of queens, following the arrangement started during the reign of Snefru.

Temple of Chephren, Giza

The main features of the temple of Chephren are (1) the quay and the lower temple, associated, it seems, with the embalming and purification rites carried out at the time of the funeral; (2) the ramp that gives access to the upper temple. This upper temple consisted of an outer temple (3); a large vestibule leading to a cloister (4), which was bordered with effigies of the king and off which five cult chapels (5) opened; and finally, the inner temple, with repositories for cult objects (6) and a false door, carved in stone, through which the dead pharaoh could come to enjoy the gifts left by worshippers.

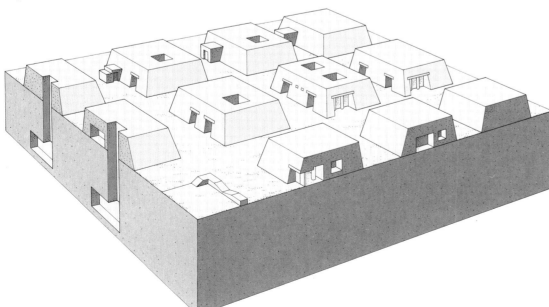

Pilasters and pillars

Pilasters imitating plant shapes first appeared under the IIIrd dynasty. The opening papyrus (campaniform) shape (1) was to be much used again during the New Kingdom. Free-standing pillars in plant forms – open palm (2), closed palm (3) and lotus (4) – are not found until the Vth dynasty.

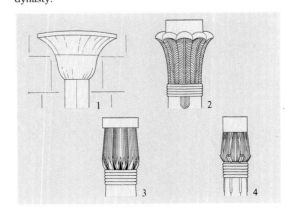

"Mastabas"

The mastaba was the typical form of Egyptian tomb for the great and famous. It consisted of a building of rectangular shape with sloping walls and was constructed of brick or stone. Richly decorated rooms were arranged in the upper parts, in particular a chapel (with a false door for the tomb's occupant and a table for offerings), and a room in which statues of the dead person were placed. A shaft, filled in after the funeral service, led to the subterranean vault, which contained the grave goods and the mummy in its sarcophagus.

121

Town planning and domestic architecture

Whereas there are numerous surviving examples of ancient Egyptian tombs and religious buildings, the reverse is the case when it comes to domestic architecture. Texts speak of a dense population, with large cities and a great many small towns built either on the edge of the cultivated region or on hills, known as *kom*, that were in the Nile valley but above flood level. But very few architectural remains have been found. This is partly a result of the materials used. Stone was reserved for the dead and then for the gods. For everyone else, raw brick was used, made from Nile mud mixed with straw, then shaped and dried in the sun. Trunks of palm trees usually supplied the beams in this country where hardwood was scarce. Reeds, palm, papyrus and lotus leaves provided additional building materials, reflecting in people's houses their closeness to and dependence on nature and its cycles. These plants were also used for small wattle buildings (sanctuaries, kiosks, shelters), in a technique employed since the earliest habitations were constructed in the Nile valley. Geographical constraints are also responsible for the disappearance of civil architecture. The deserts on both sides of the Nile have always ensured that communities would be built near the river, and so Egypt's present cities re-use the limited number of ancient sites. Even when the archaeologist has an opportunity to dig, deposits of silt have repeatedly altered historic ground levels after the annual floods, and the level of the water table can make excavation very difficult. In Memphis, for example, the New Kingdom temple is now permanently partly under water.

Some occasional but important remains have, however, been found. The site of El-Lahun, at the entrance to the great oasis of Fayum, has yielded the remains of a town – Kahun – which was inhabited by priests, managers and artisans connected with the funerary buildings of Sesostris II (Middle Kingdom). Tell el-Amarna, in central Egypt, the site of the capital of the heretical king of the

XVIIIth dynasty, Akhenaten (Amenophis IV), has also given us an image of a large city of ancient Egypt. Finally, in Thebes, where very few traces of the city have been preserved or excavated, the village built to house the artisans who worked on the necropolis of the Valley of the Kings has been discovered on the west bank.

These towns appear to have been created from nothing in response to exceptional circumstances, and may not therefore be generally representative. But the town planning experience they demonstrate cannot have been acquired overnight. The Egyptians were knowledgeable surveyors and geometricians who knew very well how to organize their available irrigated agricultural space, and we must assume they planned their towns with equal skill. This talent is seen both in their care in aligning great monuments and in the arrangement of the religious and official centres of their towns. But there can also be little doubt that, with time, these principles were negated by an unplanned proliferation of private building. In Thebes and in some other towns, texts reveal the authorities trying to clear even the temple enclosures of intrusive private housing.

Tell el-Amarna, of which the ancient name was Akhetaten ("the horizon of Aten"), provides an example of a major city in which town planning has not been disfigured by time. In fact, at the end of the reign of the heretical pharaoh, Akhenaten, the city was razed, covered with chalk and abandoned. Thus fixed in the soil it was a gift for archaeologists. Here it is possible to see the broad trends in town planning carried out by the ancient Egyptians. The town stretches along a main axis running from north to south, exemplified in the Royal Way. The axis follows the course of the nearby Nile, the great highway of ancient Egypt, on whose east bank the city had been established. A large harbour gave access to a main road leading to the palace quarter. Around this main street a number of secondary roads were arranged from north to south and east to

west according to a more or less regular grid. The centre of the city was marked by religious and official buildings.

To the north and south of the centre there were residential quarters where substantial and modest houses intermingled. This was perhaps a peculiarity of the reign, since in the Middle Kingdom at El-Lahun (Kahun) there was a definite organization of residential areas in relation to the social scale of the occupants. At the northern edge was the commercial and business quarter and at the edge of the cemetery, to the east, was the artisans' village, which was also carefully planned. This substantial city was part of a vast area sacred to the god Aten encompassing both banks of the river – its limits were defined by inscribed boundary stones.

The walls of the houses and of the palace of Tell el-Armana have been flattened, but the archaeological remains and paintings in the tombs give a fairly accurate picture of what they were like. The modest terraced houses, with a few rooms, were crowded in a very dense pattern. Their walls were covered with a coating of lime. The rich dwellings, inside surrounding walls, had open spaces with large courtyards and sometimes a garden with a pond. They consisted of the master's quarters and of common rooms and stores. (In Thebes, where building land must have been in shorter supply, even the dwellings of the rich are familiarly urban, consisting of two storeys and without gardens.)

In Tell el-Amarna, interior walls in the better houses were covered with brightly painted plaster. The ceilings of the large reception rooms were supported by columns of wood with floral decoration. The character of these houses was repeated in the palace only with greater luxury, where the walls were splendidly clad with ceramic tiles. The remains of the palace of Amenophis III at Malgatta (west of Thebes) show that it had already anticipated the freshness and elegance of the naturalistic decoration of the palace of Tell el-Amarna.

Town of the pyramid of Sesostris II, El-Lahun (Kahun; Middle Kingdom, early 19th century BC)

The town, established for the community that was to build the pyramid, was laid out on a rectangular plan in an area about 400 by 350 metres (440 by 380 yards). A wall contained the whole, which was then subdivided into residential sectors according to social status. To the west, the artisans' quarter has small terraced houses opening on to parallel roads running east to west. The main road runs north to south and is about 8 metres (9 yards) wide. The entrance to it is at the southern end. The artisans' quarter is completely cut off from that of the managers by a long brick wall.

The managers' quarter occupies the whole of the eastern part of the town. Its main road runs east to west with a gateway at the eastern end. To the north of the road are the richest dwellings, arranged around large courtyards with porticoes facing north in order to benefit from the cooling north wind. An entrance corridor leading into the courtyard separates the family's apartments from the domestic offices. The houses to the south of the main road are for junior managers.

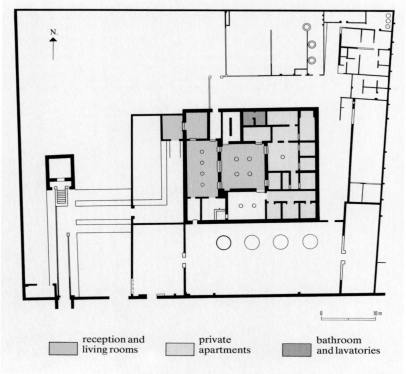

House of a nobleman (New Kingdom, about 1360BC), Tell el-Amarna

This is a spacious villa, which includes a large pleasure garden. The master's residence is reached by an entrance court. There are vast reception and living rooms, with a loggia and terrace. The private apartments include numerous bedrooms, a salon with a central column, and a bathroom and lavatories.

The other courtyards contain the grain store, stables, kennels and a poultry yard. They also give access to the servants' quarters.

reception and living rooms · private apartments · bathroom and lavatories

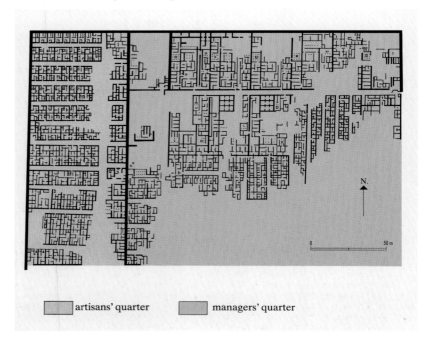

artisans' quarter · managers' quarter

Artisans' village at the royal burial site at Thebes (New Kingdom, XVIIIth–XXth dynasties), Deir el-Medineh

Contained within an almost rectangular enclosure measuring 130 by 50 metres (140 by 55 yards), the village is divided into two parts by a road running approximately north to south. The entrance to the village, with a gatekeeper's lodge, is situated at the north end. To the north and west of the village are the tombs of the artisans, which are ranged on the lower slopes of the Theban hills. The dwellings are terraced and packed in very tightly, without any gardens.

P. Barguet

Plan and section of a house, Deir el-Medineh

The houses have a characteristic plan with rooms en suite. The same plan was repeated for the artisans' village at the necropolis of Tell el-Amarna. Built in brick on a foundation of stone, the houses of Deir el-Medineh measure, on average, 10 by 3 metres (30 by 10 feet). The sequence of rooms is: reception room, living room, bedroom and kitchen. There is a staircase giving access to the terraces. One or sometimes two cellars were dug into the rocky subsoil.

Three-storey town house (New Kingdom, XVIIIth dynasty, from the tomb of Tutnefer)

House of a notable of Thebes, including a ground floor, and two floors above, on top of which there was a roof terrace where grain was stored. The upper storeys were reached by an interior staircase. The kitchen was on the ground floor, the private apartments of the master were on the first floor and the second was used as offices. Ducts were built into the ceilings so that air could circulate and cool the building.

Tell el-Amarna, capital of King Akhenaten (New Kingdom, c.1360BC)

The centre of the town consists of religious and official buildings.
To the east of the Royal Way there are, from north to south, the great temple of Aten (1), the king's residence (2), the smaller temple (3). Between these main buildings lie the temple storehouses and various workshops. Further to the east, less strictly oriented, are the administrative offices (4) and, on the edge of the desert, the barracks and stables (5). To the west of the Royal Way, on the banks of the river, is the imposing grand palace (6) with its courtyards, state rooms and, in particular, a great hypostyle hall with 544 square columns, which was almost certainly the throne room (7). The palace has a frontage of 270 metres (295 yards) on to the Royal Way, and is connected to the king's private residence by a covered brick bridge. The layout of the king's residence resembles that of the rich dwellings of the town, with courtyards and garden, though on a grander scale. The king also possessed summer and pleasure residences on the outskirts of the town.

N.

Royal Way

0   200 m

temples   palaces   annexes, stores, offices, barracks

The temples of the New Kingdom

Under the New Kingdom, Egypt was at the peak of its power. The conquering pharaohs of the XVIIIth, XIXth and XXth dynasties extended their authority from the fourth cataract of the Nile in the south up to the frontiers of Mesopotamia in the north-east. Tributes that increased considerably the riches both of the state and of the temples flowed from this great empire. On the initiative of the sovereigns, Nubia, Egypt and especially the region of the sumptuous capital, Thebes, were generously endowed with grandiose stone buildings. The quarries of the hills which bordered the country to the south and east were exploited to the full. Directed either by the State administration or by the temple authorities these great programmes mobilized huge numbers of workers.

There are two groups of monumental buildings at Thebes. On the east bank, the great temples to deities still mark the religious and official centre of the town: the most important ones are the immense temple of Amon-Re at Karnak and the temple of Luxor. On the west bank, on the edge of the desert and hard by the sites of the numerous rock tombs, a series of temples stand which were put up by the sovereigns of the New Kingdom primarily for their afterlife cult but in which the worship of Amon was very prominent too. The most important and the best preserved are the temples of queen Hatshepsut at Deir el-Bahri (XVIIIth dynasty), of Ramesses II (the Ramesseum, XIXth) and of Ramesses III at Medinet Habu (XXth).

An Egyptian temple was a vast structure. Generally a long wall of unbaked brick delimited a large enclosure. Within were first of all the house of the god, in stone, but also numerous related buildings in brick that were connected with the many activities of the temple. The cult derived its income and its staff their upkeep from agriculture, sometimes on a vast scale, and not necessarily confined to the surrounding region. Storehouses, silos, poultry yards and cowsheds are often found in temple precincts. Workshops were erected for the maintenance of the buildings, and other buildings for the preparation of daily offerings. Stewards and administrators responsible for managing the temple had their offices. Temples were also centres of intellectual activity, in which young scribes were trained, ancient manuscripts were copied and new works of theology were written. Temples were thus repositories of knowledge, with intellectual and religious roles to play in addition to their economic functions; some temples, thanks to the influence their priests had been able to acquire, also wielded considerable political influence. The numerous brick buildings that still surround the Ramesseum give an idea of the importance of these ancillary functions.

In the middle of all this activity, there stood apart the building in which the god was immanent – a massive, forbidding form of unseeing stone walls. Its resemblance to a fortress, closed to the exterior, was further accentuated by the two towers of the pylon façade. The reliefs that covered these sloping outer walls expressed both the nature and the benefits of the sacred place. Scenes of victory and of the hunt showed the pharaoh and the gods establishing order and justice in this world of chaos. The temple was the representation of a world of perfect order, thanks to the beneficial power of the god within. He came to dwell in his earthly house, in the form of a statue, in order to feed his power on the offerings of man. The architecture of the Egyptian temple was therefore, essentially, directed to the interior, to the space rendered holy by the divine presence. It constituted a calculated progress towards the sacred in the size of its chambers, from the larger to the more intimate. As one proceeded, having crossed the great peristyle courtyard preceded by the entrance gate, the halls became shorter and narrower; ceilings were set lower and floors higher. The most sacred place in the temple, the sanctuary in which the statue was placed, was both the smallest and the highest chamber in the complex. Each temple thus represented and recalled the primordial hill – the first appearance of earth rising above the waters of the ocean at the time of the creation of the world.

Light too played a role in this orderly architectural progress. The peristyle courtyard was open to the sky and flooded by the sun. The hypostyle halls were lit by high windows giving out from the central nave over the lower roofs of the aisle. The rear of the temple received only a dim light through skylights let into the roof. The sanctuary itself was in total darkness. However, at one moment during the day it received a strong light from the entrance, straight along the axis of the central aisle. When the sun passed between the twin towers of the pylon, it enabled the few privileged priests who were responsible for his cult and offerings to contemplate the illuminated revelation of the god present in his statue. The mass of the faithful, denied this vision, were able to see the god only when he left the temple. At the time of the great festivals, the god was borne on the barge which was kept in the sanctuary's antechamber and presented himself to the crowds. At Karnak, Amon-Re was taken in this manner in procession to the temple of Luxor (at the festival of Opet) or even across the Nile in order to visit each of the great temples on the west bank (the festival of the valley). The path by which the god left was marked by the avenue of sphinxes in front of the temple entrance. In Thebes, these processional avenues developed into ceremonial routes linking the main sanctuaries of the east bank. Beside the temple there was also a sacred lake where certain festivals could be celebrated, but which was used mainly for the ritual purification which the priests had to undergo before entering the temple to serve the god.

The details of sacred buildings in the New Kingdom continued to imitate, in stone, those of civil architecture. Stone cornices echoed the overhang of thatch designed to protect walls made of impermanent materials. The corners of the inward-sloping external walls were decorated with rounded mouldings imitating the reed trusses used to protect the corners of unbaked brick or clay walls. Stone columns had the papyrus or lotus ornament traditional on wooden columns. Faceted piers, which already show the sober severity of fluted Greek columns (hence the name "proto-Doric" which is often given to them), imitated simple posts of finished wood. Even tent posts were imitated in stone. Both carvings and paintings contributed greatly to the vivid impression Egyptian temples made. Outside, the carved surfaces produced a stimulating interplay of light and shade. Inside, paintings and texts both enlivened the rooms and expressed the purpose for which they were built.

Some of the more important temples have lost the initial unity that one can still see in more humble monuments. In fact, each reign tended to leave its mark by adding a new feature to the hypostyle halls, courtyards or pylons – the great temple of Amon-Re at Karnak is a veritable catalogue of monuments and styles from different periods. But the core of the temple always met unchanging needs, because the Egyptian temple of the New Kingdom was the outcome of the continual reinterpretation of immutable truths about the nature of the world and its functioning. The main characteristics therefore, as expressed in the temple of Khons in Karnak (opposite), exhibit a permanence independent of transitory notions.

The great hypostyle hall, temple of Amon-Re, Karnak

Constructed by Seti I and Ramesses II (XIXth dynasty), the hypostyle hall measures 103 by 52 metres (340 by 170 feet) and has 234 papyriform columns. The roof of the central nave is elevated and supported by campaniform (open papyrus) columns 20 metres (66 feet) in height. The lateral columns are monostyle (with closed papyrus buds) and 13 metres (43 feet) high. This variation in the level of the roof made it possible to put in clerestory windows to light the nave.

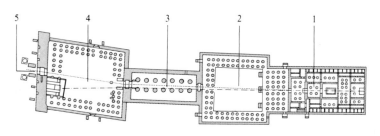

Temple of Amon, Luxor

The rear part of the temple (1) contains the sanctuary, dating from Amenophis III (XVIIIth dynasty). This king then built the great peristyle court (2 and photograph) with its magnificent lotus-shaped columns, and added a long vestibule with two rows of campaniform columns (3). During the XIXth dynasty, Ramesses II built a second peristyle court (4) on a rhomboid plan (possibly to align it with the processional way coming from Karnak) and a large entrance pylon (5). In front of this there stood six colossal statues of the Pharaoh. Only one of the two obelisks that used to frame the door is still in place; the other is in the Place de la Concorde, Paris.

Temple of Khons, Karnak

The small temple of Khons, the son in the divine trinity of Thebes (Amon, Mut, Khons), was built by Ramesses III (XXth dynasty) and is typical of the Egyptian temple of the New Kingdom. It measures 75 by 30 metres (245 by 100 feet).

The inner temple consists of the room in which the portable ceremonial barge was kept and, after a pillared vestibule, of the sanctum that sheltered the divine statue.

Skylights give a dim illumination to the vestibule.

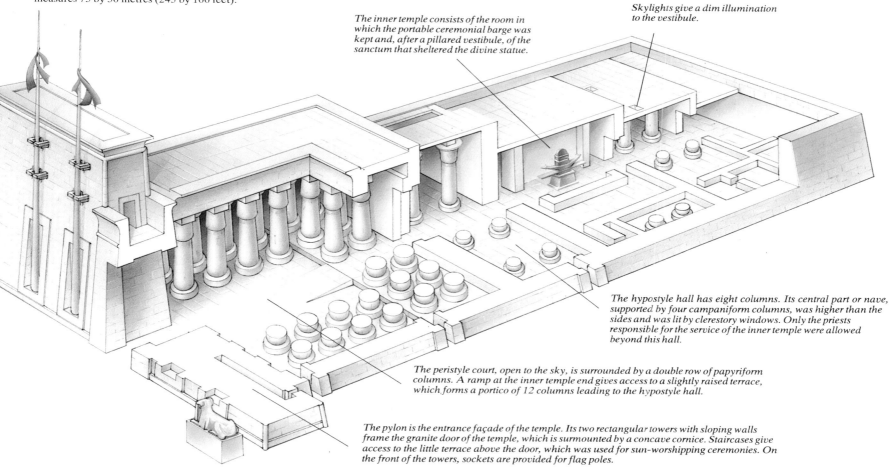

The hypostyle hall has eight columns. Its central part or nave, supported by four campaniform columns, was higher than the sides and was lit by clerestory windows. Only the priests responsible for the service of the inner temple were allowed beyond this hall.

The peristyle court, open to the sky, is surrounded by a double row of papyriform columns. A ramp at the inner temple end gives access to a slightly raised terrace, which forms a portico of 12 columns leading to the hypostyle hall.

The pylon is the entrance façade of the temple. Its two rectangular towers with sloping walls frame the granite door of the temple, which is surmounted by a concave cornice. Staircases give access to the little terrace above the door, which was used for sun-worshipping ceremonies. On the front of the towers, sockets are provided for flag poles.

Temple of Hatshepsut, Deir el-Bahri

Inspired by a funerary temple of the Middle Kingdom built by King Mentuhotep (XIth dynasty), the architect of Queen Hatshepsut (XVIIIth dynasty), Senenmout, built one of the most beautiful monuments of ancient Egypt, the style of which was never repeated.

It consists of a succession of terraces whose supporting walls are masked by long colonnades divided in the centre by monumental access ramps. On the second terrace a third portico gives entry to a peristyle courtyard leading to the sanctuary, which is cut out of the cliff. The work of Senenmout is, in the strictness of its composition, architecturally very successful and a fine example of the integration of architecture and natural site.

Avenue of the sphinxes, temple of Amon-Re, Karnak

Joining the quay to the temple, the Divine Way was bordered by sphinxes with the head of a ram, an animal sacred to Amon. The avenue was probably rearranged during the Late period, but the sphinxes themselves date from the XIXth dynasty.

R. Deschames

Temple of Segesta (Sicily)

This temple, begun in about 420BC by a Greek builder, does not seem to have progressed beyond its outer shell. The "barbarian" city of Segesta, which had long oscillated in allegiance between western Greek and eastern Carthaginian Sicily, soon after lost its independence to Carthage. Today, the columns of the peristyle, which were made of poor local limestone, stand out alone in a country which impressed Goethe by its magnificent ruggedness. The austerity of the western Doric Order is further accentuated by the absence of stucco covering and by the plain columns – their fluting was never completed. This temple has nothing provincial about it despite its proportions being slightly more extended than usual (6 × 14 columns instead of 6 × 13). The lateral and longitudinal curvature of the stylobate, and certain decorative details, indicate that the designers intended to rival the greatest temple of the era – the Parthenon.

*I*t would be difficult not to have some familiarity with Greek architecture. Ever since the 18th century, when the drawings of Piranesi and of Stuart and Revett first educated the public in the beauties of Paestum and of Athens respectively, European and American towns have abounded with Greek imitations. In Munich, Berlin, London, Paris, Washington and New York, the impersonal majesty of colonnades and pediments on public buildings seems to guarantee the importance and nobility of whatever activity is housed within. But this familiarity is deceptive. These buildings, serving as sacred repositories of power, art or money, skilful copies though they may be, discredit the reality of the Greek temple as a building with a shape and structure developed over a long period into an organic whole. If the architects of the Greek revival had visited the original buildings on site, the distortion might have been less marked. Like all great architecture, that of Greece owes its power to an intimate rapport with its environment, a rapport achieved through light, which makes the lines and volumes stand out, and through materials, with all their inherent constraints and possibilities. But Greece remained an unfamiliar country up to the end of the 19th century. Most of the artists and writers who based their ideals on it had never been there. Greece was then, and maybe still is, the East. It suggests disquiet, insecurity and the unknown because of the miscegenation and successive conquests to which it has been subject – its present reality has not very much to do with the spiritual ideal formed on the basis of its ancient texts. The study of Greek architecture has suffered from this excessively abstract approach: its scope has been restricted to Athenian classicism and to some isolated but easily accessible monuments, and it has for a long time only consisted of a dry catalogue of form – detached from all experience. Direct contact with Greek buildings was, and still is, a revelation to many people, who find that the features familiar from copies are transformed in their living reality.

The internal coherence, the clarity and simplicity, the rapport with the landscape is always perceptible despite the ruinous condition of virtually all ancient Greek architecture. There may be no more than a stylobate, some columns, one or two bare walls: in most cases this is all the harsh climate and the degradations or abuse of subsequent ages have left. But very often, that is enough; sometimes it is better like that. These gutted buildings, without a roof, stripped of all their painted decoration and sculpture, are reduced to their essentials, as is the Victory of Samothrace without arms

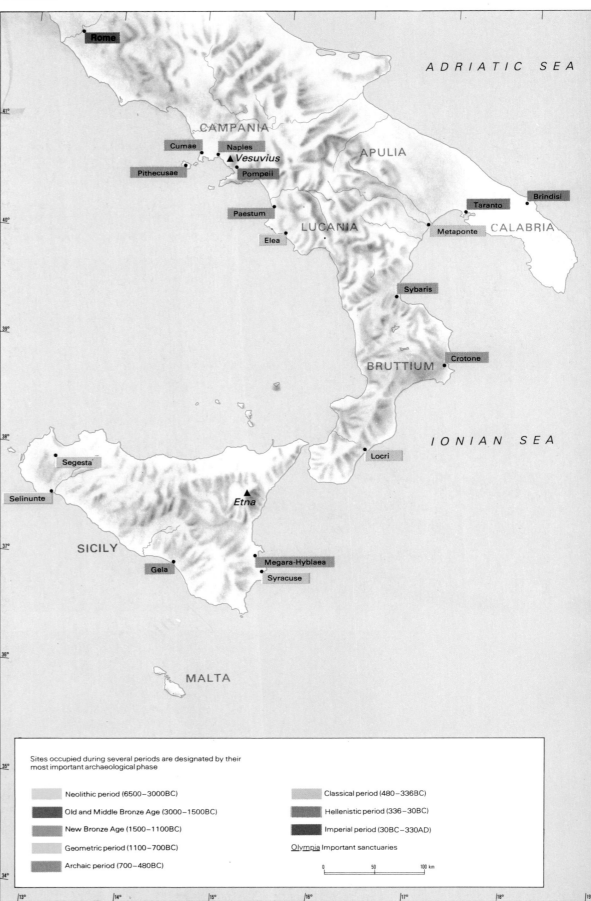

Sites occupied during several periods are designated by their most important archaeological phase

Neolithic period (6500–3000BC)

Old and Middle Bronze Age (3000–1500BC)

New Bronze Age (1500–1100BC)

Geometric period (1100–700BC)

Archaic period (700–480BC)

Classical period (480–336BC)

Hellenistic period (336–30BC)

Imperial period (30BC–330AD)

Olympia Important sanctuaries

0   50   100 km

THE GREEK WORLD

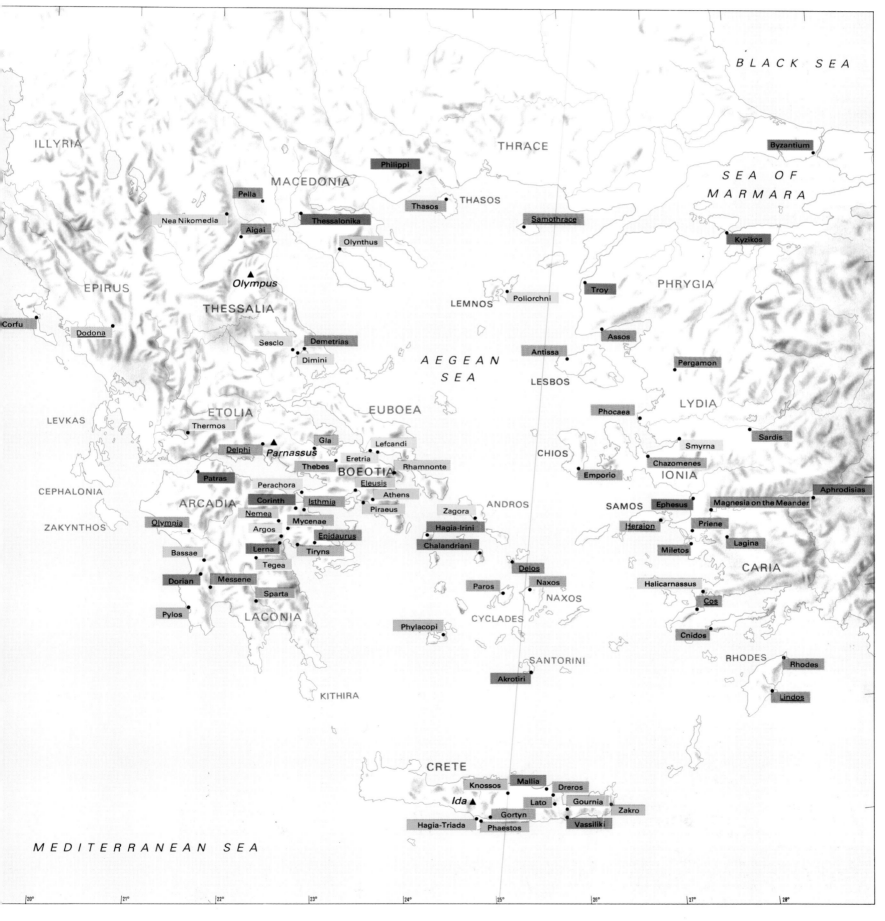

or head. This is a romantic experience, but incomplete; it is up to the archaeologist to fill in what time has destroyed by careful observation and reconstruction (considerably aided by the standardization of the elements and units of Greek architecture). The survival of a single element of each part of a building is enough to make it possible to restore its detail and elevation. This task, however, though it has been proceeding for some 150 years, is far from being finished. Excavations, which have multiplied since the Second World War in Greece, southern Italy and Turkey, never cease to produce something new. Our knowledge of Greek architecture is, therefore, in constant evolution, and now extends into time and space very far removed from the Athenian "cradle of civilization" which so fascinated the 19th century. The successive discovery of Mycenaean, Minoan and neolithic civilizations has revealed that Greek architecture was not a sudden miracle, born of nothing, as was then supposed. Through all the vicissitudes of history, forms and techniques remained the same. The interest recently shown in the later periods – the end of the Hellenistic period and the beginning of the Roman period – has made it possible to establish elsewhere that the "Baroque" current which soon permeated Roman architecture probably originated in Alexandria, and that architecture in the Greek world remained alive and original at least until the end of the 2nd century AD. From this much widened chronological perspective has emerged a much more exact understanding of the local dialects in the field defined by the terms "Ionian" and "Doric". For 20 years now we have been aware of an island "Ionic", the existence of which had hitherto been hardly guessed. At the same time newly discovered traces of Ionian buildings in the western Mediterranean colonies have led to a modification of the old idea that this region was exclusively Doric. Secondly, attention has been less rigidly fixed on religious buildings as the prime subject of aesthetic preoccupations, and has turned to aspects of architecture sometimes more directly relevant to society and history – such as defensive and domestic building. Even in the religious sphere, the systematic examination of written accounts and specifications found in the sanctuaries has made it possible to enter into the practical side of building and to restore more faithfully that most fragile part of Greek buildings, which has nearly always disappeared – the roof. The study of Greek architecture today has left Neoclassical stereotypes far behind, and offers new experiences and knowledge which have nothing academic about them.

It is only when the question of its material has been settled that architecture can become an art; then the grammar gels and can serve expression. In Greece stone had been in use from neolithic times. It reappeared in the 2nd millennium BC with the Mycenaean civilization, and again at the end of the 7th century BC. At first the softer stones were used, because easier to work. Then tufa ("poros") limestone, and then marble, the noble material par excellence, from the 6th century BC. Except for a few important buildings, for which the Greeks did not hesitate to import high-quality marble – in particular Parian and Pentelic – and with it workmen skilled in dressing it, the material used came from a neighbouring site. Transport of stone was slow, dangerous, difficult and very costly. The cost of the carriage of stone blocks

dates (BC)	history and civilization	architecture
Neolithic (6500–3000BC)		
c.4500	Settlements: agriculture, pottery. Macedonia: Nea Nikomedia. Thessaly; acropolises of Sesclo and Dimini. Troy I.	Log huts. Cabins with walls of rough brick. Megaron.
Old Bronze Age (3000–2000BC)		
2600–2100 2450–2150 2700–2000	Metalwork: first towns. Cycladic civilization: marble idols, obsidian work. Troy II and III. Lerna (Argolid). Dorion-Malthi (Messene). Crete: early Minoan civilization.	Cyclades: stone houses with apses and small fortified towns. TROY: stone ramparts. LERNA III: tiled houses. Crete: collective tombs in a tholos.
Middle Bronze Age (2000–1500BC)		
c.1700 c.1500	Continental Greece: appearance of first Indo-Europeans, agricultural feudalism. Crete: Minoan civilization, centralized power and maritime domination. Hieroglyphic writing and "Linear A". First destruction of palaces. Catastrophe of Akrotiri (Santorini) and second destruction of palaces.	Continental Greece: trench and chamber tombs; golden masks. Crete: palaces at KNOSSOS, PHAISTOS, MALLIA, ZACRO; towns at KNOSSOS, Akrotiri on Santorini.
New Bronze Age (1500–1100BC)		
c.1150	Second wave of Indo-Europeans. Mycenaean civilization: several princedoms; occupation of Crete. "Linear B" writing. Third wave of Indo-Europeans: Dorian invasion.	Acropolises fortified; palaces with megaron. MYCENAE, TIRYNS, PYLOS, GLA, and so on. Princes' tombs in a tholos.
Submycenaean period (1150–1000BC)		
	Fall of Mycenaean civilization. Colonization of Ionia by refugees. Writing lost. End of negotiations with the East and Egypt. Agricultural smallholding.	Destruction of Mycenaean towns. Return to primitive houses.
Geometric period (1000–700BC)		
proto-Geometric (1000–900) early and middle Geometric (900–750)	Athens escapes the Dorian invasion. Formation of cities. Appearance of Geometric style in ceramics. Aristocratic governments. Slow resumption of maritime trade. Phoenician writing adopted.	Villages of huts. Buildings with apses. Large sanctuaries at OLYMPIA, DELPHI, DELOS, SAMOS.
776 late Geometric (750–700)	First Olympic Games. Homeric poems reach definitive form. Small-scale statuary. Trade with East intensifies. Agricultural and population problems. Colonization of southern Italy. Decline of the Geometric style; appearance of the human figure on ceramics.	First religious buildings with external wooden colonnades.
Archaic period (700–480BC)		
7th century 670–620	Colonization of entire Mediterranean basin. Decline of aristocratic power: tyrannies, democracies. Orientalizing phase in art. Heyday of Corinthian pottery. Appearance of large-scale statuary: "Daedalic" phase in art.	Progressive change to stone in religious architecture. Elaboration of Orders.

represented a third of the total cost of a column for the temple at Didyma. The materials and so the nature of Greek buildings were to a large extent conditioned by their site. Nevertheless, economic considerations did not prevent the use of several kinds of stone in the same building: marble was often reserved for the upper parts, sometimes occasioning discreet contrast. When the local stone had too mean an appearance, as, for instance, the spongy tufa at Olympia, it was coated with a stucco made of marble dust, but this was exceptional. Rather, the frank display of its material is one of the most characteristic traits of Greek architecture. The structure of

a Greek building is apparent in every aspect of its elevation; the arrangement of the stone blocks remained visible, their joints contributed to the effect. These, however, were thin since no cement was used, and the blocks were attached to each other instead by internal vertical bolts and horizontal iron cramps.

By the 6th century BC, the arrangement and shape of the blocks in a wall were consciously used to ornamental as well as structural effect. Polygonal motifs were created using blocks with a face of at least five sides. These were either rough bond, when the blocks were of different dressing

dates (BC)	history and civilization	architecture
620–580	"Colossal" phase; appearance of monumental sculpture.	Temple of Hera, OLYMPIA. Temple of Artemis, CORFU.
6th century	Ionian heyday.	Colossal Ionic temples: EPHESUS, DIDYMA (Miletos), SAMOS.
534	First performance of tragedy in Athens. Heyday of Attic pottery.	Sanctuaries, temples and treasuries at DELPHI, OLYMPIA and on the Acropolis at ATHENS.
510–509	Democratic reforms of Cleisthenes in Athens.	Ramparts in stone become general.
522–486	Reign of Darius the Great in Persia. Conquest of Ionia by Persia; Ionian revolts.	
490	First Persian War: Athens repels the Persians at Marathon.	Treasury of the Athenians at DELPHI.
480	Second Persian war: Athenian naval victory at Salamis.	Occupation and destruction of ATHENS by the Persians.
479	Land victory by the Greeks at Plataea.	
Classical period (480–336BC)		
480–450	"Severe style" in art: poetry (Aeschylus, Pindar); sculpture (Myron, Calamis); wall paintings (Polygnotos).	Temple of Zeus, OLYMPIA.
477	Confederation of Delos, directed by Athens.	New plan of Miletos by Hippodamos.
453–429	Pericles assumes power in Athens. History: Herodotos, Thucydides. Theatre: Sophocles, Euripides, Aristophanes. Sculpture: Polykleitos, Pheidias (statues in gold and ivory in Olympia and Athens).	Reconstruction of the Acropolis in ATHENS: the Parthenon (447–432); the Propylaea (438–432); the temple of Athene Nike (427–425); the Erechtheion (421–406).
432–404	Peloponnesian War between Sparta and Athens: final defeat of Athens and end of its hegemony.	First mosaics. First arches. Temple of BASSAE (Phigalia): first Corinthian capital by Callimachos.
399	Execution of Socrates.	
387	Plato founds Academy in Athens.	Tholos of DELPHI.
377	Recovery of Athens: Second Confederation of Delos. War between the cities: Athens, Sparta, Thebes. Social and moral crisis of the cities. Decline in Attic red-figure pottery.	Building at the Sanctuary of Asklepios in EPIDAURUS.
359–336	Reign of Philip II of Macedonia, opposed by Demosthenes in Athens.	
354–332	Sculpture: Praxiteles, Scopas.	Temple at TEGEA by Scopas. Mausoleum of HALICARNASSOS.
348	Destruction of Olynthos by Philip II.	
343	Aristotle tutor to Alexander.	Reconstruction of Priene on Hippadamian town plan.
	Athens defeated by Philip II at Chaeronea: end of the cities' independence.	
336	Assassination of Philip II.	Royal tombs at VERGINA (Macedonia).
Hellenistic period (336–30BC)		
338		New temple of Artemis at EPHESUS.
336–323	Reign of Alexander: conquest of the East.	Foundation of ALEXANDRIA.
323–281	Wars between Alexander's successors; large monarchies founded; progressive Hellenization of the East. Sculpture: Leochares, Bryaxis, Lysippos; portraits. Theatre: comedies of Menander.	New temple of Apollo at DIDYMA (Miletos). New towns: ANTIOCH, PERGAMON, AIKHANOUM (Afghanistan). Development of royal patronage.
3rd century	Greece: Aetolian and Achaean confederations. Alexandria: development of the museum. Philosophy: Cynics, Stoics and Epicurians.	Civil architecture: the portico. Remodelling of the Agora in ATHENS. New developments in military architecture.
212	First war between Macedonia and Rome.	
188	Peace of Apameus: decline of the Seleucid monarchy; heyday of Pergamon and Rhodes.	Decline of religious architecture. Arrangement of the sanctuary of Athene at LINDOS (Rhodes).
166–88	Sculpture: "Baroque" in Asia Minor. Free port of Delos: Eastern and Roman communities.	Great altar at PERGAMON. Peristyle and mosaic houses in DELOS.
148	Macedonia becomes a Roman province.	
146	Destruction of Corinth by the Romans.	
133	Death of Attalos III of Pergamon who bequeathed his kingdom to Rome (an Asian province in 129).	Arrangement of the Asklepieion on COS.
	Sculpture: Neoclassicism: *Venus de Milo.*	Temple of Hecate in LAGINA (last frieze).
88–64	Wars between Mithridates VI of Pontium and Rome: ancient Greek world destroyed.	
86	Sack of Athens by Sulla.	
63	End of the Seleucid kingdom; Syria annexed by Rome.	
42–30	Marc Antony rules the Greek East.	ATHENS: Tower of the Winds.
30	Annexation of Egypt by Octavian; end of Greek independence.	

and needed wedges to fill the gaps; or with straight or curved joints of regular bond following the line of the stones without any filling. Trapezoidal and rectangular bonds were either irregular, when the blocks were not set on constant courses, or "isodome", when each course was of the same height, or "pseudo-isodome", when there were regular courses but of different heights. These bonds were not used indifferently, and went in and out of fashion; they were evidently chosen both for their statics and for their aesthetic effect. Hence the polygonal bond with curved joints (called "Lesbian"), in which all the stones were dressed to measure, but with different

curves to different templates, was used for prestigious supporting walls, both because of its great strength, and, in the case of the terrace wall of the temple of Apollo at Delphi, for the sake of the arabesque effect. But it was expensive and had gone out of fashion by the beginning of the 5th century BC. Polygonal and trapezoidal bonds with straight joints are very common in military architecture, while a rectangular bond was favoured for important religious and civil architecture. The rectangular isodome is shown to perfection in the stark rigour of certain walls on the Athenian acropolis (Propylaea and Parthenon). The regularity of these facings may conceal more diverse

patterns of assembly involving square blocks (visible on only one side of the wall) and parpens (oblong blocks visible on both sides). Here again, local variations existed and persisted; they individualize a building like a signature – for instance, the irregular Cycladic bond which arbitrarily inserted a filling of small parpens among the large blocks. The wide variety of possibilities available was extended by the free mixture of bonds, in particular in military and domestic buildings. A wall might have a polygonal and trapezoidal bond in the lower part, altering to rectangular in the higher part.

Bonds used in Greek architecture

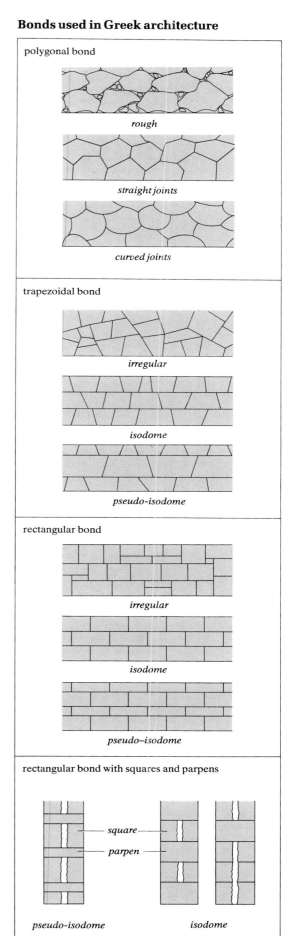

polygonal bond

rough

straight joints

curved joints

trapezoidal bond

irregular

isodome

pseudo-isodome

rectangular bond

irregular

isodome

pseudo–isodome

rectangular bond with squares and parpens

square
parpen

pseudo-isodome   *isodome*

Base and capital of an Ionic column (north of the Erechtheion). The Attic Ionic base is made up of two *tori* (convex mouldings) which surround a *scotia* (concave moulding). Only the upper *torus* is decorated, with an interlacing pattern which reappears on the echinus above a band of "egg and dart" motifs. A frieze of palmettes and a thin string of "beads" and lotus flowers encircles the top of the shaft of the column. On the abacus of the capital there is another band of "egg and dart".

Not only the bond, but also the texture of the facing was varied. Instead of simply being planed and polished, walls were often intricately worked: carving, bevelling, chamfers and rabbets emphasized corners and joints, while incisions, rustication and striations enlivened the "panels" so created. The sharp light of Greece gave this ornament, usually discreet in religious and civil architecture but more emphatic in military architecture where massive and very prominent rustication was customary, great vividness and expression.

Another element of Greek architectural decoration are the mouldings, which emphasize and refine the articulation of the building. Mouldings were no more than a modulation of a transition (base of the column and the wall; crowning of a wall; between entablature and roof, and so on) by a play of flat, concave and convex surfaces, decorated when on higher parts of the building by paintwork; they could be carved in relief with a limited range of ornamental motifs (lotus flowers and palmettes, "egg and dart", rosettes, meander, "beads") taken over from ceramic decoration. The location and number of these mouldings on a building depended on the Order. The Doric Order was austere: only a limited smooth and painted decoration was permitted. For the Ionic Order the rules were more flexible, ornament in carved relief was normal, its degree depending on the taste of the architect. As a consequence the decoration was sometimes overloaded – for example in some Archaic treasuries and some Hellenistic temples. Once again, the Athenian acropolis shows a perfect balance: the integration of relief mouldings with the shape and bulk of a building has never been more successful than on the Erechtheion. It has the lightness of refined needlework which underscores the architectural lines without drawing attention to itself. These mouldings were originally painted, then later carved – which illustrates once again the significant historic fact that Greek architecture, like Greek sculpture, was a translation into stone of procedures inherited from a technology of wood and baked earth when decoration was with paint. The survival of pictorial effects in a material which was hardly suited to them is typical of the conservative character of Greek art, particularly in architecture and in religious statuary.

A third type of decoration, reserved exclusively for sacred buildings (treasuries, temples, altars) represents another survival from this earlier painted architecture: this is the sculpture which adorned certain parts of these buildings. Here, too, the Doric Order was stricter and more parsimonious than the Ionic. Only the rectangular panels

of the frieze (metopes), the triangular space of the pediments and their ornamental summits could receive sculpture; there was never felt the need for more, indeed it was rare for all the metopes to be sculpted. In the Hephaisteion of Athens ("Theseion"), only the metopes of the façade were sculpted; in the temple of Zeus at Olympia, only the metopes of the pronaos and opisthodomos. Fragments of painted metopes of terracotta found in Thermos prove that metopes, progressively carved in increasingly high relief, were a plastic adaptation of an early painted decor. This would explain the very strong colours used for the background and the drapery of sculpted metopes. A similar evolution can be seen on the tympanum of the pediment. Fragments painted in bright colours from the pediment of the old temple to Athene on the acropolis, and others in quite high relief, also decorated with incisions, from the temple of Artemis in Corfu, take us back to the realm of painting. The ornaments (acroteria) decorating the three corners of the pediments were not always sculpted figures: geometric motifs (painted terracotta paterae from the temple of Hera in Olympia) or plants (Parthenon) could take their place. In the Doric Order, however, the pediments generally were sculpted, except in some temples in southern Italy and Sicily where austerity was taken to extremes, while the pediments of Ionic temples frequently were not – since it was up to the architect. On the other hand, in the Ionic Order, the bases of the columns could be sculpted (the temple of Artemis in Ephesus), and the frieze – the continuous ring of relief sculpture running all around the building – was not necessarily above the architrave as had long been thought: a better acquaintance with the architecture of Asia Minor has shown that this frieze could be placed at the base of the wall, half way up the wall or at the top, as was the "Panathenaic" frieze on the Parthenon. This temple-cum-treasury marks the peak of Greek architectural sculpture, both in the quantity and quality of its sculptures and in their practical and symbolic integration with the building. The iconography of this architectural sculpture is otherwise very limited – apart from the frieze of the little temple of Athene Nike in the Acropolis, some of which probably represented a battle between the Persians and the Greeks, all the scenes depicted on friezes and pediments were mythological. This did not, however, rule out a political and moral symbolism (the Amazons in eastern dress representing the Persians; the Centaurs, the primitive force . . .). The quality of Greek architectural sculpture lies above all in the precise handling of a limited repertoire, which shows unflagging inventiveness – for, with the almost complete loss of the original sculpture set

up inside their temples, it is the statues of the pediment, the acroteria and the friezes that convey to us most immediately and effectively the character of the most important ancient Greek artform.

In the monumental buildings, the internal surfaces received a treatment like that of the exterior, but this was not true of more modest constructions. Especially since sometimes they were built with a variety of materials, these were plastered and given a uniform, unarticulated surface. The plaster and stucco general in Minoan architecture were here revived. These blank surfaces called for pictorial decoration. Recent finds (Tomb of the Diver in Paestum, tombs at Kizilbel and Caraburum in Asia Minor) show that from the end of the Archaic period, plastered walls were given an elaborate figurative decoration, and the written evidence attests to the fact that the beginning of the Classical period ("Severe style": 480–450BC) was marked by the rise of mural painting. The grand compositions with numerous figures by Polygnotos of Thasos (the Stoa Poikile – a portico with paintings in the Agora in Athens, and the Lesche – meeting room of the Cnidians at Delphi) are well known to us from the descriptions of Pausanias, and paintings on vases seem to have been directly inspired by them. It is not known if these wall paintings were true frescoes in the technical sense, or what their support was: were they painted on plaster, or on panels of wood fixed to the walls (a custom known from inscriptions)? In any case, Greek painting was from the beginning a fully narrative style – linked to the Minoan taste for completely decorated walls, as illustrated by findings at Akrotiri on Santorini. This decorative painting was always the "Grand Style", even though an independent genre painting (portraits, still-lifes, genre scenes) had been developing since the end of the 6th century BC. The panels of the royal tombs in Vergina, some fragments recovered from houses on Delos and above all, paintings in the great houses

Unfinished wall (Propylaea of the Acropolis, Athens, north wing). Against the perfect polish of the main face in isodome bond, contrasts the very light rustication of the blocks which make up the upper plinth of the wall. The handling knobs which were used to hold the ropes in place while the stones were being fixed were finally allowed to remain, after the abandonment of Mnesikles' project, for the sake of their decorative effect. (The square cavities are a medieval botching.)

in Pompeii and Herculaneum, inspired by Greek models, are landmarks of the heyday of this internal pictorial decoration in the Hellenistic era. Undoubtedly such scenes were initially reserved for tombs and public buildings; then they appeared in the private dwellings of the upper classes. The example of Delos seems, however, to indicate that narrative scenes were rare in Greece proper; the decoration was usually limited to geometric motifs and to huge monochrome panels in a range of colours. Stucco decorations in relief also seem to have been quite rare, except perhaps in Alexandria.

Floor decoration developed in the 4th century BC at the same time as wall painting. Whereas stone tiles were usual in religious and public buildings, private dwellings, except those of the rich, had no more than a floor of trodden earth. But mosaics had appeared in the wealthier houses by the end of the 5th century BC; the fashion was clearly imported from the east (Anatolia and Syria). These "carpets" of figurative mosaic were initially in black and white, under the influence of ceramics, and were made of pebbles (Olynthia: early 4th century). Soon they were enriched with colours and reproduced the compositions of "grand" painting (Pella: end of the 4th century). The mosaics of Delos, dating for the most part between 166 and 88 BC, show the virtuosity acquired in this technique during the Hellenistic era, whether in the complicated framing of geometric motifs or in figurative panels, made up from now on of very small tesserae (opus vermiculatum), in which shading could be added to the pictorial effect. These mosaic carpets were confined to the reception rooms in the house, to the entrance which was decorated with an emblem representing the arms of the owner, to the impluvium of the peristyle, and the threshold and floor of the banqueting chamber.

It was quite natural that interior decoration – paintings, murals, stucco reliefs and mosaic – should boom during the Hellenistic period. A new emphasis on the individual accompanied a higher standard of living. Architecture, which had been the servant of the city-state during the Archaic and Classical periods, was dependent on personal power and private wealth.

Ever since the 6th century BC, Greek architecture had faced a problem which hitherto had kept it in check – namely roofing over large stone buildings. While the tendency to the monumental, even the colossal, is clear in the plans and elevations of some buildings at the eastern and western ends of the Mediterranean, their roofing remained traditional. The great stone temples had the same wooden framework as the small buildings of the 8th and 7th centuries BC. This seriously restricted the width of such buildings, and also explains plans in which the temple and portico are elongated, while the width remains modest. Greek architects were prevented from creating large internal spaces because transverse beams could not stretch more than 15 metres (50 feet). Intermediate hypostyle supports were always necessary for square rooms which were very rare for this reason, while the traditional lateral colonnades which flanked the temple cellas did not really serve any roofing purpose. This inability to invent a system and a technique for roofing in answer to the desire for greater volume constitutes the main weakness of Greek architecture. It was aggravated by a shortage of wood. From the 5th century BC deforestation in continental

C.N.R.S. Centre de documentation photographique

Tholos of Epidaurus: detail of the framework of a doorway. This doorway is richer in decorative refinement than that of the north porch of the Erechtheion, whose rosette motif it copies. It illustrates how the Ionic Order could be embellished even to excess by introducing carved motifs even into the smallest mouldings.

Greece had reached such proportions that it was hard to find the trees suitable for very long beams – except in the northern frontier districts of Macedonia, Thrace and Thasos and in the Anatolian hinterland. The enormous dimensions of some buildings erected near these regions were made possible by access to such wood. Also, this heavy carpentry was perishable: it was the roof of these Greek buildings that decayed first, either because it soon rotted when it was not maintained or because it burnt down – a very frequent occurrence. The use of a vault to support a stone roof was known from at least the 4th century BC (Macedonian tombs, Necromantion of Ephyra), but its use remained very limited. It never gained currency in important religious and civil buildings, perhaps because it was considered "foreign" if it is true that it originated in the northern parts of Greece.

These facts demonstrate the traditionalism of Greek architecture, which remained satisfied with its limitations. Greek art, in all its manifestations, was not an art of breakthrough and conquest; the idea of "avant-garde" is quite foreign to it. It was an art of tradition, based on a practice carried on in the workshop from generation to generation, which every craftsman learned and adopted without ever trying to alter it radically. Greek architects preferred therefore to try every possible variation of the traditional formula inherited from the 7th century BC and so make a virtue of necessity.

The importance of Orders and theoretical investigations of proportion are also explained by the same formalism. Yet the Orders, which constituted the grammar of architectural forms, did not restrain invention: offering two contrasting methods of construction and expression, they channelled design rather than strictly controlled it. They were always used with great flexibility. Local traditions, contemporary fashions and individual

initiative conferred a savour on buildings which was always different, and which banished uniformity. As in sculpture, the stereotype became unique in the execution. In order fully to appreciate a Greek building, one must place it in the class to which it belongs and so recognize the special peculiarities of an individual architect or team. For though the decorative features and the structure will be immediately clear, the abstract principles which can govern their disposition will remain imponderable so long as they are not analysed mathematically.

On the basis of a small number of ancient texts, an effort has been made to find (in buildings sufficiently well preserved) a coherent system of proportions based on the golden number, pi (π), or on the universal ratios of the Pythagoreans. Almost always, when all possible measurements have been taken, some system of geometric figures or some modular common denominator has come to light. However, the validity of this research remains uncertain: it is easy to overestimate the importance of an architectural speculation. It is not unlikely that some architects, in imitation of sculptors such as Polycleitos, should have wished to base their works on a strict system of ratios, but it would be wrong to generalize. In the conservative environment of ancient Greece, architectural activity was an empirical practice in which experience and intuition, that is to say "mastery", played a large part. As far as is known, Greek architects did not work out very detailed plans: models were made, and in the workshop workmen had full-scale templates in wood or terracotta of the different dressings for the stones. The possibilities of design were therefore somewhat limited, and perhaps these architects closely resembled shipwrights who, even today, make boats without any plan, guided only by instinct and living tradition. The small wage paid to these Greek architects indicates, furthermore, that they were generally classed as specialist artisans; design and production were not so separate from each other as they are today. One thing is certain though: in the great civil and religious buildings there was a module, often the diameter of the column at its narrowest point – a basic dimension from which all the others were calculated. This made the designing and the dressing of the blocks easier, and permitted both the application and variation of proven formulae. In most cases the architect would not venture beyond simple arithmetic proportions which would ensure the uniformity of the building.

A stone architecture, indissolubly bound by setting and by a limiting tradition, an open-air architecture, where external appearance was always the most important consideration; a sacred and a civic architecture rather than a royal one – what more can Greek architecture offer us now that the Neoclassical fashion which perpetuated its echo has passed? Everything about it is of another age: its materials, its practices, its spirit, above all the column – the very epitome of Greek architecture – seem definitely at an end. The West has moved away from its origins, however jealously it protects and maintains them. Greek architecture is no longer a model, but its exploitation of material necessity can still set an example relevant to other conditions. Integrity in the use of materials, strictness of form, care in detail and in execution – these virtues combine to make its beauty simple and lively.

Pre- and protohistoric dwellings

Since 1945, refinement in methods of digging and analysis of archaeological data have made it possible to obtain much more detailed information about prehistoric Greece. For example, it has been discovered that human habitation began much earlier than had been thought – from the middle palaeolithic period (Mousterian: 80000–35000BC). On the other hand, the change from a nomadic life based on hunting and food gathering (palaeolithic period) to a settled life based on agriculture (neolithic period), does not seem to have been rapid and irreversible as after a technological innovation. A semi-nomadic way of life persisted for a long time according to local circumstances. This would explain contemporary traces in neighbouring regions of varying degrees of settlement and nomadism.

Dating from the phase known as proto-neolithic, preceding the appearance of ceramic around 6500BC, cabins of variable plan have been found in Thessaly, notably in the deep strata of Sesclo, often buried to a slight depth in the ground and in structure directly derived from tents covered with the skins of palaeolithic animals: wooden stakes embedded in the ground support wattles of reeds or branches covered with clay.

In the early neolithic period (about 6200BC), the site of Nea Nikomedia (Macedonia), excavated in 1961–63, revealed a more developed habitat: the technique of construction was the same, but the houses, which consisted of only one room, were much bigger and were rectangular in shape: the floor of trodden earth was often insulated with a bedding of leaves and branches. During the second phase of occupation, houses with an inside partition which isolated one part of the dwelling appeared. There seems to have been no order yet in the arrangement of these primitive hamlets; but there can be no doubt that some were surrounded by wooden fencing in front of which was a ditch.

In the middle neolithic period (5500–4400BC), houses with several rooms appeared, particularly in Thessaly during the time when Sesclo was at its peak. The material changed, the plan became more complex. Rectangular houses were built with gabled roofs with two slopes, with walls of raw brick, insulated from the damp by a stone base anticipating the orthostats of classical architecture. But most importantly, in about 4600BC, the plan known as the megaron appeared. This was to have an extraordinary history lasting through every age of Greek architecture. The rectangular main room, with the fireplace dug out of the floor, was preceded by a bare vestibule open to the exterior, with one or two wooden supports forming a porch. This arrangement is found in the Balkans and in Troy, but at much later dates, which may mean that it was a Greek idea which was later to spread elsewhere. The site at Sesclo, which occupied the top and the slopes of a low hill, contains an acropolis of dry stones which constitute the first known fortifications in Greece.

In the late neolithic period (4400–3000BC), techniques of building changed little, but spatial organization reflects a more hierarchical society. The summits of the hills at Dimini and Sesclo were occupied by a very large dwelling consisting of a vestibule opening to the south and two big rooms, the largest of which housed the fireplace. Concentric stone surrounds ringed the much poorer houses on the slopes. The oldest level of occupation of Troy (Troy I: about 3500–2600BC) was of comparable character: it was a modest fortress 100 metres (110 yards) in diameter, protected by a wall of earth with square towers where nothing more than a megaron of elongated form has been found. The relative complexity of the Cretan buildings (neolithic level of Knossos below the court of the palace), which seem to owe something to the East, make a considerable contrast.

The Bronze Age is characterized by new plans and new techniques, and by the appearance of a continuously inhabited complex which anticipates the first towns of the middle and late Bronze Age in Crete and on the mainland. At Troy, levels II and III (2600–2100BC) indicate a larger agglomeration of an area of about 8,000 square metres (9,600 sq. yards) with stone ramparts reaching a thickness sometimes of 12 metres (40 feet), paved ramps and contiguous megaron-type buildings facing the south-east. In the Cyclades, where no site has been completely explored, stone houses with apses are often found (Syros, Paros, Melos) in the fortified acropolises of small area. This is the earliest appearance of a tradition of town planning in the Cyclades that has lasted to the present day. Houses with apses are also found on the continent, especially at Dorion-Malthi in Messene, at Orchomenia in Boeotia and at Lerna in the Argolid, where a house with storeys has been excavated, and can be considered the first palace to be found in Greece. There is a gap of nearly 1,000 years before such an ambitious architecture is found again on the mainland. During the Minoan Age (1900–1600BC), Crete developed an extremely refined palatial architecture, but continental Greece, shaken by an invasion by which nearly all the sites now excavated were destroyed, achieved hardly any innovation in technique or form.

Model of house found at Crannon (Thessaly)

Model in terracotta of a middle neolithic house (Museum of Volos M 5509). Notice particularly that, apart from the openings at the side and the slight overhang of the roof, there is an opening at the top to let out the smoke from the fire.

Acropolis at Sesclo (Thessaly)

Reconstruction of the middle neolithic acropolis (about 4500BC), after M. Corrès. The general use of stone for the perimeter and foundation of the houses makes it possible to get an accurate idea of the location of the dwellings: their disposition here indicates a number of independent farms rather than a village in which economic duties were divided.

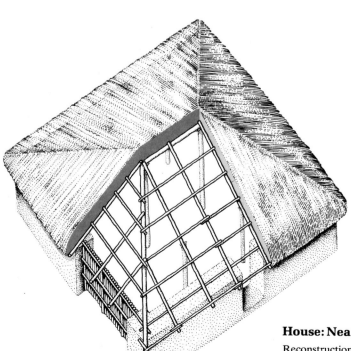

House: Nea Nikomedia (Macedonia)

Reconstruction by R. Rodden. Wooden posts support a light wooden frame, covered here with thatch. Joined with wattles, they form an inner framework for the rubble walls of varying height. Given the two supports in the middle, it is possible to restore a roof of two or four slopes.

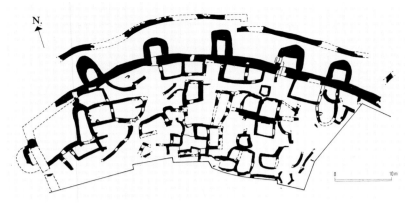

Acropolis of Chalandriani (Syros)

Plan of the acropolis (2700–2200BC) after C. Tsountas. Behind thick walls reinforced with oval towers, the stone houses were crowded together; each had one or two rooms, of different size and shape; access was gained by a network of little roads. The need for protection, both from marauding pirates and from the winds off the sea, partly explains this characteristic jostling plan of the Cyclades.

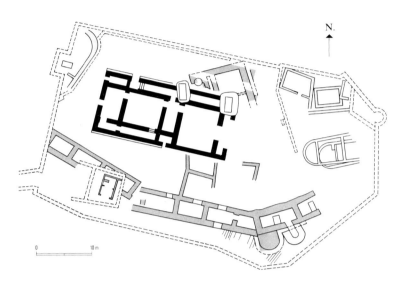

Lerna III (Argolid)

Plan of Lerna III (2450–2150BC) by J.L. Caskey. The centre of the fortified perimeter was occupied by a vast building measuring 25 by 12 metres (82 by 39 feet) made up of a row of four rooms, of which three were flanked by corridors – a complex development of the primitive megaron. The existence of an upper storey is proved by a staircase from the north corridor, and explains the thickness of the walls, made of rough brick covered with stucco on a stone base. Its American excavators gave this extraordinary building the name of the House of Tiles because of the quantity of tiles they found: they are thought to have covered the gabled roof as well as the floor of the upper storey.

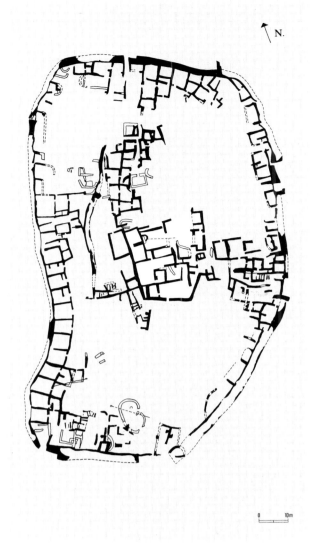

Dorion-Malthi III–IV (Messene)

Plan of Dorion-Malthi III–IV (about 1800BC) by N. Valmin. Backing on to the lower rampart, which was 2 or 3 metres (5 or 7 feet) thick, were small buildings with one or two rooms without inside support, of which the roof was probably a terrace – stores and workshops rather than dwellings. The centre was occupied by the ruler's house and by other smaller houses. The rural population of the outlying districts would have been able to collect together in the large open spaces in case of danger. A good example of a "squire and his castle" in the tradition of Dimini.

Minoan palaces and Mycenaean fortresses

The origins of Cretan civilization remain obscure. The language has not been deciphered and archaeological details dating from the early Minoan period (2700–2000BC) are few. The "House on the Hill" of Vassiliki (eastern Crete), with its irregular arrangement of rooms, seems to be an ancestor of the later larger palace complexes; but the great tombs for multiple burial (250 bodies in Hagia Triada!) dug into the side of the hills of the Messara remain, for the moment, the outstanding architectural feature of this period. Aegean history was interrupted in the middle Bronze Age (2000–1700BC). Whereas the arrival of the first Indo-Europeans in continental Greece represented a definite set-back, Crete, and with it at least some of the Cyclades (Melos and Santorini), enjoyed a sudden boom which raised them to the level of the greatest earlier or contemporary civilizations. The palaces of Knossos, Phaistos, Mallia and Zakro are the equal in size and refinement of those of Mari or Beyce Sultan. Around a vast rectangular courtyard, arranged in several storeys – from which originated the Greek legend of the Labyrinth – there were shops, studios, sanctuaries, reception rooms and living rooms, decorated with frescoes ... The Minoan palaces therefore seem to constitute a microcosm of the society of which they were the religious and political centre. Without doubt these were the residences of the king-priests who shared the sovereignty of the island. Architectural proof of the quality of Minoan life, dependent on the security derived from their mastery of the seas, was the openness of these palaces to the outside. Instead of ramparts, these megara had "salons" which looked out on to the countryside through windows along two sides. The dwellings of the aristocracy (Little Palace at Knossos and the villa in Hagia Triada near Phaistos) had similar comforts, light and freshness. Such a refined court life presupposes the kind of social differences which alone make possible urban life. Although it has not been possible to excavate the town of Knossos, it is estimated that at its peak it might have had a population of nearly 100,000.

In order to get an idea of what life would have been like in a Minoan town, it was once necessary to visit the ruins of Gournia, a small town on the side of a hill at the end of the gulf of Mirabello. Here there was a rectangular public square, on which there was situated a small palace belonging to the local magistrate, while the private houses, very variable in plan and dimension, were served by paved alleys becoming steps when the slope was too great. But, since 1967, there has been the veritable Minoan Pompeii of Akrotiri on Santorini, which rises bit by bit from the enormous mass of ash which engulfed it about 1500BC when the great volcano of which the island consisted, erupted – a cataclysm which also without doubt caused the second destruction of the Minoan palaces, already once previously destroyed in an earthquake of 1700BC. The houses with flat roofs, preserved sometimes up to the second floor, have no set plan; their small rooms are lit by large windows; the rooms on the first floor are often decorated by murals of much better preservation than any previously excavated Minoan painting. The roads vary in width, and they often change direction; under the paving, drains collected water which had been used in the houses. Akrotiri, with its dense but varied and often unexpected buildings, was a Minoan "outrider" in the Cyclades, rising just opposite the metropolis.

Crete never recovered from the catastrophe which befell it around 1500BC. But its palaces were soon reoccupied, notably at Knossos, by a different people, this time speaking Greek: the Indo-Europeans established in central Greece and in the Peloponnese since the beginning of the middle Bronze Age took advantage of the Cretan catastrophe to establish their authority on the island. But, as so often happens, these conquerors had already been won over by Minoan civilization, and it was a hybrid culture which thereafter developed in the great Peloponnesian sites until the Dorian invasion around 1150BC. Nevertheless, despite its borrowings from Minoan Crete, the essentially different, Mycenaean character of the civilization is very clear, particularly in its architecture, which expresses a state of mind as bleak and bellicose as that of the Minoans seems to have been peaceful and hedonistic.

If the fabulous objects discovered by H. Schliemann in the trench tombs of the Mycenaeans were inspired by or even imported from Minoan Crete, the tombs themselves, whether consisting of a chamber inside an isolated mound, or, later, inside a tholos with a stone dome, were original in form. Mycenaean severity reaches its peak in its "Cyclopean" walls, so called by the Greeks because of the sometimes colossal dimensions of the blocks of which they were constructed. Here, for the first time, whether against the threat of Dorian bands descending from the Balkans, or in order to defend a feudal power (successfully) against centralization, a grand architecture of dressed stone appeared in continental Greece. The Mycenaeans were obsessively concerned with defence, as is also shown by the arrangements for water supply to Mycenae, the inclusion of places of refuge in the fortified perimeter and the numerous bastions at Tiryns. The palaces themselves were much smaller than those of Crete, and even if they imitated Minoan stucco decoration, coloured murals and certain other furnishing, remained faithful to the megaron plan inherited from neolithic Thessaly. At Tiryns and at Pylos, as at Mycenae, the reception rooms open on to a central courtyard, and consist of a portico of two columns, a vestibule and a large square room with a central fireplace, under a ceiling supported by four columns. Very little is known about the domestic architecture; excavations carried out recently at Mycenae below the palace have revealed a few houses but no typical interior plan has emerged. In fact, nowhere is there any evidence of a system of small houses being grouped around their fortified acropolis in any Mycenaean town. In any case, particularly in the Peloponnese and Boeotia, the population at the end of the new Bronze Age, around 1200BC, seems to have been mostly rural, and the princely residences never became real towns – even in Mycenae, the seat of the most powerful king. Situated in the foothills of a mountain range, it has more the unsociable appearance of an eagle's nest than the spaciousness of a prosperous capital.

Staircase: Palace of Knossos (Crete)

The grand staircase leading to the royal apartments served three storeys and had five landings; its colonnade (with columns tapering to the bottom, the opposite of Greek columns) led in to a little courtyard and formed a well of light, a characteristic feature of Minoan palace architecture.

Palace of Knossos (Crete)

Plan at the level of the central courtyard. This palace, the largest known in Crete, with an area of 22,000 sq. metres (26,300 sq. yards), was excavated by A. Evans between 1899 and 1932, and spectacularly restored, sometimes excessively. It occupies the summit of a small hill, and to the east it dominates a ravine on to which the royal apartments look out, with their large megaron on the Minoan plan – open on two sides (A), reached by a large staircase (B). The three main entrances are to the north (C), the west (D) and the south (E). The western wing was occupied by extensive storerooms (F) and by official apartments – audience and reception halls (G), sanctuary (H); a large staircase (I) leads to state rooms.

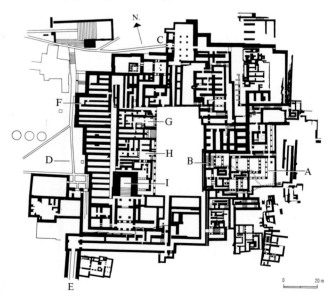

Façades of houses

Tablets of earthenware representing the fronts of houses (Heraklion museum). Found in Knossos, they formed part of the decoration of a wooden box of the middle Minoan period (1900–1600BC). The houses had one or two floors and a terrace roof. Note the timber framing, picked out in dark paint. The windows are of two types: double oblong lights or square grills.

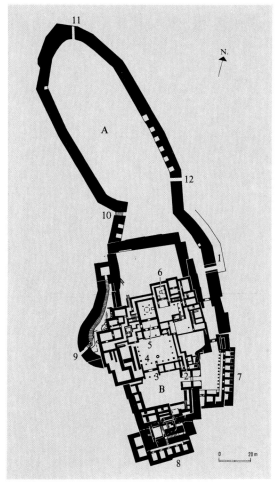

Fortress of Tiryns

Plan after K. Müller. Built on a little hillock, 18 metres (60 feet) high, not far from the edge of the Gulf of Argos, Tiryns is the best preserved Mycenaean citadel (about 1200BC). It includes, apart from the palace (B), a lower refuge zone (A). Access is gained by a ramp (1), which makes visitors expose their right side, unprotected by a shield. After having crossed various intermediate court-yards and two propylaea (2 and 3), the inside courtyard (4) is reached, on to which the great tripartite megaron (5) opens, flanked by a smaller megaron (6). The number of bastions (7 and 8) and of posterns (9–12), which were more or less hidden, emphasizes the defensive purpose of this massive building.

Treasury of Atreus, Mycenae

Plan and elevation of the "Treasury of Atreus" or "Tomb of Agamemnon" in Mycenae (about 1250BC), after P. de Jong. This tholos tomb with stone dome, the largest known, was plundered in antiquity. An access passage (dromos), bordered by a pseudo-isodome wall, leads to a façade 10.5 metres (34 feet) high. The door opens on to a rotunda, 14.6 metres (48 feet) in diameter and 13.5 metres (44 feet) high, with a masonry domed vault of 33 regular courses; some blocks bore a metal decoration, probably of "patera" form. This door has a pyramidal shape which is also found in Egypt, and which reappears in classical architecture. The lintel is made up of two enormous blocks; the inner one weighs about 120 tons. The void triangle above it is characteristic of Mycenaean architecture: it serves to deflect the thrusts of the upper part of the building on to the supports of the door. This triangle was originally masked by a polychrome marble slab flanked by two half-columns with oblique fluting, of which some fragments have been found. The door itself was flanked by two half-columns of green marble, decorated with horizontal zig-zags. A side door gave access to a second, cubic chamber measuring 6 metres (20 feet) on each side, with walls originally covered by sculpted stone decorations. No other Mycenaean building can boast such exact stone cutting, nor such refined proportions; not for another 1,000 years in Greece was such technical perfection put at the service of such a grandiose architectural design.

House in Akrotiri, Santorini

Façade of the "West House" facing on to the "Road of the Telchines" (about 1500BC). The houses, generally of one storey, were built of rough stone and loam, reinforced by timbers. The use of dressed stone was, except in the case of the houses of the rich, limited to corners and to the surrounds of doors and windows, as is seen here. The ground floor was reserved for storage and work, while the living rooms, decorated by murals and lit by the largest windows, were upstairs. Each house had a sanitary system connected to a subterranean pit in the road.

The rebirth of Greek architecture

With the coming of the Dorians, around 1150–1100BC, the Bronze Age ended disastrously for Greece; the Mycenaean civilization, which had spread from Sicily to Asia Minor, was violently dispersed; its seemingly impregnable fortresses were destroyed; its writing was forgotten and all the brilliant advances of the 2nd millennium lost. Everywhere this reverse was spectacular, even in Crete, where the Minoan minority still managed to remain active. Nowhere was it more keenly felt than in architecture. After the complexity of the Cretan palaces and the monumental austerity of the Mycenaean fortresses and tombs, there was a reversion to primitive dwellings of light materials. This stage of "zero architecture" has left only a few traces, often obliterated by later building, so that these "Dark Ages" (1100–700BC) are known almost exclusively by their ceramic remains. It is therefore the "Geometric" style, which developed in Athens and spread bit by bit throughout the whole of Greece, that has given its name to this period of very slow recovery. It was only in the 8th century BC (late Geometric) that the Greeks ventured to sea again, and set up buildings on a few sites, where the remains, to judge from the materials and techniques, might belong to the 3rd millennium BC.

On the continent, buildings were constructed in rough brick on a foundation of rubble; elongated in shape, they terminated in an apse with a gabled roof supported by wooden posts resting on flagstones. This form of house, which would hardly be appropriate to a continuous urban network, indicates a return to a rural type of habitat. In fact, such agglomerations as are known, including Athens, are only villages. The most ancient rampart known, that of Smyrna, of which the first state dates from 850BC, surrounds an urban space of 35,000 sq. metres (42,000 sq. yards) in which there is no orderly arrangement of the houses. Zagora (Andros), abandoned about 700BC, presented a different appearance, typical of Cycladic architecture throughout the ages: the village was built on a plateau measuring 850 by 550 metres (930 by 600 yards), on steep cliffs dominating two harbours, and was fortified only on the isthmus by a wall in places 7 metres (23 feet) thick. Stone houses, all quadrangular and with a terraced roof, made up dense, but distinct quarters. The centre of the plateau was occupied by a temple which survived the abandonment of the site.

There is the same discontinuity of dwelling at Emporio (Chios), a village abandoned about 600BC whose houses are spread on the side of a hill over a space of 300 by 250 metres (330 by 270 yards) between the port and the acropolis, which is the only fortification. Here there was found a temple to Athene and the residence of the governor. This building, which measured 18 by 7 metres (60 by 23 feet), had like most of the spacious houses in Emporio and Zagora the same megaron plan which had appeared in the neolithic age and developed into the Mycenaean palaces; a porch with two columns leading into a long room with axial colonnades and a gabled roof, where the fireplace is found. Very often a stone bench stood against at least one side, and was used variously as a seat, a bed and a shelf. It was in a room like this that the massacre of the suitors, described in the *Odyssey*, was carried out by Ulysses.

The earliest temples known, of the 8th century BC, were built on the megaron plan. Such buildings, which were used to house the statue of worship, while the worship itself was celebrated in the open around the altar, did not exist during the Bronze Age; the places of worship, chapels or simple niches, were then part of the palace or the house. Its appearance, which is one of the great novelties of the new era, was to have a considerable effect on the evolution of Greek architecture: the care given to these buildings made them the testing ground for new techniques and designs up to the Hellenistic period. The most modest of these temples simply reproduced private houses: they were rectangular rooms (Heraion on Delos; temples of Dreros and of Prinias, in Crete) or with apses (Heraion on Perachora, Daphnephorion on Eretria) of small dimensions, generally entered through a porch supported on columns of wood. Others were more ambitious and extended these two types of plan to enormous dimensions. Thus, the first temple to Hera on Samos (about 800BC) was a long chamber of 100 Greek feet (about 34 metres), rectangular, which was surrounded at the end of the 8th century with another colonnade – anticipating the peripteral temple. At Eretria a "hecatompedon" soon superseded the first temple, but kept the plan of the former "laurel hut", though lengthening it considerably; the space inside was again punctuated only by an axial colonnade which supported the framework of the gabled roof. Whereas the length of these rooms could be extended at will, their breadth remained limited by the length of the wooden transverse beams available, an obligation which Greek architects would have liked to discard from the 6th century BC, but which they were never really able to overcome. The sequence of buildings is of special significance in the sanctuary of Apollo at Thermos in Aetolia: the apse form disappeared during the 7th century, a period of extensive experimentation stimulated by the rediscovery of the East. It was in this period that the still disparate elements of the two Orders, Doric and Ionic, appeared, created by technical constraints and by imitation of oriental models. At the same time the single axial colonnade disappeared nearly everywhere in favour of a double one, set close to the side walls, which made it possible to give more prominence to the cult statue. Though the columns and rafters were still of wood, the walls were from then on of stone. This adoption of stone, which progressed during the second half of the 8th century, and which was also happening in sculpture, resulted in a separation of religious from domestic architecture. Domestic architecture remained for a long time almost as it began.

Ramparts of Smyrna

Reconstruction after R.V. Nicolls; about 850BC. Measuring 4.75 metres (15 feet) wide at the base, it consisted on the outside of a section of rough stone about 0.8 metres (3 feet) thick, behind which a mass of shingle was packed to a thickness of 2 metres (7 feet); it was supported at the rear by a wall of rough brick, again about 2 metres (7 feet) thick. A century later (about 750BC) this surround was strengthened by an addition to the inside wall of a thick buttress with a facing of dressed stones, the earliest appearance of the polygonal bond which was to be repeated and refined a little later at Miletos and at Antissa (Lesbos).

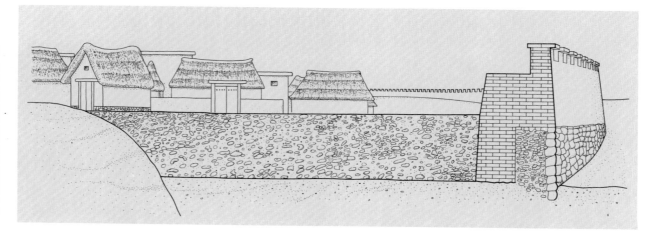

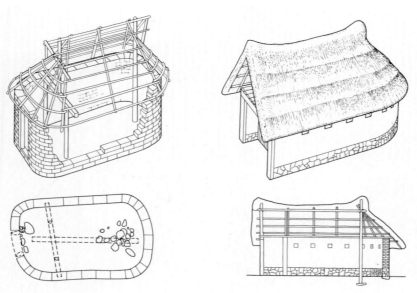

Houses, Smyrna

Plan and reconstruction of a proto-Geometric house (about 900BC) and reconstruction of an apsed house of the 8th century in Smyrna, after R.V. Nicolls. The first is an oval house, measuring 3 by 5 metres (10 by 16 feet), with rough brick walls plastered on the outside and without base or foundations: the floor inside is slightly lowered; the two internal supports of the wooden framework on the diagram are hypothetical. A larger house of the same type was found in Athens on the north slope of the Areopagos. The apsed house is more elaborate, with a stone base; it has no inside partitions, unlike other, larger apsed houses at Antissa and Mycenae.

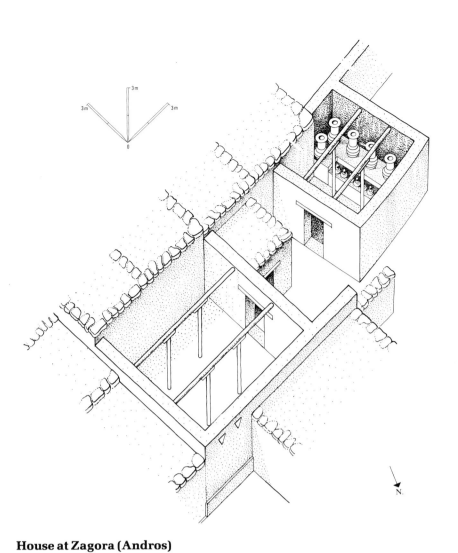

House at Zagora (Andros)

Reconstruction of house D 6-7-8-27 (8th century BC) after J.J. Coulton. This house was reached by a little courtyard, in the corner of which was a very small room in which domestic animals were probably kept. To the right opened off a small room, at one end of which stood a double stone bench on which domestic objects were arranged – in particular jars containing water, always a rare commodity on the islands. To the left of the courtyard there was a large living room, whose terraced roof was supported by four wooden posts. The top of the north wall contained two small triangular windows, an arrangement typical of Zagora; but the majority of the houses were lit only through the door and by the opening above the central fireplace.

Model of a temple

Reconstruction of a small model in terracotta, representing possibly the first apsed temple to Hera Akraia in Perachora (before 750BC), after H. Payne. Notice the twin columns at the entrance, the three little square windows above the door, and the very steep slope of the roof, slightly curved, which served to protect the tops of the raw brick walls from trickling water.

Temple of Thermos (Aetolia)

Plan of three successive temples at Thermos (Aetolia). After the apsed megaron (1), often dated to the Mycenaean era but more probably built in the 9th century, there followed, in the 8th century BC, Temple 2. This adopted the same plan but had a rear rectangular room and thicker-set proportions; the oval colonnade in wood retained a traditional appearance. Towards 625BC came Temple 3, a building with an axial colonnade, marking a transition to the peripteral temple; its elongated orthogonal plan was typical of the early Archaic period; the supports were still made of wood, as well as the framework sheathed with painted terracotta tiles.

"Laurel hut", Daphnephorion, Eretria

Restoration of the "laurel hut" of the Daphnephorion of Eretria, after P. Auberson. Around 800BC. On a base of ellipsoidal stones stood a building measuring 11.5 by 7.5 metres (38 by 25 feet); against this base, on each side were set very light wooden posts on a clay foundation. The absence of any trace of brick leads one to think that this must be a local reproduction of the mythical "laurel hut" built by Apollo at Delphi: the "walls" were simple partitions of wattling and leaves fixed on to posts. Estimated height: around 7 metres (23 feet).

Legend:
- 9th century BC
- 8th century BC
- end of 7th century BC

The Doric Order

At the close of the period of transition represented by the 7th century BC, Greek architecture rediscovered the monumental character it had lost since the Mycenaean period. In the sanctuaries great stone buildings replaced light structures. Changing materials and standardization of design went hand in hand; on the sometimes hazardous experiments of the 7th century there followed a period of consolidation when the two Orders, Ionic and Doric, destined to establish the language of Greek architecture for the remainder of its history, were defined.

The beginnings of the Doric Order are better documented than those of the Ionic Order through some archaeological good luck which has made it possible to follow the stages of its development in the continental and western regions of the Greek world (Peloponnese, central Greece, Corfu, southern Italy and Sicily). The role of Corinth and Argos in this phase of development seems to have been considerable: the first buildings in which Doric elements appeared, at Thermos, Olympia and Corfu, were all situated in regions dominated by the political and artistic influence of these two major centres of the high Archaic period.

The plan of the Doric temple originated in the megaron plan found in continental Greece since the 3rd millennium, but it was expanded to the rear of the central hall (naos or cella) where the cult statue was displayed, by the addition of an opisthodomos reduplicating the entry vestibule. Sometimes this space was accessible only from the cella, and so constituted a closed room which served as a sacristy (Corfu: temple of Artemis; Syracuse: temple of Apollo; Selinunte: temples C, D and F; Paestum: temple of Hera of Silaris and temple of Hera I). More frequently, in particular in mainland Greece, it did not communicate with the cella, but formed a rear vestibule where precious offerings were often on display. This arrangement gained ground during the 6th century and resulted quite naturally from the abandonment of the apsed plan and the adoption of a peripteral colonnade: since the front was no longer privileged, and the rear was no longer made distinctive by the apse, the duplica-tion of the entrance made it possible to avoid inertia at the rear, and to balance the building, which was provided in this way with two symmetrical façades.

The Doric Order was the direct heir of an architecture in wood. This can be seen in temple C in Thermos (last quarter of the 7th century BC), and in the temple of Hera in Olympia (around 600BC) where the remains show the process of converting to stone still in progress. Stone is here limited to the base (stylobate), and to the lower part of the walls at Olympia; the columns were still made of wood and were replaced one by one by stone columns: in the 2nd century AD, Pausanias saw one in oak still remaining in the opisthodomos of the temple of Hera. These were stumpy logs without a base, but enlivened by vertical fluting and encircled by metal at the top. A capital in the form of a slab with a bell curve marked the transition to the entablature. The architrave, made of massive wooden beams and uncarved, formed a horizontal framework on which rested the eaves and the transverse beams of the roof. The ends of the beams were protected from damp by terracotta tiles – metopes and triglyphs in alternation, together constituting the frieze. The overhanging cornice, which deflected water trickling from the roof away from the entablature and the colonnades, was also protected by terracotta tiles nailed to it at their lower part, standing vertical. All these Doric features, which played a strictly functional role in this wooden architecture, were translated into stone. Some (the guilloche, the regulae and the guttae, the frieze and the mutules) were only there for decoration. The evolution concluded with the temple of Artemis on Corfu (around 590BC), which has the first known pediment. The relief decoration, always enriched by bright colours, a relic of painting on terracotta, would always be optional; in the west, pediments were never decorated, and the metopes were often smooth, even on the most refined buildings, or were only sculpted on the façades or above the interior porches.

The Doric Order had emerged as an architecture in stone, but was still clumsy. The columns were squat; the entablatures very high; inside, space was scarce – the exterior colonnade had no base. Every-thing gave the impression of being heavy-handed and awkward. The architects set about correcting this by constant work on the proportion, on the plan and on the elevation. At the end of the 6th century, in the temple of Aphaia on Aegina, the classical equilibrium was achieved. From then on, the short sides were to be equal to half the long sides: to six columns of the front (eight in the temple of Artemis in Corfu, at temple G in Selinunte, in the temple of Hera of Silaris and in the Parthenon; nine in the first temple to Hera in Paestum) there were generally 13 on the long sides (12 in the temple of Aphaia), that is to say, a ratio of n : 2n + 1. This extra width made it possible to open up the interior, all the more since the peristyle, or external colonnade, had tended to contract. The cella itself was articulated by a double colonnade on two levels, which made a screen for the cult statue, especially when the colonnade ran round behind it (temple of Hephaistos and the Parthenon in Athens). The columns were made more slim, more space was put between them, entablatures were made lower and lighter, the entasis (tapering) was made more subtle; the echinus of the capital tended to become rectangular towards the end of the century. The new cohesion which united these austere forms, without any decorative enlivement, was based on mathematical research: when all the proportions were calculated from a single module, the Doric temple achieved an almost organic coherence. Its restraint constitutes one of the greatest achievements of classicism; the idea of order, however one may define it, here found exemplary expression.

With the end of the 5th century, the new taste for a richer and more flexible architectural language led to the rapid decline of the Doric Order, which was forced into an academic elegance, more and more enfeebled (temple of Nemea at the end of the 4th century BC). But if it was no longer the preferred Order, it remained a basic element of the eclecticism of the Hellenistic and Roman periods. It is seen, in an oversimplified form, in numerous buildings – as a portico façade or the peristyle of a house – where its austerity is a mark primarily of economic considerations.

Plans of the temple of Artemis in Corfu (about 590BC) and of the temple of Hephaistos (so-called Theseion) in Athens (449BC)

Within a century and a half, the Doric Order found its perfect balance: improved proportions, colonnades better integrated with the plan, inside space fully adapted to its function.

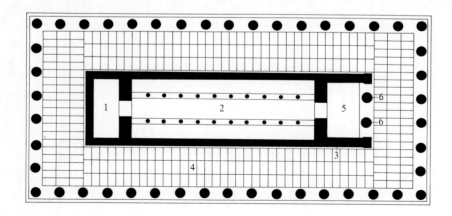

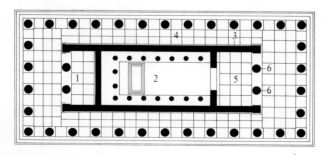

1 opisthodomos
2 naos (cella)
3 antae
4 peristyle
5 pronaos (vestibule)
6 columns "in antis"

N.

Temple of Apollo, Thermos (Aetolia)

Reconstruction of the entablature; around 620BC. In the 7th century BC the wooden beams of the roof were protected by a covering of terracotta: the triglyphs with vertical grooves mask the end of the transverse beams placed on the axis of each column, while the metopes, decorated with mythological scenes, occupy the intervening space, an arrangement which persisted after the change to stone; the metopes then often had a sculpted decoration in high relief, enriched with colours on a red or blue base.

Temple of Hera, Paestum

Western façade of the temple of Hera II (so-called temple of Poseidon, around 460BC) at Paestum (Poseidonia). The absence of any sculptural decoration increases the austerity of the building. The poor quality of the material, a local, very porous limestone, was originally concealed by a stucco of powdered marble, as at the temple of Zeus at Olympia, by which the temple of Hera seems to be directly inspired. Notice, besides the outer colonnade and the two columns of the opisthodomos, the two-tiered colonnade of the cella, which is well preserved here.

Temple of Athene Aphaia, Aegina

Reconstruction of the elevation of the temple (about 500BC). The euthynteria, which protrudes for a few centimetres, forms the transition between the foundations and the stylobate of three steps, which raise the temple in relation to the surrounding terrain; an access ramp, typical of Peloponnesian architecture, leads to the level of the stylobate on which the columns rest, each with 20 fluting-ridges. Only the roof was of wood; it was covered by large flat tiles with pentagonal or round battens, usually of terracotta.

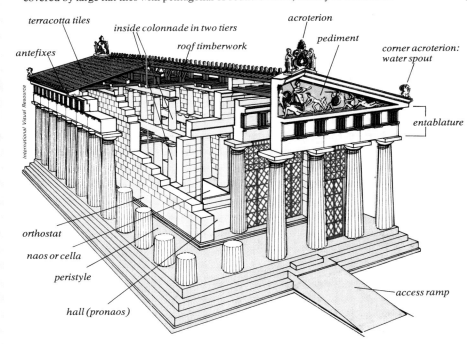

Parthenon, Athens

Restored elevation of the north corner and of the east façade of the Parthenon (447–438BC), after A. Orlandos. The column, made up of assembled drums, has a scarcely perceptible entasis (tapering) towards one end only: the echinus of the capital is almost rectangular, the architrave and the frieze are of the same height; the sima is decorated with a painted motif of palm leaves; the corner acroterion is a foliage motif in marble. Despite its Ionic peculiarities, the Parthenon, with subtleties which enliven its severity (no line is really straight), represents the peak of perfection of the Doric Order.

139

The Ionic Order

Ionic is rather more a style than an Order; it lacked the severity of the Doric Order, forms were much less standardized and regional variations were considerable. Between Cycladic Ionic, featuring small buildings decorated with carved engravings, and the Ionic of the coast of Asia Minor, where the influence of the Orient is seen in colossal temples with double colonnades and in the abundant relief decoration, the common denominator was, above all, a similar state of mind: the taste for slender form and for ornament in which the imagination of the architect could be given free rein. At all levels of the elevation – base, capital, top and bottom of the wall and frieze – the decoration could be more or less developed; secondary mouldings – often very delicate – could be combined to emphasize the lines or to articulate the surfaces. It is a great pity that the local dialects of the flexible vocabulary of the Order are today so poorly understood. In the Cyclades, the buildings have nearly all completely disappeared, and it is only recently that, thanks to some very detailed research, it has been possible to form an image of this refined architecture. On the coast of Asia Minor, and on the islands which face it, the great Archaic temples were destroyed in antiquity, and it is generally their imposing successors of the Hellenistic period which are known. Yet it is here that the Ionic Order seems to have taken shape.

The Aeolic capitals of Asia Minor, with a vertical volute, were contemporary with the first Ionic capitals, with a horizontal volute; the Aeolic variant, which endured in provincial Aeolia, was derived directly from the East. Very similar capitals were to be found in Palestine, Phoenicia and in Assyria during the 8th and 7th centuries BC. Elegant but frail, this type of capital could support only a light entablature: so it was the more functional horizontal volute capital that was used in the great temples built between 570 and 550BC. With their dimensions, colossal compared with mainland Greece, their double colonnades and their sculptured decorations, these temples at once raise Greek building to the level of Oriental achievements. Yet island Greece and continental Greece were always resistant to this kind of architecture, which smacked of the exotic: only the great colonial cities of the west (temple G in Selinunte) were tempted to take up the challenge.

This first Ionic flourish, so clearly influenced by the East, was violently interrupted by the events at the end of the 6th century, when the cities of the coast rebelled against Persia, and were sacked or destroyed. The almost complete gap that followed is only imperfectly covered by the few Ionic buildings of the 5th century in the west (Syracuse, Locri, Metaponte, Catania, Hipponion and Elea), which have been studied only recently. In fact, the Ionic Order never made a comeback until the post-Periclean period in Athens. After early experiments at mixing the two Orders (in the Parthenon and in the Propylaea, where the Ionic Order, which was more advanced, was adopted for the internal supports – a combination which had a wide following), Athens, at grips with the Dorian coalition led by Sparta (432–404BC), went back to its roots and the Ionic Order triumphed in the temple of Athene Nike and the Erechtheion. But this was not the rich Ionic of the Asian coast; it was that of the Cyclades, modest and gracious, with sculpted friezes.

At the end of the 5th century BC, when the Ionic Order seems to have expanded again in Asia Minor (the funeral temple of Xanthos, known as the "Monument to the Nereids"), a new variant appeared in the Peloponnese at the temple of Bassae. This was an exceptional temple in every respect; in its position, in its interior space, with engaged Ionic columns, above which there is a sculpted frieze, and in particular, in its single free-standing column at the rear of the cella. On top of this there is a capital which, instead of having the ordinary double scroll, has a decoration of acanthus leaves. The great advantage of this type of capital, known as Corinthian because the sculptor and goldsmith Callimachos was said to have invented it in Corinth, was that it did not have a single viewpoint, like the Ionic capital: the four faces present the same arrangement of more or less developed leaves, from which four volutes sprout obliquely at the angles. The Ionic Order with a Corinthian capital, used in the 4th century in interior spaces (the tholoi of Delphi, of Epidaurus and of Olympia and the temple of Tegea) became more and more of a competitor to pure Ionic, which, however, came back into favour during the Hellenistic period in Asia Minor, with the great temples of Sardis, Priene, Didyma and Magnesia on the Meander. During the 1st century BC the decorative richness of the Corinthian capital did, however, catch on: it was to be the dominant Order of the imperial era; the Ionic was reduced to its most simple expression and from then on was restricted to interior colonnades or to upper tiers in civil and domestic architecture.

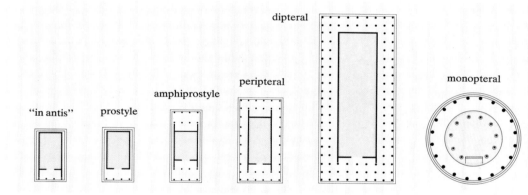

Plans of Ionic temples

The diversity of the Ionic Order is seen first in the variety of plans. The three first types are characteristic of Cycladic architecture.

Dipteral Ionic temples

The temple of Hera on Samos (top) built under Polykrates (end of the 6th century BC) is the largest of the Archaic Ionic temples (112 by 55 metres/370 by 200 feet). The two short sides consist of a triple range of columns, the one at the back being of nine columns. The pronaos is very deep, and the opisthodomos is missing as it is in most Ionic temples. The second temple of Apollo in Didyma (bottom), the construction of which lasted over five centuries, shows the resurgence in the Hellenistic period of colossal architecture: on a crepidoma of seven steps, 3 metres high (10 feet), there stands a dipteral temple (110 by 50 metres/360 by 180 feet) of which the plan recalls that of the Archaic temple of Samos, but the pronaos is here very wide and the cella consists of a courtyard to which access is gained by a large staircase or by lateral ramps over vaults; at the end of this courtyard there is a small prostyle temple which houses the cult statue. The columns of 20 metres (65 feet) in height are closer together than in any other temple, which gives an effect of density unusual in the Ionic Order.

Temple of Athene Nike, Acropolis, Athens

This small amphiprostyle temple (427–424BC), consecrated to Athene, on a bastion overlooking the entrance to the sacred rock, is the purest expression of Attic Ionian, nearer in spirit to the islands than to Asia Minor: the place of the sculpted frieze above the architrave characterizes insular Ionic (most unusually it represents the battle of Plataea against the Persians in 479BC, not some mythological episode). The columns are monolithic and very graceful; the external scroll of the angle of the capitals is placed diagonally, making it clear that a varied viewpoint was intended.

Ionic temple, Metaponte

Elevation of the Ionic temple recently discovered at Metaponte (1st half of the 5th century BC), after D. Mertens. The very bulbous tori at the base have horizontal flutings different from those of the shaft; the neckpiece is decorated with geometric motifs; very finely chiselled mouldings separate the different zones of the entablature; the architrave here has only two fascie instead of the usual three; the frieze is not figurated but decorated with a motif of palm leaves and lotus flowers; the denticulae are without doubt echoes of the ends of the wooden beams of the framework.

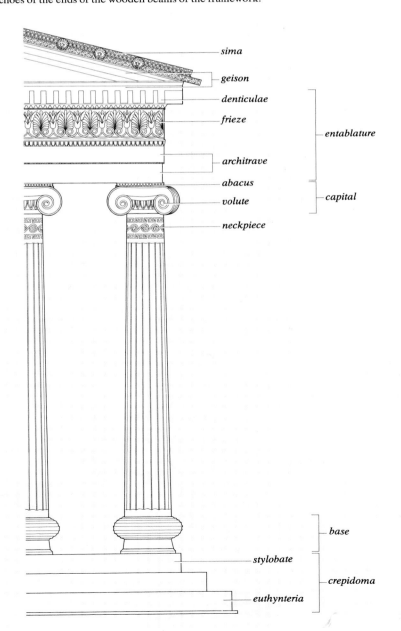

- sima
- geison
- denticulae
- frieze
- entablature
- architrave
- abacus
- volute
- capital
- neckpiece
- base
- stylobate
- crepidoma
- euthynteria

Capitals derived from the Ionic Order

Two variants of the Ionic Order: the Aeolic capital with vertical volutes (Neandria, around 560–550BC) and the Corinthian capital (Hellenistic and imperial periods). The first was too light to carry heavy entablatures and was not widely used; the second, richer and more flexible than the Ionic capital with horizontal volutes, eventually replaced it.

Temple of Artemis, Ephesus

Reconstruction of the second temple of Artemis in Ephesus (around 340–250BC). The original temple was among the Seven Wonders of the World but was burnt down in 356 by a maniac, Herostratos, on the night of the birth of Alexander. It was rebuilt on exactly the same plan, but raised by a foundation to show off its splendid proportions (115 by 55 metres/380 by 180 feet; height of columns: 19 metres/62 feet). As before, the 36 columns had reliefs above the base, one of which was executed by Skopas. Typical features of the Ionic of Asia Minor were the absence of a frieze over the architrave, and denticules.

The great sanctuaries

Since religious building was, until the 4th century BC, the main type of architecture to which the monumental upsurge which began after the end of the 7th century was devoted, it is the great sanctuaries which illustrate the most characteristic examples of Archaic and Classical Greek civilization.

A sanctuary was a place given over to a divinity in the countryside; it could be no more than a wall around an altar, visited by people in the neighbourhood; it could also be the residence of a patron of a city or of a group of cities, and if this city or confederation were important, the sanctuary would have a commensurate influence. Examples of this were the Heraion in Argos, the Athenaion of the Acropolis in Athens, the Apollonion of Delos, the Heraion of Samos and the Artemision of Ephesus. The sanctuary could also be one of the Panhellenic meeting places, where the Greeks, who were always torn by paltry but lasting differences, assembled at fixed times and arranged a "holy truce" in order to celebrate the honour of a great god with sporting or musical gatherings.

In these great sanctuaries, the cultural and votive buildings were assembled, without a plan, around a fixed place which constituted the altar. The temple, of which the façade was usually turned towards the altar, held the cult statue; in some sanctuaries, access to it was forbidden to most of the faithful. The votive chapels were known as treasuries; in Delphi and Olympia they were numerous, and took the form of small Doric or Ionic buildings, prostyle or "in antis", built by a city to protect the precious offerings made on the occasion of a public event, a victory or a prodigy. From the 4th century, porticoes were built instead. These were long halls, open on one side to a colonnade to shelter offerings and visitors. Other offerings – statues, portraits in bronze or stone, groups of lesser or greater importance, columns and pillars of increasing size – were spread around the whole of the sacred area, with each worshipper trying to claim the best place. The result was that in the Hellenistic period, Delphi and Olympia became veritable depots for masterpieces, where the Romans came to take their pick. As well as the cult buildings and countless monuments, there were administrative buildings (prytanea), buildings for physical training (palestrae and gymnasia) and for performances (theatres, stadia, hippodromes). These were usually built on the edge of the sacred area.

The Greeks had the greatest disdain for personal comfort; it was a characteristic of their architecture, up to the time of their encounter with Rome. Pilgrims came from all over the country and the Greek world to Delphi to obtain advice from Apollo through the prophecies of the Pythia, and to take part in the Pythian games, where artistic events were as important as the sports; but no accommodation was provided for them. Those who could lodged with a local inhabitant, otherwise they were obliged to camp out in the open. The same applied to those who went to Olympia to take part in the games in honour of Zeus, and where philosophers, orators and poets, certain of a large audience, gathered.

Although religious, cultural and sporting activity became more and more formal after the end of the Hellenistic period, the sanctuaries continued to be enriched for a long time afterwards with offerings and new buildings, while the ancient ones were restored. The awakening of an historicist awareness and the nostalgic Hellenism of the rulers and intellectuals of the 2nd century AD occasioned their final renaissance before Christianity put these centres of paganism in jeopardy. It was in vain that Julian the Apostate tried to prevent this decline. The oracle in Delphi replied to his messenger: "Tell the king: the magnificent building has crumbled; Phoibos no longer has a dwelling; no longer a prophetic laurel; the source is silent; the flow of eloquence is ended."

The edict of Theodosius I on November 8, 392 put an end to this long decline by proscribing paganism. The buildings remained standing, but abandoned, and did not take long to lose their roofs; churches were built on the ruins, and what remained of the offerings were melted down and hammered into different shapes, or removed.

Sanctuary at Delphi; view from the rock that overlooks it

It was the shepherd Coretas who discovered, on the steep slopes of Parnassus, occasionally shaken by earthquakes, the prophetic properties of the sulphurous gases coming from a crack in the ground. Having slain the dragon Python, which guarded the place in the name of Earth, Apollo took possession of the oracle. Its fame became universal from the 7th century BC, when it played an essential part in the programme of colonization by giving its approval to projected expeditions. Regular consultation took place once a month, even during the absence of Apollo, who retired for three months during the winter. In a crypt situated at the foot of the temple (adyton), the Pythia sat on a tripod built over the crack in the rock and, while in a delirium, delivered her prophecies. Her statements were immediately interpreted and put into verse by priests who passed them on to the pilgrim – an ordinary person or the emissary of a city. The Doric temple of the 4th century BC, of which today only ruins remain, was at least the third built on the site. It stands on an artificial terrace held in by a wall of polygonal bond on which are engraved hundreds of deeds of slave emancipation. The sanctuary, which forms a steep quadrilateral measuring 130 by 180 metres (142 by 197 yards), enclosed by a surrounding wall, is crossed by the Sacred Way (between 4 and 5 metres/approx. 15 feet wide) which leads to the temple: the paving on it is fairly late in date. Most of the treasuries built by the cities were grouped around its lower bend; the Treasury of the Athenians in Parian marble, put up in honour of the victory at Marathon in 490BC, is the only one to have been restored. Space was very restricted, and votive monuments were arranged in total disorder; the temple esplanade bristled with pillars all carrying statues. A theatre with 5,000 seats occupied the north-east corner of the sanctuary, while higher up on a flat piece of ground was the stadium of which the visible part dates from the 2nd century AD. The little town of Delphi, which made its living entirely from the sanctuary, arranged its houses in tiers all round the site.

Acropolis of Athens

A model of the Acropolis as it was during the 2nd century AD. This small plateau with steep cliffs had been occupied since prehistoric times. It was first of all the seat of the local ruler before being the home of Athene, the protector of Athens. All the buildings visible date from the second half of the 5th century BC, the Archaic Acropolis having been sacked by the Persians in 480. Under the stimulus of Pericles and the direction of Pheidias, the works' superintendent, a start was made in 447–438 on building the Parthenon (1), the most refined of all Greek temples. It was not, however, strictly speaking a temple, since the old wooden statue of Athene was never kept there. It was rather like a colossal treasury, with the treasury of the League of Delos, which was administered by Athens, in its back room (opisthodomos). Its cella housed a statue of Athene in gold and ivory, 12 metres (39 feet) high, by Pheidias – a prodigious offering dedicated by the Athenians to their patron. Immediately afterwards (438–432) work was carried out on the propylaea (2), a monumental entrance to the sanctuary, with a hall to the north in which panel paintings were later exhibited. Interrupted by the Peloponnesian War, work was resumed sporadically, but in another style. The Ionic Order was chosen, which was less majestic but more graceful. The little temple of Athene Nike (427–424) (4), and above all the Erechtheion (421–406) (5), an odd building in which the most ancient cults of Athens were regrouped, followed; it was in part of it that the cult statue of Athene was kept. Between the Erechtheion and the Parthenon is the site of the Archaic temple to Athene (6): the altar which stood in front of it is still in the same place (7). Apart from these major buildings of the 5th century, which are all that remain today, there were other buildings in the Acropolis. As soon as he had left through the propylaea, the visitor would find himself in front of the colossal bronze statue of Athene Promachos by Pheidias; he would have on his right the sanctuary of Artemis, a local copy of that of Brauron (8), then the Chalkotheke (9) where numerous precious offerings were kept. The steps in front of the west façade of the Parthenon did not lead to it – the entrance was on the other side – they were used instead for exhibiting offerings. Against the northern rampart, near the Erechtheion, was the house of the Arrephorae (10); they were the young maidens whose duty it was to weave the peplos which was to be worn by the goddess on the occasion of the Panathenaic festival. Beyond the Parthenon, the highest point of the rock was occupied by a small sanctuary of Zeus Polieus (11). Shortly after AD27, a small round monopteral temple dedicated to Rome and Augustus was built in front of the Parthenon. Finally on the south-east corner of the plateau, occupied today by the museum, there was a building in which one could visit the workshop of Pheidias. Constantly being altered, but remaining intact up to the end of the Middle Ages, the main buildings of the Acropolis suffered worst during the Turkish occupation, during which time a garrison was stationed there. The Parthenon, transformed into a powder store, was blown up in 1687 during the siege of Athens by the Venetians.

Sanctuary of Zeus, Olympia

(model seen from the south-west)

The establishment of the sanctuary seems to have followed very closely on the settlement in Elis of some Dorian cattle breeders who came from the north (Aetolia): the oldest, terracotta, votive figures date from about 1000BC. The growing numbers of offerings and their richness show the rapid rise of the sanctuary. In 776BC the first Olympic Games took place and, at first, only attracted competitors from the Peloponnese. About 650BC architectural progress began with the sanctuary around the sacred wood, the Altis (1), and with the altar (2). The oldest preserved building is the temple of Hera (3), which still had a wooden colonnade, about 600BC. An artificial terrace (4) received, during the 6th century, a number of treasures, dedicated mostly by Dorian cities in the west. It was only in the 5th century, between 470 and 457BC, that the temple of Zeus was built (5); its anonymous sculptures are masterpieces of the "severe" style. In the 4th century, the portico known as the Echo portico (6) closed off the sanctuary from the east. The votive statues scattered around the sanctuary should be noticed. Beyond the surrounding wall (7) at the end on the right there is part of the stadium (8), but the tiers of seats were never built: to the right, the administrative buildings (9); in the foreground is the Leonidaion (10), a hostel of the 6th century BC; in the rear on the left (11), the workshop where Pheidias made the statue of Zeus, in gold and ivory.

Military architecture

Defensive works – ramparts, forts and watchtowers – whose imposing remains today scan the solitude of the Greek countryside, represent the other face, long hidden, of an architecture hitherto seen only in terms of purity and spirituality – in terms of sacred buildings within the protection of sanctuaries. These military buildings, important and numerous in every phase of Greek civilization, are the eloquent witness of a historic reality dominated by war. Geography certainly assisted Greece's political fragmentation: every plain or plateau which could be cultivated, or every island, had tended to set itself up as a distinct entity since its prehistoric times; ethnic, linguistic and religious solidarity only rarely counterbalanced the Greeks' burning desire for political autonomy.

The dry stone surrounds of Dimini and Sesclo (around 4000BC), the fortifications with towers of Chalandriani in Syros (about 2500BC) and the curtain walls of Dorion-Malthi (around 1600BC) are primitive examples, both in size and in technique, compared with Mycenaean defences (1400–1200BC). Although political power had by then been divided between feudal principalities, over which that of Mycenae seems to have exercised some kind of sovereignty, the ramparts do not seem to have been built because of civil wars, but to anticipate an external danger, such as invasion by Dorian hordes coming from the Balkans. A continuous wall was built to bar the isthmus of Corinth, and vast protective surrounding walls (for example, that on the island of Gla in Boetia, which was 3 kilometres – nearly 2 miles – in circumference), were disposed round fortified acropolises. These walls were colossal: measuring between 5 and 7 metres (16–23 feet) thick and between 9 and 10 metres (30–33 feet) in height, they were made up of blocks which often weighed more than 5 tons, coarsely quarried and packed together in Cyclopean bond. This extraordinary defensive deployment, the equivalent of which has not been seen since, and which supposes the use of a considerable amount of labour, did not save the Mycenaean citadels from destruction. But they left such imposing remains that the Greeks of the Classical period assumed these walls to have been the work of giants or of mythical heroes.

From the time when these first towns began to be resettled, during the 9th century BC, fortifications reappeared: the oldest now known is that of Smyrna (8th and 7th centuries BC), made of raw bricks on a stone base, without towers except to protect the few gates. These early walls, of a very simple plan, have left few remains (Halieis or Porto Cheli), but stone ramparts dating from the end of the 6th century have been found and were punctuated, no doubt in imitation of the Orient, with projecting towers. A path sheltered by a machicolated parapet ran all the way round the top of the curtain-wall, which gradually increased in height in accordance with developments in siege technique. Siege ladders which could hardly extend beyond 8 metres (25 feet) were succeeded by the end of the 5th century by mobile wooden towers fitted with pieces of artillery. From this time on, continuous progress in techniques and tactics brought an increasing complexity to plans, and architects and engineers competed in ingenuity. A specialized literature appeared, of which something still survives: *The Manual of Siegecraft* by Aeneas the Tactician (around 350BC) being one example. Some sieges in which technology reached its peak have become famous: that of Rhodes by Demetrios Poliorcetes (305–304, which was unsuccessful) and that of Syracuse by the Romans, who succeeded in taking it in spite of some extraordinary machines built by Archimedes to repel them. The gradual conquest of all the Greek world by Rome put an end to all intercity wars, and finally led to the decline of all military architecture. Under the Empire, ancient fortifications were no longer kept up, which left the Greeks vulnerable to the Herulian barbarian invasion of AD267.

With the exception of Sparta, which built them only very late (195BC), maintaining that its citizens substituted for them, every Greek city had its ramparts. They corresponded to their resources; often a few humble remains indicate that a village, whose very name has been lost, had existed there. Contrasting with these little rustic surrounds, carelessly prepared in local stone, were the ramparts of the cities with massive arrangements of large stones, the lines of which often far exceeded the town limits in order to include some favourable ground, to surround a well or an area where the rural population could seek refuge. Syracuse, with a perimeter of 27 kilometres (17 miles) and a large area of ground within the walls that was not built on, and

Athens with its "Long Walls" connecting it with Piraeus, were extreme cases. The rise of the ballastic machine led on the one hand to an increase in the thickness of the curtain wall (on average 3 to 4 metres/10 to 15 feet, with a filling of pebbles in hard cement between the two faces) and on the other hand to a development of the towers, provided with firing platforms and with large openings for ballistae and catapults or thin loop-holes for archers and slingers. The construction of the gates, often with forecourts and flanking towers, often involved complicated devices in which a desire to achieve monumentality was combined with the need for defence (gates with sculpted reliefs at Tharos and the Arcadian gate at Messina, the Great Gate at Side). While there was a free space of at least 5 metres (16 feet) left behind the rampart to allow rapid deployment of men and equipment, some fortifications had forward embankments in the open, designed to slow down the approach of the enemy. There was a fairly wide and deep ditch preceded by a bank running at the foot of the rampart.

Beside the defensive redoubts which made up the ramparts of the town, Greek cities often put up towers or small forts within the confines of their territory. These, like those on the islands to prevent raids by pirates, were usually simply watchtowers, or forts guarded by a small permanent garrison with a place of refuge for the local population. But they might also be strongly fortified places like Phyle and Rhamnonte on the frontiers of Attica, or Eleutheria and Aegosthenes on the borders of Boetia. These large garrisons and so many fortifications within a large area deterred potential invaders, who could not risk leaving their rear unprotected.

All these fortifications, which are history's mark on the Greek countryside, garlanding the hills with their austere lines, have not only a functional and documentary value: the Greek feeling for stone is apparent here as much as in religious architecture, only differently. The art of enlivening façades with lines, rustication and pointwork, of emphasizing corners, of articulating fortified curtains and towers by courses, variations in stone and different mouldings, is again apparent; and these works have an aesthetic quality to which our age may be more sensitive than the 19th century, when the language of the Orders of religious architecture was still living.

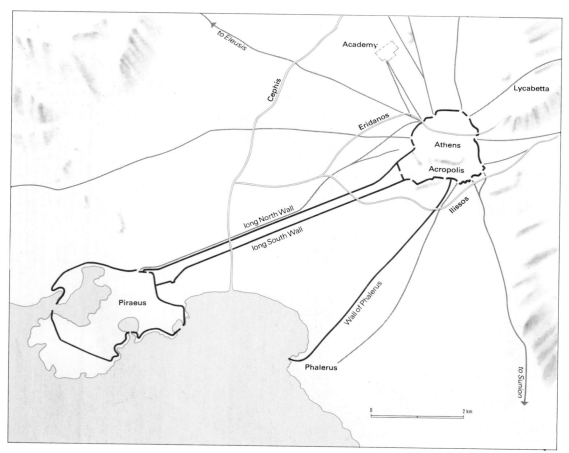

Ramparts of Athens and of the Piraeus

Defensive system of Athens during the 5th century BC, after J. Travlos. From 470BC, immediately after the defeat of the Persians at Plataea, Themistocles undertook the construction of the new ramparts around the town and its harbour, the Piraeus. Kimon then combined these two systems by two "Long Walls", thus surrounding in the defence perimeter the entire bay of Phaleros. With the building of the middle Long Wall under Pericles (445BC), a fortified corridor of 6 kilometres (4 miles) was established, which enabled Athens to resist the Spartan raids as well as keep mastery of the sea. This fortress, about 30 kilometres (19 miles) in perimeter and guarded by 14,000 men, was dismantled after Sparta's victory in 404. Restored by Konon after 394, it was strengthened at the end of the 4th century BC, and remained until Athens fell to Sulla in 86BC. From that time on Athens gave up all political ambition and remained an open town, hence it was easily sacked by the Herulians in AD267.

Fortress of Eleutheria

Situated on a height dominating a defile which allows passage from Boeotia to Attica, the fortress of Eleutheria, known today as Gyphtokastro (about 330BC), is the best preserved example of a strong control point. Its curtain wall of about 700 metres (766 yards) is buttressed every 50 metres (55 yards) by square towers, which also project into the interior. The fortified curtain is made up of two stone facings of regular courses, rusticated, on either side of an interior of pebble filling (emplecton).

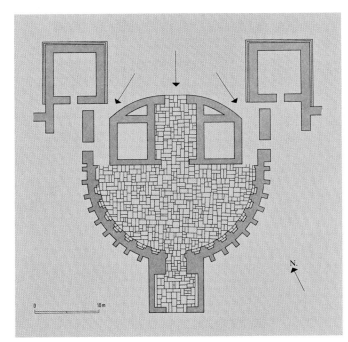

Ramparts at Thasos

Staircase to the curtain wall in pseudo-isodome bond with point work (4th century BC). The very different measurements of the blocks allowed economies in stone and time; the insertion in the marble facing of a corner block in gneiss is a typical Thasian procedure.

Tower at Chimarru, Naxos

This tower, from the Hellenistic period, is one of the best preserved of its type thanks to its very isolated position at the south of the island. Built in local white marble, it is still 15 metres (50 feet) high and had at least four floors. Flanked by a rectangular enclosure, it was probably a shelter rather than a watchtower; it is situated on a plateau from which one cannot see the sea. All the Greek islands had this system of protection from pirates, who were very active until put down by Pompey in 67BC.

Great Gate of Side

Restored plan, after A.M. Mansel (2nd century BC at the earliest). This gateway was more complicated than anything else known at the time. It consists of a vast, round, tiled courtyard, flanked on the outside by two great square towers. Two smaller towers, set back from the great towers, control the three entrances; a small, square courtyard at the rear reunites the traffic. This axial, funnel arrangement permitted filtering of the entrants through straight passages without compromising the grandeur of the plan; prestige and safety were therefore reconciled.

Ramparts of Athens

Sectional reconstruction of the rampart near Gate VII (4th century BC), after J. Travlos and A.W. Lawrence. In the front is a deep ditch and an artificial platform, faced by a parapet. The rampart is made of a homogeneous mass of stone arranged in regular courses. A staircase gives access to the top of the wall; the reconstruction of the wall in brick with windows and a sloping roof is known to be correct from an inscription.

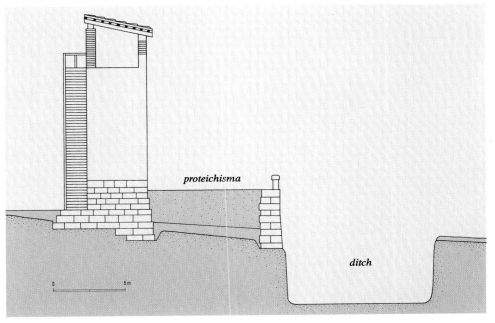

proteichisma

ditch

Public buildings and private houses

Civil and domestic architecture developed only late on in Greece. During the whole of the Archaic and the Classical periods, meeting places and houses remained unadorned in their original, traditional condition. The agora, for example, where civic and commercial activities were gradually concentrated, was for a long time put to many uses. It was in turn a market and the place for political discussion. Houses had hardly evolved since the 7th century BC, and were small, dark and had few comforts. It was not until the 4th century BC that the number of public buildings constructed increased and private houses became more spacious.

Public buildings were of two forms – the portico or stoa, a hall opened on one side by a colonnade, and the covered room or hypostyle (with internal columns supporting the roof). Cultural and sporting activities, instituted on the occasion of gatherings in honour of the gods, caused specialized buildings to be erected, either beside the large sanctuaries or, later, in all the important cities. Gymnasia (racing) and palestrae (wrestling and boxing), where professional athletes and the young men of a city came to train, were generally built in the open air around courtyards and consisted of a complex of porticoes containing tracks and covered rooms, as well as changing rooms and wash rooms. They were also meeting places, frequented by amateurs and those with time to spare, and above all they were places of education. Vitruvius expected palestrae to contain training and conference rooms in which "Philosophers, orators and all those who were interested in scientific discussion could sit down and talk"; a library was often added to the premises. As well as being responsible for the administration, in each city, of the palestrae and gymnasia, the local magistrates during the Roman and Hellenistic periods had powers which amounted to those of a minister of sport, culture and education. In a time when the great cities, led by Athens, tried to compensate for the loss of their independence by the prestige of their culture, these "houses of culture" of dual purpose were the subject of special attention

and received numerous donations: often they were the centre of life in the cities and an expression of patriotism.

At the same time, there were buildings for the staging of entertainments. While the stadia remained just oblong tracks with mounds of earth at the side until the Roman era, the theatre emerged as an architectural form at the end of the 4th century BC, contemporaneously with its decline as a religious spectacle. Theatres were built initially near sanctuaries (that of Dionysos in Athens, of Asklepios in Epidaurus, of Zeus in Dodona, of Apollo in Delphi), but by the Hellenistic period all cities of any importance had a theatre, the site of which depended on topography. In order to avoid a great deal of terracing, theatres were always in the shape of shells, with their back to a hill: the largest, at Pergamon and Argos, could seat 20,000 spectators. Furthermore, they were always open to the sky since it was impossible to vault such vast spaces. A wall, which later developed into a complex building, closed the area; it carried the scenery, and echoed sound back to the audience. When they went into decline, theatres tended gradually to be replaced by odeons, which were closed auditoriums of smaller proportions, reserved originally for music and then later for conferences. The oldest odeon known, that of Pericles in Athens (about 440–430BC), close to the sanctuary of Dionysos, was a vast hypostyle hall without tiers; but the amphitheatre form without inside supports was soon preferred for odeons and political meeting rooms (bouleuteria).

Large porticoes (stoae) appeared in public places along the main roads of the big towns during the Hellenistic and Roman periods. Their long colonnades gave a monumental appearance to the centre of the towns in which only isolated buildings had existed up to that time. This very simple, flexible architectural form gave a real unity and rhythm to an urban area. Sometimes flanked by two projecting wings, sometimes arranged in a square, but mostly simply straight, porticoes could be simple

covered alleys, but an interior colonnade might double their width. Shops could be placed inside, thereby changing them into commercial centres, and one or even two storeys gave them more space. The longest of these exceeded 150 metres (165 yards). These great halls had no real function, but it was there that people met other people. Thanks to the porticoes, the colonnade, which had until then been the preserve of religious architecture, also became a fundamental element of civil architecture; the same Orders were used, but they were simplified.

Houses were usually between 200 and 500 sq. metres (240–600 sq. yards) in area. The rooms would open on to a central courtyard, and when there was an upper storey, it was reserved for private apartments, especially for the women. Here again, it was the introduction of the peristyle colonnade around the courtyard in the early 4th century that gave houses more uniformity and more space. Thus, at Olynthos, only the north side of the courtyard had a portico, while the peristyle was in fashion in Delos in the 2nd century BC in the leisured quarter round the theatre. The north side of the yard sometimes caught the sun from the south, by virtue of a higher portico on this side (peristyle of Rhodes type), where the large reception and drawing rooms were situated. These were often decorated by mosaic on the floor and with stucco or murals on the walls painted in bright colours. In the other rooms, light generally came through the door; windows were uncommon and narrow.

No palace from the great Hellenistic capitals such as Alexandria, Antioch or Pergamon, is known today, so it is only possible to judge princely architecture from the early 3rd century by the Macedonian palaces in, for example, Pella, Aigai-Vergina and Dimitrias. These only survive in plan: the rooms decorated with mosaics and stucco were arranged round a vast square court. Only the dimensions and the absolute uniformity of the plan distinguished these very simple buildings from the bourgeois houses on Delos.

"House of the Comedians", Delos

Reconstruction of the peristyle courtyard, after P. Fister (2nd century BC). In the foreground, a well in white marble communicates with a tank (impluvium) installed beneath the courtyard pavement; the pavement itself is made of gneiss and is almost square. Twelve Doric columns, 3.6 metres (12 feet) high, fluted only from a height of 1.7 metres (6 feet), support a Doric Order with triglyphs painted blue. The upper floor, to which there was access by an arched gate giving directly on to the street, had exceptional Attic Ionic piers standing on a parapet almost 1 metre (3 feet) high. At the far side of the courtyard is the entrance to the great reception hall (measuring 9.5 by 5.5 metres/31 by 18 feet) with walls of coloured stucco and a frieze representing characters from the New Comedy.

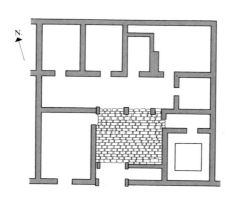

House in Olynthos

Plan of house A VII 4 (end of the 5th century BC) from Olynthos, level VIII. It was part of a building plot in which each house covered about 290 sq. metres (347 sq. yards) and cost to build about 12.5 drachmas per square metre, without counting the price of the land (daily wage of a builder: 1 drachma). All the houses in this plot faced south in order to get more light and heat. To the north of a paved courtyard measuring 6 by 5 metres (20 by 16 feet) there stretched a portico 13 metres (43 feet) in length, from which there were openings on the left to two living rooms and on the right to a bathroom and kitchen. On the left of the entrance there was a workshop or store (7 by 5 metres/23 by 16 feet), which also opened on to the street; on the right, a square reception room (andron) measuring 4.6 metres (15 feet) on each side. A wooden staircase gave access to the floor of the gallery of the portico on which the women's rooms were to be found (gynaekeon).

Theatre at Epidaurus

Built after 350BC, the theatre was not changed during the Roman era. The seating, consisting of stone tiers, could take 14,000 spectators; it is divided into two parts by an intermediary corridor (diazoma); there are twice as many stairways in the upper part. The tiers make more than a semicircle, which means that the spectators sitting at the ends would not have been able to see the stage wall at all well – the foundations of this can be seen on the left. While the chorus sang in the circular area of the orchestra, the actors spoke from the podium placed against the stage wall; the scenery was very schematic. On either side of the seating tiers are the double doors of the side entrance passages (parodoi).

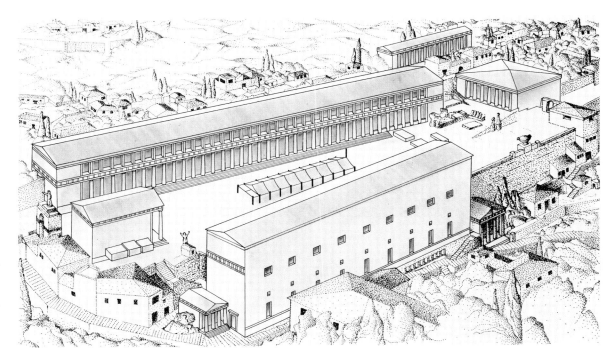

The Agora at Assos

Reconstruction of the agora during the Hellenistic period, after R. Koldewey. Two large porticoes with upper storeys form a trapezoidal terrace on sloping terrain: the portico in the foreground is 69 metres (75 yards) in length, with two storeys at the side of the agora and five on the side of the slope, where its height reaches 25 metres (82 feet). To the right the square room of the bouleuterion; to the left a small prostyle temple.

Portico of Attalos, Athens

Ground floor of the portico built at the expense of King Attalos II, around 150BC, in the agora of Athens, and rebuilt between 1953 and 1956. It is 112 metres (370 feet) long, 19.5 metres (64 feet) wide by 11.5 metres (37 feet) high. Each floor includes 21 shops, of which the entry doors are just visible on the left. An interior Ionic colonnade without fluting corresponds to the exterior Doric colonnade.

Assembly Hall at Priene

Reconstruction (around 200BC). In an almost square, covered space is a theatre with straight tiers; these are longer on the sides than at the end and are set out round a central space occupied by an altar. Staircases set at angles give access to the tiers: the end tier is higher by five rows. The piers supporting the framework have been set back along a sort of tribune, so as to free the view; this results in a span of 14 metres (46 feet) without intermediate support – one of the largest known in Greek architecture.

Greek architecture during the imperial period

The Roman conquest of Greece and her colonies during the 2nd and 1st centuries BC brought an irreversible decline in Greek art, but it was architecture which suffered most in the political turmoil which threatened the heritage of the Greeks (Athens was sacked in 86BC by Sulla) and demanded all their resources. When peace returned and regular administration was re-established, architectural activity began again in the Greek cities, either on their own initiative or as the result of gifts by the Roman government or emperors. During the 2nd century AD the Greeks recovered their elan in the eastern basin of the Mediterranean. The "Pax Romana" brought a new prosperity, reflected in ambitious and refined buildings, due in large part to the philhellenism of the Antonine dynasty, certain emperors of which – Hadrian and Marcus Aurelius in particular – felt themselves just as much Greek as Roman.

Roman influence on Greek architecture is seen in particular in the fullness and luxury of the civic buildings (stadia, libraries, odeons, fountains, baths and so on), which predominated over religious buildings and military constructions, as well as in the borrowing of some typical features. In plans and elevations there was much greater use of curves; the use of the arch, which had appeared in the 4th century BC in early tombs of Macedonian type, became more frequent, and bricks and masonry became the norm, notably for domes over large spaces. On the other hand, walls with an applied decorative colonnade, which became very common in the 2nd century AD, did not originate in Rome, as used to be thought, but in Alexandria, and so, again, were a Hellenistic creation adopted by Rome. The result of this cross-fertilization was an architecture in which Greek and Roman components varied from one region to another of the Hellenized Orient according to the availability of materials locally, the degree of Hellenization of the place, and the taste and nationality of the client and architect.

In Asia Minor, where Hellenization was well established on the coast, but was just as intense and deep on the Anatolian plateau in the Hellenistic period (3rd to 2nd century BC), where marble for buildings was also very plentiful, the architecture remained very largely Greek in form and technique. Long unknown, because of their difficult access, the great Greek sites of internal and southern Asia Minor were systematically explored only from the 1950s. Better preserved than those of Greece because they were totally abandoned by later ages, they speak eloquently of the vitality of this late Hellenism. They were less hampered by the traditions of the mother country, where architecture, just like the plastic arts, literature and thought, was fighting a rearguard action to maintain an out-of-date tradition. This tendency to look back, most pronounced in Athens because it posed as the guardian of classicism, was almost universal throughout Greece, particularly in the cities which boasted a prestigious past. Only the towns founded again by Rome (Thessalonica, Philippi, Corinth, Patras and so on), where the population was at least partially of Latin origin, attempted an architecture which was more clearly Roman. This resistance by the Greeks to assimilation is an important cultural fact: although administered by Rome, Greece retained a lively feeling of its own identity, which was to find political expression at the final severance from the Western Empire at the end of the 4th century AD.

Public latrine, Athens

This latrine from the 1st century AD (after J. Travlos) is composed of a peristyle with four columns and a central impluvium. Along the walls is a marble bench with 68 holes, each 40 centimetres (16 inches) apart, but with no partitions. The holes emptied into a sloping, subterranean channel and then into the town drains; cleanliness was maintained by a continuous flow of running water. The idea for these conveniences was taken from Rome, and they are the oldest known in Athens. A latrine of similar type with 42 seats has been found in Philippi in Macedonia.

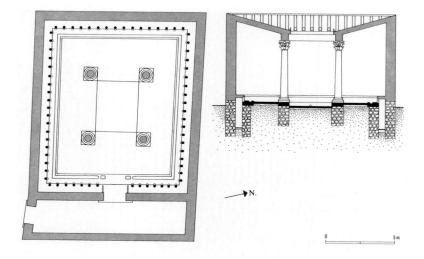

Andronikos' clock or "Tower of the Winds", Athens

This is an octagonal tower in Pentelic marble (about 45BC), opening to the north-east and north-west by two doors, each of which once had a porch with a pediment. Each external face, 3.2 metres (10½ feet) wide, carries an engraved sun-dial, as does the small tower behind; on the crown runs a frieze on which the eight principal winds are carved in the form of winged young men and old men. The roof is in the shape of a dome of straight section, with the 24 trapezoidal marble tiles kept in place by a circular keystone which supports a weather-cock in bronze representing a salamander. The inside was occupied by a waterclock supplied by the spring Clepsydra, the water of which was led to the north side of the Acropolis by an artificial conduit, the hydraulic system itself being hidden in the little cylindrical tower joined on the south side. The central part of the tower, ringed by a parapet, was occupied by a device (an anaphoric disc) indicating the hours and the seasons in the manner of an astrolabe. The "clock pavilion", a marvel of ancient technology, was situated near the oil market (Roman agora), one of the most frequented places in Athens.

Hadrian's Library, Athens
(model)

Built in AD132, the library was one of the numerous gifts made to the city by Hadrian (117–38), who came to be known as the "second founder of Athens". Like the "Roman agora" which lay on its south side, the library opened to one side of the old agora by a porch with a pediment. On this side the blind wall of marble was ornamented by 14 smooth Corinthian columns of green marble from Carystos which supported plinths on which the statues were set. The use of coloured marble, as again inside the building, and the presence of decorative columns with no bearing function, betray Roman influence. The central courtyard (82 by 60 metres/90 by 65 yards) was occupied by an oblong pool surrounded by bushes. It was ringed by a peristyle, 7 metres (23 feet) wide, of which the 100 columns were in Phrygian marble; the revetment of the poros walls was of the same marble – another Roman feature. The library itself was at one end of the building. The three sides of the central hall (23 by 16 metres/75 by 52 feet) were occupied by cupboards with shelves which contained the books; the halls at the side were used for conferences. The ceilings were in gilt wood and the walls covered with marble or decorated with paintings. Statues decorated the rooms. The library of Celsus in Ephesus (about AD120) was similarly laid out with more emphasis on decoration.

148

Stadium at Aphrodisias (Asia Minor)

Built in the first century AD, this is the best preserved of all Greek stadia. It is 262 by 59 metres (287 by 65 yards), with 30 rows of seats; the ends are semicircular with an arched entrance gate while the long sides are slightly curved. The official stand is at the centre of the north side. The meetings which were held were "Pythian", that is to say based on those of Delphi, where the artistic contests had a more important place than in the Olympic Games. The persistent vitality of these Greek institutions up to the 3rd century AD is proved by a large number of inscriptions commemorating victories. Later, the eastern part of the stadium was converted into a circus, as at Ephesus, for Roman gladiatorial games.

Odeon of Herodes Atticus, Athens

This concert hall with 5,000 seats (about AD170), the largest and the most exotic of its kind, was a gift to the city from the orator Herodes Atticus, who used his enormous fortune to rival Hadrian for generosity. Except for the fact that its roof was supported by a cedar timberwork, this was in effect a Roman theatre with a semicircular *cavea* (diameter: 86 metres/280 feet) with 33 rows of seats in marble and scenery buildings standing 28 metres (92 feet) high. The systematic use of niches and of arched windows flanked by applied columns in the three storeys of the scenery wall, gives a pronounced Roman character to the building. Statues were placed in all the niches; mosaics decorated the floor of the entry portico. The *cavea* was restored in 1952–54.

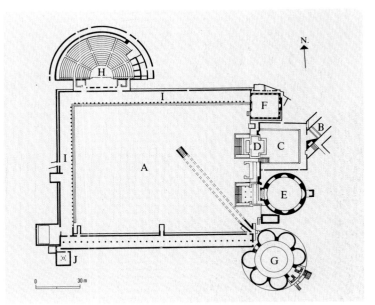

Sanctuary of Asklepios, Pergamon

Plan in Roman times (AD140–75). The buildings of the Hellenistic period, much more modest, survive only to the foundations in the middle of the court (A) (102 by 140 metres/112 by 153 yards). A paved avenue (B) with a portico at the side leads to a peristyle front court (C), which leads on to the central court (A) through monumental propylaea (D). Immediately to the south, preceded by a porch with a pediment, a pendant to the propylaea, there was a round temple to Zeus-Asklepios (E), an imitation of the Pantheon in Rome, with a brick dome 24 metres (79 feet) in diameter. The south-east corner was occupied by a rotunda on two storeys, 26.5 metres (87 feet) in diameter, with six apses (G), without doubt the hospital proper; its basement was connected by a vaulted tunnel to the centre of the court where the sacred fountain stood, and perhaps some older buildings. The three other sides of the courtyard were occupied by Ionic porticoes (I); the portico to the south had a vaulted basement; in (J) a large latrine. To the north, a theatre on the Roman plan with 3,500 seats; in the north-east corner, a library (F).

Fountain of Regilla, Olympia

The fountain was dedicated by Herodes Atticus in AD153–54 to commemorate the priestess of Demeter who cured his wife in Olympia. Terminating a long aqueduct, which was partly subterranean, the building today consists only of bricks, but these were once completely sheathed by white, grey, green and red marble. The semicircle surrounding the upper basin was decorated with an applied Corinthian colonnade and niches where there were statues of the imperial family, dedicated by Herodes Atticus, and those of his own family dedicated by the administrators of the sanctuary. On both sides of the lower rectangular basin small Ionic monopteral buildings contained basins with jets of water. In its materials and its design, this fountain 12 metres (40 feet) high resembled more the great Roman fountains than Greek fountains, which were always functional; while here there was an almost theatrical display of water in an architectural setting.

149

Porta Nigra, Trier

This monumental gateway (36 metres/120 feet wide and nearly 30 metres/100 feet high) dates from the end of the 3rd or beginning of the 4th century AD. It is representative of Hellenistic military architecture of the times; the complex arrangement of gateways fulfilled a dual role by reinforcing the defences at a very vulnerable part in the surrounding wall and by marking, architecturally, the entrance to the town. The semicircular towers are unified into the composition by repeating the motif of the engaged half-column across the entire façade.

Roman architecture is all around us: the centres of old towns, baths, amphitheatres, temples, city walls and triumphal arches, together with Roman bridges and aqueducts, often still in use, form an integral part of Western scenery. Like Latin literature, Roman architecture has never had to be rediscovered, nor reconstructed from scanty remains; it has never ceased to be alive and to inspire Western architecture, whose history can be traced by revealing the borrowings of forms, decoration and techniques. The Renaissance was only a return, more fervent and more fertile, to this "visible reserve". Europe's gradual discovery of Africa and the East since the 17th century has greatly increased the number of known buildings. Scientific examination undertaken since the 19th century makes it possible, for all their apparent uniformity, to appreciate as well the regional variations often determined by local cultures. While perception of imperial Roman architecture becomes more refined, excavations have made it possible to rebuild the long process of assimilation which led to its spreading. The archaeological exploration of Pompeii and Herculaneum, begun in 1748, has revealed the extent of the cultural cross-breeding in Italy at the beginning of the Empire, as well as the importance of figurative decoration – paintings, mosaics and sculptures – in private houses. The discovery of the Etruscan necropolises early in the 19th century revealed the early influence of Archaic Greek culture. Excavations carried out in Rome and Latium since the end of the 19th century have made it possible, if not to solve the problem of Rome's origin, at least to put it in a different light.

The history of Roman architecture as it gradually unfolds is complicated, sometimes even obscure, since few buildings of the royal and republican periods survive and those that do are difficult to interpret. What is clear, however, is the exceptional cultural receptivity of Rome. Whereas, during the 7th century, once the materials and forms

had been established, Greek architecture developed in isolation, without borrowing from outside, Rome only achieved its originality very late. During the republican period, it was more concerned with transformation than with creation. In religious and domestic architecture, neither Greek Orders nor ground plans were adopted as they were; the Tuscan Order is a debased form of the Doric, incorporating Ionic features, while the Composite Order has a capital which fuses Ionic and Corinthian characteristics. The forms obtained at first from the Etruscans and later directly from Greece were then adapted to Italian traditions. Rome confirmed its faith in these by an ostentation which was all the more marked as the influence of the Graeculi became stronger. It was only from the 1st century BC that it was possible to explore the opportunities offered by a new material. The use of blocks (opus caementicum) made from rubble soaked in a very hard cement made of volcanic sand (pozzolana) and clay, enabled Roman architecture to exceed restrictions imposed on Greek architecture by the exclusive use of stone. Massive pillars, capable of supporting vast arches, then supplanted the column as load-bearers. On the other hand, this unsightly composite material of no aesthetic value had to be covered over. Consequently different methods evolved of improving the appearance of façades; opus quadratum, made from large rectangular tiles, arranged horizontally, was followed in the 1st century BC by opus reticulatum, made up of small tiles in the form of a regular diagonal web, while brick (opus testaceum) appeared during the 1st century AD. This was an essential difference from Greek architecture: the facings were decorative veneers placed on top of a material they wished to hide, while in Greece the stones visible on the surface constituted the wall itself. Roman architecture therefore found itself gradually developing an aesthetic illusionism which distanced it from the spirit of Greek architecture; while it borrowed features, it divorced them from their functional importance.

By the middle of the 1st century AD, the Hellenizing classicism of the Augustan era had been left behind; composite blocks, bricks and the arch completely liberated Roman architecture from the Greek tradition. Subsequently the interior, freed from the restrictions imposed by transverse wooden beams, was conceived by architects in full spatial terms, a conception previously limited to the exterior. Roman buildings, unlike Greek, had from that point on to be judged and appreciated from the inside. The remains of the Domus Aurea or "Golden House", the palace-villa built by Nero in the heart of Rome after the fire of AD64, confirm that the transformation which had been going on for two centuries was at last complete. The great domed octagonal hall, which pre-dates Hadrian's Pantheon, represented the first attempt to break "the tyranny of the right angle" which had been so characteristic of Greek architecture. The emergence of this Baroque taste was to continue with the palace built by Domitian (Domus Augustana) and triumph with the alternating curves of the island pavilion in Hadrian's villa at Tivoli. From then on, Roman architecture created highly original spaces in which the curve predominated both in plan and elevation. This non-classical modernism, which was accompanied by a tendency towards the colossal, stimulated by technical achievements and the demands of imperial society, was coupled with a very lively taste for decoration. The somewhat exaggerated Baroque of these new forms was destined to survive for many years in the Mediterranean basin.

The elements of this decoration were not new, but their style and application were increasingly innovatory. The formulas which the Hellenistic world had perfected in painting, relief stucco, mosaic and marble inlay were developed in a new spirit and extended to all interior walls in a profusion which characterizes Etrusco-Italian taste. Greek mural painting has been almost completely lost, but the towns smothered by the eruption of Vesuvius in AD79 continue to provide plenty of visual

Construction methods used in Roman architecture

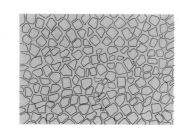

opus incertum

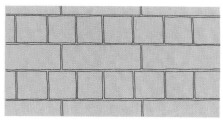

opus quadratum

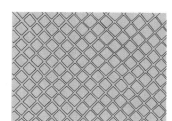

opus reticulatum

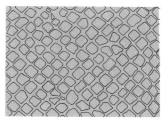

opus quasi reticulatum

ROME

information, and complement a number of discoveries in Rome (Livia's House and the Domus Aurea) and Ostia. Although Campania had long been Hellenized and had become an area in which top Roman society decided to build its country residences, so establishing a brilliant cultural environment, comparisons with Rome show that the quality of mural decoration seems to have been higher in the capital. With few exceptions, painters working in Campania were second-rate artists who made fairly professional copies of Hellenistic paintings, a practice not uncommon in Rome. The chronological sequence of four styles, which has been established for over a century, still remains valid, although the dates of each are continually being discussed and periodically adjusted. The first style is that which can be seen in houses at Delos dating from the beginning of the 1st century BC; it was an illusionistic form of decoration in

which superimposed zones of different colours simulate the appearance of a marble wall. At the base there was a dado, then an isodome elevation, finally, at the top, there was a plinth; sometimes these stones were stuccoed in relief so as to reproduce the surface quality found on walls designed by Greek architects. The second style, which appeared about 80BC, is more properly pictorial in that it gives the impression of depth by the use of architectural perspective; complex arrangements of columns, which sometimes predate the colonnade screens of Baroque 2nd century architecture, fill the foreground, while the background within this columnar framework portrays urban or pastoral scenes. The influence of theatre decoration seems to dominate this architectural illusionism; figures are depicted on a sort of stage-set designed with frail ornamental architecture, just like masques. The houses of Augustus and Livia

on the Palatine represent the end of this complex style, in which too much mystic symbolism has perhaps been sought. These architectural effects, like the theatre decoration to which they refer, represented a means of enlarging the interior by opening up views to an unreal exterior; the first style had restricted the interior by enclosing it within walls. Thus the pictorial representation of the architecture, whether imitating the theatre or fragile Alexandrine structures, completed the architecture itself by visual means. The real space was doubled by an imaginary space which extended and magnified it, thus creating a false unity between the architecture and the painted decoration.

A third style, the dates of which are very debatable, from 20BC or AD20 to AD50 or 63, marked the return to a more traditional kind of decoration in which the architectural components were reduced to the role of a

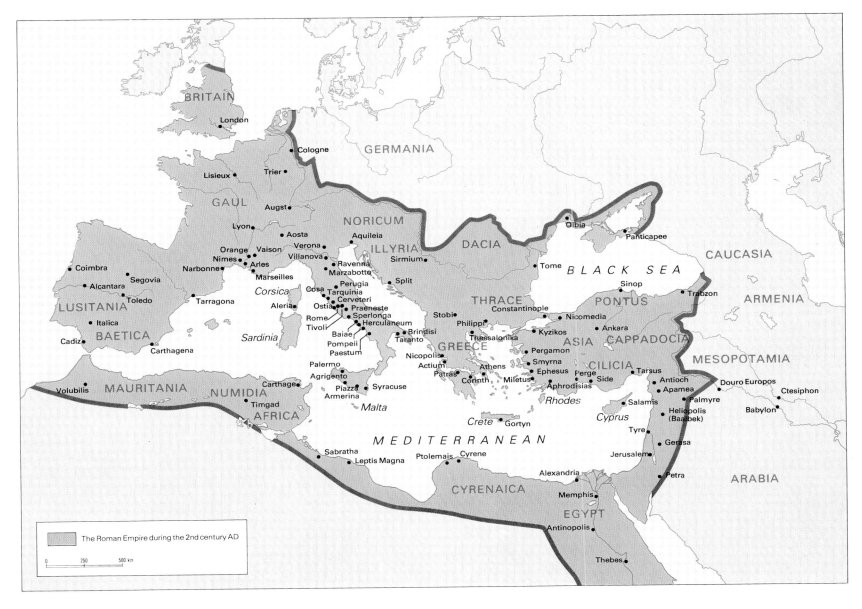

The Roman Empire during the 2nd century AD

0   250   500 km

two-dimensional frame. The centre of the monochrome panels was occupied by an isolated figure or a small, often oblong, tableau depicting an imaginary country scene in which nature and architecture were blended together. Was this a classicizing phase affecting all mural painting? Or was it merely a conservative current running parallel with the illusionism of the second style? The spatial experimentation of the fourth style certainly suggests that it can be regarded as a direct continuation of the second, even though it is fused with the severe character of the third. After the catastrophe of AD79, mural painting almost disappeared completely. Some panels in Ostia dating from the 2nd century AD show the exhaustion of this decorative architectural style; technique is simplified, and the third dimension has disappeared. The elaborate fantasies in architectural illusionism were now definitively dispensed with; mural painting returned either to large figural scenes closer to the Greek tradition, or to isolated figures on a white background which foreshadowed the style of the early Christian catacombs. Fresco painting had been temporarily replaced by mosaics.

The method of paving in mosaics which had spread throughout the Grecian East during the 2nd century BC came to Italy after Sulla's campaigns against Mithridates (87–84BC). He brought back with him the Greek mosaicists who designed the Nile scenes at Praeneste (Barberini mosaic) and the older floors of Pompeii like the celebrated Battle of Alexander (Naples museum). At this time the mosaic, despite its technical virtuosity, was still dependent on large-scale fresco and sometimes even easel painting. Now, very gradually, Rome would give it an independent character – something unknown in the Greek world. Italy, however, remained satisfied for a long time with black geometric patterns on a white background, the plainness of which contrasted with the extravagance of the second and fourth styles of mural painting. It was only with the decline of the latter, at the end of the 1st century AD, that mosaic came back to the fore as a means of decorating public buildings and houses. Stylized plant motifs in arabesques

dates	history and civilization	architecture
Bronze Age		
c.1500BC	Progressive arrival of Indo-Europeans. *Terramare* civilization in the Po valley. Apennine civilization in central Italy.	Villages on piles beside lakes. LUNI and the Forum Boarium in ROME: rectangular cabins with gravel walls and thatched roofs.
Iron Age		
1000–900BC 814BC 753BC	Villanovan civilization: geometric Italian pottery. Etruscans in central Italy. Foundation of Carthage by the Phoenicians. Traditional date for the foundation of Rome. Start of Greek colonization in southern Italy.	Etruscan towns: TARQUINIA, VULCI, VEIO etc.
Archaic period (750–509BC)		
615–509BC 600BC	Roman monarchy. Etruscan domination of Rome. Marseilles founded by the Greeks of Phocea. Etruscans in Campania.	ETRURIA: Large tombs with rooms cut into the bedrock (CERVETERI, TARQUINIA...). Podium temples.
Republican period (509–27BC)		
509BC 5th century BC 493BC 450BC 386BC c.380BC 343–291BC 312BC 300BC 270BC 264BC 264–241BC 218–201BC 212BC 200–194BC 193?BC 188BC 184BC 167BC	Republic formed. Domination of Latium. Law of the Twelve Tables. Gauls sack Rome. War with the Samnites. Domination of Italy. First gladiatorial duels in Rome. First Punic War with Carthage. Domination of Sicily, Corsica and Sardinia. Second Punic War: Hannibal in Italy. Siege and capture of Syracuse by the Romans. Death of Archimedes. Second Macedonian War; liberation of Greek cities. Peace of Apamea: Rome arbitrates between the Hellenistic kings. Death of Plautus; Cato the Elder as censor. Greek historian Polybius in Rome.	IN ROME: Temple of Jupiter on the Capitol. First arrangement of the Forum. Temple of Ceres. Servian Wall. Temple of Apollo. Via Appia from Rome to Capua. Aqua Appia: first great aqueduct. Temple C at Largo Argentina. First use of blocks. First stone arches. First bridges. "Porticus Aemilia". First basilica in the Forum.

appeared in the floors of Hadrian's villa at Tivoli, popularizing the rise of the "floral style", which was to spread throughout the West with provincial

variations. From the Flavian period (AD69–96) a parallel style developed in Africa (Libya and Tunisia), which was dependent upon the figured and polychrome characteristics of Hellenistic mosaics. It introduced a new iconography with views of amphitheatres or circuses and scenes from daily life (hunting, fishing, agriculture and so on). These vast compositions, richly framed with plant motifs, in southern Europe covered the whole floor space in large houses and villas (Piazza Armerina in Sicily). Their chromatic virtuosity and thematic originality made this the most exciting art of the period. The mural mosaic (opus musivum), on the other hand, had appeared in Pompeii during the 1st century AD where it was used for the decoration of exterior fountains (grottoes), ornamental niches and several arches. Its rise seems connected with that of the arch and of the dome: the brilliant play of the colours suited the decoration of these badly lit surfaces very well. Later adopted in Christian art, the wall mosaic had its first success in Ravenna during the 5th and 6th centuries, and was popular in Byzantium up to the 14th century. By contrast, the floor mosaic had disappeared by the end of the classical period.

Floors and walls could also be decorated in other ways which were no less sumptuous; inlays with geometric motifs (opus sectile)

Domus Aurea ("Golden House") of Nero, Rome (AD64–68). Painted decoration of a room. Transition from the third to the fourth style: simple architectural frames border panels with small, centrally placed pastoral scenes; architectural perspectives are restricted to the side panels.

dates	history and civilization	architecture
149–146BC 146BC	Third Punic War: destruction of Carthage. Annexation of Macedonia; destruction of Corinth. Greek art flows to Rome; vain resistance to Hellenism by conservatives.	Temple of Jupiter Stator by Hermodoros of Salamina. Hellenization of religious and domestic architecture: peristyle houses.
129BC	The kingdom of Pergamon becomes Roman province of Asia.	
91–88BC	Civil war: Italians given Roman citizenship.	Mural paintings of the first style with architectural decor.
90–50BC	The Greek sculptor Pasiteles in Rome.	Sanctuary of Fortuna at PRAENESTE.
87–84BC 80BC 64BC 61–55BC	Sulla in Greece: sack of Athens. Pompeii a Roman colony. Annexation of Syria and Pontus by Pompey.	First mosaics in Italy. First vaults in blocks. Theatre and porticoes of Pompey in ROME.
58–51BC	Conquest of Gaul by Caesar. Cicero, Sallust, Horace, Virgil.	Forum of Caesar in ROME.
31BC	Naval battle at Actium: Octavius sole master of the Roman world; end of civil wars.	Mural paintings of the second style: architectural perspectives.
Imperial period (27BC–AD395)		
	Augustus reorganizes the Roman state and establishes the Principate.	Pont du Gard. Maison Carrée at NÎMES. Transformation of ROME: 82 temples restored, 10 temples built. Development of architecture in the provinces.
AD14–68	Julio-Claudian dynasty: Tiberius, Caligula, Claudius, Nero.	Villas at CAPRI and Campania. Domus Aurea of Nero in ROME.
AD69–96 AD79	Flavian dynasty: Vespasian, Titus, Domitian. Eruption of Vesuvius: Pompeii and Herculaneum buried.	Mural paintings of the fourth style.
AD80		Colosseum, Arch of Titus, in ROME. Imperial palace on the Palatine in ROME.
AD96–192	Antonine dynasty: Nerva, Trajan, Hadrian, Antoninus Pius, Marcus Aurelius, Commodus. Empire reaches its peak: Pax Romana. New wave of Greek sophists: Lucian, Herodes Atticus, Aelius Aristides, Plutarch, Pausanias.	Forum of Nerva, ROME (98): first curtain- colonnade. Trajan's forum in ROME by Apollodorus of Damascus (113). Rise of OSTIA, port of Rome. Hadrian's Pantheon in ROME (118–28). Hadrian's villa at TIVOLI. Hadrian's mausoleum in ROME (c.130). Rise of Baroque, especially in the East.
AD193–235	Dynasty of Severus: Septimius Severus, Caracalla, Heliogabalus, Alexander Severus.	New monumental centre at LEPCIS MAGNA. Baths of Caracalla, ROME.
AD212	Concession of Roman citizenship to all free men in the Empire.	BAALBEK: temple of Jupiter.
AD235–84	Military anarchy; provincial emperors. Plotinus: Neoplatonism.	Aurelian defences around ROME.
AD284–305	Diocletian reforms the Empire: the tetrarchy. Trier the capital of Gaul.	Diocletian's baths in ROME. Galerius' arch and rotunda in THESSALONIKA. Diocletian's palace, SPLIT. Villa at PIAZZA ARMERINA.
AD312–37	Constantine the Great converted to Christianity.	Basilica of Maxentius in ROME transformed by Constantine.
AD330 AD375 AD392 AD395	Constantinople the new capital of the Empire. Start of the great invasions. Theodosius bans pagan worship. Final break-up of the Empire.	

pragmatists to the point of utilitarianism, were first and foremost technicians. They had been great engineers long before they were great architects. The techniques of road construction, carriage and drainage of water, heating – in short everything that the Enlightenment, in complaining of the pragmatic rationality of Rome, called "bridges and highways" – saw an extraordinary development.

The importance given to these works of public utility was paralleled by the social status of architects-engineers: director of the Roman water supply was one of the highest posts in the Roman administration (a post held by Vitruvius and Frontinius). In the provinces, engineering was one of the most highly respected of professions, as is known from an epitaph of the 3rd century, found in Arles: "Into the hands of the gods we entrust Quintus Candidus Benignus, member of the corporation of engineers in Arles, eminent builder, zealous, wise and modest, whom the great engineers have always considered their master. None were wiser than he; none surpassed him in the building of machines or the designing of aqueducts. He was an amiable companion, knowing how to entertain his friends, with a spirit desirous of learning, and a heart full of kindness. Candida Quintina to her much loved father and Valeria Maximina to her very dear husband." Further evidence of the prestige of these engineers, who had the inspiration to turn engineering into art, can be found. One engineer, in the 2nd century AD, proudly signed his name on the bridge over the Tagus, which he had designed.

The Roman mind worked in quite a different way from that of the Greeks. For

Mural painting in the house of Sulpicius Rufus, Pompeii. After the earthquake in AD63, Pompeii developed a fourth composite style which blended the tableaux of the third style with the spatial experimentation in architecture of the second style. This recently discovered panel is distinctive for its restricted palette; other examples of the same style (House of the Vettii) are much more gaily coloured.

G. Mandel, Ziolo

made of coloured marbles, often imported from distant lands (Africa and Asia). Hadrian's Pantheon shows how such revetment could ennoble an interior by articulating the wall surfaces with a pattern of large coloured panels. The same type of lavish decoration must be imagined as having once decorated the walls of large public buildings during the imperial age, like the baths of Caracalla and Diocletian in Rome. Here again, Rome had gone far beyond Greece. The latter had encouraged mosaics for practical rather than aesthetic reasons (paving of the tholos in Epidaurus); while Greek architects and merchants were always hesitant in importing marble because of high transport costs, the Roman emperors, owners of all the quarries throughout the Empire, often sought to acquire the most exotic, and therefore most valuable, marble.

The last development in the boom of decoration which concealed the structure of the buildings was architectural. Architecture itself became the decoration with the Orders fixed against the inner as well as the outer walls. The first known example of the colonnade screen which conceals the wall behind is in the Forum Transitorium of Rome, started by Domitian and opened by Nerva in AD97. The play of light and shade gives a chiaroscuro effect to the surfaces. The origin of this Baroque fashion is still very debatable; the presence

of a similar device in the Palace of Columns of Ptolemais (Cyrenaica, 1st century BC) seems to suggest an Alexandrine Hellenistic source, as for the frail architecture which figured in the mural paintings of the second style. This rich decoration, adopted with a certain amount of reticence in Western Europe and Greece, spread particularly through Asia Minor, the East and Africa, where it adorned secular monuments (marble fountains, libraries, theatres and so on) almost to excess, increasingly using marbles of different colours. Sculpture itself also participated in this decorative profusion. The niches, arranged on the walls or between the columns of these curtain-façades, housed copies of celebrated works. These famous sculptures were thus divorced from their original cultural or votive conception. The column and the entablature, which had a vital function in Greek buildings, are here reduced to the level of decorative features. They articulate the space, achieving in plastic form the essential character of the second and third styles of mural painting.

The architecture of Rome illustrates one of the essential traits of Roman character: a dynamic feeling for organization was translated into architecture by a technical mastery which remained unequalled until the 19th century. While they were not to be artists until after being influenced by the Greek school, the Romans, realists and

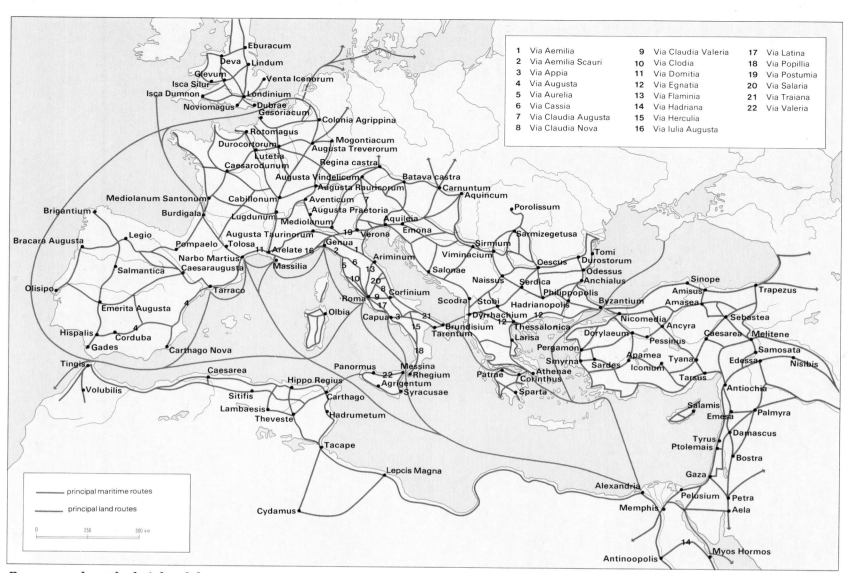

Roman roads at the height of the Empire. During the 2nd century AD, the Roman Empire was at its largest with an area of more than 5 million sq. kilometres (nearly 2 million sq. miles). In order to maintain the cohesion of a mosaic of peoples, it was not enough to establish colonies to diffuse Roman civilization. It was necessary to encourage exchange and to control provincial administration. Thus permanent and rapid communication was essential. During the winter months (*mare clausum*, from October to April) sea traffic in the Mediterranean came to a complete stop, and roads became the only method of communication. They were all the more important now that the Empire was no longer a coastal fringe. In the 2nd century, the network exceeded 100,000 kilometres (62,000 miles). It carried Roman culture from Scotland to the Sahara, and irreversibly altered civilization.

1	Via Aemilia	9	Via Claudia Valeria	17	Via Latina
2	Via Aemilia Scauri	10	Via Clodia	18	Via Popillia
3	Via Appia	11	Via Domitia	19	Via Postumia
4	Via Augusta	12	Via Egnatia	20	Via Salaria
5	Via Aurelia	13	Via Flaminia	21	Via Traiana
6	Via Cassia	14	Via Hadriana	22	Via Valeria
7	Via Claudia Augusta	15	Via Herculia		
8	Via Claudia Nova	16	Via Iulia Augusta		

principal maritime routes
principal land routes

0   250   500 km

the latter, applied science and utility were inferior to pure science and abstract thought. In Archimedes, the Greeks admired the author of the famous theorem, but the Romans looked to the inventor of the machines which worried them so much during the long siege of Syracuse. It is also probable that the great changes in architecture would not have been possible without this positive approach to technology. It was continuous experimentation, at first tentative, into the possibilities of concrete which opened the way to the great domed spaces of the 2nd century. This interest in technology is reflected in the one surviving treatise on architecture, Vitruvius' ten-volume *De architectura*, which has exercised a great influence on European architecture since the Renaissance. Vitruvius' designs combined the Greek tradition, still in vogue in Rome at the time when he was writing (early in the reign of Augustus), with a constant regard for practicality only to be found in Greece among military engineers. This pre-eminence of technique and of standardized utilitarian architecture, which does not preclude isolated achievements of great aesthetic value, brought Roman architecture close to us at a time when, paradoxically, contemporary architecture was ridding itself of its dependence on classical models. Modern architecture owes nothing to the form and decoration of Roman building, but finds itself again in an analogous situation: the adoption of an artificial material, which is malleable, cheap and easy to make – in this case, reinforced concrete – has overthrown architectural tradition as once opus caementicum did in Rome.

E. Lessing, Magnum

Pont du Gard, near Nîmes (end of the 1st century BC)

This bridge, over the river Gard, is 275 metres (900 feet) long and 49 metres (160 feet) high. It was part of an aqueduct nearly 50 kilometres (30 miles) long which supplied Nîmes with water. On its first level it carries a road and at the top of the third level, a water conduit, which is 1.8 metres (6 feet) high and 1.2 metres (4 feet) wide and has a gradient of 0.4 per cent. The three levels were built in dressed stone without mortar. The projecting blocks supported the scaffolding during construction.

Mosaic from the "House of Virgil" in Sousse

This mosaic, which dates from the beginning of the 3rd century AD, represents Virgil flanked by the Muses of History and Tragedy – Clio and Melpomene. This is an exceptional subject which shows that like the great Greek authors, who appear more frequently in mosaic, the Latin poet had become a "classic".

Mosaic from the villa of Dominus Julius in Carthage (about AD400)

Within a frame decorated with scrolls and fruit, various scenes of agricultural life are portrayed. The centre of the three layers depicts a building – the villa itself? – reminiscent, with its corner towers and great arcaded gallery, of the villa-fortress of Diocletian at Split.

155

Primitive Rome and Etruscan architecture

Archaeology has profoundly altered the image of Rome's origins as provided by literary and historic tradition (Virgil and Livy). The site had already been occupied well before April 21, 753BC, the traditional date of Rome's foundation by Romulus; the area round the Forum Boarium shows signs of Bronze Age habitation dating from 1500–1400BC. There are indications that it had been occupied by Indo-European tribes, similar to those which had been living in the Apennines. At the beginning of the Iron Age (8th century BC), two hamlets of the Villanovan type coexisted on the Palatine; other hills were also inhabited. It was their unification, in the 7th century BC, with the Forum area as a common civic centre, which gave birth to Rome, by a synthesis similar to that achieved by Theseus at Athens. The houses were primitive: rectangular or oval, they were set down a little into the ground: a post at the centre supported a wooden framework and a thatched saddleback roof. One of these huts, carefully maintained and restored, was visible beside the Palatine in ancient times; it was the house of Romulus.

The introduction of Greek columns in Campania, immediately to the south of Latium, after 750BC, and in particular the influence of the Etruscans, who had established themselves on the right bank of the Tiber and whose authority was going to be exercised directly on Rome in the 6th century BC, caused an early metamorphosis in the civilization of central Italy. The Etruscans spoke a non-Indo-European language, which has not as yet been deciphered, and seems to have come from Asia Minor – an eastern origin reflected in their culture. The influence of the East mingled with that of Greece reflects the receptivity of the Etruscan civilization.

In the cities which made up the Etruscan confederation the first building given monumental form was the temple. Generally erected on a podium and constructed of rough brick it had a deep colonnaded portico, with often two and sometimes three rows of columns. The very wide spacing of these columns leaves one to suppose an entablature of wood, protected by an elaborate terracotta facing, painted in imitation of Greek temples. These squat temples, which were almost square, were never peripteral as were Greek temples: a colonnade was never attached to the rear of a temple and rarely to the sides. The cella was often divided into three parallel rooms, consecrated to a divine trinity.

Compared with the apparent equilibrium of the Greek temple, whose short sides resemble each other, first the Etruscan and then the Roman temple had a directional and frontal emphasis. These Etrusco-Roman temples are similar to the Ionic prostyle buildings of the Cyclades. Such originality is seldom found in the elevation; the mixture of various Greek motifs, including the Aeolic capital, which harmonize more or less happily, reflects an eclectic approach to design. Columns of the "Tuscan Order", as defined by Vitruvius, consisted of an Ionic base on which sat a smooth shaft tapering slightly towards the top followed by a capital similar to that of the Doric Order with its circular echinus and square abacus. If then the entablature without a frieze and the roof extending beyond some parts of the walls are not Greek, the painted terracotta coverings improved on the Archaic Greek taste for the polychromatic. From the 6th century BC the pediments were sometimes decorated with multi-coloured reliefs, while terracotta figures on *acroteria* proliferated excessively on the sloping parts of the pediments and on the coping of the roof. While the features of this Etruscan architecture were Greek in principle, the sentiment was quite different. The notion of order with all that it implies was totally absent.

Little domestic Etruscan architecture is known. Knowledge of it is based upon Etruscan tombs excavated from the rock in which both the arrangement and decoration followed those of patrician houses. Excavations have, however, brought to light modest rectangular houses sometimes with a small latrine and a well. The plan was that of a megaron, that is to say, a building with a porch opening on to the road, a small front room and a large back room. Thatched roofs gave way to tiles during the 6th century BC. The living quarters excavated at Marzabotto, near Bologna, confirm the existence around 500BC of an orthogonal urban plan with large rectangular blocks of houses; but towns situated on raised ground, more typical of Etruscan civilization, did not have a regular plan, and the layout of roads and walls rarely corresponded to the three roads and town gates which text books give as the basic principle of Etruscan town planning.

In Rome itself, evidence of its first monumental expansion is scarce: all the buildings put up during that period have been destroyed or later rebuilt. However, fragments of painted terracotta decoration from Archaic temples show that from the 6th century Rome was affected by Hellenic styles through Etruscan influence. The Forum was only a piece of trodden ground. To the north-west there was an area where the *comitia* met, in front of the senate house. The first city walls, traditionally attributed to King Servius Tullius (578–534BC), were not in fact built until after the invasion of the Gauls (386BC); during this Etruscan period only the area between the Esquiline and the Quirinal was fortified. As at Ardea, Antium and Satricum it consisted of a simple rampart (*agger*) with a ditch in front; elsewhere, as in many Etruscan cities, terraced walls made it easy to defend the higher sites.

Following this first provincial Hellenization of Etruscan inspiration a second phase of Roman civilization left more tangible architectural evidence.

Hut on the Palatine, Rome

Excavations carried out in 1948 in front of the temple of Magna Mater revealed the foundations of three huts, of which one, dating from the 8th century BC, was complete. The arrangement of the posts on which the walls and framework were constructed make it possible to reconstruct the hut as oval in plan with a central post and preceded by a small covered porch. This primitive dwelling was destroyed during the late 7th century BC (reconstruction after A. Davico).

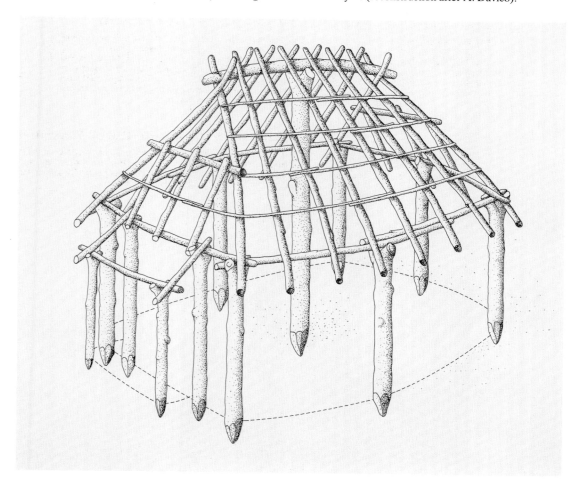

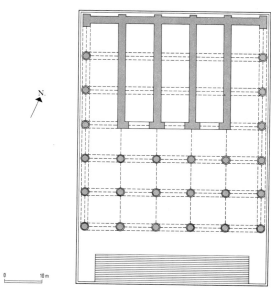

Temple of Jupiter Capitolinus, Rome

Inaugurated in 509BC, this temple, the most important of Archaic Rome, was destroyed by fire in 83BC and rebuilt in 69BC following the original plan but with a marble elevation. The podium, standing about 4 metres (13 feet) high, measured 62 by 53 metres (68 by 58 yards), that is to say a ratio of 7:6. Almost half of the ground plan is taken up by a triple row of six columns with a return at the sides. At the back, a wall extends both sides of the triple cella in which the statues of Juno and Minerva were housed. This very ambitious temple, the largest in the Italian world, reflects Rome's wealth at the end of the Etruscan era.

Capitolium, Cosa (Etruria)

Reconstruction after A. Davico of the entablature and roof of the Capitolium built around 150BC. The Etruscan taste for terracotta decoration covering parts of the timber framework was still in evidence even at this late period. It was applied to all vertical surfaces. The antefixae (1) bear, alternately, heads of Hercules and Minerva. The slopes of the pediment (2) are decorated by a high cyma with a double frieze. The longitudinal beams of the wooden framework (3) rest directly on the architrave (4), and project markedly from the façade; the transverse roof beams (5) finish in a lateral, prominent weatherboard.

Etruscan tomb, known as "The Doric Columns", Cerveteri (Caere)

The necropolis of Banditaccia comprises all the most important chamber and tumulus tombs known. Cut out of the tufa, most of these tombs echo certain characteristics of Greek architecture. In this Doric column the animated arris flutings have been reduced to a few flat surfaces common in Etruscan tomb architecture. The echinus, a very thick square slab, is very similar to Greek capitals of the early 6th century BC, but the capital seen in the background has a more extended echinus, typical, at least in Greece, of the beginning of the 5th century. In this way eclectic Etruscan architecture places two incompatible types side by side.

Tomb of the Montagnola, Quinto Fiorentino

An access passage (dromos) leads to an oblong, corbel-vaulted antechamber, from which two small side rooms open; at the end there is a circular room, the corbel vault of which is propped up by a central pillar (plan and section after M. Mannini and F. Chiostri). Dated about 600BC by a number of articles left by pillagers, this tomb resembles the great *tholoi* of the Mycenaeans.

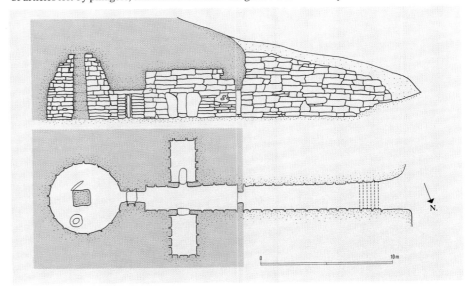

157

Roman architecture in the republican period

The five centuries between the fall of the kings and the establishment of the Principate by Augustus (509–27BC) embraced two periods of unequal interest for the evolution of architecture. From 509 to the end of the 3rd century, Rome gained control of the Italian peninsula, including the Hellenized south (Magna Graecia, Sicily). The colonies established in these regions employed a regular plan often derived from the fortified camp of the Roman legion. At this time ramparts of polygonal or pseudo-isodomic masonry appeared at Terracina, Ferentium, Praeneste, Norba and Cosa. In Rome itself, the surrounding fortified city wall, said to have been made by Servius, was built shortly after the invasion by the Gauls in 386BC. By contrast, the city was rebuilt without plan: the twisting lanes were lined with high apartment blocks into which homeless peasants were crowded (in 218, a bull fell from the third floor of such an apartment block). During the same period, the Forum rapidly lost its commercial function: from the 4th century BC only bankers and money-changers had their stalls on this site. Here, later, the balconies which had been built above shops by the consul Maenius in 338 provided vantage points for watching the first gladiatorial contests (264BC). At this point there were no theatres and the two circuses (Maximus and Flaminius) were only banks of earth around a track. The temple C in the sacred precinct of Largo Argentina, built around 300BC, shows the persistence of Etruscan forms in republican sacred architecture. While monumentality in architecture was still rare, novel techniques did appear: the first stone semicircular arches were built during the 4th and 3rd centuries in town gates (Falerii Novi) and bridges (Via Amerina), shortly to be followed by the use of concrete blocks (a mixture of mortar and small stones: *opus caementicum*). The appearance of this form and this material marked a decisive turning point in the history of Roman architecture: free from the constraints and limitations of stone, vaults were quickly exploited and became the preferred method of covering large civic buildings such as the Porticus Aemilia, a vast hall situated alongside the Tiber, to the south of the Aventine, which was built in 193BC.

In every respect, the Second Punic War (218–201BC) marked a major turning point for Rome: at the end of this "world" war on a Mediterranean scale, Rome dominated the Western basin and found it necessary to intervene directly in the East, since Philip V of Macedonia had been foolish enough to side with Hannibal (215BC). And so Rome came into contact with the great Hellenistic monarchies where Greek culture was in the process of assuming a new look. Despite the defiant conservatism of one section of the ruling classes, the modern imperialist party was soon dominant. But while the Roman state grew enormously by the annexation of the Greek world – Macedonia in 148BC, the kingdom of Pergamon (the province of Asia) in 129BC, the Seleucid kingdom (Syria) in 64BC and Egypt in 30BC – Greek culture irresistibly conquered Rome: poetry, the plastic arts and architecture were all transformed by it. By the end of the Republic, Rome had become a Hellenistic state, as the buildings erected during that period bear witness. The task of drawing the attention of Roman institutions to this fact fell to Augustus (27BC–AD14), who at the same time favoured the appearance of a mixed culture. In his autobiography (*Res Gestae*) he boasts that he found Rome a city of brick and left it a city of marble.

Even if the first temple built in marble (temple of Jupiter Stator by the Greek Hermodoros of Salamina) dates from 146BC, the use of marble in Rome remained limited until the time of Augustus, when the quarries of Luna (Carrara) were first exploited. Beforehand it had been imported from abroad, mainly Greece, and was therefore very expensive. Local tufa and travertine from Tivoli were the stones most frequently used in Hellenizing architecture, and they were normally covered up with stucco painting, as were brick and concrete walls. Thus another feature of Roman architecture was established: disguising surfaces by sumptuous decoration. This was to culminate, under the Empire, in polychrome marble facing.

As was natural, it was religious architecture which resisted Hellenization most strongly. With a few exceptions, the Roman temple remained faithful to its Etruscan origins: the podium with frontal staircase remained, as did the vast columnar portico. It was rather the rhythm and style of these which were borrowed from the Hellenistic East: the temple of Jupiter Capitolinus, rebuilt in 69BC, had marble Corinthian columns of about 16 metres (52 feet) in height, some of which were taken by Sulla from the unfinished Olympieion in Athens. Engaged half-columns often enlivened the sides of the cella, recalling peripteral Greek temples (temple of Portumnus, known as the "Fortuna Virilis" in the Forum Boarium, *c.*150–100BC; tetrastyle temple in Tivoli, of the same date). The innovations in secular architecture were more striking, where the adoption of porticoes introduced a spatial arrangement altogether new; squares (fora) adopted an axial layout, one side of which was often dominated by a temple or a basilica – a covered commercial centre with an oblong plan. The first basilica known in Rome was built in 184BC by Cato the Elder in the Forum. It was quickly followed by the Basilica Aemilia and the Basilica Sempronia. Others appeared towards the end of the century in Pompeii, Ardea, and Alba Fucens. These enormous halls with three naves were, from the 1st century BC, an essential feature of Roman urban centres, and a prestigious future was in store: their plan was adapted for the first Christian churches of the Roman West.

Hellenistic influence was still more pronounced in the great axially planned complexes where porticoes and terraces punctuated the space and framed a temple (sanctuaries of Fortuna at Praeneste, of Hercules Victor at Tivoli and of Jupiter Anxur at Terracina).

Servian Wall, Rome

Built about 375BC, the wall was constructed with alternating courses of headers and stretchers of yellow tufa; it was about 10 metres (33 feet) high and 3 to 4 metres (10 to 13 feet) thick. The total length was about 11 kilometres (7 miles). (The picture shows the inner face of the portion preserved beside the central railway station.) The wall surrounded an area of about 426 hectares (1050 acres), including the seven hills which constituted the centre of early Rome. Between the Esquiline and the Quirinal the wall gave way to a man-made bank of earth (*agger*), about 40 metres (130 feet) wide and supported on the outside by a terraced wall about 10 metres (33 feet) high. In front, there was a trench 17 metres (56 feet) in depth and 36 metres (118 feet) wide. This defensive system, which discouraged Hannibal from laying siege, was restored and modernized in 353, 217, 212 and 87BC. Rendered superfluous by the city's expansion, it was replaced in the 3rd century AD by the Aurelian Wall (271–75).

Round temple of the Forum Boarium, Rome

Dedicated about 120BC to Hercules Victor, patron of the oil merchants, by the merchant Marcus Octavius Hersenus. It was the second marble temple built in Rome, and is the oldest to survive. This *tholos* in Pentelic marble, almost certainly designed by a Greek architect, attests to the wealth of the Roman merchants who dominated Mediterranean trade. The cult statue was also the work of a Greek artist, Scopas the Younger. Built on a tufa foundation with a marble facing, the temple is peripteral in form with 20 Corinthian columns, and an east-facing portal; nine columns and eleven capitals were reworked by Tiberius in Luna (Carrara) marble. The entablature and roof are now missing.

Theatre and portico of Pompey, Rome

Built on the Campus Martius between 61 and 55BC, this was the first permanent theatre in Rome. Restored late in antiquity, it always remained the most important in Rome. Its semicircular *cavea*, with a diameter of about 150 metres (164 yards) was able to seat some 15,000 spectators; it was dominated by the temple of Venus Victrix, approached by a staircase lying on the theatre's central axis. This arrangement often found in Italy (Cagliari, Gabies, Tivoli, Praeneste) can be explained by the religious origins of the theatre. Behind the *frons scenae* stretched a garden enclosed by porticoes (180 by 135 metres/197 by 148 yards). It was the first public garden in Rome and was adorned by statues, some of which were brought from Greece. One of the rooms (*exedrae*) leading on to this garden was used for meetings of the senate; it was here that Caesar was murdered on March 15, 44BC, at the foot of the statue of Pompey. The idea of a vast promenade adjoining a theatre is Hellenistic (Athens, Pergamon . . .), but the arrangement of a garden surrounded by a peristyle encouraged an interest in garden architecture, a characteristic feature of Roman civilization. (Plan after L. Canina).

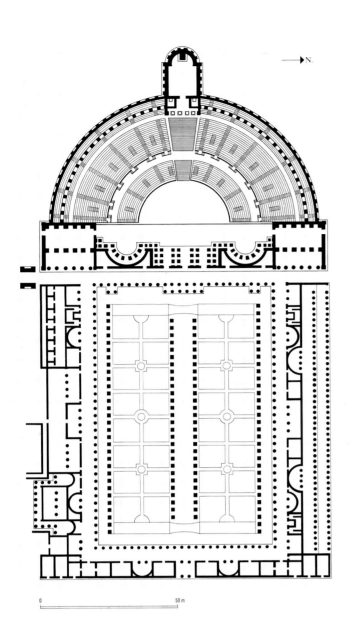

Basilica in the forum, Pompeii

Although its name suggests a Greek origin, this type of covered building, which gradually increased in size due to the introduction of concrete vaults, has no equivalent in Hellenistic architecture (could it perhaps be inspired by the great reception rooms of the kings of Egypt?). This basilica, the oldest known (120BC), has a long rectangular plan, 55 by 24 metres (60 by 26 yards), divided into three naves by two rows of stuccoed brick columns. It differs from the type described by Vitruvius: the main entrance leading to the forum occupies the short side, which creates an internal space with a marked longitudinal axis like a Greek temple. The plan is similar to that of Christian churches, except for the short sides of the internal peripteral colonnade.

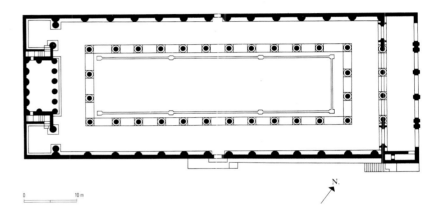

Sanctuary of Fortuna Primigenia, Praeneste
(Scale drawing and section after F. Fasolo)

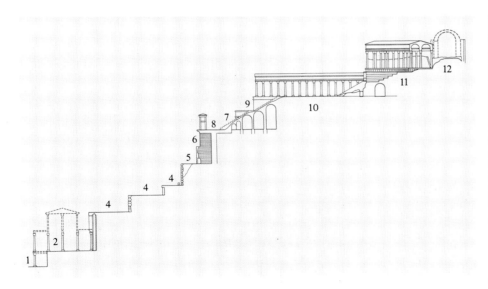

Destroyed by Sulla in 82BC, the town was later colonized by veterans from his army. It was then that the forum and the sanctuary were built on the site where today stands the town of Palestrina. Above the forum (1), flanked by a large two-storey basilica (2) and the local curia (3), the abrupt slope of the hill was remodelled in parallel terraces facing east–west. The three lower levels separate the sanctuary from the forum: there are perpendicular stairways connecting these levels. The architectural layout of the sanctuary begins with the large wall in polygonal masonry (5), which forms the base of the triangular wall supporting the two covered access ramps (6) leading to the central staircase (7). The two lower terraces of the sanctuary (8 and 9) were lined by two rows of shops. Above, a vast courtyard (10), opening towards the plain, is surrounded on three sides by a Corinthian portico. It is dominated by a theatre with semicircular tiers (11) surmounted by another Corinthian portico from which there is access to the circular temple of Fortuna (12). This elaborate composition, by introducing a rigorous axiality and dramatic focus, converted the great Hellenistic terrace systems (Pergamon, Lindos, Cos) into a complex altogether Italian in character.

159

The forum, heart of the Roman town

After Augustus, much more is known about Roman architecture: following the turmoil of the civil war, which concluded with the demise of republican institutions, the regime installed by Augustus ensured two centuries of peace for the Mediterranean world. During this period the Empire was consolidated and enjoyed a prosperity which found expression in architecture, not only in Rome and the older provinces, but also at the fringes of the Empire, regions hitherto almost unknown. More than the temples of the state religion, weakened by the influx of oriental cults, it was the civil and administrative buildings which best expressed the spirit of this mixed civilization.

The forum is the focus of this essentially urban architecture; in the colonies founded throughout the Empire as in the Romanized towns of Italy, architectural expression of the various civic functions – political (curia), religious (capitol) and commercial (basilica, market) – had a clearer structure than Rome itself where historical precedents were difficult to overcome. Because of the difficulty of giving the ancient Forum, cluttered with prestigious buildings, a monumentality appropriate for a capital of more than a million inhabitants, Caesar, Augustus, Domitian and Trajan constructed adjacent forums on its northern side. These were enclosed by porticoes, arranged symmetrically about a central axis. These were variations on the same theme: the porticoed courtyard dominated by a temple placed on the short side. However, this string of successive forums lacked unity and independence: the interconnecting passages were inconvenient and narrow. In fact, only the forum of Trajan, lying between the Capitol and the Quirinal, at the cost of massive terracing, made up a harmonious ensemble. The functions, political (equestrian statue of Trajan in the vast forecourt; column commemorating his victories between the two wings of the library and the temple to the deified emperor), cultural (library), commercial and judiciary (Basilica Ulpia and the commercial centre overlooking the great *exedra* to the north of the courtyard, around the Via Biberatica) were carefully arranged in a vast composition ascribed to Apollodorus of Damascus. Contrasting with the monumental severity of the forum is the ingenious flexibility of the markets that stand above it, using the space available on the side of the hill to the best advantage.

There was nothing like this in the provinces, where social and historic determinants were negligible or non-existent; curia, capitol and basilica occupied either the axis or the sides of a generally rectangular courtyard which was surrounded by shops. This scheme was repeated throughout the Empire. The standardization and use of ready made models, such as those outlined by Vitruvius in his treatise, reduced the role of architectural innovation. This is explained by Rome's territorial expansion: from the 1st century BC new towns and municipalities became miniature Romes, adopting Roman institutions and customs.

Some exceptions rejected the functional monotony of these civic centres. Imperial favour sometimes caused a town to be built according to above average standards. Hence Lepcis Magna, on the banks of the Sirte in Libya, home of Septimius Severus (193–211), doubled in size in a few years into a new, sumptuous town, where considerable use was made of imported marble; similarly Trier, which became one of the capitals of the Empire at the end of the 3rd century AD.

The Forum during the Empire, Rome

(Reconstruction looking to the south-west corner from the north-east.)

The foreground is occupied by a paved square with monuments to famous people. The temple to the Divine Julius, dedicated in 29BC to the deified Caesar (the first case of political deification in Rome), built in a Hellenistic style, is located in the background on the left; to the right is the temple of Vesta and the house of the Vestal Virgins, guardians of the everlasting flame (the only priestesses in Rome); further to the right is the temple of the Dioscuri, Castor and Pollux (Greek gods whose cult was brought to Rome in the 5th century BC) dedicated in AD6. Here the office of weights and measures was situated. The podiums of the temples of Caesar and the Dioscuri were often used as orators' platforms and it is in this part of the Forum that the meetings of the *comitia* took place. On the far right is the Basilica Julia built by Caesar in 54BC. Its long façade (101 metres/110 yards) occupies the entire south side of the Forum.

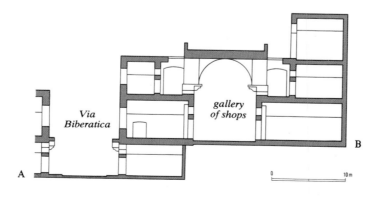

Via Biberatica

gallery of shops

A   B

0   10 m

Cross-section of Trajan's market, Rome

This commercial centre of about 150 shops and offices, backing on to the side of the Quirinal, completes the forum of Trajan, which it overlooks. Thanks to the masterly composition on five levels, the architect has used almost all the available space, while creating an original and picturesque urban scene, which flanks the lower zone of the forums to the north. While the walls are built of brick, the architectural detailing, such as the bases, capitals and door-frames leading into the shops, is made of travertine.

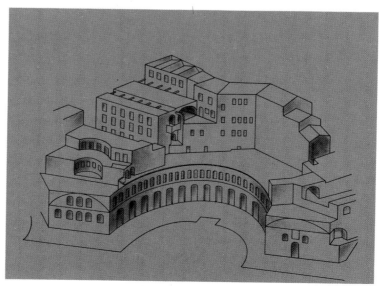

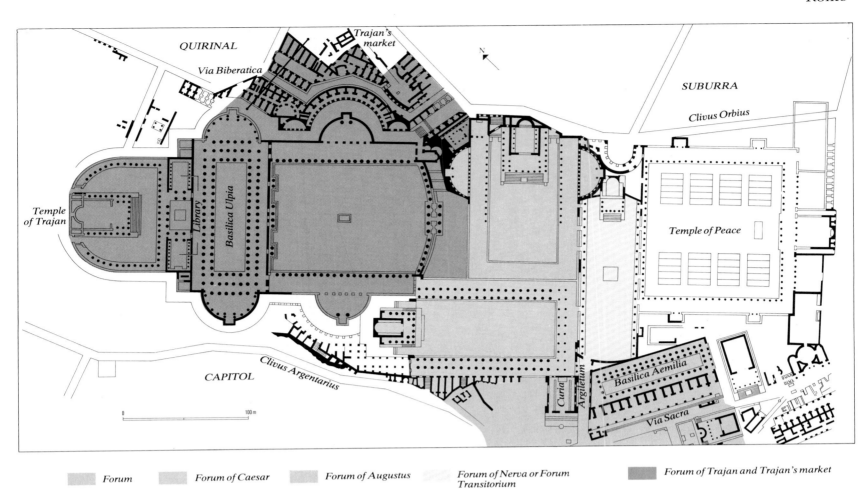

Forum	Forum of Caesar	Forum of Augustus	Forum of Nerva or Forum Transitorium	Forum of Trajan and Trajan's market

The imperial forums, Rome

In order to remedy overcrowding in the Forum, which was increasingly ill-suited for the growing metropolis, Caesar added a new forum to the north, behind the Curia, which was finished in 46BC. It is a long court with porticoes on three sides. At the end stands the temple of Venus Genitrix, the mythical ancestor of Caesar's family. In the centre of the square rises the equestrian monument to Caesar. This plan can be seen to reflect the grandeur of a man regarded as a figure of historic importance and as a god. It was to be repeated by other imperial forums, and predates the "royal squares" of European absolutism. The forum of Augustus, inaugurated in 2BC, has its axis perpendicular to that of Caesar's forum. Essentially it follows the earlier plan while embellishing it with two lateral, semicircular *exedrae*. In the middle there was the statue of Augustus standing in a triumphal chariot. The temple of Mars Ultor was built in fulfilment of a vow made before the battle of Philippi (September 42BC), a battle which Caesar's assassins lost. Statues in gilded bronze showed the continuity of Rome from the time of Aeneas and Romulus up to that of Augustus, of whom a colossal 14 metre (46 feet) statue was later erected there by Claudius. Because of its dedication to Mars, this forum became the cult centre of Roman military power. It was there that the senate decided upon questions of war and peace, and there that statues commemorated conquering generals. The Forum Transitorium, begun by Domitian and dedicated by Nerva in 97BC, is only an illusion: it is a monumental passage between the Forum and the Suburra quarter. The porticoes at the side are reduced to colonnades, placed directly against the walls. This was the first time such a decorative Baroque device, which was going to make its mark in the 2nd century, had been seen in Rome; only the temple of Minerva repeats this sumptuous decoration. The forum of Trajan, built in six years by Apollodorus of Damascus, brings the axial plan of the forum to perfection, by making the best use of covered and open spaces. The orthogonals are here softened by the curving colonnades.

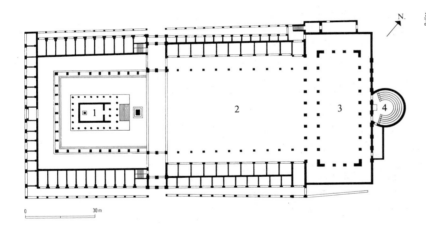

Forum, Augusta Raurica (Augst, near Basel)

This town was founded as a colony of veterans in 44BC. Situated on a plateau overlooking the Rhine, it went on developing until the 2nd century AD. The position of the forum, where two main roads intersected, was retained right from the beginning, even though the buildings were built piecemeal. Its perfect uniformity and the harmony of the various buildings associated with it make it a fine example of the colonial forum: (1) temple of Jupiter (Capitolium); (2) square for porticoes and shops; (3) basilica, both market and tribunal; (4) curia, meeting place for the municipal council.

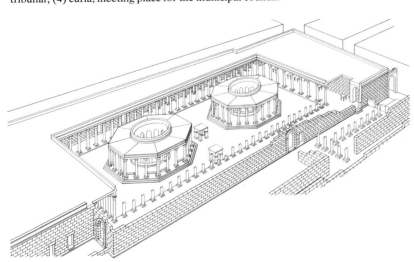

Arch of Septimius Severus: the Forum, Rome

The arch of Septimius Severus was built in AD203. A triumphal arch, often erected at one of the exits from the forum, is a typically Roman monument. By means of inscriptions and narrative reliefs which tell of an emperor's conquests the triumphal arch was one of the principal means of spreading imperial ideology. Throughout the East, these arches symbolized the provinces' patriotism to Rome. The oldest arch known is that attributed to Octavian, built in 29BC, also in the Forum.

Market, Lepcis Magna

(Reconstruction after G. Caputo)

The originality of this market, which was built far from the forum by a rich merchant Annobal Tapapius Rufus in AD8–9, lies in its two elegant polygonal pavilions. The windows are arched and the octagonal Ionic colonnades occupy the centre of the paved yard. Both were built at the end of the 1st century AD of local limestone. One of them, however, was rebuilt around AD200 in black and green imported marble. The yard and porticoes were decorated with statues of councillors. Standards of weights and measures cut in marble, as well as butchers' stalls, were also found there.

Temples of the imperial age

The form of the Roman temple had been established for a long time, but its appearance underwent a transformation with the introduction of marble during the 1st century BC. From the time of Augustus it changed little, except in the enrichment of decoration, but this is a subject reserved for those studying the development of Roman Baroque. Floral decoration, already present in the Corinthian capital, was applied gradually to the frieze, the cornice and to the framework of doors and so on. Mouldings were increased and had the effect of shaping the surfaces rather more than giving them contrast. The walls themselves, from the end of the 1st century BC, were enlivened by curtain colonnades and niches suggesting depth without it really being created. In this way, by using light and shade, plain surfaces were avoided and were made to gleam by the use of coloured marble. Thus architecture approached the illusion of the second and fourth styles of painting, the architectural perspectives of which are thought to have been borrowed from theatre decoration. But this Baroque of the 2nd and 3rd centuries was not to be found everywhere in the Empire. The West and Rome itself, at least in religious architecture, only yielded to it reluctantly. It was in Africa, Asia Minor and particularly in Syria (Baalbek, Petra) that it achieved its greatest popularity, foreshadowing Italian designs of the 16th and 17th centuries.

Augustus pointed out in his list of achievements (*Res Gestae*) that, in Rome, he had repaired 82 temples and had built, or completely rebuilt, 10 others. This resulted in a certain degree of standardization; some architects and entrepreneurs copied and varied the same formulas time and time again. Roman religion in the provinces took on a very marked civic character. The towns were anxious to set up a temple dedicated either to Jupiter Capitolinus or to Rome and Augustus in the centre of their forum, thus demonstrating their allegiance to Rome. There, too, few innovations were to be expected. The best surviving example of these dynastic temples is the Maison Carrée in Nîmes. In the eastern Empire, the cult of Rome and Augustus subsumed the tradition of the deified Hellenistic kings, but its temples followed Greek models (Acropolis in Athens, Trajaneum of Pergamon).

Alongside this precise but unoriginal sacred architecture appeared temples with vaults or domes largely dependent upon the use of concrete. This technique, which allowed larger spaces and more complex structures to be built, constituted, without doubt, Rome's most original and fertile contribution to architecture, since it lived on in Byzantium, the Muslim world and the Italian Renaissance. The dome was first used during the 1st century AD in various types of civic architecture – which was consistently more open to innovation (the baths at Baiae, the Domus Aurea of Nero and the palaces of the Flavians). At the start of the 2nd century AD it was one of the highlights of Western architecture, as Hadrian's Pantheon in Rome exemplifies. Soon afterwards it was to be imitated in Pergamon in the new temple to Zeus-Asklepios. The apse, covered with a half-dome, was used from the beginning of the imperial era and became much more popular in temples and forums in the 2nd century, when a taste for curved spaces was confirmed.

Finally, the common denominator between the temples of the Hellenized Italian tradition and the new designs in which the curve was employed in both plan and section seems to have been the growing attention given to the composition of internal space – volume and decoration – while the outer skin of the building remained conventional, even neglected. In this way Roman architecture of the imperial period distanced itself from the Greek aesthetic, which gave precedence to external volume. From this point on it became necessary to appreciate the interior of a building.

Interior of the Pantheon (Rome), by Giovanni Paolo Pannini

This temple, dedicated by Agrippa in 25BC and twice destroyed by fire (in AD80 and 110), was entirely rebuilt by Hadrian between AD118 and 128. The architect is unknown. It was without doubt dedicated to the imperial cult, and is built in two parts which are badly defined. A portico with the traditional pediment makes it clear that one is entering a temple. The cella, however, is circular. It is lined with niches and covered by a dome with five rows of poorly stuccoed coffers. At the apex there is an oculus measuring 8.7 metres (29 feet) in diameter. The diameter of the hall (43.3 metres/143 feet) is equal to the interior height. The extraordinary poverty of the exterior wall contrasts with the rich, plastic articulation of the interior. This is hollowed out with rectangular niches and apses and further enlivened by small tabernacles and marble panels. It is a magnificent example of Roman interior decoration. Generally only the skeleton, without the revetment, survives. A concrete dome reduced in thickness and weight by 140 coffers rests on a double-skinned shell. Walls with vertical and horizontal bricks together with load-bearing arches reduce the thrust. The dome's exterior was originally covered with gilt bronze. This technical masterpiece, which has only been bettered in modern times, creates a unified spherical space, which enlivens the mobile shaft of light coming through the oculus.

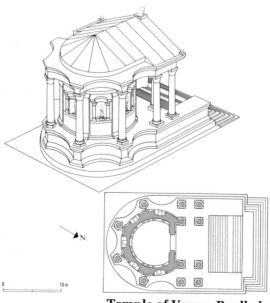

Temple of Venus, Baalbek
(Plan and reconstruction after J.B. Ward-Perkins)

A small enigmatic jewel of the 3rd century AD. The restrained façade is contradicted by the rear colonnade; the concavities, worthy of Borromini, recapitulate those of the niches on the convex cella, creating in this way a counterpoint of Baroque curves. Also worthy of notice are the four pentagonal bases and capitals at the rear.

The Maison Carrée, Nîmes

This civic Roman temple was built by Agrippa, who died in 12BC. It was then dedicated to his two sons, Caius and Lucius, heirs of Augustus who both died very young. It shows the allegiance and loyalty of the Roman colony to the imperial dynasty. It stands on the short south side of the forum, which it dominates resting on a podium which is nearly 3 metres (10 feet) high. It was built of local limestone, but without a doubt the architect and workmen came from Rome. The source of the frieze with its acanthus scrolls is the Ara Pacis in Rome, which is the best preserved example of Augustan classicism. The ratio of short to long sides approaches 1:2 (6:11 columns), and the portico takes up almost a third of the total length. The use of half-columns at the sides and the back (pseudo-peripteral) is very like Greek temples. The Roman Corinthian Order, which was by now well established, is enriched by decorative motifs, particularly on the cornice. This is the beginning of the lavish style which was going to spread, later in the next century, to the eastern provinces of the Empire.

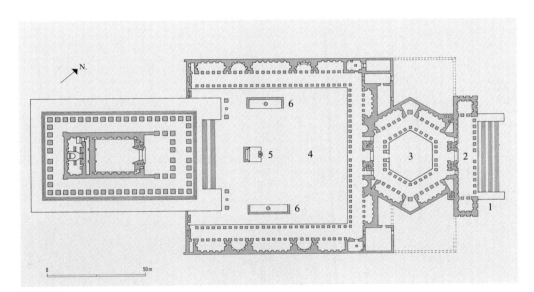

Sanctuary of Heliopolitan Jupiter, Baalbek

(Reconstruction after P. Collart)

During the 2nd and at the beginning of the 3rd century AD, the temple of Jupiter was laid out on a strictly axial plan similar to that of the sanctuary to Diana in Jerash, Jordan. This extravagant composition with steps (1), propylaea flanked by towers (2), hexagonal forecourt with double portico (3), large courtyard with double portico (4) and *exedrae* (6) framing the altar (5), although not characterized by curves, is representative of the Baroque spirit which was spreading throughout Syria during the 2nd century AD.

Façade of a rock tomb, Petra

Petra was a rich oasis situated on the caravan route between Arabia and the Mediterranean. It was annexed by Rome in AD106 and from the 1st century BC had developed an extraordinary funeral architecture. Cut into the sides of the nearby mountains, it resembles the Baroque forms found in the so-called "second style" of painting. The façade of this tomb, known as the Deir, has a broken pediment which frames a *tholos* supported by a concave architrave. The design is echoed in a fresco in the House of the Labyrinth in Pompeii. If it is true that the origin of this Baroque style can be traced back to the Hellenistic palaces of Alexandria, which have now unfortunately disappeared, there is no reason to date these tombs in Petra to the 2nd century AD: a date around the beginning of the imperial era seems more plausible.

Interior of the temple of Bacchus, Baalbek

This temple, which is smaller than its neighbour, the temple of Jupiter, is in a much better state of preservation (c.AD150). Within the Hellenizing exterior of this Corinthian peripteral temple, and raised on a podium in the Roman style, there is a vast cella. The interior wall is very sculpturally conceived. On a lower level, between Corinthian half-columns, a number of arcades support pedimented niches which once contained statues. Furthermore, arches, pediments, friezes and cornices are decorated with a profusion of plant decoration, minutely carved.

Buildings for leisure and spectacle

"*Panem et circenses*": Juvenal's famous phrase rebuking the ordinary people of Rome for being parasites ought, perhaps, to be modified. It is, however, a fact that Roman society, which lived on free corn and was only interested in the amusements of the amphitheatre and circus, enjoyed considerably more leisure under the Empire. Free entertainment gradually replaced traditional religious festivals and became a form of relaxation in which town dwellers took an ever greater part thanks to the levelling out of political inequalities as a result of Caracalla's decree of AD212. It was clearly in Rome itself that the phenomenon went furthest, influenced by the emperors' predilection for the spectacular. In the provinces the theme was echoed by the Romanized upper classes, but it was in Rome that the most impressive evidence was found of this leisure architecture. Numerous remains survive throughout the Empire; some are still in use.

Like the forums and agoras, the streets tended to become places for conducting business and leisure. This was due to the construction of porticoes, giving the main streets, particularly of towns in Asia Minor and Syria, a uniform, monumental appearance creating spacious avenues in the urban environment. Similarly in the Latin East, the basilica remained the favourite place for social activity. These open halls with their non-partitioned spaces, often situated beside the forums, served a number of purposes. They were places where business meetings and legal or political debates took place, thereby attracting a considerable crowd. To the sides were aisles, sometimes with upper levels, and in the centre a large nave with an apse above the tribunal was lit by lateral windows. In this way they foreshadowed early Christian churches. Columns and revetment of coloured marble, ceilings either flat or vaulted, adorned with painted or stuccoed coffers with their sumptuous display of colour, brought these enclosed spaces, often built on a grandiose scale, to life. The basilica of Maxentius (early 4th century AD), situated beside the Forum, marks the culmination of this type in Rome: the central nave measures 80 metres (260 feet) in length, 25 metres (80 feet) in width, with a height of about 35 metres (115 feet).

These huge halls found themselves gradually competing with a type of building which was going to become, throughout the Empire, the true symbol of Romanism – the *thermae*, or baths. The oldest known examples (Stabius, Pompeii) of this type of public building date from the end of the Republic. Without the additions which became more and more complex the three-part arrangement of the baths had already appeared in the imperial age. From the 1st century AD, sports and conference rooms, promenades and private assembly rooms gradually clustered around the changing rooms (*apodyteria*), the cold bath (*frigidarium*), the tepid bath (*tepidarium*), the hot bath (*caldarium*), as well as the steam bath (*laconicum*) and the swimming pool (*natatio*). The variety of activities that baths had to offer made them very sociable places; once the activities of the day were concluded, at about three o'clock in the afternoon, it was there that one would go for relaxation, instruction and meeting people. Even small towns had several baths of different sizes: a garrison town like Timgad had no less than a dozen for a population of about 15,000 inhabitants. In Rome, beside countless suburban baths (952 in AD354), it was the great buildings put up in the 3rd century by Caracalla and Diocletian which represented the zenith of this thermal age. It is not so much the complexity of the functions and ground plan as the richness of the decoration and the virtuosity in dealing with the technical problems posed by the roofing and heating that gives these buildings their importance.

Huge open air buildings for all forms of theatrical spectacle also fit into the category of structures designed for the pursuit of leisure. Even though drama was in decline, overtaken in popularity by dance, mime and pantomime, the classical repertoire kept its place. Every town of importance had its theatre. Its form over the centuries developed little; it remained close to that introduced into Italy during the late Republic. A high *frons scenae*, often with two or three superimposed Orders, enclosed the auditorium up to the level of the highest tier of seats. Actors and spectators were protected from the heat of the sun by means of an awning hung from poles. Later, the theatres were often converted in order to stage gladiatorial combats, animal baiting and naval battles.

These spectacles, cruel and often bloody, were of Lucanian origin. They first appeared in Rome fairly late in the Republic, and at that time purpose-built structures were not required: gladiatorial combats took place either in the Forum or on the Campus Martius, where spectators were seated on makeshift tiers. Such temporary structures were not always safe. During the reign of Tiberius, some 50,000 people were either killed or seriously injured by the collapse of one such structure in Fidenia near Rome. The oldest known amphitheatres, those of Pompeii (c. 80BC) and Pozzuoli, were already elliptical in shape. Rome's first amphitheatre was built during the time of Augustus and was destroyed in the fire of AD64. Vespasian, to make up for the loss, erected the Flavian amphitheatre on the site of a lake in front of Nero's Domus Aurea. It came to be known as the Colosseum by association with the enormous statue of Helios which had been put up nearby. It was in this amphitheatre that the most horrific massacres in Rome's history took place. The last of these gladiatorial combats occurred in 438, and the last animal baiting in 523.

By contrast with the amphitheatre, the design of the circus was less original because it followed closely the layout of Greek stadiums. It was, however, much less common, as its size and consequent cost was prohibitive; it was only seldom seen in the provinces. The vast capital expenditure, the size of the crowds and the frequent involvement of political factions made the chariot race, for which circuses were almost exclusively reserved, Rome's greatest spectacle. It was the sport most favoured by the emperors, who looked on from a high platform in direct communication with the Palatine. In its final form, the Circus Maximus in Rome, with its tiered seats, could seat 300,000 spectators and remains the largest place of entertainment ever built.

"Frons scenae" of the theatre, Sabratha

A provincial town in Tripolitania, Sabratha benefited from the wealth that came from the banks of the Sirte in the Severan dynasty. Recent restoration has rebuilt the *frons scenae* of the theatre (end of 2nd century AD) with all its Baroque spirit. A curtain colonnade on three levels, in coloured marbles, gives a sense of depth to the façade, as do the recesses penetrated by rectangular windows.

Basilica of Septimius Severus, Lepcis Magna
(Reconstruction after Vincifori)

Completed in AD216, it formed part of the vast building programme undertaken by Septimius Severus (193–211) in his native town, Lepcis Magna in Tripolitania. This sumptuous basilica has direct access to the new forum. A central nave, 19 metres (63 feet) wide and 30 metres (98 feet) high, with a two-storey colonnade, is terminated by two half-dome apses. The two central columns of each apse, set on higher pedestals, support a raised entablature.

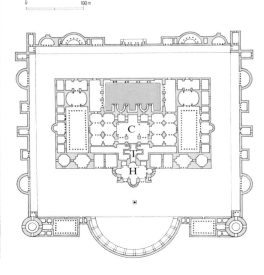

Baths of Diocletian, Rome

To the left, reconstruction of the *frigidarium* by E. Paulin; to the right, plan of the whole complex.

These baths, built between AD298 and 306, are based on those built by Caracalla (212–16) but are even larger in conception. In a vast courtyard with porticoes and *exedrae*, stands the bath building measuring 240 by 144 metres (263 by 158 yards). In the centre of the complex there are three halls: cold (C), tepid (T) and hot (H), together with a large open air swimming pool. Either side there is a porticoed *palaestra* for sports activities surrounded by various assembly rooms. This reconstruction by E. Paulin shows the scale and pomp of this architecture, which daily accommodated thousands of visitors.

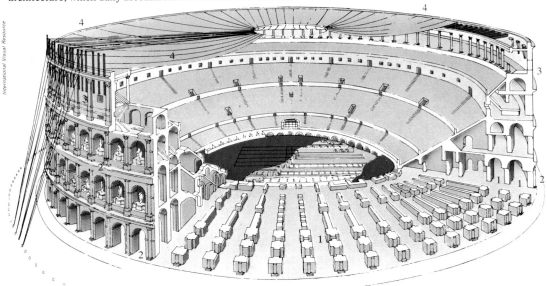

Colosseum, Rome

Built between AD70 and 80, the Colosseum is the largest of all Roman amphitheatres. It is elliptical in form, measuring 188 by 156 metres (206 by 170 yards) and could seat between 50,000 and 70,000 spectators. The external travertine shell (2) is 48.5 metres (160 feet) in height. Three Orders of arched bays, Doric at the bottom, Ionic in the middle and Corinthian at the top, are crowned by a wall articulated with pilasters (3), behind which runs a portico-promenade. The *cavea* is reached by a vaulted double corridor (1), from which a complex system of staircases leads to various seating levels. Both corporations and the various social strata of Roman society had sections reserved for them (the closer to the arena the greater the prestige). Under the wooden floor of the arena there were service areas (machinery, armoury, cages for the wild animals and so on), which were connected by an underground passage to the nearby gladiatorial school. An enormous awning (4), raised by marines detached from the base at Misenus, could be hung on poles arranged around the outside of the *cavea*. It was held in place by ropes attached to pegs set into the ground.

Circus Maximus and Palatine, Rome

Built before the creation of the Republic, in the valley lying between the Palatine and the Aventine, this hippodrome was frequently enlarged following fires up until the late Empire. In its final state it was 600 metres (656 yards) long and 200 metres (219 yards) wide. It was traversed longitudinally, as is seen in this model, by a dorsal spine (*spina*), 340 metres (372 yards) long, around which the chariots raced. This long podium was adorned with a number of works of art, among which were two Egyptian obelisks, that of Ramesses II, erected in 10BC, and that of Tutmosis III, set up in AD357. The exact design of the platform for the officials which backed on to the Palatine is still unknown. The circus was dominated on one side by the imperial palaces of the Palatine.

165

Palaces, villas and houses

The idea of a palace as a monumental symbol of supreme power located in the heart of a capital city had its origin in Rome; both the notion and the word itself were born in Rome. It was on the Palatine, close to Romulus' hut, that Augustus chose to live modestly in contrast to the dwellings of the Roman aristocracy which had become increasingly lavish since the 2nd century BC. But his successors were not to share the same scruples; gradually the whole of the hill was to be absorbed into the elaborate palatial complex. The palaces of Tiberius (Domus Tiberiana) and of Nero (Domus Transitoria, burnt down in AD64) were considered inadequate and soon disappeared. The emperors' official residence up to the loss of the Western Empire was to be the vast palace of Domitian (Domus Flavia or Augustana); a new wing was added by Septimius Severus (Domus Severiana) late in the 2nd century AD. Thus in two centuries a political acropolis was formed opposite the old religious acropolis of the Capitol.

Just as the city palace evolved from patrician residences, so the imperial villa reflected the passion of high Roman society for huge suburban dwellings. There, far from the pressure of public opinion, the emperors were able to give free rein to their interests and desires. Tiberius, for example, passed the last ten years of his reign in retirement on Capri. There he built and transformed a dozen villas, laid out swimming pools and banqueting halls, and decorated several grottoes with sculptures, notably that of Sperlonga. In Tivoli, Hadrian built a villa which was simply a collection and reconstruction of country scenes and buildings that he had admired in the East. Few of these imperial villas are well known. A late example at Piazza Armerina has a Baroque fantasy which contrasts strongly with the military severity of the fortified palace at Split to which Diocletian retired in 305 after his abdication. As for the Domus Aurea, or Golden House, erected by Nero after the fire of AD64, it was a colossal "folly" which achieved the impossible: a villa in the heart of the capital. In this structure, which the Flavian emperors were anxious to erase from the face of Rome, one sees clearly what distinguishes the villa from the palace: a very free spatial articulation of the structure and above all the integration of nature and architecture. This was not achieved merely by adding a garden, as in more modest villas, but by rearranging the entire landscape.

The same distinction between *domus* and *villa* can be seen in a less pronounced form in the homes of the managerial classes: senators, *equites* and rich citizens. Much is known about these classes from the excavations at Pompeii and Herculaneum, the towns smothered by the eruption of Vesuvius in AD79. The growing need for space and comfort gave rise to the creation, particularly in the provinces, of an intermediate type of residence: the house with a garden. The traditional Italian *domus* had a vast hall (*atrium*) with an open roof (*impluvium*). On to the *atrium* opened the reception room (*tablinum*) and other living rooms. Generally, the house had a garden surrounded by a type of Greek peristyle. When space permitted, there was a portico at the rear which opened on to a fairly large garden arrayed with pergolas, fountains and a plentiful display of statuary. The most important room was, from the 1st century onwards, the *triclinium* or dining room, where one reclined during enormous banquets. Of the rooms it was also the most decorated. The floor was laid with mosaics and the walls adorned with figure paintings or architectural designs. The complexity of their layout, the comfort, the richness of their decoration and furniture characterize these family houses. Amply provided with domestic staff, they were forerunners of the large private residences of the European aristocracy. One has to wait until the 16th century before finding such a high standard of living in the West. Outside Italy, this lifestyle had to be adapted to local climatic and social conditions. Both in Gaul and in Britain, a great number of rural properties comprising a home and a farm have been studied. Some are very large: in Montmaurin in the Haute-Garonne, a residence had 200 rooms and occupied 4 hectares (10 acres) out of a total property of 18. From the 3rd century, many of these properties were fortified.

In the large towns, on the other hand, the ordinary people lived in tenements (*cenacula*) which they rented in apartment blocks (*insulae*). In about AD350 the 14 districts of Rome consisted of 46,602 *insulae* as against 1,797 *domus*. The ground floor of these *insulae* was occupied by shops (*tabernae*) or by one single apartment which generally resembled the *domus*. The upper floors were divided into much smaller apartments with large balconies which overlooked the road. Numerous tenants were obliged to sublet parts of their apartments because the rent was so high; this gave rise to much promiscuity. Comfort was rudimentary, especially in Rome. There was no water, nor means of heating. The dread of fire precluded the use of fireplaces. The sole source of heat was the brazier permitted for cooking. Without kitchens and sanitary installations, these five-storey buildings looking on to twisting narrow roads soon became nothing more than slums. The *insulae* of Ostia, where the planning was more uniform and less dense, seem to have been more healthy and agreeable despite the crowding; some housed between 200 and 300 people. Ostia was a new town, planned to enable the Tiber port to cope with the ten million or so sacks of grain needed annually for feeding Rome.

This comprehensive town planning, so modern in conception, was however quite exceptional. Even in the West where the Roman model was accepted without protest, provincial towns, whether or not laid out according to a predetermined format, created their own social environment based largely on the family home.

Domus Augustana on the Palatine, Rome

This enormous palace, built by the architect Rabirius for Domitian (AD81–96), is neatly divided into two wings. One accommodates all the great reception halls, the audience hall (2), the tribunal (3), the banqueting hall (4), as well as the guard room (1), all accessible from the Forum to the north. The other contains the private apartments which look south over the Circus Maximus from a concave portico on two levels. The lower level is arranged around a large courtyard with a central basin (5), with two domed octagonal rooms to the north. A monumental double-ramped staircase (7) leads to the upper, largely destroyed level where a huge courtyard with porticoes and fountain balances symmetrically that of the official wing. To the east there is a large riding area (9) in the form of a stadium running alongside the palace and surrounded by a spectators' gallery on two levels. The richness of the marble decoration and the size of the rooms – the audience hall, which measures 33 by 25 metres (108 by 82 feet) was at least 20 metres (66 feet) high – boast absolute power emancipated from prudent Augustan modesty.

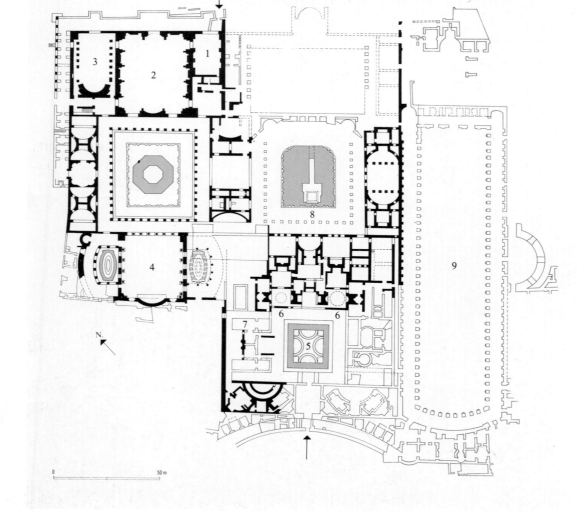

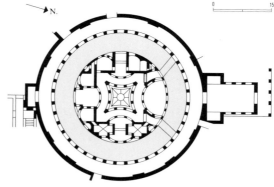

Hadrian's villa, Tivoli (Tibur)

This collection of buildings and views was put together with superb imagination. The villa represents the peak of imperial pleasure architecture (c. AD130). Near the library and private apartments there is a round marble structure surrounded by water. It creates, through the counterpoint of its curved colonnades, a complex space, Baroque in inspiration.

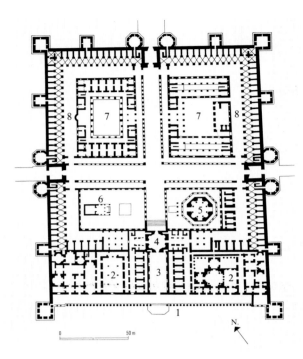

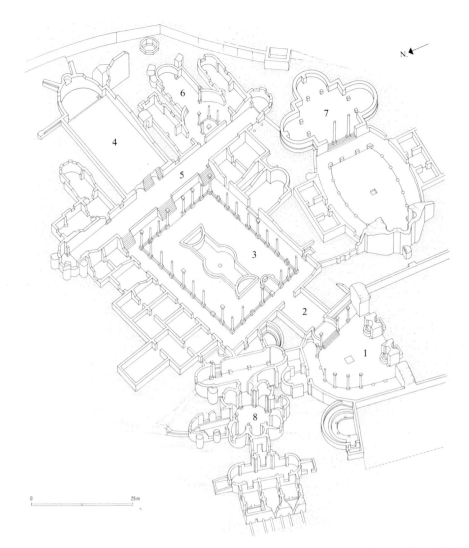

Palace of Diocletian, Split

This retreat, built about AD300 on the Dalmatian coast, resembles in plan a fortified camp, in size and luxury a palace (175 by 216 metres/190 by 235 yards). Behind the long promenade (1) overlooking the sea were the imperial apartments (2); an extended vestibule (3), ending in a rotunda (4), led to an esplanade surrounded by arcading. Behind this columnar screen rises the octagonal mausoleum of the emperor (5) and a small temple dedicated to Jupiter (6). The north part of the enclosure is occupied by two residential blocks (7), while the guards' barracks line the fortified walls (8).

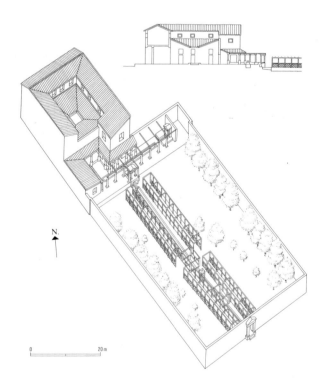

Villa of Maximian, Piazza Armerina, Sicily

This villa of Maximian, the complete antithesis of the fortified palace of his colleague Diocletian, perpetuated, c.AD300, the pleasure architecture of preceding centuries. Unlike Split, the layout of the complex was not symmetrical and the curve plays a large part in the articulation of the interior. Imaginative use is made of the slope of ground in order to give individuality to the spaces. From the forecourt (1) a vestibule (2) leads to a large courtyard (3) surrounded by a peripteral colonnade. The axis of the vestibule does not align with that of the courtyard nor that of the audience hall (4). The latter is reached through a transverse corridor, which also serves the private apartments. An oval courtyard precedes the trilobal dining hall (7). Baths (8) lead off the central court. Most of the floors were decorated with sumptuous mosaics, African in both style and subject matter. (Plan after I. Gismondi.)

House of Loreius Tiburtinus, Pompeii

This small traditional house was built on two levels around an *atrium* with *impluvium*. A small dining room at the back opens on to a terrace shaded by a pergola. From one side to the other stretches a long basin into which water flows from a number of marble grottoes. The garden repeats, perpendicularly, this same arrangement with grottoes, a fountain and a sloping channel framed by pergolas. The remaining space was planted with fruit trees and decorated with statues. (Reconstruction after J.B. Ward-Perkins.)

Model of a large tenement house ("insula"), Ostia

On the ground floor there were shops (*tabernae*), which had a mezzanine level with small windows. A balcony supported by brick arches surrounded the whole of the first floor. The three upper floors are imaginary, but probably existed. Inside, the walls were covered with bare plaster, and mosaics were rare; outside, the brick façade remained unstuccoed. Light and air were provided by the many large windows. The internal courtyards were sometimes patterned in squares.

The Greco-Roman legacy: the town

To study the achievements of Greek and Roman architecture is to follow the development of a phenomenon which has always played an important part in Western civilization – the town. Settlements are found at every stage in the evolution of Western civilization, whether they be humble centres, sometimes small political units, keenly attached to their autonomy, or proud, turbulent capitals of rival monarchies, or else cities greedy for control of the Mediterranean world. Without the pulsating life of towns, continually importing and exporting goods, ideas and men, neither Hellenistic nor Roman culture would have been disseminated throughout the known world; cities could not prevent themselves from being affected. Thus within one millennium the whole of the Mediterranean basin was influenced by Western dynamism. We see this process going on today, for better or worse, throughout the world.

The origin of the first urban centres remains a mystery. Ancient civilizations explained the beginnings of a city in terms of founder heroes who were protected by the gods (Theseus in Athens, Romulus in Rome). However, the appearance of a settlement was connected with a favoured site (spring, arable land, strategic position on a river and so on). This gave rise to the congregation of groups, which until then had been scattered around the countryside (synoecism). In such settlements there was no systematic town planning. The town developed spontaneously around two poles; an escarpment, or defensive stronghold where the local divinities could be installed, and an ill-defined piece of ground for markets and political meetings (in Athens, the Acropolis and the Agora; in Rome, the Capitol and the Forum). The streets were extensions of pre-existing roads.

In this development the accidents of geography and history play the leading roles. However, from the 8th century BC both in Greece and in Etruria, true town planning appeared. In these regions colonization was primarily an urban phenomenon. In Greece, reasons for colonization were principally social and commercial. The trading post (*emporion*) was a place of commercial and cultural exchange with the native populace while the deliberately colonized settlement (*apoikia*) relieved an over-

crowded metropolis of its homeless poor. In both types the choice of site is determined by the requirements of every Greek town: a sheltered anchorage, drinking water, a natural defensive position, with arable land nearby. Excavations carried out since 1945 in the Greek colonies on the Black Sea, in Sicily and southern Italy have shown that according to local conditions and the nature of the colony, there was a double allocation of land. Each settler received a plot of agricultural land (*chora*) from the new city, as well as an urban site on which to build his home. The latter was generally oblong, enclosed and bounded for the most part by orthogonal roads. The building did not occupy the entire plot, at least in the beginning. If the town plan was laid out first, with sites reserved for the agora and sanctuaries, it would long remain incomplete.

This systematic and uniform division of land was the subject of empirical experimentation during the colonization of the Archaic era. Hippodamos of Miletus, the first town planner, who laid out the cities of Miletus and Piraeus, put these ideas into practice when he created functional urbanism at the beginning of the 5th century BC. The basic module was the city block (*insula*), larger than the long narrow plots of new colonies. He laid out a grid with no particular axis, in which certain zones were reserved for religious, civic and commercial activities. The novelty lies not so much in the division of land usage as in the planning and design procedures, which anticipated the future development of the town. Centuries passed before Miletus and Piraeus filled the areas laid out in the original plans. Such a state of affairs is demonstrated by simple signposts like one found in Piraeus which reads "to the harbour, public area". And so the town became the outward manifestation of a rationality which attempted to overcome the anarchy of evolution just at the time that political philosophy was systematizing society. Human *logos*, not content with imposing order on to space, was also organizing time: the first example, in fact, of planning, in both senses of the word. The ideas of Hippodamos were universally adopted, because their simplicity rendered them applicable to almost every situation: the addition of a new quarter to an old town (Olynthus, *c.* 430BC), moving an old town to a new

sloping site (Priene, 4th century BC), building new towns (Alexandria, its satellite towns, and its Hellenized successors in the East).

A similar geometric design was applied to the new Roman towns. Here, however, it was used more rigidly in places where colonization was closely linked with the military organizations. These colonies which governed and Romanized the provinces were tailored to resemble Roman military camps, which borrowed their axial arrangement from Etruscan town planning. The inhabitants were, for the most part, army veterans who had received plots of land in compensation for many years of active service. Two perpendicular axes, the *cardo* (north-south) and the *decumanus* (east-west) cross in the centre of the town, usually near the forum and public buildings. The *castrum* in Ostia, built about 350BC to guard the town against pirates, is the oldest known example of this military town planning. Its tufa wall, 6 metres (20 feet) high, surrounds an area of about 2 hectares (5 acres), and it was able to house a garrison of about 300 men. This simple plan, which imposes on an almost square town (*quadrata*) a chequerboard network of roads, is found throughout the Empire but particularly in the West. In the East, this military severity is often softened by the influence of Greek town planning, which attempted to employ Hippodamos' ideas in varying the axes as well as the layout of the civic areas.

This standardization resulted in very monotonous plans: but towns had to pay this price for their comfort. Contemporary disappointment has shown that town planning and town life do not always run in double harness, and are sometimes even at odds with one another. It would perhaps be right to moderate the traditional acclaim for the uniformity of provincial Roman towns and to remember a further point – boredom. Without going so far as to praise the chaotic expansion of a large city such as Rome, or a mushroom town such as Delos, it is perfectly reasonable to prefer a more modest form of town planning which limits itself to setting an example and leaves the large towns to grow naturally, as at Athens and Pergamon.

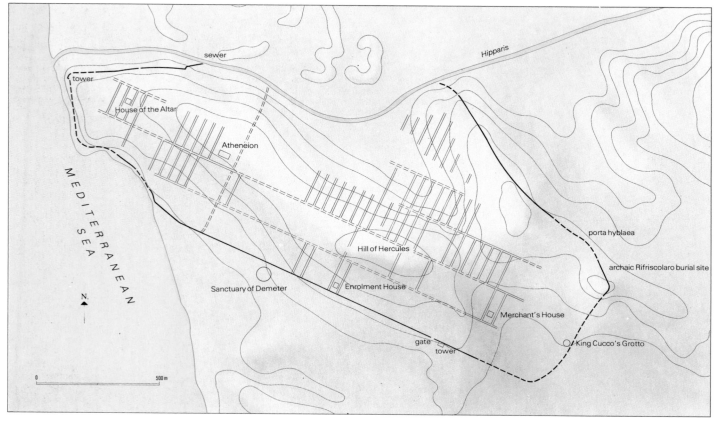

Plan of Camarina (Sicily)

(After P. Pelagatti)

This colony of Syracuse was founded about 600BC, 135 years after the foundation of the metropolis, and throughout its history it retained its original plan. It was characterized by an orthogonal grid which followed the axis of the hill overlooking the Hipparis river. The long blocks which make up the plan were not developed until the 4th century BC. By this time there was a well established artisan industry which contrasted with the agricultural character of the original settlement.

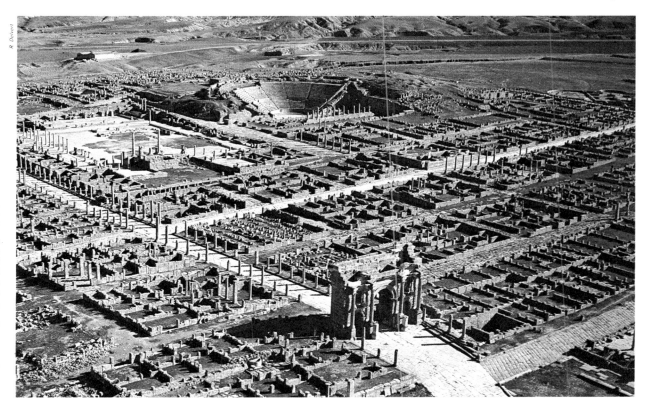

Aerial view of Timgad (Algeria)

This colony of 15,000 inhabitants was founded about AD100 for veterans of the third legion stationed in the province of North Africa. It is a perfect example of Roman military town planning. At the intersection of the *decumanus* and the *cardo*, which was lined by colonnades, there is a typical forum with porticoes, basilica, curia and temple. A small theatre with 3,500 seats is cut into a natural rise in the ground. Besides the many *thermae*, there is also a library which cost its patron 400,000 sesterces. The presence of large churches dating from the beginning of the 5th century is a reminder that Africa was one of the cradles of Christianity.

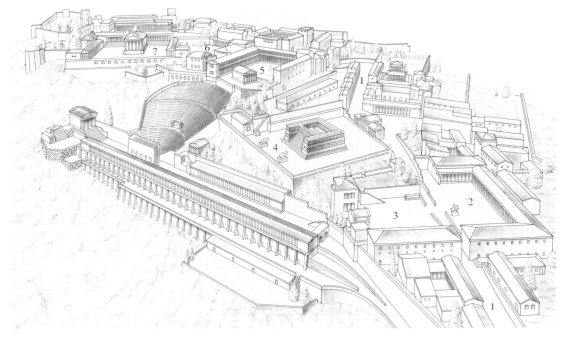

Acropolis of Pergamon

The kingdom of Pergamon, the last of the great Hellenic states, had a short history (280–133BC). During that period, the capital, which had originally been an insignificant town, became one of the most shining metropolises in the Greek world. Here, large-scale but flexible town planning developed. The layout is determined, to a great extent, by the steep sloping site. The acropolis is shaped like a fan with four terraces surrounding the auditorium of the theatre. This arrangement is emphasized by the horizontal majesty of the vast promenades. Access to it is provided by a road serving various groups of monuments situated half way up the slope (lower agora, gymnasium, sanctuary of Demeter). The first terrace of the acropolis is the upper agora. Above and to the left is the sanctuary of Dionysus whose temple faces the road. The second terrace, opening on to the countryside, is occupied by the great altar to Zeus, the frieze of which is the last great achievement of monumental Greek sculpture. Twisting behind the terraces so as to give a view of the town, the road reaches the porticoed sanctuary of Athena. Passing the library, it arrives at the last terrace, which at the time of the Romans was occupied by the temple of Trajan. To the right of the road, hidden from the town and overlooking a steep ravine, are the arsenals, barracks and royal palace.

Plan of Aosta (Augusta Praetoria)

This colony of 40 hectares (100 acres) was founded by Augustus in 25BC for 3,000 veterans of the Praetorian Guard. It is sited in a position of strategic military importance near the Alps. The positioning of the gates indicates which of the streets are the two main axes of the town, the *cardo* (AA) and *decumanus* (BB). The grid pattern of the secondary roads divides the town into 16 squares each of 130 by 165 metres (142 by 180 yards). Archaeologists have pinpointed the location of two temples (1) and some shops (2) which could have belonged to the forum, in this case curiously off-centre. The baths were situated at (3), and to the north-east of the town were the theatre (4) and the amphitheatre (5), set inside the walls for reasons of safety.

Plan of Miletus

This town was destroyed by the Persians in 494BC. It was gradually rebuilt after 480 according to the plan drawn up by Hippodamos. The new town was constructed on a peninsula running from north to south, far from the ancient acropolis (1). There were two harbours, one for the navy (2) and the other for commerce (3). Adjacent to these were two public areas (4) at right angles to each other. In between lay three residential zones (5) each with *insulae* of different forms. Three porticoed agoras (6) were located in the public zone, one in the centre and the others at the extremities. There were also two gymnasiums (7), a town hall (8) and a stadium (9). Also included in the general grid was the great sanctuary of Apollo Delphinios (10). The theatre (11) is, as usual, built against a steep hillside.

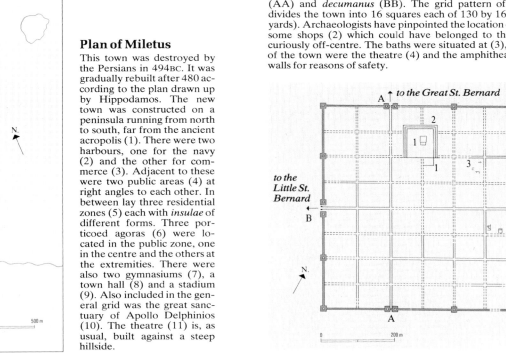
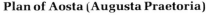

Architecture for transport: roads, bridges, aqueducts

Roman and Greek civilizations were both essentially urban, but each had had quite a different attitude to the importance of town life. The Greeks considered the city primarily as the centre of a political unit, the city-state, constantly in conflict with its neighbours. The result was a cultural fragmentation, a situation favoured by the environment. Islands, small isolated pockets of land and valleys were unsuitable for the development of towns that wished to push out their roots. The great cities and commercial centres of the classical era, Corinth and Athens, contained no more than a few tens of thousands of inhabitants. It was only with the growth of the great eastern kingdoms that large cities began to appear (Alexandria and Antioch, for example). Interurban communications did not concern the Greeks: political theories took little account of trade because the perfect city was a closed system in a state of equilibrium. It was not that the Greeks were incapable of great technical achievements in this field. There was the fountain of Megara, a subterranean aqueduct at Eupalinos on Samos (6th century BC), the *diolkos* in Corinth for hauling boats from one gulf to another. Their skill was also demonstrated by the lighthouse at Alexandria and various harbours. But these were only isolated achievements and were not conceived as part of a general project to stimulate overland trade. The roads were not constructed until the imperial era; travellers were content with paths or mule tracks, preferring to do most of their journeying by sea.

The Romans, who were engineers before they were architects, adopted quite a different attitude. Roman imperialism could only succeed if it made accessible the furthest corners of an empire which was rapidly expanding throughout the Mediterranean. It developed an increasingly large network of communications with towns as staging posts. In this way, innumerable small and distant townships, by

means of roads, bridges, ports and aqueducts, kept in touch with a distant capital. Thus the Roman macrocosm contrasted with the self-contained microcosm of the Greek world.

The Roman Empire developed road networks as a means of quickly moving large armies in times of war. The legionaries were, right from the start, road-makers as well as soldiers, and always remained so. Some of these roads still form part of the landscape. The first paved road, the Via Appia, was built in 312BC connecting Rome and Capua. By the end of the republican period the Italian road system was complete and the Mediterranean network planned. To the east, the Via Egnatia was to cross the Balkans from the Adriatic to the Black Sea. To the west, the Via Domitia, which was to run beside the sea when crossing southern France, made Spain more accessible. In the 2nd century AD, roads would extend to Scotland and to Palestine, and the plans did not end there (see map on page 154). Today, modern roads often follow old Roman routes. These freeways were to be maintained by the local communities. They were 4 metres (13 feet) wide, and paved with large flagstones on successive layers of cement and gravel. A gilt-bronze sign (*Milliarium aureum*) placed by Augustus in the Forum indicated where the system began. Milestones placed at regular intervals along the route were useful for gauging distance. Relay points with hostels and horses made travel as quick and as comfortable as possible. The imperial post, reserved for official mail, was carried non-stop in light two-wheeled chariots which could travel 200 kilometres (124 miles) a day.

A network on this scale suggests the existence of many monuments of artistic interest such as bridges, which from the beginning of the 2nd century BC would have been built in stone. Many of these bridges, whose massive piers and tall arches

make it possible to span valleys at heights structurally impossible if built of wood, are still in use. More characteristic of the Roman genius were aqueducts: bridges carrying water across deep valleys in a slightly inclined channel and bringing it to towns often many kilometres away. These strings of arches superimposed on each other are the most original and grandly conceived structures, both in form and function, that Rome ever built. Stendhal described the Pont du Gard, the most celebrated and best preserved of the aqueducts, as being like "sublime music". The aqueducts of Rome, certain sections of which still grace the Roman countryside, own much of their fame to the treatise written by Trajan's director of water services, Frontinius. Numbering nine in all, they had a combined length of more than 400 kilometres (250 miles) and delivered more than a million cubic metres (1,300,000 cubic yards) per day to the capital. Bearing in mind that the population of Rome in those days was about one million, then each Roman had 1,000 litres (220 gallons) of water per day compared with 475 litres (105 gallons) in 1968. This demonstrates the importance of the baths in Roman life.

Priority was given to the public fountains, thanks to a system of distribution from water towers. The uppermost water main served private houses; the one in the centre, public buildings (baths and so on); and the lowermost, the fountains where the majority of the public went for their supplies. Should the level have fallen, the fountains alone would have been served. The water ran continuously; the waste was considerable, but it made a contribution to public cleanliness by ensuring continuous swilling of the drains.

These feats of engineering, unsurpassed until the 19th century, give Roman architecture another dimension. They stand side by side with the scale of its great vaulted and domed spaces.

Aqueduct in Segovia (Spain)

Built in the 1st century AD, this aqueduct is nearly 900 metres (985 yards) long and 34 metres (112 feet) high, and is still in use. The austere yet slim structure with emphasized uprights is designed quite differently from the Pont du Gard. Instead of huge arches on a few piers (a precaution against sudden floods), it is a veritable lacework of stone with 128 arches. Strongly projecting mouldings break the uniformity of the very high rectangular piers.

Alcantara bridge (Spain)

The bridge was built in AD106 by 11 neighbouring towns in the province of Lusitania. (They are listed in an inscription on the triumphal arch dedicated to Trajan, which straddles the structure.) It crosses the river Tagus in six arches of different sizes; the central arches each have a diameter of 27 metres (30 yards). At one end there is a small temple and near it a dedicatory inscription ascribes the design to the architect Gaius Julius Lacer.

LATE ANTIQUITY AND THE EARLY MIDDLE AGES

A. Lonchampt, CNMHS, SPADEM

Baptistry of Fréjus

During the period of late antiquity the centralized plan was increasingly used, and for two purposes. In mausoleums it followed a traditional pattern but tended to be reserved for members of the imperial family and for saints. It was frequently used for baptistries, with a piscina in the centre, into which the neophyte was plunged. More than 400 of these have been recorded throughout the ancient Roman Empire. Some of them, like that of Marseilles, were of considerable size. The baptistry of Fréjus, of which the oldest portions date back to the 5th century, appears square on the outside but is in fact an octagon formed of eight apses, alternately flat and semicircular. It is surmounted by a cupola, subsequently reconstructed; this rests on columns which are attached by arches to the walls.

Until quite recently, the year 476 was taken as the date that marked the fall of the Roman Empire, the victory of the Barbarians and the beginning of a long period of darkness that descended on Western Europe and was to lift only with the bright new dawn of the Renaissance. Opinions about this period, however, have changed a good deal; and the judgments of classical scholars, naturally biased towards catastrophe, have been subjected to reappraisal. Recent historians, discovering a wealth of fascinating material, much of it hitherto unknown, have formed a more balanced view of this age, once conveniently, yet in their judgment mistakenly, labelled as decadent. Such a reassessment has been based not only on intensive local research, but also, and perhaps more importantly, on the recognition that here was a civilization whose criteria were not exclusively those of the ancients. Indeed, it proved to be extraordinarily complex and, in certain respects, truly original, striving towards new horizons. Yet in the main it retained strong links with the ancient world. This, at any rate, was how contemporaries saw it. The invasions of the 5th century did not sweep away a civilization, they simply took advantage of circumstances, pitting themselves against an Empire no longer at the apex of its glory. Even so, there are sufficient attested historical facts to suggest that a new period had begun.

Some of these facts, which might easily be dismissed as unimportant, prove, on closer examination, to be rather significant. Changes in costume, for example, went beyond the mere whims of fashion. The toga was no longer used except for official ceremonies and was replaced by the tunic, which seems to have originated in Asia. Clinging to the body, it permitted much more freedom of movement than the toga. Even more important, however, was the existence of a school of pagan philosophy which had its source in Plotinus (205–70) and his mystical pursuit of the One. The philosophy of Plotinus, as developed by those whom he later inspired, raised a question crucial to the understanding of this period: that of religious experience. This was the matter which brought about the split between classical and late antiquity. Since the first 30 or so years of the 3rd century there had been a new spirit evident in Roman art, and this asserted itself more strongly as time passed despite abortive attempts to turn the clock back. Christianity succeeded, not because it triumphed over a pagan religion that was no longer attracting followers, but because it emerged supreme among other religions centred on a single God rather than many gods – a concept widespread throughout

the Roman Empire, with varying local nuances. At the same time, the belief in another, eternal life took firm hold. This religious uncertainty explains the seemingly identical use of certain iconographical themes, which can be distinguished only by their context. In defining the meaning of the theme, Christian art drew freely from a vast and rich store of experience. One 3rd century artist, in his Confession of St. Peter, in the Vatican, instinctively depicted Christ as Apollo Helios driving his chariot. A common feature of these religions was the participation in a mystery, in the sense that divine celebration no longer consisted of an assembly of townspeople in front of a temple, but required the gathering of initiates inside a building especially equipped for that purpose; adherents of the cult of Mithras would worship their deity by hiding themselves in caves or underground crypts.

The Empire was thus dominated by three religions: Judaism, Christianity and Arianism. The first, and oldest, came into contact with Rome at an early date, and the second prevailed over the third and so enabled the Empire to affirm its doctrines. The victory was achieved in two stages: the first came in 313 with the Edict of Milan, when the Emperor Constantine officially tolerated Christianity, the second towards the end of the 4th century, when, as a result of a series of measures taken by Theodosius, paganism was condemned, the last temples were closed, and Christianity was recognized as the state religion. The alliance of throne and altar, thus cemented, was to endure for centuries. The secular arm of the state was henceforth sworn to defend the true faith against heretics and pagans. The "City of God" evolved, and over it ruled an "emperor by the grace of God". Once Christianity was assured of victory, edicts of tolerance in favour of Arians were abrogated. In 380, Theodosius condemned all heresies, ordering Christians to subscribe to the faith as defined by the Council of Nicaea. In the East, Arians were commanded to yield their episcopal seat to the orthodox.

The consequences were soon apparent in architecture. Constantine's conversion led to the construction of immense buildings: in Rome (basilicas of St. John Lateran and St. Peter's, and churches of Santa Costanza and Sant' Agnese fuori le Mura), in Jerusalem (Golgotha and Holy Sepulchre), in Bethlehem, and in Constantinople (Santa Sophia). This activity was continued by his family and by the clergy who followed him in becoming converted. Two types of building, which characterized the whole of the Middle Ages, made their appearance:

the rotunda, centrally planned, which undoubtedly had a funerary origin, and the basilica, which borrowed from antiquity while adapting to the needs of the new religion. Another, parallel development, likewise destined to leave its indelible mark on the Middle Ages, was monasticism, which had its roots in the East. From the 3rd century onward, anchorites are known to have lived in Syria and in Mesopotamia. St. Anthony (251–356) remained faithful to this hermit tradition while St. Pachomius (died 346) was the first to organize a community enclosed within a precinct. The success of this latter experiment was resounding. In the West, it was Athanasius of Alexandria (died 373) who revealed its existence during the course of his exile in Gaul. The first monastery proper was established by St. Martin, in 361, at Ligugé, just outside Poitiers. As originally created, these communities were simply monastic towns set up on an irregular plan, in which buildings were situated next to one another. In the West, the application of the rule of St. Benedict, which he drew up around 534 for the monks of Monte Cassino, introduced a semblance of order into the planning; and during the ensuing Carolingian period a programme was defined which was to be generally adopted from then on.

Thus were established the foundations of a new civilization – one that was solidly linked with the past, that was capable of adapting to the realities of the present, and which held out the promise of a rich and rewarding future. Although its beginnings can be fairly precisely dated, it is by no means as easy to say how long it lasted. In 1937, Henri Pirenne, in a fascinating book entitled Mahomet et Charlemagne, declared that the Arab invasion signalled the end of the ancient world; it had closed the Mediterranean and at the same time separated once and for all two civilizations that until that time had managed, or at least attempted, to live alongside one another. The question that has puzzled later historians is how to assess the Carolingian age: should it be seen as an isolated phenomenon or should this outburst of creative energy be regarded as the final spasm of a civilization directly descended from the Empire of Constantine? It is generally thought nowadays to be more closely attached to the past rather than a true harbinger of the future. Historians have recently emphasized the catastrophic results of the Norman invasions which, from the beginning of the 9th century onward, battered the Empire, leaving it split and shattered beyond repair. It was superseded by a new society based on the concept of feudalism, in which everyday relationships between individuals were decreed and determined by law. The new

LATE ANTIQUITY AND THE EARLY MIDDLE AGES

civilization that sprang up brought changes far and wide.

If we accept this span, from the 4th century to the end of the 10th century, it is realistic to recognize that such an immensely long and complex period can best be considered in successive phases. Broadly speaking, there are three: the first is the so-called palaeo-Christian, which really deserves to be called imperial; the two others, the result of the shattering of this world, continued to carry on a dialogue with each other, but this relationship was often strained and at times even violent.

In the history of the Mediterranean world, palaeo-Christian art was the first manifestation of an art form which extended far beyond its original geographic confines. In the frontier zones it came up against regional pockets of resistance (Ireland, for example, to the west). But thanks to an astonishing capacity for adaptation, it managed to integrate the various regional differences, so that these latter forms appeared relatively minor in comparison with the original, whose unity remained virtually intact. This drive against disintegration is witnessed by the facts and by writers. It was not the result of chance but of a political impetus, which, from Marcus Aurelius to Theodosius, tried to give the world a new outlook.

The earliest manifestation of palaeo-Christian art can be seen in the catacombs – long, underground galleries punctuated by niches intended as resting places for the bodies or ashes of the dead. The custom had been adopted by the pagans, and both Jews and Christians subsequently introduced the same practice. The pictorial and sculptural art which developed within the catacombs was given individual meaning by each of the religions so concerned. A striking example of this is to be found at Doura Europos, on the Euphrates, where there are three monuments, more or less contemporary, each belonging to a different religion: Mithraism, Judaism and Christianity. Wealthy Christians were eager to have themselves buried in magnificent sarcophagi with walls decorated in high relief. But the iconography might still be pagan, or sometimes was pagan and Christian mixed.

The recognition and growing acceptance of Christianity led to the construction, in the 4th century, of the first great places of worship. Although there is no documented proof of the theory, Constantine almost certainly played a personal part in selecting a suitable architectural style. Rome, after the victory over Maxentius, once more became for a while the centre of the Empire,

and it was here, apparently, that the first basilica, St. John Lateran, was built. Entered through a huge atrium, it consisted of a nave made up of five ceiled aisles, leading to a wide transept and ending in a semicircular apse. The gigantic dimensions (8 by 19 metres/24 by 62 feet) made it clear that only the emperor could have initiated the project. The absence of vaults made its construction easier, and also helped to link the side aisles more closely to the central nave. Subsequently, after the foundation of Constantinople, building activity tended to be concentrated in the East. The emperor erected enormous basilicas on the important sites of Christ's own life. In Jerusalem, the Holy Sepulchre and the Church of the Resurrection on Golgotha brought together the basilica and the rotunda; and in Bethlehem, St. Helena, Constantine's mother, built a Church of the Nativity. Analysis of these different buildings leads to the conclusion that they were devised according to a single plan. But those that originated beyond the bounds of the imperial family circle give evidence of more individual freedom afforded to the architects, and consequently have marked variations. Be this as it may, the basilica type became established throughout the Empire, from Trier to Syria, and by way of North Africa.

The gulf between West and East widened in the course of the 4th century, culminating in final separation after the death of Theodosius in 395, a date marking the beginning of what has conveniently been called Byzantine art. Before this date, the basilicas built in all the provinces and cities of the Empire had obeyed very strict rules in terms of plan and elevation. This was either because a programme had been imposed or because the basilical plan had been chosen in the certainty that it was the most suitable for the celebration of Christian worship. A large number of such basilicas survive in Rome: San Paolo fuori le Mura, Santa Maria Maggiore, Santa Pudenziana and Santa Sabina. At the same time, the first centrally planned baptistry was built at the Lateran. The circular plan reappears at St. Etienne, which incorporates two annular corridors and the Greek cross. Tentative attempts at the central plan are also in evidence at San Lorenzo, Milan, where the tetrafoil is adopted.

It is at Ravenna, however, that the finest examples are found of the wooden-roofed basilica, with columns surmounted by arches, regularly pierced windows and a projecting apse: San Giovanni Evangelista (425), Sant' Apollinare Nuovo (519) and Sant' Apollinare in Classe (549). The centralized plan was also used here in the two mausoleums of Galla Placidia and the

two baptistries – the Orthodox (beginning of the 5th century) and the Arian (c.500) – and, above all, in San Vitale (522).

In Africa, Christianity made its appearance in the 3rd century, and there was extensive building activity in the 4th and 5th centuries. The churches, often built with re-used materials, had very wide naves with several aisles, their western apses being flanked by two halls. Coptic Egypt is notable for covering oratories and small buildings with vaults. The Syrian churches are remarkable for their stereotomy (stone cut into measured forms) and their admirably balanced masses. At Qalaat Seman, where a monastery was built round the column of St. Simeon Stylites in 480, there is a series of buildings with varied plans, notable for their magnificent and elegant decoration. The imperial hallmark is even more strongly evident in Palestine than in Syria. Justinian rebuilt the Church of the Nativity in Bethlehem and raised a shrine in Jerusalem in honour of the Virgin. Palestine was famous, too, for its Memoria; these have since disappeared but were frequently mentioned in texts. In Asia Minor, as well, there were many buildings with different types of plan, sometimes quite novel. The transept is strongly emphasized and materials include large blocks of admirably dressed stone; vaulting is common, and the façades are usually characterized by two towers. Certain examples appear to be the distant prototypes of Romanesque architecture.

A varied architecture sprang up around the Aegean Sea and in Constantinople. There are hundreds of listed monuments which provide a multitude of solutions. The ambulatory made its appearance at Miletus; at St. John there are four basilicas encircling a courtyard, as at Qalaat Seman. In St. Demetrius at Salonika, the central nave leads to a lower apse, and the side aisles are flanked by a series of arcades springing from enormous, rectangular piers or slender columns of marble; the church is flooded with light through three levels of bays – aisles, galleries and clerestory windows.

Constantinople was part of the same sphere of influence, but had its own particular style. To protect his capital, Theodosius II between 413 and 440 ringed the city with a powerful defensive wall, and this structure was to keep the town secure for centuries. In the towers, enormous halls with stone vaults provided an exciting new field of experience for architects. They throw light, too, on the extraordinary brick vaults of Santa Sophia, the Church of the Holy Apostles, St. John, and St. Sergius and St. Bacchus.

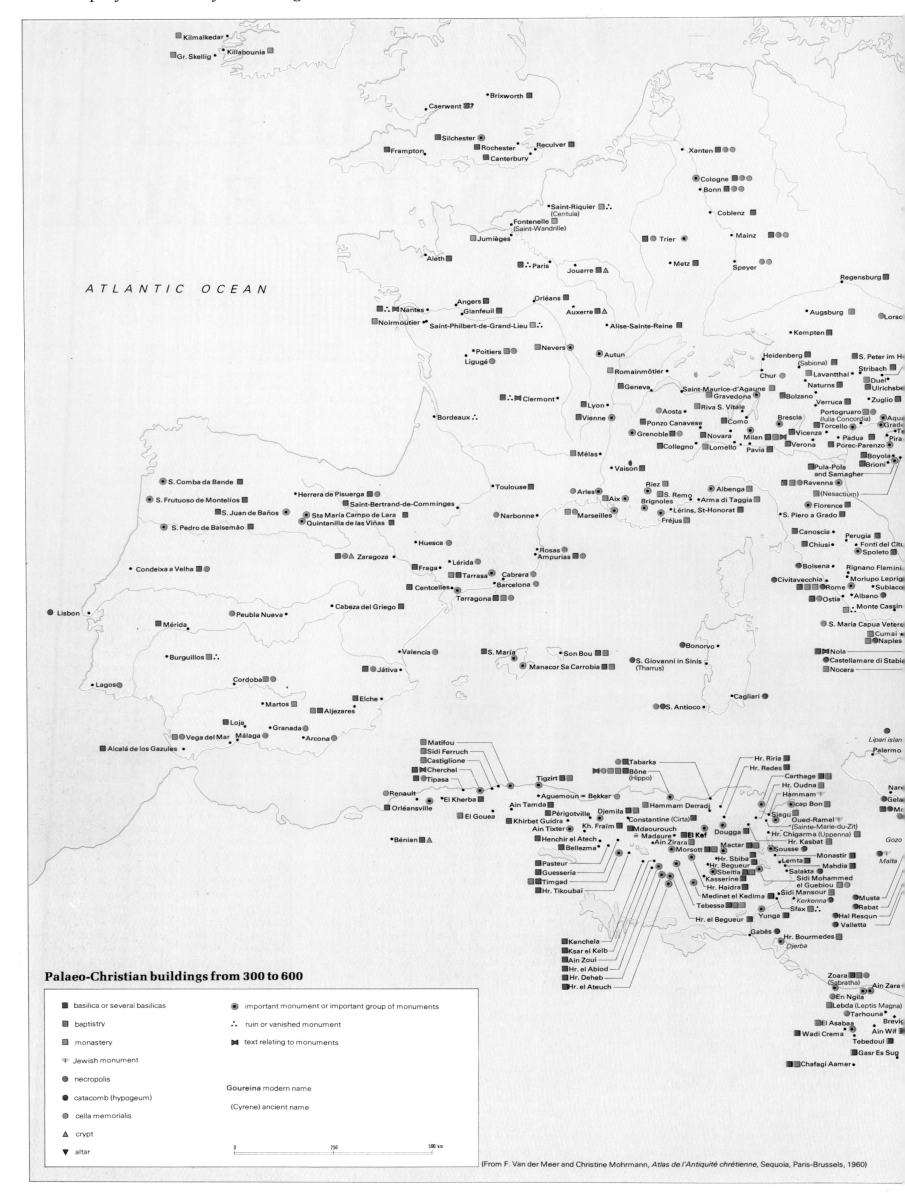

Palaeo-Christian buildings from 300 to 600

■ basilica or several basilicas	● important monument or important group of monuments
▣ baptistry	∴ ruin or vanished monument
▢ monastery	⋈ text relating to monuments
▽ Jewish monument	
● necropolis	
● catacomb (hypogeum)	**Goureina** modern name
● cella memorialis	(Cyrene) ancient name
△ crypt	
▼ altar	0 250 500 km

(From F. Van der Meer and Christine Mohrmann, *Atlas de l'Antiquité chrétienne*, Sequoia, Paris-Brussels, 1960)

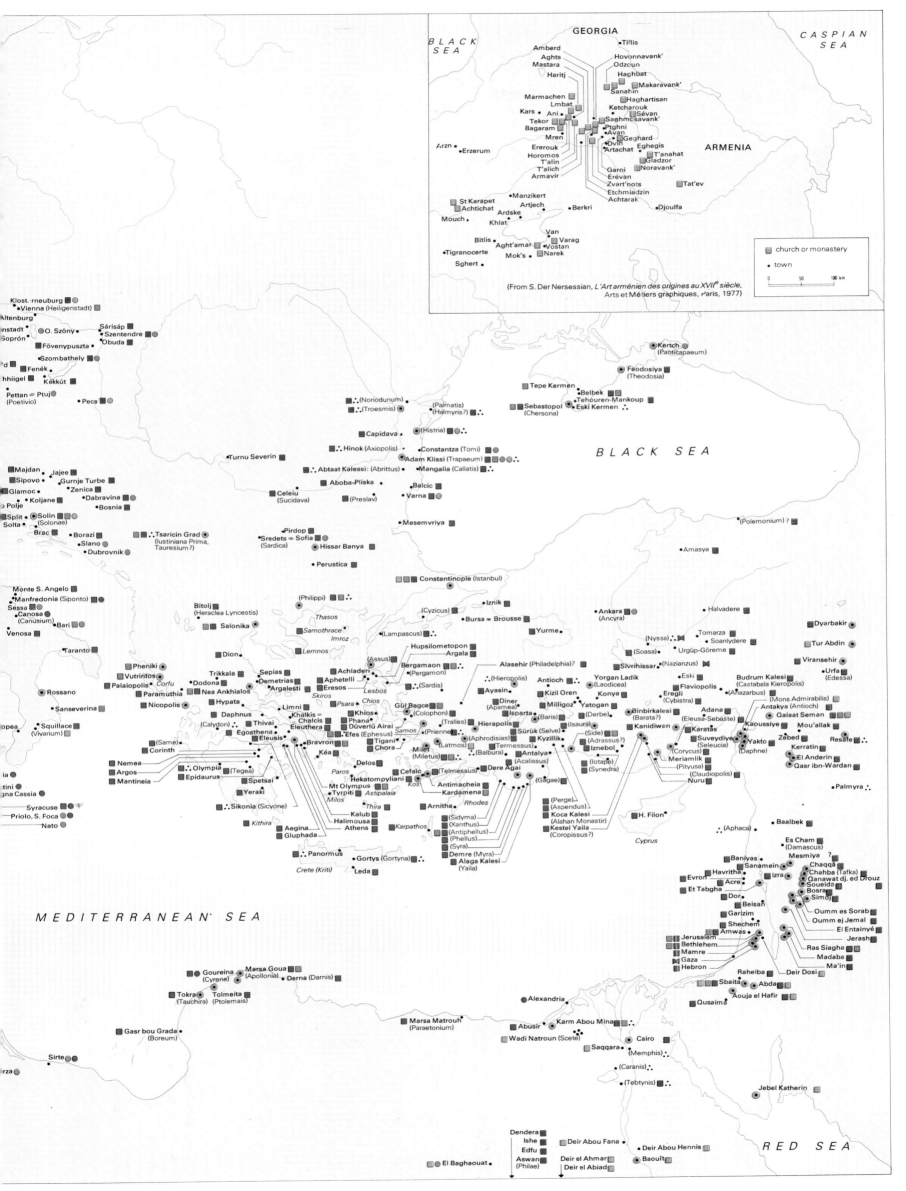

The creation of the basilica: Rome

Constantine's victory over his rival Maxentius in 312 gave him possession of Rome, which for a brief period emerged again as the centre of the Empire. The edict of tolerance that was proclaimed in Milan granted Christianity a civil statute and the same privileges as the institutions of the official state religion. Now that it was tolerated, the Church received immediate protection and places of worship could openly be built. The architectural plan which was imposed, and adopted throughout the Empire with modifications according to local usage, was that of the basilica. The choice was undoubtedly approved by the emperor himself, who showed keen interest in religious matters and was aware that the most ancient basilicas had been constructed in Rome. It is probable that the first in the series of Christian basilicas was St. John Lateran, set up by Constantine in the Domus Faustae. Although it was only consecrated in 324 by Pope Silvester I, it was certainly older, contemporary with the triumphal arch erected in honour of Constantine's victory. St. Peter's was built a little later, even if the actual dates are not known. The original appearance of both basilicas can be reconstituted in spite of subsequent upheavals. The fresco of San Martino ai Monti depicts St. John Lateran as it was before the work of Borromini in 1650. The church contained a five-aisled nave, leading to a projecting transept and a semicircular apse. The central nave, wider than the aisles, was flanked by a wall supported by arches which sprang from marble columns with capitals; this wall was decorated with marble plaques in various colours. The original appearance of St. Peter's, which harboured the tomb of the first apostle, is known from different drawings and paintings,

prior to its transformation by Bramante from 1506 onward, the central one being 20 metres (65 feet) wide. The walls were supported on columns, surmounted by an architrave between the central nave and the first aisles, and by arcades betwen the first and second aisles. The windows at the top of the walls flanking the central nave let in a little light.

San Paolo fuori le Mura, founded by Valentinian II and completed c.440, has happily escaped such transformations and preserved its original appearance, in spite of the fire of 1823. The magnificently illuminated central nave makes a stunning impression; its architect followed the example of St. John Lateran's lofty arcades, whereas Santa Maria Maggiore was modelled on St. Peter's. Built by Pope Liberius (352–66), Santa Maria Maggiore was rebuilt by Sixtus III (432–40). The architect simplified the basilical plan, only retaining one aisle; the mosaic decoration, partly preserved, stands out splendidly against the veined grey of the columns. Santa Sabina, built at the beginning of the 5th century on the Aventine, adopts the same simplified plan; here the arches spring from fluted columns of exceptional beauty that are topped by equally elegant Corinthian capitals.

One very strong principle observed in all these basilicas was to concentrate interest on the interior. The outsides consist of simple masses of brick, juxtaposed but not merging with one another. The walls are bare, broken only by bays, and fairly thin because they do not have to support much weight. Inside, what is immediately striking is the way the eye of the worshipper is drawn towards the altar by means of receding lines: columns, guttered walls

and floors all contribute to this effect, which is reinforced by the covering. Breaking with Roman traditions, which had made general use of the vault, these architects covered their buildings with a frame that was hidden from view by a wooden ceiling. This gave an impression of lightness which was transmitted to the walls and further reinforced by the use of columns. The other surprising feature was the poor integration of the respective masses. This is particularly evident at the junction of nave and transept, though the dislocation is attenuated by the light.

Contrasting with the basilical plan are the centrally planned *martyria* and baptistries, the oldest example of which is in the Lateran palace. The primitive baptistry, built in the reign of Constantine, was completely renovated under Sixtus III and the rotunda transformed into an octagon. A central colonnade, topped by architraves, supports eight more columns which originally must have carried the dome. In the centre is the piscina, in which the future Christian was immersed; and surrounding this is a corridor covered by a ring-shaped barrel vault. This pattern was adopted for Santo Stefano Rotondo, built by Pope Simplicius (468–83), but with different proportions. Because of the size of the rotunda, other parts had to be scaled down.

The centralized plan is seen again in the two mausoleums built for the imperial family: Santa Costanza, with its double colonnade supporting curious cushions, and Santa Elena. The two buildings adopt the same principle of vaulting and vestibules with side apses, but in other respects differ considerably: Santa Costanza has 12 pairs of columns, arcades and a ring vault; Santa Elena, eight columns, entablature and transverse ribs.

Sant' Agnese fuori le Mura

Built by Constantine in 324, the church of Sant' Agnese was renovated by Pope Honorius I (625–38). It is a rare example of a basilical church transformed into a building with tribunes; these surmount each of the side aisles.

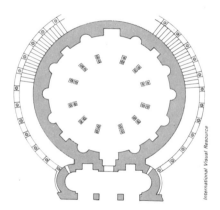

Santa Costanza

The mausoleum was designed to accommodate the body of Constance, daughter of Constantine, and was only converted into a church in 1256. The architect therefore adopted a circular centralized plan, frequently used in ancient buildings. A narthex with a double exedra leads by three entries into the rotunda. The dome is supported by 12 paired columns.

Santa Sabina

Under Sixtus III (432–40), two important basilicas were built in Rome: Santa Maria Maggiore and Santa Sabina. They are both longitudinal buildings, without transepts, which further accentuates the impression of depth. Rhythm is conveyed by close-set columns. In Santa Sabina, the fluted columns are of Parian marble and surmounted by Corinthian capitals which support the arcades; recent reconstruction has restored the illumination originally afforded by the enormous windows of the apse.

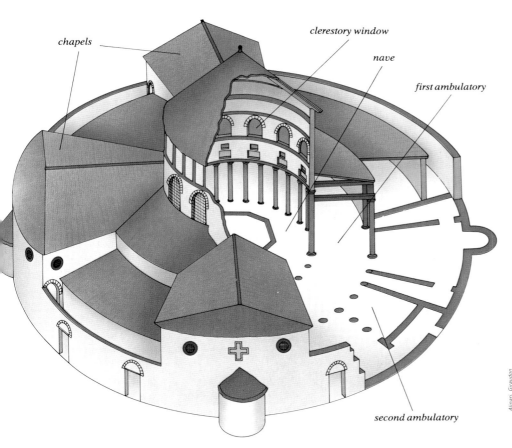

chapels

clerestory window

nave

first ambulatory

second ambulatory

Santo Stefano

Founded by Pope Simplicius (468–83) to house the relics of St. Stephen, discovered in 415, Santo Stefano Rotondo was built on a circular plan, like the ancient mausoleums. However, it includes an annular ambulatory, containing a cross. The elevation remains archaic, with squat proportions and a timber-framed roof. In size, it is clearly related to the Holy Sepulchre.

Alinari, Giraudon

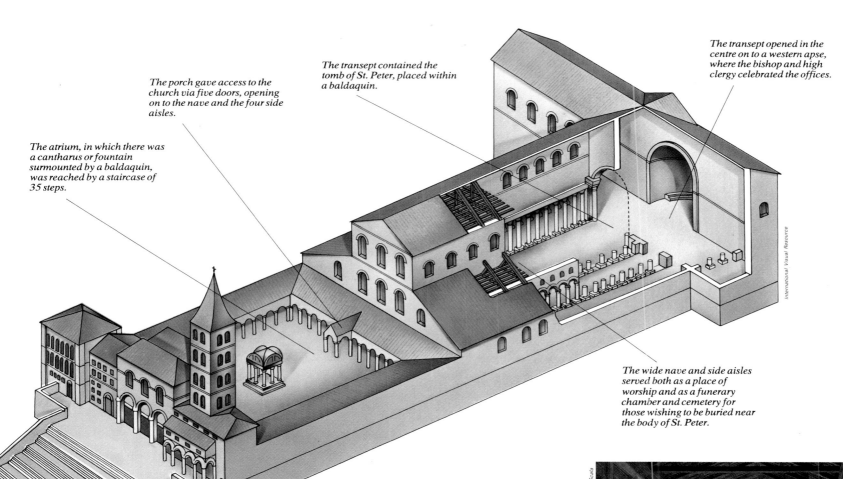

The transept opened in the centre on to a western apse, where the bishop and high clergy celebrated the offices.

The transept contained the tomb of St. Peter, placed within a baldaquin.

The porch gave access to the church via five doors, opening on to the nave and the four side aisles.

The atrium, in which there was a cantharus or fountain surmounted by a baldaquin, was reached by a staircase of 35 steps.

The wide nave and side aisles served both as a place of worship and as a funerary chamber and cemetery for those wishing to be buried near the body of St. Peter.

International Visual Resource

St. Peter's

Scala

None of the churches built by the Emperor Constantine has survived in its original form. Nevertheless, it is possible to reconstruct the basilicas of St. John Lateran (after 313) and St. Peter's (324–35), thanks to documents dating to the years prior to their transformation. They originally consisted of a closed atrium, the centre of which was occupied by a fountain, serving as a meeting point for the worshippers. Access to the basilicas was through several doors: the grandiose plan envisaged a central nave flanked by double side aisles which gave on to a large transept that took on a rounded form in the apse. The dimensions were considerable: the nave of St. John Lateran measured 75 by 19 metres (246 by 62 feet), and that of St. Peter's 100 by 27 metres (328 by 88 feet). The most noticeable difference between the two buildings was that in the Lateran there were arcades above the columns, whereas in St. Peter's the columns supported an architrave between the nave and the first side aisle, and arcades between the first and second side aisles. There was also far less light in St. Peter's because the small bays were set very high.

Conservative architecture: Ravenna

Ravenna's chapter of glory, short-lived and violent, opened in 405 when the Emperor Honorius made the city the capital of the Empire in place of Milan. Odoacer established himself there after 476, and Theodoric, king of the Ostrogoths, made it his capital in 493. The reconquest of the city by the Byzantines in 540 brought to an end a flourishing age which had seen the construction of a precinct, and the building of the Santo Spirito cathedral and its baptistry, as well as the mausoleum of Theodoric. The Emperor Justinian kept careful watch over the city, which in 550 was made an archiepiscopal seat. Within a few years, other important monuments were built by Julian the Treasurer. In 568, the arrival of the Lombards reduced the importance of the city.

Ravenna had thus developed both as a state whose destiny was no longer assured and as a focus of attraction for barbarian tribes. It was this privileged and yet perilous situation that explained the role it played at that time and also the fascination it continues to exert. Encircled by forces of dissolution, Ravenna counteracted by remaining conservative, and by perpetuating art forms that were essentially elitist. Here then was the close fusion, already achieved in Rome and Constantinople, of antique art and Christian faith.

Architects nevertheless remained loyal to the formulas that had already been tested in Milan and Rome. Their basilicas, framed or with ceilings, sometimes had five naves (the cathedral), but more often three (San Giovanni Evangelista, Sant' Apollinare Nuovo, Sant' Apollinare in Classe), separated by columns surmounted by arcades. Bricks were in general use, gradually becoming smaller in size as time passed. The bays pierced in the side aisles and the walls of the central nave gave out a light that showed off the splendour of the marvellous mosaics adorning the inner walls. The contrast with the outside was all the more striking, for that was deliberately left bare, except for the blind arcades at the top of the walls and the flat pilasters on the façades. One of the most original features of these basilicas was the presence of a semicircular crypt, a motif apparently borrowed from Rome.

More characteristic are the centrally planned buildings, even though they reproduce some of the features already mentioned in the basilicas: bricks, thin walls and lightweight masses, as in the Galla Placidia mausoleum, the Orthodox and Arian baptistries, and San Vitale. The principle of juxtaposed masses is especially striking in the mausoleum of Galla Placidia and in San Vitale: they are intended to define the interior space, not to support very heavy vaults as in Roman monuments, for example the basilica of Maxentius. Although the buildings are covered by vaults or cupolas, the materials are very light and do not weigh upon the walls: the Galla Placidia mausoleum has a semicircular flattened dome, the Orthodox baptistry a cupola on pendentives, and San Vitale a dome on squinches. San Vitale, begun in 532 and completed in 547 when it was consecrated by Archbishop Maximian, represents the culmination of these endeavours. The octagon provides a surprise in the interior: the central area is expanded by eight apsidal niches (the eighth is the apse proper), which lead to the ambulatory through three rows of three superimposed arcades. The desire to integrate inner masses had never been so completely expressed: the only separations between them are the thin partitions that let in the light. The roofing is no less original: half-domes over the apsidal niches, and a central dome borne on eight tall pendentives resting on piers linked by semicircular arches.

The mausoleum of Theodoric (died 526) stands out strikingly among these Ravenna buildings, which are homogeneous in appearance and period. Constructed of huge stone slabs, it is astonishingly weighty. It also exhibits another conception of exterior mass, with very deeply hollowed, shadowy arcades. Between the ground floor and first storey the stonework abruptly contracts to coincide with a change in plan – from octagonal to circular. The same strength is evident in the ornamental cordon running round the upper part, concealing the point where the stone dome begins. This strange edifice in fact retains links with ancient architecture and underlines the taste for the past of a barbarian king addicted to Roman traditions.

San Vitale

Begun in 532 and consecrated in 547 by Archbishop Maximian, the church of San Vitale is the last building in Ravenna with an octagonal plan. The construction is mainly of brick, and its architectural merit is the arrangement of geometric masses. On the outside they are enlivened only by buttresses, between which large bays are cut. Inside, communication between the different parts is attained by a double series of arcades. The dome – made of interlocking terracotta tubes – is mounted on eight pendentives which are supported on piers linked by arcades.

Arian baptistry

Built c.500, it adopts the centralized plan which is also to be found in the baptistry of the Orthodox cathedral. The octagon is transformed at the base into a square by the addition of four apsidal niches. The mosaic decoration of the dome shows the apostles who appear to be approaching, in hieratic order, the empty throne adorned by a cross.

Sant' Apollinare in Classe

Consecrated in 542, the church of Sant' Apollinare in Classe was completed under Archbishop Maximian. It is decorated with Lombard bands on the outside. The apse, polygonal on the outside, is circular inside. The ancient narthex, with its main entrance and two side bays, still survives; it is surmounted by an upper storey. The architect tried to break up the walls by hollowing out openings. The nave, timber-framed, is notable for its 12 columns topped by arcades which lead the eye towards the apse.

Scala

Mausoleum of Galla Placidia

Built between 425 and 433, this small mausoleum adopts a cruciform plan, and the crossing is covered by a dome. On the outside, the architect simply juxtaposed masses. However, in contrast to Romanesque architecture, the mausoleum walls give the impression of being simple partitions designed to mark off the interior spaces. Blind arcades are its only decoration. The inside is relatively small and extremely simple. The mausoleum was intended from the very start to be covered with mosaics, and these are the oldest in Ravenna. The eye is seduced by the brilliance of the colours, which mask the architecture and create an illusionistic effect. The principal scene depicts the martyrdom of St. Lawrence at the moment when the saint approaches the red-hot gridiron. The other niche represents the Good Shepherd, and on the upper walls are the apostles.

A work of light: Santa Sophia, Constantinople

Santa Sophia in Constantinople is without any doubt one of the most important and lasting achievements in the history of religious architecture. To understand the building, it is essential to know the reasons behind its construction. In the aftermath of the popular Nika insurrection, when the ancient church was burned down (532), the Emperor Justinian decided to build, to the glory and honour of the Almighty, a "great new church" on the site of the one that since the time of Theodosius had borne the name of Divine Wisdom (Hagia Sophia). When this basilica was consecrated five years later, on December 27, 537, he is reputed to have cried out in pride: "Solomon, I have surpassed you." The admiration was shared by his contemporaries and reaffirmed by posterity. Justinian's historiographer, Procopius, included in one of his works a description of the church that was not only enthusiastic but also very precise, showing himself sensible to the lightness of the construction, the interior effects of lighting and the dome that "dominates the whole world". As a result of an earthquake (December 6, 557), the dome collapsed (May 7, 558). It was rebuilt by Isidore of Miletus, and the church was again consecrated on December 26, 562. From then on it was the focal point of the city's religious and political life, the site of imperial festivals and of major political decisions.

Justinian spared no expense on Santa Sophia, making major financial contributions himself and commissioning raw materials from every part of the Empire. The work force was placed under the command of two of his official architects, Anthemius of Tralles and Isidore of Miletus. The choice of plan was certainly not theirs; it was decided and imposed by Justinian himself. Santa Sophia does not have the basilical plan generally adopted for large buildings, but is on the centralized pattern. The outer square, one side of which consists of an apsidal niche, encloses another square bounded by four powerful piers to support the dome, and shouldered to north and south by side buttresses. To east and west, the central space is prolonged by a half-domed apse, the sides of which are enlarged by a similarly half-domed niche. This succession of graded vaults leads the eye upwards to the dome, the heart of the church, both aesthetically and symbolically. The transition from the square to the upper parts, on the one hand, and from the square to the side sections, on the other, is further facilitated by an astonishing interplay of marble columns and arcades. Their effect is both to reduce the wall area and to create, on the two levels, easy transitions between the masses, while concealing the pendentives and the four enormous piers of the crossing. At the same time, the many openings which appear at seven levels add character to the building: on the ground floor, bays are set into the outer wall; higher up are tribunes, in the semidomes of the niches; and in the north and south walls beneath the relieving arch of the dome, there are two levels of apertures, the higher one extending east and west into the calottes above the pendentives and into the extrados of the dome. Because of the exceptional number of bays, light floods freely into the church at every hour of the day and at all seasons of the year. Procopius, entranced by this brightness, felt bound to remark: "It is full of light and reflections of the sun." The architects succeeded in obtaining the very effect at which Justinian had aimed: to make what was material immaterial. Such an impression must have been even stronger before the collapse of the first dome in 558. The present dome, with a shorter radius and thus more convex, is nevertheless quite as remarkable from the architectural viewpoint. Use of a lighter material, brick, made this greater height possible; but inside it is held firm within a casing of stonework, strengthened by buttresses to prevent any yielding. Furthermore, it is relieved by four wide-spanned brick arches which rest upon four ashlar piers with strong perpendicular pointing. The transition from a square to a vertical plan is effected by means of enormous pendentives, not squinches, which make the structure look more airy.

The architectural form of Santa Sophia is concealed by the richness of decoration. The walls, from the ground up, are covered in identical manner. Plaques of red, yellow and green marble blend with the mosaics, and these are further embellished by the capitals, imposts, architraves and friezes.

The contrast between the inside and outside is thus all the more surprising. The architects made no attempt to give a pleasing aspect to the exterior; on the contrary, they appeared deliberately to reject all those elements that might have given balance to the building: the buttresses are huge and very heavy, the span of the relieving arches seems insufficiently wide, and the roofing is clumsy.

E. Lessing, Magnum

The vaulted side aisles, 15 metres (50 feet) wide, surmounted by galleries, run round the whole building, except for the eastern side of the nave, where they are separated by a beautiful screen of marble columns.

M. Levassort

In 1453 Santa Sophia was transformed into a mosque; the building was then provided with four minarets which lightened the heavy, massive effect of the exterior. In order to open up the interior, the architects decided to transfer to the outside the elements needed for balancing the building and supporting the vault. Massive buttresses bear the thrusts and are interlinked by prominently projecting arches on the walls. On the upper storey, the dome, pierced by many bays, is held up by a series of close-set buttresses which prevent it from spreading.

The entrance to Santa Sophia is via a double narthex or porch. The lower floor of the main narthex was reserved for catechumens and penitents.

The interior of the building, in contrast to the exterior, is astonishingly light: the walls are partitions which enclose a space and likewise vanish behind the seven tiers of bays. The plan is a rectangle of 77 by 72 metres (250 by 235 feet), divided into three vessels, the central nave terminating in a small apse. Four enormous piers support the dome by means of gigantic pendentives. The dome is 31 metres (100 feet) in diameter and 65 metres (213 feet) high.

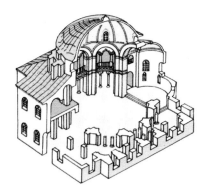

Church of St. Sergius and St. Bacchus, Constantinople

The church was founded in 527 and was apparently the work of Anthemius of Tralles, the architect of Santa Sophia. From the outside it is a cubic mass topped by a flattened dome. The transition from a square to a circle is achieved by means of a shallow drum which is similar to that of Santa Sophia. Inside, the ribbed dome rests directly on heavy, massive piers, linked by niches with high arcades. One of the features of the church is the heavy entablature around the central nave.

The Pantocrator

Basil I (867–86) was evidently responsible for part of the mosaic decoration of Santa Sophia, Constantinople. The dome is dominated by Christ Pantocrator. The iconographical scheme is completed in the apse by the Virgin and, on the walls of the nave, by the prophets.

Pendentives occupy the corners of the square: composed of four big arches, they rear up to form a circle which supports the shallow dome, 33 metres (108 feet) wide.

Four arches borne on massive pillars support the entire structure of the enormous brick dome, buttressed by 40 ribs. Half-domes, supported by the main pillars and by huge buttresses, take the thrusts of the dome to the north and south.

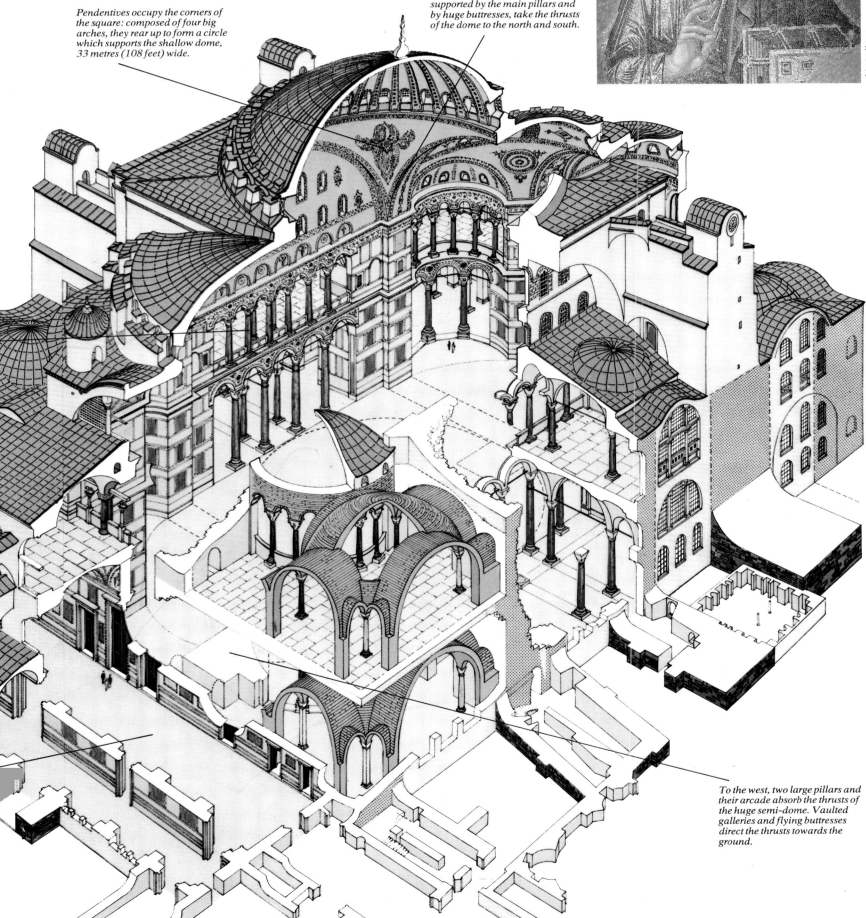

To the west, two large pillars and their arcade absorb the thrusts of the huge semi-dome. Vaulted galleries and flying buttresses direct the thrusts towards the ground.

181

Greece and the Balkans: the impact of liturgy

In Greece and the Balkans, an extremely original style of architecture appeared towards the end of antiquity, and this can be explained both by geographical situation and by the emphasis placed on liturgy. Here the influence of Western, Roman architecture clashes with that of Constantinople. The former is especially marked in the basilicas with five-aisled nave and transept, modelled upon St. John Lateran or Santi Apostoli in Rome, as at Epidaurus and Nicopolis. However, this plan is not adopted everywhere; there are three-aisled naves at Lokris, at Corinth and in St. Demetrius, Nicopolis, and in St. Demetrius, Nicopolis, and the transept disappears at Eski Djouma (Acheiropoietos) in Salonika and the Stobi church in Macedonia. Many buildings exhibit local variations of considerable originality, such as arcades running the length of walls and columns and plinths based on Roman models.

A second group of churches departs entirely from the basilical plan with its three- or five-aisled nave. In these the emphasis is placed on the choir, which is broader towards the transept. Examples of this are found in St. Demetrius, Salonika, and in the terraced basilica of Philippi. The extension of the choir is the result of a difference in the form of worship. In Rome, relics were placed below the altar, in an area accessible to the faithful, and this encouraged the development of the relic cult. In the East, however,

each altar possessed its own relics, and the latter were not within reach of the worshippers. Thus the choir and transept were separated from the nave by a tripartite structure. Oriental liturgy therefore played an important role in determining the layout of the eastern portions of such churches, and could be conducted in the grandiose ceremonies staged in the 4th century by St. Basil and in the 5th century by St. John Chrysostom.

At Ephesus, alongside the basilica built within a gymnasium, there are two large churches offering different solutions. St. John, a martyrium raised in the 5th century over the empty tomb of the saint, adopts the style of St. Simeon Stylites: four arms cross one another, leaving a vaulted square in the centre. The Seven Sleepers is a basilica with a single brick-vaulted nave, brick being used for the whole building. The thick walls contain deep niches and the vault seems to overwhelm the low interior structure.

Salonika provides a wealth of information about the churches originally built there. St. Demetrius, much transformed over the centuries and largely restored after the fire of 1917, is a typical example of a building with a very broad nave flanked by double aisles, brightly lit through four groups of windows: in the first and second aisles, the tribunes of the central nave and the clerestory windows. This

feature of pierced walls is also seen in the apse and in the western façade, formed of three superposed levels. The overall impression is one of airiness, reinforced by the rhythm of the supports – four columns followed by a rectangular pier – both in the central nave and the tribunes. The inner side aisles, on the other hand, are separated from the outer ones by simple columns which support the semicircular arcades. The ornamentation of coloured marble is scrupulous and the sculpted capitals are unusually elegant. The so-called Acheiropoietos church, also in Salonika, has numerous windows pierced in the walls, likewise allowing an extensive play of light to flood the interior.

The centralized plan is just as frequent. St. George of Salonika is a mausoleum of the Emperor Galicius adapted for Christian worship. The plan of the oratory of Christ Latomos, also in Salonika, is more unusual: an apse opening to the east contains a cross, while the centre of the church is vaulted by a dome, the arms by barrel vaults and the corners by smaller domes.

Before Justinian came to the throne, Constantinople was in the sphere of Egyptian influence. St. John the Baptist, Studios, built in 463, had two levels of superposed columns. Even more unusual was the overall plan, with no transept and the nave leading directly to the polygonal apse.

Church of the Holy Apostles, Salonika

The Church of the Holy Apostles, completed between 1312 and 1315, is a characteristic building of the Palaeologus period, by virtue of its height. The narthex is perforated by arcades and the church has a decorated brick exterior. Inside, the dome rests on four slender columns and is surrounded by four other domes. The apse, semicircular in plan, is flanked by semicircular niches.

Church of Ohrid

Many churches and monasteries were built in Macedonia under the Byzantine domination (11th to 13th centuries). Ohrid (a town in Yugoslavia) was then a very creative architectural centre; this little church, with its painstaking exterior construction, is evidence of that fact.

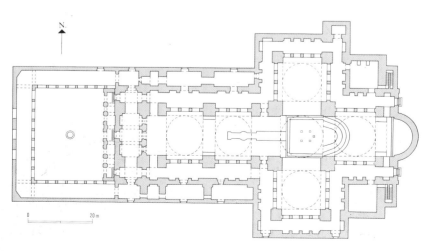

St. John of Ephesus

The martyrium of St. John of Ephesus was built in the 5th century over the empty tomb of the saint, based on a cruciform plan in which four basilicas form the cross. The building was considerably modified in the 6th century, in accordance with a basilical plan in which six domes are held up by pillars.

The Seven Sleepers, Ephesus

The basilica of the Seven Sleepers, dating from the mid-5th century, comprised a single nave on which was set a beautifully structured brick vault. The walls, likewise of brick, were pierced with deep niches (*arcosolia*) which were supposed to enshrine the bodies of the seven sleepers.

St. Irene, Constantinople

St. Irene was begun by Constantine and completed under Constantius II. The church then possessed a dome over the crossing of the transept, and a vaulted nave. It was twice transformed, after the Nika insurrection of 532, when it was badly damaged, and after a fire in 564. The new building was influenced by the principles introduced by Anthemius of Tralles and Isidore of Miletus, of a succession of spaced-out areas with walls between. The enormous dome rests on four longitudinal piers by means of pendentives.

St. Demetrius, Salonika

The immense central nave of St. Demetrius, vaulted by conspicuous timberwork, is further extended by side aisles and tribunes, which in their turn open out widely. The principle of alternation, one pier to every four columns, was adopted for both the first and second storeys, creating an individual rhythm which is reflected, too, in the clerestory windows. The broadly pierced walls – side aisles, gutters of the central nave, apse and façade – produce fascinating effects of light on the walls themselves.

Monuments of stone: Armenia

The recognition, by King Tiridates III in about 314, of Christianity as the official state religion, was a landmark in the history of Armenia, and provides a partial explanation for the extraordinary blossoming of architecture – a phenomenon for which no otherwise satisfactory answer exists. Between the 5th and 7th centuries, a large number of monuments were built – now in ruins or even vanished – which display or once displayed certain constant features. The most striking characteristic is the use of dressed stone, either calcareous tufa in a variety of colours (yellow, red, pink and grey), which local architects handled with great skill, or stone neatly cut into small squares in the traditional ancient fashion. On the outside, simple squares and rectangles of stone combine to convey a monumental impression to buildings that are often of very modest proportions. The austerity is softened by pierced bays, the variegated colours of the bonding and the contrasted forms of roofing. The bays, arranged symmetrically, throw shadows that lighten the appearance of the masonry, and are surmounted by string-courses that are generally sculpted (T'alich, 661–82). The use of polychrome stone, with contrasting brick-reds and grey-greens, has a ravishing effect in the case of the 7th century cathedral of T'alin; and the diverse lines of the roof give a soaring impression to St. Stephen of Lmbat.

This exterior harshness is offset by a highly original inner structure, particularly as regards the stone roofing. The oldest buildings with a single nave are covered by a vault resting directly on the walls. It is sometimes strengthened by transverse arches supported by engaged piers. The absence of a transept leads the eye in the direction of the apse which, often flanked by chambers, does not project on the outside. However, from the 4th century onward, naves with side aisles made their appearance, as at K'asagh; and during the 5th and 6th centuries both the central and side aisles tended to be of equal height, thus reducing the illumination (Dsiravanor church at Achtarak, 548–57).

Not content with throwing semicircular vaults over the naves and half-domes over the apse, Armenian architects displayed great ingenuity in building cupolas. At first these were placed at the crossing of the church, and later over centrally planned buildings. The T'alich church is one of the most typical with its four piers supporting the dome, the transition to a circular plan being achieved by pendentives. Centrally planned churches became the norm in the 7th century: the dome was then shouldered by barrel vaults directing the thrust towards the side walls, and the change from a square to a circle was accomplished by squinches. Architects often punctuated the drum with long bays and gave emphasis to the calotte by means of arches (cathedral of Mren, 629–40). Such technical prowess was evidently matched by skill in stonecutting – something that did not reappear in the West until the 12th century. All the domes were, in fact, assembled from small squares of stone. St. John of Mastara (mid-7th century) is one of the most beautiful examples of this type of church architecture; two superposed rows of eight squinches support the 16-sided drum of the dome, reinforced by 12 ribs. At Vagharchapat, St. Hrip'simé (618) exhibits an astounding plan which set a model. A tetrafoil, rectangular in shape with niches and corner chapels, is covered by a dome with two rows of squinches – eight large ones surmounted by 16 smaller ones.

The Arab conquest put a violent stop to this building activity between the 7th and mid-9th century. The succession of Ashot I in 886 heralded a fresh start which was already evident in local architecture. In 961 Ashot III transferred the capital to Ani and converted it into a flourishing city until its capture in 1064 by the Seljuks. The architect Trdat began to build the cathedral there in 989 and it was completed in 1001. The building was distinguished from those of the preceding period by the soaring grace of the exterior and by the use inside of bundles of colonnettes and ribs, which some see as the distant forebears of the Gothic ogee.

Church of the Redeemer, Ani

The Church of the Redeemer, Ani, built in 1036 by Ablgharib, is probably also the work of the architect Trdat, who had already provided plans for the cathedral. Here, too, he adopted the centralized plan with eight apses, and a dome that added size to the whole building before it partially collapsed. The principle of the high blind arcade springing from small columns was readopted, but on two levels. There is also the same policy of not revealing the interior details on the outside.

Cathedral of T'alin

Built in the 7th century, with particularly large dimensions, the cathedral of T'alin is in the form of a rectangle, three of the sides being expanded by an apse, so giving it the appearance of a trefoil. The transept is marked in the centre by the presence of four strong pillars which supported, prior to its collapse, an ovoid dome resting on pendentives. The exterior is very beautiful thanks to the clear arrangement of the geometric masses, whose austere effect is relieved by varicoloured stones and the interplay of blind arcades over the apses and archivolts of the bays.

Church of T'alich

Founded by Grigor Mamikonian (661–82), the church of T'alich (Aroutj) has the characteristic plan of a long rectangular hall with a non-projecting apse and a central dome. The latter is supported by four strong pillars, surmounted by squinches which thus turn the square into a circle. On the outside, the long side of the rectangle is broken over the transept by a gabled wall which interrupts the lines of the roof over the nave and side aisles. Splendidly proportioned and positioned bays form hollows in the very smooth walls.

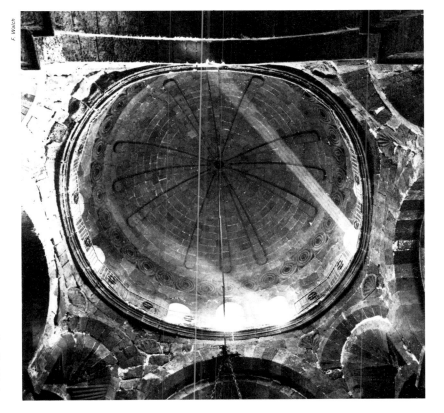

St. Hrip'simé, Vagharchapat

Built in 618 over the primitive martyrium of the saint by the Catholicos Komitas, the church is built to a square plan, the centre of which is occupied by an immense dome that rests on the walls. The space is expanded by four apses that form a tetrafoil, and in the corners by small niches. Two series of squinches convert the square into a circle.

Church of the Holy Cross, Aght'amar

King Gagik Ardsrouni established the island of Aght'amar on Lake Van, and built on it a palace and a church dedicated to the Holy Cross, having commissioned the plans from the architect Manuel between 915 and 921. The plan, a tetrafoil with corner niches, is similar to that of St. Hrip'simé. The centre consists of a dome resting on pendentives.

Cathedral of Ani

King Smbat, in 989, requested plans from the architect Trdat for a cathedral in his new capital; it was completed in 1001 under his successor, Gagik I. The adopted plan is a long rectangle, the centre of which is taken up by four pillars to support the dome, now collapsed. The choir consists of a deep apse, flanked by two closed chapels. The architect underlined the vertical elements of the interior by using small clustered columns as supports for the arches of the vault. The exterior plan is very simple: four magnificently constructed walls in warm shades of stone and in various colours ascend higher than the cross to form a gable. The entire building is encircled by high blind arcades supported by slender colonnettes. A few long, narrow windows cut in the walls bring a little light to the interior.

View of the nave towards the west, church of Odzoun

The plan of the church of Odzoun (6th–7th centuries) is particularly remarkable: it is a long rectangle, enclosed on three sides by a corridor that opens out into six semicircular arcades. The central nave is flanked by narrow side aisles which lead to rectangular side chapels. The transept is notable for four piers, cruciform in plan, that support the double curves of the large arcades. Admirably worked squinches transform the square into an octagon supporting the dome. Four small bays are situated at the base of this dome. The outside is striking for its geometric severity, with its masses superimposed on one another.

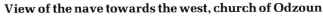

Religious architecture

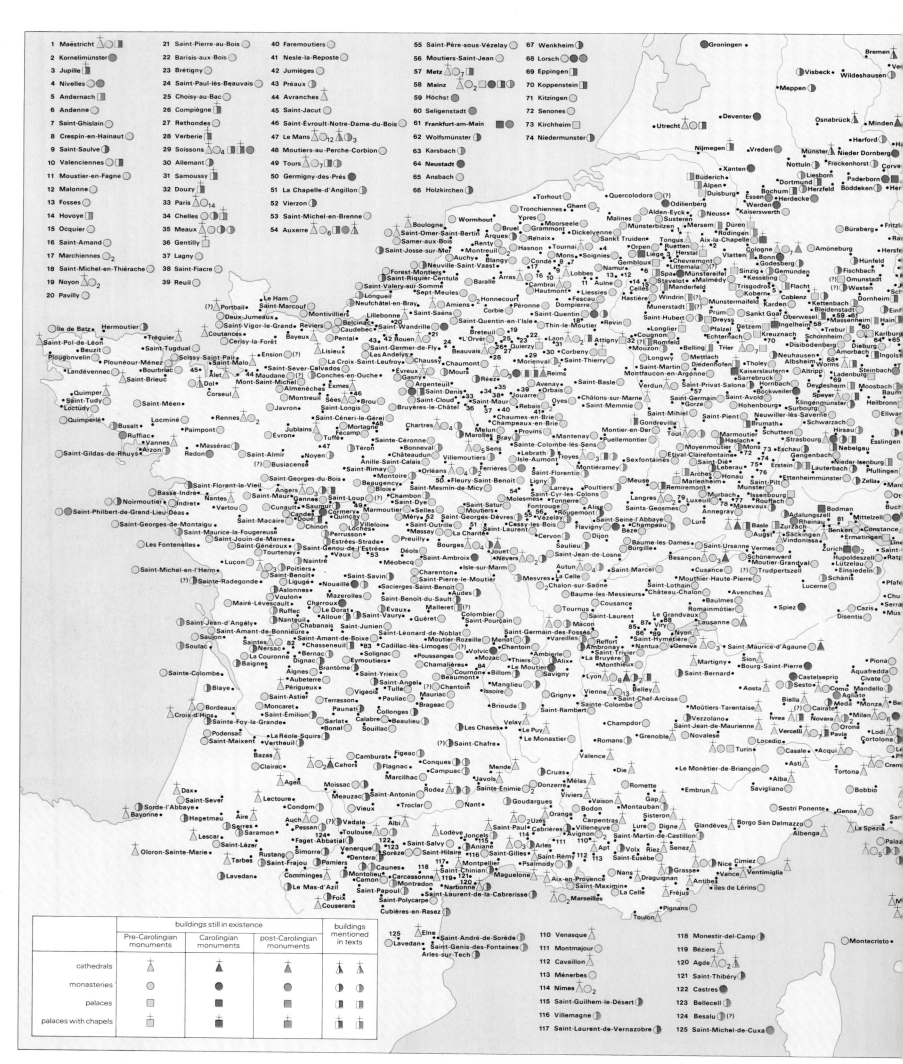

The Carolingian renaissance cannot be understood without taking into account the surge of monastic activity in 7th century Europe. In Ireland, Britain and north-western Gaul, monasteries set a cultural example which the Carolingian kings endeavoured to extend throughout Gaul. The surviving monuments are too few in number for its effect on architecture to be fully judged; often the crypt is the only remaining testimony to the newly discovered skill in stonecutting. Two events were to reinforce this movement yet further: the appearance at the beginning of the 8th century of monasteries founded on a regular plan instead of the previous pattern of scattered buildings, and the reform introduced by Chrodegang, bishop of Metz, around 754, whereby the organization that already existed in Benedictine monasteries was extended to the secular clergy. Charlemagne devoted great energy to the diffusion of these reforms.

A perfect illustration of this is the history of the monastery of Centula, today St. Riquier. Angilbert, the founding abbot, was a learned, cultured man who had links with the emperor; thanks to Charlemagne's financial support, he was able to complete its construction by 799, in less than ten years. The plan adopted was that of a triangle, in homage to the Trinity; each of the corners was occupied by a church, and these were linked to one another by galleries. The principal church, dedicated to the Saviour, the Virgin and St. Riquier, was planned to face the west, and the main sanctuary, raised above a crypt and topped by a tower, was also turned in that direction. The second church, dedicated to the Virgin, was in the shape of a rotunda, and the third was in the form of a basilica. Similar diversity of plan is to be found in other monuments that have escaped ruin. At St. Denis, consecrated in 775, Abbot Fulrad, on returning from a mission to Rome, adopted the idea of a ring crypt, namely a winding corridor around the confessio. Associated with the cult of relics, crypts assumed new importance during the 8th and mid-9th century; at St. Philibert in Grandlieu, St. Germain in Auxerre and St. Médard in Soissons. This development was to have a lasting effect on Western architecture.

In addition to such remarkable originality in plans, it is worth drawing attention to the quality of the drafting. Although this is rather difficult to judge at St. Denis, where the external wall is barely visible, it can be seen in all its perfection at St. Médard, Soissons. The beautifully drafted walls support equally fine groined vaults. Not until the 12th century do we again come across such perfect technique, for it was not inherited by successive generations. Even so, this dexterity was by no means general. At Grandlieu, the architect modelled himself clumsily on the ancient technique of *pastourelles* (small cubic stones), separated at regular intervals by rows of bricks. At Auxerre, the semicircular vault of the crypt rests on a wooden beam which forms an architrave. The taste for polychromy often conceals this defect. The triumphal door at Lorsch exhibits a variety of squares, some of them placed on their tip, and of hexagons in different colours.

This architectural development, characterized, according to scholars, by 27 new cathedrals, 417 monastic establishments and 100 royal residences built between 768 and 855, was supplemented by hospitals, schools, towns, bridges and fortifications too numerous to count. This immense achievement, which received its impetus from the king and his courtiers, was to be wiped out by the subsequent Norman invasions.

The Ottonian and Salian emperors (until *c.*1070) resurrected the artistic policies of the Carolingians and built a number of monuments, some of which escaped ruin. The Carolingian influence, apparently predominant in the cathedral of Magdeburg (now vanished) and the abbey church of Essen, is nevertheless tempered by Byzantine features. The architects of St. Bartholomew, Paderborn, were described as *operarii graeci*. The originality of Ottonian architecture is nevertheless manifest in the striking interplay of interior and exterior masses, more often juxtaposed than fused. Additional features are dominant towers on the outside and, inside, the smooth surfaces of the walls which rest either on piers or columns. To accentuate the horizontal impression, the nave is covered by a wooden ceiling. Buildings on this model were to be found in Saxony, at Cologne and at Trier, the masterpiece being St. Michael of Hildesheim (1010–33), the work of Bishop Bernward.

St. Médard, Soissons

The crypt of St. Médard, Soissons, is the only surviving part of the abbey church built between 817 and 841. The plan consists of a corridor opening on to three oratories that face east and six others that face west. Besides this original feature, the whole structure is very beautiful. Transverse and wall ribs spring directly from pillars on a cruciform plan. The same goes for the vaults, the groins of which are lost in the corners.

Lauros, Giraudon

The architectural renaissance of the 7th to 10th centuries

(after Albrecht Mann and Theodor Strauss.)

Palaces

It was not only religious architecture that blossomed so spectacularly under the Carolingians. In a revival of antique tradition, the emperors built palaces and residences for their personal use, for their families and for the members of their court. The pattern of these buildings depended on the specific use to which they were put. Many obviously served as homes and for entertainment, but others were designed for more public purposes: for administration and the dispensing of justice, and as schools and places of worship (for religious life was closely associated with the person of the emperor).

Charlemagne was responsible for building numerous palaces, the most famous of them being those of Ingelheim and Nijmegen. The one at Aix-la-Chapelle has in large part survived, and excavations carried out in the 19th century have made it possible to reconstruct it completely. Its ground plan was a rectangle 180 metres (590 feet) in length, bordered on the north by an *aula* and to the south by the chapel. Extending between the two buildings was a courtyard, and the buildings themselves were linked by a porticoed gallery. There was a door in the centre of the western gallery, the upper storey of which was occupied by the courtroom. The *aula* to the north was extended to the west by an apse accommodating the imperial throne, and by two others to the north and south.

The southern end comprised the religious buildings in the form of a Latin cross; in the centre was the famous octagon which subsequently became the cathedral. One has to ignore the elements added in the Gothic period and the 19th century in order to comprehend the original significance of the chapel, begun prior to 798, and its architecture. In the centre, eight huge piers prop up the broad arcades which lead to the ambulatory. Above is a second row of arcades, broken halfway up by marble columns supporting an architrave, and an upper line of columns rising somewhat awkwardly to the top of the arch. The third level contains windows through which the light floods in; and topping it all is the dome. The ambulatory is covered by groin vaults in greywacke (dark sandstone) which merge into the wall ribs. Massive square pillars, surmounted by heavy abaci, support the springers. Finally, it is worth remarking on the absence of transverse ribs, which facilitates the interlinking of the bays. On the first storey, the tribunes are covered by rampant barrel vaults. Eudes de Metz, who built the chapel, owed nothing to Byzantine example, but created here a powerfully original work.

Aix-la-Chapelle, which exerted considerable influence, was not the only building of this type. Halfway between Orléans (of which he was bishop) and St. Benoît-sur-Loire (of which he was abbot), Theodulf, friend of Charlemagne and a man of great culture, built in 806 a centrally planned chapel in his villa at Germigny, which has survived after radical restoration in the 19th century. Each side of the square (10.4 metres/34 feet) is prolonged by an apse, and the square itself encloses yet another apse, bounded by four pillars. Here, too, is the variety of roofing already seen at Aix: five domes, groin vaults and semicircular vaults. Yet although they are both based on the central plan, the two buildings are far removed from each other. Ottmarsheim, however, which was consecrated in 1049, has obvious links with Aix-la-Chapelle. Here, too, is the octagonal framework and a similar interior elevation, with the arcade likewise broken halfway up by columns.

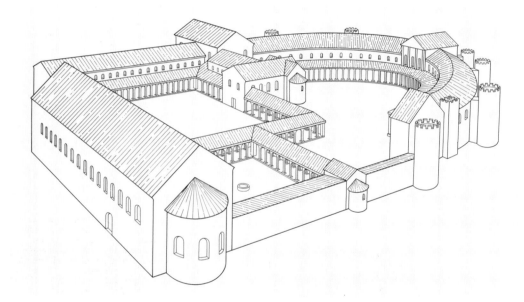

Palace of Ingelheim

Begun in 777 by Charlemagne, the palace of Ingelheim was completed by his successor, Louis the Pious. The dimensions (100 metres/330 feet square) – with a semicircular entrance to the east – are less imposing than those of the palace of Aix-la-Chapelle. However, Ingelheim is conceived on much the same lines as far as the plan is concerned, with an *aula* which likewise terminates in an apse; as at Aix, the church is cruciform and is separated from the *aula* by a courtyard. The difference lies in the arrangement of the other buildings which follow a semicircular pattern. Wooden galleries enable visitors to move about under cover (based on K. Weidemann).

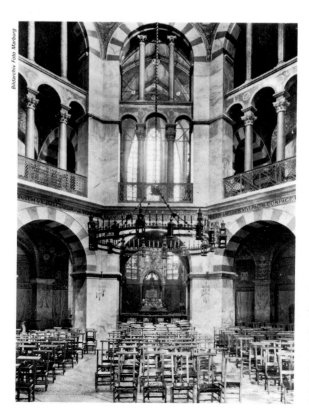

Palatine chapel, Aix-la-Chapelle

The original height of the octagon is not precisely known, since the upper parts of the chapel have been twice restored. It was approximately 36 metres (118 feet).

Palace of Aix-la-Chapelle

The palace of Aix-la-Chapelle covers a rectangle of about 20 hectares (50 acres), divided by a "highway" which passes beneath the porch (1). Two galleries (2) provide access on the north to the *aula* (3), preceded by a porch (4), and on the south to the places of worship, arranged on a cruciform plan. In the centre is the octagon (5), flanked on the north and south by annexes (6) and on the west by an atrium (7).

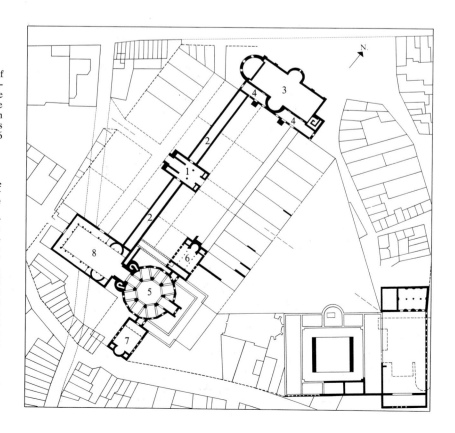

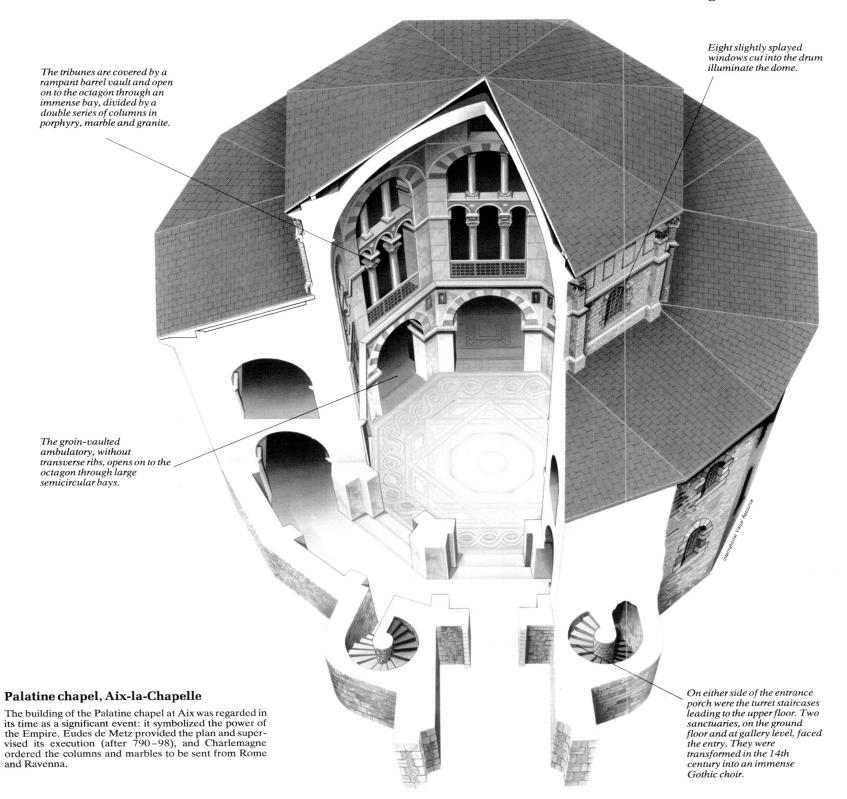

Eight slightly splayed windows cut into the drum illuminate the dome.

The tribunes are covered by a rampant barrel vault and open on to the octagon through an immense bay, divided by a double series of columns in porphyry, marble and granite.

The groin-vaulted ambulatory, without transverse ribs, opens on to the octagon through large semicircular bays.

Palatine chapel, Aix-la-Chapelle

The building of the Palatine chapel at Aix was regarded in its time as a significant event: it symbolized the power of the Empire. Eudes de Metz provided the plan and supervised its execution (after 790–98), and Charlemagne ordered the columns and marbles to be sent from Rome and Ravenna.

On either side of the entrance porch were the turret staircases leading to the upper floor. Two sanctuaries, on the ground floor and at gallery level, faced the entry. They were transformed in the 14th century into an immense Gothic choir.

Ambulatory, Aix-la-Chapelle

The architectural structure of the ambulatory of Aix-la-Chapelle reveals a technical prowess rivalled a few years later by the crypt of St. Médard, Soissons. It is covered by groin vaults without transverse ribs, which disappear far above the abacus. By contrast, the very large wall ribs serve as draining arches and enable bays to be pierced.

Dome, Aix-la-Chapelle

Over the octagon, Eudes de Metz had the original notion of a dome made up of a series of groin vaults which give it a tapered appearance. Since 1870–73 it has been covered by a mosaic that replaced the original one depicting Christ blessing, surrounded by the Elders of the Apocalypse offering him their crown.

An ideal plan for a monastery

A precious and unique document in the library at St. Gall, Switzerland, testifies to the imperial desire to organize Carolingian monasteries on a regular pattern. Slightly earlier than 829 an architect drew a detailed plan, on five pieces of parchment stitched together, for Abbot Gozbert of St. Gall, who wanted to rebuild his monastery. The plan shows a complex of buildings extending to a length of more than 230 metres (755 feet), with a gigantic abbey church, apparently envisaged in stone, surrounded by other buildings which were doubtless to be constructed in wood. What the architect presents is, in fact, a small, self-contained town, admirably organized, with its religious life ordered around the cloister, which is the extension of the abbey church to the south. To the east is the dormitory, to the south the refectory and to the west the cellar with the pantry above. The other buildings are grouped round like islands inside neatly drawn rectangles. To the east, behind the apse of the abbey church, is a second church, flanked on the south by the con-vent for novices and to the north by the infirmary. Near by are the doctor's house, a sanatorium and a herb garden. The cemetery is situated south-east of the abbey church, next to the garden. To the north, from west to east, are the hospice for outsiders, the school and the abbot's house; and to the south-east, the hospice for the poor. Farther south are the barn and the building for the trade associations. To the west are the farm buildings. The wish to organize the different parts of the monastery on a regular basis is reflected in the interior structure as well. In the hospice for outsiders, the hearth is placed in the middle and the desire for comfort is evident, as is shown by the number of rooms allotted for baths and the heating by hypocaust.

This project furnishes valuable information about the apparently wealthy homes of the Carolingian period and the running of model farms. It was presumably too ambitious and was never carried out, but it became a model for Cistercian architects of the 12th century.

"Centula" (St. Riquier, Somme)

The abbey of Centula, built at the end of the 8th century by Abbot Angilbert, served as a model throughout the Carolingian era. The plan of St. Gall is a later and much more elaborate illustration of this. The chosen plan was a triangle, the corners of which were occupied by three churches, in honour of the Trinity. (Engraving after Petau, 1612.)

Plan of St. Gall (reconstruction by Dom Cabrol)

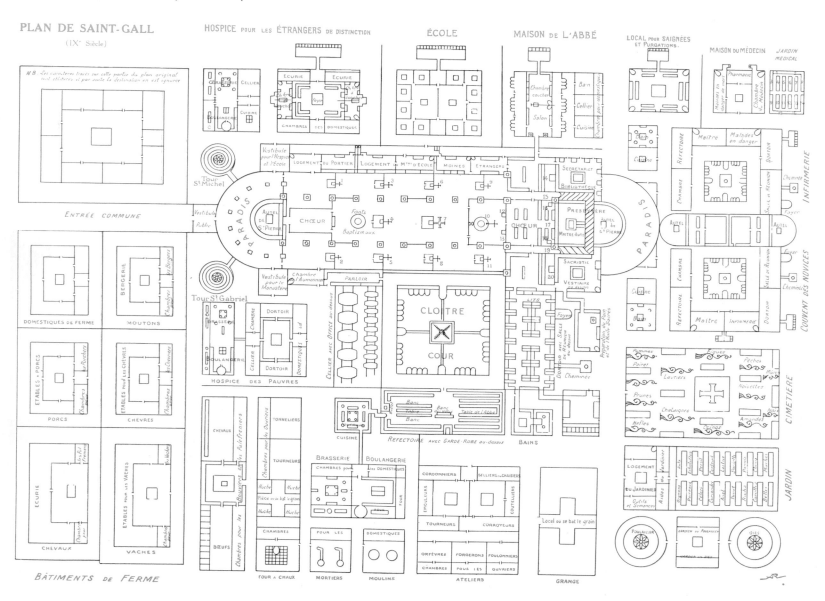

THE MIDDLE AGES

Church of St. Nectaire

Auvergne is notable for its beautiful Romanesque architecture; the landscape seems as if expressly fashioned for such buildings. Around Clermont-Ferrand and within a radius of 30 kilometres (18 miles), these churches have a family resemblance not wholly explained by the fact that they are constructed from the same materials; among the largest of them are Notre-Dame-du-Port at Clermont, St. Paul at Issoire, St. Nectaire, Orcival, and St. Saturnin. The plan of these churches is often very similar: an ambulatory with an odd or even number of radiating chapels, a two-level elevation with tribunes, and varied types of roofing – groin vaulting on the side aisles, half-barrel vaulting in the tribunes, semicircular vaulting over the central nave, dome on squinches over the crossing, half-domes in the apse and niches, and an annular barrel vault over the ambulatory. On the outside the notable feature is the extraordinary equilibrium of the ranged masses of the apse, culminating in the transept tower.

Charlemagne's ambitious dream of unifying the Empire was shattered by the repeated bloodthirsty raids of the Normans. The Empire emerged from these invasions splintered into kingdoms which were in turn subdivided into individual domains: France, Germany, Italy, Lotharingia, Burgundy. Only Spain and England escaped this fate. Yet in the face of these destructive forces, others appeared to rebuild those states that were only a shadow of their former selves. In France, the Capetians achieved this from the end of the 10th century. In Spain, Castile, Navarre and Aragon proceeded to conquer the peninsula, now in the hands of the Muslims. In southern Italy, the Normans drove out the Greeks and Arabs; in England, William the Conqueror seized the crown (1066) and set up a new kingdom across the Channel. Within the Empire, fortunes did not fluctuate to this extent, for the Ottonian and Salian emperors remained in power, extending their possessions to Lorraine and Italy.

While the boundaries of the new states (which were to be those of the modern world) were being established, the links with antiquity were finally sundered. This affected all walks of life: trade, communications, town planning, law, religion and art. Society was gradually changing, due in large measure both to a new network of roads, which, unlike that of ancient times, was not centred on Rome, and to waterways, now in abundant use. At the same time, the medieval town sprang up, not, as in olden times, created as much for politics as for pleasure, but a town of traders, with markets and fairs sponsored by lords, either secular or ecclesiastical. The relationships between people were no longer based on rights but on individual ties – a wholly new conception in western medieval society, where feudalism was established. Religion was carried along on this new wave; aware of its strength, it set off to regain pagan lands: Sicily, Corsica and Sardinia for Italy; the Hungarians and western Slavs for central Europe. In Spain, the struggle was more bitter and only came to an end in the 13th century. This religious reconquest was extended overseas and was sanctioned by the First Crusade (1096) with the setting up of the Latin kingdom of Jerusalem. At the same time, the Church was reformed, thanks to the activity of Gregory VII. The religious orders, spearheaded by Cluny, played a crucial role everywhere.

Reacting against the architecture of late antiquity and the early Middle Ages, the Romanesque period embarked on a number of experiments which, in spite of obvious local variations, indicated a definite sense of cohesion. As always in religious architecture, this universal approach was conditioned both by necessities and by liturgical demands, which had a strong bearing on the evolution of forms. During the Romanesque era, the building was very much the product of the ceremonial conducted within its walls; consequently, a number of new features emerged, firstly in respect of the ground plan, subsequently in respect of elevation.

The plan that had been inherited from the period of late antiquity was markedly more elaborate than before, and this complexity was associated both with the cult of relics, which became more widespread, and with the need to increase the number of altars so that the clergy could celebrate mass. In other words, the entire development of religious architecture changed direction. During the Carolingian age, which in this respect was the inheritor of the Merovingian world, the accepted policy was to multiply the available places of worship; the Romanesque policy, on the other hand, was to reduce the number of churches, but to make these individual buildings very big. The abbey of Fleury, today St. Benoît-sur-Loire, is a striking example of this tendency, exhibiting as it does the transition, at the end of the 11th century, from a group of several buildings to a single building consisting of a rotunda, crypts and church. This is by no means a unique phenomenon, and the process can be seen in a number of other monuments which have been preserved. Undoubtedly it explains the increased size of churches, which, when built on the basilical plan, were comparatively small, but which now consisted of an apse opening out into a large transept. When the basilica of St. Denis was reconstructed and consecrated in 775, Fulrad adopted a plan whereby the worshippers were able to walk around a corridor that completely encircled the recess for relics. The Carolingian era went the same way but found it reached an impasse (at St. Philibert de Grandlieu and at Soissons); nor did architects have any greater success in adding an eastern rotunda, which was adapted awkwardly from the traditional basilical pattern (St. Germain at Auxerre and St. Pierre at Flavigny). These experiments, albeit interesting, had no chance of success for the simple reason that the places of worship were too widely dispersed. In this respect, the Romanesque period broke fundamentally with the past, even though it did readopt a large number of other schemes from former days. All these endeavours culminated in a plan which featured an ambulatory with radiating chapels; but the date of its appearance and the earliest example have long been matters of conjecture. It used to be thought that St. Martin in Tours, wrongly dated around the end of the 10th century, was the first church to exhibit such an arrangement, which then set the fashion for the rest of the western Christian world. It is now recognized that St. Martin cannot be dated earlier than the end of the 11th century. Another formula, seemingly older, was to prove equally successful; this was the echelon plan. It made its appearance, if one can go by the excavations that have been carried out at Cluny, in the church constructed by St. Maïeul, in 981. Although very different from the preceding plan in that there was no ambulatory, it similarly incorporated a number of altars. Nevertheless, when at the end of the 11th century it was decided to rebuild the abbey church of Cluny, the plan incorporating an ambulatory and radiating chapels was retained.

Whereas the eastern parts of the church were extended and altered in extraordinary fashion, the western parts tended to be much simplified. Once again, this transformation came about as a result of liturgical development. In comparison with the Carolingian period, there was a marked reduction in religious ceremonial, which made the western transept and first-storey tribune obsolete. Nevertheless, there was no discernible regular pattern in the formal development of the church, and many buildings show obvious signs of hesitation, not to say retraced steps, on the part of architects. Yet the movement proved to be irresistible, culminating in what has been conveniently described as the harmonious façade, perfected by the Norman architects of the late 11th century: here the façade is framed by two towers situated on the same vertical plane. In this instance, too, the date when the innovation first appeared is uncertain. Some have claimed to see in it the slow evolution of Ottonian architecture which was taken up in Normandy before it extended to the larger part of western Europe. The question is not easily resolved if it is considered only in relation to the structural plan, not taking into account its liturgical use. It is clear that the trend towards simplification was in line with the wish to provide an easily accessible entrance for the worshippers. The evolution was the same, whether it applied to monasteries or to churches located in and around towns. Even so, there is evidence of some groping towards a solution. At Cluny, the nave of the abbey church built at the end of the 11th century is preceded by a pronaos consisting of five bays and flanked by two towers. This narthex, which apparently served as a church for the laity, led into the church proper by way of three principal doors. The same arrangement is found soon afterwards at Vézelay, but displaying less

ROMANESQUE ARCHITECTURE

grandiose proportions. Eventually this appendage, having become useless, was abandoned, though at a later date it was reconstituted in the form of the porch.

Between this broadly developed choir and the pronaos, which gradually disappeared, were the nave and the transepts. Here too there is an obvious simplification of forms, culminating in the disappearance of the western transept in favour of a homogeneous interior space. In the case of the nave, the plan is especially simple, generally consisting of a central vessel flanked by side aisles. As for the transept, this can be seen to evolve in accordance with a principle which is constant in Romanesque architecture and subsequently in Gothic architecture: the transept itself is conceived as a kind of church, set at right angles to the church proper, and conforming to it both in height and elevation.

It goes without saying that the definition of the Romanesque building as outlined above does not hold true for a number of churches which conform to other principles. The centralized plan is perpetuated but is not as common as it was during the period of late antiquity and the early Middle Ages. Furthermore, crypts, which in the course of the Carolingian age occupied a privileged place in association with the cult of relics, now became an integral part of the building, an essential ingredient of its plan.

As far as elevation is concerned, Romanesque architecture shows much originality, this being manifested particularly in the exterior arrangement of masses. Harking back to Roman traditions, Romanesque architecture was bent on covering its constructions with stone vaults, this technique having been abandoned late in antiquity in favour of the framed ceiling, which made it possible to reduce the thickness of the outside walls and multiply the number of windows. The result was a building that was splendidly illuminated by two levels of windows – in the nave and in the aisles – and whose interior and exterior volumes were strongly accentuated. The unity of the interior space was further reinforced by doing away with the transverse ribs that were a frequent feature of antique architecture. The gaze of the spectator was thus guided by means of perspective towards the sanctuary. The architects of the Carolingian age, followed by those of the Ottonian period, remained faithful to this tradition at least in churches built on the basilical plan. In those monuments constructed on the centralized pattern, where framework covering was ruled out from the beginning, stone vaulting had been retained.

The 11th century provides an uncommonly wide variety of examples in this area of church construction, and the broad outlines of these developments can today be traced. This evolution would have been easier to analyse had not so many of the major buildings meanwhile disappeared. In France, where such architectural activity was most pronounced, St. Martin of Tours, St. Martial of Limoges, and Cluny are no more than memories, with only a few stones or the odd drawing to convey any idea of what they looked like. But these abbey churches were undoubtedly important stages in the process. The earliest churches were, as in the Carolingian era, quite small: and since crypts or sanctuaries were of modest dimensions, they could be covered by a stone vault without risk of collapse. There were several reasons why the principle of vaulting was subsequently extended to the entire building. The first, as is evident from the writings of chroniclers, was a purely technical and practical matter.

The huge timbered buildings of the Carolingian age or those that were built in the 11th century were particularly vulnerable to fire, because of the large amount of wood involved. Such a fire might accidentally break out in the sanctuary, with its hangings, and the flames would rapidly spread to the ceiling and the timbers of the nave. The stone walls would be next, and within a few hours the whole church would be reduced to a heap of ashes. This was what happened on numerous occasions, according to chroniclers who actually witnessed such catastrophes or heard tell of them. The stone vault, on the other hand, could act as a firebreak between the interior of the building and the timber of the roof, so preventing an absolute disaster. There was an additional reason, however, for stone being used, although this does not emerge so clearly from contemporary texts: this was the difficulty of finding enough wooden beams of adequate length to be stretched across the central body of the

The influence of the abbey of Cluny
(Based on *Histoire générale des églises de France*, Robert Laffont, Paris, 1966.)

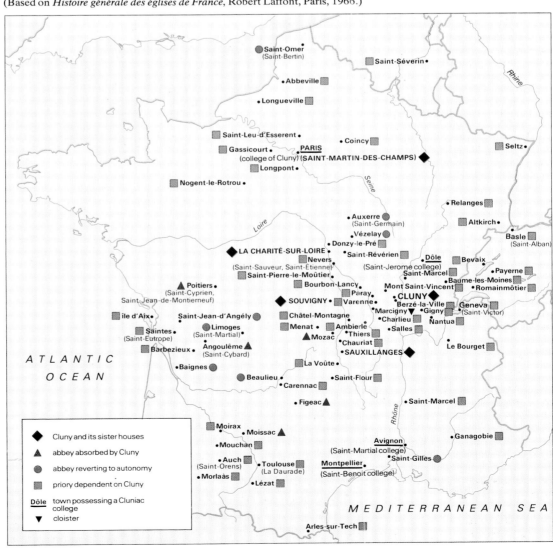

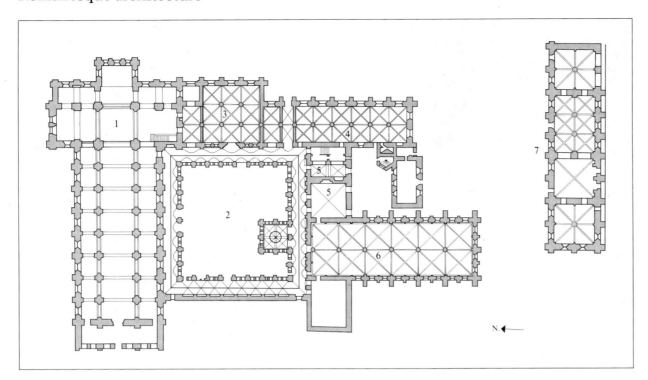

Plan of a Cistercian abbey: Fontenoy, in Burgundy

(Based on *Histoire générale des églises de France*, Robert Laffont, Paris, 1966.)

It is certain that Cîteaux set the early pattern for the plan of a Cistercian abbey wherever the site permitted it to be realized. It was not binding in its entirety but was based both on a realistic appraisal of the needs of an enclosed community and also on an analysis of the ancient villa. On the north is the church (1), of which the apse was, originally, flat. In the centre is the cloister (2), around which all community life revolved, with buildings extending along each wing. To the north are the chapter house (3) and the great hall (4) which was built over the dormitory. To the south are the boiler-room (5) and the refectory (6). To the west are the cellar and the stores, above which was the dormitory for lay brothers. Farther off, near the river, are the forge and the mills (7). There were also a number of barns, associated with the farming activities, at various distances from the abbey.

Vaulting of the Romanesque church

(Based on *Histoire de l'architecture*, vol. II, Vincent, Fréal et Cie., Paris, 1955.)

The architects of the Romanesque period had to resolve a double problem: to counter the risks of fire, they undertook to vault the entire building, and to increase interior lighting, they decided to enlarge the windows. These procedures proved difficult to reconcile and the solutions proposed were many and varied. The dome has the advantage of being easy to set above vast spaces and of exerting lesser thrusts. It is thus possible to reduce the interior space to a single nave and to pierce the thrust-carrying walls with clerestory windows, as in the cathedral of St. Pierre, Angoulême. St. Ours of Loches is a unique case with its "dubes", which are, in fact, an original conversion of the dome above a single nave into a hollow pyramid. The problem of direct lighting is a determining factor in planning a building. To achieve it, in a church with semicircular vaulting over the nave, the architect of St. Étienne, Nevers, provided buttresses in the form of tribunes, some of them with quarter-circle vaults. This buttressing is facilitated by the use of a pointed vault with minimal thrusts; the tribunes are thus rendered useless and clerestory windows can be pierced, as at Paray-le-Monial and St. Sernin, Toulouse. Another possibility is furnished by buildings with a nave covered by a semicircular vault, without direct light into the nave, as at St. Savin. The substitution of very high side aisles for tribunes achieves the same result.

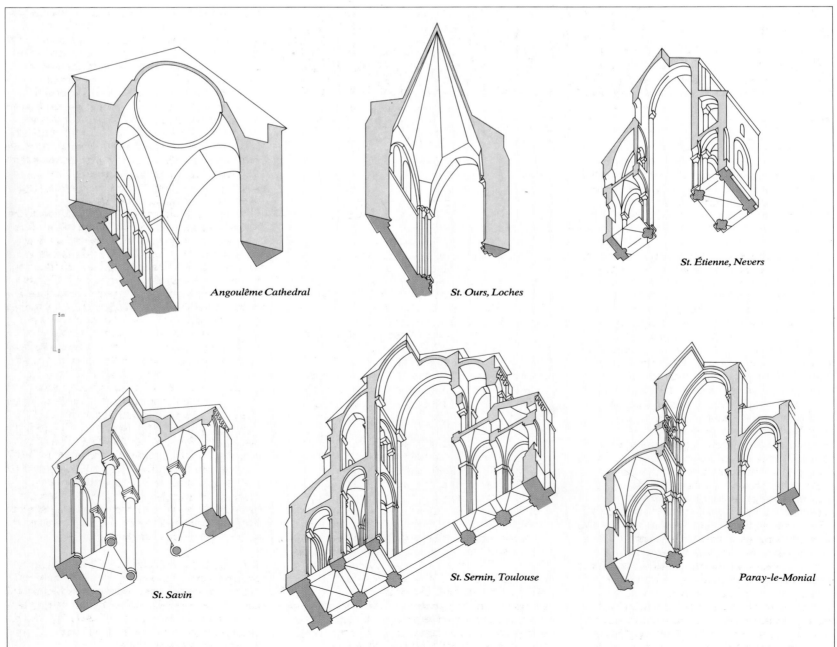

Angoulême Cathedral

St. Ours, Loches

St. Étienne, Nevers

St. Savin

St. Sernin, Toulouse

Paray-le-Monial

St. Michael, Hildesheim. Thanks to its restoration after the Second World War, the church of St. Michael, Hildesheim, has recovered its 11th century appearance. The bare walls of the nave, with the ceiling, form a kind of box. They are only broken low down by large arcades that communicate with the side aisles, and higher up by windows. This austerity does not lack beauty and is tempered by the rhythm of the supports, in which a square pier alternates with two columns topped by cubic capitals.

church from wall to wall. During the 11th century forests were literally ransacked in order to find sufficient raw material for building churches, ships and, above all, wooden castles.

Taken individually these reasons might not seem all that convincing, but there were others more intimately related to structure. It was not only the roofing that had to be considered, but also the bay, which now assumed new importance. In palaeo-Christian buildings walls had been virtually continuous; now, in contrast, the tendency was increasingly to provide vertical and projecting supports which extended from the base to the top of the wall. Such supports, admittedly, had existed even before stone vaulting, but the tendency now was to combine column and pier in a regular alternation, "ab, ab" (unlike earlier, more complicated groupings), and Norman architects at the end of the 11th century were particularly adept in this respect. This structure of bays was further reinforced by the practice of piercing openings above the large arcades (big apertures when applied to the tribunes over the central nave, smaller ones when it was merely a matter of providing air for the upper parts of the church) or even blind arcades to adorn a wall that would formerly have been left bare. These same arcades would surround the windows pierced in the walls. So the outcome was a kind of grid: the supports

emphasizing the vertical plane – large arcades, tribunes, triforium and clerestory windows – and cordons, projecting to a lesser or greater degree, accentuating the horizontal.

At the same time as the interior was undergoing such transformation, the outside of the building was also radically modified, in comparison with that of the Carolingian period. Until that time, the preference had been for square or rectangular masses that were juxtaposed rather than fused. On this point, as in so many others, Romanesque architects went back to Roman tradition, in which as much care had been given to the outside as to the inside. The western front of the building was established as the principal façade with broad entry doors for the worshippers. Its twin surmounting spires could be seen from quite a distance, and with its sculptural decoration it served both as symbol and catechism. Inside it was the belfry, and the regular tolling of the bells could be heard from afar, marking the prescribed intervals of religious observance and also, possibly to a greater extent, controlling the everyday affairs of ordinary folk. The belltower soon became synonymous with the church itself. Cluny III, with its six towers, appears to have inaugurated the fashion. These towers were built not only on the façade but also at the crossings of the large and small transepts, and at the ends of the arms of the large

transept. So many towers tended to give the church a spiky effect, and one of the most successful examples of such a structure is Tournai Cathedral. In contrast to these vertical lines, more or less emphatic according to the regions concerned, were horizontal lines, either straight or curved. Here was one of the greatest triumphs of Romanesque architecture – the graduated construction of apses or rounded forms one above the other, culminating in the spire over the crossing.

This overall effect was not immediate and general; it came about as a result of all the various experiments made in the course of the 11th century and the pattern was not finally established more or less everywhere until the 12th century. As always, the different elements tended to be exhibited gradually before they came together to form a coherent picture in the 12th century; they are apparent in a series of contemporary buildings, scattered over Western Europe, but all bearing witness to a newly acquired technical mastery on the part of the architects concerned. The principles which they enshrine characterize the Romanesque world of the 12th century. Having reached a point of perfect equilibrium, the Romanesque place of worship emerges as unique by reason of its subtle arrangement of vertical forms, curves (apse) and rectangles (central nave, side aisles and transept). The unification of all these elements made it possible to build monuments that until the 16th century were to remain the largest in Western Europe (Cluny). In order to obtain such a result, there had to be a meeting between two men: the client, who had got together the necessary money to finance his project, and the architect, who could be relied upon to support the conception. The former was generally an abbot but sometimes an important nobleman, like William the Conqueror; in either case, they would have some interest in architecture. Bernward, who ordered the building of St. Michael of Hildesheim shortly after the year 1000, was, in the words of his biographer, "eminent in scholarship, experienced in painting, excellent in the art and science of casting bronze, as well as in all kinds of architectural enterprises". Aethelwood, an English bishop, was versed in the building and repairing of monasteries; and Berno, bishop of Osnabrück in the 11th century, was "a first-class architect, very skilled in carrying out projects in masonry". There are numerous other examples that could be mentioned in this context, providing further evidence of the key role played by men of the church or nobles in stamping their personality on architecture of the day. Such men possessed the expertise and had a good notion of the technical possibilities available. As for the architect proper, he would seem to have been, despite meagre reference in texts, a man brimming with self-confidence and prepared to tackle all the difficulties involved in stone vaulting. It is certain, however, that the appearance of well cut, well drafted stone, in place of stone broken by hammer, could never have happened had it not been for the progress achieved in other techniques, such as better hardened steel, the technique of centring and the construction of scaffolding.

Thus it was that the classic Romanesque architecture of the end of the 11th century and the 12th century, parting company with that of the first half of the 11th century (truly an age of experiment and discovery), was to hold its own until the day when new ideas were to render it obsolete.

The first Romanesque age

From the end of the 10th century onward, Western Europe was gripped by what amounted to architectural fever. The ruins caused by the Norman and Hungarian invasions had to be restored, and new buildings made available to a rapidly growing population. Lombard masons played an important role in this reconstruction work. Traditionally experienced in the art of building, they were commissioned to carry out numerous projects. Texts refer to the workshops which they set up everywhere and detailed study of monuments makes it possible to trace their presence in Lombardy, Catalonia, Roussillon, Languedoc and Provence, extending up the Rhône valley into Burgundy and beyond as far as the Rhineland. These buildings are characterized by certain common features. The plan is simple, with a nave flanked by side aisles and separated by columns or pillars. It is prolonged by an apse, with half-domed apsidal niches on either side. On the outside, the wall reverts to a principle already observed at Ravenna in 5th century brick architecture. Along the top of the wall runs a line of little arches, supported at regular intervals by slender buttresses or lesenes built from the base: arches and lesenes,

not projecting far from the wall surface, define it and catch the light. A few carefully placed windows are cut into the wall, casting shadows and allowing a little light to penetrate the interior of the building. Apart from these stylistic features, a very obvious technical characteristic is the use of ashlar, broken by hammer and laid flat.

Catalonia offers many examples of this international style. At San Martin of Canigó, consecrated in 1028, the architect covered the two superposed storeys with shallow vaults. A single belltower, with openings that increase in number with height, tends to dominate such churches, one example being San Clemente at Tahull. Abbot Oliva, a very remarkable man who was bishop of Vich and also abbot of San Miguel of Cuxa and Ripoll, proved himself a determined partisan of the new style and left behind him characteristic buildings at all these places.

There are more examples of the architecture of the first Romanesque phase in Burgundy than in Languedoc and Provence. Superb churches bearing witness to this are St. Vorles at Châtillon, St. Martin at Chapaize, and Uchézy. St. Philibert, Tournus, whose dates are still uncertain but which obviously

goes back to before the fire of 1019, displays the peculiarity of combining the Lombard technique, for the external structure and decoration, with local practice in the shape of the huge porch terminated to the west by two belltowers. On the ground floor, strong round piers, crowned by a simple stringcourse, support transverse ribs and groin vaults in the side aisles, and diaphragm arches support transverse barrel vaults in the main vessel of the nave. The result is truly astonishing, the pillars giving majestic definition to an interior brightly illuminated by windows cut high in the walls. The overall effect is of great severity but considerable grandeur, and a touch of colour is provided by the pink stone.

In other regions, as in the Loire valley where stone is easy to cut, the technique is quite different. There are attempts at drafting and experiments in vaulting, initially in the bay in front of the sanctuary. In the north, Notre-Dame, Melun, and the crypt of Étampes exhibit the architectural decadence that characterized the rule of Robert the Pious (beginning of the 11th century). In fact, the architectural revival was to discover its source elsewhere and not in these abortive experiments.

St. Philibert, Tournus, France

Following a fire, Abbot Bernier (1008–28) undertook the reconstruction of the abbey church, this work continuing during the 11th century and early years of the 12th century. The nave was vaulted under the abbacy of Pierre I (1066–1107) and the dome was erected between 1107 and 1120. The pronaos, for which Bernier was responsible, underwent an important change in plan while being built. The adoption of stout bonded pillars as supports for the transverse barrel vaults is repeated in the nave, but on a much less grandiose scale.

St. Vorles, Châtillon-sur-Seine, France

Apparently it was the bishop of Langres, Brun de Roucy, who built the church of St. Vorles, Châtillon-sur-Seine, just before the year 1000, to accommodate the body of the saint. One of the original features of the building is the presence of a western block which accords with Carolingian tradition. The church displays Lombard influence, not only in the interplay outside of bands and blind arcades, but also in the heavy, massive structure of the interior, with no attempt at decoration.

Santa Maria, Barbera, Spain

Santa Maria, Barbera, built at the end of the 11th century and at the beginning of the 12th century, was consecrated between 1116 and 1137. Its plan is simple: a single nave which opens on to a transept and terminates in an apse flanked by two niches. To the north is a tall belltower. The exterior decoration follows the Lombard principle of a blind arcade running along the top of the walls, with lesenes.

San Clemente, Tahull, Spain

The church of San Clemente, famous for the sumptuous painted decoration of its interior before the latter was transferred to the museum of Catalonian art in Barcelona, was consecrated in 1123. The nave and aisles are covered by a single timbered frame resting directly on the outer walls. The gutters of the central nave are carried on masoned columns, without intermediate capitals. The apse is more elaborate, with its blind arcades of superposed arches and its engaged columns. To the south, as an annexe, is the very fine belltower with six levels of openings.

San Paragorio, Noli, Italy

The church of San Paragorio, Noli, built c.1040–60, marks a phase in the evolution of early Romanesque architecture. The nave is still timbered, but the piers adopt a quadrangular plan in response to the large double-tiered arcades. In addition, small niches are hollowed into the walls of the apse. On the outside, the Lombard adornment of blind arcades and lesenes affords a more striking relief, and the bonding is more carefully done.

Santa Maria Maggiore, Lomello, Italy

The church of Santa Maria Maggiore, Lomello, dates from 1025–40. The timbered nave is flanked by bonded piers which support diaphragm arches, on the principle of alternation. In contrast, the side aisles have groin vaults, like the choir and apses. The strongly projecting transept, lower than the nave, breaks the unity of the building. The outside, formed of very sober geometric masses, is decorated with Lombard bands and a blind arcade.

197

France: the vaulted church

The overriding preoccupation of architects of the last third of the 11th century was to extend a covering of stone over the entire building. Until then only those parts with smaller dimensions had been vaulted: apse, aisles and crypt. To construct a vault over more than 10 metres (33 feet) demanded complete mastery of a technique which entailed replacing wooden beams with heavy stone. Vaulting also necessitated thicker walls and stronger supports, as well as exterior buttressing. Towards the end of the 11th century so many buildings of this kind appeared, some of them exhibiting such close similarities, that it is tempting to discover a common link among the churches that culminate in Santiago de Compostela. Thus St. Remi of Reims, St. Martin of Tours, St. Martial of Limoges, Ste. Foy of Conques, St. Sernin of Toulouse and, beyond the Pyrenees, Santiago de Compostela, all possess similar plans and elevations: a nave flanked by side aisles (sometimes double), a transept likewise flanked by side aisles, which sometimes continue to the ends of the arms, and a deep choir surrounded by an ambulatory opening into radiating chapels. The elevation is notable for the presence of very broad tribunes that open on the nave and for the absence of any direct lighting on the central part of the nave. The church is therefore entirely vaulted: semicircular over the nave (lightened by transverse ribs), groins over the side aisles, half-barrel in the tribunes and a half-dome in the apse and chapels. The tribunes make a considerable contribution towards overall equilibrium by shouldering the central nave. The architects concerned have broken up the masses by the positioning at regular intervals of

the transverse ribs that span the vault; these rest on engaged columns ascending from the bottom to incorporate large tribunes and arcades, like a colossal order. The pattern of the interior structure can be traced on the outside; the masses are juxtaposed without fusing, the most spectacular success being the proportions of the apse.

Founder of the biggest monastic empire in Christendom, Cluny embarked in 1088 on the rebuilding of its abbey church, which emerged as the largest building in the Christian world, 130 metres (425 feet) long, rivalling St. Peter's in Rome. The plan was equally grandiose in conception: a pronaos as big as a church, a nave with double side aisles, two transepts each enlarged by orientated chapels and an ambulatory with five radiating chapels. The boldest stroke was to vault these immense masses which soar to a height of 28 metres (92 feet) in the central vessel of the nave: slightly pointed barrels, groins, domes and ringed barrels were all used for the vaulting. Just as audacious was the decision to cut windows in the tops of the walls. Because of its enormous size, Cluny only had a modest impact on other buildings: Paray-le-Monial followed the pattern, but on a more ordinary scale, and there are dull echoes at Autun, Beaune and Langres.

In Burgundy there was a marked preference for another architectural feature, illustrated by the nave of Vézelay. Here the two-level elevation, with direct illumination, was adopted; and the nave was covered by groin vaults. This vaulting has the advantage of dividing the thrusts more effectively, and at the same time facilitates the piercing of windows in the upper part of the elevation. The bay, further-

more, is strongly articulated by engaged columns on piers, which rise up to accommodate very prominent transverse ribs. St. Martin of Autun, St. Lazare of Avallon, Pontaubert and Anzy-le-Duc have the same architectural feature.

In the regions of Poitou, Berry and Saintonge, the hall-church was popular, as in Germany and Spain. The three naves, all of the same height, balanced one another but the central one, by contrast, was not directly lit. The round-arched vaulting of the central nave was either in the form of groins (Notre-Dame-la-Grande at Poitiers, and Chauvigny), in a quarter-circle (Preuilly, Montmorillon and St. Eutrope at Saintes) or even transverse barrels (St. Gontier). However, the churches with a single nave did not follow this rule.

Provence reflects ancient influences, not only in decoration and outline but also in general planning. At St. Gilles du Gard the façade is treated like an antique wall. Masses are, as a rule, fairly simple, the architects showing a clear preference for the single, low, dimly lit nave and a semicircular or polygonal apse. A dome on squinches covers the crossing of the transept, which is higher than the nave. The vaulting generally consists of the pointed barrel and the ribbed semicircle. These geometrically planned buildings are dominated by imposing belltowers.

In the south-west, over an area ranging from Cahors to Saintes and including Périgueux and Angoulême, the dome is common. Set on pendentives, it exerts a vertical thrust which is counterbalanced when the cupolas are in a row. St. Front of Périgueux, St. Étienne of Cahors and the abbey of Souillac are masterpieces of this type.

St. Étienne, Périgueux

The church provides the oldest example of a single nave vaulted by a line of domes, but following later destructions, only two of them survive. The earliest of them, dating to the end of the 11th century, is the western one, massive and squat, supported by strong piers and thick arches. The foundation of the dome (15 metres/50 feet in diameter) rests on high pendentives.

La Madeleine, Vézelay

The present abbey church was rebuilt after the fire of 1120 which ravaged the Carolingian church. Renaud of Semur began the work with the nave, which was completed around 1135–40, continuing with the pronaos, finished about 1150. The Gothic choir was started some time after 1185, and the transept completed in about 1215. The architect adopted a covering of groin vaults, separated by striped transverse arches.

Ste. Foy, Conques

Begun by Abbot Odolric (1030–65), the abbey church was, in fact, completed at the start of the 12th century, being then based on a different plan, especially for the apse, than that originally envisaged. The six-bayed nave with side aisles leads to a large transept, itself bordered by aisles and provided with two chapels on either arm; it terminates in an apse surrounded by an ambulatory with three radiating chapels. The elevation is equally impressive: tribunes open on to the central vessel of the nave through twin bays. They are covered by half-barrel vaults which shoulder those of the nave. The already considerable amount of light is increased still further by the lantern tower of the crossing, whose original dome was replaced in the 14th century by a rib vault.

1 *nave*
2 *transept*
3 *ambulatory*
4 *radiating chapels*
5 *double aisles*

Abbey church of Cluny

Built between 1088 and 1130, the abbey church rivals St. Peter's, Rome, in its architectural scope and its dimensions (187 metres/614 feet). Novelties that appeared in the course of its construction undermined contemporary architectural thinking – especially the 30-metre-high (90 feet) stone covering. The nave, 68 metres (223 feet) long and flanked by double side aisles, was on three levels. At the transept crossing, extending to a height of some 40 metres (130 feet), there was a dome carried by pendentives. After the French Revolution all that survived of the building was the southern arm of the transept.

St. Étienne, Caen

Around 1063, William the Conqueror decided to establish a Benedictine abbey outside Caen. The church was consecrated in 1077. In the 13th century the choir was reconstructed. The elevation of the nave is on three levels, the clerestory windows having been substantially modified, when, in the 1130s, stone vaults replaced the primitive timber framing. The overall clarity of conception is reflected in the façade topped by its two magnificent belltowers with their powerful vertical lines.

Norman church-building in England

Even before the battle of Hastings (1066) and the seizure of the throne by William the Conqueror, Norman architecture had made its mark in England. Edward the Confessor, in fact, had been responsible for building an abbey church at Westminster which adopted the Norman principle, already widespread in that French province, of alternation. The new king and the prelates who accompanied him initiated constructional work, repairing destroyed churches or building new ones (Rochester and Durham). The generally adopted basilical plan was extended eastward either by graduated apses (Canterbury, Lincoln, St. Albans, Rochester, Ely and Durham) or by an ambulatory with radiating chapels (Battle, St. Augustine of Canterbury, Bury St. Edmunds, Winchester, Worcester, Gloucester, Tewkesbury, Chichester and Norwich). All these buildings date from before the year 1100; after this date the flat apse became more general.

The elevation was on three levels: large arcades, tribunes and clerestory windows, in front of which, thanks to the thickness of the walls, there was a continuous passage. Alternating supports are frequently encountered, but this system has no real function because the covering consists of a wooden ceiling. The interior impression of heaviness derives from the considerable thickness of the walls, abetted by the squat proportions, powerful pillars and

semicircular arches. But in contrast to this, the architects obtained a most satisfying rhythmic effect by means of apertures which threw shadows and underlined the horizontal elements of the central nave. One original feature of Romanesque architecture in England is the presence of the lantern tower at the crossing of the transept (Durham, St. Albans, Tewkesbury and Southwell).

English architects were quick to tackle the problems of roofing. As a rule, they retained the wooden framework over the central nave, as at Peterborough, Ramsey, Worksop and Southwell; the stone barrel vault was much rarer (Tower of London, chapter house of Gloucester). They normally confined vaulting to the side aisles, with half-domes over the first and groins over the second aisles. However, they made very early experiments with a new type of covering, the rib vault: the first example of this was at Durham Cathedral in 1096, soon followed by Peterborough in 1118.

The arrangement of the exterior masses did not lack grandeur, in spite of a somewhat squat appearance, like the inside. The lantern towers were sheltered on the outside within rectangular blocks which strongly emphasized the articulation of the roofing (Winchester, Tewkesbury, Durham and Southwell). Sometimes two towers were added on the façade (St. Albans, Norwich and Durham).

This architectural activity, due to the Benedictines, was soon emulated by the Cluniacs and the Cistercians. The former introduced the double transept which they had used at the end of the 11th century for their new church at Cluny (Canterbury and York). It was to become a specific feature of English architecture.

As a reaction against the luxury of the Cluniacs, the Cistercians encouraged a more austere style, with flat apses, no triforium, bare walls and no belltowers. The earliest foundation of the order in England was at Waverley (1128); the nave without side aisles, with a transept and flat apse, was adopted soon afterwards at Tintern (1131). This plan was subsequently replaced by that of the Burgundian abbey of Fontenay: at Rievaulx (1132), Fountains (1135) and Kirkstall (1135). However, in the last two cases the architects, despite official prohibition, retained the central towers. The Cistercians played a not inconsiderable role in the formal evolution of other buildings. The English had a marked preference for heavy structures: at the abbey church of Kirkstall, the Cistercians, in the second half of the 12th century, adopted the clustered pier, which spread elsewhere. At the same time, they were responsible for the increasing use of rib vaulting: this appears in the choir of Kirkstall, pointing the way to a new style – the Gothic.

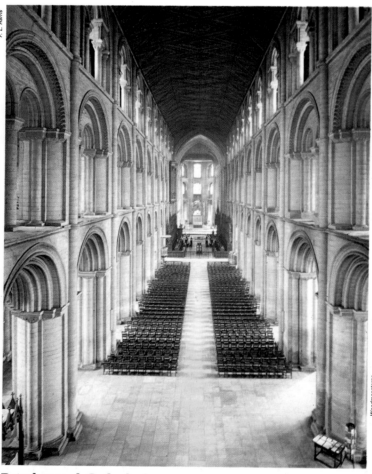

Fountains Abbey

Fountains Abbey, a Cistercian foundation, was established by the Benedictine monks of St. Mary's Abbey in York (1132), to which St. Bernard sent the monk Godfrey. After 1135 they set about building a monastery. It was abandoned in 1539 and then fell into ruin. The plan is typical of Cistercian monasteries, particularly that of Fontenay in Burgundy. The abbey church consisted of a nave with single aisles, a transept on to which opened a number of rectangular chapels, and a flat apse. According to local tradition the crossing of the transept was surmounted by a tower.

Peterborough Cathedral

The ancient abbey church of St. Peter, St. Paul and St. Andrew, Peterborough, was only established as a cathedral in 1541. The monastery was founded by the king of Mercia in 653. After a fire that occurred in 1116, work began on the rebuilding of the church. In 1143 the choir, the transept and two bays of the nave had been completed. In the middle of the 12th century eight bays of the nave were added, and in 1180 two more. Although the work proceeded slowly, a certain unity was achieved. Strongly articulated by the massive piers, by the powerfully moulded arcades of the tribunes and by the clerestory windows with a passage in front, the nave is covered by a painted ceiling.

St. Anselm's crypt, Canterbury Cathedral

The rebuilding of the cathedral coincided with William the Conqueror's occupation of England. Lanfranc, abbot of St. Étienne, Caen, was appointed archbishop in 1070; he quickly embarked on the reconstruction of the cathedral, which was consecrated in 1130. The plan – nave with aisles, transept and choir with three apses – was modified by his successor, St. Anselm (1093–1104), who considerably enlarged the apse.

Hereford Cathedral

The plan adopted at the end of the 11th century for the rebuilding of the cathedral was based on that of Caen: a single-aisled, eight-bayed nave, a transept with a lantern tower over the crossing, and a three-bayed choir with a triple apse. Time proved unkind to the building. The choir has retained its three-level elevation. The massive cylindrical piers of the nave are flanked towards the central vessel by engaged colonnettes.

Castle Acre Priory, Norfolk

Castle Acre was the second priory founded by Cluny in 1090. The priory church originally comprised a single-aisled nave with six bays, a transept with two oriented chapels and a choir with tiered apsidal niches. The façade, built around 1150, is characteristic of Romanesque architecture in England, with its interplay of blind arcades constructed on rigidly horizontal lines.

Tewkesbury Abbey

The abbey church, begun at the very end of the 11th century and consecrated in 1123, was built in Caen stone. The nave, dating from a second building phase, was provided, in the 14th century, with rib vaults to replace the original ceiling. Here, the architect did not aim, as in Gloucester Cathedral, for plastic effects, but allowed the light to flood bare walls. However, the cylindrical piers are less squat.

Gloucester Cathedral

The rebuilding of the abbey church – to become a cathedral in 1540 – was due to the Abbot Serlo, the first Norman abbot. His is also the crypt with its ambulatory and radiating chapels. It extends beneath the eastern part of the church which repeats the same layout. The nave displays the original elevation, except for the rib vaults, which replaced the wooden ceiling in 1242. The squat columns, surmounted by a large torus, support the strongly moulded arcades. Above is a narrow gallery and then the clerestory windows, with a passage in front.

Early appearance of the rib vault: Durham

Durham, more than any other English city, symbolizes, in its castle and cathedral, the full flowering of Romanesque architecture. Both were built in the late 11th and 12th centuries, and they testify to the contribution made by the Normans in both politics and religion. It was the monks of Lindisfarne who, in 995, settled on this horseshoe-shaped strip of rocky terrain. In 1093, the abbey church, from that date a cathedral, was rebuilt on the initiative of William of Calais, who in 1083 had invited the Benedictines of Wearmouth and Jarrow to take over the monastery. The cathedral is enormous, with two towers on the west front, a single-aisled nave, a large transept with a lantern tower over the crossing, a long choir opening into the second transept, and a flat apse. William of Calais did not live to see his project completed for he died three years after work commenced in 1096, but there was no interruption in the building. In 1099 the choir and the transept were finished; in 1104 the relics of St. Cuthbert were solemnly placed in the apse; and in 1133, at the time of the consecration, the nave and

lower parts of the towers were completed. The pronaos was constructed in 1175 and the western towers in 1226. At the beginning of the 13th century, the Romanesque apse was demolished so that it could be extended by a Gothic bay and a second transept completed.

In the nave, with its six bays, a system of alternate supports was adopted. The weak support consists of a thick column with a carved shaft, the strong one of a clustered pier, with the column facing the central nave rising to the level of the springing of the ribs. The elevation is on three levels: large arcades, tribunes and clerestory windows. The technique of thick walls, which accounts for the extraordinary dimensions of the piers, made it possible for a continuous passage to be cut at the height of the clerestory windows. The lines of the bay are thus strongly emphasized by the articulations of the strong piers and by the decoration of the round columns, which seems to lack architectural significance. Nevertheless, there is, at each level, a binary rhythm which gives meaning to the whole building.

Then, too, the thickness of wall lends itself to a wealth of decoration which covers the archivolts and deep apertures, creating a powerful interplay of shadows. English architects have always been highly sensible of plastic effects and here they are particularly in evidence.

Durham's great originality, in the history of Romanesque architecture, is that of being the first large building conceived in terms of stone vaulting. In order to do this, the architect decided to use the rib vault, which, by virtue of its very prominent diagonal arches, could articulate forms better than the groin vault. One of the major achievements of Romanesque architecture was the autonomous bay, and the rib vaulting reinforced that effect. The crown of the vault became the centre of the unified bay. However, although this is certainly so in the side aisles, where each bay is clearly separated from the next by a transverse rib, it is not quite so successful in the main nave, where the transverse rib only spans the strong piers; the intermediate ribs spring somewhat awkwardly from a console.

Durham Cathedral

The rib vault covering of Durham Cathedral is the oldest example that has survived. The plan of the building was Romanesque and the architect decided to adopt this procedure from the first. Between 1093 and 1104 the choir and the apse were similarly vaulted, and subsequently the rest of the cathedral. Plan and elevation nevertheless remain Romanesque, the structure being particularly weighty. The "thick" wall that was traditional in Normandy is pierced by a passage in support of the clerestory windows.

The interior parts of the western towers have retained their Romanesque character as have portions of the nave, the choir and the east and west walls of the main transept. The rest of the outside has many Gothic features.

The cathedral is preceded by a porch or galilee which must have been completed around 1175. On a rectangular plan, the architect built five vessels of four bays, which were most elegantly decorated. The supports, formed of four bonded or false-bedded columns, bear semicircular arcades, adorned with chevron mouldings. The handling of space already looks forward to the Gothic conception.

The central tower, built between 1465 and 1490 in the late perpendicular Gothic style, replaces the original tower, damaged in 1429 by lightning.

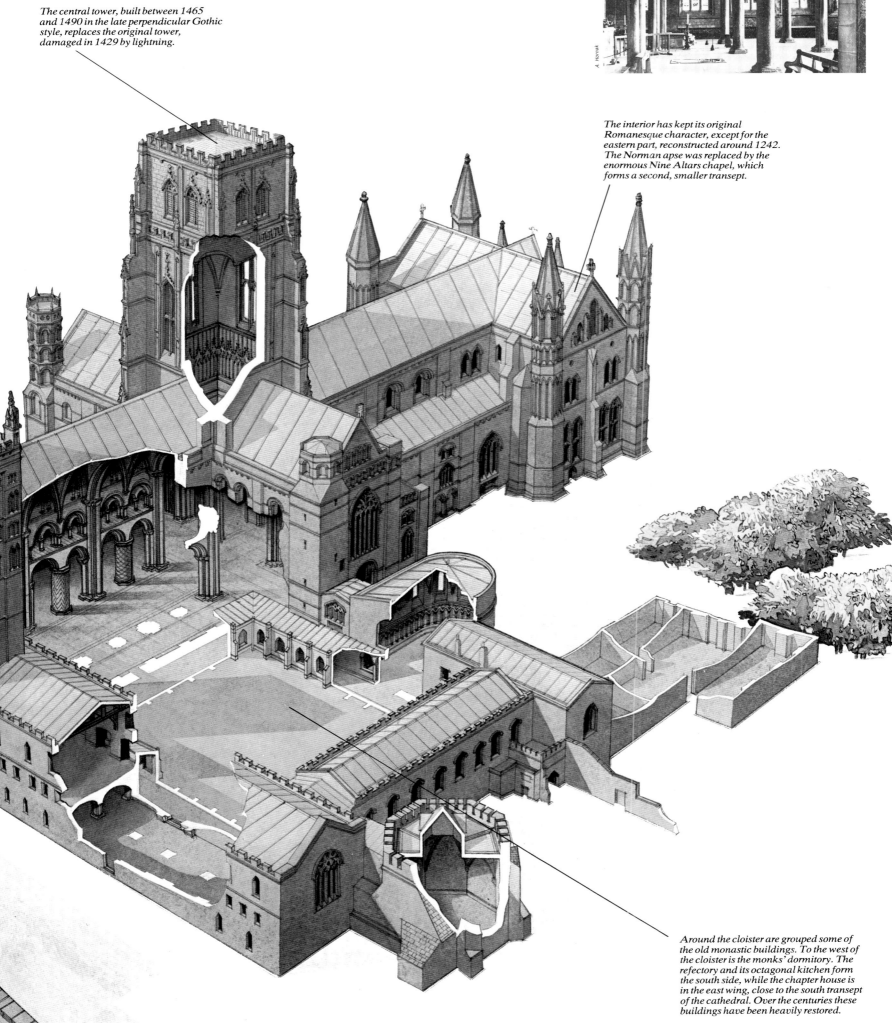

The interior has kept its original Romanesque character, except for the eastern part, reconstructed around 1242. The Norman apse was replaced by the enormous Nine Altars chapel, which forms a second, smaller transept.

Around the cloister are grouped some of the old monastic buildings. To the west of the cloister is the monks' dormitory. The refectory and its octagonal kitchen form the south side, while the chapter house is in the east wing, close to the south transept of the cathedral. Over the centuries these buildings have been heavily restored.

Architectural diversity in Italy

Romanesque architecture in Italy reflects the political structure of that country, split into regions each of which is strongly individualized. Additional factors also colour local styles in varying degrees: the influence of antiquity, the continuity of Byzantine tradition, the impact of the Muslim world and the assimilation, to a lesser or greater extent, of western examples. But the astonishing wealth of building activity that was so marked in France, Spain, England and the Empire was not nearly as evident in Italy.

In the north, Lombardy and neighbouring regions displayed their vitality in the construction of broad naves and the extension of stone vaulting to the entire church. Vaults, however, were heavy, so necessitating sturdy supports. In planning, architects were quick to abandon the ambulatory in favour of enormous crypts. A typical example of this Romanesque vision is Sant' Ambrogio in Milan, a strongly articulated building with strikingly contrasted effects of shadow. The centralized plan, of ancient tradition, appertained everywhere in the case of baptistries (Florence, Pisa, Cremona and Parma), and also in the north, as, for example, in Brescia Cathedral.

In Tuscany, San Miniato of Florence, begun in 1018 and completed at the end of the century, is wholly traditional in its basilical plan. Supporting the ceiling at regular intervals are diaphragm arches resting on engaged pillars which break up the long nave, where horizontal masses remain dominant. The width of the central nave in comparison with the side aisles emphasizes the architect's debt to palaeo-Christian monuments; the conservative instinct is evident in the use of marble columns and capitals. The immense crypt and raised choir bear witness to Carolingian tradition. In contrast, the 12th century front introduced a new element by being divided into tiers and by virtue of its vertical elements: there are already hints here of a new concept.

The architects of Pisa were much more forward-looking, both in terms of the arrangement of the cathedral buildings and also of architectural forms. Belltower, cathedral and baptistry are aligned on an east-west axis. The cathedral adopts the plan of the cross, and there is a remarkable development in the transept, where the crossing is surmounted by an oval dome. The three-level elevation (large arcades springing from columns, tribunes whose arcades rest on pilasters, and clerestory windows) follows horizontal principles, which also underlines the presence of a ceiling. Here again, the palaeo-Christian tradition is very marked, and accentuated by the presence of double side aisles. By contrast, the treatment of the exterior was innovative, with dissembled walls beneath marble slabs: in their decoration and play of colours they lend a very individual rhythm to both sides and façades. The four levels of blind arcades on the main front likewise convey a sense of upward movement which is not suggested by the rest of the building.

The eclecticism to be found in southern Italy is explained by its contacts with the outside world. Here, too, conservative tendencies are seen in the taste for unarticulated flat walls. The nave remained timbered (Monte Cassino, Cefalù, Palermo, Monreale, Bari and Trani). There was more experiment with decoration, with the use of all known techniques for covering the wall or for concealing it. The culmination of this trend is found in the chapel of the royal palace at Palermo.

Colour Library International

St. Mark's, Venice

St. Mark's basilica majestically symbolizes the lagoon and enshrines the city's history. Possession of the saint's relics enabled the Republic to establish its authority, from 828 onward, over Grado and Aquileia. In 1063, under Doge Domenico Contarini, it was decided to rebuild the church on the same Greek cross plan as the previous one. In 1096 it was finished, but the decorative work continued until the beginning of the 19th century. The model had been furnished by the Church of the Holy Apostles in Constantinople (536–46): five domes covering the crossing and each of the arms, supported by large piers linked by arches. The light was thus directed towards the centre of the basilica, leaving the side aisles in comparative shadow.

Monreale

The cloister adjoining the cathedral, built after 1172, is one of the architectural and sculptural masterpieces from the end of the 12th century. The architect adopted the principle of twinned columns and pointed arcades, giving an impression of great lightness. The sculpture of the capitals, done by several artists, shows a number of influences, not the least that of antiquity.

Cefalù Cathedral

Begun in 1131 by Roger II, the cathedral stands at the foot of an enormous rock that dominates the town. The original project, of considerable dimensions, was not executed: around 1160 the nave was built on a more modest scale. It is nevertheless gigantic, 74 metres (242 feet) long, with a colonnade and raised arches. The façade extends sideways, with two towers and a porch, built in 1471, between them.

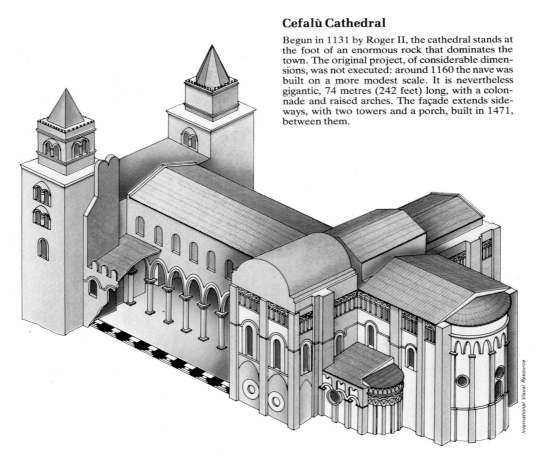

International Visual Resource

Sonia Halliday

C.M. Dixon Photo Resources

Pisa Cathedral

Pisa provides a rare example of a marvellously preserved complex designed on an east-west axis, consisting of belltower, cathedral and baptistry. It reflects the immense prosperity of the city which, in 1063, embarked upon the rebuilding of the cathedral, planned by the local architect Buscheto. The plan is an original one, with a strongly projecting transept terminating in an apse, and the nave and choir both provided with double aisles. The elevation is equally impressive, with its beautiful rhythm of columns supporting arcades and tribunes. The outside is no less elaborate, with a luminous covering of marble. The architect Diotisalvi followed the same decorative principle in 1153 for the baptistry, as did Bonanno for the tower.

St. Nicholas, Bari

The basilica was built in order to accommodate the relics of the bishop-saint. Work started in 1087; the crypt was consecrated in 1089, the cathedral not till 1197. The plan was quite standard, with its nave flanked by groin-vaulted side aisles, and its transept. Two features seem more original: the long, flat façade dominated by two towers, and the enormous dome over the crossing. Unfortunately, as a result of later modifications, the latter is not visible on the outside.

San Miniato, Florence

San Miniato, which dominates the city of Florence, is a Carolingian foundation, restored in 1018 with the assistance of Emperor Henry II. It was renovated in about 1140–50, and the façade was built around 1170. The decoration of the flat façade shows innovative ideas, with its interplay of colours and geometrical designs.

Verona Cathedral

Begun in 1139 and completed in 1187, Verona Cathedral was drastically renovated in the 14th century. With its long bands, it still has a strikingly individual effect.

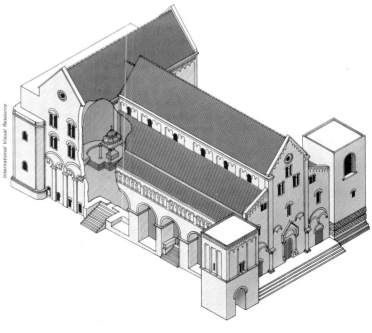

205

Local traditions and French influences in Spain

At the end of the 11th and the beginning of the 12th century, Spain changed course abruptly and adopted a foreign art style. It broke with the strongly implanted local tradition of small buildings constructed with hammer-crushed stones. Such a transformation was the result of fundamental changes, political, economic and religious, as well as artistic. The unconquered Christian states were completely passive, subject to the all-powerful Umayyad caliphate of Cordoba. However, at the beginning of the 11th century, this empire crumbled, and the Christian states took advantage of the situation to make contact with the countries on the other side of the Pyrenees. Cluniac monks played an important role in rescuing the Peninsula from its isolation, encouraging it to renounce its religious traditions in favour of those accepted by the rest of Europe, now influenced by Rome, and for almost a century filling most of the Spanish bishoprics.

Cluny's contribution was even more marked in the area of pilgrimages. The monks managed to draw a group from the north to Santiago de Compostela, and what was formerly a modest place of pilgrimage soon developed into one of the greatest shrines of western Christendom. At the same time, this route, the *camino francés*, emerged as a major commercial artery for northern Spain, widely used by the French. All this led to the decision to rebuild the cathedral of Compostela. The grandiose plan, adopted at the end of the 11th century (1075–78), broke with regional traditions, for it was based upon the pattern established around that time in a number of French churches, such as St. Remi of Reims, St. Martin of Tours, Conques and St. Sernin of Toulouse. The nave, preceded by a pronaos and flanked by side aisles, features 11 bays and leads to a large transept, likewise bordered by aisles, the arms of which are each furnished with two chapels. The semicircular apse is surrounded by an ambulat-

ory with five radiating chapels. The elevation is no less novel, with large tribunes, above high arcades, buttressing the central vessel of the nave. The entire cathedral is vaulted: groins over the side aisles, quarter-circles in the tribunes, flat domes elsewhere. The building, sponsored by Alfonso VI, king of Castile, was too exceptional to set a model for others, which tended to be far simpler and less costly, not requiring the services of the 50 stonecutters employed for the cathedral.

At San Martin at Fromista, at the beginning of the 12th century, the architect was also manifestly inspired by foreign example. The vaulted nave is buttressed by side aisles of virtually equal height; the non-protruding transept, covered by a dome on pendentives, opens on to three successive apses. Although it has been much restored, the church retains a certain elegance by virtue of the beautifully rhythmical arcades of the nave and the shape of the central apse. San Isidoro of León adopts a very similar plan, but a different elevation, with clerestory windows in the central vessel of the nave; outside, the buttresses are in the form of columns. The church at Jaca is notable for its alternation, with a column as the weak support.

After this period, during which Spanish architecture was subservient to French, the 12th century saw an emphasis on regional styles and an expansion of Romanesque art. Catalonia stands out for its use of cut stone but still remains loyal to 11th century traditions: churches with tribunes are rare, and the ambulatory is infrequent, except in the case of San Pedro in Roda. The principal building is the cathedral at Urgel, known to be the work of the architect Peter the Lombard; it has in the apse a gallery of the type common in northern Italy. At San Pedro de Galligans in Gerona, the nave has a barrel vault and the side aisles, lower, quarter-circle vaults. San Andrés of Soreda displays a more origi-

nal feature, with the side aisles covered by transverse barrel vaults.

Western Spain exhibits two types of very different monuments: one group of French inspiration, initiated by kings, bishops and important abbots, the other, more modest, conserving the memories of Mudéjar architecture. The influence of the big churches of the late 11th century is to be seen at San Vicente and San Pedro at Avila. The influence of Santiago de Compostela is to be found in Galicia in the presence of tribunes (cathedrals of Lugo and Tuy), as well as in Portugal (old cathedral of Coïmbra). One group of buildings, with groin vaults, is reminiscent of Vézelay: these include the old cathedral at Salamanca and the cathedral of Zamora, and the relationship is further accentuated by the presence of lantern towers.

In the Sahagún region, by contrast, Mudéjar traditions remain alive. Naves are covered by a decorated ceiling and exhibit horseshoe arches. Many other features are of Muslim origin, like the multifoil arch, used in many portals in Navarre (Cirauqui and Estella). It is also evident in the excessive use of ribs below domes, the function of which is decorative rather than architectonic; examples include the chapel of Torres del Rio, San Miguel church at Almazán, and the Vera Cruz church at Valladolid. Many other Spanish churches possess no less original forms of vaulting, such as the tapered half-dome of San Juan at Rabanera and the rib vaults at the entrance to the choir of San Juan at Duero. The masterpiece is the *cimborio* in the old cathedral of Salamanca: the dome, formed of a series of small arches, rests on pendentives and rises above two levels of bays, relieved by ribs radiating around a crown that rests on columns attached to the masonry by two string-courses. The highly original effect is not very dissimilar from that of Toro.

Outside of the lantern tower, Zamora Cathedral

Begun in 1151, Zamora Cathedral was conceived on a grandiose scale, consisting of a nave leading to a slightly projecting transept and originally terminating in three staggered apses, later replaced by a new apse. Over the transept crossing was a magnificent *cimborio* supported by 16 branches of ribs abutting on a crown and themselves supported by engaged columns with bays cut between them. The interior structure is perfectly visible from the outside.

"Cimborio", old cathedral of Salamanca; Holy Sepulchre of Torres del Rio

Salamanca Cathedral (left) was begun in 1152 on a plan of staggered apses and a projecting transept whose crossing is covered by a *cimborio*, which does not form part of the original concept. The architect was apparently inspired by Zamora Cathedral, but added a second level of bays. Like many churches dedicated to the Holy Sepulchre, that of Torres del Rio is centralized. It has the shape of an octagon, with a semicircular apse and, facing it, a turret with staircase. The church is roofed with a dome supported by multiple arches, based on a plan borrowed from the Muslim world.

Santiago de Compostela

The destination of the best-known pilgrimage of medieval western Christendom, the cathedral of Compostela is a masterpiece of Romanesque architecture, although later additions have made original features hard to detect. Begun in 1078, it was almost complete by 1122. The three great portals, north, south and east, were then in position. The architect, Bernard le Vieux, apparently a Frenchman, adopted the plan of St. Sernin, Toulouse, modifying it by adding a side chapel that does not exist at Toulouse, and a supplementary bay in each arm of the transept.

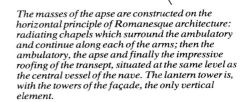

Over the transept crossing is a lantern tower with two levels of bays.

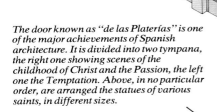

The door known as "de las Platerías" is one of the major achievements of Spanish architecture. It is divided into two tympana, the right one showing scenes of the childhood of Christ and the Passion, the left one the Temptation. Above, in no particular order, are arranged the statues of various saints, in different sizes.

Toro Cathedral

Toro Cathedral adopts the plan of staggered apses with, at the crossing, a dome on pendentives with two levels of bays, the archivolts of which are decorated, both inside and outside, with many-lobed arches. On the outside, it is flanked by four circular skylights, also on two levels.

The masses of the apse are constructed on the horizontal principle of Romanesque architecture: radiating chapels which surround the ambulatory and continue along each of the arms; then the ambulatory, the apse and finally the impressive roofing of the transept, situated at the same level as the central vessel of the nave. The lantern tower is, with the towers of the façade, the only vertical element.

La Seo, Urgel

The apse reflects Lombard influences, notably in the gallery situated above the bays, as is found again at Pavia, Bergamo and Modena. The name of the architect, Raymond the Lombard, is known from a contract of 1175 between the bishop, the canons and himself. He was assisted in his work by four Lombard artisans.

207

Romanesque architecture in Germany: continuing traditions

In the Germanic lands Romanesque architecture is seen in most highly developed form in the Rhine-Moselle region. A number of grandiose buildings, too often maltreated by time and human agency, still evoke memories of the Carolingian era and show hardly any signs of evolution until the mid-13th century. The churches of Trier, Mainz, Maria Laach and Bonn retain the plan of two opposed apses. There is no transept at Trier, but Worms has one transept and Maria Laach, Mainz and Verdun have two. At Speyer, the single transept is particularly large. The trefoil plan, of ancient tradition, is especially developed at Cologne (St. Mary in Capitol, St. Martin, Holy Apostles). The rotunda reappears, or reappeared, in imitation of that of Aix-le-Chapelle, at Ottmarsheim, Liège, Bruges, Louvain and Mettlach. Even so, traditional plans were not ignored. In Cologne, the choir of St. Mary in Capitol is surrounded by an ambulatory. At St. Godard at Hildesheim, there are three additional radiating chapels.

In those buildings where the plan is still traditionally Carolingian, the outside appearance also remains archaic: masses are clumsily combined and there are very marked breaks between rounded forms and those based on right angles. However, the number of towers at the crossing, over the arms of the transept and on the front tend to lighten the overall massive effect: this is evident at Mainz, Maria Laach and Trier. Very often the nave appears merely as an obligatory link between the elaborate western wing and the large apse. This respect for tradition is equally evident in the use of material, with Lombard bands being retained (as at Trier, Cologne and Neuss) until late in the 13th century; and at Maria Laach the architect produced a splendid decorative effect by using stones of different colours. This technique provides variety and individuality to each region, with a mixture of pink, grey or blue sandstone, tufa, trachyte and brick. Reverting to an even older tradition, architects adopted the gallery that ran along the upper part of the wall and opened on the outside in a blind arcade. At Maria Laach, Neuss, Cologne, Trier and Schwarz-rheindorf, this helps to relieve the weighty masses.

The Carolingian conception lingers on inside, in the form of parallelepiped blocks which are clearly demarcated and well separated from one another. At St. Gertrude of Nivelles and at St. Michael of Hildesheim, the roof is a flat ceiling which looks strangely like a lid. In fact, most of these buildings were not vaulted; where they are, it tends to be a later addition or a change of plan in the course of construction. This is the explanation for the very characteristic long walls above large arcades. The side aisles, on the other hand, are generally covered by groin vaults. Alternating supports are sometimes adopted in order to break the monotony, but their rhythm is variable. At St. Peter in Utrecht, the architect reverted to an ancient arrangement of columns. Nevertheless, many architects took care to provide a bay in the central nave: in Cologne, although it is not a feature of St. Mary in Capitol, it makes a striking effect in the church of the Holy Apostles. St. Mary in Capitol, one of the most famous churches, is notable for its impressive choir. It is extremely large and most beautifully and successfully designed. Encircled by an ambulatory which continues along the arms of the transept, it provides the illusion of a centralized plan with the fourth side missing: the square crossing enables the viewer to take in the three apses at a single glance.

Westphalia is interesting architecturally for its output of hall-churches, the first example of which, dating from the beginning of the 11th century, is to be found at St. Bartholomew at Paderborn. In other respects the regional style remains loyal to the Ottonian tradition of a ceiled roof, sometimes replaced at a later date by vaults (Abdinghof church at Paderborn). However, in contrast to the Rhineland, the walls are not articulated, the supports consisting of square slabs of stone. The architects also paid particular attention to the western part of the building. At Paderborn Cathedral it takes on the guise of an enormous square tower flanked by two circular towers containing staircases. Elsewhere, older buildings were modified, as at Corvey and at Minden.

In Lower Saxony, architects turned their skills to the delicate problem of alternating supports, which preoccupied them for two centuries: column-column (Jerichow and Paulinzella); pier-column (Drübeck, Ilsenburg, Bursfelde, Clus and Hecklingen); pier-column-column (St. Michael of Hildesheim). The flat ceiling is the characteristic form of roofing. Even more typical are the western wings, with large, simple masses which often form a screen. At Goslar and at Brunswick, they take on the appearance of long transverse blocks, flanked at either end by a lateral tower. The architect of Havelberg Cathedral simply constructed an enormous rectangular box, the central portion of which emerges at the top.

In southern Westphalia, the southern part of Lower Saxony and to the north of the Alps, there is a vast region where the ceiling is retained as a covering for the central nave, together with the tradition of the smooth wall. The ruined abbey church of Hersfeld and Würzburg Cathedral exhibit these features. The city of Regensburg (Ratisbon), which once rivalled Cologne, preserves many examples of such traditions, the finest being the western transept of St. Emmeran. More curious is the group of so-called "niched buildings": the architectural masterpiece of Regensburg is the chapel of All Saints, situated in the cathedral cloister, where the architect shows himself to have mastered perfectly the technical difficulties of the quadrifoliate plan.

Worms Cathedral

Bishop Conrad II, in 1171, undertook the rebuilding of St. Peter's Cathedral at Worms, while retaining the plan and certain features of the old church. Thanks to the enormously long nave, the emphasis throughout is on the horizontal, although there are three major vertical elements, the apse, the crossing and the western front.

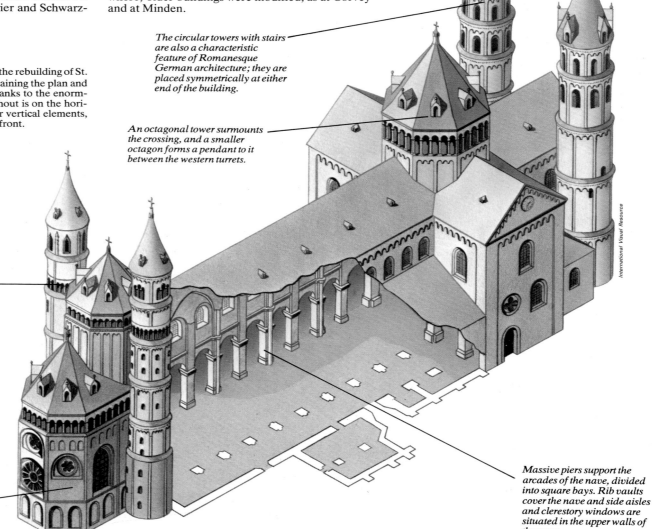

The circular towers with stairs are also a characteristic feature of Romanesque German architecture; they are placed symmetrically at either end of the building.

An octagonal tower surmounts the crossing, and a smaller octagon forms a pendant to it between the western turrets.

An open blind arcade encircles the towers in the Lombard manner, and bands give rhythm to the walls.

The polygonal western apse, begun in 1234, is an addition. It contrasts with the older apse on the east, which is flat. Here, as was the custom, there are apses at either end, which are entered through the side aisles.

Massive piers support the arcades of the nave, divided into square bays. Rib vaults cover the nave and side aisles and clerestory windows are situated in the upper walls of the nave.

St. Michael, Hildesheim

Bishop Bernward (1007–33) was responsible for the building of the church of St. Michael at Hildesheim, which was later severely damaged by fire. It was restored in 1162, the work being finished in 1189 when it was reconsecrated. The plan, in the Carolingian tradition, provides for a double apse with two transepts that are juxtaposed.

Jerichow Church

The church of the Premonstrants, Jerichow, built out of brick some time after 1200, is an astonishingly simple construction. Circular piers are surmounted by cubic capitals with blunt corners, and the large arcades are edged by a sharply groined cordon, an element also found in the transept and apse. The wall, which is undecorated, is pierced by unmoulded clerestory windows.

Maria Laach

The church of Maria Laach has been much affected over the years: begun in 1093 as a result of a gift from the Count Palatine Henry II, it was well advanced by 1152, except for its western portion. In the first third of the 13th century it was vaulted and the "paradise" added. The plan provides for an apse and a western block. The juxtaposed cubic masses underline the existing geometrical pattern.

St. Mary in Capitol, Cologne

The plan of the gigantic church of St. Mary in Capitol comprises a trefoil apse, a nave and a western block, the building of which dates from the start to the middle of the 11th century. The outside is notable for its heavy masses and strong plastic effects.

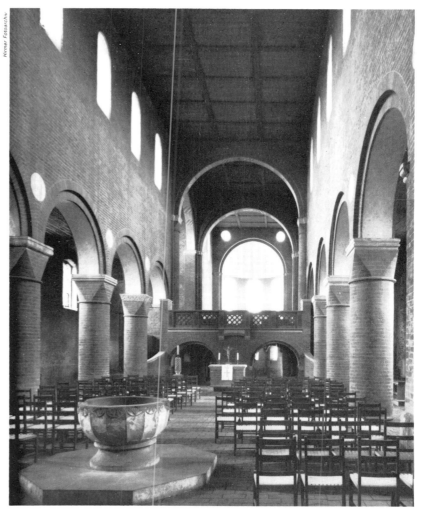

J. Feuillie, Arch. phot. Paris. S.P.A.D.E.M.

Amiens Cathedral

Gothic architecture is defined not only by interior space in which the light filtering through the stained glass plays a particular part, but also by exterior appearance. The masses of the earliest Gothic buildings still remain within the Romanesque tradition, being placed alongside one another without any particular emphasis on vertical elements: St. Denis (1140), Notre-Dame, Paris (1160) and Laon (1160) remain faithful to this principle, and English architects continued to adopt it. Things were different, however, in France after the mid-13th century: the apses of Reims, Beauvais, Amiens and Le Mans pointed out a new path for contemporary architecture. Vertical elements predominated as horizontals vanished behind a mass of pinnacles. Flying buttresses, with their slender lines, reinforced this dynamic effect.

Gothic architecture is without doubt one of the most brilliant inventions of the Western spirit, even though it constitutes a kind of parenthesis in the history of form. Without precedent in the ancient world, it had no successor, even if one takes account of its brief revival during the 19th century. It began to affect Western Europe in the 12th century, spread to the Holy Roman Empire and central Europe the following century, to some extent pushed its way into the countries conquered by the Crusades, and even spread into the Scandinavian countries. Italy alone remained relatively unaffected, pursuing other directions which were to transform architecture more permanently. In some countries, Gothic architecture was to rule for three centuries or more until, at the end of the 16th century, France, England, Spain and the Holy Roman Empire hesitated before adopting the new language of the Renaissance. The remarkable success of Gothic can be explained quite convincingly by practical reasons – better mastered techniques in stonecutting, improved cement bondings, more sophisticated lifting apparatus – but it was also and above all the result of a new perception of symbolic values, leading to the idea that Gothic architecture was better suited than any other style to the Christian religion. This identification was not brought about by chance, but reflects a long evolution of the collective human will. The ribbed vault, which is often pointed to as the characteristic feature of Gothic art, does not give a sufficient idea of the revolutionary transformation which Gothic architecture constituted. It was an invention of Romanesque architects at the end of the 11th century, in response to the difficult problem of roofing their broad naves in stone. It was generally used by Gothic architects – though not always – and contributed to the Gothic style; but it only represents one of the many elements of this new architectural era.

It is a fact of considerable significance that the first Gothic monument – the choir of St. Denis in France, completed in 1143 and consecrated in 1144 – was the work of an abbot who played an important role in France at the time and who was deeply influenced by the philosophical doctrine of Plotinus, to which Christian thought was now adding a new dimension. In the two treatises which allude to his work as a builder, Suger clearly expresses the idea he wanted to carry out – to render immaterial all that is material by means of sanctified light. After a long period of searching for a religious architecture which would answer to an eschatological vision, the Gothic style emerged as the solution. There is no other explanation for this remarkable

development, profoundly bound up with strong religious feeling, which changed Western Europe. The way in which the style endured, though undergoing changes over the course of the years, is exceptional in the history of Christian art. However, we must not forget that the problem solved by these Christian architects had already been encountered by two architects – Isidorus of Miletus and Anthemius of Tralles – many years previously at Hagia Sophia in Constantinople. They had already conceived of the role of light in the definition of architecture, even though this went contrary to the art of their own era.

Architecture can be defined as the treatment of internal space and the manipulation of exterior volumes. In this sense the Gothic style was applied not only to architecture itself, but to all the arts – stained-glass windows, sculpture and church furniture. For the first time in religious art, there was a single style to which everything concerned with church building belonged. In order to appreciate Gothic art now we have to reconstruct imaginatively the true nature of churches as they were in the Middle Ages: the Hundred Years War, the Wars of Religion, the Counter-Reformation, the vandalizing "embellishments" of 18th century canons and various liturgical "reforms" have all profoundly altered their original appearance by removing or transforming their furnishings. Originally, everything in the church combined to produce a single effect. Subsequently there came a breaking point, as each of the techniques employed necessarily pursued its own lines of development. Architecture, stained glass and sculpture together defined the Gothic edifices of the 12th century: the removal of any of these three elements would have been enough to destroy the nature of the monument.

Nevertheless, the Gothic conception, arising from the aspiration of contemporary religious thought, could not have been realized without the technical means required to achieve this extraordinary architectural feat. Viollet-le-Duc, confronted in the middle of the 19th century with the crucial problem of restoring buildings from the Middle Ages, tried to define the Gothic principle as follows: "Everything is a function of constructional requirements, tribune, triforium, pinnacle and gable; there is no architectural form in Gothic art, it is founded on free fantasy." The principle of the ribbed vault is an example of this kind of "functionalism": the ribbed vault is a vault whose groins have been reinforced by ribs which facilitate its construction and, at the same time, lead the thrust of the vault to defined points.

Transverse and lateral ribs complete the structure. The vertical supports have only to be set at certain precise points to receive the thrusts and the wall between them is rendered unnecessary for the bearing of the load. However, the thrust exerted by the vaulting and consequently by the arches and ribs is, because of their curve, not vertical but diagonal. Therefore, to avoid sliding masonry, the Gothic architect at first loaded his buttresses with pinnacles whose weight was calculated in relation to the thrust. Another even more efficient system was invented shortly afterwards: a flying buttress was thrown out in the direction of the thrust and the angle calculated exactly to match the diagonal of the thrust. With these solutions to the problems of load bearing, and the widespread use of the pointed arch, Gothic architects created a style which was dynamic as opposed to the static engineering of the Romanesque period. Walls were no longer structurally necessary, and could now serve simply to enclose the volume, and, in this role, could be replaced without difficulty by a transparent partition which would let in coloured light. Hence the astounding success of stained glass, an essential ingredient in Gothic buildings. From the middle of the 13th century to the mid-16th century, there was a battle between the stone wall and the stained glass "curtain" which resulted in the victory of the latter. When summed up in this way, Viollet-le-Duc's definition may appear tainted by the scientific approach of the 19th century. It applies more to the fully developed architecture of the 13th century, and fails to account for the experimentation of the 12th century. Moreover, it does not explain the new spatial vision of the Gothic architect.

The proportions of the Gothic church differ both from those of early Christian buildings and from those of the Romanesque basilica, since now height is greater than width. At Sens, the ratio between height and width is 1:1.4; at Noyon, it is 1:2; at Chartres, 1:2.6; at Paris, 1:2.75; at Amiens, 1:3 and at Beauvais, 1:3.4; the height of the vault of these churches being 24.4 metres (80 feet), 26 metres (85 feet), 37 metres (120 feet), 35 metres (115 feet), 43 metres (140 feet) and 48 metres (155 feet) respectively. The building gives the impression of soaring upwards, which the pointed arches can only increase. Romanesque architects, concerned with the problem of the roof span, had built their engaged columns right up to the springing of the vault; thanks to ribbed vaulting, their Gothic successors advanced far beyond this hesitant attempt. They extended the vertical pier visually into the vaulting, by continuing it into the diagonal and transverse ribs. Finally, at the beginning of the 13th century, the alternating rhythm of

GOTHIC ARCHITECTURE

the piers of sexpartite vaults was replaced by the uniformity of the identical supports of the quadripartite vault. The nave then appeared to be built of a succession of uniform component elements, along both wall and vault. Further evolution towards even greater refinement took place in the 13th century by a narrowing of the piers and an increase in the height of the aisle arcades. There was a danger that the highly stressed pattern of the vaulting would create a diffuse impression of the interior. Sensitive to this problem, the Gothic architects unified the volume by stressing repetitive horizontal elements – broad arcades, tribunes, triforia and tall windows led the eyes of the congregation towards the choir, whose rounded form closed off the space. Taking this idea even further, the architect tried to merge the various volumes. This was one of the most characteristic inventions of Gothic architecture, one which makes clear its originality in relation to previous periods. Until then, compartmentalization was the rule, each separate section being treated as a volume in its own right – the central nave, the aisles, the transepts, the choir, the chapels and the tribune. Carolingian and Ottonian architects had put this principle to original effect by making clearly defined juxtapositions. Although generally faithful to this tradition, Romanesque architects had to a certain extent reacted against it by building "hall" churches: nave and aisles seemed to merge into one, because in this type of church the aisle vaults rise to the same height as the nave. Gothic architects sought to achieve the same effect by very different means. They raised the nave arcades to the highest possible limit in order to eliminate any division between the aisles and the central nave; they narrowed the supports, and, above all, they learnt to exploit the unifying role of light. The wide windows cut into the aisle-walls, in the clerestory and, from the middle of the 13th century, in the triforium too, diffused the light on three levels without it being obstructed by any heavy stonework. About 1140, the architect of St. Denis had solved this problem in the ambulatory. In spite of the exceptional proportions he had created by dividing it in two, he succeeded in uniting the space of this double ambulatory with the radiating chapels. The use of piers cut en délit (on a diamond rather than square plan), remarkably slender for the weight they have to carry; the small depth of the chapels, encompassed in an undulation of the wall; the addition of an extra diagonal rib to the external ambulatory to cover each chapel; all these devices enabled him to solve this tricky problem. It was further resolved by having two very wide and high windows in each chapel, which allowed the light to filter through to the choir.

The introduction of the transparent partition was of major importance: the new structure of the Gothic bay would have absorbed light and upset the interior space, if it had not been transformed by the delicacy of stained-glass windows. Gothic architects devoted considerable attention to this problem, even if, over the years, they did not come up with identical solutions. In the 12th century and the first half of the 13th, stained-glass windows were extremely rich in colour; after that, grisaille (literally, "grey") glass gradually took over, together with lighter colours and silver sulphide staining. Parallel and even in counterpoint to this development, the technique of split wall construction made it possible to set in front of the window an arch-frame divided from it by a passage, this second frame repeating the pattern of the window proper. Consequently, the passage of light was filtered across this shadow-generating corridor, and through the design of the interior tracery. The perception of light inside the building was transformed by this and at the same time its diffusion was regulated. Gothic architects realized the effects that could be achieved with this arrangement from the middle of

the 13th century. Still at St. Denis, in the choir begun in 1231 and then in the nave, the architect created an amazing effect (in a way which would continue to be developed) by manipulating the way in which the light enters from the clerestory and triforium windows: he placed the windows in two different positions, set out towards the exterior on the middle level and brought back towards the inside wall on the upper level. The resulting visual effect is noteworthy, since the light, whose source seems distant at the first level because of the ambulatories and aisles, becomes stronger at the intermediary level and finds its full strength at the top; the effect of distance is therefore annihilated.

The evolution of the Gothic window over the ages is also instructive. It consisted of the gradual extension of the clerestory window, which, by the late Gothic period, had dropped right down to the top of the main arcades, incorporating the triforium. In the middle of the 13th century, the Sainte Chapelle in Paris marked an important stage: here the architect managed to bring the window right down to the dado arcading of the lower level of the upper chapel. The

Stained glass window in Bourges Cathedral. Around 1390, the duke of Berry had the rose window in the west front of Bourges Cathedral replaced by this magnificent piece of fenestration, henceforth called the *Grand Hous-teau*. It was made by Guy de Dammartin. Two immense lights further divided into three lancet windows support the rose window set in a diamond. Its upper rim is closed in, decorated with a pattern of trefoils on the outside; round the rest of the window the quatrefoils are perforated. The extremely ingenious filling out of the area with tracery recalls the early Gothic style, whereas many contemporary constructions by this architect were already in the Flamboyant style.

211

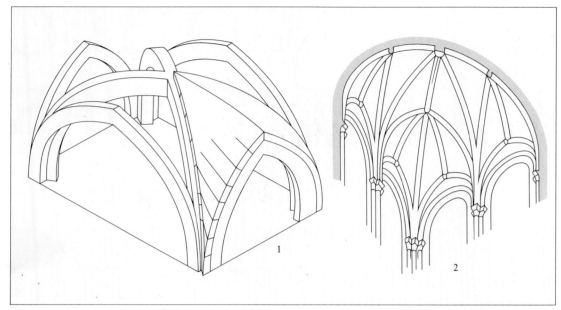

Vaults. The success of ribbed vaulting was due partly to its greater ease of construction compared to Romanesque vaults. The difference lay in using the diagonal arch round which the elements of the vault were built, rather than the arches round the sides. When the principle had been perfectly mastered the groins and the ribs were built separately. The result was an overall elasticity, and the movements of the two independent masses of stone no longer had awkward consequences. The vault could be reduced to a single, thin veil of little weight (1). The "Angevin" vault is given as an example because it combines classic ribbed vaulting with a dome, from which it takes its raised shape. The ribs play no constructive part, but have become a stylistically essential element of roofing (2). (From A. Choisy, *Histoire de l'architecture*, Vol. II, Vincent, Fréal et Cie., Paris, 1955.)

size of the glass "curtain" is such that the spectator has difficulty in assessing the exact dimensions of the pillars, which jut out by more than a metre into the interior of the building.

Another important feature of Gothic development was the transepts – not that they had been neglected before, but from now on they had a particular significance. Most churches, though not all, had transepts – a sort of counter-nave at right angles to the nave and of the same height. From the middle of the 13th century they were given their own light, through the presence of a rose window at the top of the wall. This was extended underneath by a perforated triforium, aligned with the triforia of choir and nave. Handled in this

way, the transepts no longer seemed to be a separate volume juxtaposed to the volumes of the nave and choir, forming a barrier between the two, but became incorporated in the whole.

The same effort to integrate volumes was made in the case of the west front, or façade, and the entrance to the nave. The general adoption of the Norman front with its two towers always posed difficult problems at the junction of the vault under the belltower with that of the nave. Romanesque architects had overcome the difficulty by building a narthex beyond the nave, of no real liturgical necessity. It had the advantage of enclosing the east piers of the towers which would otherwise have marred the lines of the nave. In 1140 at St. Denis, the

architect could find no other way of solving the problem than by building a narthex in the traditional way. His successors at Laon and Paris did away with it, but without sorting out the problem of the bulky piers. At Reims an answer was finally found: the piers are barely any thicker, so as to merge in, and the first bay has vaults of the same height as the rest; the homogeneity of the interior space is at last perfected.

From the outside, the silhouette of a Gothic church is no less original. The Gothic architects preferred a certain amount of movement rather than the static and well-ordered forms of the Romanesque edifice. Vertical lines dominate over horizontal, as in the interior. The effect is achieved primarily by the height given to the towers and spires; in this the Gothic architect adhered to a Romanesque tradition strongly asserted in the Holy Roman Empire and even in France (Tournai). Laon cathedral is a good example, especially since in addition to the five existing towers two more were planned for the east arms of the transepts. At Chartres, eight or even nine towers were planned; at Reims, six. However, this idea, still impregnated with memories of the past, was abandoned early on, in the first 30 years of the 13th century; the four transept towers at Chartres were left incomplete and the same applies to Reims a little later. The cathedrals of Paris and Bourges were forerunners of the new approach. The architect of the former, which was begun in 1160, planned only two towers on the west front, and the spires were never built. The absence of transepts in Reims cathedral, built at the very end of the 12th century, eliminated the towers usual at either end of it. Whereas the vertical element began to disappear in favour of a single, unified façade, another element was emerging – the flying buttress. Indispensable for counter-balancing the thrust of the vaults, from the beginning of the 13th century it became a stylistic feature in the external design of the building. Sometimes sent up beyond the level of the double aisles or ambulatories, the flying buttress joined together the varying levels of the building by the repetition of its diagonals over each vault. The resulting tension set up between the vertical buttresses built on the outside of each bay and these diagonals is staggering. The dynamic quality transmitted to the whole building by this repetitive effect is carried through from earth to sky and often culminates in a spire placed at the junction of the nave and transept roofs. Furthermore, this ascending movement is accentuated by pinnacles, which give some chevets a spiky look; the cathedrals of Le Mans and Beauvais offer the most remarkable examples.

Buttressing. The flying buttress was an essential element in Gothic architecture, serving to guide the diagonal thrust of the vaults to a specific point, the buttress proper. The difficulty lay in establishing the exact location of the thrust, and the architects of the Middle Ages were constantly experimenting. Another difficulty arose when it became necessary to project a flying buttress over a building with several aisles. The architect had to plan intermediary stops for the flying buttress projecting at right angles to the nave and another flying buttress to counteract the thrust of the inner aisle. (From A. Choisy, *Histoire de l'architecture*, Vol. II, Vincent, Fréal et Cie., Paris, 1955.)

However, although its broad characteristics may be quite simply defined, the long life of Gothic architecture, as well as its wide diffusion, produced important variations in the course of its evolution. This evolution was not identical in every country; it advanced in several stages which reflect deeper changes as well as formal updating. The Gothic revolution affected not only architecture, but all the arts. At the same time, the style born in the heart of the church extended to the art of building in general: military and civil architecture absorbed the principles of Gothic architecture on a small scale and without the same drive. At the end of the 15th century, Western Europe knew only one language, the Gothic language, which, however, was shortly to be supplanted.

Chartres Cathedral

Beauvais Cathedral

Poitiers Cathedral

Church of the Jacobins, Toulouse

Axonometric drawings. The ribbed vault and flying buttress helped to solve the tricky problems caused by thrust and enabled windows to be built in the outside walls. At the end of the 12th century in Chartres Cathedral, the system had already been perfectly mastered, but remained sober. Thirty years later at Beauvais, the architect pushed the technical possibilities to their limits. At Poitiers, the problem of counter-balancing the nave was solved by building the aisles to the same height. In the Church of the Jacobins, Toulouse, the ribs sprang audaciously from a row of central piers, so as to cancel out the thrust. (From A. Choisy, *Histoire de l'architecture*, Vol. II, Vincent, Fréal et Cie., Paris, 1955.)

Early Gothic in France

The period from 1130 to 1190 is one of the most exciting in the history of architecture: highly talented architects were confusedly aware of the potential of a new technique of vaulting linked to a new style. Experiments of all kinds bear witness to this at every decade. Two buildings opened the way in two different directions which, in the end, proved to be opposed: Sens Cathedral and the abbey church of St. Denis. The former, planned by Bishop Henri Sanglier (from 1130), adhered to the Romanesque tradition, with its enormous nave without transepts, an ambulatory (seemingly) without radiating chapels, and a three-tiered elevation – arcade, triforium, clerestory – and sexpartite vaulting. The main piers are remarkably solid in effect, whereas the secondary piers are divided into two slender columns, surmounted by magnificent capitals beneath the same abacus. The ribbed vaulting, which is 25 metres (80 feet) high over a width of 15 metres (50 feet), springs from very low. The delicacy of the chancel of St. Denis, completed in 1143 and consecrated in 1144, is in marked contrast to the chancel of Sens Cathedral and to its own crossing, completed in 1140 still under the influence of the Anglo-Norman style. For the chancel, the help of a new architect was sought, and he produced a design of prodigious delicacy both in plan, with seven radiating chapels opening onto a double ambulatory, and in elevation. The use of piers *en délit* (in diamond plan) gives the supports a greater lightness as well as facilitating the flow of air and circulation of light.

In the 1150s, experiments were no less revolutionary. At St. Germain-des-Prés in Paris, the architect opted for an elevation in three tiers in the choir, free-standing cylindrical piers and highly individual radiating chapels leading off the ambulatory. At Senlis Cathedral, which has no transepts, the elevation is also in three tiers with large triforia and strongly emphasized alternation of piers; the

radiating chapels are quite compact. Noyon Cathedral is the first of a series of large buildings whose initial plan is not known for certain because of the degree of modification undergone during construction. The choir, with its elevation in four tiers, was the forerunner of a design which would be used until the end of the century. Its main characteristics are alternating supports, triforia opening onto the central nave, then blind arcades, then clerestory; the horizontal divisions are formed by cordons which run across the columns as though attaching them to the wall. The transepts are of the next decade and introduced a new feeling to the building: the arms are rounded, lit by windows on three different levels, and the walls are hollowed out in linking passages. The effect obtained by the wave of light that flows in is that of making the very thick walls appear to be mere partitions. The whole is a kind of architecture of illusion.

The generation active in the 1160s, having already shown its colours with the transepts of Noyon, was even more audacious in the building of two more huge edifices – the cathedrals of Laon and Paris. The former is important for the development of the transepts, with a lantern tower at the crossing, aisles under a gallery and a two-storey chapel in each arm. The elevation remains in four tiers and the vaulting is still sexpartite. However, for the first time, the architect gave up the principle of alternating supports, at least in the western nave, in favour of cylindrical columns. The very large galleries open onto the central nave through twin arches in each bay. Above this runs a triforium hiding the walls which, with the help of the galleries, support the nave vaulting, which soars up to 25 metres (80 feet). The genius of Laon's architect is apparent in his "Baroque-style" experiments in the violent contrasts of light and shade and in the powerfully articulated wall areas. The Parisian plan shows a marked contrast to these experiments in the clarity

of its design, the simplicity of its elevation and the refusal to exploit the walls. The design consists of a double aisle which continues, without the interruption of transepts, into a double ambulatory with no radiating chapels. The elevation is in four tiers, the third of which consists of rose windows serving to open up the clerestory. As at Laon, alternating piers have disappeared in favour of cylindrical columns, except between the two aisles, where 12 shafts ring every other column. Notre-Dame, Paris differs both in its flat elevation and in its stress on horizontals, inside as well as outside. Indeed, the silhouettes of these two great buildings are entirely different.

In the early 1170s, the new but now assured style began to conquer neighbouring regions. First in Champagne, St. Quiriace, Provins received an octopartite vaulting over the chancel. At St. Remi in Reims, where the abbot, Pierre de Celle, was in charge of the reconstruction of his church, the elevation was in the traditional four tiers, but the architect increased the number of windows and closely tied the clerestory level to that of the triforium by letting down to it linking columns framing the windows. At the entrance to the circular radiating chapels, he placed two small piers *en délit* of unusual elegance; at the same time, he made a passage beneath the sills of the windows in the walls of the chapels in order to emphasize the lightness of the structure. Notre-Dame-en-Vaux in Châlons-sur-Marne and the south transept of Soissons Cathedral continued this line of refined experiments, where the wall is excavated away in perforated stonework. The trend reached Burgundy; the choir of Vézelay, with its three-tiered elevation, is extremely beautiful; the removal of the partitions between the radiating chapels, above a certain level, permits free circulation of the air. Normandy was conquered: the nave at Lisieux reproduced the Laon plan in an elevation of three tiers.

Abbey church of St. Denis

The crypt and ground levels are the only remaining parts of the church built by Abbot Suger between 1140 and 1143 and consecrated in 1144; the upper part was rebuilt in the mid-13th century. We do not know how the choir originally terminated, although it probably did not have a triforium. On the foundation of a traditionally styled crypt, the architect built an exterior wall of undulating plan and placed a buttress between each apsidiole, leaving himself free to open out large bay windows in the apsidioles.

St. Etienne Cathedral, Sens

Sens Cathedral, one of the most original buildings of early Gothic art, was probably built slightly earlier than St. Denis. The elevation is in three tiers with very high nave arcades, in contrast to the small triforium and clerestory (enlarged in the 13th century when the vault was raised). The vaults, which were originally deeply curved, with a better balance, are sexpartite, and spring from a "strong" pier of 16 shafts alternating with a "weak" pier of twin columns.

St. Germain-des-Prés, Paris

The chancel of the abbey church of St. Germain-des-Prés was completed well before 1163, when the altars were consecrated by Pope Alexander III. The elevation is in three tiers, the two upper levels having been altered in the 17th century when the clerestory was lowered. One of the special features of the building is its cylindrical columns surmounted by superb capitals. Contrary to the principle of St. Denis, the architect has favoured each of the volumes equally without attempting to merge them into a whole.

Notre-Dame Cathedral, Laon

Laon Cathedral was begun at the same time as Notre-Dame in Paris, but based on a very different conception. Luminous, where Notre-Dame in Paris is dark, it exhibits a certain mannerism in its very distinctive wall decoration. The effect is striking in the highly sculpted façade which allows the shadows to play freely. Its external appearance, with its towers, two of which were not built, still harks back to Romanesque themes.

Notre-Dame Cathedral, Noyon

Work on Noyon Cathedral, begun in 1145–1150 at the chancel, continued around 1170 at the transepts and around 1180 in the last section of the nave. This cathedral is one of the major constructions of early Gothic art. The architect rounded off the transept arms, which he gave three tiers of windows, making a passage in front of them on the first two levels and behind them on the third. He also lowered the triforium: this is architecture in the service of light.

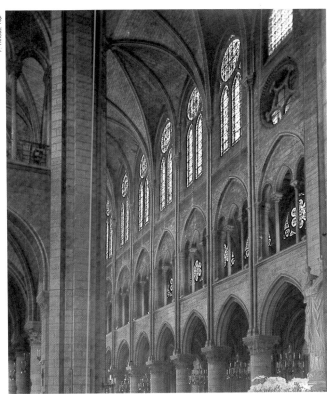

Notre-Dame Cathedral, Paris

Notre-Dame in Paris differs markedly from its contemporary namesake in Laon. It fails in comparison as far as lighting is concerned, for, despite the windows having been enlarged in the 13th century to the detriment of the rose window, it is a dim church. Although it has sexpartite roofing which should have alternating supports, the cylindrical column is repeated in a regular pattern in the nave and the choir.

Chartres and Bourges

After 1190, a kind of architectural exhaustion becomes noticeable in the Île-de-France, following the advances made in the preceding period in supports, openings and walls. Two major edifices built in the last decade of the century would give renewed vigour and spirit to Gothic architecture: the first, Chartres, has enjoyed fame due to its incredible simplicity; the second, Bourges, has never been repeated because its design was too original to be reproduced elsewhere. They both feature a complete mastery of a technique of which the full potential had at last been realized – the flying buttress. In the great Romanesque and earliest Gothic buildings, the nave was buttressed by the gallery, but beneath the roofs of the aisles, there were other arches serving the same purpose. At some point, an architect was bold enough to bring this supporting structure out of the roofing. In 1180, the architect of Notre-Dame in Paris, who was modifying the plans for the nave, planned buttresses from the ground level, but still retained the gallery though it was now redundant, in fact, doomed; future architects did not make this mistake. At the same time, they stopped using sexpartite vaulting in favour of quadripartite vaulting, and this allowed them to do away with alternating piers. A tendency towards uniformity, which was already apparent in Notre-Dame, Paris, would become the norm.

At Chartres, the plan presents a number of characteristic traits. The nave is bordered by one single aisle which is extended into the transepts, while the choir is surrounded by a double ambulatory opening onto five radiating chapels. As at Paris, the transept is midway between the choir and the front. This desire for regularity can also be seen in the elevation where the nave arcades and the clerestory are noticeably of the same height. The rhythm given to the nave is achieved by the alternating piers, though the sensation is purely visual: a column flanked by four straight-sided piers is followed by a straight-sided pier flanked by four columns. The articulation on each bay is strongly delineated by the bundles of colonnettes which rise to the springing of the transverse, diagonal and lateral ribs, but it is tempered by the horizontal line of the continuous triforium and by the two cordons which form a projection on the colonnettes. The architect succeeded in finding a happy balance by means of the precision of his proportions, which eschew the gigantic. However, the vaults rise to 37 metres (120 feet) whereas those at Notre-Dame, Paris are only 30 metres (100 feet) high. The quality of the mouldings and the magnificent geometry of the design add even more grandeur to the building. The exterior is no less majestic, with an immense transept cutting at right angles across the nave and a fabulous play of flying buttresses. Two superimposed arches are linked by an open arcade, then surmounted by a third even higher up, to dampen the force of the high winds in the Beauce region.

Bourges Cathedral, begun in 1195, reflects a different approach in Gothic architecture, first in its design, since the double aisles extend without interruption to the ambulatory, from which five small radiating chapels open out; secondly in the absence of transepts, since the architect wanted to emphasize the lengthening effect on the interior as well as the exterior; thirdly in its elevation, which is pyramid-shaped – nave vaults 38 metres (125 feet), inner aisle vaults 21 metres (70 feet), outer aisle vaults 9 metres (30 feet) high. In order to reach such heights, the engineer of Bourges had to raise the piers of the nave to a height of 17 metres (55 feet); this enabled him to set the nave arcades even higher and to broaden the openings between the nave and the inner aisle. Thus he managed to make the various sections of the building interpenetrate. The elevation of the nave and the inner aisle is in three tiers, although the architect remained faithful to sexpartite vaulting. Nonetheless, there is no alternation in the piers, which all consist of a single column with eight engaged shafts, except at the upper level where there are five shafts at the springing of the transverse rib, otherwise three. As in early Gothic architecture, the architect also seems to have hesitated between emphasis of the verticals of the bay and horizontals. The outside of the cathedral is just as spectacular. Behind a huge front with five doorways, an immense roof stretches back to cover the structure right up to the sanctuary. The various masses are tiered one above the other regularly; but this horizontal stress, foreign to the Gothic tradition, is tempered by the extraordinary thrust of the flying buttresses which soar from the exterior buttresses up to the clerestory. The ideas of the master-builder of Bourges were too personal to be followed. The choirs in the cathedrals of Le Mans, Coutances, Burgos or Toledo retained only their dim echo.

Bourges Cathedral

In 1195, the master mason of Bourges designed an extraordinary building, but his plans were not entirely followed. Above the crypt which allowed him to make up the difference in level between the floor and foundations, he built a choir to which five chapels were added that had not been planned originally, attached to the buttresses. These chapels enabled the architect to amplify the window surface considerably. In the chevet, the balance of the masses sticks to Romanesque traditions: the three volumes of the first and second ambulatories and of the choir are clearly defined. The buttresses and their pinnacles create a strongly opposed vertical line with flying buttresses taking up the momentum: the first line of these is on the second aisle; the second, with two arcs, is on the choir. They impart to the building a very distinctive dynamic.

The richly decorated north spire, added in 1507 in the Flamboyant style, forms a contrast to the austerity of the tower it stands on and to the quiet elegance of the south spire.

The south spire dates from the 12th century. A beautifully simple octagon ensured the transition from the square tower to the spire.

The west façade with its royal portal survived when the church was destroyed by fire in 1194.

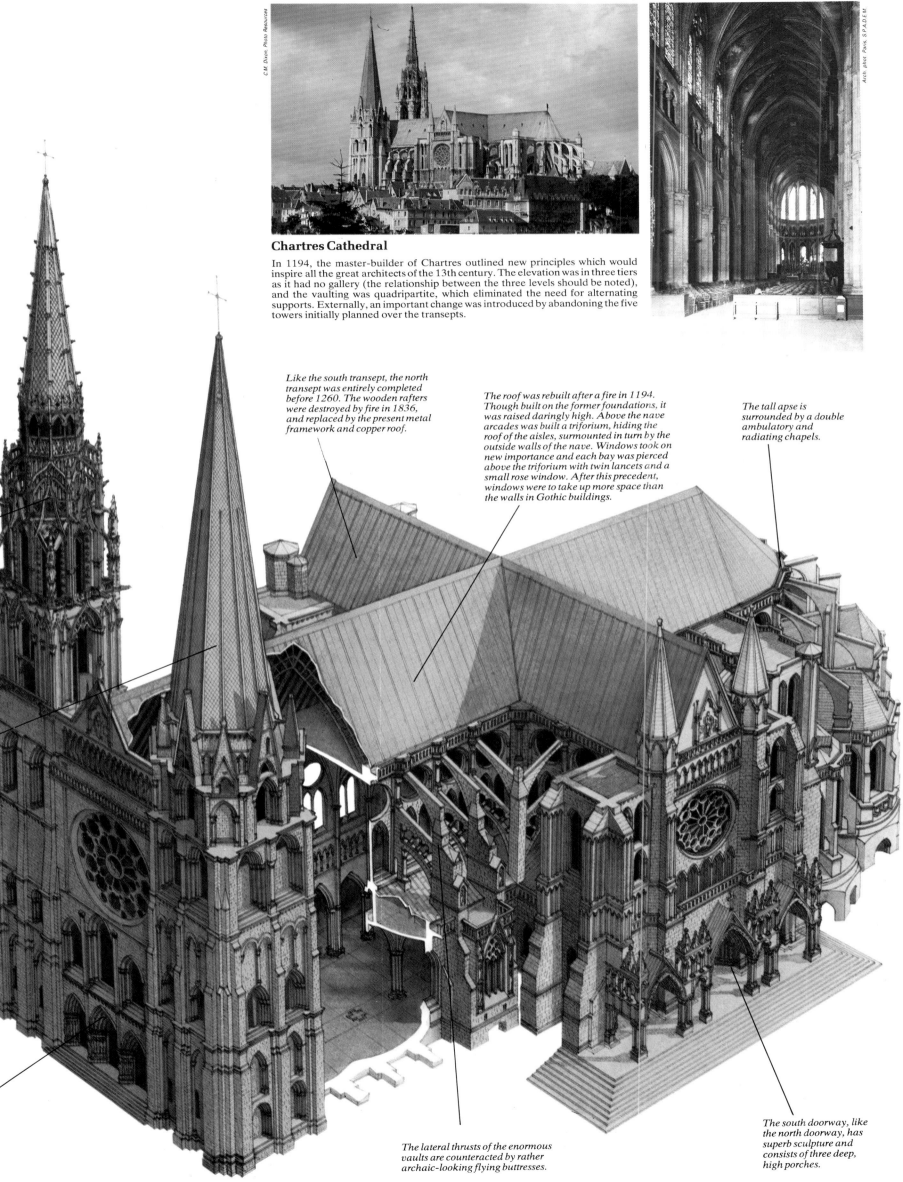

Chartres Cathedral

In 1194, the master-builder of Chartres outlined new principles which would inspire all the great architects of the 13th century. The elevation was in three tiers as it had no gallery (the relationship between the three levels should be noted), and the vaulting was quadripartite, which eliminated the need for alternating supports. Externally, an important change was introduced by abandoning the five towers initially planned over the transepts.

Like the south transept, the north transept was entirely completed before 1260. The wooden rafters were destroyed by fire in 1836, and replaced by the present metal framework and copper roof.

The roof was rebuilt after a fire in 1194. Though built on the former foundations, it was raised daringly high. Above the nave arcades was built a triforium, hiding the roof of the aisles, surmounted in turn by the outside walls of the nave. Windows took on new importance and each bay was pierced above the triforium with twin lancets and a small rose window. After this precedent, windows were to take up more space than the walls in Gothic buildings.

The tall apse is surrounded by a double ambulatory and radiating chapels.

The lateral thrusts of the enormous vaults are counteracted by rather archaic-looking flying buttresses.

The south doorway, like the north doorway, has superb sculpture and consists of three deep, high porches.

217

Three 13th century French cathedrals

Chartres Cathedral set a trend which the architects of the first 30 years of the 13th century followed, with modifications, at Soissons, Reims, Beauvais and Amiens. Here the language is more or less the same and the variations between these buildings are less than those between the constructions of the early Gothic period. However, in order to reach the dizziest heights, each architect brought in individual solutions, refining the treatment already prescribed by a pre-established model. Soissons Cathedral, which must date back to 1197–1198, and the cathedrals of Reims, Amiens and Beauvais, begun in 1211, 1220 and 1235 respectively, were the main landmarks of this period. The influence of Chartres can be seen in the elevation on three tiers, in the shape of the piers – a column surrounded by four smaller engaged pillars – in the triforium which runs all round the building, in the double lancet windows surmounted by a rose window and in the quadripartite vaulting. Furthermore, the unit of the bay is strongly emphasized by the engaged columns which meet the spring of the vault, and the feeling for plasticity is increased. On the outside, the front with two towers retains its prestige and flying buttresses of two flights are adopted.

However, the architects brought new elements into their constructions which distinguished them from Chartres and led them inevitably towards a new perception of interior volume. The first sign of this was in the supports for the nave arcades. At Reims, the decoration of the capital extends onto the shafts, creating a horizontal interrupted only by the nave arcades. At Amiens, the shafts towards the nave are interrupted only by a narrow projecting band. Beauvais Cathedral is fairly similar. The major differences lie in the treatment of light: Beauvais marks an important advance over Reims, since the triforium is no longer blind, but perforated. This device was taken up on a large scale in the chancel of Amiens. Against this, Reims Cathedral featured a new kind of window which was no longer perforated but built on a stone armature. The heights of the vaults are more impressive: 38 metres (125 feet) at Reims, 43 metres (140 feet) at Amiens; the 48 metres (155 feet) of Beauvais set a limit to this desire to conquer space. The interior volume was modified both by the relation between height and width and by the infiltration of light. By building his chancel 48 metres (155 feet) high, with the aisles 20 metres (65 feet) high, and by opening up the triforium, the architect of Beauvais organized the interior space in an individual fashion. The areas of shade at Chartres, Orbais, Reims and St. Quentin are restful to the eye; the pierced triforium assists its upward movement; the connection between the two upper tiers, initially only visual, later materialized when the colonnettes and mullions of the windows descended right down to the sill of the triforium. The Chartres conception based on the balance of light and shade was broken at Beauvais in favour of a dynamic style whose potential was soon grasped by the architects of the High Gothic period.

The evolution of the exterior of the buildings was equally significant. The horizontal and vertical divisions at Laon and Paris dominated the façade; now they were tending to merge. At Reims, the gables are so overpowering that the central one even blocks off the rose window. The only horizontal is relegated to the top level where the towers begin. At ground level, five gables of descending height blur the horizontal lines. Amiens Cathedral is more sober in style, at least on first impression, but on analysis some strange features emerge. The verticals of the buttresses are strongly emphasized, but they recede at each level. Nevertheless, they soar up, interrupting the horizontals of the arcade and of the kings' gallery. At ground level, three immense porches seem to reach right into the interior of the cathedral. The initial outline of horizontals and verticals disappears in the confusion.

The treatment of the apse and aisles is governed by the same tension between verticals and horizontals. At Chartres, an equilibrium had been maintained between the varying heights of the rooftops, united by the flying buttresses and the powerful verticals of the towers. At Reims, the balance is destroyed by the raised roofs of the choir and the spiky pinnacles. At Amiens, the rupture between ground level and the upper sections is confirmed on the outside in the varied spacing of the pinnacles necessary to provide a view of the chevet. The flying buttresses are loaded with a display of arcades which make a contrast with their diagonal lines. Beauvais Cathedral keeps to the Reims tradition, retaining gracefully formed pinnacles.

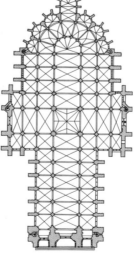

Beauvais Cathedral

The cathedral of St. Pierre, Beauvais, begun in 1235, was never completed in spite of the work being taken up again in the 16th century. The choir and the east transept are the only parts belonging to the 13th century. A terrible disaster whose causes have never really been ascertained befell the high vaults above the choir, which collapsed in 1284. Intermediary piers then had to be raised in order to receive the new sexpartite vaults. The architect had in fact pushed his daring too far by building the choir vaults 48 metres (155 feet) high and the ambulatory vaults 20 metres (65 feet) high.

Amiens Cathedral

The cathedral of Notre-Dame, Amiens was begun in 1220 with the nave, followed by the transepts and finally the choir, of which the upper sections were completed in 1269. Meanwhile, in 1236, the west façade was built following a changed design. The sheer size of the building was achieved by the extraordinary height of the nave arcades. The vaults are 43 metres (140 feet) high and the cathedral is 150 metres (490 feet) long. The plan is very similar to that of Reims, but the chevet is different, with seven radiating chapels, the axial chapel being prominent. An important development is apparent when comparing the triforium of the nave, which is dark, with the triforium of the choir, which was built later and is lighter. Gothic architecture was entering a new phase, marked by close liaison between the two upper tiers.

Reims Cathedral

Work on the cathedral of Notre-Dame, Reims, begun in 1211, did not proceed unhindered: in 1233 it was temporarily interrupted by a revolt. Building began at the choir, which was not roofed until 1241. This long period explains the differences to be detected behind a façade of apparent unity. The plan underwent many changes, first on the exterior, since, as at Chartres, seven towers had been planned – two on the front, two on either arm of the transepts and one on the crossing; only the two west towers were built. The elevation is based on Chartres: three tiers with a continuous blind triforium, and a clerestory which, though not identical, is similar. Its forms are much lighter thanks to very elegant mouldings and to a new type of decoration, notably in the capitals, which contrasts with the severity of Chartres. To this is added a perfect sense of balance and skilful juggling of proportions which makes Reims Cathedral the most classic building of Gothic architecture in France.

The plan is grandiose, with a nave bordered by single aisles. The nave consists of nine bays which open onto a particularly developed transept of three bays bordered by double aisles. These double aisles run beside the bays of the choir before reducing down to a single ambulatory from which open five radiating chapels, the axial one being slightly more prominent. The vaults of the nave, 38 metres (125 feet) high, are quadripartite and have remarkable decorated bosses.

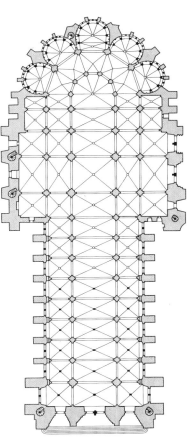

The originality of English Gothic

In spite of its precocious use of ribbed vaulting, England discovered Gothic architecture relatively late. It was introduced by Cistercian art and by a single French architect. The Cistercian abbeys of Roche and Furness can hardly conceal their Continental origins. After the fire in Canterbury Cathedral in 1176, a French architect, Guillaume of Sens, was brought in, and he introduced the new style of cathedral architecture, while giving it from the beginning a particular originality that has survived the centuries. Strange though it may seem, the choir, which is all that remains of what he designed, shows nothing of Sens Cathedral apart from the three-tier elevation. The insistent presence of columns of black Purbeck marble rapidly became a characteristic of English Gothic architecture. A new architect, William the Englishman, adopted the principle of twin columns in the Trinity chapel. Elsewhere the Purbeck marble, permeating to the highest levels and capitals, is clear evidence of the architect's great originality.

This originality can also be seen in the plans of the cathedrals which retain the double transepts that originated in Cluny – Canterbury, Lincoln, Wells and Salisbury. This choice is significant because, in comparison to the Gothic style of the Île-de-France, where spatial concentration was sought, English architecture favoured smaller volumes (Salisbury, Lincoln) and had a distinct partiality for horizontals. This concept reappears in the design of the west fronts, which extend endlessly without any attempt to correspond to the interior of the building. At Lincoln and Wells, they are really screens. The entrance for the congregation is often pushed out to the north or south aisle and is given a huge doorway.

The treatment of interior space is also completely different from the French, and the concept of the bay, gradually evolved in the French early Gothic style, is not the same. At Lincoln, begun in 1192, the bays are surprisingly wide and seem to be all the more so because of the slenderness of the piers. They consist of a single column surrounded by shafts of Purbeck marble. The rhythm above is equally unusual: the nave arcade gives way to twin arches at the level of the triforium and divides into three at the clerestory. The respond carrying the spring of the ribs descends quite far – to the abacus of the main arcades. At Salisbury, where the nave is contemporary with the nave of Amiens, it stops a little higher, at the level of the triforium.

The dilution of the bay element is even more striking in the vaulting. In the Gothic architecture of the Île-de-France, the roof is the logical end of the piers and visually prolongs their movement. The English vault is governed by different principles and has no close relation with the lower portions. At Lincoln, the transverse rib is a linking element between the diagonal ribs, which are symmetrical over two bays. The split comes in the centre of the bay and is marked by a thinner rib attached to the walls by smaller ribs (tiercerons). A central lierne rib is also added, so as to make the roofing appear uniform. The discord between the rhythm of the piers and that of the vaulted roof is very marked.

Finally, the two-tone colouring plays an important part in the perception of the interior space: the use of Purbeck marble accentuates the lines of the building by emphasizing the horizontals. In the nave at Lincoln, the columns of the main arcades stand out very clearly.

Another original feature of English architecture is the chapter house, which has no analogy on the Continent. This often has a centralized plan. At Salisbury (c.1275), it is octagonal, and the deeply rounded vault springs from a central pier which seems thin in comparison. The walls are pierced by enormous glass windows above a blind arcade.

Lincoln Cathedral (left)

A reconstruction of Lincoln Cathedral was undertaken after an earth tremor in 1185. The plan, with two transepts, was inherited from Cluny, and had been already introduced at Canterbury and Worcester. The elevation is in three tiers and is remarkable mainly for the richness of its mouldings, which obscure the walls.

Westminster Abbey (right)

Built in the mid-13th century, Westminster Abbey shows the influence of French architecture – ambulatory with radiating chapels, an elevation of 34 metres (110 feet) which emphasizes the narrow nave, and high windows. However, some of its features are particularly English, for example the use of Purbeck marble for the columns.

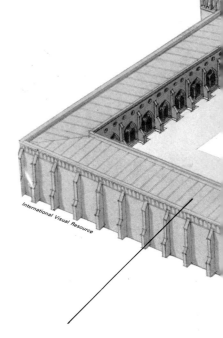

The west front of Salisbury Cathedral was almost certainly inspired by the screen-façade of Wells. However, it is less impressive than its model.

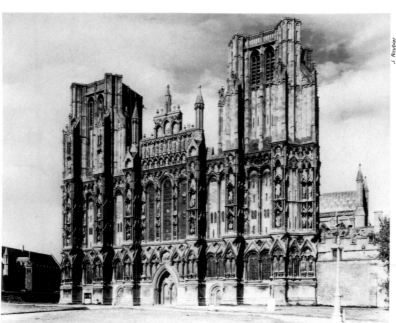

Wells Cathedral

Begun between 1183 and 1192, the construction of Wells Cathedral was completed in 1260 with the nave, the north porch and the west front. It has strongly marked English characteristics, such as the stress on horizontal lines. From this point of view, the west front is typical: it unfolds impressively in width, punctuated by six buttresses which are obscured in the luxurious sculpture.

The cloister was completed in 1284. It is richly furnished in the "Decorated" style. This cloister is the biggest and best preserved of English cloisters annexed to a cathedral.

Salisbury Cathedral

Built between 1220 and 1280, with the exception of the steeple and its spire (14th century), Salisbury Cathedral has a double transept and a flat-ended chevet. It is distinct from other English church buildings because of its extraordinary simplicity and stylistic unity; it has quadripartite vaulting and piers much less complex than those of Lincoln.

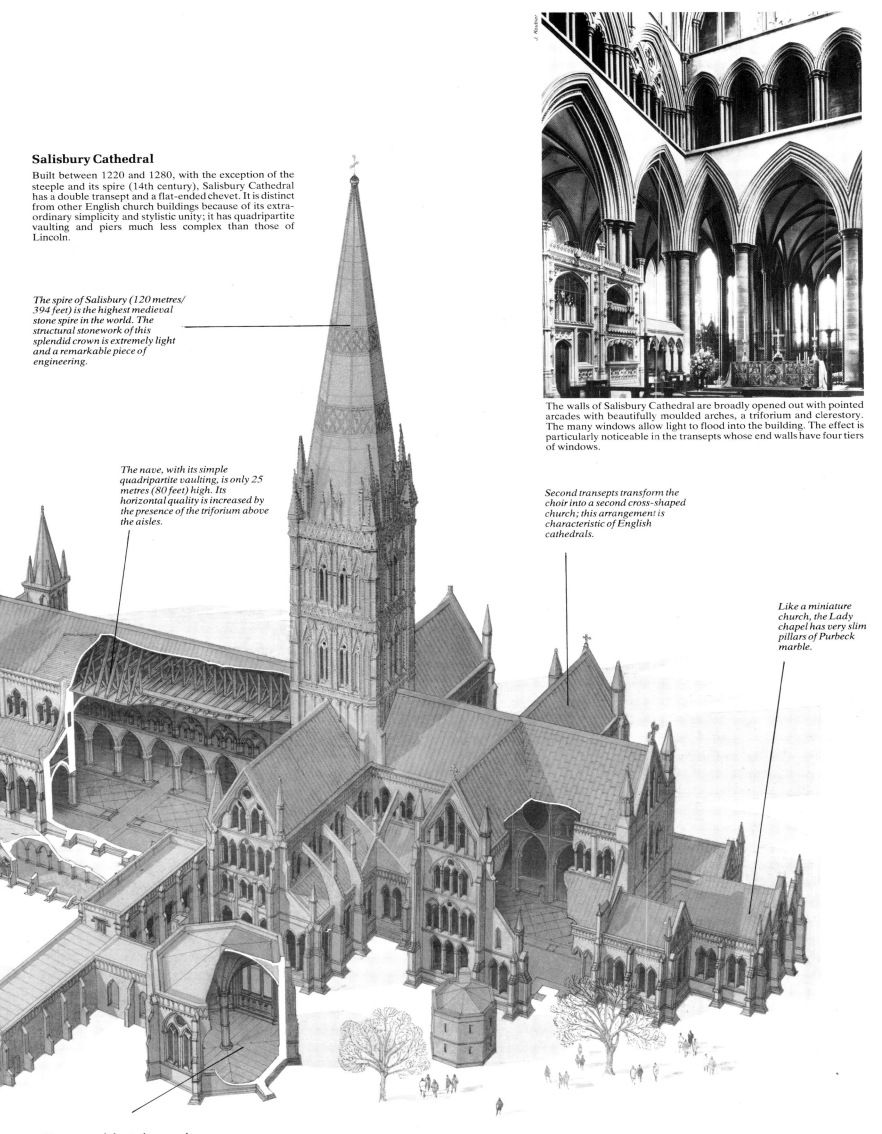

The walls of Salisbury Cathedral are broadly opened out with pointed arcades with beautifully moulded arches, a triforium and clerestory. The many windows allow light to flood into the building. The effect is particularly noticeable in the transepts whose end walls have four tiers of windows.

The spire of Salisbury (120 metres/ 394 feet) is the highest medieval stone spire in the world. The structural stonework of this splendid crown is extremely light and a remarkable piece of engineering.

The nave, with its simple quadripartite vaulting, is only 25 metres (80 feet) high. Its horizontal quality is increased by the presence of the triforium above the aisles.

Second transepts transform the choir into a second cross-shaped church; this arrangement is characteristic of English cathedrals.

Like a miniature church, the Lady chapel has very slim pillars of Purbeck marble.

The octagonal chapter house and its beautiful vault were begun in 1263. The geometric tracery of the windows is characteristic of the early Decorated period.

221

Spanish Gothic

It was more than half a century before Spain came to accept the new Gothic style, the first experiments by the Cistercians having come to nothing. But the building of the cathedrals of Toledo, Burgos and León changed the course of Spanish architecture. Their plans were probably drawn up by French architects, but the fabric was raised by the local work-force and completed under architects from the north of Spain. At Toledo, Archbishop Rodrigo Jiménez de Rada had been granted the financial assistance of the papacy for the new building works. The architect, Master Martin, adopted the design of Bourges – a double aisle running without interruption round the choir into a double ambulatory with seven radiating chapels, between which he placed small rectangular chapels. The arrangement of the double ambulatory is copied exactly from Bourges, but there is not the same ascending movement; the spaces have been widened at the expense of height. Moorish influence combines with northern in the triforium, where the arcades are multilobed.

At Burgos, the influence of Coutance Cathedral is apparent in the choice of plan, although the elevation is reminiscent of Bourges. However, the great originality of the cathedral results from the huge triforium with its multilobed arcade. Again, as at Toledo, the width has been enlarged.

Later, at León (c.1255), the plan adopted was that of Reims, though that was already archaic by this period – ambulatory with five radiating chapels, vast transept with aisles. The front, however, with its projecting towers, observes the principle of the harmonious façade, and indeed develops it. The interior elevation is in three tiers with the clerestory of the same height as the nave arcade. The architect, who copied the Reims arrangement of a passage below the aisle windows, brought light into the triforium, which at Reims had been left blind. The colonnettes which ring the piers of the nave rise straight from the floor to the springing of the vault ribs, with two horizontal cordons protruding at each storey: the effect is to emphasize the verticality of the interior and strongly define the bays. This building, the closest in Spain to the French tradition, was not influential, Spanish architects preferring the less accomplished but more prestigious model of Burgos – as at Burgo de Osma, Sasamón and Castro Urdiales.

In Catalonia, the mendicant orders residing in the villages played an important role in the definition of Catalan Gothic. Its basic plan, which is to be found throughout the western Mediterranean (Italy, France and Spain), and which dates from the mid-13th century, consists of an aisleless nave with ribbed vaulting, a polygonal apse, with chapels set between the buttresses, and a large clerestory through which light pours into the church. However, a variant, to be explained by lack of funds, is wooden roofing over parts of the building.

The aisleless nave rapidly became established in Spain, not only in parish churches, since it was easy to build and economical, but also in prestigious buildings such as the cathedrals. It appears at San Bertrand in Comminges in 1304, at Santa Maria del Mar in Barcelona in 1322, at San Justo y San Pastor, also in Barcelona, in 1329, at San Francisco in Palma de Majorca, completed in 1349, and at Perpignan in 1324. Work on the cathedral of Gerona, begun in 1320 with the aisles, was interrupted in 1416 when it reached the nave, there being an idea to broaden this out into a single space.

However, buildings with aisles, ambulatory and radiating chapels were not entirely abandoned. At Barcelona, in 1328, the architect of the cathedral chose an original solution which allowed him to shed the flying buttresses. The arcades, rising very high, pushed up the triforium and the rose windows, placed in the cove of the vault, while the aisles were widened at ground level by chapels set between the buttresses. The ample, unencumbered space of the interior was flooded with light from huge aisle windows. Palma Cathedral in Majorca, started at the beginning of the 14th century, was subjected to several changes of design over its long period of construction. With a vault 46 metres (150 feet) in height, it uses the same principle of opening the nave on to the aisles by means of very high arcades, but also has a clerestory of the usual size. The severity of the octagonal pillars imparts a certain dryness. The exterior is quite different, with its dense throng of buttresses, on top of which flying buttresses are thrown at wider intervals.

León Cathedral

The plan of León Cathedral, begun about 1255, was inspired by Reims, with a five-bay nave and single aisles, a gigantic transept with single aisles on the west and double aisles on the east, and a choir with straight bays followed by an ambulatory with five radiating chapels. On this basic scheme the architect made a number of variations, proving that he was up to date with the developments of his time: hence, the triforium is not blind as in Reims, but admits light. The vaulting is quadripartite, with raised coves to allow greater room for the clerestory windows.

Gerona Cathedral

In 1320, Gerona Cathedral was planned as an aisled church. But although the plan was put into effect in the choir, the nave aisles were never built.

Santa Maria del Mar, Barcelona

Begun in 1328, Santa Maria del Mar presents an original arrangement in the elevation of its east end. Radiating chapels are enclosed within the thickness of the buttresses and there is a very high ambulatory with tall windows. Equally tall windows appear in the rounded section of the choir, while the straight section has rose windows.

Burgos Cathedral

Burgos Cathedral, begun in 1221 or 1222, was inspired by French designs, especially those of Bourges Cathedral. The first master-builder was soon replaced by a second, who was influenced in the alterations he made by Reims Cathedral.

Toledo Cathedral

Archbishop Rodrigo Jiménez of Toledo set about building a cathedral a little before 1226, having preached until then in a mosque. The architect, Master Martin, was inspired by Bourges Cathedral as regards the choir – double aisles leading into a double ambulatory and opening onto seven radiating chapels between which eight little square chapels were placed.

The Holy Roman Empire: new directions

The Holy Roman Empire accepted the Gothic style reluctantly, being strongly attached to its Romanesque traditions. It was not until 1230 that the new style was allowed in at Strasbourg, Trier, Marburg and then at Cologne. It immediately took on a colour of its own, apparent first in the shape of the piers. The angel pier in the south transept of Strasbourg Cathedral is an unexpected illustration of this. The choice of plan for these buildings was also unusual. At Trier, the architect adopted a plan based on a Greek cross set within a circle. At Marburg, the trefoil shape of the choir was continued into the nave, where the vaults of all three aisles are of the same height. However, as compared to hall-churches where stress is given to the horizontal elements, the huge circular columns encircled by four smaller ones emphasize the vertical. Two tiers of windows set in the outside walls bathe the interior of the building with light. The choir of Cologne Cathedral, begun later, in 1248, shows French influence in the adoption of an ambulatory with radiating chapels; the model chosen was Amiens Cathedral, although Cologne surpassed Amiens in the height of its vaults and had a much stronger vertical emphasis. The engaged columns of the nave rise without obstruction to the springing of the vault, the windows have become longer and thinner and the arches more pointed. Altenburg

Cathedral is an exact replica of Amiens but simplified, as if made to a draft plan.

The taste for sobriety apparent in this Cistercian church recurs in the buildings erected by the mendicant orders, the Dominicans and Franciscans. Ratisbon Cathedral, contemporary with Cologne, shows the direction which Gothic architecture would take in the Holy Roman Empire. The elevation is in two tiers: the nave arcades are higher and the windows run to the full height of the walls, creating a "curtain" effect hardly interrupted by the springing of the supports. Since the articulation of the bay was so minimal, only the vault guided the eyes of the congregation towards the chancel, which formed merely an extension of the nave. Sometimes, the mendicants were happy just to cover the nave with a wooden ceiling. In the 14th century, their growing success led them to abandon their original ideals of simplicity in favour of more imposing buildings.

At the end of the 13th century, Gothic architecture had a second wind, and highly varied buildings were constructed. At Lübeck, where the design of an ambulatory with radiating chapels was repeated, the architect used brick, which explains the flat elevation of the nave. The cathedrals of Freiburg im Breisgau, Cologne and Strasbourg are all representative of the first stages of an evolution which

explains the extraordinary choir of Aachen, which is treated as a glass cage. Supports were reduced to the most slender dimensions possible to allow the glass curtain to stretch in height as well as in width.

A dynasty of architects – the Parlers – pushed these experiments even further. At Schwäbisch-Gmünd, built to the design of Henry Parler I, the plan adopted was that of the hall-church. The building is particularly significant in its tendency towards simplicity – the use of very tall columns to open out the volumes and to unite them. Light contributed to this effect, thanks to the very high windows which allowed it to diffuse freely. In the choir (1351) ribbed vaulting is used in a surprising way, purely as a decorative feature and not as a structural one. Peter Parler, who took over from Matthieu d'Arras at Prague in 1356, pushed these radical tendencies even further. Within a structure which remained traditional, he treated the triforium and clerestory in a new fashion: the dense tracery with emphasized horizontals is set at an angle to the shafts bearing the vault. In the vault itself, the removal of transverse ribs and the deflected lines of the diagonal ribs, which only travel two thirds of their proper length, eliminate any upward movement. The close connection between the vault and its supports disappears, leaving an independent roofing.

Cologne Cathedral

When he laid out the plan in 1248, the architect tried to rival the greatest French cathedrals. But the building as we know it today was completed between 1842 and 1880. The desire for height is apparent in the choir with its huge arcades whose movement is continued through to the clerestory.

Strasbourg Cathedral

The style of the cathedral was altered in 1220 to Gothic, which first appeared in the transepts, and was continued in 1240 down the nave. The architect, under the influence of the High Gothic style of France, adopted the shafted column, the lit gallery and clerestory windows rising to the full height of the vault.

St. Martin, Landshut

The church of St. Martin, Landshut was built between 1389 (the choir) and 1459 (the vault). The tower, one of the great masterpieces of Bavarian Flamboyant architecture, was not built before 1500. The interior resembles a hall-church, with vaults supported on extremely elegant polygonal piers.

St. Mary, Lübeck

Between 1260 and 1290, an alteration transformed the original plan of the choir of St. Mary, Lübeck. The elevation is in two tiers – nave arcades and clerestory with blind stone tracery occupying its lower part. The extraordinary weightlessness of the stonework was to serve as an example for many other monuments.

Prague Cathedral

In 1344, Matthieu d'Arras started building the choir for the cathedral. On his death in 1352, Charles IV sent for another architect, Peter Parler. Tied to a pre-established plan and partly built structure, Parler erected a choir which introduced a new aesthetic: the triforium became an independent element, breaking away from the planar quality of the elevation. In its play of lierne and tierceron ribs, the vaulting is no longer linked to the piers.

Church of the Franciscans, Salzburg

The choir of the Franciscan church in Salzburg was added between 1408 and 1450 to the 12th century nave; the architect was Hans Stetheimer. He adopted the design of an apsed hall-church with an ambulatory with square chapels and vaults resting on tall cylindrical columns.

Decorated and Perpendicular in England

The reconstruction of Westminster Abbey, possibly planned since 1245, was felt by contemporaries to be a break from a firmly established tradition. The architect, Henry of Reynes, adopted a French plan by providing an ambulatory with radiating chapels and a transept with aisles, as well as an elevation in which the bay was strongly emphasized. The originality consisted in the use of Purbeck marble, emphasizing the horizontal lines, and in the highly pointed arches of the nave arcades, triforium and clerestory. However, this aspect is secondary to the handling of space which makes Westminster a truly exceptional monument in English Gothic architecture.

The example set by the abbey was not sufficient to turn taste in a different direction. Up until now, England had remained faithful to its accustomed proportions: hence the cathedrals of Exeter and York, the choirs of Lichfield and Wells and the towers of Ely and Salisbury. Exeter Cathedral, begun between 1280 and 1290, was, however, innovatory in its vaulting and in the strong definition of its bays. The diagonal ribs sprout from the pier, blossom into the vault and then retreat onto the opposite pier. The pattern given to pier and rib prevails over any functional necessity. York Minster, where the double transept was abandoned for an abnormally long choir, shows a tendency to integrate the different volumes, a tendency which the square tower over the crossing helps to emphasize. By setting back the two upper tiers of the nave (triforium and clerestory) the architect has attempted visually to unite them. The same intention is apparent in the west front, which is framed by two towers. At Lichfield, the effect is achieved through a happy synthesis in the west front between the emphasized verticals and the screen which reveals nothing of the interior divisions. The blind arcades of the screen, between which are placed statues, highlight this wonderfully inventive piece of mural architecture.

In the vaulting of its chapter house (completed in 1306), Wells Cathedral displays the extraordinary talent of the English masons: the ribs shoot out of a central pillar, but the movement is interrupted at regular intervals by a ring at the top of the pillar and octagonal ribbing where they blossom out. This concern to break up movement is characteristic of English architecture, which shies away from forms that are too regular.

An undoubted masterpiece of this period is the tower of Ely Cathedral (1328–1340), where the use of the rib as a decorative rather than an architectonic element reaches its climax. It serves as a line of force which leads the eye of the beholder from the piers to the centre. Above, a two-tiered octagon rises: one of the levels is blind, the other is very well lit; the whole is covered with a vault which seems to prolong the windows and bring the complex web of ribs to a central point. An astonishing dialectic of contradictory movements is created, to be resolved by the eye.

The extraordinary freedom shown by English architects on many occasions was further demonstrated in the middle of the 14th century by what is called the Perpendicular style. It is the window tracery that defines this point in the history of architecture. The arrangement of the windows within a rectangle imposed itself to such an extent as to become the main decorative motif of the whole church. Curved lines were eliminated, and a much simpler language took over in reaction to the previous style. The earliest example is Gloucester Cathedral, first in the transept, then in the choir (1337–1378). The flat east end has a huge curtain of window with very strong tracery lines. In contrast to this assertion of right angles, the roofing displays a stupefying freedom: transverse, diagonal, lateral, lierne and tierceron ribs seem to have been thrown together into an extraordinary dance which annihilates the true form of the structure – a barrel vault.

It was in the 15th century that the English architects were at their most daring. In the chapel of King's College, Cambridge, and in many other buildings, a very simple plan – a long rectangle – contrasts with an elevation in which windows occupy the whole width of the wall, descending very low and rising right up to the vault, and with a very busy vault design. Taking a pattern already adopted in the chapter houses, architects made full use of fan vaulting. From a technical point of view, the principle is simple, but the entirely functionless intricate web of ribs makes for a very rich effect. English architects made special use of the Flamboyant style of architecture, grasping that they could use the design of the vault not only to play "games" in stone, but also to create exciting spatial effects.

F.L. Harris

Exeter Cathedral

Exeter Cathedral was probably started a little before York, between 1280 and 1290, the nave being completed in 1300 and the choir around 1325. The plan followed the early Gothic precedent with double transepts and a flat-ended choir. The elevation, too, was traditional, in three tiers; its novelty lay in the adoption of corbels for the springing of the ribs. The imposing piers made up of a series of engaged columns are proportionate to the nave arcades, whose width is toned down by roll mouldings of very sharp outline.

Ely Cathedral

After the lantern tower collapsed in 1322, a new tower was erected between 1328 and 1340, following a different design, which obscured the corners of the crossing with tracery panels. Above this, a wooden tower was built by the master carpenter, William Hurley.

Michael Kaufman

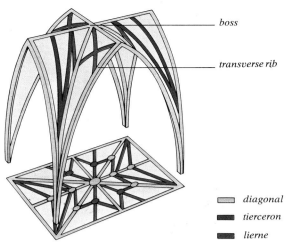

boss

transverse rib

diagonal
tierceron
lierne

Vault and ribbing

The vault plays an important role in the perception of interior volume. The attaching of tierceron ribs, which do not spring from the pier, is not a functional but a purely decorative feature; that is to say, the cells of the vault still rest only on the diagonal ribs. The same is not true of the liernes, which bind together and strengthen the diagonal and transverse ribs upon which the vaulting cells are based.

Wells Cathedral

The chapter house of Wells Cathedral, which dates from the beginning of the 14th century, is one of the most amazing examples of the skill of English architects. The central support disappears behind a circle of shafts which is interrupted by an ornate capital. The ribs then spring from an abacus following a strict pattern which allows room for wide windows in the walls.

Lincoln Cathedral

Reconstruction of the building was undertaken in 1192 starting with the choir and transepts; the plan was ambitious with double transepts and a long, flat-ended choir. The nave, front, and central tower were built between 1225 and 1255, with the "Angel Choir" following between 1256 and 1280. The luxury and quality of the interior, for which Purbeck marble was used, was completed by "crazy vaults" which deliberately disturb the rhythm of the bays. On the west front a long, drawn out screen again deliberately masks the arrangement of the interior.

Gloucester Cathedral

This ancient Romanesque abbey, which did not become a cathedral until 1541, was restored at the request of King Edward in 1327; the Norman choir was entirely rebuilt (1337–1377) and the Romanesque walls were decorated with a network of rectangular panels. At the east end, the wall was knocked away to make room for a huge window with geometric tracery which allows light to stream in, barely filtered by the stained glass. The distinctive, emphatic design of the verticals in the tracery is continued into the complex web of ribs in the vault, where diagonal, lierne, and tierceron ribs follow an equally strict pattern. The architect of the cloister developed the possibilities of vaulting further, with the invention of the fan vault (1315–1412). The ribs burst into a semi-cone shape which covers part of the vault, the spaces being filled with diamonds decorated with elegant rose tracery.

A new architectural vision in Italy

Gothic architecture never really became established in the Italian peninsula. When monuments were built there in the new style, they looked very strange in a country impregnated with older traditions. As in the rest of Europe, the Cistercians were the first propagators of the Gothic style – at Fossanova, begun in 1187, and at Casamari (1203–1207); these two sister houses of Pontigny were very influential in making known the new architectural style. Then the Dominicans and the Franciscans took up the formula when they built their convents in the towns, but with a different conception which was more fitting in the Mediterranean context. Contrary to the northern Gothic style, which articulates the building in bays, Italian architecture remained faithful to the unbroken wall and never adopted the "curtain" window. In this sunny country, such an abundance of light was not desirable. Moreover, the Italian conception of interior volume, founded on the principle of the basilica, was contradictory to the ideas of the northern countries where the proportions were fixed from the 13th century on in favour of height over width. The external appearance of Italian buildings is equally distinctive – strictly organized geometric masses in which horizontals powerfully dominate the verticals. The determining role of the mendicant orders only reinforced this tendency in the architecture of the 13th and 14th centuries.

The basilica of San Francesco at Assisi, begun in 1228 and consecrated in 1258, is the first evidence of these distinctive tendencies. It was on two levels, like a Palatine chapel, and had a very simple plan – single nave, projecting transepts and polygonal apse. The design – with the exception of the protruding transepts – was taken over from the Sainte Chapelle in Paris, with which it is almost contemporary; on the other hand, the elevation is radically different in spite of the presence of ribbed vaulting over prominent piers. Up to a certain height, the wall is reserved for the free application of wall paintings. Above this, it is set back to leave room for a passage; there are two long narrow lancet windows in each bay. The frescoes, organized in rectangular panels, help to stress the horizontal nature of the interior volume, which the slender supports scarcely interrupt.

The Dominicans began work on their abbey church, Santa Maria Novella, in Florence in 1279. The basic plan was inspired by the Cistercians: nave with aisles, transepts with two rectangular chapels in the arms, flat-ended choir; however, the elevation is derived from different sources. The interior volume opens out freely thanks to arcades which establish easy communication between the very high aisles and the nave. The wall remains the predominant element, with few windows either in the aisles or in the clerestory, where they are small and round. The ribbed vaulting bears no relation to contemporary technique; the deeply curved vaults spring from very low, a feature which allowed the architect to avoid flying buttresses.

Florentine architects continued to progress in this very distinctive direction, hence the Franciscan church of Santa Croce, rebuilt from 1295 on a plan attributed with some justification to Arnolfo di Cambio. In order to lessen the mass of the walls and piers, the architect abandoned stone vaulting in favour of a visible wooden structure. Polygonal piers support very pointed arcades; above this, there is a row of consoles supporting a balustrade, and finally the clerestory. The bay divisions are marked only by flat pilasters which rise from the capitals to the wooden ceiling and are masked by the balustrade. Horizontal lines are strongly emphasized, as at Santa Maria Novella. The architect greatly increased the space – 115 metres (380 feet) long by 38 metres (125 feet) high – by raising the nave as high as possible. In this way, he created a nave with an entirely homogeneous space which ends suddenly in the apse. In effect, the dynamic concept of Gothic architecture has been renounced, and an older tradition observed – that of the early Christian basilica. The organization of the interior and exterior volumes, both strongly outlined, is governed by the same conception: the same applies to the avoidance of mass and to the windows, which flood the interior with light, chasing away the shadows so dear to Gothic architecture.

A new stage was reached with Florence Cathedral whose construction was undertaken in 1294 by Arnolfo di Cambio before he left the city in 1302. After that, work went on at irregular intervals until Brunelleschi completed the building by enlarging the choir and erecting the dome (1420–1436). Arnolfo had planned a nave much larger than its aisles, a trilobed choir, and a crossing to be covered by an octagonal dome. Brunelleschi considerably amplified the original plan to the east. However, the nave was constructed according to Arnolfo's plans in which the methods employed at Santa Croce were further developed – polygonal piers, galleries on consoles and arcades establishing free communication between the nave and the aisles. The difference lay in the deeply curved ribbed vaulting and the piercing of *oculi* in the walls. The heritage of classical antiquity was strongly evident in this building, which belonged already to the Renaissance.

Siena Cathedral

The construction of Siena Cathedral is linked with the development of this independent commune. It was originally a Romanesque building with nave and aisles, on which construction had begun in the middle of the 12th century, but the present appearance of the monument owes much to the work done under the supervision of monks from the abbey of San Galgano. However, the building is still Romanesque in its volumes and in the use of alternating layers of black and white marble, even though moulded Gothic piers were employed. In 1264, work was begun on the hexagonal dome. From 1284 to 1299, Giovanni Pisano was in charge of the façade: he adopted a new design by making deep, gabled doorways. From 1339, further impulse was given to the construction work by Lando di Pietro, who tried to give the building a more slender shape.

San Francesco, Assisi

Pope Gregory X founded the basilica of Assisi in 1228 above the tomb of St. Francis, placed in the crypt. The plans were the work of Friar Elia. For the lower church, he adopted an aisleless nave with four bays, preceded by a narthex. The plan was identical for the upper church, consecrated in 1253. The cylindrical buttresses and multi-coloured effect on the exterior are characteristically Italian features.

Santa Croce, Florence

Begun in 1252 and rebuilt from 1295 onwards, the church was not consecrated until 1443 by Cardinal Bessarion. The plan which Vasari attributed, probably correctly, to Arnolfo di Cambio, was inspired by early Christian buildings in Rome: its dimensions of 90 metres long, 19 metres wide and 36 metres high (295 feet by 62 feet by 118 feet) are very similar to those of the Old Basilica of St. Peter's. The wooden roofing derives from the same architectural conception, reacting against the ascending movement of Gothic architecture.

Santa Maria Novella, Florence

Initially, the Dominicans intended to build a church in the Cistercian style (1278); during the course of construction, major alterations took place which considerably transformed the interior space of the original plan – two rectangular chapels on each end of the transept arms, a flat-ended choir, and six bays with quadripartite vaulting in the nave.

The technical perfection of late Gothic

The term "late Gothic" is used to denote the period in the development of the Gothic style that commenced in the late 14th century; but a single term can hardly cover the rich and varied developments of the period. In France, the term used is "Flamboyant", describing the play of undulating arches which enlivened the windows of churches, but it is not enough to define the extraordinary inventiveness shown in Europe during the 15th and the first half of the 16th centuries, everywhere except Italy. "Late Gothic" is also misleading as a blanket term. In fact, there was a fundamental rupture in European architecture during this period in favour of regional styles developing independently in England, Spain, France, Portugal and the Holy Roman Empire, and within each of these countries, too, there was again considerable variation. Parallel to this fragmentation, remarkable technical advances were made which partly explain the spectacular successes of the Renaissance period: these advances ranged from a considerable reduction in the size of piers, whose forms now varied from the most simple (column) to the most elaborate (undulating or facetted piers); to a streamlining of ribs, which now disappear into the piers without the intermediary of a capital; to the construction of vaults of an incredible lightness, significantly reducing their weight on the walls; to the evolution of the four-centred arch; to the elimination of the triforium, reducing the elevation to two tiers, and boldly extending the clerestory windows from the top of the vault down to the level of the nave arcade. Such technical progress, the reasons for which have not yet been elucidated, was probably linked to the improvement of tools and a greater mastery of architectural geometry.

However, contrary to what is usually claimed, the internal and external structure of the building remained very simple, as surviving designs make clear. The structure is concealed from the onlooker behind the elaborate ornament, which though it is responsible for the slight respect accorded to the style, is evidence of a prodigious inventive talent.

This ornament not only pervaded the whole exterior of the building, loading it with buttresses, flying buttresses and pinnacles, but even affected the front façade, which was often amplified by vast porches. The same went for the interior: the vault disappeared behind a web of diagonal ribs supplemented by liernes and tiercerons, producing the most diverse and daring effects. In the Holy Roman Empire and in England, the vaulting lost its role as the definition of the bay as all logic was defied and the ceiling became entirely independent of the walls. There was sometimes extraordinary dislocation between the bay and the vault.

France, however, was less daring than a number of other countries and stuck to its own traditions. This makes the origins of the Flamboyant style even more difficult to define since it is hard to say whether it was imported or whether it was the result of native evolution. Both theories have been put forward, but neither carries complete conviction, since the style was very much more than a more or less elegant game of pinnacles and cusps. The crossing of Amiens Cathedral (c.1270) was vaulted with lierne and tierceron ribs, but it was not until the very end of the 14th century that the new style was truly established. The most successful and coherent example of the style is the chapel of Riom, built on the commission of the duke of Berry by Guy de Dammartin and completed in 1380, but it had been preceded by promising attempts at Paris and elsewhere. The plan and elevation of the Sainte Chapelle at Vincennes, which was not completed until the 16th century, belongs to the 1370s; it seems that the team of architects brought together at this time by Charles V played a decisive role and that the diffusion of the new style can be attributed to them. But even if architectural development was not entirely halted during the Hundred Years War, there was a downturn before the acceleration of the second half of the 15th century. This development, whose significance has still not been properly appreciated, continued until the middle of the 16th century. It was certainly fostered by the recovery of the economy and by urban development. The buildings were not so grand as those of the 13th century; often it was a question of adding to an existing building but there were new constructions too. Originality is apparent first of all in the choice of plan, which varies enormously: at St. Nicolas-de-Port (1481–1530), the architect built two transepts side by side. At Cléry, on the other hand, the plan is extremely simple. The apse was also subject to a variety of treatments, with a distinct preference for the polygon. A tendency to greater spaciousness resulted in the integration of nave and aisles.

This same construction fever affected England, with the Perpendicular style, and the Holy Roman Empire, where a large variety of building was undertaken. The Spanish peninsula was no longer merely on the fringe, and monuments were built there of great beauty. The taste for decoration took on stupefying proportions, especially in the façades (Valladolid). However, besides these highly ornate monuments, such as the remarkable Chapel of the Constable, built onto the choir of Burgos Cathedral (1482–1494), there were others whose lines were still clearly perceptible – San Juan de los Reyes at Toledo, the new cathedral in Salamanca (1510) and the cathedral at Segovia (1524), the last two being the work of Juan and Rodrigo Gil de Hontanon respectively.

Portugal adopted the Flamboyant style at a relatively late date, in the façade and the "unfinished chapels" of the church at Batalha (1433–1438), but architecture there took a highly original turn at the end of the 15th century and the beginning of the 16th century, with the Manueline style. This further exaggerated the decorative style of Isabella's reign, adding greater relief and motifs borrowed from landscape and the sea. The effect first appeared in the cloister of Batalha, but became established in the Hieronymite convent at Belem (after 1500) and in the cloister of Santa Cruz at Coimbra (1520); its most characteristic example is the window at Tomar. Nonetheless, in their interior space these buildings remained traditional.

Chapel of the Holy Spirit, Rue

The Chapel of the Holy Spirit at Rue, endowed by Louis XI in 1480, is characteristic of the Flamboyant style, with its walls and vaults overrun by luxurious decoration which obscures the simplicity of the plan. The space is very bright, with light streaming in.

St. Nicolas-de-Port

The choir and nave of St. Nicolas-de-Port were built from 1495 to 1514, and the façade from 1514 to 1551. This is one of the most beautiful examples of Flamboyant architecture. The very high arcades establish easy communication with the aisles, and the windows rise through the three tiers of the elevation. In the apse, they rise uninterrupted to the vaults.

Church at Brou, Bourg-en-Bresse

Margaret of Austria carried through the intentions of her parents-in-law in 1505 to construct a monastery at Brou. The plan and elevation belong to Brabant Gothic style. While retaining an elevation on three levels, the architect has managed to set huge windows into the walls. The apse consists of superimposed tiers, scarcely separated by the ornate frieze. The pillars rise without obstruction from the floor to receive the ribs directly, without capitals.

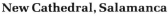

New Cathedral, Salamanca

The new cathedral was begun in 1513 under the supervision of Juan Gil de Hontañón. In spite of its late date and several additions, it is still Gothic in spirit. The architect succeeded in imparting an extraordinary sense of space to the interior of his building while maintaining a correct balance of proportions.

The Trinity, Vendôme

Erected at the beginning of the 16th century, the façade of the Trinity remains faithful in principle to the medieval tradition. The vertical divisions are respected by the three doorways which correspond to nave and aisles, but the horizontals disappear behind a tracery gable. The buttresses are lost beneath the impressive pattern of mouldings.

Window of the chapter house of the Hieronymite convent, Tomar

Since Eugenio d'Ors published *On the Baroque*, the window at Tomar has become a point of reference, all the more difficult to define because it belongs to the beginning of the 16th century. In it, Ors could see "one of the essential symbols of the Lusitanian spirit".

Notre-Dame, Cléry

The collegiate church of Notre-Dame, Cléry is a perfect illustration of the ambiguity of Flamboyant architecture. Begun a little before the middle of the 15th century, it shows strict simplicity in its elevation of two tiers. A high, bare wall has been retained between the nave arcades and the clerestory. The piers, which merge into ribs, lend movement to the nave without disturbing the flat character of the wall.

Château-Gaillard

This hilltop castle is closely adapted to its site, whereas on the plain a military architect was free to adopt the plan he considered best suited to defence. In a case such as this, ingenuity was required to supplement the natural advantages of the hilltop site. Château-Gaillard can be fully appreciated if it is compared to the contemporary fortress of the Louvre, built on the banks of the Seine, where the plan was chosen purely to maximize defensive strength. At Château-Gaillard (from 1196 onwards) Richard the Lionheart's architect was obliged to adapt his design to a promontory with sides which fell away sheer down to the Seine. He built a series of concentric structures – the outer bailey, the inner wall, and the keep, which forms the last line of defence. The most curious feature is undoubtedly the form of the inner wall, made up of a series of half-round towers.

T he question of defence has always faced man, ever since he first recognized the dangers that surround him – most of them originating in his fellow beings. Every generation has responded in a different way. There have always been dissident voices denying the existence of these dangers, or alternatively exaggerating them. Even those who have considered defence indispensable have not been unanimous: their view has been based either on a collective view of society, advocating defence for everyone, or else on an individualistic attitude, advocating defence of the clan, more or less broadly conceived. The means of defence has therefore varied according to the group defended – from a city wall to an isolated keep, the castle surrounded by a bailey being somewhere between the two. The selection of means of defence is clearly linked to social position: the peasant defended his farm, the rich landowner his villa, the lord of the manor his domain, the head of state his realm. From the end of the 4th century AD to the end of the Hundred Years' War, Western Europe was inevitably obsessed by the problem of defence, and responded to it in very different ways. This variety resulted in an extraordinary diversity of defensive structures – of which the majority, unfortunately, have disappeared. Only in France can one study in full the evolution of military architecture from the 4th to the 16th centuries.

Obviously the nature of each castle depended on the financial resources of its builder. But throughout the Middle Ages there was a constant concern to make invulnerable whatever fortification was under construction. Invulnerability was clearly not absolutely defined, but was conceived in relation to certain factors. The most important was that the strength of the defence need be only just superior to that of the attack; overkill was not indulged, for reasons of economy. This explains differences in construction technique during the same period – defensive systems of earth and timber, for example, continued to be built at a time when stone had been universally adopted for religious architecture. Tradition and innovation followed one another on parallel routes without ever meeting, since their objectives were not the same.

The circumstances of Gaul at the end of the 3rd century were unusual. Under the earlier Roman Empire it had been defended by frontier lines, but these had by now been breached, so a prodigious amount of stonework was newly erected around cities anxious for protection. The great walls that were built, supplemented on the outside by glacis (earthworks) formed by the

demolition of neighbouring structures, protected public buildings and ensured the survival of the State and public security. Meanwhile, everyday life continued outside.

From the 4th century onwards defensive systems burgeoned everywhere. These were of earth, timber, or even stone, depending on the resources of the builder and the importance of his territory. It was not long before elaborate fortifications were constructed which had a precise military function and were generally sited where defence was aided by the terrain. They frequently included a bastion which could serve both as a residence and as a refuge in case of attack. A period of anarchy ensued, as a result of the declining powers of the State – a situation against which the Carolingian monarchs reacted forcefully. In 864 Charles the Bald ("le Chauve") ordered the destruction of all private fortifications: From this date onwards, fortifications were built only by order of the emperor, and were directed principally against Norman incursions. They are nevertheless little different in appearance from those of the preceding period, whether protective walls around monasteries, houses and farms, or fortifications of exclusively military purpose.

The 11th century saw a marked break from previous periods with the appearance of the "motte and bailey" castle, that is, a castle comprising a central tower on a mound (motte) surrounded by a wall forming a courtyard (bailey). To begin with, only earth and timber were used. The motte was created by heaping up the earth excavated in the process of digging the surrounding ditch, and the keep built on its summit served as a lookout post. An outer line of defence followed the same pattern – a ditch, a dyke formed from the spoil, a palisade of wood. This ring gave protection to the outbuildings of the castle and at the same time served as a refuge for the neighbouring population in times of immediate danger. The lord and his family usually occupied the first floor of the keep, while the household and garrison occupied the upper levels; livestock was kept on the ground floor. The first floor was often reached by means of an external ladder which could be withdrawn to deny access to the enemy. The same principle operated inside, where communication between the different floors was effected by the same means – rudimentary, but easy to remove: in the last analysis, defence was paramount. During the 11th century, the need for protection became still more compelling and was reflected in a reduction in the size of the bailey, which thus became easier to defend. The insecurity and political anarchy of the

age explain the astonishing number of these structures of earth and wood.

Technical progress, social evolution and the concentration of power in the hands of a few important individuals led, together with the introduction of masonry, to the transformation of military architecture. The first examples appeared in the middle of the 11th century, and the new pattern became general by the end of that century, echoing the progress of religious architecture. Initially, the layout was the same as that of timber fortifications. Attention was primarily directed to the keep, which remained the residence and ultimate retreat. In the west of France and in England the plan of the keep was generally rectangular, like that of the Tower of London. The shell was of stone, the rest – stairs, floors – still of wood. The principal entrance was still on the first floor, sometimes reached by means of a masonry addition, and the tendency was towards the greater use of stone. At the end of the 11th century, the first stone stairs appeared – at Loches, for instance. Fitted into the thickness of the walls, the stairs were staggered from side to side, so that any assailant who had penetrated the keep would have to cross each floor in order to continue his ascent.

The main weakness of the rectangular plan inherited from timber construction was its blind outer corners, which made defence more difficult. Other formulas were tried, though none proved entirely satisfactory. At Gisors, an octagonal keep; at Châtillon-sur-Loing, a keep with 16 faces on a square base; at Provins, an octagonal keep on a square base. In imitation of ancient architecture, the circular plan was rapidly adopted, for example at Fréteval in the mid-11th century, then at Château-Renault, Neaufles-St. Martin, Château-sur-Epte. The interior arrangement remained the same, however, except that stone stairs now became the rule. No attempt was made at flanking, and defensive action was restricted to the upper parts of the keep. From the 12th century these terminated in hoardings, or timber galleries cantilevered out from the walls which enabled the foot of the keep to be "covered". Defence remained mainly passive, and those under siege were content to seek refuge behind thick walls, to keep the enemy's movements under observation and to drive them off with bombardments of stones and arrows when they approached, confident of the strength of their keep. Castles could not be destroyed except by famine, fire, undermining or treachery.

Defence was governed by the nature of attack, which remained anarchic and

MILITARY ARCHITECTURE

unskilful during this period. Passive defence was sufficient until the attack became more threatening, due partly to better arms but also to a more resolute spirit on the part of certain lords. In response to this new reality, not always clearly understood, new defensive theories were developed. They were based on the reading of ancient authors, particularly Vegetius, whose Stratagems became a standard reference work. The consequence was a rediscovery of the role of the flank. Hitherto a simple wall had been considered a sufficient defence against attackers. Now defence was made more concentrated, the walls being "covered" or guarded by salients. But an uncertainty noticeable in their construction shows that the importance of the flank was not immediately understood. At Houdan, in the first third of the 12th century, the cylindrical keep was reinforced by four turrets, which could not, however, be used for guarding the walls because of the curved plan. At Provins, an irregular octagonal plan was adopted, with turrets on the four smaller faces. At Etampes the composition was a great deal more elaborate but also somewhat ineffective, with four interlocking towers.

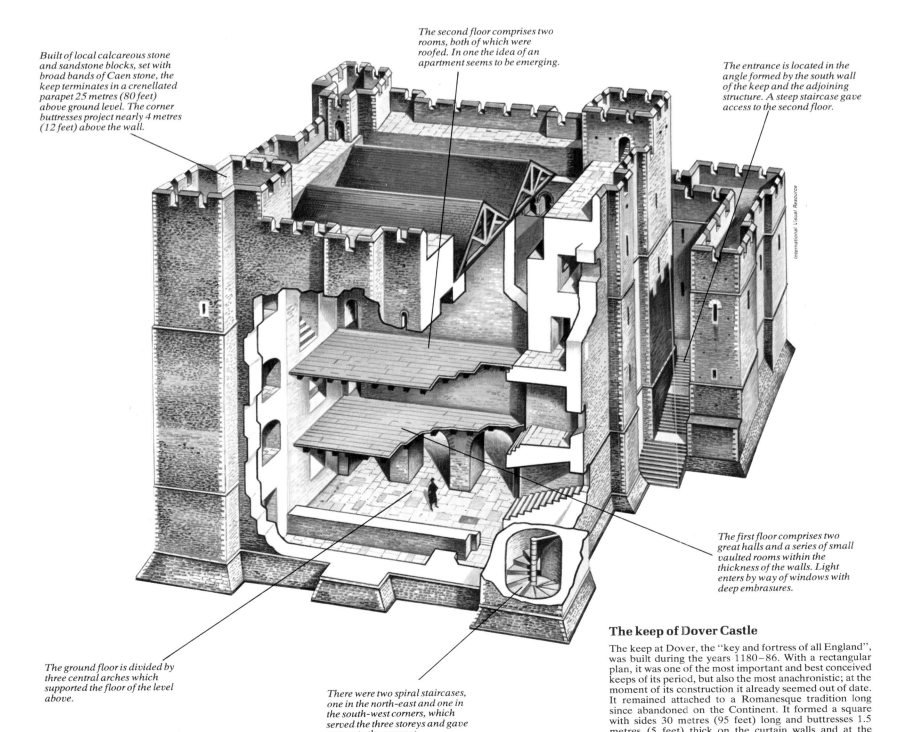

Built of local calcareous stone and sandstone blocks, set with broad bands of Caen stone, the keep terminates in a crenellated parapet 25 metres (80 feet) above ground level. The corner buttresses project nearly 4 metres (12 feet) above the wall.

The second floor comprises two rooms, both of which were roofed. In one the idea of an apartment seems to be emerging.

The entrance is located in the angle formed by the south wall of the keep and the adjoining structure. A steep staircase gave access to the second floor.

International Visual Resource

The ground floor is divided by three central arches which supported the floor of the level above.

There were two spiral staircases, one in the north-east and one in the south-west corners, which served the three storeys and gave access to the parapet.

The first floor comprises two great halls and a series of small vaulted rooms within the thickness of the walls. Light enters by way of windows with deep embrasures.

The keep of Dover Castle

The keep at Dover, the "key and fortress of all England", was built during the years 1180–86. With a rectangular plan, it was one of the most important and best conceived keeps of its period, but also the most anachronistic; at the moment of its construction it already seemed out of date. It remained attached to a Romanesque tradition long since abandoned on the Continent. It formed a square with sides 30 metres (95 feet) long and buttresses 1.5 metres (5 feet) thick on the curtain walls and at the corners.

Military architecture

At the end of the 12th century new circumstances revolutionized the nature of defence, which until then had remained detached from other issues. The city now became an essential element in commercial, political and intellectual life, and began to play a more important part in military considerations. The initiative was taken by Philippe Auguste, who understood what a powerful support the city could be in his struggle against the Plantagenets. At his command, and in imitation of what the burghers of Paris had already achieved, the more important cities in France were surrounded with powerful defence works, consisting of a high thick wall punctuated at regular intervals by round towers, projecting in such a way that they could protect the wall. At the same time the king resolved the problem of manpower by making it the duty of the population to ensure the guarding and protection of the wall against possible enemies. To reinforce this system further, Philippe Auguste ordered a specially formed body of engineers to build forts beyond the walls. These were all conceived along the same lines, hardly varying from the north of the kingdom to Berry in central France: they were round towers protected on the outside by a broad deep ditch and reinforced on the inside by rib vaults which also acted as fire-breaks; defence proper was restricted to the summit of the walls. In Paris the precautionary measures taken were even greater, with the construction on the right bank of the river (facing Normandy) of a powerful fortress, the Louvre. Its rectangular plan was used as a model elsewhere in France, at Dourdan and at Yèvre-le-Châtel. This type of fortress was strategically placed and required only a limited number of men to assure its protection; it resulted from the study of ancient monuments, from the recognition of the weakness of contemporary constructions, and from a deeper knowledge of ancient texts, especially the Stratagems of Vegetius.

The formula perfected by Philippe Auguste and his engineers rapidly became established throughout the kingdom: Carcassonne, Coucy, Boulogne, Angers and Najac are the most famous surviving examples. It continued in use for a very long time, appearing at the beginning of the 14th century at Villandraut, the native region of Pope Clement V, who ordered a castle to be built there that was faithful to the general conceptions of the beginning of the 13th century. This system was not, however, adopted in Germany or England for some time: the Norman castles in the Marches of Wales, for instance, were of the old "motte and bailey" type.

The early 14th century also saw the appearance of the first residential castles, in which the lord could live comfortably with his court. Avignon offers the best example. Having decided to establish himself in this town, Pope Benedict XII (1334–42) resolved to build a palace that could also serve as a fortress. The impressively bare walls of his castle were capped by corbelled battlements. Clement VI (1342–52) considerably enlarged the work of his predecessor, preserving its external severity, while providing the interior with a decorative programme of

Castle of Saône, Syria

Following their capture of the fortress of Saône at the beginning of the 12th century, the Franks made haste to improve its defences, for the site commanded the route which led from Latakia to the Orontes. The fortifications extended for nearly 730 metres (800 yards).

Mehun-sur-Yèvre

The castle of Mehun-sur-Yèvre is characteristic of castles built in the 12th and 13th centuries and later substantially remodelled (the Louvre is another example – a military fortress of the late 12th century which lost its function when a new wall incorporated it into the city). Charles V (1364–80) turned the austere 13th century fortress into an agreeable princely residence, calling in the greatest architects and sculptors of the age. The count of Anjou effected a similar transformation at Saumur and the duke of Berry at Mehun.

Constantinople

The construction by Thedosius II of a new wall to protect Constantinople (413–40) was an important moment in the history of military architecture. Two parallel walls were built and reinforced by numerous vaulted towers. The technique of bonding stone with bands of brick formed part of a perfectly mastered ancient tradition.

Fortress, Armenia

Military architecture in Armenia followed its own line of development and produced innovations in many ways superior to what was being built in Europe at the same time. Ashlar walls appeared very early, together with strongly projecting round towers which protected the curtain walls. On the plains, castles were built on a regular plan and with smaller dimensions, while mountain fortresses continued to be adapted to their sites, whose irregularities they followed.

rare elegance. At that time there was nothing to suggest that the war between France and England would last a hundred years. But as the need became felt, other fortresses were built in areas where danger threatened. Elsewhere the king and lords contented themselves with reinforcing older structures by the addition of up-to-date defensive improvements.

New formulas which came into use can be seen in two imposing structures built by Charles V (1364–80), the Bastille and Vincennes. The purpose of the former was to protect Paris on the east as well as to keep watch for any signs of insurrection; Vincennes was to act as a forward defence. The Bastille, with its polygonal plan of six unequal sides, was very novel in conception: the curtain walls rose to the same height as the towers, which allowed the formation of a continuous path around the summit, following the curvature of the walls and making movement easier for the defenders. This principle was widely adopted until the beginning of the 16th century. Vincennes was even more unusual:

disgusted with Paris, the king envisaged the establishment of an administrative capital there, as Louis XIV was later to do at Versailles. A huge enclosure (335 by 175 metres/360 by 190 yards), with rectangular towers at its four corners, sheltered the carefully preserved 13th century manor house. To this the king added only a large chapel on the ground floor. To strengthen the defences he built a keep on the west curtain wall, protected by its own outer wall. Within the keep were the apartments of the king and queen. Another return to Romanesque ideas was the raising of the entrance from the ground floor back on to the first floor. Many other contemporary castles imitated this feature to strengthen their defence. On the other hand, earlier structures which no longer served a military purpose were fitted out extraordinarily luxuriously. Charles V showed the way with the Louvre which, now sheltered within an extension of the city walls, became a pleasure palace. The duke of Berry at Mehun-sur-Yèvre and the duke of Anjou at Saumur followed the royal example. Only Louis of Orléans undertook the

construction of huge fortresses, such as that at Pierrefonds, which was completed, and La Ferté-Milon, which never was. During the second half of the 15th century castles were built which definitely, if rather late, reflected a response to progress in techniques of attack. Cannon, barely mastered at the beginning of the century, gradually became more effective. Battlements lost their function and tended therefore to disappear; the height of fortifications was reduced; the number of gun-slots was markedly increased.

Bridges were also an important element in defence. From the end of the 9th century Charles the Bald built a number of wooden bridges so that he might keep the Normans back. In the 13th century the gate tower reappeared, linking the bridge to a larger fortified complex: an example is the Valentré Bridge at Cahors. The principle had been carefully worked out by the engineers of Philippe Auguste, who protected the head of the bridge with a fort and linked its fortification closely with that of the city.

Carisbrooke Castle, Isle of Wight

Built on a mound, Carisbrooke Castle is a 12th century example of the traditional pattern of English military architecture, which did not develop significantly until the 13th century.

The Krak des Chevaliers

The capture by Tancred in 1110 of what was to become the Krak des Chevaliers made it possible to guard the pass of Homs and ensured the survival of Tripoli. New construction work was immediately undertaken, which in turn underwent important modifications until the time of the capture of the castle by the Muslims in 1271. A vast outer ward protected by round and square towers surrounds the castle proper, which is protected by an inner wall and composed of a number of buildings. At the centre is the courtyard on to which the great hall faces, with a gallery running along it. The quality of the stonework in this complex structure shows that the best masons were employed. On the right, in the western part, is a hall 120 metres (130 yards) long, with a barrel vault which is illuminated at regular intervals by openings in the vault.

Passive defence: rectangular stone keeps

The Bayeux tapestry, dating from the end of the 11th century, supplements other evidence that the substitution of stone for wood in the construction of military fortresses took place gradually. Of the five castles represented in the tapestry, four are still of timber. This helps us to understand why structures that were technically more modern in conception remained tied to older traditions, their architects remaining content simply to translate into stone what they had previously known in wood – which, together with earth, they continued faithfully to use throughout in the construction of palisades.

The first generation of keeps are distinguished by their square or, more generally, rectangular plans; in effect these continue the plan, imposed by their timber constructions, of wooden keeps. They have the same characteristics – very thick, high walls with few openings, to avoid weakening the wall, and an entrance set at least 5 metres (16 feet) above ground level, on the first floor, either by means of a removable ladder, or by a planked bridge linked to the outer walls, or even sometimes by an outer construction built of stone and called the "little keep" (Loches, Montbazon). Inside the principal keep there were several floors, originally made of planks. The unlit ground floor, where there was a well, was generally used as a cellar. The first floor was reserved for the master of the house and his immediate family, and the upper levels for the rest of the household and for everyday life. The top of the keep – where our attempts at reconstruction are always complicated by transformations of the original – was used as a lookout and, when necessary, for

defence. Concern for defence also extended to the communication between the floors inside. Communication between the ground and first floors was by means of a ladder passing either between the floor timbers or, after the introduction of vaulting, through an oculus. The same went for the upper levels, and this permitted the occupants to retreat from floor to floor once the enemy had succeeded in entering. When the first stone stairs appeared, fitted within the thickness of the walls, they were always located on opposite sides on each floor, to force assailants to cross the rooms. Comfort remained limited, and examples of chimneys and latrines are rare. The powerful masses of masonry constituted an adequate means of resistance; even so, they were strengthened by careful construction when their master had the means. Furthermore, to counter attempts at undermining, which led to the capture of many fortresses, the foot of the keep would be buried in a mound of earth.

There were notable differences between these structures, even if the main principles – which survived in certain areas until the end of the 12th century, as the example at Dover shows – were constant. Originally walls were smooth, without buttresses. These were added as an afterthought at Langeais and Loches, but later were built together with the walls, playing a significant part in strengthening them. They were of very varied shape – flat at Langeais, Montbazon (two out of six) and Beaugency; half-round at Montbazon (four) and Loches; flat but with two facets at Falaise. This last fortress had a further peculiarity in its two con-

joined corner buttresses, hollowed out at the centre to form rooms and staircases. Nevertheless, such buttresses were not a means of providing flanking, nor were there any flanking arrangements in the castles built by the Normans in England. Differences also appear in internal arrangement. At Langeais, which certainly dates from as early as the end of the 10th century, the floor of the first storey was supported by a central pillar, and at Loches and Falaise by a partition wall.

The keep developed both in plan and in construction during the course of the 11th and 12th centuries. The walls of the first stone keeps were extremely thick, but the thickness was to increase still further: 1.5 metres (5 feet) at Langeais and Loches (west), 2.5 metres (8 feet) at Beaugency, Montbazon and Loches, and up to 3 metres (10 feet) at Chambois and Falaise. The height of the keep, however, did not change so dramatically – Montbazon was 28 metres (90 feet) high, Loches 37 metres (120 feet) and Beaugency 36 metres (118 feet). The dimensions of the ground plan also increased.

The second stage in this evolution was the progressive abandonment of these enormous masses of stone, which were difficult to build and had obvious points of weakness. Profiting from the study of ancient texts and structures, engineers tried to adopt a principle of defence from every angle. They therefore set about building fortresses on a circular plan, of which one of the oldest examples is Fréteval, dating from the middle of the 11th century.

Falaise

Falaise was easily defensible, perched on its sandstone rock and separated from Mount Mirrha to the west by a ravine. A number of building programmes succeeded one another: the great round tower was the work of the military engineers of Philippe Auguste after his conquest of Normandy. The keep has two additional elements – the chapel of St. Peter on the south and the "little keep" on the west. Entrance was from the east by way of a door cut through the wall at first floor level.

Beaugency

The keep of Beaugency is one of the best preserved in France, now standing at a height of 36 metres (118 feet); it originally rose a little higher. Traces of the mound that surrounded it until the 19th century can be seen around the base. The broad flanks are supported by four flat buttresses which taper inwards at the top. Access was by way of a door in the curtain wall preceded by a drawbridge. The ground floor had a double barrel-vault.

B. Barbey, Magnum

Loches

Loches had a succession of fortifications from the 11th century onwards. The rectangular stone keep is one of the oldest parts, dating back to the end of the 11th century: originally it had no buttresses. Construction was resumed at the beginning of the 12th century: the walls were given buttresses, and the west wall was thickened on the inside and given buttresses at the corners. The buttresses, applied to piers, have a half-round form that can also be found at Montbazon and on certain keeps in Normandy.

Arch. phot. Paris. S.P.A.D.E.M.

Langeais

The keep of Langeais was one of the fortifications due to Folque Nerra, count of Anjou (987–1040). He had it built on the promontory which dominates the Loire. Originally the walls, which enclose an internal space of 16 by 7 metres (52 by 23 feet), carried neither buttresses (these were added a little before the middle of the 11th century), nor vaults, nor a stone staircase. They are built of stone blocks laid in mortar and crudely covered by a facing of smaller stones.

Loudun

The keep of Loudun was built in the 12th century at the summit of the hill and at the time marked the furthest extent of Anjou in the direction of Poitou. The dimensions of the plan are small (9 by 4.5 metres/30 by 15 feet), especially in relation to the height of the building (30 metres/100 feet). The stone coursing is very carefully laid, and the narrowly spaced buttresses (three on the narrow faces, four on the broad) taper into the wall at the top.

Arch. phot. Paris

Montrichard

The keep of Montrichard rises above the town and looks out over the valley of the Cher. Built in 1110–20, it is of fairly modest dimensions (15 by 5 metres/50 by 16 feet), and its present height is 20 metres (65 feet). The buttresses are applied in an irregular fashion against piers on the south and south-west faces. The regular stone facing conceals rubble walls.

Ciccione, Rapho

Active defence: round towers

The determination of Philippe Auguste after 1180 to reconquer his kingdom from the Plantagenets, whose possessions extended widely throughout it, resulted in a revolution in the principles of defence, in terms of both strategy and architecture. Until then an uncoordinated system had prevailed, in which isolated fortresses were built without links between them and requiring very substantial garrisons to guard them in case of attack. This was succeeded by a strategic vision founded on new principles – the need to hold territory once conquered from a population whose loyalty could not be relied on; and the integration of several fortresses in a homogeneous defensive system. To achieve these objectives the king of France set up a team of military engineers unique for the period; 13 of their names are known to us. Their task was to direct construction, for which they were responsible to the king. Thanks to certain documents which have survived, the course of each operation can be traced. The choice of site was always dictated by tactical imperatives decided on by the king and his council; a study of the terrain and the exact siting was left to the engineer. As for the general layout, this was decided once for all and is identical in all known fortresses.

Philippe's constructions were, however, of several types: city walls, generally built at the expense of the inhabitants, who were also responsible for their maintenance and surveillance; additions to existing older fortifications; and, finally, new structures. In this last category Philippe Auguste was most original. Enough examples survive to permit some sure conclusions. They consisted of round towers of similar dimensions (exterior diameter between 14 and 19 metres/46 and 62 feet; thickness of walls between 4 and 7 metres/13 and 23 feet; height, though more difficult to assess, generally around 30 metres/100 feet). The tower was protected externally by a deep, broad ditch constructed of stone like the bottom of a barrel. The walls were pierced on the ground floor by two doors on opposite sides, guarded by drawbridges light enough to be operated by one or two persons. The tower contained three levels supported on rib vaults. On the ground floor there was a fireplace with hood and chimney, and a recess lined with tiles to serve as a bread oven, together with a well and latrines. A spiral staircase fitted into the thickness of the wall rose from the bottom of the tower to its summit, which was covered by a projecting timber roof.

This new disposition offered several advantages; in particular, it allowed easy horizontal and vertical circulation. Under siege, it was easy to take refuge inside, with the drawbridge raised. Access to the summit was rapid, thanks to the broad, well-lit staircase: the presence on the ground floor of a well, a chimney and, very probably, livestock, made it possible to withstand a long siege. The circular plan, the thickness of the walls, and the rib vaults which helped to bind the walls together, enabled the tower to resist the engines of war which by then had reached a peak of development. Finally, the broad ditches reinforced with stone gave protection from undermining.

Depending on its location, the tower played a varying role. Abandoning the attempt to defend the countryside, which had until then been the role of all defensive works of stone, the king tied his fortifications closely to the cities. The towers constituted a formidable addition to defence. The first ones, at Vernon and Gisors (1196), were still integral with the castle, and the city walls abutted them, but they were soon made free-standing. At Villeneuve-sur-Yonne, the alignment of the walls was even altered so that the tower did not become attached to them. This detachment allowed the garrison to take refuge in the city if the tower should fall, and to shelter in the tower should the enemy overrun the city.

At the time of their construction, these towers enjoyed another advantage, new to the medieval West – that of standardization. As a result, a considerable amount of construction time was saved, which explains the extraordinary speed with which they were built. At the same time, their cost could be estimated reasonably accurately.

Towers were no more than one part of Philippe Auguste's military strategy – a defence system in which all the parts lent one another support. Another factor should be mentioned, the psychological dimension, of which the importance should not be underestimated. The towers reproduced almost exactly the tower of the Louvre; they thus became the visible symbols of the newly acquired royal power.

Caen Castle

The castle at Caen constitutes an important complex which testifies to the long and varied history of the city. Excavations undertaken within the complex since the Second World War have made it possible to work out the plan in more detail and thus to establish the role of the castle in the 13th century. In fact it followed the principles laid down by the architects of Philippe Auguste, as exemplified by the Louvre: a square enclosure – slightly irregular at Caen – at whose angles stand markedly projecting round towers from which to guard the curtain walls.

Editions Publitotal

Lauros-Giraudon

Gisors

The conquest of Normandy was the principal objective of Philippe Auguste. In 1196 Gisors was ceded to him by Richard the Lionheart, and he immediately set about improving its defences. The keep, dating from the end of the 11th century, dominating the Epte from its mound, was abandoned in favour of a new defensive structure closer to the river. As at Rouen, the tower was directed against the city, of uncertain loyalty.

Joan of Arc's Tower, Rouen

Soon after the conquest of Rouen (1204), Philippe Auguste's engineers decided to relocate the ducal castle, which stood on the banks of the Seine. They built it above the town over which it was intended to keep watch. At the same time it could be easily secured in case of siege. Despite a major restoration, the tower still has more or less its original appearance.

Villeneuve-sur-Yonne

At this town standing on the extreme tip of the Île-de-France, and therefore facing the county of Champagne, Philippe Auguste's engineers built a defensive tower. They located it outside the walls, whose course was altered for the purpose. It stood on the east side of the town, near the royal castle, which was within the walls.

Arch. phot. Paris. S.P.A.D.E.M

Carcassonne

Carcassonne is a unique example of a double fortification. The older part dates from late antiquity, the more recent part from the 13th century. The first without doubt inspired the second. The projection of the towers from the wall, and the fact that they therefore commanded it, made possible a more flexible system of defence.

Arch. phot. Paris. S.P.A.D.E.M

Pictor

A new civic spirit: bridges

The new spirit of the medieval West was expressed not only in churches and monasteries, and in the fortifications of castles and cities, but also in civic achievements. The study of this last category presents grave difficulties, for most examples no longer exist, having been replaced by others in the cause of technical progress. Yet there is no doubt that medieval engineers excelled in the construction of bridges and demonstrated a clear technical superiority over their Roman predecessors.

In antiquity, the construction of bridges was accompanied by religious rites performed by priests. The Middle Ages respected this tradition, and examples abound of members of the clergy encouraging the construction of a bridge, invoking the assistance of the Almighty or his saints. An ancient tradition held that bridges were often the work of the devil or resulted from divine intervention. This explains the frequent presence of a shrine or chapel mid-way along the span. The maintenance of bridges could be entrusted to brotherhoods, who often also built them. Thus the Pontive friars built bridges at Bonpas, Lourmarin, Mallemort and Mirabeau. The brotherhood of the Holy Spirit, founded in 1265, was responsible for the construction of the Bridge of the Holy Spirit over the Rhône, not completed until 1307. Bishops well understood the importance of bridges: Humbert, archbishop of Vienna, rebuilt the Roman bridge there in 1219. Many other examples could be cited to illustrate the concern of the civil and religious authorities in such projects.

During the long period stretching from the end of antiquity to the beginning of the 16th century, the construction of bridges underwent important modifications. In the Carolingian era, bridges were made of wood. Eginhard, a kinsman of Charlemagne, had such a bridge built to span the Rhine. These wooden bridges also had another role in that they could be used to prevent invaders from advancing up rivers and streams. With the commercial developments of the 11th and 12th centuries, these timber bridges, which a strong flood could carry away, became extremely inconvenient and were therefore replaced by bridges of stone. The engineers who undertook this difficult enterprise rediscovered and improved the techniques of antiquity. The biggest problem of all was the foundations, which had to be laid either under dry conditions, after diverting the watercourse or damming the stream and pumping the water out, or by specialist divers.

Another innovation concerned the shape of the abutments, which were henceforth pointed, both upstream and downstream, a form well suited to cutting through the descending flow, to breaking up ice-floes, and to reducing the upstream erosion of the stonework by the action of the water. A constant preoccupation of engineers in the Middle Ages was to prevent the bridges holding back too much water: this risked causing floods, as recent cases have shown. The build-up of water could also result in the bridge being carried away. It was therefore of fundamental importance to reduce obstructions to the flow of water to a minimum. Broad spans were employed and openings contrived in the mass of masonry above the abutments. In this respect the pointed arch was a crucial advance. High, pointed openings could let through even the most swollen floods. The technical innovations of the Gothic era also included the adoption of a pointed span heightened by inclined approach ramps. The central arch, thus enlarged, allowed a better flow of river traffic. At the same time, the sharper pitch of the bridge allowed flood and rain water to drain off more quickly.

The individual nature of a bridge depended very much on its position: it was of urban character when in the centre of a city – in which case houses were often built on it, as on the Ponte Vecchio in Florence – and military if outside. Numerous fortified bridges were conceived primarily as means of defence: each head was protected by defensive features (gatehouses or towers) which overlooked the approaches. Sometimes defensive works were added to the full span of the bridge. To improve resistance to attack still further, in some cases the stone roadway was cut through and space left for long timber planks, which could easily be withdrawn to prevent access to the opposite bank.

Valentré Bridge, Cahors

Built between 1308 and 1380, this bridge spans the Lot at Cahors. It is protected by three tall towers, one at each end and a third at mid-point, between its six arches. It was originally linked to the walls of the city, forming part of the defensive system and enabling the hills on the opposite bank to be kept under surveillance.

St. Savin

The old bridge which spans the Gartempe at St. Savin dates back to the 14th century. It was so narrow that refuges were provided so that pedestrians could get out of the way when vehicles crossed. The abutments of the slightly pointed arches are rectangular downstream, but prow-shaped upstream.

Airvault

The bridge at Airvault, dating back to the 12th century, has half-round arches formed of parallel ribs. This system has the double merit of economy and lightness. The roadway crosses on paving over the arches. The piers are pointed upstream and rectangular downstream.

Giraudon

Ponte Vecchio, Florence

The Arno's floods have on numerous occasions carried away the bridges which span the river at the point where the banks come closest together. After a disastrous flood in 1333 a new bridge was built which, despite the precautions taken, again held back the waters in 1966 and caused Florence to be flooded once more. Following a medieval practice abandoned only in the 17th century, shops were built on the bridge, cantilevered on wooden props.

J. Feuille, Arch. phot. Paris, S.P.A.D.E.M.

Orthez

The bridge which spans the torrent of Pau at Orthez was fortified by a tower, constructed saddle-back between the two unequal arches.

Lauros-Giraudon

Bridge of the Holy Spirit, Pont St. Esprit

In 1265 Jean de Tessanges ordered the construction of the Pont St. Esprit ("Bridge of the Holy Spirit") over the Rhône; it took some 40 years to complete. Its length of 1 kilometre (over half a mile) explains some of the difficulties encountered. The spandrels of its 28 segmental arches were pierced to allow flood waters through. The town of Pont St. Esprit takes its name from this magnificent piece of engineering.

241

Columns of a pavilion in the Court of the Lions, Alhambra, Granada (14th century)

Islamic architecture is characterized by both subtlety and rigour, in the handling of space, the fall of light, and the articulation and disposition of each building. The gateway to the great Ghorid mosque of Herat (12th century), below, and the later Nasrid polychrome decoration (14th century), shown opposite, recall in their increasing use of colour an aspect of medieval Islamic work that is too often forgotten. The development of Islamic architecture was towards the use of bolder masses and more monumental plans, but always it retained the outlook of the early Middle Ages when a taste for ornament and finesse threatened almost to overwhelm it.

The art of Islam seems familiar enough to the Westerner, who might well feel he knows its essential qualities and has a clear picture of it based on direct observation. But as soon as he tries to give those qualities precise definition the impression dissolves. Taking buildings alone, and thinking for example of the various forms of mosque, all sense of consistency disintegrates. What does an Ottoman mosque in Istanbul have in common with the great mosque of Cordoba? Can an Afghan palace and a Moroccan madrasa in any sense be regarded as manifestations of a single culture? (For those who know Morocco and Afghanistan, the earth fortifications of the two countries do in fact present many similarities.) In the face of a reality too diverse to admit of easy classification, this first impression of consistency, which seems so well to reflect the doctrinal uniformity of Islam, is extremely difficult to explain.

In the effort to discover the essence of Islamic architecture, a good number of obstacles arise. We are dealing with a world which is still alive and changing, so much so that its present appearance can obscure 15 centuries of constant evolution. This was a major pitfall for some researchers on the subject. They interpreted the "backward" appearance of Islamic cities at the beginning of this century as a relic of the Middle Ages. The foreign researcher is liable to be more conscious of what is closest to himself, noticing what Islam inherited from the civilizations it in part conquered rather than what it injected of its own. This new civilization, born out of little-known Saudi Arabia, can easily appear as a poor relation beside the Byzantine and Sassanid empires. Furthermore, in trying to define too exactly the role of Islam, whose sphere of influence has stretched for more than one and a half thousand years from the Atlantic to eastern Asia, do we not run the risk of overlooking its capacity for diversity and flexibility whilst staying true to essentials, which is among its major qualities?

We feel at heart that Islamic monuments, in that very diversity which surprises us, are the best and certainly the most objective evidence of the coherence of the Muslim community. We shall try in the pages that follow to point out – imperfectly, because the subject is immense – the essential geographical and historical features of this remarkable architecture. We may sense that there is a European, African and, in particular, an Asian Islam – quite rightly. But the best avenue of approach is to discover as far as possible those elements which from century to century have given focus to the life of all the Islamic communities. We shall try to follow this architecture in the hope of understanding how it continuously adapted itself in time and space to the needs of Islam and its way of life. Over and above the Islamic religion, born in Arabia and constantly centred on Arabia though geographically dispersed, over and above the world of the cities in which Islam developed, we must first examine what were the types of building the Islamic peoples developed and how Islamic society responded in the face of more and more diverse environmental conditions and architectural traditions. The main Western idea of Islamic life was formed from their cities – from the reports of travellers and invaders. These were presented as a stereotype of urban anarchy, with warrens of crooked alleyways that were an affront to the idea of orderly planning which was so much part of the classical and Renaissance tradition. Certainly this kind of medieval city, untouched by any attempt at municipal organization, can be found from Damascus to Fez. The nature of its streets is significant as far as urban life is concerned; the houses that border the streets are conceived as turned towards an inner world in which outer façades and approaches matter little. Yet truly monumental compositions do exist.

Conquering Islam, spreading out from its Arabian bases of Mecca and Medina, was soon, like its predecessors, in debt to its own conquests. The character of the first Islamic cities is linked directly to that of the pre-Islamic cities: the boundaries and the two great axes of the ancient city of Damascus owe little to Islam, and its mosque, as we shall see, takes the place of a temple to Zeus, which had itself given way to a church. But where building was ex novo, very deliberate planning is apparent. From the plan of Anjar with its insulae (tenement blocks) to the circular layout of Baghdad, inaugurated when the Abbasid caliphate established itself in Mesopotamia, Islam could adapt with equal mastery typically Asian and typically Mediterranean plans. And in every case the town was adapted to the terrain, climate and function as much as to the location or culture. Certain places were from the beginning open cities – Marrakesh, for example – but more often they were protected by walls, or included a citadel, an acropolis or a high qasaba, as was appropriate to the site. We would not expect to find the same pattern of streets on the steep banks of the river at Fez as on the flat site of Bust. But it is most important to emphasize how far Islam was able, as we shall see, to carry out vast architectural and urban-planning projects. Life in the cities was intense, so a full analysis of their growth, the incorporation of suburbs and so on, would be long and complicated. But we can at least appreciate the richness of an endlessly vital and varied tradition. There is no model Islamic city: there are, rather,

The Ghorid gateway of the great mosque of Herat (Afghanistan). The older parts of this structure, preserved inside a mosque which has since been completely altered, show in their contrasted decoration of turquoise and brick the early stages of a trend towards the use of rich colour, which is characteristic of all Islam.

numerous rich agglomerations of superb monuments – such as the great mosque of Damascus or that of Cordoba. Numerous monumental designs were developed in response to the varying needs and tastes of the peoples of Islam, whether "patrons" or "architects". These we must now trace.

The building which seems at first sight to typify Islamic architecture is the mosque. But the word itself in English is ambiguous, since it is applied to different buildings with distinct functions. For the prayer repeated by the faithful five times daily, no particular building is necessary. But when the whole community gathers together for the Friday midday prayers, at which a sermon (khutba) is given, it must be in a space whose purity reflects that of the believers. This is the structure which for convenience we call the great mosque (jami). It should be distinguished from the simple oratory (masjid), which serves a quite different function, and is in a way the only Islamic building designed for collective use.

The architectural history of the great mosque is that of a continuing search for harmony between the structure, its plan, and its liturgical functions. The believers, arranged in parallel rows, pray facing Mecca: one wall, the qibla, whose name expresses its orientation, provides for the requirements of prayer. A shallow apse is hollowed out of it – the mihrab. Near to this is a pulpit, the minbar, from which the sermon is given. This constitutes the basic mosque. It was surrounded at first (as at Kufa) by a ditch, then by a wall, and then covered over in one part, the zulla, which became the prayer-hall. Only the faithful were given shelter; the rest of the enclosure was a form of outdoor courtyard (sahn) surrounded with porticoes (riwaq) of varying plan. This basic arrangement continued to evolve in response to other functions of this place of weekly assembly. The political and social structure which, like justice and education, cannot be dissociated from religion, played its part in the process as well as stimulating the development of other architectural forms altogether. Thus, for instance, a small chamber was built in the courtyards of Umayyad mosques to serve as a treasure house.

The original architecture of the first mosque – the house of the Prophet – is not known, nor is that of any of the earliest sanctuaries of Arabia. Its rapid conquests soon brought Islam into contact with other civilizations and its builders were able to make use of the elements of the Roman basilica, for example – first at Damascus, where a broader and higher nave leads from the

court to the mihrab. Though its primary function was to indicate the direction of Mecca, such a nave might also, through its secular associations, have drawn attention to the political role of the great mosque. Islam, which could assimilate and re-diffuse what it gathered from all sides, frequently reverted to such dominant naves, later punctuated by one or more domes.

It is always important to relate the two essential roles of the mosque. As we have said, it often had a political role: the name of the ruler featured in the khutba, and he – or his representative – was soon provided with a private enclosure next to the mihrab, the maqsura. But in the 9th century a desire seems to have been felt for a larger space round the qibla, without abandoning the axial nave inherited from the basilica. A T-shaped plan was the result, which enjoyed remarkable favour in Mesopotamia, Egypt, and Hispano-Maghrebi territories. The significance of the "transept" in front of the qibla is not clear, nor that of the dome which surmounted the crossing of the two naves. But whether secular or religious, these features were quickly accepted throughout Islam. It was doubtless the prestige of these forms, developed at the very centre of the empire, which established them even in the most remote provinces and under different caliphates.

Architectural innovations, developing always within local building traditions, reflected a constant search for harmony between structure and liturgy. Certain examples will be given later. The evolution of the mosque in Iran is particularly instructive. The mosques of this area incorporated a classical type of prayer-hall such as that, for example, at Nayin: it combined an emphatic axial nave with a courtyard with porticoes of considerable scale. At Isfahan, the basis was a great mosque of the Mesopotamian type, to which was added a maqsura in the form of a detached domed pavilion in imitation of the Sassanid temples of fire, and finally a courtyard with four iwans. This represented a return, typical of the whole Islamic world, to the most persistent features of the architecture of the region. A different type of mosque was developing at the same time in the West: the progressive enlargement of the great mosque at Cordoba, which was of the classic Umayyad type, by the extension of the qibla and by the introduction in the 10th century of the T-plan, stimulated the taste for mosques with a longitudinal plan with arcades of columns perpendicular to the qibla. In the 12th century the desire to imitate the East seems to have curtailed this

development and even led to a revival, as at Rabat, of archaic forms deriving from Mesopotamia. But the type nevertheless remained current, and the latest Maghrebi mosques prove that this regional variation of completely Mediterranean origin was never forgotten.

Dado of enamelled tiles ("zellij") at the Alhambra in Granada. This polychrome geometric decoration shows a further stage, later than Herat, in the late medieval development of a taste for the play of increasingly vivid colours.

In Anatolia, two original types became established in succession. Due to the harsh climate of the region, together perhaps with the memory of pre-Islamic forms, from Seljuk times onwards the courtyard was reduced to a simple open bay. In other respects however – such as carpentry and stone vaulting – Seljuk architecture was extremely sophisticated. The huge domed sanctuaries of Byzantium, of which Santa Sophia is the best example, stimulated the Ottoman architects to a long series of experiments, the fruits of which are well known in the south-east Mediterranean. And so the very building which every week symbolized the unity of the community of believers also illustrated the diverse vitality of Islamic architecture. The great mosques, whose very orientation recalled to

243

Gateway of the "ribat" at Sousse (Tunisia).
The projecting gatehouse of this barracks for the soldiers of the Faith has a concealed portcullis; it shows a typical re-use of classical fragments.

urban ring, and at Samarra, to where the royal residence was moved, there was evidently a need for protection from possible uprisings. But there were other factors: the very concept of authority had been influenced by Sassanid Asia, and the growing complexity of palace ceremonial, merging with local traditions, had brought about a complete change in the architecture of a princely residence.

Westerners are astonished today by these palace-cities which, it must be said, were quite exceptional architectural performances. Their massive vaults of unbaked brick, faced with a skin of carved plaster, clearly reveal that those who built them could draw on the resources of an immense empire. And each sovereign in turn left his mark on the palace complex with his own monuments to his power. Vast courtyards led the visitor in sequence on a slow progress round the official quarters which, at Samarra, opened on to tended gardens along the banks of the Tigris; the complex included a mosque and an oratory. Plans were sufficiently rigorous to imply the presence of an architect, but too extended and too little documented for us to be able to trace the steps in their creation as we should like.

Palaces were frequently deserted and allowed to decay. As a result, we do not know the details of how they were run and used, as we do with the great mosques. There is the same story, however, of both local tradition and exchange between East and West. At Cordoba, for example, we know nothing of the first palace of the emirs and Umayyad caliphs who achieved independence from the authority of Baghdad, except that it was a building of moderate dimensions adjacent to the great mosque and linked to it by a private passage that allowed the caliph to go directly from his residence to the maqsura reserved for him in the sanctuary.

The same arrangement existed at Madinat al-Zahra, the only city of government to have been explored. Adjacent to the great mosque, the palace buildings were arranged around a series of patios, containing gardens, pools and fountains. The main reception rooms were basilical in plan; attached to them were secondary and service rooms, and sometimes baths. Corridors and ramps provided the means of circulation through the sequence of buildings and patios. Only the inward-facing façades received any architectural decoration. The cities of government in Morocco – the Qasba of Marrakesh (12th century), Fez Jdid (13th–14th century), and above all the Alhambra at Granada, which will be discussed later – faithfully followed this tradition. Only Alaouid Meknes, built by Moulay Ismail, shows any variation in the basic pattern. Everywhere Islamic architecture seems committed to a life turned inwards.

On the southern shore of the Mediterranean the influence of the Asian East on the princely cities appears, to the best of our knowledge, to have been more marked. Tlemcen and Mansura, to the west of present-day Algeria, are examples of the Hispano-Maghrebi style, but eastern North Africa developed its own harmoniously proportioned stone architecture, characterized by a moderate scale, complicated entrances through chicanes and niched walls. With the 10th century, under the Fatimids, we can feel the influx in Tunisia of eastern ideas – for example in the

group of buildings in Kairouan, where a dar al-imara was fitted into the apse of the great mosque. A palace at Raqqada, an Aghlabid city of government to the south of Kairouan (9th century), was extended by the addition of apartments arranged in long lines, which though their date is still unclear, suggest a change in attitude; but the rooms retained the Mediterranean basilical plan. In the 10th century clear evidence of change can be found in the 100 hectares (250 acres) of the Fatimid city of al-Mansuriya – for example in the audience chambers of one of its palaces, measuring nearly 5,000 sq. metres (5,980 sq. yards), in which the usual basilical plan has been replaced by a room of "Iranian" plan. Also, the development there of a commercial quarter, drawing economic activity away from the neighbouring metropolis of Kairouan, shows that when, as at Baghdad, the government at a moment of insecurity withdrew, it quickly reorganized an urban life around itself: one that was much more under control because it was near the seat of authority.

all the common centre and symbol of unity – Mecca – also bore witness to the strength of local traditions. The sheer size of the Islamic empire allowed local traditions to exist; its religion held them in check.

A second type of building was set beside the great mosque by early orientalist scholars, the "centre of government". The seat of authority, the residence of the caliph himself or of his representatives or rivals, gave rise to increasingly ambitious architectural programmes. Governors and local potentates, who little by little acquired effective independence, developed the architecture of the palace as a sign of their power. At the same time the qasr, which originally formed part of the town itself, came to be separated from it because of the need for security. Autonomous cities developed, centred on rulers and the services they required, royal towns or cities of government that very much reflected the mentality of the Islamic world.

The earliest known royal city of this type is without doubt Anjar in Lebanon, which had a wide influence. Its walls enclosed palaces, a great mosque next to one of them, baths, market buildings and a series of blocks which, if they can be identified, will give us a complete picture of the facilities then thought necessary to the entourage of a sovereign. These services were a microcosm of civic life, commerce and manufacture; official architecture and buildings for everyday life were intimately associated.

At the beginning of the Abbasid period there was rapid change – in less than a century – in the design of the royal palace and city. This evolution was due first of all to the transfer of the seat of the caliphate to Baghdad. It can be charted from the theoretical plan of the round city of al-Mansur, which has been reconstructed from texts, and from the better known plans of the gigantic constructions raised at Samarra along some 36 kilometres (22 miles) of the banks of the Tigris. Both at Baghdad, where the palace was originally inserted within an

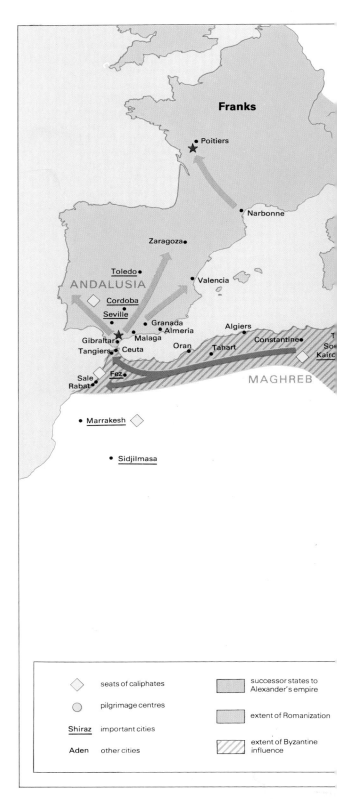

◇ seats of caliphates	successor states to Alexander's empire
○ pilgrimage centres	extent of Romanization
Shiraz important cities	extent of Byzantine influence
Aden other cities	

The provinces of central Asia, such as al-Andalus or the Maghreb, also had their sumptuous palaces though they were of more modest dimensions. The palace of Ghazna (Afghanistan) shows that, from the 11th century, formulas originating in Iraq were known and adopted. An enormous entrance opened on to a monumental courtyard of cruciform plan, and led, beyond the iwan that faced it, to the audience chambers and private apartments; a mosque, ranged across the western corner of the courtyard at an angle to the rest of the complex, completed the usual set of facilities.

The same arrangement on a larger scale can be found in the palace built by the Ghaznavids at Lashkari Bazar (Afghanistan): it consisted of several groups of buildings, with gardens and apartments arranged on a linear plan. But the presence of the type of layout featuring four iwans shows that the design, though originating in the heart of the empire, had been altered by local traditions.

A common conception of palace life inspired common solutions among architects of the medieval period; every region was in close touch with the centre of the empire, first Syria, then Mesopotamia. But little by little resurgent local traditions gained ground over the communal models which had been most influential in the first centuries of the empire. The new diversity became clearly apparent in the modern era. If Morocco, which always remained faithful to the Hispano-Maghrebi tradition, seems to have been affected by eastern influence in the scale of the constructions at Meknes, the points of similarity go no further. We have only to compare the Ottoman palace of Topkapi in Istanbul to Safavid architecture in Isfahan or to the Mughal palaces of Fatehpur Sikri, for example, to feel that henceforth regional or imperial traditions are the significant factors: we can now speak only of Ottoman Safavid, Mughal or Alaouid architecture, even if it was all produced within the broad context of the Islamic world. They remained to some extent tributaries of the Islamic way of life;

but this was no longer the unifying factor it had been for six centuries.

The mosque and the palace were two major fields in which Islamic architecture developed. But our consideration should not be restricted to them alone, since so many other monuments, either by their number or by their function, also influenced the life of the umma and the evolution of the art of building in the lands of Islam. The medina, for instance, the city proper, was enclosed by a wall furnished with towers, monumental gateways and posterns, which could be closed off in times of siege. The arrangement served other purposes than simply the defence of the city: it was useful for policing and necessary for the control of the economy. The walls were much simpler than those of the later Roman empire or of Byzantium, and frequently consisted of no more than a single ring; wall, ditch, and outer wall are found only occasionally.

Although these fortifications usually offered only one line of defence, they were

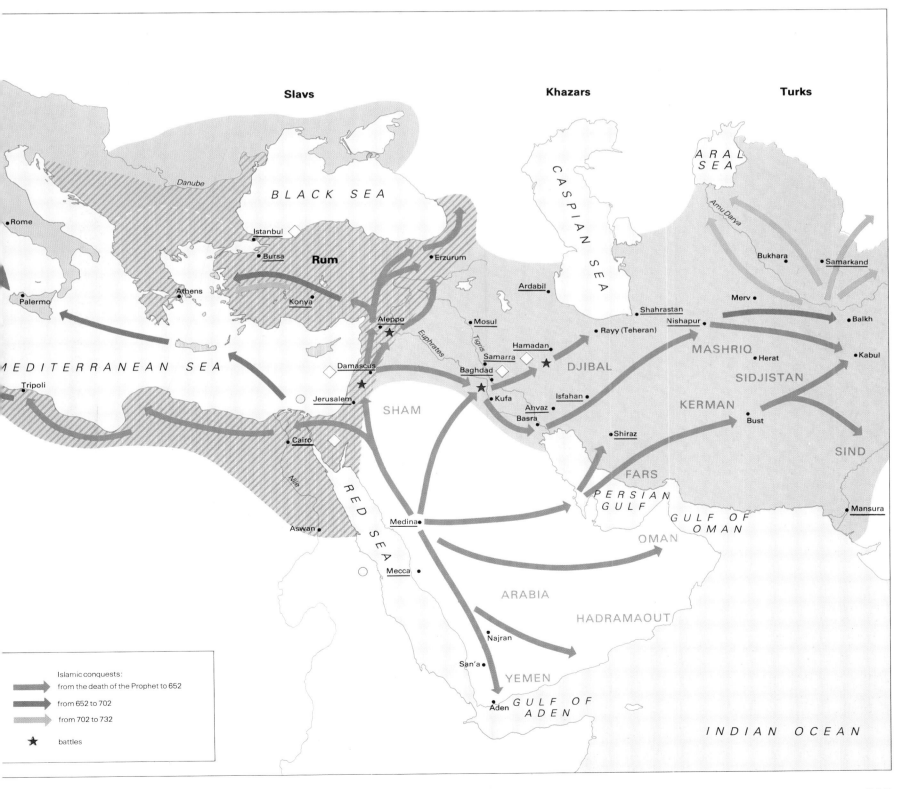

Islamic conquests:
from the death of the Prophet to 652
from 652 to 702
from 702 to 732
★ battles

Dates	The Christian West and Byzantium	Hispano-Maghrebi world	Near and Middle East	Iranian provinces
622			Hegira.	
629	Dagobert. Unification of Visigothic Spain.			
632			Death of Mohammed.	
634-642			Conquest of Syria and Mesopotamia.	
638			Foundation of *Basra* and *Kufa*.	
642			Conquest of Egypt. Foundation of *Fustat*.	
647		First raids on the Berbers.		
651				Conquest of Iranian provinces.
654				Conquest of Seistan.
660			UMAYYADS at Damascus.	
663	Constantine in Italy.			
670		Foundation of *Kairouan*.	Rebuilding of the great mosque of *Kufa*.	
673-678	Siege of Constantinople.			
680	Lombard domination in Italy.			
685	Justinian II.			
691			Dome of the Rock built in *Jerusalem*.	
705			Caliphate of al-Walid I.	Raids beyond the Oxus.
705-715		Capture of Ceuta.		
709			Great mosques of *Damascus*, *Aleppo*, *Jerusalem*, *Medina*.	
710			Royal palaces.	
710-716		Conquest of Spain. Raids into France.		Conquest of region beyond the Oxus.
714				
716	Last siege of Constantinople.		Castles in Syria.	
724				
725	Occupation of Narbonne.			
730		Kharijite rebellion among the Berbers.		
732	Battle of Poitiers.			
740-775	Constantine V.			
750			ABBASIDS.	Great mosque of *Damghan*.
751	Capture of Ravenna by the Lombards.			
754	Byzantine iconoclasm.			
754-775		UMAYYADS at Cordoba.	Caliphate of al-Mansur.	
756				
762			Foundation of *Baghdad*.	
771	Charlemagne king of the Franks.			
775	Consecration of St. Denis in France.			
785		Great mosque of *Cordoba* built.		
787	Council of Nicaea.			
c.790	St. Riquier built.	*Ribat* of *Monastir* built. Enlargement of the great mosque of *Cordoba*.		
796	Palatine chapel at *Aix-la-Chapelle*.			
800	Coronation of Charlemagne in Rome.	Foundation of *Fez*. AGHLABIDS in Ifriqiya.		
800-909				
814	Death of Charlemagne.			
817	First translations of relics to churches in *Rome*.	*Ribat* of *Sousse*.		
821				TAHRIDS in Khurasan.
821-873			Foundation of *Samarra*.	
836		Rebuilding of the great mosque of *Kairouan*.		
836-874				
843	Treaty of Verdun. End of iconoclasm.			
847-861			Caliphate of al-Mutawakkil. Great mosques and palaces of *Samarra*.	
850		Great mosque of *Sousse*.		
867-911			TULUNIDS in Egypt.	SAFFARIDS (Sistan, Khurasan).
868				
875	Charles the Bald emperor.			SAMANIDS (Trans-Oxus region, Khurasan).
876		Aghlabid palace of *Raqqada*.	Great mosque of Ibn Tulun in *Cairo*.	
879	Second Council of Constantinople.			
883			Samarra abandoned as capital.	
907				Mausoleum of Ismail the Samanid at *Bukhara*.
909-1171		FATIMIDS in Ifriqiya.		
910	Foundation of the abbey of *Cluny*.			
911	Naval defeat of the Byzantines.			
912		Reign of Abd al-Rahman III in Cordoba. Foundation of *Mahdiya*.		
916				
929-1004			HAMDANIDS (Djazira, Syria).	
932-936				BUYIDS.
935-969			IKHSHIDIDS in Egypt.	
936	Otto I king of Germany.	Foundation of *Madinat al-Zahra*.		
945-1055			BUYIDS (Iraq, western Iran).	
960				Mosque of *Nayin*.
969			FATIMIDS in Egypt. Foundation of *Cairo*.	
987	Consecration of Hugues Capet.			
998-1186				GHAZNAVIDS. Palace of *Lashkari Bazar*.
c.1000		Mosque of Bib Mardoum in *Toledo*.		
1001	Truce between Basil II and al-Hakim.			Conquest of the Punjab.
1001-1021				
1002	St. Benigne, *Dijon*, built.			
1003			Great mosque of al-Hakim in *Cairo*.	
1010		Andalusia divided amongst petty kings.		
c.1015	Crypt of St. Michael of *Hildesheim* built.			
1032				SELJUKS in Trans-Oxus region.
1036-1147		ALMORAVIDS in the Maghreb.		
1037	County of Castile becomes a kingdom. Abbey of *Jumièges* built.			
1038	Treaty between Byzantines and Fatimids.			Capture of Nishapur.
1038-1157			Seljuk movement (Iran, Near East).	
c.1040-1063	St. Mary of the Capitol built in *Cologne*.			
1049	Consecration of the church of *Ottmarsheim*.			

Dates	The Christian West and Byzantium	Hispano-Maghrebi world	Near and Middle East	Iranian provinces
1051				Capture of Isfahan.
1055			SELJUKS in Baghdad.	
1063-1073	St. Mark's built in *Venice*.			
1065	Consecration of *Westminster* Abbey.			
1066-1071	Abbey of *Monte Cassino* built.			
1067			Nizamiya *madrasa* in *Baghdad*.	
1070	William the Conqueror in England.	Foundation of *Marrakesh*.		
1071	Turkish victory at Manzikert.			Reign of Malikshah.
1073-1092				
1075-1128	Santiago de *Compostela* built.			SELJUKS OF RUM.
1077-1307			SELJUKS in Syria.	
1078-1117				
1080-1096	Choir of St. Sernin built in *Toulouse*.			
1085	Capture of Toledo by Alfonso VI.			
1086		ALMORAVIDS in Spain.		
1088				Work on the great mosque of *Isfahan*.
1088-1121	Cluny III built.		City walls of *Cairo* rebuilt.	Mosque of *Diyarbakir* (Anatolia).
1091				
1093-1133	*Durham* Cathedral built.			
1095	First Crusade.			Konya capital of the Seljuks.
1097				ARTUQIDS (Diyarbakir).
1098-1232			Capture of Jerusalem by the Crusaders.	
1099		Complete annexation of Spain by the Almoravids.		
1103				ARTUQIDS (Mardin).
1104-1408		Mosque and palace of Ali ben Yusuf in *Marrakesh*.		
1106				Mosque of *Qazwin*.
1116			Frankish and Muslim fortifications (Syria, Palestine). SELJUKS in Iraq.	
1118-1194				Caravanserai of *Ribat i-Sharaf*.
1119		Walls of *Marrakesh* built.	Al-Aqmar mosque in *Cairo*.	
1125			ZANGIDS (Djazira, Syria).	
1127-1181		ALMOHADS in the Maghreb.	*Madrasas* in Syria.	
1130-1269	Consecration of the choir of *St. Denis*.	Capture of Marrakesh by the Almohads.		
1144	Frederick Barbarossa.		Reign of Nur al-Din.	
1146		ALMOHADS in Spain.		
1146-1174		Mosque of *Tinmal* and Kutubiya mosque in *Marrakesh*.		
1147				
1153				Mosque of *Silvan*.
1155	Notre-Dame in *Paris*, Notre-Dame in *Laon* built.		Mosque of Salib Talai in *Cairo*.	
c.1160			AYYUBIDS (Egypt, Syria).	
1169-1260			End of Fatimid rule in Egypt.	
1171			Reign of Saladin.	
1174-1193	Reign of Philippe Auguste.			Frederick Barbarossa occupies Konya.
1180-1223	Third Crusade.			
1190	*Chartres* Cathedral begun.			Minaret of *Djam* (Afghanistan).
1194	*Bourges* Cathedral begun.	Almohads victorious in Spain.		
1195		Great mosque of Hasan at *Rabat*.		
1204	Capture of Constantinople.		Citadel of *Damascus*.	
1209	*Magdeburg* Cathedral begun.		Citadel of *Aleppo*.	
1210	*Rheims* Cathedral begun.			
1212		Defeat of the Almohads in Spain (Las Navas de Tolosa).		Qutb-Minar at *Delhi*.
1226-1270	Reign of St. Louis.			Building by the Han Sultans near *Konya* and at *Kayseri*.
1228-1253	Basilica of St. Francis built in *Assisi*.			
1229				
1230	*Burgos* Cathedral begun.	NASRIDS at Granada.		
1230-1492			"Firdaus" *madrasa* at *Aleppo*.	
1236	Capture of Cordoba.	HAFSIDS at Tunis.		
1237-1574				
1242-1253	Notre-Dame of *Trèves* built.			MONGOLS in Anatolia.
1243				
1245	Rebuilding of *Westminster* Abbey.			
1248-1269	Capture of Seville. Sainte Chapelle in *Paris* built. *Cologne* Cathedral begun.			
1249			MAMLUKS in Egypt.	
1250		MERINIDS at Fez.		
1251				Karatay *madrasa* at *Konya*.
1255	*León* Cathedral begun.		MONGOLS in Syria and Iraq.	
1258	Choir of St. Nazaire at *Carcassonne*.		ILKHAN MONGOLS in Iraq.	ILKHAN MONGOLS in Iran.
1261-1327		MERINIDS at Marrakesh.		
1269		First Merinid *madrasa*.		
1271		Foundation of *New Fez*.		
1276			Reign of the Mamluk Qala'un.	
1281-1291			Conquest of the Latin kingdom in Syria.	
1291	*Florence* Cathedral begun.			
1295		Generalife at *Granada*.		
early 14th century		Moroccan *madrasas*. Necropolis of *Chella*.		
1307				Foundation of the *Sultaniya of Qazwin*.
1308-1327	Choir of *Exeter* Cathedral.			
1312	Choir of *Gerona* Cathedral.			
1313				Sultaniya capital of the Mongols.
1326				MONGOLS in Anatolia, with Bursa as their capital.
1329	Santa Maria del Mar and choir of *Barcelona* Cathedral begun.			
1333-1354		The Comares group of buildings at the Alhambra in *Granada*.		
1334	Palazzo Vecchio in *Florence* begun.			
1337	Beginning of the Hundred Years' War.			
1348-1349		Bu Inaniya *madrasa* at *Fez*.		
1352	Arrival of Peter Parler in *Prague*.			
1354-1392		The Court of the Lions group of buildings at the Alhambra in *Granada*.		
1356			*Madrasa* of Sultan Hasan in *Cairo*.	OTTOMANS at Edirne.
1362				Conquests of Tamerlane.
1365				
1366	Château of *Vincennes* begun.			
1377	Chartreuse de Champmol begun at *Dijon*.			
1389				Accession of Bayezid I.

Dates	The Christian West and Byzantium	Hispano-Maghrebi world	Near and Middle East	Iranian provinces
1399				Bibi Khanum *madrasa* at *Samarkand*.
1400				
c.1400	Choir of *York* Cathedral. Incomplete chapels of *Batalha*.		Tamerlane in Iraq and Syria.	
1402				Edirne, Ottoman capital.
1405	Start of work on Notre-Dame de l'Epine.			Death of Tamerlane; TIMURIDS.
1410				"Green Mosque" at *Bursa*.
1413				
1415		Portuguese masters of Ceuta.	Mosque of Sultan Muayyad in *Cairo*.	Renewed Ottoman expansion under Murad II.
1421-1451				
1429	Joan of Arc.			
1447	King's College chapel, *Cambridge*.			
mid-15th century				"Blue Mosque" of *Tabriz*.
1453	OTTOMANS masters of Constantinople.			
1471		Portuguese capture Tangiers.		
1475			Funerary mosque of *Qa'itbey*.	
1481				Bayezid II.
1484				Complex at *Edirne*.
1490	St. John the Baptist of *Tomar*.			
1492	Christopher Columbus discovers the New World. Château of *Blois* begun.	Conquest of Granada by the Catholic kings.		
1508				
1513		Portuguese at Mazagan and Azemmour.	SAFAVIDS in Baghdad.	
1517			OTTOMANS in Cairo.	
1520				
1525	Battle of Pavia.	SAADIANS at Marrakesh.		Reign of Suleiman the Magnificent.
1530	Charles V emperor.			
1534			OTTOMANS in Baghdad.	
1545	Council of Trent.			

UMAYYAD: dynasties; *Kairouan:* foundation of cities, also Islamic terms; *Kufa:* sites and monuments.

the proud symbol of the town, proclaiming the status of its lord – the monumental gateways, of powerful design and frequently rich decoration, make this eloquently clear. Even the improvement of their military capability, by access galleries or salients, portcullises or battlements, served ornamental purposes just as much as those of defence. Suburbs were sometimes provided with walls of their own. These could be of very varied materials, depending on the resources available – baked or unbaked bricks, dressed or undressed stone – but were similarly governed by aesthetic as well as technical considerations. The fortifications did not prevent cultural exchange with the enemies they were built to exclude: it is curious that in the struggles of the Crusades, eastern and western rivals enjoyed a kind of architectural symbiosis across the very lands on which their armies were opposed.

Within these walls the principal monuments of the city were erected, even if the rest of the city – its markets, its musallas (open-air oratories), its cemeteries, its pleasure gardens and its new districts – sprawled freely beyond them when space became constricted. The monuments often included the commercial quarters – the bazaar or souk sometimes consisted of ordinary streets bordered by shops, often in the neighbourhood of the great mosque, but was sometimes laid out deliberately as an architectural complex. The qaysaria, the official market for luxury or imported goods such as fabrics, was sometimes housed in a structure of simple plan, which grouped booths behind galleries or porticoes on several storeys around an oblong courtyard. Khans or funduqs were both storehouses and hostels for the accommodation of merchants; sometimes they became substantial works of architecture, especially in the Mediterranean area.

Mosques and oratories were provided with water for washing, and the centres of cities and their districts were furnished with baths. These public hammams, which complemented the private baths of the largest houses, derived from ancient baths of the kind described by Vitruvius. Dressing rooms and rest areas preceded the sequence of three rooms – hot, tepid, cold – which were each of distinct plan. They were sometimes arranged in linear sequence, as in the West after the 11th century, or else were grouped more compactly. There was a system of service rooms, and heat from the furnaces was circulated by means of underground hypocausts and channels in the walls of the tepid and hot rooms; the steam bath, derived from the ancient laconicum and still extant in the Middle Ages, seems thereafter quickly to have disappeared. The baths, which were frequently funded by bequests, were the object of considerable architectural elaboration. The vaults and roofing, the entrance and tepidarium, were often of high quality. The baths were obviously very important in the social life of the community.

So too were the institutions related to teaching and forms of religious life. The sabil-kuttab, usually found in the vicinity of a local oratory, combined a Koranic school with a public fountain. This type of building was the occasion of some modest but charming pieces of design, especially in Egypt. But of much greater importance were the madrasa and the zawiya, which were developing rapidly at the peak of the Sunnite reaction and in its aftermath.

The madrasa was a foundation devoted to the teaching of religious and juridical knowledge; the zawiya was intended either for religious fraternities or simply for the reception of travellers. The architecture which housed the madrasa and the zawiya reflected these functions: it combined with cells for the accommodation of the students an oratory and a varying number of related rooms and, in the East only, the tomb of the founder. These foundations can be found at different dates and in different regions of the Islamic world: common in the eastern Mediterranean during the 12th century, they did not reach Morocco until the second half of the 13th century, and only developed there and in Spain during the following century. The form of the madrasa in every region was governed by local architectural tradition, and although the institution is common to the whole Muslim world, its architecture is very varied.

This point can be illustrated particularly well in the last provinces to be reached by the madrasa. Whereas in the Asian regions, in Syria and Iran, its plan had reached an advanced state of development, the first madrasa in Fez, built near the mosque of al-Qarawiyin in 1271, consisted simply of an oratory and cells grouped around a courtyard, without any refinement; a monumental gateway and a minaret of stubby silhouette were the only attempts at aesthetic expression in an ensemble astonishingly lacking in sophistication. But very soon its architecture developed under the constraints on space imposed by the central location of the madrasa. A longitudinal axis from the entrance to the oratory defined the basic symmetry of the courtyard, surrounded on two or three sides by porticoes, which took up the irregularities of the site; the site was sometimes so small that the cells around the small lateral courts were omitted. Elsewhere, larger sites and therefore better conditions led to the planning of more regular compositions, whose central and lateral courtyards recall the palace plans known throughout Islam, from Ukhaidir in Iraq to the Zirid palace of Achir. But it was above all from the private house that the madrasa derived: it adapted the plan of the private house to collective life and added an oratory. Lavish decoration was reserved for key points such as the entrances, the oratory, and the façades facing the courtyard, in the centre of which there was often a pool.

Architects eventually created out of this institution born of the Sunnite reaction a masterpiece of harmony. The plan of the madrasa Bu Inaniya (which can be found on a later page) shows how even this formula was capable of evolution: if there was no funerary architecture to be accommodated, the madrasa tended towards a cruciform plan, and was endowed with a handsome minaret and a set of clocks. A monument such as this reveals clearly how religious politics, piety and a refined aesthetic sensibility informed a wholly local architecture, renewed and revived through contact with the East.

The unity of Islamic life can be felt everywhere despite its diversity. Places of pilgrimage, common to all Islam, were a focus for the perpetual desire to gather together, which is a fundamental part of the life of the believer. Mecca and the Kaaba are very well known; the Dome of the Rock, in Jerusalem, which represents the birth of Islamic architecture, is a better example of a place of pilgrimage of early Islamic times. But other kinds of sanctuaries were developed, often linked to a funerary monument. The many "tombs" of Ali were often, like the tombs of Christian saints, focal points of local religious life. The East, like the West, developed its own abundant funerary architecture. Evolving in parallel, by the end of the Middle Ages both had created virtual cities out of their sanctuaries. The Timurid necropolis of Gazurgah, near Herat in Afghanistan, can be compared with the Merinid funerary city of Chella, at the gates of Rabat in Morocco. Everywhere these "little cities of God" exhibit an intriguing ambiguity of meaning in that their religious function was the pretext for rich worldly creations which, for us, are a highpoint in the development of Islamic ornamental architecture. The emergence of aesthetic preoccupations marks in Islam, as it does in Christianity, the end of the Middle Ages. The modern era, if perhaps with less refinement, developed these preoccupations further, consciously elaborating decorative patterns and rejoicing in the play of mass and light.

Less well known is Islamic architecture specific to the countryside and the coasts. The unceasing development of rural architecture for 15 centuries from the time of the Umayyad dynasty shows the same peculiarly Islamic adaptation to the forces of history and necessity.

The study of rural Islamic architecture was first understood to mean that of the country retreat. Within rectangular turreted enclosures little castles, recalling the "castelli" of the later Roman empire, were discovered in Syria, dating from the medieval period. Miniya near Jericho is an excellent example of these small fortified structures, arranged around a courtyard, often with a portico. More ambitious structures also existed, as is attested by remains at Khirbat al-Mafjar, east Qasr al-hayr, west Qasr al-hayr and Mchatta. If the baths at Khirbat al-Mafjar suggest almost royal pretensions, those at Qusayr Amra show that elaborate architecture could well be accompanied by more humble structures. In the vicinity of these country properties, dams and systems of irrigation have been found – evidence of a desire to exploit the land around what were at first called "desert" villas. There might also have been commercial premises.

A good number of poets over the centuries have sung of the charms of the muniya, a country property, an almost palatial residence as well as a centre of agriculture. We know that these existed in the 10th century around Umayyad Cordoba and in the 11th century in Toledo. A single muniya has been preserved intact, despite the activities of the Catholic kings and Romantic restoration: the Generalife in Granada. Recent excavations in Morocco have proved a close link between

medieval descriptions and the actual buildings: small dwellings built around sometimes diminutive courtyards were dotted along the slopes overlooking the sea near Ceuta; rooms decorated with enamelled mosaics and frescoes were set amidst gardens, pools and running water. Simplicity and refinement were delicately combined in the harmony of monumental architecture with nature.

Nevertheless, the beauty of the countryside was not the only stimulus to rural architecture. In Iran, as in Morocco and Anatolia, the authorities were concerned to build roads and facilities for commerce as well as for official business. On a later page the plan of the Iranian caravanserai on the road from Nishapur to Merv, Ribat i-Sharaf, is given: it is one of the most impressive examples, testifying to a remarkable organization about which too little is known. It can be compared to the khans of Anatolia, of which a typical plan is also included. To illustrate the point more fully, we should also mention an example from the West: the road that led from Marrakesh, capital of the western caliphate in the 12th century, to Seville, the Andalusian metropolis and a base for the holy wars of Spain and the Maghreb. We know its stages, which ranged from simple halts equipped with tanks and water storage, to a huge camp-city, Rabat, to the port of Qasr al-Saghir on the straits of Gibraltar. So, a taste for rural pastimes, politics, economics and the holy war conditioned in their various ways the birth and evolution of a rural architecture whose importance should not be under-estimated.

Similar factors exerted their influence on the development of coastal architecture, notably along the coasts of the Mediterranean, which appeared sometimes to be an Islamic lake, sometimes a battle ground with Christendom. At intervals

along the Islamic coastline, as along the frontiers of the empire, can be found ribats. Several examples are known on the Tunisian coast, that at Sousse showing clearly how its enclosure, fortified with round and half-round towers, incorporated at one corner a square bastion with a tower serving as both a minaret and a lookout. A courtyard with a portico at the side gave access to the cells of the soldiers of the Faith, and an oratory at a higher level dominating the entrance was itself surmounted at the level of the battlements by a reminder of the orientation of Mecca: prayer and battle could thus both be pursued without one obstructing the other.

Maritime architecture had to serve many other functions as well: there were fortified harbours, preceded by the monumental gateways of naval construction yards, whose parallel vaulted roofs are known to us from Malaga to Turkey and Egypt; almost all have disappeared, but engravings from the early modern era show an architecture and technology rooted in the inheritance of the Hellenistic world but long since absorbed by Islam.

It is above all the interchange between the three continents bordering the Mediterranean that seems to have informed Islamic architecture, from the 8th century to our own day. We have seen how its architecture responded to the needs of a world both so close and so completely different to our own. The pages that follow show how the architecture of each region of the empire reflected the great events in Islamic history without abandoning its own identity. It may be that the adoption of similar techniques unites rival worlds in spite of their political and religious differences. A work of architecture can remind us by its forms and colours that these people of a very different civilization often had tastes similar to our own.

Arcades of the mosque at Baalbek (Lebanon), seen from an oculus in the apse. Who among the innumerable visitors to Baalbek is familiar with the great mosque of the city? As can be seen here, Lebanon has preserved the heritage of many different communities: the interest of pre-Islamic antiquity should not obscure more than a millennium of subsequent history.

The two sources of Islamic architecture

Islam, ruling regions as diverse as the western coasts of the Mediterranean and the lands of Iran and Iraq, came into frequent contact with other civilizations. Certainly, its native Arabia was never forgotten, remaining the focal point of the life of the *umma*, the community of believers. But the transfer of the seat of power, first to Syria, then to Mesopotamia, accelerated the creation and evolution of an Islamic architecture rich in local traditions and adapted to the realities of the new empire.

The prime characteristic of this architecture was its responsiveness to the country in which it took root. In Syria, which was rich in building stone and in valleys suitable for the cultivation of cereals and olives, the architecture appeared still very Mediterranean. In the broad alluvial plains of Mesopotamia, by contrast, vast constructions had long been built in baked or unbaked brick. Yet these two modes were readily embodied in the Islamic architectural tradition.

In certain cases, however, the Islamic conquerors did affirm their own building traditions, particularly where they were unable or unwilling to make use of existing structures. From Kufa to Kairouan, fortress towns were created (many of which were subsequently rebuilt or enlarged); the pattern of the great mosque and the *dar al-imara*, the centre of government, also emerged in this period. But one is principally impressed by the speed with which Islam made use of the existing traditions. When the first Umayyad caliph established the seat of power of the first Muslim dynasty at Damascus, the assimilation of the Byzantine heritage was most apparent; but Islam was aware too of the heritage of other succes-

sors to Alexander's empire, far or near. The traditions of the Parthians and the Sassanids were not only familiar to the Umayyads, but were also a profound influence on Islamic art after 750, when the new Abbasid caliphs moved their capital to Mesopotamia. The courts of Baghdad and Samarra, where a new ceremonial tradition developed with the presence of an increasing number of Iranians, were well able to adapt their architecture to the Asian way of life. Thus history as well as geography contributed in the mingling of different sources of inspiration which led to the creation of an Islamic architecture.

The evolution of the mosque, illustrated by the three plans shown on the opposite page, reflects this process. The mosque at Kufa, where the sanctuary was at first protected from defilement simply by a ditch, was rebuilt without altering the design. It is worth noting that protection against the sun was provided for the faithful only, as they lined up in rows parallel to the wall facing Mecca; porticoes along the remaining walls of the court completed what was a very austere building. At Damascus, an axial nave indicated the direction of prayer, and the transept of the Christian basilica was thus converted to new use. Finally, at Samarra, the scale of the building and the techniques employed have undergone a complete change; although the treatment of space at first recalls Kufa, the enormously long coloured brick walls, enlivened with buttresses and openings, are in striking contrast to the stone architecture of Syria. The spiral form of the minaret of the Malwiya recalls the ziggurats of Babylon. Islam propagated in the Mediterranean world the lessons

of as much of Asia as it had brought into the Faith.

But there was never any question of sterile copying, and the 7th century mosque of Damascus proclaims its quality as a masterpiece. The space of the temenos of the converted temple was remodelled: the rhythmic array of its arcades, covered with mosaic, and the façade of the prayer-hall displayed both the richness appropriate to a great caliphate mosque and the simplicity required of a place of prayer. Inside the oratory, a sober clarity was achieved through the suppression of all ornament. The powerful lines alone of this building typified an architecture that was both faithful to its regional heritage and responsive to the needs of the Umayyad community.

The sense of invention working within continuity can be felt everywhere. The centralized plan of the cupola on the summit of Mount Moriah at Jerusalem clearly recalls the Church of the Ascension (the Anastasis), just as the plan of Anjar with its *insulae* recalls that of Split (Spalato) and Hellenistic ideas of organization. But in each case the architects, like the designers of ornament who knew how to purify the formal repertory of Byzantine mosaics, affirmed their enthusiastic adherence to Islam, its laws and its daily obligations. In the development of towns and the management of the country, Mesopotamian Asia as much as Syria brought together the opposing modes of the Asian and Mediterranean worlds – a synthesis which from the early Middle Ages onwards was disseminated by Islam throughout its huge empire.

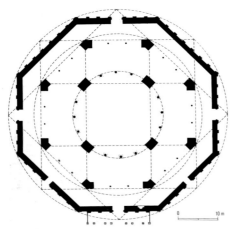

Plan of the Dome of the Rock
(after Creswell)

This plan is dictated by a geometrical scheme like those of San Vitale in Ravenna or the Church of the Ascension in Jerusalem.

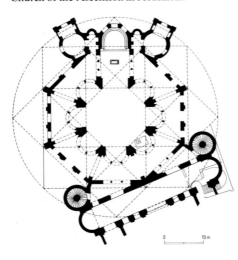

Superimposition of the plan of the Dome of the Rock on that of San Vitale in Ravenna
(after Ecochard)

The geometry of these two plans shows clearly how faithful the architect of the Dome of the Rock (above) remained to local traditions derived from the Byzantine world.

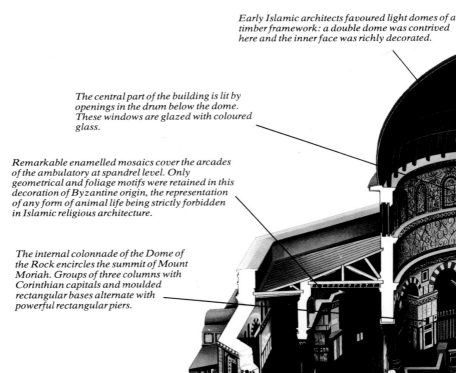

Early Islamic architects favoured light domes of a timber framework: a double dome was contrived here and the inner face was richly decorated.

The central part of the building is lit by openings in the drum below the dome. These windows are glazed with coloured glass.

Remarkable enamelled mosaics cover the arcades of the ambulatory at spandrel level. Only geometrical and foliage motifs were retained in this decoration of Byzantine origin, the representation of any form of animal life being strictly forbidden in Islamic religious architecture.

The internal colonnade of the Dome of the Rock encircles the summit of Mount Moriah. Groups of three columns with Corinthian capitals and moulded rectangular bases alternate with powerful rectangular piers.

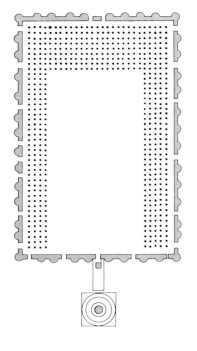

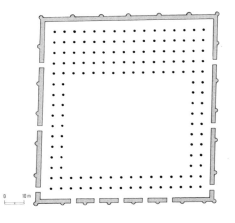

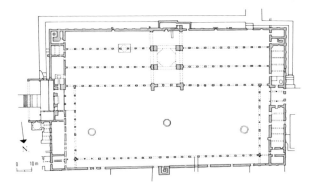

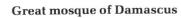

Great mosques of Kufa and of Samarra (or al-Mutawakkil)

A comparison between the two plans shows how the sanctuary of Kufa type (above) was modified under the Abbasids in Mesopotamia. The first great mosque of Samarra (below and above left), built on the banks of the Tigris in the 9th century, was a portico-mosque whose gigantic brick architecture (157 by 240 metres/170 by 260 yards) shows the influence of eastern Asian traditions on early Islamic architecture.

Great mosque of Damascus

The great mosque of Damascus (plan above) owes its proportions and dimensions (100 by 180 metres/110 by 200 yards) to the temenos of the temple of Zeus which it occupies. A courtyard surrounded by arcades (below left) precedes a prayer-hall on a basilical plan: the two arcades that support the simple framework of the roof form a nave and aisles. This arrangement and the light (see the photograph below) make it clear that Islam could often match the achievements of Byzantine architecture.

The Dome of the Rock marks the summit of Mount Moriah with a dome surrounded by a double ambulatory: it made Jerusalem the third pilgrimage centre of Islam. Sacred to the Jews, the site of this monument is also sacred to the Muslims, who see it as the place of the Prophet's ascent to Heaven. The "Dome" was built by the Umayyads in 691 at a time when Mecca and Medina were in the hands of a rival of the caliph. This already mature creation signals the rise of a specifically Islamic architecture.

The Barada panel (detail), great mosque, Damascus

This extensive Umayyad sequence of mosaics shows how Islam had adopted the Byzantine technique of enamelled mosaics, while excluding – but only in religious architecture – all figurative decoration.

Anjar (Lebanon)

Anjar, an Umayyad royal city, had a regular plan with rectangular housing blocks divided by arcaded avenues. Through the arcades that once bordered one of its streets are visible the remains of a shop in stone and brick and, beyond that, the principal palace of the city.

Break-up of the empire and architectural regionalism

The huge size of the Islamic empire made it inevitable that the architecture developed in the Umayyad and Abbasid periods should be subjected to ever more diverse conditions. First there was the task, with each new conquest, of adapting to local conditions. Then in the 9th and 10th centuries a degree of political independence gave way to secessionist tendencies linked to religious dissension, which put the unity of the empire in question. The examples of Egypt, which was rapidly reconquered, and of Tunisia, where Kairouan was founded in 670, show well how architecture was stimulated by the formation of regional schools; this decentralization poses the question of the artistic relationship between the various regions of the empire.

Ifriqiya – present-day Tunisia and eastern Algeria, or in ancient times the Roman and then Byzantine province of Africa – in the 9th century became an independent emirate, remaining nevertheless in the fief of the caliph of Baghdad. The great mosque of Kairouan was therefore rebuilt. Its columns were salvaged from an earlier structure and the sculpture remained close to pre-Islamic traditions, but the enamelled ceramic tiles which adorned the *mihrab* were in the latest Mesopotamian fashion. The naves perpendicular to the *qibla* marked the beginning of a tradition in western Islam, while the T-shaped plan was taken up by the mosque of Abu Dulaf in Samarra. The silhouette of the minaret of Kairouan, with its three successive stages, may even recall the lighthouse of Alexandria. Original invention and interchange between architectural centres could thus perfectly well co-exist.

This situation became more marked in the 10th century and, curiously, even after the Fatimids – heterodox Shiites – had seized power in Ifriqiya and established a caliphate opposed on religious grounds to that of Baghdad. Their hatred was inexpiable. And yet it was at this moment that Tunisian art underwent a profound change. The conquest of the East remained the first objective of the Fatimids, and the palace city that they built on the peninsular of Mahdiya had the appearance of a naval installation; nevertheless, a new architecture was developed for the mosque, showing a fresh interest in monumental façades, for the palaces and government buildings, and for the fortified harbour and arsenal. Alongside conquered Kairouan the Fatimids then founded the immense round city of al-Mansuriya-Sabra: the brick material and the plan of its powerful walls and vast palaces show an Asian architecture being unveiled in the western Mediterranean. Tunisia was confirmed in its role as the port of the West.

For centuries Tunisia would remain the essential staging post for traditions originating in Egypt. Even before the Fatimids founded Cairo in about the year 1000, the cities of Fustat and al-Qatai demonstrated the vigour of an architectural tradition which had very early taken root on the banks of the Nile. The mosque of Ibn Tulun shows that, here as elsewhere, artistic exchange followed political power with alacrity; moderate proportions still similar to those of the period of conquest, and lateral wings and a minaret recalling the monuments of Samarra, cannot disguise the synthesis that had taken place. Cairo became the main link in the east-west chain.

Cairo was also, from its foundation under the Fatimids to the period of Ottoman domination, one of the great centres of Islamic art. The great mosques of Cairo, such as those built by al-Hakim or Baybars I, were largely responsible for the evolution of new plans determined by function; after the orientation of the nave towards the wall known as the *qibla*, it was the enclosure reserved for the sovereign, the *maqsura*, which received more emphasis, roofed by an ever more monumental dome. Later, the architecture of the *madrasa* and the tomb underwent in their turn an equally fruitful regional development: the complex projects carried out by Sultan Hasan and Qala'un are examples. Finally, the walls of the city and their gates, such as Bab al-Futuh and Bab al-Nasr, show that alongside buildings almost hidden by a welter of fine ornament, there could develop from the 11th century a powerful stone architecture revealing considerable mathematical sophistication. Egypt, whether Fatimid, Ayyubid or Mamluk, neighbour both to Syria and to Asian Mesopotamia, contributed perhaps more than any other region to the renewal and diffusion of eastern Muslim art.

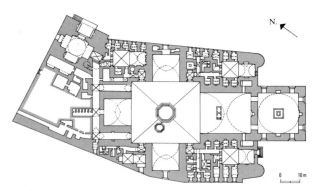

"Madrasa" of Sultan Hasan (14th century), Cairo

A courtyard with four *iwans* leads into an oratory and to small subsidiary courtyards surrounded by cells. The institution of the *madrasa* and the plan shown here are excellent examples of Cairo's role in Islamic architecture: it was a creative centre often open to influences from Asia, which it transmitted to the western provinces.

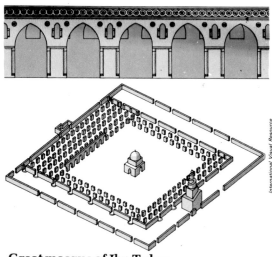

Great mosque of Ibn Tulun, al-Qatai (Egypt)

This mosque, which was built after 876, almost a century before the foundation of Cairo, was the work of a Turkish officer of the Abbasids who was able to assume almost independent authority; the city of al-Qatai (which today is part of Cairo) is further evidence of this. The mosque nevertheless remained subject to the Mesopotamian caliphate, and so to its architecture. Although this mosque does not have the grandeur of its models in Samarra, it has similar additional wings and a spiral minaret. Its proportions are reminiscent of Kufa. Beautiful carved decoration lightens the brick arcades on heavy piers.

Courtyard of the great mosque, Sousse (Tunisia)

The façade of the prayer-hall visible on the right dates from the original mosque. The simple and vigorous style of the frieze of Kufic script which is terminated at the junction of the staircase dates the building to the 9th century. The angle-tower behind recalls the necessity at that time of defence against raiders along the Tunisian coastline. The mosque was enlarged in the 10th century by the Fatimids.

Remains of a Fatimid palace, Mahdiya

Excavations on the peninsula of Mahdiya between Sousse and Sfax have revealed the remains of a palace of the first city of government founded by the Fatimids in the 10th century: the gatehouse building visible here gave access via a dogleg passage to a square courtyard. This structure of small dressed stones is one of the rare remains of Fatimid secular architecture – another, very similar example is the palace of Ashir in present-day Algeria.

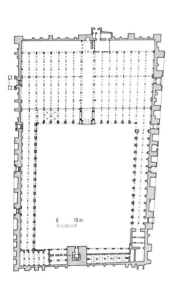

Plan of the great mosque, Kairouan

The sanctuary of Kairouan was the first great mosque to be built in the western lands of Islam; the plan of the existing structure, rebuilt in all essentials under the Aghlabids between 836 and 874, initiated the Maghrebi tradition. The T-plan of the prayer-hall, the proportions of the vast arcaded courtyard and the axial minaret were all widely imitated.

Groined vaults, great mosque of Sousse

Tunisian architecture in the early Middle Ages made use of many kinds of vault: the great mosque of Sousse has good examples of groined vaults covering the bays of a prayer-hall. Such vaults can be seen in the *ribat* as well as here, in the only old part of the great mosque of Mahdiya to have been preserved.

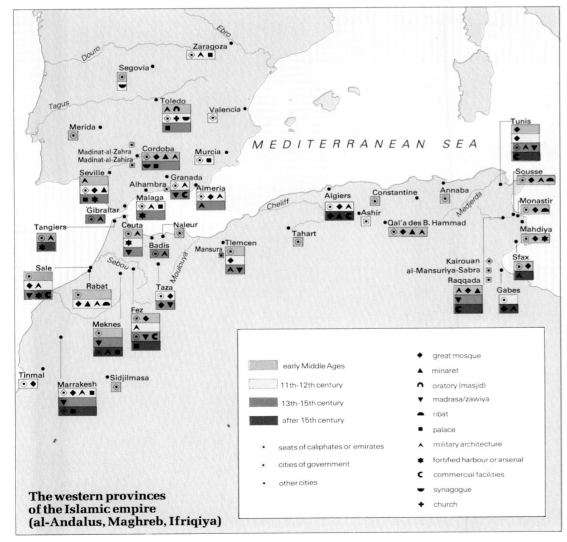

The western provinces of the Islamic empire (al-Andalus, Maghreb, Ifriqiya)

early Middle Ages
11th-12th century
13th-15th century
after 15th century

· seats of caliphates or emirates
· cities of government
· other cities

◆ great mosque
▲ minaret
∩ oratory (masjid)
▼ madrasa/zawiya
◖ ribat
■ palace
Λ military architecture
✶ fortified harbour or arsenal
C commercial facilities
◡ synagogue
+ church

Sunnite reaction
and the renewal of form

The 11th century was an important period in the history of the Islamic world. This was first of all due to the increasing role of the Turcoman populations from central Asia. The Seljuk movement imposed its dominion east to west, from the territory of the Ghaznavids (Afghanistan) to the shores of the Mediterranean. In 1055 these partisans of Islamic orthodoxy – Sunnism – replaced the Shiite Buyids as guardians of the caliphate of Baghdad. The regions of central Asia thus once again influenced the fate of Islam and its civilization; it has often been stated that the Seljuks, with the assistance in turn of the Mongols, were in part responsible for East and West "turning their backs on one another". This was not the whole story, however.

At the same time as the Turks were becoming dominant in the East, the Berber dynasties, coming originally from the edges of the Sahara and then from the Moroccan Atlas, managed to unify the Maghreb and a Muslim Spain perpetually threatened by Christian reconquest. The Berbers were also under the influence of a religious reform movement favourable to Sunnism. These political developments, which led relatively recent converts to Islam to the seats of the eastern and western caliphates, were to alter the direction of architectural development, though without obstructing – rather the opposite – exchange between the regions of Islam.

The importance of the architecture developed in Irano-Afghan Asia by the Samanids and the Ghaznavids is well known: its scale and quality can be seen in the city of Bust and the nearby palaces of Lashkari Bazar, which together form a wholly Asiatic complex extending 10 kilometres (6 miles) along

the banks of the river Hilmend. The buildings, arranged around rectangular courtyards with four *iwans*, were roofed by massive vaults of unbaked and (more rarely) baked brick. In the southern palace of Lashkari Bazar one such courtyard, preceded by a vestibule also of cruciform plan, gives access to the audience chamber overlooking the river and, alongside the official rooms, to several groups of apartments. The interweaving arcades, which were the *leitmotif* of decoration of the external and internal façades, are famous; there was once painted and sculpted ornament to accompany them. This vast structure was originally no more than a small fraction of the complex: commercial and agricultural buildings once demonstrated as clearly as the mosques and palaces the vigour of the Asiatic traditions that were henceforth to influence Islamic architecture on the coasts of the Mediterranean.

It was not until the end of the 12th and the beginning of the 13th centuries that the Ayyubids in Syria built a significant quantity of architecture on this vast scale; it was usually under royal, but sometimes under private patronage. The traveller who contemplates today the huge water-wheels of Hama, on the Orontes, should realize that they belong to a tradition of enlightened husbandry, making full use of technology, dating from the Umayyad era. Military architecture experienced an unprecedented development, as is clearly demonstrated by the citadel of Aleppo, whose fortifications are as beautiful today as they were effective then. In religious architecture, as we have seen, the development of the *madrasa* was the most important event of the period. Thus the Sunnite reaction, promoted by the Seljuks and their heirs, led to a

complete renewal of eastern Islamic architecture.

A parallel evolution occurred in western Islamic architecture in the 12th century. The conquest of al-Andalus by the Almoravids brought the Hispano-Maghrebi world under a single authority, ensuring the diffusion in Africa of the artistic legacy of the Umayyads of Cordoba: the ribbed dome of the Almoravid great mosque of Marrakesh, its sole remaining vestige of any importance, is a direct imitation of Cordoba. At the same time the adoption and development of the decorative motif of the "stalactite" confirms the permanence of links between the caliphates amongst whom the Islamic world was divided.

These links are perhaps still clearer in the second half of the 12th century under the Almohads. Alongside the advance in military architecture, which is comparable to that of Syria, they are apparent in the great mosque of Rabat, the Moroccan city-encampment for the soldiers of the Faith. If its square minaret built of local stone is formally within the Hispano-Maghrebi tradition, the dimensions and T-shaped plan of its sanctuary, surrounded by *ziyadas*, deliberately recall the Abbasid East, even if in this deliberate homage the usual pattern of an Almohad mosque is still perceptible and its long naves still echo Cordoba. The return to forms originating in Sunnite Baghdad was a political gesture: the Almohads were proclaiming themselves both caliphs of the West and, like heirs of the 11th century Seljuks in the East, ardent defenders of orthodoxy. Religious reform and political ambition had transformed the architecture of all Islam.

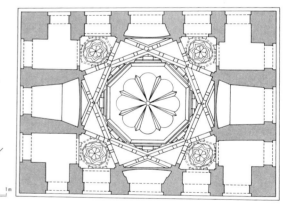

"Qubba" of Ali ben Yusuf, Marrakesh (Morocco)

This domed structure was an annexe to the great mosque built shortly after the foundation of Marrakesh by the ruler Ali ben Yusuf: the reign of this Moroccan prince, whose mother was Andalusian, marks the flowering of a new Hispano-Maghrebi art. The skilful arrangement of the windows enabled the architect to vault the building with a ribbed dome whose geometrical framework was decorated with flowers and stalactites.

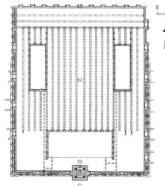

Mosque of Hasan, Rabat

At the end of the 12th century the Almohads founded a camp-city on the Atlantic coast of Morocco to gather the soldiers of the Faith for an attack on Muslim Spain, and conceived a mosque on a scale appropriate to this vast project. Its rubble walls enclosed a space of 180 by 140 metres (196 by 153 yards), once extended with *ziyadas*; powerful cylindrical piers demarcated the long Cordoban-style aisles as they extended outwards from the "transept" across the *qibla*. Both the minaret and the scale of this incomplete mosque recall Abbasid examples, and it was their grandeur that the western caliph clearly wished to rival.

254

Gateway of the citadel, Aleppo (Syria)

The same taste for clarity and power asserted itself in all fields of architecture and in all countries of Islam in the late 11th century. In the West as here in Syria, complex plans and powerful gatehouse structures testify to aesthetic as well as technical progress in military architecture. Such complex gatehouses with curving passages and portcullises were set in huge bastions whose stone façades recall the architecture of Ayyubid Syria.

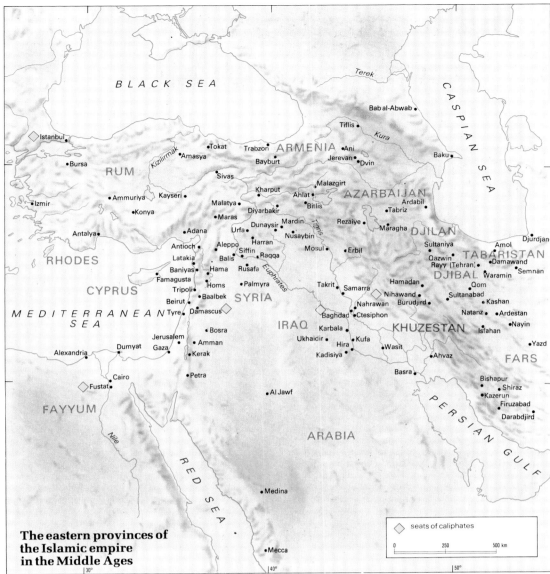

The eastern provinces of the Islamic empire in the Middle Ages

◇ seats of caliphates

0   250   500 km

Water-wheel on the Orontes, Hama

One should not overlook the outstanding technical capabilities of Islamic architects and builders. In every province, hydraulic engineering was remarkable: dams, locks and water-wheels are everywhere in evidence.

Courtyard of the al-Firdaus (Paradise) "madrasa", Aleppo (Syria)

This *madrasa*, founded in 1237 by the widow of an Ayyubid sovereign, has a rectangular plan of 44 by 55 metres (48 by 60 yards). Shown here is a corner of the central courtyard, against the north side of which was placed an external *iwan*. On the opposite side was the oratory. Though the plan was Iranian, the building material – dressed stone, used notably for the domes – was typically Syrian.

Southern palace, Lashkari Bazar (Afghanistan)

This south-facing façade of the southern palace of Lashkari Bazar once opened on to a vast courtyard containing a mosque, which in turn was preceded by a long shopping street. The articulation and the arcades with their characteristic curvature are, like the carving that once covered the façade, good examples of the art of the eastern provinces on the eve of the Sunnite reaction.

Combined traditions in Turcoman Anatolia

The defeat of Byzantium at Manzikert in 1071 opened the way for the Seljuks to penetrate Anatolia. Between the end of the 12th and the beginning of the 14th century, Turcoman dynasties installed themselves in upper Mesopotamia and in Anatolia: the Seljuks "of Rum" and the Artuqids thus provoked the confrontation of eastern Islamic traditions with those of Byzantine Christianity. Their architecture in fact benefited both from Iranian influences and from forms and techniques deriving from Syria and Armenia. A second phase of architecture, also developed from the legacy of Abbasid art, was to be born from the encounter with the Christian world of the Crusaders. From this richness of sources emerged forms of striking originality.

Certain techniques of construction were common throughout. Dressed stone was used for the walls and the vaults, on façades and for portals and gateways; sometimes walls were infilled with rubble or vaults were built of brick – as in the mausoleum of Tokat – but these were exceptions. The predominance of dressed stone, and also of two-toned patterning, place these buildings in an unbroken eastern Mediterranean tradition. The variety of vaulting methods testifies to the skill of the masterbuilders: pierced barrel vaults, domed or groined vaults, stellar vaults, all kinds of dome rising from stalactitic squinches as well as from the pendentives that are characteristic of the Seljuks, even ribbed vaults covering bays sometimes of very complex form – the mosque and hospital at Divrigi provide a good example. The buttressing that went with these vaults should also be noticed: the way in which it is used to articulate the façades demonstrates how closely technical knowledge and aesthetic intention were related in medieval Anatolia.

The art of fortification, served by such skill in building, attained a high level of excellence, especially in exploiting the landscape: Afyon, Kayseri and Mardin are good examples. But chief among the characteristics of Seljuk architecture was the adaptation of its mosques to the climate. Their interior spaces are variable in number, with regular use being made of a three-naved plan; a dome covers the space before the *mihrab*; there is sometimes a second dome over the nave but more often it is open to the air, constituting the sole reference to the idea of a courtyard. A portico on the façade, often flanked by two rooms, marks the entrance to the building. The resemblance of such a plan to that of a windowless church has sometimes been remarked: Islam was able here again to adapt the traditions of local craftsmen to its own needs, as the decoration confirms.

Other building types were also transformed by the creative powers of the Anatolian architects. The numerous *madrasas* were usually planned round a courtyard with arcades; a principal axis linked the entrance *iwan* with the oratory housed in the far *iwan*, and a secondary axis sometimes appeared in the lateral arcades. The addition of a second storey permitted an increase in the accommodation for students – though this was an innovation found throughout Islam. A tomb was often included in an annexe, according to the common eastern tradition; but detached mausoleums were also built, and the two illustrations on this page bear witness to the variety of style characteristic of the Turcoman synthesis.

Secular architecture, whether of palaces or private houses, has not usually been so well preserved, and is in fact scarcely known: in Konya itself, which was the capital of the Seljuks of Rum, the great mosque and several *madrasas* are relatively well preserved, as well as other remains, but only a few vestiges survive to remind us that a palace once stood at the centre of the medieval town. On the other hand, numerous clues to the organization of commerce and the trade routes have come down to us. Bridges, as shown here, were structures of high quality, and reveal frequent reference to the many varied examples of bridges in the Mediterranean area. The structure of arsenals, with long parallel vaults identical to those in Spain, Morocco, Egypt and Turkey, proves again that, Christian or Muslim, the countries of the Mediterranean shared in the same technical heritage. Seljuk Anatolia nevertheless housed traditional Islamic institutions in monuments of its own invention. The caravanserais or *khans* still mark out the trade routes of the economic life of Anatolia: their plans and the treatment of their façades confirm the very special place that medieval Anatolian architecture holds within the Islamic tradition. The perfection of their construction explains their survival long after being abandoned; the vigour of their decoration in brick or stone, ranging from incised ornament to sculpture in such high relief as almost to be in the round, bears witness once again to the meeting of two architectures, the perennial symbiosis of East and West.

Mosque and hospital, Divrigi (Turkey)

One building houses on the left a great mosque and on the right, against the *qibla*, a hospital. The oratory of distinctively Anatolian plan is similar in style to the *iwans* that surround the central vaulted space of the hospital. These first complex structures founded an entire Anatolian tradition.

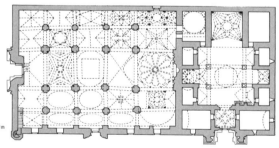

"Türbes" (mausoleums) at Tokat, left, and at Erzurum, right

Funerary architecture has always played an important part in Islam, from east to west, whether integral with another building, grouped in necropolises or in the form of the *türbe*. One can clearly see here the contrast between the *türbe* of Tokat, with its quadrangular base and pyramidal brick roof, and the circular structure at Erzurum, ornamented with blind arcading and topped by a conical stone roof with the same coursing as the walls.

Portal of the mosque of 'Ala 'ad-Din, Konya (Turkey)

Konya was the capital of the Seljuks of Rum; the entrance to its great mosque makes an impact above all by its polychromy and the very precise dressing of the two different types of stone that decorate the façade. Geometrical interlace patterns ornament the rectangular surround, which frames a design of interlacing lobes; the scale of this decoration contrasts with the slender engaged columns at the angles of the door. The lintel is a remarkable piece of stone-dressing and supports a decorated tympanum. Both Anatolian tradition and Syrian affinities are present here.

An Anatolian "khan" (caravanserai)

The systematic organization of the trade routes in Anatolia has left numerous remains, such as this caravanserai on the road from Konya to Beysehir: a sturdy, stone-dressed structure offering travellers and merchants a refuge for the night. Below can be seen the plan of a larger *khan*: this one is very modest but the rooms are still grouped around an arcaded courtyard. The façade shows that stone coursing was the primary decoration of the architecture of Seljuk Anatolia.

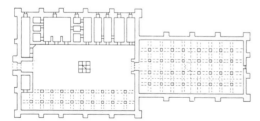

Details of the decoration on the Sircali "madrasa" at Konya and on the Turumtay "türbe" at Amasiya (Turkey)

Many types of decoration enlivened walls in medieval Anatolia. On the left one can see that even in far western Asia, play was made with the different tones of enamelled bricks: this delicate polychromy recalls the architecture of Seljuk Iran. On the other hand, carved stone floral ornament was often deployed, and its relief could be so high (right) as to be almost in the round, suggesting not so much Fatimid Egypt as the work of Anatolian sculptors using imported Seljuk motifs. This is different again from the low-relief decoration shown on the right, from a gateway in Divrigi, which has the appearance of embossed ornament originally formed in plaster and somehow translated into stone.

Sculpted doorway, Divrigi

This doorway to the monument shown in the plan that appears opposite sets decorative detail off against strongly defined mouldings and unexpected effects of scale; it is a busy design but none the less striking.

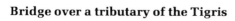

Sultan Khan, caravanserai on the route from Konya to Kayseri

This staging post groups within a wall of deliberately military character a veritable microcosm: an oratory (above a kiosk at the centre of the courtyard) and vaulted baths were among the facilities offered, besides secure shelter, storage and extensive accommodation for pack animals.

Bridge over a tributary of the Tigris

This medieval bridge has the classic hump-back profile, in which the bold arch thrown across the river contrasts with the necessary weight of the abutments. Such structures were necessary to allow caravans and travellers to cross, at all times of the year, rivers whose currents were often too strong to be fordable.

The Hispano-Maghrebi provinces and new formulas

When in the 8th century the last fugitive Umayyad established his emirate at Cordoba in the Muslim province of Spain, he introduced Syrian traditions to the once Visigoth kingdom. In the 10th century the ruler of al-Andalus resumed the title of caliph, but once again political independence did not preclude architectural exchange. From the great mosque of Cordoba to the later medieval Granada of the Nasrids, there was a constant search for an original architecture adapted to the needs and climate of the Iberian peninsula and of the western Maghreb; but it was never forgotten that they belonged to the community of Islam.

From the beginning, the great mosque situated next to the Roman bridge in Cordoba attested to the encounter of East with West. The *qibla* faces an imaginary Mecca to the south of Andalusia, as if it were still in the Syria that so many of its elements recall – the plan with its enlarged axial nave and such details as the pointed battlements that crown the façade. On the other hand, pre-Islamic Spain is present in the extensive re-use of materials – Roman and Visigoth columns and capitals support the arcades of the first prayer-hall and the structure itself, with its two superimposed arches, recalls Hispanic aqueducts of the Roman era. For a while this arrangement was maintained, but the enlargement carried out for al-Hakam II in the 10th century transformed it: a play of interlaced cusped arches covered with rich decoration replaced the plain horseshoe arches with their memories of Syria and the Visigoths. The form that now appeared was Mesopotamian, and the ribbed domes and enamelled mosaics reveal other ties with both Asia and Byzantium. The capacity for synthesis and a constant desire for invention characterize western

Muslim art at all periods. When in the 12th century it became Hispano-Maghrebi, it gradually moved towards a greater sobriety, and the Almohads in the second half of the century imposed a puritanical monumentality. From the 13th to the 15th centuries the loss of Cordoba, reconquered by the Christians in 1236, deeply affected the Muslim art of Spain and the Maghreb and its memory excited a profound but fertile nostalgia. Faithful to their past, dislocated and threatened by the reconquest, the regions of the caliphate were nevertheless active in the search for new ideas.

The Morocco of the Merinids is an early and clear example. It was at Fez that an art developed, soon after 1250, in which the architecture was better integrated than ever before with the dense fabric of the city. Innovations were stimulated by the recollection of lost Andalusia: the great mosque of Fez Jdid, the government city of the Merinids, repeated the dimensions of the palace-city of the Umayyads at Cordoba. But the minaret was of Maghrebi form, and the interlace patterns on its faces and enamelled tiling (*zellij*) at its summit expressed a growing taste for verticality, ornament and colour. A similar taste for polychromy was developing at the same time in Timurid Asia.

New formulas were appearing. The fortified harbours of Sale and Tangier, for example, introduced ideas into Merinid Morocco that were known throughout the Islamic Mediterranean: we know from contemporary texts that "specialists" were hired in Spain to carry out these technically demanding tasks. But the *madrasa* shows how, paradoxically, the adoption of an eastern institution engendered a reversion to Hispano-Maghrebi architectural tradition. The *madrasa* of Sale, of very

modest dimensions, is a masterpiece of balance and elegance: coloured *zellij* tiling, carved plaster and cedarwood once heightened by painting, express on the façade the principal lines of the plan. This all-pervasive decoration in no way compromises architectural quality, as can be seen even better at the *madrasa* Bu Inaniya at Fez: the cruciform plan recalls eastern examples, but a great mosque is substituted for the usual simple oratory. New functions, plans and styles show that Morocco was developing its own architectural formulas.

Even in the final years of Muslim Spain, a threatened al-Andalus remained a centre of art worthy of its Umayyad and Hispano-Maghrebi predecessors. The Alhambra remains without equal, despite restorations carried out in the 19th century in a romantic spirit, which altered it as well as preserving it. This fortress town dominating the double valley of Granada seems at an early date to have converted its defensive walls to pleasurable use. The palace zone, which is shown here, was attached to its northern line, and the Ambassadors' Hall occupies one of its largest bastions – the tower of Comares. The exploitation of light is supreme: the dappled light of rooms with murmuring fountains contrasts wonderfully with the overpowering brightness of Andalusia and the south-east. The patios, with their gardens and running water, around which the buildings are arranged, again show faultless skill: the columns, arches, and decorations of the Court of the Lions, though so rich, give no impression of heaviness. Rhythms and colours are such that "architecture resolves itself into music". The kingdom of Granada, like Merinid Morocco, participated in true Islamic fashion in the decorative passion of the end of the Middle Ages.

Enlargement of the great mosque (10th century), Cordoba (Spain)

The work of al-Hakam II furnished the great mosque of Cordoba with a rich axial nave whose entwined lobed arches suggest, paradoxically, a renewal of the exchange between East and West; the art of al-Andalus, which here reached mastery, was an inspiration for many Hispano-Maghrebi architects.

Courtyard of the Merinid "madrasa" (14th century), Sale, Morocco

Although the Maghreb adopted the eastern institution of the *madrasa* at the end of the 13th century, its architecture remained true to local tradition. Here, the narrowness of the arcaded courtyard is determined by the restricted nature of the site. The door into the oratory can be seen across the courtyard, whose decoration combines enamelled tiling, plaster and carved wood in refined harmony.

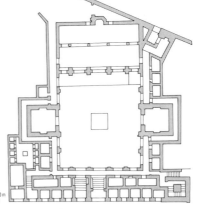

Bu Inaniya "madrasa", Fez (Morocco)

The latest of the Merinid *madrasas* in Fez shows important innovations. A great mosque has replaced the traditional oratory, while the lateral rooms may derive from the cruciform plans more common in the East than in the Maghreb. But above all it signals a renaissance in Moroccan architecture.

Palace of the Alhambra: plan and view of the Court of the Lions, Granada (Spain)

The Court of the Lions has long been considered an outstanding example of the virtuosity of Islamic architecture. It is, at the very least, the finest element in a palace complex disposed along the northern wall of the "city of government" which dominated Granada. The essence of the palace of the Alhambra appears in the plan below. Of the earliest part, arranged around a courtyard with a long pool (1), only the Ambassadors' Hall has been preserved, fitted into the so-called Comares tower (5), from which the whole group is named; an antechamber flanked by alcoves, the Sala de la Barca (4), and a portico with seven bays give the impression of a classical palace complex. This is skilfully reflected in the façade. A similar group, destroyed at the time of the construction of Charles V's palace, repeated the design to the south. This first "palace", in which the simplicity of the long sides contrasts with the richness of the north and south façades, is flanked on the west by the Mechouar Hall (2) and the Cuarto Dorado suite of rooms (3), and on the east by the royal baths (6), which are situated, like the garden they adjoin (7), on a lower level. In the Court of the Lions (8), as can be seen, a cruciform pattern of water channels divides the garden housing the famous 11th century fountain into four parterres. The scents of the garden and the splash of running water are as much a part of the architecture as the columns and pavilions; it is an architecture that very much reflects the splendid lifestyle of the last years of Islamic Spain.

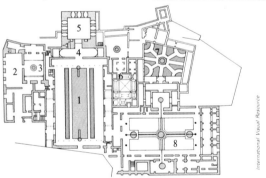

Overall view of the north wall of the Alhambra (from Albaicín)

The Alhambra was also a fortress; one can see on either side of the powerful Comares tower the citadel of the city on the right, and the church of Santa Maria on the left, in place of its great mosque.

Decoration of a window, Alhambra, Granada

The internal walls of the rooms are covered with rich ornament yet overstatement is avoided: surfaces are outlined and framed by bands, often bearing poetic inscriptions. Two planes of carving stand out from backgrounds that are often coloured, and set up a play of light. Stylized foliage extends into the interior the walled garden over which this paired window looks out.

Iranian architecture

The eastern provinces of the Islamic world had, as we have seen, a unique influence over the life of the empire. Endowed from the earliest days with their own architectural tradition, they constituted a regional school that endured from century to century, even overwhelming forms emanating from the centre of the caliphate immediately after conversion to Islam. This is well shown by the architectural history of the city of Isfahan.

There is plentiful evidence that soon after conquest the whole region, corresponding approximately to present-day Iran, Afghanistan and the Islamic provinces of the U.S.S.R. beyond the Oxus, experienced a period of intense architectural creativity. The tomb of Ismail the Samanid at Bukhara, marking the beginning of a long tradition of funerary architecture, demonstrates two key elements of the local tradition: the body of the mausoleum, in the form of a parallelepiped, is built in a patterned brickwork that articulates and animates the façades; and the roof of the structure asserts the primordial and unchanging importance of the dome. Other buildings, such as the mosques at Damghan and Nayin (Iran) or even the simple oratory with nine domes near Balkh (Afghanistan), reveal the links of this early Iranian architecture with the rest of the Islamic empire. The mosque at Nayin, for example, is decorated with stucco ornament that appears to be 10th century, and shows that a classical plan used to emphasize both the axial nave and the wall of the *qibla* was already familiar at this period.

The same is true of the earliest Friday Mosque at Isfahan, even though its plan is more suggestive of the sanctuaries of Samarra. Recent research has demonstrated the nature of the initial plan beneath successive transformations. The enlargement of the portico and the introduction of clustered piers soon marked a departure from the original scheme, but the decisive step was taken in the 11th century: a domed pavilion, dated by an inscription to the reign of Malikshah, was placed in front of the *mihrab*, isolated from the prayer-hall by an open space. This was the first stage in the complete reconstruction of the building. The creation of the domed pavilion, in imitation of pre-Islamic temples of fire, was a re-assertion of local architectural traditions. Many further alterations and additions over the centuries have distorted the regularity of the monument – particularly the relatively late insertion of four *iwans*, which constitute a renewed input of Iranian tradition. This basic scheme, which can be found in all the styles of the region and was adopted, as we have seen, by many other Islamic provinces, was continued under the Safavids but with a completely different aesthetic.

It would be impossible here to give a complete picture of a city which has so fascinated European travellers. Gobineau saw in Isfahan "the triumph of elegance and the model of beauty", while Tavernier in about 1679 saw no more than "a large ill-shaped village". Chardin, at the end of the 17th century, counted in the city no less than 162 mosques, 48 "colleges", 1,802 caravanserais and 273 baths. Even if his figures are exaggerated, this illustrates the extraordinary architectural patronage of the Safavids, after the fifth monarch, Shah Abbas I, made Isfahan his capital. Even if we know nothing

of the organization of the Seljuk city, we can be certain that the huge royal square (*maydan-i-shah*) measuring 484 by 155 metres (530 by 170 yards) was surrounded by blind arcading. The new great mosque was built facing the royal bazaar which occupied the narrow south side of the square; the plan of the mosque was once again cruciform, and was dominated by the *iwan*, increased in scale and flanked by minarets, and by the powerful dome of the prayer-hall. The sanctuary was embellished near the apse with porticoed courtyards. Palaces and the oratory of Sheik Lutfullah were situated on the east and west sides of the square, indicating again the vast extent of the project.

Particularly striking in Isfahan is the long perspective of an avenue of water and vegetation, a perfect expression of that taste for grand vistas which had already created the royal square. Several bridges replaced the old pontoon bridge that had linked the two banks of the city since the Middle Ages. The weight of their construction contrasts with the lightness of the palace architecture, but the arches of the Khadju bridge show that the same aesthetic informed this Safavid work. Certain themes, such as the vast areas covered by sumptuous but fragile faience decoration, so often a feature of the architecture of modern Iran, are undeniably repetitive. But these do reveal the revival of local traditions, which determined the evolution of Islamic architecture in the lands it conquered: every people within the community of believers was able to build monuments suited to its own purposes. Thus Iran, while remaining faithful to Islam, was able to return to its own roots.

Minaret of the great mosque of al-Mutawakkil, Samarra (Iraq)

The spiral form of this minaret and the first great mosque of Samarra (9th century) are among the best examples of influence from the Arabian peninsula and Mesopotamia upon the eastern provinces of the empire.

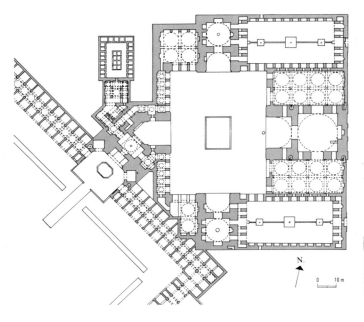

N

0   10 m

The "masjid i-shah" or royal mosque, Isfahan (Iran)

The composition of four *iwans* that was achieved in stages at the Friday mosque in Isfahan was here created at one stroke in a sanctuary built *ex-novo* in the Safavid era. One is at first surprised by the oblique entrance to the mosque: it was forced on the architect by the difference between the alignment of the royal square and the direction of Mecca, which it was necessary to respect in the construction of the new great mosque. The desire to respect the demands of piety in no way interfered with the symmetry of the plan: the courtyard combines two storeys of arcades with four *iwans* on a cruciform plan, a familiar design of Iranian architecture. The prayer-hall occupies no more than a small part of the monument: two rooms with small domes are linked awkwardly with the great *iwan* and the central dome of the composition; but the spaces on either side of them are more felicitously filled by two courtyards surrounded by arched alcoves. The monument exemplifies the perfect clarity and slightly insipid charm of Safavid architecture.

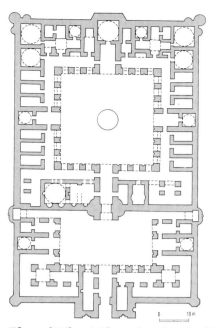

Plan of Ribat i-Sharaf and Safavid portico of the great mosque of Isfahan

These two images are clear enough illustration of the constants and the evolution of Iranian architecture. The caravanserai of Ribat i-Sharaf, built in the 12th century, has two courts in succession, each of cruciform plan and each having an oratory; the larger of the two, for official use, has apartments on either side of the principal *iwan*. Decorative stone-dressing and carved ornament contributed to a refined but vigorous architecture of domes and vaults. In the great mosque at Isfahan an alternative form of decoration clothes and colours the architecture: this kind of pervasive ornament doubtless owes its appeal to the play of warm colours, but it can be a little wearying to anyone who analyses the repertoire of designs, which are as luxuriant as they are monotonous.

The conception of the central courtyard of the royal mosque is distinctly Iranian and combines four "iwans" at the centres of the façades with two storeys of arcades flanking them; a pool occupies the centre of the composition.

It should be noted that the "iwan" giving access to the prayer-hall is, like the entrance "iwan", broader and higher. It also is flanked by minarets whose twisted shafts form part of the decoration.

This Safavid mosque, like the 11th century Friday mosque at Isfahan, was provided with a large dome in front of the "mihrab"; this dominates the whole building, underlining the importance that was accorded to the "mihrab" and the "maqsura". It is very brightly coloured, as are the most important façades.

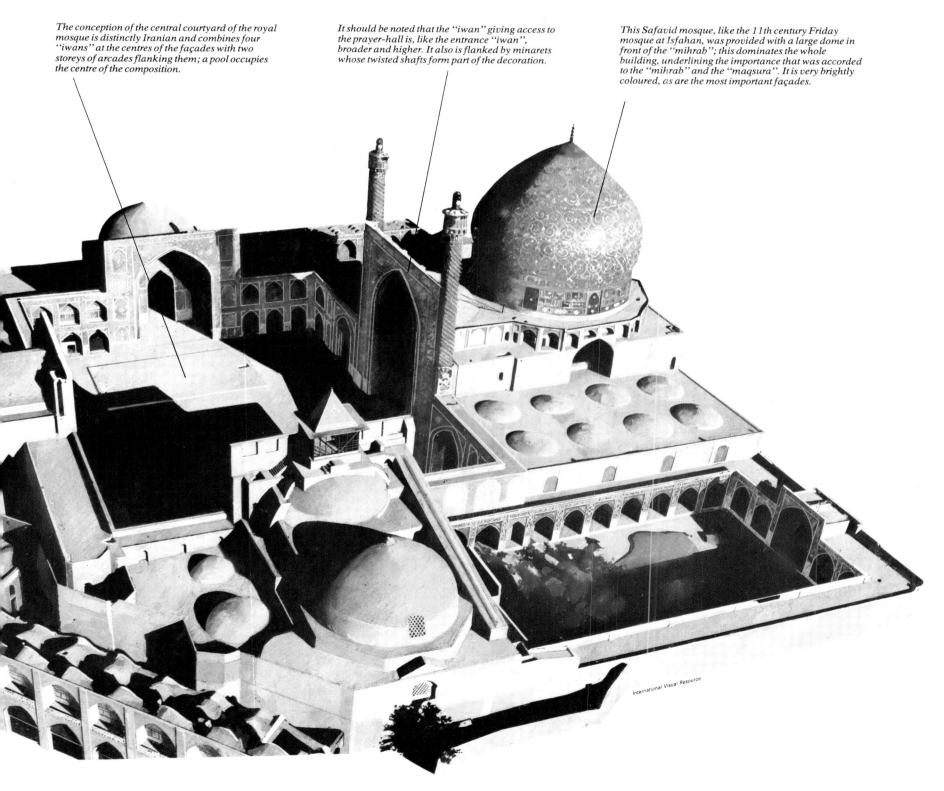

International Visual Resource

Ottoman Turkey

The Ottoman empire, alongside that of Safavid Iran and Mughal India, was one of the great empires of Islam. Its architecture, however, was the fruit of an evolution beginning in the 14th century, before the empire itself was established. It began when a group of Turcomans benefited from a decline in the power of the Mongols to expand their territory towards Europe from the sea of Marmara. The defeat which Tamerlane inflicted on them in central Anatolia in 1402 failed to stop them completely and in 1453 they captured Istanbul. While Islam was retreating in Andalusia, it was advancing in eastern Europe. The architecture of the new empire was thus the heir both of Seljuk Anatolia and of the Byzantine empire. After an initial period in which the Seljuk tradition can still be detected, the example of Byzantium and particularly of Santa Sophia began to exert an influence over Ottoman architecture.

It is important to remember just how extensive the domain of the Ottoman empire was: it covered the entire territory that the Mamluks could no longer defend, beyond Syria and Egypt as far as present-day Algeria. A colossal empire stretching from Baghdad to North Africa and the Balkans, coupled with the organizational and administrative skill of the Ottomans, gave their architecture immense financial resources. Their monuments seem as much to reflect their method as their power. In their details they do not perhaps have the aesthetic qualities and skill of the medieval architects. But the decline of Islamic art in the modern era, which is often exaggerated, should not obscure the artistic achievement of this new Turkish development.

Edirne in Europe exemplifies many characteristics of the evolution of Ottoman architecture. The Selimiye mosque, built between 1569 and 1574, was the masterpiece of the architect Sinan. The thrust of its minarets, and its dome 31 metres (100 feet) in diameter, sit beautifully in the landscape. If the façades remain a little uninteresting, the plan is extremely skilful: the arrangement with eight piers is the culmination of a long search for the best means of lighting and opening out the space of a large prayer-hall. After the cluttered space of Bursa or the still restricted Green Mosque at Iznik, Selimiye represents a conspicuous improvement. Stages in the search for lightness and grace in the buttressing of the dome are well illustrated by the Sultan Bayezid mosque or the Sulaymaniye of Istanbul.

A different compositional formula appeared between 1484 and 1488 in the work of the architect Khayr al-Din on the banks of the Tunja in Edirne, a complex commissioned by Sultan Bayezid II; grouped around the mosque and the two rooms for charitable purposes on either side of the domed space were a hospital, a *madrasa*, an *imaret* (a religious foundation for the distribution of foods – as much to students as to the indigent), baths and a granary. This complex has been described as the greatest "socio-religious" foundation in 15th century architecture. It shows that the end of the Middle Ages had already initiated a new Ottoman architecture in which the use of mass and façade invested a certain frigidity of conception with a classical power.

Courtyard of the great mosque, Edirne

The solemnity of the internal volumes, verging on frigidity, is immediately apparent: only the discreet use of coloured stone in the arches of the portico animates the façade of the prayer-hall facing the courtyard. But the transition from the slender columns of the portico to the mass of the dome is skilfully controlled.

Selimiye great mosque, Edirne (Turkey)

The great 16th century mosque, the work of Sultan Selim, dominates the city without overwhelming through excessive mass. The architect was able to unify the horizontal plane of the mosque and its auxiliary buildings with a spreading dome and four thin minarets which give vitality to the composition.

Bayezid II's complex, Edirne

The side pictured here illustrates the balance and the "classicism" of this complex, in which are combined a mosque (1), a hospital (2), a *madrasa* (3), an *imaret* (4), shops (5) and a drinking fountain (6).

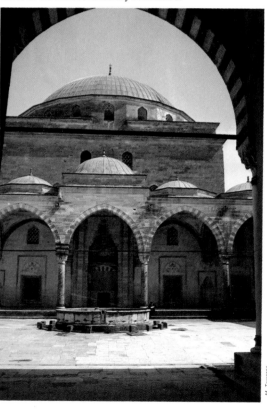

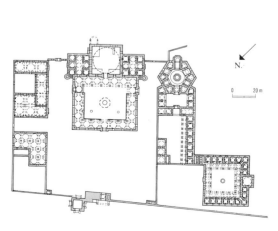

THE
AGE OF CLASSICISM

The Charterhouse of Pavia
(detail)

Amadeo produced the model for the marble façade affixed to the great Gothic body of the church in 1490, and supervised the execution of the lower Order (one bay of which is shown). Two Orders of pilasters, each crowned by a small gallery, make up the façade; the strikingly abundant ornament obeys an impeccable logic, with each architectural member characterized by a specific ornament – medallions on the base; narrative reliefs on the plinths; sculptured statues in the pilaster niches; medallions surrounding each bay; decorative reliefs on the surrounds.

The history of Renaissance architecture coincides only partially with that of European architecture as a whole in the 15th and 16th centuries. Far from showing signs of exhaustion, Gothic architecture, which its contemporaries called "modern", continued to produce new masterpieces. At the same time the "antique" style which had appeared in Florence at the beginning of the 14th century spread through Italy and, during the course of the 16th century, throughout Europe (though not without resistance). Historians, instead of attempting to generalize the history of European architecture in the 15th and 16th centuries, have juxtaposed two distinct histories: one traces what in retrospect appear as the last manifestations of the Gothic style; the other, the progress of the new style, the architectural expression of which has been known since the 19th century as the Renaissance.

The architecture of the Renaissance is distinguished by a new architectural language based on the use of the ancient Orders, by a new conception of the handling of mass and surface, and by the appearance of new types of church, public building and residence; but it was also part of a much wider cultural movement, which hoped to revive, after centuries of neglect and decay, the whole of ancient culture.

Italians of the 16th century used the term rinàscita to describe this impassioned return to the classical Greco-Roman world, which was seen as both the source of and the model for a civilization which, as it grew more remote from its origins, had degenerated rather than progressed. The contrast between the Italy of the time, ravaged by barbarians, and the splendid image of ancient Rome served as a painful reminder. The desire for such a revival was first expressed in the middle of the 14th century in the work of Petrarch. By the careful study of the Greek and Latin languages, and the indefatigable quest for manuscripts, inscriptions and monuments, followers of Petrarch strove to revive the antico valore, and to rediscover ancient knowledge, which showed a way to civic and human liberation, a way out of the Dark Ages.

The bipolar picture of history – pagan era and Christian era – now had to be substituted by a three-phase picture – antiquity, the Middle Ages and the age of the Renaissance. The architecture of the Renaissance rejected the maniera tedesca, the Gothic style, and adopted the new principles of the antica e buona maniera moderna, the "good modern antique style", but it did not simply repeat; it emulated. The intention was to take up the antique again, not in order to copy it in a servile manner, but to surpass it, building on its achievements. This renovatio antiquitatis was only one aspect of the new modern culture that was slowly developing during the 15th and 16th centuries.

The architects of the Middle Ages had not ignored ancient architecture, but they adapted it to their own style and needs. The Renaissance architects wanted to rediscover the true appearance of the ancient buildings which had been defiled by the barbarians. To do this it was necessary to study at first hand both the ancient texts (especially Vitruvius), and the ruins. Andrea Palladio states this clearly in the preface to his treatise (I Quattro Libri d'Architettura, Venice, 1570), which was the synthesis of a century and a half of architectural humanism: "Guided by my natural inclination, I devoted myself from my earliest years to the study of architecture, and since I considered that the ancient Romans had, in architecture, as in so many other fields, far surpassed their successors, I proposed as my master and guide Vitruvius, the only ancient to have spoken of architecture, and I set myself to examine the remains of ancient buildings".

Vitruvius's treatise De Architectura, dedicated to Augustus, is the only ancient architectural treatise to have come down to us complete, and it was immediately

Ospedale Maggiore, Milan. The plan of this hospital, built by Filarete from 1456, was inspired by Florentine principles of regularity, but the windows of the elevation do not align with the arcade and their surrounds retain a pronounced Gothic flavour.

THE RENAISSANCE

seized on as an essential tool in this
renovatio antiquitatis – but a tool which
only patient philological study proved
able to render usable. In the preface to a
translation of Vitruvius undertaken in
about 1532, Giuliano da Sangallo the
Younger clearly describes the difficulties of
the enterprise: "Our Vitruvius has not yet
been well understood, for numerous
reasons: first, artists made use of his work
who were quite ignorant of literature; then
writers turned their attention to him who
had no practical knowledge of art".
Nevertheless, architects and humanists
soon began to work together on the texts; the
contact made between Filippo Brunelleschi
and Leon Battista Alberti, between Fra
Giocondo and Guillaume Budé, between

Palladio and Daniele Barbaro, between
Philibert de l'Orme and Rabelais, and
between Jean Goujon and Jean Martin,
shaped the development of Vitruvianism.
Copies of the manuscript began to circulate
from 1414. Vitruvius' treatise was able to
benefit from the increase in distribution
made possible by the advent of the printing
press. The first printed edition appeared in
1486, and in 1511 Fra Giocondo published
the Latin text illustrated with engravings.
There were numerous Italian translations:
Francesco di Giorgio was responsible for
one produced before the end of the 15th
century; another was prepared under the
direction of Raphael, and others by the
Sangallo family. Cesare Cesariano, a pupil
of Bramante, printed one at Como in 1521.

In the following decades Spanish and
French translations followed.

Other ancient technical treatises also
received attention, such as the treatises on
agriculture by Varro and Columella, or that
on hydraulics by Frontinius. The bucolic
poetry of Horace and Virgil, and the
histories of Caesar and Tacitus played a less
obvious, but no less influential, role in
weaving around the life of court and villa
an antique aura in which the actors of the
Renaissance could play their parts. The
long descriptions that Pliny the Younger
gives of his villas in Tusculum and
Laurentinum, together with the first
excavations of Hadrian's Villa at Tivoli and
the first reconstructions of the villas on the

Map of Renaissance Italy (from A. Chastel, *Le Grand Atelier d'Italie*, Gallimard, Paris, 1965).

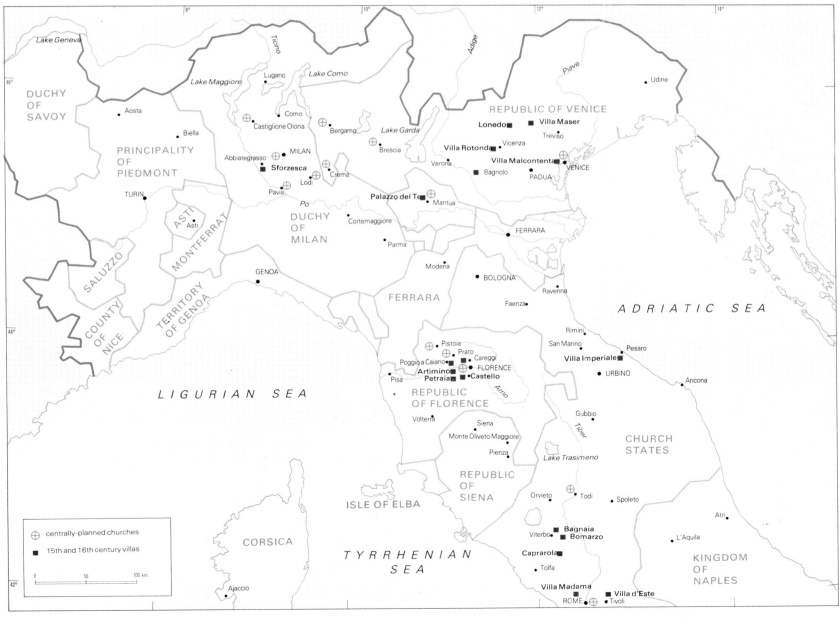

265

Temple of Fortuna Virilis, Rome. In his commentary on this engraving, published in 1570 in his treatise on architecture (Book IV), Palladio remarked that he had come across no building that used the Ionic Order described by Vitruvius.

hills of Rome, provided a climate favourable for the revival of the grand villa in the ancient manner, such as the Belvedere in the Vatican, by Bramante, and the Villa Madama by Raphael.

Study of texts was complemented by the survey and restoration of ruins: while Vitruvius gave written rules for the design of the Orders, the ruins provided real examples of columns, capitals and friezes. Pliny described the courts and rooms of his villa in Laurentinum; at Hadrian's villa, the original nymphaeum and reception rooms could actually be seen. Vitruvius described the decoration of Roman houses ("landscapes are painted in the galleries . . . and at significant points there are grand paintings of the gods as they are described in poetry, or of important events such as the Trojan War or the journeys of Ulysses"); the vaults of the Domus Aurea of Nero displayed this very kind of stucco decoration and painting. These decorations, discovered hidden beneath the earth, as though in grottoes (hence the term "grotesque"), were greatly admired. Albums of motifs were built up, at first in the form of manuscripts – invaluable sources of reference for architects and studios; then, during the 16th century, many were published. Sebastiano Serlio took many of the elements for his books of architecture from the portfolio of drawings owned by Baldassare Peruzzi, and in 1570 Palladio published some of his archaeological surveys.

But it took the enthusiasm of several generations of architects and humanists to overcome the problems of interpreting Vitruvius accurately, and to piece together the jigsaws of the ruins. The architecture of the Renaissance nevertheless drew a certain strength from this lack of understanding of both texts and monuments: the design of a capital or an entablature could not be resolved by a simple, tried and tested formula; it required inspiration and enthusiasm. Misunderstandings, incorrect reconstructions and the mixing of old designs with new research gave birth to a

variety of forms, which resulted in the originality of these two centuries. A history has yet to be written of the forms arrived at through misunderstanding or incorrect reconstruction. The best example is, without doubt, the colonnaded vestibule, such as that of the Palazzo Farnese, born out of an incorrect interpretation of the alae (wings) of the atrium described by Vitruvius.

This period of research reached fruition in the second half of the 16th century. The treatises of Serlio (1537–70), Vignola (1562) and Palladio (1570) in Italy, and those of Jean Bullant (1564) and Philibert De l'Orme (1567) in France, coordinated and systematized the research of the previous years. The architects of the Renaissance had little understanding of the historical time-span of antiquity although they were aware of the obvious disparity between the text of Vitruvius and the evidence of the ruins and between the ruins themselves. The choices made between these diverse examples by Serlio, Vignola and Palladio led to a confusion in differentiating between works of antiquity and those of the modern period. This confusion even occurred within the treatises themselves – Bramante's Tempietto and St. Peter's in Rome were included by Serlio in his book Dell'antichità.

Thus one sees the revival of a whole architectural repertoire – of ornament (Greek key, festoons, ribbons), of motifs (pilasters, columns, inscriptions, pediments, medallions, thermal windows) and of compositions (superimposed Orders, as at the Colosseum or the Theatre of Marcellus; open colonnades, as at the Septizonium; alternating bays, derived from triumphal arches). At the same time, ancient technology was rediscovered. Breaking with Gothic tradition, which saw architecture as a system of linear forces, the architects of the Renaissance began again to conceive of structures in terms of mass. Walls were seen as forms that could be modelled with niches (Santa Maria degli Angeli in Florence, St. Peter's in Rome).

Theatre of Marcellus. Engraved by Serlio in his third book Dell'Antichità (1540), the theatre of Marcellus was one of the Roman ruins that, together with the Colosseum, was most highly regarded by architects of the time. The theme of regular arcades decorated with two superimposed Orders became one of the patterns for Renaissance architecture.

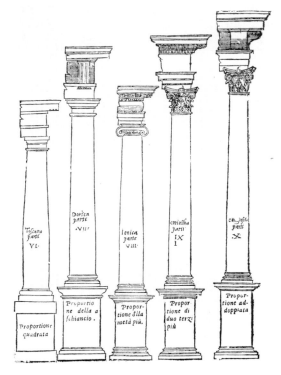

The five Orders according to Serlio. In Book IV of his treatise on architecture (which was in fact the first to be published, in 1537), Serlio presented on the first plate the five Orders side by side, "like the characters in a comedy", as he put it. The correct handling of the Orders is indeed the foundation of the architectural language of the Renaissance.

Brunelleschi studied the ancient methods of vaulting, and they contributed to his design for the dome of Florence Cathedral. The coffered vaults of ancient baths and temples inspired Alberti and Bramante in the vaults they designed for their own churches (Sant' Andrea in Mantua and St. Peter's in Rome), and triumphal arches were the model for their façades (Tempio Malatestiano in Rimini).

The re-creation of certain types of ancient building soon became more ambitious: the revival began of triumphal arches for festivals and solemn entries, peristyle temples (Bramante's Tempietto), ancient villas (the Villa Madama, the Belvedere), the ancient type of theatre (the Teatro Olimpico at Vicenza) and mausoleums (project for the palace of Urbino, tumulus in the garden of the Villa Medici). Houses, too, without imitating literally the dwellings of the ancient Romans, incorporated certain of their characteristics; for example the

Courtyard of the Palazzo Farnese, Rome
Begun in 1534 by Antonio da Sangallo the Younger, the courtyard was inspired, like that of the Palazzo Venezia half a century earlier, by the superimposed Orders of the theatre of Marcellus and the Colosseum, the highest expression of Roman grandeur. Michelangelo, who completed the palace after 1546, designed the third storey with less dependence on ancient models.

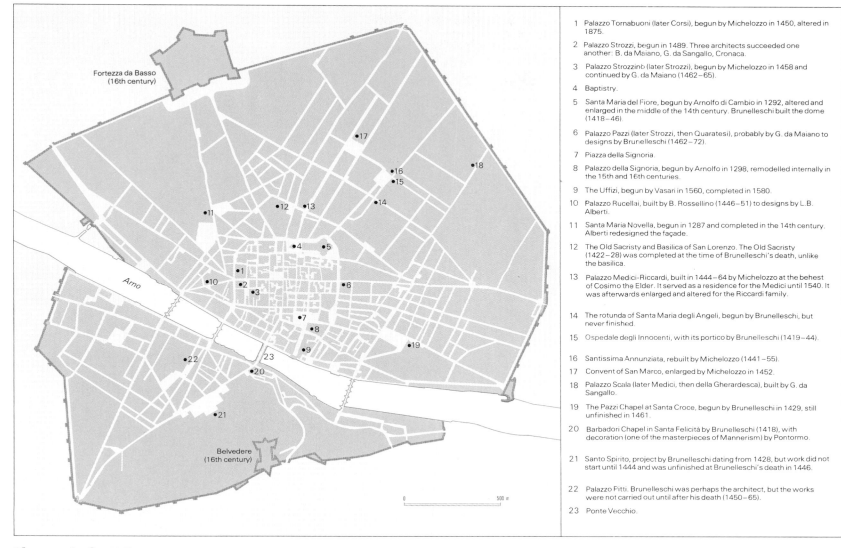

1   Palazzo Tornabuoni (later Corsi), begun by Michelozzo in 1450, altered in 1875.

2   Palazzo Strozzi, begun in 1489. Three architects succeeded one another: B. da Maiano, G. da Sangallo, Cronaca.

3   Palazzo Strozzinò (later Strozzi), begun by Michelozzo in 1458 and continued by G. da Maiano (1462–65).

4   Baptistry.

5   Santa Maria del Fiore, begun by Arnolfo di Cambio in 1292, altered and enlarged in the middle of the 14th century. Brunelleschi built the dome (1418–46).

6   Palazzo Pazzi (later Strozzi, then Quaratesi), probably by G. da Maiano to designs by Brunelleschi (1462–72).

7   Piazza della Signoria.

8   Palazzo della Signoria, begun by Arnolfo in 1298, remodelled internally in the 15th and 16th centuries.

9   The Uffizi, begun by Vasari in 1560, completed in 1580.

10   Palazzo Rucellai, built by B. Rossellino (1446–51) to designs by L.B. Alberti.

11   Santa Maria Novella, begun in 1287 and completed in the 14th century. Alberti redesigned the façade.

12   The Old Sacristy and Basilica of San Lorenzo. The Old Sacristy (1422–28) was completed at the time of Brunelleschi's death, unlike the basilica.

13   Palazzo Medici-Riccardi, built in 1444–64 by Michelozzo at the behest of Cosimo the Elder. It served as a residence for the Medici until 1540. It was afterwards enlarged and altered for the Riccardi family.

14   The rotunda of Santa Maria degli Angeli, begun by Brunelleschi, but never finished.

15   Ospedale degli Innocenti, with its portico by Brunelleschi (1419–44).

16   Santissima Annunziata, rebuilt by Michelozzo (1441–55).

17   Convent of San Marco, enlarged by Michelozzo in 1452.

18   Palazzo Scala (later Medici, then della Gherardesca), built by G. da Sangallo.

19   The Pazzi Chapel at Santa Croce, begun by Brunelleschi in 1429, still unfinished in 1461.

20   Barbadori Chapel in Santa Felicità by Brunelleschi (1418), with decoration (one of the masterpieces of Mannerism) by Pontormo.

21   Santo Spirito, project by Brunelleschi dating from 1428, but work did not start until 1444 and was unfinished at Brunelleschi's death in 1446.

22   Palazzo Pitti. Brunelleschi was perhaps the architect, but the works were not carried out until after his death (1450–65).

23   Ponte Vecchio.

Florence in the 15th century (from Giovanni Fanelli, *Firenze, architettura e città*, Vallecchi, Florence, 1973).

atrium, cryptoporticus or nymphaeum. The idea of the regular organization of space was developed at this time: courtyards and façades were based on strict proportional relationships and on a regular rhythm of columns and bays. The humanist architects discovered in Vitruvius the fundamental idea that beauty consisted in the rational coordination of the proportions of all parts of a building, so that every part was of a clearly defined size and shape, and so that nothing could be added or taken away without destroying the harmony of the whole.

It is clear that in this search for regularity the discovery of linear perspective was of great importance; indeed, it was an essential aid to the establishment of the new architectural ideal. However, it would be wrong to see this ideal as a purely aesthetic concept, or even as the manifestation of man's self-assurance now that he was freed from the oppression of religious dogma and was once more master of his own world. The search for harmonious proportions and the preference for pure forms – the circle and the square – had a strong religious and symbolic significance. In their quest to find rationes *(ordered proportions), Brunelleschi, Alberti and Palladio studied Pythagoras and the Bible, Vitruvius and St. Augustine. The mystique of Pythagorean numbers was matched by the wisdom of Solomon, who declared that God had defined the dimensions, number and weight of all things; the* concinnità *(harmony) of Vitruvius was paralleled by the vision of St. Augustine, who saw in the regular arrangement of architectural elements such as doors and windows an image of divine order. Humanism and Christianity, cosmology and astrology all combined to promote the mystique of numbers, an essential aspect of Renaissance religious*

Palazzo Branconio dell'Aquila, Rome. Like the Palazzo Caprini, this work by Raphael (*c*.1518), now destroyed, was a variation on the theme of the ancient *insula* (block), but was treated with more elegance and variety. The simplicity of the Tuscan ground floor contrasts with the variety of the first floor, with its alternating rhythm of niches and aedicules (with segmental or triangular pediments), and with that of the attic storey (with its rich stucco decoration).

PALATIUM ET HABITACULUM RAPHAELIS SANTII DE URBINO

267

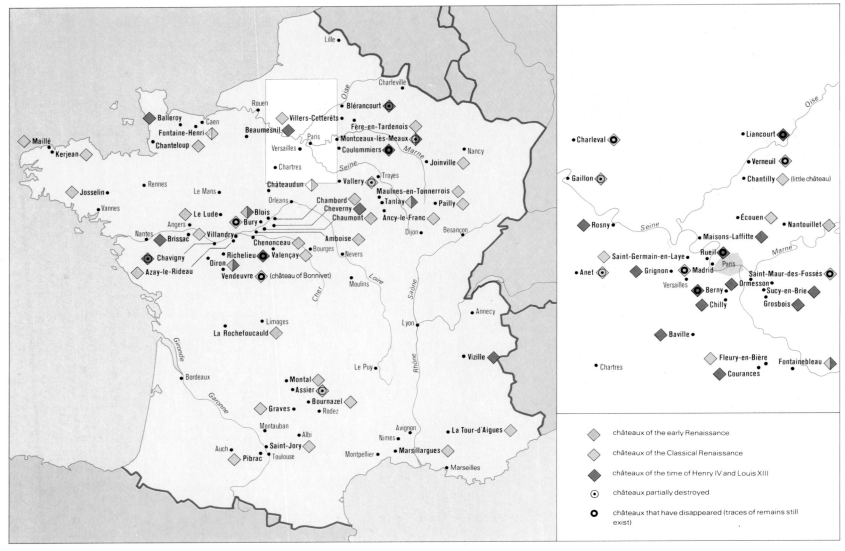

châteaux of the early Renaissance

châteaux of the Classical Renaissance

châteaux of the time of Henry IV and Louis XIII

châteaux partially destroyed

châteaux that have disappeared (traces of remains still exist)

architecture which soon extended to the secular domain. The beauty of Palladio's villas owes much to the fact that he conferred on these buildings the sacred harmony associated with the temples of antiquity.

The Orders of pilasters and columns also played an essential role in the definition of the new architecture. Though ornamental, they provided the basis for the geometric and harmonic control of all parts of the building: the module, that is to say the width or half the width of the column or pilaster, determined the dimensions of all other elements of the structure. (One of the earliest examples is without doubt Alberti's façade of the Palazzo Rucellai in Florence.) Each of the three Orders (Doric, Ionic, Corinthian) differed not only in their proportions and their capitals, but also in their character – severe Doric, gracious Ionic, majestic Corinthian: a difference of "mode", in the musical sense of the term, which is one of the principal themes in the architecture of the 16th century.

The Renaissance movement was clearly recognized by contemporary artists and intellectuals, and Vasari, in his monumental work, Lives of the Most Excellent Painters, Sculptors and Architects of Italy, gives a brilliant picture of it. This book was published in 1550, revised with additions in 1568, and remains an essential work of reference. It traces the development of the Renaissance through the contributions of a succession of great artists; in the field of architecture these were Brunelleschi, Bramante and Michelangelo. In retrospect, the Renaissance may appear as a homogeneous movement, but in fact these two centuries were full of changes and contrasts. One can follow the progress of architectural humanism as it re-created ancient architecture, with greater and

greater audacity, and ended by surpassing it, and as it spread from Italy to the rest of Europe. But there is a striking contrast between the fragmented, essentially Florentine architecture of the 15th century, reflecting the turmoil of rival princely courts, cities and families, and the architecture of the 16th century, in which the new Roman language established its universal character. This language itself was used in different ways: some wished to copy antiquity, others to surpass it; some took their models from ancient classical architecture, others from that of the later imperial period.

The rejection of the Gothic style, which was the starting point of the new architecture, certainly came more naturally to Florence and Rome, where Gothic was regarded as a foreign import. The return to the style of antiquity, to the style destroyed by the barbarian hordes, was thus a return to the national style. The Italian cities, and Florence in particular, looked to the Roman past for the origins of their self-assurance, for the foundations of their success in banking, commerce and craftsmanship. This nationalist flavour is especially clear in the architecture of Brunelleschi, the earliest manifestation of the new style. In returning to the Roman past, to the unsullied image of Roman architecture, Florence was asserting herself as a successor to the Roman republic. In Rome, architects preferred as models the buildings of the imperial period. A clear contrast can be seen between the columns of the courtyards of Florentine palaces, based on Tuscan models, and the arcades of the Palazzo Venezia in Rome, with their attached half-columns recalling those of the nearby Colosseum. In Milan, where architectural activity centred on the construction of the cathedral – one of the last great Gothic cathedrals of Europe –

Filarete wrote a treatise to convince his patrons of the superiority of ancient architecture. When drawing up the designs for a projected Venetian palace, he incorporated cusped windows in homage to the maniera veneziana, which maintained its identity until the beginning of the 16th century.

In northern Europe Gothic was the modern, national style, which explains the very strong resistance that was put up to the new antique manner. Gothic religious architecture was almost untouched by the new ideal, and the French nobility remained attached to its prestigious feudal past. Throughout the 16th century an architectural syntax was preserved which played on the contrasting masses of a building rather than on its surfaces and which favoured vertical subdivisions rather than horizontal ones. This continuity helped to establish the characteristic "French manner", even more than did the high roofs and dormer windows observed with interest by Italian travellers. However, it was not difficult to reconcile a Gothic taste for ornament with the classical repertoire, which merely became one more variety. Also, the rustic French were open to seduction by the urbane splendour of the Italian style (on his return from Naples, Charles VIII no longer prized Amboise so highly, though he had just had it rebuilt); and the memory of the Roman empire lent architecture a universal character. To build in the ancient manner was to cast oneself in the role of an emperor. Pope Julius II was the first to understand the power of the new architectural language. Even if in general northern Europe was too attached to its own culture to accept without resistance the revival of the antique style, the kings of France and the emperor of Germany could still be tempted to assume a classical rhetoric for their own benefit.

Courtyard of the ducal palace, Urbino. The great courtyard was an enlargement to a monumental scale of the Florentine arcaded courtyard. An elegant Latin inscription glorifying Duke Federico runs around the frieze. The attic is a 16th century addition.

Palazzo Raimondi, Cremona. Varying colours are used here to supplement the mouldings in shallow relief, in order to emphasize the rigour of the façade and the regular rhythm of the pilasters.

Palace of Charles V, Granada. Earlier than the Louvre of François I and Henri II, the palace of Charles V in Granada (1528) makes grand use of the new architectural rhetoric – the façade with a rusticated podium, the circular courtyard with a portico.

The Florentine Renaissance

The first signs of a Renaissance of the architecture of antiquity appeared in Florence a little before 1420. This Renaissance was encouraged by the rather exalted cultural climate of the "Florentine Republic", which modelled itself on the republic of ancient Rome, of which it saw itself as the heir. Filippo Brunelleschi (1377–1446), who turned to architecture after his setback in the competition with Ghiberti to make the bronze doors of the Baptistry, proposed a radical renewal of the language of architecture, based on a return to the vocabulary of Romanesque and pre-Romanesque architecture in Tuscany, by which means he thought he would regain the beauty of classical architecture. His mastery of linear perspective (which enabled exact control to be established over the dimensions of a building and their proportional relationships), and his use of contrasting grey (*pietra serena*) for the articulating elements and white for the walls and vaults, lent to this purification of medieval forms a visual force that impressed all his contemporaries. The juxtaposition of elementary volumes – the cube and the sphere – from which all the dimensions were derived by means of a single module, realized the Renaissance ideal of perfect harmony.

The portico of the Ospedale degli Innocenti or Foundling Hospital (1419–20) displayed the elements of this new architectural language – in the regular rhythm of its arcades which spring from slender Corinthian columns (similar to those of the 4th century Florentine church of Santi Apostoli), and in its classical entablature carried by elegant pilasters fluted and abutted at the corners like those of the Baptistry (a 10th century building, which was imagined by contemporaries to be a converted ancient temple). Brunelleschi developed this new style at San Lorenzo (Old Sacristy, 1422; reconstruction of the basilica, 1425), and remained loyal to it in the Pazzi chapel (*c.*1429) and at Santo Spirito (1444), the culmination of his study of the Christian basilica. In this final work, the modular pattern was applied with extreme rigour, and the columns regained greater authenticity of proportion – evidence of a better understanding of ancient art. Brunelleschi's visits to Rome and his conversation with Alberti during the 1430s doubtless contributed to this.

A new feeling for the plasticity of Roman architecture is particularly apparent in the church of Santa Maria degli Angeli (1434–37, incomplete), in which the walls were conceived as solid masses from which the chapels appeared to have been hollowed out, and in the "blind tribunes" of the cathedral (1438–44) with their heavier articulation of niches and half-columns.

To Vasari, Brunelleschi may have appeared in retrospect as the first architect to revive the *bella architettura dell' antichità*, but by his contemporaries he was admired as an inventor of genius, whose "miraculous skills as an engineer" had made possible the construction of the dome of the cathedral (1420–34). This dome dominates the city with its 42 metre (140 feet) diameter and its swelling form clearly supported by buttresses – their white marble cladding standing out clearly from the red tiled roofs. It stands as a living symbol of the cultural and technical supremacy of Florence. Brunelleschi's confidence – he built the dome without the benefit of a timber framework – indicated a more theoretical approach to architecture. To succeed he made use both of the experience of the Gothic masters, in conceiving the dome as a network of ribs, and of his own observations of ancient domes, in ensuring that there was complete integration of ribs and shell. To lift materials rapidly to the summit of the dome, he invented numerous machines, cranes, hoists and engines. At his death in 1446 Brunelleschi was one of the most famous men in Italy. The first of the architect-engineers of the Renaissance, he gave architecture a new rationality and rediscovered the essential elements of the classical Orders.

In Florentine sculpture classical elements had been exploited for some time, and Ghiberti (*c.*1380–1451), like Donatello (1386–1466), developed in his reliefs an ideal classical architecture of sometimes greater purity than that of Brunelleschi. But Brunelleschi's only true rival remains Michelozzo (1396–1472), who established himself in the field of secular architecture where Brunelleschi's contribution remains obscure, and who in the Palazzo Medici (1446–60) produced the prototype for the Florentine Renaissance palace. Although he broke with Gothic tradition perhaps less cleanly than Brunelleschi, he endowed the convent of San Marco with a fine Ionic Order and in the rotunda of the Santissima Annunziata produced an exact copy of the temple of Minerva Medica.

The achievements of the Florentine architects were acknowledged throughout Italy; called upon to practise their skills elsewhere, they soon spread the new style abroad.

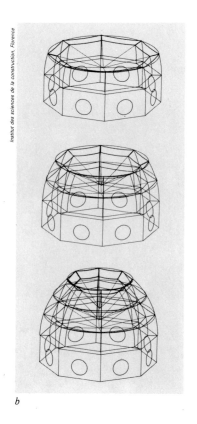

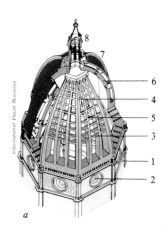

1 octagonal drum
2 round windows (tondi)
3 horizontal ties
4 principal ribs
5 secondary ribs
6 inner shell
7 outer shell
8 lantern

Dome of Florence Cathedral (Santa Maria del Fiore)

The dome was erected under the direction of Brunelleschi between 1420 and 1436; the lantern, for which Brunelleschi left a model, was not finished until 1471. The dome has eight faces and was built on a system of ribs crossed by eight concentric circles, on which were supported two light vaults; between them run stairs for access, while the thinner outer shell affords protection (diagram *a*). To erect the dome without the traditional use of timber "centring," which the width of the span made impossible, Brunelleschi constructed the dome as a series of concentric self-supporting rings, laying the brick and stone courses in a herringbone pattern on inclined surfaces converging towards a single centre, which was progressively raised to produce a "five point" curvature (diagram *b*). He thus obtained the advantages both of light, ribbed Gothic structures and of the ancient structures of solid mass, which he had studied in Rome.

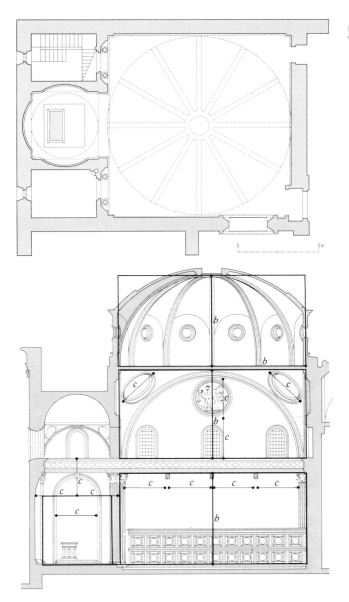

Old Sacristy, San Lorenzo

The Old Sacristy was the first funerary chapel of the Medici. Possibly begun in 1422, it was completed in 1428. The spatial composition depends on the contrast, repeated in the choir, between the elementary volumes of cube and sphere. The network of pilasters, the surrounds to the openings and the ribs of the dome, all made of *pietra serena*, contrast with the white rendered walls and underline the simple proportional relationships that link the different elements (see cross section). This chapel, which demonstrates all the elements of the new architectural poetry, was to have considerable influence. The choir of Santa Maria delle Grazie by Bramante and the New Sacristy of San Lorenzo by Michelozzo were influenced by this first masterpiece of the Florentine Renaissance.

Santo Spirito

Santo Spirito was the last work of Brunelleschi, begun in 1444, two years before his death, but not completed until after 1486. It remains a perfect example of composition by the addition of identical units, a method typical of early Renaissance culture. All dimensions are derived from the measurement of the radius of the nave arches; by the arithmetical multiplication of this module the dimensions are obtained for the depth of the niches, the width of the aisles, the height of the small Order, the height of the aisles to the keystone and the width of the nave. Despite fierce polemic, Brunelleschi's successors shrank from the ultimate conclusion of this repetitive scheme and built a façade with three doors, instead of the four bays which the scheme demanded. Brunelleschi was able to combine here the medieval Latin cross plan with the early Christian basilica. The archaeological accuracy of the capitals crowned by a fragment of entablature should be noted, as should the way in which Brunelleschi uses two orders – a small Order of columns in the arcades and a large Order of pilasters on the crossing piers.

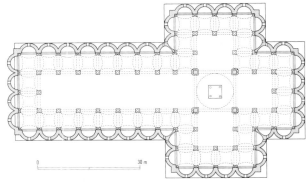

Pazzi chapel

The Pazzi chapel, situated in the cloister of Santa Croce, was begun in 1429, but not finished until much later (the dome was vaulted in 1461). Brunelleschi repeated in it the architectural conception of the Old Sacristy of San Lorenzo, but since the chapel was required to serve as a chapterhouse, the central domed square was extended laterally with two barrel vaults. Here again the structural framework is picked out and the elements of the building are linked by the same repetition of simple numerical relationships, but the rhythm of the pilasters is more insistent and the decoration – by della Robbia – is more refined. The exterior – the outcome of various restorations – does not necessarily correspond to Brunelleschi's design.

A new type of palace

In Florence, the tower form of house was gradually abandoned during the 14th century in favour of the courtyard form. The courtyard, at first small and irregular (Palazzo Davanzati, beginning of the 14th century), became at the beginning of the 15th century the central element, around which the rest of the building was organized (Palazzo Busiri-Bardi). Vasari rightly hailed the Palazzo Medici, built for Cosimo the Elder between 1446 and 1460 by Michelozzo, as "the first to be built in a modern style and on a good plan". Geometrical rationality, introduced into religious architecture by Brunelleschi, now also overtook the grand urban dwelling, which became an object of civic and family pride, and which by its mass and regularity stood out prominently from the fabric of the medieval city.

The regular, generally square courtyard, surrounded by porticoes on its four sides, enclosed within the mass of the building and linked to the street by an arched vestibule, is the basis of the plan of the Renaissance palace. "The principal member of the whole edifice is the courtyard with its porticoes," wrote Leon Battista Alberti in his *De Re Aedificatoria* (Book V), and Francesco di Giorgio echoed him: "The house of a gentleman should have a hall and a courtyard". Around the latter were arranged all the rooms and the means of access, especially the great staircase.

This plan derived more from medieval merchants' houses, with their ground-floor shops and living accommodation above, than from the ancient *insulae*, which became models only for the later Roman palaces of Bramante and Raphael. The ground floor, whose only openings on to the street were small square windows placed very high up, contained shops, offices, and service and guest rooms. The living and bedrooms of the "family" were on the first floor, the *piano nobile*, reached by a monumental staircase with two straight flights – an essential feature for reasons of prestige. These rooms were linked by glazed passages or sometimes by open porticoes, set above the colonnade of the ground floor. On the second storey were less important rooms, including food and furniture stores.

This new regularity of plan was also expressed in the elevation. The public palaces of the 13th and 14th centuries (Bargello, Palazzo Vecchio) had been built in thick courses of *pietra forte*, a calcareous stone, roughly dressed. Inspired by this, Florentine architects of the Renaissance developed a gamut of more or less emphatic rustication, which they contrasted from storey to storey: very pronounced rustication on the ground floor, less so on the first, and less again on the second, while the regular rhythm of the bays was underlined by the radical pattern of the keystones. This formula, developed at the Palazzo Medici, enjoyed considerable popularity in Florence until the end of the century (Pitti, Gondi and Strozzi palaces). For reasons of economy, sometimes only the ground floor was treated in this way (Palazzo Gerini), the upper floors receiving painted decoration over rendering. At the Palazzo Rucellai, on the other hand, Alberti made skilful use of a different solution, framing the rustication with the classical motif of three superimposed Orders.

During the second half of the 15th century, this new type of palace spread throughout Italy. At Pienza, Rossellino built a variation of the Palazzo Rucellai for Pope Pius II Piccolomini (1459); Florentine architects worked at Naples and Urbino (where a new tower was constructed in 1465). Even in Venice, where building design remained faithful to a completely different plan dictated by local conditions (the living rooms were arranged around a long central hall, not around a courtyard), the Palazzo Corner-Spinelli (1480) is evidence of the penetration of the new ideas, with its rustication and symmetrical arrangement of windows.

Nevertheless, a certain regional variety can be seen. In Rome, the courtyard of the Palazzo Venezia (1460), with its half-columns attached to massive piers, was inspired by the nearby Colosseum, and not by Florentine palaces; in Bologna and Ferrara, diamond-faceted rustication was preferred to the Florentine type; in Milan, the use of cast terracotta for all mouldings (arcading, friezes and cornices) lent the façades and courtyards a totally different colouring. Soon, the interest of the architects seems to have focused on decorative motifs (portals, friezes, capitals), and buildings received a delicate ornamentation with increasing reference to antiquity. Even in the 16th century, when new designs were appearing in Rome, Verona and Genoa, the old form of palace continued to enjoy success; in Rome, Antonio da Sangallo the Younger remained faithful to it, even if he used rustication only on the corners of his buildings and gave the courtyards a very Roman flavour (Palazzo Baldassini, Palazzo Farnese).

Palace of Urbino

The ducal palace of Urbino was built by Federico da Montefeltro (1426–82), humanist *condottiere* and duke by a papal decree of 1474. The first project, organized in a linear pattern around an arcaded courtyard, was modified in 1465 by Luciano Laurana who built a monumental staircase and audience hall to the north, and moved the ducal apartments towards the south-west. Superimposed loggias facing the valley and the approach road, framed by two stair towers that allowed the duke rapid access to all floors, formed the new triumphal façade dominating the valley. Francesco di Giorgio, who succeeded Laurana in 1472, arranged the apartments of the duchess, completed the decoration of the courtyard, and installed ingenious hydraulic and acoustic systems. The façade facing the city, which was meant to be clad with marble, remained unfinished.

The apartments of the duchess, with living room (a), bedroom (b), garderobe (c) and oratory (d).

Corbelled out from the wall of the garden, this gallery links the duke's apartments with those of the duchess.

This secret garden (created above the vaulted rooms of the cistern, ice store, cellars and riding school), is bordered on the east by a loggia (a) and on the west by a wall pierced by windows (b) which give a view of the surrounding countryside.

Plan of the Palazzo Medici (restored)

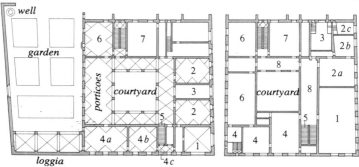

Palazzo Medici, Florence

The Medici palace, built between 1446 and 1459 by Michelozzo for Cosimo the Elder, was the prototype of the *palazzo signorile* of the Renaissance. Planned around a regular courtyard, the palace is presented on the exterior as a cube, whose mass is emphasized by elaborate rustication.

Ground floor

1 *Loggia opening on to street, converted into a room in 1517*
2 *office and bedroom*
3 *vestibule*
4 *guest suite: (a) living room; (b) bedroom; (c) closet. Charles V stayed here.*
5 *main staircase*
6 *the great bedchamber ("of Lorenzo"). Behind it there was a steam bath.*
7 *servants' quarters*

First floor

1 *great hall*
2 *apartment of Piero di Cosimo, later of Lorenzo the Magnificent: (a) bedchamber; (b) garderobe; (c) scrittorio (closet)*
3 *chapel frescoed by Benozzo Gozzoli (1459–63)*
4 *apartment of Cosimo*
5 *stairs*
6 *apartment of Giuliano de' Medici*
7 *service room*
8 *corridors*

Palazzo Rucellai, Florence

The Palazzo Rucellai, built in two stages by Bernardo Rossellino, perhaps to a design by Alberti (courtyard 1448–55; façade after 1457, before 1469), is distinct among Florentine palaces in having a grid of three superimposed Orders of pilasters, applied over the traditional rusticated stonework. A base with an *opus reticulatum* design (in front of which runs a continuous stone bench), sculpted friezes above, and a heavy classical cornice enhance the plasticity of this façade.

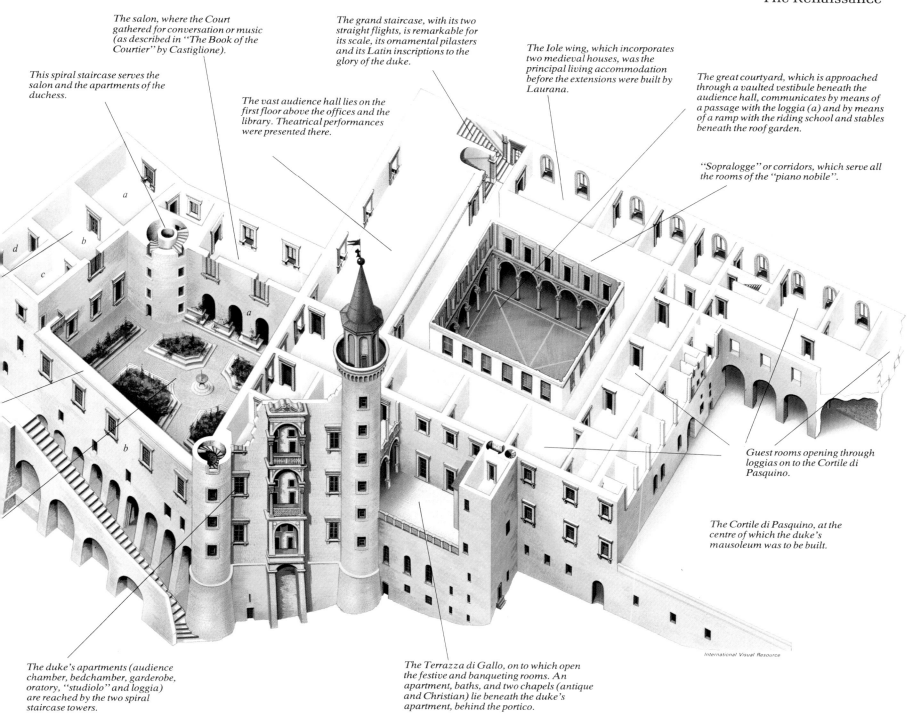

The salon, where the Court gathered for conversation or music (as described in "The Book of the Courtier" by Castiglione).

This spiral staircase serves the salon and the apartments of the duchess.

The grand staircase, with its two straight flights, is remarkable for its scale, its ornamental pilasters and its Latin inscriptions to the glory of the duke.

The vast audience hall lies on the first floor above the offices and the library. Theatrical performances were presented there.

The Iole wing, which incorporates two medieval houses, was the principal living accommodation before the extensions were built by Laurana.

The great courtyard, which is approached through a vaulted vestibule beneath the audience hall, communicates by means of a passage with the loggia (a) and by means of a ramp with the riding school and stables beneath the roof garden.

"Sopralogge" or corridors, which serve all the rooms of the "piano nobile".

Guest rooms opening through loggias on to the Cortile di Pasquino.

The Cortile di Pasquino, at the centre of which the duke's mausoleum was to be built.

The duke's apartments (audience chamber, bedchamber, garderobe, oratory, "studiolo" and loggia) are reached by the two spiral staircase towers.

The Terrazza di Gallo, on to which open the festive and banqueting rooms. An apartment, baths, and two chapels (antique and Christian) lie beneath the duke's apartment, behind the portico.

International Visual Resource

Palazzo Bevilacqua, Bologna

The Palazzo Bevilacqua was begun around 1480. The façade facing the street, with its diamond faceting is an elegant variation of Florentine rustication. The courtyard with its fluted columns on the ground floor and colonnettes (two per bay) on the first floor shows the same careful refinement.

Palazzo Strozzi, Florence

The palace of the Strozzi, the great rivals of the Medici family, was begun by Benedetto da Maiano in 1489 and completed after 1504 by Cronaca, who crowned the façade with a colossal cornice inspired by ancient ruins. The building derives directly from the Medici palace.

Palazzo dei Diamanti, Ferrara

In 1492 Biagio Rossetti drew up designs for a new quarter of Ferrara for Ercole I d'Este, envisaging numerous palaces at the crossing of the two principal axes. The Palazzo dei Diamanti, built for Sigismondo d'Este, was the only one to be realized.

Humanist architecture

After 1450, a group of architects, the second generation of the Renaissance (Antonio Manetti, 1405–60; Pagno di Lapo, 1408–70; Maso di Bartolomeo, 1406–56; Bernardo and Antonio Rossellino, 1409–63 and 1428–79), began to spread the new style throughout Italy, from Castiglione d'Olona to Pescia and from Genoa to Pienza. Florentine rationalism reached Milan through the work of Antonio Averlino, known as Filarete (c.1400–after 1465). At the behest of Ludovico Sforza, Filarete built the Ospedale Maggiore (c.1456–65), its rooms of cruciform plan inspired by the famous Ospedale degli Innocenti in Florence. The functional grid on which it was based was later much imitated.

When, after 1442, Leon Battista Alberti (1404–72) concentrated his multifarious activities on architecture, the Renaissance took a new direction. Descended from a great Florentine family of merchants, bankers and intellectuals, to whom he owed a meticulous classical education, Alberti was the incarnation of the humanist ideal of the "man of letters", being at the same time philosopher, artist and scholar. Like Brunelleschi, he had studied the remains of ancient Rome and the 1st century AD architectural treatise of Vitruvius. From this knowledge he derived the principles of the new architecture (definition of the Orders' proportions derived from the human body, and so on) which he expounded in his *De Re Aedificatoria* (c.1447–52). He also made observations on practical problems, on town planning, philosophy, aesthetics and history. For Alberti, architecture could not be reduced simply to a problem of technique and style. His objective was to create an environment for man which was not only aesthetic, but also adapted to his activities. He regarded the architecture of antiquity as a model to be adapted to new circumstances.

Around 1450, Sigismondo Malatesta, tyrant of Rimini, entrusted Alberti with the transformation of the church of San Francesco into a mausoleum to his glory. The reconstruction was interrupted in 1458 and never completed, but Alberti took a decisive step in adapting the motif of the ancient triumphal arch (for instance, the arch of Augustus in Rimini and that of Constantine in Rome) to the façade of a Christian church. In a letter to his assistant in which he summed up all the aspirations of the Renaissance towards perfection of proportion, he urged him to respect the dimensions and proportions of pilasters. "If you modify these in any way," he wrote, "the music will be reduced to utter discord." In the dedication which Alberti carved on the architrave of the mausoleum, he revived for the first time the lettering of Roman inscriptions; similar lettering can also be found on the façade of the Florentine church of Santa Maria Novella (1457–58), where he was obliged to work with the existing Gothic elements. Here he recalled by the use of coloured marble cladding the Baptistry of the city and the church of San Miniato al Monte.

In 1460 and 1471 Alberti finalized the plans of two churches in Mantua, San Sebastiano and Sant' Andrea, which represent his own interpretations of the centralized plan and the Latin cross plan. If linear elegance is the characteristic of Brunelleschi's buildings, those of Alberti are notable for their spatial qualities. The façade of San Sebastiano, whose overall proportions are square, is an adaptation of the classical temple front to a large expanse of flat wall. Four pilasters support a triangular pediment above an entablature, which is broken at the centre by an arched opening. It is difficult, however, to know exactly what Alberti's intentions were for this building, since work continued long after his death.

As the modern style spread throughout Italy, it merged with local traditions of building and decoration. There was thus great variety of plan and form. In Umbria the façade of the little church of San Bernardino in Perugia, built between 1457 and 1461 by the Florentine sculptor Agostino di Duccio, was decorated in a fantastical style combining Tuscan and classical motifs with a very delicate polychromy. In Venice, where architecture was strongly influenced by the particular local conditions and by the close contacts maintained by the republic with the old Byzantine world and the East, the new style at first made little headway, but became more prominent around 1470 in the work of such architects as Pietro Lombardo and Mauro Codussi. In the Po valley, the appearance of buildings was conditioned by surviving Romanesque and Gothic examples and by the use, since antiquity, of baked brick for building, decorated with marble or terracotta. The charterhouse of Pavia (c.1429–c.1473) by Giovanni and Guiniforte Solari, and the Colleoni chapel in Bergamo Cathedral (1470–73) by Giovanni Antonio Amadeo, are representative of this period in Lombard architecture.

With Donato Bramante (1444–1514), the brick architecture of Milan acquired a new simplicity and monumentality. A native of Urbino, he owed his extensive knowledge of the problems of perspective to an initial training as a painter. He had studied the writings of Vitruvius and was familiar with the works of Alberti. In Milan, where he worked for Ludovico Sforza from 1482 to 1499, he came under the influence of the local early Christian architecture. He was responsible for major enlargements at Santa Maria presso San Satiro and Santa Maria delle Grazie, where he came into contact with Leonardo da Vinci (whose *Last Supper* is in the refectory of the convent). Leonardo's extensive research in the field of architecture and town planning ran parallel to his own, and greatly influenced him. Bramante's choir at Santa Maria delle Grazie is an interpretation of Brunelleschi's Old Sacristy at San Lorenzo in Florence, but on a more imposing scale and with refined Lombard decoration. In Rome Bramante was inspired by the ancient remains to develop a more monumental architecture. The cloister of Santa Maria della Pace (1500–04), whose elevations derive from the Colosseum, marks in its austere grandeur the transition from the early to the High Renaissance.

Apart from Bramante, two other Tuscan architects contributed to the development of a new style in the second half of the 15th century. The Sienese Francesco di Giorgio Martini (1439–1501) revived a simple and powerful classical vocabulary in the construction of the cathedral at Urbino (beginning in 1482); and the Florentine Giuliano da Sangallo (1443–1516) chose for his own designs the most elegant classical details, creating for Lorenzo the Magnificent at Poggio a Caiano the prototype of the humanist villa, with a clear and rational plan (c.1480–85).

Tempio Malatestiano, Rimini

The temple is a memorial built in honour of Sigismondo Malatesta and his humanist court. Around 1450 the despot asked Alberti to reclad the Gothic church of San Francesco with a classical façade and to renovate the interior – a huge dome was proposed to span the crossing. The project was never completed, but the existing work clearly shows Alberti's ability to make fresh use of the forms and details borrowed from antiquity. He employed the triumphal arch motif for the monumental entrance façade, and formed niches and arcades in the side walls to house the sarcophagi of the men of letters at the Court.

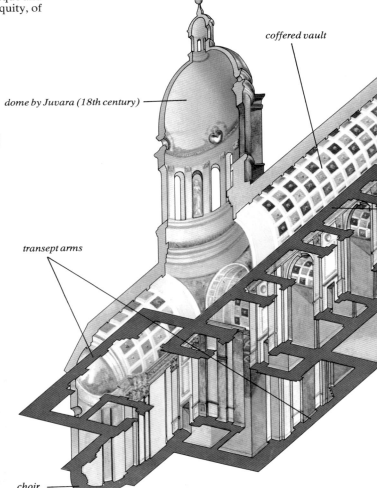

coffered vault

dome by Juvara (18th century)

transept arms

choir

Cloister of Santa Maria della Pace, Rome

Built between 1500 and 1504, this cloister was the first work of Bramante in Rome. On the ground floor, the arches supported on piers ornamented by Ionic pilasters were inspired by the Colosseum. The upper storey is lighter, and the bays are subdivided by single columns.

Colleoni chapel, Bergamo

Situated alongside the cathedral, the Colleoni chapel was built around 1470–75 by Giovanni Antonio Amadeo, who later became Bramante's collaborator in Milan. Its dome rests on an octagonal drum inspired by the one built by Brunelleschi for Florence Cathedral. The polychrome façade is overloaded with decoration borrowed from the classical Lombard repertoire and from the Gothic style (rose windows, pinnacles, gallery with colonnettes). This challenge to the rigour and purity of Tuscan architecture is a manifesto of local traditions.

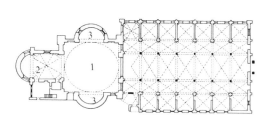

Santa Maria delle Grazie, Milan

During the 1490s Bramante added the centrally planned eastern section to the Gothic nave. The light, spacious crossing (1) is covered by a dome resting on pendentives pierced by oculi. Its geometrical scheme, based on a play of circles, is taken up again in the choir (2) and in the chapels with half-dome vaults (3). It is inspired by the Old Sacristy in Florence by Brunelleschi. The delicate painted and stuccoed decoration is typical of Lombardy. In his Roman work Bramante turned away from this style to a greater austerity and grandeur.

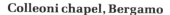

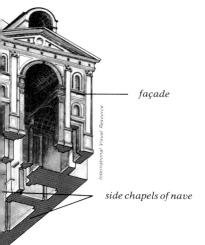

façade

side chapels of nave

Sant'Andrea, Mantua
(axonometric view)

Begun by Alberti in 1472, the year of his death, Sant'Andrea was completed in the 18th century by Filippo Juvara, who built the dome. The plan initiated the Latin cross type with a single nave flanked by chapels, which was later adopted in numerous churches. The majestic façade, combining a triumphal arch with a temple front, is the most distinctive feature of the exterior. The overall conception indicates a very free attitude towards ancient models.

Sant'Andrea, Mantua
(interior view)

Alberti's debt to the architecture of ancient Rome is clearly visible in the imposing coffered barrel vaulting which gives the interior of Sant'Andrea a quality of grandeur. The side chapels, also with coffered barrel vaults and lined with pilasters, repeat on the same scale the scheme and rhythms of the façade, thus adding to the impression of unity.

The new St. Peter's in the new Rome

The return of the papacy to Rome at the beginning of the 15th century, after its exile in Avignon, initiated a new campaign of building in the city. During the reign of Nicholas V (1447–55), Leon Battista Alberti, as adviser to the pontiff on questions of architecture and town planning, was made responsible for preparing plans for the reconstruction of certain parts of the Vatican, for the restoration of the Acqua Vergine aqueduct and for the construction of the Trevi fountain.

At the beginning of the 16th century the papal states came to have an exceptional importance throughout Europe, largely as a result of the personalities of popes Julius II (1503–13) and Leo X (1513–21). By his choice of papal name, Julius II declared himself not only the successor of Peter, but also the heir of the Caesars, and recalled thereby the supremacy of Rome, *caput mundi*. The presence of the greatest artists (Bramante, Raphael, Michelangelo, and their pupils), the beauty and extent of the ancient remains, augmented by new archaeological discoveries encouraged by the popes, made Rome from now for nearly two centuries the artistic capital of Europe.

Old St. Peter's, the largest and most famous church in Christendom, was at that time more than 1,100 years old and showing signs of its age. In the pontificate of Nicholas V, Bernardo Rossellino began the construction of a new choir beyond the old basilica, but this work was never finished. Julius II finally entrusted Donato Bramante (1444–1514) with the complete rebuilding of St. Peter's to a new design. Bramante had recently completed the cloister of Santa Maria della Pace, and he alone seemed capable of emulating the grandeur of imperial Roman architecture, that of the baths and the Pantheon. The basilica housed the tomb of St. Peter; it was thus a commemorative church or martyrium, like the Tempietto of San Pietro in Montorio which Bramante designed at the same time, and which was intended to recall the site on the Janiculum where the martyrdom of St. Peter was traditionally held to have taken place. A centralized plan, a symbol of divine perfection, was frequently adopted for this kind of building.

In practice, however, churches with centralized plans did not lend themselves well to grand cere-monies, and the central St. Peter's was increasingly compromised during the century. The medal by Caradosso (1506) and the partial plan drawn by Bramante (in the Uffizi, Florence), probably represent the earliest stage of the design, before the difficulties appeared which obliged the architect and his successors to propose, and in some cases implement, numerous changes. These changes related not only to the general conception of the plan – first a Greek cross, then a Latin one – but also to the plan of the transepts, which at one time were to have ambulatories; to the role of the Orders, first purely decorative (Bramante), then structural (Raphael, Michelangelo); and to the construction and shape of the dome, first with a single masonry shell (Bramante), then a double one (Sangallo, Michelangelo). The piers at the crossing, which were intended to support the dome, were one of the biggest problems; too slender in Bramante's plan, they were frequently reinforced. Because of these hesitations, and because of the Sack of Rome in 1527 with its disastrous financial consequences for the Holy See, construction, which had started in 1506, lasted until the end of the century. Raphael, who succeeded Bramante, returned at one point to a Latin cross plan. The huge timber model made after plans by Antonio Sangallo the Younger (who died in 1546) was a further compromise; it resolved a number of problems by combining the centralized with the basilical plan, but it did not have the heroic grandeur of Bramante's design. Michelangelo, who was in charge of construction from 1547 onwards, returned to the centralized plan; like Bramante, he was capable of conceiving a design on a monumental scale in keeping with the importance of the building. He speeded up construction work, which had made little progress by the time of his arrival, to such an extent that on his death in 1564 a great part of the building could be seen in its final state. The dome, nevertheless, had not risen above the drum; it was completed and slightly altered by Giacomo della Porta and Domenico Fontana. We know of Michelangelo's precise intentions from various drawings and from another great wooden model (though this has undoubtedly been altered). In 1607 Maderno extended the nave to increase internal space, and as a result altered the entire relation-ship between the façade and the dome. In the 17th century further important modifications were made by Bernini when he created the great colonnade that encircles the Piazza San Pietro.

In addition to the work at St. Peter's, in about 1505 Julius II entrusted Bramante with the construction of the courtyard of the Belvedere and the Loggias in the Vatican. The buildings of the *cortile*, which extended for more than 300 metres (nearly 1,000 feet), were intended to link the old papal palace with the villa built by Innocent VIII between 1485 and 1487 on the north slope of the Vatican hill. The ensemble formed a grand perspective, the architecture combining with the steep landscape. Although this type of composition was not unknown in the Quattrocento, Bramante was directly inspired by ancient models – the Circus of Maxentius on the Palatine, Hadrian's villa at Tivoli, and the Domus Aurea of Nero, known from its remains and from the descriptions of Tacitus and Suetonius. The Loggias, which today form the west side of the Cortile San Damaso, were intended to form the principal façade of the palace facing the city. Above the ground floor, treated as a basement, rose three storeys of galleries, the lower two arcades, the upper a colonnade. The Orders were arranged in the normal sequence: Doric, Ionic, Corinthian. This design introduced a new type of palace façade.

The grand Roman style of the years 1500–30 was intended to rival ancient imperial architecture. In building new palaces, churches and villas, Bramante, Raphael and their pupils therefore made use of the ancient forms most suited to the expression of "grandeur and magnificence". Plans were borrowed from the baths, the remains of the Palatine, and Tivoli (as in the Villa Madama, built by Raphael for Lorenzo de' Medici from 1516). Elevations and the details of the Orders were taken from the Colosseum, the theatre of Marcellus, the Septizodium, and the massive structures of the Forum. Heavily modelled profiles replaced the shallow mouldings of the early Renaissance. Frequent use was made of rustic detail and coffered vaults. The Domus Aurea provided Raphael and his pupils with models of the fantastic style of decoration known as "grotesque", which enjoyed immense popularity in the 16th century.

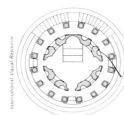

Tempietto of San Pietro in Montorio, Rome

The Tempietto in the cloister of San Pietro in Montorio was built by Bramante after 1502, on the commission of the Spanish monarchs, Ferdinand of Aragon and Isabella of Castile. The emphasis here is on the harmony of proportions, the simplicity of volumes (cylinder, hemisphere) and the sobriety of the Doric Order. The circular plan symbolizes divine perfection. Inspired by ancient temples, the Tempietto is both a homage to antiquity and a Christian memorial.

St. Peter's, Rome

Model by Sangallo

The wooden model of St. Peter's, made from the drawings of Antonio da Sangallo the Younger in the 1530s, no longer has the classical simplicity of Bramante's project. It appears to be a compromise between the centralized and the Latin cross plans. Its most original feature is the "bridge" that links the front section with the nave.

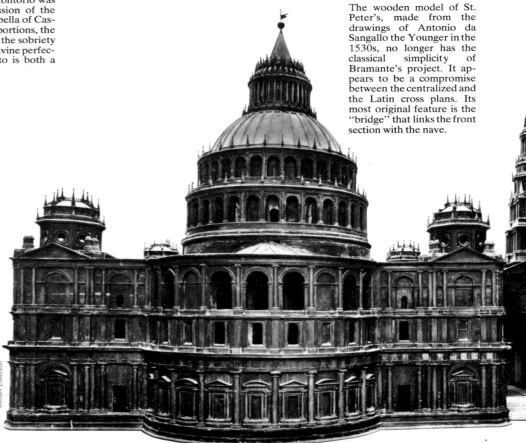

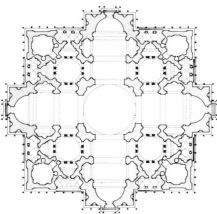

Bramante's plan

Bramante's plan for St. Peter's was centralized and probably in the form of a Greek cross (the original drawing preserved in the Vatican shows only half the building). Four smaller Greek crosses fill the space between the arms of the principal cross, creating an effect of harmonic repetition and a subtle gradation between the different elements of the building. This project was approved by Julius II in 1506 but never carried out.

Interior of St. Peter's

The internal space of St. Peter's is uniform, articulated by the regular rhythm of pilasters, arcades and niches. The jutting profiles of the entablature and the massive Order of pilasters emphasize their load-bearing function and accentuate the sense of the colossal in this enormous building. The crossing is abundantly lit by the windows of the drum and by the central lantern of the huge dome which is wider than the nave. The coffered barrel vaults and the polychrome marble decoration were inspired by ancient palaces, basilicas and baths.

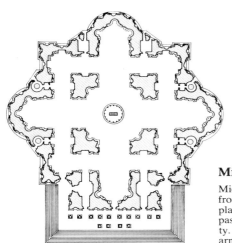

Medal by Caradosso

The medal by Caradosso (1506) shows the elevation of Bramante's first project for St. Peter's. As in the Pantheon, the volumes rise by degrees towards the central dome. Four smaller domes surmount the spaces between the arms of the Greek cross. Two belltowers flank the façade.

Dome

The dome of St. Peter's rises 123 metres (400 feet) above pavement level and, from the outside, dominates the whole building. Begun by Michelangelo, it was completed by Giacomo della Porta between 1585 and 1593. The elongated form differs from Bramante's original design inspired by the Pantheon. Michelangelo himself had envisaged a hemispherical shell, but it is possible that he later chose the solution finally adopted by della Porta. The dome is buttressed by the apses and supported internally by four massive piers more than 18 metres (60 feet) thick. The rhythm of its colonnade harmonizes with that of the pilasters on the external wall.

Michelangelo's plan

Michelangelo's plan for St. Peter's dates from 1546. He returned to a centralized plan, as envisaged by Bramante, but surpassed that project in clarity and simplicity. By opening up the aisles linking the arms he created a cross inscribed in a square and achieved a more homogeneous interior space. A double colonnade and a stepped platform lent the façade a new nobility.

Courtyard of the Belvedere

The buildings of the Belvedere court or *cortile*, shown here in an engraving by Etienne Dupérac, were begun by Bramante in 1505 at the command of Julius II. They linked the old papal palace with the villa of Innocent VIII and created a grand perspective, destroyed at the end of the 16th century by the construction of the library of Sixtus V. The sloping site made it necessary to build terraced gardens; these are dominated by the great exedra of the upper wing, which resembles the backdrop of a vast ancient theatre.

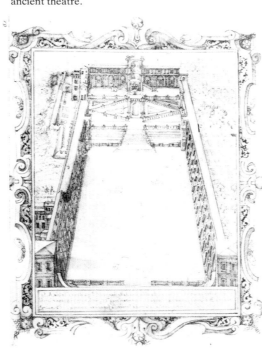

The classical heritage and Mannerism in Italy

After 1520 the grand Roman manner, developed by Bramante and Raphael and their circle, spread throughout Italy, hastened in 1527 by the Sack of Rome which dispersed the pupils and associates of these two artists. These pupils shared in the general admiration for the creations of their masters, which were considered as worthy of imitation as the ancient ruins whose grandeur they had succeeded in reviving. But while some, such as Antonio da Sangallo, consolidated the achievements of the Roman Renaissance, others, such as Giulio Romano, Sanmicheli, Sansovino and Peruzzi, took to an extreme form certain tendencies which had germinated in the second decade of the century. The term "Mannerism" is used to describe this reaction, where the architect drew his inspiration not directly (*di natura*) from the ancient buildings but from the "manner" (*maniera*) of his masters. The sensibility of these new perceptions varied greatly, from the heavyweight style derived from Bramante's Palazzo Caprini, to the sophisticated decorative style derived from the Palazzo Branconio dell'Aquila of Raphael (destroyed).

Giulio Romano (1492–1546), Raphael's principal collaborator, left Rome for Mantua in 1524, and remained there for the rest of his life in the service of the Gonzaga, for whom he built the Palazzo del Te (his best-known work). Working primarily in the severe Doric mode, he exploited the possibilities of rustication. Following certain ancient examples, particularly the Porta Maggiore in Rome, he revived the rusticated Order, in which the columns and entablature appear partially masked by blocks left in an uncut state.

Sanmicheli and Sansovino, who left Rome for northern Italy in 1527, also knew how to handle this powerful style when it was appropriate (city gates, arsenals, treasuries), but they also explored the path opened up by Raphael at the Palazzo Branconio (a complex rhythm of bays and decorative arabesques in counterpoint). Sanmicheli (1484–1559), based in Rome from 1500, returned to his native city of Verona and built there the new gates of the city and a number of palaces, elegant variations on the theme of Bramante's Palazzo Caprini and Raphael's Palazzo Branconio (Palazzo Pompei, 1530; Canossa, 1537; Bevilacqua, c.1540). The Florentine Jacopo Sansovino (1486–1570), who had arrived in Rome with Giuliano da Sangallo in 1505, went to Venice where he established himself virtually as city architect. In the Palazzo Corner della Ca' Grande (1537), he gave the traditional Venetian palace a classical organization, but his true masterpiece is the Library in the Piazzetta di San Marco.

After the Sack of Rome in 1527, Serlio (1475–1554) also went to Venice, after pausing on the way in his native city of Bologna. With the aid of a portfolio of drawings which he had inherited from his friend Peruzzi, Bramante's principal assistant, he began to prepare the publication of his treatise on architecture (1537–76); this was to play a considerable part in the diffusion of the new style, especially in France, where Serlio settled in 1540, and in northern Europe. Peruzzi (1481–1536), who had returned to Siena in 1527, did not re-establish himself in Rome until 1535; there his last work, the Palazzo Massimo alle Colonne, testified once more to his independence of the classical tradition.

In Rome, meanwhile, continuity was ensured above all by the Florentine Antonio da Sangallo the Younger (1484–1546), nephew of Giuliano. Competent, though without great imagination, he drew on his wide experience to create models whose clear plans found popularity. The Palazzo Farnese, begun in 1513 (it was completed by Michelangelo), combined the clarity of a Florentine plan with the new monumentality of the Roman Orders. The church of Santo Spirito in Sassia offered a modern version of the façade of Santa Maria Novella in Florence, with two superimposed Orders.

Michelangelo (1475–1564) advanced in a different direction, seeking to give architectural elements a new tension and plasticity that owed much to his experience as a sculptor. In the New Sacristy of San Lorenzo in Florence (1520–27) – the pair of Brunelleschi's Old Sacristy, whose plan it adopted – the framework of *pietra serena* is lent a Roman grandeur, but the mouldings retain the sharpness of Brunelleschi's. Michelangelo's most innovative building was the Biblioteca Laurenziana, begun in 1524, where the columns, recessed into the walls of the vestibule, are treated like sculptures, and the mouldings are freely redesigned – the sign of a new freedom of attitude to classical antiquity.

In the second half of the century an effort at clarification became apparent, which resulted in the publication of several treatises – including the classics of Vignola (1562) and Palladio (1570). Following the path opened by Serlio, they offered rules that were easy to follow and pre-selected the best fragments of antiquity. At the same time the divergence in objectives was becoming more marked: in Florence, Vasari (1511–74), immortalized by his *Lives of the Most Excellent Painters, Sculptors and Architects*, and above all Buontalenti (1536–1608), both conscious of the lessons of Michelangelo, revealed considerable inventiveness in abstract architectural ornament. In Rome, Pirro Ligorio (c.1510–88) obtained his effects at the *casino* of Pius IV in the Vatican by the interplay of sculpture. Active in Genoa and Milan, Alessi (1512–72) gave architectural elements a sculptural appearance, and multiplied them at will in the Palazzo Marino in Milan, and in a number of palaces that he built in Genoa. It took the genius of Palladio (1508–80) to assimilate these different styles and modes. From the robustness of the Palazzo Thiene to the simple elegance of his villas, in a sense his work summarized the experience of a century.

Palazzo Caprini, Rome

In this palace, built around 1510, Bramante established a striking contrast between the ground floor, occupied by shops and faced with heavily rusticated stonework, and the first floor, occupied by the apartments and articulated by paired Doric columns. An elaboration of the Roman *insula*, this type of palace with a rusticated ground floor was exceptionally popular; Raphael, Sansovino and Sanmicheli in particular introduced a number of variants.

Palazzo del Te, Mantua

Between 1526 and 1534 Giulio Romano built this palace by the gates of Mantua, a grandiose re-creation of the Roman suburban villa, and an expression of the political ambitions of Federico Gonzaga, who became duke in 1530. On the external wall and in the courtyard Giulio Romano deployed all the resources of the rusticated style, while opening a grandiose loggia towards the garden.

Palazzo Pitti, Florence

Cosimo I de' Medici bought the Pitti palace in 1549; Ammanati enlarged it for him between 1558 and 1570. The courtyard is a rusticated variation on the theme of the courtyard of the Palazzo Farnese, using the local Tuscan Order. The heavily rusticated Quattrocento façade explains the adoption of the rustic mode here.

New Sacristy, San Lorenzo, Florence

In the New Sacristy of San Lorenzo (1520–27; 1530–34), which is, like the Old Sacristy, a mortuary chapel in honour of the Medici family, Michelangelo repeated the basic structure of Brunelleschi's Sacristy, but modernized it (aediculed windows and a coffered dome instead of arched windows and ribbed dome), amplified it by introducing a second Order, and above all created a powerful architectural tension between the framing of *pietra serena* and the white marble cladding.

Vestibule, Biblioteca Laurenziana, Florence

The first projects by Michelangelo for the Laurentian Library date from 1524, but it was not until 1558–59 that the wax model for the staircase in the vestibule was handed to Ammanati, who supervised the construction. Taking advantage of the technical constraints (the limited thickness of the walls, hence the columns in niches; the need to go high to obtain daylight, hence the unusual relationship between height and width), Michelangelo gave the vestibule an exceptional dramatic tension, which contrasts with the calmer rhythm of the actual libary. The freedom with which he applied the architectural elements inspired the later anticlassical movement.

Palazzo Marino, Milan

Alessi built this palace for the Milanese banker Tommaso Marino from 1558. The contrast between the severe and light-filled ground floor with its smooth columns and the more delicate and ornate upper floor recalls the classical superimposition of Ionic on Doric, here transformed by biomorphic architectural language – lion consoles on the ground floor, caryatids above. The multiplication of small elements and the profusion of ornament are typical of Lombard taste, but also of the second generation of Mannerists.

Library, Piazzetta di San Marco, Venice

The library, which stands on the Piazzetta opposite the Doges' Palace, was begun by Sansovino in 1537 to receive the books bequeathed to the Venetian Republic by Cardinal Bessarion. It was not until 1588 that it was completed, by Scamozzi. A severe Doric portico supports the grand Ionic Order. It is notable for the plasticity of its treatment of the windows, the ornamental richness of the frieze and the elaboration of the balustrade that crowns it.

Palazzo dei Conservatori, Campidoglio, Rome

In 1538 Michelangelo presented a proposal for the reorganization of the Capitol along monumental lines: the trapezoidal square, dominated by the Palazzo Senatorio, was to be flanked by two palaces at an angle to one another. For the Palazzo dei Conservatori (1568–80) he established a regular rhythm of giant pilasters and inserted beneath them a small Order of columns whose entablature corresponds to the floor of the upper storey.

The villas

The precocious development of the city in Italy encouraged the early growth of a nostalgia for the pleasures of the countryside. Since the 14th century, as numerous stories of Boccacio testify, many rich Florentines had acquired the habit of taking refuge in the countryside during the heat of summer or during epidemics. In his *Chronicles* Giovanni Villani says that in a six mile radius around the city there were "so many rich and noble houses that they could not be contained within two Florences".

Ancient treatises on agriculture (Columella, Varro), bucolic poetry (Virgil, Horace), and the long descriptions by Pliny the Younger of his villas at Tusculum and Laurentinum soon gave this idea a humanist aspect. There were two kinds of villa – suburban, intended only for intermittent occupation, and rural, which were centres of agriculture – a distinction drawn by all Renaissance theoreticians from Alberti onwards, following the ancient writers. But the earliest villas of the 15th century were still no more than small *casinos* of irregular plan, giving by way of a loggia on to a garden (villa of Cardinal Bessarion in Rome, *c*.1450) or on to a particularly attractive view (villa of Giovanni de' Medici at Fiesole, *c*.1455).

The villas at Poggio a Caiano near Florence, for Lorenzo the Magnificent (1485, but not completed until 1519), and at Poggio Reale near Naples for Alfonso II (1487–88) were the first monumental villas boasting regular plans. The former, built adjacent to a model farm on a large agricultural estate, stands on its ground floor rather as on a podium; it is planned around a grand living room and was suit-able for long periods of occupation. The villa at Poggio Reale, which no longer exists, was built on a hill above the bay of Naples; four little pavilions were arranged around a galleried and stepped courtyard, which served as an open-air banqueting hall. Gardens, fountains and a swimming pool completed the attractions of this suburban villa, which was intended for occasional pleasure outings. These two types of buildings were constructed throughout the 16th century but, unlike city palaces, villas did not adhere to set models, and a great variety of approaches was tried.

The rediscovery of Nero's Domus Aurea in Rome and of Hadrian's villa at Tivoli, which were assiduously studied, particularly after 1490, enabled a more concrete form to be given to literary visions. In Rome, the climate of archaeological fervour, which was particularly noticeable in the pontificates of Julius II and Leo X, encouraged various attempts to revive the ancient type of suburban villa: the courtyard of the Belvedere in the Vatican by Bramante (1505), with its sequence of terraces and its exedra, was inspired by the imperial villa of Albano and the gardens of Lucullus on the Pincio. The Villa Lante on the Janiculum by Giulio Romano (1517) is a small *casino* whose loggia commands an impressive view of the "seven hills of Rome". The Villa Madama by Raphael (1518) on Monte Mario is a careful reconstruction of Pliny's villa at Laurentinum. But at the Palazzo del Te in Mantua Giulio Romano was able to create a quite different effect, illustrating the great freedom of imagination in architects who were apparently fol-lowing the same texts and archaeological examples.

During the course of the 16th century, the design of the gardens of the suburban villas that grew up in and around Rome and other major cities became more and more sophisticated – water games, fountains, cascades, nymphaeums and grottoes grew increasingly popular. The Villa Giulia (1550–55), recalling the Villa Madama, was organized around a spectacular nymphaeum, and at the Villa Lante, Bagnaia (1566), two *casinos* were situated above an artificial landscape, as at Hadrian's villa at Tivoli. The undistinguished Villa d' Este at Tivoli, like the castle at Caprarola, owes its character to the spectacular development of its gardens, its profusion of fountains and cascades, and its great loggias, which allow a fine view of the landscape.

Rural villas, which had attracted the interest of the architects of the early Renaissance, did not achieve any striking architectural expression until the second half of the 16th century when, in the Veneto, Palladio developed an idea possibly first explored by Sanmicheli at the Villa La Soranza (now destroyed). In the new model he put forward, which was to have a considerable following, Palladio arranged the farm buildings majestically and symmetrically around the principal villa, linking them by walls and porticoes. He attempted to give the *casa padronale* a great many different forms, though (as at Poggio a Caiano) the principal living rooms are generally raised above a ground floor devoted to services, and entered through a grand loggia – often resembling the peristyle of a temple – which dominates the surrounding agricultural land.

Villa Medici, Poggio a Caiano

The villa of Poggio a Caiano, between Florence and Pistoia, was built from 1485 for Lorenzo de' Medici, to plans by Giuliano da Sangallo, at the centre of a huge agricultural estate. Completed between 1515 and 1519, it is raised in the ancient manner on a square podium pierced by arcades, and opens on to the countryside by way of a loggia. The principal room, with a vast coffered barrel vault, links the front and rear apartments.

1	*original staircase*	5	*principal room*
2	*terrace*	6	*dining room*
3	*loggia*	7	*apartments*
4	*vestibule*	8	*salon*

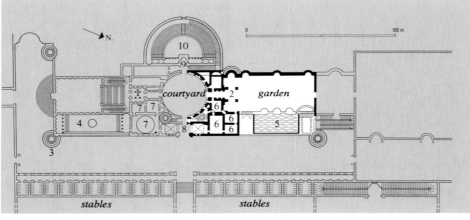

1	*vestibule-atrium*	6	*apartments*
2	*loggia used as summer dining room*	7	*apartments adjoining the grand salon*
3	*fish pond*	8	*loggia opening on to the countryside*
4	*secret garden*	9	*nymphaeum*
5	*glazed winter garden room*	10	*theatre based on a classical model*

Villa Madama, Rome

The Villa Madama on Monte Mario was begun in 1518 to designs by Raphael for Cardinal Giulio de' Medici, the future Pope Clement VII. The detailed description which Raphael gave in a long letter and the plans drawn up in the Sangallo studio allow us to understand this ambitious project to re-create a Roman villa (Pliny the Younger's villa at Laurentinum, in particular). Only about a third was actually built (shown in white on the plan); the stucco and fresco decoration in the main loggia, executed by Raphael's pupils, was directly inspired by study of the vaults of the Domus Aurea of Nero.

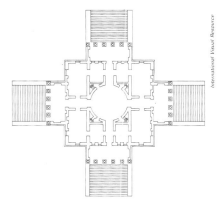

Villa Rotonda

This villa, begun between 1567 and 1569, is situated on a hill near Vicenza. Unlike other villas by Palladio, it was a suburban villa and not a farm. There are porticoes on every side. Centred on a circular *salon* lit from above and covered by a dome, the symmetrical plan of this villa is completely original: the four temple fronts preceded by their great flights of stairs, and the single dome, removed from their original functions, have become pure symbols of ancient majesty.

Villa Barbaro, Maser

The Villa Barbaro was built between 1560 and 1568 for Daniele Barbaro, humanist aristocrat and editor of Vitruvius, and his brother Marcantonio, who like many Venetian aristocrats re-invested their fortune in large agricultural estates. The villa functions as a farm set in the middle of fields of rice and maize, but the residence proper, decorated with frescoes by Veronese, dominates the symmetrical working wings.

Villa Medici, Rome

The Villa Medici, built in the second half of the 16th century, turns a severe face towards the city, but the garden façade is encrusted with ancient fragments and is opened up with a great loggia designed by Ammanati. An engraving by Falda (below right) records the original design of the gardens.

Villa Giulia, Rome

The Villa Giulia, built between 1550 and 1555 for Pope Julius III by Vasari, Vignola and Ammanati, recalls the Villa Madama. Behind the little *casino* with its severe façade extends a semicircular portico. Two loggias face one another on either side of the nymphaeum, which is hollowed out of the centre of the garden.

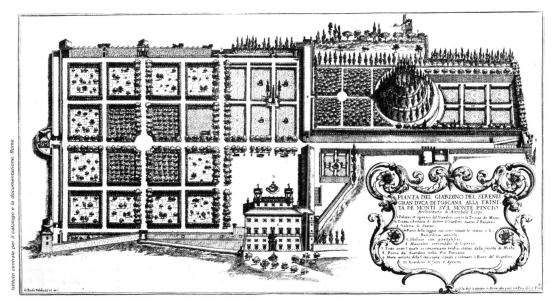

Churches of the Counter-Reformation

In the second half of the 16th century, the Counter-Reformation stimulated a rapid development in religious architecture. The Council of Trent (1545–63) defined the doctrine and codified the pastoral life of the Church, but it did not rule on matters of religious architecture and decoration. Nevertheless, prelates and theologians began to take a more active part alongside patrons and architects in the development of plans.

Architectural evolution was determined by new demands. Although the centralized plan was the most representative of the Renaissance ideal of harmony, it was in conflict with the needs of the liturgy and for this reason was soon restricted to commemorative churches such as Bramante's Tempietto in Rome, which were not expected to accommodate a large congregation at major ceremonies. Nevertheless, the superiority of the centralized plan was not disputed by architects, and in 1573 Palladio still saw in the circle the ideal form for a Christian church, in as much as it was the image of the "unity, infinite essence, uniformity and justice of God". Vignola worked on some variations of this theme in his little domed or oval churches, which heralded the work on a grander scale of Borromini and Bernini. Meanwhile in 1577 Carlo Borromeo, archbishop of Milan, took up the cause, in his *Instructiones*, of the longitudinal plan, as being better adapted to the liturgy. Palladio in turn justified the Latin cross plan because of its analogy with the cross of Christ. By way of compromise a new type of church became established, derived from a prototype built by Alberti a century earlier, Sant' Andrea in Mantua. A large nave, flanked by chapels or aisles, was attached to a wide transept and the crossing was crowned by an ample dome, evidence of the technical mastery which the architects of the age had attained.

The treatment of the façade was also reviewed. The difference in height between the nave and the chapels or side aisles made the adaptation of an ancient temple façade to a Christian church particularly difficult. Furthermore, unlike the façade of a church, the portico of a temple was a three-dimensional feature, which stood away from the building proper. The solution adopted by Alberti at Santa Maria Novella in Florence – the linking of the central bay to the lower side bays by volutes – was taken over by Leonardo da Vinci (project, c.1515), by Antonio da Sangallo at Santo Spirito in Sassia near Rome (1537–45) and by Vignola in his project for the façade of the Gesù (c.1568). This last was executed a little later by Giacomo della Porta following the same principles. With its composite Order on both storeys, its use of double pilasters (as in the interior), its engaged columns and its pediments and powerful volutes, the Gesù façade has considerable majesty. Rich decoration underlines the vertical thrust of the central bay. The solution adopted by Palladio in his Venetian churches overcame the same problem by superimposing two façades of the ancient type, but of differing width, with the central element slightly projecting. Alessi at Santa Maria di Carignano in Genoa (1549) and Palladio at the Maser chapel (1579–80) reintroduced into their compositions the twin belltowers envisaged by Bramante in his project for St. Peter's in Rome.

Vignola (1507–73) was one of the most innovative architects of the Counter-Reformation period. He codified the use of the Orders, choosing proportions that seemed to him "the most beautiful and the most satisfying to the eye". His research into the oval plan type, which was to have considerable impact, is evidence of his powers of free invention, since this form was dictated neither by the site nor by the function of the building (dome of Sant' Andrea in Via Flaminia in Rome, c.1550–53; the oval plan inscribed in a rectangle at Sant'Anna dei Palafrenieri, 1565). In 1568 Vignola was entrusted with the construction of the Gesù, the mother church of the new order of the Jesuits, the principal agents of the papacy in imposing the Counter-Reformation. The plan of the Gesù, dictated by the preaching mission of the order, was adopted and modified by Giacomo della Porta (c.1533–1603) at Santa Maria dei Monti and at Sant'Andrea della Valle (1590–c.1600) in Rome. Della Porta brought in a resolutely modern architecture which no longer took its classical forms from ancient remains, but from Michelangelo. At Sant'Andrea della Valle he created a dynamic and clearly articulated space by using pilasters, projections in the entablature and the arches of the vault in such a way as to give a vertical accent.

Galeazzo Alessi (1512–72), a native of Perugia who worked in Genoa and Milan, built the church of Santa Maria di Carignano in Genoa (started in 1549) to a design adapted from Michelangelo's project for St. Peter's. The façade of Santa Maria presso San Celso in Milan, begun by Alessi before 1570, recalls the designs of Antonio da Sangallo and Michelangelo for San Lorenzo in Florence, but it also shows the Lombard decorative tradition to be still very much alive. Alessi declared his adherence to the longitudinal plan in the church of Santi Paolo e Barnaba, built for the Barnabites between 1561 and 1567 in Milan. The architecture of the Counter-Reformation in Milan was also developed by Pellegrino Pellegrini, who built San Fedele (begun in 1569) on a longitudinal plan and San Sebastiano (begun in 1577) on an oval plan.

Andrea Palladio (1508–80) was without doubt the greatest and most influential architect of his time. His art was based on a profound knowledge of ancient architecture, derived from the study of Vitruvius and ancient remains in Rome, southern Italy and southern France. It could be said that Palladio wished to revive, in the full sense of the word, the architecture that he considered to be the most beautiful and the most perfect. Although pagan in origin, the classical forms seemed to him to be the most suitable for expressing the grandeur of God in a Christian church. In Venice he built the façade of San Francesco della Vigna (c.1565) and two churches – San Giorgio Maggiore, designed in 1565 for the Benedictines, and the Redentore, built as a thanksgiving for the city's release from the plague of 1575–76.

Sant'Andrea in Via Flaminia, Rome

Sant' Andrea was one of the most innovatory churches of the 16th century. It was built in 1554 for Pope Julius III by Vignola. Inspired by the Pantheon, small in size and logical in conception, it has an elliptical dome (1) carried on a Corinthian cornice (2) and pendentives (3); the overall plan is square (4). The oval of the dome anticipates small Baroque churches. The elegant entrance façade imitates that of a temple, with a pediment and Corinthian pilasters.

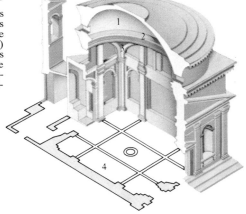

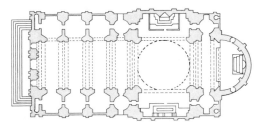

Gesù, Rome

The plan of the Gesù, designed by Vignola in 1568, recalls that of Sant'Andrea in Mantua by Alberti. Adapted to the preaching vocation of the Society of Jesus, it comprises a vast nave, 18 metres (60 feet) wide, flanked by side chapels, and a transept of the same width as the nave and aisles. The grandiose character of the church is particularly striking at the crossing, which is surmounted by a large dome from which abundant light streams down. The nave is lit by windows set in the lower part of the barrel vault. Unlike those of Sant'Andrea in Mantua, the low side chapels have no part in the grand spatial effect produced by the nave and crossing. The original austerity of the interior was transformed in the 17th century by sumptuous painted decoration. The walls were originally distempered in white, from which the arcades, entablature and double pilasters were picked out in grey travertine (substituted by marble in the 19th century), generating a unifying rhythm. Unfinished at the death of Vignola, the façade was finally built by Giacomo della Porta between 1573 and 1584, to a design derived from Vignola and recalling that of Alberti for Santa Maria Novella in Florence.

San Giorgio Maggiore, Venice

San Giorgio Maggiore was begun in 1566 by Palladio for the Benedictines. The church achieves a compromise between the centralized and the basilical plans. Aisles run parallel to the nave, and continue beyond the transept. The liturgical choir opening into the monks' choir through a columnar screen, the deep transepts with half-dome vaults, and the high dome over the crossing, all contribute to a feeling of great spaciousness. Palladio made use of two Orders of different heights: a monumental Order for the nave and transepts, a smaller one for the aisles. He also varied the type of column – free-standing or engaged – and pilaster, in order to establish a hierarchy between the elements of the building. As at the Redentore, the structural elements in grey stone stand out from the whitewashed walls.

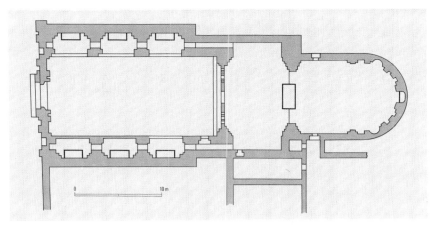

Santi Paolo e Barnaba, Milan

The church of Santi Paolo e Barnaba was built by Galeazzo Alessi between 1561 and 1567 for the Barnabites. Its longitudinal plan comprises a nave flanked by chapels (as in the Gesù), a slightly recessed transept, and a deep choir for the use of the religious community. The nave is barrel vaulted. The crossing piers project prominently, forming a double triumphal arch which emphasizes the position of the high altar.

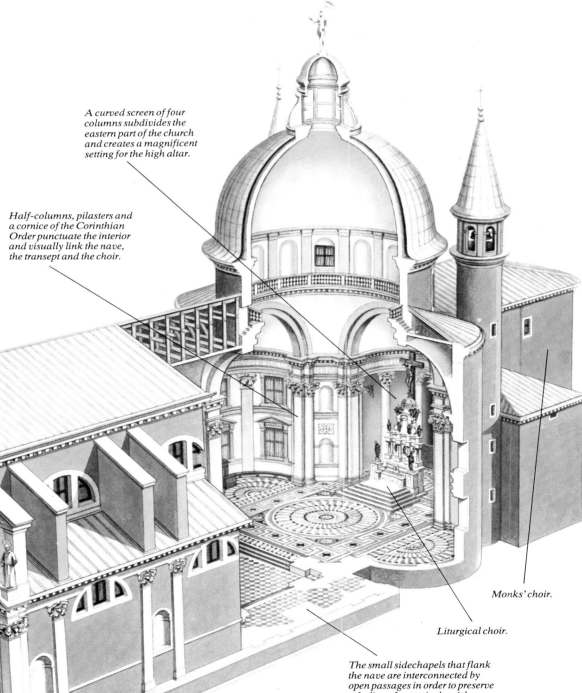

A curved screen of four columns subdivides the eastern part of the church and creates a magnificent setting for the high altar.

Half-columns, pilasters and a cornice of the Corinthian Order punctuate the interior and visually link the nave, the transept and the choir.

The pitch of the roof echoes that of the pediments on the main façade.

Monks' choir.

Liturgical choir.

The small sidechapels that flank the nave are interconnected by open passages in order to preserve a feeling of space in the aisles.

Balustraded steps lead up to the front entrance of the church, which is raised upon a podium.

Il Redentore, Venice

The church of the Redeemer is a glorious expression of gratitude by a city saved from the plague in 1575–76. The work, begun in 1577, was completed after the death of Palladio by Antonio da Ponte. The plan is cruciform, but the centre is accentuated by the three apses – choir and transept arms – which open off the central space of the crossing. The progression from the entrance through different spaces recalls the organization of ancient baths (with their frigidarium, tepidarium and caldarium). The plan was well adapted to the great ceremonies of thanksgiving, presided over by the doge, which were held there every year. Giant engaged columns and pilasters support a cornice that runs all round the interior of the church. In the choir, four freestanding columns form a semicircular screen around the altar, through which the monks' choir can be seen. Whitewashed walls accentuate throughout the feeling of space and light. The façade is an ingenious interpenetration of three pediments, stressing the division between the nave and aisles as well as unifying them.

The early Renaissance in France

The Italian wars waged by Charles VIII, Louis XII and François I between 1494 and 1525 gave the French the opportunity to discover the art of the world beyond the Alps. However, artistic contact between France and Italy had been made before this time. In 1445 the painter Jean Fouquet travelled to Rome, where he painted a portrait of Pope Eugenius IV, studied geometrical perspective and acquired a repertoire of classical decoration. Between 1475 and 1485 King René of Anjou, a patron of artists and men of letters (and a painter in his own right), employed Francesco Laurana, architect of the ducal palace at Urbino, to build the chapel of St. Lazare à la Major in Marseilles. During the 15th century in Rome the pope had a French entourage who were in touch with the new direction in the arts, and who became more numerous at the time of the invasion under Charles VIII. This group gave work to the great Roman artists, but it is difficult to know whether their patronage had any real repercussions in France. An awareness of antiquity was brought about to some extent by the study and publication of Greek and Latin texts by the French humanists Robert Gaguin and later Lefèvre d'Etaples and Guillaume Budé.

In Italy the French, who under Louis XII and François I had made themselves masters of Genoa and Milan, were more impressed by the ornamental richness of Lombard and Venetian architecture than by Florentine purity or Roman monumentality. Lombard architecture offered, notably in the Charterhouse of Pavia, a synthesis of local tradition and classical forms that to some degree anticipated the style of the early French Renaissance, a style which owed its originality to its hybrid character. One can see in it, alongside the undeniable persistence of medieval planning and building practice, to which even Italian architects in France adapted, not only the use of the new decorative repertoire – quickly assimilated by the French – but also the application of the new rules of regularity – in the design of plans, the balance of masses and the rhythm of bays. However, although one can detect Italian ideas from time to time, archival sources show that most buildings built in France at this time were the work of French master masons, who were technicians and not architects in the Italian sense of the word.

The artists brought to France from Italy by Charles VIII and Louis XII worked at the châteaux of Amboise and Blois, but none of their work survives. It is also difficult to define the influence of the Italian architects Fra Giocondo and Giuliano da Sangallo who were in France at this time. The Loire valley was the centre of the greatest activity, due to the presence there of the Court. The Court style was spread to other regions by prelates, by the great families of the nobility and by the bourgeoisie who made up the royal entourage. In Normandy between 1500 and 1510, the cardinal of Amboise (also archbishop of Rouen, prime minister of Louis XII and viceroy of Milan), rebuilt the château de Gaillon, employing both French master masons and Italian sculptors, such as Girolamo Pacchiarotti (Jérôme Pacherot) and Antonio di Giusto Betti (Antoine Juste), and also the painter Andrea Solario. Certain decorative features, such as the fountain of the central courtyard, came from Genoese workshops, others from Milan. Gaillon, which has been partially demolished, was in plan and structure a medieval building, built in several stages. The sculptural decoration, of exceptional richness, mixed Gothic and Italian forms, but the façades already showed a certain regularity.

Three châteaux in the Loire valley – Bury, Chenonceaux and Azay-le-Rideau – built between 1510 and 1530 by rich bourgeois families, were novel in the regularity of their plans. Bury (1511–24, now destroyed) was the most revolutionary of the three, and created a new type that was to last until the 17th century. Its buildings formed a square with four round medieval towers at the corners. The principal living quarters (*corps de logis*) were crowned by a high central pavilion. One wing comprised a long gallery; the main entrance was in the centre of the fourth wing. The windows and dormers, flanked by pilasters, formed vertical bays symmetrically arranged on the façades, broken by horizontal bands at each storey level. The façades were thus clearly articulated but relatively flat. It was an arrangement that already existed at Gaillon and was to reappear, with variations, in other buildings of the period.

In the François I wing of the château of Blois (c.1515–24) and in the château of Chambord (begun in 1519), the special requirements of a royal residence and palace were met. At Blois, the façade facing the courtyard of the François I wing is famous for its projecting octagonal staircase: with ornamentation in the Italian manner, this transformed the old Gothic type of spiral staircase, such as the *Grand' Vis* (The Great Spiral) of Charles V's Louvre (destroyed), with a new sense of space. The façade facing the city, a more modern design, was inspired by Bramante's Loggias in the Vatican. Nevertheless, the use of the Orders is irregular, and Bramante's elegant bays with their round-headed arches are here replaced by flattened arches. These are not so much loggias but, rather, deep frames around glazed windows. This design is characteristic of French architecture of the period, which tended to adapt Italian models rather awkwardly.

The original plan of Chambord (around 1519) was certainly the work of Domenico da Cortona, based on ideas by Leonardo da Vinci and subsequently modified by French masons. Construction continued into the 1550s. The fat, round towers with pointed roofs gave the château a medieval silhouette. The principal innovation lay in the plan of the "keep", which was divided by two corridors into a Greek cross, at the centre of which was the staircase. At the corners were four identical apartments, which recall the villa at Poggio a Caiano (c.1480–85), built for Lorenzo the Magnificent by Giuliano da Sangallo, Domenico da Cortona's master. The double spiral staircase, a magnificent technical triumph, is attributed to Leonardo da Vinci, who worked for François I between 1516 and 1519.

In the first half of the 16th century the evolution of French religious architecture was closely analogous with that of secular architecture. The east end of the church of St. Pierre at Caen (1528–45) by Hector Sohier, and St. Eustache in Paris (begun 1532), both retain their Gothic structures, but Italianate decoration (Lombard ornament in one, pilasters and attached columns in the other) was substituted for or combined with the old Flamboyant style.

Entrance pavilion of the château of Gaillon

Although it was built in 1509, the structure of this pavilion resembles that of the medieval fortified gatetowers. Nevertheless, the windows are symmetrically arranged, the surfaces are regularly divided by pilasters and horizontal bands in low relief and the decorative carving is inspired by the Lombard Renaissance (with the exception of the Gothic balustrade that once surmounted the entablature). In the central bay on the first floor there are statues of Louis XII as a Roman emperor, and the cardinal of Amboise. As this photograph shows, the château has recently undergone complete restoration.

Chenonceaux

This château owes its fame to its exceptional siting on the river Cher. The right hand section was built from 1515. Italian influence can be seen in the decoration, the symmetry of the façades and the straight flights of the internal staircase. The bridge was built to plans by Philibert De l'Orme between 1555 and 1559 and the gallery from 1559 onwards by Jean Bullant, architect to Catherine de Médicis.

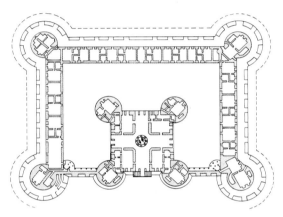

Chambord

This château was built for François I from 1519 onwards. Many different influences are evident at Chambord, typical of the hybrid character of French architecture at the beginning of the 16th century. With its round towers and high roofs, Chambord has a medieval aspect. But the plan is modern: the great quadrangle appears to develop from the inner "keep". In the keep itself, four identical apartments are divided by the arms of a vestibule in the shape of a Greek cross. The double-spiral central staircase is a *tour de force*. Its lantern crowns the roof of the keep, which is a forest of dormers and chimneys, richly decorated with classical ornament and panels of polychrome marble and slate.

Blois

The external octagonal staircase of the François I wing was built between 1515 and 1524 to replace a medieval tower. Its structure is entirely Gothic, comprising a spiral stairway covered by a ribbed vault with round bosses, on the model of the *Grand' Vis* of Charles V's Louvre. Its novelty lies in the Italianate decoration, the combined power of its different elements, and the spatial eloquence of the whole.

Azay-le-Rideau

The château of Azay was built between 1519 and 1527 on the banks of the Indre. The plan is L-shaped, but it is probable that a complete quadrangle was originally envisaged. The dormers and high roofs lend it a thoroughly Gothic soaring quality but, as at Gaillon, the façades are symmetrical and clearly articulated. The open staircase with straight flights – one of the first to be built in France – is expressed on the principal façade by an *avant-corps* that prefigures the porticoes of Anet and Ecouen.

285

The classical Renaissance in France

At the end of the 1520s the Île-de-France, where the king took up residence, became the principal centre of cultural life. Three royal châteaux built from 1528 onwards but since destroyed – Madrid in the Bois de Boulogne, La Muette at St. Germain and Challuau – plus the great château of St. Germain itself, which was transformed by Louis XIV and subsequently inexpertly restored to its original state in the 19th century, marked a clear step on the road to Italianization by the novelty of their plans, elevations and decoration. But these examples were little copied.

In 1528 François I decided to renovate the old hunting lodge at Fontainebleau. The master mason Gilles Le Breton built to the north-west the so-called Cour de l'Ovale, attaching these buildings to the medieval keep, which explains their slight irregularity of plan. He also began the construction on the west of two further groups: the Cour de la Fontaine, closed on the north side by the Gallery of François I, and the Cour du Cheval Blanc. Le Breton's style seems to have been typical of the Loire valley, but was novel in its use of pediments over the windows and of polychromy in the façades. After 1540 two important elements of a more classical nature completed the Cour de l'Ovale: a chapel, and a portico attributed to Serlio and inspired by classical triumphal arches. The second half of the century saw the completion of the Cour de la Fontaine (the Belle Cheminée wing by Primaticcio, 1568) and the continuation of work on the Cour du Cheval Blanc. But Fontainebleau was above all a setting for the activities of painters and sculptors: between 1530 and 1570 the Italian artists Rosso, Primaticcio and Niccolò dell'Abate worked on the interior decoration.

At the beginning of the 1540s, the arrival of the architect and theoretician Sebastiano Serlio (1475–1554), summoned by François I, and the establishment in Paris on his return from Italy of Philibert De l'Orme (1505/10–70), initiated a new phase in French architecture. The treatise of Vitruvius and Leon Battista Alberti, translated into French by the humanist Jean Martin (in 1547 and 1553), and that of Serlio, publication of which started in 1537 (the third book was dedicated in 1540 to François I), played an equally decisive role. French architects were by now no longer simple masons, but cultivated men, true humanists, who were capable of creating an original architecture from ancient and Italian models.

Around 1546, Serlio undertook the construction of the château of Ancy-le-Franc for the count of Clermont-Tonnerre. Built on a square plan, it consists of four wings linked at the corners by four square pavilions. The outer façades are articulated by pilasters; those facing the courtyard follow the elevation adopted by Bramante for the *cortile* of the Belvedere in the Vatican. Serlio's initial design, inspired by the *castelli* of the Quattrocento, underwent numerous modifications once construction started, and its Italian character was thereby weakened.

The reconstruction of the Louvre for François I in 1527 was entrusted to Pierre Lescot (*c.*1500–78). He seems never to have made the journey to Italy, but to have owed his knowledge of ancient architecture to a study of the illustrated treatises published at the time, and perhaps also to a study of ancient remains in the south of France. His work at the Louvre from 1546 onwards reveals a concern to achieve variety in the choice of classical elements.

The full flowering of the classical period came under Henri II (1547–55) and owed much to his mistress, Diane de Poitiers. Philibert De l'Orme built for her the château of Anet (*c.*1547–55), in which he adapted Italian ideas to French tradition in an original way. In 1541, at the behest of the king, the architect undertook the construction of the Château-Neuf, St. Germain. Its plan – a single block (*corps de logis*) set off at each corner by a pavilion – was, in its new sense of massing, a precursor of the great châteaux of the 17th century (Blérancourt, Maisons, Vaux). De l'Orme's very modern ideas were expounded in a lively fashion in the nine volumes of his *Architecture* (1567), in which he discussed the theoretical and practical problems of his profession in the light of his own experience. Asserting the originality of French architecture, he recommended the invention of new Orders based on those of antiquity. His research into the geometry of volumes would be pursued further in the 17th century. The provinces also enjoyed an architectural revival in the mid 16th century. Toulouse in particular was an influential intellectual and artistic centre.

In the second half of the century new trends emerged – complex plans conceived on a larger scale, a less regular use of the Orders, and a taste for polychromy in mixed brick and stone and for fantastic decoration. Some of these characteristics were already noticeable in the works of Lescot and the last projects of Philibert De l'Orme. In 1563–64 Catherine de Médicis entrusted De l'Orme with the construction of the palace of the Tuileries, at the western end of the Louvre. De l'Orme decided on a grid plan with five courtyards, a very elaborate design, but had time to build no more than one pavilion flanked by two wings (in a style markedly more decorative than before). The work at the Tuileries was carried on for a time by Jean Bullant (*c.*1520–78) and continued in the following century, but De l'Orme's ambitious project was never more than partially completed.

Bullant, who had been to Rome, possessed a solid knowledge of ancient architecture, as can be seen from his *Reigle générale d'Architecture des cinq Manières de Colonnes*, published in 1563. The works that he carried out between 1555 and 1565 for the Montmorency family at Ecouen, Fère-en-Tardenois and Chantilly, display a sophisticated Mannerist approach in their use of the classical elements (broken entablatures, non-alignment of the Orders and storeys, pediments broken or extended beyond their bays). In the portico of the south wing at Ecouen, Bullant initiated the use of the giant Order, inspired by the Pantheon in Rome.

Jacques Androuet Du Cerceau (*c.*1520–after 1584), who is famous for his two illustrated volumes *Les plus excellents Bastimens de France* (1576 and 1579), an essential source for French Renaissance architecture, was nevertheless more of a decorator than an architect. But two châteaux since destroyed are attributed to him: Verneuil (begun 1568) and Charleval (begun 1570 and never finished). The originality of his work lay in the fantasy of his decorative sculpture, which was to herald the work of the first half of the 17th century.

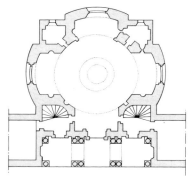

Chapel of Anet

The plan of the chapel of Anet is centralized, but more complex than that of Bramante's Tempietto in that it combines a circle and a square. It would seem that this arrangement was inspired by northern Italian models. The arcades that support the dome cannot be seen on the plan but are applied to the internal surface of the central cylinder. The marble paving repeats the motif of the curved coffers of the dome – a masterpiece of geometry, recalling ancient mosaics.

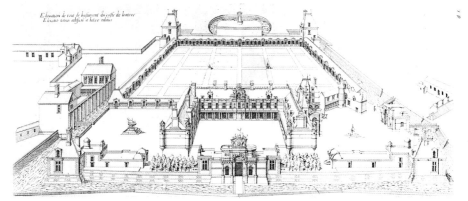

Château of Anet

As can be seen from this bird's-eye view by Jacques Androuet Du Cerceau, the plan of this château, built by Philibert De l'Orme for Diane de Poitiers about 1547–55, followed French examples of the beginning of the century – three wings round a courtyard closed on the fourth side by a lower building. Only the gatehouse, the left wing and the chapel remain. The central wing was fronted at ground level by a portico supported on columns, which continued along the right wing. The focus of the composition was a three-storey *avant-corps* at the centre, which was re-erected in the 19th century in the courtyard of the École des Beaux-Arts in Paris. It comprised three superimposed Orders in the regular sequence – Doric, Ionic, Corinthian – very correctly treated. The façades were divided in a regular rhythm by pilasters, and the windows carried alternating segmental and triangular pediments. The gateway was one of the most original works of the French Renaissance.

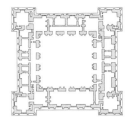

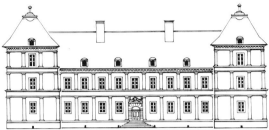

Château of Ancy-le-Franc

Begun by Serlio around 1546, the château was designed for the use of the count of Clermont-Tonnerre, an important member of the court of François I. Its plan is perfectly regular: four wings linked by four square pavilions. The external façades are punctuated by Doric pilasters. The elevations facing the courtyard were inspired by those of Bramante in the *cortile* of the Belvedere in the Vatican. The steep roofs, suited to the French climate, are ornamented with dormers. This sober and elegant composition is noticeably different from Serlio's initial project which was inspired by the *castelli* of the Italian countryside and involved the use of rusticated detail.

Château of Fontainebleau

The château was built from 1528 onwards around the keep of a small medieval château, the work being carried out in several stages that lasted until the 18th century; hence the irregularity in plan and lack of unity in style. Even so, the initial plan, which was probably the result of successive decisions under François I, was largely adhered to. The Gallery of François I, with its frescoes framed in stucco by Rosso, of between 1533 and 1540, is the first great decorated gallery built in France.

Courtyard of the Hôtel d'Assezat, Toulouse

The façade, built between 1552 and 1562, is one of the most successful examples from the classical period of the French Renaissance. The elevation with its three superimposed Orders – Doric, Ionic, Corinthian – was doubtless inspired by Book IV of Serlio's treatise, devoted to the Orders. It also recalls in its purity the *avant-corps* built by Philibert De l'Orme at the château of Anet. The architect remains unknown.

Square court of the Louvre, Paris

In 1527 François I decided to rebuild the old château of the Louvre. The work, which did not begin until 1546, was entrusted to Pierre Lescot, who built the wing shown here. He created an effect of variety in the façade by breaking it forward in projections that were dramatized by pediments, niches and columns (as opposed to the pilasters applied to the rest of the building), and by establishing a vertical gradation in the decoration; the horizontals were weakened by breaks in the entablatures. Between 1551 and 1559 the plan was developed to create a huge square court enclosed by four buildings twice as long as the wing already built and having at their centres a great pavilion like the one shown on the right. The execution of this project was not undertaken until the 17th century and was only completed in the 18th century. Lescot's wing served as a model throughout, giving the elevations a certain unity.

1 *keep of old château*	4 *Serlio's portico*	7 *chapel*	10 *Cour du Cheval Blanc*
2 *Cour de l'Ovale*	5 *chapel*	8 *vestibule*	11 *Cour de la Fontaine*
3 *Porte Dorée*	6 *Gallery of François I*	9 *"horseshoe" staircase*	12 *Belle Cheminée wing*

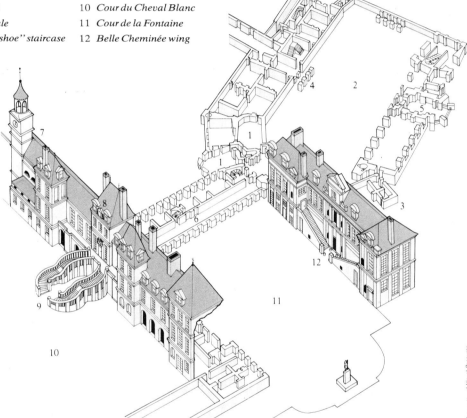

Château of Verneuil

Built from 1568 for Philippe de Boulainvilliers, a rich landowner, this château was demolished after the Revolution but is recorded by the engravings of Jacques Androuet Du Cerceau the Elder, who was probably its architect. Sculptural decoration was abundant and the treatment of the Orders very free (broken entablatures and pediments, fantastic capitals). This type of design was very influential at the beginning of the 17th century.

Polychromy and Mannerism in northern Europe

Between 1580 and 1630 there appeared throughout northern Europe an increasing number of buildings whose polychrome detailing of brick and stone, frequent use of rustication and fondness for dormers and gables show a basic similarity. The system of division of their façades and their Italianate decoration link these buildings to a kind of international Mannerism. But while some were heavily ornamented (château of Brissac in Anjou, the Old Butchers' Hall in Haarlem), others were comparatively plain (Place des Vosges in Paris, Swakeleys near London). Regional characteristics are discernible – vertical bands of stone quoining in France, huge gables in Flanders, large bay windows in England; each country developed related but distinct formulas.

By crossing the traditional constructional device of quoining (which reinforces a brick or plastered rubble wall at its corners and around openings) with the Italian motif of rustication, the architect of the château of Vallery (1550–55) developed the essential feature of the French rusticated style dominant under Henri III, Henri IV and Louis XIII. Façades were organized in vertical bands, rising from ground to dormer, of regular ashlar quoins, which emphasized corners and defined the bays. The width of the bands, the rhythm of more or less ornamental dormers and more or less elaborate window frames, allowed all kinds of variation on this basic theme, which could be adapted with flexibility to all kinds of commission. The striking contrast in colour between the stone quoining and the intervals of brick (or red or pink stone) gave the motif a seductive visual appeal. This style, often referred to in France as the style of Louis XIII because it can still be seen in the first château of Versailles, was very common from 1580 onwards and became the dominant style under Henri IV. It is evident in the *hôtels* (town mansions) of Paris (Hôtel des Abbés de St. Germain-des-Prés, 1586; Place des Vosges, 1605; Hôtel de Transylvanie, 1622; Hôtel Tubeuf, 1634) as well as in châteaux (Wideville, 1580; Rosny, 1600; Balleroy, c.1628).

In Flanders, gables and dormers became the main decorative features, and other elements were handled rather differently. The quoins that defined the bays were thinner and did not extend the height of the building. Broad horizontal bands, edged with volutes and reverse volutes of stone, counteracted the vertical emphasis of the gables. The Old Butchers' Hall in Haarlem is a characteristic example. In England, stone quoining and large dormers can be seen on certain country houses, but the huge bay windows projecting from the façades have their own distinct attraction.

Because of this diversity of forms, one should perhaps speak less of a style than of a cultural movement, whose unity lay in the deliberate assimilation to local building traditions of an Italianizing repertoire (known through engravings, and particularly through Serlio's compilations). The direct and indirect influence of Serlio's treatise on architecture was enormous: its various parts were published in Italy and France between 1537 and 1575, and soon translated into Flemish, German and English, and it was in fact the principal channel of communication between the new architectural culture of Italy and northern Europe. It made known not only the grammar of the Orders but also freer inventions, notably those in a rusticated style by Giulio Romano. Serlio's *Libro Estraordinario* (1554) was particularly influential: it contained a collection of patterns for doorways, some "refined" (with classical mouldings), others "rusticated" (with the Orders distorted by extravagant rustication). Imitated by Androuet Du Cerceau, Hans Vredeman de Vries and Wendel Dietterlin, it encouraged a taste for unrestrained ornament and heavy moulding that masked the clarity of the Orders. The success of these collections, which gave useful patterns for doorways and dormers – such themes were then the central concern of architects – was an essential factor in the coherence of the movement.

Even though it may have persisted here and there, the Mannerist rusticated style went out of fashion in serious architecture around 1630–40, when a classical reaction set in all over northern Europe. Even the houses of the Grand' Place in Brussels (after 1695), in which can be seen the last manifestation of the Mannerist style, show a much more classical sensibility.

Old Butchers' Hall, Haarlem

The hall of the butchers' guild was built by Lievin de Key in 1602–3. The architect's design for the façade was traditional – a stepped gable with decorative finials – but he gave it great animation by combining brick and stone and by the rustication of the door, window surrounds and quoins.

Houses in the Grand' Place, Brussels

Reconstructed after a bombardment in 1695, these were the last guild houses to be built around a square in the manner that was once common to all Flemish cities.

Engraving by Dietterlin

In 1593 Wendel Dietterlin (1550–99) published under the title *Architectura* a series of engravings – doors, windows and fountains – treated in accordance with the five Orders. They were very influential in central and northern Europe.

Place des Vosges, Paris

Originally called Place Royale, the Place des Vosges (1607–12) was the first regular square in Paris. Two higher and more elaborate pavilions – the King's Pavilion above the passage that links the square to the Rue St. Antoine, and the Queen's Pavilion opposite – form a discreet axis across the square. This is lined with houses of four almost identical bays: an arcaded gallery with round arches on the ground floor, two storeys adorned with bands of stone quoining, and two rectangular dormers framed on each side by an oculus (these last have in many cases been altered).

Château of Brissac, Anjou

The principal façade of the château of Brissac shows a virtuoso use of all the resources of the architectural language of the Renaissance in the rusticated mode. The central pavilion brings into play all the Orders, from Tuscan to Corinthian, and the mouldings free themselves progressively from rusticated blocking. In the wings on either side the more modest motif of the rusticated bay also becomes progressively lighter, with the surrounds freeing themselves little by little from the bands of quoining. The multiplicity of small elements, typical of the taste of the period, was to be condemned by the following generation.

Model of an early 17th century house

The album of Jacques Gentillâtre (1578–c.1623) which records "everything he saw and remarked upon both in Paris and elsewhere", gives a good picture of the architectural language common in France at the beginning of the 17th century. It contains numerous variations on the theme of the rusticated bay (rusticated quoining, that is to say bands of alternating long and short dressed stones framing the openings and rising from the basement lights to the dormers). This theme, developed in the 1550s, enjoyed great popularity.

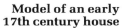

Brick houses, England

In England, brick houses became much more common in the 16th century and were especially fashionable in the 17th century, particularly in regions which did not have good building stone. Flemish influence became marked in the decoration of façades, in which gables with classical elements were a common feature. Kew Palace (above), 1631, has fine curbed gables, brick pilasters, and decorative door and window surrounds. The brickwork at Swakeleys (right), 1629–38, is decorated in stone; the curved gables carry pediments.

Spain and Portugal

Thanks to the influx of precious metals from America and the flourishing wool economy of Castile, the 16th century was for Spain and Portugal a period of great prosperity and unprecedented architectural activity. In Spain, furthermore, the unification of the country under the Catholic kings made necessary the construction of numerous palaces and churches in the territory conquered from the Moors (fall of Granada, 1492). This prosperity, centred on Seville and Lisbon, also touched Toledo and Valladolid (royal residences) and the great religious and intellectual centres – Tomar, Coïmbra, Alcalá de Henares, Granada and Salamanca. Conjoined with the Hapsburg empire under the rule of Charles V (1516–56), Spain maintained artistic contacts with the various regions of this vast domain, in particular with Italy (Lombardy) and the Low Countries. French artists, working for the princes and the Church, also contributed to the development of a new style. Under Philip II (1556–98) Italian influence became dominant in Spain. As for Portugal, it had for many years received French, Flemish and Spanish artists; Italian ideas spread there, particularly in the second half of the century, after the annexation of the country by Spain (1581).

At the end of the 15th century late Spanish Gothic of the kind that had evolved under Isabella still persisted, certainly as regards structure and fabric, although some change was evident in plan and elevation. This particularly rich decorative repertoire brought together Flamboyant and Hispano-Moorish motifs, and even occasionally Italian elements. The principal figures of the period were Juan Guas, an architect of French origin (church of San Juan de los Reyes, Toledo, c.1480; palace of the Infanta at Guadalajara, 1480–83), and Lorenzo Vázquez, the "Spanish Brunelleschi", architect of the College of Santa Cruz at Valladolid (begun 1487). The Medinaceli palace at Gogolludo (1492–95) is also attributed to Vázquez; its rustication and paired Flamboyant lancet windows recall Filarete's Banco Mediceo in Milan.

The term "Plateresque", describing the sculptured relief ornament favoured by Spanish architects until the second half of the 16th century, derives from the word *platería* (silverware). However, it is used only in figurative sense, denoting richness and profusion, and does not imply a close relationship with Spanish silverware, which remained Gothic until the 1540s. Plateresque ornament is Italianate. Free, animated, dense, sometimes gross or extravagant, it takes scant notice of the structure of buildings, and conglomerates around doors and windows and in the upper reaches of façades. The gateway of Salamanca university (1525–30) and the entrance to the church of Santa Maria La Mayor at Calatayud (1528) offer good examples of this decoration as it was applied in the first decades of the century. What is called the Cisneros style combined Italian elements with the Hispano-Moorish tradition (*paraninfo* or central hall of the university of Alcalá de Henares by Pedro Gumiel, 1498–1508; chapter house of Toledo Cathedral by Enrique Egas and Pedro Gumiel, 1504–12).

Although it is customary to use the term Plateresque to cover virtually all Spanish architectural output between the years 1500 and 1560, the picture was far from uniform. Important progress in plan, structure, elevation and even decoration is noticeable from one decade to the next, and differences also exist according to region and the personality of the architect. Thus in newly reconquered Andalusia progress was more rapid than elsewhere, due to the prestige of the building projects and the presence of Italian architects such as Jacopo and Francesco Florentino and Michele Carlone (Castillo de Calahorra, province of Granada, c.1509).

For the Royal Hospital at Santiago de Compostela, Enrique Egas, an architect of Flemish origin, chose a Greek cross plan, which was both practical and symbolic, and was apparently inspired by Italian models (Ospedale Maggiore in Milan by Filarete). In 1523 he began the construction of the cathedral at Granada, to a Gothic design. It was continued in 1528 by Diego de Siloé, who built the Corinthian piers and the semicircular east end (Capilla Mayor), topped by a dome and with round arcades. This insistence on the circle, symbol of divine perfection, recalls the ideas of Alberti and Bramante. The publication at Toledo in 1526 of the treatise by Diego de Sagredo, *Medidas del romano*, inspired by Vitruvius, and the translation of Serlio's book on architecture by Francesco de Villalpando (1552) disseminated a better knowledge of classical architecture, particularly of the Orders. At the end of the 1530s a new concern for regularity and harmony emerged in the plans and elevations of Plateresque buildings. Decoration also became more sober (Alonso de Covarrubias: Alcázar of Toledo, begun in 1537; Rodrigo Gil de Hontañón: façade of the university of Alcalá de Henares, begun in 1537, and plan of the Monterrey palace in Salamanca, 1539, in collaboration with Fray Martin de Santiago). Another significant factor was the reorganization of the royal building works on a larger scale.

Inspired by the grand Roman style of the beginning of the century (Bramante, Raphael), the palace built from 1527 onwards by Pedro Machuca for Charles V at Granada marked a complete break with national tradition, but one which had no sequel. The Italianate Hospital "de Afuera" in Toledo, built in the middle of the century, was another isolated case. The forms and rules of classical composition did not become established until the reign of Philip II, with the construction of the Escorial. They appealed to the taste of the sovereign and his entourage, who were tired of the excessive fussiness of Plateresque architecture. The Escorial was begun in 1562 by Juan Bautista de Toledo, who laid out its grid plan. It was completed by Juan de Herrera, who built, most notably, the church with its centralized plan and dome. The austere grandeur of the new style well reflected the mood of Spain at the time of the Counter-Reformation.

In Portugal, the style at the beginning of the century was one of applying Italianate sculptural ornament to Gothic structures, in which a new sense of space was nevertheless evident (Diogo Boytac and João de Castilho: cloister of the Jeronymite Monastery at Belém, 1502–19). Diogo Arruda made use of an original sculptural repertoire, inspired by the sea and navigation, for the decoration of the church and chapter house of the Convent of Christ at Tomar (1510–14). The great cloister of this convent, built by Diogo de Torralva between 1557 and 1562, is the purest example of Portuguese Renaissance classicism.

During the second half of the century Italian influence spread to the south of the country, just as that of the Low Countries reached the north. Between 1567 and 1574 Manuel Pirés and Alfonso Alvares built the church of the Espírito Santo at Evora for the Jesuits; its side chapels and tribunes, like those of the Gesù in Rome, reflected the special liturgical requirements of the order. In 1582 the Bolognese Filippo Terzi, a pupil of Vignola, began the construction of the church of São Vincente at Fora: the classical façade surmounted by two bell-towers created a type that was to be imitated countless times in Portugal and Brazil. For the Jesuit church in Oporto (the "Grilos", 1614–22), Baltasar Álvares built a façade distantly derived from that of the Gesù, but its accentuated relief and tortured forms are dependent on a "Baroque Mannerism" in which the influence of the northern decorator Wendel Dietterlin can be traced.

The Jeronymite Monastery, Belém

Begun in 1502 by Diogo Boytac, an architect who came from the south west of France, the monastery was completed between 1517 and 1519 by the Spaniard João de Castilho. The most impressive feature of the cloister is a series of deep recesses, behind which lie the aisles of the lower cloister. The very rich Italianate decoration is characteristic of the Manueline style.

Granada Cathedral

The cathedral was begun in 1523 by Enrique Egas, on a Gothic plan with double aisles. In 1528 Diego de Siloé took over the site and added the semicircular apse with radiating chapels and ambulatory; above the sanctuary he built a dome intersected by powerful ribs. This combination of a basilica and a rotunda was inspired by the Holy Sepulchre in Jerusalem. Siloé was also responsible for the piers, which are Gothic in proportion but classical in detail, and support vaults with elaborate ribs.

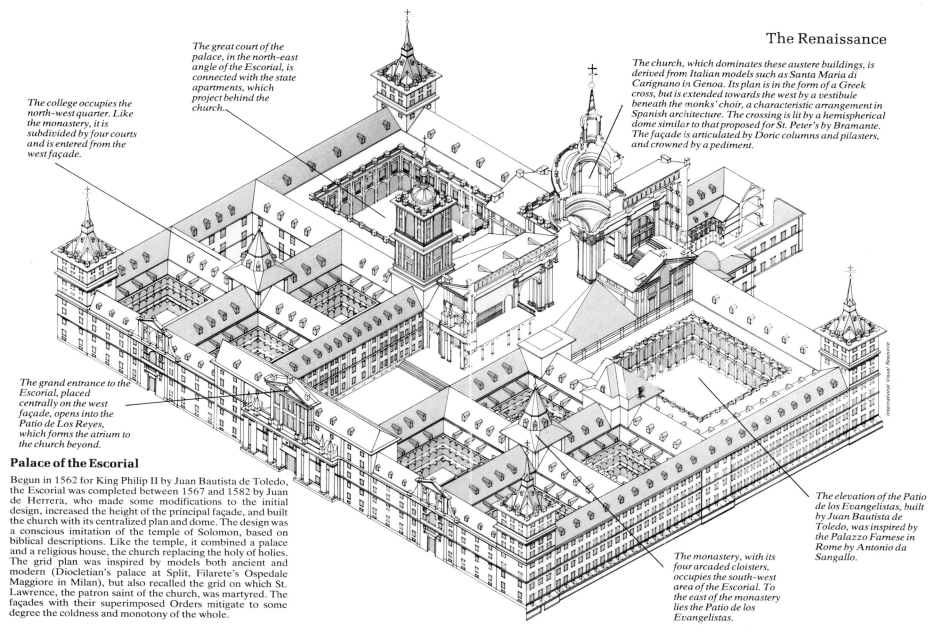

The great court of the palace, in the north-east angle of the Escorial, is connected with the state apartments, which project behind the church.

The college occupies the north-west quarter. Like the monastery, it is subdivided by four courts and is entered from the west façade.

The church, which dominates these austere buildings, is derived from Italian models such as Santa Maria di Carignano in Genoa. Its plan is in the form of a Greek cross, but is extended towards the west by a vestibule beneath the monks' choir, a characteristic arrangement in Spanish architecture. The crossing is lit by a hemispherical dome similar to that proposed for St. Peter's by Bramante. The façade is articulated by Doric columns and pilasters, and crowned by a pediment.

The grand entrance to the Escorial, placed centrally on the west façade, opens into the Patio de Los Reyes, which forms the atrium to the church beyond.

The elevation of the Patio de los Evangelistas, built by Juan Bautista de Toledo, was inspired by the Palazzo Farnese in Rome by Antonio da Sangallo.

The monastery, with its four arcaded cloisters, occupies the south-west area of the Escorial. To the east of the monastery lies the Patio de los Evangelistas.

Palace of the Escorial

Begun in 1562 for King Philip II by Juan Bautista de Toledo, the Escorial was completed between 1567 and 1582 by Juan de Herrera, who made some modifications to the initial design, increased the height of the principal façade, and built the church with its centralized plan and dome. The design was a conscious imitation of the temple of Solomon, based on biblical descriptions. Like the temple, it combined a palace and a religious house, the church replacing the holy of holies. The grid plan was inspired by models both ancient and modern (Diocletian's palace at Split, Filarete's Ospedale Maggiore in Milan), but also recalled the grid on which St. Lawrence, the patron saint of the church, was martyred. The façades with their superimposed Orders mitigate to some degree the coldness and monotony of the whole.

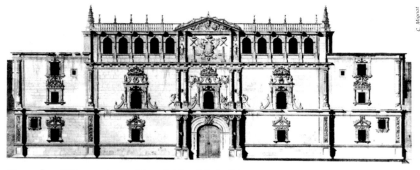

Façade of the university of Alcalá de Henares

Built by Rodrigo Gil de Hontañón from 1537, the façade has three storeys, although the two lateral wings are slightly lower than the centre. Its rigorously symmetrical composition is based on an assembly of squares which define the various horizontal and vertical bays. In keeping with Spanish tradition, the accent is placed on the upper part of the principal block, with its colonnaded gallery, and on the central entrance bay, which is framed by paired columns and enriched by particularly extravagant decoration. A light balustrade, adorned with a flame motif, crowns the façade.

Cloister of the Convent of Christ, Tomar

Begun by Diogo de Torralva between 1557 and 1562, the cloister was completed by Filippo Terzi; it is the purest example of the Renaissance style in Portugal. The use of the Serlian device – an opening of three lights, the central one arched and the two lateral ones rectangular – and of two superimposed Orders (Doric and Ionic) sets up a different rhythm on each storey and lends the composition a great sense of plasticity.

University of Salamanca

The gateway of the university, begun in 1525, is a masterpiece of the mature Plateresque style. The Italianate decoration ("grotesque" ornament taken from the painted decoration of ancient Rome, shells, medallions, pilasters) is combined with heraldic devices to produce an effect of exceptional richness. In the upper part, statues in niches of Venus and Hercules unexpectedly surround a religious scene.

Hospital of San Juan Bautista ("de Afuera"), Toledo

The hospital was built at the instigation of Cardinal Tavera in the middle of the 16th century. It was the result of a collaboration between Bartolomé de Bustamante and Alonso de Covarrubias. The most interesting feature is the double cloister formed by two storeys of arcades, with Doric columns on the ground floor and Ionic on the upper. Its restrained elegance recalls Florentine architecture.

291

Germany and England

In Germany the new style spread gradually, finding expression primarily in secular architecture, since the Reformation had to some extent disrupted the construction of religious buildings. For a long time it was restricted to the application of Italianate ornament to Gothic structures. Arcaded ground floors (*Lauben*), oriels (*Erker*), gables (*Giebel*) and great dormers or "cross-houses" (*Querhauser*) gave a persistent Gothic physiognomy to town halls, houses of the merchant class and princely residences. There was, nevertheless, a perceptible evolution in plan, elevation and carved ornament.

The free cities of the south and west – Augsburg, Nuremberg, Frankfurt – maintained direct commercial links with Italy and therefore absorbed the new style fairly rapidly. In Augsburg, the house of the Fugger bankers (1512–15) was given classical columns in the great entrance hall and an arcaded loggia of Florentine inspiration in the "ladies' court". Sometimes the Italian style merged with memories of the Romanesque; the sculptural decoration on the tower of the church of St. Kilian at Heilbronn (after 1520) is an example. Bavaria, because of its ducal patronage, was one of the most advanced centres. The palace of Landshut (1536–37), built by German masons from the plans of an Italian architect, is a rather hybrid pastiche of the style of Giulio Romano, with its rusticated detail, pilasters, pedimented windows and attic storey. But this avant-garde manifesto made very little impact. In 1560 Duke Albert V undertook the reconstruction of a large part of the Residenz in Munich; the spatial conception of the Antiquarium, built in 1569 by Willem Eckel, was inspired by the Roman vaulted cryptoporticus, and the great hall on the upper floor recalls Michelangelo's Biblioteca Laurenziana in Florence. The Electors Palatine introduced the new style to their capital, Heidelberg, with considerable splendour. The wing added to the castle at Heidelberg by Count Ottheinrich in 1556 derives from a Ferrarese model.

In the north and east of Germany the Gothic style persisted more obstinately. The wing added to the castle of Hartenfels at Torgau (Saxony) in 1537 by Konrad Krebs, with its external spiral staircase rising from a twin-ramped approach, and its vast hall running the full length of the building, recalls the palace of Coudenberg in Brussels by Philip the Good (c.1455), although the buttresses of the staircase are decorated with classicizing pilasters.

After 1580 a new generation of architects, informed by the treatises of Vitruvius and Serlio and by travel to Italy, attempted to achieve a more complete synthesis of traditional and classical forms. Bavaria was the bridgehead of the Catholic and Roman world, and the church of St. Michael, Munich, begun in 1583 for the Jesuits, was a building of completely classical appearance even though still of Gothic structure. The *Lusthaus* (banqueting hall) of the castle at Stuttgart (Georg Beer, 1580–90) was a rectangular structure with a round tower at each corner and a portico recalling that of the Belvedere of Hradschin in Prague (1536).

The taste for fantasy and decorative abundance, inherited from the Gothic, found a new source of inspiration at the turn of the century in the plates of the *Architectura* of the decorator Wendel Dietterlin (1598). These introduced variations on the customary decorum of the Orders, permitting some expression of the function of a building. Their influence can be seen in the façade of the Friedrichsbau at Heidelberg Castle, built between 1601 and 1607 by Johannes Schoch.

English Renaissance architecture, like that of Germany, was essentially secular, because of the Anglican schism (1530) and the Reformation. French artists from the Loire valley and Italians summoned by Henry VIII to build the tomb of his father at Westminster (Torrigiano, 1512) spread a new decorative repertoire that was quickly taken up by the English (the screen of King's College chapel, Cambridge, 1533–35), but they do not seem to have played much part in architecture. The palaces built in the first half of the century in brick or stone, with irregular plans, were still Gothic despite some Renaissance decorative features. Examples are Richmond (built for Henry VII in 1501, destroyed), Hampton Court (begun in 1515) and Whitehall (1530–36, destroyed) – the last two both begun by Cardinal Wolsey and enlarged by Henry VIII. Two of their characteristics were frequently to reappear: the emphasis given to the entrance (usually a pavilion with turrets at the corners) and the development of the long gallery. The manor houses of the nobility remained fundamentally Gothic, but frequently had symmetrical façades (Hengrave Hall, c.1525–39) and a regular plan (Barrington Court, c.1525–30). Nonsuch (destroyed), begun in 1538 by Henry VIII, was novel in its stucco decoration similar to that which Rosso and Primaticcio were carrying out at Fontainebleau at the same time.

A decisive step was taken in the reign of Edward VI with the house of the Protector Somerset in London (1547–52, destroyed), clearly influenced by French models. The façade was articulated by three projecting blocks decorated with pilasters, and by a triumphal arch at ground level on the central block. Although they had not yet been translated, the theoretical works of Vitruvius, Alberti, Serlio and De l'Orme began to circulate from 1550 onwards, and to play an increasingly important role, essentially as handbooks of ornament. In 1563 John Shute published a treatise inspired by Serlio, *The First and Chief Groundes of Architecture*. In the reign of Elizabeth I the commercial and religious ties that united England and the Low Countries stimulated an influx of Flemish artists who brought with them the model books of Vredeman de Vries and Dietterlin – the source for the new "grotesque" decorative strapwork.

The "prodigy houses" built by the aristocracy between 1570 and 1590 (Longleat, Burghley, Wollaton) show a certain diversity in their plans and elevations. The numerous windows, the pavilions breaking forward from the façades and the flat roofs give these buildings an original appearance yet, despite the use of classical forms, they still recall the great Gothic houses of the preceding period. They are the work of masons and carpenters following plans given them by the owners, and not of "architects" in the French or Italian sense of the word. The organization of rooms varied little; but an evolution is noticeable in the conception of the hall, which tended to become simply a vestibule on an axis with the entrance, and of the staircase, which became more and more spectacular. Great houses built between 1590 and about 1620, such as Hardwick Hall, Montacute House, Audley End, Bramshill House, Hatfield House and Blickling Hall show a fine simplicity, grandeur and regularity in their plans (often E- or H-shaped).

Longleat, Wiltshire

Built from 1572 onwards, this house is one of the great achievements of Elizabethan architecture. Its rectangular plan encloses one large and two small internal courtyards. The smaller courtyard belongs to a previous house, begun in 1554 but destroyed by fire in 1567. The façades, whose symmetry is underlined by the projecting bays with their paired windows and three superimposed Orders (Doric, Ionic, Corinthian), recall those of the Protector Somerset's house in London.

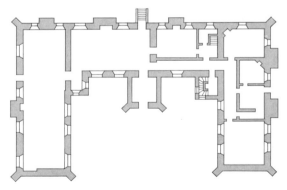

Barrington Court, Somerset

Built probably a little before 1530 by Henry Daubeny (a member of the household of Henry VIII), Barrington Court is a manor house of medieval character. The internal layout of rooms is more or less traditional, but a desire for symmetry is apparent in the U-plan. The entrance pavilion is placed centrally on the principal façade, and the stair tower in the left-hand corner of the courtyard mirrors the oriel of the hall in the right-hand corner. This type of plan was often followed in later years: for example, at Wimbledon House, Surrey (begun 1588, destroyed) and Hatfield House, Hertfordshire (1611).

Hardwick Hall, Derbyshire

Built between 1590 and 1597, probably by the mason Robert Smythson, Hardwick Hall is a characteristic rural mansion of the late Elizabethan period. Designed on an H-plan with projecting pavilions and a central hall serving as a vestibule, it is strictly symmetrical. Contemporary critics mocked its predominance of windows with the quip: "Hardwick Hall, more glass than wall". Decoration on the façade is restricted to an ornamental balustrade at roof level and a gallery with banded columns on the ground. The interior is one of the most sumptuous of the period.

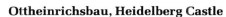

St. Michael's Church, Munich

This church was built by the Jesuits between 1583 and 1599. The original plan is not known; the choir is the work of Friedrich Sustris. The nave is covered by a broad, high vault, whose upper portion forms a barrel vault. This is carried on massive piers, adorned with giant pilasters and niches, between which there are chapels, also barrel vaulted and surmounted by a tribune gallery. This arrangement recalls that adopted by Alberti at Sant'Andrea in Mantua and by Vignola at the Gesù in Rome. The church was badly damaged in the Second World War, but has been brilliantly restored.

Ottheinrichsbau, Heidelberg Castle

This wing was built for the Electors Palatine from 1556. The architect is unknown, but a Dutch sculptor, Alexander Colin (or Hollins) is known to have worked there. The façade resembles Italian models, such as the Palazzo Rovarella at Ferrara, but its composition is more complex and decorative. The sculpture displays a rich allegorical and mythological repertoire. The use of the Orders is imaginative: for example, rusticated pilasters with Ionic capitals are combined with a Doric entablature. The entrance in the form of a triumphal arch is approached by two straight ramps, typical of German architecture of the Renaissance.

Antiquarium in the Residenz, Munich

The Antiquarium was built between 1569 and 1571 by Willem Eckel to house the collection of works of art of the duke of Bavaria, Albert V. With its low barrel vault pierced by window openings, the room has a very unusual shape. It is inspired by Roman cryptoportici. In 1586 the painter Friedrich Sustris was commissioned to decorate the vault with "grotesque" ornamentation similar to that which adorned ancient palaces, such as the Domus Aurea of Nero. The fashion for this kind of decoration, a combination of painting and stucco, was started in Rome by Raphael and his pupils (Loggias of the Vatican, Villa Madama).

Montacute House, Somerset

This house, built for a lawyer named Edward Phelips, was completed in about 1599. Its plan is U-shaped, with very short wings which carry Flemish gables. On the principal façade, bow windows form vertical bays on the ground and first floors. Stringcourses emphasize the horizontal lines. The entrance bay on the rear façade, shown here, is older (1546) and in the Gothic style, having been brought in the 18th century from Clifton Maybank (Dorset). The heraldic panel over the door is typical of Tudor architecture.

J.-L. Princelle

Collège des Quatre-Nations, Paris (now the Institute of France)

Founded according to the instructions in Mazarin's will, the Collège stands in a small square overlooking the Seine. Two short wings, decorated with superimposed Orders, connect the chapel to the two angle pavilions; the colossal pilasters of the pavilions echo the columns of the massive projecting entrance to the chapel. The system of Orders evokes classical grandeur, and divides up the façade in regular fashion, in accordance with the disposition of the space behind.

The division of history into centuries is an artificial device. Sometimes useful, often misleading, it can become ludicrous to try to force the history of an idea into the span of a century. Even when we take an overall look at the history of European architecture, it is impossible to sum up the 17th century as the age of the Baroque, succeeding Renaissance and Mannerism, or even as the age in which classical and Baroque opposed each other, without severely distorting the facts.

It is useful to remember the history of the word "Baroque". It was originally a term used by jewellers to describe irregularly shaped pearls. From this precise, technical meaning (the only one given in Furetière's dictionary of 1690) was derived the figurative sense of "irregular" or "bizarre" listed in the dictionary published by the French Academy in 1718. The word was used in this latter sense during the second half of the 18th century to describe all those idiosyncratic architectural forms so abhorred by current academic taste and by Neoclassical rationalism: it was applied to Gothic tracery; to the overlapping, broken pediments of Pietro da Cortona and Carlo Rainaldi; to the complex geometry of Francesco Borromini; to Guarino Guarini's domes; and to Rococo ornament. Here "Baroque" did not describe a specific age or style, but referred to any irregular form which – according to the definition given in Antoine Joseph Pernety's Dictionnaire des beaux-arts (1757) – "follows not the proportional norms but the caprice of the artist".

The term was taken up again in the 19th century by art historians who used it in various senses, often contradictory and far removed from its original meaning. In 1888 Heinrich Wölfflin defined it in his essay Renaissance and Baroque as "the style which marked the dissolution of the Renaissance" and which predominated until the triumph of Neoclassicism. Wölfflin divided it into two phases, the first from 1520 to 1630, the second from 1630 to 1750. His study concentrated on the first phase, tracing its formation from 1520 onwards until its full flowering around 1580; since 1910, however, the word has most often been used to describe the second phase. It is sometimes reserved for the florid style of the 17th century papal court; here, the special characteristics of Roman art correspond reasonably well to the etymological meaning. But it is usually used to cover anything approaching this grand Roman style in either England or France – Greenwich Palace or the Palace of Versailles, the Val de Grâce or St. Paul's Cathedral. The word "classical" which is used to oppose "Baroque" is perhaps equally ambiguous. At times it is used to refer to any architecture that employs the classical Orders; on other occasions it is used to describe all harmoniously proportioned architecture inspired by a few revered prototypes. The multiple meanings of these two words reflect the fundamental dilemma of 17th century architecture: whether to continue the formal system consolidated between 1520 and 1550, or whether to explore new avenues.

It would obviously make more sense to give up using such terms and to construct a history of 17th century architecture based on the fundamental question to which they confusedly refer: is the language of the classical Orders, defined during the Renaissance according to the models of antiquity, an eternal and universal one? The unity of the century stems from the fact that all its architects replied in some way to this question; its diversity from the fact that the answers varied according to generation, social milieu and nationality.

There is no clear dividing line between the 16th and the 17th centuries. The great architects admired the same models, used the same works of reference and employed the same architectural language. Such differences as there were resulted principally from the variety of local building techniques – which, during the 17th century, constituted a far more important factor than did the simple passage of time. Despite the widespread popularity of Italian Mannerism, national and regional methods remained very much alive throughout the century – a fact which did not escape the notice of the theoreticians. In 1691 in his Cours d'architecture Charles d'Aviler wrote that "the different nations build according to their particular taste and their needs", and in 1721 Fischer von Erlach declared that "national tastes vary no less in architecture than in the manner of dressing".

These differences are especially apparent in construction methods. European builders continued to use the best local materials available – wood, brick, granite, limestone – and to work in the vernacular tradition of their towns and villages. Tradition sometimes overruled ecological factors; for example, the distribution of steep roofs (the so-called "French roofs" that were built in northern France until c. 1640–50) does not correspond with the distribution of rain- or snowfall. In 1673 François Blondel noted that it was the custom of Parisian builders to mark on the façade of a building both the level of the floorboards and the level of the window sills, while in Roman houses there was only one stringcourse. With this single string-course, and with their ochre-painted walls and small windows with travertine surrounds, Roman houses of the 17th century were similar in all respects to those of the 16th; they differed markedly from 17th century Parisian houses, which had double string-courses, large rectangular windows and limestone or plaster walls covered in white rough-cast.

A similar geographical variety is apparent in grander forms of architecture. At least between 1540 and 1640, Venetian, Genoese and Roman palaces, French châteaux and mansions, remained unchanged in style, but fundamentally different from each other. Mid-16th century buildings such as the Palazzo Corner della Ca' Grande in Venice, the Palazzo Farnese in Rome and the Palazzo Doria in Genoa, the Hôtel de Ferrare at Fontainebleau and the Château de Verneuil were greatly admired throughout the period and gave rise to a certain continuity of style. Their successful synthesis of national or local traditions of planning and the new Renaissance ideal provided a model for future generations. Thus 17th century French châteaux such as the Palais du Luxembourg and even Maisons-Laffitte are closer in design to those of the 16th century, like Ecouen and Verneuil, than to their Italian contemporaries; the same observation can be made about Venetian and Genoese palaces. In this respect, Bernini's failure in Paris is important: in 1665 Louis XIV invited him to supervise the completion of the Louvre, but Bernini was unable even to get the work started. The French builders objected to Italian construction methods, and Colbert criticized Bernini for not being able to make the best use of the equipment available in France. The argument was about technique and method, not about aesthetic values.

In the 17th and 18th centuries, as in the 16th, ideas about style were very different from our own. In those days style was defined according to the classical Orders – Doric, Ionic, Corinthian, Tuscan and Composite. Each constituted a "mode" in the grammatical or, rather, the musical sense of the word: each harmonized with a particular scheme and produced a particular effect – severe Doric for prisons and city gates, elegant Ionic for villas and convents, and majestic Corinthian for

Baroque Rome, 1623–79
(opposite)
From S. Pressouyre, Rome au fil du temps, Boulogne-sur-Seine, 1973.

THE 17th CENTURY

Public places and monuments

1　Porta del Popolo (Bernini)
2　Piazza San Pietro (Bernini)
3　Piazza Navona, Fontana dei Fiumi (Bernini)
4　Fontana del Tritone (Bernini)
5　Fontana della Barcaccia (Bernini)
6　Fontana delle Api (Bernini)
7　Piazza di Trevi
8　Le Quattro Fontane
9　Campidoglio

Palaces and villas

10　Vatican Palace, corridor and Scala Regia (Bernini)
11　Palazzo Pamphili (Rainaldi)
12　Palazzo Spada, restorations and additions (Borromini)
13　Palazzo Chigi, now Odescalchi (Bernini)
14　Palazzo Barberini (Maderno and others)

Religious buildings

15　San Carlo al Corso (dome by Pietro da Cortona)
16　Santa Maria del Popolo, restoration (Bernini)
17　Santa Maria in Montesanto and Santa Maria dei Miracoli (Bernini)
18　Santa Maria della Pace, restoration and façade (Pietro da Cortona)
19　Sant' Agnese in Agone, reconstruction (Borromini and Rainaldi)
20　Santa Maria in Vallicella, façade (Rughesi)
21　Oratorio di San Filippo Neri (Borromini)
22　Santa Maria delle Sette Dolori, church and convent (Borromini)
23　San Carlo ai Catinari
24　Santa Maria in Campitelli (Rainaldi)
25　Santa Rita (Carlo Fontana)
26　Sant'Ignazio (Maderno and others)
27　Chapel of the Magi (Bernini followed by Borromini)
28　Collegio di Propaganda Fide (Borromini)
29　Sant'Andrea delle Fratte, campanile (Borromini)
30　San Nicola da Tolentino
31　Santa Maria della Vittoria (Maderno and Soria)

32　Sant'Andrea al Quirinale (Bernini)
33　San Carlo alle Quattro Fontane (Borromini)
34　Santi Vincenzo e Anastasio, façade (Martino Longhi the younger)
35　Santa Maria in Via Lata, façade (Pietro da Cortona)
36　San Martino ai Monti, renovation and façade (Pietro da Cortona)
37　San Gregorio (Soria)
38　San Giovanni in Laterano, renovation (Borromini)
39　Oratorio di San Giovanni in Oleo, restoration (Borromini)
40　Santi Luca e Martina (Pietro da Cortona)
41　Sant'Ivo della Sapienza (Borromini)
42　Sant'Andrea della Valle, completion (Maderno and Rainaldi)

**1 Het Loo Palace,
Netherlands, around 1700**

The palace, completed in 1686, was built
for William of Orange in the heart of a vast
hunting estate. The symmetry of the
buildings and gardens laid out around a
central axis recalls the plans for the enlargement of Versailles. (From an engraving published by P. Schenk.)

**2 The Great Gallery,
Royal Palace, Stockholm**

The "Versailles" style was introduced to
the Royal Palace (1690–1754) by the
Swedish architect Nicodemus Tessin the
Younger. A French team assisted with the
interior decoration. The Great Gallery,
flanked by the Halls of Peace and War,
recalls the work of Lebrun.

SATELLITES OF VERSAILLES

**6
Royal Palace and Park,
La Granja, Spain**

The palace was the work of T. Ardemanns
(1719–23), though the statues decorating
the gardens were by a team of French
sculptors. As at Versailles, their subjects
followed an allegorical programme.

3
Peterhof Palace

This summer residence was built in 1715 by Leblond at Peterhof (now Petrodvorets, 30 kilometres/18 miles from Leningrad) and enlarged by Rastrelli in 1750; the façade is 268 metres (nearly 900 feet) long.

4 The Residenz, Würzburg

Begun in 1710 by Balthazar Neumann, the plans for this episcopal palace were submitted to Boffrand and R. de Cotte, and subsequently altered by L. von Hildebrandt. The central part of the building, with its three bays around a "cour d'honneur" facing towards the town, recalls the Cour de Marbre at Versailles.

5
The Chapel of Caserta

Caserta, the country residence of the Bourbons of Naples, was the work of L. Vanvitelli. The palace chapel has a structure reminiscent of that of Versailles, although the rich decorations are in the Neapolitan Baroque style.

palaces and large churches. The differences that we believe we can detect between certain buildings are often the simple result of passing from a Composite to an Ionic mode; and what we call "High Baroque" is often nothing but a majestic Corinthian. There is no real break between one century and the next, but there are changes of register; as poetry may be composed in the epic or the lyric style, so architecture may be designed in the Ionic or the Corinthian. In the second half of the 16th century, Sebastiano Serlio, Andrea Palladio, Giacomo Vignola, Jean Bullant, Philibert De l'Orme and others had tried to bring some order to the lavish experimentation of the Renaissance, and to establish a compromise between the visible ruins of antiquity and the writings of Vitruvius. The architects of the 17th century wrote nothing new about the Orders (the last work of importance was by Vincenzo Scamozzi in 1615) but looked upon the 16th century treatises as essential reference books; these were translated and re-issued in every European language throughout the century. Two important examples are a four-language edition of Vignola, published in 1619 in Amsterdam and re-issued in 1642; and a French "Vignola", published in Paris in 1631, and re-issued in 1657 translated into English, Dutch and German.

Designs evolved in the 16th century also continued to be used as models, and Italian formulas can be traced throughout the century – church fronts with Orders superimposed or graduated; façades divided into storeys by string-courses or decorated with a giant Order; monumental porticoes flanked by classical columns and crowned by a balcony; or rusticated portals. The first decades of the 17th century can be seen only as the final phase of the new Italian style of architecture.

Inigo Jones in England and Jacob van Campen in the Netherlands introduced their respective countries to the grand Mediterranean style based on the Orders, imposing it on cultures that had hitherto resisted the Italian fashion. In the work of both men a close relationship can be seen with that of Palladio and Scamozzi. In France, too, although the country had its own classical tradition, civil architecture came closer during the 1640s to the grand classical style of the Renaissance. In Paris, for example, the façade of the Hôtel de Léon facing the Rue Garancière and the court façade of the Hôtel d'Avaux are curiously reminiscent of Michelangelo's designs for the palaces of the Campidoglio in Rome and Palladio's designs for the Palazzo Valmarana in Vicenza, while the Hôtel de Vendôme (now demolished) resembled Bramante's Palazzo Caprini.

The same phenomenon can be seen in religious architecture. Although the Gothic style survived during the 17th century due to a sentimental attachment to the famous works of the Middle Ages or in continuation of earlier plans (as with the cathedrals of Milan and Orléans), the classical church of the Italian Counter-Reformation became standard throughout Europe. This is especially apparent in France, above all in Paris, where, considering first St. Joseph-des-Carmes (1612) and then the Val de Grâce (1645) we can see the Italian and French styles coming closer to one another. The façade and plan of the former, a Jesuit seminary (now demolished), recall those of Giacomo della Porta's churches, and the dome and altar of the Val de Grâce recall those of St. Peter's in Rome.

Yet at the heart of this Italian tradition, which thus imposed itself as a model throughout Europe, though subject to very appreciable local variations, two fundamental attitudes stood out and opposed each other during the century. For some, the language of the Orders, based on a few universally known examples from antiquity, was enough to express everything; but for others, the architect was expected to be more than a perpetual copyist. The first group, taking Vignola and Palladio as their examples, wanted to establish a set of universal rules and to select from the Renaissance tradition a few models and formulas. The others, following the example of Michelangelo, wanted to escape from well-trodden paths and to invent new, "modern" forms. It was not so much a question of two styles as of two attitudes towards the Renaissance tradition.

In 1570, in his treatise on architecture, Palladio condemned the excessive use of detail, the abuse of scrolls and projections and the taste for novelty. Indeed, during the first decades of the 17th century a purist reaction can be seen in Italy, both in Rome and in Venice, where Scamozzi systematized Palladio's theories. The reverberations would soon be felt everywhere, in England with Inigo Jones, in France with Jacques Lemercier, and in the Netherlands with Van Campen.

In France, during the years 1630–40, a small group of doctrinaire purists, supported by the Superintendent of Buildings, François Sublet des Noyers, attacked "the grotesque masks, ugly scrolls and similar bizarre fantasies which contaminate the whole of modern architecture". In his Parallèle de l'architecture antique avec la moderne, written during the 1640s and published in 1650, Roland Fréart de Chambray attacked "architects who want to compose everything according to their fantasy and believe that imitation is the art of the apprentice and that to be a master one has necessarily to produce some novelty. These poor folk believe that by fantasticating some particular type of cornice or some other thing, they have created a new Order".

This stance was the opposite of that taken by Borromini, who wrote that he was not born to be a "copyist"; far from wishing to limit his experience to a few universally approved buildings, he admired the variety of late Roman architecture. Borromini's love of the spectacular and his unusual personality encouraged the development of this trend in Rome from 1630 onwards. Yet Italian Baroque should not be set against French classicism. Within every culture there arose a conflict between those who supported a strict Vitruvianism or, at least, a moderate use of decoration and a simple vocabulary of Orders, and the partisans of a modern architecture that would open up new paths. Bernini was just as critical of "heretical" architecture (like that of Borromini) as Fréart de Chambray, and Guarini was censured both by the Parisian Germain Brice and by the Italian Giovanni Pietro Bellori.

But between the most purist members of the doctrinaire school, like Scamozzi and Fréart de Chambray, and the most free-thinking of the modernists, like Borromini and Guarini, there was room for a centre party who rejected the extravagances of a style that made too free with tradition as well as the austerity of a style that was over-pure. Their handling of a whole range of elements refined since the Renaissance succeeded in producing results that were both pleasing and magnificent, and from 1660 onwards a sort of grand international style came into being, exemplified in the work of Bernini, Christopher Wren and Jules Hardouin Mansart.

Individual regions nevertheless retained relative autonomy, following local building traditions and drawing on the local reputation of particular buildings like Pierre Lescot's Louvre, Michelangelo's Campidoglio and Inigo Jones' Banqueting House. Thus, in France, during the second half of the century, a kind of national grand style was born. It was characterized by a taste for light avant-corps or projections discreetly and effectively drawing attention to the centre of a building – like the principal figure in a pictorial composition; these would be flanked simply by partitions forming pilasters (as in the Hôtel de Rohan) or divided by pilasters, half-columns and columns (as in the Place Vendôme). The ground floors were given horizontal partitions to form a lower ground floor and mezzanine, and a deliberate contrast was created between bays of different design: the central bays were curved, the recessed bays, rectangular. There was a limited but effective repertoire of decoration: the only permitted ornaments were masks, vases, foliage and sculptured figures – on pediments or on the bases of balustrades. Admiration for some of the great buildings celebrated in Marot's prints helped to ensure the homogeneity of this French style. It had no influence in Italy, but spread throughout the rest of Europe during the 18th century.

In England the Baroque style was the creation virtually of one man – Sir Christopher Wren. He followed not only French example, but, to a lesser degree, Netherlandish (particularly for his London churches) and Italian models (he was in Paris at the same time as Bernini, whom he met). Although native resistance prevented him putting into effect the kind of grandiose schemes of urban and palace planning with which he was inspired by French example, he established in England the fundamental vocabulary of French classicism.

It is perhaps this grand international style that is primarily denoted today by the word "Baroque". Its most significant achievements were for Court and Church, expressive of royal absolutism or of Counter-Reformation expansionism. Its self-confident and highly articulate rhetoric could be developed in a severe classicism or in a more exuberant mode, but its most magnificent creations – Bernini's Piazza of St. Peter's, Versailles, Wren's St. Paul's – embraced something of both. Sometimes this architecture seems designed to overwhelm by its sheer scale, since in this period programmes were successfully carried through that dwarfed even the dreams of the previous century; or the spectator cannot fail to be impressed by its complexity, its richness or its dramatic intensity. Baroque architecture is consistent in its desire to impress, to transform the environment of the viewer, to make the viewer a participant. There is often mention of Baroque "theatricality" – and this was the age that invented opera. The great monuments of the Baroque are certainly "theatrical" in that sense, but as a result not so much of deceit, as of a sincere belief in the power of art – and architecture – to inspire us.

Portal of the Collegio Propaganda Fide, Rome

Here Borromini completely rethought the scheme of the classical portal (an opening flanked by classical Orders and surmounted by a pediment). His tapering pilasters recall some of Michelangelo's motifs, but the slant is accentuated, and the pediment is quite novel.

Church of the Sorbonne, Paris, court façade (top left)

Faced with the task of creating two façades for the church of the Sorbonne (1636–42), Lemercier used the two standard approved models. For the street front he designed a somewhat austere façade with superimposed Orders in the Italian style. Overlooking the court (shown here) he composed a simple variation on the theme of the portico of the Pantheon in Rome.

Oratorio di San Filippo Neri, Rome (centre left)

For the Oratorian fathers of Rome, Borromini, by contrast, transformed the old theme of superimposed Orders by building the façade in a gentle curve. He also invented a totally original pediment by amalgamating the two classical forms, curved and triangular, and freely redesigning the capitals. This freedom of invention was not just an artistic whim; the convex part of the façade represented the body between the two arms of the wings, while the capitals were reminders of Oratorian simplicity.

St. Etienne-du-Mont, Paris, façade
(far right)

The portico, built between 1611 and 1622 by Claude Guérin in the classical style, was added in front of the great Gothic nave, only partly concealing it, although it succeeds in integrating the elements of the older building. The wealth of detail and mass of ornamentation are typical of architectural taste in Henri IV's reign. The rusticated pillars recall those by Philibert de l'Orme at the Tuileries.

Church of St. Gervais, Paris, façade
(right)

Faced with a similar task five years later (1616–20), Salomon de Brosse majestically disguised a high Gothic nave with three superimposed Orders. The sober monumentality of the façade, whose only decoration consists of coupled columns, is a statement of strict classicism.

The new classicism in England and the Netherlands

During the first decades of the 17th century there was a reaction in both England and the Netherlands against excessive forms of Mannerism and a corresponding swing towards a more sober and classical style. Its chief protagonists were Inigo Jones in England and Jacob van Campen in the Netherlands. The two men shared an admiration for Palladio, but his influence was stronger on Jones, who came to know his work at first hand in Italy. In Van Campen can be seen primarily the influence of Palladio's disciple Scamozzi, whose treatise, *Idea dell'architettura universale* (1615), codified the master's thinking somewhat rigidly. Van Campen's work came slightly after that of Jones, who therefore provided an intermediate step; Dutch classicism was, in turn, to have an influence in England slightly later.

In this classical style, buildings are composed of clearly defined masses, ground-plans take on a harmonic symmetry, and façades are unified, without heavy ornamentation. An effect of grandeur is brought about by the use of the Orders, giant or superimposed, and by the regularity of the bays. A feeling for bulk, more noticeable in the work of Jones and his pupil Webb, echoes some of the "Mannerist" tendencies to be seen in Palladio's work. The somewhat mechanical spacing of Van Campen's pilasters, resulting in a dryer effect, is certainly due to his purely graphic study of Scamozzi's prints and, in a less obvious way, to the moral climate of the young Protestant republic.

Inigo Jones (1573–1652) probably began his career as a painter and draughtsman; from about 1605 he designed costumes and scenery for the royal masques. His mastery in the arts was recognized at Court, and designing scenery must have contributed to his decision to take up architecture. In 1613 he was appointed Surveyor to the King's Works, a post he held until 1642. Before taking office, he completed his training with a journey to Italy, which he had already visited before 1603, in the company of the art-lover and collector Lord Arundel. He took as his guidebook Palladio's *Quattro Libri dell' Architettura*, which he annotated in detail; he was the first Englishman to make a critical study of ancient Rome and the great Italian tradition. It was in Italy that he learned to think of a building as a whole, arranged by rational rules.

His first works were the Queen's House at Greenwich, begun in 1616, the Banqueting House, Whitehall, built between 1619 and 1622, and the Queen's Chapel in St. James's Palace, of 1627. For the first time there rose on English soil a Quattrocento villa, a Palladian palace and a Cinquecento chapel. With the Piazza of Covent Garden (1631–38) Jones designed the first regularly planned London square. His buildings were to play a key role in the formation of English Neoclassicism.

This architectural reformation received the support of a whole group of connoisseurs, including Sir Balthasar Gerbier, Sir Roger Pratt and John Evelyn, whose ranks were later swelled by a number of master builders. Yet John Webb (1611–72) remained loyal to Palladianism when the grand French and Italian manner arrived. Webb was Jones' son-in-law, pupil and assistant. He received numerous private commissions, including Lamport Hall, Northamptonshire (1654–67); in 1654, at The Vyne in Hampshire, he added the first classical portico on any house in England, and in 1665 he built the King Charles block of Greenwich Palace. The work of Hugh May (1622–84), who visited Holland and built Eltham Lodge in Kent (1664), is more strongly marked by the influence of Dutch Palladianism.

In the Netherlands, the death of Prince Maurice of Nassau in 1625 marked the end of one period, which had been in essence a continuation of the 16th century, and the birth of another, in which the young, prosperous republic would adopt a classical style strongly influenced by the academic prototypes of Vincenzo Scamozzi. The definitive step was taken in 1633 when Jacob van Campen (1595–1657), a painter and architect from Haarlem, designed a private house for Maurice of Nassau, the Mauritshuis in The Hague. It is not clear exactly how the classical style reached the Netherlands. Van Campen had visited Italy in his youth, but his mind was then on painting rather than architecture. The humanist diplomat Constantin Huygens (1596–1687) may have oriented Dutch architecture in this direction; he had visited Venice, Vicenza and London (where he attended a masque in Inigo Jones' Banqueting House) before becoming artistic adviser to the Stathouder. His house at The Hague, built in 1634 and now demolished, was another example of the new style, which found its most monumental expression in the Town Hall of Amsterdam (1648).

The path opened up by Van Campen was soon followed by Pieter Post (1608–69), Arent van Gravesante (c.1600–62) and Philip Vingboons (1607–78) in numerous private houses.

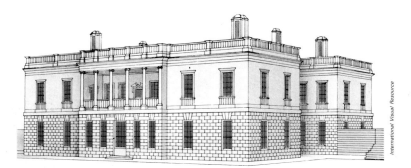

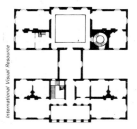

The Queen's House, Greenwich

The Queen's House, begun in 1616, was the first English villa in the Italian style. Its plan bears some resemblance to that of the Medici villa at Poggio a Caiano. The building consists of two separate wings connected by a covered bridge across what was originally the main Dover road. Each half is a simple rectangle, though one contains a cubical galleried hall, 12 metres (39 feet) square and high. The elevation owes a great deal to Inigo Jones' close study of the treatises of Palladio and Scamozzi.

The Double Cube Room, Wilton House, Wiltshire

The Double Cube Room, one of the most beautiful private rooms to survive from the 17th century, dates from about 1649. It was designed by Inigo Jones to display a collection of portraits by Van Dyck. The French influence can be seen in the rich gold and white decor. The most prominent features are the enormous coved ceiling and the fireplace with its Corinthian columns and a pediment close to some of Jean Barbet's designs.

The Banqueting House, Whitehall, London

The Banqueting House (1619–22) is Inigo Jones' masterpiece. Its design derives from Palladio's plan for an "Egyptian hall". The interior of the building is a double cube occupying both storeys; the ceiling is decorated with paintings by Rubens. In the simple façade, with its superimposed Ionic and Composite Orders, there is gentle emphasis on the three central bays, from which columns and entablature project. Beneath the upper cornice, garlands and masks symbolize the festivities associated with a banqueting hall.

Town Hall, Amsterdam

The Town Hall, now the Royal Palace, was begun by Van Campen in 1648, when the Dutch Republic was given its independence at the end of the war with Spain. The original design was inspired by Palladio's reconstructions of Greek and Roman buildings. The great central hall, which runs the entire width of the building, is placed between two courts, making it particularly light. The steep roofs, the projecting centre and corner pavilions and the emphasis on the vertical, echo the town halls of the 16th century, such as those at Antwerp and Augsburg; however, the two colossal Orders of pilasters, Composite and Corinthian, like the interior decoration derive directly from Scamozzi, creating an effective expression of the civic pride of the victorious city.

Portico of The Vyne, Hampshire

This doorway was designed by John Webb in 1654. The columns and pilasters, of brick faced with stucco, are surmounted by a wooden pediment.

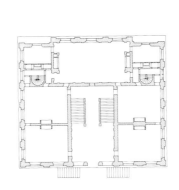

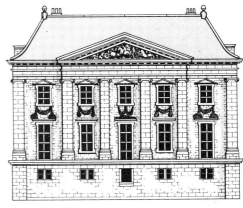

The Mauritshuis, The Hague

This small palace, built around 1633 by Maurice of Nassau from designs by Van Campen, is an expression of the new Dutch classical ideal. The arrangement of well-proportioned giant pilasters gives it an imposing character. The symmetrical plan is similar to that of Palladio's villa at Ghizzola, while the details are taken from Scamozzi.

King Charles block, Greenwich Palace

The King Charles block was to have been the main wing of Greenwich Palace, begun in 1665 but never completed. Webb's major work, it was inspired by Inigo Jones' unrealized designs for Whitehall Palace of 1647. The monumental façade, divided horizontally by two bands of stone, is unified by the group of four central columns surmounted by a pediment and by the groups of giant pilasters at each end.

The Baroque in Rome

During the first decades of the 17th century, Roman architects such as Domenico Fontana (1543–1607) concentrated on being good craftsmen without deviating from the prototypes set up by their predecessors. The predominant style was a strict classicism, represented, for instance, by the façade of Santa Susanna by Carlo Maderno (1556–1629), a simple variation on the theme of two superimposed Orders; with its rhythm of closely spaced pilasters, this church stands out in strong contrast to contemporary compositions like Santa Maria in Vallicella and San Gregorio.

Under the Barberini Pope Urban VIII (1623–44) a new generation of architects emerged. Chief among them were Bernini (1598–1680), Borromini (1599–1667), Pietro da Cortona (1596–1669), Longhi (1602–60) and Rainaldi (1611–91). These architects revived the experimental approach of the Renaissance, handling the classical Orders in a free and exuberant manner which contrasted strongly with the strict austerity of their predecessors, and which came to be known – incorrectly – by the generic title of "Baroque". They had in common an admiration for antiquity and a reverence for the great creations of Michelangelo; however, their interpretations of this dual tradition and their conceptions of spatial values differed widely.

Gianlorenzo Bernini, like Michelangelo a brilliant sculptor and master of all the arts, created a rich and theatrical style of architecture, distinguished by its use of gold and different coloured marbles (as in Sant'Andrea al Quirinale) and dramatic lighting effects (as in the Scala Regia of the Vatican, 1663–66). The favourite of two popes, Urban VIII and Alexander VII, Bernini worked on a grand scale. While he had a liking for the dynamism of the oval plan (as in Piazza San Pietro and Sant'Andrea al Quirinale), his work is characterized by extreme clarity of line and the perfect regularity with which he used the classical Orders. It is not surprising that he regarded his rival Borromini as a "heretic". From Michelangelo's work he took grandeur, as exemplified in the Campidoglio, but not freedom of invention.

Unlike Bernini, and like Michelangelo, whose heir he was in this respect, Francesco Borromini refused to be restricted by the rules laid down by his predecessors, and to copy slavishly the classical features of the Colosseum and the Theatre of Marcellus. "I was not born to be a copyist," he wrote. His knowledge of antique architecture was certainly more extensive than Bernini's; he was connected with a circle of learned antiquaries and was interested in the complex spatial ideas of late antiquity, whose variety was a spur to his imagination. The fantastic *campanile* of Sant'Andrea delle Fratte is a variation on an antique mausoleum, the Conocchia, which existed near Capua; the capitals with their inverted volutes – for which he was criticized by academics – were taken from those of the Villa Adriana, and the complex coffering in San Carlo alle Quattro Fontane, his first masterpiece, is copied from an antique pattern published by Serlio. He rejected the unifocal and orthogonal geometry of the early Renaissance, creating complex plans for his buildings, structured around several centres. His plans and decorations, always meticulously worked out, often had emblematic, even esoteric references. Although he enjoyed the patronage of one pope, Innocent X (Pamphili), for whom he restored the church of the Lateran in 1550, his main body of work was carried out for religious orders. His major works, San Carlo alle Quattro Fontane (1638–67),

Sant'Ivo della Sapienza (1642–50) and the Oratorio di San Filippo Neri (1640), were built in modest materials – brick and stucco – and their effect therefore derives solely from the ingenuity of the designs.

An intermediate position was occupied by Pietro da Cortona, who worked mainly as a painter, and by Longhi and Rainaldi. Lacking the rich inventiveness of Borromini, they nonetheless used the language of the Orders with greater freedom than Bernini. This is particularly apparent in their numerous church façades with superimposed Orders. The façade of Santi Luca e Martina (1635–50) by Pietro da Cortona, one of the foremost expressions of the new style, is designed as a convex screen curving gently across the front of the church. In 1656 at Santa Maria della Pace, Pietro further distanced himself from tradition by creating a two-tiered, curved façade which appears somehow detached from the main body of the church. Martino Longhi il Giovane, at Santi Vincenzo e Anastasio (1646–50), articulated a design of six columns supporting three interlocking pediments, and for Santa Maria in Campitelli (1663–67) Carlo Rainaldi created a series of recessing bays.

The next generation was less daring, more affected by the influence of Bernini than by Borromini. Carlo Fontana (1634–1714) was the first exponent of the grand Roman style, of which the final masterpiece was the Trevi Fountain, completed 30 years after Salvi's design for it of 1732. Of Borromini's work in Rome little was retained but the inventive details: but his decorative vocabulary lived on in popular architecture, and during the first half of the 18th century, encouraged by the spread of French and German Rococo, it underwent a revival which extended far beyond Rome.

Scala

Piazza Navona

This piazza, which follows the plan of an ancient circus, was built in monumental style by the family of Pope Innocent X (Pamphili). It sums up the Roman style of the 17th century. The church of Sant' Agnese was designed by Borromini and Rainaldi, the two fountains are by Bernini, and Pietro da Cortona painted the gallery in the Pamphili palace.

Piazza San Pietro

The piazza of St. Peter's was built by Bernini for Pope Alexander VII between 1656 and 1667. It was intended as a grand extension of the basilica, where the faithful could gather to receive the papal blessing.

Sant' Andrea al Quirinale

Bernini regarded Sant' Andrea as his most perfect creation. The church was built for the Jesuits in 1678, on an unusual ground plan: an oval with the altar on the short axis. The façade is set between two concave walls, curving outwards from the elegant convex portico. The façade itself was inspired by Michelangelo's Palazzo dei Conservatori. The porch is flanked by two smaller columns to the scale of the door, set within a giant Order of pilasters to the scale of the nave. The interior walls are covered in delicate pink marble, and the dome is richly coffered. Here Bernini used his idea of "extended action" to great effect. An altarpiece depicts the *Martyrdom of St. Andrew*; above it, a sculpture shows the saint being carried up to heaven.

Santa Maria della Pace

Pietro da Cortona added this façade to a 15th century church from 1656 to 1657. Curved screen walls conceal the different style of the building itself, and a semi circular portico projects boldly into the little medieval piazza. Beyond the side doors, alcoves provide room for coaches to turn round. Note the interlocking pediments and the elegant use of travertine.

Sant'Ivo della Sapienza

This is Borromini's masterpiece. The courtyard had already been completed when, in 1642, the architect began the building, so he had to fit it in behind the double-storeyed arcade. Borromini chose a centralized plan, based on two interlocking equilateral triangles forming a six-pointed star with a single centre. The arms of the star are intersected by circular chapels, alternately convex and concave. The ground plan and decoration of the church are an allusion to the Temple of Solomon, seat of wisdom. The star of the ground plan recalls the Star of David; the dome is again decorated with stars, with winged putti heads and pomegranates. The *campanile*, crowned by the Flame of Truth, is reminiscent of a ziggurat. It is the antithesis of the Tower of Babel, a magnificent climax to the concave *exedra* of the courtyard, the many-lobed drum and the stepped dome.

France: the spirit of classicism

Under Henri IV, French architecture deviated little from the formulas established between 1560 and 1570. Between 1620 and 1650 a new generation of architects appeared: Jacques Lemercier (*c.*1585–1654), Pierre Le Muet (1591–1669), François Mansart (1598–1666) and Louis Le Vau (1612–70). They introduced schemes based on a stricter form of classicism, using the Orders with greater sobriety and ornament with greater economy. There was considerable development in the interior planning of châteaux and other secular buildings, while in ecclesiastical architecture the Italian style of the Counter-Reformation was widely adopted.

In the 16th century the façades of châteaux and *hôtels* came to conform with the new Italian ideal, but composition was still based on the contrast between the central *corps de logis* and the side pavilions with their high-pitched roofs. At the same time there was greater stress on the vertical lines of the bay-divisions than on the horizontal lines of the entablature and string-courses. In the 17th century, architects did away with these features and came closer to Italian design. During the 1630s there was a trend towards continuous roof-lines and after 1640 these decreased in size with the spread of the two-angled roof known as the "Mansard". During the 1660s, high-pitched roofs disappeared completely from important architecture.

Although traditional methods continued to be used in smaller buildings, with their timber frames, brick or stone walls and ashlar facing, in large buildings the picturesque colour contrast of brick and stone went out of fashion. Dormer windows and quoins rising from the foundations through the entablatures to the roof-line were dropped, and the classical Orders once more became the key element in the articulation of the façade. Just as poets and orators were simplifying their language and working on a broader scale, architects gave up elaborate groupings, artful spacing and the accumulation of small details and elaborate decoration. Instead they favoured the regular and majestic repetition of a single theme, or of carefully graduated schemes leading the eye to the centre of the composition. Like paintings of groups in which the composition is based on a central figure supported by secondary figures, the designs of Mansart, Le Muet and Le Vau were formulated around the central part, employing a play of simple contrasts – columns and pilasters, giant Orders and superimposed Orders, niches and porticoes. Ornaments, including masks, relief sculpture and decorative statuary, were used with discretion and incorporated only to accentuate the focal points of the design. A comparison between the riverside gallery of the Louvre, built by Jacques Androuet Du Cerceau and Louis Métézeau under Henri IV, and the Collège des Quatre-Nations built by Le Vau under Louis XIV, clearly illustrates the new French classicism and its sober use of the Orders; an even clearer example is provided by the alterations made to the façades of the Tuileries, again by Le Vau.

There were, however, great differences between the dry, austere style of Lemercier, the rich inventiveness of Mansart, whose façades are notable for their monumental solidity, and the sometimes rather confused surface effects of Le Vau.

Although there is no very clear link, this move into formality was accompanied by technical innovations and developments in interior arrangement. Mansard roofs made it possible to cover larger areas, encouraging the spread of the double *corps de logis*, which permitted more complex interior arrangements. Rectangular rooms with beamed ceilings were replaced by Italian-style salons with coved and painted ceilings.

Throughout the 16th century the Gothic tradition had remained very much alive in the building of large parish churches and some cathedrals, and at the beginning of the 17th century Gothic roofs were still frequently employed. However, the extraordinary blossoming of monasteries and colleges, resulting from the religious fervour of the Catholic reform movement in France, encouraged architects to look to the example of Italy. The men who built for the Jesuits, Oratorians, Ursulines and numerous other reformed orders, created churches with single barrel-vaulted naves; façades with superimposed Orders; centralized ground plans; and classical porticoes. In Paris, St. Joseph-des-Carmes (1612), St. Louis-des-Jésuites (1626–40), the church of the Sorbonne (1634–50) and the Val de Grâce (1644–66) mark the principal stages in the progress towards the definitive adoption of the classical style.

Church of Les Invalides, Paris

This church was built between 1679 and 1691 by Jules Hardouin Mansart, François Mansart's great-nephew, behind the "soldiers' church" of the hospital of Les Invalides. The architect had as his main inspiration his great-uncle's abortive plans for a Bourbon mausoleum in the church of St. Denis. Above the two-storeyed portico, the upward thrust of the dome, achieved by doubling the height of the drum, stands as a tacit criticism of the proportions of the dome of the Val de Grâce.

Church of the Val de Grâce, Paris

Begun in 1645, the church was commissioned by Anne of Austria in fulfilment of a vow. It was designed by François Mansart who directed the work until 1646, when he was replaced by Lemercier. The dome was not completed until after 1655 when Pierre Le Muet built it to a new design; he supervised the decoration of the interior until 1667. Standing well back in the symmetrical forecourt and with a wide stairway leading up to it, the façade is an original combination of the Italian themes of superimposed Orders and classical portico. The marked contrast between the projecting portico and recessed bay of the lower storey is reminiscent of similar attempts by Roman architects to enliven the traditional façade.

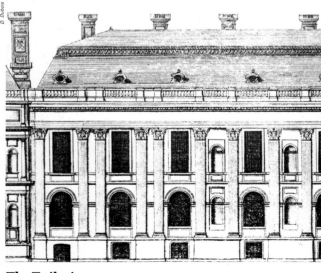

The Tuileries

In 1664 Louis Le Vau redesigned the façade of the west front of the Tuileries. A comparison between the original state of the *petite galerie* built by Jacques II Androuet Du Cerceau in the reign of Henri IV, and the new look created by Le Vau, clearly illustrates the new classical ideal. Du Cerceau's design is heavy with decoration and detail; Le Vau has simplified the giant Order of pilasters and drawn the composition together with a unified entablature.

Château of Maisons

(now Maisons-Laffitte)

François Mansart built this château to the north-west of Paris between 1642 and 1651 for René de Longueil, President of the High Court and later Superintendent of Finance. The composition is based on trios (three superimposed Orders, three pavilions and a triple design of two windows flanking niches and the central portal) and on a systematic gradation: the fairly low porticoes at each end balance the upward thrust of the centre, while the dormer windows of the pavilions balance the great triangular pediment.

Château of Vaux-le-Vicomte

To create this château Nicolas Fouquet brought together all the artists who were later to create Versailles. The architect was Louis Le Vau, the painter Charles Lebrun, and the gardens were laid out by Le Nôtre. The château (1656–61) is raised up on a rectangular platform. The traditional wings have been discarded and their places filled by two terraces. The service quarters in the basement look out over a false moat. The ground floor contains the reception rooms; the second floor, private apartments. The composition, unified by a series of horizontal courses, is enlivened by the contrast between the giant Order of pilasters on the corner pavilions and the two Orders of columns on the centre pavilion.

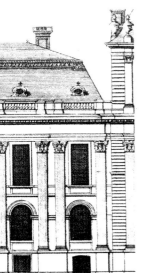

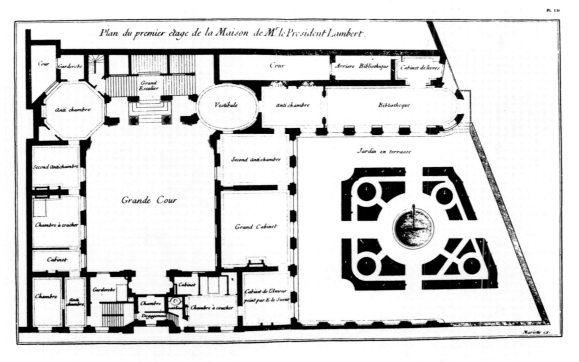

Plan du premier étage de la Maison de Mr le Président Lambert.

Hôtel Lambert, Paris

Built on the angle of the Ile St. Louis from 1640, the Hôtel Lambert is an example of the ingenuity of its architect Louis Le Vau in house planning. In the traditional layout (as in the Hôtel Sully) the *corps de logis* was placed at the far end of the court, with gardens behind it, and the wings were occupied by the service quarters and secondary apartments. Here the main apartment is set on the first floor of the right wing, overlooking the court and above the service quarters; on the other side it gives directly on to a terraced garden overlooking the Seine, with a large gallery running along its north flank. The left wing is occupied by private apartments. At the far end of the court a splendid staircase is set in a loggia.

Italian variations

Outside Rome, Italian architecture of the 17th century took a great variety of forms of which the generic label of "Baroque" simply does not take account. There is clearly nothing in common between the façades of Lecce, where luxuriant decorations conceal an archaic structure, and the dignified portico of the Superga, nor between the Salute in Venice, a brilliant variation on the centralized plan of the Palladian church, and Santa Sindone at Turin, where Guarino Guarini created his completely original conception of the dome.

Throughout Italy, developments in architecture paralleled those that have been described in Rome. During the early decades of the century a kind of classical reaction began in several cities. This was particularly noticeable in Venice with the work of Vincenzo Scamozzi (1552–1616), who turned the Palladian style into an inflexible system; it can also be seen in Milan in the work of Fabio Mangone (1587–1629) – for instance, his uniform colonnade around the court of the Collegio Elvetico. During the 1630s Baldassare Longhena (1598–1682) in Venice, Bartolomeo Bianco (c.1590–1657) in Genoa and Cosimo Fanzago (1591–1678) in Naples, like their Roman counterparts, inclined towards grandeur and pomposity, but their influence was only local. In Turin, on the other hand, the work of Guarino Guarini (1624–83), with its numerous innovatory experiments, stands out strikingly from the general scene. At the end of the century the grandeur of Bernini and the classicism of Carlo Fontana came together in the predomination of a more sober style of which the chief exponent was Filippo Juvara (1678–1736).

In many places, architectural activity was dominated by a reverence for the great works of the 16th century. This phenomenon was particularly noticeable in cities that had suffered economic difficulties, for which this era became a kind of Golden Age. In Florence, when the Pitti Palace was to be enlarged, Giulio Pangi's designs, reiterating Quattrocento themes, were chosen in preference to the more novel proposals of Pietro da Cortona. In Milan, an admiration for Pellegrino Tibaldi can be seen in the works of Lorenzo Binago (1554–1629) and Francesco Maria Ricchino (1583–1658), though the latter possessed more originality.

Even the works of the greatest architects, Longhena and Bianco, were designed along revered traditional lines, although they did achieve a new tension. Thus in Santa Maria della Salute, Longhena's masterpiece (begun in 1631), we can see the effects of his close study of Palladio's great works of San Giorgio and the Redentore. There is emphasis on the harmonic proportions between different elements of the church. However, the dramatic enlargement of the volutes and the wealth of sculptural decoration are in keeping with the new taste. Likewise, Ca' Rezzonico and Ca' Pesaro are brilliant variations on earlier palaces by Sansovino and Sanmicheli – even though the rustication and pillars have a slightly newer plasticity.

Similarly, in Genoa, Bianco took his inspiration from the Palazzo Strada Nuova. His masterpiece, the Jesuit College (1630), now the university, owes a great deal to such models, though the way in which the vestibule connects with the court, and the key role of the staircase, show a remarkable sense of scenography. In the palaces and villas of the period, there was a striking development in the deployment of staircases with a number of divergent flights. This seems to have been a general trend: it can be seen in Venice in Longhena's cloisters at San Giorgio Maggiore and in Naples in the work of Ferdinando Sanfelice (1675–1750). Between these works and those of Guarini there is a distance similar to that between the works of Bernini and of Pietro da Cortona and Borromini. Guarini's designs, which, according to the Neoclassic critic Milizia, could only appeal to madmen, can justifiably be described as "Baroque" in the sense of "bizarre". Guarini, born in Modena in 1624, became a member of the Theatine Order. He studied theology, mathematics and astronomy in Rome, which gave him the opportunity to study Borromini's early works. While teaching philosophy, he drew up designs for the Theatine churches of Parma, Messina, Paris and Lisbon – all now demolished. In 1666 he settled in Turin where he built his masterpieces, in particular San Lorenzo, the Santa Sindone and the Palazzo Carignano. Like Borromini, the liberties he took with tradition were grounded in an advanced knowledge of mathematics and the desire to create elegance. However, whereas Borromini looked to the examples of late antiquity and was most interested in mural surfaces, Guarini's greatest interest was in vaulting, and he made a comparative study of the Roman, Islamic and Gothic systems. His masterpieces at Turin reconcile the majesty of Roman architecture with the lightness of Gothic vaulting and the illusion of infinity created by Islamic domes.

Certosa di San Martino, Naples

This charterhouse was built between 1623 and 1631 by Cosimo Fanzago, who worked for the monastery for 30 years. He began the decoration of the church – combining paintings, stucco and marble – but the building was not finished until the mid-18th century.

Santa Maria della Salute, Venice

Santa Maria della Salute, built in thanksgiving after a plague epidemic, was begun by Longhena in 1631 but not finished until half a century later. The dedication has a dual meaning: *salute* refers to both physical and moral health. Set on an island at the entrance to the Grand Canal, the church is approximately equidistant from St. Mark's, San Giorgio Maggiore and the Redentore – the last two by Palladio – but we cannot be sure whether Longhena was conscious of the scenic effect of this site. The geometrical elements of the church, notably the octagon, are stressed and it presents a homogeneous view from all sides. At the lower level of the façade, which echoes the themes and proportions of the interior, Longhena demonstrates something of a Palladian severity, but the great volutes that support the lateral thrust of the dome create a lively centrifugal movement.

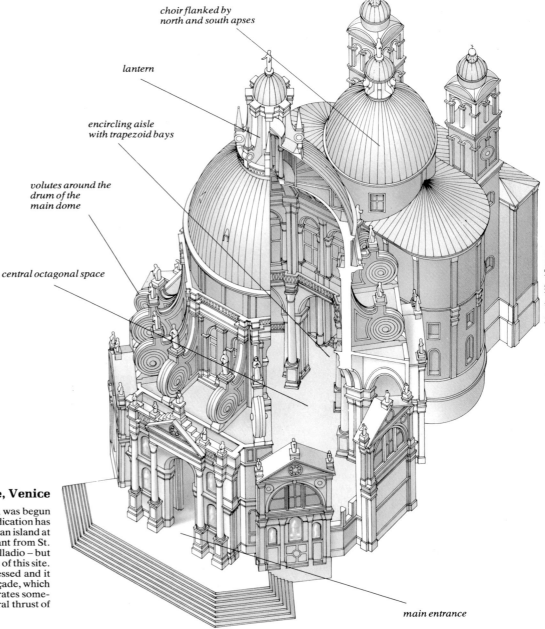

choir flanked by north and south apses

lantern

encircling aisle with trapezoid bays

volutes around the drum of the main dome

central octagonal space

main entrance

San Lorenzo, Turin

This church was begun in 1668 by Guarino Guarini for the Theatine Order, to which he belonged. Its plan is remarkable for the series of curved bays converging on the central domed space, an idea developed from Borromini. It is a masterpiece of construction: the system of ribs carries the lantern and creates a dramatic contrast of light and shade.

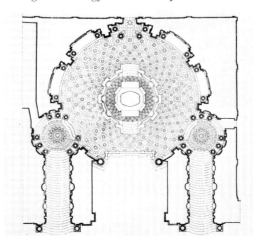

Cappella della Santa Sindone, Turin

Santa Sindone in Turin, Guarini's most dramatic creation, is a Palatine chapel housing the precious relic of the Holy Shroud. Built between 1667 and 1690, it has an unusual triangular plan, clearly an allusion to the Trinity. The chapel is sheathed in black marble, over which plays the pure white light that floods through the multiple ribbing of the dome. It provides the perfect setting for the liturgy of Good Friday.

The Superga, Turin

The church was built by Filippo Juvara between 1716 and 1727, in thanksgiving for the liberation of the city after the siege by the French in 1706. It stands high on a hill, 450 metres (1500 feet) above the city, and the dome and portico are designed to be seen from a distance. The centrally-planned church is fronted by a portico and adjoins a monastery. The heavy ribs of the dome, and the drum with its coupled columns, were inspired by St. Peter's in Rome. However, Juvara increased the height of both drum and dome, thereby arriving at extremely simple proportions in which dome, drum and the body of the church are all equal in height. The austerity of the portico is characteristic of Juvara's leaning towards classicism, but the crowning features of the monastery towers derive from Borromini's "Baroque" style. This combination is typical of the late international Baroque.

San Giorgio, Ragusa, Sicily

San Giorgio was built by Rosario Gagliardi between 1744 and 1766. Gagliardi, who had the same feeling for volume as the great Roman architects, produced some of the few genuinely Baroque churches on the island. Here the stairway, set at an angle to the church, leads down to a square. The façade is divided into three bays and the whole design draws the eye towards the central section, whose curve is accentuated by the columns. The surrounds are Rococo in style.

Santa Croce, Lecce

Despite the fact that the church, begun in 1582, took 60 years to build, the overall impression is one of stylistic harmony. It is an amalgam of local (Apulian) tradition, classical vocabulary and strikingly exuberant decoration, all merging into one another with no visible break.

Versailles: a classic residence

The spectacular and theatrical aspects of Versailles are well known: its façade 415 metres (450 yards) long, and its vast acreage landscaped with a sense of dramatic grandeur into terraces, water-gardens, shrubberies and walks. But most striking is the cohesiveness with which buildings and spaces are articulated. The palace lies between two zones which extend from the centre of it all, the King's bedroom. Towards Paris lies the town where the houses of courtiers and the quarters of administrative staff, servants and soldiers were re-grouped in a town-planning scheme. On the opposite side the park is surrounded by vast forests, once devoted to hunting and leisure pursuits and connecting with other royal residences, including Marly.

At Versailles the architectural decoration and garden statuary are designed to express the symbolic association of the Sun King with the sungod Apollo; the entire scheme was a manifestation of Louis XIV's absolute monarchy. As seen in the garden elevation, the play of forms is based on repetition and a controlled sobriety. In many ways it is the high point of what is known as French classicism. Most of the major talents in architecture, the fine arts and the decorative arts were placed in the service of Versailles, and this immense building, where work was constantly in progress, became one of the centres of the French art world until the end of the Ancien Régime. Versailles originally won royal favour for the game in its marsh-surrounded forests. Louis XIII had a hunting lodge built in 1623, which was rebuilt in 1634. It was then a small building of brick and stone with a slate roof, surrounded by moats. This typically French château still exists today, enclosed by the Cour de Marbre, at the centre of the palace. When he came to power in 1661, Louis XIV chose Versailles as a setting for his sumptuous fêtes; to improve it he summoned the men who had created Fouquet's great residence at Vaux-le-Vicomte. The architect Le Vau decorated the façades with statues, and Le Nôtre designed the gardens, landscaping the great axis of the Tapis Vert (Green Sward) and Grand Canal. Pavilions were built to house courtiers during the King's visits, and these formed the beginnings of the new town, between three avenues radiating out from the palace.

After 1668, at the time of his first military victories, Louis XIV transformed Versailles into a truly royal residence. The painter Le Brun was summoned to coordinate proceedings, a key role which he fulfilled for 15 years. Le Vau drew up a plan which was followed after his death in 1670 by François D'Orbay. It consisted of enclosing the old château on three sides, leaving open its brick and stone façade towards the town. On the garden side, by contrast, the façade was to be of stone; it comprised a rusticated ground floor decorated with arcades, a main storey decorated with Ionic pilasters and with pillars on the projecting portions, and an attic floor crowned by a balustrade concealing the roof. The whole design was clearly inspired by Italian palace façades. To the north, the Grand Appartement, of which the marble decorations have survived in part, and the King's apartment were served by the famous Escalier des Ambassadeurs, decorated by Le Brun (and demolished in the 18th century). To the south lay the Queen's apartment (redecorated in the 18th century) with its marble staircase. Between the two, the centre of the façade was taken up by a terrace overlooking the garden.

In 1682 Louis XIV, who refused to live in Paris (the Louvre was not yet finished) decided to settle permanently at Versailles and to turn it into a centre suitable for a capital. From 1678 Jules Hardouin Mansart was in charge of the building works. He replaced the terrace with the Galerie des Glaces and built two large wings to the south and the north to house courtiers and senior officials. The decoration of the façade had to be modified to adapt to the new length of the elevation: on the main storey, arches were added to all the bays. However, Mansart failed to persuade Louis XIV to do away with the slate-roofed brick and stone building on the town side. On the Place d'Armes in front of the palace he built the two sets of stables from which the three avenues lead. In 1684 he built the huge Orangerie below the Parterre du Midi (South Terrace) and in 1687, with the assistance of Robert de Cotte, he constructed at the far end of the park a secluded pavilion where the sovereign could relax: the Grand Trianon, a one-storey marble building whose walls extend to the surrounding shrubbery. Finally, again with the help of de Cotte, Mansart designed the chapel, which was finished in 1710.

Under Louis XV, the interior decoration was altered with the introduction of elegant and elaborate Rococo schemes. Jacques-Ange Gabriel, the King's chief architect, embarked on a huge project to rebuild the palace on the town side in "classical" style, but it was only possible to complete one wing, in 1772. Despite the state of the Treasury, in 1770 he managed to complete the Salle de Spectacle, taking as his main inspiration Palladio's inner colonnade at the Teatro Olimpico in Vicenza. On the eve of the Revolution, architects succeeded in introducing Neoclassical taste to the interior decoration, while the Hameau du Petit Trianon, built by Richard Mique from 1783, was a triumph of the picturesque.

Galerie des Glaces

Created between 1678 and 1684 by Jules Hardouin Mansart in the main storey of the central building, the gallery overlooks the park and is 73 metres (more than 200 feet) long. Opposite the 17 windows, 17 arched mirrors reflect the light, creating a radiant effect that was much sought after in the châteaux of this period. The decoration – like that of the Halls of War and Peace at each end – was designed by Le Brun who used a wealth of green marble, trophies of gilded bronze, and antique busts and statues. The ceiling consists of nine great paintings illustrating the life of Louis XIV, 12 medallions and six cameos, all painted by Le Brun; the programmes were by Boileau and Racine. Here Court functions took place, lit by crystal chandeliers. There were carpets on the floor and a rich collection of silver furniture (melted down in 1789).

Interior of the Chapel

This was the last building to be completed at Versailles at Louis XIV's command. It was begun in 1689 by Hardouin Mansart and finished by Robert de Cotte in 1710. It is barely visible from the exterior, and from the garden side only the roof can be seen. It consists of a very high, very light nave, terminating in a chapel at the court end. There are two storeys: the lower level is bordered by columns and arcades and the upper by tall Corinthian columns supporting a vaulted ceiling decorated with paintings. The gallery level, with the King's pew facing the altar, connects with the royal apartments. The decoration is outstandingly elegant, with its marble pavement and structure of finely grained white stone, permitting the carving of delicate reliefs.

The palace and the park

In the distance can be seen Jules Hardouin Mansart's long façade, its monotony broken by projecting bays with columns crowned by statues. The U-shaped centre section follows the outline of the Cour de Marbre (the remains of Louis XIII's château); the King's bedroom lies at the centre, and the Galerie des Glaces and Halls of War and Peace overlook the park. On the terrace the palace is reflected in the waters of the Parterre d'Eau. The axial plan chosen by Le Nôtre corresponds with the rising and setting of the sun. Below the palace lie the Parterre de Latone (Latona was Apollo's mother), and the long Tapis Vert (Green Sward) lined with statuary, which descends to the Bassin d'Apollon (not visible here), in which rises Apollo's chariot in gilded lead. In the foreground (again, out of view) is the Grand Canal. Le Nôtre was responsible for the combination of clumps of woodland and shrubbery, waterways decorated with marble statues and water-pieces with their painted or gilded sculpted groups. It achieves its full effect when the great fountains are playing. To the right of the Tapis Vert are the Bosquets du Midi (South Shrubbery) harbouring the Colonnade, and to the left, the Bosquets du Nord (North Shrubbery) enclosing among other things the Bains (Baths) d'Apollon, a conceit in the picturesque taste created in 1778 by Hubert Robert around a sculpted group by Girardon. On a level with the palace extend the Parterre du Midi (right), bordered at the lower edge by the Orangerie and the Escalier des Cent Marches, and the Parterre du Nord (left), leading to the Allée d'Eau and the huge Bassin de Neptune (not visible here).

The Petit Trianon

This small private house, set at a distance from the Court in the middle of the old botanical gardens, was intended for the mistresses of Louis XV but was actually lived in by Marie Antoinette. It was built by Jacques-Ange Gabriel between 1761 and 1764, possibly inspired by a design by Chalgrin. This small, square, isolated pavilion has something of the Palladian villa about it; the structure conforms to the model of the French château, yet the exterior elevations conceal an ingenious interior arranged for the greatest possible domestic comfort. Although it appears to open out on to the garden, the reception floor is actually placed above a basement floor which opens on to a little *cour d'honneur* facing towards the town. One side of the façade is decorated with columns, the other with pilasters, and there are half-columns on the side walls. The exterior decoration is very subdued, and is characteristic of Gabriel's approach to the new classicism.

The Colonnade

Hardouin Mansart built this circular structure in 1685 in one of the shrubberies landscaped by Le Nôtre. It consists of 36 columns in violet, blue and red marble, reinforced by pilasters and supporting delicate arcades and an entablature crowned with vases. This airy structure is completed by the play of the fountains – one under each arch. In the centre there was once a group sculpted by Girardon, *The Rape of Proserpina*.

England:
Wren and his contemporaries

Compared with architectural developments in the rest of Europe – especially in Italy and France – English architecture was characterized by its continuing individuality. Although it shared certain general trends with the great Continental models, they were subject to considerable variation and do not emerge clearly. On the English side of the Channel the eternal question of the difference between classicism and Baroque has become inextricably complex, and probably pointless. We are dealing here with a particular religious and historical situation. In England, with its Protestant, Puritan tradition, there was a natural resistance to the excesses of the Baroque. Side by side with official architecture, which had absorbed some French and Italian elements, domestic architecture continued to be greatly influenced by Dutch models.

A generation before, architectural innovation had crystallized around the work of an undoubted leader, Inigo Jones. But his Palladianism, linked more or less exclusively with a Stuart monarchy isolated from the rest of the nation, had had little influence outside Court circles. The second half of the 17th century, and the beginning of the 18th, were dominated by the outstanding figure of Sir Christopher Wren (1632–1723), whose great achievement was that he created a new and contemporary style more in tune with the traditions and character of the English nation.

Wren was a contemporary of Descartes and, more importantly, a colleague of Sir Isaac Newton in the Royal Society. He spent his youth studying physics and mathematics and became Professor of Astronomy at Oxford. He came late to architecture, but his scientific background had trained him to solve technical problems such as the stability of buildings and the construction of domes. From the start he put this experience into practice, building some time before 1665 the Sheldonian Theatre at Oxford; here, by means of a triangular system of grids, he succeeded in roofing a very large interior without using piers. Wren only left England once, to visit Paris, where he stayed for a few months between 1665 and 1666. This was at the time when the work on the Louvre was being completed, and he was able to meet Bernini.

Not long after his return to London in 1666 the Great Fire broke out, ravaging the City. As a member of the Commission set up to deal with the situation, Wren proposed an entirely new scheme of town planning, drawing up a plan based on a regular grid system of streets radiating from large squares. The citizens, however, objected, and rebuilt their houses on their former sites. Nevertheless, Wren was to have a fundamental impact on the London landscape: he was commissioned to rebuild St. Paul's Cathedral and was also responsible, to a greater or lesser extent, for the building of some 50 churches. The variety in the treatment of the plans of St. Lawrence Jewry, St. Mary le Bow, St. Clement Danes and St. Stephen's, Walbrook, bears witness to his originality. In designing these churches Wren was looking for a compromise between the traditional, longitudinal Gothic church and the centralized plan of the Renaissance and the 17th century, while at the same time referring to the Vitruvian style of basilica. He combined a Gothic structure – the spire – with classical architectural vocabulary to produce a wide range of steeples which herald the appearance of a "Protestant" style of Baroque.

In 1669 Charles II appointed Wren Surveyor General to the Crown. Around this time began the long and complicated story of the building of St. Paul's Cathedral. The architect had to abandon his original plan in the form of a Greek cross and from 1675, when the first stone was laid, until the completion of the dome in 1710, he continued to introduce hundreds of modifications to enhance the monumental character of the building. On the exterior, the great "Roman" dome was allied to a classical façade of superimposed colonnades, surmounted by towers of Baroque inspiration. In his official capacity, Wren also built a large number of secular buildings, including Trinity College Library, Cambridge (1676–84), a perfect example of the use of classical Orders, and the Royal Hospital, Chelsea (1681–91). The new king, William III, commissioned him to rebuild Hampton Court Palace, where he was able to exploit the contrast between brick and stone to break the monotony of the long façades. But his masterpiece was Greenwich Hospital (1696–1702), where he conceived a highly original structure to frame the Queen's House, built by Inigo Jones.

With the arrival of the Hanoverian dynasty in 1714, Wren's career took a downward turn. Like Jones, he had not founded a genuine school of architecture, but his friends and colleagues included Robert Hooke (1635–1703), the architect of Montagu House in Bloomsbury, famous for its French-style *cour d'honneur*; William Talman (1650–1719), who was influenced by Roman architecture and built Chatsworth and Dyrham Park; and finally William Winde (died 1722) whose masterpiece, Buckingham House (demolished in 1825) was to be the epitome of the Baroque country house during the reigns of George I and George II.

Hampton Court Palace

The palace was built around 1520 for Cardinal Wolsey, who presented it to Henry VIII in 1526. The north and south wings, the Great Hall and the chapel were added by John Molton between 1531 and 1536. Wren at first suggested rebuilding the palace entirely; his plan was rejected as being too large and costly, so he compromised by rebuilding the eastern part between 1689 and 1701, respecting the Renaissance style of the original.

Chatsworth House, Derbyshire

Rebuilt between 1687 and 1696, this imposing mansion of the late English Renaissance is the work of William Talman, one of Wren's pupils. It consists of a superbly decorated suite of apartments placed round a central court. The east façade is notable for the fine quality of its decorative sculpture.

Tom Tower, Christ Church, Oxford

In 1681 the dean of Christ Church asked Wren to complete Tom Tower, the main entrance to the quadrangle, which had been begun by Cardinal Wolsey. The two lower storeys had been put up at the beginning of the 16th century in the late Perpendicular style. Wren decided on a Gothic style to harmonize with the original work, but in a simplified version. The octagonal tower with its "Tudor" dome is an original recreation of Gothic, with more style than a mere pastiche.

St. Paul's Cathedral, London

Old St. Paul's, a Gothic cathedral, had a Palladian portico added from 1634 to 1635 by Inigo Jones, but had to be pulled down after the Great Fire of London in 1666. It was rebuilt between 1675 and 1710. The plan is a Latin cross 140 metres (460 feet) long by 30 metres (100 feet) wide. At the crossing, eight piers carry the dome. The wooden model for Wren's earlier design has been preserved.

The drum of St. Paul's, London's most famous landmark, is an extremely complex structure. The huge, ovoid, outer dome was skilfully constructed above an inner, lower dome. Between the two, Wren placed a tall cone of bricks, reinforced by two iron chains; on this cone rests the lightweight timber dome covered in lead sheeting which in turn carries the heavy stone lantern, globe and cross. Light falls on to the crossing through eight triple openings in the dome.

Thirty-two buttresses surround the drum, finishing in engaged columns to create the effect of a peristyle. Every fourth inter-columniation is filled in by a wall decorated with a niche, reinforcing the stability of the dome. The balustrade around the top of the first drum was added against Wren's wishes; he considered it to be in poor taste.

The two Baroque towers flanking the west front and framing the dome are more than 60 metres (200 feet) high. They were not included in Wren's early designs, being added only in 1708. There is a clock in the southern tower and a belfry in the northern one.

The portico on the west front has a two-storey design of coupled Corinthian columns, echoing the theme of coupled pilasters which is repeated around the exterior of the building.

International Visual Resource

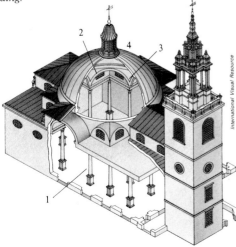

International Visual Resource

St. Stephen's, Walbrook

Built between 1672 and 1687, this church is one of the most interesting examples of Wren's work prior to St. Paul's. The interior plan is a perfect rectangle, broken into five unequal spaces by four rows of Corinthian columns (1), eight of which support eight arches around the crossing (2), which support the octagon. Pendentives (3) support the circular base of a lightweight dome in wood and stucco (4), possibly the first of its kind in England. Here the complex treatment of the interior space approaches the Baroque.

Sheldonian Theatre, off Broad Street, Oxford

Gilbert Sheldon, Bishop of London, former Warden of All Souls College, wanted to endow Oxford with a new secular building where university ceremonies could be held; he asked Wren to be the architect. Wren took his plan from the Theatre of Marcellus in Rome, which he knew from Serlio's prints. He solved the problem of roofing by inventing a truss on a triangulation system, which supports the huge painted ceiling. The exterior eschews classical monumentality; the flat façade is simple, with superimposed Orders; the curved part consists of arches supporting an upper storey containing large windows.

A.F. Kersting

311

Bastioned fortifications

In Europe, from the middle of the 16th century, the simple stone curtain walls of the Middle Ages were no longer a sufficient defence against siege, either for castles or for towns. Until then, although cannons had been invented in the 14th century, the art of fortification had changed relatively little, apart from the reinforcement of walls, the building of artillery platforms or casemates housed in the escarpments, and the installation of cannon towers pierced with numerous firing holes and of bulwarks or battery platforms in front of the ramparts (also, false screen walls at the foot of the main walls). With the invention of the cast-iron cannon ball in the 16th century, a new kind of fortification was needed, and military engineering became a specialized branch of architecture. Cannons could now be considerably reduced in calibre, and the heavy medieval mortar, which was hard to move around, was replaced by smaller, more mobile versions. At the same time, firing range was increased, so that the besieged had to find new ways of defending themselves against the ever-more powerful effects of cannon fire; this led in particular to the development of bastions.

Changes to existing buildings were slow to come about during the 16th century, for tradition imposed heavy constraints. However, the foundations for change had been laid in the work of Italians such as Francesco di Giorgio Martini (1439–1501) and even Leonardo da Vinci (1452–1519); in their treatises and works on architecture they had included several designs for fortifications surrounded by star-shaped outer defensive walls. Similar ideas can be seen in the work of Antonio da Sangallo (1455–1535) at the Castel Sant' Angelo in Rome and at the fortresses of Civitavecchia and Florence. These Italian models mark the beginnings of bastioned fortification, but their structures, although geometrical, were still simple. This system of defence was intended primarily for towns, which were easier to adapt to military requirements, rather than for existing castles, which were more difficult to modernize.

Completely effective flanking was not created until the years 1530–40 by the engineer Paciotto, at Turin, Cambrai and finally Antwerp. This type of fortress was surrounded by a rampart or a large earthen parapet covered with masonry, laid out in a broken line outside which were placed a whole series of types of "outworks", separated by ditches.

These outworks, usually built of masonry-covered earth like the rampart, at least doubled the depth of the defence, and could more effectively resist the cannon of the attacker. For two centuries European military engineers worked at adding to these outworks in order to increase the number of obstacles facing the enemy. Including the glacis, the area of fortification now extended several hundred metres in front of the main wall. In addition, the defence works were given a triangular outline, to offer less of a target for frontal attack. Firing galleries, placed at escarpment level, kept any approach under constant threat of fire, or cross-fire, from one bastion or another. The triangular shape of the fortifications is not always easy to make out today, due to demolition or deterioration.

Eventually these methods were adopted all over Europe: in Spain by P. Navarre at Lerida and Barcelona, in the Netherlands by S. Stevin, and in Germany by D. Speckle, who worked at Basle and Strasbourg and also at Oslo. In France these methods were initially applied tentatively and partially, for example at Thérouanne where a bastion was added to the western corner of the medieval keep. The building of Vitry-le-François by François I in 1545 was more significant, although the bastions were too far apart and there were no outworks. This building also underlines the pre-eminence of Italian engineers employed in France (in this case Girolamo Marini) for several decades to come. Only at the end of the century did the French school begin to develop, thanks to theoreticians like Jean Errard of Bar-le-Duc (1544?–1610), Antoine de Ville (1596–1657) and Blaise de Pagan (1604–65) who set themselves the task of solving the problems of flanking.

These investigations continued during the first half of the 17th century, and the tradition was continued by Sébastien Le Prestre de Vauban (1633–1707) and his rival, the Dutch Menno van Coehorn (1641–1707).

Vauban, an outstandingly skilled engineer, based the principles of his military work on the tactical and strategic requirements of his day. His work falls into three stages, referred to by his successors as his "three systems"; a study of these enables us to appreciate the improvements brought about by the French marshal. Their evolution is marked by the decision to increase the defensive area by arranging the works, particularly the outworks, at the front, in a series of zig-zags. The surface area of towns was reduced in relation to that of the fortified zone; at Huningue on the Lower Rhine, one of Vauban's creations, the fortifications were eight times larger than the town. Increasing the number of defence works or earthworks covered in masonry had the effect of keeping the enemy at a distance. The fortified citadel inhabited by the garrison was placed at a distance from the centre of the town, as at Lille where Vauban also enlarged the fortified area to encompass all the defence works within the same line of bastions.

Another imperative was that the town wall should be as regular as possible, as can be seen above all in Vauban's work at Huningue, Neuf-Brisach and Sarrelouis. Vauban levelled off mountain sites like Mont-Dauphin, Toul and Bayonne. His treatment of towns was based on strictly military principles; he favoured a grid layout, with public buildings and houses placed functionally around a large, rectangular central square, and with the barracks next to the walls. Vauban was an architect, but one who was always alert to tactical considerations. A man of his times, he was able to adapt himself to the aesthetic demands of classical architecture and also, often, to transcend them.

Vauban's posthumous reputation improved the standing of his successors in the 18th century, Louis de Cormontaigne (1697–1755), Jean-Claude d'Arçon (1733–1800) and Marc-René de Montalembert (1714–1800). This last, unlike Vauban, recommended an offensive line made up of forts standing free of the town walls and a flanking of batteries set in trenches. The artillery, instead of being in the open air, was to be enclosed in domed fireproof casemates. Montalembert's theories received only limited acceptance in France (for example at Lyons, where the town was surrounded by detached forts around 1830). By contrast they received a favourable welcome in the German states, where they were often put into practice, as at Cologne.

The development of grooved artillery after 1860, especially at the time of the 1870 Franco-Prussian War, forced military engineers to adopt different methods. The age of the bastioned fortification was over, and the age of the armoured underground fort had begun. This type of defence persists today, with concrete bunkers buried more and more deeply in the earth against the possibility of nuclear attack.

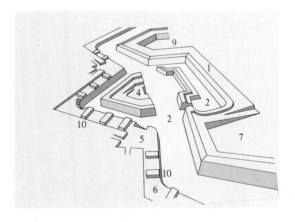
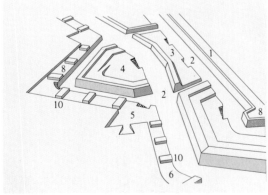
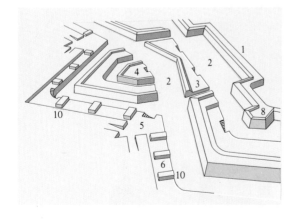

1 *curtain*	3 *tenaille*	5 *battery*	7 *orillon bastion*	9 *straight-sided bastion*
2 *trench*	4 *demi-lune*	6 *open path*	8 *bastioned tower*	10 *cross walls*

Vauban's "three systems"

Vauban's chief aim was to adapt his fortifications to the topography of the site. His first system was not very different from earlier bastioned lines. The bastions are large in size and a third of the length of their sides is taken up by an orillon, a rounded section protecting the bastion walls from enfilading fire. The curtain is surrounded by a parapet and protected from the front by a bastioned tenaille. The outworks are relatively undeveloped and all the defence works are linked to each other by trenches. In the second system the defence works are extended and set out in two independent lines. The exterior one is composed of bastions detached from each other; the second, the safety enceinte, consists of bastioned towers linked by long curtains. The third system is simply a refinement of the second, with improvements to details such as broken curtains and redoubts added to the demi-lunes.

Castel Sant' Angelo, Rome

Built as a mausoleum in the reign of Hadrian (died AD138), it was turned into a citadel between 1544 and 1565, with four orillon bastions at the corners, and connected with the city walls of Rome so that it could be used as a refuge in a surprise attack. It was further altered in the 17th century.

Citadel of Besançon, Doubs

Besançon was handed to the French by the Treaty of Nimègue in 1678. It was immediately fortified by Vauban, who improved the earlier fortifications, in particular the citadel which dominated the town. The bastions were connected to the gates by bastioned lines and a bridge was built over the ravine below the eastern walls.

Mont-Dauphin, Hautes-Alpes

An example of a mountain site, Mont-Dauphin was built by Vauban from 1693 on a plateau over 1,000 metres (3,000 feet) up, at the junction of the three largest valleys of the Queyras. To the left, one of the north-eastern bastions is crowned by a watch tower. In the centre is a wide trench about ten metres (33 feet) deep, and to the right is a counterguard.

The Porte de France, Mont-Louis, Pyrénées-Orientales

In 1679 Vauban recognized the importance of this site for guarding the Franco-Spanish frontier. The fortifications took ten years to build. The noble appearance of the gateway contrasts with the rough finish of the curtain, built of uncut stone. In the background can be seen an orillon bastion topped by a look-out turret.

Neuf-Brisach, Haut-Rhin

The town of Neuf-Brisach was built entirely by Vauban, from 1699. The regularity of the terrain enabled him to create an octagonal plan, to which he applied his third system. The bastioned towers on the wall are nearly 300 metres (330 yards) apart, protected by wide counterguards and by tenailles. The outworks surround the walls in a regular plan; the casemates and demi-lunes are equipped with redoubts. Inside, the layout is functional, with a church overlooking the central square and civic buildings; the houses are built in large square blocks and the barracks are next to the wall. The building works were completed in 1712.

View of the port of Bordeaux

This detail of a landscape painted by Joseph Vernet in 1758 shows the quays of the Place Royale from the gardens of the Château-Trompette. The opening up of town on to waterfront is one of the major themes of urbanization in the 18th century. The economic rise of Bordeaux at this time is manifested in particular by the doubling in area of the town and the embellishment of the outskirts of the old city centre. The Place Louis XV (nowadays called the Place de la Bourse), the work of the Gabriel family, father and son, is a mark of the town's affection for the monarchy, and at the same time testifies both to the progress of the arts and to the prosperity of the century. This painting by Vernet forms part of a series of views of French ports, which were officially commissioned, clearly showing the renewed interest in "portraits" of urban architecture. (Musée de la Marine, Paris.)

Among all the different stages of civilization, the 18th century stands out as an era of dazzling brightness. From enlightened despotism to the "Declaration of the Rights of Man and the Citizen" (1789); from the founding of the French East India Company (1719) and the monetary system of John Law to the independence of the colonial states of America (1776) and the birth of the modern economy in England; from Voltaire to Goethe, from Marivaux to Sade, from Bach to Mozart, from Tiepolo to David; from Diderot's Encyclopédie (1751) to the discoveries of Lavoisier and the inventions of James Watt (who perfected the steam engine around 1780): the impressive development of the arts and sciences in the 18th century is reminiscent of the intellectual brilliance and decline of dogma at the dawn of the modern era. The remains of the feudal system were destined to

some kind of nostalgia, represents a rediscovered and promising continuity.

Insatiable curiosity, a thirst for greater knowledge, the spirit of enterprise and a belief in a better social order to come, all combined to triumph over obscurantism. Religion declined sharply. A wave of rationalism attempted to redefine the rules of humanism. Genuine freedom of expression vanquished the dark forces of the soul: sentiment, sensitivity, instinct – in short, human behaviour – seemed able to break loose from moral restraint.

Man was presented with the concept of universal relativism. He worshipped Newton and made a veritable liturgy of philosophical thought that was rich in paradoxes. The spread of knowledge, the new freedom of thought and discussion, gave direction to the ideals of the

the earliest years of study, in his Plan d'une université for Catherine the Great (1775).

The art of drawing was considered the absolute basis of sound education. It became one of the most highly-developed branches of professional apprenticeship, not only for the architect, but also for the workman and artisan in the building professions and applied arts. In France, the academics of course played a leading role, as did the newly-established schools of civil and military engineering; these in turn were complemented by the new schools of drawing – the first example of free primary education in France. As at the end of the 16th century, but on a much larger scale, decorative and architectural prints were produced in great abundance. At the same time, theoretical texts attracted unprecedented interest. Periodicals devoted an increasing number of articles to architectural and urban "achievements", thereby showing that theory was not the prerogative of architects alone. The enlightened aristocrat, the meddlesome philosopher, the critic, the essayist, the politician, the magistrate and the Jesuit father showed themselves "disinterested citizens" – according to the title of an essay on town planning dating from the middle of the century – and theorized about architecture and the embellishment of towns. One of the bestsellers of the period – indeed, a remarkable work – was the Essai sur l'architecture, published in 1753 by Père Laugier.

The Renaissance spawned the architect-humanist. The Age of Enlightenment created the architect-philosopher, poet and painter. The Frenchman Claude-Nicolas Ledoux perhaps best represents the ideal "Enlightened" type. His masterpiece of 1804, L'Architecture considérée sous le rapport de l'art, des moeurs et de la législation, a vast collection of his buildings (constructed, planned or dreamed of), is a pure product of the old century – although the text, unique in its high-flown originality, foreshadows a number of Romantic traits.

The theory of architecture, however far-reaching and revolutionary it might be, must not cause us to forget other new aspects of the architecture of the Enlightenment. One of the reasons for the infatuation of the period with the art of building was without doubt a changing perception of the surrounding world. An analysis of perception and understanding, broadly developed by the empirical philosophy of Locke and Condillac, was at the root of this new-born science, to be known as aesthetics. The critic, the spokesman for public opinion (another

Façade of an Andalusian chapel. This graceful façade of a Baroque chapel in Estepa, a village situated near Antequera, shows a harmonious fusion of abundant yet clearly structured ornamentation and a taste for polychrome stone set against a plain white plaster background, typical of Andalusia.

disappear. The whole century worked towards the goal of creating a new society, but in fact this society was not properly established until after the French Revolution. The prospect of happy and grateful future generations spurred on the enthusiastic reformers who identified with the sages of ancient Greece and Rome. Western civilization, as if undergoing a second Renaissance, forged new direct links with its origins. The columned architecture of the 18th century, far from expressing

Enlightenment, of which the decisive tools were the book, the press and teaching in all its forms, both theoretical and practical. Art itself and the theatre – the rage of the century – became didactic. Architecture was clearly not forgotten in this path towards greater knowledge. Like the pictures of Greuze and Hogarth, it became a source of education, the vehicle for private and public ethics. In fact, Diderot included the teaching of architecture, or rather the art of building, as a compulsory subject, from

THE AGE OF ENLIGHTENMENT

creation of the century!), held forth about the effect produced by works of art or monuments; his pursuit of an ideal beauty was untiring, although in reality he knew it to be unattainable.

18th century architecture has a theatrical, playful quality that draws its inspiration from a long tradition of graphic and pictorial representation. In this period opera sets, etchings, vedute or view-paintings and painted and drawn architectural "caprices" became a major influence on actual building. Paintings of towns, architectural landscapes and ruins by artists such as Pannini, Canaletto, Bibiena and Hubert Robert conditioned the way architects wanted their buildings to be seen although new techniques and effects were also evolved by the architects themselves. The influence of Piranesi,

although his architecture in all its mystery and grandeur exists only on paper, was of prime importance and underlines the power of images in the 18th century.

One of the main characteristics of the period was awareness of the environment, past, present and future, and the capacity for architectural fantasy, at home, in the city and in the country. Formal gardens in the grand French manner were gradually replaced by landscaped gardens in the English fashion. The dairymaid frolics of Marie Antoinette reflected a general enthusiasm for country matters, although the artificial convention of the pastoral was soon to be swept away by the naturalism of Rousseau. This was the period in England when the beauties of the Lake District were discovered, and when "Gothic" ruins were causing flutters in hearts of sensibility. The

"picturesque" taste invaded not only gardens, but also the mansions that they surrounded – an English country house could be consciously modelled on a castle in the background of a painting by Claude. There was a movement away from the Sublime, away from the pomp of Louis XIV's Versailles; the "picturesque" included a taste for a little wilderness, for Dutch genre painting, for Chinese pavilions, for druids, for the weird and for the fresh.

In general, comfort and elegance were the keynotes of the new way of life. Towns were transformed by the provision of malls, urban walks and public gardens; nature was introduced into the city, while the countryside became more urbane.
In England and France in periods of peace fortifications might be converted into

Baroque architecture in Spain, Portugal and their colonies

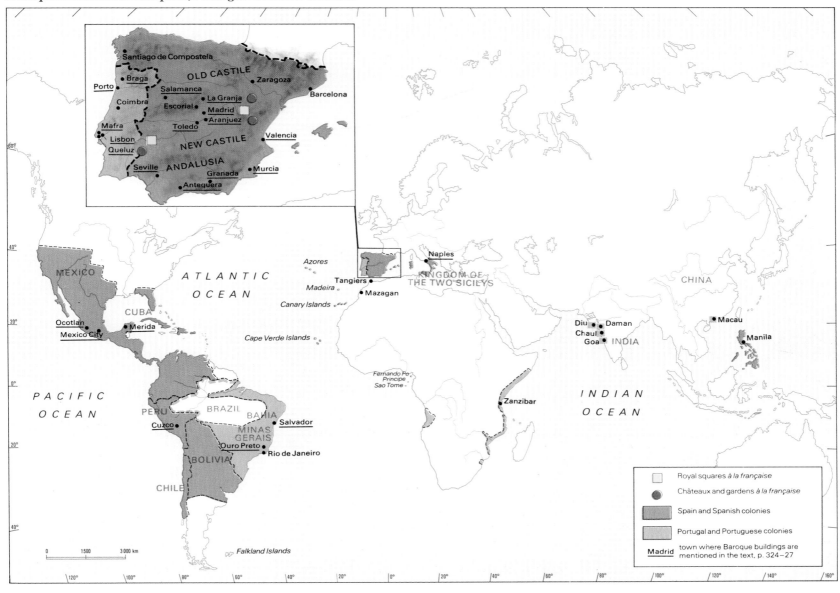

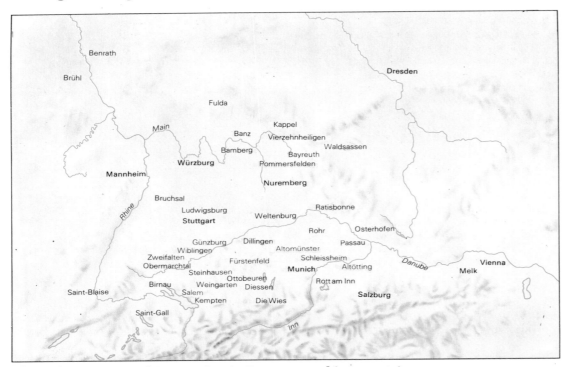

The main Baroque and Rococo sites in German-speaking countries

avenues lined with elms and lime trees. In towns the garden, an enclosed space, subservient to domestic needs since the Middle Ages, began in this period to develop and to become one of the essential features of the urban landscape. The river banks on which so many cities were built were also now exploited: grand façades rose along the quays, while houses disappeared from the bridges. Above all, streets and squares were systematized, creating new relationships between private buildings (which tended towards mansion blocks as we know them) and public ones. Water supplies were improved – more water hydrants, aqueducts and fountains; granaries, covered markets, slaughterhouses, theatres and hospitals were erected, illustrating the general need for greater comfort but also the important role of public building in the 18th century. The increasing complexity of local

administration was due to an increase in population; the exchange of goods, facilitated by the improvement of roads and the expansion of shipping and international trade, forced new relationships between the urban and rural worlds.

In the industrialized 19th century the triumph of the middle classes ("the new order, and they pay," commented Louis-Sébastien Mercier at the end of the reign of Louis XV) would be evident to all in the slum districts and suburbs: in the 18th century, outskirts were incorporated into the city but remained economically agricultural. The middle classes, however, had made themselves at home. The patronage of bankers, merchants, dancers and the doyennes of fashionable salons rivalled that of the nobility, the Court and the Church. The architect could even become his own client as a result of speculation and a rise in his social status. Some historians have discerned in Daniel Defoe's Robinson Crusoe (1719) symbols of the new era, describing the book as "a novel celebrating the energy and optimism of self-sufficient man".

It would, however, be simplistic to judge the 18th century in terms of progress and change only. Many different nuances, even exceptions, varied the main trends in different countries, regions and decades. The concept of Enlightenment is a label for a general movement which culminated, without any decisive break, in a total upheaval of civilization in the 19th century. The 18th century, however, was aware only of carrying on the tradition of the Renaissance and the Baroque, though renewing its methods and aims. It was not until the second half of the century, and only in one or two countries, that the irreversible effects of changing attitudes towards architecture became apparent. Economic expansion, philosophical and scientific curiosity, the taste for the "grand tour" and other forms of travel, to say nothing of recurrent wars (though this era is traditionally thought of as peaceful), all encouraged a cosmopolitan climate which was to be crucial to the blossoming of literature, art and, in particular, architecture.

The Royal Crescent, Bath, England. This town, very fashionable in the 18th century, still exemplifies the harmonious blending of urban architecture with surrounding countryside. The picturesque layout of squares and avenues, according to a strict pattern of curves, was largely the work of the architect John Wood and his son, between 1754 and 1770.

But the internationalism of art in the 18th century, the pervasive spread of Neoclassicism, did not mean the eradication of local characteristics. We should not obscure the distinctions of place and time, or see the birth, development and extinction of different styles at different moments as being merely the manifestations of a general trend. Such is the diversity of architectural forms in the 18th century that it is all too easy to over-simplify the concept of "style", which has nothing to do with the spirit of the time. Gothic, for example, was regarded as incorrect only where the classical style was appropriate – it would do very well for a garden shed. The traditional labels – Baroque, classicism, Rococo, rocaille, Neoclassicism, Palladianism, Régence, Louis XV, Louis XVI – must therefore be applied carefully, or we shall get lost.

The Baroque tradition partially influenced European architecture of the period and totally dominated most of Latin America. 18th century Baroque, however, does not have the dynamic, strained yet solemn qualities that the Counter-Reformation had brought about in the 17th century. To grand plastic effects and fullness of forms, the 18th century preferred diversity, grace and lightness of contour; to a well-defined subordination and gradation of spaces, a smooth and harmonious sequence. But this did not exclude seriousness of purpose, as revolutionary Neoclassicism shows. And what was true in Paris or Turin might not be true in London or Madrid at the same time. Typical of the first half of the century, for instance, are elegantly light panelling, wrought-iron balconies, apparently weightless ceilings, and endless arabesques; equally typical of the same period are the pure or composite geometric masses of the "frozen Baroque" and the dazzling displays of relief sculpture on façades. London churches have nothing in common with those of Turin, and those in turn have no connection with the churches of Paris.

Heaviness and airiness can both be found in Piranesi, restraint and laxity in Ledoux, neo-Gothic and Palladianism in James Wyatt, rocaille and classicism in Boffrand – one of the neglected geniuses of the century. Choice of form was governed by sensibility rather than by academic system, although there was a common pattern of inspiration throughout the 18th century, despite the diversity of styles. A strong feeling of individuality was partially responsible for this stylistic wealth, but also the simultaneous availability of a great number of models.

A melting pot of ideas, forms, experiences and men: such is the cosmopolitan current that runs through the 18th century. The artistic imperialism of the Spanish and Portuguese colonies was gradually diluted by local characteristics. How could it have been otherwise when Madrid and Lisbon welcomed artists and architects of French, Italian, Dutch, German or English training and extraction? But two nations exerted the predominant influence on the period: one was Great Britain, newly constituted, proud of her efficient parliamentary system and set on a path of mercantile expansion; the other was France, with a long established nationhood, a language used by the whole of Europe, and the memory of the recent splendours of the Grand Siècle.

Architecturally, England asserted a fierce, insular originality which slowly but surely penetrated both the old and new continents. Anglomania spread through northern Europe and around the Mediterranean. At the same time, the artistic influence of France was gradually becoming ever more evident and forceful: all continental Europe came to employ artists trained in Paris. These artists seem to have settled easily in their adopted countries, ably responding to the mania for embellishment shown by the Enlightenment monarchs and propagating a courtly art inspired by Versailles. The architect Pierre Patte summed up a situation which remained true even with the development of international Neoclassicism. "Travel through Russia, Prussia, Denmark, Würtemberg, the Palatinate, Bavaria, Spain, Portugal and Italy – everywhere you will find French architects in key positions. In St. Petersburg, M. La Mothe is first architect; in Berlin, M. Le Geay; in Copenhagen, M. Jardin; in Munich, M. Cuvilliés; in Stuttgart, M. La Guêpière; in Mannheim, M. Pigage; in Madrid, M. Marquet; in Parma, M. Petitot." In Russia, the first – and best – architects of the reign of Catherine II were trained in Paris; one of their masters, Charles De Wailly, whose works are engraved in the Grande Encyclopédie, was asked to run the newly formed art academy in St. Petersburg.

Thanks to the quality and importance of these simultaneous influences, cold uniformity was avoided. In the Iberian peninsula, with its unshakable Catholicism, various tendencies coexisted: Italian Baroque and local tradition blended with an increasing taste for things French. To take another example, the rocaille brought to most of the German courts by Cuvilliés about 1740 merged completely with Austrian and Italian currents in religious architecture.

Rococo, which reached its apogee in the churches of Bavaria, consists of a merging of numerous borrowed elements, such as French rocaille, Roman Baroque and the very different Baroque of Piedmont. For a long time it was regarded as a kind of luxuriant offshoot of Baroque in general, but it is now considered an autonomous style. Parisian rocaille of the Régence, furthermore, together with its remote Venetian and Portuguese derivatives, resembles German and Austrian Rococo only superficially. This Rococo questioned the very principles of Baroque (movement and decoration applied in strong relief over an imposing mass and the counterplay of space and light); it rejected the plastic role of the wall in favour of a visually unified fabric, created entirely by ornament. This absolute organic principle was at the root of the Bavarian inclination for bright, radiant harmonies. Once the debt of Rococo to Borromini, Guarini, Meissonnier, Boffrand and Cuvilliés has been admitted, the transformation that takes place in the journey from the Rhine to the Danube becomes even more clear. The strongest, most striking currents of 18th century architecture all have in common the same

or Boullée in France, via the Grecian picturesque of the Adam brothers or Bélanger, the range is infinite. The essence of Neoclassicism, however, was not so much formal, depending on historical models, as ideal. References to nature and to the artistic perfection of the Greeks and Romans, a quest for balance, a desire for visual harmony subordinating ornament to structure and governed by ideal principles, all these gave reason pre-eminence over mere effect: there is feeling, but it is rationalized. Such had been the major characteristics of classicism since the Renaissance; the tradition of Alberti, Bramante and Palladio had been maintained, even at the height of the Baroque period, by Inigo Jones in England and by the Royal Academy of Architecture in France.

Naturally the 18th century, enriched by its own experience, brought a new diversity to the resurgence of classicism. New archaeological knowledge and the discoveries at Herculaneum and Pompeii once again focused attention on classical Rome. France and England shared the highest achievements of the Enlightenment, but it was Rome that reigned over international culture, her unique classical wealth and importance attracting artists of every kind to the Eternal City. Rome was the forcing-house of Neoclassical theory as developed by Caylus and Winckelmann; colonies of architects from all over Europe shared an admiration for Piranesi and met on the most prestigious sites, which they explored and revived in their drawings. The Forum, the Baths, Paestum, Praeneste and Hadrian's villa at Tivoli were the inspiration of the new style. The

Project for public baths at a spa. This detail from a large ink-and-wash drawing by Alexis Bonnet, which won second prize in an architecture competition in 1774, makes us realize the importance of drawing in 18th century academic training. The plan for the baths also shows a new concern for comfort and leisure but, at the same time, we should not forget the obvious references to ancient Rome.

tendency to transform their influences, whatever their formal vocabulary.

Even Neoclassicism, which began to unify all Europe under its white colonnades after 1780 (but which had already appeared in France and England as early as 1750–60), was much more diverse than is generally believed. From English Palladianism, established at the beginning of the century, to the revolutionary tendencies of Ledoux

intellectuals of the Enlightenment encouraged its diffusion. With considerable foresight, Voltaire wrote: "Those after me will achieve what I have imagined.... Your theatres will be worthy of the immortal works they will show. New squares and public markets built under colonnades will adorn Paris and recall ancient Rome." From London to Lisbon, Paris to Leningrad, Dublin to Trieste, urban architecture has proved this prophecy right.

The Rococo and its interpretation in France, Italy and Russia

It is generally accepted that the most characteristic ornamental features of Rococo were created in France. *Rocaille* is a mixture of spiky shells, barks and corals with free vegetable arabesques, often asymmetrical. Chicory leaves, twisted branches, palm fronds and flexible stems replace the acanthus, foliage and garlands of classicism and Baroque. Natural forms replace geometrical shapes while a taste for exotica, particularly *chinoiserie*, introduces a vocabulary of grotesque dragons and chimeras. Ornamental panels take on a life of their own, freed from their architectural framework; the eye is bamboozled in an intricate pattern of curves and countercurves. The French Régence (1715–23), with its love of grace and comfort and its intellectual and moral freedom, turned its back on the ordered affluence that prevailed at the end of Louis XIV's reign.

Reproduced in countless volumes of etchings, *rocaille* was adopted by the whole of Europe, from Portugal to Russia; but its influence during the Age of Enlightenment varied according to the country and the strength of native traditions. In Bavaria and Austria, Rococo was universal; in France, Italy and Russia, it blended with long-established classical and Baroque tendencies. If Rococo is ambiguous in these countries, this is because of the relationship between the ornamental and monumental in the creation of public or private spaces. In France, Rococo was generally limited to interiors – panelling in bedrooms or *salons*, sometimes vaults in churches and church furniture – although it occasionally showed through on façades. It even influenced monumental architecture by submitting classical order to the combined effects of sculpture and wrought iron. Façades were enlivened by cantilevered balconies resting on consoles, sculptured trophies, cartouches and palms inserted at the divisions of the wall. Rhythms were set by tall arched windows, and a perfectly balanced structure was no longer required; columns and pilasters were de-graded to the role of mere ornament. At first a strong academic movement, jealously guarding classical principles, attempted to protect official architecture from the seductive charms of Rococo decorators; it was only after the middle of the century that, despite their frivolity, their virtues were finally admitted.

It was in Paris that *rocaille* began, in the studio of Jules Hardouin-Mansart (1646–1708), first architect to the king. The vogue of *petits appartements* with large windows, mirrors and sculptured panels permitted the varied use of an ornamental repertory which was soon to spread to jewellery, ceramics and, in particular, furniture, becoming synonymous with the Louis XV style. Without forgetting their master's repertoire of châteaux and grand urban compositions, Mansart's pupils – Gilles-Marie Oppenord (1672–1742), architect to the regent, Germain Boffrand (1667–1754), architect to the duke of Lorraine, and, above all, the decorator Juste Aurèle Meissonnier (1653–1750) – succeeded in creating an elegant style better suited to the comfortable flats of Parisian society. Other artists equally famous in their time, such as Pierre Lassurance, Jean-Michel Chevotet, Robert de Cotte, Jean Aubert and Jacques Gabriel (1667–1742, father of Ange-Jacques Gabriel) all left numerous masterpieces in which traditional forms are interwoven with *rocaille* decoration – buildings like the former Palais Bourbon in Paris, the château of Champlâtreux, the Palais Rohan in Strasbourg, the stables at Chantilly and the Hôtel Peyrenc de Moras-Biron (now the Rodin Museum in Paris). Some of the façades for houses in Paris by the architect Pierre de Vigny (1690–1772) are remarkable for their picturesque sculptures, above all the former *Cour du Dragon* of the Hôtel Chenizot on the Ile St. Louis, of which fragments are in the Louvre. Had Meissonnier's project for the façade of St. Sulpice been built, it would have been a masterpiece of religious Rococo; as it is, the sculptures in the transept by Gilles Oppenord and the sumptuous panelled vestry are the only surviving remnants of Rococo taste. But numerous Gothic cathedrals were adorned at this time with choir screens, furniture and tombs in which *rocaille* flourishes.

In Italy, from Rome to the Kingdom of the Two Sicilies, Baroque influence was sustained until the middle of the 18th century. *Rocaille* was, however, important in the decorative arts. It is apparent in the fashion for inlays of rich, multicoloured motifs in mother-of-pearl, tortoiseshell, ivory and terracotta. A Rococo taste for illusionism – white stucco or gold arabesque frames creating a radiant, dazzling setting for airy frescoes – can be seen in the gallery of the archbishop of Udine, painted by Giambattista Tiepolo (1696–1770). Tiepolo's later works in the palaces of Würzburg and Madrid are prime examples of the wide influence of Venetian Rococo in the middle of the 18th century. It is, however, in Piedmont, in the circle of Filippo Juvara (1678–1736), that the Italian Rococo style found its most original architectural expression: Juvara's daring combinations and light-filled spaces are an enrichment of the personal Baroque of Guarini in Turin. Italian Rococo was soon exported to Russia, by Domenico Trezzini (who built the basilica of Sts. Peter and Paul) and above all by Bartolomeo Rastrelli (1700–71), who was responsible for the Winter Palace, the Smolny convent and several palaces for the Empress Elizabeth – notably Tsarskoye Selo, and the Strogonov Palace. But French Rococo also had its influence on the architecture of St. Petersburg as, with the accession of Catherine the Great, did French Neoclassicism. The famous interior decorator Nicolas Pineau stayed there for many years, with the architect Le Blond: his carved oak panels in the palace of Peterhof and the sculptures and fountains in the park there illustrate, with considerable panache, the Régence style outside France.

The Oval Salon, Hôtel de Soubise, Paris

Built by Germain Boffrand in 1737–40, this is the principal feature of a noble ensemble of several communicating *salons* and bedrooms overlooking the main colonnaded courtyard by Pierre-Alexis Delamair. The most famous painters of the time – Boucher, C. Van Loo, Trémolières, Restout and Natoire – decorated the panels above the doors with mythological and pastoral scenes in rich gold *rocaille* frames. Emphasizing the plan of the *salon* and accentuating the rhythm of the panels, mirrors and arched windows that open on to the garden, eight corner panels painted by Natoire illustrate the story of Cupid and Psyche after La Fontaine. The combination of painting and architecture is here brilliantly successful. Italy, with Tiepolo, would give more importance to frescoes, while Rococo Germany, with Cuvilliés, would exalt pure ornament – as in the Amalienburg Pavilion near Munich.

"Rocaille" façade, Nantes

City planning developed in Nantes in the second half of the 18th century, where one of the most beautiful Neoclassical urban landscapes was created. The superb façades in the Ile Feydeau and along the Quai de la Fosse, built around 1730–40 for slave-traders and rich ship-owners, deserve greater recognition. Here is a remarkable example, in which the wrought-iron balconies are arranged in a pyramidal sequence, the windows show a variety of patterns, and the flat wall is articulated by rich framing elements. Other façades in Nantes are decorated with luxuriant carvings evoking the oceans and continents, sources of their owners' wealth.

Façade of the Winter Palace, Leningrad

The Czar's former residence, built beside the Neva in 1754–64 by Rastrelli, is one of the largest palaces in Europe. It is now the home of the Hermitage Museum. A tranquil Order of white columns articulates the long, uninterrupted line of apartments, which are painted pale green. Luminous, contrasting colours are one of the characteristics of Russian Rococo, outliving Neoclassicism and continuing late into the 19th century.

Grand Salon, Stupinigi

The Versailles of Turin, Filippo Juvara's masterpiece, was conceived as a gigantic hunting lodge. Its flattened X-plan is extended on each side of an enormous *salon* by two wings containing apartments and domestic quarters. The main compositional feature is the central dome, surmounted by a large statue of a stag. Inside, arcades and galleries create light, picturesque spaces. The power and imagination of the decorative play are equalled only in the churches of Bavaria.

Railings and fountain, Place Stanislas, Nancy

These wrought-iron railings, together with spouting water and glittering gold paint, illuminate the architecture of the square; they open up views, revealing the surrounding greenery.

View of the three squares, Nancy

This space, adorned with colonnades, triumphal arch, fountains, gates and statues, stands as a symbol of the brilliance of the Ancien Régime. Stanislas Leszczyński, Louis XV's father-in-law, who "reigned" over Lorraine between 1737 and 1766, commissioned this splendid complex as a link between the old and new towns. The squares are conceived as promenades lined with trees (Place de la Carrière) and quiet places of contemplation (the present Place Stanislas, formerly Place Louis XV). Many official buildings line them, including the town hall, theatre, medical college, stock exchange and government offices. The architect, Emmanuel Héré (1705–63), was much influenced by his master G. Boffrand, who had already worked for the duke of Lorraine in Nancy and Lunéville. His exquisitely graceful architecture was a foil for the display of ironwork and statuary – the fountains and the statue of Louis XV (now destroyed) by the sculptors Cyfflé and Guibal, the famous golden gates by Jean Lamour. The Place Royale was begun in 1755.

The Austrian Baroque

There may have been a German "High Baroque" in the 17th century, but Austrian art was shaped after the pattern of Roman Baroque, above all that of Bernini and Borromini. In 1614, Solari began a vast project for the reconstruction of Salzburg cathedral, with three naves and a large cupola, and in 1627 he began the façade of the University church in Vienna, which recalled Jesuit façades in Rome.

But it was only at the end of the 17th century – mainly between 1690 and 1720 – that an original Baroque architecture emerged in the Austrian countries. The Catholic renewal following the Counter-Reformation and the assertion of power by the land-owning aristocracy caused buildings – especially pilgrimage churches and monasteries – to spring up all over the country; in the towns, the houses of the gentry were given new façades. With the end of the Turkish threat in 1683, the Hapsburg monarchy became confident of its power and patronized an art which, though still influenced by the Baroque of Rome and Turin, became very much indigenous. The most famous Austrian architect, Johann Bernhard Fischer von Erlach, lived over ten years in Rome; his first works, Holy Trinity (1694) and the Collegiate Church (1696), both in Salzburg, show a very striking interpenetration of volumes reminiscent of Borromini. Called to Vienna, he was given the title of first architect to the Court and soon made himself the leading exponent of the "Imperial Baroque". His vast project for Schönbrunn was intended to surpass Versailles, and envisaged a comprehensive monumental treatment of the entire

site. Fischer von Erlach sought grand effects: forms are majestic, spaces vast, the plan is clearly expressed and there are numerous references to the ruins of Rome. The façade of the Bohemian Chancery (1711), and above all the church of St. Charles Borromeo, are good examples. His sense of the colossal and his ability to reflect on the great buildings of the past are expressed in the book he published in 1721: *Entwurf einer historischen Architektur* (Essay on a Historical Architecture), a complete survey of the art of building from Stonehenge to his own day. His illustrations seem to have caught the imagination of European architects: they have influenced more than one academic project and have inspired some of the most famous Neoclassical "visions".

The other great architect of Baroque Vienna, Lukas von Hildebrandt, was born in Genoa and had visited Rome and Turin. He was trained as a military engineer and his work is less formal than Fischer von Erlach's. He did not work for the Court but for the aristocracy surrounding Prince Eugen. In Vienna he built the Daun-Kinsky Palace (1713–16), the staircase of which, decorated with putti, he later reproduced in the Mirabell Palace in Salzburg, and the famous Belvedere ensemble. Hildebrandt also built churches, such as Jablone (1699) in Bohemia. From Italian Baroque he derived his undulating surfaces, his refined choice of decorative elements and his interpenetration of spaces.

Meanwhile, in the Danube valley and in the Tyrol, the great abbeys were embarking on recon-

struction programmes. Jakob Prandtauer, a local master builder who had never visited Italy and who worked all his life for religious communities, produced some of the most powerful of all monastic Baroque architecture. He completed the Abbey of St. Florian, placing the staircase in a pavilion with open arcades, and began the Abbey of Durnstein (1717); but his masterpiece was at Melk, where he crowned a rocky peak overlooking the Danube with long façades opening up at the front, and conceived rich and refined interiors where details are strictly subordinated to the structure.

In Bohemia and Franconia religious buildings followed the tradition of the Piedmontese Baroque of Guarini, with complex vaulting and plans dominated by oval spaces. Noteworthy are the buildings of Christian Dientzenhofer and G. Santini-Aichel (a naturalized Italian) and, in Prague, of J.B. Mathey, who tried to maintain a more monumental version of Roman Baroque. Generally, architects tended to revert to a central, oval plan, stressing the movement of volumes with diagonal lines of columns or undulating cornices along the naves and emphasizing every crossing with a dome. Fischer von Erlach's son, Josef Emmanuel, attempted to carry on the "Imperial Baroque" tradition, using his father's plans for the Library and Chancellery of the Hofburg; at Schönbrunn, however, Pacassi's façades became more and more severe while in Vienna French influence is evident in the new wing of the University built in 1753 by Nicolas Jadot.

The Belvedere, Vienna

On a vast site on the outskirts of the capital, Hildebrandt created a grandiose residence for Prince Eugen, all-powerful conqueror of the Turks. He built the lower Belvedere first, in 1714, then in 1721 added the upper Belvedere on top of the hill. The entrance side of the latter, shown here, is reflected in an ornamental lake, which compensates for the slight heaviness of the proportions and the lack of well-defined articulation. On the garden side, the palace seems larger, since the ground floor (concealed by rising ground on the entrance side) is here fully revealed. In the centre, a vast, "transparent" hall pierces the façade. Hildebrandt made subtle play with the different levels and with the supple movement of the exterior walls. Sculpture took on an important role (in the illustration, the Atlas figures of the vestibule).

St. Nicholas of Malá Strana, Prague

Christian Dientzenhofer built the façade and the nave (1703–11) and his son Kilian Ignace, the choir, vault and cupola (1739–52), demonstrating the evolution of "Imperial Baroque". The plan recalls the church of the Gesù in Rome (this was to be the Jesuits' seminary) and the stucco pillars are built along a diagonal (reminiscent of Guarini); the movement extends to the galleries above the arcades. The large cupola is visible on the right, supported on columns, a luminous shaft of light counteracting the horizontal rhythm of the nave and chapels.

320

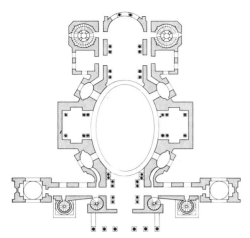

St. Charles Borromeo, Vienna

The church was built from 1716 to 1737, to the plans of J.B. Fischer von Erlach, in fulfilment of a vow made by the emperor during the plague of 1713. The votive character of the building, and the power of the emperor, are both expressed by the use of twin columns, inspired by Trajan's Forum in Rome. The façade, as is frequently pointed out, has no connection with the central plan of the church. The dome is ovoid, raised on a high drum. This highly original work successfully brings together Roman elements, a taste for vertical emphasis and a Baroque sense of theatre.

Imperial Library (now the National Library), Vienna

The front elevation and the plan are the work of Fischer von Erlach but the rest was completed by his son, from 1723 to 1735. Instead of a long rectangular gallery the architect has designed a series of niches, lightly accentuated by the balconies above, which permit access to the higher shelves. In the centre, the space opens out and is brightly lit from the cupola. The decorations of wood, gold stucco and frescoes emphasize the unity of the whole.

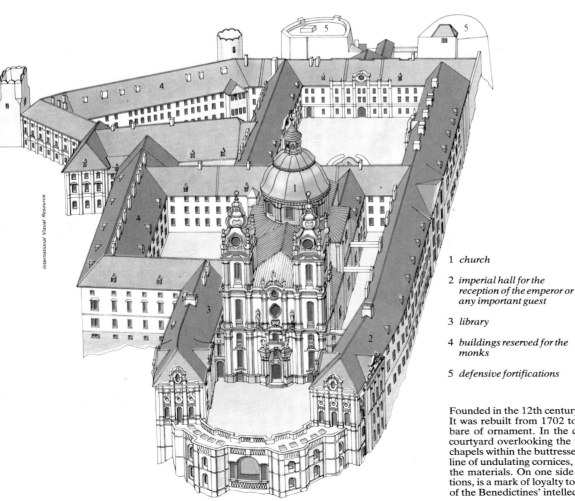

1 church

2 imperial hall for the reception of the emperor or any important guest

3 library

4 buildings reserved for the monks

5 defensive fortifications

Melk Abbey

Founded in the 12th century, the Benedictine abbey stands on a hill above the Danube valley. It was rebuilt from 1702 to 1740 to the plans of J. Prandtauer. The external elevations are bare of ornament. In the centre, the vast church crowned by a cupola faces on to a small courtyard overlooking the valley. The plan is longitudinal, and the nave is lined with small chapels within the buttresses. On both sides of the nave, rhythms are created by a continuous line of undulating cornices, galleries and arcades and reinforced by the richness and colour of the materials. On one side of the church the Emperor's Room, with its sumptuous decorations, is a mark of loyalty to the Hapsburgs; on the other, the magnificent library is a reminder of the Benedictines' intellectual achievements.

Baroque and Rococo in Germany

The great diversity of 18th century architecture in Germany was the result not only of political fragmentation, but also of local individualism under French, Italian and Austrian influences. The southern states were the most active in the 18th century but some important projects in the north should not be overlooked: in Prussia, for example, the now-destroyed Schloss Berlin, built by Andreas Schlüter in 1689 and, in Saxony, the astonishing Zwinger in Dresden, conceived by Pöppelmann at the beginning of the 18th century.

Remarkable developments in secular architecture took place during this period. Many of the princes wanted to create around them brilliant courts of artists and intellectuals, following the example of the great European capitals. Residences such as those at Mannheim and Ansbach and some palaces have formal suites where the "Emperor's Room" symbolizes loyalty to the Holy Roman Empire; the main staircase becomes a focal point and is decorated with theatrical extravagance (as at Pommersfelden or Brühl). Private apartments are decorated in a precious, often exotic, manner with the inevitable mirrored room. The Elector of Bavaria, an admirer of Louis XIV who was fascinated by Versailles, commissioned the building of Schleissheim by Zuccali and then Effner, to whom he also entrusted the creation of the Nymphenburg outside Munich, a summer residence set in a nature park.

The most important building project, however, was that of Würzburg, the creation of Balthasar Neumann, a foundry-worker turned military architect. In 1723 he went to Paris to present his plans to Robert de Cotte and Boffrand. In 1731 and 1736, the Austrian Hildebrandt came to work at Würzburg. Finally, in 1753, the prince-archbishop summoned the famous Venetian painter, Giambattista Tiepolo, to decorate the staircase ceiling and the Emperor's Room.

The major achievements in religious architecture are to be found in the Catholic states of southern Germany, where a strong popular faith encouraged the renovation and decoration of places of pilgrimage, often completely isolated in the middle of the countryside. The traditional hall-church plan, with chapels on each side of the nave framed by responds, was gradually replaced by a composite plan, a fusion of centralized and longitudinal elements. The building, often very simple on the outside, was flanked by a tall, bulbous belltower, while the dome above the crossing disappeared. The internal space was the most interesting feature, with daring arrangements, dynamic forms, and striking effects of lighting and colour. This kind of spatial drama, reminiscent of Bernini, can be found in the work of the Asam brothers, stuccoists and architects who used natural light and plaster reliefs to achieve spectacular effects. Their work shows a marked resistance to the Rococo tendencies which were first to triumph in Munich at the end of the 1730s. Here, French *rocaille* was reinterpreted by Cuvilliés, who decorated the apartments of the Munich Residenz (1730) and created the Amalienburg Pavilion and the extraordinary Residenz Theatre. He also published engravings of the new style of ornament. Decorators and architects were seduced by these and, rejecting Baroque monumentality, chose a lighter, almost abstract formal vocabulary where even structure became immaterial. Here sculpture dominates, and stucco reaches its apogee. At Zwiefalten and Ottobeuren, both by J.M. Fischer and the stuccoist Feichtmayr, or in the church of the Wies, by the Zimmermann brothers, architectonic elements tend to take second place, columns disappear into the walls and the walls themselves seem to vanish into the painted vault. Points of transition and articulation are denied; all is subservient to an ornamentation which transforms structural function by means of striking light effects and deceptive colours and materials. "The unfinished represented with perfect polish", Rococo maintained its impetus until Neoclassical forms took over, first in northern Germany, then in the south, with, for instance, the enormous cupola built by P.M. d'Ixnard from 1768 at St. Blasien in the Black Forest.

Church of St. John Nepomuk and the Asams' House, Munich

This complex was built by the stuccoist and architect Egid Quirin Asam with the help of his fresco-painter brother Cosmas Damian. The presbytery stands on the right of the small church and the architect's house on the left. The façade of the latter is richly decorated with stucco motifs glorifying architecture and the fine arts while the base of the building seems to emerge from the rock. The church – built from 1733 to 1746 – occupies a narrow space (only 9 metres/30 feet wide) and communicates with the architect's house. The façade has been conceived as a vast glass wall – it had to be, since there could be no windows at the sides; it emphasizes the structural elements – base, columns, entablature and cornice. The interior is famous for the expressive power of its plasterwork, both overwhelming and mysterious, a true *tour de force* of the Baroque sense of theatre.

Abbey of Ottobeuren, Bavaria

The architect J.M. Fischer had to build on a plan already drawn up by his predecessors. In 1748, when he took charge of the work, the foundations and the base of the walls were already laid. The longitudinal plan shows the influence of Roman Baroque through Fischer von Erlach. The façade is flanked by two tall towers. The building is vast, and the interior is remarkable for its light effects and ingenious spatial solutions; the stucco, imitating coloured marble and set off by the whiteness of the walls, is the work of J.M. Feichtmayr. At the crossing, the columns give way to pilasters; one of these bears the pulpit (commonly given a prominent position in Baroque churches, since preaching was at the heart of the Catholic revival).

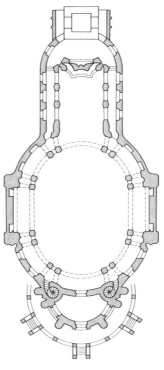

Staircase, Schloss Brühl

This staircase was designed in 1740 by Balthasar Neumann for the prince-archbishop of Cologne. As at Würzburg, the architect has created a highly theatrical perspective with a long, central corridor opening on to a brightly lit landing. The conception is Baroque but the decor, with its mixture of caryatids and columns, stucco in imitation marble and delicate wrought-iron railings, is typically Rococo.

Pilgrimage church of the Wies

Built literally in "the field" (die Wies), near Steingaden, south of Munich, the church is a place of pilgrimage centring on a wooden statue of the *Flagellation* (in a niche above the altar). The architect Domenikus Zimmermann built it between 1745 and 1754, and finally decided to live near his creation. The plan responds to the needs of the pilgrim: the nave, flanked by free-standing piers, forms a vast, bright oval while the choir, lined with arcades supporting high Corinthian columns, is narrower. The lower part of the church is dazzlingly white and sparsely decorated but the higher part is alive with cherubs, *trompe l'oeil* decorations and more. Here Rococo defies the rational, air and light pierce the walls, the tangible envelope disappears to focus attention on the altar and the celestial world beyond.

Margrave Theatre, Bayreuth

Built between 1745 and 1748 for the Margrave Wilhelmina, sister of Frederick II of Prussia, this small Rococo theatre shows foreign influences at work in the German courts. The architect and decorator Giuseppe Galli, known as Bibiena, has tried to link the stage and auditorium in an original manner, using the piers supporting the galleries as articulating elements.

Amalienburg Pavilion, park of the Nymphenburg

The Electress of Bavaria had the pavilion built by François Cuvilliés from 1734 to 1739, in the park of the summer residence outside Munich. In the centre, the large Hall of Mirrors projects forward; it is articulated by pilasters and a pediment and broken entablature, and is surmounted by a small belvedere for shooting pheasants. The façade is decorated with stucco reliefs above the windows and with busts in the niches. Inside is a truly magnificent Baroque decor, with stucco by J.B. Zimmermann – the architect's brother – and sculptures by Verhelst. In the Hall of Mirrors, the splendid ensemble is reflected endlessly from the walls.

The Iberian peninsula

In the 18th century, the cosmopolitan atmosphere of the Iberian peninsula – already in lively contact with the New World – seems to have had very little influence on provincial art in Spain and Portugal. The power of the Baroque tradition in these two countries, where Catholicism was strained but immovable, prevented the full impact of the Enlightenment, and Rococo, and later Neoclassicism, did not transform architecture as they did in other European countries. The decorative arts – encouraged by the courtly art of Lisbon, Madrid and Naples – reflected the influence of France, the Netherlands and (in the case of Portuguese furniture) England, while architecture followed the tradition of the Italian Renaissance.

Religious architecture was the most important area of development. Here, a feeling for moulded form took precedence over spatial arrangements, harmony of proportions or elegance of design. From Sicily to Mexico, Iberian Baroque reflected the strength and vigour of Latin American culture, and for two centuries maintained its essential and distinctive quality – exuberance. In a sense this exuberance had been there, animating plateresque Gothic and the 16th century Renaissance, since the time of the Arab occupation. Iberian Baroque lacks the qualities of movement and dynamism characteristic of Roman and other styles of Baroque. It is essentially sculptural and dramatic; tension is generated by solid but never uniform masses; the desire to accumulate decoration is seemingly insatiable. Generous and bold in its aspirations, Iberian Baroque always seems to dissipate itself amidst swarming forms.

Altars reveal the same characteristics, glittering in agglomerated gold in the darkness of choirs or chapels. Façades are pierced by vast circular windows and niches overflowing with sculpture;

framed by massive towers and crowned by crowds of angels and saints disappearing in clouds of stone, they prepare the visitor for the sparkling inner space of the wide, single nave. Many Gothic churches were newly adorned in the 18th century; the façades of the cathedrals of Valencia, Murcia and Compostela are vivid examples of the hybrid results, although none of them can equal the amazing ensemble of bronze, stucco, multicoloured marble and filtered light in Toledo cathedral (1721–32) by Narciso Tomé. Even foreign architects employed in the peninsula were receptive to local traditions – architects such as the German Konrad Rudolf, known as Rodolfo, in Valencia, the Dutchman Jaime Bort in Murcia and the Italian Nicaulo Nasoni in Porto (Dos Clerigos church, 1732–63). In Spain two native families of architects added something of their own genius to local traditions: the Figueroa in Andalusia (San Telmo Seminary in Seville, 1724–34) and the Churriguera, whose name has become synonymous with Castilian Baroque. Born in Madrid, José Churriguera (1665–1723) worked in Salamanca: his retable in San Esteban is undoubtedly one of the greatest masterpieces of religious art of the 18th century. His brother, Alberto Churriguera, adapted this powerful religious style to secular ends, designing the Plaza Mayor in Salamanca (though it was completed in 1755 by Andrés García de Quiñones), one of the most beautiful squares in Europe.

Official architecture in the peninsula owes its development to two major events: the earthquake that razed the centre of Lisbon in 1755 and (to a lesser degree) the fire that destroyed the Royal Palace in Madrid in 1734. The Portuguese and Spanish courts looked to European examples, very different from local traditions, for inspiration. In Lisbon, where the reconstruction was closely super-

vised by the marquis of Pombal, the Praça do Comércio (1760) was conceived by Manuel da Maia and Eugenio dos Santos in the manner of French *places royales*. The marvellous Royal Palace in Queluz (1747–52) by Mateus Vicente de Oliveira and the Frenchman Robillon is a rare but perfect example of Portuguese Rococo. In contrast, the vast palace-convent of Mafra by the German Federico Ludwig (or Ludovici) attempted a synthesis of the Escorial and Roman Baroque. In time, forms became quieter, restraining the tendencies to over-decorate of the first half of the century, and finally influencing religious architecture. Orders reappear, though Portuguese artists show a marked preference for blue, white and yellow *azulejos* surfaces. The basilica of La Estrela, built in Lisbon by Mateus Vicente, one of Ludwig's best disciples, illustrates this new northern taste; in Porto, English architecture was influential (hospital of La Misericordia by John Karr, 1770–93). In Spain, royal residences show an extraordinary mixture of French (Versailles) Baroque, European Rococo and Italian Baroque. The reconstruction of the enormous Palacio Real in Madrid to the plans of the Piedmontese Filippo Juvara had a longlasting influence in the capital: new avenues, gardens, fountains and public monuments attest to the advent of a new generation of architects led by Juan Bautista Sachetti, Francisco Sabatini and, above all, Ventura Rodríguez (1717–85) and Juan de Villanueva (1739–1811). But the Spanish style of the Enlightenment, so rich in contrasts, is probably best represented by the vast royal palaces of Aranjuez, in the heart of the arid Castilian plateau, and of La Granja de San Ildefonso, at the foot of the majestic Sierra de Guadarrama.

Sacristy of the Carthusians, Grenada

The decoration of the sacristy by Luis de Arévalo (1727–64) is the architectural equivalent to altars by the Churriguera brothers. The brilliantly lit ornamentation cannot disguise the static quality of the structure. It makes an instructive comparison with Rococo churches of the same period in Bavaria and Austria, where undulating walls and flowing spaces create perpetual movement.

Retable, Toledo Cathedral

Placed behind the choir, in the Gothic ambulatory, the ensemble is transfigured by the skilfully controlled fall of light from above, exalting the multitude of carved figures and forms out of this world.

Cathedral, Santiago de Compostela

This composite but strongly structured façade, started in the 17th century, is one of the most imposing in Spain. The central part respects the form of the high medieval nave even though it resembles a giant altar-back. The symmetrical towers flank a grand staircase. The whole was completed between 1738 and 1750 by Fernando Casas y Novoa.

Entrance to the palace of the marquis of Dos Aguas, Valencia

Designed by the painter Hipólito Rovira Brocandel, the entrance was sculpted by Ignacio Vergara (1715–76). The fact that no architect was involved may explain the extraordinary way in which the whole façade, consisting only of picturesque window frames, centres around this extraordinary *rocaille*. Even the Atlas figures have lost their architectural function. The symbolic, or rather, emblematic ornament (the aquatic decoration illustrates the owner's name) consists of uncontrolled forms regulated only to the extent that they are centred on a door.

Palace of Queluz

The palace, situated north of Lisbon, was built from 1747 to 1752 by Mateus Vicente de Oliveira for one of the sons of King João V. Like a small, more graceful and more colourful Versailles, the house testifies to the influence of the Enlightenment in Portugal. The Order is classical, but the disproportionate central pediment, the rather stiff rhythm of the bays and the decorative accents above the windows show an orientation somewhere between German Rococo and Italian Baroque.

Bom Jesus, Braga

Built to the plans of the Portuguese architect Carlos da Cruz Amarante, between 1784 and 1811, this church is above all famous for its magnificent *Stations of the Cross* set on either side of a seemingly interminable staircase leading up to the façade. Small oratories occupy each landing: each station is represented by life-size sculpture in the round. Fountains also enliven this grandiose religious ensemble.

Colonial architecture

Because of the area it covers and its exceptionally long duration – nearly three centuries – Latin American Baroque is one of the most important movements in Western art. The very size of the continent makes a detailed study difficult: stylistic changes and national schools are not easily defined; the personal role of artists, dates of buildings and precise influences are difficult to establish outside the main centres. Also, colonial architecture has its own set of rules. When one country conquers another or when a group of people leave their country to settle in another, the newcomers are faced with a different climate, new materials and often uneasy cohabitation with the native population. Thus a need for protection and control dictates the planning of towns; the employment of local craftsmen who have their own artistic tradition has a great or small, short- or long-term influence on imported architecture.

The Spanish and Portuguese embarked upon the first great campaign of colonization in Central and South America in the 16th century. Their dominion, centred on the inexhaustible mines of the conquered countries, lent heavily on the efforts of the missionaries, the Jesuits and the Inquisition, who sought to impose Christianity. The discovery of the New World coincided with the Reformation in Europe; while North America was being settled by northern European Protestants, South America witnessed the triumph of the Catholic Counter-Reformation. The ceremonial and theatrical tendencies of Mediterranean religious art became virulent in these tropical and sub-tropical countries; within a century the mingling of European, Indian, Creole, half-caste and (in Brazil) African black peoples introduced local elements into the new official religion. The basic idiom of Iberian Baroque was transformed according to the landscape, the people and the period. However, two main tendencies and two main periods can be roughly estab-

lished, distinguishing the 17th century from the 18th century and Brazil from Mexico.

In Brazil, the Portuguese discovered a complete absence of stone buildings and a local artistic tradition that was extremely primitive. The Spanish, on the other hand, conquered two countries where architecture had been flourishing for centuries. The Aztec empire in Mexico and the Inca empire in Peru had long mastered stone construction and sculpture – as pre-Columbian temples and palaces still testify – and the Spanish had no difficulty in finding craftsmen. At first, Aztec and Inca influences were strongly resisted by the imperialists, who were eager to establish their own style. For example, the cathedral of Mexico City, one of the richest and most imposing sanctuaries in the New World, was symbolically built on the site of the Temple of the Sun, sacred centre of the ancient capital Tenochtitlán. Both the Portuguese, who had no choice, and the Spanish obtained the plans for their new buildings from Court architects at home. At the end of the 16th century the Iberian Renaissance, with its Islamic undertones and Gothic survivals, dominated. The austere classicism of Juan de Herrera seems to have influenced Jesuit building and sometimes that of other religious orders, particularly in Brazil. Although the relative simplicity of church façades in Brazil during this first period is not typical of Baroque building in Peru, Bolivia and Mexico, the richly decorated naves, chapels and choirs are similar in both zones of influence. The display of colossal and limitless wealth in the name of religion, already apparent in the European home countries, knew no limits in the lands where gold and silver were actually mined. Here, stupendous altarpieces and carved gilt wooden relief sculptures (*talha*) surpassed all European precedents. To make a stronger impact on the imagination of a people used to precious idols, the Church transformed the Christian temples into "golden caves"

(V.L. Tapié). Façades, with their vast overdecorated doors and their huge towers crowned with spires and domes, made a backdrop to frequent outdoor ceremonies and sumptuous processions. The 18th century marked the climax of an eclectic, truly delirious Baroque, in which native influences became increasingly strong. This second phase of colonial Baroque nevertheless retained the fundamental characteristics of Spanish and Portuguese architecture.

At first restricted to coastal towns, the Portuguese-Brazilian style spread inland with the discovery of new gold and diamond mines. The camps of the early prospectors became settlements, then well laid-out towns with elegant houses. A distinctive local school of architecture developed in the region of Minas Gerais, with Ouro Preto as one of its most representative centres. Certain architects and sculptors, such as the half-caste Antonio Francisco Lisboa, known as Aleijadinho, introduced a new flavour to Brazilian architecture, which until then had been closely dependent on Portugal. Similarly, in Mexico, Indian craftsmen and artists were given greater opportunity to exercise their own invention. Many of their carvings re-use motifs found in pre-Columbian embroidery and decoration, adapting them to the Baroque idiom. A taste for brilliant, sensual colours is often apparent, as at San Francisco d'Acatepec (Pueblo), where the entire façade of the church is covered with multicoloured ceramics. Public architecture followed the pattern of religious architecture; the arcades of the Spanish *plaza mayor*, palaces, fountains and even aqueducts display the glory of the new empire. The beautiful fountain of Salto de Agua in Mexico and the Remedios Aqueduct are two famous examples.

Chapel of the Blessed Sacrament, Mexico Cathedral

The chapel of the Blessed Sacrament was added to the cathedral by the Spanish architect, Lorenzo Rodríguez. Decorated columns are the main feature; the moulding around the door derives from wooden sculpture.

San Francisco, Ouro Preto (Brazil)

Located in the centre of the mining region of Minas Gerais, San Francisco was built by Antonio Francisco Lisboa between 1766 and 1794. The two round towers of the façade are unusual, but the decorated door is the most remarkable feature of the building. The son of an émigré architect, Lisboa was the only really original Latin American architect of the period; he is better known under the name Aleijadinho – the little cripple. Born in Ouro Preto in 1738, he lived until 1814, perpetuating a Baroque style which had long been abandoned in Europe.

Shrine of Ocotlán, near Tlaxcala

This church, built in 1745, is unique in Mexico for the scale, richness and elegance of its towers and for the materials used in their construction. The brickwork of the bases is unglazed, and the bricks themselves are unusually shaped and pointed with white mortar, which makes them look like fish scales. The upper parts, with two symmetrical tiers, have a greater elegance than the similarly styled but unfinished façade of the more famous church of Tepozotlán.

Mexico Cathedral

Mexico Cathedral is the largest and most impressive church in the country; the chapel dedicated to the Three Magi (detail, right) is its richest ornament. Built between 1718 and 1737 by Jerónimo Balbas, an architect who probably came from southern Spain, it presents a delirious vision of statues and decorated columns in gilded wood.

La Compañia, or Jesuit Church, Cuzco (Peru)

The church was begun in 1651 but it seems likely that its remarkable façade was completed much later. The design of the towers, with four turrets encircling a dome, does not recall any familiar European model; nor does the centre of the façade, with tall arches broken by windows set beneath a crowning trefoiled arch. Above this dynamic tableau, the entablature follows the curve of the central arch.

San Francisco, Salvador (Brazil)

The façade offers only a foretaste of the magnificent decorations of gilded wood and plaster that entirely cover the inside of the church.

The great phase of the Baroque in England

Both in Italy and in Germany, Baroque was the outcome of a slowly matured aesthetic movement which lasted more than a century and was practised by a wide variety of architects. This was not the case in England. Baroque had a brief development in the early 18th century in the hands of a few totally original architects; then, extinguished by the sudden fervour for Palladianism, it ended abruptly about 1730. While English Baroque architects were aware of the Italian mastery of increasingly daring spatial arrangements, and of the Eastern European taste for combining architectural elements into an extravagance of ornamentation, their style was essentially founded on the treatment of volumes *per se*. Its geometric purity, both massive and austere though still with many Gothic and Elizabethan references, often appears strangely modern. Nicholas Hawksmoor and Sir John Vanbrugh were the main protagonists of this style and it is often difficult to determine their respective contributions to some of the buildings they collaborated on.

Nicholas Hawksmoor (1661–1735) joined Wren as draughtsman and later became his main assistant during the construction of St. Paul's Cathedral and Greenwich Hospital. In 1699 he formed a partnership with Vanbrugh to build the aristocratic country seats of Castle Howard and Blenheim Palace. At the same time, he saw through some projects of his own, for example Easton Neston in Northamptonshire, with its remarkably free plan. Following an Act passed in 1711 to provide for the building of 50 new churches in London, Hawksmoor was commissioned to build six of them. St. Alfege, Greenwich (1712–14), St. Anne's, Limehouse (1715–30) and Christ Church, Spitalfields (1719–29) all followed the plan of a classical basilica. But the façades, with their turrets, lanterns and transparent crowning elements show a brilliant interpretation of Gothic formal vocabulary. In the church of St. Mary, Woolnoth (1716–27), in the City, Hawksmoor created an entirely new design, achieving a striking and vigorous effect by strongly accentuated mouldings. But his most original church was St. George's, Bloomsbury (1716–31) where he brought together a rather literal interpretation of the portico of the Pantheon in Rome with a pyramidal element based on the mausoleum of Halicarnassus, creating a compositional antithesis similar to the techniques of *collage*. In Oxford, he drew up vast projects for several colleges, including All Souls College (1716–35), alternately classical and Gothic with interesting attempts to integrate the new buildings into the old. In both Oxford and Cambridge, he proposed plans for the ideal city. Finally, special mention should be made of the mausoleum he built, towards the end of his career, for the Carlisle family at Castle Howard: a vast Doric tholos with a strictly classical exterior.

Hawksmoor seems to have shared a taste for "eccentric forms" with Sir John Vanbrugh (1661–1726), a disconcerting character of many talents, who was associated with both the aristocracy and the London bourgeoisie. Vanbrugh abandoned a military career to become a successful playwright; it was only late in life that he began to show an interest in building. His first work was Goose Pie House (1699), which he built for himself, and where his style was immediately apparent: strict geometric masses decorated in an idiom recalling Italian Mannerism. Castle Howard, in Yorkshire, is undoubtedly his most harmonious creation (1701–15). The clearly articulated plan follows the Palladian pattern of the central element linked by curved wings to the service quarters. A giant Order of plain pilasters maintains the rhythm of the elegant façades. But it is at Blenheim Palace that he displays his "wildest powers of imagination" (Reynolds). It has been said that this colossal palace, built by Queen Anne and the English nation as a reward for John Churchill, duke of Marlborough, was a grand riposte to Versailles. The complex plan creates an even more complex elevation of jumbled volumes, accentuated by strange pinnacles that give the vast building a fantastic and theatrical quality. In his "castle" at Greenwich (1717), Vanbrugh produced an austere, almost romantic interpretation of Gothic, but at Seaton Delaval, he built a sort of manifesto of his architectural style. This house daringly synthesizes a number of discordant elements, but its exciting new hybrid vocabulary was to remain without direct imitators.

Thomas Archer (1668–1743) travelled through Europe gathering direct experience of the Baroque. His London churches, St. Paul's, Deptford and St. John's, Smith Square, as well as Heythrop House in Oxfordshire (1707–10), show precise references to the great works of Bernini and Borromini.

The Catholic Scotsman James Gibbs (1682–1754) was the favourite architect of the Tory aristocracy. Following the Act of 1711, he was commissioned to build St. Mary-le-Strand (1714–17), with its façade on two levels and circular portico (recalling Gibbs' apprenticeship in Rome with Carlo Fontana, a leading architect of the late Baroque). With St. Martin in the Fields, his approach was more classical and more in keeping with Wren's idiom. The Radcliffe Camera, a library in Oxford, represents the conclusion of his development: it is a masterful synthesis of Mannerist complexities with Baroque mass.

Niche, St. Mary's, Woolnoth, London

St. Mary's was the smallest of the 50 new churches built in London after the Act of 1711, and one of the six designed by Nicholas Hawksmoor. The ground plan is almost square to fit the tiny site. The massive, blind façade is enlivened by rustication, while the side walls are articulated with elaborate niches such as the one shown here.

Seaton Delaval, Northumberland

This is the best example of the dramatic "compactness" characteristic of Vanbrugh's style. The central part of the building, overlooking the main courtyard to the north, borrows the Tudor motif of corner turrets – contrasting them perfectly with the central pediment and the freestanding columns on either side of the monumental entrance steps. Vanbrugh's defiance of classical rules is absolute. An arcaded gallery links the main reception rooms to the stables on the left and the kitchens on the right.

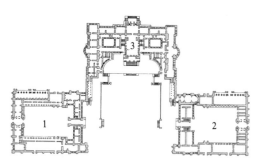

Blenheim Palace, Oxfordshire

The palace was built between 1705 and 1724 to commemorate the victory of the battle of Blenheim and as a reward for its victor, the duke of Marlborough. Its scale alone indicates that it is more a monument than a residence. Sir John Vanbrugh conceived a vast plan in which the service courtyard (1) is symmetrical with the stable yard (2) on either side of a high central building. A classical peristyle leads, on the entrance side, to an enormous hall (3) decorated with trophies. A large park landscaped with an arcaded bridge and a column of Victory surrounds the palace.

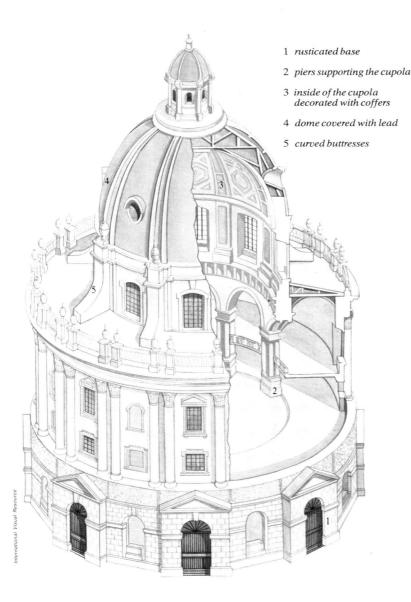

1 *rusticated base*

2 *piers supporting the cupola*

3 *inside of the cupola decorated with coffers*

4 *dome covered with lead*

5 *curved buttresses*

Radcliffe Camera, Oxford

Dr Radcliffe's library was built between 1737 and 1749 according to a design by James Gibbs. The circular plan permitted the architect to create a tall, monumental structure of two concentric cylinders. The central cylinder is crowned by a cupola inspired by Michaelangelo's dome for St. Peter's, Rome, while the curved buttresses recall those of Santa Maria della Salute by Longhena in Venice. The compact, densely rusticated base (originally an open vestibule) contrasts with the elegant Corinthian Order above, in which pairs of semicircular columns create complex rhythms of light and shade.

St. George in the East, Stepney, London

The basilical plan of this church, built between 1715 and 1718, reflects Hawksmoor's interest in primitive Christian churches. A "medieval" ensemble is created from purely classical elements. The two lower levels of the façade, the doorway framed by twin Ionic pilasters, and the tall cubic tower contrast with the lightness of the crowning octagonal lantern. Four octagonal turrets, picking up the motif of the lantern, are a vertical counterpoint to the dense horizontality of the nave.

Ragley Hall, Warwickshire

Ragley Hall was rebuilt for the earl of Hertford by James Gibbs from 1750 to 1755. The saloon shows a taste for exuberant ornamentation in the Italian style: for his private commissions, Gibbs employed the stuccoists Artari and Bagutti.

St. Martin's in the Fields, London

This elegant church (1721–26) dominates Trafalgar Square. It is perhaps the finest example of that typically English combination of a classical portico surmounted by a single spire derived from Gothic models. Originally, James Gibbs had conceived a rotunda flanked by a peristyle and a semicircular choir. The final plan was a vast rectangle. Two rows of Corinthian columns support the side galleries. The fine stucco work of the central nave was executed by Italian craftsmen.

The Palladian revival and Neoclassicism in England

The period between 1715 and 1830 in England was one of political stability and economic prosperity. The country was dominated by the aristocracy, whose power was founded on new sources of wealth (commerce, the growth of industry) as well as on the land. This was the golden age of the country house, that supremely English institution which served not only as the managerial headquarters of a vast estate but also as a symbol of family prestige. Neighbourly competition stimulated an insurgence of new building up and down the country.

This very specific type of architecture was at first identified with a single style: Palladianism. Palladio's artistic theory and forms had been introduced to England by Inigo Jones in 1617; reinterpreted in England in the second quarter of the 18th century, they were to spread across Europe. The revival was mainly due to the enthusiasm of a rich amateur, Lord Burlington, but the first buildings in the new manner were the works of a Scotsman, Colen Campbell (died 1729). His book, *Vitruvius Britannicus* (1715), was very influential in the Palladian rout of the Baroque and remained the "bible" for supporters of this form of twice-rejuvenated classicism (first by Palladio and then by Inigo Jones). After Wanstead House in Essex (1715, destroyed 1822), the best example of an almost literal imitation of Palladio's Venetian models is to be found in Mereworth Castle, Kent (1723). This is an almost archaeological reproduction of the Villa Rotonda near Vicenza, with its four identical porticoes and crowning cupola. The Palladian qualities of restraint and proportion, essential to an elegant way of life, are also present in the work of William Kent (1685–1748), who often collaborated with Richard Boyle, Lord Burlington (1694–1753). This wealthy aristocrat brought back from his Continental "grand tour" numerous drawings by Palladio, including studies of Roman baths. His most famous work is Chiswick House (1720–25), which he built for himself. The garden, designed by Kent, is one of the first examples of the new picturesque style, with its "return to nature" expressed in reminiscences of the Italian countryside and in classical quotations. Holkham Hall in Norfolk (1734) is the climax of the collaboration between Burlington and Kent. Here, the use of numerous classical motifs, the juxtaposition of masses, the "Roman" austerity of the elevations and the sumptuous interior decorations combine to achieve an almost theatrical grandeur. Other artists, such as Isaac Ware, adopted the same architectural types, but with less panache.

While these developments were taking place in country house architecture, John Wood (1704–54) was creating brilliant urban variations in Bath, the fashionable spa town of the aristocracy; his vocabulary ranged through "circuses", crescents and curving, rising streets. Meanwhile Edward Lovett Pearce introduced Palladianism to Ireland and built some important public buildings in Dublin.

The next generation of architects still followed the Palladian tradition but tended not to respect its doctrines so strictly. It included Sir Robert Taylor (1714–88), James Paine (1716–89) and John Carr (1723–1807).

Some of their contemporaries (Hogarth and his friends, for instance) considered Palladianism an aristocratic dogma opposed to the expression of life and the independent development of the arts. But they were advocating a rather outdated return to Rococo. It was Neoclassicism that interrupted the universal spread of Palladianism, while adopting certain of its characteristics. In England, as in the rest of Europe, Neoclassicism was founded on two tendencies, one archaeological, the other philosophical; both of these were explored in the forcing-ground of Rome by the leading architects of the new movement, William Chambers and Robert Adam.

William Chambers (1723–96), friend of King George III, theoretician and founder-member of the Royal Academy (1768), was given important responsibilities. Long studies in France and Italy and travels to the Far East inspired his varied and original works. At Kew (1757–63) he brilliantly illustrated the English taste for landscape architecture, creating ornamental buildings of both classical and oriental inspiration. His main work, Somerset House in London (1776–80), a monumental undertaking with a complex programme, demonstrates his refined eclecticism, with references chiefly to the Italian Renaissance and to French classicism. Robert Adam (1728–92), on the contrary, championed a stricter return to antiquity, though he also experimented with Gothic. His prolific inventiveness soon made his style dominant in England, from 1760 to the end of the century. After a long stay in Italy, where he met Piranesi, Adam built numerous country houses, some with magnificent "Etruscan" or "Pompeian" decorations (Syon House). He also designed urban buildings in London (the Adelphi complex) and in Edinburgh.

Neoclassicism, however, was given many interpretations in England. George Dance (1741–1825) gave it dramatic strength in Newgate Prison (1769, destroyed in 1902). There was also a Gothic revival (though Gothic had never quite disappeared), at Strawberry Hill by Horace Walpole (1748) and in some works by Adam and by James Wyatt (1746–1813). The second generation of Neoclassical architects included Robert Milne (1734–1811), Thomas Hardwick (1752–1829), Henry Holland (1745–1806) and Sir John Soane (1753–1837). Soane was an eccentric genius who displayed, in the Bank of England and in his own house in Lincoln's Inn Fields, a brilliant handling of internal light and space. His ability to absorb stylistic currents resulted in an entirely original sense of form, in which can be traced "the mysterious origins of modern architecture".

The later part of the 18th century saw the development of the "picturesque" school with John Nash (1752–1835) as its most important representative. George IV's favourite architect, he created disconcerting buildings, more "visual" than solid, like the Brighton Pavilion. The turn of the century coincided with the Greek revival: Thomas Hope, William Wilkins, Decimus Burton and Robert Smirke insisted on a strict emulation of archaeological models, favouring the Doric Order in particular.

Chiswick House, Middlesex

Lord Burlington, assisted by William Kent, built this house for himself on the outskirts of London. In it, he wanted to revive the Roman model of the suburban villa. The main inspiration was not therefore the Villa Rotonda but Palladio's studies of Roman baths (vaults and lighting). Nevertheless, Lord Burlington kept the main lines of the plan of the Villa Rotonda, adapting it to the requirements of both comfort and contemporary fashion. The rooms radiate from a central space, an octagonal Palladian salon covered with a cupola (1); they include anterooms (2), studies (3), libraries (4) and a state room with semicylindrical ends (5) opening on to the garden. (The diagram in fact shows the ground floor, or service quarters, but the *piano nobile* above follows the same layout.) The treatment of details on the elevation – "thermal" windows on the drum of the dome, a variety of façades, only one of which is preceded by a portico – shows a certain freedom with Palladian models. The inside, highly coloured and luxurious, seems closer to Inigo Jones and the Baroque than to Venetian originals.

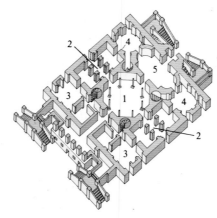

Fonthill Abbey, Wiltshire

Built by James Wyatt between 1795 and 1807 (and shortly afterwards destroyed), this house was produced by an architect described as a "weathervane, turned by the changing winds of fashion" and a patron, William Beckford, who was the most extravagant representative of the early Romantic taste in England. Beckford wanted a composite neo-Gothic house evoking cloister, church and castle. Here, archaeology became the servant of fantasy.

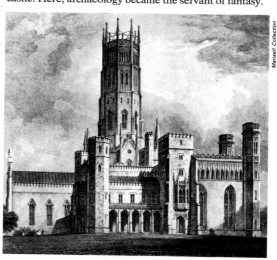

Somerset House, London

Sir William Chambers' main work, this vast building – one of the largest in England – was started in 1776. It was designed to house not only a number of state administrative departments but also the Royal Academy and the Royal Society of Antiquaries. Situated between the Strand and the Thames, it was planned around three large courtyards. The elevations as well as the general decor display a refined eclecticism, a result of the cosmopolitan training of the architect – his travel journals were full of references to Florentine, Roman and French buildings. Inside, an open circular staircase (the Navy Staircase) is a fine example of his virtuosity in the handling of space.

Syon House, Isleworth

This Tudor house, constructed around a square courtyard, was totally transformed inside by Adam between 1762 and 1769. Among the succession of rooms of varied geometrical form, the large "Roman" anteroom deserves special mention for its sumptuous mixture of gilding and green marble and stucco. Twelve columns (some are of antique marble and were found in the Tiber while others are stucco replicas) carry gilt copies of the most famous ancient statues, above a frieze. Trophy panels, a marble fireplace and a marvellous floor, well preserved, give the room a splendid solemnity: it is one of the grandest examples of the Adam style.

Palladian bridge and pantheon, Stourhead, Wiltshire

Stourhead has one of the most beautiful landscaped parks in England. Once the house had been built in the Palladian manner by the Scottish architect Colen Campbell, the owner, banker Henry Hoare, concentrated on the natural surroundings. The focal point is a large central lake which replaced a succession of ponds at the source of a small river. Walking through the park, one discovers a series of *tableaux* inspired by classical landscape painting (Claude and Salvator Rosa). Follies, a temple of Apollo, a grotto, a rustic cottage, a medieval keep, even a toy Roman Pantheon, blend easily with the flowers, shrubs and trees.

Dining room, Sir John Soane's house, London

Soane's house, completed between 1812 and 1837, is a perfect manifestation of eclecticism at its best. Walking through the rooms, one is led from classical antiquity to Egypt and on to the Middle Ages, encountering, among other things, the ruins of a monastery, a mastaba and a monk's cell. The spatial treatment is highly original (suspended ceilings, free from the walls) and creates special light effects which give the house an otherworldly feeling; this is particularly apparent in the dining room, where mirrors reflect the light let in by the lantern in the centre of a saucer dome.

331

Neoclassicism in France at the end of the 18th century

Though in complete opposition to Rococo and the decorative freedom of *rocaille* which had prevailed in the first half of the century, Neoclassicism rapidly gained strength in France after its first appearance in artistic circles in Paris from 1750. Taken up by the court and in the great provincial centres, it became widespread from about 1770, gradually evolved for the next 50 years and lasted well into the 19th century. But Neoclassicism was less an evolving fashion – though one may detect within it the phases of Louis XVI, Directoire and Empire – than an aesthetic ideal founded on theory. Since this was a theory of absolute beauty, imitating nature, it went beyond the very notion of style. The return to the balanced forms of classical antiquity was also the result of a renewed curiosity for Greco-Roman civilization. Neoclassicism was an international movement, typical of the "enlightened" society of the 18th century, and the French version must be seen in the wider context of English and German Neoclassicism. English Palladianism and, later, Winckelmann's theories share a single artistic ideal with France at the time of Montesquieu and Voltaire: revival of the antique.

The deliberate classicism characteristic of the end of Louis XIV's reign, of which Perrault's Louvre colonnade is the most famous example, prepared the way for an official "return to origins". Even an artist like Ange-Jacques Gabriel, first architect to Louis XV, untouched by Neoclassical theory, was influenced by the fashion for the antique. Two of his buildings are among the masterpieces of what is called Louis XVI style (despite being built before the death of Louis XV in 1774) – the church of the Ecole Militaire in Paris (1768–75), conceived like the nave of a Corinthian temple, and the Petit Trianon in Versailles (1762–64), a Palladian villa "in French disguise". This movement was widely publicized in books and prints before it came to influence the decorative arts, but already the furniture fashionable at the end of the reign of Louis XV had a completely different decorative vocabulary, with "Greek" friezes, consoles, mouldings and garlands. Artists became obsessed with straight lines, archaeological motifs and an idealized vision of nature; architects attempted to reproduce the solid permanence of the classical Orders. A great debate began about the appreciation of architecture, great importance being attached to a kind of visual logic: the sensual pleasure of the beholder was to be counterbalanced by his reason. Like Palladio in the 16th century, the Neoclassicists therefore stressed the load-bearing function of their Orders. Free-standing columns carrying an entablature became the main architectural elements of a building: the Greek temple was the undisputed model.

Neoclassicism was more than a reaction against *rocaille*, it was also the end of two centuries of Mannerism and Baroque (in their broadest sense). The champions of the new style were directly influenced by the philosophy of the Enlightenment – by its rationalism, its high moral tone and the emphasis it placed on historical precedent. Their aims were clarity, balance and simplicity of form. According to theoreticians and philosophers like Marc-Antoine Laugier, Germain Soufflot, Marie-Joseph Peyre, David Leroy, Nicolas le Camus de Mézières and Diderot, moral sentiment uplifted by universal, clear, balanced forms, could transform artistic creation into an instrument of communication and education. The strength of the revival of the antique, supreme symbol of civilization, lay in its didactic example. This aspect of Neoclassicism is fundamental and explains why a variety of tendencies and styles existed within an apparently uniform aesthetic.

The work of Soufflot under Louis XV, of Claude-Nicolas Ledoux under Louis XVI and of Charles Percier and Pierre Fontaine under the Empire all stemmed from the same aesthetic and from the same formal patterns derived from antiquity but the execution varied with the artist and the time. For example, Soufflot's architecture displays an inventive spirit and a dignity which the architects of the Directoire and Empire lack in their concern for decorum and historical faithfulness. The heaviness of his interior decoration contrasts with his serene exteriors and seems a far cry from the gracious harmony of the elegant mansions built by Jacques Cellerier, Alexandre Théodore Brongniart, François Joseph Bellanger and Jacques-Guillaume Legrand, in which Attic finesse melds with Pompeian charm. In Paris, Neoclassicism was patronized by the wealthy *haute bourgeoisie* and the "enlightened" aristocracy. It transformed the districts where vast speculative building projects were underway – for example, Roule, Chaussée-d'Antin and around the Grands Boulevards. The church of St. Philippe-du-Roule, built by François Chalgrin from 1769 to 1774, shows that the new ideals had even infiltrated religious architecture. Neoclassical architecture also flourished outside Paris, particularly in the great ports: architects such as Mathurin Crucy in Nantes, and Louis Combes and Victor Louis in Bordeaux, erected splendid colonnades and set a style of urban grandeur hitherto unknown. Finally, another tendency, towards both the symbolic and the "picturesque", and strongly influenced by Piranesi's drawings, brought a very individual sense of theatre to both public and private architecture. On the one hand there is "revolutionary" architecture, of which Boullée, with his projects of pure invention, was the greatest theoretician; on the other, "moralist" architecture, which can be both austere and brilliant, as practised by Ledoux, Charles De Wailly, Peyre, Jacques Gondoin, Bernard Poyet and their rivals.

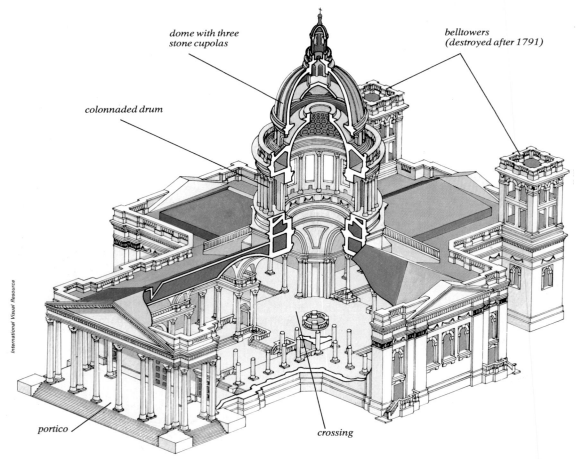

dome with three stone cupolas

belltowers (destroyed after 1791)

colonnaded drum

portico

crossing

International Visual Resource

Colonnaded aisle of the Panthéon

This picture of the interior of St. Geneviève suggests the poetic effect that Soufflot wanted his colonnade to evoke. Originally, the wall was pierced by tall windows which filtered the space with bright light. Soufflot here recalls the emotion he felt when, in 1750, he discovered and drew the Doric temples in Paestum – but the richer Corinthian Order was better suited to a royal monument.

C. Rose, C.M.H.S, SPADEM

The Panthéon in Paris (formerly the basilica of St. Geneviève)

The building, Soufflot's crowning achievement, was completed only after his death in 1780. It was one of the most important projects undertaken during the reign of Louis XV. Begun in 1757, it was intended as a monument to the divine right of monarchy and was dedicated to the patron saint of Paris, St. Geneviève, whose tomb was to be erected under the huge dome. The nature of the site, at the top of a hill, as well as a commitment to create an ideal religious building, determined Soufflot on some bold innovations. Denying the plastic role of the wall, so typical of the Baroque, with its pilasters and niches, the architect reinstated the colonnade in the place from which it had long been supplanted. Paradoxically, he managed to obtain the miraculous lightness of this classical Order by employing some Gothic engineering techniques. A new technique of reinforced stonework was worked out with the help of the engineer Rondelet. In 1791, the building became a deconsecrated monument dedicated to the country's heroes.

Château of Moncley

Built around 1780, in the *département* of Doubs, this large mansion is one of the best examples of provincial Neoclassicism. The architect, Claude Joseph Bertrand (1734–1811), was the main exponent of the style in Besançon, where he built several town houses and the church of St. Pierre. Conceived in the manner of a classical villa, the château opens out on either side of a central portico and clearly displays Palladian influence.

Staircase of the Grand-Théâtre, Bordeaux

Victor Louis' masterpiece was later to inspire Garnier in the Paris Opéra. Conceived a few years after the Paris Odéon by Peyre and De Wailly but opened two years earlier (1780), the Grand-Théâtre in Bordeaux is one of the best examples of public architecture under Louis XVI and its interior has been almost perfectly preserved. The magnificent portico of 12 Corinthian columns, the grandly arcaded exterior and the spacious approach illustrate the importance given to the theatre during this period.

Maison Acquart, Bordeaux

Urban development in Bordeaux, at its height under Louis XV, continued during the Neoclassical period. Louis Combes, a disciple of Boullée, was an engaging and original character: a Revolutionary architect, he conceived many utopian projects but also designed buildings in his native town. This beautiful house in the Cours de l'Intendance, built in 1785 for an alderman, is evidence of the wealth of contemporary Bordeaux society. A touch of fantasy softens the classical composition of the whole: two Atlas figures in the shape of Tritons support the balcony. The imposing cornice, with consoles and rosettes, has Roman overtones.

Chinese pavilion, Cassan

At L'Isle-Adam (Val d'Oise), the recently restored Chinese pavilion is the only "folly" left on the estate of the wealthy connoisseur M. Bergeret, patron of Fragonard. The taste for exotica could give Neoclassicism a picturesque charm. The landscaped parks which appeared in France in the second half of the 18th century transformed the appearance of estates: they show Anglomania, but also the insatiable urge for novelty of the Age of Enlightenment.

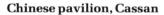

House of the director of the salt works, Arc-et-Senans

This is the first example in France of monumental industrial architecture and one of the masterpieces of Claude Nicolas Ledoux. Built between 1775 and 1779 on a semicircular plan, the royal factory was conceived as an ideal workers' city. The director's house is situated at the centre of the whole composition. Its outline is Palladian, but it also recalls the rusticated neo-Mannerism much in vogue among Revolutionary architects; this is particularly evident in the blocked columns, accentuating the massive and imposing austerity of the ensemble.

International Neoclassicism

Neoclassicism emerged in Rome in the mid-18th century and eventually influenced architecture throughout Europe. In terms of actual construction, little work was undertaken in Italy before the French Revolution, but the movement was very much alive there in theory, in both academic and artistic circles. Rome was the capital of the new style: connoisseurs and artists alike flocked there and fell under the spell of her classical ruins (particularly the Pantheon) and the grandeur of her Baroque. Nourished on archaeology, poetry and rationalist theory, a new language of architecture evolved. An entire generation of architects responded to Piranesi's brilliant etchings; from Rome they circulated the European courts, spreading the new "language". In 1746, Le Geay designed a rotunda church (based on the Pantheon) in Berlin;

in 1755, Jardin projected an enormous domed church for Copenhagen; in 1766, Victor Louis redesigned the royal palace in Warsaw in Neoclassical style. Architects in those days could also be responsible for interior decoration and furnishings, and even for town planning, as can be seen in Petitot's work in Parma and, later, in Nicolas de Pigage's work in the Palatinate.

At this time, Palladio's work became better known in its homeland, thanks to Bertotti-Scamozzi's publications; it inspired sophisticated works, also showing English influence, such as Schloss Wörlitz by Erdmannsdorff and, in Russia, the buildings of Cameron and Quarenghi (for instance, Peterhof). In the United States, Jefferson imposed Palladianism on the official buildings of the new nation and modelled his plantation at Mon-

ticello as a Palladian villa.

Around 1780 Neoclassicism came to favour external austerity, stressing the geometry of volumes and articulating façades with colonnades. There was a tendency towards "architecture for effect", to the detriment of historicism. The Doric Order, newly revealed in the 1750s in the temples of Paestum, became almost mandatory in northern Europe, in Berlin in the work of Langhans (Brandenburg Gate, 1788) and Gentz, in Sweden in that of Ehrensvärd. Academies had become very important by the end of the 18th century (San Fernando in Madrid) and in the wake of the French Revolution grand projects were undertaken: in Germany by Friedrich Gilly and Weinbrenner, in Napoleonic Italy by Cagnola in Milan, Valadier in Rome and Selva in Venice.

Prado Museum, Madrid

Transformed into an art museum in 1819, the Prado was begun in 1785 by Juan de Villanueva and originally intended as a natural history museum. Situated in the residential district of the Prado, it formed part of a programme to embellish the capital undertaken by King Charles III. The sparsely decorated façade uses repetitive elements to stress the columniation. A stepped pediment gives the central portico added grandeur.

Palace of Taurida, Leningrad

Between 1787 and 1789, Starov, former pupil of De Wailly in Paris, built a small palace for Potemkin, prince of Taurida. This is one of the finest monuments of Neoclassicism in Russia. The very simple façade is accentuated in the centre by a portico surmounted by a flat dome. Under the dome, a large vestibule with splayed corners and with bays decorated with Ionic columns recalls the monumental space of Roman baths. Beyond is a vast colonnaded hall for receptions, and a small winter garden.

Royal Church of Frederic V, Copenhagen

Jardin was invited to Denmark in 1755, but his plans for the Royal Church were not completed until the 19th century. The church takes the form of a rotunda in the centre of a Greek cross. It has colonnaded porches at the east and west ends and two corresponding chapels north and south. The project was a typical Enlightenment attempt, with the help of a range of examples from the Pantheon to St. Peter's, to create the perfect domed church. It is exactly contemporary with Soufflot's plan for St. Geneviève, now the Panthéon, in Paris. Built in a new district, the church was to be set off by the other buildings of a "Place Royale", in a scheme very similar to the Place de la Concorde (with the church of the Madeleine) in Paris.

Monticello Estate (United States)

Thomas Jefferson, American statesman and amateur architect, drew up the first plans for his estate in 1767, but continued to embellish them for more than 50 years. The house stands in a commanding position on top of a hill, amid grounds laid out in the picturesque manner. The architecture is Palladian – a style which Jefferson helped to introduce to America – but is also influenced by modern buildings he had seen in Paris, such as the Hôtel de Salm. The central salon is announced externally by an octagonal dome recalling Chiswick House in England. The disposition of the service quarters in an L-shape on either side of the house, and on a lower level to let the house stand out and be closer to nature, clearly illustrates the influence of Palladio and the rational taste of the Age of Enlightenment.

THE MODERN ERA

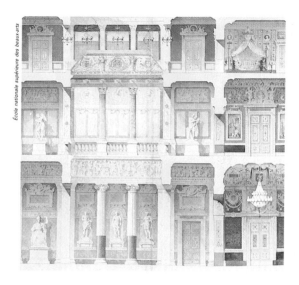

Ecole nationale supérieure des beaux-arts

Proposed imperial residence in the city of Nice

Drawing by Joseph Louis Achille Joyau, winner of the Architecture Grand Prix in 1860. The art of drawing, picturesque, precise, colourful, was fundamental in the training of 19th century architects. In this the Ecole des Beaux-Arts in Paris played a crucial role and its influence was felt as far away as the United States. The programme for the 1860 competition expressed specific contemporary concerns: glorification of imperial power and a new taste for restful country retreats. The young architect, brought up on classical precepts, adapted his knowledge of antiquity to the needs of an official style. (Detail of section, pen-and-ink, wash tint and water colour. Library of Ecole des Beaux-Arts, Paris.)

*T*he 19th century does not have a "period style" like the preceding centuries of Western civilization (characterized as Romanesque, Renaissance, Baroque, and so forth). The history of styles, a by-product of the development of history into a science, was invented at a time when the main preoccupation, not to say obsession, was to create a style. This new urge had many causes, which were all reactions against the traditions of the 18th century but are not all immediately apparent as such. The industrial, economic and social revolution which transformed Europe and the world relegated political and cultural events to second place. This revolution has continued to develop, sometimes spasmodically, sometimes smoothly, and we may consider the end of the 20th century as no more than a further, advanced phase. The age of machinery, of vast conurbations, growing with the proliferation of mechanized transport, marked a fundamental break in the secular evolution of our civilization. It is essential to understand the gradual consequences of this break in order to form a balanced judgment of the 19th century, particularly of its architecture.

The historian may choose to date the beginning of modern times from the dawn of scientific rationalism, the beginnings of the industrial revolution in England, from the French Revolution or the growth of imperialism. At the other extreme, the First World War is often seen as the turning point between the 19th and 20th centuries. But why not choose the impact of Picasso's Demoiselles d'Avignon (1907), or the Great Exhibition held in London in 1851, or the Paris Exhibition of 1889 which was a triumph of industrial architecture, with its Machine Hall and Eiffel Tower? The symbolic role of these exhibitions, or world fairs, has rightly been recognized; so it is all the more interesting to note that the 1900 Paris Exhibition showed a marked stepping back from previous progressive tendencies, or at least a sort of nostalgic loitering or hesitation which is also clearly visible in contemporary academic and historicist movements. There was an anxious reaction against a loosening of aesthetic ideas which had gained acceptance during the last decade of the century. Artistic freedom and audacity became the privilege of the "avant-garde", another kind of modern creation! Evolution ceased to be linear in any sense, periods overlapped, movements appeared and re-appeared, merging, clashing, growing, through individual initiative and political and economic conditioning.

The 19th century saw the end of the age of certainty. The humanist ideals of architects were deeply affected by materialism, which crystallized the old conflict between art and function, pleasure and utility. The very essence of architecture is called into question when the main output of a period has no clear parallel in contemporary literary or artistic movements. Did anyone refer to Romantic, Realist, Impressionist or Symbolist architecture? Not generally, and certainly not with complete conviction. The problem of architectural style needs to be stated in other terms. The acute stylistic crisis of the 19th century reflects a change of attitudes to ideas that were themselves changing.

What, in architectural terms, are neo-Gothic, neo-Romanesque, neo-Renaissance, Greek revival, neo-Byzantine, neo-Moorish, neo-Indian, historicism, eclecticism, rationalism, and the other "styles" of the 19th century? No answer can be given which denotes a precise period; one can only say generally that all these "movements" preceded the ephemeral Art Nouveau, and were associated with architecture throughout the 19th century, and that they also survived Art Nouveau. Such diversity is unknown in any other period: it is especially disconcerting when one considers the serenity of the last years of the 18th century. For it would be easy to prove that the picturesque "Gothic", "Chinese" or "Egyptian" follies built in English and English-style landscapes towards the end of the 18th century were mere poetical embellishments to international Neoclassicism. Between 1740 and 1800 the taste for archaeology, history and the Orient prepared the ground for the eclecticism of the bourgeois age, but without anticipating the effect to which these tastes would be applied.

In a final humanistic outburst, the 18th century had revived the ancient myth of universal civilization and added to it the myth of progress through Art. Enlightenment thinking was dominated by an ideal of absolute culture. One had "style" but did not attempt to produce "a style". The artist sought to obey the rules of Beauty through the means peculiar to his art. Imitation of Nature and classical ideals were his bywords. At that time imitation meant re-creation and not reproduction. The idea of pastiche, so often associated with 19th century architecture, is usually thought to be quite foreign to the 18th century. Yet we have the fashion during the late 18th century in which women draped themselves in "classical" garb. Was this any less a pastiche than 19th century architecture? But while admitting the absurdity of labelling any style a pastiche, one should also attempt to explain the unshakable belief in the classical revival shown by the Enlightenment and in the early 19th century.

In the 18th century, artists and architects subscribed to the idea that art was a universal means of communication. The classical Orders constituted the basis of their formal system, but the thinking of the revolutionaries (Etienne-Louis Boullée, Claude-Nicolas Ledoux, Charles De Wailly and their disciples, influenced by Locke, Condillac and the Encyclopédistes) gave rise to new spatial effects which were not strictly classical, achieved through the manipulation of contrasting masses, and encouraging an appeal to the senses which is the hallmark of Romanticism. Even the deliberate rationalism of Neoclassical architects, and their tendency to make the structure of the fabric visible, were new principles. Some of the characteristic tendencies of Romanticism were germinating rapidly at the end of the 18th century. Enlightened Neoclassicism went beyond its model: it founded a shared culture based on the idea of the constancy of human nature.

The moral teaching of the Age of Enlightenment was certainly one of the most important factors in the overthrowing of the old social order and in the revolution in political ideas in the late 18th century. The weakening of the Church and the monarchy – traditional pillars of patronage – had considerably increased the power of the middle classes, and this altered the status of the artist and the purpose of his work. The vague notion of social change, so fashionable nowadays, involves at least two factors: a change of attitudes and a change of social and economic structure. As far as patronage is concerned, continual changes in regimes and the awakening of nationalism had only a superficial influence on architectural production. But the new industrial building techniques, the financing and forward planning of capitalist enterprises, the change of scale of urban projects in the 19th century, are crucial factors which caused new problems in architecture. The change of attitudes was also fraught with contradictions: on one hand there was a desire to remain faithful to the legacy of the previous century, on the other a need to exploit the new inventions of the time.

For the first time in architecture, the problem of ornament was considered independently from that of structure or space. This independence created two antithetical positions: ornament could be deprived of its symbolic value and become an overlay or "frill" or, on the contrary, it could be put to the service of the constructive logic of new materials (this

THE 19th CENTURY

was Labrouste's approach in France and it is apparent in England in Paxton's Crystal Palace and its successors). The remarkable Houses of Parliament in London, begun in 1840 to the plans of Charles Barry and Augustus Welby Pugin, are a perfect illustration of the change in the significance of ornament. The Gothic outer skin of the building and its sharp silhouette do not conceal the classical conception of the whole (clear plan, symmetry, interacting masses): the care taken to achieve a spectacular reflection in the water of the Thames was not a medieval concern. Did the Victorian nouveaux riches feel closer to this superficial, nationalistic, Gothic revival, or to the Greek revival of the British Museum (begun in 1823)? It is impossible to answer such a question, since the symbolic value of any historical style can only be understood, in the 19th century, in relation to the particular use the architect makes of it. The Doric or Ionic columns of a grand railway station, the vertical pinnacles and gables of a neo-Gothic law court, cannot be called pastiches because in scale, silhouette – in the case of a station with a glass roof – or articulation these buildings have no real precedent: the link between the purpose of the building and its ornamental "style" is purely arbitrary. Another, even more ambiguous, example is the church of the Madeleine in Paris, completed during the July Monarchy. The extreme classicism of the exterior, which looks just like a true

peripteral Corinthian temple, is very close to pastiche; but the interior calls to mind another set of references (for instance, Roman baths) which destroy any feeling of stylistic unity: the interior contradicts the exterior, the pastiche is only apparent.

During this period the purpose of a building became the determining factor; this is especially true of all the results of competition projects, both academic or real, which the 18th century had already made use of for their didactic value. The revolutionary concept of architecture parlante in France could be seen as a consequence of this but it did not extend into the 19th century, although the German Neoclassical school represented by Friedrich Gilly, Carl Friedrich Shinkel and Leo von Klenze came under its influence. On the other hand this expressive type of utilitarianism, where a suitable form could be found for a building thanks to the variety of styles from which an architect or patron might choose, can be seen as a spearhead of progressiveness and modernity in the 19th century. It even led to the suppression of decoration, and thus to the elimination of any stylistic references at all, thanks to the expressive use of new materials (cast iron, steel, glass and then concrete). The cautious way in which the term "architecture" was applied to bridges and viaducts, for example, and the fact that a frankly industrial appearance was restricted to

structures of purely economic necessity (factories, workshops, depots, covered markets, warehouses), demonstrates the results of this.

To understand the rise of eclecticism in the 19th century is to realize that the study of historical "styles" cannot be separated from that of industrial functionalism. Instead a more considered and analytic approach to buildings is needed. It is not simply a question of being satisfied with the history of façades or external decoration – one must perceive the contrasts, or rather the antitheses, which, more than ever before, characterize the 19th century. The turn of the century writer J.K. Huysmans stressed this fundamental dichotomy. In his opinion, the Eiffel Tower was merely a structure (a piece of scaffolding) revealing an "absolute artistic absurdity", whereas the Machine Hall was deserving of extravagant, though subtle, praise. "From an artistic point of view," he said, "this hall constitutes metallurgy's most admirable achievement. But I repeat: as in the Hippodrome [architect, Rohault de Fleury], as in the Bibliothèque Nationale [architect, H. Labrouste], this achievement is confined to the interior. The Machine Hall is impressive as a nave, as an interior, but non-existent as an exterior, as a façade. Architecture has not progressed in this direction: no genius has yet created a complete work with iron, a true work."

The British Museum, London. Built between 1823 and 1847, to house its collection of antiquities and the National Library, the British Museum is one of the richest cultural institutions in Europe. The architect, Robert Smirke, deployed an uncompromising classicism which is typical of the first half of the 19th century.

Giraudon

His hatred for the "Second Empire" or so-called *pompier* style demonstrates the passionate judgment of this committed critic. The verdict of posterity might be different: whether one likes it or not, the Paris Opéra by Garnier is generally regarded as an absolute masterpiece. This is both a very personal building, in which even the tiniest details were selected by the architect, and a monument with a clearly expressed social and cultural function. A judgment of such a building is a matter of taste: arguments about such matters have degenerated since the disappearance of classicism. In art history, the passion for the Impressionists has been such that all the (quantitatively) important works of any other kind during the second half of the century were (until recently) almost completely overlooked. In the history of architecture, emphasis on technical innovation and new theories, until recently, similarly distorted our understanding of the century. With the perspective which a greater time lapse allows, it is now possible to give the unpopular buildings of the 19th century their proper place again as part of the culture of the period.

Creativity and tradition are always inextricably combined in the works of the period. Attitudes to progress are never clearly defined; the careful attempt to "adapt" which seemed to be responsible for a slow evolution led in the end to a radical break. For instance, it is only for the sake of easy analysis that two parallel currents are usually distinguished during the 19th century – academicism and industrial functionalism. Between these two extremes, architects were making stylistic compromises which now appear almost unnecessary. This is probably because we have now abandoned one of these extremes: Art Nouveau and the more recent Art Deco have been forgotten, and economic functionalism has been the main approach since the Second World War.

A history of architecture should perhaps dispel the notion, to paraphrase J.M. Richards, that "modern" architecture is for the use of "modern" men. We are, after all, of the same human type as our ancestors. According to Richards, this error arises from seeing architecture as being in the service of man as an individual, whereas in fact architecture aims above all to serve society, and the needs of society have changed utterly over the last 100 years. It is probably more accurate, however, to say that "the needs of society" have had to obey the new rules of the machine age and consequently those of industrial profit, to the detriment of any humanist culture. This is undeniably an important constituent of our present cultural crisis: the history of architecture in the 19th century sheds light on its first beginnings.

Finally, we must try to suggest some of the underlying causes of this unprecedented architectural crisis. Is it possible to explain dissatisfaction with the cultural heritage – a tendency which has always been present throughout the ages – in terms of the emerging superiority of the new building techniques? Three factors may help us to understand the formal disorder of 19th century architecture: political changes marking the end of the old social order, with accompanying economic expansion and colonialism; the provision of a new educational system including, in particular, the teaching of architecture and the fine arts; and finally the particular role of the architect within society which

acquired at this period the new status of the liberal professions.

The first of these factors explains the ever-increasing gap between the desire to maintain a dignified official architecture and the need to adapt it to the demands of modern materialism. The persistence of Neoclassicism in certain countries in the 19th century (Russia, Germany, Italy, Greece) is another sign of this. Running in parallel to this, we see new techniques making an early appearance in countries such as England, France, the Netherlands and the United States. The first industrialized country, England, was also responsible for the destruction of French supremacy and the collapse of Napoleonic Europe in 1815. Even after this collapse, the new political structure established in Europe by the Congress of Vienna, with powerful political capitals behind it, encouraged the spread of an international Neoclassicism – dignified, legitimate, authoritative. The ruling classes found it perfectly tailored to their needs for a long time before other styles seduced them. In London, around the great parks, in Berlin, in Munich, in Turin and particularly in St. Petersburg (now Leningrad), vast spaces punctuated by public monuments seemed to vaunt the ideals of the European Enlightenment. Nevertheless, this 19th century Neoclassicism was soon confronted by new historical, nostalgic and nationalist tendencies, as well as new archaeological perspectives. The discovery that the buildings of ancient times had originally been brightly coloured, and the very desire to conform strictly to classical models somehow debased the notion of imitation: the re-creation of the spirit of antiquity, which was the heritage of the previous century, shifted into the re-creation of archaeological forms. This shift from imitation to reproduction coincided with the advent of new industrial building techniques. Neoclassicism changed its character: it ceased to be an art for contemplation and became an art for consumption.

The academicism which grew up in the 19th century can be seen not as the safeguard of an ideal, but as an elitist form of culture. Academic architecture was particularly preferred for law courts and museums. But even within academicism there were contrasts. The neo-Greek style of the German Romantics influenced official architecture in Athens, capital of a new kingdom. English neo-Palladianism affected France and became the dominant style in the United States before being partially replaced by Gothic and Romanesque. One of the problems encountered in this century was to create some sort of order out of the vast fund of historical precedents now known.

The second factor, the growth of the teaching of fine arts, encouraged the spread of historicism through the development of scientific archaeology and the strengthening of national identity: education now gave an important place to the monuments of classical times: their study was institutionalized and even became a proper activity for the architect. Developments in philosophy and science deeply affected cultural attitudes. Cataloguing, classifying, experimentation, production – these were the key words of the capitalist society. The study of the history of styles, though soon ossified by conservatism, could be considered as a first glimmering of the social sciences.

The third factor, that of the architect's new professional status, probably accentuated some aspects of the architectural crisis: architects as artists probably felt threatened by their colleagues, the engineers, at a time when the ambitions of the ruling class were being asserted through engineering. This hidden conflict between architects and engineers has not been fully examined, but it is central to the history of architecture, considered as an activity both broadly cultural and specifically artistic. It could partly explain the return to the Gothic style on the part of so many 19th century architects.

In fact, the new Gothic churches show all three of these factors at work. Their building was occasioned by urban expansion and social change, and in them 19th century architects often took on medieval engineering at the point where it had left off. They were also conceived as part of a programme of both spiritual growth and moral and cultural regeneration. Particularly in England, the development of Gothic church architecture was closely bound up with liturgical ideas, which were in continual conflict and evolution; although today these ideas may seem pompous and even banal, the sincerity remains, and one should not neglect in the free development of the neo-Gothic tracery of so many east-end windows the early tendrils of Art Nouveau.

Ornament was vital to the 19th century. The mastery of new materials was accompanied by a desire in the artist, or in the engineer aspiring to that status, to adapt ornament to structure. The prestige of architecture in decorated metal, whether in municipal or in more utilitarian buildings such as department stores, gives some idea of the feverish search for "harmony" between the art of building and the impulse to make a show. In everyday life, where domestic comfort was of greatest concern, any contradiction between pleasure and utility was avoided – except in working-class districts. Haussmann's apartment blocks in Paris served the same desire for "aestheticism" as the majority of manufactured objects. The environment of the middle classes was made more dignified by rediscovered styles, which do not appear to follow any logical pattern and seem to be chosen quite arbitrarily – except that there is an implicit will to mask social imbalances. The ridiculous scale of official architecture of this period has often been criticized for mocking the deep divisions within society, but there is also something rather moving, even tragic, about such a grand show of pretence.

An aesthete asserted rather oddly in 1900: "Electricity, which can adapt to any shape, from a Louis XV chandelier to a Venetian lantern, from a helmet to a flower, does not itself suggest any form." Such a statement would have seemed naive in academic circles: however, functionalism, having run through so many disguises, would eventually triumph over rationalism. The stylistic hysteria which raged from 1900 to the First World War shows that Viollet-le-Duc's warning was not heeded except by a very few true innovators, whether of the Arts and Crafts movement in England – heir to the theories of William Morris – or of the Art Nouveau movement on the Continent. "It is time that architects ceased to believe," wrote Viollet-le-Duc, "that style consists in setting Greek columns or Gothic belfries on a façade, without being able to give a reason for the use of these forms . . ."

Admiralty, St. Petersburg (Leningrad)

The Admiralty was built by Andreyan D. Zakharov, who had studied with Chalgrin during a long stay in Paris (1782–86). This vast building on the banks of the Neva is marked at its centre by a tall golden mast. Built between 1805 and 1819, it is one of the most beautiful public monuments of the Neoclassical period in St. Petersburg.

Albert Memorial, London

Built in 1872 in memory of Queen Victoria's husband, this monument glorified not only Albert but also civilization and the Arts. Its architect, George Gilbert Scott, was the most celebrated of all English neo-Gothic architects.

St. Michel fountain, Paris

This fountain (1858–60) is a good example of collaboration between architect and sculptor in Haussmann's Paris. Gabriel Davioud (who also designed the fountain of the Observatoire, sculpted by Carpeaux) used the motif of an imperial triumphal arch to frame Duret's colossal bronze. This huge composition, situated at the heart of the Latin Quarter, represents the struggle between Good and Evil, with St. Michael at the centre victorious.

339

Technical progress in Great Britain

Under the stimulus of its early industrial revolution, British society had to adapt simultaneously to rapid economic development and population growth. Industrial districts, workers' towns and great ports developed at such speed that traditional patterns could no longer be observed: the all-powerful machine soon played its part in architecture, and architecture in turn served the new capitalist order. New types of buildings were created to respond to the new functional demands of production, circulation and exchange. Materials and processes were new; even work on the building site had to adapt to a quicker pace, to the pre-fabrication of components in a factory. But this new architecture, rational and functional, was deprecated by the guardians of "aesthetic architecture", which was strongly influenced by the classical tradition and the Gothic revival. Yet it is in "industrial" architecture that the beginnings of modern architecture have been discerned. Even when historicism appeared to predominate, in façades of brick or stone, as at the University Museum, Oxford, by Deane and Woodward (1853), the spirit of the new buildings, in conception, use of materials and treatment of space, was clearly innovatory. Paxton's Crystal Palace was an amazing *tour de force* – it showed that a building need no longer be a system of enclosing space within opaque surfaces, and that its structure and form could be generated by a completely new assembly system.

The architects of the new buildings were in some cases distinguished figures of the industrial revolution; the engineer became an architect – as in the case of Boulton and Watt, who invented the steam engine, or Brunel, a naval engineer. Joseph Paxton, the creator of the Crystal Palace, was originally a gardener: self-taught, he became famous for his greenhouses before being offered the chance to build the largest building in the world. Industrial techniques and architectural output were closely linked: for example, Abraham Darby, the first man to produce cast iron with coke rather than charcoal, was also the first man to build a cast-iron bridge, near his factory at Coalbrookdale (1777–79). Cast iron soon took over from wood and stone and became a building material in its own right. England, the first country to open a railway, in 1825, soon had a network of both railways and canals which involved the construction of many bridges and aqueducts, appearing like symbols of the industrial age all over the British countryside. Technical progress made possible more and more daring projects – with vast spans – like the beautiful Firth of Forth Bridge in Scotland, constructed in steel by Baker and Fowler from 1883.

Metal and glass had been used since the end of the 18th century for the construction of covered spaces. With greater fire resistance and also taking up less room, cast-iron posts and metal sheeting replaced wooden posts and laths, as in the Philips and Lee cotton mill near Manchester (1799–1801). There was almost a fashion for metal, which explains the fact that even Neoclassical architects – Nash, for example – used cast iron (as in the Royal Pavilion, Brighton, 1818).

The new techniques and forms were also used in urban architecture, even if brick and stone and a traditional architectural vocabulary were used for façades. Through the use of metal spanning arches the central halls in railway stations were freed of piers, as in Newcastle (1846–50) and in St. Pancras in London (1863–76), conceived by Barlow, with a 75 metre (240 feet) span. Ports such as London and Liverpool were equipped with vast warehouses and docks, constructed of metal thinly clad with brick walls.

The role of metal and the new techniques was crucial in the creation of new building forms, not only in Europe and the United States, but all over the world, and particularly in the colonial empires.

Clifton Suspension Bridge

Built over the gorge of the River Avon, the bridge was the work of the famous railway engineer Isambard K. Brunel. He drew up the plans in 1836 but the bridge was not completed until 28 years later. It has a span of 214 metres (700 feet).

Cysyllte Aqueduct, Wales

The aqueduct was designed by the Scottish engineer Thomas Telford in 1795 to take a canal across the river Dee. It is 300 metres (980 feet) long and built of cast iron supported on 19 masonry piers. Behind the parapet, a tow-path allowed boats to be pulled up the canal.

Central Railway Station, Newcastle-upon-Tyne

The station, the work of John Dobson, was built between 1846 and 1850. It was conceived as a vast, luminous tunnel, using circular cradle-vaults to support a metal and glass roof (used in many stations afterwards). The structure follows the bend in the railway line. The Neoclassical façade of the station, facing on to the town, was also designed by Dobson.

Crystal Palace (destroyed by fire)

For the occasion of the first world fair, the Great Exhibition of 1851, Prince Albert and Henry Cole decided to erect the largest building in the world; but neither time nor available techniques made it possible to build it in brick or stone. Paxton was called in, and proposed a gigantic cast-iron, glazed armature, made from prefabricated elements. It was an enormous transparent box, over 500 metres (1,600 feet) long, of welded cast-iron posts with wooden glazing bars. First erected in Hyde Park, the vast building was taken down and rebuilt on Sydenham Hill, where it was destroyed by fire in 1936.

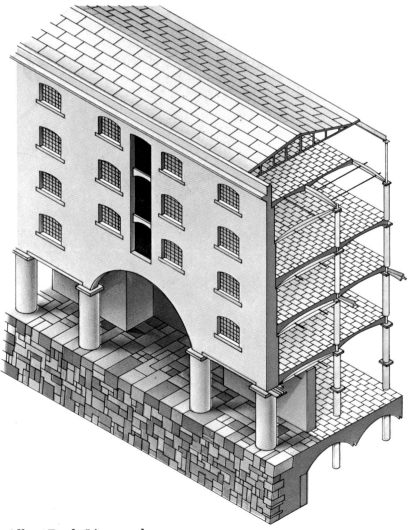

Great Hall, University Museum, Oxford

Built between 1854 and 1860 by the architectural partnership B. Woodward and T. Deane, the museum has a symmetrical stone façade with twin Gothic windows. Inside, the Great Hall is like a Gothic nave in metal, strongly lit from above and with arches which produce a cloister-like effect along the sides. This is a good example of the Victorian Gothic so praised by John Ruskin.

Albert Dock, Liverpool

Built in 1845 by Jesse Hartley, inspector of the Liverpool Docks, the Albert Dock was probably inspired by St. Catherine's Dock in London. It was surrounded on four sides by a vast warehouse on five floors. The structure of the warehouses was entirely of cast iron, including the Doric columns on the ground floor, which formed a covered gallery on the quay. The outside walls and arches were of red brick.

341

The Paris Exhibition, 1889

The first world fair, the Great Exhibition, took place in London in 1851 to celebrate industry, commerce and the arts. Organized by the business world under royal patronage, it was a kind of consecration of the development of industrial capitalism. To house the numerous exhibitors (whose exhibits ranged from simple artefacts to railway engines), a vast pavilion had to be erected: the Crystal Palace, whose glass and iron construction became a prototype. Other exhibitions were to follow in Europe, America, Australia: New York in 1853, Munich in 1854 (the Glass Palaast), Paris in 1855 (then in 1867 and 1878), Vienna in 1873, and Philadelphia in 1876. The buildings had to be large, they had to be put up quickly and be easily dismantled, and they needed to be as cheap as possible. The use of glass and iron, the prefabrication of component parts, and the simplicity and speed of assembly — all these factors contributed to the success of this new building type.

These extremely functional structures (their only aesthetic was achieved by repetition of elements) were often made more attractive by the addition of bricks, stucco or enamel panels or painted sheets of metal. The eclectic vocabulary of official architecture found some channel of expression in this decorative veneer, but the structure and overall design was a functional matter of pure engineering. The eclecticism of the decor was reflected in the exhibits, which included architecture itself: all the participating countries put up their own small pavilions, which bore witness to both their colonial successes and the supremacy of Western art.

The 1889 Exhibition in Paris, exceptional for its size and political significance, was staged by the Third Republic to celebrate the centenary of the 1789 Revolution and to assert to a monarchic Europe the power of France and its ideals. At the end of the Champ-de-Mars, alongside the Ecole Militaire by Gabriel, was set up (soon to be dismantled) the famous Machine Hall, a huge covered space (420 by 115 metres/1,380 by 380 feet) designed by Dutert, holder of the Prix de Rome for architecture, and the engineer Contamin. A structure of 20 steel arches established a central nave and two aisles, leaving a vast area of free, uninterrupted, covered space. Such a space was without precedent and reversed all traditional architectural concepts: the sheer size of the building transformed architecture, the art of enclosing, by creating a luminous space without any apparent limits. The centuries-old laws of statics had been overthrown. The beams supporting the gallery, spanning 115 metres (380 feet), shrank into thin points at their base.

But the most popular building of the 1889 Exhibition – and its symbol – has survived, in spite of its apparently frivolous function. The idea of a "300 metre tower" was then circulating in Europe and the United States, and it was seen by the Third Republic as a good means of impressing visitors. A competition for the design of such a monument was set up, and Gustave Eiffel's project was chosen from the many entries.

Eiffel had begun to design his 300 metre (984 feet)-high tower in 1884, with the help of the engineers Nougier and Koechlin and the architect Sauvestre. He himself supervised the construction, and produced the metal elements in his own factory in Levallois. The building of the tower was a triumph of mathematical calculation and site organization. Eiffel developed original techniques to secure the foundation of the building and to ensure the horizontality of the first floor. He devised a system of wind-breaks and managed to keep the whole construction amazingly light (the thrust on the ground is equal to that of a man sitting on a chair). However, if the Eiffel Tower presents an entirely novel profile in its upper part, the lower part had to compromise with current architectural prejudice: perforated arches, with no supportive function, were added between the four "legs" simply to reassure the eye. The Eiffel Tower has since become the most instantly recognizable symbol of the city of Paris.

Bird's eye view of the 1889 Exhibition

Situated between the Seine and the Ecole Militaire, the Champ-de-Mars, where the festivals of the Revolution had taken place, was chosen as the Exhibition site in 1867. The vast central palace (with a rotunda built by Fermigé) was linked to the foreign industrial galleries and the large Machine Hall (on the right). The Eiffel Tower, facing the Trocadéro, marked the entrance to the site. A few years after the 1900 Exhibition, all the buildings were destroyed, apart from the Eiffel Tower.

The Eiffel Tower

Today the Eiffel Tower is known all over the world as a part of the Parisian landscape and is one of the city's most visited monuments. Its transparent, soaring frame reflects all the moods of the Parisian sky.

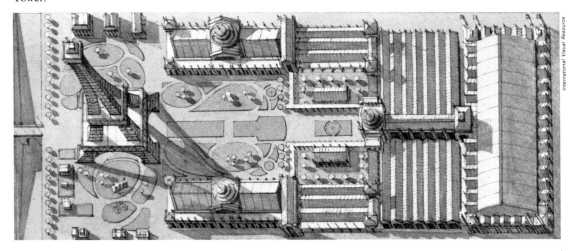

The Machine Hall

Built by Dutert and the engineers Contamin, Piétron and Charton, this iron and metal structure was not unlike contemporary German railway stations, but the beams spanned an unprecedented distance (115 metres/380 feet): the height of the arches (43 metres/140 feet at the apex) permitted the installation of large industrial machines which the visitors could see functioning from the gallery above. The success of the exhibition was such, and its organization so efficient, that one day, 100,000 visitors were able to file through the hall. It was said that the visitor could "take in at a glance the infinite variety of appliances devised by modern science to serve the worker", and the "bold movement of the graceful curves soaring through the air, like the wings of a bird in flight" was also praised. The hall was demolished in 1910.

The 1900 Exhibition, Paris

The photograph shows the display of machines in the centre of the 1900 hall. Galleries at the sides allowed for the display of smaller pieces of machinery. This type of architecture seems entirely in harmony with its purpose and contents: it has become a sort of temple to the Machine.

The emergence of new techniques

The economic and demographic development of the 18th century, together with the beginnings of mechanization, generated a complete transformation of urban civilization in the 19th century, the age of industrialization and capitalism. The new exploitation of coal, particularly in England, transformed the production of metal: as early as 1750, coke had replaced charcoal in the processing of iron ore, making possible the production of cast-iron girders. In the middle of the 19th century, the invention of laminated-iron beams resulted in considerably lighter structures and greater economy in construction techniques.

Wrought iron had been used extensively in some masonry buildings in the 18th century: the classical architect Soufflot introduced reinforced stone in the construction of the church of Ste. Geneviève in Paris (now the Panthéon, 1755–90). The metal dome built by François Joseph Bélanger over the Paris Corn Exchange (now the Bourse) in 1810 shows a serious response to new economic and technical imperatives. In England, a new industrial architecture made its appearance, whose strictly functional character allowed any amount of audacity in its construction. In 1801, Matthew Boulton and James Watt built a seven-storey cotton mill in Salford in which traditional masonry was combined with an internal structure of cast-iron columns and beams.

Cast iron and, later, steel were at first only used in the construction of industrial buildings, bridges and other utilitarian structures. The Pont des Arts in Paris (1801–4) by Louis Alexandre de Cessart and Jacques Dillon is a famous example. Rapid progress was made in certain areas – for example, in suspension bridges, first built with chains and later with steel cables: after Thomas Telford's work at Conway Castle (1822–26) and Marc Seguin's on the Rhône at Tournon (1824), the engineer Isambard Kingdom Brunel spanned the River Avon with a bridge 214 metres (700 feet) in length (1836).

For a long time, aesthetic considerations prevented the new materials from being acceptable in the sphere of official architecture. At the beginning of the century, the famous Royal Pavilion in Brighton, built by Nash in the "Indian" style, used metal in the construction and in certain decorative elements: this exception was justified by the picturesque effect intended – more in the nature of garden follies. But soon advances in the glass manufacturing industry occasioned the proliferation of light, luminous constructions, of which greenhouses and shopping arcades were the forerunners – the Galerie d'Orléans in Paris by Pierre Fontaine (1829); the Palm House at Kew Gardens by Decimus Burton and Richard Turner (1844). The Crystal Palace, created by Joseph Paxton for the Great Exhibition of 1851 in London, was one of those revolutionary buildings which exerts lasting influence on future generations of architects. Erected in six months and covering an area of 98,000 sq. metres (117,000 sq. yards), this vast hall of glass and iron was completely without ornament. Later, new techniques of glass moulding were to enable glazed roofs to become more than a mere covering, and to form an integral part of the structure itself, supported by pillars whose vegetal ornamentation announced Art Nouveau. Alternatively, some architects tried to adapt classical decoration to the new structures, without concealing their "modern" nature. Henri Labrouste was one of the most distinguished representatives of a rigorous classicism applied to structures built undisguisedly in the new materials.

The progress of industry and commerce – in particular the development of the railway and of commercial distribution centres – required a new type of public architecture well suited to the new techniques – railway stations, for example, which inspired painters and writers (Monet, Huysmans) with their smoky naves, as well as covered markets or big department stores. With the prosperity of the Second Empire and the Victorian era, these cathedrals of iron and glass become hymns to the materialist civilization. Even great churches in Paris were affected by this fashion, of which certain utopian architects, such as Hector Horeau, had been the prophets or instigators. Victor Baltard, architect of the old Les Halles in Paris, also built the church of St. Augustin (1860) which is a strange, but poetic compromise between the eclecticism of the "Beaux Arts" and the expressive language of the new techniques.

Ushering in an architecture for crowds on the move and goods on display, most of the new techniques received a first seal of approval in the great central staircases of the big new stores. At first iron and steel were employed mainly for the vaulting of large spaces; but soon they pervaded other types of construction as a result of a frenzy of speculative building, the intensification of industrialization and the appearance of new production techniques (1856: the Bessemer converter; 1864: the Martin-Siemens furnace; 1878: the Thomas process). Structures made of articulated beams, which meant that supporting walls and columns could be abandoned, together with the invention of the lift (New York Fair, 1853), made the skyscraper possible. The most famous architects of the Chicago school, from William Le Baron Jenney to Louis Sullivan, designed the first examples of this symbol of the modern city.

Reliance Building, Chicago

This is one of the ancestors of the modern skyscraper. The design, by Daniel H. Burnham and John W. Root, is modular (based on proportions) and the elegance of the building is due to the economy of its steel structure. Four storeys were completed in 1890, and another nine were added in 1894, the whole being faced with terracotta.

Ste. Geneviève Library, Paris

Designed in 1843 by Henri Labrouste and built between 1845 and 1850, this is a very early example of a classical building provided with a large interior space by the use of iron. While the outside walls are of traditional masonry, the double-vaulted roof and the columns supporting it independently of the walls are made of wrought and cast iron. The long building, rectangular in plan, has a reading room on the first floor, like a vast double nave, and on the ground floor, a lobby and book stacks. Labrouste's masterpiece was the model for the Boston Public Library, completed in 1893 by McKim, Mead and White.

Victor-Emmanuel Arcade, Milan

This is a vast covered arcade with shops and cafés. The plans, dating from 1861, were by Giuseppe Mengoni but the construction was completed, between 1865 and 1877, by an English firm. It is the largest arcade of its kind. The plan is cruciform, and the octagonal intersection is surmounted by a large cupola.

"Au Bon Marché" department store, Paris

Built in 1876 by Louis Auguste Boileau and Gustave Eiffel, the Bon Marché was one of several department stores which made use of the new industrial materials to create vast and well-lit interior spaces. The cheapness of these materials permitted rich decoration, notably of the extraordinary stair-well, top-lit through the glass roof and flanked by suspended gangways. In later constructions the metal decoration became even more exuberant as, with reinforced concrete, the structural elements became more slender – a tendency well demonstrated by the main hall and staircase of the Galeries Lafayette in Paris, built by Ferdinand Chanut in 1912; the staircase was pulled down in 1974.

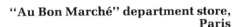

St. Jean, Montmartre, Paris

This novel building (1894–1904) was the work of one of the most influential disciples of Labrouste and Viollet-le-Duc, Anatole de Baudot (assisted by the engineer Contamin). A teacher and architectural historian, he designed important projects in reinforced concrete. This church illustrated his ideas on the use of the new material, within an aesthetic approach influenced by neo-Gothic rationalism.

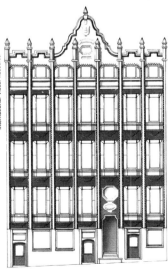

Oriel Chambers, Liverpool

Built in 1865 by Peter Ellis, this office block – an unusual type of building at that time – clearly displayed its structural skeleton. It was made of cast iron, with iron panels hung between the thin stone piers of the façade at each storey. Each panel had shallow oriel windows with flat panes set in a delicate iron frame.

Historicism: tradition and antiquity

The first half of the 19th century appears to be dominated by historic styles, particularly those of ancient Greece. Neoclassicism had appeared in the previous century and now became firmly entrenched, with a proliferation of historical references and archaeological borrowing; classical forms were then considered the only rational architectural vocabulary. "We are the descendants of the Greeks and Romans. The cult of antiquity is for us the cult of our ancestors," declared Quatremère de Quincy, a proponent of strict Neoclassicism, in 1820. And yet antiquity shone out more as an ideal than as an actual model. The most important principle of the day was the "Enlightened" idea of a total architecture, with a formal vocabulary inspired by ancient Greece, and this led to the creation of a new official architecture, found throughout Europe, of hospitals, museums, law courts, prisons, town halls, universities and cemeteries. Napoleon's initiatives in town planning, as seen in the creation of the Rue de Rivoli, the monumental façade of the Palais Bourbon, the Temple of Victory (the Madeleine) and the buildings of his architects, Percier and Fontaine, were typical.

The dominant and most coherent movement was the Greek revival, founded on a good knowledge of classical monuments (thanks to a series of published studies following that of Athens made by Stuart and Revett in the 18th century) and making frequent use of the Doric Order. Impressively pure, solid and massive, the Doric Order was dominant in England

and Germany and was even used in Italy with the "temple" built at Possagno by Canova. We now know of the important part played in the Greek revival by the measured drawings and sketches brought back by archaeologist travellers: also, at the height of the Romantic period, the impact of the Greek War of Independence was considerable. The Greek revival was enshrined in some of the best-known buildings in London: the Bank of England by John Soane (1788–1833), who had a spectacular and visionary conception of architecture; the Ionic façade of the British Museum by Robert Smirke (1823–47); the caryatids of St. Pancras Church in Euston Road; and, of course, the work of John Nash, who re-shaped the entire West End from Regent's Park (begun in 1813) – with its long, white, colonnaded façades – down through crescents and circuses to Regent Street, Carlton Terrace and the Mall.

Archaeology continued to yield fresh knowledge during the 19th century, with ever-increasing excavations and new publications and museums. Sharp conflicts developed about the true nature of classical architecture. The debate as to the original colour of Greek buildings, which Hittorff raised as early as 1824, is well known. Reconstructions formed the basis of the architect's training and students' designs had to conform to strict principles of archaeological accuracy; the technical standard of drawings and watercolours was exceedingly high. In France, an official career was impossible without

first passing through the Ecole des Beaux-Arts. The Prix de Rome and study at the Villa Medici were keystones of the academic tradition.

In the first half of the 19th century, Greek Neoclassicism was especially fashionable in Germany. K.F. Schinkel, painter, decorator, town-planner and architect, transformed Berlin into a monumental classical showcase, a new Arcadia of the North, the main features of which were the New Royal Guard (1816), the Altes (Antique) Museum (1822) and the theatre, a massive abstract building, stripped bare of decoration. Later, in Bavaria, Ludwig I started building an urban dream: Leo von Klenze created the Königsplatz with its Propylaea (1817–46) and Glyptotheka (1816): his Walhalla was a Doric temple set solemnly in a magnificent woodland site.

The fact that Greece had a sovereign of Bavarian origin explains the strange character of present-day Athens, in which the official buildings are in Bavarian neo-Greek style, designed by German and Danish architects. Finally, Neoclassicism was particularly successful in the United States after the arrival, in 1796, of Benjamin Latrobe, who worked in Richmond, Philadelphia and Baltimore, and began the Capitol in Washington (1803–14). Latrobe was responsible for the New World we know today, populated by white buildings, with domes, porticoes and colonnades, all monuments to the triumph of official Neoclassicism.

B. Holtzmann

National Library of Athens

Theophil von Hansen (the Younger) was the architect of this Doric building, made of tufa and marble. Even though it is of late date (1888–1902), it remains characteristic of Greek Neoclassicism in Greece. The Library formed the western completion of a remarkable ensemble begun in 1839 by Hansen the Elder, with the University in the centre, and the Academy to the east built in the Doric Order from 1859 by Hansen the Younger.

Law Courts, Lyon

The long façade with 24 giant Corinthian columns stretches along the Saône. The building is successfully integrated into the site: the longitudinal stress helps to create the monumental effect required when this bank is seen from the other side of the river. The work is by Louis Pierre Baltard, one of the scholars of academic Neoclassicism (he published the *Grands Prix d'Architecture* with Vaudoyer and taught at the Ecole des Beaux-Arts) and was built between 1835 and 1847. Inside, the vast, solemn vestibule is reminiscent of Roman baths, which were the subject of numerous imaginary reconstructions by architects of the period.

Cliché Inventaire général J.M. Refflé

Schauspielhaus, Berlin

K.F. Schinkel built the Schauspielhaus (theatre) between 1818 and 1821. The building consisted of a concert hall in the left wing, administrative and backstage rooms in the right wing and the theatre itself in the centre. The architect has adapted a classical vocabulary to a highly functionalist style. In the wings, for instance, the repetition of windows set very close together creates a sort of open grid, in which the supporting elements are essential both to the structure and to the form.

Temple of Possagno

The great Neoclassical sculptor, Canova, undertook the rebuilding of the parish church of his native village in the hills north of Venice. He designed the "temple" himself, though he was advised by Selva and Antonio Diedo. Set among wooded hills, the white temple with its pure and confident lines appears to have been inspired by both the Roman Pantheon (the rotunda) and the Greek Parthenon (the Doric portico).

St. Pancras Church, London

The church was built on the Euston Road from 1818 to 1822, to designs by William Inwood and his son William Henry, a Greek scholar who published a book about the Erechtheum in 1827. The classical façade is decorated with an interpretation of the famous caryatids of the Erechtheum and the spire is inspired by another Greek monument greatly admired in the 19th century: the Tower of the Winds at Athens. The ground plan, however, has no archaeological precedent, answering only to the requirements of Anglican worship, and is quite similar to that of St. Martin-in-the-Fields.

Stock Exchange, Philadelphia

William Strickland, a pupil of Latrobe's, built the Stock Exchange (1832–34) on a triangular site. He exploited the shape of the site with a circular façade, enlivened by Corinthian columns and a small belvedere on top recalling the famous Lysikrates monument in Athens. The building is of brick with marble dressings. It forms part of an urban development characteristic of early Greek Neoclassicism in the United States.

347

Neo-Gothic architecture

The revival of Gothic architecture in the 19th century was preceded by a wave of interest in the most famous medieval buildings. In the 18th century, even when classicism held absolute sway, architects and theoreticians started to analyse and admire the structural boldness, the soaring effects and the qualities of light in medieval cathedrals. One of the major works of the Age of Enlightenment, the Panthéon in Paris, shows that its architect Soufflot's thinking had been influenced by the techniques of Gothic architecture. A fascination with things medieval had been at the origin of a rather exotic fashion in England, which produced that monument of the picturesque style, Strawberry Hill. Gothic follies in gardens, ruins or not, served as counterpoints to classical temples; their fantastic shapes appealed to the imagination rather than to reason. In the case of Fonthill Abbey, built by James Wyatt between 1796 and 1807 for the eccentric William Beckford, an entire building was conceived as a half-ruined monastery. Gradually the fashion became a movement: in literature, the "Gothick novel" was replaced by the historical novel, preluding a new interest in national history. As early as 1772, Goethe saw Strasbourg Cathedral as the achievement of a specifically German architecture. The explosion of nationalism which so strongly shaped the 19th century explains the significance attributed to the great Gothic buildings of the past, resulting in Germany in the completion of Cologne Cathedral in 1840.

In France, during the Revolution, Alexandre Lenoir had set up a museum of French monuments, an archaeological evocation of the nation's past.

With the Restoration and an official return to Christianity, there was a movement demanding the repair of chapels, resistance to the vandalism of the speculators, even a fleeting success of a "troubadour" style in the decorative arts. In England, when it was decided to rebuild the Houses of Parliament, the competition conditions specified Gothic architecture. A.W.N. Pugin, who was selected with Charles Barry, was already an ardent enthusiast of Gothic architecture, which he had compared favourably to contemporary (classical) architecture in his book *Contrasts*, published in 1836, with the slogan that form must follow function. For Pugin, Gothic architecture was the proper expression of true function in the service of the true faith (he was a Catholic) and the nation's own genius. This amalgam of the functional and the picturesque became the Gothic revival, reaching its apogee about 1870 in "High Victorian" architecture. During this development, the pure, slender forms of 14th century Gothic were gradually replaced by more solid ones, and given a polychromy inspired by medieval Italian architecture; design was also influenced by the Anglican form of worship, as is apparent in All Saints in London (1849–59), by William Butterfield. The desire to unite form and materials reached its peak with William Burges' work. His originality can be seen in the book he published in 1865, *Art Applied to Industry*, and he displayed his decorative talent at Cardiff Castle (1868–81). An important role was played by the critic John Ruskin, an influential champion of Gothic architecture, who voiced in books like the *Seven Lamps of Architecture* (1849)

a reaction against Victorian mercantilism and an ideal of craftsmanship founded on moral and spiritual values.

In France, a policy to restore medieval buildings – with the creation in 1837 of the Commission for Historical Monuments – had a marked influence on new building, in spite of strong opposition from the Academy and the Ecole des Beaux-Arts. Official architecture began to move simultaneously in two contradictory directions. Pioneering architects, such as F. Debret at St. Denis and J.A. Alavoine, who rebuilt a Gothic spire on Rouen Cathedral out of cast iron (1823), led the way to important restoration programmes, as at the Sainte Chapelle in Paris, redecorated by a pupil of Labrouste's, J.B.A. Lassus. Viollet-le-Duc joined Lassus in 1840 and carried out numerous restorations which have since been much criticized, although his work has recently been re-assessed – for instance at Vézelay, Notre-Dame (Paris), Carcassonne and Pierrefonds. When necessary, Viollet-le-Duc used modern techniques and materials; but his historicism was much more subtle than has been supposed: "The monuments of the past have to be studied," he wrote, "not to be copied but to discover their original principles . . . A form cannot be beautiful if it is impossible to explain it." His rational approach, ingenious technical solutions and inventive forms deserve to be appreciated. His *Dictionnaire raisonné de l'architecture française du XIème au XVème siècle*, published in ten volumes from 1854 to 1868, and his *Entretiens sur l'architecture* (1858–72) were a general survey of his experience and set out his system.

Royal Chapel, Dreux, France

This building was commissioned by the dowager duchess of Orléans as a funeral chapel for her family in the pro-monarchy, pro-Catholic aftermath of the French Revolution and the Empire. It was built as a Neoclassical rotunda by Cramail from 1816 to 1822. When the duke of Orléans became King Louis-Philippe, he wanted to have the chapel enlarged, and it was given a Gothic covering from 1839 by P.B. Lefranc. Lefranc also created an ambulatory to house the family tombs and, without giving the building the vertical impulse it needed, he multiplied the Gothic references, adding turrets, gables, crocket pinnacles and lacework balustrades.

Lestrade, Fondation Saint-Louis

Popper Foto

Votivkirche, Vienna

One of the largest and most homogeneous neo-Gothic churches of the 19th century, the Votivkirche was built by H. von Ferstel and completed in 1879. The building as a whole and its ornamentation recall Cologne Cathedral, but also later (14th century) Gothic. The towers are reminiscent of the famous spire of St. Stephen's Cathedral in Vienna.

Houses of Parliament, London

The reconstruction of the palace of Westminster, following a fire in 1834, was dictated by what was left behind – the medieval Westminster Hall and Westminster Abbey – and by the site itself, with its long frontage overlooking the Thames. The new building was also required to have a national character appropriate to the seat of British democracy. Charles Barry won the competition: the rational solution he proposed reflected his Neoclassical training. But the architectural vocabulary and the interior decor were the work of Pugin, who surpassed himself in the invention of Gothic-inspired forms, from the Tudor period in particular. Begun in 1840, the work was completed in 1865, and it represents the triumph of neo-Gothic architecture in public monuments.

Trinity Church, New York

Built by Richard Upjohn, the church was completed in 1846. It is one of the most characteristic buildings of early neo-Gothic in the United States. The symmetrical façade, with its tower-porch enhanced by a tall steeple, was chiefly inspired by English Gothic.

Bedroom in the château of Roquetaillade, Gironde

Viollet-le-Duc supervised the restoration of this small fortified castle between 1864 and 1879, though the work was carried out by his pupil Edmond Duthoit. The building is a well-preserved manifesto of Viollet-le-Duc's ideas, particularly concerning interior planning (it has a beautiful staircase) and the importance of furniture and decoration. The quality and originality of the work, its colour schemes, and its elegance illustrate the fascination that the relationship between architecture and craftsmanship held for this industrial age.

St. Eugène, Paris

Designed in 1854 by Louis Auguste Boileau, St. Eugène is an exercise in self-supporting vaulting, independent of walls. These are used merely to enclose space while a framework of wrought and cast iron (the pillars recalling the refectory in St. Martin-des-Champs in Paris) supports vaults of reinforced plaster. Boileau's architecture is characterized by lightness and economy, and his ideas were strongly criticized by Viollet-le-Duc and César Daly, who accused him of lack of sophistication.

The Paris Opéra

Théophile Gautier called it admiringly "a secular cathedral of our civilization", and the Paris Opéra is regarded today as one of the masterpieces of 19th century architecture. It represents a style which, after years of criticism, is now better understood – eclecticism. It is important to consider the building in its urban context – the Paris of Haussmann – and as the product of three and a half centuries of architectural evolution, of which it is in many ways a synthesis.

The word "Opéra" now means for the Parisian and the tourist a whole district, with *grands boulevards*, smart shops, international banks and department stores. From a distance this enormous building with its imposing silhouette seems to stand as a bulwark against the busy life that takes place around it, enclosing its own life inside. From close up, the majestic façade with its sumptuous decoration speaks of the changing spectacles which are staged within. For the architect, Charles Garnier, the façade was so important that he thought it "the most typical and personal part of the whole building". The subsequent development of theatre architecture proves him right: the façade was to become an archetype.

Theatres were an important part of Greek and Roman architecture, but it took a long time for them to reappear as monuments in modern cities. At first thought of merely as interiors, they were for a long time no more than parts of palaces or public buildings. The chief models in Europe in the 16th and 17th centuries were Italian. Then, in the 18th century, French architects turned their attention for the first time to the exterior appearance. The theatre became a public monument, as important as the town hall and destined to remain one of the permanent focuses of urban life, to the point of becoming a symbol of the Age of Enlightenment. The Grand Théâtre in Bordeaux by Victor Louis (opened in 1780) and the former Comédie Française by Marie Joseph Peyre and Charles De Wailly (the present Théâtre de l'Odéon in Paris, opened in 1782) are good examples. During the reign of Louis XVI and throughout the Neoclassical period (of which Schinkel's Schauspielhaus in Berlin, 1818–21, is a superb example), theatres were built as temples dedicated to Apollo, the Muses or the great playwrights.

The Paris Opéra (Royal Academy of Music and Dance, founded by Louis XIV) burned down in 1781 and numerous projects were drawn up for its reconstruction, incorporating it into various town-planning schemes. Lack of funds and constant changes in the political climate prevented any of these projects from going ahead, and from the Revolution to the Second Empire the Opéra was a collection of temporary buildings. In 1857, Napoleon III proposed the reconstruction of a vast Opéra in the centre of the new districts recently remodelled by Baron Haussmann. The site was chosen by Haussmann himself; in 1858, an officially appointed architect, Charles Rohault de Fleury, made plans and even designed suitable elevations for the buildings surrounding the theatre. The whole district was orchestrated on a grand scale in accordance with Haussmann's theories and Napoleon III's wishes. Haussmann declared: "I have never planned even an ordinary street, let alone one of the main avenues in Paris, without thinking of the vista." The Opéra had to be suited to the layout and style of the whole area, but it also had to stand out, symbolizing the triumph of the Empire, in a style which still had to be invented. Facing the Louvre and the Tuileries, Napoleon III's residence, the new building was a natural continuation of the enormous programme of work started around the Carousel by the architect Hector Le Fuel; it also had to be a sort of society salon where the Court would meet the town, in the tradition of the Ancien Régime. Consequently, the silhouette of the building, its façade and its state rooms had to have pomp and an architectural clarity. Rohault de Fleury's project was rejected, though he built the richly fronted mansions around the square, and an open competition was held in 1860.

Viollet-le-Duc was one of the 70 unlucky competitors. The winner, Charles Garnier (1825–98), was 35 years old, winner of the Grand Prix de Rome in 1848, a precocious and romantic genius. Finally opened in 1875, the Opéra was a gigantic undertaking which the architect himself constantly supervised, for he wanted it to be his own personal work, down to the last detail. His drawings were translated into paintings, mosaic, bronze, marble and stucco by the finest artists of the time. On no other building had the creative will of an architect been imprinted with such force, boldness (particularly with regard to the relationship between the metal structure and the sumptuous interior spaces), and meticulousness. We cannot but admire the absolute unity of architecture and ornamentation; the quality of execution testifies to the talent of artists and craftsmen at the end of the 19th century.

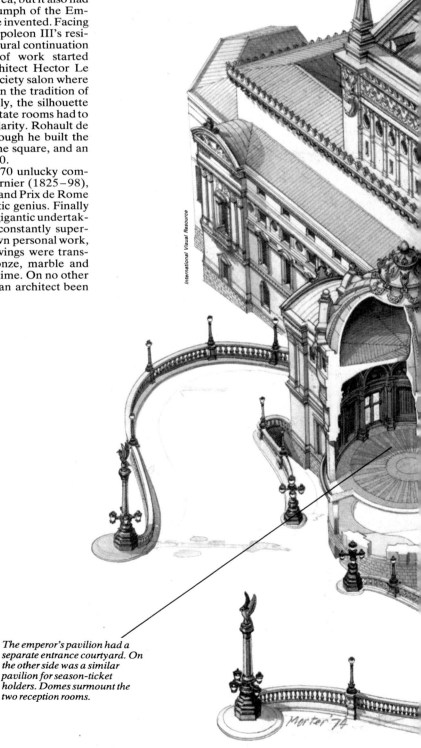

International Visual Resource

Bernard Cox

The main façade

Garnier's eclecticism is clearly seen in the composition of the façade. His training at the Ecole des Beaux-Arts was classical, but he wanted his "masterpiece" to include some of the motifs used so successfully by the great architects of the Renaissance and the Baroque. His spiritual masters were Michelangelo, Perrault, Palladio and Sansovino. But the symbolism is nevertheless subordinate to function: the façade consists of a large open gallery, or loggia, which welcomes the visitor from the square into the foyer. As one approaches, the polychromy and spatial variety emerge into focus while the general outline disappears; from a distance, the flattened dome surmounting the auditorium and the pediment above the stage reveal the main divisions of the building. Sculpture is not only used for decoration or symbolic representation: it affects the reading of masses and lines of force, directing the verticals towards the sky and thickening the horizontals. But Garnier avoids pastiche and produces a completely rational building whose form is exuberant but subservient to function. However, the structure itself is still masked (and why not, since this is the Opéra?): the building's steel supports are never seen. Garnier was a rationalist rather than a functionalist: his conception of art was one of the last manifestations of humanism.

The emperor's pavilion had a separate entrance courtyard. On the other side was a similar pavilion for season-ticket holders. Domes surmount the two reception rooms.

The great staircase

Here, as in contemporary department stores, the staircase was the focus of a building erected for the purpose of social parade. But the Opéra demanded the most sumptuous ornament: the metal structure was hidden by a skin of marble, onyx and bronze. The architecture of commerce exploited the nature of new materials in a way that Garnier's formal staircase could not. An adaptation of the staircase of the Grand Théâtre in Bordeaux by Victor Louis, swelling like one of Piranesi's visions, it has a decorative splendour which is in sharp contrast with its Neoclassical models.

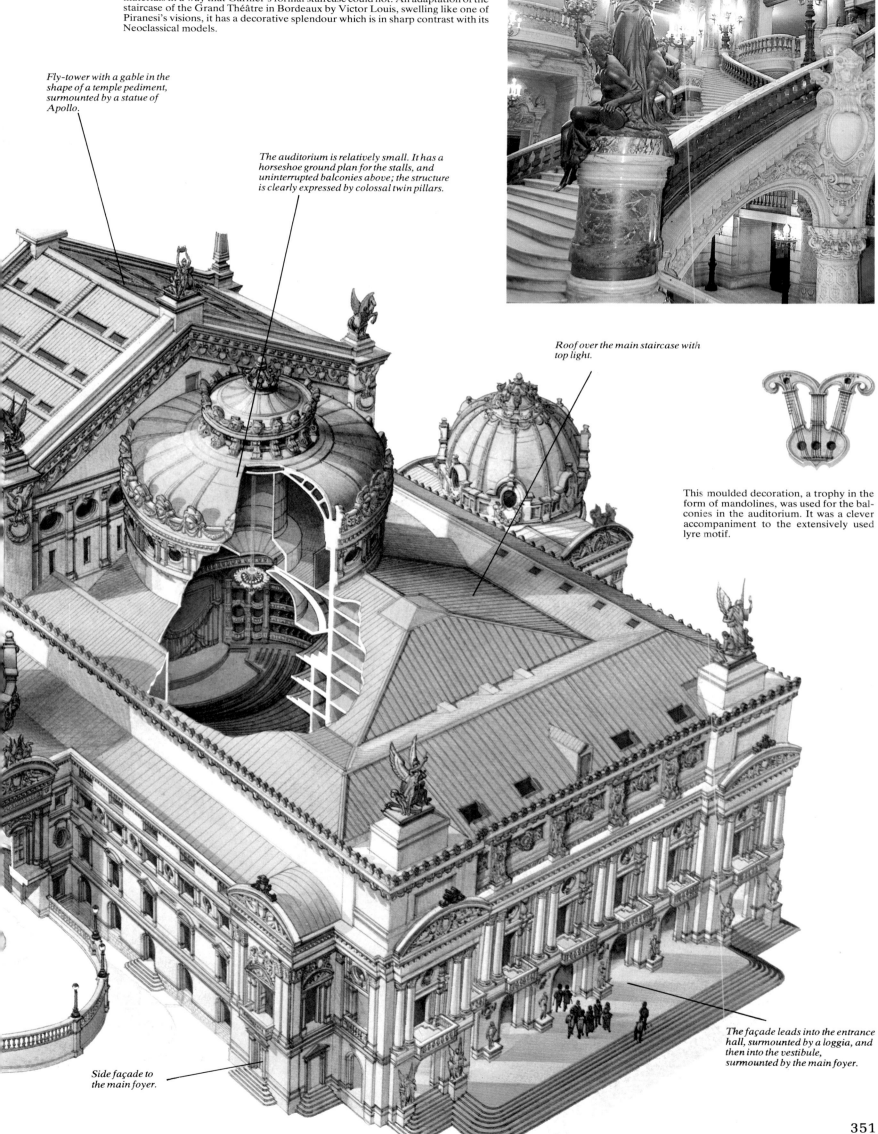

Fly-tower with a gable in the shape of a temple pediment, surmounted by a statue of Apollo.

The auditorium is relatively small. It has a horseshoe ground plan for the stalls, and uninterrupted balconies above; the structure is clearly expressed by colossal twin pillars.

Roof over the main staircase with top light.

This moulded decoration, a trophy in the form of mandolines, was used for the balconies in the auditorium. It was a clever accompaniment to the extensively used lyre motif.

Side façade to the main foyer.

The façade leads into the entrance hall, surmounted by a loggia, and then into the vestibule, surmounted by the main foyer.

351

Eclecticism and stylistic uncertainty

The word eclecticism aptly describes 19th century architecture as a whole, implying both the stylistic uncertainties of the period and its determination to produce a style. For architects and their official patrons such a style had to express and assert a new era in Western civilization. Eclecticism reflects the concerns of a strongly conservative academic current determined to put across a cultural and ideological message through a traditionally "noble" activity, architecture – something different from the constructions of engineers. But architecture was also beholden to the new industrial techniques and, above all, to the laws of capitalism. The classical ideal, which had dominated the cultural world from the Renaissance to the Enlightenment, and persisted, at least in Russia and Germany, beyond 1850 – had no place in the new order of things.

Eclecticism seems also to be the outcome of a new assertion of the spiritual value of art, displaced in a world ruled by machines. Aesthetics, extolled in the previous century by philosophers, theoreticians and politicians, was replaced by history and the cataloguing of styles. The birth of nationalism as well as the Catholic revival seemed to favour a return to the styles of the past. The classicism of the 18th century had attempted to imitate nature and antiquity (the Greeks after all were the inaugurators of Western civilization). Modern artists, eclectic but not revolutionary, were to build up a vocabulary of historical forms with the aim of continuing their development. The setting up of commissions for historic monuments and the Romantic taste for the Middle Ages illustrate this phenomenon perfectly. A new "pure" Gothic evoked the vision of an unchanging Christian world, a new

Baroque reflected the ambition and wealth of the bourgeoisie, and a new "Italian Renaissance" lent a note of distinction to cultural aspirations. It seemed that the period, like its department stores, had a comprehensive catalogue of styles ... Indian and Moorish styles also appeared, encouraged by the growth of colonialism, and were favoured for buildings associated with leisure pursuits and fashionable society. Casinos in spas and seaside resorts used exotic styles in a truly original manner. Disgruntled critics have too often identified eclecticism with pastiche. In isolation, forms often are close to pastiche, but when the new buildings are considered as a whole their scale and context reveal an unexpected stylistic unity.

Whatever their style, the railway station, the theatre, the exhibition pavilion or the town hall are not to be mistaken for the church, the palace or the university. The specific functions of buildings within grandiose urban projects (as in Paris under Napoleon III or Vienna under Franz-Joseph) often explain the taste for stylistic variety. In France, Hector Le Fuel, Charles Garnier, Victor Baltard, Jacques Espérandieu, Pierre Bossan and Victor Laloux sought to create a style suited to the Second Empire and the Third Republic through the combination of borrowed elements. Yet the best representatives of the Beaux-Arts favoured particular styles: Léon Vaudoyer and Auguste Vaudremer defended a rationalist neo-Romanesque style, Paul Avadie a picturesque neo-Byzantine one and Gabriel Davioud a quiet neo-Renaissance. But the particular style seems to have been much less important to an architect than the determination in any particular commission to build an exemplary monu-

ment. As a result, an architect like Théodore Ballu could, simultaneously, build in Paris a pure neo-Gothic church (Ste. Clothilde) and another in a Renaissance manner (La Trinité). There were two, very distinct, eclectic currents: one used historical styles for their symbolic value or for their appropriateness to the particular programme in hand; while the other picked and chose motifs and juxtaposed or combined them in the same building. Thus, in the 19th century, eclecticism embraced both an approach (a kind of historicism) and a style.

Historical styles were easily recognizable, easily understood and spectacular. In Anglo-Saxon countries, Romanesque stood for justice, Gothic was thought suitable for educational buildings, the Greek style was for government buildings, and Venetian for commerce. Every building told a story and carried some moral implication. Norman Shaw (1831–1912) was one of the masters of eclecticism in England. His brilliant handling of surfaces and perspective in commissions for wealthy patrons did not prevent him from using wrought iron and glass. In France, the architects of the Beaux-Arts school worked on similar lines and had a long-lasting influence on the Chicago school. The glazed roofs of railway stations, the factories and department stores of the industrial age and the first skyscrapers were all abundantly decorated. But official buildings, which reflected the power of the State, were colossal hymns to sculpture, monumental in both scope and scale – consider the Law Courts in Brussels and Rome, Le Fuel's Louvre, or the Victor Emmanuel monument in Rome.

Monument to Victor Emmanuel II, Rome

The monument consists of a vast stepped platform, faced in marble and supporting a huge equestrian statue of the king; it stands in front of the Capitol. The design by Giuseppe Sacconi dates from 1884. After his death, in 1905, work continued under Manfredi, but was not completed until 1922. The monument was intended as a great altar to patriotism, based on Hellenistic models. Unfortunately, its over-sized, dazzling-white appearance is very much out of keeping with the ancient ruins of the Eternal City.

Rijksmuseum, Amsterdam

This vast building, erected between 1877 and 1885, was the work of the architect Petrus Josephus Hubertus Cuijpers, who until then had designed only religious buildings. It was a compromise between neo-Gothic (in the windows, roofline, dormer windows, gables) and 17th century public architecture. The two main entrances are openings in the enormous mass formed by a pair of towers standing on either side of an arcaded courtyard. The exhibition rooms are vaulted with roofs of wrought iron and glass.

Pappier Foto

Law Courts, Brussels

Built by Joseph Poelaert, the gigantic building towers over the upper part of the city. Its massive elements form a pyramid rising towards the central dome, which is elongated like a lantern tower. Polaert produced here a brilliant version of the "Babylonian" style, otherwise mainly limited to academic drawing exercises: the overwhelming mass crowns the city with the dignity of classical temples, fantastically enriched and on a gigantic scale.

Westminster Cathedral, London

In a neo-Byzantine style, the church was begun in 1895 by John Francis Bentley. The nave and choir, surmounted by brick domes, present a solid mass on the exterior. All the walls have the same pattern of alternating bands of white stone and red brick, giving uniformity to the conglomeration of different volumes. A high tower soars to the north-west, balancing the ponderous effect of the body of the cathedral.

J.-C. Vaysse

Inventaire général, Jacques et Malnoury

A. F. Kersting

Gare d'Orsay in Paris (left) and the station at Tours (below)

The two stations, built in 1900 and 1895–98 respectively, illustrate the varied inspiration of Victor Laloux, one of the masters of the Beaux-Arts. The station at Tours, using in a lighter idiom the formula of the Gare de l'Est in Paris, is an extremely elegant combination of visible metal structure and sculpture. It is one of the most balanced and inventive creations of its kind. Conversely, the Gare d'Orsay plays with contrasts in the dramatic mass of the stone façade which overlooks the river and the airy transparency of the vast interior space. The station is no longer in use, but is destined to become the Musée d'Orsay.

Doors for the Willow Tea Rooms, Glasgow

This beautiful detail from the entrance door to the Willow Tea Rooms, designed by Charles Rennie Mackintosh (1868–1928), illustrates the equivocal nature of Art Nouveau. In spite of the evident desire for simplicity, rationality of form and economy of means, there was still considerable scope for the craftsman to play a creative role.

The last decade of the 19th century, the fin de siècle *so often discussed in connection with literature*, has generally been seen as a watershed between the classical and contemporary periods. Inventions as marvellous as electricity, the telephone, the internal combustion engine and the aeroplane do indeed make the contemporary age profoundly different from anything in the past. In retrospect, the 19th century with its oil-lamps, coal fuel and steam engines seems hopelessly obsolete. But to isolate one historical moment as a decisive break with the past, whether the French Revolution, the invention of the railway, the Commune, the Paris Exhibition of 1889, the Eiffel Tower, the First World War or the Russian Revolution, is to ignore a process of evolution that has been going on now for nearly two centuries. In fact, the entire 19th century was a watershed. The industrial revolution ushered in a new age, both culturally and economically. The modern mentality, way of life and culture it produced were anti-classical, opposed both to the rigid social structures that accompanied the classical outlook, and to the conception of art as a mere symbol of power. On the economic front, industry took over from agriculture on a global scale, just as decisively as agriculture had taken over from the pastoralism of primitive civilizations. The origins of the transformation are discernible in the mercantilism of the 15th century. It gathered momentum with the beginning of industrialization in the 18th century and reached its climax in the technological revolution of the end of the 19th century. The sheer number of historic landmarks that punctuate the period bears witness to the continuity of change.

The coming of industrialization transformed European civilization in three principal areas, sociological, ecological and technological. There was a restructuring of social classes and of relations between them, a fundamental change in man's relationship with nature and, of course, an immense increase in mechanization. With mechanization, work became routine and dull, and the people doing it were no longer artisans but "workers", members of the proletariat. Meanwhile, the development of capitalism vastly increased the profits accruing to the ruling classes and enabled them to live in a manner comparable to that of the old aristocracy. As the rich were getting richer and the poor poorer, possible solutions to the inequalities of wealth became more elusive and class antagonism all the more pronounced. The operation of the free market made the situation more explosive every day. A less iniquitous distribution of wealth was only achieved after great intellectual and political struggles and a vast amount of bloodshed.

Alongside the growth of poverty came the impoverishment of man's relationship with nature. The majority of the population lost the direct contact with the land involved in agricultural labour and lived an urban life that was entirely artificial. For the first time in history, the town expanded to the point where it was completely independent of natural rhythms and limitations. The proliferation of suburbs and the related growth of public transport destroyed all sense of distance as something that could be walked and made the town infinitely extendible. Artificial illumination, especially street lights, usurped the natural sequence of day and night which had formerly governed the towndweller's pattern of life and institutions. The urbanization of society affected family life as well. Here the changing relationship with the environment revealed itself in people's expectations of comforts and amenities. The 19th century brought running water to the home, gas-light, central heating and the modern bathroom. And with the coming of electricity, telephones and cars at the end of the century, the break from the rhythms of nature was complete.

Industrialization brought about equally profound changes in architecture and design. The building industry evolved rapidly with increasing mechanization. Methods of construction were improved; masonry, carpentry and earthmoving were all revolutionized; and there was a massive increase, as methods of manufacture developed and prices fell, in the use of glass and iron. Glass became widespread from the end of the 18th century with the popularity of covered walks, conservatories and winter gardens. As full of light as an exterior space yet protected from the elements, such structures embodied an architectural paradox that was to become a touchstone of modernism. At the same time, the use of cast iron made it possible to reduce dramatically the mass of weight-bearing members, replacing a stone pier by a cast-iron column as little as a thirtieth of the width. An important development of the 1870s was the use of prefabricated steel girders which could simply be riveted together as a constructional framework; a completely steel "skeleton" was first used in 1871 by Jules Saulnier in the Meunier Chocolate Factory at Noisiel-sur-Marne. The already extraordinary pace of technological progress accelerated towards the end of the century. Reinforced concrete, for instance, which began to be used in 1893, spread rapidly throughout Europe and America.

Remarkable though the evolution of building techniques may have been, even more important changes were happening in the sphere of manufactured objects. The production of everyday items such as clothing, furniture and tableware was expanded to a prodigious degree. In 1830 the enjoyment of quality goods remained largely the privilege of the upper classes; by 1850 the situation was quite different. Thanks to the reduction of prices brought about by mass-production, the rising middle class could afford any quantity of material possessions – indeed, the high level of consumption was one of the most characteristic features of the new culture. Improvements in wages and living conditions won by the working classes in the last quarter of the century enabled them to enter the market as well. A major aspect of Art Nouveau was the mass-production of objects for the working class, a trend that culminated with Art Deco in the 1920s. The continuing transformation of life and society seemed to demand new forms of expression; the cultural tradition that had held sway since the Renaissance was first questioned, then rejected. Art played a fundamental role in giving form to the values of the new society. The possibility of a "new art" had been the subject of debate since the 18th century but it was only in the last years of the 19th century that it found its realization. But this proved more an end than a beginning. Art Nouveau was the legacy of three-quarters of a century of critical thought; but it offered no viable prospect for the future, as its extremely rapid decline within ten years would suggest.

The world-view of classicism rested on the concepts of order and perfection. It was permeated by platonic idealism, the belief in divine absolutes of which the creations of mankind could be no more than pale imitations. It was an intellectual construct that succumbed to pragmatic criticism. And when classicism in architecture lost its metaphysical significance, as a system of perfect proportions, it was reduced to a mere formal exercise, just one of many systems equally worthy of attention and emulation. As the classical language of design was decaying, other, non-European cultural influences were coming into play. The status of classicism was all the more strongly challenged with the growing feeling that it was a cold, inhuman style. Beginning with debates over the subjectivity of Beauty at the end of the 17th century, and continuing through the Romantic period, there had been a shift away from metaphysical ideas as the basis for art towards the expression of emotion. But this is a simplification. In fact, the basic tendencies towards feeling on the one hand

THE TURN OF THE CENTURY

and thought on the other naturally continued to coexist within the human mind and, setting aside all metaphysics, the fact remained that reality could be perceived just as well in terms of logic as in terms of emotion. These are the two approaches – sometimes complementary, sometimes conflicting – between which the contemporary world has constantly fluctuated. The "new art" had to take account of this problem.

Neoclassicism traditionally aspired to become a great public art at the service of the State. Dismissed by Romantic artists as academic, it was replaced from the 1830s by a more personal, subjective approach, of which Tuscan ruralism, the neo-Greek elegance of the Etruscan manner and the smooth, picturesque "troubadour" style were among the many and various expressions. The dissolution of classical culture and the triumph of the Gothic Revival might suggest that a wholly new sensibility had been born, the architectural equivalent to the bourgeois dramas of Sedaine. In fact, nothing could be further from the truth. There was an emotional Gothic and a rational Gothic and each attacked the other, the first for being uncontrolled, the second for being dry. In other words, there was another dividing-line beyond the opposition of Gothic and classical, Romantic and academic. And in the course of the century, the roles reversed: the traditionalists were led by their love of beauty into the highly subjective realm of aestheticism, while the opposite camp sought to establish their work on a rigorously rational basis. Soon it mattered little what style an architect adopted as his point of reference. Joseph Louis Duc and Henri Labrouste professed exactly the same opinions on the art of their time as Viollet-le-Duc, the leader of the Gothic Revival. A little later, with the dissolution of classicism continuing, the same kind of discrepancy arose within the Romano–Byzantine school of architects: it was only on the most superficial level that Paul Abadie and Jean-Camille Formigé had anything in common with Pierre Bosan.

The opposition of reason and feeling appears at the end of the century in the constant criticism levelled by rationalists against Art Nouveau for its lack of restraint. With feeling, individuality and subjectivity as its supreme considerations, art was drowning itself in a flood of narcissism and self-indulgence. Art Nouveau was a bourgeois art-form doomed by its own ideological shallowness. Art must be more than mere pleasure!

The basis on which a truly "new art" would be established was the urge to link art and

the community, to express in heroic style the great wave of technology that was sweeping through modern society. The major theoretical positions had been defined since 1860, by Gottfried Semper in Germany, Ruskin in England and Viollet-le-Duc in France. They provided a basis for the Art Nouveau of the 1890s but also for the modernist pronouncements of Le Corbusier after the First World War.

The 19th century has been called the century of the bourgeoisie, of historicism, of

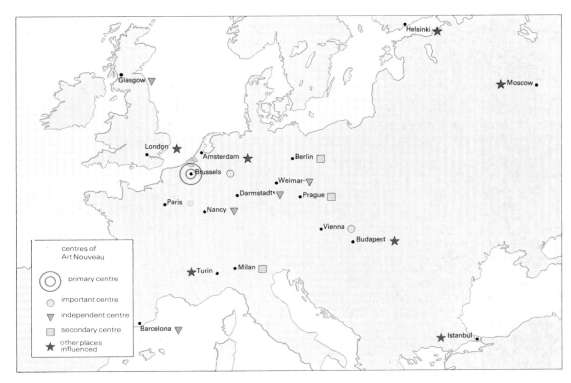

eclecticism. Yet running through the period there was a strain of self-criticism, a longing for art that would transcend all these things, an art that would be social, not historical or contradictory but expressive of a society in flux, an art of reconciliation and hope as opposed to egoism, isolation, corruption and conflict. In a sense, the notion of an art nouveau was present throughout the century, though referred to until the 1890s as "modern" rather than "new". As a movement of that last decade of the century, Art Nouveau was a late attempt to resolve problems posed over several generations. But too many hopes were invested in it, too important a symbolic role expected of it, and inevitably it proved a disappointment. Soon it was itself challenged and superseded with the rise of modernism.

The story of Art Nouveau is ultimately the story of a failure. Of all the 19th century attitudes weighing art down, it managed to throw off only one, that of historicism.

Despite all its attempts to reach ordinary people, it remained essentially bourgeois, the art of the ruling class. It remained eclectic, too, individualistic in its allusions, contradictory in its forms and theories. Art Nouveau was all about departure from the norm. As in the world of politics, there was never any real consensus, never a collective message that would be acknowledged by everyone involved.

The great value of Art Nouveau, like Post-Impressionism in painting, was that it

cleared away the outworn notion of dependence on the past. The 19th century, its cultural institutions shaken to the foundations, suffered from a nostalgic eclecticism, an insistent referring-back to history. There was no faith in the ability of the age to develop its own style. Artists of the 1890s finally dared break the habit of historical allusion. They opened up whole new possibilities for decorative design. They felt the excitement of modernity and were full of hope for art and the future, a quality that had been conspicuously lacking for the preceding half century. No matter that their hopes were disappointed. It was vital that they believed what they did in order to release art from the trap in which it had been caught, to forge the all-important concept of an art for the future, an art for the industrial society that was in the process of being born.

The house

By upsetting the relationship between man and nature, industrialization brought about a cultural as well as a technological revolution. The economic development of towns had already engendered patterns of behaviour that were remote from the rhythms of rural life. Urbanity may have been the image of elegance and politeness, but it also meant the fragile artificiality of everyday life in the great cities. With industrialization, the town became synonymous with noise and vastness, the confrontation of luxury and poverty, night life and modernity. If the fascination of urban luxury (symbolized by the manufactured objects that spread far and wide during the 19th century) was universal at the time when Napoleon III's Paris and Queen Victoria's London were the capitals of the universe, nostalgia for the rural world and provincial life was also developing, leading to a profound ambivalence in tastes and attitudes.

This ambivalence is demonstrated in 19th century attitudes towards construction in metal, which was seen as a symbol both of the benefits and of the evils of industrial production. The 19th century may have been a century of history, but it was also one of reaction against the past. As early as 1830, the idealist Saint-Simonians had agreed with the aristocratic "ultras" in their condemnation of industrial society and its train of upheavals. Philosophers and artists joined with moralists in deploring the dissolution of traditional values and in calling for their reinstatement. Architecture was increasingly bound up with politics and the inflammatory acts of the Commune were no less important culturally, in their desperate reaction against the Paris bourgeoisie, than the neo-Gothic châteaux of the legitimists or the phalansteries of the utopians.

In retrospect, rural architecture seems free from the defilement of the industrial Babylon; there was a tendency to turn towards the values it symbolized in an emotional rediscovery of regional and popular culture. All part of the same movement were the antiquarian and archaeological studies of the pro-

vincial schools of Romanesque art in the Auvergne and Poitiers, the writing of histories of costume and furniture, and the renaissance of regional languages such as Flemish, Breton and Provençal. The movement led to a new appreciation of the local heritage, which had until then been virtually overlooked in favour of the imposing architecture of public monuments; and, finally, it brought about a reappraisal of the traditional values of craftsmanship and family life.

Industrial society, in changing man's relation to work, had seriously modified the structure of the family group, reducing it to the parent-child unit and eliminating the extended family and servants. The basic urban apartment failed to respond adequately to the needs of the smaller family group. But the individual house, in itself a symbol of the nuclear family, tried to adapt itself to the demand, giving rise to the Domestic Revival movement in Great Britain, and effecting a profound change in Western concepts of housing.

The doubt that industrial society had cast upon cultural values had already manifested itself in the practice of eclecticism in architecture, a debasement of a formal system which brought ideological content down to a simple question of "appropriateness", suitability to an overall scheme, a commission or the surroundings. But the demise of the grand style could only lead to some form of renewal by a departure from pure formalism. Only an ethical renewal could bring about such an important aesthetic transformation.

Industry, through its formidable range of technical possibilities, allowed – even favoured – the attitude of "anything goes". The return to craftsmanship was a reaction against this trend, as it was a means of determining form and message. Simplicity, efficacy, and suitability to function were set against the emptiness and soullessness of the industrial object. The English Domestic Revival went hand in hand with the Arts and Crafts movement in reviving artisan work, and with the Pre-

Raphaelite movement in painting in its condemnation of the artificial seductions of formalism and its frantic search for meaning in pictorial art.

Philip Webb in the Red House he built for William Morris in 1859, then C.F.A. Voysey, Norman Shaw, Baillie Scott and Ernest Newton were to give the renewal of domestic and popular architecture (sometimes called the "cottage style") an international importance. The style made an impact on American architecture at the end of the century (in the work of Henry Hobson, and even Frank Lloyd Wright) and has even influenced the more mundane forms of resort and suburban architecture of our own time. It was a style made up of simple, freely-distributed forms, expressed through a lively interplay of volumes at roof level, and it could adapt itself to the most complex of conditions. It revealed the internal organization of the building and allowed the details to show up by simplifying everything else. With its roots in the tradition of post-medieval rural architecture, as preserved on the fringes of the industrial world, it forbade all reference to classical culture.

This refusal of the urban world to adopt the classical tradition inevitably led to the creation of a new type of dwelling, the suburban villa, whose birth may be dated towards the end of the 18th century. The outcome of all this was the garden city, the London prototype being Bedford Park designed by Norman Shaw from 1875 onwards. This experiment in residential architecture drew on the theories of the town-planner Ebenezer Howard, whose ideas lay behind all the great garden city projects in industrial towns in the first half of the 20th century. In the trend towards garden cities and in the related Domestic Revival movement, the dominance of English architectural theory was paramount. It is hardly surprising that the oldest of the industrialized countries should have played a major role in this renewal of a culture and way of life that began in the mid-19th century.

The Red House, Bexley Heath

The Red House was built in Kent in 1859 by the architect Philip Webb for his friend Wiliam Morris. A founder of the Arts and Crafts movement (which stood for the renewal of craftsmanship in the face of the ravages inflicted by industrialization on artistic production in Great Britain), William Morris wanted to break with the learned tradition of public architecture, whether it was the art of the court under royal patronage, or bourgeois art, with its great civic monuments. In choosing to draw upon the popular tradition of rural architecture of the 17th century, Philip Webb succeeded in avoiding both Gothic pastiche and the classical tradition. With its simple forms and lack of decorative detail, the building is expressive of the life of its inhabitants. It is precisely this correlation that the architect wished to achieve.

1 outbuildings
2 courtyard
3 laundry
4 kitchen
5 lavatory
6 pantry
7 dining room
8 staircase joining the two wings
9 hall
10 north porch
11 waiting room
12 bedroom
13 exit to the garden

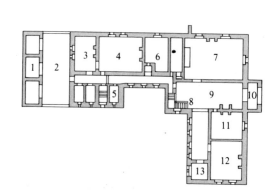

356

CORNER PROS=PECT OF ONE OF THE NEW ROA=DS ON THE BEDF=ORD PARK ESTATE

Bedford Park, London

Prototype of the 20th century garden cities, Bedford Park was created in a London suburb from 1875, at the same time as the opening of a new railway station at Turnham Green. The architects Norman Shaw, E.W. Godwin, E.J. May and Maurice Adams systematized the individual dwellings – detached or terraced, but all with gardens – in the prevailing Domestic Revival style. Inspired by Webb's Red House, they offered their clients the Queen Anne style, deemed to be the least formal of architectural traditions and the best adapted to England's climate. It was also the style most geared to the external expression of the interior layout of the building – the function of each room, its lighting requirements, and its relation to the whole house. Differing widely in price, the houses of Bedford Park were conceived as individual houses, the most beautiful of which were those built by Godwin in 1876 in The Avenue (above left).

HOUSE TO BE BUILT AT GARTMEL FELL GILLHEAD BY WINDERMERE FOR J.W. BUCKLEY ESQRE — C.F.A. VOYSEY ARCHT

Bloemenwerf, Brussels

The house that Henry van de Velde built in the English manner for his young wife, Martha Sèthe, in the elegant Uccle area of Brussels in 1896, showed him to be as much of an architect as he was a painter and interior designer. The "Bloemenwerf" villa remains one of the great testaments of Belgian Art Nouveau and Domestic Revival architecture.

The Orchard, Chorley Wood

Charles F.A. Voysey, one of the greatest architects of the Art Nouveau period in England, built himself a large house, "The Orchard", in Hertfordshire in 1899. The extreme starkness of form and the emphatic sense of materials may not, as was previously thought, be the beginning of modernism, but rather the culmination of the purity of spirit of the Arts and Crafts movement.

Sherman House, Newport

Unnoticed on the Continent, the influence of the English Domestic Revival was felt mainly in the United States. The most brilliant of the American architects of the 1880s, Henry Hobson Richardson, brought to the American East Coast a type of villa midway between the rationalism of Viollet-le-Duc and the English Domestic Revival, developing the so-called "shingle style".

357

Art Nouveau in Europe

Ever since de Laborde's famous pronouncement on the aesthetic of manufactured objects, prompted by products on show at the Great Exhibition in London in 1851, the whole world had realized that the 19th century lacked its own style. Though as common as it was practical, eclecticism had few supporters on a theoretical level because everyone was hoping for a transformation of style, for the creation of a formula that would be truly expressive of a new society.

Art Nouveau was the result of half a century of effort to renew the language of ornament, to adapt it to the techniques and forms brought into being by the industrial revolution. It drew upon a rich stylistic heritage passed on by the English Neoclassical architects (the most prominent of whom was Sir John Soane), the French rationalists (Henri Labrouste, Alfred Normand, Auguste Vaudremer and Léon Vaudoyer) and finally by the exceptional figure of Viollet-le-Duc. It was Viollet-le-Duc who made the disconcerting identification between Gothic and modern. He divorced the forms of the Gothic Revival from their sentimental and nostalgic associations, using incisive logical analysis to show how they were determined by their function. This rather Darwinian view of historical evolution, this formal determinism, underlined the irrationality of historicism and led to its replacement by a new concept of style based on the principle that form should always speak for a building's function.

Classicism, the manifesto of a past epoch, had no future. Since 1830, attacks against it and its ideology of academicism had been multiplying. As an aesthetic system, the idealist philosophy of classicism hardly corresponded with the requirements of a society whose values were realism and pragmatism. The very principle of proportion was condemned during the 19th century because it made architecture into an object of pure aesthetic contemplation, and not the expression of technical, economic or social dynamism.

From the moment classicism was rejected as a system of reference and no longer thought to be appropriate to the ideological needs of the time, the only option left was to break with the past. A new style must be created, perhaps one as audacious as medieval architecture had been when it first appeared eight centuries before. Gothic acted as an intermediate stage, a provisional cloak for the evolving style. The fundamental problem for the 19th century was to get rid of the Orders (columns and entablatures) and the classical system of proportions, and to develop a repertoire of ornament that was free of idealist reference and sufficiently flexible to be used on different scales and in different situations.

If it had only been a question of form, the classical vocabulary would have been able to adapt itself to meet the demand. Charles Garnier showed this brilliantly in the very personal style he used for the Paris Opéra, which was a perfect example both of structural rationality and of the ostentation of the triumphant bourgeoisie in the first era of industrial capitalism. But for the creation of the *new* art that had been called for over several decades, the connotations of classical form were too powerful. Gothic had the great advantage of a sense of distance, as did the other exotic styles of orientalism and *japonisme* which also contributed elements to the new style.

Yet Gothic was more than just rationalism, since part of its ornamental content was derived directly from nature. This second aspect of Art Nouveau, the use of floral motifs, developed more rapidly and caught on more widely than the principle of rationality. The cult of nature was bound to touch a society menaced by its own technical progress. The search for roots led at once to a communion with mother nature and towards the investigation of the newly-revealed unconscious mind.

Such diversity of often contradictory intentions could not lead to a unified style. To start with, there was a bewildering variety of historical and cultural references. The "Louis XV Gothic" of Art Nouveau in Nancy co-existed with the mixture of Japanese masks and suburban design (rough stonework, brick and wood-panelling) beloved of Hector Guimard; the Chinese dragons of August Endell with the symbolism of Gauguin; the bare geometry of Josef Maria Olbrich with the floral flourishes of Otto Wagner. But there were even wider disparities of approach. The mystical direction taken by Antonio Gaudi in his Sagrada Familia was far removed from the prodigious decoration that Victor Horta used at the Hôtel Solvay and Van Eetvelde house in Brussels, and had little in common with the rigorous search for economy of means pursued by Paul Hankar.

For this reason, Art Nouveau as we generally think of it – a style of curves and floral decoration – must be considered as only one tendency in the art of the period. Perhaps not the most decisive trend, the *style nouille* was born around 1893 and came to an end as early as 1902. Its last testament – and confirmation of its premature obsolescence – was the exhibition of decorative arts held in Turin in 1902. In this respect, the fashion for Art Nouveau was really only a flash in the pan.

Castel Béranger, Paris

Hector Guimard drew his inspiration for this block of flats at 15, Rue La Fontaine, Paris 16 ème, from the neo-Gothic style. His discovery of Belgian Art Nouveau led him to redesign entirely the external ornamental detail of the building. Completed in 1898, Castel Béranger is still one of the most famous examples of French Art Nouveau or, as Guimard himself modestly put it, the "style Guimard".

Huot houses, Nancy

The twin houses at 92 and 92A Quai Claude-le-Lorrain, Nancy, were built in 1902 by Emile André for the town's university. They represent a rather late but very successful example of the fusion that took place in French Art Nouveau between the neo-Gothic of rationalist inspiration and the picturesque style beloved of the French bourgeoisie. This lyrical form of flamboyant architecture, with its hints of resort buildings and rich floral ornament stemming from Gallé vases, is a typically French amalgam, where ornament elegantly overrides architectural expression.

Studio Elvira, Munich

The shop of a famous German photographer, Studio Elvira was designed in 1896 by August Endell. The decoration of the façade draws upon Japanese design, enlarging the motifs to an architectural scale. Hitler hated the building, seeing it as a symbol of the degeneracy of modernism, and had it destroyed when he came to power.

Van Eetvelde house, Brussels

Victor Horta, who co-founded Belgian Art Nouveau with Paul Hankar, influenced the whole of his generation in the freedom of his decorative schemes, based on stylized plant forms. This virtuosity, and the use of the most luxurious materials, are the very essence of European Art Nouveau.

Artists' Colony, Darmstadt

Financed by the Grand-duke of Hesse and centred around Josef Maria Olbrich, the Darmstadt Colony was a group of artists inspired by the Viennese Secession, which they introduced into Germany. The artists' hall (1899–1901) was conceived of as a permanent exhibition space for their works.

Secession Art Gallery, Vienna

In the imperial capital of Austria, this exhibition gallery for the anti-academic avant-garde, built by Olbrich in 1896, seems less like a work of Art Nouveau than a humorous commentary on the vocabulary of classical form; the dome, an incongruous ball of boxwood, deflates any architectural pretensions.

Exhibition of Decorative Arts, Turin

The Exhibition of Decorative Arts in Turin in 1902 marked the end of the floral phase of Art Nouveau. Here the Secessionist trend triumphed, especially in the central pavilion designed by the Italian Raimondo d'Aronco. Monumental forms, hieratic figures, ornamental pylons and bands of incised decoration were in evidence all over the building.

Behrens house, Darmstadt

The Berlin architect Peter Behrens, who later became a pioneer of industrial design, built his own house in 1901 while a guest of the Darmstadt colony. It represented a reaction against the ornamentalist trends of Art Nouveau in its cruciform plan, the discreet expression of function by a few carefully calculated asymmetries, and the modulations of the openings. Ornament is restricted to the outlines of the structure and to a few key points.

Critical rationalism

Art Nouveau was a movement of various tendencies and it is difficult to contain its often contradictory strands under this one title. The problem of how to relate to history may have been solved by the end of the century but that is not to say that ideological differences concerning the role of art and its means of expression had been settled. On the contrary, the opposition that had existed for half a century between the academics and the rationalists was still current. It was the confrontation of two utterly antipathetic views of form, not just a difference of opinion over its external treatment but a fundamental disagreement on what its underlying intention should be.

During the 1890s when Art Nouveau was triumphant in Europe, becoming all the rage among the leisured classes who thought it heralded the art of the 20th century (and who tried, like Proust's Saint-Loup, to transform their interiors accordingly), another current was developing, that of critical rationalism. This new movement rejected the facile aspects of Art Nouveau, and introduced a deeper level of reflection on the question of style.

Art Nouveau was only a fashion, a repertoire of formulae as deprived of meaning as the outdated resources of historicism. It could be seen as the last manifestation of eclecticism, showing not only a debt to historicism but, worse still, a willingness to lend itself to formal hybrids that were accepted as the "right style" for commercial purposes – in the same way that Romanesque art was adopted as the style for religious communities, Gothic for parish churches and Louis XVI for bourgeois mansions.

Looked at from the sociological point of view, Art Nouveau can be associated with the liberal *haute bourgeoisie* of leading lawyers, politicians, and enlightened industrialists, as Victor Horta's clientele would suggest. In France, there was a curious alliance between Art Nouveau and the secularist movement, which subtly transformed the ideological content of the style into a political message. The conflicts in the architectural world indeed came to reflect the power struggle between several different groups within the bourgeoisie, rather as parties might in the world of politics.

This adulteration of its content was particularly noticeable when Art Nouveau first became known to a wider public, around 1894–95. Publications on the decorative arts dating from this period were set on conquering a profoundly traditional market. The reviews saluted each new building as a victory in the war that Art Nouveau was supposedly waging against historical styles. By 1896–97 criticism was mounting against fraudulent imitations of the style, its superficial applications and its use in an advertising and commercial context. Finally, after 1900, architects increasingly sought to free themselves from the dependence of their style on a given social class, and ended up by associating floral motifs so strongly with the *haute bourgeoisie* that they inhibited the free expression of their own temperaments. This happened to both Horta and Hector Guimard, who sought a less flamboyant formula that would be more suited to the wider clientele they envisaged.

The formalism of Art Nouveau was counterbalanced by the more exacting aesthetic analysis of the rationalists, which stood in a direct line of descent from Viollet-le-Duc's *Entretiens* in its relation of form to function. Here too there was little stylistic unity; but the intellectual direction was clear, very assertive, and perfectly convincing. The Amsterdam Stock Exchange by Hendrik Petrus Berlage owes a great deal to the influence of Henry Richardson and the neo-Romanesque trend in American architecture. But it is still allowed to reveal the nature of its construction: the masonry is left exposed, the subtle, natural colours of the materials are much in evidence and ornament is restricted to a few key positions. There is a considerable difference between this building and the rival designs of Anatole de Baudot, which included rooms of pre-fabricated metal construction or reinforced concrete. However, the search for form led in both cases to an expression of structure, prefiguring later designs such as those in reinforced concrete by Pier Luigi Nervi.

Modern architects have well understood this rationalist trend in the age of Art Nouveau. Certain analyses of Gaudi's works have emphasized not only his mystical intentions but also his insistence on the appropriateness of surface design to underlying structure. Gaudi's apparently fantastic creations always relate to the facts of their construction and work with rather than against it. Horta's buildings, on the other hand, are no more than theatrical productions in which the astonishing facility of his design makes one forget the incongruity of the end result.

The works of Paul Hankar in Brussels, Otto Wagner in Vienna and Charles Rennie Mackintosh in Glasgow seem more traditional, following in the rationalist line that still owed a great deal to Viollet-le-Duc. This is due to the basically realist approach of these architects and to the everyday context in which they worked, apparently without the slightest concern about innovation but with a strong desire for maximum economy of formal means. The extreme purity of their designs derived from their refusal to be sidetracked by cultural and literary intentions. An art of sobriety, this critical form of Art Nouveau carried the richest possibilities for the future, totally escaping from the dead-end of formalism.

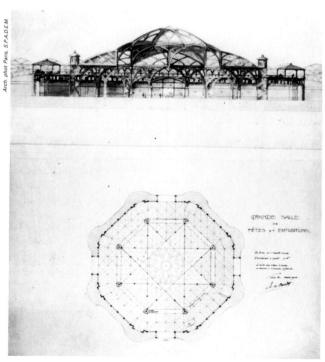

Concert hall

In this unrealized plan for a large space covered by reinforced concrete, dating from 1913, Anatole de Baudot took stock of 15 years of reflection on new structures in architecture. He employed a language stripped of ornament, following in the tradition of French rationalism as upheld by his master Viollet-le-Duc.

Stock Exchange, Amsterdam

Built between 1897 and 1909 by Hendrik Petrus Berlage, the Stock Exchange is a rationalist manifesto, forming a critique of the designs of the Frenchman Louis Cordonnier; these had won the original competition for the building, held in 1884, and were in a Flemish nationalist style. The strength of Berlage's design lies in its lack of ornament and in its very distinctive sense of atmosphere.

The Majolika Haus, Vienna

Going against both the floral style beloved of Horta, Guimard and Majorelle and the sophisticated re-writing of Neoclassicism that was the Viennese Secession, the Majolika Haus was designed in 1898–99 by Otto Wagner, whose background was in the most official academic tradition. Consisting of a metal frame clad with a ceramic facing, this building inaugurated an architectural language completely adapted to the needs of industrial construction. The decoration does not reveal the structure but is purely ornamental and indeed contradicts the disposition of doors and windows. It takes up the traditional theme of the painted façade and plays upon the tension between naturalistic representation (the climbing vegetation) and geometric structure (the masques and medallions of the upper storey).

Glasgow School of Art

Forming a parallel to the experiments of Wagner in Vienna, Charles Rennie Mackintosh based his work upon the tradition of Scottish baronial architecture, arriving at a simplified style stripped of all formal ornament and profoundly expressive of interior organization. The Glasgow School of Art (1896–1909) was, in its starkness, inspired as much by medieval dungeons as by industrial workshops. Its spiritual kinship with Voysey and the Domestic Revival is pronounced.

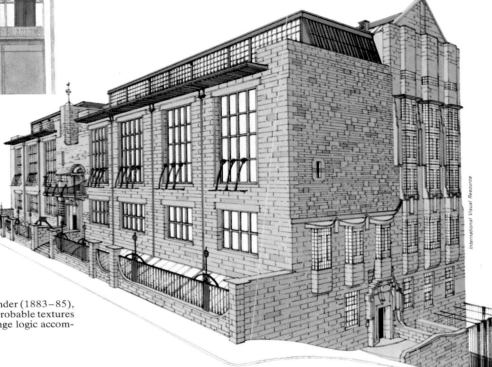

International Visual Resource

Capricho, Santander

...ne of the works of Gaudí's youth, the villa Díaz de Quijano at Comillas, near Santander (1883–85), ...lights in a mad profusion of material, a repetitive geometry of moulded forms, improbable textures ...d a typically Catalan symbiosis of Gothic rationality and wild exoticism. A strange logic accom-...nies this most extravagant of fantasies.

Hôtels Ciamberlani and Janssens, Brussels

These two adjoining houses, built in the Rue Defacqz in 1897 and 1898 by Paul Hankar for painter friends, are exactly contemporary with Horta's famous Hôtel Solvay. Repudiating the lyrical formalism of Horta, Hankar was trying to re-establish a dialectical relationship between architecture and decoration that went beyond the botanical forms of Art Nouveau.

Archives de l'architecture moderne

The search for pure form

An essentially decorative art, Art Nouveau lost its credibility among architects as soon as the style, transmitted through manufactured objects, became too popular. After 1900 the formal facility of items decorated with interlace and floral borders came to be thought vulgar and middle-class. Parallel to the fashion for the floral style, more discreet tendencies were emerging in England, America and Belgium. They prolonged and developed the spirit of the Arts and Crafts movement, and established a close link between craftsmanship and economy of means. The Refreshment Room at the Victoria and Albert Museum in London, by William Morris and Philip Webb (1867), was a model of restraint in the face of the excesses of Art Nouveau. Even when it encompassed historicism (as, for example, in the Queen Anne style that was so fashionable during the last 20 years of the century), English architecture always kept a sense of restraint that had its roots in a tradition going back to the work of Inigo Jones and John Soane.

The English Domestic Revival, whose works were published in *The Studio* magazine, provided a model that became known throughout the world. Whistler's "Peacock Room" and the house that Edward William Godwin designed for him in Chelsea developed tendencies originating in the preceding generation – for example, in the work of William Butterfield and Philip Webb. The "cottage style" had been too closely linked to the forms of the individual suburban house. The originality of this new style created by the Pre-Raphaelites and their successors lay in its assimilation of *japonisme* and post-Gothic, which was comparable to the re-creation of Gothic by Viollet-le-Duc but carried out by different plastic means.

The influence of the English school was most directly felt during the first few years of the 20th century in America, in the work of Frank Lloyd Wright, a young Chicago architect fresh from the studio of Louis H. Sullivan. The "prairie houses" that Wright was building in Chicago at the turn of the century made ingenious use of the traditional forms of Japanese architecture, and absorbed something of its spirit in their fluid spaces, transparent compartments and acute feeling for materials and atmosphere. At a time when Europe was tackling stylistic problems almost exclusively from an ornamental perspective, Wright was working towards the recreation and redefinition of space. It is easy to assess Wright's inventiveness by comparing his work with the refined but too narrowly Japanese-influenced buildings of Charles and Henry Green in California.

This search for purity of form was the logical outcome of rationalist thought, and was not always absent from even the most lyrical manifestations of Art Nouveau, including the works of Victor Horta. But its effects are more clearly felt in the bareness of works such as those by Van de Velde, which exhibit a sobriety as rigorous as it was efficient. One might almost call such work "geometric" Art Nouveau: certainly, after 1900 the influence of critical rationalism became more evident, opposing itself against the "excesses" of Art Nouveau.

The 1902 Turin Exhibition clearly marked the breaking point: the conversion of the Belgian decorators Léon Sneyers, Antoine Pompe and Georges Hobé to a geometric style shows the influence of Paul Hankar's designs of the last ten years of the 19th century, contemporary with the better-known work of Horta. Furthermore, the discovery of Horta's furniture in 1897 had converted Otto Wagner to Art Nouveau and led him to found the Viennese Secession.

The year 1910 marked the final break with Art Nouveau. The German publisher Wassmuth brought out a major edition of the work of Frank Lloyd Wright, which was to exert a considerable influence on the birth of the modern movement. It was also in this year that Antoine Pompe built the Van Neck clinic in Brussels, a rather nostalgic exercise in rationalism in the manner of Hankar. Meanwhile, Josef Hoffmann was finishing the interior of the sumptuous Stoclet house. The capital of Art Nouveau had become that of the Secession. At the same time, Henri Sauvage was drawing up plans for the terraced house in the Rue Vavin, Paris; Van de Velde and Perret were designing the Champs-Elysées Theatre, and Eliel Saarinen was working on the Central Station for Helsinki.

There were divergent tendencies in all these works but certain common themes emerged: a move towards simplification, a hieratic quality (rather like the Ballets Russes whose productions began in 1909 at the Châtelet Theatre) and a taste for large, powerful and expressive forms. It is nonetheless true that there is a world of difference between Van de Velde's proposed plans for the Champs-Elysées Theatre and those actually realized by Auguste Perret, couched in a Neoclassical language full of ambiguities. Once the problem of ornament had been resolved, the question of a relationship to history returned to the forefront, with implications both cultural and ideological.

Whistler's House, London

The British Arts and Crafts movement was one of the tendencies that led to a questioning of Art Nouveau. E.W. Godwin, one of the masters of the Domestic Revival during the 1870s, designed a house for the painter Whistler in Chelsea. He did two versions, of which the first was quite bare of ornament, relying upon the interplay of wall and roof, the rich patterns of the roof timbers, the animation of the empty spaces and the harmonious proportions of the front door and its surroundings. This composition was softened in the second version by the addition of suitable decorative detail, although the result still avoids being merely picturesque.

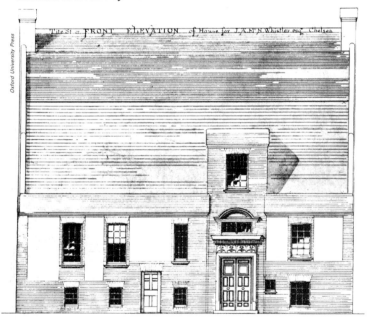

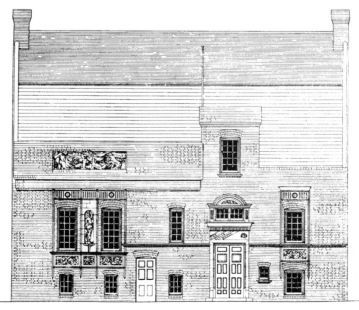

Robie House, Chicago

Frank Lloyd Wright, the most outstanding figure of the 1910s, built the Robie house in 1909. It became one of the most famous "prairie houses" for its experimentation with a new type of space created by the mingling of interior and exterior, an architectural ideal that was absorbed into modern art of the Thirties.

Stoclet house, Brussels

A temple to industrial luxury, the cold architecture of the "Palais Stoclet" (1904–11) is the tomb of Art Nouveau in the capital of its birth. Designed by the Viennese Josef Hoffmann, it affirms both an extreme attachment to geometric form and a condemnation of all purely ornamental virtuosity.

Champs-Elysées Theatre, Paris

Inaugurated in 1913 and made famous by *The Rite of Spring* produced there that year, this theatre by the brothers Auguste and Gustave Perret, adorned with sculptures by Bourdelle, had originally been designed by Van de Velde. The Perret brothers used reinforced concrete, retaining a careful Neoclassicism that repudiated all the excesses of modernity. The influence of the first plan by Van de Velde can still be detected, however, even in the detailing.

Van Neck Clinic, Brussels

In 1910 this posthumous homage to Paul Hankar presented itself as a manifesto of modernity. Its exaggerated rationalism, the fact that the whole façade is determined by the interior arrangement, may not have been what was expected of the architect Antoine Pompe, but it nonetheless revealed how radical the reaction against Art Nouveau was, and how decisive the influence of critical rationalism on the birth of the new art.

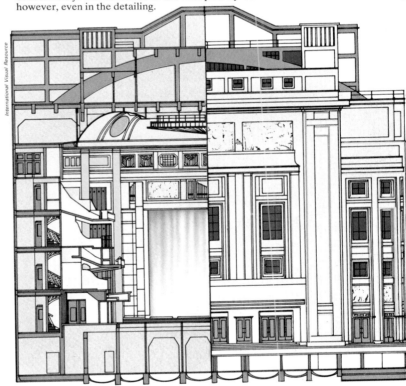

Central Station, Helsinki

Though the first of the great post-Art Nouveau monuments, Helsinki Central Station (1904–14), like the Stoclet house, still draws upon the lessons of Art Nouveau, its architect, Eliel Saarinen, having been one of the most appreciated Finnish masters of the movement. Bathed in the architectural atmosphere of the Germanic world, it owed as much to the Secessionist experiments of Olbrich at Darmstadt and Wagner in Vienna as to the Wertheim Store in Berlin by Alfred Messel (1896–1904). But the end result was a synthesis without nostalgia.

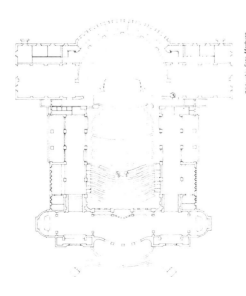

Theatre of the Werkbund Exhibition, Cologne

Ousted from Paris in 1914, Van de Velde went to Cologne to design an unusual theatrical project, where a projecting hall and triple diorama-stages made an ideal space for the performance of spectacles. The exterior is entirely determined by the building's function and shows an interplay of flattened and softened forms that anticipates the aesthetics of the Thirties.

The birth of modernism

At the very moment when the most brilliant manifestations of Art Nouveau were appearing in Europe, stylistic reaction against the movement began to develop in the advanced industrial society of the United States. Louis H. Sullivan came back from his stay in Paris, where he had been a pupil of the rationalist architect Auguste Vaudremer, fascinated by the experiments with mural painting made by Viollet-le-Duc in his decorations at Pierrefonds during the last years of the Second Empire, and equally convinced of the theory he later summed up in the famous dictum "form follows function". In his interior of the Trading Room in the Stock Exchange Building, Chicago (1893–94) he pushed the principles of decoration shown at Pierrefonds to their limit, using a rational basis of balancing motifs. In an article of 1892, however, he had suggested that it would be a good thing to give up all ornament for a few years and design buildings pleasing in their nakedness.

During the last decade of the 19th century, Sullivan carried through an architectural experiment that was not only technically exciting, in the application of steel skeleton-construction to the building of skyscrapers, but aesthetically adventurous as well. The prolific decoration that characterized the Wainwright Building in St. Louis (1890–91) became chastened in the large expanses of glass and stately rhythm of the arches in the Guaranty Building in Buffalo (1894–95) and disappeared altogether, in favour of structural clarity, in the great Carson, Pirie, Scott department store in Chicago (1899).

Sullivan's work was to have a profound effect on European architects who saw it. First among these was that legislator of modern architecture, Adolf Loos. He spent three years in America, before settling in Vienna in 1896. There he met artists of the Vienna Secession – Gustav Klimt and the architects Josef Maria Olbrich and Josef Hoffmann. But this served only to enable him to criticize more effectively their formalistic, purely decorative approach to design, their lack of any technical, economic or social commitment, and their escape into an aristocratic aestheticism. Alongside Otto Wagner, Loos waged a war of theory against Art Nouveau. He summed up his views in a series of articles in the *Neue Freie Presse* in 1897–98, later published together under the title *Ins Leere gesprochen* ("In Place of Emptiness"), then in the seminal *Ornament und Verbrechen* ("Decoration and Crime") of 1908, which became the bible of the modern movement between the wars. In its total absence of decoration, his Steiner house of 1910 was a deliberately provocative manifesto.

Determined to evolve an architectural language that was non-decorative and anti-Art Nouveau, Loos used pure, abstract forms that could not be understood either figuratively or ornamentally. He condemned symbolism as roundly as he condemned decoration. The emerging spirit of modernism, heir to critical rationalism, pushed the search for purity of form to the highest possible degree of abstraction. The expressive possibilities of form, reduced to its essentials, lay exclusively in the play of volumes, the relationship of solid to void. Design in terms of spatial flow was not to be trusted, because it lent itself too easily to sentimentalism. Loos's almost obsessional reductionism and avowed adherence to the most rigid symmetry could never be fully realized in practice. The back and front of the Steiner house are quite different and played off

against each other. Its main attraction as a design lies in the unexpectedness of the curved side elevation, the blocky façade having prepared the spectator for an unrelieved rectilinearity.

The same path towards modernism was followed by Otto Wagner, whose refined, eclectic style of the 1880s gave way without warning in his last works – above all in the Postal Savings Bank, Vienna, of 1904–12 – to the most extreme purism. Peter Behrens in Berlin and Auguste Perret in Paris made their contributions to the new architectural language, too, developing particularly the use of reinforced concrete. The Parisian engineer François Hennebique had erected numerous industrial buildings with exposed reinforced concrete skeletons since the invention of the material in 1893, but when commissioned to build some offices he brought in the architect Eugène Arnaud to design the façade, also in reinforced concrete but moulded into decorative mock-Rococo forms. Modernism, however, insisted on the frank expression of structure in all cases. In architecture as in the design of cars, the display of technology would take precedence over considerations of style.

Along with the idea of architectural truth, simplicity of form and the rejection of ornament, there grew up almost undetected the notion that the forms of modern architecture should imitate modern technology, that they should be machine-like. Machines were new and seductive; they also suggested a new formal vocabulary. The tradition of rationalist discourse associated with Gottfried Semper and Viollet-le-Duc carried on more or less unchanged. But a new tendency arose for writers of rationalist treatises to illustrate their ideas with machine-made objects and industrial structures.

Carson, Pirie, Scott Department Store, Chicago

Mentor of Frank Lloyd Wright and Adolf Loos, both of whom collaborated with him, Louis H. Sullivan was the greatest American architect of his time and a pioneer in the development of the skyscraper. He worked initially under the influence of the French architects Viollet-le-Duc and Vaudremer, and absorbed the American transcription of their style in the work of H.H. Richardson. But in the Carson, Pirie, Scott building, built between 1899 and 1904, he forged an utterly new approach to design. Only the window-frames are decorated, in a style inspired by the interlaced patterns of Celtic art. The rest of the ceramic-covered façade is strictly determined by the underlying framework of steel girders.

Wainwright Building, St. Louis

From 1890 the direction of Sullivan's work was clear. In the Wainwright Building the expression of the skeleton-structure takes priority over ornamentation. There are still allusions, inspired by Michelangelo, to a giant Order of columns and cornices. But the significant features are the naked, stripped-down look of the pilasters and the emphasis on texture rather than on definite motifs.

A.E.G. Turbine Factory, Berlin

Peter Behrens, architect and designer to the A.E.G. company, built this vast hall for the construction of electric turbines in 1909. Its powerful character comes from the simplicity and massiveness of its forms, the use of giant steel piers and the hard edges to the window-walls. This is an architecture that disdains detail, recognizes only mass, proclaims its allegiance to the machine aesthetic and welcomes the gigantic scale demanded of buildings for the industrial age.

Centenary Hall, Breslau (now Wroclau)

The fascination of the industrial megastructure, foreshadowed in the exhibition buildings of the mid-19th century, was here indulged to an unprecedented degree. The main hall of this colossal concrete structure, built in 1911–12 by the German engineer Max Berg, was more than 70 metres (230 feet) in diameter.

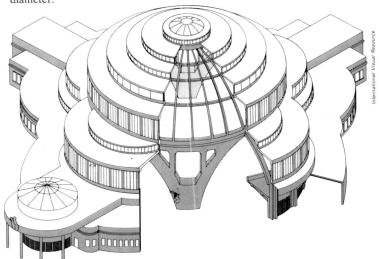

Model Factory, Cologne

As part of the Werkbund Exhibition of 1914, and situated not far from the theatre by Van de Velde, Walter Gropius's model factory was designed like a giant workman's hut made of steel. This monument to schematic form, conceived entirely in terms of mass, is rightly regarded as the first fully "modern" building. It is still influenced in its detailing by Frank Lloyd Wright but otherwise reflects the new architectural ideals very faithfully.

Steiner house, Vienna

In 1910 Adolf Loos, pioneer of the unadorned style, built an extraordinary villa which, in its adherence to rigid symmetry and proportion, and in its powerful masses and unexpected relationship of front view to profile, anticipated "cube" architecture. Echoes of this design are to be found throughout the 1920s.

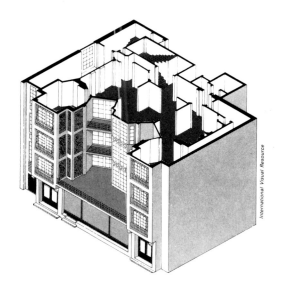

Perret flats, 25A Rue Franklin, Passy

This building of 1903 by Auguste Perret was constructed over a reinforced concrete skeleton. The front was faced with panels of glass and ceramic (featuring Japanese motifs); the back, with its glazed brickwork, was more traditional. The courtyard-like recession of the central façade, the regular arrangement of balconies and bow-windows and the large expanses of window-surface are part of an architectural vocabulary free from all reference to traditional masonry.

The Chrysler Building, New York

Art Deco in France found its American equivalent in the design of the New York skyscrapers of the 1920s. The Chrysler Building of 1930 by William Van Alen was one of the most accomplished essays in the style. While modernism was still an avant-garde movement, Art Deco enjoyed popular success. As a result, its artistic merits have been underestimated and are only now beginning to be recognized.

*D*id the modern movement originate in that apocalypse of iron and blood, the First World War? There are certainly some connections, even if they fall far short of a complete explanation. The trauma of the war brought attitudes and values out into the open and destroyed the cocoon of convention in which society had been enveloped. The striving for the most efficient production methods during the war, and the total disregard for artistic concerns, took industrial design to new levels of brutalism. To some, indeed, military machines, products of pure technology, seemed to point the way forward for architecture and design in general. As a possible solution to the problem of how to create a truly "modern" art, industrial design had tended to be overlooked. This was because, since the beginning of the industrial revolution, contemporary art had been regarded as inseparable from history. The desire to maintain and enrich the cultural heritage, not only through art-historical knowledge but also through new works that paid homage to the past, imposed a crushing burden upon architects. With the "period style" architecture that proliferated from the middle of the 19th century, creativity had taken second place to history and the very existence of art as a living force in society had seemed under threat.

Modernism tended more and more to oppose itself to history, insisting that the world of artistic creation had nothing to do with that of the museum. Art Nouveau had embraced both worlds – indeed, museums had been prominent patrons of the artists associated with the movement and had collected their works. Now the relationship became uneasy. Avant-garde artists defiantly resisted the artificial values, commercial and aesthetic, that museums placed upon the works they displayed. Duchamp's "readymades" and the works of the Dadaists were hardly designed to go in the Louvre! The years between the wars were a time of extremes, of caricature, intolerance and violence, both verbal and physical. It was quite in the spirit of the age that the stances adopted by the advocates of past and present should have become increasingly fixed and aggressive. For some, the only way forward was to throw off the yoke of history and bury the past as if it were a corpse. Others believed that the creation of anything new was impossible, that it could be no more than a negation or mockery of the past, that the only true artistic values were traditional, that the cultural heritage was the last line of defence against the invading forces of a new obscurantism. War was declared between traditionalism and futurism in art as in politics. There was a mass retrenchment in

the attitudes of architects and their clients. In the 1920s the idea of pastiche became acceptable again and certain architects were prepared to renounce their own pre-war work, devoting themselves to the imitation of classical buildings. Their work is largely forgotten now but in the 1920s they were a force to be reckoned with. Art Nouveau had been just a moment of euphoria. Even before 1914, all genuine hope of reconciling the art of the present to the past had faded. Discourse on art had long been dominated by the conflict between the old guard and the new, and those artists who were neither one nor the other, the "juste milieu", tended to be caught in the cross-fire.

But the reality of the inter-war period was far more complex than this schematic picture suggests. The fight between revolutionaries and reactionaries did not fill the whole stage, only the foreground, and the adversaries often exhausted themselves in pointless internal wrangles: the disputes over "urbanism" among the Russian avant-garde in the 1920s, for instance, and the personal antagonisms within the Bauhaus. The actual practice of architecture was meanwhile taken over by those who were the least outspoken about their theoretical positions. The structure of the artistic world, like that of the political world, reflected the nature of contemporary society: the more advanced the theoretical position, the less it had popular acceptance.

Paradoxically, the movement that was most doctrinaire and narrow, in every sense of the word, was the new historicism, which rejected everything except a scrupulous pastiche of great works of the past. Encouraged by the higher echelons of society, the "establishment", it attracted a particular type of architect, culturally sophisticated and anxious about the status of architecture in the society of the future. Towards this position of doubt and nostalgia, the modernists took up a particularly virulent critical stance. The traditionalists were their rivals on a purely professional plane, depending upon the same elite patronage. However, the modernists did not yet constitute a single movement. That was to take another decade. At the beginning of the 1920s their aesthetic attitudes were far from unified, showing quite divergent and mutually exclusive tendencies. Historical accounts of the avant-garde usually describe a simple opposition of modernist against expressionist, the first concerned with purity of form, the second with its emotional value. The situation was in fact quite otherwise. From the outset, there was a section of the modernist movement that put its faith in an amalgam of japonisme,

Hinduism and neo-Platonic philosophy. It regarded perfection of form as a supreme expression of man in his relationship with the Absolute, an idea that had been part of Art Nouveau theory as well. Put into practice, this formal purism evolved towards a geometric abstraction that slowly lost its idealist content. A very professional attitude developed, geared to industrial production; and the machine, given a mythical status, came to take the place of the divinity.

It is easy to see this happening in the history of the Bauhaus: first came Walter Gropius's idealistic proclamation of 1919, composed under the influence of Johannes Itten, Lyonel Feininger, Wassily Kandinsky, Oskar Schlemmer and Paul Klee; next, the technological emphasis of the generation of Marcel Breuer, László Moholy-Nagy and Josef Albers; then the political involvement of Hannes Meyer, Ludwig Hilberseimer and Ludwig Mies van der Rohe. These represent three distinct phases, three different ideologies, all unfolding within the short period from 1919 to 1933. Such a linear account still fails to do justice, however, to the rich ambiguities of modernist theory in the decade after the war. It was during this period that the Secessionist movement produced some of its best work, notably that of the young Robert Mallet-Stevens in France. Leaving that aside and considering just the modern movement proper, there were two radically opposed tendencies within the Berlin context alone. The purist line represented by Mies van der Rohe was under attack from what could be called "modernist expressionism" in the architecture of Hans Scharoun and Hermann Finsterlin, as well as the utopian publications of Bruno Taut. Mies van der Rohe's famous monument to Karl Liebknecht and Rosa Luxemburg shows that he himself could not entirely escape their influence. The same is true of Erich Mendelsohn's "Einstein Tower", the celebrated scientist's observatory at Potsdam. When architects themselves vacillated between styles, it would be misleading to see architecture as moving in one direction, even if hindsight might show one tendency to have been more significant than the others.

It was in the Dutch avant-garde of the 1920s that the conflicting currents within modernism revealed themselves most clearly. Around Mondrian the De Stijl group forged a purist ideology under the banner of "neo-Plasticism", an obvious adaptation of neo-Platonism. From traditional Japanese architecture, they assimilated a way of structuring space through the play of forms and planes, which inevitably had a profound influence on their contemporaries. Their work went far beyond Frank Lloyd Wright – his style was altogether too compromising, too responsive to the physical environment for this rising generation of abstractionists. For them, it mattered not at all whether a building bore any relation to its setting or to established cultural traditions. Indeed, the less integrated it was, the more impact it would have, and the more effective it would be as an aesthetic manifesto. A building such as Gerrit T. Rietveld's Schröder house, built in the suburbs of Utrecht in 1923, has little or nothing in common with contemporary works in Amsterdam such as Michael De Klerk's Eigen Haard housing estate of 1920–21 or Piet Kramer's De Dageraad estate of 1923. The Amsterdam school was at its height at precisely this time. But the outlook of its exponents was quite opposite to Rietveld's. They conceived of architectural forms as analogous to human emotions, a theory

based on a Freudian interpretation of culture as expressive of psychological forces. Modernism as conceived by the purists was by definition independent from history and culture. The expressionist movement insisted that, on the contrary, it was the task of architecture to confirm the cultural identity of the individual and express the collective destiny to which he was subject.

The modern movement was of marginal importance as far as the construction of actual buildings was concerned, and from the ideological point of view quite contradictory. Although from 1925 it expanded, and purism emerged as a dominant tendency, resulting in an architecture of ever-increasing homogeneity eventually dubbed "the International Style", the fact remains that initially, around 1920, modernism was pulled in several different aesthetic

directions and in any case accounted for only the tiniest fraction of the total output of architecture. Furthermore, it had to contend with very strong competition from the reviving historicist movement, with its painstakingly archaeological reconstruction of period styles. Modernism owed its survival to the many publications it spawned and the theoretical debates carried on within their pages, which were as lively in content as they were outrageous in tone. This was the heyday of the avant-garde reviews, short-lived and narrow in circulation but later to be acknowledged as the guiding lights of modern art.

The contrast between expressionism and neo-Plasticism in the Netherlands shows how simplistic it is to conceive of modernism as a unified movement. Another tendency that belies that view, and perhaps the most dynamic force within the modern movement during the 1920s, is

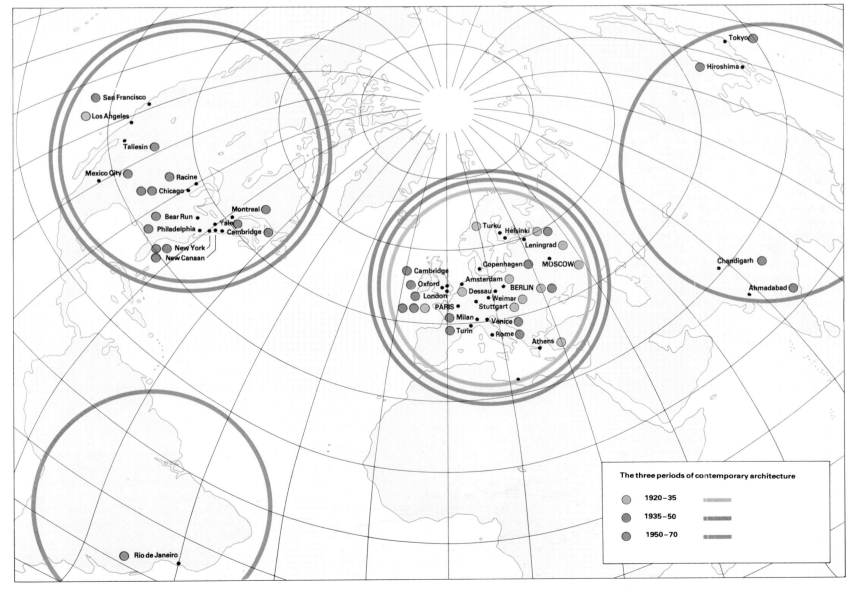

The three periods of contemporary architecture

● 1920–35
● 1935–50
● 1950–70

regionalism. This was to be denounced by advocates of the International Style, conveniently labelled as "culturalist" by modernist critics from Françoise Choay onwards and lumped together with the most retrogressive historicism. But the work of figures such as Antoine Pompe and Fernand Bodson, the leading Belgian representatives of the movement, can hardly be written off as simple traditionalism. Deliberately misrepresented by modernist ideology, regionalism has remained relatively obscure. Primary sources of information are few and far between, and a great deal of research will have to be done before we can gain a rounded view of the movement. What is undeniable is that it did occupy a central position, often overlapping with Art Deco, in the architectural world of the inter-war years.

The vast majority of run-of-the-mill architects were quite oblivious to the rise of modernism. As far as they were concerned, the most stimulating new movement in architecture was regionalism. This was particularly the case in northern and eastern parts of France that had been ravaged by the war. Lying somewhere between strict modernism and traditionalism, the regionalist view was widely adopted and disseminated by the professional journals. An architecture of ideas, created largely by men from the most prestigious architectural schools, was thus popularized among ordinary surveyors, engineers, technicians and entrepreneurs involved in everyday building, who adapted original designs to bring them within the financial range of clients from the middle classes.

It is all too easy to ridicule the architectural pretentiousness of suburbs and resorts. There is certainly little connection between these typically bourgeois environments and the rural traditions they purport to follow. Nevertheless, it would be unjust to condemn them without taking into account the simple fact that they do seem to work. Resorts such as La Baule, not to mention parts of Deauville, the towns that were rebuilt in Flanders and garden cities such as Tergnier, Stains and Drancy (built on the model established by Ebenezer Howard in England) possess a power and unity that are indisputable. The phenomenon was far from being particular to France. It is increasingly clear that Welwyn Garden City in England, the "Logis Floréal" in Brussels and Vreewyk near Rotterdam are works of primary importance in the history of architecture and town planning in the 1920s. The rehabilitation of this kind of architecture will probably restore it eventually to the important position it occupied in its own time. It will also enhance our understanding of the greatly underestimated regionalist movement. In the context of the 1920s, publications with titles like Life in the Country had an altogether greater impact on the public at large than Le Corbusier's L'Esprit Nouveau!

There were points of contact between regionalism and that other essentially middle-class architecture, the late form of Art Nouveau known as Art Deco. This flourished prodigiously in the first half of the 1920s, its success culminating in the Paris Exhibition of 1925. Regionalism was closely tied to considerations of setting and as such was a logical extension of the Domestic Revival. Art Deco was more an urban style. It principally affected manufactured goods, fashion design, furniture, jewellery and interior decoration, quickly spreading to commercial architecture as well. The great works of Art Deco were in the fields of applied arts and in the architecture of shops and skyscrapers.

Paris was the capital of Art Deco. The collection of the Musée des Arts Décoratifs contains the most precious examples of the style. But the capital of the Art Deco skyscraper, which left its mark so forcefully upon the history of American architecture, was of course New York, at least until the Crash of 1929. Regarded as a single, continuous movement running from 1890 to 1930, Art Nouveau and Art Deco occupy an extraordinarily important position in the history of architecture in general, enjoying great popularity, passing on a great legacy to the future, giving expression to those twin periods the "Belle Epoque" and the "Roaring Twenties". The sumptuous interiors of buildings such as the Tuschinski Theatre in Amsterdam (Jaap Gidding, 1921), the "De Bijenkorf" store at The Hague (Piet Kramer, 1926) or the annexe to the "Bon Marché" store in Paris (Louis-Charles Boileau, 1924) are memories that might well fill us with nostalgia for that great feast of architecture and ornament. So too might the few relics that have survived, such as the Chrysler Building in New York or René Lalique's restaurant-car for the Orient Express.

Regionalism and Art Deco were variations on the same architectural thought and together they constituted what was beyond doubt the dominant movement of the 1920s. It is a curious fact that, co-existing with such prominent and distinctive forms of expression as these, the modern movement generally refrained from directly attacking them, saving its polemics for academicism and pastiche. Perhaps it respected Art Deco as an authentically popular architecture; or perhaps it simply ignored it on the grounds that it was a kind of vernacular style, aimed at the middle classes and so outside the modernist range of interests. We have suggested that the dissemination of different approaches to architecture and the degree to which they were avant-garde were inversely proportional. The elitist nature of the modern movement undermined its credibility: could revolutionary declarations really be compatible with serving the most aristocratic clientele? Architects cannot be held responsible for the nature of contemporary society but they cannot ignore it either. Without their almost messianic faith in the future of art, the gap between the avowed aims of modernist architects and their actual practice would have been intolerable. Today, as we try to form a balanced view of the period, we must recognize that the part played by the modernists was innovative but limited, that the overwhelming consensus in society as a whole was in favour of Art Deco.

The question of classicism is an issue quite separate from those we have so far discussed. Part of the problem is that classicism was no longer a single formal language. The eclectic borrowings of architects had thrown up a multiplicity of different "classicisms", whether Napoleonic, Louis XIV, Louis XVI, Renaissance or Greek Revival. Classicism was now only tied to academicism in as much as it was one of the sources upon which eclectic architecture, increasingly a mere matter of pastiche, would draw. The single classical tradition that did continue was that of the "Grand Hotel" in the Louis XVI style, a facile formula very much in fashion just before the First World War. The work of the military circle around Charles Le Maresquier, whom Le Corbusier attacked with such contempt and savage irony, is a perfect example of this official style. Imitated throughout the world, it kept alive, with slight modifications, the played-out forms of Second Empire Baroque. For the Gare d'Orsay, Victor Laloux took Hector Lefuel's New Louvre, revised it, improved it and added just a dash of Art Deco.

Other forms of classicism survived in close relation to the Art Deco movement. There was a 1925 Neoclassicism that was strongly tinged with Art Deco, a fusion between the Neoclassical ideas reintroduced from the United States after the war and the trend towards geometric ornamentation. There was also the related movement of Secessionist Neoclassicism, which adopted the basic formal language of Otto Wagner and Josef Hoffmann but retained classical references, columns, pilasters, capitals and even stylized figures borrowed from early Greek vases, Mycenaean and Minoan art. It should be said finally that a whole aspect of modernism itself was bound up with classicism. Le Corbusier's taste for mathematics and proportion, and his constant reference to the ideal forms developed in the Renaissance illustrate how deeply the modern movement was indebted to Alberti's neo-Platonism.

It was for this reason that the war between modernism and academicism was a war of words not deeds. The professional concerns of architects lay entirely elsewhere. The Academy had abandoned its dogmatic stance long ago, after the death of Quatremère de Quincy in 1849, and historicism had been discredited since the triumph of Art Nouveau in 1893. It was against Art Deco and its variant forms that the real battle was being fought. Adolf Loos had been quite right to concentrate his efforts against architectural ornamentation but now modernism had to maintain hostilities on another front as well. Formal abstraction had developed in the modern movement as a reaction against iconographic, figurative decoration, the possibilities of which were exhausted by Art Nouveau, but equally against the insidiously attractive forms of Art Deco at its most banal. The modernist diatribes against pastiche came directly out of a sense of rivalry with architects aiming at the same clientele, and they have the great advantage of being easy to follow. But the real threat to the movement was the seduction of public taste by Art Deco and the general popularity it enjoyed – even if no one ever talked about it!

From 1925 a major campaign was undertaken to destroy Art Deco and the aesthetic cult that had grown up around it, and it came from the right as much as the left, from academicism as much as modernism. It was the coming to a head of antagonism between the champions of official art, national, public and didactic, and those who saw the future of industrial society in the machine aesthetic.

In the sphere of domestic architecture, the ideological implications of different styles took on a particular importance, especially in relation to authoritarianism. In the 1930s an identical conception of the public role of art arose in Nazi Germany, Fascist Italy and Soviet Russia. The development of large-scale industrial production methods turned the house into a consumer product. It destroyed the sense of home as a personal space until the idea of impressing an individual personality upon it seemed futile if not incongruous. The disappearance of private architecture as such left room for whole new ideologies of housing to grow up and architects all set about formulating their own theories. A few borrowings from the classical tradition in the composition or ornament turned a building into a great Neoclassical monument. A dynamic interplay of volumes or the occasional nautical-looking detail were enough to suggest a modern, progressive approach. Around 1935 modernism was the predominant style, even if sometimes in "classic" guise. The profoundest changes had occurred in the building industry, encouraged by the spread of mass-production techniques. As time went on they became more pronounced and soon the industrialized nations were building several hundreds of millions of dwellings every year to standard patterns.

The triumph of modernism expressed itself most conspicuously through the industrialization of building. The rationalization of production methods favoured simplified forms and lack of ornament, which eventually left both Art Deco and regionalism artistically bankrupt. But as opposition to modernism on formal grounds fell away, its champions found themselves a little embarrassed. The success of the movement went beyond all expectations but as it grew, so did anxieties about its consequences. Mass-produced housing soon began to spoil the landscape, to create spaces that were inhuman and ugly, completely lacking the abstract beauty the modernists had envisaged. The housing of maximum economic efficiency revealed all too clearly the brutal face of industrial enterprise.

There were two courses of action open to modernism in the 1930s if it was not simply to admit defeat: to ennoble technology, giving the severely rational forms of industrial products an artistic veneer, making architecture a branch of "design", or to provide those forms with a sound ideological justification. With the first option, the use of expensive industrial materials – steel, glass and aluminium – was a guarantee of success. It went together with the most sophisticated experimentation with systems of proportion, undertaken by Jean Prouvé in France, for example, and Mies van der Rohe in the United States. The second option admitted that gestures towards decoration, whether Neoclassical pilasters or tile roofs, had long been no more than minimal, but maintained that even the slightest such references were contrary to the spirit of industrial production. There must be even more economy. The hesitancy that marked the modernism of the 1930s reflected doubts as to the significance of the movement. The strong humanist reaction had created Art Deco, from which architecture and design were only just emerging, and was now becoming associated with the spirit of craftsmanship of Art Nouveau. The "resurrection" of Frank Lloyd Wright and the spectacular change of style in the work of Le Corbusier demonstrate this clearly. Technology continued to dominate the United States but European architecture, under the influence of Wright and Le Corbusier, took on a different, more original character. Concentrating on the mass of a building and its interior space, their work met the toughest demands of industrial production, the simplification and repetition of forms. It avoided the pitfall of ornamentation and the ever-increasing difficulties of relating surface decoration to uncompromisingly rational form underneath. The triumphant modernism of the half century from 1925 to around 1975 was in a state that was, to say the least, contradictory. Having defeated its rivals, it could no longer vent its critical energies on them and turned with greater and greater virulence upon itself, constantly harping on the failure of the theory of functionalism. Modernism was supposed to have been the salvation of the working class but met only with indifference and hostility. Phrases such as "architectural complex" and "prefabricated structure" came to trigger off a whole negative vision of the movement. And the typical architectural forms of the big city, the skyscraper office block and the airport, so overwhelmingly dominated the environment that they too inspired deep public resentment.

The rehabilitation of contemporary architecture had to be based on a fundamental rethinking of principles. The new plasticity of Le Corbusier's treatment of space denied the theory of functionalism. (The disparity between Le Corbusier's theory and his practice was a constant source of perplexity and embarrassment to critics.) The same goes for the "empiricism" of Alvar Aalto and the "organic" approach of Frank Lloyd Wright. With the return of symbolic architectural forms, the concern with the idea of the monument shown by third-generation modernists such as Eero Saarinen, Louis I. Kahn and Jørn Utzon, the break with the functionalist ideology was complete. Belief in modernity as the supreme consideration was dead. Architecture appeared once again in an historical perspective, as part of the cultural life of Western civilization. It took on a symbolic charge inescapably.

From the 1960s the disintegration of modernism was accomplished by a rediscovery of alternative styles. Robert Venturi, for example, reassessed the importance of American vernacular architecture, setting it against its horrendous antithesis, the "consumer" architecture of Las Vegas. Like a breath of fresh air, there came a great questioning of modernism and its myths, indeed, a shift in the whole concept of architecture. The rejection of the industrial product, sometimes even the rejection of industrial civilization as a whole, served to highlight the problem of relating architecture to environment, the individual house to the townscape. Most important of all, it stimulated new ideas about the ideological significance of this relationship.

The architecture of the late 20th century, as developed since the 1970s, has sought ways out of the technological dead-end in which modernism, rather naively equating industry with the proletariat, imprudently allowed itself to become trapped. It has aimed to infuse the products of our time with a solid, distinctive, yet popular character. From the prestige monument to the humblest private home, it has replaced anarchy with a sense of clarity and order. It has rejected the idea of competition and the showiness that characterized the key projects of the Sixties. Buildings have become less spectacular in order to share equal prominence as parts of the urban environment, a principle followed with exemplary success in the 18th century. In addition, the language of architecture has become simpler so that it can be assimilated everywhere and by everyone, reproduced even outside the charmed circles of the leading architects. Reviving the doctrines of the European tradition and disavowing modernism as such has brought about a fusion of old and new, rich and poor, intellectual and popular. Today we are rediscovering the qualities of Haussmann's ideas on town planning – for example, his success at unifying urban spaces and creating a sense of community life. A new approach has been taken towards articulation and decoration, in which detail is used to diversify and individualize the structure to which it is applied. Modernist

World Trade Center, New York. The tallest blocks in Manhattan (420 metres/1,378 feet high, with 104 storeys, built by Minoru Yamasaki in 1969–74) were among the last manifestations of the International Style in New York. At the same time, the monumental treatment of the lowest storeys, their flamboyance reminiscent of the Doge's Palace in Venice, represents a slight gesture towards the ideas of post-modernism.

architecture tends to consist of a multiplicity of buildings that are uniform but relatively casually disposed; recent projects put more emphasis on the structuring of public spaces and allow greater freedom as far as individual detailing is concerned, not following any kind of socio-aesthetic theory. The revaluation of Hendrik Petrus Berlage's plans for southern Amsterdam and the hitherto much-reviled contemporary village of Port-Grimaud shows clearly which direction today's architecture has taken. Eclecticism has become acceptable, much practised and welcomed as a way of investing a project with individual expression. It is a weapon against the brutality of the industrial norm, which we have come to realize was a worse tyranny than the frilly ornamentation it replaced.

Modern architectural thought has been caught in the same dilemmas since the end of classicism in the 18th century. The concepts it has thrown up have all testified to an uneasy relationship with technology and power. In architecture as in other fields, art and politics are in constant interaction.

From expressionism to Art Deco

The First World War did not cause the deep rift in people's attitudes that might have been expected. Its effect was purely that of a terrible blood-letting forced upon a whole generation: it was the dead of 1914 who bore the brunt, not the survivors, for whom peace meant a return to normal life. Artistic movements that originated before the war accordingly continued afterwards. Many of their practitioners were dead but others simply took over, quite often merely completing projects begun by their predecessors.

The great exhibition of the Deutscher Werkbund in Cologne in 1914 had defined two attitudes towards industrial civilization, both positive yet absolutely contradictory in effect. The first – that of the dawning modernism – saw a path to the future in the marriage of a formal language with the technical possibilities of industrial machinery. It allowed for the re-establishment of a perfect correspondence between means of production and product – much more than between function and form, whatever may have been said, for "function" can be defined any number of ways. The second viewpoint, a much more humanist one, saw in architectural form a projection of the psyche, a transposition of man's relationship with the world, seeing the question of technique as altogether of secondary interest.

If the model factory of Walter Gropius can be considered a manifesto of mechanization as an architectural ideology, then its most obvious counterweight was the influence of Henry van de Velde. A Homeric antagonism must have divided the two architects even within the framework of the exhibition on the subject of man's relation to machine, with Van de Velde vigorously defending the principle of the dominance of form over factors of production. But the disagreements were much deeper, though less clearly expressed, between Gropius's position and that of another branch of the modern school represented by Bruno Taut.

Strictly humanist in attitude, Van de Velde tended to see the relation of form to manufacture as analogous with that of thought to matter, an idealistic principle which rejected modernity as a particularly subversive form of nihilism. But the artistic debate would have proved much more revealing if it had centred on differences among the champions of modernism, bringing Gropius's pragmatic viewpoint up against Taut's social and political messianism. The world of magic and light, the technological fairyland of Taut's imagination, made the advent of industrial production an era of liberation for the entire working class; the prospect of "triumphant tomorrows" had infused the whole history of socialism and its battle for political recognition.

It was the very same prospect that inspired the movement which has often been called, rather too formally, "expressionism". This architectural movement was certainly not exempt from interaction on or sympathy with the literary and artistic movements of its day: occasionally it shared with them the distinctive attitude towards humanity – a blend of irony and affection – which ran through the greater part of artistic output between the wars. Yet the relationship with other artistic manifestations surely had a deeper basis than the simple borrowing of ideas from a particular group or artistic circle. It was the mark of a world-view in which culture was an essential element in the exchange between man and nature – it was a reflection of man, his testimony and confession in the face of reality.

Expressionism had sources deep in the historicist tradition and in its most recent manifestation, Art Nouveau. The Gothic allusions of Peter Vilhelm Jensen Klint, the Scandinavian architect, and the primitivism of the "Amsterdam School" are witness to this. But its real significance does not lie there. If its repertory of forms looks back to a precedent, it is not in order to extol some dream of cultural heritage, or to exalt the nationalist message of the prewar "Heimatstyl". Using culture (and ultimately modernism) as its means, expressionist art used forms, spaces and ornament as a projection of human personality that was often quite emotional.

Its difference from the forms of classical art lay in the fact that this projection was not that of an individual. Taking a somewhat neutral stance, expressionism seeks to embody the collective spirit of an epoch or of a social group.

Semantic confusion may have arisen between the lyrical aspect of expressionism and the ornamental language of Art Deco, despite the great difference between their respective aims. It was only certain forms that they might to some extent have in common. Art Deco, the direct heir of Art Nouveau, aimed for nothing other than to create a popular style, an art accessible to all both financially (its social preoccupations were often explicit, as, for example, when it produced furniture specifically designed for working-class families) and aesthetically. It was important that everyone should understand the same language of design, independently of the differences of class and culture which so profoundly marked the beginnings of the industrial epoch. Art Deco was a call for reconciliation. Judging by the extraordinary success of the Paris Exhibition of 1925, the call was heard largely by the middle strata of society. It was similarly well received as what the Americans call the "skyscraper style", so characteristic of New York and Chicago.

Of the three architectural currents of the 1920s, Art Deco might well be the most underestimated. It was certainly the most brilliant and the most accessible – whilst modernism and expressionism were only comprehensible to the intellectual classes of Europe. In obvious contradiction to its stated intentions, avant-garde art remained a vehicle of expression for the elite, even at the moment when the great decorators of 1925 were finding ways of appealing to a wide public. Must we condemn the movement because of its success? It is to answer this that we are now looking much more closely at the work of Henri Sauvage, Pierre Patout, Charles Plumet and Maurice Dufrêne.

Grundtvig Church, Copenhagen

Often called expressionist, the church built by P.V. Jensen Klint in Copenhagen dates from 1920. This monumental construction of bricks is inspired, in its mass and plan, by French 13th century cathedrals, notably by Notre-Dame in Paris. But it has an unexpected vigour in its treatment of a traditional detail of northern rural architecture (the stepped gable animated by vertical stripes) on a colossal scale. The "organ-pipe" façade is a completely stylized rewriting of neo-Gothic whose exaggerated verticality is extremely expressive.

Eigen Haard housing estate, Amsterdam

Built between 1913 and 1922, the Eigen Haard complex is a kind of miniature village with modifications. The great tiled spire marks the social centre of the estate. Borrowing many details from the Flemish tradition, particularly its materials, Michael De Klerk sought to infuse the whole place with the simplicity and power of popular imagery. In this he was profoundly expressionist, reminiscent even of Gaudi.

The Paris Exhibition of 1925

Installed on the Alexander III bridge, the gallery of boutiques by Maurice Dufrêne is one of the most characteristic ensembles of the Art Deco style that dominated the great Exhibition of 1925. This geometric form of Art Nouveau, skilfully combining modern simplicity and precious detail, carries on the spirit of the pre-war Secession movement in an original way. It was bound to be a great popular success.

The House of Glass, Cologne

The contribution of the young architect Bruno Taut to the Werkbund Exhibition in Cologne in 1914, the House of Glass, brought a new dimension to the idea of modernism which is often underestimated by the critics. The magic world of light and colour modulations, now possible through new technology, was at least as important in the years 1910–20 as the idea of functionalism.

Offices of the I.G. Farben Company, Frankfurt

Built in 1920–25 the paint factory of the I.G. Farben Company features, in its administration building, a large hall around which offices are arranged, on the model of the Larkin Building by Frank Lloyd Wright. Peter Behrens' version is strongly marked by Dutch expressionism, turning the well of light into a very dynamic space both by the theatrical play of light and by the systematic use of slanting rafters which serve to disrupt the overall rectilinearity. The work of Behrens, Poelzig and Bonatz in Weimar Germany deserves a great deal more attention than it has so far received.

Grosses Schauspielhaus, Berlin

In 1919 Hans Poelzig was commissioned to transform an old circus into a round theatre to be used for concerts and plays. This vast public hall was decorated with imitation stalactites and made to look like some immense grotto, a modern version of Aladdin's cave.

The elaboration of a language

Faced with the dominant style of 1925, modernist architecture constructed its own system of forms as a weapon to be used in its struggle against the *status quo*. But it was not without difficulties and hesitations that the new style emerged from a number of different and, at the outset, concurrent models.

There is no doubt that the feeling for mass, so characteristic of works by Frank Lloyd Wright such as the Larkin Building, the Unity Church and the Mason City Hotel, profoundly influenced the birth of modernism in Europe. The model factory of Walter Gropius in Cologne, the Modern City of Victor Bourgeois at Berchem-Sainte-Agathe, the villa at Huis ter Heide by Robert van't Hoff, as well as numerous works of the "Amsterdam School", the late work of Hendrik Petrus Berlage, Peter Behrens and Paul Bonatz in Germany, the style of Auguste Perret and Tony Garnier in France all witness their dependence on Wright's formal vocabulary.

The monumental, Babylonian character of Wright's aesthetic placed no value on machine production. If he represented its power symbolically in his "silver temples" he could hardly have conveyed the same message through the less ambitious forms of his private houses. These were social habitats and as such the object of lively interest in this period of political ferment. As for the "prairie houses", their refined vocabulary of interior-exterior relationships turned out to be prohibitively costly. Economical construction demanded simple forms and volumes, without subtle spatial definition and interpretation.

The experiments of Ernst May in the Bruchfeldstrasse estate and the Römerstadt district of Stuttgart, and Bruno Taut's at the Hufeisen Siedlung in Berlin-Britz, show how difficult the transposition of grand architecture into the field of housing proves to be. An impoverishment of means goes almost necessarily hand in hand with an impoverishment of form. So with considerable skill and courage the modernist architects searched for a new vocabulary. They considered questions of scale and the disposition of voids with a view to making the quality of the urban space compensate for what was lacking in individual buildings where economy made for monotony of design. Thanks to the use of a strong polychromy directly inspired by Cubism, austere masses could create a powerful effect. But the fact remained that abstract forms, however seductive to the eye, were often perishable. Time and the elements soon conspired to destroy their pristine harmonies.

The period of hesitancy that was the early 1920s therefore witnessed the transposition of Cubism into architecture. The plastic arts asserted themselves so strongly that they broke out of the fictitious space of the canvas or poster to enter the real, habitable space of architecture, with sculpture tending to become concerned with environment, even spectacle. This disruption of the boundaries between artistic domains, summed up in the very word "Constructivism", benefited architecture by offering new formal models, notably in the work of Mondrian. His simple arrangements of lines and planes translate unexpectedly happily into architectural terms, as shown in that manifesto of the modernist vocabulary, the 1924 Schröder-Schräder house by Gerrit Rietveld in Utrecht. At the same moment "revolutionary" architecture triumphed among the Russian Constructivists, El Lissitzky, Mart Stam, the brothers Vesnine and Konstantin Melnikov.

From the outset the formation of the new style, which soon became the "International Style" was in serious competition with the aesthetic of Frank Lloyd Wright and with the rival expressionist school. In Holland the opposition between the Amsterdam School expressionists and the De Stijl modernists was especially strong. In Berlin, the capital of architectural innovation at this time, the lyrical movement represented by the utopian publications of Bruno Taut, Hermann Fisterlin, Hans Scharoun and Erich Mendelsohn contrasted strongly, in its formal freedom and acute sense of architectural symbolism, with the incredibly rigorous approach of Ludwig Mies van der Rohe, so passionately enamoured of formal rationality.

There is no doubt that the projects designed by Mies van der Rohe between 1919 and 1924, and exhibited in the architectural section of the Novembergruppe, constituted the most coherent plastic system elaborated by any of the modernist architects between the wars. His skyscrapers of glass and steel, his concrete office-blocks and the famous "country houses" were theoretical models no less effective than the ideal cities, centralized town plans or the scenographic spaces of the Renaissance imagination four centuries earlier. This corpus of modern architecture, patiently elaborated during five years in the stimulating intellectual milieu of Berlin in the 1920s, remains today an accepted pattern-book of architectural composition, even though since the 1970s critical opinion has turned against the constraints of such a language. From 1925 modernism no longer existed just as an idea but as an established plastic system. This was, moreover, the year of Le Corbusier's *Esprit Nouveau* pavilion at the Paris Exhibition. The triumph of Art Deco is also a key date in the history of modern art!

Villa at Huis ter Heide, Utrecht

The publication of Frank Lloyd Wright's works by Wassmuth met with a considerable response in Europe, where the "prairie houses" inspired a number of modernist architects. The villa built by Robert van't Hoff in 1916 at Huis ter Heide near Utrecht, clearly shows Wright's influence. This precocious manifestation of the modern movement was much admired by the De Stijl group.

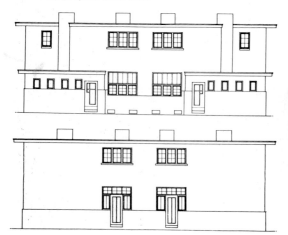

Town Hall, Hilversum

Willem Dudok, working under the influence of both Berlage and Frank Lloyd Wright, went his own way during the period between the wars, affected less by the Cubist aesthetic of fragmentation than by the monumental sobriety of the generation of the 1910s. The powerful play of volumes in the Hilversum Town Hall (1930) is an example of this. It was much admired on the other side of the Channel, where Dudok's work found a considerable following in the 1930s.

The Modern City, Berchem-Sainte-Agathe

The modern movement was very active in Belgium thanks to those architects who, during the occupation of their country by the Germans in the First World War, had sought refuge in Holland and established contacts with the intellectual circles of Amsterdam. The housing estate built by Victor Bourgeois in Berchem-Sainte-Agathe near Brussels between 1922 and 1925 was one of the most advanced projects of its time.

Bruchfeldstrasse, Frankfurt

The Weimar Republic was favourably disposed towards experiments with housing estates. In Frankfurt the architect Ernst May was able to practise the town-planning theories of the modern school on a large scale. His work calls to mind the contemporary debate on town planning among Soviet architects. The 1925 Bruchfeldstrasse complex is one of his first major achievements in this vein before 1933, the year in which he was driven into exile, first to the U.S.S.R. and later to South America. The repetition of units reveals certain weaknesses, however, such as the Neoclassically inspired loft which, in accordance with Dutch practice, is divided up into individual store-rooms for the use of tenants.

The Einstein Tower, Potsdam

The Einstein Tower (1919–21), commissioned by Einstein from the architect Erich Mendelsohn, was an observatory specializing in the study of spectro-analytical phenomena. The sophisticated technical organization of the interior was complemented by an architecture aimed at suggesting the scientific theories of its user. Mendelsohn's dynamic style, with its curvilinear movement, derives quite evidently from the formal vocabulary of Rudolf Steiner and the theosophical architecture of the "Goetheanum" in Dornach – but it is marked by a greater simplicity and unity. There is, nevertheless, a striking contrast between this monumental sculptural exterior and the technical complexity of the interior. Around the 1920s the machine aesthetic and the Constructivist style which embodied it were by no means the only features of modern architecture. Symbolism and spiritualism played an equally large part.

Cover of the "Frühlicht" review

The modernist utopia of the early 1920s expressed itself in an architectural messianism, which saw in the architecture of the future a field for popular reconciliation and communion, with technology as the means to this end. Bruno Taut, apostle of *glass-architectur* as demonstrated in his 1914 design for the House of Glass at the Cologne exhibition, published numerous utopian drawings such as this review cover of 1920 and the famous "alpine architecture" projects.

Hufeisen Siedlung, Berlin

Bruno Taut could become quite a realist when faced with definite commissions. This horseshoe-shaped estate in Berlin-Britz was built between 1925 and 1931 at the instigation of the town-planner Martin Wagner. It takes up May's experiment in Frankfurt, notably in the beautiful polychromatic facings which give this highly individual architecture its character. The icy perfectionism so often criticized in modern architecture is absent here.

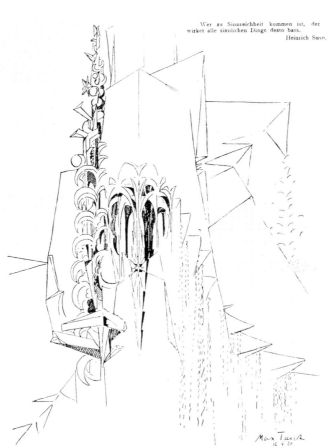

The triumph of modernism

Having evolved as a style that was easy to recognize, modernism promised to become the great success of the 1930s. The idealistic hope of collaboration between art and technology, man and machine, now had an adequate form of expression at its disposal. The advocates of the new direction in architecture could now rally round under the banner of purism: they had found a common language. It is striking that this new language was primarily the negation of another, just as it was (or strove to be) a negation of a political system and a society.

Modernist architects, identifying with the purified forms of industrial production, turned the machine aesthetic into a double-edged symbol. Firstly it stood for the new civilization and attitudes towards the past that ranged from indifference to hostility. It was between the two world wars that an iconoclastic mentality was formed that rejected the past in the name of the future of architecture and even encouraged its destruction. The burning of the library at Alexandria was no longer considered one of the great crimes in the history of humanity but, on the contrary, as an act of courage and faith in the future! Secondly it was the herald of political and social action. The question of whether the new architecture was acceptable to the lower classes was not raised often enough (the story of Le Corbusier's Frugès quarter in Bordeau-Pessac proves that it should have been) but it was believed that the exemplary character of the latest architectural achievements would eventually win general approval like the automobile and the aeroplane.

The consensus which emerged among the modernist architects of the 1920s to adhere to a purist aesthetic is due on the one hand to the extreme novelty of the language. It took no interest in the restricted field of ornament, it denied itself at the same time the rhetoric of allegory and symbolism and set itself up as a simple aesthetic treatment of technical means. A large part of its appeal, on the other hand, lay in the reassuring nature of this "other" language, so easy to understand and to apply, a language which calls for no individual expression from its author beyond the correct application of norm, a language which carried rich and positive connotations in its proclaimed avant-gardism.

It followed that purism, as a formula for modernity, was from the beginning based upon uncertain foundations. Was it to be the cultural foundation for a future society, that of the budding industrial era, prefiguring the language of a future socialist society and becoming the expression of an egalitarian morality? Or was it to be a symbol of a society enslaved by the power of industrial mechanization, a symbol of money and the predominance of capitalism in the contemporary world?

The two images were quite distinct, with just a few nuances in common. On the one hand there was the ambiguous relation between modernism and Fascism (Le Corbusier, Giuseppe Tarragni) and, on the other, its dependence on the moneyed aristocracy. For modernism was also the fashion of the international elite, something comparable to the luxury train or the French Line cruiser.

Modern art was something of an attempt to square the circle. How was it to cater to a clientele of the world's richest industrialists, the most sophisticated elite of intellectuals, and still build housing that was good for the community as a whole? Had they not been guided by a prophetic vision of their message, the modernists would certainly have failed to achieve such an incredible compromise in a class society. It was faith in the future of industrial architecture and its formulas that sustained all their experiments.

Normalization and prefabrication, the systematic use of industrial products and the mechanization of the building site were their incessant themes. Their aim was above all to develop the appropriate tool of production for a mechanized society, to design forms suited for mechanical production and reproduction, simple forms to be realized in new materials such as glass, iron and concrete.

There emerged a kind of expression which was at once very powerful in its coherence, demonstrative in its intentions and sometimes even profoundly lyrical in the ease with which entirely new spatial forms were conceived and realized without the least trace of nostalgia. This was the heroic period of modern art and the Schröder house (Rietveld), the Villa Savoye (Le Corbusier), the Bauhaus buildings (Gropius) and the Lovell house (Neutra) are all there to prove as much.

The Bauhaus, Dessau

Walter Gropius, the director of the Bauhaus school of art – the most important school of architecture and the applied arts in the modern world – built in Dessau in 1925 a series of school buildings with glass façades, markedly influenced by the Constructivist spirit. At the time they were seen as one of the great manifestos of international modernism.

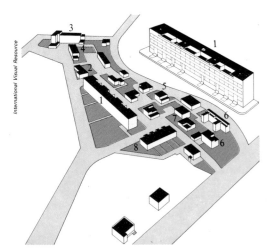

1 block of flats by Mies van der Rohe
2 house by Adolf Rading
3 villa by Behrens
4 houses by Mart Stam
5 villa by Poelzig
6 apartments and villas by Le Corbusier and P. Jeanneret
7 prefabricated houses by Gropius
8 houses by J.J.P.Oud

The Weissenhof, Stuttgart

For the Werkbund exhibition of 1927, Ludwig Mies van der Rohe was commissioned to build a model modern housing estate. He designed the plan and a sample block of houses whose apartments were fitted out with mobile partitions. All the greatest modernist architects of the time were called in to contribute at least one building each to this exceptional ensemble.

Schröder-Schräder house, Utrecht

In 1924 the Dutch architect Gerrit Rietveld designed a house on the outskirts of Utrecht demonstrating the theories expounded by the neo-Plasticists of the De Stijl group formed around Mondrian and Van Doesburg. This architecture based on intersecting planes and pure colours (which owe a great deal to the Japanese house) is directly opposed to the Dutch expressionist school.

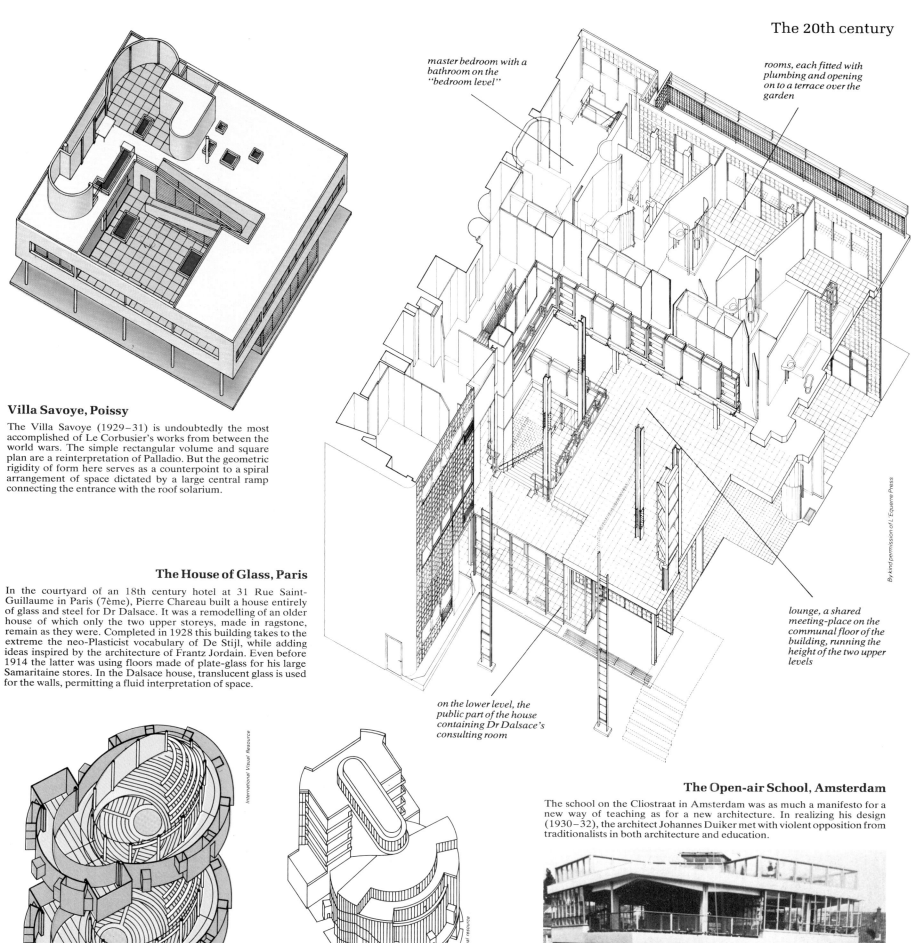

master bedroom with a bathroom on the "bedroom level"

rooms, each fitted with plumbing and opening on to a terrace over the garden

By kind permission of L'Equerre Press

lounge, a shared meeting-place on the communal floor of the building, running the height of the two upper levels

on the lower level, the public part of the house containing Dr Dalsace's consulting room

Villa Savoye, Poissy

The Villa Savoye (1929–31) is undoubtedly the most accomplished of Le Corbusier's works from between the world wars. The simple rectangular volume and square plan are a reinterpretation of Palladio. But the geometric rigidity of form here serves as a counterpoint to a spiral arrangement of space dictated by a large central ramp connecting the entrance with the roof solarium.

The House of Glass, Paris

In the courtyard of an 18th century hotel at 31 Rue Saint-Guillaume in Paris (7ème), Pierre Chareau built a house entirely of glass and steel for Dr Dalsace. It was a remodelling of an older house of which only the two upper storeys, made in ragstone, remain as they were. Completed in 1928 this building takes to the extreme the neo-Plasticist vocabulary of De Stijl, while adding ideas inspired by the architecture of Frantz Jordain. Even before 1914 the latter was using floors made of plate-glass for his large Samaritaine stores. In the Dalsace house, translucent glass is used for the walls, permitting a fluid interpretation of space.

International Visual Resource

International visual resource

▨ *stage*		▨ *floor*	
☐ *seating*		▨ *projection screen*	

The "total theatre"

Conceived for Erwin Piscator, the "total theatre" (1926) by Walter Gropius aims to satisfy the demand for flexibility expressed by modern directors. It offers an auditorium with a revolving platform which combines a number of functions: a central orchestra circle, an amphitheatre with or without a back stage and an Italian-style auditorium with a traditional stage. This formula was not put into practice till much later, in 1968 for the cultural centre in Grenoble.

The Open-air School, Amsterdam

The school on the Cliostraat in Amsterdam was as much a manifesto for a new way of teaching as for a new architecture. In realizing his design (1930–32), the architect Johannes Duiker met with violent opposition from traditionalists in both architecture and education.

Nederlands documentatiecentrum voor de Bouwkunst

Challenges to the "International Style"

In most Western countries, modernism found itself in conflict with local architectural traditions and, especially between the wars, with a powerful regionalist movement. This had grown out of Art Nouveau and Art Deco but drew on different, purely local sources of inspiration. It derived its ideology from the Domestic Revival and Arts and Crafts movements of half a century before, although that kind of art had by now lost its impact, having been vulgarized and stereotyped *ad nauseam*. Alongside regionalism, there also developed a reactionary taste among the most affluent classes for pastiche, the exact reproduction of "period styles" that could supposedly never look out of date. The rapid obsolescence of Art Nouveau and Art Deco showed how ephemeral contemporary styles could be, and the imitation of the past seemed the safest alternative.

In the 1930s modernism (or rather the most superficial and easily recognizable features of the movement, the reduction of ornament and the use of simple geometric forms) was embraced by Art Deco. The idea of adapting modernism to the world of popular design was quite alien, of course, to its original avant-garde status. As a militant minority, the modernists were profoundly elitist. Only a very restricted circle of wealthy amateurs could afford to indulge themselves in an art that was so perfectly sophisticated, so intellectual in its purism and economy of means. True modernism was anything but popular.

From 1932 modernism was generally called the "International Style", a term coined by the historian Henry Russell Hitchcock and the architect Philip Johnson for a retrospective exhibition at the Museum of Modern Art in New York. Its appropriateness was obvious. A certain architectural formula had been adopted throughout the Western world, producing buildings that were astonishingly alike, from Moscow (the Centrosoyus) to Los Angeles (the Lovell house), from London (Ember-ton's Yacht Club at Burnham on Crouch) to Athens (the Koletti Street school by Nicolaus Mitsakis). This uniformity had long been apparent, and contemporary critics had reasonably objected to the sheer artificiality of a theory that took the industrially-produced object as its sole point of reference and was oblivious to the importance of local conditions. Modernism, they argued, took no account of the differences between building steel skyscrapers in America and relatively primitive structures in poor countries from stone hand-cut by local masons. It gave no consideration to market factors, climate or indigenous culture. In its insistence on formal purity, it was not adaptable to people's actual needs.

The debate between modernists and traditionalists became increasingly complex. Traditionalism no longer meant quite the same as it had before. There were now few who declared themselves completely opposed to any kind of contemporary expression, or who considered the pastiche of past styles the only acceptable course. Confusingly, the advocates of Art Deco, the "modernized" Art Deco of the 1930s, stressed how modern they were and dismissed the International Style as an extremist movement that could not possibly last. Indeed it was Art Deco that the modernists principally attacked, considering its way of appealing to the masses to be spurious. The main debate, in other words, was not between those looking to the past and those looking to the future, as some have suggested, but between camps that both laid claim to modernity.

In the U.S.S.R. and Germany, modernism was condemned on political grounds. Technical considerations took second place to the need to establish an architecture that expressed the power of the State. For the Nazis, this could only be achieved by a return to the great classical tradition. The Stalinists despised modernists for their intellectualism, reverted to the narrowest academic dogma and pronounced classicism to be essentially a popular culture, which the proletariat must take over as their rightful inheritance from the bourgeoisie. The interaction of art and politics in these countries raised questions that affected architectural thought everywhere. What was the relevance of modernism as an aesthetic determined by purely technical concerns? What was its relationship to the general culture and to history?

The ideological disparateness of the movement showed itself clearly in countries that were traditionally rural, whether underdeveloped like Brazil or just less urbanized like Finland. Figures such as Alvar Aalto, Lucio Costa and Oscar Niemeyer played a leading role in architecture from 1930 to 1960 exactly because they were able to make modernism compatible with local materials and building methods. They constituted a movement sometimes called "empiricism", which went beyond questions of style and history and sought to ally itself with the living heritage of indigenous cultures.

Their approach was very similar to that of the Arts and Crafts Movement. The important difference was that it was free from nostalgia, not imitative of past forms but compatible with them. Aalto took the limitations imposed upon him by any given project as the starting-point for his design. This was the essence of empiricism. With him it was not a matter of modernism pitted against traditionalism, or purism against academicism, but empiricism against "culturalism". Empiricism cared nothing for history, taking its point of departure from the existing culture. Its opponents pointed to the way industrial civilization was destroying cultural traditions and insisted that these should be preserved intact. The question of the cultural heritage was once again to the fore – the relationship of the industrial age to its past, with all the problems that that very complex relationship raises.

Concert Hall, Halsingborg

The success of modernist architecture turned an audacious avant-garde into a recognized movement. What had been a fashion among intellectuals of the most privileged classes in Europe spread throughout the world and, for better or worse, came to be known as the International Style. The Concert Hall at Halsingborg (1932) by the Swedish architect Sven Markelius illustrates how readily the formal vocabulary of modernism was assimilated in places far removed from the creative centres of Paris, Berlin and Moscow. The conventional arrangement of circular auditorium, here entirely glazed, with rectangular blocks containing the entrance hall and upper seating areas, is treated in a manner obviously influenced by Constructivism.

San Francisco, Pampulha

Built by Oscar Niemeyer in 1943, the church of San Francisco at Pampulha in Brazil represented a nationalist reaction against the International Style. It denied the purism that was so much part of the modernist aesthetic. The curving shapes of the concrete walls contradicted the principle of absolute rectilinearity, while the large figurative decorations in majolica by Paulo Werneck challenged the insistence of the De Stijl group on pure abstraction. Here was an architecture of feeling, emerging from a complex ideological and cultural background and calling modernist internationalism into question.

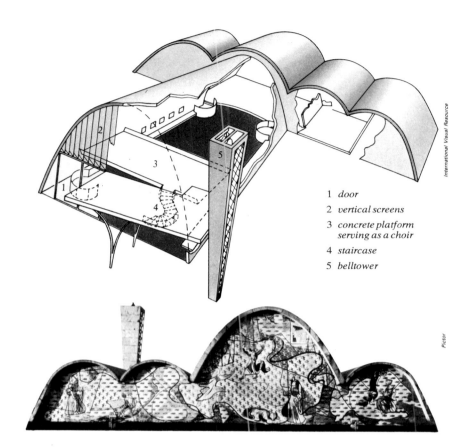

1 *door*
2 *vertical screens*
3 *concrete platform serving as a choir*
4 *staircase*
5 *belltower*

Philadelphia Savings Fund Society Building, Philadelphia

Built by the American architects Howe and Lescaze in 1932, this office block recalls the language of forms developed by the Constructivists in the preceding decade, not least in the giant sign placed diagonally across the roof.

University Library, Mexico City

Seeking to fuse their own cultural traditions with the modernist aesthetic, Latin-American architects incorporated symbolic designs into their work. The most impressive example is the vast mosaic entirely covering the storage tower of the University Library in Mexico City, by Juan O'Gorman, of 1953. The architecture itself conforms absolutely to modernist ideas: the reference to the national culture is really no more than window dressing.

Woodland Crematorium, Stockholm

The propylaea of the Stockholm cemetery, containing funerary chapels and a crematorium, were designed by Erik Gunnar Asplund in 1940. Exhibiting the most refined sense of scale and respect for the landscape, they present a challenge to the machine aesthetic that goes far beyond considerations of national culture.

From Wright to Aalto: organic architecture

As the modernist desire to bring architecture into line with machine production began to be attacked and its purism criticized as a stylistic strait-jacket, the great dream of the international architectural congresses was dissipated. The dogmatic tone of the congresses had undoubtedly been what was required. The preliminary declaration of La Sarraz (1928) and the famous "Athens Charter" (1933) were the basis for every great architectural and town-planning project executed in the Western world for almost half a century. But in the process of examining and defining itself, the modern movement had become a new kind of academicism.

The formal repertoire developed over ten years by Gerrit T. Rietveld under the auspices of the De Stijl group, then by Le Corbusier, Ludwig Mies van der Rohe, Rudolph Schindler and many others, was erected into a rigid theoretical code. Modern architecture became a cult with its own temples and, in the form of the "Athens Charter", its own catechism. Faced with the rise of an architectural dictatorship, it is not surprising that the opposition to modernism changed tactics, one of the most effective forms of resistance being empiricism. Otherwise, the chief threat to the International Style was the occasional wave of extreme reaction, the closing of the Bauhaus by Hitler and the flight of German architects abroad, and the rejection of modernism in the U.S.S.R. As a result, it flourished exclusively in liberal democracies, Great Britain, the United States, France, Belgium, the Scandinavian countries and South America. The fact that empiricism developed with particular vigour in these same countries was no accident.

The men who breathed much-needed new life into architecture had, curiously perhaps, been closely associated with modernism in its first stages. They were Frank Lloyd Wright in America, the "forerunner" of the movement, Alvar Aalto in Finland and Le Corbusier in France, two of its originators. Aalto's development showed from the beginning a complete freedom from dogma. By contrast, Le Corbusier was the great polemicist who had been responsible for the "Athens Charter" (which he published in 1933). His taste for invective should not blind us, however, to the subtlety of his work as an architect, which in fact undermined the notion of modernism as a fixed system.

But the (somewhat unlikely) key figure was to be Frank Lloyd Wright, a leader of American Art Nouveau whose career as an architect of real conviction seemed to have come to an end with the Imperial Hotel in Tokyo (1922) and the Millard house in Pasadena (1923). He was now an old man, founder of a private school of architecture at which his wife gave dancing lessons. Yet here it was, at his school in Taliesin West, deep in the Arizona desert, that Wright threw himself into a far-reaching critical appraisal of modernist architecture, bringing to bear his acute sensitivity to the relation of building to setting, and the concern with fluidity and diversity of space so admirably demonstrated in his "prairie houses".

Wright was not particularly interested in mass-produced materials, the exact repetition of forms or the idea that the design of a building should suggest its function. What did interest him was the relationship of interior to exterior, the character of every

space and, anticipating Bachelard, its psychological effect. Rigorously excluding the ornamentation that had been so fashionable in his youth, he worked, like the modernists, in terms of volumes and spaces. These he infused with an emotional power, exploiting natural elements such as the water and fire at "Falling Water" and the diffused light at the Johnson Wax Building in Racine.

All his life, Wright had been an enthusiastic admirer of Japanese architecture, which indeed had influenced his work at the beginning of the century. It helped him even more in developing his later style, just as it had helped Bruno Taut and Theo van Doesburg in their contributions to the development of modernism. Finding his new means of expression was a matter of following modernism just so far as to suppress unnecessary ornamentation.

Wright called his work "organic architecture" to express his antipathy to the machine aesthetic and all theories of purism. He was attempting to create a new relationship between man and architecture, no longer through ornamentation as in the 19th century, but through a highly controlled treatment of space. Aalto believed in making the constraints of a project determine the final design, so that every work was entirely unique and original. Hoping to reconcile modernism with popular culture, Le Corbusier introduced the kind of irregularity associated with things made by hand. Wright forged a wholly individual conception of man in his emotional relationship to life and to nature. Though formally quite distinct, Wright, Aalto and Le Corbusier were together in their denial of the aesthetics of industry as the basis for architecture.

Sanatorium, Paimio

Developing at the very heart of the modern movement, Alvar Aalto's "empiricism" was in fact a challenge to the machine aesthetic it seemed to follow. The Sanatorium at Paimio (1931) is spider-like in plan, the different blocks expressing the diversity of functions performed by the sanatorium and the cyclical nature of the daily work carried on inside. These open-air galleries for patients to catch the sun and see the view were entirely original.

M. Kapanen, Alvar Aalto Museo

"Falling Water", Bear Run, Pennsylvania

In this poem of air, water and fire, Frank Lloyd Wright pushed to the very limits the possibilities offered by reinforced concrete for building cantilevered structures. Attached to a masonry stem, platforms are placed crossways at different heights to create terraces. At the lower level, immediately above the waterfall, which is seen through a glass panel set in the floor, the main living area (1) is arranged around the hearth, extending into the dining area (3) and the kitchen (2). The room opens out on to the great terraces (4) and a concrete pergola (7) which diffuses the light and leads down to the level of the waterfall. The bedrooms (5) are on the top level opening on to an immense flat roof on which is a belvedere used as an art gallery (6).

E. Stoller

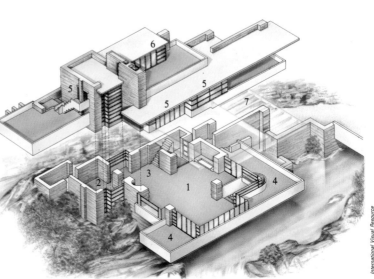

International Visual Resource

The International Exhibition of 1939, New York

The Finnish pavilion at the New York International Exhibition was designed by Alvar Aalto. Its fascinating interior was enclosed within undulating and inclining walls made of wooden boards, a symbol of the Finnish timber industry. At ground level the space opened out for the display of objects; higher up were posters representing national activities. The originality of the design lay in the successful harmony it achieved between the two displays.

Price Tower, Bartlesville, Oklahoma

The design Frank Lloyd Wright used for the Price Tower was conceived as early as 1929 but executed only in 1956. There is a vertical core containing stairs and lifts, and four radial supporting structures. The areas between are occupied alternately by apartments and offices, the former distinguished by struts giving a vertical emphasis, the latter by horizontal projections defining the storeys.

Johnson Wax Building, Racine

Like "Falling Water", the Johnson Wax Building at Racine, Wisconsin (1936–39) won Wright tremendous acclaim. Contemporaries were impressed above all by the use of natural illumination diffused by translucent tubes of Pyrex glass. Spaces were bathed in an even, non-directional light, which creates a calm atmosphere highly conducive to work. Wright had used the same principle of natural illumination for a closed space in the Larkin Building of 30 years earlier, where the interior courtyard was a well of light.

Bands of Pyrex glass tubing transmit as much natural light as possible into the laboratory tower. Immediately under the tower is a recreational area and a car park.

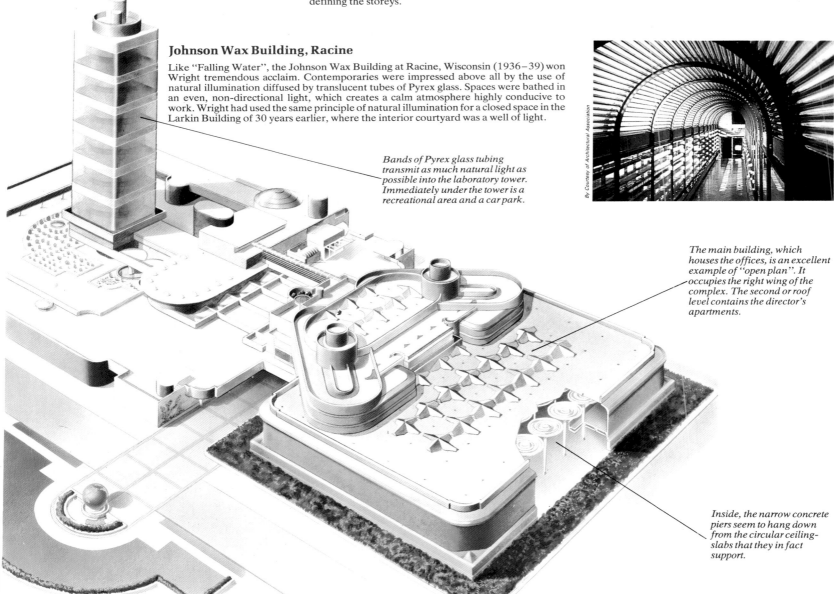

The main building, which houses the offices, is an excellent example of "open plan". It occupies the right wing of the complex. The second or roof level contains the director's apartments.

Inside, the narrow concrete piers seem to hang down from the circular ceiling-slabs that they in fact support.

379

Brutalist Europe

The debate about contemporary architecture that had gone on in the 1930s became all the more important in the state of political and economic disruption that was the aftermath of the Second World War. The cultural situation was becoming clearer. The nostalgic, traditionalist trend, which had produced the architecture of pastiche, had gone out of fashion; Art Deco was a thing of the past as well, leaving modernism very much in control. The question was, should the movement adhere to the standard established by 20 years of theory and practice as the "International Style"? Or should it move towards the experimental, fundamentally anti-dogmatic architectural current favoured by culturalists and humanists and known as "empiricist" or "organic"?

Once again, the relationship of architecture to technology was at the heart of the debate, at least to the extent that the countries involved had been industrialized. The situation was complicated by the fact that major cultural groups had evolved in such different ways. Germanic Europe was quite distinct from Latin Europe, with its orientation towards Africa, the Middle East and South America. The Anglo-Saxon countries followed procedures and models that were different again, though still within the modernist language. The works of great figures such as Hans Scharoun and Alvar Aalto were seminal as far as Europe north of the Rhine was concerned, but had only the slightest effect on France and England. Finally, a new American school had formed during the war around Ludwig Mies van der Rohe and Walter Gropius, which was to exercise a lively influence over Europe after the liberation.

There were two main cultural tendencies that affected architecture during the technological and economic changes of the 1950s. Firstly, the assertion of national identity no longer carried the same ideological significance as it had in the crisis years immediately before the outbreak of the war. Now it was merely a matter of language differences. There was a freer interaction between countries: the Italians became enthusiastic about Frank Lloyd Wright, thanks to the publications devoted to him by the critic Bruno Zevi, while the British showed themselves very open to Le Corbusier. Secondly, there arose a distinction, essentially technological and going beyond traditional cultural structures, between "steel countries" and "concrete countries". Steel and concrete represented different architectural languages but more than that, different levels of industrial production and different standards of living, respectively affluent and not so affluent.

Concrete was the material of the poor, involving only a small quantity of iron but plenty of stones and a high level of manual work. It was possible, using industrial methods, to reduce the number of workers and the skills required of them without increasing the cost of the raw material. Lacking the precise lines of steel and often showing all too clearly the imperfections of the workmen using it, concrete was yet to be invested with any real dignity in its own right. It was in this area that the ideas of Le Corbusier were to be of decisive importance for European architecture as a whole. Completely abandoning the purist aesthetic of the 1920s, that of the Salvation Army Building and the Centrosoyus, he began after the war to use concrete in all its roughness and irregularity of texture and form. The *pilotis* of the Swiss Hostel of 1931 in the Cité Universitaire, Paris, are an early example. Taking up the idea again in 1947 at the Unité d'Habitation, Marseilles, he transformed what had been merely a matter of architectural detailing into an all-over feature of great sculptural power.

Avoiding all reference to the machine aesthetic, Le Corbusier developed a style that was monumental, not only in the overwhelming sense of mass, enhanced by the setting, but also in the graphic play of forms and spaces, which made the façade an extraordinary framework of contrasted darks and lights. To this outer skin, the rough, rugged, almost savage material brought a richness of texture that caught the light to stunning effect. With its bold colours – large expanses of unmodulated primaries – the style had an austere grandeur that was powerful if equally inhuman.

The new aesthetic has been called "brutalist". Admittedly, it made little concession to prettiness, created an overpowering, megalomaniac effect by its scale and used the most aggressive materials and colours. What made brutalism more than just a wilful gesture, however, was its acute sensitivity to light. On the exterior this is used in a sculptural way to outline and subtly model volumes. The interior lighting, whether dazzling natural light or the diffused illumination from what Le Corbusier called his "light cannons", was designed to appeal on an emotional level to the sense of space and movement. This concept, of which Ronchamp was the fascinating revelation, brought the world of Le Corbusier close to that of the last works of Frank Lloyd Wright.

Le Corbusier's ideas were taken up to a considerable extent in Latin America but his main sphere of influence remained Europe. By the vigour of his rhetoric, he became standard-bearer to the "Team Ten" generation (Georges Candilis, Alison and Peter Smithson, Aldo van Eyck, etc.) in their struggle against the academicism of the modern movement as represented by the tenth C.I.A.M. conference at Dubrovnik in 1956. Against the growing influence of the new American school and its architecture of glass and steel, Europe became identified with brutalism. It was a defence mechanism against the cultural colonialism of the richest country in the world. But it was also an original language developed by a Europe that was still of central economic and cultural importance.

Orphanage, Amsterdam

A member of the "Team Ten" group, Aldo van Eyck sought to adapt Le Corbusier's formal vocabulary to the demands of prefabrication. His Amsterdam Orphanage of 1960–61 is constructed from the basic elements of posts, girders and concrete domes enclosed within brick walls, following a pattern inspired by Islamic architecture. The systematic repetition of the same unit makes the composition infinitely extensible. Van Eyck's work has been much imitated, its versatility being especially suited to school architecture. Twenty years after its construction, it remains a major example of what we can for convenience call brutalism.

United Nations Building, New York

When Le Corbusier came to New York in 1947 to put forward his plans for the United Nations skyscraper, Manhattan was still what it had been in the 1930s. His design of glass and steel, a stark rectangle overlooking the East River, impressed contemporaries by the power of its mass. Its 39 storeys made it taller than any neighbouring buildings. Winner of the competition for the League of Nations building 20 years earlier, a project that was never realized, Le Corbusier had in the meantime acquired an international reputation. His design for the U.N. was accepted but the execution and detailing were handed over to the American office of Wallace K. Harrison and Max Abramovitz. This masterpiece of industrial technology contained the germ of the late Le Corbusier in all its power, as he moved further and further away from the elegant refinement of purism towards a purely sculptural sense of mass and texture.

House of the Millers, Ahmedabad

While at work at Chandigarh, Le Corbusier was also invited to design the headquarters of the millers' union at Ahmedabad, which was built in 1954. Surrounded by landscape, the building is a concrete cube, virtually blind on its eastern and western sides, transparent to the north and shaded on the south by a monumental screen orientated to cut out the direct sunlight. The sculptural effect of the oblique partitions of the screen, which create triangular shadows, is dramatically interrupted by a deep central opening penetrated by the sloping form of the entrance ramp. This was a rethinking of the Villa Stein at Garches combined with the Villa Savoye at Poissy.

The Unité d'Habitation, Marseilles

Claudius Petit, "Ministre de la Reconstruction" under the Fourth Republic, was bold enough to call upon Le Corbusier to build an apartment block that would realize all his theories of architecture. The result was the Unité d'Habitation, or Cité Radieuse, built 1947–52. At the very moment when the spirit of the "Athens Charter", which he had edited, was reigning supreme, Le Corbusier turned his back on functionalism in architecture and town planning to propose a gigantic structure that would be a crushing, dominating presence in the banal setting of the Marseilles suburbs. This vast communal dwelling, reminiscent of a ship, a shoebox or a blockhouse, was to contemporaries quite bewildering. Should it be analysed and appreciated exclusively in terms of functionality, as advocated by the architect himself? Or should it be condemned as an inhuman conglomeration of pigeon-holes, which was how his detractors described it? Or perhaps it should be regarded as an enormous abstract sculpture, a colossal ornament to embellish the Avenue du Prado?

Duplex apartments interlock in a back-to-back arrangement designed to allow part of the living space and the balcony to occupy the full two storeys. They are served by an "internal street" in the centre. At the heart of the building, on the seventh and eighth floors, is a shopping centre.

The southern and western façades are animated by the play of light and shade on the balconies. The effect of the roughcast concrete, vibrant in the sunlight, is enriched by a vivid polychromy in the primary colours of the balcony dividing-walls. The northern side of the building, by contrast, is completely blind as a protection against the mistral.

The 18 main levels of the Unité d'Habitation contain 337 duplex flats of 23 different types, from the one-room studio to the large family apartment. Each one has a deep balcony which acts as a shield against the sun.

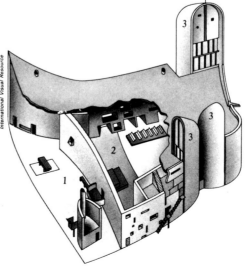

Notre-Dame-du-Haut, Ronchamp

Called upon in 1955 to rebuild a pilgrimage chapel in the Vosges region out of war-damage funds, Le Corbusier used one of the strangest, but also one of the most sculptural forms it is possible to imagine. A thick concrete form, like a sail but turned up to resemble a three-cornered hat, floats over curving walls orientated and punctuated in a way that follows the course of the sun. The southern "wall of light" is pierced by a multiplicity of holes containing stained glass, acting as a kind of projector and filling the interior with coloured light. Meanwhile, a ray of light penetrates through the roof; and "cannons", rather like the air vents on a ship, transmit light down from above into the chapels (3). A place for private prayer, holding only 50 people, the main chapel (2) is enlarged on the east side by an exterior altar (1) for the use of pilgrims.

The voice of America

The Second World War made the United States conscious of its own power. With Germany being crushed under the Allied bombardment, Great Britain faced with the serious threat of invasion and France paralysed by the Occupation, the United States undertook an enormous industrial effort in preparation for their landing in Europe and in the process became the most technologically advanced country in the world. The Yalta Agreement, by which the Americans divided Europe with the Russians, consolidated their pre-eminence.

The United States had already made a vital contribution to the history of modern architecture by inventing the skyscraper, that symbol of the power of money, that "cathedral of Mammon" which turned business accommodation into prodigious, monumental complexes such as the southern tip of Manhattan. Initially torn between the ideals of modernism and the revaluation of "high culture", between Chicago and New York, American architecture had arrived at a coherent formula in the 1920s that brought together the strange bedfellows of Gothic verticality and Art Deco ornament. The crash of 1929 brought a premature end to this original movement.

By the 1940s the vagaries of fashion had put the Art Deco skyscraper beyond the pale. Meanwhile, the Cubist aesthetic of the Daily News Building and the Rockefeller Center in New York had unsuccessfully been presented as an alternative formula, a modernized version of the rich play of volumes that Art Deco rightly prided itself upon. The simultaneous attempts of William Lescaze and George Howe to introduce the International Style into the United States was also a failure and the Philadelphia Savings Fund Society Building was an isolated case. It looked as if American architecture would follow its own course, quite independently.

But that would have been to overlook the importance of politics. Great architects such as Walter Gropius and Mies van der Rohe fled to the United States from Nazi Germany and made it the most important gathering-place for modernist architects of the time. Gropius became director of the famous M.I.T. (Massachusetts Institute of Technology) at Harvard, and Mies van der Rohe took charge of I.I.T. (Illinois Institute of Technology) in Chicago. They brought up a generation of architects on the experimental teaching of the Bauhaus, where Gropius and Mies had been the masters, winning them over completely to the purist aesthetic of German modernism as a new, disturbing yet fascinating idea.

In this stimulating atmosphere, Mies perfected his own distinctive graphic language. A cross between the Japanese tradition and Prussian Neoclassicism, this found its definitive expression in a few works that rapidly achieved "classic" status. One of his buildings on the I.I.T. campus, the Alumni Memorial Hall, a structure entirely of glass, brick and steel, was the most rigorous display of technological purism. Its steel pillars, with their sophisticated detailing, have been compared with the monumental power of the Parthenon.

In the American context, Mies's highly technological conception of architecture took on a new significance. It became a symbol of the industrial power of the country. Avoiding the overt commercialism of Art Deco and indeed any form of crude showiness, his spare, intellectual, refined style perfectly suited the triumphant spirit of the United States at this time. The idea of the United States as guardian of culture was beginning. The country felt itself to be entering a great cultural era in which it would become the radiant centre of world thought. All this was far removed from the radical political message conceived in the 1920s by young Berlin architects on the fringes of nihilist circles. The links

between art and politics are close but they are also subject to the most curious reversals.

Now the architect of American high capitalism, Mies van der Rohe created the most accomplished essays in modernism, the ultimate symbols of the union of art and technology. His apartment blocks on Lake Shore Drive in Chicago (1948–51) and the Seagram Building in New York (1958) are the realization of ideas the Chicago School had begun to conceive three-quarters of a century earlier, and which the German utopians had dreamt of during the great days of the Weimar Republic.

Around Mies a whole school formed, including Philip Johnson, Pietro Belluschi, the Skidmore, Owings and Merrill group (notably Gordon Bunshaft) and Eero Saarinen. These efficiently pursued the modernist theme of the great steel and glass block and, with detached pavilions within an open campus of the hospital or university type, the theme of the model factory too. The spectacular regeneration of the American school also allowed for the emergence of an isolated figure such as Richard Neutra, whose designs for individual houses of steel and glass show the influence of both purism and the work of Frank Lloyd Wright in their treatment of space and use of interpenetration.

The impact of American architecture was so great in the 1950s that certain European architects came completely under its spell. Arne Jacobsen in Denmark, the Smithsons in England (who tried to fuse the technological approach coming from the United States with the brutalism of Le Corbusier) and many lesser architects imported patterns into Europe that they discovered on architectural pilgrimages to New York and Chicago. Oscar Niemeyer in South America interpreted the work of Le Corbusier in a strictly aestheticizing way, but even his lyricism does not conceal an underlying purism and emphasis on technique.

Alumni Memorial Hall, Chicago

Mies van der Rohe took refuge in the United States in 1938 and became director of the Armour Institute, later the architectural school of the Illinois Institute of Technology. During the war he undertook the reconstruction of the campus of I.I.T. and the Alumni Memorial Hall of 1944–46 was one of the first buildings to be finished. In this architecture of brick, cast concrete and industrial rectilinearity, he at last found the means to express his own purist vision. Rarely has an architectural style so aptly corresponded with the dominant outlook of a country, in this case the richest in the world at a time of victory.

Lake Shore Drive, Chicago

These apartment blocks at nos. 860–80 Lake Shore Drive on the edge of Lake Michigan were built betwen 1948 and 1951 to the designs of Mies van der Rohe. The entirely steel skeleton and the curtain-wall façades were the latest in luxury and technical refinement. The perfectly rectangular blocks are animated by being set at right-angles to each other, by the random pattern of open and closed curtains in the windows and the play of sunlight on the glass.

The Equitable Building, Portland

Built in 1948 by Pietro Belluschi, the Equitable Savings and Loan Association in Portland, Oregon, is one of the most perfect realizations of American post-war purism. The façade is a strictly regular pattern of mullions and horizontal bands, all flush with the window surfaces. This kind of flat façade, lacking even the slightest modelling, projection or recession, is one of the most characteristic formal elements of modernist purism, used sometimes in a way that goes against both truth to materials and plain logic. Here the graphic effect is what counts and architecture reduced to the drawing out of grids.

Pepsi Cola Building, New York

From the 1950s onwards, Gordon Bunshaft of the firm of Skidmore, Owings and Merrill popularized a particular type of glass office block in New York. The prototype was the Lever Brothers Building but here the form reached a pitch of exceptional elegance.

Seagram Building, New York

Built between 1954 and 1958, this was the most perfect of all Mies van der Rohe's works. The combination of smoked glass and black, anodized aluminium made it a luxury object, mysterious and perfect, overlooking a marble plaza provided for the people of New York (a generous gesture in view of the value of real estate in Manhattan!). The mirror-like façade is crowned by a blind attic storey containing the air-conditioning equipment.

Kaufmann house, Palm Springs

This "house in the desert" was built by Richard Neutra, the Californian architect, for the same client who ten years earlier had commissioned "Falling Water" from Frank Lloyd Wright. A similar spirit suffused his designs of a breathtaking technological perfection.

Johnson house, New Canaan

Friend and admirer of Mies van der Rohe, the architect Philip Johnson built this "house of glass" for himself in 1949 in a rural setting in Connecticut. It was the first of its kind and the undisputed masterpiece of the genre. Completely transparent except for a central bathroom in the form of a plain cylinder, it is wholly open to the landscape. The view can be altered at will by moving screens as in traditional Japanese houses. In its lightness, this architecture of glass and steel conforms absolutely to the canons of American purism.

Palace of the Alvorada, Brasilia

The development of Oscar Niemeyer towards a dynamic style incorporating curves has often led to his being called Baroque. A less superficial examination of his work shows that he was in fact adhering to the technical purism of North American architecture, using the same technical and spatial devices but dressing them in a more plastic, less graphic guise. His sculptural approach to articulation is particularly striking in the presidential Palace of the Alvorada of 1958. Here an upside-down arcade of cast concrete covered with polished marble serves to shelter a wall of glass behind.

Christensen Factory, Aalborg

American purism met with immense success, above all in Northern Europe, where its cold elegance was in tune with an ancient cultural tradition. The Carl Christensen car factory was built in 1957 by Arne Jacobsen in Denmark – a centre of Fifties "design". In its reduction of form to the simplest rhythm of mass and space, it shows a sense of proportion and graphic elegance that recall Neoclassicism, although the system of harmonies is based more on the Japanese principle of pairing than on the usual European practice of grouping by threes.

The third generation

The friendly rivalry between Le Corbusier and Mies van der Rohe, representing opposite sides in the economic and cultural struggle between Europe and the United States, hardly left much room during the 1950s for any creative innovations in the language of architecture. Pitting technology against culture, the Latin against the Germanic, wealth against poverty, the architectural modes of steel and concrete were locked in a sterile conflict. It seems all the more futile when we remember that metal construction was a luxury that would have been impossible outside countries of extreme affluence such as the United States. The proliferation of this expensive material in the United States was in fact the result of a surplus following the Korean War, and it was even used when concrete would have been more suitable.

Meanwhile, a "third generation" of modern architects arose who stood quite apart from the debate over steel versus concrete. The term "third generation" was coined by Siegfried Giedion to distinguish them from the first generation of the 1920s purists, and from the second generation of the empiricists and champions of organic architecture. The architects of the 1960s were concerned to reduce the ideological antagonism between brutalism and technological architecture, to rescue the work of Mies van der Rohe and Le Corbusier from the silly labels that had been placed upon them. They admired the Seagram Building and Chandigahr with equal enthusiasm, not seeking at all to make them into rallying points for particular ideologies or cultures. On the other hand, there was a lively concern to establish a set of priorities regarding architectural programmes and urban structures. The question of the *monument* was indeed at the centre of their interests.

Modernist architecture had despised the town. It had advocated anti-urban types of building such as the isolated house and the tower-block. It had rejected the street in favour of the walkway, the monument in favour of the functional structure. After 30 years it had become obvious that the new architecture was undermining the whole fabric of town life. It was time to re-examine the idea of the "urban organism", to question existing values. Should the contemporary space be dominated by individual houses and office blocks, or should these give way to other types of building that were beneficial to the community as a whole? The issue became all the more urgent as the spectacular economic development of the Sixties transformed the urban environment, with ever-increasing rapidity, and a veritable law of the jungle began to hold sway.

A theoretical hierarchy of institutions was established, with a premium on monumentality. New buildings that were churches, theatres, auditoriums, sports centres, airports or universities were to be given special prominence. The obvious intention was to emphasize architecture that stood for cultural, as opposed to economic and social values.

Against the immense skyscrapers and gigantic housing complexes produced by industrial technology, it was important to accentuate buildings by means of scale. Auguste Perret was the last architect to have tried this in the rebuilding of Le Havre, which is dominated by a belltower over 100 metres (300 feet) high. Distinguishing features other than scale had to be developed, such as reduction of size, isolation by surrounding green areas, richness of form and outline, and stylistic originality.

It was through the reconsideration of the old 19th century problem of covering a large space that a way out of the *impasse* was found. The architectural form would express the structure of the building in accordance with the rationalist principles of the preceding century – what was new was the systematic abrogation of established laws of proportion. When a technical detail is blown up to a huge scale, it takes on an emphatic, monumental character which turns the building into a technological gesture. What are called "megastructures" in architecture are closely akin to works of art in which meaning is conveyed through sheer size.

At the same time, a new architectural style grew up, formally distinct from most architecture of the day in its stress on curves and movement as opposed to rectilinearity. The great concrete forms designed by Pier Luigi Nervi over the past 30 years began to enjoy enormous popularity and esteem, as did certain lyrical works of Aalto and the very personal, dynamic style of Hans Scharoun in Germany. Sometimes regarded as a Baroque revival and associated in the most derogatory terms with the work of Oscar Niemeyer, this development was above all an attempt to reintroduce a sense of order and hierarchy into architecture, encouraging great artists to produce great works, unique personal achievements such as Hans Scharoun's Philharmonie in Berlin, Saarinen's Washington airport or Aalto's church of Vuoksenniska, Le Corbusier's convent of La Tourette and certain buildings by Tange Kenzō and Louis I. Kahn.

The rethinking of architectural values resulted in one of the most significant monuments of this century, the Sydney Opera House. Designed by the Danish architect Jørn Utzon in 1956, this combines a lyricism in keeping with its beautiful waterside setting, with the most rigorous technical rationality, its great overhanging skull-cap forms having been constructed entirely from prefabricated elements. Fascinated by the work of Antonio Gaudi, Utzon attempted an all but impossible fusion of spatial poetry, austere form and audacious technology. The partial failure of his project (he was dismissed while it was still in progress) was no doubt an indication that the bold synthesis he envisaged was far in advance of its time.

1 *gallery* 3 *glass panels* 5 *exhibition space*
2 *prefabricated elements* 4 *semicircular dome* 6 *basement*

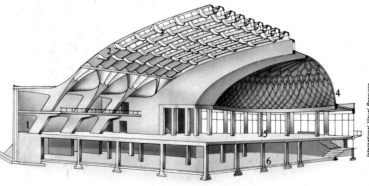

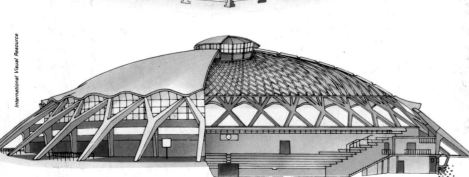

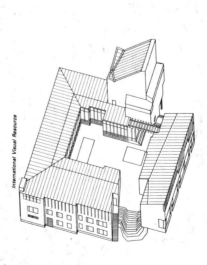

Exhibition Hall, Turin, and Sports Arena, Rome

A specialist in reinforced concrete, Pier Luigi Nervi made his name in the 1930s building immense aircraft hangars inspired by the constructional methods perfected by Eugène Freyssinet in France. Critics were surprised by the similarity between his work and the theoretical projects of Anatole de Baudot but this can be explained by the close links that existed at the end of the 19th century between certain engineers and rationalist architects. The monumental, entirely prefabricated forms conceived by Nervi are among the most accomplished in the field of contemporary architecture. Above is the exhibition hall built for the Turin exhibition in 1947 and below it the smaller sports arena built in 1960 in Rome.

Town Hall, Säynätsalo

With the civic centre of Säynätsalo in Finland (1950–52), Alvar Aalto sought above all to infuse his design with a strong sense of individuality. The tower containing the council chamber and the elevated courtyard are transcriptions of the medieval themes of keep and dungeons. They are pivotal points around which the whole building functions, determining the arrangement of blocks and the gaps between them that allow access to the courtyard and internal walkways.

Opera House, Sydney

Masterpiece of the Danish architect Jørn Utzon, the Sydney Opera House was the outcome of a competition in 1956. The building was immediately recognized as something quite exceptional, becoming one of the most telling symbols of the 1960s. To the traditional opera house pattern, Utzon brought techniques generally used to cover vast spaces. The structure consists of large shell-like forms with ribs of prefabricated concrete and a white ceramic facing, in some parts matte and elsewhere shiny. The effect is that of immense birds' wings skimming across the surface of Sydney harbour. The interior is a labyrinth with occasional touches of architectural theatricality.

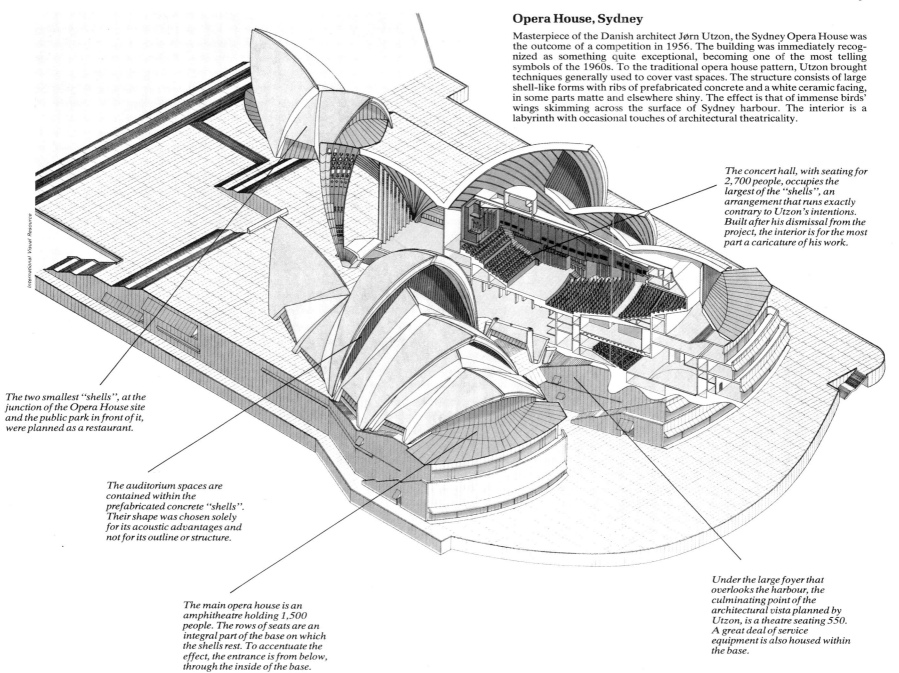

The concert hall, with seating for 2,700 people, occupies the largest of the "shells", an arrangement that runs exactly contrary to Utzon's intentions. Built after his dismissal from the project, the interior is for the most part a caricature of his work.

The two smallest "shells", at the junction of the Opera House site and the public park in front of it, were planned as a restaurant.

The auditorium spaces are contained within the prefabricated concrete "shells". Their shape was chosen solely for its acoustic advantages and not for its outline or structure.

The main opera house is an amphitheatre holding 1,500 people. The rows of seats are an integral part of the base on which the shells rest. To accentuate the effect, the entrance is from below, through the inside of the base.

Under the large foyer that overlooks the harbour, the culminating point of the architectural vista planned by Utzon, is a theatre seating 550. A great deal of service equipment is also housed within the base.

Student housing, Yale

The Samuel F.B. Morse and Ezra Stiles College at Yale University, New Haven, Connecticut, was one of the last works of Eero Saarinen before his premature death in 1961. Though less celebrated than his great projects in the "Jet" style, it is still remarkable in its relaxed relationship with the setting.

Philharmonie, Berlin

Standing at the end of a long career interrupted by the Nazi period, Hans Scharoun's Philharmonie of 1963 shows the kind of integration of effect that might have characterized the Sydney Opera House. Designed very much with the function of its interior in mind, this "cathedral of music" focuses attention on the octagonal orchestra pit at its centre.

The triumphant Sixties

Set against the development of prestige architecture in the 1960s, the drive towards monumentality evident in certain culturally-orientated buildings appeared corrective rather than excessive. The economic expansion of the Western bloc brought a new lavishness and expansiveness to architecture, a new level of conspicuous consumption. Even in the everyday world of domestic housing, architectural pretension became the *sine qua non* of a high social status. And in the realm of the office block, which symbolized the avidly sought-after success of companies, the prestige function of architecture became positively blatant.

Modern architecture, concerned with efficiency and technical rationality, was not particularly adaptable to this function, which had been fulfilled so perfectly by the repertoire of ornaments and rhetorical effects that characterized mid 19th century academicism. A "modernist rhetoric" had to be invented to respond to the demands of capitalism and commerce. The work of a whole generation of architects was there to be used as a pattern-book, a "grammar of ornament" – this was what the modern movement had become through a process of vulgarization. In addition, there were international reviews that spread the latest architectural trends from Japan to America, America to Europe and *vice versa*. The fashionable "review architecture" was the type most readily suited to the demands of business patronage. Unlike 19th century academicism, which was a matter of imitating great models of the past consecrated by history, this was an architecture drawing on models that were contemporary and of the moment. Fashion had been an essential ingredient of culture since the beginning of the industrial age.

The great architectural firms, who dominated the available patronage, became more and more concerned with the public image their buildings projected. Their work became little more than an advertising exercise on behalf of their clients. They constantly revised their styles in accordance with market conditions. After having worked in the style of Mies van der Rohe, for example, the Skidmore, Owings and Merrill group discovered the merits of concrete at exactly the moment when steel became expensive again, inventing ways of turning it into a luxury material as well, notably the *schokbeton* process used for the first time at the Lambert bank in Brussels.

In the 1960s American architecture, having exhausted the repertoire of technologically-inspired forms, established itself more and more as an official art, erecting modernist ideas into an academic syntax of masses, symmetry, articulation and proportion. The use of *schokbeton* could become the pretext for a lively composition of columns and arcades at basement level. At the Beinecke Library at Yale University, Gordon Bunshaft did not hesitate to use marble – which, over a cast concrete armature, forms a facing so thin as to allow a diffuse light to pass through it into the interior. Even when there were no classical references, academicism was still in evidence. Paul Rudolph has often been accused of being a sweetened version of Le Corbusier, but he is by no means the only one to whom the description could be applied. Boston City Hall (Kallmann, McKinnell and Knowles) and the Simon Fraser University in Canada (Erickson and Massey) show that North America assimilated Le Corbusier as quickly as Mies van der Rohe.

In the domain of the skyscraper, American ingenuity still reigned supreme. It gave the basic formula a vigour free from all trace of academicism. Architectural thought of the period concentrated mainly on the variables of mass, height and means of construction. As far as mass was concerned, there was a movement away from the elementary rectangular block towards more complex, sculptural forms. Sometimes a sense of dialogue between separate blocks was introduced, as with the beautiful twin towers of the Marina City apartments in Chicago by Bertrand Goldberg. The evolution of technology as applied to air-conditioning and computer-controlled lift systems, allowed architects to go far beyond the previous height limitation of about 30 storeys. The result was buildings of 150, then 200 and even 250 metres (800 feet) in height. The 100-storey barrier was broken first by the John Hancock Building in Chicago in 1969 then by the World Trade Center in New York five years later. As buildings shot rapidly upwards, so the pace of evolution in constructional techniques increased. The concrete façade was abandoned and experiments were made with new kinds of articulation, especially bracing elements that formed immense St. Andrew's crosses covering as many as a dozen storeys each. Then sloping façades and moulded plinths came in, creating the effect of monstrous columns on bases that were themselves several storeys high. Perhaps the culmination of experiments to find a new formula for the skyscraper was the technique of piling up prefabricated units, which was pioneered by Moshe Safdie with Habitat 67 at Montreal. The Nagakin Capsule building by the Japanese architect Kurokawa Kisho is one of the most striking examples.

A means of salvation for architecture that avoided the dangers of academicism was technological innovation. The British group Archigram pushed this virtually to the limit, designing a futuristic town that represented the apogee of the technological look, derived its inspiration from the complex forms of oil refineries and was worthy of a comic-book fantasy. It was only much later that the British architects of the Pompidou Centre in Paris brought this style to realization, and in the meantime it had been christened "high tech". A passion for the latest technology also marked the work of engineers such as Richard Buckminster Fuller and Frei Otto, and all the utopian projects that everyone enthused over in the Sixties. It was a tendency that showed how hidebound the official language of modernism was becoming.

The spirit of the Sixties, the taste for the technological extravaganza, has really only survived in the specialized field of hotel architecture. The work of John Portman, for example, includes fantastic abstract forms of glass and steel and huge interior spaces with transparent lifts moving up and down, which create an effect of dizzy monumentality that Gaudi himself would have admired and which do undeniably have a certain grandeur. This very sophisticated style developed out of the work of American designers who embraced industrial technology but brought to it a certain leaven of humour, as in the building conceived by Cesar Pelli in the form of a giant classical moulding. There is always an element of incongruity or irony in contemporary technologically-inspired architecture. American "technologism" lives on in a state of ambiguity.

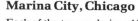

Marina City, Chicago

Each of the towers designed by Bertrand Goldberg for Chicago's Marina City (1964) consists of 18 storeys of garages conceived as a spiral ramp, surmounted by blocks of large luxury apartments opening out on to balconies shaped like flower petals.

Olympic Village, Munich

Inspired by the ideology of progress, the architects of the Munich Olympic Games complex of 1972 enlisted the help of the engineer Frei Otto. The arenas he designed were covered by vast awnings stretched with steel cables and covered with transparent polyester.

Moshe Safdie and Assocites, Inc.

Habitat 67, Montreal

Designed by the Israeli Moshe Safdie, this pyramid of dwellings was the outcome of the utopian theories promulgated by Sixties groups such as Archigram in England. It was a triumph of heavy prefabrication, which the structure makes no attempt to hide, and a *tour de force* that was as beautiful as it was impractical. The total cost was actually much greater than that of an equivalent building of the more traditional type. The prefabricated units, each containing a single apartment, were placed in position on a concrete megastructure with the aid of an immense movable scaffold. Access to them is gained by means of lifts and external moving staircases protected by perspex "bubbles".

E. Stoller, Esto

Art Center, Des Moines

When the project did not lend itself to a display of technology, American architecture could take on a preciousness full of erudition. The Des Moines Art Center (Iowa) by Ieoh Ming Pei is the most formal essay in the Bauhaus tradition as transmitted by figures such as Marcel Breuer. The incessant reference to models in the past was justified by the new level of technical perfection American architects brought to them.

Pompidou Centre, Paris

For a long time, French architecture held out against American influence, always translating new ideas from across the Atlantic into "Beaux-Arts" terms, emphasizing and sometimes over-emphasizing effects of monumentality. Only with the Pompidou Centre of 1976 did "high tech" come upon the French scene, thanks to an international competition won by Renzo Piano and Richard Rogers, who were Englishmen of Italian origins. A late monument to the movement, out of date as soon as it was finished, the Centre will nevertheless go down in history as a symbol of architecture before the economic recession.

Bonaventure Hotel, Los Angles

The strong point of John Portman, a commercial architect specializing in prestige hotels, was by no means aesthetic subtlety. Taking up the forms developed in the great days of the 1960s, however, he arrived at arrangements of geometric masses that were quite telling, changing their relationships according to viewpoint in a highly sculptural manner. Portman is also noted for his immense entrance halls, going up through dozens of storeys and featuring transparent external lifts that create the most spectacular effects.

J. Portman

B. Vincent

New directions in the modern movement

The monumentalist movement of the Sixties left only academic works behind it. The new ideas introduced by the "third generation" were of vital importance, calling this international, official style into question. The problem of internationalism, first raised in the 1930s with the rise of empiricism, could only become more intense as time went on. It ended in a kind of explosion which destroyed the formal unity of the modern movement and opened up a whole range of different new possibilities to choose between. The way became clear after the 1956 international architectural congress in Dubrovnik and in the following decade it broadened out.

Different points of view had already become defined by the turn of the 1940s. The principle of sparseness and simplicity survived, and ornament was still considered a crime as it had been since Adolf Loos. The desire for "economy of means" that paralleled the work of Malevich in painting remained throughout. But the tendency to speak of the modern movement in terms of geographical areas – a Nordic school, an American school, a Latin school – proved that modernist internationalism was slowly waning.

The break-up was not entirely a matter of geography and ethnography, although the nationalist impulse before the war was certainly a factor. The approach advocated by Frank Lloyd Wright was to make architecture responsive to its own position, both geographical and cultural. Like a Lazarus raised from the dead, it would suddenly become conscious again of its surroundings, its past and its roots in common human experience. As soon as these were accepted as valid considerations, the whole face of modernism was changed. The concept of the machine as an ideal, a perfect object, was smashed. Another alternative approach was provided by the Germanic or Nordic attitude (related to the spiritualism of Rudolf Steiner, founder of Theosophy) in which lyricism of form created emotive spaces where architecture was handled as a vehicle of expression. Meanwhile, the relationship to indigenous traditions brought Western modernism into contact with other cultures. All these different forces at work upon the movement created a wide gap between younger architects and the old order, the Bauhaus figures now in America, who were advocating an even deeper involvement with technology.

Each of the new directions grew into a broad tendency in its own right. The influence of Frank Lloyd Wright, along with that of Hans Scharoun and Alvar Aalto, deeply affected the "third generation" in its rejection of object-architecture and its constant search for meaning in form. The cultural experiment begun by Le Corbusier gained currency with extraordinary speed. It was the inspiration behind post-war architecture not only in South America but also in Japan. In Japanese architecture a fusion took place between the syntax of brutalism and native traditions, between concrete and wood. Dominated by the personality of Tange Kenzō, it concerned itself first with adapting models from the work of Le Corbusier, just giving them a Japanese accent. Then in the Sixties it severed this link and evolved a kind of technological lyricism reminiscent of Eero Saarinen in the United States. Little by little, its original nationalist ambitions dissolved in an all-pervasive formal eclecticism close to the American style of the same period. In the meantime Japan had become one of the great modern industrial powers and it was symptomatic that its architecture should have merged with "industrial design".

Brutalism could still be taken in an unexpected direction, marrying the language of Le Corbusier with its antithesis, that of Mies van der Rohe. This was the path taken in England, where Alison and Peter Smithson defined brutalism as "reactivated Mies". With James Stirling in particular, there was a mixing together, highly intellectual and at times sarcastic, of insistent technology and brutalist derision. His stance towards technology, which generated formal and spatial ideas yet was used by him to the most wilfully repulsive effect, is an obvious case of the mannerist ambiguity that seems to lie at the contradictory heart of Sixties architecture. Wright, Aalto and Le Corbusier had hoped to redirect the modern movement towards a new future and new hope but the Sixties saw the growth of serious doubts. The problem of ideological significance, having failed to resolve itself, ended up as a destructive force. The only escape was by means of an elegant sidestep, as Stirling so admirably demonstrated.

It was a rather marginal figure of American architecture of the Sixties, Louis I. Kahn, a professor at the University of Pennsylvania, who showed modernism a way forward that avoided the double dead-end of academicism and intellectual mannerism. With a certain amount of daring, he adopted formal models from 18th century French Neoclassicism, created a repertoire of pure, geometrically severe forms (sphere, pyramid and cube) and combined them according to systems of symmetry and axiality derived from the "Beaux-Arts" tradition. Out of this totally academic language, he evolved telling volumes and spaces in a manner reminiscent of Wright. It was a purification of the modernist vocabulary, freeing the movement from technological excess, the window-dressing of "design" and all the nostalgic, decorative touches that were invading official architecture. The principle of taking formal geometry as a point of departure went together with a functional and technical rationalism into which humanity was finally admitted. This was a reversal of the relationship of form and function. In the elaborate thought and planning that went into each project, equal attention was paid to beauty and efficiency. For Kahn, architecture was not to be confused with mere design.

Richards Medical Center, Philadelphia

The forms of the Richards Medical Center at the University of Philadelphia by Louis Kahn (1958–60) stress the contrast between the vertical ventilation shafts and the expansive areas of the laboratories: closed and open spaces, the services and the functions to which they are auxiliary.

Sher-e-Banglanadar Hotel, Dacca

In his last works, Louis Kahn restricted himself to elemental volumes whose rectilinear lines contrasted with the circular and arched shapes of the openings. Here a solid envelope contains living-spaces that are far more free and open in form, creating dynamic contrasts inside, contrasts very much justified by the climatic conditions. The building takes a middle course between the architecture of spectacle and that of doubt. Reversing the relationship of form to function, it takes pure forms and works a function into them.

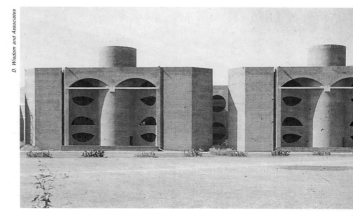

Indian Institute of Management, Ahmadabad

Inspired by Muslim monastic schools, the Indian Institute of Management is arranged around an interior courtyard shaped like a cloister and refreshed by a fountain and a pool. It is contained within great concrete and brick superstructures which act as sun-shields and set up a lively interplay of different scales, from the huge principal masses down to the most intricate detailing in the brickwork. His ability to set up a balanced relationship between ensemble and detail was the basis of Louis Kahn's high reputation.

Engineering School, Leicester

The work of James Stirling is permeated by a mannerist taste for distortion and paradox, especially at the Engineering School in Leicester (1960–63), where the diversity of forms, expressive of the internal functions of the building, is a pretext for the liveliest interplay of masses.

Sports Arena, Tokyo

Built for the Olympic Games of 1964, the Sports Arena in Tokyo was an incredibly ambitious gesture towards technology. The covering, suspended by steel cables, was the largest structure of its kind in the world. It is a work of abstract sculpture justified on symbolic grounds, alluding to the awnings over ancient circuses, only on a colossal scale. But the work is more than a hymn to technology or a childish imitation of a historic building type. The severe treatment of form gives it an uncompromising power. It is a dinosaur of a building that demands respect.

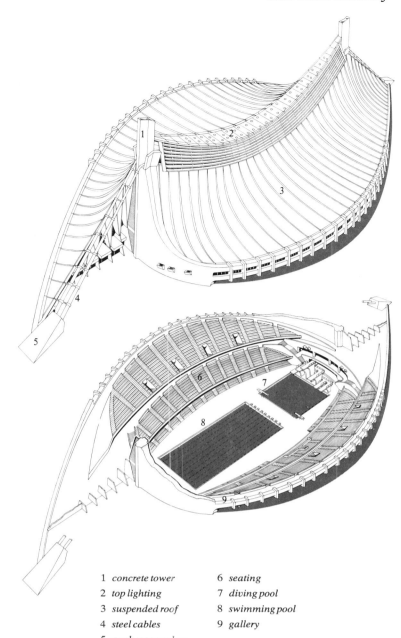

1	concrete tower	6	seating
2	top lighting	7	diving pool
3	suspended roof	8	swimming pool
4	steel cables	9	gallery
5	anchorage pylon		

Festival Hall, Tokyo

Expressive of the formalist strain in Sixties architecture, this municipal assembly hall in Tokyo was built in 1958–61 by Maekawa Kunio, a former collaborator of Le Corbusier. Set on a large square platform, complex volumes reflect the different functions of the interior. Somewhat surrealistic, though in fact purely functional (note the theatre with its arches towards the back), the massing of the blocks creates different effects from different viewpoints.

Columbus office block

The formalism of the modern movement at the turn of the 1970s showed itself in the continual striving to come up with something new within the terms of the traditional glass and steel skyscraper. For this block at New Haven (Connecticut), Kevin Roche and John Dinkeloo, former collaborators of Saarinen, designed a stool-like structure, the "legs" containing the lift shafts and waste disposals. This made the offices themselves immense open spaces: Louis Kahn writ large!

Modernism in question

Since the 1970s, especially since the oil crisis of 1974, the position of architecture has been radically transformed. First of all, there have been obvious material changes in the shrinking of the market and the abandonment of great building programmes, whether housing, offices or new towns. At the same time, the sense of the architectural heritage has expressed itself in the fitting up of derelict buildings such as the "lofts" of the United States and the general rehabilitation of old housing. The question of modernity has necessarily taken second place to the need to supply demands as complex as they are diverse.

But changes in patronage cannot fully explain the stylistic evolution taking place in our time. With the systematic challenging of modernist assumptions and the widespread condemnation of its heroes, we are witnessing a wholesale change of attitude. Today the work of Le Corbusier, Alvar Aalto and Ludwig Mies van der Rohe tends to provoke hostility, accusations of academicism, totalitarianism, fascism or collaboration with capitalism! This ideological critique, which would have horrified the generation of the 1920s, reflects the fact that 50 years of modernism in practice has made the movement's inherent weaknesses obvious. The phrase "post-modern" was coined by Charles Jencks in his brilliant essay *The Language of Post-modern Architecture* (1977) and it clearly expresses the sense of a break with the modernist tradition.

Admittedly, this post-modern architecture is still very much on the drawing-board, yet to find its full realization. It tends to wallow in a depressing eclecticism, mixing up historical and cultural sources with the most incoherent results, from Robert Venturi's homages to American vernacular, to Quinlan Terry's all too clever pastiches, to the wayward follies of Ralph Erskine and Lucien Kroll. In French architecture, the Gabriel-like classicism developed by Ricardo Bofill co-exists surprisingly happily with the refined 1930s-revival style of Christian de Portzamparc. Post-modernism has yet to find its aesthetic identity. It is still a movement of

reaction, a lively but confused search for a new style.

Another sign of the trend against modernism is the renaissance of utopian architecture. Nothing is more clearly indicative of burgeoning new attitudes than the ideal, but none the less very definite, architectural scheme that ignores the constraints of the real world. The revival of utopia is characteristic of periods in which the prevailing architectural language is being challenged. Its essential role is to stimulate a multiplicity of designs which, by being free of the kind of restrictions imposed upon real projects, take the realization of the architect's ideas to their absolute limit. The utopian scheme is at once an opportunity for reflection and a vital phase of experimentation, the elaboration of new formulae.

The spirit of technology had its moment of glory at the beginning of the 1960s because it offered an alternative to the insipidity of a banal empiricism. At that time Yona Friedman, Paul Maymont and Walter Jonas were written off as "architectural visionaries". Today a new wave of important utopian architects has risen up in the shape of Massimo Scolari, Aldo Rossi and Léon Krier, architect-artists for whom the construction of actual buildings would involve unacceptable compromises. The "theoretical landscapes" of Scolari are spaces whose evocative power lies partly in their unreality, and partly too in the quality of the draughtsmanship. More practical, Rossi and Krier take the same didactic line as Mies van der Rohe two generations earlier, making precise and buildable designs but refusing to take responsibility for their realization, on the grounds that today's market conditions would make this impossible.

Such theoretical projects are once again deeply polemical in tone. Just like the modern school of the 1920s, the "rationalist" or post-modern tendency of the 1980s believes in the close relationship of form and meaning, architecture and ideology. Its projects are combative, a deliberate corrective to the work of other, less ideologically correct

architects. Krier's designs for Bremen and Luxembourg and those of the A.R.A.U. for Brussels, are fundamentally political projects. Following through the cherished ideas of "the reconstruction of the European town", restoration and the provision of public spaces, they are calling into question the whole modernist notion of subservience to the machine. They respect instead the human implications of architecture, the fact that urban spaces, streets and squares are points of social contact. They condemn the vast scale of the metropolis, the volume of traffic, the division of labour and the fragmentation of people's activities. They represent a resistance movement against industry and as such a source of constant bewilderment to the traditional political parties.

The tendency is worldwide but more noticeable in Europe than in the United States, even though public opinion there is very sensitive to the problems of urban planning. Recent projects in the United States seem marked with scepticism and mannerism. The fantastic Neoclassical grottoes of Charles Moore in New Orleans are extremely witty in the application of sophisticated synthetic materials to the clichés of Roman classicism – arches, columns, orders and grotesques – but their significance remains limited. As for the admirable designs of Richard Meier and Michael Graves, these are no more than aesthetic meditations on the formal repertoire of the great purist architects, half-way between the Le Corbusier of the 1920s and Rudolph Schindler or Richard Neutra. American post-modernism, though drawing upon a wider theoretical base than before, hardly seems to be developing a way forward. The works of the Dutchman Aldo van Eyck, late of the "Team Ten" group of the Fifties, of Oswald Mathias Ungers at Magdeburg and the great Internationale Bauausstellung project in Berlin (which involved Moore, Vittorio Gregotti, Arata Isozaki, Rob Krier and others) represent a much securer prospect in the stress they place upon the image of the town as the starting-point for theories of architectural form.

Douglas house, Harbor Springs, Michigan

In the debilitating cultural context of the individual house in the United States, architects such as Richard Meier and the Group of Five have introduced a tone of intellectual speculation reminiscent of the ivory tower of contemporary art. Supported by a closed circle of patrons from the intelligentsia, these highly cultivated architects have indulged in a reworking of characteristic expressions of modernism between the wars. Sophisticated though this exercise may be, it spells the end of modernism as a progressive ideology.

Pacific Design Center, Los Angeles

This strange construction by Cesar Pelli (1976) was the outcome of that keen sense of the object that characterizes the tradition of American "design". It is a hangar made of mirror-glass, with a profile like a classical moulding and strikingly incongruous forms that seem to have no logical explanation. Unable to affirm any kind of optimism or faith in the future of civilization or architecture, the American post-modernists use formalism to express the opposite, as a meaningless image reflecting all their anxiety about the very relevance of architecture.

National Gallery of Art, Washington

Even commercial architecture has discovered the attractions of post-modernism, which has been rapidly vulgarized by architectural books and journals. Along with Philip Johnson, Ieoh Ming Pei is today developing a pleasantly stylish manner somewhere between the naïvety of the preceding decade and the over-sophisticated questioning of the elitists. As time goes on, we are seeing architecture tend more and more towards a love of effect, a generosity and a respect for proven formulae that place it squarely in the "Beaux-Arts" tradition.

Chestnut Hill Villa

This combination of a Palladian villa-plan and a gabled roof, designed by Robert Venturi in 1962, is a typical work of post-modernism. It is an architecture of trickery and false leads. The Palladian layout is in fact a shallow rectangle, the gable roof is broken by a central slit, the apparent symmetry turns out to be false and a narrow staircase is unexpectedly placed at the exact centre of the composition.

.es Hautes-Formes, Paris

Christian de Portzamparc and Giorgia Benamo have opened the way to a new tradition of Parisian architecture which is typified by the complex in the Rue des Hautes-Formes in the 13th arrondissement (1978). The atmosphere, scale and planning have a sense of everyday practicality that recalls the reworking of the Flemish house by Van Eyck around the same time.

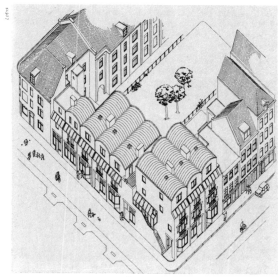

Jordaan district, Amsterdam

Though abandoning the technological will-o'-the-wisp that prefabrication turned out to be in the Sixties, Aldo van Eyck stuck to the idea of "additive architecture". The communal housing project of the Jordaan district in Amsterdam (1976–80) is based on the pattern of the individual house with dividing walls separating it from its neighbours.

Benacerraf house, Princeton, New Jersey

The sophisticated work of the Group of Five (in this case Michael Graves in 1969) is quite alien to that of European architects concerned with cultural relevance and the urban environment. Behind the formal similarities, these are two radically opposed currents within post-modernism.

Bibliography

The following lists begin with general books and series, all published in English, and continue with more specialized publications relating to specific chapters.

Reference

COLVIN, Howard, *A Biographical Dictionary of British Architects 1600–1840*, 1978
FLEMING, John, HONOUR, Hugh and PEVSNER, Nikolaus, *The Penguin Dictionary of Architecture*, 3rd edition, 1980
HARRIS, John and LEVER, Jill, *An Illustrated Glossary of Architecture 850–1830*, 1966
HATJE, Gerd (ed.), *Encyclopaedia of Modern Architecture*, 1963
PLACZEK, Adolf K. (ed.), *Macmillan Encyclopedia of Architects*, 4 vols, 1982
RICHARDS, J.M. (ed.), *Who's Who in Architecture, from 1400 to the Present Day*, 1977

Technique

COWAN, Henry J., *The Master Builders–A History of Structural and Environmental Design from Ancient Egypt to the Nineteenth Century*, 1977
FOSTER, Michael (ed.), *The Principles of Architecture: Style, Structure and Design*, 1983
HODGKINSON, A. (ed.), *Handbook of Building Structure*, 1974
SALVADORI, Mario and HELLER, Robert, *Structure in Architecture*, 1963

Theory

GAULDIE, Sinclair, *The Appreciation of the Arts: Architecture*, 1969
GIEDION, Siegfried, *Space, Time and Architecture*, 5th edition, 1967
NORBERG-SCHULZ, Christian, *Meaning in Western Architecture*, revised edition, 1980
RASMUSSEN, S.E., *Experiencing Architecture*, 1959
SAINT, Andrew, *The Image of the Architect*, 1983
SCOTT, Geoffrey, *The Architecture of Humanism*, new edition with a preface by David Watkin, 1980
SCRUTON, Roger, *The Aesthetics of Architecture*, 1979
SUMMERSON, John, *The Classical Language of Architecture*, revised edition, 1980
WATKIN, David, *Morality and Architecture*, 1977
ZEVI, Bruno, *Architecture as Space*, 1975

General histories

COPPLESTONE, Trewin (ed.), *World Architecture*, 1963
FLETCHER, Banister, *A History of Architecture*, 18th edition, 1975
FURNEAUX JORDAN, Robert, *A Concise History of Western Architecture*, 1969
KOSTOF, Spiro (ed.), *The Architect: Chapters in the History of the Profession*, 1977
PEVSNER, Nikolaus, *An Outline of European Architecture*, 7th edition, 1963; *A History of Building Types*, 1976
RAEBURN, Michael (ed.), *Architecture of the Western World*, 1980

National histories

GODFREY, F.M., *Italian Architecture up to 1750*, 1971
KIDSON, Peter, MURRAY, Peter and THOMPSON, Paul, *A History of English Architecture*, 2nd edition, 1979
LAVEDAN, Pierre, *French Architecture*, new edition, 1979
WHIFFEN, Marcus and KOEPER, Frederick, *American Architecture: 1607–1976*, 1981

General series

These three excellent series cover virtually the whole of world architecture and together form a massive collection of information and illustrations. The Pelican History of Art series, still incomplete, is particularly valuable, being the most comprehensive and authoritative history of art ever published in the English language; many of its volumes are classics in their fields.

The Great Ages of World Architecture (George Baziller Inc./Studio Vista)

ALEX, William, *Japanese Architecture*, 1963
BRANNER, Robert, *Gothic Architecture*, 1961
BROWN, Frank E., *Roman Architecture*, 1961
HOAG, John D., *Western Islamic Architecture*, 1963
LOWRY, Bates, *Renaissance Architecture*, 1962
MACDONALD, William, *Early Christian and Byzantine Architecture*, 1962

MILLON, Henry A., *Baroque and Rococo Architecture*, 1961
ROBERTSON, Donald, *Pre-Columbian Architecture*, 1963
SAALMAN, Howard, *Medieval Architecture*, 1962
SCRANTON, Robert L., *Greek Architecture*, 1962
SCULLY, Vincent, Jr, *Modern Architecture*, 1961
WU, Nelson I., *Chinese and Indian Architecture*, 1963

History of World Architecture, edited by Pier Luigi Nervi (Abrams)

BUSSAGLI, Mario, *Oriental Architecture*, 1974
GRODECKI, Louis, *Gothic Architecture*, 1977
GUIDONI, Enrico, *Primitive Architecture*, 1978
HEYDEN, Doris and GENDROP, Paul, *Pre-Columbian Architecture of Mesoamerica*, 1975
HOAG, John D., *Islamic Architecture*, 1979
KUBACH, Hans Erich, *Romanesque Architecture*, 1975
LLOYD, Seton, MÜLLER, Hans Wolfgang and MARTIN, Roland, *Ancient Architecture: Mesopotamia, Egypt, Crete, Greece*, 1974
MANGO, Cyril, *Byzantine Architecture*, 1975
MIDDLETON, Robin and WATKIN, David, *Neoclassical and 19th Century Architecture*, 1980
MURRAY, Peter, *Renaissance Architecture*, 1979
NORBERG-SCHULZ, Christian, *Baroque Architecture*, 1974; *Late Baroque and Rococo Architecture*, 1974
TAFURI, Manfredo and DAL CO, Francesco, *Modern Architecture*, 1980
WARD-PERKINS, J.B., *Roman Architecture*, 1977

The Pelican History of Art

BLUNT, Anthony, *Art and Architecture in France: 1500–1700*, 4th edition, 1980
BOËTHIUS, Axel and WARD-PERKINS, J.B., *Etruscan and Roman Architecture*, 1970 (reissued in separate revised volumes as BOËTHIUS, Axel, *Etruscan and Early Roman Architecture*, 1979, and WARD-PERKINS, J.B., *Roman Imperial Architecture*, 1981)
CONANT, Kenneth J., *Carolingian and Romanesque Architecture: 800–1200*, 4th edition, 1978
FRANKFORT, Henri, *The Art and Architecture of the Ancient Orient*, 4th edition, 1970
FRANKL, Paul, *Gothic Architecture*, 1962
GERSON, Horst and TER KUILE, E.H., *Art and Architecture in Belgium: 1600–1800*, 1960
HAMILTON, George Heard, *The Art and Architecture of Russia*, 3rd edition, 1983
HEMPEL, Eberhard, *Baroque Art and Architecture in Central Europe*, 1965
HEYDENREICH, Ludwig H. and LOTZ, Wolfgang, *Architecture in Italy: 1400–1600*, 1974
HITCHCOCK, Henry-Russell, *Architecture: Nineteenth and Twentieth Centuries*, 4th edition, 1977
KALNEIN, Wend Graf and LEVEY, Michael, *Art and Architecture of the Eighteenth Century in France*, 1972
KRAUTHEIMER, Richard, *Early Christian and Byzantine Architecture*, 3rd edition, 1979
KUBLER, George, *The Art and Architecture of Ancient America*, 2nd edition, 1975
KUBLER, George and SORIA, Martin, *Art and Architecture in Spain and Portugal and their American Dominions: 1500–1800*, 1959
LAWRENCE, A.W., *Greek Architecture*, 4th edition, 1983
PAINE, Robert Treat and SOPER, Alexander, *The Art and Architecture of Japan*, 3rd edition, 1981
ROSENBERG, Jacob, SLIVE, Seymour and TER KUILE, E.H., *Dutch Art and Architecture: 1600–1800*, 3rd edition, 1977
ROWLAND, Benjamin, *The Art and Architecture of India: Hindu, Buddhist, Jain*, 4th edition, 1977
SICKMAN, Laurence and SOPER, Alexander, *The Art and Architecture of China*, 3rd edition, 1971
SMITH, W. Stevenson, *The Art and Architecture of Ancient Egypt*, 3rd edition, 1981
SUMMERSON, John, *Architecture in Britain: 1530–1830*, 7th edition, 1983
WEBB, Geoffrey, *Architecture in Britain: The Middle Ages*, 2nd edition, 1965
WHITE, John, *Art and Architecture in Italy: 1250–1400*, 1966
WITTKOWER, Rudolf, *Art and Architecture in Italy: 1600–1750*, 3rd edition, 1973

NON-EUROPEAN CIVILIZATIONS

China

BLASER, W., *Courtyard House in China*, 1979
BOYD, A., *Chinese Architecture and Town Planning*, 1962
GRANET, M., *La Civilisation chinoise*, 1978

KESWICK, M., *The Chinese Garden*, 1978
PIRAZZOLI-T'SERSTEVENS, M., *Living Architecture: Chinese*, 1972

Korea

ADAMS, E.B., *Korea Guide*, 1977
BUREAU OF CULTURAL PROPERTY, SEOUL, *The Arts of Ancient Korea*, 1974
KIM, Chewon, *Birmanie, Corée, Tibet*, 1964
LI, Ogg, *Histoire de la Corée*, 1979

Japan

FUJIOKA, M., *Shiro to shoin* (Castles and the Shoin style), 1973
INAGAKI, E., *Jinja to reibyo* (Shinto shrines and mausoleums), 1968
KAWAKAMI, M. and NAKAMURA, M., *Katsura rikyu to shashitsu* (Palace of Katsura and tea pavilions), 1967
MASUDA, T., *Living Architecture: Japanese*, 1971
NAITO, A. and NISHIKAWA, T., *Katsura, un ermitage princier*, 1978
NAKANO, G., *Byodoin Hoodo* (The Pavilion of the Phoenix at Byodoin), 1978
OTA, H., *Japanese Architecture and Gardens*, 1966
SANSOM, G.B., *A Short History of Japanese Architecture*, 1957
SUZUKI, K., *Horyuji to Ikaruga no tera* (Horyuji and the temples of Ikaruga), 1978

India

BATLEY, C., *The Design Development of Indian Architecture*, 4th edition, 1954
BROWN, P., *Indian Architecture*, 2 vols, 1959
COOMARASWAMY, A.K., *History of Indian and Indonesian Art*, 1927
GOETZ, H., *Inde*, 1960
KRAMRISCH, S., *The Hindu Temple*, 1946
NILSSON, Sten, *European Architecture in India*, 1968
SECKEL, D., *The Art of Buddhism*, 1964
SIVARAMAMURTI, C., *L'Art de l'Inde*, 1964
VOLWAHSEN, Andreas, *Living Architecture: Indian*, 1969

South-East Asia

BERNET-KEMPERS, A.J., *Ancient Indonesian Art*, 1959
DUMARÇAY, J., *Borobudur*, 1978
FRÉDÉRIC, Louis, *The Art of Southeast Asia: Temples and Sculpture*, 1965
GROSLIER, B.P., *Art of the World: Indo-China*, 1962
NAFILYAN, G., *Angkor Vat*, 1969
RAWSON, Philip, *The Art of Southeast Asia*, 1967
STERN, P., *L'Art du Champa*, 1942
THAW, Aung, *Historical Sites in Burma*, 1972

Black Africa

CHITTICK, N., *Kilwa, an Islamic Trading City on the East African Coast*, 2 vols, 1974
DENYON, Susan, *African Traditional Architecture*, 1978
DEVISSE, J., ROBERT, D.C. et al., *Tegdaoust III. Recherches sur Aoudaghost. Fouilles de 1960 à 1965*, 1981
FASSASSI, M.A., *L'Architecture en Afrique noire*, 1978
GARDY, R., *Maisons africaines*, 1974
GARLAKE, Peter, *Great Zimbabwe*, 1973
PRUSSIN, L., *Architecture in Northern Ghana. A Study of Forms and Functions*, 1969; *The Architecture of Djenne, African Synthesis and Transformation*, 1973
VANACKER, C., *Tegdaoust II. Recherches sur Aoudaghost. Fouille d'un quartier artisanal*, 1979
WILLETT, Frank, *African Art*, 1971

Pre-Hispanic America

BINGHAM, H., *Machu-Picchu. A Citadel of the Incas*, 1930
GASPARINI, Graziano and MARGOULIES, Luise, *Inca Architecture*, 1980
HARDOY, J., *Urban Planning in Pre-Columbian America*, 1968
KELEMAN, P., *Medieval American Art*, 2 vols, 1956
KOSOK, P., *Life, Land and Water in Ancient Peru*, 1965
STIERLIN, H., *Living Architecture: Mayan*, 1964
WILLEY, G.R., *An Introduction to American Archaeology*, 2 vols, 1966 and 1971

Pacific Ocean

BELLWOOD, P., *Man's Conquest of the Pacific*, 1978
GARANGER, J., *Pierres et rites sacrés du Tahiti d'autrefois*, 1968

HEYERDAHL, Thor et al., *Archaeology of Easter Island*, 1962
SUGGS, R., *The Island Civilizations of Polynesia*, 1960

THE ANCIENT WORLD

The Near East

AMIET, Pierre, *Art of the Ancient Near East*, 1980
CAUVIN, J., *Les Premiers Villages de Syrie-Palestine, du IXe au VIIe millénaire avant J.-C.*, 1978
DESHAYES, Jean, *Les Civilisations de l'Orient ancien*, 1969
GARBINI, Giovanni, *The Ancient World*, 1966
GARELLI, P., *Le Proche-Orient asiatique, des origines aux invasions des Peuples de la mer*, 1969
GARELLI, P. and NIKIPROWETZKY, V., *Le Proche-Orient asiatique, les empires mésopotamiens, Israël*, 1974
LLOYD, Seton, *Art of the Ancient Near East*, 1961
NAUMANN, R., *Architektur Kleinasiens von ihren Anfängen bis zum Ende der hethitischen Zeit*, 1971

Egypt

ALDRED, Cyril, *Egyptian Art*, 1980
BADAWY, A., *A History of Egyptian Architecture*, 3 vols, 1954–68
CHOISY, A., *L'Art de bâtir chez les Égyptiens*, 1904
CLARKE, S. and ENGELBACH, R., *Ancient Egyptian Masonry*, 1930
DE CENIVAL, J.-L., *Living Architecture: Egyptian*, 1964
LAUER, J.P., *Le Mystère des pyramides*, 1974
VANDIER, J., *Manuel d'archéologie égyptienne*, 1954–55

The Greek world

COULTON, J.J., *Greek Architects at Work*, 1977
DINSMOOR, W.B., *The Architecture of Ancient Greece*, 3rd edition, 1950
GRUBEN, G., *Die Tempel der Griechen*, 1980
LAWRENCE, A.W., *Greek Aims in Fortification*, 1979
RICHTER, Gisela M.A., *A Handbook of Greek Art*, 8th edition, 1983
ROBERTSON, D.S., *A Handbook of Greek and Roman Architecture*, 2nd edition, 1943
THEODORESCU, D., *Le Chapiteau ionique grec*, 1980
WINTER, F.E., *Greek Fortifications*, 1971
WYCHERLEY, R.E., *How the Greeks Built Cities*, 2nd edition, 1962

Rome

ASHBY, T. and RICHMOND, J.A., *The Aqueducts of Ancient Rome*, 1935
GAZZOLA, P., *Ponti romani*, 1963
HENIG, Martin (ed.), *A Handbook of Roman Art*, 1983
MACDONALD, William L., *The Architecture of the Roman Empire: An Introductory Study*, revised edition, 1982
MACKAY, A.G., *Houses, Villas and Palaces in the Roman World*, 1975
PERCIVAL, J., *The Roman Villa*, 1976
ROBERTSON, D.S., *A Handbook of Greek and Roman Architecture*, 2nd edition, 1943
SEAR, Frank, *Roman Architecture*, 1982
WHEELER, Mortimer, *Roman Art and Architecture*, 1964

LATE ANTIQUITY AND THE EARLY MIDDLE AGES

FERNIE, Eric, *Anglo-Saxon Architecture*, 1983
GRABAR, A., *The Beginnings of Christian Art: 200–395*, 1967
HAMILTON, J.A., *Byzantine Architecture and Decoration*, 2nd edition, 1956
KIDSON, Peter, *The Medieval World*, 1967
RICE, David Talbot, *Byzantine Art*, revised edition, 1968
STEWART, Cecil, *Early Christian, Byzantine and Romanesque Architecture*, 1954

THE MIDDLE AGES

Romanesque architecture

ARTS COUNCIL OF GREAT BRITAIN, *English Romanesque Art: 1066–1200*, 1984
BUSCH, Harald and LOHSE, Bernhard, *Romanesque Europe*, 1960

GRODECKI, L., *L'Architecture ottonienne*, 1958
OURSEL, R., *Living Architecture: Romanesque*, 1967
TIMMERS, J.J.M., *A Handbook of Romanesque Art*, 1969
ZARNECKI, George, *Romanesque Art*, 1971

Gothic architecture

BONY, Jean, *The English Decorated Style*, 1979
BRANNER, R., *St Louis and the Court Style in Gothic Architecture*, 1965
EVANS, J., *English Art 1307–1461*, 1949
FITCHEN, J., *The Construction of Gothic Cathedrals*, 1961
FOCILLON, H., *Art d'Occident*, 1938
HARVEY, John H., *The Gothic World 1100–1600*, 1950; *The Perpendicular Style*, 1978
LAVEDAN, P., *L'Architecture gothique religieuse en Catalogne*, 1938
MARK, Robert, *Experiments in Gothic Structure*, 1982
SANFACON, R., *L'Architecture flamboyante en France*, 1971
SEYMOUR, C., *Notre-Dame of Noyon in the 12th century*, 1939
SIMSON, O. von, *The Gothic Cathedral*, 1956
SWAAN, Wim, *The Gothic Cathedral*, 1969

Military architecture

ANDERSON, William and SWAAN, Wim, *Castles of Europe from Charlemagne to the Renaissance*, 1970
BOASE, T.S.R., *Castles and Churches of the Crusading Kingdom*, 1967
CHATELAIN, A., *Donjons romans des pays d'Ouest*, 1973
FINO, J.-F., *Forteresses de la France médiévale*, 3rd edition, 1977
FOURNIER, G., *Le Château dans la France médiévale*, 1978
GARDELLES, J., *Les Châteaux du Moyen Âge dans la France du Sud-Ouest 1216–1337*, 1972
GEBELIN, F., *Les Châteaux de France*, 1962
HUGHES, James Quentin, *Military Architecture*, 1974
LAVEDAN, P. and HUGUENEY, J., *L'Urbanisme au Moyen Âge*, 1974
RITTER, R., *L'Architecture militaire du Moyen Âge*, 1974
ROCOLLE, P., *Deux Mille Ans de fortification française*, 3 vols, 1973
TOY, Sidney, *A History of Fortification from 3000 BC to AD 1700*, 1955

Islam

ASLANAPA, O., *Turkish Architecture*, 1971
CRESWELL, K.A.C., *A Short Account of Early Muslim Architecture*, 1958; *The Encyclopaedia of Islam*, 2nd edition, 1960; *A Bibliography of the Architecture [. . . .] of Islam*, 1961, supplement 1973
GALDIERI, E., *Isfahan, Masjid i-Juma*, 1972
GOODWIN, Geoffrey, *A History of Ottoman Architecture*, 1971
GRABAR, Oleg et al., *City in the Desert, Qasr al-Hayr East*, 1978
HAMILTON, R., *Khirbat al-Mafjar*, 1959
HILL, Derek and GRABAR, Oleg, *Islamic Architecture and its Decoration*, 1967
MARÇAIS, Georges, *Architecture musulmane d'Occident*, 1954
MICHELL, George (ed.), *Architecture of the Islamic World*, 1978
POPE, A.U. and ACKERMAN, P., *A Survey of Persian Art*, 1939
RICE, David Talbot, *Islamic Art*, 1965
SCHLUMBERGER, D., and SOURDEL, J., *Lashkari Bazar, une résidence royale ghaznévide et ghoride*, 1978
TERRASSE, H., *L'Art hispano-mauresque des origines au XIIIe siècle*, 1932; *Islam d'Espagne, une rencontre de l'Orient et de l'Occident*, 1957; *La Mosquée al-Qarawiyin à Fès*, 1968

THE AGE OF CLASSICISM

The Renaissance

ACKERMAN, James, *Palladio*, 1966; *The Architecture of Michelangelo*, 1970
BENEVOLO, Leonardo, *The Architecture of the Renaissance*, 2 vols, 1978
BRUSCHI, A., *Bramante*, 1977
GRANVEAUD, P. and MOSSER, M., *Filippo Brunelleschi*, 1979
HITCHCOCK, Henry-Russell, *Renaissance Architecture in Germany*, 1981
HUGHES, James Quentin and LYNTON, Norbert, *Renaissance Architecture*, 1962
LEES-MILNE, James, *Tudor Renaissance*, 1951

MURRAY, Peter, *The Architecture of the Italian Renaissance*, 1969
SHEARMAN, John, *Mannerism*, 1967
VASARI, G., *The Lives of the Artists*, 1550, 2nd edition 1568 (Penguin edition 1971)
WITTKOWER, Rudolf, *Architectural Principles in the Age of Humanism*, 3rd edition, 1962
WÖLFFLIN, Heinrich, *Renaissance and Baroque*, 1888

The 17th century

BLUNT, Anthony (ed.), *Baroque and Rococo: Architecture and Decoration*, 1978
BRAHAM, A. and SMITH, P., *François Mansart*, 1973
BUSCH, Harald and LOHSE, Bernhard, *Baroque Europe*, with an introduction by James Lees-Milne, 1962
GEBELIN, F., *Versailles*, 1965
HELD, Julius S. and POSNER, Donald, *17th and 18th Century Art: Baroque Painting, Sculpture, Architecture*, 1972
KITSON, Michael, *The Age of Baroque*, 1966
PORTOGHESI, P., *Borromini*, 1964
SUMMERSON, John, *Inigo Jones*, 1966
TAPIÉ, V.-L., *The Age of Grandeur*, 2nd edition, 1966

The Age of Enlightenment

BRAHAM, A., *The Architecture of the French Enlightenment*, 1980
DU COLOMBIER, P., *L'Architecture en Allemagne au XVIIIe siècle*, 1956
GRISERI, A., *Le Metamorfosi del barocco*, 1967
GUINNESS, Desmond and SADLER, Julius Trousdale, Jr, *The Palladian Style in England, Ireland and America*, 1976
HAUTECOEUR, L., *Histoire de l'architecture classique en France*, 7 vols, 1943–57
HITCHCOCK, Henry-Russell, *Rococo Architecture in Southern Germany*, 1968
KAUFMANN, Emil, *Architecture in the Age of Reason*, 1955
RÉAU, L., *L'Europe française au siècle des Lumières*, 1971
ROSENBLUM, Robert, *Transformations in Late Eighteenth Century Art*, 1967
VILLEGAS, V.M., *El Gran Signo formal del barroco*, 1956

THE MODERN ERA

The 19th century

BENEVOLO, Leonardo, *History of Modern Architecture*, vol 1, 1971
CLARK, Kenneth, *The Gothic Revival*, 1975
COLLINS, P., *Changing Ideals in Modern Architecture, 1750–1950*, 1965
DIXON, Roger and MUTHESIUS, Stefan, *Victorian Architecture*, 1978
GERMANN, Georg, *Gothic Revival in Europe and Britain*, 1972
MIDDLETON, Robin (ed.), *The Beaux-Arts and Nineteenth-Century French Architecture*, 1982
PEVSNER, Nikolaus, *Pioneers of Modern Design from William Morris to Walter Gropius*, 3rd edition, 1974

The turn of the century

BORSI, F. and WIESER, H., *Bruxelles, capitale de l'Art Nouveau*, 1971
DAVEY, Peter, *Arts and Crafts Architecture*, 1980
GUERRAND, R., *Art Nouveau en Europe*, 1965
MADSEN, S.T., *Sources of Art Nouveau*, 1956
PEVSNER, Nikolaus, *Sources of Modern Architecture and Design*, 1968
RUSSELL, Frank (ed.), *Art Nouveau Architecture*, 1979
SCHMUTZLER, R., *Art Nouveau*, 1964
SERVICE, Alistair, *Edwardian Architecture*, 1978

The 20th century

BANHAM, Rayner, *Theory and Design in the First Machine Age*, 1960
BENEVOLO, Leonardo, *History of Modern Architecture*, vol 2, 1971
CURTIS, William J.R., *Modern Architecture since 1900*, 1982
FRAMPTON, Kenneth, *Modern Architecture: A Critical History*, 1980
JENCKS, Charles, *Modern Movements in Architecture*, 1973
RICHARDS, J.M., *An Introduction to Modern Architecture*, 9th edition, 1962
SHARP, D., *A Visual History of Twentieth-Century Architecture*, 1972

Index/glossary

For reasons of convenience and intelligibility this index is a selective one. It makes no attempt to provide an inventory of all the names and ideas referred to in the book or to list the maps and charts accompanying individual chapters.

So that the reader need consult only one list, the index and glossary are combined. The glossary entries do not list every occurrence of the term described, and not every term defined is followed by a reference. Well known building types (church, theatre, etc.) are not defined; nor, at the other extreme, are rarely used terms which have been defined in the text.

Roman numerals refer to the text, and italic numerals to illustrations and their captions. To help the reader identify the illustration referred to, page numbers may be followed by a brief reference within brackets – for example, **ADAM**, Robert (1728–1792) 330, *331 (Syon House)*.

Only architects' and artists' names are followed by their dates.

Entries followed by "See . . ." indicate that the reader is being referred either to the same entry under a different spelling or name (e.g. **LI** (dynasty) see **YI**) or to an equivalent term (e.g. **BONDSTONE** see **HEADER**) or that a term is defined within the subsidiary definitions under a different main heading (e.g. **IONIC** see **ORDER**). Entries followed by "See also . . ." refer the reader to complementary information.

ABU SIMBEL, colossi on the façade of the temple of Ramesses II, XIXth dynasty.

ALTERNATING SUPPORTS, abbey church, Jumièges.

APSIDIOLES at the church of St. Benoît-sur-Loire.

BAKHENG, Angkor.

ABYDOS, interior of the temple of Seti I, XIXth dynasty.

Victor BALTARD, Les Halles, Paris.

ASA DAL (7thC) 36 (Tabotap, Pulguk-sa)

ASAM, Cosmas Damian (1686–1739) and Egid Quirin (1692–1750) 322, 322 (Church of St. John Nepomuk)

ASPLUND, Eric Gunnar (1885–1940) 377 (Woodland Crematorium)

ASSISI, Umbria; San Francesco basilica 228, 229

ASSOS, Troade; agora 147

ASSUR (archaeological site), Iraq 110

ASSURBANIPAL, king of Assyria 110, 111 (Babylon)

ASSURNASIRPAL II, king of Assyria 110

ASTRAGAL Circular-section moulding, usually with beading 130

ASUKADERA or HOKOJI 45

ASWAN, Egypt 118

ATHENS Parthenon (Acropolis) 130, 138, 139, 140; Erechtheion (Acropolis) 130, 130, 140; Propylaea (Acropolis) 130, 140; temple of Athene Nike (Acropolis) 130, 140, 141; Acropolis 143; temple of Hephaistos 130, 138, 138; ramparts 144, 144, 145; Odeon of Pericles 146; Portico of Attalos 147; public latrine 148; Andronikos' clock 148; Hadrian's Library 148; Odeon of Herodes Atticus 149; National Library 346

ATHENS CHARTER 378

ATRIUM Open central court in Roman houses, from which the other rooms open off; an open, colonnaded court in front of a church. By extension, a vestibule 166, 167 (house of Loreius Tiburtinus), 177, 266, 291

ATTIC In classical architecture, decorative horizontal element, sometimes including a cornice, at the top of an entablature; attic storey Top storey, of less height than the rest, above the main entablature of a building 146 ("House of the Comedians"), 269 (courtyard at the ducal palace, Urbino)

AUBERT, Jean (died 1741) 318

AUDAGHOST see TEGDAOUST

AUGSBURG, Germany; house of the Fugger bankers 292

AUGUSTUS (Caius Julius Caesar Octavianus Augustus) 158, 160, 162, 166

AUXERRE, Yonne; St. Germain 187

AVIGNON, Vaucluse; papal palace 234

AXONOMETRICS 12

AYYUBIDS 254, 255 (citadel of Aleppo; courtyard of al-Firdaus "madrasa")

AZAY-LE-RIDEAU, Indre-et-Loire; château 284, 285

AZTECS 90, 91 (Tenochtitlán), 326

AZUCHI-MOMOYAMA (period) Japan 44

BAALBEK, Lebanon; temple of Venus 162; sanctuary of Heliopolitan Jupiter 163; temple of Bacchus, interior 163; great mosque 249

BABYLON (archaeological site) Iraq; the neo-Babylonian city 104, 110, 111

BACTRIA, Afghanistan 106

BAGHDAD, Iraq 242, 244, 250

BAILEY Open court of a castle 232, 232

BAKHENG, Angkor 68

BAKONG, Angkor 68

BALBAS, Jerónimo (18thC) 327 (Mexico Cathedral)

BALLU, Théodore (1817–1885) 352

BALTARD, Louis Pierre (1764–1846) 346

BALTARD, Victor (1805–1874) 344, 352

BANCO Term used in East Africa for clay/sand material used for the construction of dwellings, and, refined, for wall decoration. Also known as daga, tub, etc. in different regions of the continent 78, 79 (Mabas houses, Cameroon), 83 (Marka granaries, Upper Volta)

BANDITACCIA (necropolis) Cerveteri 157 (Etruscan tomb)

BANNAJI, Tochigi 49

BANPO, China 24

BAPHUON, Angkor 68

BAPTISTRY 172, 176, 178, 200, 204, 205 (Pisa Cathedral)

BARBERA, Spain; Santa Maria 197

BARCELONA, Spain; Santa Maria del Mar 222, 223

BARI, Italy; St. Nicholas basilica 205

BARREL VAULT see VAULT

BARRINGTON COURT, Somerset 292

BARRY, Sir Charles (1795–1860) 349 (Houses of Parliament)

BARTLESVILLE, Oklahoma; Price Tower 379

BASILICA In ancient Roman architecture, a large apsed meeting hall, also used as law courts and money exchange 158, 159 (Pompeii), 160, 161 (imperial forums), 164, 280 (Villa Medici). In church architecture, primitive Christian church with rectangular plan, having a nave and two or more aisles 172, 173, 176, 177, 178, 182, 200, 204, 228, 270, 271, 276, 276, 283 (San Giorgio Maggiore), 290 (Granada Cathedral), 307 (the Superga), 329 (St. George in the East)

BASSAE, Peloponnese 140

BASTION Projecting part at the angle of a fortification from which the garrison can defend the ground before them 120 (Zoser, Saqqarah), 255 (citadel, Aleppo), 312, 312, 313, 321 (Melk Abbey); orillon bastion One in which the walls themselves form the angle projections 312, 313 (Porte de France)

BATH, Avon; Royal Crescent 316

BATHS 164, 165, 170, 257 (Sultan Khan), 259 (Alhambra), 317

BAUDOT, Anatole de (1834–1915) 345 (St. Jean, Montmartre), 360, 360 (concert hall)

BAUHAUS 366, 374, 378

BAY Uniform division of a building as in a section of an arcade 198, 202, 207 (Santiago de Compostela), 208, 216, 220, 226, 230, 288, 289, 300, 304, 307 (San Lorenzo, Turin), 308

BAYON, Angkor 69, 70

BAYREUTH, Germany; Margrave Theatre 323

BAZAAR 248

BEAM see TIE-BEAM

BEAR RUN, Pennsylvania; "Falling Water" 378

BEAUGENCY, Loiret; keep 236, 236

BEAUVAIS, Oise; cathedral 213, 218, 218

BEDFORD PARK, London 356, 357

BEHRENS, Peter (1868–1940) 359 (Behrens house), 364, 365 (A.E.G. turbine factory), 371 (Farben offices)

BEIKHTANO (monasteries) Burma 65

BÉLANGER, François Joseph (1744–1818) 344

BELÉM, Portugal; Jeronymite monastery 290

BELLUSCHI, Pietro (born 1899) 382, 382 (Equitable Building)

BELVEDERE (roof) 323 (Amalienburg Pavilion), 347 (Stock Exchange)

BENEDETTO DA MAIANO (1442–1497) 273 (Palazzo Strozzi)

BENG MEALEA, Cambodia 65

BENI HASAN, Egypt 118

BENTLEY, John Francis (1839–1902) 353 (Westminster Cathedral)

BERCHEM-SAINTE-AGATHE, Belgium; housing estate 372 (the Modern City)

BERG, Max (1870–1947) 365 (Centenary Hall)

BERGAMO, Lombardy; Colleoni chapel 274, 275

BERLAGE, Hendrik Petrus (1856–1934) 360, 360 (Amsterdam Stock Exchange)

BERLIN New Royal Guard 346; Atlas Museum 346; Theatre 346, 347, 350; A.E.G. turbine factory 365; Schauspielhaus 371; Hufeisen Siedlung 373; Philharmonie 385

BERNIER, abbot of Tournus 196

BERNINI, Gian Lorenzo (1598–1680) 276, 298, 302, 302, 303

BERNWARD OF HILDESHEIM (c.960–1022) 187, 195

BERRY, Jean de France, duke of 234 (Mehun-sur-Yèvre)

BERTRAND, Claude Joseph (1734–1811) 333 (Château of Moncley)

COLOSSI OF MEMNON, *western Thebes, Amenophis III, XVIIIth dynasty.*

CONE, *wall of clay cones, Uruk, c.3000BC.*

CONSOLE, *room in the Kyongbok palace, Seoul.*

CUICUILCO, *main pyramid. Constructed in several phases up to c.500BC.*

CLUNY (abbey) Saône-et-Loire 192, *193*, 198, *199*, 200, 206

COB Clay and straw mixture used for walling

COFFERING Decoration of a ceiling, vault or dome with segmental panels in relief 35, *162 (Pantheon)*, 164, 266, *275 (Sant'Andrea)*, *277 (St. Peter's)*, *279 (sacristy, San Lorenzo)*, *280 (Villa Medici)*, *286*

COGOLLUDO, Spain; Medinaceli palace 290

COLA (dynasty), India 60

COLOGNE, Germany; St. Mary in Capitol 208, *209*; cathedral 224, *224*, *348*; Werkbund Exhibition Theatre *363*; model factory *365*; House of Glass *371*

COLONNADE 136, 140, *159 (basilica, Forum)*, 161 *(imperial forums)*, *167 (Hadrian's Villa)*, 266, 271, 276, 310, *334*

COLOSSAL (style or Order) Using pillars which rise through the height of several stages; also referred to as giant or Babylonian 150, *293 (St. Michael, Munich)*, 300, 304, 306, 320, 328, *346 (Law Courts, Lyon)*, 351, *353 (Law Courts, Brussels)*, *365 (A.E.G. turbine factory)*

COLOSSUS Monumental statue representing the sovereign and placed at the entrance to Egyptian temples or in their courts 119

COLUMN A round member, usually bearing a masonry load, but also used ornamentally *37 (cross-section of a building with galleries)*, *49 (evolution of plans)*, 153, *326, 327, 332, 332 (Pantheon)*; campaniform (bell shaped) An Egyptian column whose shaft and capital represent a papyrus stem with open umbel *121 (columns)*, 124, 125; closed lotus Egyptian column in which the shaft and capital represent the closed lotus flower and stem *121 (columns)*, 124; closed papyrus Egyptian column whose shaft and capital take the form of a closed papyrus flower *121 (columns)*, *124*; engaged Column which is attached to a wall *121 (columns)*, 140, 150, 158, *163 (temple of Bacchus)*, 176, *176 (Santa Sabina)*, 198, 212, 276, *283*; monostyle Egyptian column, a simplified version of the closed papyrus column 119, *124 (temple of Amon-Re, Karnak)*, 125; palmiform Egyptian column crowned with a capital of palm leaves *121 (columns)*; sistrum Column representing a sistre, a musical instrument linked with the cult of the goddess Hathor 119; twin Columns placed side by side, sharing the same plinth and abacus

COMBES, Louis (1754–1818) 332, *333 (Maison Acquart)*

COMPOSITE See ORDER composite

CONE A flat-based wedge with tapering sides, found in Mesopotamian archaeology, made from clay, or, more rarely, stone. Placed side by side so that only the base can be seen, these cones protected the walls from erosion, as well as being decorative 105, 108

CONQUES, Aveyron; Ste. Foy 198, *199*

CONSOLE Ornamental bracket *48 (console systems)*
See also BRACKET

CONSTANTINE I (THE GREAT) Roman emperor 172, 176

CONSTANTINOPLE (formerly Byzantium, now Istanbul) 182; St. Sophia 180, *180*, *181*; St. Sergius and St. Bacchus *181*; St. Irene; fortifications 234

CONSTRUCTIVISM 372, *373 (Einstein Tower)*, 376, *376*

CONTAMIN, Victor (1840–1893) 342, *343 (Machine Gallery)*, 345 (Montmartre)

COPÁN, Honduras 90; ball game ground 90

COPENHAGEN Royal Church of Frederick V *334*; Grundtvig Church *370*

CORBEL Projection from the wall to provide support for another part of the building
See also BRACKET

CORBELLING Courses of a building built one above the other to form a support. In the Far East, wooden beams or consoles supporting the roof 33, *42*, 44, *47 (Kasugado and Hakusando of the Enjoji)*, 48, *49 (Jizodo)*, 50 *(Yakushiji Pagoda)*, 54, 57, *58*, 65, 66, *84 (Labná Arch)*, 86, 92, 94, 98, *121 (cross-section of pyramid, Cheops)*

CORDOBA, Spain 244, 254; great mosque 243; enlargement of the great mosque (10thC) *258*

CORFU Temple of Artemis 138, *138*

CORINTHIAN see ORDER Corinthian

CORMONTAIGNE, Louis de (1697–1755) 312

CORNICE Top section of an entablature, or decorative moulding projecting along the top of a building 49 *(Jizodo)*, *139*, 160, *163*,

272, *282, 283*; concave In Egyptian architecture, a cornice with a large semicircular moulding, in imitation of a crown of palms 118, 124, *125*

COSA, Etruria; Capitolium *157*

COSTA, Lucio (born 1902) 376

COTTAGE (style) 356

COTTE, Robert de (1656–1735) *297 (Residenz, Würzburg)*, 308, *308 (chapel interior)*, 318, 322

COUNTERSCARP External wall of a moat next to the ramparts and facing towards assailants. The part of the counterscarp between the parapet and the moat forms a gallery or covered way

COVARRUBIAS, Alfonso de (1488–1570) *291 (Hospital of San Juan Bautista)*

CRANNON, Thessaly; model of a house *132*

CREMONA, Lombardy; Palazzo Raimondi *269*

CRENELLATION Parapet with openings, at the top of ramparts 144, 145, *233*, 258

CREPIDOMA Stepped base of a Greek temple 126, *139*, *141*

CRESTERIA Decorative roof ridge in Mayan architecture, running parallel to the façade and often of great height 86

CRONACA, IL (Simone del POLLAIOLO) (1457–1508) *273 (Palazzo Strozzi)*

CROSS-BEAMED (roof construction) Primitive form of timber roof structure found in the Far East, made up of spaced horizontal beams whose dimensions decrease towards the ridge 19, 22, *23*, 41, 42, 44, *49*

CROSS WALLS (fortification) *312*

CROSSING Intersection of the nave and transepts in a church *179*, 198, 204, *208*, 214

CRUCY, Mathurin (1749–1826) 332

CRYPT 178, *187 (St. Médard, Soissons)*, 193, *200 (St. Anselm's crypt)*, 204

CRYPTOPORTICUS 292, *293 (Antiquarium)*

CRYSTAL PALACE (Great Exhibition, 1851) 340, *341*, 342, 344

CTESIPHON (archaeological site) Iraq 106, *113*

CUELLO, Belize 84

CUICUILCO, Mexico 86

CUIJPERS see CUYPERS

CULEBRAS, Peru 87

CUPOLA A vault which in plan is circular, oval or polygonal *11 (Invalides, dome)*, 60, 62, 106, 148, *149 (Pergamon)*, 150, 162, *162*, 204, 228, 243, 250, 252, *255 ("madrasa" al-Firdaus)*, 256, 260, 277, 320, *321 (Library, Vienna)*, *329 (Radcliffe Camera)*, 330 (Chiswick House), *331 (Sir John Soane's house)*, *332 (Pantheon)*, *334*, 384
See also DOME

CURIA A building for meetings of the senate in ancient Rome, and in the Roman empire for meetings of the municipal authorities *159 (sanctuary of Fortuna Primigenia)*, 160

CURTAIN COLONNADE 148, *149*, 151, 153, 162, *164*

CURTAIN WALL Wall of a fortification between two bastions 144, *145*, *234 (fortress, Armenia)*, 235, *236 (Beaugency)*, *238*, *312*. In modern architecture, a non-load-bearing cladding wall in use from 1937 but now replaced by concrete blockwork *382 (Lake Shore Drive)*

CUVILLIÉS, François de (1695–1768) 317, 322, *323 (Amalienburg Pavilion)*

CUYPERS or CUIJPERS, Petrus Josephus Hubertus (1827–1921) *352 (Rijksmuseum)*

CUZCO, Peru 92, *92 (wall bonding)*; La Compañia 327

CYRUS II (THE GREAT) 112

CYSYLLTE, Wales; aqueduct *340*

DACCA, Pakistan; Sher-e-Banglanadar *388*

DACIEN SI Temple of Benevolence, Xi'an 29

DAGA see BANCO

DAHCHUR, Egypt *117*, 120

DAIBUTSUYO ZUKURI Buddhist style of architecture introduced into Japan in the Kamakura period, originally from China 44

DAIHOONJI, Kyoto 48 *(console systems, B)*

DAMANG GONG (palace) Chang'an 25

ÉCOUEN, *portico, south wing.*

Jacques Henri ESPÉRANDIEU, *Palace of Longchamp, Marseilles.*

DOGON, *granaries attached to the cliff face.*

FLORENCE, *portico of the Ospedale degli Innocenti by Filippo Brunelleschi.*

399

Giraudon

HERCULANEUM, *a street.*

A.F. Kersting

William KENT, *staircase of Holkham Hall, Norfolk.*

Bildarchiv Foto Marburg

Leo von KLENZE, *the Walhalla near Ratisbon.*

Bibl. nat., Paris

LATTE, *Tinian, Marianas Islands. Detail of an illustration from "A Voyage Round the World in the Years 1740–1744" by Lord George Anson.*

Léon KRIER, *design for a school for 500 children.*

Archives de l'Architecture moderne, Bruxelles

MARAE, "Arahurahu", Tahiti.

MACKINTOSH, Charles Rennie (1868–1928) 360, *361 (Glasgow School of Art)*

MADERNO, Carlo (1556–1629) 276

MADI see **MEDINET MADI**

MADINAT AL-ZAHRA, Spain 244

MADRID Royal Palace 324; Prado Museum *334*

MAEKAWA, Kunio (born 1905) *389 (Festival Hall)*

MAFRA, Portugal; palace-convent 324

MAGOBISASHI Japanese porch or supplementary peripheral passage *49 (crosssection)*

MAHABALIPURAM, India 54, 56, 57, *61*; Draupadi ratha 54, *61*; Shore Temple 57

MAHABODHI, Bodh Gaya 57

MAHDIYA (peninsula), Tunisia 252, *253*

MAIA, Manuel de (1688–1768) 324

MAÏEUL (953–994) 192

MAISONS-LAFFITTE, Yvelines; château of Maisons 12, *305*

MALATESTA, Sigismondo Pandolfo 274

MALGATTA, Thebes West 122

MALLAHA (archaeological site) Israel 103

MALLET-STEVENS, Robert (1886–1945) 366

MALWIYA (minaret) Samarra, Iraq 250

MANDARA (African people) *82*

MANGONE, Fabio (1587–1629) 306

MANSART, François (1598–1666) 304, *304 (church of the Val de Grâce), 305 (château of Maisons)*

al-MANSURIYA, Tunisia 244, 252

MANTUA, Lombardy; Sant' Andrea 266, 274, *275*; San Sebastiano 274; Palazzo del Te 278, *278,* 280

MANUELINE (style) *290,* 324

MANWOL DAE (palace) Kaesong 35, 36

MAORIS (New Zealand people) 97

MAQSURA Enclosure reserved for the ruler in the prayer-room of a great mosque 243, 252

MARAE Socio-religious monument of central Polynesia 94, 96, *96,* 100, *100*

MARBURG, Germany 224

MARIA LAACH, Germany 208, *209*

MARKA (African people) 82, 83

MARKELIUS, Sven (1889–1972) *376 (concert hall)*

MARRAKESH, Morocco 242, 244, 254; *qubba* of Ali Ben Yusuf *254*

MARSEILLES, Bouches-du-Rhône; chapel of St. Lazare à la Major 284; Unité d'Habitation *381*

MARTINI, Francesco di GIORGIO (1439–1502) 272, *272 (palace of Urbino),* 274, 312

MARTYRIUM Building, often a church, erected over the tomb of a martyr 176, 182, *182 (St. John)*

MARZABOTTO, province of Bologna, Italy 156

MASER, Veneto; Villa Barbaro *281*

MASJID 243

MASSA (African people) 82

MASTABA 116, 117, *121*

MASTARA, Armenia; St. John 184

MATHEY, Jean-Baptiste (1630–1695) 320

MATTHIEU D'ARRAS (died 1352) 224, *225 (Prague Cathedral)*

MAUSOLEUM 176, *176 (Santa Costanza), 177 (Santo Stefano),* 178, *179*

MAY, Ernst (born 1886) 372, *373 (Bruchfeldstrasse)*

MAY, Hugh (1622–1684) 300

MAYA (civilization) 84, 86, 90

MAYDAN I-SHAH (royal square) Isfahan 260

ME'AE see **MARAE**

MEDICI 272, 278, 280 286

MEDINET HABU, Thebes West 118, 119, 124

MEDINET MADI, Egypt 118

MEGALITHIC Constructed of great stones 32, 94

MEGARON In Greek architecture, room with a projecting columned porch or vestibule 132, *133,* 134, 135, 136, 138, 156

MEHUN-SUR-YÈVRE, Cher; château *234*

MEIDUM, Egypt 117, 120

MEIER, Richard (born 1934) 390

MEIREKI (period) Japan *53 (Omote "shoin" of Samboin)*

MEISSONNIER, Juste Aurèle (1693–1750) 318

MEKNES, Morocco 244, 245

MELK (abbey) Austria 320, *321*

MEMNON (Colossi) Thebes West 119

MEMPHIS (now Mit-Rahineh) Egypt 118, 120, 122

MENDELSOHN, Erich (1887–1953) 366, 372, *373 (Einstein Tower)*

MENGONI, Giuseppe (1829–1877) *345 (Victor-Emmanuel Arcade)*

MENTUHOTEP (funerary monument) XIth dynasty, Deir el-Bahari 117

MEREWORTH CASTLE, Kent 330

MERINID 249, 258, *258 (Sale "madrasa")*

MERLON Raised portion of battlement, see **CRENELLATION**

MESOAMERICA 84–87, 90–91

METAPONTE (Ionic temple) *141*

MÉTÉZEAU, Louis (1572–1615) 304

METOPE Part of the frieze of a Doric Order 130, 138, *138, 139*

MEURTRIÈRE Small opening in a fortification from which to fire under cover

MEXICO cathedral 326, *326, 327;* fountain of Salto de Agua 326; University library *377*

MICHELANGELO, Buonarroti (1475–1564) *266 (courtyard of the Palazzo Farnese),* 268, 276, *277,* 278, *279*

MICHELOZZO DI BARTOLOMMEO (1396–1472) 270, 272, *272 (Palazzo Medici)*

MIES VAN DER ROHE, Ludwig (1886–1969) *13 (Illinois Institute of Technology),* 366, 372, *374 (Weissenhof),* 378, 380, 382, *382 (Alumni Memorial Hall; Lake Shore Drive), 383 (Seagram Building),* 388, 390

MIHRAB A prayer niche in the centre of the *qibla* wall in a mosque, indicating the direction in which to pray 243, 252, 256, *261*

MILAN, Lombardy; Sant' Ambrogio 204; Ospedale Maggiore *264,* 274; Santa Maria delle Grazie 274, *275;* Santa Maria presso San Satiro 274; Palazzo Marino *279;* Santa Maria presso San Celso 282; San Fedele 282; San Sebastiano 282; SS. Paolo e Barnaba 282, *283;* Victor-Emmanuel Arcade *345*

MILETUS (Greek town in Asia Minor) plan *169*

MINARET Mosque tower from which the muezzin calls the people to prayer 62, *62, 63,* 250, *254,* 258, *260*

MINBAR Wood or stone pulpit in a mosque, from which the *khutba* was read 243

MING (dynasty) China *20 (Great Wall),* 23, 24 *(Tumulus of the Valley of the Thirteen Tombs),* 26, 27 *(evolution of the plan of Peking),* 28, 29 *(Temple of Heaven, Peking)*

MINGUN (temple) Burma 66

MINIYA, Syria 249

MINOANS 134, 136

MI-SÖN A 1 (style) Vietnam 65

MITESAKI, Japan 48, *48 (console systems)*

MITLA, Mexico *91*

MIXTEC (civilization) *91 (Mitla)*

MOAI Giant statues in the Easter Islands 96–98, *99*

MOCHICA (civilization) 89

MODULE Unit of measurement regulating the proportions of a building; often half the diameter of a column or pilaster

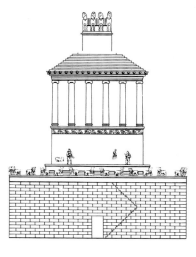
MAUSOLEUM *of Halicarnassus (after K. Jeppesen).*

MI-SON A 1, *Vietnam, south-west façade.*

MEGALITHIC, *temple of Tarxien, Malta, c.3000–2500BC.*

MUDHIF, *in the salt marshes of the Euphrates.*

403

PAVIA, Lombardy; Charterhouse *264, 274, 284*

PAXTON, Sir Joseph (1801/1803–1865) *340, 341 (Crystal Palace), 344*

PEARCE, Sir Edward Lovet (1699–1733) *330*

PEDIMENT Triangular element crowning the façade of a classical building; can also head a window or door. A pediment is often curved *130, 138, 148 (Hadrian's Library), 156, 157 (Capitolium), 163, 267 (Palazzo Branconio dell'Aquila), 283, 286*

PEI, Ieoh Ming (born 1917) *387 (Art Center), 391 (National Gallery of Art)*

PEKING, China *23, 26, 27, 30;* Forbidden City *18, 25, 27, 28, 28, 29;* Pavilion of Introspection, Fragrant Hills *20;* Yuanming yuan *28, 30;* Temple of Heaven *29;* pavilion, garden of the Summer Palace *30*

PELLEGRINO DE' PELLEGRINI see **TIBALDI**

PENDENTIVE see **DOME**

PERACHORA, Boeotia; model of a temple *137*

PERCIER, Charles (1764–1838) *332*

PERGAMON, Mysia *162;* sanctuary of Asklepios *149;* acropolis *169*

PERICLES *143 (Athens Acropolis), 144 (Athens ramparts)*

PÉRIGUEUX, Dordogne; St. Étienne *198*

PERIPTERAL Term describing buildings surrounded by a row of columns *137, 138, 140, 158 (round temple), 163 (temple of Bacchus)*

PERISTYLE Continuous colonnade around the perimeter of a building or an open court; also the space between such a colonnade and the walls of the building *119, 124, 125, 131, 146, 146, 148, 149 (sanctuary of Asklepios), 159 (theatre of Pompey), 166, 167, 328 (Blenheim Palace), 332*

PERRET, Auguste (1874–1954) *362, 363 (Champs Élysées Theatre)*

PERSEPOLIS (archaeological site) Iran *102, 106, 112, 112–113*

PERUGIA, Umbria; San Bernardino *274*

PERUZZI, Baldassare (1481–1536) *278*

PESHAWAR, India *57, 58*

PETERBOROUGH cathedral *200, 200*

PETRA, Syria; façade of a rock tomb *163*

PETRODVORETS (Peterhof), U.S.S.R.; palace *297*

PEYRE, Marie-Joseph (18thC) *332, 333 (theatre staircase), 350*

PHIDIAS (c.500–c.430BC) *143 (Athens Acropolis)*

PHILADELPHIA, Pennsylvania; Stock Exchange *347;* P.S.F.S. Building *377;* Richards Medical Center *388*

PHILIP II, king of Spain *290*

PHILIPPE II (Philippe Auguste), king of France *238*

PIAZZA ARMERINA, Sicily *152, 166;* villa of Maximilian *167*

PICTURESQUE (style) *330, 358 (Huot houses)*

PIENZA (formerly Corsignano), Tuscany *272*

PIER A buttress or abutment *212 (buttressing), 257 (bridge over a tributary of the Tigris), 237 (Loches; Montrichard)*

PIETRO DA CORTONA (Pietro BERRETTINI) (1596–1669) *302, 302, 303 (Santa Maria della Pace)*

PIKILLACTA, Peru *92*

PILASTER Rectangular pillar or pier projecting only slightly from the wall *15 (Ancy-le-Franc; Louvre), 54, 64, 65, 165 (Colosseum), 204, 264 (Palazzo Raimondi), 270, 271, 272 (Palazzo Rucellai), 274, 277 (St. Peter's), 279, 282, 286, 299 (Portal of the Collegio Propaganda Fide), 301, 304, 304 (Tuileries), 323 (Amalienburg Pavilion)*

PILLAR *56, 57, 58, 59, 68, 69, 70, 117, 118, 150, 180, 180, 181, 183, 196, 196 (St. Philibert), 201, 208, 214, 215, 220, 222, 224, 226, 290, 322 (Ottobeuren church);* **engaged** Pillar which forms part of the wall *184, 184;* **Osirian** Pillar incorporating a monumental statue of the Pharaoh *114, 119;* **shafted** *200, 202, 224*

PILOTIS Stilts or pillars on which a building is raised *30, 39 (Kyonghoe pavilion), 40, 41, 46, 47, 50 53 (palace of Katsura), 380*

PINEAU, Nicolas (1684–1754) *318*

PINNACLE Small pyramidal or conical tower, usually topping a buttress *210, 210, 212, 216, 218, 230*

PIRANESI, Giovanni Battista (1720–1788) *315, 317, 334*

PISA, Tuscany; cathedral *205*

PISAC, Peru *92 (wall bonding)*

PISÉ Building material made from bonded earth or clay *19, 38, 102, 104, 132, 254 (mosque of Hasan)*

PLATERESQUE (style) *290, 291 (Salamanca University), 324*

PODIUM *156 (Temple of Jupiter Capitolinus), 159 (Basilica, Pompeii), 160 (Forum), 163 (Maison Carrée), 165 (Circus Maximus)*

POELART, Joseph (1817–1879) *353 (Law Courts)*

POELZIG, Hans (1869–1936) *371 (Grosses Schauspielhaus)*

POGGIO A CAIANO see **FLORENCE**

POGGIO REALE see **NAPLES**

POISSY, Yvelines; Villa Savoye *375*

POITIERS, Vienne; cathedral *213*

POLONNARUVA, Sri Lanka; Anuradhapura, Thuparama, Vatadage *58, 59*

POLYNUCLEAR PRINCIPLE (Africa) *74*

POMPE, Antoine (1873–1980) *363, 363 (Van Neck Clinic)*

POMPEII, Campania *130, 150, 152, 164, 166;* murals in the house of Sulpicius Rufus *153;* basilica of the forum *159;* house of Loreius Tiburtinus *167*

POPCHU-SA (temple) Korea *32, 35, 37*

PÖPPELMANN, Matthäus Daniel (1662–1736) *322*

POROS *128, 145, 148, 149*

PORTICO Covered entrance to a building, colonnaded or arcaded on the open side. (Originally a ceremonial door leading into a building) *23, 57, 58, 59, 68, 107, 112, 118, 125, 143, 147, 149, 158, 159, 161, 163 (sanctuary of Heliopolitan Jupiter), 164–66, 188, 250, 251, 257, 264, 269, 270, 272, 287, 301, 303, 304, 305 (château of Maisons), 307 (the Superga), 329 (St. Martin's in the Fields), 332 (Pantheon), 333*

PORTLAND, Oregon Equitable Building *382*

PORTMAN, John (born 1924) *386, 387 (Bonaventure Hotel)*

POSSAGNO, Veneto; temple (19thC) *346, 347*

POST, Pieter (1608–1669) *300*

POST-GUPTA *60 (Kailasa)*

POST-MODERNISM *390, 391*

POSTERN Rear entrance to a castle *135 (Tiryns)*

POTSDAM, Germany; Einstein Tower *366, 373*

POYET, Bernard (1742–1824) *332*

PRAENESTE see **PALESTRINA**

PRAGUE cathedral *224, 225;* St. Nicholas of Malá Strana *320*

PRAMBANAN (Chandi Lara Jonggrang) Java *64, 68*

PRANDTAUER, Jakob (1658–1726) *320, 321 (Melk Abbey)*

PRE-COLUMBIANS *84–93*

PREFABRICATION *341 (Crystal Palace), 342, 369, 380 (Amsterdam Orphanage), 384, 384 (Turin Exhibition Hall), 386, 387 (Habitat 67)*

PRÈ RUP (temple) Angkor *68*

PRINCETON, New Jersey; Banacerraf house *391*

PRONAOS Outer vestibule preceding the body of a temple or church *138, 140, 192, 198, 206*
See also **NARTHEX**

PROPYLAEUM In Egyptian and Greco-Roman architecture a gateway to a sacred enclosure *112, 113, 135, 135 (fortress of Tiryns), 142 (Acropolis), 149 (sanctuary of Asklepios), 163 (sanctuary of Jupiter), 377 (Woodland Crematorium)*

PROSTYLE Temple with a colonnade *140, 147, 156*

Matthäus Daniel **PÖPPELMANN**, *the Zwinger, Dresden.*

RABAT, *12th century Almohad portal.*

PEKING, *gardens of the Yuanming Yuan, to the north-west of the Summer Palace.*

PLATERESQUE, *façade of Santa Maria la Mayor, Calatayud.*

Henri **SAUVAGE**, *Primavera pavilion, Paris Exhibition of 1925.*

SHANGHAI, *tea pavilion, 18th century.*

SIDE AISLE, *Bourges Cathedral.*

Sir John SOANE, *Mausoleum, Dulwich College Art Gallery, London.*

TRILITH, *"Ha'amonga-a-Maui", Tonga.*

TEPE Persian word for an artificial hill, site of an ancient settlement 104

TESSIN THE YOUNGER, Nicodemus (1654–1728) *296 (Great Gallery, Royal Palace)*

TETI, VIth dynasty 117

TETRAFOIL Building, or part of a building, with four apses 173, 184, *185 (Church of the Holy Cross)*

TEWKESBURY, Gloucestershire; abbey *201*

THAMUGADI see **TIMGAD**

THASOS ramparts *145*

THEATRE 146, *147 (Epidaurus), 159,* 164, *164,* 169, 266, *266 (Theatre of Marcellus),* 323, 333, *347 (Berlin),* 350, 363, *371 (Grosses Schauspielhaus),* 375, *385 (Sydney Opera House)*

THEBES, Egypt 117–25; Ramesseum 114, 124; temple of Mentuhotep, Deir el-Bahari 117; temple of Hatshepsut, Deir al-Bahari 118, 124; colossus of Memnon *119;* Luxor 119, 124; Artisans' village, Deir el-Medineh 123; temple of Ramesses III, Medinet Habu 124; temple of Amon-Re, Karnak 124

THEMISTOCLES *144 (Athens ramparts)*

THEODOSIUS II Eastern emperor 173, *234 (Constantinople)*

THEODULF (c.750–821) 188

THERMOS, Aetolia 130, 136; temples *137;* temple of Apollo *138*

THESSALONICA (now Salonika); St. Demetrius 173, 182, *183;* Acheiropoietos church 182; St. George 182; oratory of Christ Latomos 182; Holy Apostles *182*

THIRTEEN TOMBS, China *24, 28*

THOLOS Dome-shaped tomb
See also **ROTUNDA**

THREE KINGDOMS (period), Korea *32, 36*

THUPARAMA, Polonnaruva, Sri Lanka 58, *59*

TIAHUANACO, Peru *89, 92*

TIBALDI, Pellegrino (1527–1596) 282, 306

TIBERIUS (Tiberius Claudius Nero), Roman emperor 166

TICHITT, Mauritania 77

TIE-BEAM Timber beam crossing the base of the roof structure and taking the weight of the principals at the wall plates 19, *23 (evolution of roof structure, China),* 47 (*"honden", Kamitani jinja)*

TIES Metal or wooden braces incorporated into masonry to strengthen the wall 102, *234 (Constantinople),* 311 *(St. Paul's Cathedral)*

TIERCERON Secondary rib of a Gothic vault 226, *227,* 230

TIKAL, Guatemala 86, 90

TIMBER FRAMING Building method in which the weight is borne by a timber frame rather than by the walls. The walls are an infill, usually of wattle and daub 24, 54, 57, 64, *120 (step pyramid)*
See also **CROSS-BEAMED, HALF-TIMBERING, HOOPED, RAFTER, TIE-BEAM**

TIMGAD (formerly Thamugadi), Algeria 164, *169*

TIMURIDS 248
See also 62, *62 (Humayun's tomb)*

TIRYNS, Argolis 134; fortress *135*

TIVOLI (formerly Tibur) Latium; Hadrian's villa 150, 152, 166, *166,* 265, 266; tetrastyle temple 158; Villa d'Este 280

TOCHIGI, Japan; Bannaji *49 (cross-sections, C)*

TOD, Egypt; Montu Temple 118

TODAIJI, Nara-ken 42, *42,* 45

TOFUKUJI, Kyoto *50*

TOHUA Ceremonial constructions on the Marquesas Islands 96

TOKAT, Turkey; Türbe *256*

TOKONOMA Japanese name for an alcove or niche in a wall, a place reserved for a painting or precious objects and adorned with flowers 44, *53*

TOKYO, Japan; Ksitigarbha Pavilion at Shofukuji *49;* Festival Hall *389;* Sports Arena *389*

TOLEDO, Spain; cathedral 222, 223; Hospital of San Juan Bautista 290, *291;* retable, cathedral 324, *324*

TOLEDO, Juan Bautista (died 1567) 290, *291 (Escorial)*

TOMAR, Portugal; window in the Jeronymite monastery 231; cloister in the Convent of Christ *291*

TOMÉ, Narciso (1721–1732) 324

TORI Ringed column bases 102, *102 (residential palace of Cyrus),* 107, *118 (Kiosk of Sesostris),* 124, 130, *130 (base and capital of an Ionic column),* 141

TORO, Spain; cathedral *207*

TORRALVA, Diogo de (1500–1566) 290, *291 (cloister of the Convent of Christ, Tomar)*

TORRES DEL RIO, Spain; Holy Sepulchre 206, *206*

TOSHODAIJI, Nara 41, 48

TOULOUSE, Haute-Garonne; St. Sernin *194 (Romanesque vaulting),* 198; courtyard of the Hôtel d'Assezat *287*

TOURNAI, Belgium; cathedral 195

TOURNUS, Saône-et-Loire; St. Martin 192, 198; railway station *353*

TOWN PLANNING 19, 21, 24, *25, 26, 27,* 32, 42, 86, 89, *89,* 90, 92, *93,* 104, *110, 111, 113,* 122, *122,* 156, 160, *160,* 161, 163, 168, 169, 234, 242, 244, *295,* 330, 340, 346, 356, 368, 369, 384, 390

TRAJAN Roman emperor 160

TRANSEPT The cross-piece of a cruciform church, or one of its "arms" considered separately 177, 182, 192, 212, 214, *217,* 228, *275 (Milan),* 282, *283;* **double** 198, *199,* 200, 201

TRANSVERSE ARCH Arch which separates one bay of a vault from the next 184, *187,* 195, 198, 202, 210, 214, 216, 220, *227*

TRDAT (10thC–11thC) 184, *184 (Church of the Redeemer, Ani)*

TREFOIL Building or part of a building having three niches or apses in the shape of a clover leaf *184 (cathedral of T'alin), 209 (St. Mary in Capitol)*

TREZZINI or **TRESSINI,** Domenico (1670–1734) 318

TRIBUNE A raised platform or gallery in a room; in a church, the gallery *176 (Sant' Agnese fuori le Mura), 183, 189 (Palatine Chapel),* 195, 198, 200, 202, 205, 210, 214, 216, *320 (St. Nicholas of Malá Strana)*

TRIER, Germany 160, 224; Porta Nigra *150*

TRIFORIUM A straight, arcaded wall passage in a church, above the main arcades (or tribunes when they exist) *183 (St. Demetrius),* 195, 200, 210, 211, 214, *214,* 216, 217, 218, 222, *222,* 224, *225,* 230

TRIGLYPH Element in Doric frieze *139*

TRILITH Monument in the Pacific islands, consisting of two massive pillars supporting a heavy horizontal stone 96

TRIUMPHAL ARCH; of Septimius Severus, Rome 161; Renaissance 266–74

TROY 132

TS'EU-HI, empress of China see **CIXI**

TS'IN (dynasty) see **QIN**

TS'ING (dynasty) see **QING**

TSUKESHOIN In Japan, work table placed beneath a window in a *Shoin* residence; one of the four decorative elements characteristic of the style 44, *53 (Guests' pavilion)*

TUB see **BANCO**

TUGHLUQ (sultans) India 62

TUI TONGA (empire) Oceania 96

TUKOUZOU, MOUNT, Korea; General's Tomb 33

TUMULI (period) Japan 40

TUMULUS Mound of earth covering a burial place *24, 32,* 33, 40, 58, *59 (Anuradhapura),* 96, *157*

TURIN, Piedmont; Santa Sindone 306, *307;* Palazzo Carignano 306; San Lorenzo 306, *207;* the Superga *307;* Exhibition of Decorative Arts (1902) *359, 384*

TUSCAN see **ORDER**

TUTMOSIS III, XVIIIth dynasty 118

TUTUB see **KHAFADJE**

TYMPANUM The area between the lintel of a doorway and the arch above it; the triangular area between the mouldings of a pediment 54, 56, *58*

TAMBO COLORADO, *an Incan centre on the coast of Peru. The buildings are of unbaked brick dressed with clay.*

TEOTIHUACÁN, *the "Citadel" and pyramid of Quetzalcoatl,* AD200–450.

TOULOUSE, *basilica of St. Sernin.*

TRIBUNE, *the tribunes of Notre-Dame, Paris.*

TYMPANUM, *Chartres Cathedral.*

UGARIT, *postern in the ramparts, Hittite style, 14th–13th centuries* BC.

Sir John **VANBRUGH**, *Vanbrugh Castle, Greenwich, London.*

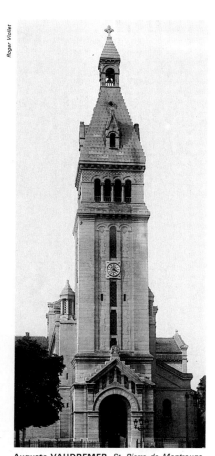
Auguste **VAUDREMER**, *St. Pierre-de-Montrouge, Paris.*

XANTHOS, *façade of the Monument to the Nereids.*